Media Law

PEARSON

At Pearson, we have a simple mission: to help people make more of their lives through learning.

We combine innovative learning technology with trusted content and educational expertise to provide engaging and effective learning experiences that serve people wherever and whenever they are learning.

From classroom to boardroom, our curriculum materials, digital learning tools and testing programmes help to educate millions of people worldwide – more than any other private enterprise.

Every day our work helps learning flourish, and wherever learning flourishes, so do people.

To learn more please visit us at www.pearson.com/uk

Media Law
Text, Cases and Materials

Eric Barendt, Lesley Hitchens, Rachael Craufurd-Smith
and Jason Bosland

PEARSON

Harlow, England • London • New York • Boston • San Francisco • Toronto • Sydney
Auckland • Singapore • Hong Kong • Tokyo • Seoul • Taipei • New Delhi
Cape Town • São Paulo • Mexico City • Madrid • Amsterdam • Munich • Paris • Milan

Pearson Education Limited
Edinburgh Gate
Harlow CM20 2JE
United Kingdom
Tel: +44 (0)1279 623623
Web: www.pearson.com/uk

First published 2014 (print and electronic)

ISBN: 978-1-4082-2161-7 (print)
         978-1-4082-2162-4 (PDF)
         978-1-292-00344-3 (eText)

British Library Cataloguing-in-Publication Data
A catalogue record for the print edition is available from the British Library

Library of Congress Cataloging-in-Publication Data
Barendt, E. M., author.
  Media law: text, cases, and materials/Eric Barendt, Lesley Hitchens, Rachel Crauford-Smith, and Jason Bosland.
    pages cm
  ISBN 978-1-4082-2161-7
  1. Mass media–Law and legislation.   2. Mass media–Law and legislation–Europe.   I. Hitchens, Lesley, author.
II. Crauford-Smith, Rachel, author.   III. Bosland, Jason, author.   IV. Title.
  K4240.B37 2014
  343.09′9—dc23

10 9 8 7 6 5 4 3 2 1
18 17 16 15 14

Print edition typeset in 10/12pt Minion Pro by 35
Print edition printed and bound by Ashford Colour Press Ltd, Gosport

NOTE THAT ANY PAGE CROSS REFERENCES REFER TO THE PRINT EDITION

Brief contents

Contents

14
Investigative journalism: access to information and the privilege not to disclose sources *647*

Companion Website

For open-access **student resources** specifically written to complement this textbook and support your learning, please visit **www.pearsoned.co.uk/legalupdates**

ON THE WEBSITE

Acknowledgements

We are grateful to the following for permission to reproduce copyright material:

Text

Extract 1.2.2 from *The Sunday Times* v *United Kingdom* (1979) 2 EHRR 245, at 280–1 (European Court of Human Rights); Extract 1.2.3 from *Jersild* v *Denmark* (1995) 19 EHRR 1, at 215–18 (European Court of Human Rights); Extract 1.2.4 from *Informationsverein Lentia* v *Austria* (1994) 17 EHRR 93, at 112–14 (European Court of Human Rights); Extract 1.3.1 from L.C. Bollinger, 'Freedom of the press and public access: toward a theory of partial regulation' (1976) 75 Michigan Law Review 1, at 10–11, 13–16 © 2013 Michigan Law Review. All Rights Reserved; Extract 1.3.2 from E.M. Barendt, *Broadcasting Law: A Comparative Study* (Oxford: Clarendon Press, 1995), at 5–9. By permission of Oxford University Press; Extract 1.4.2 from J. Lichtenberg, 'Foundations and limits of freedom of the press', in J. Lichtenberg (ed.), *Democracy and the Mass Media* (Cambridge University Press, 1990), chapter 3, at 102–5, © Cambridge University Press 1990, reproduced with permission; Extract 1.5.2 from *Dow Jones and Company, Inc* v *Gutnick* (2002) 210 CLR 575, [2002] HCA 56, paras 86–9, at 123–5, from Commonwealth Law Reports, reproduced with permission of Thomson Reuters (Professional) Australia Limited. This publication is copyright. Other than for the purposes of and subject to the conditions prescribed under the Copyright Act (Australia) 1968, no part of it may in any form or by any means (electronic, mechanical, microcopying, photocopying, recording or otherwise) be reproduced, stored in a retrieval system or transmitted without prior written permission. Enquiries should be addressed to Thomson Reuters (Professional) Australia Limited. PO Box 3502, Rozelle NSW 2039. www.thomsonreuters.com.au; Extract 1.5.3 from J. Rowbottom, 'Media freedom and political debate in the digital era' (2006) 69 *Modern Law Review* 489, at 508–12, Copyright © 2006, John Wiley and Sons; Extract 1.6.1 from *The Observer and The Guardian* v *United Kingdom* [1992] 14 EHRR 153, at 191 (European Court of Human Rights); Extract 1.6.5 from *Wingrove* v *United Kingdom* (1997) 24 EHRR 1, at 36–7 (dissent of Judge De Meyer); Extract 2.3.1 from Editors' Code of Practice (December 2011), http://www.pcc.org.uk/assets/696/Code_of_Practice_2012_A4.pdf; Extract 2.3.2 from *Burrell* v *News of the World*, PCC Report No 78 (18 November 2008); Extract 2.3.3 from *The Queen* v *Business Age*, PCC Report No 34 (1996), at 5–8; Extract 2.3.4 from *McGuiness* v *Sunday World*, PCC Report No 74 (2006); Extract 2.3.5 from *Full Fact* v *Daily Mail*, PCC Report (2011); Extract 2.3.6 from *Ramblers' Association* v *Sunday Express*, PCC Report No 15 (1992); Extract 2.3.7 from *El-Atar* v *Evening Standard*, PCC Report No 74 (2005); Extract 2.3.8 from *Blom-Cooper* v *Daily Telegraph*, PCC Report No 37 (1997); Extract 2.3.9 from *Sheridan* v *Scottish Sun*, PCC Report No 75 (2007); Extract 2.3.10 from *Allason* v *Daily Mirror*, PCC Report No 37 (1996); Extract 2.3.11 from *Goble* v *The People*, PCC Report No 80 (2009); Extract 2.3.12 from *Fortier* v *Sunday Mirror*, PCC Report No 68 (2004); Extract 2.3.13 from *Thomson* v *Daily Record*, Press Complaints Commission (2011); Extract 2.3.14 from *Palomba* v *Evening Standard*, PCC Report No 72

(2006); Extract 2.3.15 from *Waller* v *Daily Star*, PCC Report No 42 (1998); Extract 2.3.16 from *Sharon* v *The Independent*, PCC Report No 62 (2003); Extract 2.3.17 from *Thames Valley Probation Area* v *The Mail on Sunday, PCC Report No 74 (2007)*; Extract 2.3.18 from *Various* v *The Daily Telegraph*, PCC Report No 43 (1998); Extract 3.4.1 from L. Hitchens, *Broadcasting Pluralism and Diversity: a comparative study of policy and regulation* (Oxford: Hart Publishing, 2006), at 142–3; Extracts 3.5.1 and 3.5.10 from T. Gibbons and P. Humphreys, *Audiovisual Regulation under Pressure: Comparative cases from North America and Europe* (London: Routledge, 2012), at 95–6 and 101–2, Copyright © 2012 Routledge. Reproduced by permission of Taylor & Francis Books UK; Extract 4.4.7 from C. Munro, 'The Banned Broadcasting Corporation' [1995] *New Law Journal* 518, at 519–20, reproduced by permission of Reed Elsevier (UK) Limited trading as LexisNexis. Copyright © 1995 New Law Journal; Extract 4.4.8 from *Scottish National Party* v *Scottish Television plc and another*, 15 April 1997, LEXIS (Court of Session, Outer House), reproduced by permission of Reed Elsevier (UK) Limited trading as LexisNexis. Copyright © 1997 LexisNexis; Extract 4.5.1 from ATVOD, *Determination that the Provider of the On Demand Programme Service 'English Milf' was in breach of Rule 11*, 2 July 2012, at 1, 4, 6–7; Extract 4.5.2 from ATVOD, *Determination of ATVOD on a complaint that the On Demand Programme Service 4OD included unsuitable or harmful content. Complaint AT126WSPBY (Mr Woodcock)*, 29 March 2012, at 1–4; Extract 5.2.1 from Statute of the Council of Europe, London, 5 May 1949, ETS no 1, art 1 © Council of Europe; Extract 5.2.2 from Groppera Radio AG and Others v Switzerland (1990) 12 EHRR at 321, at 337, 338–9, 340, 342–3; Extract 5.2.3 from F. Hondius, 'Regulating transfrontier television – The Strasbourg option' (1988) 8 *Yearbook of European Law* 141, at 148 and 159–60, by permission of Oxford University Press. © Oxford University Press; Extract 5.7.4 from Jackie Harrison and Lorna Woods, *European Broadcasting Law and Policy* (Cambridge University Press, 2007) at 185–6; Extract 5.8.1 from Thomas Gibbons and Peter Humphreys, *Audiovisual Regulation Under Pressure: Comparative Cases from North America and Europe* (Routledge, Abingdon, 2012) at 140, copyright © 2012 Routledge. Reproduced by permission of Taylor & Francis Books UK; Extract 5.9.2 from Case E-8/97, *TV 1000 Sverige AB* v *Norway*, EFTA Court Report 1998, p. 68 at paras 24 and 26, © EFTA Secretariat, 2011; Extract 6.2.1 from *Casado Coca* v *Spain* (1994) 18 EHRR 1, at 20, 23–4 and 25 (European Court of Human Rights); Extract 6.3.1 from *R* v *Advertising Standards Authority, ex parte Charles Robertson* (Developments) Ltd [2000] EMLR 463, 475–6; Extract 6.3.2 from The UK Code of Non-broadcast Advertising, Sales Promotion and Direct Marketing on Non-Broadcast Advertising (12th ed., 2010) Rule 7, © Committee of Advertising Practice (CAP); Extract 6.3.4 from *R* v *Advertising Standards Authority, ex parte Matthias Rath BV* [2001] EMLR 22, paras 19, 26–8; Extract 6.4.1 from The UK Code of Non-broadcast Advertising, Sales Promotion and Direct Marketing, 12th edition, 2010, Rule 01 Compliance, © Committee of Advertising Practice (CAP); Extract 6.4.2 from The UK Code of Non-broadcast Advertising, Sales Promotion and Direct Marketing, 12th edition, Rule 03 Misleading Advertising, © Committee of Advertising Practice (CAP); Extract 6.4.3 from ASA Adjudication of 16 December 2009: Procter & Gamble (Health and Beauty Care) Ltd., © Advertising Standards Authority (ASA); Extract 6.4.4 from The UK Code of Non-broadcast Advertising, Sales Promotion and Direct Marketing, 12th edition, Rule 04 Harm and Offence, © Committee of Advertising Practice (CAP); Extract 6.4.8 from Adjudication on Channel 4, 3 October 2012, © Advertising Standards Authority (ASA); Extract 6.4.9 from The UK Code of Non-broadcast Advertising, Sales Promotion and Direct Marketing, 12th edition, 2010, Rule 06 Privacy, © Committee of Advertising Practice (CAP);

Extract 6.4.10 from *Director General of Fair Trading* v *Tobyward Ltd and Another* [1989] 2 All ER 266, at 270–1, reproduced by permission of Reed Elsevier (UK) Limited trading as LexisNexis. Copyright © 1989 All England Law Reports; Extract 6.5.2 from ASA Adjudication on Marie Stopes International, 4 August 2010, © Advertising Standards Authority (ASA); Extract 6.5.3 from The UK Code of Non-broadcast Advertising, Sales Promotion and Direct Marketing Code, Rule 32 Scheduling, rules 32.5–32.11, © Committee of Advertising Practice (CAP); Extract 6.7.1 from *VgT Verein gegen Tierfabriken* v *Switzerland (VgT)* (2002) 34 EHRR 4, paras 74–7; Extract 6.7.2 from *R* (on the application of Animal Defenders International) v *Secretary of State for Culture, Media and Sport* [2008] UKHL 15, [2008] 1 AC 1312, paras 28–34; Extract 7.2.1 from C.E. Baker, *Media Concentration and Democracy. Why Ownership Matters* (Cambridge University Press, 2007) pp. 7 and 16; Extract 7.2.2 from M. Gentzkow and J.M. Shapiro, 'Competition and truth in the market for news' (Spring 2008) 22/2 *Journal of Economic Perspectives (JEP)*, at 133–54; Extract 7.2.3 from P. Seabright and H. Weeds, 'Competition and market power in broadcasting: where are the rents?' in P. Seabright and J. Von Hagen (eds) *The Economic Regulation of Broadcasting Markets* (Cambridge University Press, 2007), pp. 47–80 at p. 50; Extract 7.3.10 from Cases 1095/4/8/08 and 1096/4/8/08, *British Sky Broadcasting Group plc, Virgin Media Inc* v *(1) The Competition Commission, (2) The Secretary of State for Business Enterprise and Regulatory Reform* and *Virgin Media Inc* v *(1) The Competition Commission, (2) The Secretary of State for Business Enterprise and Regulatory Reform* [2008] CAT 25, at paras 262 and 263; Extract 7.5.4 from Craig Arnott, 'Media mergers and the meaning of sufficient plurality: A tale of two acts', (2010) 2/2 *The Journal of Media Law* 245–75 at 269–70; Extracts 7.5.6 and 7.5.7 from R. Craufurd Smith and D. Tambini, 'Measuring media plurality in the United Kingdom: policy choices and regulatory challenges' (2012) 4/1 *The Journal of Media Law* 35–63, p. 48 and 35–63, pp. 50–1; Extract 7.6.1 from *Centro Europa 7 S.R.L and Di Stefano* v *Italy* Application no. 38433/09, 7 June 2012, paras 133–4 © Council of Europe; Extract 7.6.2 from G. Doyle, 'From "pluralism" to "ownership": Europe's emergent policy on media concentrations navigates the doldrums' (1997) (3) *Journal of Information Law and Technology*, http://elj.warwick.ac.uk/jilt/ commsreg/97_3doyl/; Extract 7.6.3 from P. Valcke, R. Picard, M. Sükösd, B. Klimkiewicz, B. Petkovic, C. dal Zotto and R. Kerremans, 'The European Media Pluralism Monitor: bridging law. Economics and media studies as a first step towards risk-based regulation in media markets', (2010) 2/1 *Journal of Media Law* 85–113, pp. 88–9; Extract 8.3.4 from K. Lefever, *New Media and Sport, International Legal Aspects* (TMC Asser Press/Springer, The Hague, 2012) at p. 145; Extract 9.2.1 from R. Wacks, 'Privacy in cyberspace: personal information, free speech, and the Internet' in P. Birks (ed.), *Privacy and Loyalty* (Clarendon Press, 1997), pp. 93 and 95–6, PRIVACY AND LOYALTY edited by Peter Briks (1997) Ch. 4 "Privacy in Cyberspace: Personal Information, Free Speech, and the Internet" by Raymond Wacks pp. 93–112. Excerpts from pp. 93, 95 & 96. By permission of Oxford University Press; Extract 9.2.2 from A. Guadamuz, *Networks, Complexity and Internet Regulation. Scale-Free Law* (Edward Elgar, Cheltenham, 2011), pp. 211–14; Extract 9.2.3 from R. Benson, 'Futures of the news: international considerations and further reflections' in N. Fenton (ed.) *New Media, Old News: Journalism and Democracy in the Digital Age* (Sage, London, 2010), p. 188 © Sage Publishing; Extract 9.2.4 from Y. Benkler, *The Wealth of Networks: How social production transforms markets and freedom* (Yale University Press, New Haven, 2006), pp. 30 and 32–3; Extracts 9.3.1 and 9.3.5 from T. Gibbons, *Regulating the Media*, 2nd ed. (Sweet & Maxwell, 1998), pp. 301–2 and 304; Extract 9.3.10 from YouTube, *Community Guidelines* (accessed 2 May 2013). Available at:

http://www.youtube.com/t/community_guidelines?gl=GB&hl=en-GB; Extract 9.3.11 from D. Tambini, D. Leonardi and C. Marsden, *Codifying Cyberspace: communications self-regulation in the age of internet convergence* (Routledge, 2008) pp. 284–5, Copyright © 2008 Routledge. Reproduced by permission of Taylor & Francis Books UK; Extract 9.2.12 from N. Helberger, 'Exposure diversity as a policy goal' (2012) 4/1 *Journal of Media Law*, pp. 65–92 at 74–5; J. Zittrain, *The Future of the Internet and How to Stop It* (Yale University Press, 2008), pp. 245–6, Extract from The Future of the Internet and How to Stop It by Jonathan Zittrain reprinted by permission of Peters Fraser & Dunlop (www.petersfraserdunlop.com) on behalf of Jonathan Zittrain; Extract 10.3.1 from *Charleston v News Group Newspapers Ltd* [1995] 2 AC 65 (HL) 73–4; Extract 10.3.2 from *Lewis v Daily Telegraph* [1964] AC 234 (HL) 258–60; Extract 10.3.3 from *Cassidy v Daily Mirror Newspapers* [1929] 2 KB 331; Extract 10.3.4 from *Thornton v Telegraph Media Group Ltd* [2011] 1 WLR 1985; Extract 10.3.6 from *Berkoff v Burchill* [1997] EMLR 139 (CA) 151, 153; Extract 10.3.7 from *Hulton v Jones* [1910] AC 20 (HL) 24; Extract 10.3.8 from *Newstead v London Express Newspapers Ltd* [1940] 1 KB 377 (CA) 388; Extract 10.3.9 from *O'Shea v MGN Ltd and Free4Internet.net Ltd* [2001] EMLR 40; Extract 10.3.10 *Knupffer v London Express Newspaper Ltd* [1944] AC 116 (HL) 124–5; Extract 10.3.11 from *Loutchansky v Times Newspapers Ltd [No 2]* [2002] QB 783; Extract 10.3.16 from *Crookes v Newton* [2011] 3 SCR 269; Extract 10.3.17 from *Jameel v Wall Street Journal Europe Sprl* [2007] 1 AC 359; Extract 3.4.3 from *Silkin v Beaverbrook Newspapers Ltd* [1958] 1 WLR 743 (QB) 746–7; Extract 10.4.4 from *London Artists Ltd v Littler* (1969) 2 QB 375 (CA) 391; Extract 10.4.5 from *British Chiropractic Association v Singh* [2011] 1 WLR 133; Extract 10.4.6 from *Spiller v Joseph* [2011] 1 AC 852; Extract 10.4.11 from *Reynolds v Times Newspapers Ltd* [2001] 2 AC 127; Extract 10.4.12 from *Jameel v Wall Street Journal Europe Sprl* [2007] 1 AC 359; Extract 10.4.13 from *Roberts v Gable* [2008] QB 502; Extract 10.4.14 from *Horrocks v Lowe* [1975] AC 135 (HL) 149–50; Extract 10.5.1 from *Bonnard v Perryman* [1891] 2 Ch 269 (CA) 284; Extract 10.5.2 from *Greene v Associated Newspapers Ltd* [2005] QB 972; Extract 10.5.3 from *Broome v Cassell & Co* [1972] AC 1027 (HL) 1071; Extract 10.5.4 from *Sutcliffe v Pressdram Ltd* [1991] 1 QB 153 (CA) 182–184; Extract 10.5.5 from *Steel and Morris v United Kingdom* (2005) 41 EHRR 22; Extract 10.5.6 from *Elton John v MGN Ltd* [1997] QB 586 (CA) 53–5, 57–8; Extract 10.5.7 from *Kiam v Neil (No 2)* [1996] EMLR 493 (CA) 507–508, 510; Extract 11.2.1 from D. Solove, 'A Taxonomy of Privacy' (2006) 154(3) *University of Pennsylvania Law Review*, pp. 477–564, Copyright © University of Pennsylvania Law School, 1945; Extract 11.3.2 from *Von Hannover v Germany* (2005) 40 EHRR 1; Extracts 11.3.3 and 11.4.7 from *Von Hannover v Germany (No 2)* (2012) 55 EHRR 15; Extract 11.4.1 from *Attorney General v Guardian Newspapers (No 2)* [1990] 1 AC 109; Extract 11.4.2 from *Campbell v MGN Ltd* [2004] 2 AC 457; Extract 11.4.5 *Browne v Associated Newspapers Ltd* [2008] QB 103; Extract 11.4.8 from *Murray v Express Newspapers plc* [2009] Ch 481, 26; Extract 11.4.16 from *Douglas v Hello!* [2006] QB 125; Extract 11.4.18 from *Campbell v MGN Ltd* [2004] 2 AC 457; Extract 11.4.20 from *A v B plc and C* [2003] QB 195; Extract 11.5.3 from *Campbell v MGN Ltd* [2003] QB 633; Extract 11.7.3 from *R v Broadcasting Complaints Commission, ex parte Granada Television Ltd* [1995] EMLR 163 (CA), 167–9; Extract 12.1.1 from *Worm v Austria* (1998) 25 EHRR 454, paras 50–1, 54; Extract 12.2.2 from *Attorney-General v English* [1983] 1 AC 116, at 141–4 (HL); Extract 12.2.3 from *Attorney-General v MGN Ltd and Others* [1997] 1 All ER 456, at 460–1, 466 (DC), reproduced by permission of Reed Elsevier (UK) Limited trading as LexisNexis. Copyright © 1997 All England Law Reports; Extract 12.2.5 from *Attorney-General v MGN Ltd and News Group Ltd* [2011] EWHC 2074 (Admin) 2074, [2012]

EMLR 9, paras 17–21, 31–6; Extract 12.2.6 from *A-G v Guardian Newspapers Ltd* [1999] EWHC Admin 730, [1999] EMLR 924–5, paras 68–73; Extract 12.2.8 from *Attorney-General v Random House Group Ltd* [2009] EWHC 1727 (QB), [2010] EMLR 9, paras 103–10; Extract 12.3.2 from *Attorney-General v Sport Newspapers Ltd* [1991] 1 WLR 1194, at 1207, 1209 (DC); Extract 12.3.3 from *Attorney-General v Punch* [2002] UKHL 50, [2003] 1 AC 1046, paras 43–4, 47–53, 61–3; Extract 12.4.2 from Practice Direction (Criminal Proceedings: Consolidation) [2002] 1 WLR 2870, para 1.3.2; Extract 12.4.3 from *Ex parte The Telegraph plc* [1993] 1 WLR 980, at 984–5, 987–8 (CA); Extract 12.4.4 from *Ex parte Telegraph Group plc* [2001] EWCA Crim 1075, [2002] EMLR 10, paras 19–22, 32–4; Extract 12.4.5 from *R v Clerkenwell Stipendiary Magistrate, ex parte The Telegraph* [1993] QB 462, at 470–1 (DC); Extract 12.5.1 from *R v West* (1996) 2 Cr App Rep 374, 388–9; Extract 12.6.2 from *Attorney-General v Associated Newspapers* [1994] 2 AC 238, at 259–60 (HL); Extract 12.6.3 from *Attorney-General v Seckerson and Times Newspapers Ltd* [2009] EWHC 1023 (Admin), [2009] EMLR 20, paras 45, 50, 52–6; Extract 13.2.1 from *Scott v Scott* [1913] AC 417, at 437–9 (HL); Extract 13.2.2 from *Attorney General v Leveller Magazine* [1979] AC 440, at 450–3 (HL); Extract 13.3.1 from M. Dockray, 'Courts on Television' (1988) 51 *Modern Law Review* 593, at 598–602; Extract 13.4.1 from *R v Legal Aid Board, ex parte Kaim Todner* [1998] 3 All ER 541, at 550–1 (CA), reproduced by permission of Reed Elsevier (UK) Limited trading as LexisNexis. Copyright © 1998 All England Law Reports; Extract 13.4.2 from An Application by Guardian News and Media Ltd, Re [2010] UKSC 1, [2010] EMLR 15, paras 63–76; Extract 13.5.2 from *Spencer v Spencer* [2009] EWHC 1529 (Fam), [2009] EMLR 25, paras 49–55, 59–66; Extract 13.6.1 from *Re S (A child) (Identification: Restriction on publication)* [2004] UKHL 47, [[2005] 1 AC 593, paras 30–8, HL; Extract 13.6.2 from *R (On the Application of Y) v Aylesbury Crown Court* [2012] EWHC 1140 (Admin), [2012] EMLR 26, paras 18–19, 39–55; Extract 13.7.1 from *Re Webster (A Child)* [2006] EWHC 2733 (Fam), [2007] EMLR 7, paras 73–8, 99–104, 115; Extract 13.7.2 from *Re X (A Child) (Residence and Contact – Rights of Media Attendance)* [2009] EWHC 1728 (Fam), [2009] EMLR 26, paras 51–9; Extract 14.1.1 from *R v Shayler* [2003] 1 AC 247, paras 18, 20–4, 27, 29–31, 36 (HL); Extract 14.2.1 from *T2rsas2g A Szabads2gjogokê´ rt v Hungary* (2011) 53 EHRR 3, paras 26–9, 35–9; Extract 14.2.2 from *Sugar v BBC* [2012] UKSC 4, [2012] EMLR 17, paras 75–9; Extract 14.2.4 from *R (On the application of Guardian News and Media) v City of Westminster Magistrates' Court* [2012] EWCA Civ 420, [2012] EMLR 22, paras 72–7, 85; Extract 14.2.5 from *R (on the application of BBC and Dominic Casciani v Secretary of State for Justice)* [2012 EWHC 13 (Admin), [2012] EMLR 18, paras 42–5, 76–82, 97; Extract 14.4.2 from *X Ltd v Morgan Grampian Ltd* [1991] 1 AC 1, at 40–5 (HL); Extract 14.4.3 from *Goodwin v United Kingdom* [1996] 21 EHRR 123, at 143–5 (ECHR); Extract 14.4.4 from *Mersey Care NHS Trust v Ackroyd* (No. 2) [2008] EMLR 1, paras 17–24, 28–32, 80–5; Extract 14.5.2 from *R v Bristol Crown Court, ex parte Bristol Press and Picture Agency Ltd* (1987) 85 Cr App Rep 190, 195–6 (DC); Extract 14.5.3 from *Sanoma Uitgevers BV v Netherlands* [2011] EMLR, paras 64–72.

Preface

This book provides a comprehensive course-book for students of media law, an increasingly popular optional subject for study – at both undergraduate and graduate levels – at many universities and colleges in the UK and in other Commonwealth countries. It builds on the earlier *Media Law: Cases and Materials*, written by two of us and published in 2000. But this book does much more than update the earlier work. It contains a full discussion of the fundamental principles of media law, as well as a commentary on the leading cases, statutory provisions, and other materials from which the extracts are taken. Our intention has been to write a core text book with extracts, rather than the more usual cases and materials book generally used as a supplement to other books.

Inevitably the selection of topics has been difficult. We have included some discussion of the principles of data protection and freedom of information law, which were not covered at all in the earlier book. There is a much fuller treatment of the Internet and video on demand, particularly in relation to the principles of broadcasting regulation. But this book does not attempt to cover aspects of Internet law such as electronic commerce, which are entirely unrelated to the topics of media law. Nor does it deal with topics such as pornography, incitement to racial, etc. hatred, and incitement to or encouragement of terrorism, which do apply to the mass media; they are well covered in books on civil liberties. Further, their practical impact on the media is relatively slight compared to the laws of libel, privacy, contempt of court and concerning restrictions on court reporting, all of which are covered at length in separate chapters (Chapters 10–14). We have also not covered in this book copyright law, an important part of media and entertainment law in practice, but one which is well served by works on intellectual property and which is taught in separate university courses.

For better or worse, media law is subject to rapid change. Largely for this reason the particular content of most chapters in this book bears relatively little resemblance to that in the corresponding chapters in the book published in 2000, even if the overall structure of some chapters is not dissimilar to that of their predecessors. Further important changes are imminent. We have been able, in Chapter 2, to discuss the principal recommendations in the Report of the Inquiry conducted by Lord Justice Leveson into the Culture, Practices and Ethics of the Press. That Report was published in November 2012; it is not yet clear how its recommendations will be implemented, in particular, whether the draft Royal Charter agreed by the three political parties or instead that put forward by the press will be adopted. At some stage in the next year or two a new Communications Bill will probably be introduced to supplement, if not replace, the regime for broadcasting regulation discussed in Chapters 3 and 4; provisions in the Bill may also concern the regulation of the Internet (see Chapter 9). Reform of contempt of court law is likely, following the issue by the Law Commission of a Consultation Paper (No 209) towards the end of 2012.

Despite the difficulties occasioned by the constant stream of case law and proposals for the reform of media regulation, we have endeavoured to take account of all material available to us by 31 December 2012. We have, however, been able to incorporate references to a few developments during the production process.

This book has been written by four authors, and most chapters have been read and commented on by at least two of us. However, it may be helpful to indicate the author of particular chapters. Eric Barendt is the author of Chapters 1, 6 and 12–14; Jason Bosland is the author of Chapters 2 and 10–11; Rachael Craufurd-Smith wrote Chapters 5 and 7–9, and Lesley Hitchens wrote Chapters 3–4. We would like to thank Luke Cesare, Sophie Walker for helpful comments on the defamation chapter and Claire Richardson for proof-reading and assisting with the referencing in Chapters 2, 10 and 11. We are also grateful for the encouragement of Cheryl Cheasely, who commissioned this book, and to the work of her colleagues at Pearson during the production process. We would also like to thank Luke Cesare.

Eric Barendt
Jason Bosland
Rachael Craufurd-Smith
Lesley Hitchens
January 2013

Abbreviations

ASA	Advertising Standards Authority
AVMSD	Audiovisual Media Services Directive
ATVOD	Association for Television on Demand
Broadcasting Code	Ofcom Broadcasting Code 2011
CCA	Contempt of Court Act 1981
DA	Defamation Act 1996
ECHR	European Convention on Human Rights
HRA	Human Rights Act 1998
ODPS	On-demand Programme Service
Ofcom	Office of Communications
PCC	Press Complaints Commission
Aplin *et al.*	*Gurry on Breach of Confidence*, Aplin, T., Bently, L., Johnson, P. and Malynicz, S. (eds) (Oxford: OUP, 2nd edn, 2012).
Barendt, E.	Barendt, E., *Freedom of Speech* (Oxford: OUP, 2nd edn, 2005).
Carter-Ruck on Libel and Privacy	*Carter-Ruck on Libel and Privacy*, Doley, C. and Mullis, A. (eds) (London: Lexis Nexis, 6th edn, 2010).
Fenwick and Phillipson	Fenwick, H. and Phillipson, G. *Media Freedom under the Human Rights Act* (Oxford: OUP, 2006).
Gatley	*Gatley on Libel and Slander*, Milmo, P. and Rogers, W.H.V. (eds) (London: Sweet & Maxwell, 11th edn, 2008).
Robertson and Nicol	Robertson, G. and Nicol, A., *Media Law* (London: Penguin Books, 5th edn, 2008).
The Law of Privacy and the Media	*The Law of Privacy and the Media*, Warby, M., Moreham, N. and Christie, I. (eds) (Oxford: OUP, 2nd edn, 2011).

Table of cases

Table of statutes, statutory instruments and conventions

1 The principles of media law

1.1 THE IMPORTANCE OF MEDIA FREEDOM

Freedom of speech may be regarded as the most important of the fundamental rights which everyone should enjoy in a liberal society. For without this freedom, a state would find it harder to claim legitimacy for the restrictions it imposes on the conduct of its citizens, including restrictions on the exercise and enjoyment of other rights such as privacy or property rights. Only citizens free to contest the wisdom of state laws can be expected to comply with the obligations they impose. Commitment to a liberal democracy, therefore, entails respect for freedom of speech not only during election campaigns, but at all times. Furthermore, freedom of speech enables the discovery of truths about social, economic and other matters, thereby making progress possible, while its exercise is vital for the arts and for individual intellectual development.

In a modern democracy free speech is primarily exercised through the mass media, principally the press and the broadcasting media. Other media, however, are, or have been, very important. For example, during much of the eighteenth century, stage plays at the theatre provided many of the radical ideas which led to the French Revolution and other challenges to established authority. A similar role might be claimed for the cinema in the twentieth century. The Internet and social media may have enabled the spread of democratic ideas, notably in the Arab spring in early 2011. The Net can be used by everyone with access to a computer or mobile phone to disseminate their ideas throughout the world, without the consent of a newspaper editor or a radio or television controller – often referred to in this context as 'gatekeepers'.

Despite the important cultural role played by other media and the advent of the Internet, newspapers and broadcasting, particularly television, channels are the key media for the communication of information and the spread of political and social ideas and opinion. Surveys have often shown that, despite the increasing use of the new electronic media, most people still rely on television as the principal source of news and for coverage of important events such as the Queen's Jubilee or the Olympic Games.[1] It is expression in the press and on the broadcasting media which forms the principal subject matter of this book. At first glance media law seems to consist largely of restrictions on the freedom of the press and broadcasters. However, that perspective can be misleading. It is important to emphasise the central place of media freedom: their freedom to report and discuss matters of public interest. Without that freedom newspapers, broadcasters and other branches of the media could not perform their vital role in the political and social life of a liberal society; moreover, individuals, whether in political, social or cultural life would find it much harder to disseminate their views to the general public. The media provide a platform for political and other types of discussion.

---

[1] The House of Lords Select Committee on Communication reported that 67 per cent of adults over the age of 16 use television as their main source of news about the UK: *The ownership of the news* (1st Report for Session 2007–8, HL Paper 122–1), para 75. There has been a marked decline in newspaper readership, particularly among younger age groups: ibid., paras 13–14, 33.

Media freedom has been recognised in many national constitutions (see Extract 1.1.1) and by the European Court of Human Rights (see Section 1.2). Its position in English law has been more ambivalent. Two hundred years ago William Blackstone wrote in his *Commentaries on the Laws of England* that press freedom 'consists in laying no *previous* restraints upon publications and not in freedom from censure for criminal matters when published'.[2] The presumption against previous, or prior, restraints is discussed in the final section of this chapter (Section 1.6). Dicey, the influential nineteenth-century constitutional lawyer, agreed that the absence of any system of licensing was central to freedom of the press. However, he also emphasised other aspects of English press law, notably that liberty of discussion – another term for freedom of speech – really meant no more than the freedom to say or write what a jury in a criminal (or then a civil) case would consider lawful, in that it was not proscribed by, for example, the laws of sedition, blasphemy or defamation. Further, there was no difference between the legal freedom of a letter writer on the one hand, and that of a journalist or editor on the other. Indeed, a specific liberty or freedom of the press was not recognised by English law.[3] That remained a general perspective for much of the twentieth century.

This account now seems very complacent. Furthermore, it has clearly been superseded by recent legal developments. First, it is surely wrong to rely on juries to safeguard freedom of the media; their members may be unsympathetic to the opinions of minorities or to the radical press and magazines.[4] Second, a number of restraints on the media may be imposed without their involvement. It is judges who determine whether to grant an injunction to restrain breaches of confidence or privacy (see Chapter 11) and whether to uphold applications to commit editors for contempt of court (Chapter 12). Further, the broadcasting media may be subject to some censorship (see Section 1.6).

Most importantly, even before the enactment of the Human Rights Act 1998, incorporating into English law the right to freedom of expression under the European Convention on Human Rights (ECHR) the courts in England had recognised a common law principle of freedom of speech. That principle was invoked to place a narrow interpretation on legislation which appeared to curtail freedom of speech and related rights to demonstrate,[5] and in the context of media law was used to develop and expand existing common law defences to defamation actions[6] (see further, Chapter 10, Section 10.4(a)–(c)). In two leading House of Lords decisions shortly before the Human Rights Act came into force, Lord Steyn emphasised the constitutional character of freedom of expression;[7] it was in his view as strongly protected in English law as it was under the ECHR. There is no doubt now that English courts reject the view of Dicey that freedom of expression (or speech) is no more than a residual liberty, allowing only the freedom to discuss ideas which are tolerated by juries or for that matter the judges themselves.

However, Dicey's final point that there is no difference between the free speech rights, say, of individual letter writers and of the press merits further discussion. It enjoys some judicial support. For example, in the famous *Spycatcher* case, Sir John Donaldson, MR, in

---

[2] 4 Bl Comm (London, 16th edn, 1825), 151.

[3] A.V. Dicey, *An Introduction to the Study of the Law of the Constitution* (Macmillan, 10th edn, 1961), 246–7.

[4] Moreover, juries have been responsible for the award of extravagant damages in libel cases: see Chapter 10, Section 10.5.

[5] *Brutus* v *Cozens* [1973] AC 854.

[6] See *Silkin* v *Beaverbrook Newspapers* [1958] 1 WLR 743, Diplock J (Extract 10.4.3) (fair comment defence), and *Reynolds* v *Times Newspapers Ltd* [2001] 2 AC 127, HL (Extract 10.4.11) (qualified privilege).

[7] *R* v *Home Secretary, ex parte Simms* [2000] 2 AC 115; *Reynolds* v *Times Newpapers Ltd* (n 6 above).

the Court of Appeal said that the right of the media to know and publish information 'is neither more nor less than that of the general public'.[8] This is an attractive view, for it is not obvious why press editors, or television channel controllers or other broadcasters, should have wider free expression rights than individual authors, speakers at Hyde Park Corner, or anyone else. Moreover, if press or media freedom is different from the freedom of expression of individuals, we must ask hard questions what further rights a distinctive press (or media) freedom entails, beyond the freedom of expression of individual journalists and correspondents, and how the press or media should be defined for these purposes. For example, are monthly periodicals or academic journals entitled to claim the same freedom of the press as newspapers, and what is the position of the regular bulletins issued by financial advisers, investment trusts, or professional firms of solicitors or architects? Should citizen journalists taking photographs of a public event on their mobile phone be entitled to the same media freedom as the broadcasters who then redistribute these images on their television channels?

While English law may be able to avoid these awkward questions, the same is not so true of other legal systems where a specific press freedom is explicitly stated in the Constitution. The best-known constitutional provision in this context is without doubt the First Amendment to the Constitution of the United States of America (1791) which states that 'Congress shall make no law . . . abridging the freedom of speech, or of the press . . .'. In fact, the Supreme Court of the United States has not generally given the 'free press' limb of this First Amendment any specific content, clearly distinct from the coverage the media enjoy, as do ordinary individuals, under the free speech clause – although one Justice of the Supreme Court writing extra-judicially has argued that the Free Press guarantee should be given a distinct interpretation (see Extract 1.4.2 below). More generally, although the Supreme Court has never taken the absolutist approach that no regulation at all of the media is permissible, the First Amendment does mean that all types of regulation – the laws of libel and privacy, contempt of court and other reporting restrictions, broadcasting and cable regulation – can be reviewed by the courts to see that they do not infringe the freedoms guaranteed by it. The equivalent provision in the post-war German Basic Law (or Constitution) is much fuller than the First Amendment.

Extract 1.1.1
Article 5 of the German Basic Law (1949)

(1) Everyone shall have the right freely to express and disseminate his opinion by speech, writing and pictures, and freely to inform himself from generally accessible sources. Freedom of the press and freedom of reporting by means of broadcasts and films are guaranteed. There shall be no censorship.

(2) These rights are limited by the provisions of the general laws, the provisions of law for the protection of youth, and by the right to inviolability of personal honour.

(3) [*Omitted*].

A few points may be made about this provision as they are of general relevance for discussion of media law. First, freedom of expression confers a right on the general public to *receive* information, as well as to express its opinion. Whether it also confers a right to obtain information from public authorities unwilling to disclose it is doubtful; this

---

[8] *Attorney General v Guardian Newspapers (No 2)* [1990] 1 AC 109–83.

topic is discussed in Chapter 14, when the part played by freedom of information law in investigative journalism is examined. It is important here to point out that when discussing media freedom we should also consider the interest or right of the public to receive information and ideas the media wish to impart. Second, the German provision also guarantees the freedom of broadcasters and the cinema, an unusual explicit recognition in a constitution of the modern media. The final point is that the third sentence of article 5(1) totally outlaws censorship, a provision understood to preclude systems of administrative censorship, under which material must be submitted to an authority before its publication or release. Media law is generally hostile to censorship systems. The ban does not, however, preclude judicial orders to stop a publication of an article infringing personal privacy (see Chapter 11, Section 11.4(f) for discussion of injunctions to protect privacy in English law).

Media freedom is closely related to freedom of expression, a right which is enjoyed by all individuals and is now often protected by national constitutions. It is also guaranteed by the European Convention on Human Rights, provisions of which have now been incorporated into English and Scots law by the Human Rights Act 1998. The significance of the Convention right to freedom of expression for media law in the United Kingdom is explored in the next section of this chapter, which discusses a few important rulings of the European Court of Human Rights in Strasbourg and important terms of the Human Rights Act. Section 1.3 looks at the special regulation of the broadcasting media, and asks whether there is any justification now for that regulation, under which television and radio are subject to legal restraints which do not apply to the print media and to the Internet. The relationship between freedom of expression and press (or media) freedom is further explored in Section 1.4, which outlines a number of perspectives on that relationship, and introduces the concept of media plurality or pluralism, which is now a key idea in media law. Section 1.5 looks at the position of the Internet and its implications for media regulation, while Section 1.6 discusses the legality of systems of censorship and prior restraint in UK media law and under the European Convention.

1.2 THE EUROPEAN CONVENTION AND THE HUMAN RIGHTS ACT 1998

(a) The Convention and the European Court of Human Rights

Press and media freedom are not explicitly guaranteed by the European Convention of Human Rights and Fundamental Freedoms (ECHR) but they are covered by the right to freedom of expression guaranteed by ECHR, art 10. Many areas of UK media law cannot now be understood, without an appreciation of the terms of article 10, so it is set out in full.

Extract 1.2.1
European Convention on Human Rights and Fundamental Freedoms, article 10

(1) Everyone has the right to freedom of expression. This right shall include freedom to hold opinions and to receive and impart information and ideas without interference by public authority and regardless of frontiers. This Article shall not prevent States from requiring the licensing of broadcasting, television or cinema enterprises.

> (2) The exercise of these freedoms, since it carries with it duties and responsibilities, may be subject to such formalities, conditions, restrictions or penalties as are prescribed by law and are necessary in a democratic society in the interests of national security, territorial integrity or public safety, for the prevention of disorder or crime, for the protection of health or morals, for the protection of the reputation or rights of others, for preventing the disclosure of information received in confidence, or for maintaining the authority and impartiality of the judiciary.

Unlike the equivalent provision in the European Charter of Fundamental Rights,[9] there is no mention of the press or other media in ECHR, art 10. Indeed, on one view, it would be odd to protect powerful press and broadcasting institutions in a Convention intended to protect *human* rights, largely against overbearing or totalitarian governments. But this view, however defensible in theory, would make no practical sense, given the crucial role played by the media in the dissemination of ideas and information. The media provide a platform for individual voices as well as being themselves powerful players in open democratic and social debate. The importance of ECHR, art 10 for the press (and the mass media generally) was made plain in the *Sunday Times* case, the first important ruling of the Strasbourg Court on freedom of expression. The House of Lords had granted an injunction to stop the publication of a newspaper article discussing the responsibility of the drugs company, Distillers, for the deformities caused by its thalidomide drug (see Chapter 12, Section 12.1 for discussion of the House of Lords decision). A majority of the European Court of Human Rights held that this restraint could not be justified as 'necessary in a democratic society . . . for maintaining the authority of the judiciary'.

Extract 1.2.2
The Sunday Times v United Kingdom **(1979) 2 EHRR 245, at 280–1 (European Court of Human Rights) (footnotes omitted)**

As the Court remarked in its HANDYSIDE judgment,[10] freedom of expression constitutes one of the essential foundations of a democratic society; subject to paragraph 2 of Article 10, it is applicable not only to information or ideas that are favourably received or regarded as inoffensive or as a matter of indifference, but also to those that offend, shock or disturb the State or any sector of the population.

These principles are of particular importance as far as the press is concerned. They are equally applicable to the field of the administration of justice, which serves the interests of the community at large and requires the co-operation of an enlightened public. There is general recognition of the fact that the courts cannot operate in a vacuum. Whilst they are the forum for the settlement of disputes, this does not mean that there can be no prior discussion of disputes elsewhere, be it in specialised journals, in the general press or amongst the public at large. Furthermore, whilst the mass media must not overstep the bounds imposed in the interests of the proper administration of justice, it is incumbent on them to impart information and ideas concerning matters that come before the courts just as in other areas of public interest. Not only do the media have the task of imparting such information and ideas: the public also has a right to receive them.

To assess whether the interference complained of was based on 'sufficient' reasons which rendered it 'necessary in a democratic society', account must thus be taken of any public

---

[9] Article 11.
[10] *Handyside* v *United Kingdom* (1979–80) 1 EHRR 737. The case involved an unsuccessful challenge to the application of UK obscenity legislation to a booklet addressed to adolescents, which advocated sexual freedom and liberal use of drugs.

interest aspect of the case. The Court observes in this connection that, following a balancing of the conflicting interests involved, an absolute rule was formulated by certain of the Law Lords to the effect that it was not permissible to prejudge issues in pending cases: it was considered that the law would be too uncertain if the balance were to be struck anew in each case . . . Whilst emphasising that it is not its function to pronounce itself on an interpretation of English law adopted in the House of Lords, the Court points out that it has to take a different approach. The Court is faced not with a choice between two conflicting principles, but with a principle of freedom of expression that is subject to a number of exceptions which must be narrowly interpreted. In the second place, the Court's supervision under Article 10 covers not only the basic legislation but also the decision applying it. It is not sufficient that the interference involved belongs to that class of the exceptions listed in Article 10(2) which has been invoked; neither is it sufficient that the interference was imposed because its subject-matter fell within a particular category or was caught by a legal rule formulated in general or absolute terms: the Court has to be satisfied that the interference was necessary having regard to the facts and circumstances prevailing in the specific case before it.

The Court concluded that the House of Lords decision fell outside the 'margin of appreciation' which states enjoy in determining whether a restriction on the exercise of the freedom is necessary in a democratic society. Another important decision of the European Court of Human Rights was its ruling that Austrian defamation law violated the Convention when it required the defendant, the publisher of a satirical magazine, to prove the truth of an expression of opinion on the political manoeuvres of the Chancellor, Bruno Kreisky; the Court emphasised the importance of the press in fostering political debate.[11] It was the first of many rulings of the Strasbourg Court in the area of defamation law. In one of them it held that an award of £1.5 million damages in an English libel case amounted to an infringement of article 10, as such an enormous sum was a disproportionate restriction on the exercise of freedom of expression.[12] Indeed, a large number of defamation cases have been taken to the European Court, as an application may be brought by either the media complaining that their freedom of expression under ECHR, art 10 has been infringed, or by individuals arguing that a national judgment in a defamation case has failed to protect their rights under ECHR, art 8. Article 8 of the Convention guarantees the right to respect for private life, and the Court has ruled in a number of cases that this privacy right covers the right to reputation, at least if the defamatory allegations were sufficiently serious to injure the individual's integrity:[13] for further consideration of this topic, see Chapter 10, Section 10.2.

There have also been important European Court decisions on the compatibility of state privacy law with the right guaranteed by ECHR, art 8. Among them is its famous ruling in the *Von Hannover* case,[14] when it held that the German courts had failed to protect Princess Caroline of Monaco's right to respect for her private life, when they allowed the publication by tabloid magazines of several pictures of her out alone in public or dining with friends. The Court distinguished the publication of stories of real public interest, which are protected under ECHR, art 10, and celebrity gossip or photographs, which make

---

[11] *Lingens* v *Austria* (1986) 8 EHRR 407.
[12] *Tolstoy* v *Miloslavsky* v *UK* (1996) 20 EHRR 442, [1996] EMLR 152.
[13] For a review of the complex European Court judgments in this area, see A. Mullis and A. Scott, 'The swing of the pendulum: reputation, expression, and the re-centring of English libel law' (2012) 63 *Northern Ireland Law Quarterly* 27.
[14] [2005] EMLR 21 (Extract 11.3.2).

no real contribution to public debate. The impact of this decision, and of judgments of the European Court concerning English privacy law is discussed in Chapter 11, Section 11.3.

In one much cited decision, the Court ruled that journalists enjoy freedom under the Convention to report offensive speech in respect of which the speaker himself could be prosecuted. The applicant, a Danish journalist, had conducted a television interview with a youth group ('the Greenjackets'), in the course of which members of the group made racist remarks. The Court held that the journalist's conviction for aiding the spread of racist speech infringed article 10.

Extract 1.2.3
Jersild v *Denmark* (1995) 19 EHRR 1, at 215–18 (European Court of Human Rights) (footnotes omitted)

A significant feature of the present case is that the applicant did not make the objectionable statements himself but assisted in their dissemination in his capacity of television journalist for a news programme . . . In assessing whether his conviction and sentence were 'necessary', the Court will therefore have regard to the principles established in its case-law relating to the role of the press . . . In considering the 'duties and responsibilities' of a journalist, the potential impact of the medium concerned is an important factor and it is commonly acknowledged that the audio-visual media have often a much more immediate and powerful effect than the print media . . . The audio-visual media have means of conveying through images meanings which the print media are not able to impart.

At the same time, the methods of objective and balanced reporting may vary considerably, depending among other things on the media in question. It is not for this Court, nor for the national courts for that matter, to substitute their own views for those of the press as to what technique of reporting should be adopted by journalists. In this context the Court recalls that Article 10 protects not only the substance of the ideas and information expressed, but also the form in which they are conveyed . . .

News reporting based on interviews, whether edited or not, constitutes one of the most important means whereby the press is able to play its vital role of 'public watch-dog' . . . The punishment of a journalist for assisting in the dissemination of statements made by another person in an interview would seriously hamper the contribution of the press to discussion of matters of public interest and should not be envisaged unless there are particularly strong reasons for doing so . . .

There can be no doubt that the remarks in respect of which the Greenjackets were convicted . . . were more than insulting to members of the targeted groups and did not enjoy the protection of Article 10 . . . However, even having regard to the manner in which the applicant prepared the Greenjackets item . . . it has not been shown that, considered as a whole, the feature was such as to justify also his conviction of . . . a criminal offence under the Penal Code.

The *Jersild* decision, and other Court rulings highlighting the crucial role of the media to public political debate,[15] indeed may suggest that the press and broadcasting channels enjoy stronger protection under ECHR, art 10 than ordinary individuals do when communicating their views to other people.[16] On the other hand, it is clear that individual pamphlet writers are as entitled as the institutional media to claim the protection of article 10,[17] while in a number of recent cases the Court has stressed that the press and other media must

---

[15] For example, *Lingens* v *Austria* (n 11 above).
[16] See the views of Fenwick and Phillipson, 65–72.
[17] *Steel and Morris* v *UK* [2005] EMLR 314, (2005) 41 EHRR 403.

exercise their freedom in a manner consistent with their responsibilities.[18] The crucial point in *Jersild* is that the journalist was *reporting* the expression of extreme racialist views; the decision might have been different had he adopted them, or expressed them himself.[19]

The interpretation of article 10 poses problems in the context of the broadcasting media and the cinema. Under the third sentence of its first paragraph, states may establish licensing systems for these media. A relevant question is the relationship between this sentence and the terms of paragraph (2), which appears to allow restrictions on freedom of expression only when they are necessary for the protection of the rights and interests set out in that paragraph. In *Groppera* v *Switzerland* the Court upheld a ban on the retransmission in Switzerland of programmes broadcast from an unlicensed station in Italy; the station had been set up to evade the Swiss licensing system.[20] The Court ruled that a state is entitled to use its licensing system for technical reasons, for example, to prevent overcrowding on the wavelengths, but it must observe the other requirements set out in article 10(2).

The Court addressed these issues more fully in *Informationsverein Lentia*, where the issue was the compatibility of the Austrian public broadcasting monopoly with the Convention.

Extract 1.2.4
Informationsverein Lentia v *Austria* **(1994) 17 EHRR 93, at 112–14 (European Court of Human Rights) (footnotes omitted)**

As the Court has already held, the purpose of [the third sentence of paragraph 1] is to make it clear that States are permitted to regulate by a licensing system the way in which broadcasting is organised in their territories, particularly in its technical aspects. Technical aspects are undeniably important, but the grant or refusal of a licence may also be made conditional on other considerations, including such matters as the nature and objectives of a proposed station, its potential audience at national, regional or local level, the rights and needs of a specific audience and the obligations deriving from international legal instruments.

This may lead to interferences whose aims will be legitimate under the third sentence of paragraph 1, even though they do not correspond to any of the aims set out in paragraph 2. The compatibility of such interferences with the Convention must nevertheless be assessed in the light of the other requirements of paragraph 2.

The monopoly system operated in Austria is capable of contributing to the quality and balance of programmes, through the supervisory powers over the media thereby conferred on the authorities. In the circumstances of the present case, it is therefore consistent with the third sentence of paragraph 1. It remains, however, to be determined whether it also satisfies the relevant conditions of paragraph 2.

The Court has frequently stressed the fundamental role of freedom of expression in a democratic society, in particular where, through the press, it serves to impart information and ideas of general interest, which the public is moreover entitled to receive. Such an undertaking cannot be successfully accomplished unless it is grounded in the principle of pluralism, of which the State is the ultimate guarantor. This observation is especially valid in relation to audiovisual media, whose programmes are often broadcast very widely.

Of all the means of ensuring these values are respected, a public monopoly is the one which imposes the greatest restrictions on the freedom of expression, namely the total impossibility of broadcasting otherwise than through a national station and, in some cases, to a very limited

---

[18] In particular, see *Pedersen* v *Denmark* (2006) 42 EHRR 24, para 71; *Flux* v *Moldova (No 6)* Decision of 29 July 2008; *Lindon* v *France* (2008) 46 EHRR 35, para 62.
[19] See *Pedersen* v *Denmark* (n 18 above), para 77.
[20] (1990) 12 EHRR 321.

extent through a local cable station. The far-reaching character of such restrictions means that they can only be justified where they correspond to a pressing need.

As a result of the technical progress made over the last decades, justification for these restrictions can no longer today be found in considerations relating to the number of frequencies and channels available; the Government accepted this . . .

The Government finally adduced an economic argument, namely that the Austrian market was too small to sustain a sufficient number of stations to avoid regroupings and the constitution of 'private monopolies'.

In the applicant's opinion, this is a pretext for a policy which, by eliminating all competition, seeks above all to guarantee to the Austrian Broadcasting Corporation advertising revenue, at the expense of the principle of free enterprise.

The Court is not persuaded by the Government's argument. Their assertions are contradicted by the experience of several European States, of a comparable size to Austria, in which the coexistence of private and public stations, according to rules which vary from country to country and accompanied by measures preventing the development of private monopolies, shows the fears expressed to be groundless.

In short, like the Commission, the Court considers that the interferences in issue were disproportionate to the aim pursued and were, accordingly, not necessary in a democratic society. There has therefore been a violation of Article 10.

In a subsequent case the Court has held that the Swiss broadcasting authority was entitled to refuse a broadcasting licence for a commercial channel, Car TV, on the ground that its primary purpose was to promote car sales.[21] A state could use its licensing powers to promote the quality and balance of television programmes, even though that goal is not specified among the aims for which restrictions on freedom of expression may be imposed under ECHR, art 10(2).

Recently, the Grand Chamber has held that freedom of expression requires diversity of programmes, reflecting a variety of political opinion, in broadcasting – in other words, media pluralism.[22] Another important point is that the Court has held incompatible with the right to 'receive . . . information and ideas', conferred by ECHR, art 10(1), restrictions on the use of satellite dishes for the receipt of television programmes from foreign countries.[23]

Questions for discussion

1. Does the *Jersild* case suggest that journalists and broadcasters have a right under the Convention to express, say, racist views, the expression of which by members of the public would be a criminal offence? Should the media enjoy a wider right to freedom of expression than ordinary individuals, on the ground that they have special responsibilities to promote open public debate in a democracy?

2. What was the basis of the Court's decision in *Informationsverein*? Is it legitimate for states to license broadcasting or cinema enterprises on grounds not stated in article 10(2)?

3. What do you think the Court had in mind in referring to 'the principle of pluralism'? (Pluralism is discussed below in Section 1.4.)

---

[21] *Demuth* v *Switzerland* (2002) 38 EHRR 20.
[22] Application 38433/09, *Centro Europa 7 SRL* v *Italy*, Decision of 7 June 2012, paras 129–30: see Section 1.4.
[23] *Autronic* v *Switzerland* (1990) 12 EHRR 485; *Khurshid Mustafa* v *Sweden* (2011) 52 EHRR 24.

(b) The Human Rights Act 1998

The European Convention on Human Rights was incorporated into UK law by the Human Rights Act 1998 (HRA). Under the Act which came into force in October 2000 it is unlawful for any 'public authority' to act incompatibly with the Convention rights set out in Schedule 1 to the Act, including of course the right to freedom of expression: HRA, s 6. The term 'public authority' includes courts and tribunals and any person 'certain of whose functions are functions of a public nature ...'.[24] Legislation must be interpreted and applied compatibly with Convention rights;[25] if that proves impossible, the High Court and appellate courts may declare legislation incompatible with the Convention.[26] However, they have no power to invalidate an Act of Parliament for this reason. In considering the scope of Convention rights, UK courts must take account of, but are not bound by, decisions of the European Court of Human Rights.[27]

Incorporation of the Convention has significant repercussions for media law in the United Kingdom.[28] Courts must interpret legislation restricting media freedom, such as the Defamation Act 1996 (see Chapter 10), Contempt of Court Act 1981 (Chapters 12–14) and provisions in the Children Act 1989 (Chapter 13) compatibly with the right to freedom of expression, which in these contexts includes the freedom of the press fully to report legal proceedings. The courts have also considered, but rejected, the argument that a provision in the Communications Act 2003 banning political advertising on the broadcast media was incompatible with the guarantee of freedom of expression in ECHR, art 10.[29] Under HRA, s 6, the decisions of regulatory authorities such as the Office of Communication (Ofcom), the Association for Television On-Demand (ATVOD), and the Advertising Standards Authority must not infringe Convention rights, in particular in this context the rights of broadcasters and advertisers to disseminate information and ideas. It is less clear that the Press Complaints Commission (considered in Chapter 2) has been bound to observe Convention rights, although the better view is that it does discharge a function of a public nature, viz, press self-regulation, and so must act compatibly with Convention rights: freedom of expression and the right to respect for private life. Certainly any successor body set up in the wake of the Report of the Leveson inquiry would be bound, at least if its existence was recognised or underpinned in statute. The BBC and Channel 4 (but not Channel 3) might also be regarded as 'public authorities', since they discharge specific public broadcasting responsibilities imposed on them by Royal Charter in the case of the BBC and statute in the case of Channel 4.[30]

Initially it was unclear whether the HRA would have much impact on purely private bodies, such as newspapers, magazines and book publishers. Unlike public authorities, they are not *directly* bound to act compatibly with Convention rights; the HRA does not have full horizontal effect, so that the right to respect for private life, guaranteed by ECHR, art 8, cannot as such be claimed in UK courts against newspapers or other private bodies. However, the courts are bound under HRA, s 6 to act compatibly with Convention rights.

---

[24] HRA, s 6(3).
[25] Ibid., s 3.
[26] Ibid., s 4.
[27] Ibid., s 2.
[28] For a comprehensive analysis of the impact of the HRA on media law, see Fenwick and Phillipson, ch 3.
[29] *R (Animal Defenders International)* v *Secretary of State for Culture, Media and Sport* [2008] UKHL 15, [2009] 1 AC 1312 (Extract 6.7.2 below).
[30] See Fenwick and Phillipson, 114–22 for a full discussion of the arguments for and against treating these broadcasters as covered by HRA, s 6.

In a number of important privacy cases, they have accepted that they must develop the law of breach of confidence in conformity with the Convention rights under articles 8 and 10.[31] It remains unclear whether this obligation requires them only to take account of Convention rights or the values underlying these rights (weak *indirect* horizontal effect), or requires them to develop the common law compatibly with these rights (strong *indirect* horizontal effect).[32] In more recent decisions they appear to have adopted the second approach.[33] Indeed, Lord Steyn in *Re S (A Child)* seems to have taken an even stronger view, when he said that after the HRA came into effect, the courts' jurisdiction to restrain publicity in cases concerning children came from the rights under the European Convention, rather than the inherent jurisdiction of the courts under the common law.[34] As later chapters in this book will show, the HRA has had a significant impact on the development of privacy law in the UK and on the powers of the courts to limit media access to, and reporting of, sensitive cases, particularly when they concern children; it has also influenced, albeit to a lesser extent, defamation law and the law on the privilege of journalists not to disclose their sources.

During the passage of the HRA through Parliament, the press expressed anxiety that it would inevitably lead to the development of a right to privacy which English law hitherto had not recognised.[35] Largely to meet this anxiety, the measure was amended to give special treatment to freedom of expression. HRA, s 12 applies whenever a court considers whether to grant any remedy in a civil case which might affect the exercise of the right to freedom of expression.[36] Two provisions concern interim relief and are set out in Section 1.6, but HRA, s 12(4) applies in all circumstances.

Extract 1.2.5
Human Rights Act 1998, section 12(4)

(4) The court must have particular regard to the importance of the Convention right to freedom of expression and, where the proceedings relate to material which the respondent claims, or which appears to the court, to be journalistic, literary or artistic material . . . to—

   (a) the extent to which—

      (i)   the material has, or is about to, become available to the public; or

      (ii) it is, or would be, in the public interest for the material to be published;

   (b) any relevant privacy code.

There has been some debate whether this provision should be interpreted to give priority to freedom of expression over other Convention rights, as opponents of privacy laws doubtless hoped. That view was firmly rejected by Sedley LJ in *Douglas v Hello! Ltd*, the first case to go to the Court of Appeal after the HRA came into effect.[37] Regard to the Convention right to freedom of expression entailed, in his view, attention also to the qualifications to the exercise of that freedom which are set out in ECHR, art 10(2)

---

[31] In particular see *Douglas v Hello!* [2001] QB 967, *Venables and Thompson v News Group Newspapers Ltd* [2001] Fam 430, *Campbell v MGN* [2004] 2 AC 457 (Extract 11.4.2).

[32] For a full discussion of this distinction, see Fenwick and Phillipson, 123–44, and G. Phillipson, 'The Human Rights Act, "horizontal effect" and the common law: a bang or a whimper?' (1999) 62 *Modern Law Review* 824.

[33] See the judgments of Lord Phillips MR in *Douglas v Hello (No 6)* [2006] QB 125, paras 52–3, and of Buxton LJ in *McKennitt v Ash* [2008] QB 73, paras 8–11.

[34] [2005] 1 AC 593, para 23 (Extract 13.6.1).

[35] For further discussion, see Chapter 11.

[36] HRA, s 12(1).

[37] Note 31 above, paras 133–5.

(see Extract 1.2.1) – including restrictions to safeguard the rights (among them privacy) of others. Second, section 3 of the HRA requires the courts to interpret all legislation, including the Human Rights Act itself, compatibly with Convention rights; further, the ECHR does not give priority to freedom of expression over other rights. So it would be wrong to understand HRA, s 12 as giving priority to freedom of expression. It simply directs the attention of the courts to the importance of the freedom. This view of the limited impact of section 12(4) has been accepted by the Joint Committee of the House of Lords and House of Commons in its recent review of privacy law.[38]

Questions for discussion

1. Should the HRA be interpreted in such a way that newspapers (and other private persons) are bound to respect Convention rights, for example, to respect for private life?
2. Do you agree with Sir Stephen Sedley's interpretation of HRA, s 12(4)?

1.3 THE SPECIAL REGULATION OF THE BROADCASTING MEDIA

This section introduces the special regulation of the broadcasting media – radio and television – and discusses whether this regulation can now be justified. The position of the print media should be outlined first. The publication of newspapers, magazines, and books has not been subject to a licensing system since the end of the seventeenth century. Indeed, the introduction of any licensing system would be strongly resisted as contrary to a long tradition of press freedom. This freedom is limited only by the general law, notably the laws of defamation, privacy and contempt of court, which impose significant restrictions on the press (and other media); these laws are discussed in Chapters 10–13. (Laws prohibiting the dissemination of hate speech, incitement to terrorism and to commit other criminal offences, and the publication of obscenity apply to the press and other media just as they apply to ordinary individuals; but they are invoked very rarely against the institutional media, so they are not discussed in this book.) Newspapers and magazines (but not book publishers) have also been subject to a system of voluntary regulation operated by the Press Complaints Commission (see Chapter 2).

In addition to the constraints imposed by the general criminal and civil law, broadcasters are also subject by statute to a number of special restrictions. First, the company operating an independent broadcasting channel or providing content services must obtain a licence.[39] Second, programme restrictions go beyond the constraints imposed by the general laws, say, of obscenity, hate speech and defamation. For example, offensive and harmful material should not be included in licensed television and radio services. Broadcasters must show 'due impartiality' or observe comparable standards in their programmes, while public service channels are required to include news bulletins and serious programmes, for example original drama, in their schedules.[40] Political advertising is banned on radio and television.[41] There are no restrictions of these kinds on the press.

---

[38] *Privacy and Injunctions*, Session 2010–12, HL Paper 273, HC 1443, paras 54–9.
[39] See Chapter 3, Section 3.4.
[40] For full treatment of these topics, see Chapter 3, Sections 3.4 and 3.7 (public service obligations), and Chapter 4, Section 2(c) (impartiality) below.
[41] See Chapter 6, Section 6.7.

A newspaper, for instance, is free to support a political party, take as much political advertising as it likes, and may wholly ignore foreign affairs or other stories which in its view are of no interest to its readers.

Is there any justification for this radical divergence in the regulation of the principal branches of the mass media? This question has been extensively discussed in both academic literature and official reports. In a famous law review article, Lee Bollinger, a leading commentator on freedom of speech and media law in the USA, explored the issues against the background of two apparently conflicting Supreme Court decisions.[42] In *Tornillo*[43] the Court struck down a law providing for a 'right of reply' to newspaper columns as incompatible with freedom of the press and the editor's freedom to determine the contents of his paper, while in its previous ruling in *Red Lion* (discussed in the extract from Bollinger's article) it had upheld the reply right granted by the Federal Communications Commission to personal attacks on radio and television.[44] The Court was persuaded that it was legitimate to regulate the latter because of the scarcity of frequencies for broadcasting.

Extract 1.3.1
L.C. Bollinger, 'Freedom of the press and public access: toward a theory of partial regulation' (1976) 75 *Michigan Law Review* 1, at 10–11, 13–16 (footnotes omitted)

It is clear that the Court has not made explicit just what is so 'unique' about the broadcast media that justifies legislative action impermissible in the newspaper context. It is doubtful that the so-called scarcity rationale articulated in . . . *Red Lion* provides an explanation. Certainly the scarcity rationale explains why Congress was justified in devising an allocation scheme to prevent the overcrowding of broadcasting frequencies. It may also serve to explain in part why the television industry is so concentrated. The scarcity rationale does not, however, explain why what appears to be a similar phenomenon of natural monopolization within the newspaper industry does not constitute an equally appropriate occasion for access regulation. A difference in the cause of concentration – the exhaustion of a physical element necessary for communication in broadcasting as contrasted with the economic constraints on the number of possible competitors in the print media – would seem far less relevant from a first amendment standpoint than the fact of concentration itself. Thus, it might be argued that a person 'attacked' in the *Washington Post*, or one who holds a different viewpoint than that expressed in that newspaper, is able to publish a pamphlet or his own 'newspaper' in response. But does this have any more appeal than a similar argument with respect to the Columbia Broadcasting System?

It is true, of course, that a person with the requisite capital and inclination could, theoretically, always establish his own newspaper if the local print media refused to publish his point of view, whereas it is highly unlikely that he could establish his own broadcast station if the local stations refused to cover his viewpoint. But this seems a slim basis on which to predicate such dramatically different constitutional treatment. Even if we assume greater ease in entering the print media, however, the question remains why the purported openness of the newspaper market should not be considered an important factor in assessing the significance of concentration in the broadcast media. Why, this analysis asks, did the Court in *Red Lion* treat the broadcast media as separate and discrete? Why did the Court, in an exercise similar to defining the 'relevant market' in an antitrust case, narrow its focus to a particular segment of the mass media? Why did the Court not say that, so long as people can gain access somewhere within the mass media, there

[42] Also see his book, *Uninhibited, Robust and Wide Open* (New York: OUP, 2010), 29–42.
[43] *Miami Herald Publishing Co v Tornillo*, 418 US 241 (1974).
[44] *Red Lion Broadcasting Co v FCC*, 395 US 367 (1969).

is no need for legislative action in any concentrated branch? The treatment of the broadcast media as discrete constitutes at least implicit acknowledgement that the newspaper and other major print media are also highly restricted. If anyone could set up a major newspaper, would we really care if entry into the broadcast media was physically precluded? Or is the explanation somehow hinged to the nature of the regulatory scheme itself? . . . In many important respects, television is today the most pervasive medium of communications in our society. Not only does virtually everyone have access to a television set, but more people watch it, even for purposes of obtaining news, and for longer periods, than read the publications of the print media. In addition, television is frequently considered to have a 'special impact' on its audience. Thus, many courts and commentators believe television is today the dominant means of influencing public opinion, not only because more people watch it than read newspapers, but also because it possesses some undefined and unquantifiable, but nevertheless unique, capacity to shape the opinions of the viewers in ways unrelated to the merits of the arguments presented. The television medium, it is also said, offers the opportunity to thrust information and ideas onto the audience. Unlike printed publications, which can be avoided by 'averting the eyes', television provides the opportunity to force extraneous messages onto audiences gathered for other purposes. This medium, in short, may be the preeminent forum for the discussion of ideas and viewpoints in the society and it may offer opportunities to persuade that cannot be matched elsewhere within the system of expression. The greater concentration of power in television, therefore, may arguably represent more serious social and first amendment problems than the situation in the print media.

This line of argument, promising though it may seem, contains several serious problems. First, the analysis fails to explain why the current level of concentration in newspapers, even assuming that it is not as high as that in television, is not sufficiently troublesome by itself to justify governmental intervention . . .

Even more problematical, however, is the alleged special impact of television. Quite apart from any natural suspicions concerning the validity of the claim, given the frequency with which it seems to confront each new medium of communications, the impact thesis is a dangerously amorphous justification for regulation. It provides no clear limits to official authority and invites censorship as well as affirmative regulation. Further, in so far as the thesis rests upon the premise that regulation is more acceptable the greater the audience and the impact, it seems inconsistent with the underlying purpose of the first amendment, which presumably is to protect effective as well as ineffective speech . . . Finally, there is simply no evidence at the present time to support the proposition that television shapes attitudes and ideas in ways so unprecedented as to require urgent remedial regulation. Thus, until more evidence exists to support the theory, or perhaps until a much wider consensus is formed in its support, it seems wise to avoid relying on the special impact theory.

It is at this point that conventional thinking about broadcast regulation largely stops. Once it is determined that the broadcast and print media are constitutionally indistinguishable, then it is concluded that the Court's theory of access regulation is without rational foundation and should be discarded at the earliest opportunity. Such a conclusion possesses a certain legalistic appeal, but it also may be an oversimplification. The very weakness of the scarcity rationale suggests that there is something more here than first meets the eye. The dual treatment of the press has been so long accepted even by persons known for their sensitivity to first amendment values, that the scarcity rationale may in fact be a convenient legal fiction covering more subtle and important considerations.

It is helpful, therefore, to adopt a less formalistic approach to the problem and to probe beyond normal legal analysis to account for this remarkable constitutional development. For even if broadcasting and the printing press are essentially the same, they nevertheless have different origins, have existed for different periods of time, and one has been controlled from its beginnings while the other has been left unrestricted. It is important, in short, that our analysis be sensitive to the historical process through which the present system has developed.

In a later Supreme Court decision, *FCC v Pacifica Foundation*[45] (mentioned in Extract 1.3.2) the uniquely powerful character of television, intruding into the home, was regarded as justifying the special regulation of the broadcasting media. However, the crucial point, so far as Bollinger is concerned, is not whether broadcasting is really different from the print media, but the fact that they are generally considered to be different.[46] However, we will see from the next extract that he also attempted to justify the diverse treatment of the two mass media.

The arguments have also been considered in the UK, though here they lack the constitutional dimension they have in the USA and in Germany.

Extract 1.3.2
E.M. Barendt, *Broadcasting Law: A Comparative Study* (Oxford: Clarendon Press, 1995), 5–9 (some footnotes omitted)

The [scarcity] argument is, however, less clear than appears at first sight. Does, for example, the scarcity of frequencies refer to the limited number *allocated* by the government as available for broadcasting or to the actual *numerical shortage* of broadcasting stations? If the former, it can be argued that the scarcity is an artificial creation of the government (rather than a natural phenomenon) since it reserves a number of frequencies for the use of the army, police, and other public services; government is then not in a good position to argue for restrictions on broadcasters' freedom. Further, economic liberals contend that if broadcasting licences were sold to the highest bidders (as happened in Britain in 1991), and they were then free to sell them, there would probably not be an excess of those wishing to broadcast over the supply of frequencies. That problem arises when a government chooses to award licences for nothing (or at below market price). On the alternative formulation of actual scarcity, it has been pointed out that in the United States there has been an increase in the number of broadcasting stations during the last twenty years, while there are fewer newspapers than there used to be.[i] Comparable developments have occurred in European countries in the same period, especially since the advent of cable and satellite.

The scarcity argument cannot easily be divorced from economic considerations. The German Constitutional Court, for instance, coupled them when it held positive regulation of the broadcasting media constitutionally necessary. The shortage of frequencies and the high costs of starting up broadcasting channels explained their dearth in comparison with the numbers (in 1961) of newspapers and magazines.[ii] However, it is now probably as difficult to finance a new newspaper as it is a private television channel, if not more so. Certainly that is true if a comparison is made between the costs of setting up a national newspaper and a local community radio station. Yet anybody rich enough to afford the former is free to publish what he wants, while there are (in most countries) limits on what the latter may broadcast. If, on the other hand, it is relatively easy to enter the press market, it may be hard to see why policy-makers should be so concerned about the prohibitive costs of instituting a broadcasting station: those unable to afford that would be able to communicate effectively in other ways.[iii]

Finally the scarcity argument is much less tenable now than it used to be. Cable and satellite have significantly increased the number of available or potentially available channels, so that there are more broadcasting outlets than there are daily newspapers (national and local), though it is harder to calculate the respective numbers of television or radio stations and specialist magazines . . .

[Another] major argument for the differential treatment emphasizes the character of the broadcasting media. Television and radio, it is said, are more influential on public opinion than the press, or at least are widely thought to be. In the *Pacifica* case the United States Supreme Court majority said that they intrude into the home, are more pervasive, and are more difficult to

[45] 438 US 736 (1978).
[46] Extract 1.3.1 at 20.

control than the print media.[iv] In particular, it is hard to prevent children from being exposed to broadcasts, while it is relatively easy to stop them looking at magazines and papers (which in any case they may not be able to read or purchase) . . .

A somewhat different version of this argument has been formulated by the German Constitutional Court in the *Third Television* case:[v] regulation is necessary to guarantee pluralism and programme variety, whether or not there is now a shortage of frequencies and other broadcasting outlets. The free market will not provide for broadcasting the same variety found in the range of press and magazine titles. It follows that programme content should be regulated and that media monopolies should be cut down by the application of anti-trust laws. The implications of these propositions may differ from those which flow from the *Pacifica* rationale; but both the United States and German arguments lay stress on the power of television and its unique capacity to influence the public.

The arguments are difficult to assess. Broadcasting does not intrude into the home unless listeners and viewers want it to. From the point of view of constitutional principle, it is not easy to justify the imposition of greater limits on the medium on the ground that it is more influential than the written word. It cannot be right to subject more persuasive types of speech to greater restraints than those imposed on less effective varieties. On the other hand, the Court majority in the *Pacifica* case was probably right to regard broadcasting (particularly television) as a 'uniquely pervasive presence' in the lives of most people. Regrettable though it may be, much more time is spent watching television than reading; further, the presence of sound and picture in the home makes it an exceptionally potent medium. It may also be harder to stop children having access to 'adult material' on television than to pornographic magazines . . .

These . . . justifications for broadcasting regulation are inconclusive. There may still be something to the scarcity rationale, and it is probably true that broadcasting is the most influential medium of communication. But it is doubtful whether the case is powerful enough to justify the radically different legal treatment of the press and broadcasting media. A separate question is whether it is appropriate to continue to treat radio in the same way as television. There is generally a large choice of local, if not national, radio programmes, and it is hard to believe that they exercise a dominating influence on the formation of public attitudes. A similar question arises for cable television.[vi] Although a permit must be obtained from a licensing authority, several franchises may be physically accommodated and a wideband cable system may be able to carry up to thirty or forty or even more channels. The scarcity rationale therefore seems inapplicable to cable, and, further, it is hard to believe that this mode of broadcasting exercises such a strong influence that stringent programme regulation is justifiable.

The last argument for the divergent treatment of the press and broadcasting media has been made by a leading American scholar, Lee Bollinger.[vii] He admits that there is no fundamental difference in the character of the two mass media. But they have been perceived as different, a phenomenon to be explained in terms of their history. Broadcasting is still a relatively new means of mass communication, and it is understandable that society has wanted to regulate it, just as it has treated the cinema with more caution than it has the theatre. Bollinger's case is, however, not based solely on tradition. He justifies the divergent treatment of the two media on the ground that society is entitled to remedy the deficiencies of an unregulated press with a regulated broadcasting system. That may be preferable to attempting to regulate both sectors. Regulation poses the danger of government control, a risk which is reduced if one branch of the media is left free. This seems an unsatisfactory compromise. It does not appeal to the advocates of broadcasting deregulation. If regulation of the press is always wrong (and perhaps unconstitutional) and if there is no significant difference between its position and that of the broadcasting media, it follows that the latter should also be wholly unregulated. On those assumptions, Bollinger's case would appear to lack coherence,[viii] for it attempts to justify the unequal treatment of the liberties of broadcasters and newspaper proprietors and editors, when in all material respects their position is identical.

The argument is also unconvincing from the opposite perspective that regulation of the broadcasting media compensates for the weaknesses of an unregulated press. Suppose one shares Bollinger's view that there are powerful arguments for regulating the press, for example, by mandating in some circumstances rights of reply or access to it. His argument is that we have become used to an unregulated press and that there are good reasons for only regulating one part of the mass media. The question is then whether it makes sense to correct the (alleged) shortcomings of the press by regulating the broadcasting media to ensure that they are not repeated there. This is doubtful. In Britain, for instance, the press is overwhelmingly sympathetic to the Conservative Party, while broadcasters must not express their views and their programmes must be impartial. These latter restraints will only remedy a lack of balance in the newspaper industry on the assumption that otherwise broadcasters would also present predominantly Conservative programmes. However, the government imposed a tougher impartiality requirement in the Broadcasting Act 1990, because (some of) its supporters felt television and radio programmes were too left-wing!

Source: Broadcasting Law: A Comparative Study by E.M. Barendt (1995). pp. 5–9. By permission of Oxford University Press.

[i] See Powe, [*American Broadcasting and the First Amendment*, Berkeley, California, 1987], 204–8.
[ii] See 12 BVerfGE 205, 262 (1961).
[iii] See Bollinger, 'Freedom of the Press and Public Access' [Extract 1.3.1 above], 11.
[iv] *FCC v Pacifica Foundation* 438 US 736 (1978) . . .
[v] 57 BVerfGE 295, 322–3 (1981).
[vi] The United States courts have been unsure whether to treat cable as similar to the press or to terrestrial broadcasting when ruling on the constitutionality of its broadcasting: see P. Parsons, *Cable Television and the First Amendment* (Lexington, Mass, 1987) . . .
[vii] See Bollinger, 'Freedom of the Press and Public Access' [Extract 1.3.1 above] . . .
[viii] For the requirement of coherence and integrity in law, see R.M. Dworkin, *Law's Empire* (London, 1986), ch 6.

The scarcity argument for broadcasting regulation is now further weakened by the development of digital technology which enables many more channels to be transmitted, whether this is done terrestrially over broadcasting frequencies or by cable or satellite. The arguments in the preceding extracts must also be considered in the changed circumstances of media convergence, when, for example, newspaper content may be disseminated online as well as in print, and when broadcasting programme content may be watched on a computer or via a mobile phone. These developments call into question the meaning of 'broadcasting'; there is perhaps no good reason for distinguishing the regulation of conventional television programmes viewed at a particular time in a broadcasting schedule and videos viewed on demand, whether they are received over the Internet or a mobile phone. But as the law now stands, comparable content may be regulated by different authorities under separate regulatory regimes.[47]

In the view of many commentators, particularly in the United States, broadcasting regulation should be more or less abandoned, save perhaps for rules against the showing of violent or sexually explicit material; the free market will provide viewers and listeners with an adequate choice of programmes, just as it provides readers with a range of books, newspapers, and magazines.[48] This view may also have been held by James Murdoch when he said that the profit motive was the only guarantee of a free media.[49] However, it was not

[47] See Chapter 4, Section 4.5, and Chapter 6, Section 6.6 below.
[48] See R. Coase, 'The Federal Communications Commission' (1959) 2 *Journal of Law and Economics* 1; L. Powe, *American Broadcasting and the First Amendment* (Berkeley, CA, 1987); T. Krattenmaker and L. Powe, 'Converging First Amendment Principles for converging communications media' (1995) 104 *Yale Law Journal* 1719.
[49] MacTaggart Lecture at Edinburgh TV Festival (full text at http://www.guardian.co.uk/media/video/2009/aug/29/james-murdoch-edinburgh-festival-mactaggart (accessed 21 September 2012)).

shared by the UK government in its White Paper, *A New Future for Communications*,[50] which heralded the enactment of the Communications Act 2003. Public service broadcasting, and implicitly therefore the special regulation of broadcasting, could be justified, even after the end of spectrum scarcity. The market may not provide the range of programmes viewers want, as channel controllers tend to produce schedules of mass appeal. Further, there are important democratic and cultural arguments for ensuring that broadcasters provide news, and offer challenging documentaries and other serious programmes.[51] In her book, *Broadcasting Pluralism and Diversity*, Lesley Hitchens, drawing on the concern for a public sphere in which the community can exchange information and ideas about government and social affairs, has argued that 'regulation of the media can be justified by reference to the role it can and should play within the public sphere'.[52] Without public broadcasting, or at least some regulation of broadcasting, whether public or commercial, there would be no platform for, say, the discussion of political and social issues which everyone should have an opportunity to hear and consider. The need for such a platform is perhaps now the best argument for the special regulation of broadcasting, for most people still rely on radio and television for news, particularly at times of crisis or during election campaigns. Perhaps, as Hitchens argues, the question is not so much whether the specific regulation of broadcasting can be justified, but whether it is right to leave other media, notably newspapers, as unregulated as they are.[53] This question is discussed in Section 1.4.

Questions for discussion

1. Which, if any, of the arguments considered in this section justify the special regulation of the broadcasting media?
2. Are you persuaded by Bollinger's argument that, as the print and broadcast media have distinctive histories, it is right to treat them differently?
3. Would it be better to leave the broadcasting media, as well as the print media, to the free market?

1.4 MEDIA FREEDOM AND FREEDOM OF EXPRESSION

As was mentioned in Section 1.1, media freedom is intimately connected with freedom of expression. Indeed, the traditional view in English law has been that freedom of the press and the freedom of individual writers are substantially the same. On this view press freedom is essentially the freedom of editors and journalists to express their views; similarly, broadcasting freedom is the freedom of radio and television commentators and producers to speak and make programmes. There is something to be said for this simple perspective. If the government bans a television programme or libel damages are awarded against a newspaper, both freedom of speech and freedom of the media are implicated. Moreover, there is no need to define the press or the media for the purpose of determining which bodies are entitled to a discrete freedom.

---

[50] Cm 5010, December 2000.
[51] Ibid., paras 5.3.5–5.3.12.
[52] Oxford: Hart Publishing, 2006, at 60.
[53] Ibid., 60–1.

However, this perspective may fail to do justice to the complexity of media freedom. The difficulties can be exposed by posing some questions. Does an instruction by an editor to a journalist not to publish an article amount to an infringement of free speech, or is it an exercise of editorial freedom, an aspect of press freedom? Does a rule requiring broadcasters to show 'due impartiality' on matters of controversy, and not to express their own views, interfere with broadcasting freedom? Or should such a rule be defended as enhancing the access of viewers to a range of opinion and so protecting their freedom of speech? Further, as Potter Stewart points out in the article from which Extract 1.4.1 is taken, the traditional view fails to give any distinct meaning to the 'Free Press' limb of the First Amendment, or, it might be said, to the separate provision for broadcasting freedom in article 5 of the German Basic Law (see Extract 1.1.1). The author was a member of the Supreme Court when he wrote this article, though of course he was expressing here a personal view.

Extract 1.4.1
P. Stewart, 'Or of the press' (1975) 26 *Hastings Law Journal* 633–4

It seems to me that the Court's approach . . . has uniformly reflected its understanding that the Free Press guarantee is, in essence, a *structural* provision of the Constitution. Most of the other provisions in the Bill of Rights protect specific liberties or specific rights of individuals: freedom of speech, freedom of worship, the right to counsel, the privilege against compulsory self-incrimination, to name a few. In contrast, the Free Press Clause extends protection to an institution. The publishing business is, in short, the only organized private business that is given explicit constitutional protection.

This basic understanding is essential, I think, to avoid an elementary error of constitutional law. It is tempting to suggest that freedom of the press means only that newspaper publishers are guaranteed freedom of expression. They *are* guaranteed that freedom, to be sure, but so are we all, because of the Free Speech Clause. If the Free Press guarantee meant no more than freedom of expression, it would be a constitutional redundancy . . .

It is also a mistake to suppose that the only purpose of the constitutional guarantee of a free press is to insure that a newspaper will serve as a neutral forum for debate, a 'market-place for ideas', a kind of Hyde Park corner for the community. A related theory sees the press as a neutral conduit of information between the public and their elected leaders. These theories, in my view, again give insufficient weight to the institutional autonomy of the press that it was the purpose of the Constitution to guarantee.

. . .

The primary purpose of the constitutional guarantee of a free press was . . . to create a fourth institution outside the Government as an additional check on the three official branches. Consider the opening words of the Massachusetts Constitution, drafted by John Adams:

The liberty of the press is essential to the security of the state.

The relevant metaphor, I think, is the metaphor of the Fourth Estate. What Thomas Carlyle wrote about the British Government a century ago has a curiously contemporary ring:

Burke said there were three Estates in Parliament; but, in the Reporters' Gallery yonder, there sat a Fourth Estate more important far than they all. It is not a figure of speech or witty saying; it is a literal fact – very momentous to us in these times.

A similar approach seems to have been advocated in the Report of the Royal Commission on the Press in 1977, the third Commission set up to investigate the position of newspapers in the UK after the Second World War. It pointed out that press freedom had different meanings for different people: for owners it meant the freedom to establish and market their publications, for editors the freedom 'to decide what shall be published', and for individual journalists and others the freedom to communicate their views in the pages of a newspaper. These freedoms were all elements in the right to freedom of expression.[54] But the claims made by different groups may conflict. No claim to freedom of expression or press freedom should be treated as absolute. So the Commission treated press freedom as bearing distinctive meanings, but was unsure how they related to freedom of expression.

In the following extract Judith Lichtenberg offers a different perspective on media freedom. In her view, this freedom is valuable only in so far as it promotes the values underlying the fundamental human right to freedom of speech.

Extract 1.4.2
J. Lichtenberg, 'Foundations and limits of freedom of the press', in J. Lichtenberg (ed.), *Democracy and the Mass Media* (Cambridge University Press, 1990), chapter 3, 102–5

I confess that I do not entertain that firm and complete attachment to the liberty of the press which is wont to be excited by things that are supremely good in their very nature.

A. de Tocqueville, *Democracy in America*[i]

Freedom of the press is guaranteed only to those who own one.

A.J. Liebling, *The Press*[ii]

Tocqueville and Liebling notwithstanding, freedom of the press in democratic societies is a nearly unchallengeable dogma – essential, it is thought, to individual autonomy and self-expression, and an indispensable element in democracy and the attainment of truth. Both its eloquent theoreticians and its contemporary popular advocates defend freedom of speech and freedom of the press in the same stroke, with the implication that they are inseparable, probably equivalent, and equally fundamental.

At the same time, we know that the press in its most characteristic modern incarnation – mass media in mass society – works not only to enhance the flow of ideas and information but also to inhibit it. Nothing guarantees that all valuable information, ideas, theories, explanations, proposals, and points of view will find expression in the public forum.[iii] Indeed, many factors lead us to expect that they will not. The most obvious is that 'mass media space-time' is a scarce commodity: Only so much news, analysis, and editorial opinion can be aired in the major channels of mass communication. *Which* views get covered, and in what way, depends mainly on the economic and political structure and context of press institutions, and on the characteristics of the media themselves.

These are some of the most important factors: (1) More often than not, contemporary news organizations belong to large corporations whose interests influence what gets covered (and, what is probably more central, what does not) and how.[iv] (2) News organizations are driven economically to capture the largest possible audience, and thus not to turn it off with whatever does turn it off – coverage that is too controversial, too demanding, too disturbing.[v] (3) The media are easily manipulated by government officials (and others), for whom the press, by simply reporting press releases and official statements, can be a virtually unfiltered mouthpiece. (4) Characteristics of the media themselves constrain or influence coverage; thus, for example, television lends itself to an action-oriented, unanalytical treatment of events that can distort their meaning or importance.

It is not surprising, therefore, that a great range of opinion and analysis outside the narrow mainstream rarely sees the light of the mass media. This lack of diversity manifests itself in two ways. One is simply lack of adequate exposure to information and ideas that are true or interesting or useful, that help us to understand the world better or make life more satisfactory

---

[54] Cm 6810, 1977, para 2.2.

in one way or another. The range of views considered respectable enough to appear regularly in the American mass media is extraordinarily narrow.[vi] As a result, we are more ignorant and more provincial than we could be, and we may be worse off in other ways as well.

The other consequence more directly concerns justice. The press, once thought of as an antidote to established power, is more likely to reinforce it, because access to the press – that is, the mass media – is distributed as unequally as are other forms of power. It is not, of course, that the less powerful never speak in the mass media or that their doings are never reported, or never sympathetically. But the deck is stacked against them, because the press is itself a formidable power in our society, allied intimately (although not simply) with other formidable powers. Displacing the attention of the media from the usual sources of news – the words and deeds of public officials and public figures – often demands nothing less than the politics of theater, for which those using such tactics may also be blamed.[vii] . . .

        . . .

I believe that we have misunderstood what a modern democratic society's commitment to freedom of the press means and should be. Unlike freedom of speech, to certain aspects of which our commitment must be virtually unconditional, freedom of the press should be contingent on the degree to which it promotes certain values at the core of our interest in freedom of expression generally. Freedom of the press, in other words, is an instrumental good: It is good if it does certain things and not especially good (not good enough to justify special protections, anyway) otherwise. If, for example, the mass media tend to suppress diversity and impoverish public debate, the arguments meant to support freedom of the press turn against it, and we may rightly consider regulating the media to achieve the ultimate purposes of freedom of the press.

[i]   vol. 1, chap. 11.

[ii]   (New York: Ballantine Books, 1964), pp. 30–1.

[iii]   This formulation is neat, but misleading. Viewed in purely quantitative terms, information is plentiful; indeed, the problem is that we are flooded with it and must take measures to stem the tide. When we are talking about enhancing or inhibiting the flow of ideas and information, then, we are thinking about quality and diversity, not mere quantity. Our concern is that we find less diversity in the mass media than we could and should, and than we found in the absence of *mass* media altogether.

[iv]   See, e.g., Ben Bagdikian, *The Media Monopoly* (Boston: Beacon, 1983), esp. chap. 3; Tom Goldstein, *The News at any Cost* (New York: Simon & Schuster, 1985), chap. 5; Peter Dreier and Steve Weinberg, 'Interlocking Directorates,' *Columbia Journalism Review* (November–December 1979).

[v]   For an extensively illustrated discussion of this and the third factor, see Jeffrey Abramson, 'Four Criticisms of Press Ethics,' this volume.

[vi]   As compared, for example, with the European press . . .

[vii]   Especially for a nonjournalist, specifying what of importance is not reported is fraught with paradox because it requires independent access to news sources. How do you know what is news except by following the usual sources? . . .

It may follow from Lichtenberg's argument that it is legitimate to regulate the media to foster the value of media pluralism and other values such as transparency and openness associated with the fundamental right to freedom of speech (or expression).[55] For example, it suggests that limits should be imposed on the freedom of press proprietors to own a number of newspapers and on the freedom of broadcasting companies to acquire controlling shares in other channels; too great a concentration of media ownership might mean that readers or viewers no longer had access to a range of different sources of information and opinion – the value of media pluralism, as it is generally known.[56]

[55] Also see E.M. Barendt, 'Press and broadcasting freedom; does anyone have any rights to free speech?' [1991] 44 *Current Legal Problems* 63, at 64–67, and Barendt, 419–24.

[56] For an excellent discussion of the values underlying media pluralism, see R. Craufurd-Smith and D. Tambini, 'Measuring media plurality in the United Kingdom: policy choices and regulatory challenges' [2012] *Journal of Media Law* 35, 36–41.

Regulation to protect media pluralism may therefore be necessary to protect freedom of expression, even though it inhibits the freedom of media owners to expand their business. Indeed, in a recent major ruling the Grand Chamber of the European Court of Human Rights has held states have a positive obligation to guarantee effective pluralism in the audiovisual media sector, particularly where the national broadcasting, as in Italy, is characterised by an effective duopoly.[57]

Questions for discussion

1. This section has outlined three perspectives on media freedom: that it is identical to freedom of expression; that it confers separate rights for owners and editors; and that it is an 'instrumental good'. Which of these perspectives on media freedom do you agree with, and why?
2. On Lichtenberg's perspective, would it be legitimate to legislate for rights of reply to personal attacks in the press and broadcasting media? Or more radically for rights of access to publish or present articles or programmes which balance the coverage of the newspaper/television channel?
3. On her perspective, does the case for differential treatment of the press and broadcasting media collapse? Should the press be regulated in much the same way as broadcasters?

1.5 THE INTERNET AND MEDIA REGULATION

We should now consider the impact of the Internet on media law and regulation. Although some forms of communication on the Net – emails and small discussion groups – cannot be equated with the traditional mass media, others such as the BBC and other much visited websites, the online versions of newspapers, and videos and other television-like material transmitted over the Net may be. For many people they are an important source of news and entertainment, as are social media such as Facebook and Twitter. There are two fundamental questions, although many others are treated in books on Internet law and regulation, notably how particular areas of law such as copyright or defamation law apply to the Net.[58] The first major issue is how, if at all, the Internet is to be regulated – in particular, should it be subject to special regulation comparable to that to which broadcasting is subject, or should it, like the press, be subject only to the general criminal and civil law, perhaps modified to take account of its characteristics.[59] The second question is whether the advent of the Net has implications for the coherence of the existing law governing the traditional mass media. It may make no sense to continue with a special regime for the broadcasting media (see Section 1.3) in an era of media convergence, when programmes can be transmitted over the Net and received on personal computers.

---

[57] Application no 38433/09, *Centro Europa 7 SRL v Italy*, Decision of 7 July 2012, para 134.
[58] For example, A. Murray, *Information Technology Law* (Oxford: OUP, 2010), and L. Edwards and C. Waelde (eds), *Law and the Internet* (Oxford: Hart Publishing, 3rd edn, 2009).
[59] J. Rowbottom, 'To rant, vent and converse: protecting low level digital speech' (2012) 71 *Cambridge Law Journal* 355 discusses how freedom of expression principles and the criminal and libel law should be applied to casual speech on the Net.

Some commentators used to argue that the Internet should not for reasons of principle, and technically could not easily, be regulated by systems of national law.[60] This Cyber-libertarian creed is no longer commonly held. Governments can, and do, control access to the Net and impose restrictions on what can lawfully be communicated on it.[61] It may be difficult for a national legal system to impose effective controls, when, say, anonymous bloggers put their messages up on websites subject to another jurisdiction, but it is not impossible.[62] There is also general agreement that controls are necessary, for example, over the dissemination by Internet of incitement to terrorism, child pornography, and some extreme obscenity. However, there is disagreement over the application of other areas of law, for example, defamation law, to communications on the Net. In the United States Internet Service Providers (ISPs) and other facilitators of communication cannot be sued for libel, because Congress wanted to encourage freedom of expression on the Net.[63]

In an early seminal ruling on the legal status of the Internet, the US Supreme Court held unconstitutional provisions of the Communications Decency Act of 1996 (CDA), which penalised the communication over the Net of 'indecent' or 'patently offensive' material to persons under the age of 18. In its view these vague provisions would inevitably curtail the freedom of expression right of adults to view sexually explicit material. In its argument the government relied on previous rulings of the Court in which it had upheld broadcasting regulation.

Extract 1.5.1
Reno v American Civil Liberties Union, 521 US 844, 867–70 (1997) (footnote omitted)

In *Southeastern Promotions, Ltd.* v. *Conrad*, [1975] USSC 53; 420 U.S. 546, 557[1975] USSC 53; 95 S.Ct. 1239, 1245–1246, 43 L.Ed.2d 448 (1975), we observed that '[e]ach medium of expression . . . may present its own problems'. Thus, some of our cases have recognized special justifications for regulation of the broadcast media that are not applicable to other speakers, see *Red Lion Broadcasting Co.* v. *FCC*, [1969] USSC 141; 395 U.S. 367, 89 S.Ct. 1794, 23 L.Ed.2d 371 (1969); *FCC* v. *Pacifica Foundation*, [1978] USSC 176; 438 U.S. 726, 98 S.Ct. 3026, 57 L.Ed.2d 1073 (1978). In these cases, the Court relied on the history of extensive government regulation of the broadcast medium, see, *e.g., Red Lion*, 395 U.S., at 399–400, 89 S.Ct., at 1811–1812; the scarcity of available frequencies at its inception, see, *e.g., Turner Broadcasting System, Inc.* v. *FCC*, [1994] USSC 47; 512 U.S. 622, 637–638[1994] USSC 47; 114 S.Ct. 2445, 2456–2457[1994] USSC 47; 129 L.Ed.2d 497 (1994); and its 'invasive' nature, see *Sable Communications of Cal., Inc.* v. *FCC*, [1989] USSC 139; 492 U.S. 115, 128[1989] USSC 139; 109 S.Ct. 2829, 2837–2838[1989] USSC 139; 106 L.Ed.2d 93 (1989).

Those factors are not present in cyberspace. Neither before nor after the enactment of the CDA have the vast democratic fora of the Internet been subject to the type of government supervision and regulation that has attended the broadcast industry. Moreover, the Internet is not as 'invasive' as radio or television. The District Court specifically found that '[c]ommunications over the Internet do not "invade" an individual's home or appear on one's computer screen unbidden. Users seldom encounter content by accident".' 929 F.Supp., at 844 (finding 88). It also found that '[a]lmost all sexually explicit images are preceded by warnings as to the content',

---

[60] For the classic exposition of this view, see D. Johnson and D. Post, 'Law and borders: the rise of law in cyberspace' (1996) 48 *Stanford Law Review* 1367.
[61] See J. Goldsmith and T. Wu, *Who Controls the Internet?* (New York: OUP, 2006).
[62] A. Murray and C. Scott, 'Controlling the new media: hybrid responses to new forms of power' (2002) 65 *Modern Law Review* 491.
[63] Communications Decency Act of 1996, s 230. See Chapter 10, Section 3(c)(iv) for discussion of this issue in English law.

and cited testimony that 'odds are slim' that a user would come across a sexually explicit sight 'by accident.' Ibid.

We distinguished *Pacifica* in *Sable*, 492 U.S., at 128, 109 S.Ct., at 2837–2838, on just this basis. In *Sable*, a company engaged in the business of offering sexually oriented prerecorded telephone messages (popularly known as 'dial-a-porn') challenged the constitutionality of an amendment to the Communications Act that imposed a blanket prohibition on indecent as well as obscene interstate commercial telephone messages. We held that the statute was constitutional in so far as it applied to obscene messages but invalid as applied to indecent messages. In attempting to justify the complete ban and criminalization of indecent commercial telephone messages, the Government relied on *Pacifica*, arguing that the ban was necessary to prevent children from gaining access to such messages. We agreed that 'there is a compelling interest in protecting the physical and psychological well-being of minors' which extended to shielding them from indecent messages that are not obscene by adult standards, 492 U.S., at 126, 109 S.Ct., at 2836–2837, but distinguished our 'emphatically narrow holding' in *Pacifica* because it did not involve a complete ban and because it involved a different medium of communication, *id.*, at 127, 109 S.Ct., at 2837. We explained that 'the dial-it medium requires the listener to take affirmative steps to receive the communication'. *Id.*, at 127–128, 109 S.Ct., at 2837. 'Placing a telephone call', we continued, 'is not the same as turning on a radio and being taken by surprise by an indecent message'. *Id.*, at 128, 109 S.Ct., at 2837.

Finally, unlike the conditions that prevailed when Congress first authorised regulation of the broadcast spectrum, the Internet can hardly be considered a 'scarce' expressive commodity. It provides relatively unlimited, low-cost capacity for communication of all kinds. The Government estimates that '[a]s many as 40 million people use the Internet today, and that figure is expected to grow to 200 million by 1999'. This dynamic, multifaceted category of communication includes not only traditional print and news services, but also audio, video, and still images, as well as interactive, real-time dialogue. Through the use of chat rooms, any person with a phone line can become a town crier with a voice that resonates farther than it could from any soapbox. Through the use of Web pages, mail exploders, and newsgroups, the same individual can become a pamphleteer. As the District Court found, 'the content on the Internet is as diverse as human thought'. 929 F.Supp., at 842 (finding 74). We agree with its conclusion that our cases provide no basis for qualifying the level of First Amendment scrutiny that should be applied to this medium.

This reasoning is open to criticism.[64] On one view the Internet is just as invasive as broadcasting in exposing vulnerable people to indecent or other unsuitable material; the fact that it requires a minimal effort and skill to log on hardly justifies the different treatment of the two media. The Court appeared for the most part to rely on historical arguments to explain why broadcasting has uniquely been subject to special controls, but that does not *justify* the immunity from comparable regulation of similar material on the Net.

Another perspective is provided in the judgments of the High Court of Australia in *Dow Jones and Company* v *Gutnick*, when it held that the courts in Victoria had jurisdiction over a libel action brought by a business man, resident and domiciled there, in respect of defamatory allegations uploaded by the appellant on a website in New Jersey; further the courts could apply the law of Victoria, the place where the allegations had been published. The libel law aspects of this important ruling are discussed in Chapter 10; the point to bring out here is that the High Court rejected the argument that the law should be refashioned to take account of the new means of communication provided by the Internet.

---

[64] See M. Price, 'The newness of new technology' (2000–1) 22 *Cardozo Law Review* 1885, 1904–12.

Extract 1.5.2
Dow Jones and Company, Inc v *Gutnick* **(2002) 210 CLR 575, [2002] HCA 56, paras 86–9, 123–5 (footnotes omitted)**

KIRBY J:

86. In addition to these difficulties of controlling access to a website by reference to geographic, national and subnational boundaries, the Internet has recently witnessed a rapid growth of technologies ('anonymising technologies') that enable Internet users to mask their identities (and locations). By reason of these developments, the provision of cost effective, practical and reliable identity verification systems, that could afford a universally reliable recognition of the point of origin of an Internet user, has not emerged. This is why the nature of Internet technology itself makes it virtually impossible, or prohibitively difficult, cumbersome and costly, to prevent the content of a given website from being accessed in specific legal jurisdictions when an Internet user in such jurisdictions seeks to do so. In effect, once information is posted on the Internet, it is usually accessible to all Internet users everywhere in the world. Even if the correct jurisdiction of an Internet user could be ascertained accurately, there is presently no adequate technology that would enable non-subscription content providers to isolate and exclude all access to all users in specified jurisdictions.

87. These special features of the Internet present peculiar difficulties for the legal regulation of its content and, specifically, for the exclusion of access in defined jurisdictions. Such difficulties may have a bearing on the question of whether a particular jurisdiction has an advantage in regulating content published and accessed on the Internet . . . This does not mean (and no party before the Court suggested) that the Internet is, or should be, a law-free zone. However, in considering what the law, and specifically the common law of Australia, should say in relation to the contents of the Internet, particularly with respect to allegedly defamatory material on a website, the appellant argued that regard had to be taken of these elementary practical features of the technology.

88. *Novel features of the Web*: The crucial attributes, so it was said, include the explosion in the availability of readily accessible information to hundreds of millions of people everywhere, with the consequent enhancement of human knowledge, and the beneficial contribution to human freedom and access to information about the world's peoples and their diverse lives and viewpoints that the Internet makes available, thereby contributing to human understanding. It was argued that the law should generally facilitate and encourage such advances, not attempt to restrict or impede them by inconsistent and ineffective, or only partly effective, interventions, for fear of interrupting the benefit that the Internet has already brought and the greater benefits that its continued expansion promises.

89. This Court has made reference to the fact that modern development in mass communications and particularly the electronic media may influence the continued relevance or reformulation of established legal principles. The appellant contested the respondent's suggestion that the Internet was merely the latest of many technologies that have enhanced the spread of information. It submitted that the Internet involved a quantum leap of technological capacity and the ubiquitous availability of information that demanded a root and branch revision of some of the earlier legal rules in order to take into account the Internet's special features.

. . .

123. *Limits to judicial innovation*: The foregoing considerations present a persuasive argument for the formulation of a new rule of the common law that is particular to the publication of allegedly defamatory matter on the Internet. For myself, I do not regard them as mere slogans. They present a serious legal issue for decision. Judges have adapted the common law to new technology in the past. The rules of private international law have emerged as a result of, and remain alive to, changes in the means of trans-border communication between people. The Internet's potential impact on human affairs continues to expand and is already enormous. Later

judges, in a position to do so, can sometimes reformulate the law in order to keep it relevant and just. Specifically they may re-express judge-made rules that suit earlier times and different technologies. For a number of reasons I have concluded that this Court would not be justified to change the rules of the Australian common law as would be necessary in this case to respond to the submissions of the appellant.

124. First, a starting point for the consideration of the submission must be an acceptance that the principles of defamation law invoked by the respondent are settled and of long standing. Those principles are: (1) that damage to reputation is essential for the existence of the tort of defamation; (2) that mere composition and writing of words is not enough to constitute the tort; those words must be communicated to a third party who comprehends them; (3) that each time there is such a communication, the plaintiff has a new cause of action; and (4) that a publisher is liable for publication in a particular jurisdiction where that is the intended or natural and probable consequence of its acts. Where rules such as these are deeply entrenched in the common law and relate to the basic features of the cause of action propounded, their alteration risks taking the judge beyond the proper limits of the judicial function.

125. *Rules should be technology-neutral*: Whilst the Internet does indeed present many novel technological features, it also shares many characteristics with earlier technologies that have rapidly expanded the speed and quantity of information distribution throughout the world. I refer to newspapers distributed (and sometimes printed) internationally; syndicated telegraph and wire reports of news and opinion; newsreels and film distributed internationally; newspaper articles and photographs reproduced instantaneously by international telefacsimile; radio, including shortwave radio; syndicated television programmes; motion pictures; videos and digitalised images; television transmission; and cable television and satellite broadcasting. Generally speaking, it is undesirable to express a rule of the common law in terms of a particular technology. Doing so presents problems where that technology is itself overtaken by fresh developments. It can scarcely be supposed that the full potential of the Internet has yet been realised. The next phase in the global distribution of information cannot be predicted. A legal rule expressed in terms of the Internet might very soon be out of date.

The judgment of Gleeson CJ (and three other Justices) doubted whether the World Wide Web was significantly different from satellite broadcasting in its reach.[65] The decision in the *Dow Jones* case is the major common law authority (outside the USA) for the proposition that in the absence of statutory reform the Internet should not be treated more generously than the other media. It is for the legislature to decide whether and how to regulate the Internet, for example, to stop the dissemination of pornography or hate speech.

An important set of questions now concerns how the Net may be most effectively regulated without impairing the greater freedom of expression for individuals it has clearly promoted. It may be easier to regulate the conduct of ISPs by requiring them to take down illegal material on the Net than it is to penalise the conduct of its producers. Informal systems of self-regulation by ISPs may also be encouraged as an alternative to legal control.[66] Arguably the Internet should be lightly regulated because it enables individuals

---

[65] (2002) 210 CLR 575, para 39.
[66] See the excellent discussion of these techniques to limit the control the dissemination of pornography on the Net in M. Birnhack and J. Rowbottom, 'Shielding children: the European way' (2004) 79 *Chicago-Kent Law Review* 175.

as citizen-journalists to communicate their ideas, and provide information, including important news developments, as an alternative to the traditional media. Moreover, the need for mass media regulation, in particular the special regulation of the broadcasting media, is open to question in view of the opportunities for individuals to 'compete' with the mass media as news providers. Jacob Rowbottom addressed these issues in the article from which the next extract is taken. In the pages before the extract he argued that the Internet is dominated by elite players, for example, much-visited websites such as those of the BBC and the most popular newspapers, and search engines, notably Google.

Extract 1.5.3
J. Rowbottom, 'Media freedom and political debate in the digital era' (2006) 69
Modern Law Review **489, 508–12 (footnotes omitted)**

This article has focused on the way the established media, influential websites and search engines help determine the success of online expression in reaching a wide audience. A range of other private actors also impact on the opportunities for online expression, including software companies that produce user-friendly applications, ISPs and non-state regulators such as ICANN [the body which oversees domain name registration]. Instead of eliminating the chance of private barriers to expression, digital technologies can increase the range of potential barriers. Regulation should not be ruled out, if it can help facilitate democratic expression by controlling the private power and should not automatically be prohibited by the courts. The stricter regulations associated with the broadcast model of regulation need not be rejected, but may require adaptation to some online communications if it would serve the values of freedom of expression. The difficulty is defining the boundaries between the tier of mass media entities and the tier of smaller speakers and forums outlined above.

   One approach may be to find that those entities already subject to media regulations offline be subject to similar regulations online. Under this approach, the current terrestrial broadcasters would be subject to their public service duties on online, and other licensed broadcasters would have to meet the basic tier of broadcast regulations online. Such a strategy reflects the current approach and is only likely to be workable in the short-term. As the media technologies converge and more people watch programmes online it will be possible for companies and groups to distribute audiovisual programmes solely through online channels. If such newcomers gain a significant share of the audience, then it may undermine the purpose of the current regulations, as a wide range of online content similar to that found on the broadcast media will command a mass audience but remain exempt from the regulations. Furthermore, as is currently the case with cable television, the licensed broadcaster will argue that they need to be less regulated to compete with the other unregulated outlets. If such a relaxation of the regulations is not possible, then the regulated broadcaster may find that it is in their long term interests to distribute their content through the lesser-regulated online channels, in other words to opt-out of the broadcast sector. An alternative strategy could be to subject certain types of content to a particular regulatory regime. For example, the regulations applied to broadcasters could apply solely to audiovisual content. Initially this may seem appealing as it fits with current audience expectations, but it does beg the question why audiovisual content should be subject to stricter controls. Given the relative inexpense of video and audio equipment and software, audiovisual content will be used by many individuals, such as videobloggers, and not solely by media elites.

   The boundary could be drawn instead between commercial and amateur entities. This could still cause difficulties, for example, a company website or content produced by an interest group should not be equated with mass media, nor should a small scale website that makes a small amount of income on advertising. It may be necessary to target those online speakers that are commercial and whose primary content is the provision of media, whether as an aggregator or provider, and which has a particular share of the market or turnover. Distinguishing the sphere of regulated mass media from other types of communication has parallels in existing law. For example, in media merger rules, newspapers are distinguished from other types of communication by reference to the frequency and content of the publication. Similarly elections laws distinguish newspaper and broadcaster reports from the communications of political campaigners, exempting the former from third party expenditure limits. Distinguishing online media outlets that are the equivalent of modern day mass media may not be a clear cut task, but has a precedent in the UK.

A further difficulty with regulating online media entities is the global nature of the Internet. The requirements of UK democracy should not be imposed on media outlets based abroad and targeting a different country, yet Internet users are still free to access this content. This raises a situation similar to that of cable television where foreign broadcasts, such as Fox News and Al-Jazeera, are thought to be straining the regulations applied to licensed broadcasts. Furthermore, European Union law imposes restraints on the capacity to regulate media providers based outside jurisdiction. Given the global environment of the media, traditional rules of impartiality and accuracy are being increasingly questioned, a trend that is likely to increase in relation to the online media. However, it would still be possible to single out those media entities whose content is targeted at an audience within jurisdiction, especially in relation to the coverage of news and politics. Those outlets focusing on UK based news are most likely to command a broad audience in the UK, and are unlikely to face greater competition from outlets covering the news and politics of a different country. In any event, as outlined below, some more partisan media content from abroad may be unproblematic, but simply should not represent the whole media landscape. The global context also raises issues of enforcement and the possibility of evasion. However, it is likely that those sites that are the equivalent of mass media would want to maintain a base in the UK, for example for its reporters or advertising, and are likely to conform to such national rules. Furthermore, the development of geographical location technology may also make it possible to limit the dissemination of material to and from foreign countries. A full consideration of the problem of jurisdiction and enforcement is beyond the scope of this paper. The point is merely that the global nature of online expression does not eliminate the role for the regulation of certain media entities to serve the broader needs of democracy.

If it can be established that such media entities may be the subject of regulation, it still raises the question of what regulations are necessary to serve democratic needs. So far reference has been made to broadcast media regulations for impartiality and balance in political coverage, but such regulations are not imposed on the print press. It may be argued that partisan online content serves democratic needs in the same way the partisan press does. This need will probably be found with many speakers on the new media, such as bloggers or interest group sites. While it is important, such partisan content associated with the print model need not be the norm for all online content. Rather than reflecting one model of democratic expression, the regulated tier of online expression could be designed to permit different regulatory regimes. Prior to the prominence of the Internet, Lee Bollinger argued that the different regulatory regimes for print and broadcast media are justified by balancing one another. Similarly, James Curran [in *Media and Power* (London, Routledge, 2002)] has advocated different media sectors serving separate democratic needs. The regulation of the new media could be designed to promote the various different functions of the media in a democracy, with different elements of the print and broadcast model to be found in different media sectors. Some areas of the web, such as original news reporting and the largest gatekeeper sites, could reflect the republican concern with balance, impartiality, and differing viewpoints, while some elements of a partisan media reflecting the liberal pluralist approach could be permitted in commentary sites such as blogs. However, even in a sector that recognises the importance of partisan content, different points of view need to be accessed and the various gatekeepers referred to above may need to act to promote access to diverse opinions. It would be unsatisfactory if the only partisan sites that could easily be found online all supported the same perspective, whether left or right.

If regulations to promote impartiality, balance, accuracy, and quality content associated with the public service function of the media are applicable to some online media, then a further question arises as to how best to achieve these aims. One method has been to propose state funded websites to act as civic forums. This approach represents an attempt by the state to set up an elite site of its own that will promote democratic values and reflect a public service rationale, rather than constraining private entities. The danger with setting up such a website purely for political debate is that it may draw few visitors. With such a wide range of options, people are more likely to go to the sites that are most entertaining. Possibly the most successful example of this type of site is the BBC, which has regularly been praised for its online services. It attracts many visitors, not just because of its well-known name, but also its wide range of content, such as entertainment or sports pages. However, dangers exist in placing all public interest requirements on one media entity. A variation of the public service site is the proposal by Blumler and Coleman [in *Realizing Democracy Online: A Civic Commons in Cyberspace* (London: IPPR, 2001)] of a public agency to promote and publicise online deliberation. The agency would act as a gatekeeper to some online expression, be the moderator of discussion and help facilitate the interaction of civic networks online. Such a role could be allocated to the Public Service Publisher that has been proposed by Ofcom to promote and distribute content on digital television and through broadband that fulfils public service requirement. As above, the danger with such an agency is that its success would be dependent on regular use and interest from the public.

For as long as the BBC remains the most popular website in the UK, the public service model will partly define political expression online by shaping user expectations. For example, current broadcast regulations on news coverage create an expectation, so that a blatantly partisan audiovisual news bulletin would have little credibility with those accustomed to the norms of impartiality and balance. However, as greater convergence with the technologies occurs and significant developments in what can be done continue, the BBC site may face greater competition in future years and may lose its share of the market. As, and if, this occurs, then some regulation of privately run sites may be necessary to ensure the system of expression and media reflects our democratic values. This may include the types of proposal such as rights to reply or must carry rules, as outlined by Sunstein. Rules could be introduced to require some content providers to provide balance and impartial political coverage, as well as access for political parties at election times. In addition incentives could be designed to promote the production of educational and cultural content. The search engines and other gatekeepers could be encouraged to give priority to the impartial/balanced news providers and ensure that the access to partisan content does not give disproportionate emphasis to one slant or viewpoint. These goals could be achieved not only through legal direction in some cases, but through codes of practice, possibly drawn up by Ofcom, or through subsidy and tax relief for those fulfilling these goals.

The approaches outlined above seek to regulate the use of existing technology to ensure the provision of particular types of expression, rather than determine what it is possible to do online. However, there may be other areas of online technology that can promote democratic goals. As Balkin points out [in 'Digital speech and democratic culture' (2004) 79 *New York University Law Review*, 1, 52] the design and architecture of the digital technology must also be considered as a possible area of regulation. This area of regulation could be used to benefit the small scale speakers discussed above. An important element of free expression is the development of user-friendly applications that make media production possible for those with minimal technical expertise and fewer resources. Promoting such applications could serve the goal of public service regulations to encourage widespread participation in politics and media production. An approach to media regulation that also considers issues of design and architecture will help to promote expression at all the different tiers described above.

Questions for discussion

1. Should the Internet be immune from the special regulation to which the broadcasting media are subject?
2. Do you agree with Kirby J's view in *Dow Jones* that in principle the law should treat the Internet in much the same way as other media?
3. Is Rowbottom right to conclude that some regulation of the Net is justified to promote open political debate?

1.6 CENSORSHIP AND PRIOR RESTRAINTS

Blackstone and Dicey defined press freedom in terms of the absence of prior restraints: see Section 1.1. A newspaper or book publisher might be liable to a criminal prosecution or civil action for damages in respect of a work which has already been published, but pre-publication censorship is incompatible with the freedom.[67] It is objectionable since an official or committee is given authority, exercisable in private and on the basis of imprecise standards, to stop publication of a book or newspaper. In these circumstances, the public has no opportunity to debate the wisdom of its proscription. In contrast, a criminal trial or civil action does involve a publication which has seen the light of day; further, in principle liability can only be imposed if there is a clear breach of relevant legal standards.[68]

(a) Judicial prior restraints

There is no provision in English law for the licensing or official censorship of newspapers and other printed media. However, in some circumstances the courts may grant an injunction to prevent a publication, on the ground, for example, that it would amount to a breach of confidence or contempt of court. In these cases there is a *judicial* prior restraint, which can be contrasted with the absence of provision for *administrative* censorship. The former is a less serious infringement of press freedom than the latter, since there is at least an opportunity to contest the grant of an injunction in open proceedings before an impartial tribunal.[69] The courts are very reluctant to grant interim relief to restrain publication of material alleged to be defamatory: see Section 10.5. On the other hand, they have been more willing to prevent publication by the media of confidential or personal information, and so protect privacy. The point is that once personal information, for example, about intimate sexual or family matters has been published, privacy is lost, so a judicial prior restraint may be the only effective remedy.

We return to this issue after briefly examining the position under the European Convention and a provision in the HRA which makes it more difficult than it used to be to obtain an interim injunction against the media. The compatibility of prior restraints with the ECHR was considered by the European Court of Human Rights when two newspapers complained that injunctions granted against them on the basis of breach of confidence to prevent publication of allegations made in a book, *Spycatcher*, violated

---

[67] See Robertson and Nicol, paras 1-020–1-025, for the view that the rule against prior restraints is a fundamental principle of media law, albeit one which is far from absolute in practice.

[68] For fuller discussion, see Barendt, 118–24.

[69] Ibid., 124–8. The European Human Rights Court has ruled that an administrative ban on the circulation of a foreign book could not be justified under ECHR, art 10(2) in the absence of prompt and effective judicial review of the decision: *Association Ekin v France* (2005) 35 EHRR 1207.

article 10 of the Convention.[70] The Court held that the maintenance of these injunctions after the time when the book became available in the USA could not be justified, as the allegations then ceased to be confidential.

Extract 1.6.1
The Observer and The Guardian v United Kingdom (1992) 14 EHRR 153, at 191
(European Court of Human Rights) (footnote omitted)

For the avoidance of doubt . . . the Court would only add to the foregoing that Article 10 of the Convention does not in terms prohibit the imposition of prior restraints on publication, as such. This is evidenced not only by the words 'conditions', 'restrictions', 'preventing' and 'prevention' which appear in that provision, but also by the SUNDAY TIMES judgment of 26 April 1979[71] and its MARKT INTERN VERLAG GmbH AND KLAUS BEERMAN judgment of 20 November 1988.[i] On the other hand, the dangers inherent in prior restraints are such that they call for the most careful scrutiny on the part of the Court. This is especially so as far as the press is concerned, for news is a perishable commodity and to delay its publication, even for a short period, may well deprive it of all its value and interest.

[i] MARKT INTERN VERLAG AND BEERMAN V GERMANY (1990) 12 EHRR 161 [where the Court upheld the grant of an injunction by the German courts to restrain breach of unfair competition law.]

However, five members of the Court said that prior restraints on publication, whether administrative or judicial, permanent or temporary, could never be justified outside wartime and national emergency.[72]

(b) Human Rights Act 1998

As discussed in Section 1.2, the HRA has incorporated the rights guaranteed by the European Convention on Human Rights into UK law, so courts will be required to consider their significance for media law. As a result of the press anxiety about the implications of incorporation, in particular of the Convention right to respect for private life (see Chapter 11), the measure was amended to ensure that courts paid particular regard to freedom of expression. A key provision has already been set out (Extract 1.2.5); others limit the availability of interim relief against the media.

Extract 1.6.2
Human Rights Act 1998, s 12(1)–(3)

12.— (1) This section applies if a court is considering whether to grant any relief which, if granted, might affect the exercise of the Convention right to freedom of expression.
(2) If the person against whom the application for relief is made ('the respondent') is neither present nor represented, no such relief is to be granted unless the court is satisfied—
  (a) that the applicant has taken all practicable steps to notify the respondent; or
  (b) that there are compelling reasons why the respondent should not be notified.
(3) No such relief is to be granted so as to restrain publication before trial unless the court is satisfied that the applicant is likely to establish that publication should not be allowed.

[70] The grant of interlocutory injunctions (now interim injunctions) had been approved by a majority of the House of Lords (*Attorney General v Guardian Newspapers* [1987] 1 WLR 1248), but the House subsequently refused permanent injunctions: *Attorney General v Guardian Newpapers (No 2)* [1990] 1 AC 109, discussed in Chapter 11, Section 11.4.
[71] (1979–80) 2 EHRR 245: see Extract 1.2.2.
[72] This was also the view of two members of the Supreme Court in the leading modern US case on prior restraint: *New York Times v US*, 403 US 713 (1971).

The effect of section 12(2) has been to make it harder to obtain an interim injunction against the media without an opportunity for them to contest its grant. Under section 12(3) courts are directed not to grant relief unless they are satisfied that a claimant's case is likely to succeed on full trial.[73] In *Greene* v *Associated Newspapers*,[74] the Court of Appeal held that this provision did not affect the strict common law principle classically stated in *Bonnard* v *Perryman*[75] that a prior restraint will not be granted in libel proceedings, unless it is clear that no defence could succeed at full trial. The extract from the Court of Appeal's judgment brings out the reasons for the hostility to prior restraints in this context, and contrasts the legal position with that in confidentiality and other cases.

Extract 1.6.3
***Greene* v *Associated Newspapers Ltd* [2004] EWCA Civ 1462, [2005] QB 972, paras 74–7, 78**

BROOKE LJ:
74. If a claimant were able to stop a defendant from exercising its ECHR Article 10 right merely by arguing on paper-based evidence that it was more likely than not that the defendant could not show that what it wished to say about the claimant was true, it would seriously weaken the effect of Article 10. In *The Observer and The Guardian* v *UK* (1992) 14 EHRR 153 the court at Strasbourg said (at para 60):
  . . . '[T]he dangers inherent in prior restraint are such that they call for the most careful scrutiny on the part of the Court. This is especially so as far as the press is concerned, for news is a perishable commodity and to delay its publication, even for a short period, may well deprive it of all its value and interest.'

75. Scoops, as Mr Caldecott [counsel for the newspaper] observed, are the lifeblood of the newspaper industry. He might have added that stale news is no news at all. If Mr Spearman [counsel for the claimant] was correct, people with a fair reputation they do not deserve could stifle public criticism by obtaining injunctions simply because on necessarily incomplete information a court thought it more likely than not that they would defeat a defence of justification at the trial.

. . .

78. In cases involving confidential documents, the confidentiality of the documents will be lost completely if an injunction against disclosure is not granted when appropriate. In cases involving national security, great damage may similarly be done if an injunction is not granted when appropriate. In a defamation action, on the other hand, while some damage may be done by permitting the publication of what may later turn out to be false, everyone knows that it is at the trial that truth or falsehood will be tested and the claimant vindicated if the defendant cannot prove that the sting of the libel is justified or that he has some other defence the law will recognise. The damage that may on occasion be done by refusing an injunction where a less strict rule would facilitate its grant pales into insignificance compared with the damage which would be done to freedom of expression and the freedom of the press if the rule in *Bonnard* v *Perryman* was relaxed.

The significance of these principles for the laws of defamation and privacy are considered further in Chapters 10 and 11.

---

[73] For discussion of *Cream Holdings* v *Banerjee* [2004] 4 All ER 617, the leading ruling on the interpretation of section 12(3), see Chapter 11, Section 11.4(f)(i).
[74] [2004] EWCA Civ 1462, [2005] QB 972.
[75] [1891] 2 Ch 269, CA.

Questions for discussion

1. Do the arguments against administrative censorship apply as strongly to Court injunctions?
2. In what circumstances, if any, might it be reasonable for a court to impose a prior restraint on publication of a newspaper, magazine or book?
3. Are you persuaded by Brooke LJ that the courts should be much less willing to grant prior restraints in defamation than in confidentiality cases?

(c) Films, video, and broadcasting

Theatre censorship was finally abolished when the Theatres Act 1968 removed the power of the Lord Chamberlain to ban or demand cuts in stage plays. However, films, radio and television, and videos have all been subject to various censorship schemes. While pre-transmission censorship has been abolished for broadcasting, it remains for cinema films and for videos. By statute local authorities must impose restrictions prohibiting the admission of children to 'unsuitable' films, while they have a general power to impose conditions on the use of licensed cinemas.[76] In practice, these responsibilities are delegated to the British Board of Film Classification (BBFC), which classifies films on the basis of their suitability for various age groups. Local authorities, however, must retain power to take the final decision; occasionally they permit a film refused a certificate by the BBFC or, more often, prevent its exhibition in their area, although it may be available in a neighbouring area where the council takes a different view.[77]

The principle of film censorship was approved by the Williams Committee which was set up to examine the law of obscenity and film censorship.

Extract 1.6.4
Report of the Williams Committee on Obscenity and Film Censorship, Cmnd 7772 (1979), paras 12.1–12.2, 12.7–12.8, 12.11

12.1. The effect of the [censorship] system is broadly that what is regarded as objectionable, for reasons only partly connected with what the law prohibits, is never allowed to gain a showing in a public cinema, so that those who are responsible for enforcing the laws on obscenity and indecency on a 'subsequent punishment' basis scarcely have to concern themselves with investigating whether the law is being broken. The system therefore combines prior restraint with extra-legal control . . .

12.2. Despite the system's haphazard origins and despite the fact that this style of control is in this country peculiar to the cinema, it has many friends and few enemies. It has operated for a long time with a remarkable degree of public acceptance. Objections of principle to any idea of pre-censorship have to a large extent been suspended in favour of film censorship. It has undoubtedly been an effective system, both making it fairly certain what cinemas can legally show and under what conditions, and providing fairly watertight procedures to ensure that the rules are kept . . .

---

[76] See now the Cinemas Act 1985, s 1. For fuller treatment of film censorship, see Robertson and Nicol, paras 15-001–15-007, and 15-025–15-045.
[77] An example of this phenomenon was the ban by Westminster Council of West End cinemas showing David Cronenberg's film *Crash*; it was, however, shown in cinemas licensed by Camden and other London boroughs.

12.7. . . . We think that the aim of treating all the media uniformly is misconceived; there is no reason why one solution should be expected to apply equally to a series of different problems. That the problems are different we have no doubt at all. No one can dispute that reading a magazine, watching a live show and watching a film are three very different experiences. We suggest that it is sensible and reasonable to apply three different standards of control, and not to hope, unrealistically, that the same control can be stretched to cover all three.

12.8. This conclusion, in rejecting the argument for parity of treatment, removes one type of objection to accepting the pre-censorship of films. We are taken further towards accepting it by the facts that the major part of our evidence supported the continuation of film censorship, that the present system has, in the main, worked effectively and well and that most other countries appear to regard film censorship as acceptable and desirable. What clinched the argument for some of us at least was the sight of some of the films with which the censorship presently interferes. We feel it necessary to say to many people who express liberal sentiments about the principle of adult freedom to choose that we were totally unprepared for the sadistic material that some film makers are prepared to produce. We are not here referring to the explicit portrayal of sexual activity or to anything which simply attracts charges of offensiveness. Films that exploit a taste for torture and sadistic violence do raise further, and disturbing, questions.

. . .

12.11. . . . We freely admit . . . that we are in part encouraged to favour pre-censorship by the fact that it is what already exists. What we have to consider is, realistically, not whether we would institute a system of censorship if it were a novelty but whether we should abandon a functioning system; or rather, to put it more exactly, whether we should continue to use the system for the protection of young audiences (as almost all our witnesses considered necessary), but at the same time refuse to use the system to control films for adult viewing. We were very much impressed, moreover, by a different kind of argument. The impact of a film can depend on very subtle factors, which will not at all be caught by simple statements of what is being shown on the screen, and because of this the law is too inflexible an instrument through which to impose a control. An *ad hoc* judgment, grounded on certain guidelines, is a more efficient and sensitive way of controlling this medium. All these considerations together led us to the conclusion that films, even those shown to adults only, should continue to be censored.

However, the Committee did propose transferring statutory film censorship powers from local authorities to the BBFC. Its recommendation has never been adopted.

The BBFC does enjoy statutory powers over videos. It is the authority designated under the Video Recordings Act 1984 to determine whether they are suitable for the issue of a classification certificate, 'having special regard to the likelihood of video works in respect of which such certificates have been issued being viewed in the home'.[78] A refusal to grant a certificate in effect bans distribution; it is an offence to supply a video for which none has been issued.[79] There is a right of appeal from BBFC decisions to a Video Appeals Committee.

The BBFC refused to grant a certificate for a short video, *Visions of Ecstasy*, on the ground that it might be liable to a prosecution for blasphemy as offensive to Christians. It depicted the erotic arousal of a nun as she caressed the body of the crucified Christ. The majority of the European Court of Human Rights held the ban compatible with the Convention; Judge De Meyer dissented on the ground that it amounted to a prior restraint.

[78] Video Recordings Act 1984, s 4. For further discussion, see Robertson and Nicol, paras 15-008–15-020.
[79] Unless it is an 'exempted work', e.g. because it is designed to inform or educate, or it is concerned with sport, religion, or music: Video Recordings Act 1984, s 2.

Extract 1.6.5
Wingrove v United Kingdom **(1997) 24 EHRR 1, at 36–7 (dissent of Judge De Meyer)**
(footnotes omitted)

This was a pure case of prior restraint, a form of interference which is, in my view, unacceptable in the field of freedom of expression.

What I have written on that subject, with four other judges, in the OBSERVER AND GUARDIAN V THE UNITED KINGDOM case applies not only to the press, but also, *mutatis mutandis*, to other forms of expression, including video works.

It is quite legitimate that those wishing to supply video works be obliged to obtain from some administrative authority a classification certificate stating whether the works concerned may be supplied to the general public or only to persons who have attained a specified age, and whether, in the latter case, they are to be supplied only in certain places.

Of course, anything so decided by such authority needs reasonable justification and must not be arbitrary. It must, if contested, be subject to judicial review, and it must not have the effect of preventing the courts from deciding, as the case may be, whether the work concerned deserves, or does not deserve, any sanction under existing law.

Under the system established by the Video Recordings Act 1984 the British Board of Film Classification and the Video Appeals Committee may determine that certain video works are not suitable for being classified in any of its three categories, and they can thus ban them absolutely *ab initio*.

This was indeed what actually happened in respect of the piece at issue in the present case.

For reasons examined earlier in this chapter (Section 1.4), broadcasting is subject to special regulation. While broadcasting channels and programme services must be licensed, the regulatory authority, Ofcom, has no authority to preview or censor programmes before transmission.[80] On the other hand, the government does have power under the Communications Act 2003 to require Ofcom to direct broadcasting licensees to refrain from including any matter or type of matter in their schedules.[81] (It also has power to require Ofcom to direct them to include public service announcements – a power exercised during times of national crisis or emergency.[82])

In fact, the government has rarely used its censorship power. It did use it rather controversially in 1988 when it prohibited the BBC and the commercial channels from broadcasting the voices of members and supporters of terrorist organisations in Northern Ireland. In *R v Home Secretary, ex parte Brind* the House of Lords held this decision by the Home Secretary could not be regarded as unreasonable; it limited the freedom of terrorist supporters to communicate their views to the public through the most influential of the mass media. At that time the government was not required to consider whether the ban was compatible with the right to freedom of expression, now guaranteed by the HRA. The European Commission later held a complaint by Brind, a broadcasting journalist, inadmissible; in its view the ban was clearly justified under article 10(2) of the ECHR in the interests of national security and to prevent disorder. However, it was lifted in August 1994, and there has been no threat, so far as is known, that a government will exercise its

---

[80] The Independent Broadcasting Authority (IBA) used to have power to preview programmes, though it is unclear whether this amounted to censorship: see Barendt, *Broadcasting Law* (Oxford: OUP, 1995), 37–8. Under Broadcasting Act 1990, s 11(3) the Independent Television Commission (which replaced the IBA) did not have such power.

[81] Communications Act 2003, s 336(5). The Secretary of State has a similar 'censorship' power over the BBC under its Agreement: see Chapter 3.

[82] Communications Act 2003, s 336(1)–(2).

censorship powers on a subsequent occasion. However, the existence of the power may inhibit the freedom of the BBC and the commercial channels, which, it should be noted, did not themselves challenge its exercise in 1988. The power to ban a broadcast would clearly be unconstitutional in the USA as contrary to the First Amendment and would probably contravene article 5 of the German Basic Law (see Extract 1.1.1).

Questions for discussion

1. Could the UK film censorship system be challenged under the Human Rights Act 1998?
2. If the government were now to issue a broadcasting ban similar to that at issue in *Ex parte Brind*, could it be challenged successfully under the Human Rights Act 1998?

Selected further reading

Freedom of expression and the media

E. Barendt, *Freedom of Speech* (Oxford: OUP, 2007). Chapter 12 examines how freedom of speech principles apply to the mass media.

J. Lichtenberg, 'Foundations and limits of freedom of the press' in J. Lichtenberg (ed.), *Democracy and the Mass Media* (Cambridge: CUP, 1990) argues that press freedom is valuable as an instrumental right, that is, in so far only as it promotes the values of freedom of speech.

P. Stewart, 'Or of the press' (1975) 26 *Hastings Law Journal* 631 is the classic statement of the view that press freedom gives the media rights beyond those covered by freedom of speech/expression.

European Convention, HRA and the media

H. Fenwick and G. Phillipson, *Media Freedom Under the Human Rights Act* (Oxford: OUP, 2006). Chapters 2–3 provide a full analysis of the implications of the ECHR and HRA for media law.

The special regulation of broadcasting

L. Bollinger, 'Freedom of the press and public access: toward a theory of the partial regulation of the mass media' (1976) 75 *Michigan Law Review* 1–42 explains the different treatment of the mass media from an historical perspective.

T. Krattenmaker and L. Powe Jr, 'Converging first amendment principles for converging communications media' (1995) 104 *Yale Law Journal* 1719–41 argue there is no justification for any special regulation of broadcasting.

J. Weinberg, 'Broadcasting and speech' (1993) 81 *California Law Review* 1103–206 defends broadcasting regulation, while admitting that there are dangers to government intervention.

Regulation of the Internet

J. Balkin, 'Digital speech and democratic culture: a theory of freedom of expression for the information society' (2004) 79 *New York University Law Review* 1–58 argues that the Internet expands the opportunities for individuals to participate in public debate, without providing a substitute for the mass media.

A. Murray, *Information Technology Law* **(Oxford: OUP, 2010).** Chapters 4 and 6 discuss regulation of freedom of speech on the Internet.

J. Rowbottom, 'Media freedom and political debate in the digital era' (2006) 69 *Modern Law Review* **489–513** doubts whether the Internet undermines the arguments for media regulation.

2 Regulation of the press

2.1 INTRODUCTION

Essential to any working democracy is a free media. At least historically, this applies with particular force to freedom of the press: more so than any other media form, newspapers have been – and continue to be – committed to the important pursuit of keeping the citizenry informed and politically engaged, in addition to holding those who wield power to account by exposing government and corporate corruption and impropriety. As Jeremy Tunstall wrote in 1996:

> It is the newspapers, not television, which go for the politician's jugular. Typically it is the newspaper which first spills the politician's blood; only then does television swoop in for the action replay.[1]

Apart from the general law (i.e. defamation, privacy, contempt), the activities of the press are not subject to state regulation. Unlike broadcasting, for example, where state regulation is imposed on the basis that broadcasters use a scarce public resource (the radiofrequency spectrum) and that broadcasting, as a medium, is particularly invasive and influential, the operation of the press is not restricted in terms of access, content or influence. This, however, has not always been the case. It was only once the licensing system for the use of the printing press was abolished in 1695 that the press was free to publish newspapers without the permission of the state or the church. Even so, the last vestige of state control over newspapers did not cease until the mid-1800s with the abolition of the 'taxes on knowledge', a special tax imposed on newspaper sales.[2] This was said to mark the beginning of freedom of the press in the United Kingdom and it was at this time that newspapers began to flourish.

According to Lord Justice Leveson, the history of the struggle for press freedom over the centuries 'provides an essential background to understanding the commitment of modern democratic society to freedom of the press'.[3] However, it must be acknowledged that the existence of a free press in a democracy is sometimes a double-edged sword. While the press is to be valued for actively sniffing out and exposing stories of legitimate public interest, the press itself wields a vast amount of power and political influence. Newspapers are, almost by nature, politically partisan.[4] They reflect the ideological beliefs of their proprietors and/or editors, all the while catering to, and reinforcing, the biases and fears of their readers. They have the freedom to select what is newsworthy (and what is not), and the manner in which such stories are presented. This, of course, raises legitimate concerns about whether the exercise of such power is always compatible with democracy and, moreover, whether it should go unregulated.[5]

---

[1] Jeremy Tunstall, *Newspaper Power: The New National Press in Britain* (Oxford University Press, 1996), 1.
[2] Geoff Ward, 'UK National Newspapers' in Peter J. Anderson and Geoff Ward (eds), *The Future of Journalism in the Advanced Democracies* (Ashgate, 2007), 74, 78.
[3] The Leveson Inquiry, *An Inquiry into the Culture, Practices and Ethics of the Press: Report* (HC 2012–13, 780-I), 58.
[4] Ibid., 79.
[5] Jeremy Tunstall, *Newspaper Power: The New National Press in Britain* (Oxford University Press, 1996), 2.

Contrasting newspapers with the broad appeal of television, Tunstall also recognised that newspapers tend to operate at the extremities: '[t]he press has its main strength not in this broad middle range but at the most serious extreme and at the least serious, most sleazy, and most disreputable end of the range'.[6] There is no doubt that scandal, sex and celebrity gossip sell newspapers; and there is equally no doubt that some newspapers have gone to extreme lengths to satiate the prurient appetites of their audiences, including gross violations of privacy, harassment and, in the case of News International's now defunct *News of the World*, illegal phone hacking. As discussed below, such excesses of the press – particularly invasions of privacy – have been scrutinised in numerous official inquiries, and are among the key issues which faced the recent Leveson Inquiry, established in the wake of the *News of the World* phone hacking scandal.[7] To date, however, no government has been prepared to impose a system of statutory regulation on the press. Rather, the press has enjoyed a system of self-regulation to ensure that it abides by its own standards of acceptable conduct.

This system, including the Editors' Code of Practice and the complaints mechanism, is considered in detail in Section 3. The following section examines the history of self-regulation of the press and explores Lord Justice Leveson's proposal for a new system of self-regulation with statutory backing.

2.2 VOLUNTARY REGULATION AND THE PRESS

(a) History of press self-regulation

The self-regulation of the press has a relatively long history. The General Council of the Press was established in 1953 upon the recommendation of the first Royal Commission on the Press[8] (although the body that was eventually formed differed substantially from that which was recommended). Its principal functions were to promote press freedom and to consider complaints against its members. Initially it was composed entirely of journalists and editors, with the owner of *The Times* as chairman. However, following criticism by a second Royal Commission in 1962 regarding the General Council's lack of lay membership,[9] it changed its name to the simpler 'Press Council'; Lord Devlin, a retired Law Lord, was appointed as the first lay (non-press) chairman and its lay membership was increased to 20 per cent (as recommended by the first Royal Commission). Its treatment of complaints, however, was considered unsatisfactory. The Council often took months to reach a decision, while many complainants thought it was biased in favour of newspapers. The criticism continued unabated despite the change in 1978, on recommendation of a third Royal Commission, to parity of press and lay members.[10] Adjudications were inconsistent and poorly reasoned, and newspapers sometimes failed to report adverse rulings or buried them in an inside page.

In 1989 the government invited Sir David Calcutt to chair a committee (the 'Calcutt Committee') to consider whether to provide further protection for privacy against the press. Its report recommended the replacement of the Press Council by a Press Complaints

---

[6] Ibid., 184.

[7] See The Leveson Inquiry, *Terms of Reference*, <www.levesoninquiry.org.uk/about/terms-of-reference/>.

[8] Royal Commission on the Press 1947–9, *Report* (Cmd 7700, 1949).

[9] Royal Commission on the Press 1961–2, *Report* (Cmnd 1811, 1962).

[10] Royal Commission on the Press 1974–7, *Final Report* (Cmnd 6810, 1977). See also criticisms of the Younger Committee: Younger Committee, *Report of the Committee on Privacy* (Cmnd 5012, 1972).

Commission ('PCC') to give 'one final chance to prove that voluntary self-regulation can be made to work'.[11] The PCC should differ from the Council in a number of respects; most importantly, it should no longer be concerned to defend press freedom but concentrate on the adjudication of complaints. Moreover, the membership of the PCC should not be nominated by the press, but should be 'independent and of high calibre'; to this end, appointments should be made by a dedicated Appointments Commission.[12] Complaints should be dealt with swiftly through clear conciliation and adjudication procedures, with conciliation the preferred route where practicable;[13] and a fast-track procedure for the correction of significant factual errors should also be available.[14] It also recommended that the PCC 'publish, monitor and implement a comprehensive code of practice for the guidance of both the press and the public'[15] as well as provide a 24-hour hotline to assist complainants who are facing unwanted media attention.[16]

In line with the recommendations made by the Calcutt Committee, the PCC replaced the Press Council at the beginning of 1991. Rather than acting as an industry body and defending press freedom (as the Press Council had done), the PCC's role was to promote the Editors' Code of Practice and to provide an independent dispute resolution procedure for complaints arising from possible breaches of the Code. But its institution did not end the debate on the effectiveness of self-regulation. When it accepted the recommendation of the Calcutt Committee that the industry be given a final opportunity to make voluntary regulation work, the government intimated that it would review the new system after 18 months to determine whether a regime of statutory regulation was required. Sir David Calcutt was subsequently asked to review the working of the PCC in 1991–2 (the 'Calcutt Review'). He concluded that it was not sufficiently independent to be an effective regulator. In particular, its members were not appointed by a fully independent Appointments Commission (as had been recommended),[17] while the Code of Practice had been drafted by a Code Committee comprised entirely of press representatives rather than the PCC itself. Moreover, the contents of the Code differed in significant respects from that drafted by the Calcutt Committee and did not 'hold the balance fairly' between the interests of the press and the interests of individuals.[18] Finally, on occasion, tabloid newspapers had shown contempt for the PCC's adjudications.[19]

In light of his findings, Sir David concluded that it would be right to replace the PCC with a statutory press tribunal with the power to draw up its own code of practice, to impose fines, to award compensation, and to require the printing of apologies and corrections. However, the National Heritage Committee of the House of Commons (since renamed the Culture, Media and Sport Committee following the renaming of the Department in 1997) disagreed. It did not think it necessary to abandon voluntary regulation; the Committee recommended that the PCC have broader responsibilities and powers – in particular, the power to award compensation and issue fines[20] – and that its work be supported by a statutory Press Ombudsman.

---

[11] Home Office, *Report of the Committee on Privacy and Related Matters* (Cm 1102, 1990), 14.38.
[12] Ibid., 15.20–15.22.
[13] Ibid., 15.24.
[14] Ibid.
[15] Ibid., 15.7.
[16] Ibid., 15.11.
[17] Department of National Heritage, *Review of Press Self-Regulation* (Cm 2135, 1993), 3.32–3.33.
[18] Ibid., 3.62.
[19] Ibid., 4.24–4.28.
[20] National Heritage Select Committee, *Privacy and Media Intrusion* (HC 1992–3, 294), 74–8.

The government did not react to the Heritage Committee's proposals for two years. On one view, it held back its response to see how the press and the PCC would react to these proposals and to those in the Calcutt Review. A less charitable interpretation is that the government was anxious not to jeopardise its relations with the press before the General Election, eventually held in 1997. Alternatively, there may have been divisions within the government as to how to handle the proposals of the Calcutt Review and the National Heritage Select Committee Report. In any event, the government eventually concluded that voluntary regulation should continue:

> A free press is vital to a free country. Many would think the imposition of statutory controls on newspapers invidious because it might open the way for regulating content, thereby laying the Government open to charges of press censorship. Furthermore, the Government does not believe that it would be right in this field to delegate decisions about when a statutory remedy should be granted to a regulator such as a tribunal. It believes that, in principle, industry self-regulation is much to be preferred. That conclusion applies equally to Sir David Calcutt's statutory complaints tribunal and to the National Heritage Select Committee's statutory Press Ombudsman proposal.[21]

The government placed much reliance on various changes in procedure and practice that the PCC had announced and/or implemented in the period following the National Heritage Select Committee's report.[22] These changes included: a majority lay representation on the PCC; an additional independent member to be recruited to the Appointments Commission; changes made to the Code of Practice; the incorporation of the Code of Practice into the contracts of all journalists and editors; the establishment of a 'press hotline' to assist members of the public in handling anticipated breaches of the Code; and lastly, a great willingness to consider third party complaints and to initiate independent PCC investigations.

The past ten years has witnessed a series of parliamentary inquiries into the regulation of the press, usually in response to particular events or public outrage over press behaviour. None, however, have followed Calcutt in recommending a system of statutory regulation. In 2003, the Culture, Media and Sport Committee made a series of recommendations as to how the current system of self-regulation could be improved.[23] These included: minor revisions to the Code of Practice; changes to the appointment process and an increase in the lay membership of the Commission; a recommendation that a publication be required to reference any adverse PCC adjudications on its front page; greater proactivity in investigating potential breaches of the Code; and, lastly, power for the PCC to award compensation to successful complainants. Another inquiry into the regulation of the press, conducted by the same committee in 2007, denounced a series of failures in newsgathering activities by the press but found that such lapses did not justify statutory intervention.[24] One of the matters considered by the 2007 Committee was the outcome of Operation Motorman, an investigation undertaken by the Information Commissioner's Office. That investigation focused on the activities of a private investigator, Stephen Whittamore, who was found to be supplying data obtained in breach of the Data Protection Act to journalists from many newspaper and magazine titles. As a result of its investigation and after raising with the PCC the fact that 'certain newspapers and magazines were behaving in an

[21] Secretary of State for National Heritage, *Privacy and Media Intrusion* (Cm 2918, 1995), 2.5.
[22] Ibid., 2.6–2.15.
[23] Culture, Media and Sport Committee, *Privacy and Media Intrusion* (HC 2002–03, 458-I).
[24] Culture, Media and Sport Committee, *Self-regulation of the Press* (HC 2006–07, 375), 35.

unacceptable way',[25] the Information Commissioner recommended that the PCC 'should take a much stronger line to tackle any involvement by the press in the illegal trade in personal information'.[26] Despite the evidence obtained by the Information Commissioner, no attempt was made to prosecute any of the individual journalists concerned. The 2007 Committee, however, did not see this as an excuse for the PCC's failure to proactively investigate the issue and warned that '[i]f the industry is not prepared to act unless a breach of the law is shown to have occurred already then the whole justification for self-regulation is seriously undermined'.[27]

Two years later the Committee once again considered the merits of self-regulation in the context of a wide-ranging inquiry into press standards, privacy and libel.[28] This inquiry was sparked by a series of events, including the gross violation of Max Mosley's privacy by *News of the World*, the reporting of a spate of suicides in Bridgend in 2007 and 2008, and the treatment of Kate and Gerry McCann by the British press following the unresolved disappearance of their daughter from a Portuguese hotel in 2008. Other longer-term developments also prompted the inquiry, including 'the rise of the Internet' and the introduction of the Human Rights Act.[29] In its report published in 2010, the Committee recommended the retention of self-regulation but that the PCC should do more to 'effectively regulate, not just mediate'.[30] It also recommended that the PCC increase its lay membership to a two-thirds majority[31] and repeated its past recommendation that the PCC should take a more proactive approach in investigating potential breaches of the Code.[32] The Committee was also concerned that some publications did not subscribe to the PCC system, or had refused to pay their subscription, and highlighted the need for greater incentives to subscribe, possibly in the form of a reduction of cost burdens in defamation cases.[33] It was further recommended that corrections and apologies should be printed on either an earlier, or the same, page as the page on which an offending article originally appeared,[34] and, to increase the PCC's credibility and public support, that it should have the power to impose financial penalties on offending publications,[35] and even suspend publication for the duration of one issue for especially serious breaches of the Code.[36]

(b) The future of press self-regulation: the Leveson Inquiry

In July 2011, the Prime Minister, David Cameron, appointed Lord Justice Leveson, a judge of the Court of Appeal, to conduct the most extensive inquiry into the culture, practices and ethics of the press ever undertaken to date. The inquiry was instigated in response to the revelation that there had been widespread phone hacking at News International's *News of the World*.

---

[25] Information Commissioner's Office, *What Price Privacy?* (HC 2005–06, 1056), 7.19.
[26] Ibid., 7.20.
[27] Culture, Media and Sport Committee, *Self-regulation of the Press* (HC 2006–07, 375), 19.
[28] Culture, Media and Sport Committee, *Press Standards, Privacy and Libel* (HC 2009–10, 362-I).
[29] Ibid., 2.
[30] Ibid., 531.
[31] Ibid., 542.
[32] Ibid., 552.
[33] Ibid., 558.
[34] Ibid., 573.
[35] Ibid., 575.
[36] Ibid.

In 2007, Clive Goodman, Royal Editor at *News of the World*, and Glenn Mulcaire, a private investigator paid by Goodman, were both convicted of unlawfully intercepting telephone voicemail messages of staff at Buckingham Palace; Mulcaire was also convicted of unlawfully intercepting voicemail messages of various public figures. Allegations of phone hacking at *News of the World* had already been considered by the Culture, Media and Sport Committee in 2007 and 2010; however, the 2010 Committee was not convinced (nor was its 2007 predecessor) by assurances then given that phone hacking was isolated to a single 'rogue reporter' nor that there was no one else at the newspaper who was aware of what was occurring.[37] Allegations that there had been a cover-up regarding the extent and knowledge of phone hacking at *News of the World* appeared in a July 2009 article published by *The Guardian*.[38] The PCC responded by initiating its own investigation. In its report issued in November 2009, the PCC accepted the explanation given by *News of the World* that the Goodman case was isolated. It then admonished *The Guardian* for publishing the allegations. The 2010 Media, Culture and Sport Committee, in turn, was critical of the way the investigation was handled by the PCC:

> The *Guardian's* fresh revelations in July 2009 . . . provided good reason for the PCC to be more assertive in its enquiries, rather than accepting submissions from the *News of the World* once again at face value. This Committee has not done so and we find the conclusions in the PCC's November report simplistic and surprising. It has certainly not fully, or forensically, considered all the evidence to this inquiry.[39]

In light of the events that followed, the PCC subsequently withdrew its report, and serious doubt was cast over the PCC's ability to act as an effective regulator.

Little by little, as more was revealed during the course of civil litigation brought against News International by victims of phone hacking, it became apparent that phone hacking was not confined to the actions of Goodman. Matters came to a head in July 2011 when it was reported in *The Guardian* that the voicemail messages of Milly Dowler, a 13-year-old girl who was murdered on her way home from school in 2002, had been intercepted by reporters at *News of the World*. The fallout was almost immediate. The *News of the World* announced its closure two days later and its final issue was printed on 10 July 2011. Three days after that, Prime Minister David Cameron announced the Leveson Inquiry, with one of its principal aims to consider 'the failure of the current system of regulation' and to 'make recommendations for a new, more effective way of regulating the press'.[40]

In November 2012, more than twelve months after the Leveson Inquiry first received evidence, Lord Justice Leveson delivered his Report. He found that the PCC was neither an effective nor an independent regulator.

---

[37] Culture, Media and Sport Committee, *Press Standards, Privacy and Libel* (HC 2009–10, 362-I), 399–442. See also Culture, Media and Sport Committee, *News International and Phone-Hacking* (HC 2010–12, 903-I) (where the Committee found that the 2010 Committee had been misled in evidence given to it by those associated with *News of the World* regarding knowledge of phone hacking and the nature and extent of the internal investigation conducted by the newspaper).

[38] See Nick Davies, 'Murdoch papers paid £1m to gag phone-hacking victims', *The Guardian* (online), 8 July 2009 <www.guardian.co.uk/media/2009/jul/08/murdoch-papers-phone-hacking>.

[39] Culture, Media and Sport Committee, *Press Standards, Privacy and Libel* (HC 2009–10, 362-I), 472.

[40] HC Deb, 13 July 2011, vol 531, cols 311–12.

Extract 2.2.1
The Leveson Inquiry, *An Inquiry into the Culture, Practices and Ethics of the Press:*
***Executive Summary* (HC 2012–13, 779)**

41. Turning to the Press Complaints Commission (PCC), I unhesitatingly agree with the Prime Minister, the Deputy Prime Minister and the Leader of the Opposition who all believe that the PCC has failed and that a new body is required. Mr Cameron described it as *'ineffective and lacking in rigour'* whilst Mr Miliband called it a *'toothless poodle'.* The Commission itself unanimously and realistically agreed in March 2012 to enter a transitional phase in preparation for its own abolition and replacement.

42. The fundamental problem is that the PCC, despite having held itself out as a regulator, and thereby raising expectations, is not actually a regulator at all. In reality it is a complaints handling body. Scarcely any less profound are the numerous structural deficiencies which have hamstrung the organisation. It lacks independence. The Editors' Code Committee which sets the rules is wholly made up of serving editors and is separate from the PCC. Its members are appointed by the Press Standards Board of Finance ('PressBoF'), itself entirely made up of senior industry figures, which also controls the PCC's finances and the appointment of the PCC Chair. Financially, the PCC has been run on a tight budget and without the resources to do all that is needed.

43. Voluntary membership and the concentration of power in relatively few hands has resulted in less than universal coverage. Whatever the reasons and whether or not justified, the departure of Northern & Shell was a major blow to the purpose and credibility of the PCC. The absence of Private Eye from membership, however, is the understandable consequence of the organisation's lack of independence from those so often held to account by that publication. Furthermore, in reality, its powers are inadequate, especially regarding the right to conduct an effective investigation: the PCC is at the mercy of what it is told by those against whom complaint was made.

44. In any event such powers as the PCC has appear to have been under-utilised. Further, even when complaints are upheld, the remedies at its disposal are woefully inadequate and enforceable only by persuasion. In the light of all that I heard during Module One, I do not consider that the power to issue adverse adjudications holds quite the fear that the editors suggest (save, perhaps, only to their pride). I have already referred to the lack of disciplinary action against journalists following criticism by the PCC but neither is there any comeback or criticism of the editors who are ultimately responsible for what is published.

45. In practice, the PCC has proved itself to be aligned with the interests of the press, effectively championing its interests on issues such as s12 Human Rights Act 1998 and the penalty for breach of s55 Data Protection Act 1998. When it did investigate major issues it sought to head off or minimise criticism of the press. It did little in response to Operation Motorman; its attempts to investigate phone hacking allegations, which provided support for the *News of the World*, lacked any credibility: save for inviting answers to questions, no serious investigation was undertaken at all. It may be that no serious investigation could be undertaken: if that was right, it was of critical importance that the PCC said so.

46. The PCC has not monitored press compliance with the Code and the statistics which it has published lack transparency. Even what the organisation undoubtedly was able to do well, namely complaints handling and anti-harassment work, was restricted by a lack of profile and a reluctance to deal with matters that were the subject of civil litigation. That latterly high profile complainants almost invariably turned to the courts instead of using the PCC speaks volumes.

In light of Lord Justice Leveson's findings, he recommended that the PCC be replaced with a system of voluntary independent self-regulation underpinned by legislation. Under the proposal, an independent Board, comprised entirely of lay members but set up by industry, would have four principal functions:

- establish a standards code;
- hear complaints regarding breaches of the standards code;
- promote high standards of conduct within the industry (including the investigation of serious or systemic breaches of standards); and
- operate an arbitration service for the resolution of civil disputes arising from press publications.[41]

To ensure the independence of the Board, the Chair and the members of the Board should be appointed in an 'open, transparent and independent way, without any influence from industry or Government'.[42] The Chair, in particular, should be independent of the press and should demonstrate a commitment to both freedom of expression *and* the rights of others, and should be able to balance those rights 'in precisely the way that Articles 8 and 10 of the European Court of Human Rights (ECtHR) identify that balance'.[43] The Chair of the independent Board should be appointed by an appointment panel, independent of the press and of government; in turn, the members of the Board should be appointed by the appointment panel and the Chair (once appointed).[44] The fees required to fund the operation of the Board should be set by the Board itself, rather than an industry dominated body such as the current Press Standards Board of Finance (discussed in Section 2.3).[45] The standards code should be ultimately approved by the Board but would be on the advice of a Code Committee, which may be comprised of both independent members of the Board and members of industry. The code should, at the very least, cover standards of conduct, 'especially in relation to the treatment of other people in the process of obtaining material', as well as respect for privacy and matters to do with accuracy.[46]

In order to be an effective regulator, the Board should be vested with the power to deal with individual complaints regarding breaches of the standards code *and* the power to examine, on its own initiative, 'serious or systemic breaches of the code and failures to comply with directions of the Board'.[47] In a departure from the existing system, individual complaints should be able to be made by those who are directly affected by a purported breach *as well as* by third parties who question the accuracy of material published by the press.[48] Perhaps most importantly, however, the Board should have greater powers in relation to remedies and sanctions. In particular, it should be able to award appropriate remedies to individuals directly affected by breaches of the code and to direct the publication of corrections and apologies;[49] in addition, it 'should have the power to impose appropriate and proportionate sanctions (including financial sanctions up to 1 per cent of turnover, with a maximum of £1 million)'.[50] The Board should not, however, have the power to impose prior restraints on the publication of any material whatsoever;[51] rather, the Board should be willing to provide a pre-publication advice service to editors relating to compliance with the standards code.

---

[41] The Leveson Inquiry, *An Inquiry into the Culture, Practices and Ethics of the Press: Report* (HC 2012–13, 780-IV), 1759.
[42] Ibid.
[43] Ibid.
[44] Ibid., 1761.
[45] Ibid., 1761–2.
[46] Ibid., 1763.
[47] Ibid., 1766.
[48] Ibid., 1765.
[49] Ibid., 1766.
[50] Ibid., 1767.
[51] Ibid.

As well as handling individual complaints and investigating serious and systemic breaches of the code, a key recommendation made by Lord Justice Leveson is that the Board should also operate a 'fair, quick and inexpensive' arbitration service in relation to civil claims brought against the press.[52] This could be staffed by legal experts (including retired judges and senior members of the legal profession) and should be provided on a costs-only basis.

Lord Justice Leveson acknowledged that in order to be effective, any system of voluntary regulation needs to have wide industry participation, and should be open to online news publishers such as blogs (although requirements may vary depending on the nature of the publisher).[53] The need for broad participation means that there should be appropriate incentives to encourage newspapers and magazines to subscribe to the system. Leveson puts forward a number of ways of achieving this, but the incentive central to his proposed regime is in shifting the allocation of costs in the resolution of civil disputes involving the media. Thus, as recommended in the Report:

> [I]t should be open to any subscriber to a recognised regulatory body to rely on the fact of their membership and on the opportunity it provides for the claimant to use a fair, fast and inexpensive arbitration service. It could request the court to encourage the use of that system of arbitration and, equally, to have regard to the availability of the arbitration system when considering claims for costs incurred by a claimant who could have used the arbitration service. On the issue of costs, it should equally be open to a claimant to rely on failure by a newspaper to subscribe to the regulator thereby depriving him or her of access to a fair, fast and inexpensive arbitration service. When that is the case, in the exercise of its discretion, the court could take the view that, even where the defendant is successful, absent unreasonable or vexatious conduct on the part of the claimant, it would be inappropriate for the claimant to be expected to pay the costs incurred in defending the action.[54]

Another way of encouraging participation put forward in Leveson's Report is to allow the court to award exemplary or aggravated damages against an unsuccessful defendant who does not subscribe to the voluntary system.[55] Giving effect to these incentives would require statutory recognition that the body established by the industry satisfies the requirements of an effective and independent regulator, along with statutory changes that would permit exemplary and aggravated damages to be awarded in defamation and privacy cases in the circumstances described by Leveson.[56] It is in these ways that the proposed system is said to require 'statutory underpinning'.[57]

According to the proposal, the law must set out the criteria for a body to be considered an independent and effective regulator (based on the system of self-regulation just described) and the 'responsibility for recognition and certification of a regulator shall rest with a recognition body'.[58] It was recommended that this role should be undertaken by Ofcom (which is clearly experienced in media regulation) or an independent Recognition Commissioner appointed by Ofcom, and should be carried

---

[52] Ibid., 1768–9.
[53] Ibid., 1761.
[54] Ibid., 1770.
[55] Ibid., 1771.
[56] Note that the current availability of exemplary and aggravated damages in defamation cases is discussed in Chapter 10.
[57] The Leveson Inquiry, *An Inquiry into the Culture, Practices and Ethics of the Press: Report* (HC 2012–13, 780-IV), 1771–2.
[58] Ibid., 1772.

out on a periodic basis (two years after certification and thereafter every three years).[59] Leveson described this 'statutory underpinning' as the 'most controversial' part of his recommendations.[60]

However, as demonstrated in the following extracts – and despite the way the recommendations have been portrayed by certain media interests[61] – Leveson was at pains to stress that the proposal is not for a system of statutory regulation; nor is it a step towards such as system.

Extract 2.2.2
The Leveson Inquiry, *An Inquiry into the Culture, Practices and Ethics of the Press: Executive Summary* (HC 2012–13, 779)

70. . . . In order to give effect to the incentives that I have outlined, it is essential that there should be legislation to underpin the independent self-regulatory system and facilitate its recognition in the legal processes.

71. It is worth being clear what this legislation would not do. The legislation would not establish a body to regulate the press: it would be up to the press to come forward with their own body that meets the criteria laid down. The legislation would not give any rights to Parliament, to the Government, or to any regulatory (or other) body to prevent newspapers from publishing any material whatsoever. Nor would it give any rights to these entities to require newspapers to publish any material except insofar as it would require the recognised self-regulatory body to have the power to direct the placement and prominence of corrections and apologies in respect of information found, by that body, to require them.

72. What would the legislation achieve? Three things. First, it would enshrine, for the first time, a legal duty on the Government to protect the freedom of the press. Second, it would provide an independent process to recognise the new self-regulatory body and reassure the public that the basic requirements of independence and effectiveness were met and continue to be met; in the Report, I recommend that this is done by Ofcom. Third, by recognising the new body, it would validate its standards code and the arbitral system sufficient to justify the benefits in law that would flow to those who subscribed; these could relate to data protection and the approach of the court to various issues concerning acceptable practice, in addition to costs consequences if appropriate alternative dispute resolution is available.

73. Despite what will be said about these recommendations by those who oppose them, this is not, and cannot be characterised as, statutory regulation of the press. What is proposed here is independent regulation of the press organised by the press, with a statutory verification process to ensure that the required levels of independence and effectiveness are met by the system in order for publishers to take advantage of the benefits arising as a result of membership.

➡

---

[59] Ibid., 1773.
[60] The Leveson Inquiry, *An Inquiry into the Culture, Practices and Ethics of the Press: Executive Summary* (HC 2012–13, 779), 70.
[61] See, e.g., Fraser Nelson, 'Leveson Report: Cameron's Tory principles are protecting our ancient liberties', *The Telegraph* (online), accessed 29 November 2012 <www.telegraph.co.uk/news/uknews/leveson-inquiry/9711698/Leveson-Report-Camerons-Tory-principles-are-protecting-our-ancient-liberties.html>.

The Leveson Inquiry, *An Inquiry into the Culture, Practices and Ethics of the Press:* *Report* **(HC 2012–13, 780-IV), 1780**

Protection of freedom of the press

6.38. It has been argued that any legislation touching on press regulation would be the beginning of the slippery slope; that any Government would find it easier to amend an existing Act than to bring forward new legislation to shackle the press; that Parliament is itching to control the press and that this would be an opportunity to do so. I do not accept any of these arguments. If the history of the last 50 years on press regulation tells us anything, it tells us that Parliament wants nothing less than to pass legislation to regulate the press. There may have been the occasional siren voice expressing a contrary view but, in truth, Parliament has managed to avoid many opportunities to do so, despite real (and repeated) public concern about press behaviour and the consequences of failing to deal with it.

6.39. There is no foundation in the suggestion that it is easier to amend an existing Act than to bring in a new one. Any statute only gives Government, or anyone else, the powers that are stated on the face of the legislation. If a statute simply provides for a recognition process for a press regulatory body then it can only be used for that purpose. Any attempt to introduce further legislation of the press would require a new Act of Parliament which could make new provisions or amend an existing Act, but it would need to be a new Act, and go through exactly the same processes that an Act establishing a recognition process would need to do today.

6.40. Having said that, I recognise the concern expressed by many and, in order to address the slippery slope argument, it would be possible to use a statute setting up a recognition process for a regulatory body to also place an explicit duty on the Government to protect the freedom of the press. I have already referred earlier to an example of just this, drawing heavily from s3 of the Constitutional Reform Act 2005, which would look like this:

GUARANTEE OF MEDIA FREEDOM

(1) The Secretary of State for Culture, Media and Sport and other Ministers of the Crown and all with responsibility for matters relating to the media must uphold the freedom of the press and its independence from the executive.

(2) The Secretary of State for Culture, Media and Sport must have regard to:

   (a) the importance of the freedom and integrity of the media;

   (b) the right of the media and the public to receive and impart information without interference by public authorities;

   (c) the need to defend the independence of the media.

(3) Interference with the activities of the media shall be lawful only insofar as it is for a legitimate purpose and is necessary in a democratic society, having full regard to the importance of media freedom in a democracy.

6.41. Without necessarily suggesting that the clause should be worded in exactly this way, as I am sure there would be benefit from further consideration around the precision with which the intention is expressed, this seems to me to be an admirable proposal, which should provide some comfort to those who have any concerns about the risk of Government decisions impacting adversely on the freedom of the media . . .

In the event that the press is unable or unwilling to set up a self-regulatory body that satisfies the criteria set out above, Lord Justice Leveson recommended that Ofcom should act as a backstop regulator.[62]

---

[62] The Leveson Inquiry, *An Inquiry into the Culture, Practices and Ethics of the Press: Report* (HC 2012–13, 780-IV), Pt K, ch 8.

As was to be expected, the responses to Leveson's recommendations have varied widely. While supporting the requirements set out by Leveson for an independent self-regulatory body, Prime Minister David Cameron expressed caution over the statutory element of the proposal: '[i]n this House, which has been a bulwark of democracy for centuries, we should think very, very carefully before crossing that line'.[63] The Deputy Prime Minister, Nick Clegg, did not share David Cameron's concerns and endorsed Leveson's proposed model in its entirety: '[i]t is a voluntary system, based on incentives, with a guarantee of proper standards. It is not illiberal state regulation'.[64] The Leader of the Opposition, Ed Miliband, characterised the proposed model as 'measured, reasonable and proportionate' and encouraged its implementation without delay.[65] The press, of course, dismissed the statutory element as an affront to democracy and called for another chance to put its own system of self-regulation in place without statutory oversight. Many of the victims of media intrusion who gave evidence to the Leveson Inquiry, on the other hand, were critical of David Cameron's quick dismissal of the statutory element of Leveson's proposal.[66]

At the time of writing, a number of options for reform were being considered and negotiated in response to the Leveson Inquiry. A short inquiry by the Culture, Media and Sport Committee to consider Leveson's proposals commenced on 11 December 2012. The day before this the Labour Party published a draft Bill, the Press Freedom and Trust Bill, to give effect to Leveson's statutory underpinning.[67] The Conservatives, on the other hand, have agreed to produce an alternative Bill only in an attempt to demonstrate that a system of self-regulation underpinned by statute cannot be achieved.[68] In the meantime, Oliver Letwin, a Conservative MP and the Prime Minister's policy adviser, has put forward a proposal that the recognition body recommended by Leveson be set up by Royal Charter rather than by legislation.[69] This has been criticised by those on both sides of the debate as undemocratic and is said to give power to cabinet to control the press 'through the back door'.[70] Letwin and Cameron have sought to allay these concerns by preparing legislation that would ensure that the Royal Charter could only be changed by a super majority vote in the House of Lords and the House of Commons rather than by the Privy Council.[71] At the same time, the press and Lord Hunt, the current Chairman of the PCC, have been attempting to devise various solutions that would meet the concerns highlighted in the Leveson Report but without the need for statutory backing.

---

[63] HC Deb, 29 November 2012, vol 554, col 449.

[64] Ibid., col 471.

[65] Ibid., col 451.

[66] Patrick Wintour, 'Leveson report: JK Rowling left "duped and angry" at PM's response', *The Guardian* (online), 30 November 2012 <www.guardian.co.uk/media/2012/nov/30/leveson-victims-press-intrusion>; Josh Halliday and Patrick Wintour, 'David Cameron accused of dismissing Leveson report too quickly', *The Guardian* (online), 30 November 2012 <www.guardian.co.uk/media/2012/nov/30/david-cameron-accused-prejudging-leveson>.

[67] Labour Party, *Labour Publishes Draft Press Freedom and Trust Bill* (10 December 2012) <www.labour.org.uk/labour-publishes-draft-press-freedom-and-trust-bill>.

[68] Dan Sabbagh, 'Oliver Letwin finalises plan for press regulator enshrined in royal charter', *The Guardian* (online), 13 December 2012 <www.guardian.co.uk/media/2012/dec/13/oliver-letwin-finalises-press-regulator>; Lisa O'Carroll, 'David Cameron considers royal charter on press backed by legislation', *The Guardian* (online), 20 December 2012 <www.guardian.co.uk/media/2012/dec/20/david-cameron-royal-charter-leveson>.

[69] Dan Sabbagh, 'Oliver Letwin finalises plan for press regulator enshrined in royal charter', *The Guardian* (online), 13 December 2012 <www.guardian.co.uk/media/2012/dec/13/oliver-letwin-finalises-press-regulator>.

[70] Ibid.

[71] Ibid.; Lisa O'Carroll and Dan Sabbagh, 'Oliver Letwin outlines new thinking on Leveson reforms', *The Guardian* (online), 20 December 2012 <www.guardian.co.uk/media/2012/dec/20/oliver-letwin-leveson-reforms>.

> ## Questions for discussion
>
> 1. Do you think the press has a special claim to freedom of expression?
> 2. What did Lord Justice Leveson see as the main problems with the PCC?
> 3. Does the proposal for self-regulation underpinned by statute raise concerns about government control of the press? Do you accept the 'slippery slope' argument?
> 4. Should the press be given one final chance to implement its own system of self-regulation without statutory underpinning?
> 5. Should the PCC be able to fine its members for breach of standards? What about awarding compensation to complainants?
> 6. Does Lord Justice Leveson's proposal deal appropriately with online publishers (such as blogs)?
> 7. Are the 'incentives' proposed by Lord Justice Leveson appropriate? Are they likely to work?

2.3 THE CODE OF PRACTICE AND PCC ADJUDICATIONS

(a) Composition and complaints procedure of the PCC

The PCC has 17 members, 10 of whom, including the chairman, are lay members, the other seven being editors of national or regional newspapers or of magazines. They are chosen by an independent Nominations Committee under the chairmanship of the present chairman of the PCC, Lord Hunt. As mentioned above, the PCC is financed by the Press Standards Board of Finance (PressBoF), which collects a levy from the newspaper and magazine publishing industries and is comprised of industry representatives.

The PCC procedure for the processing of complaints regarding breaches of the Editors' Code of Practice is as follows. Complaints, which are only accepted in writing, are first evaluated to see whether they fall within the PCC's remit. The remit of the PCC covers complaints about 'editorially-controlled material' published in UK newspapers and magazines, and on their associated websites (including audio and audiovisual material). The complaints procedure, therefore, does not deal with broadcast material, books, or advertising; nor will the PCC consider complaints relating to matters not dealt with in the Code – for example, issues of taste and decency. Moreover, the PCC will not accept complaints made by third parties (except where they raise important issues of public interest previously not dealt with by PCC adjudication)[72] or those lodged more than two months after the date of publication (except online material). In 2011, of the 7,341 complaints made to the PCC, 847 related to matters not covered by the Code, 13 were made after unreasonable delay and 106 were lodged by third parties. A further 2,125 complaints were abandoned.[73]

If a complaint raises a possible breach of the Code, a letter is sent to the editor of the relevant publication, with a view to resolving the complaint without the need for adjudication. If a satisfactory resolution cannot be brokered between the editor of the publication and the complainant, the PCC will then formally adjudicate on whether or

---

[72] On occasion, however, the PCC will initiate its own investigations if it believes that it is in the public interest to do so: see, e.g., *PCC v The Guardian*, PCC Report No 78 (2009).

[73] Press Complaints Commission, *PCC 2011 Complaints Statistics*, 4 <www.pcc.org.uk/assets/80/PCC_Complaints_Statistics_for_2011.pdf>.

not the Code has been breached. Adjudications are made on the basis of written complaints and replies; however, the Commission retains the right to ask the complainant and the editor to attend for an oral hearing, but this course is rarely, if ever, adopted. The PCC is required to adjudicate in only a small minority of cases; most complaints are resolved to the complainant's satisfaction. For example, in 2011, of the 719 complaints judged by the PCC to involve a likely breach of the Code, only 20 required a formal ruling by the PCC against the publication in question. In a further 102 instances, the PCC found that the publication had offered to take sufficient remedial action – for example, the publication of a suitable correction or apology.[74]

Where the PCC does adjudicate, the newspaper or magazine in question will be obliged to publish any decision made against it in full and with due prominence in a manner agreed by the PCC, including a headline reference to the PCC.[75] The PCC, however, lacks formal powers to compel enforcement. Nor can it award damages in favour of a complainant or issue fines for breaches of the Code, no matter how egregious. Furthermore, the PCC will not entertain a complaint which is also the subject of prior or concurrent legal proceedings, but the complainant is free to pursue a legal remedy if he or she is not satisfied with the outcome of the PCC process.[76]

One of the criticisms most frequently made of the PCC's predecessor, the Press Council, was that it took months to reach a decision. In contrast, the PCC emphasises the speed with which it deals with complaints. In 2010, the average time between a complaint being lodged and it being concluded was 32.8 working days;[77] however, in 2011 that figure saw an unexplained increase to 50.4 working days,[78] far in excess of its target of 35 working days.

In addition to the complaints procedure, the PCC also offers a 24-hour telephone hotline to assist those who believe that they are being harassed by the media.[79] If the PCC is satisfied that the complainant is subject to unwarranted media attention and that such a notice is 'genuinely necessary', it will issue a 'desist request' to its list of editors (and also to broadcasters who have voluntarily agreed to participate in the system of desist requests).[80] The PCC takes care to ensure that the system is not abused 'to prevent legitimate scrutiny or to protect exclusive deals with one media outlet over another'.[81] In 2011, the PCC issued 60 desist requests, down from just over 100 in 2010.[82] The PCC also offers pre-publication advice and assistance, both to potential complainants who believe material is about to be published about them as well as to editors seeking guidance on the application of the Code. Any concerns that a potential complainant may have are

---

[74] Ibid.

[75] The requirement that the PCC agree to the manner of publication was added to the Editors' Code of Practice in January 2012: see Press Complaints Commission, *The Evolving Code of Practice* <www.pcc.org.uk/cop/evolving.html>.

[76] PCC decisions appear to be subject to judicial review: see *R v PCC, ex parte Stewart-Brady* [1997] EMLR 185. However, there is some uncertainty as to whether the PCC can be classified as a 'public authority' for the purposes of the HRA and, hence, whether it is required to act compatibly with the Convention rights: see Takatsuki and Christie, *The Law of Privacy and the Media*, 11.135–11.143.

[77] Press Complaints Commission, *Statistics 2010: Speed of Service* <www.pcc.org.uk/review10/statistics-and-key-rulings/complaints-statistics/speed-of-service.php>.

[78] Press Complaints Commission, *PCC 2011 Complaints Statistics*, 4 <www.pcc.org.uk/assets/80/PCC_Complaints_Statistics_for_2011.pdf>.

[79] Press Complaints Commission, *Code Advice for Complainants* <www.pcc.org.uk/code/advice_for_complainants.html?article=Mzg2Mw>.

[80] Press Complaints Commission, *PCC 2011 Complaints Statistics*, 5 <www.pcc.org.uk/assets/80/PCC_Complaints_Statistics_for_2011.pdf>.

[81] Ibid.

[82] Ibid., 6.

passed on to the editor of the publication involved. While the PCC does not have the power to prevent a publication involving a potential breach of the Code, it is claimed that '[c]ountless stories never appear – or appear in a considerably different format – as the result of this invisible part of the Commission's service'.[83]

(b) The Code

Central to any evaluation of the PCC is the quality of the Code and the decisions which apply it. The Calcutt Committee's Report had recommended that the PCC should adjudicate complaints on the basis of a published code. Ideally, its decisions should be coherent and well-reasoned, providing clear guidance to editors and journalists on the standards set out in the code.

The Code is drafted by a committee of senior editors, called the Editors' Code of Practice Committee. The Code is regularly reviewed and, since it was first introduced in 1991, has undergone a series of revisions, both in response to public concerns about press behaviour and as a result of technological advances in information gathering and publication techniques.

Extract 2.3.1
Editors' Code of Practice (December 2011)

The Press Complaints Commission is charged with enforcing the following Code of Practice which was framed by the newspaper and periodical industry and was ratified by the PCC in December 2011 to include changes taking effect from 1 January 2012.

The Code

All members of the press have a duty to maintain the highest professional standards. The Code, which includes this preamble and the public interest exceptions below, sets the benchmark for those ethical standards, protecting both the rights of the individual and the public's right to know. It is the cornerstone of the system of self-regulation to which the industry has made a binding commitment.

It is essential that an agreed code be honoured not only to the letter but in the full spirit. It should not be interpreted so narrowly as to compromise its commitment to respect the rights of the individual, nor so broadly that it constitutes an unnecessary interference with freedom of expression or prevents publication in the public interest.

It is the responsibility of editors and publishers to apply the Code to editorial material in both printed and online versions of publications. They should take care to ensure it is observed rigorously by all editorial staff and external contributors, including non-journalists, in printed and online versions of publications. Editors should co-operate swiftly with the Press Complaints Commission in the resolution of complaints. Any publication judged to have breached the Code must publish the adjudication in full and with due prominence agreed by the Commission's Director, including headline reference to the PCC.

1. Accuracy

i)   The Press must take care not to publish inaccurate, misleading or distorted information, including pictures.

ii) A significant inaccuracy, misleading statement or distortion once recognised must be corrected, promptly and with due prominence, and – where appropriate – an apology published. In cases involving the Commission, prominence should be agreed with the PCC in advance.

---

[83] Ibid., 5.

iii)   The Press, whilst free to be partisan, must distinguish clearly between comment, conjecture and fact.

iv)   A publication must report fairly and accurately the outcome of an action for defamation to which it has been a party, unless an agreed settlement states otherwise, or an agreed statement is published.

2. Opportunity to reply

A fair opportunity for reply to inaccuracies must be given when reasonably called for.

3.* Privacy

i)   Everyone is entitled to respect for his or her private and family life, home, health and correspondence, including digital communications.

ii)   Editors will be expected to justify intrusions into any individual's private life without consent. Account will be taken of the complainant's own public disclosures of information.

iii)   It is unacceptable to photograph individuals in private places without their consent.

Note – Private places are public or private property where there is a reasonable expectation of privacy.

4.* Harassment

i)   Journalists must not engage in intimidation, harassment or persistent pursuit.

ii)   They must not persist in questioning, telephoning, pursuing or photographing individuals once asked to desist; nor remain on their property when asked to leave and must not follow them. If requested, they must identify themselves and whom they represent.

iii)   Editors must ensure these principles are observed by those working for them and take care not to use non-compliant material from other sources.

5. Intrusion into grief or shock

i)   In cases involving personal grief or shock, enquiries and approaches must be made with sympathy and discretion and publication handled sensitively. This should not restrict the right to report legal proceedings, such as inquests.

*ii)   When reporting suicide, care should be taken to avoid excessive detail about the method used.

6.* Children

i)   Young people should be free to complete their time at school without unnecessary intrusion.

ii)   A child under 16 must not be interviewed or photographed on issues involving their own or another child's welfare unless a custodial parent or similarly responsible adult consents.

iii)   Pupils must not be approached or photographed at school without the permission of the school authorities.

iv)   Minors must not be paid for material involving children's welfare, nor parents or guardians for material about their children or wards, unless it is clearly in the child's interest.

v)   Editors must not use the fame, notoriety or position of a parent or guardian as sole justification for publishing details of a child's private life.

7.* Children in sex cases

1.   The press must not, even if legally free to do so, identify children under 16 who are victims or witnesses in cases involving sex offences.

2.   In any press report of a case involving a sexual offence against a child –

   i)   The child must not be identified.

   ii)   The adult may be identified.

   iii)   The word 'incest' must not be used where a child victim might be identified.

   iv)   Care must be taken that nothing in the report implies the relationship between the accused and the child.

8.* Hospitals

i) Journalists must identify themselves and obtain permission from a responsible executive before entering non-public areas of hospitals or similar institutions to pursue enquiries.

ii) The restrictions on intruding into privacy are particularly relevant to enquiries about individuals in hospitals or similar institutions.

9.* Reporting of crime

i) Relatives or friends of persons convicted or accused of crime should not generally be identified without their consent, unless they are genuinely relevant to the story.

ii) Particular regard should be paid to the potentially vulnerable position of children who witness, or are victims of, crime. This should not restrict the right to report legal proceedings.

10.* Clandestine devices and subterfuge

i) The press must not seek to obtain or publish material acquired by using hidden cameras or clandestine listening devices; or by intercepting private or mobile telephone calls, messages or emails; or by the unauthorised removal of documents or photographs; or by accessing digitally-held private information without consent.

ii) Engaging in misrepresentation or subterfuge, including by agents or intermediaries, can generally be justified only in the public interest and then only when the material cannot be obtained by other means.

11. Victims of sexual assault

The press must not identify victims of sexual assault or publish material likely to contribute to such identification unless there is adequate justification and they are legally free to do so.

12. Discrimination

i) The press must avoid prejudicial or pejorative reference to an individual's race, colour, religion, gender, sexual orientation or to any physical or mental illness or disability.

ii) Details of an individual's race, colour, religion, sexual orientation, physical or mental illness or disability must be avoided unless genuinely relevant to the story.

13. Financial journalism

i) Even where the law does not prohibit it, journalists must not use for their own profit financial information they receive in advance of its general publication, nor should they pass such information to others.

ii) They must not write about shares or securities in whose performance they know that they or their close families have a significant financial interest without disclosing the interest to the editor or financial editor.

iii) They must not buy or sell, either directly or through nominees or agents, shares or securities about which they have written recently or about which they intend to write in the near future.

14. Confidential sources

Journalists have a moral obligation to protect confidential sources of information.

15. Witness payments in criminal trials

i) No payment or offer of payment to a witness – or any person who may reasonably be expected to be called as a witness – should be made in any case once proceedings are active as defined by the Contempt of Court Act 1981.

    This prohibition lasts until the suspect has been freed unconditionally by police without charge or bail or the proceedings are otherwise discontinued; or has entered a guilty plea to the court; or, in the event of a not guilty plea, the court has announced its verdict.

*ii) Where proceedings are not yet active but are likely and foreseeable, editors must not make or offer payment to any person who may reasonably be expected to be called as a witness, unless the information concerned ought demonstrably to be published in the public interest and there is an over-riding need to make or promise payment for this to be done; and all reasonable steps have been taken to ensure no financial dealings influence the evidence those witnesses give. In no circumstances should such payment be conditional on the outcome of a trial.

*iii) Any payment or offer of payment made to a person later cited to give evidence in proceedings must be disclosed to the prosecution and defence. The witness must be advised of this requirement.

16.* Payment to criminals

i)   Payment or offers of payment for stories, pictures or information, which seek to exploit a particular crime or to glorify or glamorise crime in general, must not be made directly or via agents to convicted or confessed criminals or to their associates – who may include family, friends and colleagues.

ii) Editors invoking the public interest to justify payment or offers would need to demonstrate that there was good reason to believe the public interest would be served. If, despite payment, no public interest emerged, then the material should not be published.

The public interest

There may be exceptions to the clauses marked* where they can be demonstrated to be in the public interest.

1. The public interest includes, but is not confined to:
    i)   Detecting or exposing crime or serious impropriety.
    ii)   Protecting public health and safety.
    iii) Preventing the public from being misled by an action or statement of an individual or organisation.
2. There is a public interest in freedom of expression itself.
3. Whenever the public interest is invoked, the PCC will require editors to demonstrate fully that they reasonably believed that publication, or journalistic activity undertaken with a view to publication, would be in the public interest and how, and with whom, that was established at the time.
4. The PCC will consider the extent to which material is already in the public domain, or will become so.
5. In cases involving children under 16, editors must demonstrate an exceptional public interest to over-ride the normally paramount interest of the child.

In 2010, of the issues raised in complaints with merit, 87.2 per cent related to accuracy and opportunity to reply (clauses 1 and 2), 23.7 per cent related to privacy (clauses 3–9 and 11), and 3.3 per cent related to discrimination (clause 12).[84] In 2011, the figures were, respectively, 90.7 per cent, 29.2 per cent and 1.1 per cent. Furthermore, complaints under clause 10 (clandestine devices and subterfuge) comprised 1.6 per cent of all complaints with merit in 2011, up from 0.9 per cent in 2010.[85]

The following sections consider adjudications under clauses 1 (accuracy), 2 (opportunity to reply), 3 (privacy), 4 (harassment), 5 (intrusion into grief or shock), 10 (clandestine devices and subterfuge), 12 (discrimination) and 16 (payment to criminals).

---

[84] Press Complaints Commission, *Statistics 2010: What Do People Complain About?* <www.pcc.org.uk/review10/statistics-and-key-rulings/complaints-statistics/what-do-people-complain-about.php>.
[85] Press Complaints Commission, *PCC 2011 Complaints Statistics* <www.pcc.org.uk/assets/80/PCC_Complaints_Statistics_for_2011.pdf>.

(c) Clauses 1 and 2: Accuracy and the opportunity to reply

Although at first glance the four obligations under clause 1 seem clear enough, some of them allow room for movement. When, for instance, is an inaccuracy sufficiently 'significant' to give rise to a duty of correction, and does a newspaper publish a correction 'with due prominence' if it is printed on an inside page when the inaccurate or misleading material appeared on the front page?

While clause 1 is concerned with accuracy, it is not the role of the PCC to make formal findings of fact; rather, its role is to consider whether 'sufficient care has been taken [by the press] not to publish inaccurate material'.[86] Where the accuracy of the reported facts is a matter of disagreement between the parties, attention will turn to the evidence provided by the publication that it took care not to publish inaccurate or misleading information. Thus, the publication will provide evidence that either the factual allegations are correct, that there is a reasonable factual basis for them, or that it had otherwise engaged in appropriate conduct in seeking their verification. Where the publication cannot satisfy the PCC that it took satisfactory care, the PCC will consider whether, in light of the inaccuracy, the publication has fulfilled its obligation under the Code to publish an adequate correction 'promptly and with due prominence'.[87] This is the approach of the PCC even when the publication cannot establish that it took sufficient care because it wants to maintain the confidentiality of its sources.[88]

The following adjudication demonstrates the general approach of the PCC in assessing whether sufficient care was taken not to publish inaccurate information. In a newspaper article published in *News of the World* in 2008 it was alleged that Paul Burrell, the late Princess of Wales' long-standing butler, had had sex with the Princess. Burrell, who denied the allegation, complained to the PCC under clause 1.

Extract 2.3.2
***Burrell v News of the World*, PCC Report No 78 (18 November 2008)**

The complainant strongly disputed the central allegation in the article. He said that the sole basis for the allegation was Mr Cosgrove's claim that the complainant confided the secret to him in a pub in 1993, and denied that such a conversation had occurred. He accepted that the PCC was not the appropriate body to determine whether or not the conversation had taken place, or whether the allegation was true, and restricted the complaint to two issues:

- whether or not the newspaper had taken care not to publish inaccurate information, by investigating the claims properly, including putting them to the complainant for his comment before publication;
- whether or not readers would have been misled by the lack of a denial from Mr Burrell.

The complainant argued that the claim by Mr Cosgrove was inherently improbable and likely to be motivated by the financial reward offered by the newspaper. This meant that there was a greater need for the newspaper to go to Mr Burrell for comment. He said that the article referred to the complainant and Mr Cosgrove discussing the Princess's use of the phrase 'her rock', but said this phrase was not current in 1993. Mr Cosgrove had never previously shared his lurid claims with his wife or sister, and had waited fifteen years to raise them.

---

[86] *Macleod and Ors v Sunday Mail*, PCC Report No 52 (2001).
[87] Editors' Code of Practice, cl 1.
[88] See, e.g., *Cassidy v Woman*, PCC Report No 78 (2008).

The newspaper argued that it had credible evidence to publish the story. It had three sources at the time of publication. The first was a confidential source, a former associate of Mr Burrell, who approached the newspaper several months before the story was published. He made detailed allegations on tape and in an affidavit. The newspaper did not publish anything at that time because there was no further corroboration. Months later, and entirely separately, Mr Cosgrove volunteered his account. His version of events was tested several times in interview, and he swore an affidavit in support of his position. This affidavit was then confirmed by his son Stephen (who signed and witnessed it prior to publication, and subsequently signed his own affidavit). Stephen Cosgrove indicated that he had heard the story himself from Mr Burrell at a later event. The newspaper provided the PCC with redacted versions of the two Cosgrove affidavits, but it did not supply the initial source's affidavit because it wished to respect that source's anonymity . . .

ADJUDICATION:

Given that, as the complainant had conceded, it was not possible for the Commission to make a finding of fact as to whether the alleged conversation had ever taken place, the principal task for the Commission was to consider whether the newspaper had taken care not to publish misleading information in the way it had presented the story. This boiled down to an assessment as to whether readers would have been misled by the omission of Mr Burrell's position on the matter, which was that he strongly denied either having had the conversation with Mr Cosgrove or ever having a sexual relationship with Princess Diana.

The newspaper had argued that it was not necessary to go to the complainant for a comment before publication because his comments would have been worthless as he was a proven liar, and because it had three sources for the claim that he had boasted of a sexual relationship with his former employer.

The Commission has previously said that failure to contact the subjects of articles before publication – while not obligatory – may constitute a lack of care under Clause 1 in some circumstances. It has never said that people have no right ever to comment on a story, or to be offered a right of reply, if they have misled people in another context.

The Commission was also aware of the newspaper's concerns about an undeserved injunction being granted. However, it did not consider that this meant that the requirements of the Code did not apply. Given the nature of the story, and how the newspaper wished to present it, the inclusion of the complainant's comments was necessary to avoid breaching the Code.

There were several reasons why the Commission considered that Mr Burrell's denial of the allegations should have been made clear in the article. The claims about him were significant and substantial, and published with great prominence. The information came from the recollection of a fifteen-year-old conversation, and was not corroborated on the record by anyone outside Mr Cosgrove's immediate family (as the earlier source remained anonymous). It was clear to the Commission in these circumstances that there was a strong likelihood that the omission of any denial from Mr Burrell may have misled readers into believing that he accepted Mr Cosgrove's allegations. Given the startling nature of the claims, and the narrow basis for them, the newspaper should have contacted the complainant and published his position on the matter. Readers could then have made their own assessment as to the value of his comments in the context of the piece and in light of his reputation. But they were not given this opportunity. Another way of dealing with the problem would have been to offer Mr Burrell a prompt and proportionate right of reply immediately following publication. The offer to include the denial on the website, made at the end of the PCC investigation, was neither prompt nor proportionate.

It has never been an absolute requirement for newspapers to contact those who are about to feature in articles. This would be impractical for a number of reasons: often there will be no dispute about the facts, or the information will be innocuous; the volume of people mentioned in straightforward stories would make it impossible; and legitimate investigations might on some occasions be compromised by such a rule. However, in this case the newspaper made the wrong decision and the complaint was upheld.

The PCC's approach to resolving complaints relating to inaccuracies was also highlighted in *The Queen* v *Business Age*. In that case, Charles Anson, the press Secretary to The Queen, complained that an article in *Business Age* magazine had inaccurately estimated The Queen's personal wealth.

Extract 2.3.3
***The Queen* v *Business Age*, PCC Report No 34 (1996), 5–8 (appendix omitted)**

COMPLAINT:
. . . In correspondence, *Business Age*'s solicitors raised a number of procedural matters with the Commission. They suggested that the matter should only proceed after a measure of disclosure from the Palace had been provided and an opportunity given to their clients to present their case, examine the complaint and tender expert evidence after its experts had been given the facility to inspect and value properties and other assets associated with The Royal Family. They also asked to be able to cross-examine the author of a letter (a copy of which had been provided by the Palace Press Office) who had personally written the previous year's article on the Queen's wealth.

ADJUDICATION
The Commission rejected all these requests. While the PCC is prepared to consider oral submissions, expert evidence and cross-examination where appropriate, the approach set out below does not, in its view, require any procedural change from the normal practice of considering complaints only on the basis of the written documentation submitted. In considering the complaint the Commission did not consider the letter mentioned above as being of any assistance to it as the author appeared to have no current knowledge of how the magazine arrived at its conclusions and the basis for the calculations adopted.

While complaints may be required to supply necessary information to satisfy the Commission that a complaint is well founded, the PCC did not accept the solicitor's contention that their clients and their representatives should be able to conduct a roving expedition into the facts and background. Such a course might not only cause inconvenience and expense to complainants but would also allow newspapers and other media to print speculation under the guise of being factually correct as a means of flushing out information if a complaint was subsequently made. This cannot be right. It must be for the publication concerned to satisfy the Commission that either its statements are true and accurate, or that there is a reasonable factual basis for the material printed.

The Commission had considered carefully the approach which it should adopt in this case. The PCC is concerned not to inhibit investigatory journalism in the public interest, nor does it wish to criticize proper speculation by the press about matters which are unclear. Mr Anson did not contend that any investigation into the Queen's wealth was not a matter of public interest but he did argue that the magazine's conclusions had been reached without properly checking the facts with the relevant people concerned, were riddled with inaccuracies and presented supposition as authoritative fact.

The Commission accepted the magazine's contention that there were complicated matters of a legal and factual nature which may be the subject of legitimate discussion and argument in any assessment of the Queen's wealth. The Commission was pleased to note that the magazine had agreed to consult with the Buckingham Palace Press Office and others during the course of [the] investigation and trusted that this may enable the differences between the two sides to be narrowed. In considering the current complaint the Commission confined itself to a consideration of whether the magazine's claim that its research on the subject was exhaustive was justified and whether it may have indulged in speculation disguised as fact and without checking its conclusions with the relevant officials at Buckingham Palace.

The Commission considered that in increasing the total figure from £158m in 1994 to £2.2bn for 1995 the magazine should clearly have explained the basis on which the new figure was calculated. Only a limited breakdown was given in the magazine article without a clear description of how the final figure has been reached. However the magazine had supplied the Commission with a lengthy document together with a number of appendices which sought to set out the basis of the figures selected. The Commission agreed with a contention made by the Buckingham Palace Press Office that if there was insufficient information and understanding on which to base a valuation of the Queen's personal wealth, this should have been reported, rather than presenting purely speculative numbers as established facts . . .

In respect of a number of other items the magazine did admit that a number of errors had occurred and said it would correct these in its next valuation. In the view of the Commission this is unsatisfactory as periodicals have a clear obligation under the Code to correct promptly any errors which have occurred. In this case the magazine should have corrected any admitted errors in the next issue of the magazine. It did not do so . . .

The Commission concluded that to the extent set out above, the article presented speculation as established fact, the magazine failed adequately to check its facts and it made a number of errors which were not properly addressed.

On this basis, the complaint is upheld.

Questions for discussion

1. Do you think the PCC should be able to make determinations of fact?
2. Do you agree with the decision in *The Queen* v *Business Age*? Should the PCC be prepared in these circumstances to consider oral evidence and allow cross-examination of witnesses?

In some instances, the PCC will reject a claim that the publication has not taken sufficient care in relation to the accuracy of the material on the basis that the allegation is expressed as opinion rather than as fact, or where it is made clear that the allegation is simply that: an allegation.[89] In *McGuiness* v *Sunday World*, McGuiness complained to the PCC regarding a newspaper article published on 28 May 2006 in the *Sunday World*. The article contained an allegation, which McGuiness denied, that he was a British spy.

Extract 2.3.4
McGuinness v _Sunday World_, PCC Report No 74 (2006)

The article contained the claims of Martin Ingram, a former agent handler in the Force Research Unit. He said that a transcript of a conversation between 'J118' and 'G', published in the newspaper, was between the complainant and his M16 handler.

The complainant was concerned that the headline had stated as fact he was a spy, and that the newspaper did not contact him in advance of publication for an opportunity to comment. The headline, the complainant said, was not justified by the contents of the article, in which Mr Ingram was quoted as speculating that the complainant was a spy. The transcript document was clearly not authenticated by anyone in a position of knowledge.

The newspaper said that the full headline was actually 'Spook's shock claims: McGuinness was a Brit Spy'. It was therefore clear that the article concerned an individual's opinion on the subject. The article was based on a document which Martin Ingram claimed was a transcript of a conversation between the complainant and his handler, and which had been authenticated by other intelligence sources. Mr Ingram – who the newspaper said was a credible source and

---

[89] See, e.g., *Messrs Manches on behalf of the Tolkien family* v *Sunday Mercury*, PCC Report No 62 (2003); *McGuinness* v *Sunday World*, PCC Report No 74 (2006).

the man who had previously identified the FRU agent 'Stakeknife' – also gave a detailed account of the complainant's alleged co-operation with the security services. The newspaper did not contact the complainant in advance of publication, as it was aware that he had not previously been willing to offer a comment to it on any issues of controversy. It published a follow-up article containing Gerry Adams' dismissal of the claims in the follow week's edition, and offered to publish an interview with the complainant or a statement of his vehement denial.

The complainant considered that the headline 'Spook's shock claims' appeared to be separate, and was in a different box, to the main headline. This gave a misleading impression.

DECISION: Not Upheld

ADJUDICATION:
It was clearly not within the scope of the Press Complaints Commission – which does not have legal powers of investigation or sub-poena – to establish the veracity of the claims contained in the article. Nor was it necessary for the Commission to do so, in order to come to a decision on this complaint under the terms of the Code. The central question was whether the newspaper had clearly distinguished the claims of Martin Ingram as comment rather than fact. The Commission considered that it had. Above the main headline of the front-page was a reference to the 'shock claims' contained within the article. Although this was in a separate box to the headline, the Commission considered that it was clear that it referred to the main article. Furthermore, the Commission noted that the second paragraph of the front page made clear that 'the revelations are made by . . . Martin Ingram' and the opening paragraph of the page 4 article began: 'a British Army whistleblower today names Sinn Fein chief Martin McGuinness as a high-ranking MI6 agent'. The banner headline for this story was 'allegations about Republican chief's past'.

Taking all this into account, the Commission considered it likely that readers would have recognised that the reference to the complainant as a spy was not a statement of fact but a claim from an intelligence source.

The second issue related to the newspaper's failure to contact the complainant for comment prior to publication. The Commission considered that, in view of the nature of the allegations, the newspaper should have done so, and included the complainant's denial in the first article published on the subject. Nevertheless, the newspaper had taken care to ensure that readers would be aware that the article was based upon information from an alleged official document and a former member of a security organisation, but that the claims had not been otherwise corroborated. The Commission also noted that the newspaper had published the complainant's dismissal of the allegations as 'total and absolute rubbish' the following week. In these circumstances, the Commission considered that the failure to contact the complainant did not in itself mean that the newspaper had failed to take care over the accuracy of the reporting of the allegation.

Question for discussion

1. Is the PCC right to make this distinction between comment and fact in its adjudications under clause 1?

Clause 1 obliges a publication to publish a correction 'promptly and with due prominence' when it becomes aware of a published inaccuracy. This, of course, raises questions over when a correction will be considered to have 'due prominence'. Much will turn on the prominence given to the inaccuracy and the seriousness of the allegations. Sometimes publication of the correction on the 'letters page' will be sufficient; in other cases – for example, where the original allegations appeared on the front page – such a correction will be inadequate.[90] In *Full Fact* v *Daily Mail*, a complaint was made to the PCC regarding the accuracy of two articles published on separate occasions on the front page of the *Daily Mail* and also on the newspaper's website. The first alleged that Britain spent more on foreign aid as a percentage of national income than any other nation; the second stated that the violent behaviour in British classrooms had doubled in the previous year. The newspaper accepted that the articles contained factual errors and offered to publish corrections. The complainant accepted the wording of the draft corrections, but argued that their publication on page 2 in a dedicated 'Corrections and Clarifications' column, as the newspaper had proposed, would not be with 'due prominence'. Because the original articles had been published on the front page of the newspaper, Full Fact was of the view that the corrections should also receive front page treatment. The PCC took the opportunity in this adjudication to outline its approach to the 'due prominence' requirement in Clause 1.

Extract 2.3.5
Full Fact v Daily Mail, PCC Report (2011)

ADJUDICATION:

. . . When considering the issue of 'due prominence', the Commission has strong regard for the location of the original article. However, this cannot be the only determining factor. The Commission will consider the full circumstances surrounding the complaint: the nature of the breach of the Code; the scale of the error; the full context of the story; and the existence or otherwise of a designated corrections column. Whatever the circumstances, however, the appearance on two separate occasions of significant inaccuracies on the newspaper's front page was a matter of serious concern to the Commission. It was incumbent on the newspaper to correct the record in an appropriate way.

The Commission welcomed the newspaper's indication that it intended to institute a corrections column. A regular (and appropriately prominent) location for corrections can mean additional prominence for the rectification of mistakes, and the Commission considered that it was good practice for newspapers and magazines to make use of this facility.

. . . [G]iven the nature of the inaccuracy [in the first article], the Commission considered that it was appropriate for it to be clarified online and in the newspaper on page 2 as part of a new Corrections and Clarifications column. In the Commission's view, the error was not of such import that the Code required a front-page correction.

The second article – in the Commission's view – contained a more straightforward inaccuracy . . . Given the context of the error, and the steps the newspaper had taken prior to publication, the Commission concluded that the corrections column on page 2 represented a sufficiently prominent location for this item.

It may be appropriate, on some occasions, for a correction to a front page story to be published on the front page, and the PCC has negotiated such texts in the past. The Commission does not believe that every front-page error, in whatever context, must be corrected in the same location. In these cases, the Commission had to have regard for the full context of the errors. While the mistakes were sloppy, the issues were not personal to the complainant and had not caused personal harm. In addition, in the Commission's view, the errors did not render the coverage of either story to be wholly inaccurate, including on the front page. In the full circumstances of the complaints raised on this occasion, page 2 corrections (within a new column) were proportionate.

---

[90] See, e.g., *Binley* v *The Daily Telegraph*, PCC Report No 79 (2009); *Wright* v *The Sunday Times*, PCC Report No 79 (2009).

Sometimes a charge of inaccuracy is accompanied by a complaint that the newspaper has refused the complainant an opportunity to reply, so violating clause 2 of the Code of Practice. These are, however, much less common than those brought under clause 1. The drafting of clause 2 should be noted: there is an obligation to provide a '*fair* opportunity for reply to inaccuracies . . . when *reasonably* called for'.[91] This amounts to a more modest obligation than that recommended by Sir David Calcutt in the Report of 1990, let alone that imposed by the legally enforceable right of reply law that is commonly found in continental European systems. Calcutt's draft Code provided for a 'proportionate and reasonable opportunity to reply to *criticisms or alleged inaccuracies*'.[92]

Whether or not a particular opportunity to reply is sufficient will depend on the nature and severity of the allegation.[93] The PCC's approach is exemplified in the following three extracts.

Extract 2.3.6
Ramblers' Association v Sunday Express, **PCC Report No 15 (1992)**

COMPLAINT:
The Ramblers' Association, of 1/5 Wandsworth Road, London, SW8, complain that in the preparation of a report for the *Sunday Express* on April 19th 1992 there was a failure to take care not to publish inaccurate, misleading or distorted material, contrary to Clause 1 of the Code of Practice and a breach of the duty to maintain the highest professional and ethical standards, in that subsequently a fair opportunity to reply was not given, in breach of Clause 2.

ADJUDICATION:
The *Sunday Express* published an article 'Family lose home built across forgotten path . . . Rambler's rights . . . Couple and son on the street.' The article states that a family unknowingly built their house across an ancient footpath and despite support from the local borough council, had failed to have the footpath removed because of opposition from the Rambler's Association. Due to personal financial difficulties, the family tried to sell their house but said the decision that the footpath should be maintained deterred potential buyers. The house was subsequently repossessed and the article claimed that the house was not likely to be sold for less than half its original value . . .

The newspaper published a letter from the complainant a week after the article appeared which set out its objection to the article. The Association complained that the effect of its rebuttal was nullified by the newspaper including a footnote to the letter stating that *Sunday Express* stood by its original story . . .

The Commission find that the article wrongly gave the impression that the family had become homeless as a result of the objections of the Ramblers' Association, whereas the report of the inspector made it clear that the Association was only one of a number of objectors. The substance and position of a quotation ascribed to a 'rambler' (in fact a *Sunday Express* reporter) further suggested that he was associated with the complaint. In the view of the Commission, there were errors and misleading statements in the article which deserved to be corrected. The publication of a letter by the newspaper containing the Ramblers' Association replies was largely negated by the footnote added by the newspaper.

---

[91] Emphasis added.
[92] Home Office, *Report of the Committee on Privacy and Related Matters* (Cm 1102, 1990), App Q (emphasis added).
[93] *Brown* v *Nottingham Post*, PCC Report No 42 (1998).

The newspaper has made a number of technical points concerning the application of the Code of Practice to the facts of this case, all which the Commission rejects. The newspaper argues that the duty, set out in the introduction to the Code, to maintain the highest professional and ethical standards is not to be imported into each individual Clause of the Code. This is plainly wrong. It also argues that the Code does not prevent the newspaper placing its own comment after a corrective letter. The Commission holds that it will depend on the circumstances of each case as to whether such a comment will negate the effect of a fair reply provided under Clause 2 of the Code, as it does in this case.

The complaint is upheld.

Extract 2.3.7
El-Atar v *Evening Standard*, **PCC Report No 74 (2005)**

COMPLAINT:
Mr Samir El-Atar, Managing Director of Dar Al-Taqwa bookshop, complained to the Press Complaints Commission that an article headlined 'Terror and hatred for sale just yards from Baker Street', published in the *Evening Standard* on 28 July 2005, was inaccurate and misleading in breach of Clause 1 (Accuracy) and that he had been denied an opportunity to reply under Clause 2 (Opportunity to reply) of the Code.

The complaint was upheld.

The article focussed on allegedly extremist literature which was on sale in Islamic bookshops in the aftermath of the London bombings. The complainant's bookshop featured prominently in a photograph, alongside pictures of three of the titles that the newspaper said advocated terrorism and which were said to be sold at premises 'such as Dar Al-Taqwa'. The complainant made clear that the shop had never stocked the books or the DVD pictured. The article was therefore misleading since it led people to believe that the shop sought to promote and incite terrorism . . .

The newspaper . . . offered to publish an abridged letter from the complainant or his representative together with an editorial footnote which apologised for any misunderstanding. The complainant was unhappy with the remedial action both taken and offered by the newspaper.

ADJUDICATION:
Clause 1 requires newspapers to 'take care not to publish inaccurate, misleading, or distorted information'. In this case – given the seriousness of the allegations and the sensitive time at which they were published, shortly after the terrorist attacks – there was an over-riding need to ensure that the information gathered by the paper was accurately presented.

While the newspaper was doubtless acting in the public interest when researching the article, it had subsequently conceded that the books and DVDs pictured prominently in the piece were not sold in the shop. Although there was no dispute that the pamphlet quoted in the article was sold by the bookshop, the Commission concluded that the pamphlet provided insufficient corroboration to support the extremely serious claims contained in the headline. Sufficient care had not therefore been taken by the newspaper over the accuracy of the story. In upholding the complaint the Commission was mindful that, in the climate of anxiety following the attacks, the consequences of the misleading allegations – particularly given the fact that the shop's contact details had been prominently displayed – could have been extremely serious for the complainant. It did not in these circumstances consider that the offered remedies were adequate to resolve what was a clear breach of Clause 1. There was also therefore a breach of Clause 2 of the Code.

Extract 2.3.8
Blom-Cooper v Daily Telegraph, PCC Report No 37 (1997)

Sir Louis Blom-Cooper QC, Chairman of Victim Support, London, SW9 complained that an article in the *Daily Telegraph* of 26 September 1996, headlined 'Women must be forced to return to Room 101', contained significant inaccuracies, misleading statements and distortions in breach of Clause 1 (Accuracy) of the Code of Practice. In considering the complaint the Commission also had regard to Clause 2 (Opportunity to reply) of the Code of Practice.

A named writer had put forward her views on the work of Victim Support organisations, focussing on its witness service. The complainant alleged that a number of statements in the article misrepresented or distorted the position of the group. There were also significant inaccuracies including the writer's statements that the group had been started up by a grant from an anonymous American donor and that it was funded entirely by the Home Office. In correspondence with the editor the complainant had asked for space for an article in reply by Victim Support. While not ruling this out the editor offered publication of a letter responding to the points made, an offer which the complainant did not regard as satisfactory . . .

ADJUDICATION:
The Commission noted that the article was clearly presented as a comment piece. It considered that most of the complaints made concerned matters which were clearly presented as the named writer's personal opinions, which she was entitled to make, as they related to the interpretation and critique of Victim Support's work. The terms of the comparison between the system in the United States and the UK were clear. With regard to the factual complaints the Commission did not find any errors significant within the context of the article taken as a whole.

Any complaint about the article could have been dealt with through the newspaper's offer to publish a letter from the complainant. There was no obligation on the newspaper to give space to a reply article.

The complaint under Clause 1 was rejected.

Questions for discussion

1. Are these adjudications consistent? Do you think that the PCC provides complainants an effective opportunity to reply to misleading or inaccurate articles?
2. When is it reasonable for an editor to state that he does not agree with a letter sent in reply to 'inaccurate' allegations?
3. Should a breach of clause 2 only arise where the complainant requests an opportunity to reply, or should a reply be *sought* from the complainant in all circumstances where inaccurate material is published?
4. Is it possible for the PCC to find that clause 2 has been breached without also finding a breach of clause 1?

(d) Clause 3: Privacy

The legal regulation of privacy is dealt with in Chapter 11. However, as an alternative to expensive and lengthy litigation, complaints can be made for invasions of privacy to the PCC under clause 3 of the Code. The downside to this route, of course, is that the PCC does not have the power to prevent the publication of private information; rather, as explained above, a complainant can only seek prior restraints through the courts. Moreover, the PCC cannot award post-publication damages or a final injunction to enjoin repeated publication.

It was for these reasons that the ECtHR held in *Peck* v *United Kingdom* that regulatory bodies without the power to award damages cannot afford an effective remedy for violations of article 8 (the right to a private life)[94] and why, in order to satisfy articles 8 and 13 (the right to a remedy) following the introduction of the Human Rights Act, the courts have been required to develop an effective *legal* remedy for the misuse of private information (see Chapter 11). While the PCC is not able to afford a legal remedy to a complainant, it should be noted that clause 3 of the Editors' Code of Practice is legally relevant to the extent that courts are required under section 12(4) of the HRA to have regard to 'any relevant privacy code'.

Clause 3(i) incorporates the wording of article 8 of the ECHR: '[e]veryone is entitled to respect for his or her private and family life, home, health and correspondence', with the reference to 'digital communications' added in 2004. It is beyond the scope of this chapter to provide a comprehensive review of what has been held by the PCC to fall within clause 3(i). Suffice to mention that it includes matters related to a person's intimate relationships and sex life,[95] information concerning health (including pregnancy),[96] personal correspondence[97] and information about a complainant's home (including address and pictures of the interior).[98] Importantly, the PCC has held that the *mere fact* that someone is a public figure or a celebrity does not justify invasions of their privacy under the Code unless the intrusion is warranted on public interest grounds.[99] It will not, however, be a breach of the Code to publish material in relation to which the victim has previously sought media publicity (see clause 3(ii)), or where the information has otherwise already entered the public domain to such a degree that it can no longer be regarded as private.[100] This will be the case even where the information entered the public domain as a result of a prior invasion of privacy about which the alleged victim did not complain at the time. For example, in *Maclean* v *The Mail on Sunday*,[101] two articles were published in the newspaper in 2002 claiming that David Maclean MP had had an affair with a senior civil servant. When the newspaper re-published the allegations two years later in the context of Boris Johnson lying about his own affair with Petronella Wyatt, it was able to successfully defend its actions on the basis that the information was already in the public domain. This was despite the fact that the original stories were small and were described as 'diary pieces'. The PCC said: 'It is . . . important for people who are the subject of such pieces to realise that not to complain about them may limit their ability to complain about future articles which repeat the same thing'.[102]

The PCC, however, has held that the re-publication of private information posted on social networking sites (such as Facebook, MySpace, Bebo and Twitter) may amount to a breach of clause 3, even if the information is publicly available and not protected by

---

[94] See *Peck* v *United Kingdom* (2003) 36 EHRR 41, 108–109.
[95] *Charters* v *Scottish Sun*, PCC Report No 48 (1999).
[96] *Minogue* v *Daily Record*, PCC Report (2010); *Miliband* v *The Mail on Sunday*, PCC Report No 69 (2005); *A woman* v *OK! Magazine*, PCC Report No 76 (2007); *Spencer* v *News of the World*, PCC Report No 29 (1995).
[97] *Shipman* v *Daily Mirror*, PCC Report No 56 (2001); *McNicholl* v *Scottish News of the World*, PCC Report No 75 (2007).
[98] *Craig* v *The Mail on Sunday*, PCC Report No 78 (2009); *A woman* v *Barking and Dagenham Recorder*, PCC Report No 77 (2008); *Popple* v *Scarborough Evening News*, PCC Report No 77 (2008); *Rowling* v *Daily Mirror*, PCC Report No 72 (2005); *Dynamite* v *Islington Gazette*, PCC Report No 63 (2003).
[99] *Allason* v *Daily Mirror*, PCC Report No 37 (1996).
[100] See, e.g., *Coonan* v *News of the World*, PCC Report No 74 (2007).
[101] PCC Report No 72 (2005).
[102] Ibid.

available privacy settings. In *Mullan, Weir and Campbell* v *Scottish Sunday Express*,[103] the complainants were the parents of three teenagers who had survived the Dunblane school shooting in 1996. Based on information and images obtained from social networking sites, the newspaper published a story claiming that the teenagers 'had "shamed" the memory of the deceased with "foul-mouthed boasts about sex, brawls and drink-fuelled antics"'. The PCC held that it will be acceptable, in some circumstances, to use information taken from social networking sites – usually when the person has attracted publicity through their own actions, or where the information is relevant to a matter currently in the news. Moreover, the PCC said that 'if the images used are freely available (rather than hidden behind strict privacy settings), innocuous and used simply to illustrate what someone looks like it is less likely that publication will amount to a privacy intrusion'. In this instance, however, the PCC upheld the complaint because the teenagers had done nothing to warrant media attention and the images that were published to accompany the article were taken out of context and their use was 'designed to humiliate or embarrass them'.[104] The media, however, will be justified in publishing photographs where they have been widely circulated on the Internet. In *A woman* v *Loaded*,[105] for example, the PCC refused to uphold a complaint against a magazine which published pictures of a woman it had taken from the Internet. The magazine offered its readers a reward of £500 to encourage the woman to do an official photo shoot. The pictures were originally uploaded to the woman's Bebo site when she was 15 and had been widely distributed on the Internet. While the PCC expressed sympathy for the complainant, it held that the photographs had been so widely distributed prior to their publication in the magazine that it would be 'untenable' to find that the Code had been breached.[106]

Clause 3(iii) makes it a breach of the code to 'photograph individuals in private places without their consent', with 'private places' defined as 'public or private property where there is a reasonable expectation of privacy'. The PCC has held that a person has a reasonable expectation of privacy in quasi-public places such as such as restaurants[107] and hotels,[108] the workplace (such as an office, even if accessible to the public)[109] and places of worship.[110] Depending on the circumstances, a person may even have a reasonable expectation of privacy in relation to photographs of them in a public street. For example, reminiscent of the facts in *Campbell* v *MGN Ltd* (see Extract 11.4.2), it was held in *A woman* v *OK! Magazine* that the publication of a photograph of a woman leaving an Alcoholics Anonymous meeting was intrusive, subsequently breaching the Code.[111] Similarly, in *McCartney* v *Hello!*,[112] the magazine was held to have breached the Code by publishing photographs of Sir Paul McCartney and his family on the streets of Paris, taken during their period of mourning following the death of Sir Paul's wife, Linda.

Conversely, as the following extract demonstrates, a person may not necessarily have a reasonable expectation of privacy in relation to photographs taken of them on private property.

[103] PCC Report No 79 (2009).
[104] Ibid.
[105] PCC Report (2010).
[106] Ibid.
[107] *Tunbridge* v *Dorking Advertiser*, PCC Report No 58 (2002).
[108] *Ryle* v *News of the World*, PCC Report No 53 (2001).
[109] *Kisby* v *Loaded*, PCC Report No 73 (2006).
[110] *McCartney* v *Hello!*, PCC Report No 43 (1998).
[111] *A woman* v *OK! Magazine*, PCC Report No 76 (2007).
[112] PCC Report No 43 (1998).

Extract 2.3.9
Sheridan v *Scottish Sun*, PCC Report No 75 (2007)

COMPLAINT:

Mrs Gail Sheridan complained to the Press Complaints Commission, through solicitors Bannatyne Kirkwood France & Co, that an article in the *Scottish Sun* of 11 October 2006 headlined 'Gail's pain' was illustrated by a photograph of her taken in a private place in breach of Clause 3 (Privacy) of the Code.

The complaint was not upheld.

The complainant said the photograph showed her in her back garden, a place where she had a reasonable expectation of privacy, and was taken with a long lens. There was no public interest in its publication, particularly as she had appeared in public at a press conference the previous day . . .

ADJUDICATION:

In considering whether individuals have a reasonable expectation of privacy in particular locations, the Commission applies a common sense test that is not confined simply to whether or not the land someone is on is privately owned. For instance, there are publicly accessible places such as cafes, churches or offices where there is a reasonable expectation of privacy, while ground which is privately owned but completely visible to passers by may be considered less private.

In this case, it seemed from the evidence provided that the complainant would have been visible and identifiable from the street when the photograph was taken. She was standing to the side of her house in relative proximity to an opening onto the road and was not hidden from public view in an enclosed back garden. Had she been hidden from view in an enclosed space, the Commission may well have come to a different decision. It further noted that the photograph did not appear to show the complainant engaging in any particularly private activity. In circumstances where the complainant was outside and visible to passers by – and where the photograph was innocuous – the Commission found no grounds to uphold the complaint. This was the case even though the photograph appeared to have been taken with a long lens. The Code does not distinguish between long lens and other types of photography. It is the location of the individual – in this case, whether the complainant was visible and identifiable from the street – that is important, not the means by which a photograph is taken.

Compare *Sheridan* v *Scottish Sun* with the PCC's adjudication in *Khan* v *The Daily Mail*.[113] A photograph of the Aga Khan and his wife lounging on the deck of a private yacht were published in the *Daily Mail*. The newspaper argued that the couple did not have a reasonable expectation of privacy because the yacht was 'in full sight of casual observers and . . . had been in the Mediterranean in the height of summer'.[114] The PCC nevertheless decided that the publication of the photograph was a breach of the Code; this was on the basis that 'when the photograph was taken they had been on the deck of their private yacht, moored near a private island on which the general public was not allowed'.[115] On the other hand, in *Ford* v *OK! Magazine*,[116] the PCC refused to uphold a complaint brought by BBC newsreader Anna Ford and her partner, David Scott. The photographs in question, taken while the complainants were on holiday in Majorca, showed the couple on a public beach in their swimwear. They argued, believing that it was a private beach, that they

---

[113] *Khan* v *The Daily Mail*, PCC Report No 46.
[114] Ibid.
[115] Ibid.
[116] *Ford* v *OK! Magazine*, PCC Report No 52 (2000).

had a reasonable expectation of privacy. The PCC, however, accepted the magazine's submission that the beach was not private property, was accessible to the general public and was overlooked by numerous apartments. As such, the complainants did not have a reasonable expectation of privacy.

> ### Questions for discussion
>
> 1. Do you agree with the PCC's conclusions in these adjudications under clause 3?
> 2. Can they be reconciled or are they inconsistent?

A newspaper can defend an invasion of privacy if it can demonstrate that it is justified in the public interest. According to the Code, the public interest includes, but is not limited to:

(i)   detecting or exposing crime or serious impropriety;
(ii) protecting public health and safety; and
(iii) preventing the public from being misled by an action or statement of an individual or organisation.[117]

Furthermore, the Code explicitly recognises that there is 'public interest in freedom of expression itself'.[118]

Importantly, however, any intrusion into privacy must be in proportion to the degree of any public interest. It was held in *Popple* v *Scarborough Evening News*,[119] for instance, that publishing video footage and a photograph of the inside of the complainant's house taken during a drug raid by the police amounted to breaches of the Code. While, according to the PCC, it was in the public interest for the newspaper 'to illustrate the police campaign against drugs', the degree of intrusion was disproportionate to any such public interest.[120] However, the PCC arrived at the opposite conclusion where similar photographs accompanied a story about a woman's trial for conspiracy to supply cannabis; the publication of the photographs were justified considering the grave public interest in reporting on the 'whereabouts of the proceeds of a multi-million pound drug smuggling ring'.[121] The importance of proportionality can be seen in another example where two newspapers separately reported the same scandal concerning the affair committed by the wife of an aristocrat. In *A woman* v *News of the World*,[122] it was considered disproportionate to the (limited) public interest in reporting on the adultery to include intimate sexual details; however, the PCC found that the *Daily Mail* had 'struck the right balance' between the interests at stake by refraining to include such intimate details in its report.[123]

The following two extracts provide examples of the PCC's approach to the public interest defence to invasions of privacy.

---

[117] Editors' Code of Practice.
[118] Ibid.
[119] PCC Report No 77 (2008).
[120] See, also, *Bourne* v *Sunday Mercury*, PCC Report No 72 (2006).
[121] *Tomlinson* v *Peterborough Evening Telegraph*, PCC Report No 60 (2002).
[122] PCC Report No 74 (2007).
[123] *A woman* v *Daily Mail*, PCC Report No 74 (2007).

Extract 2.3.10
Allason v Daily Mirror, PCC Report No 37 (1996)

COMPLAINT:

. . . On 9 May 1996 the [Daily Mirror] newspaper published a story about the complainant over the whole of the front page and covering five inside pages, alleging that he was conducting an affair with a named woman. It published a number of photographs of the couple on holiday, together with one of the accommodation in which it said they had stayed. It alleged that Mr Allason's 1992 General Election Address pictured him with his wife and children, and described him as being married with two young children. In later interviews the MP was quoted as saying that he was a family man and one who did not maintain a mistress. The newspaper also carried remarks in a later article from a number of his constituents in which they said they believed him to be happily married. In an editorial the newspaper described him as a hypocrite who had misrepresented his position and who should resign.

The complainant said that there was no public interest justification for invading his privacy. The newspaper's defence relied on the complainant's election address in 1992, and on an interview given by the complainant to *The Tatler* in 1994 which contained material regarding his family life and information from constituents. The complainant replied that the newspaper had not suggested he was guilty in 1992 of any of the offences cited in the editorial or that he had said anything untrue or hypocritical in 1996, and therefore had no defence for invading his privacy. The complainant said that knowledge of his current marital status had been made known for some considerable time to appropriate individuals within his constituency, but that he had not made any public announcement.

The newspaper did not allege that the impression given by the Election Address and quotations from the article were untrue at the time they were issued. Instead, it argued that there was a public interest justification for its story to prevent Mr Allason's constituents and (to a lesser extent) the electorate at large from being misled. It argued that as soon as Mr Allason ceased to be the happily married man that had been portrayed in his election literature, he had a duty to inform the electorate accordingly. His failure to do so, along with subsequent public remarks about his marital status, justified publication. It noted in addition that Mr Allason was still appearing with his wife in his constituency as late as December 1995 and pointed to the material, in the original newspaper article, that his constituents still believed him to be happily married . . .

ADJUDICATION:

As a matter of principle, the Commission strongly believed that the mere fact that a person is a public figure did not in itself justify publication of intimate details of his or her private life unless the story could be demonstrated to be in the public interest – although Members of Parliament, as representatives of their constituents, clearly had to expect a greater degree of public scrutiny. The Commission did not believe it could plausibly be argued that a Member of Parliament had an absolute duty publicly to correct facts or impressions conveyed in interviews or an Election Address when they ceased to be accurate, especially when this might occur some time after the election concerned, provided that the MP did not appear to be continuing to foster that impression.

In this particular case, the Commission noted that there was no allegation that the Election Address was untrue at the time it was published. However, in testing the newspaper's public interest defence, the Commission had to judge whether the complainant – by his words and actions – was either intentionally or unintentionally continuing to give the impression to his constituents up to the time the article was published that his marital status had not changed since 1992.

The complainant said that he had informed 'those he believed appropriate to do so' about his separation from his wife. However, according to the newspaper's evidence, he had appeared with his wife at a constituency function as recently as Christmas 1995. Similarly, a number of those questioned by the newspaper – including some of those who said they knew the complainant well – appeared to believe that the impression given by the Election Address about his marital status had not changed.

The Commission found that the complainant – whether intentionally or not – had left at least some of his constituents with the continuing impression that he was still happily married. The interviews with *The Tatler* and the *Evening Standard* in 1994, the fact that the complainant and his wife were still living together part of the time in London and that his wife was continuing to make appearances in the constituency, continued to reinforce that impression.

The Commission found that in the particular circumstances of this case, the newspaper had sufficient public interest justification . . . for its intrusion into the complainant's privacy.

Extract 2.3.11
Goble v *The People*, PCC Report No 80 (2009)

COMPLAINT:
Phyllis Goble complained to the Press Complaints Commission, on behalf and with the signed authorisation of her son-in-law, John Hayter, that an article published in The People on 26 April 2009 headlined 'My lot have murdered someone again. S*** happens' invaded Mr Hayter's privacy in breach of Clause 3 (Privacy) of the Code of Practice. . . .

The article reported that a serving police officer, John Hayter, had posted a message on Facebook about the death of Ian Tomlinson during the London G20 protest in April 2009. His message said: 'I see my lot have murdered someone again. Oh well, shit happens.' The complainant said that publication of this comment, along with two others from Mr Hayter's profiles on social networking sites, showed a lack of respect for his privacy. The profiles on Facebook and Friends Reunited, from which the comments were taken, were not publicly accessible. Mrs Goble also complained that the newspaper had also intruded into Mr Hayter's privacy by taking and publishing a picture of him on his private driveway, and by publishing a picture taken from his sister's Friends Reunited profile showing him in uniform.

The newspaper said that Mr Hayter's comments had been brought to its attention by a third party with whom he was acquainted. The third party had legitimate access to Mr Hayter's online profiles. In addition, Mr Hayter had accepted the newspaper's journalist as an online 'friend' for a period of around an hour, before deleting her. She also, therefore, had legitimate access to the information. The newspaper argued that it was reasonable to publish the comments in question because there was a public interest in showing how serving police officers regarded incidents such as the death of Ian Tomlinson.

In terms of the photographs, the newspaper said that the first picture was taken from a public road where Mr Hayter did not have a reasonable expectation of privacy. The other image had not been taken by the paper but been passed to it by a source whose identity could not be revealed.

ADJUDICATION:
The Commission has recently made clear that it can be acceptable in some circumstances for the press to publish information taken from social networking websites, even when the material is originally intended for a small group of acquaintances and not publicly accessible. However, this will generally be only in cases where the public interest overrides the individual's right to privacy.

The Commission was persuaded that this was such a case. The individual in question was a serving police officer, commenting on a matter that was the subject of considerable media and public scrutiny. He had done so in a way that made light of a person's death and the role apparently played by the police. There was a clear public interest in knowing about police attitudes (whether publicly or privately expressed) towards the incident. In any case, posting such controversial comments to people who were not obliged to keep the information secret was likely to involve an element of risk on Mr Hayter's part, given his job. The Commission considered that any intrusion into privacy was justified by the public interest, and there was therefore no breach of Clause 3 of the Code. Additionally, the Commission considered it reasonable for the newspaper to have published two further comments also relating to his work, since they provided additional context to his remarks about Mr Tomlinson.

Complaints about the pictures of Mr Hayter were also rejected. The main image showed him standing in his drive and was taken from a public road. He was not in a place where he had a reasonable expectation of privacy, and the picture did not show him engaged in any private activity. The second image, which had been obtained from a confidential source, simply showed Mr Hayter in his uniform.

Questions for discussion

1. Do you agree with the conclusions reached in each of these cases on the question of public interest?
2. Can they be reconciled, or are the PCC's adjudications inconsistent?

(e) Clause 4: Harassment

The law regarding protection from harassment is dealt with in detail in Chapter 11. Complaints regarding harassment at the hands of the media, however, can also be made to the PCC under clause 4 of the Editors' Code of Practice, amended following concerns about the involvement of the paparazzi in the death of Princess Diana.

It is important to note that the reference in clause 4(i) to 'intimidation' and 'harassment' is clearly intended to cover instances of information gathering where the subject suffers a degree of fear, apprehension or annoyance as a result of the journalist's conduct. The reference to 'persistent pursuit' in clause 4(i), on the other hand, is 'designed to prevent journalists or photographers from chasing individuals, usually in vehicles, in a way that may endanger the individual's safety'.[124] It does not have the broader meaning of referring to, for example, persistent investigation or undercover investigation.[125] Nor does it cover harassment by repeated publication of news stories about a person.[126]

Clause 4(ii) does not prohibit journalists from asking questions or even 'door-stopping' a complainant; rather, it requires that journalists must not persist in their efforts to obtain information where they have been asked to desist[127] (or where it would be obvious according to common sense that repeated approaches are not welcome).[128] Where there is conflicting evidence about whether a request to desist was made or whether a journalist persisted to contact a claimant following such a notice, the case will be resolved in favour of

---

[124] *Caplin v News of the World*, PCC Report No 72 (2005).
[125] Ibid.
[126] *Arani v The Daily Telegraph*, PCC Report No 78 (2008); *Entwistle v Worksop Guardian*, PCC Report No 77 (2008). Cf harassment under the Protection from Harassment Act 1997 (see Chapter 11, section 11.6).
[127] *Cunningham and Ferris v Daily Record*, PCC Report No 76 (2007); *Cousins v The Sunday Times*, PCC Report No 73 (2006); *Fortier v Sunday Mirror*, PCC Report No 68 (2004); *A Woman v Scottish News of the World*, PCC Report No 60 (2002).
[128] *Kimble v Bucks Herald*, PCC Report No 53 (2001).

the newspaper[129] (except, so it seems, where the complaint has been brought on behalf of a member of the Royal Family).[130]

In the following adjudication, *Fortier v Sunday Mirror*, the PCC outlined its approach to clause 4(ii) and (iii), both in general and in the particular context of the taking and publication of photographs. In that case, the complainant had been the subject of press attention following the revelation of her affair with the then Home Secretary, David Blunkett. At the time that the story broke, the complainant contacted the PCC to complain about harassment she was receiving at the hands of the press; the PCC contacted the relevant newspapers and the harassment ceased. On 26 August 2004, two weeks after the news of the affair first broke, the complainant was approached and photographed while she was walking in public in Los Angeles. According to the complainant's version of events, she had asked the photographer not to take her photograph. The *Sunday Mirror* published the photograph on 29 August 2004. In light of the prior warnings given to the newspaper and the photographer in question, the complainant alleged that clauses 4(ii) and (iii) had been breached.

Extract 2.3.12
***Fortier v Sunday Mirror*, PCC Report No 68 (2004)**

ADJUDICATION:

Noting that no complaint had been lodged about the more general coverage of the complainant's alleged affair with the Home Secretary, the Commission's central task in this case was to decide whether the taking and publication of the particular photograph under contention was in breach of the Code of Practice – and, if it was, whether there was a public interest justification for that breach.

Clause 4 (Harassment) requires journalists not to engage in 'intimidation, harassment or persistent pursuit', and there was no evidence that those responsible for taking the picture in question had behaved in this way. Similarly, there did not appear to have been questioning or telephoning of the complainant in a way that would infringe the requirements of the Code. While the complainant had apparently been distressed by the approach, something that the Commission regretted, it did not appear that the photographer had 'persisted' in taking her photograph after having been asked to desist. The photographer had asked the complainant if she wished to pose for a picture and she had indicated that she did not. At some point – either before he spoke to her or afterwards – he took a photograph. Neither account of the incident led the Commission to conclude that there had been a breach of the Code.

However, the matter under Clause 4 did not end there, because the Commission had to consider the further argument that the request of the 16th August to journalists and photographers to desist from approaching the complainant was still relevant on the 26th August. The solicitors had contended that this was the case, and that any approach made after the 16th August would therefore breach the Code.

The Commission found this argument difficult to accept. It was certainly not disputed that the newspaper was aware of the complainant's earlier request, and was also aware of her request – made after the photograph was taken – that any resulting image not be published. However, the purpose of Clause 4 is to protect individuals, and provide relief, from physical intrusion by journalists and photographers, whether they are on their own or in a group. The Commission responds quickly and flexibly to any complaints under Clause 4 because it recognises the immediacy of any problem, and it is well placed to organise the disbanding of press packs by passing on messages to desist.

---

[129] See, e.g., *Cousins v Sunday Times*, PCC Report No 73 (2006) (although the claim based on clause 4 was rejected, the newspaper was found to have breached clause 6).

[130] *HRH Prince William v OK! Magazine*, PCC Report No 52 (2000).

The Commission does not consider it appropriate – or within the meaning of Clause 4 – to assume that a request for journalists and photographers to desist from approaching a complainant lasts in perpetuity. It would be artificial not to recognise that circumstances change. The Commission judges each case on its merits, and on this occasion it noted that the approach had taken place ten days after the request to desist, during which time there had been demonstrable developments in the story. Indeed, the article which accompanied the photograph had reported the news that the complainant had contacted the Home Secretary in order to bring an end to their alleged relationship. In these circumstances, the Commission found no breach of the Code in the photographer's approach to the complainant, which took place in public and without any physical intimidation. It followed that there was also no breach of Clause 4(iii) regarding the use of non-compliant material.

Questions for discussion

1. Do you agree with the conclusion reached by the PCC in *Fortier* v *Sunday Mirror*?
2. Is it justified that a request to desist be ignored where a certain amount of time has lapsed or where there are new developments to a story?

(f) Clause 5: Intrusion into grief or shock

Among the most sensitive aspects of journalists' work is the reporting of accidents, sudden deaths, and tragedies such as road accidents, terrorist attacks and the like. Thankfully, such reporting gives rise to relatively few complaints under clause 5(i), which requires that reporters act sensitively in circumstances where they are reporting on matters involving personal grief or shock. Examples of conduct which may amount to a breach of clause 5(i) include the following:

- a reporter directly notifying family and close friends that a person is deceased or has been involved in an accident or other incident;[131]
- publication of the fact that a person is deceased or has been involved in an accident before family and close friends have been notified;[132]
- the insensitive portrayal of a recently deceased person either in a light-hearted[133] or disparaging manner;[134]
- publication of a graphic description or photograph of a tragic event, such as a death or accident;[135] and

---

[131] See, e.g., *McKeown* v *Evening Chronicle*, PCC Report No 40 (1997).
[132] See, e.g., *Oliver* v *Manchester Evening News*, PCC Report No 43 (1998).
[133] See, e.g., *Napuk and Gibson* v *FHM*, PCC Report No 48 (1999).
[134] *Hemley* v *Herald & Post (Luton)*, PCC Report (2012) (description of the deceased as a 'pervert' was held to be 'unacceptable and gratuitous'). Cf *Brown* v *The Citizen (Gloucester)*, PCC Report (2011) (description of the complainant's son as a 'dog killer' in the headline of an article reporting his suicide was acceptable in light of the fact that he had been convicted of causing the death of a dog in 2006); *Cowles* v *Daily Mail*, PCC Report (2010) (where an allegedly offensive, homophobic and inaccurate article by Jan Moir commenting on the death of Boyzone singer Stephen Gately did not breach the Code because it was not flippant or gratuitously explicit, despite causing grief to the complainant).
[135] *Kirkland* v *Wiltshire Gazette & Herald*, PCC Report No 77 (2008) (photograph of the complainant's mother-in-law receiving treatment following a car accident); *Thomson* v *Daily Record*, PCC Report (2011) (publication of a photograph showing a body covered with a sheet where the outline of the deceased was visible); *Blows* v *The Northern Echo*, PCC Report (2012) (photograph of the complainant's husband receiving treatment after his glider crash-landed).

- publication of photographs of people in mourning, including unwanted media coverage of funeral services.[136]

The PCC has consistently maintained that newspapers are entitled to report on public interest stories and tragic events and, as explicitly recognised in clause 5(i), the press is also entitled to report on legal proceedings, including inquests. However, in doing so, the press is subject to an overriding obligation that journalists approach subjects with sympathy and discretion and that any resulting publication is handled sensitively and is not gratuitous in its content. This will always involve, by its very nature, a subjective judgment.[137] As the purpose of the clause is to 'minimise the risk of gratuitously aggravating people's vulnerability' during times of grief and shock,[138] much will turn on the amount of time which has elapsed since the event in question and the degree to which the complainant is considered to be vulnerable at the time of the publication.[139]

One of the difficulties, however, is that PCC adjudications on the breach of clause 5(i) are often difficult to reconcile, as the following two cases demonstrate. In *Thomson* v *Daily Record*, a complaint was made in relation to a newspaper report that a body had been found close to Arthur's Seat in Edinburgh, which was accompanied by a photograph of the body wrapped in a sheet. The outline of the body could be discerned. The deceased's aunt complained to the PCC, arguing that the article was insensitive and had caused distress to the family.

Extract 2.3.13
***Thomson* v *Daily Record*, (2011)**

COMPLAINT:
. . . The newspaper apologised to the complainant and her family for the distress and upset caused by the publication of the photograph, which had been removed from the online version of the article. It did not accept a breach of the Code, however: its duty was to inform the public of such tragic events and there was always a difficult balance to strike. In this case, the decision to publish was not taken lightly; rather, the body was covered and visible to the public and, in those circumstances, the publication was a matter of editorial judgement. Such photographs were unfortunate, but not uncommon. That said, the newspaper was willing to publish an apology to the family.

The complainant did not accept the sincerity of the newspaper's apology. She did not take issue with the reporting of the tragedy: it was the graphic photograph which had caused the upset. In addition, she said that the body was not publicly visible as it was 300ft up on the side of a cliff, which, she said, led the police not to erect a privacy screen.

DECISION: Upheld

ADJUDICATION:

Newspapers are fully entitled to report on tragic events which take place in public, some of which – by their very nature – will cause distress and upset to family and friends. This will often include the taking and publishing of photographs. The overriding requirement under Clause 5 of the Editors' Code is that publication must be 'handled sensitively' at times of grief or shock.

---

[136] *Cattermole* v *Bristol Evening Post*, PCC Report No 80 (2009).
[137] *Rundle* v *The Sunday Times*, PCC Report (2010).
[138] *Manchanda* v *The Independent*, PCC Report (2008).
[139] *A Boy* v *The Sunday Times*, PCC Report No 74 (2007); *A Man* v *Chat*, PCC Report No 76 (2007); *The mother of Hannah Sharp* v *Chester Chronicle*, PCC Report (2009).

The Commission recognised that the choice of photographs to accompany stories of deaths can be an extremely difficult editorial decision. The full context of the article and level of information contained in the image will generally be key factors. In this case, it agreed that it was legitimate for the newspaper to report that a body had been found, and noted that it had occurred at a well-known location, in a public place.

However, in all the circumstances, it did not think that this was sufficient to justify the specific nature of the photograph. In the Commission's view, the outline of the body through the sheeting would have been visible to readers. It quite understood why this had caused the complainant and her family such distress. The Commission considered that the use of this type of explicit image did not meet the Code's requirement of handling publication 'sensitively'.

While the Commission welcomed the newspaper's offer to apologise, it upheld the complaint.

The outcome in *Thomson* v *Daily Record* can be compared to the PCC's adjudication in *Palomba* v *Evening Standard*.[140] In that case, a complaint was made to the PCC regarding an article published in the *Evening Standard* reporting that Katherine Ward, a successful lawyer, had jumped to her death from a London hotel room. Two photographs accompanied the article: one showing Ward standing on the ledge moments before she jumped and another of her during the fall. A second article published two days later repeated the information. Ward's friend claimed that the publication of the images was unnecessary and that the articles had been published before the victim's death had been made widely known and before her identity had been publicly confirmed; moreover, the images were distressing and voyeuristic.

Extract 2.3.14
***Palomba* v *Evening Standard*, PCC Report No 72 (2006)**

ADJUDICATION:
The Commission has already considered a similar complaint against *[T]he Sun*, which was the first newspaper to publish the images. It found no breach of the Code in that instance. While the complaint against the *Evening Standard* was different in one important respect (see below), the decision remained that the complaint was not upheld. . . .

The role of the Commission as a whole was to assess under the Code whether the publication of the images constituted a failure by the newspaper to 'handle publication sensitively' at a time of grief and shock. Although it is not explicit in the Code of Practice, the Commission also considers in such cases whether publication has broken the news of the death to a victim's immediate family.

Against that background, the Commission first dealt with the broad question of whether publication was handled sensitively under the terms of Clause 5 of the Code. While accepting that this would to some extent inevitably be a subjective judgement, it concluded that there was no breach of the Code on this point.

It started from the position that the simple fact of publishing photographs of what was a public incident did not, in itself, constitute a failure to be sensitive. The Commission considered that it should be slow to restrict the right of newspapers to report newsworthy events that take place in public. This includes the right to publish photographs. This tragic case concerned an unusual death, which had taken place in public. As such, it was a newsworthy event.

This did not mean, though, that the newspaper was free to publish the information in an insensitive manner, such as by making light of the incident or including unnecessarily explicit details. Had the newspaper done so, there would have been a breach of the Code. The fact was,

---

[140] PCC Report No 72 (2006).

however, that it had not sought to trivialise or sensationalise the death of Ms Ward, and had not – in common with other newspapers – presented the photographs in a gratuitously graphic manner.

This part of the complaint under Clause 5 was not therefore upheld.

The Commission next turned to the question of whether publication in the *Evening Standard* had broken the news of the death to the victim's immediate family.

Firstly, the Commission noted that there was no evidence that any of Ms Ward's immediate family – who were apparently all abroad – had actually learned of her death through reading newspaper coverage of it. Indeed, in seeking to demonstrate that it had not thoughtlessly published the photographs regardless of whether the family of the victim were aware of the death, the newspaper pointed to the fact that it understood that the police had known the woman's identity when it published the piece.

That said, the Commission was concerned that the *Evening Standard* had made no further checks to establish unequivocally whether the family had, in the event, already been informed. In the Commission's view, its responsibility was greater than that of the Sun as one of the photographs it published (of Ms Ward on the hotel ledge) would have made her more clearly identifiable to those that knew her.

The newspaper had not demonstrated to the Commission's satisfaction that it had taken enough care before publication to establish that printing the picture would not have identified Ms Ward to her family. It had seemingly not made specific checks, but rather assumed from the fact that the police were aware of the woman's identity that the family must have known. In the event, the fact that publication did not lead to identification seemed to the Commission to be more a matter of luck than judgement. Greater steps should have been taken to verify the position before the decision to publish such a clear picture was made.

While it had been stated that the coverage revealed the news to some of her friends – something that, if true, was a matter of regret to the Commission – the Commission has never taken the view that its position that newspapers should not generally break the news of a death to a victim's immediate family can reasonably extend to all those connected to the victim.

The Commission, taking into consideration all of the above, did not consider there to have been a breach of the Code raised by this aspect of the complaint.

Questions for discussion

1.   Can these cases be reconciled?
2.   Do you agree with either decision?

The requirement under clause 5(ii) that care be taken in reports of suicide to prevent the publication of excessive detail about the method used was introduced in 2006 and is intended to limit the potential for 'copycat' suicides. It will often be a 'difficult judgment call'[141] as to whether details are excessive. In *PCC v The Guardian*,[142] it was held that it was not a breach of the code for the newspaper to publish an article about a man who cut his own head off with a chainsaw, including details about how it had been activated. Some other publishers reporting on the story, however, went too far by including detailed information about the apparatus used by the victim. In another example, *A Woman* v

---

[141] *PCC v The Guardian*, PCC Report No 78 (2009).
[142] Ibid.

The News (Portsmouth),[143] the PCC found that a newspaper article reporting the death of a woman by suicide had breached the Code by naming the anti-depressant medication taken by the victim, the number of pills missing and the dosage she had ingested. The amount of alcohol in the victim's blood was also reported. This was 'sufficient information to spell out to readers the precise method of death'.[144] Similarly, in the first adjudication under the new sub-clause, the PCC found that a report of an inquest into a teacher who electrocuted himself was in breach of the Code.[145] The PCC said that although newspapers are free to report proceedings conducted in public, the article included too much detail in describing the method used.

Question for discussion

1. Should there be limits on the amount of detail included in a report on a person's suicide?

(g) Clause 10: Clandestine devices and subterfuge

It is currently a breach of clause 10 of the Code to obtain information by subterfuge or misrepresentation, through the use of clandestine devices or interception of communications, or by the unauthorised removal of documents or photographs.[146] Such journalistic techniques, however, will be acceptable where they are justified in the public interest.

In order to justify the use of clandestine devices and subterfuge in the public interest, the editor must establish, first, that such techniques are not being used in furtherance of a 'fishing expedition'.[147] In other words, there must be a reasonable basis for believing that the investigation will result in obtaining information in the public interest and not simply on the off chance that such information *might* be uncovered.[148] Second, the use of the clandestine methods must be proportionate to the public interest in question. In *A man v Sunday World*, for example, a complaint was upheld by the PCC where a newspaper was unable to demonstrate that the story in question had a high level of public interest justifying the use of intrusive footage obtained by a hidden camera.[149] Third, the impugned techniques must be necessary; as recognised explicitly in clause 10(ii), the material must not be available by other means. In *A man v The Observer*,[150] for instance, the PCC upheld a complaint where a journalist pretended to be a shooting enthusiast in order to obtain information from the complainant who was said to be developing a revolver that would avoid regulation under the Firearms Act. While the PCC agreed that the story was in the public interest, the newspaper was not able to establish that the subterfuge was necessary in light of the fact that no other efforts were made to obtain the material.

---

[143] PCC Report No 80 (2010).
[144] Ibid.
[145] *A Woman v Wigan Observer*, PCC Report No 76 (2007).
[146] This is in addition to the legal regulation of such activities under, for example, the Data Protection Act 1998 and the Regulation of Investigatory Powers Act 2000.
[147] *Munro v Evening Standard*, PCC Report No 54 (2001); *Ryle v News of the World*, PCC Report No 53 (2001).
[148] Ian Beales, *The Editors' Codebook* (Press Standards Board of Finance, 2012), 65.
[149] *A man v Sunday World*, PCC Report (2010).
[150] PCC Report No 44 (1998).

The necessity requirement, however, has been treated generously in cases where the press can demonstrate that the information *might* not be available by more direct means. In *HH Saudi Research & Marketing (UK) Limited* v *The Sunday Telegraph*,[151] a journalist posed as a potential customer of a Saudi-owned printing company to find out whether it published the British National Party's 'anti-Muslim' newspaper, *The Voice of Freedom*. A subsequent conversation with a spokesman for the company confirmed this as correct, but only after the journalist said he had irrefutable evidence. In dismissing the complaint, the PCC held that it will not breach the Code in circumstances where material is otherwise *potentially* available if there are reasonable grounds to believe that seeking information by direct means would 'compromise the ability of reporters to investigate matters subsequently'. This will also be relevant 'where any subterfuge is not serious and causes little harm'. On the facts, the PCC found that because the information had the potential to cause embarrassment, it was reasonable for the newspaper to suppose that the company might not have otherwise divulged the information to the journalist. Moreover, the reporter did not intrude into the privacy of the complainant, the subterfuge was 'of a less serious order' and it was not a 'fishing expedition'.[152]

Question for discussion

1. Do you think it can ever be justified for a journalist to obtain information by subterfuge or by using clandestine devices? If so, in what circumstances?

(h) Clause 12: Discrimination

The PCC has repeatedly stressed that clause 12(i) is aimed at censuring discrimination directed at particular individuals, rather than discrimination or abuse directed at groups or categories of people.[153] According to *The Editors' Codebook*, extending clause 12 to cover generalised comments about groups or categories of people would 'involve subjective views, often based on political correctness or taste, and be difficult to adjudicate upon without infringing the freedom of expression of others'.[154] In other words, the Code should not be interpreted in such a way as to stifle opinions and debate about issues of race, religion, sexuality or gender, even where views are expressed in a way that may shock, disturb or offend.

In 1996, the PCC held that two anti-German headlines ('Let's Blitz the Fritz' and 'Here We Go – Bring on the Krauts') published in the context of the European football championship did not breach the Code. The PCC issued a statement, pointing out that clause 12 (then clause 15) is concerned with the pejorative treatment of individuals on the basis of their race, not abuse of national groups.[155] This view was confirmed shortly after in a complaint about a tabloid leader concerning the allocation of World Cup tickets. In this context, and in that of complaints concerning payments to criminals (discussed below), the PCC frequently exercises its discretion to consider complaints by third parties (that is, individuals not directly concerned by the press article).

---

[151] PCC Report No 71 (2005).
[152] Ibid.
[153] See, e.g., *Terziu* v *Sunday Times*, PCC Report No 73 (2006).
[154] Ian Beales, *The Editors' Codebook* (Press Standards Board of Finance, 2012), 72.
[155] PCC Report No 35 (1996).

Extract 2.3.15
Waller v *Daily Star*, PCC Report No 42 (1998)

COMPLAINT:

Dr R. Waller, of The University of Liverpool, and six others complained that a short leader comment, 'Frogs need a good kicking', in the *Daily Star* of 2 March 1998 was discriminatory in breach of Clause 13 [now clause 12] (Discrimination) of the Code of Practice. The comment said that the way in which the French had 'grabbed the lion's share of World Cup tickets is typical of their slimy continental ways . . . As we proved at Agincourt and Waterloo, a good kicking on their gallic derrieres is the only language the greedy frogs understand.' The complainant said the comment was racist, offensive and likely to incite violence . . .

ADJUDICATION:

The Commission had considered a number of similar complaints about discrimination and incitement of football fans to violence during 1996. Then, three newspapers had covered the Euro 96 football tournament in a way which many people found tasteless and offensive. On that occasion, the Commission did not censure any newspaper for a breach of the Code. It believed that a considerable amount of nationalist fervour and jingoism was inevitable at a time of any significant international sporting event, and that newspapers were reflecting those emotions. However, the Commission had believed the reporting shrill and poorly judged, and a far cry from the tradition of tolerance and fair play that had previously characterised reporting of such events: editors themselves had recognised much of it as in bad taste and rightly apologised for the offence they had caused. The Commission asked all editors to bear in mind the strong public reaction to this coverage in reporting in the future.

The principles which underlay the Commission's decision then remain unchanged. Sporting events – and matters relating to them, such as ticketing arrangements – are bound to excite considerable emotion. Newspapers will inevitably reflect that – even if they do so in a way which some people will find offensive.

The Code is not intended to stop such robust comment. Indeed, the purpose of Clause 13 is to protect *individuals* from prejudice – not to restrain partisan comment about other nations. The Commission has noted before on a number of occasions that the Clause is rightly defined in this way to allow the press to make pointed and critical comment, if necessary, about events and people in a variety of circumstances. The leader comment on this occasion – reflecting partisan concern in a clearly tongue-in-cheek manner – had not therefore breached the Code, although its tone had been misjudged.

In order to breach the Code under clause 12(i), a publication must refer to an individual's race, colour, religion, gender, sexual orientation or to a physical or mental disability, in a prejudicial or pejorative manner, and must therefore be discriminatory of the person on that basis. A mere reference to a person's race, colour, gender, sexual orientation or physical or mental disability will not be sufficient. In *Dale* v *Daily Mail*,[156] for example, a 'snide' reference to a parliamentary candidate as 'overtly gay' was not pejorative. The PCC said that 'where it is debatable – as in this case – about whether remarks can be regarded solely as pejorative and gratuitous, the Commission should be slow to restrict the right to express an opinion, however snippy it might be'. Despite the distress cause to the claimant, the PCC went on to reiterate that 'the right to freedom of expression that journalists enjoy also includes the right – within the law – to give offence'. The PCC came to a similar conclusion in *Cowles* v *Daily Mail*,[157] where Stephen Gately's civil partner, Andrew Cowles, complained to the PCC regarding a column by Jan Moir published in the *Daily Mail* and

[156] PCC Report No 80 (2009).
[157] PCC Report (2010).

on the newspaper's website. The complainant alleged that the article attributed Gately's death (otherwise found to have resulted from natural causes) to vices associated with 'a gay lifestyle'. The article said that his death, along with the then recent death of Matt Lucas's civil partner, Kevin McGee, both struck a blow 'to the happy-ever-after myth of civil partnerships'.[158] The PCC held that, while tasteless and offensive, the article did not breach clause 12(i) because the columnist did not use 'pejorative synonyms for the word "homosexual" at any point'.[159] While finding the article tasteless and offensive, it was reported that the PCC stressed the importance to be attached to freedom of expression enjoyed by journalists:

> [T]his part of the Code was not designed to prevent discussion of certain lifestyles or broad issues relating to race, religion or sexuality. There was a distinction between critical innuendo – which, though perhaps distasteful, was permissible in a free society – and discriminatory description of individuals, and the Code was designed to constrain the latter rather than the former.[160]

However, the *Sunday Times* was said to have crossed the line where TV presenter Clare Balding was referred to as a 'dyke on a bike'.[161] This was, according to the PCC, 'a pejorative synonym relating to the claimant's sexuality' and was used in a 'demeaning and gratuitous way'.[162] Similarly, referring to a male-to-female transsexual as a 'tranny' has been held to be in breach of the Code.[163] While the newspaper was entitled to air concerns about the complainant's role as a rape counsellor, the use of the term 'tranny' was a 'needless abbreviation' and was clearly pejorative.[164]

Questions for discussion

1. Do you agree with the reluctance to extend the operation of clause 12 to discrimination of groups? Why/why not?
2. Is the PCC right to limit breaches of clause 12 to prejudicial or pejorative references to a person's race, colour, religion, gender, etc.? Do you agree that *Cowles* v *Daily Mail* was correctly decided on this basis?

It is not a breach of the Code, however, for the press to publish material which is pejorative, but not discriminatory on the basis of an individual's race, colour, religion, gender, sexual orientation or physical or mental disability. In *Sharon* v *The Independent*,[165] a cartoon depicting the former Israeli Prime Minister Ariel Sharon eating an infant was published in *The Independent* one day before the Israeli general election and two days after an Israeli attack on Gaza City. The cartoon was said to be 'tainted by anti-Semitism', it being argued that the depiction of Sharon eating the infant was a reference to the so-called 'blood libel', the false accusation that Jews preyed on Christian children. The newspaper denied the allusion to the blood libel, claiming instead that the 'baby in the figure represented the Israeli electorate being ruthlessly devoured by its Prime Minister'.[166]

---

[158] Ibid.
[159] Ibid.
[160] Ibid.
[161] *Balding* v *The Sunday Times*, PCC Report (2010).
[162] Ibid.
[163] *McCormack* v *Sunday Life*, PCC Report No 80 (2010).
[164] Ibid.
[165] PCC Report No 62 (2003).
[166] Ibid.

Extract 2.3.16
Sharon v *The Independent*, PCC Report No 62 (2003)

ADJUDICATION:

Having made that general point [that political leaders are often the subject of depiction in cartoons], the Commission nonetheless dealt with the substance of the complaint under Clause 13 and considered whether the cartoon amounted to a prejudicial or pejorative reference to Mr Sharon's race or religion. It rejected the complaint for a number of reasons. At its heart, this complaint concerned an allegation that the cartoon had alluded to the 'blood libel' – and it was clear that a number of readers had inferred this too. However, it was also clear from the feedback that the newspaper itself published that other readers and commentators had not. In view of this, and for other reasons set out below, the Commission was not prepared to make a connection between the cartoon and the alleged blood libel. The Commission regretted any offence that had been caused to the individual concerned and to others who had complained, but this in itself was not enough to conclude that a breach of the Code had occurred.

. . . There was no reason for the Commission to disbelieve the cartoonist's position – published in the newspaper and submitted as part of its evidence – that he had taken the view that the attack on Gaza City was a form of 'macabre electioneering' whose equivalent in a less fraught situation might be the more traditional stunt of kissing babies. He explained that this thought brought to mind the Goya painting and its depiction of the insanity of Saturn who is driven by paranoia into consuming his own children. The Commission accepted this explanation. It represented an approach which could apply equally to other governments and politicians. It did not consider that there was anything particularly prejudicial to Mr Sharon's race or religion about satirising him in this way – especially as there is nothing inherently anti-Semitic about the Goya image or about the myth of Saturn devouring his children, which has been used previously to satirise other politicians accused of sacrificing their own 'children' for political purposes.

The solicitors had said that the absence of any Jewish emblems or Israeli insignia in the cartoon was irrelevant, and that the association of someone who was a known Jew with a hostile image of a practice commonly attributed by anti-Semites to Jews was sufficient to conclude that the image was discriminatory. The Commission did not agree with this position – having already accepted the cartoonist's explanation it could not ignore the fact that there was nothing in the cartoon that referred to Mr Sharon's religion at all. Of course it is well-known that the Israeli Prime Minister is Jewish, but he is also a public figure of the sort that newspapers frequently satirise or criticise, and it is not the Commission's job to interfere with newspapers' rights to comment on individuals in this way unless there is an issue under the Code.

Clearly some people had felt strongly that the cartoon had made a direct reference to the blood libel – a position that might have been more justifiable without a convincing explanation from the newspaper. The fact remained, however, that the newspaper's explanation was accepted by the Commission and it considered that it would be unreasonable to expect editors to take into account all possible interpretations of material that they intend to publish, no matter what their own motive for publishing it. That would be to interpret the Code in a manner that would impose burdens on newspapers that would arguably interfere with their rights to freedom of expression.

Questions for discussion

1. Do you find the PCC's reasoning in *Sharon* v *The Independent* convincing?
2. Is it satisfactory that editors should not be required to take into account all possible interpretations of material that they publish? Is this different from the approach taken by the law of defamation as to whether a publisher is liable for defamation?

Clause 12(ii) requires that details of an individual's race, colour, religion, sexual orientation, physical or mental illness or disability can be included only where genuinely relevant to the story. Gender is not covered because it is not seen as discriminatory to refer to an individual's gender. In *Bishko* v *Evening Standard*, for example, it was held to be a breach of the Code to refer to the complainant as a 'Jewish South African' where it had no relevance in an article about the complainant's business activities.[167] However, it was found to not be a breach of clause 12(ii) in *Haji-Ioannou* v *Financial Times* where a columnist referred to the complainant's Greek Cypriot origins.[168] This was because the complainant had, in the past, been happy for his background to be discussed in the public domain, he had himself referred to his Greek origins (on his website) and it formed part of his public persona. The PCC further said that 'such brief references to the nationality of a public figure, in a descriptive article about him, were not irrelevant'.[169]

In *Arani* v *The Daily Telegraph*,[170] references to the complainant as a 'Muslim lawyer' were considered relevant in the context of articles discussing the complainant's representation of Islamic terrorist suspects and her regular appearances at various Islamic events, including her speech at a controversial rally that had prompted the articles in question. Similarly, an article with the headline 'Gay BBC weather girl is having DIY baby' was held to not breach the Code by referring to the sexuality of a pregnant woman.[171] This was because the non-pejorative reference to the complainant's sexuality was relevant to a discussion in the article that made 'comparisons with the childbearing of other same-sex couples'.[172]

(i) Clause 16: Payment to criminals

Among the most controversial decisions of the PCC have been those interpreting clause 16 (previously clause 17, and prior to that, 16(ii)), which prohibits payment, except in certain circumstances, to confessed or convicted criminals and their family members and associates for stories, photographs or information. The clause was amended in June 2004 to make it clear that it is only intended to apply where the payment for the material will lead to the exploitation of a particular crime, or will glorify or glamorise crime in general. Since this time, only 5 complaints have been adjudicated under clause 16, far fewer than the 25 adjudications that spanned a similar length of time between September 1996 and June 2004. It is possible that this reduction can be attributed to the fact that it is now clear that there will be no breach of clause 16 where the material is not sought by the press to 'exploit a particular crime or to glorify or glamorise crime in general',[173] compared to the pre-2004 position where *any* payment amounted to a *prima facie* breach of the Code and the burden was on the press to establish a public interest defence.

(i) Exploiting a particular crime, or glorifying or glamorising crime in general?
According to *The Editors' Codebook*, the burden rests on the editor to establish that there 'was genuinely no intentional exploitation of a particular crime or of glamorising or glorifying

---

[167] *Bishko* v *Evening Standard*, PCC Report No 40 (1997).
[168] *Haji-Ioannou* v *Financial Times*, PCC Report (2011).
[169] Ibid.
[170] PCC Report No 78 (2008).
[171] *A Woman* v *Scottish News of the World*, PCC Report No 60 (2002).
[172] Ibid.
[173] Editors' Code of Practice, cl 16.

crime generally, and [to] demonstrate that it was not reasonable to expect that to be the outcome'.[174] This will usually be evident on the face of the resulting publication.

In *Moffatt* v *Chat*,[175] the PCC considered for the first time the question of whether payment was made to a convicted criminal in order to exploit a particular crime. Sylvia Payne had been convicted of unlawful sex with her son; *Chat* magazine paid the woman, through an agency, for her story. The article described the criminal act and quoted the woman as saying that she did not regret what she had done but that she regretted that she had been caught. The PCC ruled that the woman had 'had a right to express this view', but that payment to her 'was a clear breach of the Code on the part of the magazine'.[176] Thus, it was obvious that the payment was for a story that sought to exploit the particular crime in question. In *Fleming* v *Pick Me Up*,[177] it was similarly held that a magazine article focusing on a woman's first-person account of discovering that she had slept with a man on the same night that he had committed a murder was, without doubt, a story that exploited the murder. The magazine's payment to the woman, therefore, was a breach of clause 16.

It is apparent from these adjudications, therefore, that a particular crime will have been 'exploited' where information is obtained for the purpose of an article or story that reports or focuses on the crime in question. In contrast, the PCC found in *Thames Valley Probation Area* v *The Mail on Sunday* that interviews with convicted criminals for the purpose of a story about a community service scheme was not information that was sought in exploitation of a particular crime.[178]

Extract 2.3.17
Thames Valley Probation Area v The Mail on Sunday, PCC Report No 74 (2007)

The article followed news that the Lord Chief Justice, Lord Phillips, had done some undercover community service in order to test the merits of non-custodial sentences. It quoted three individuals who were said to have been carrying out their own sentences on the same day as Lord Phillips. They discussed their experience of the Lord Chief Justice, their opinion of him and their approach to community service . . .

The complainant . . . asked the Commission to consider whether there had been a breach of Clause 16. One of the interviewed men, Shane Campbell, was on a stand-alone Curfew Requirement and was wearing an electronic tag at the time of the interview.

The newspaper said that it had initially spoken to Mr Campbell – who appeared to possess a large amount of information about the session – without an offer of payment. It soon became apparent that a full interview would not have been obtained without payment. The newspaper gave him a total of £460 in three payments. He, in turn, supplied pictures and information about the two other individuals who, he said, had taken part . . .

DECISION: Not Upheld

ADJUDICATION:
For the purposes of this complaint – even though both parties to the complaint agreed that those interviewed had not, after all, carried out community service with the Lord Chief Justice – the Commission proceeded on the basis that Shane Campbell, who received £460 from the

---

[174] Ian Beales, *The Editors' Codebook* (Press Standards Board of Finance, 2012), 83–4.
[175] PCC Report No 73 (2006). See also *Wishart* v *Take a Break*, PCC Report No 79 (2009) (involving an interview with a woman convicted of arson).
[176] *Moffatt* v *Chat*, PCC Report No 73 (2006).
[177] PCC Report (2011).
[178] *Thames Valley Probation Area* v *The Mail on Sunday*, PCC Report No 74 (2007).

newspaper, had been convicted of a crime. Certainly that must have been the assumption of the newspaper when it made the payments, for two reasons: he had claimed to have been carrying out community service, and he had told the newspaper that he was the subject of a curfew order which entailed him wearing an electronic tag.

Clause 16 of the Code says that payments must not be made to convicted criminals for information which seeks 'to exploit a particular crime or to glorify or glamorise crime in general'. There is, however, a public interest defence for making such payments. The Code does not outlaw payments to people with criminal records in all circumstances.

The information clearly could not have been in the public interest if it was fictitious. However, before the Commission considered whether the information would have been in the public interest had it been true, there was a simpler consideration: did the information exploit a particular crime, or glorify or glamorise crime in general?

The Commission concluded that it did not. The Code deliberately refers to a 'particular crime' so that it does not amount to a blanket ban on paying anyone who has a criminal record. Campbell's crimes were not referred to in the piece – so 'a particular crime' had not been exploited. The fact that a crime would have had to have been committed in order for someone to talk (honestly) about their experiences on a community service scheme was not sufficient, in the Commission's opinion, to engage the terms of the Code. Otherwise, the definition of exploiting crime would be unduly restrictive so that stories about general prison life – or other information from the perspective of a criminal – would be caught by the Code.

There was also nothing in the article that glorified crime in general terms, and the descriptions of the life of a petty criminal undertaking community service did not glamorise it.

The Commission appreciated that there would be people who would have strong views about payment to such people in any circumstances. However, the Commission must adjudicate under the terms of the Code – and its decision, for the reasons set out above, was that it had not been breached.

(ii) Public interest

It is a defence to a payment or offer of payment otherwise in breach of clause 16(i) to show that it was justified because it resulted in the publication of material considered to be of public interest. This requires, under clause 16(ii), that the editor demonstrate 'that there was good reason to believe the public interest would be served'. Clause 16(ii) further provides that if the information for which payment was made does not, contrary to the editor's expectations, turn up any material of public interest, then the material that is obtained should not be published.

While there has not been a detailed adjudication focussing on the public interest defence since it was revised by the introduction of clause 16(ii) in 2004, a number of guiding principles set out in the PCC's earlier adjudications would appear to have continuing relevance. First, the PCC has held that the payment must be *necessary* to secure the publication of the material.[179] This was an explicit requirement in the pre-2004 incarnation of the public interest defence but does not appear in the current version. Nevertheless, *The Editors' Codebook* assumes that it is still a requirement: '[t]his means a newspaper which pays a criminal, in the genuine and reasonable belief that it would *be the only way* to elicit information of public interest, is covered'.[180] Necessity, according to the pre-2004 adjudications, will usually be satisfied where the payee is not willing to provide the information other than for a fee[181] or where payment is required in order to ensure

---

[179] See, e.g., *Various* v *The Daily Telegraph*, PCC Report No 43 (1998); *Bright* v *Daily Mail*, PCC Report No 44 (1999); *Barlow* v *The Daily Telegraph*, PCC Report No 47 (1999).

[180] Ian Beales, *The Editors' Codebook* (Press Standards Board of Finance, 2012), 85.

[181] See, e.g., *Cupit* v *News of the World*, PCC Report No 50 (2000); *McInnes* v *Daily Record*, PCC Report No 62 (2003).

exclusivity.[182] In the case of book serialisation, the PCC readily considers that payment for the right to serialise is necessary to ensure that the public interest material is made available to as wide an audience as possible (i.e. beyond those who buy the book itself).[183]

Second, the information resulting from the payment must be *new*, or it at least must provide a new perspective on the issue said to be in the public interest. Indeed, this must be right; except in the case of book serialisation, it is difficult to see how it could be considered necessary to make a payment to extract information from a payee where that information is already in the public domain. However, the question of whether payment has generated the production of new material has been the subject of confused treatment in the PCC's adjudications. Sometimes it is considered as part of the question of necessity;[184] in some adjudications it is seen as relevant to the question of whether there is public interest in the material;[185] and, in others, it is treated as a stand-alone 'test'.[186]

The third principle – whether or not the payment has been made to its recipient for profit – has also given rise to contradictory and confused treatment. In some adjudications, the profit motive of the payee has been considered relevant to the question of necessity;[187] in other cases, it has been treated as a stand-alone consideration.[188] Under either approach, a payment will be much more likely to be considered acceptable in the public interest where it is made to a charity or where it is needed to support a bid for freedom or to clear a convicted criminal's name.[189] On the other hand, a payment which allows a criminal or an associate to profit from their story is particularly frowned upon.[190] In other cases, however, the profit motive of the payee has been treated as irrelevant. In *Cupit* v *News of the World*,[191] for example, the newspaper made a payment of £1000 to a convicted criminal (who shared a prison cell with the complainant) for the story that the complainant was faking her religious beliefs at the early stages of her sentence in order to obtain favourable treatment. The PCC held that the payment was necessary to obtain the public interest information and appeared to treat the profit motive of the informant as irrelevant: 'the manner in which Ms Gibson intended to spend the money was not a matter that would have had any bearing on the Commission's decision under the Code'.[192] Similarly, payments made to nurses Deborah Parry and Lucille McLauchlan, convicted in Saudi Arabia of killing a fellow nurse, were justified in the public interest, even though the PCC acknowledged that they were made for profit.[193]

The following extract provides a number of examples of when payment to criminals (or their associates) will be justified in the public interest.

---

[182] See, e.g., *PCC* v *Daily Mirror*, PCC Report No 63 (2003); *Bright* v *Daily Mail*, PCC Report No 44 (1999); *Various* v *The Daily Telegraph*, PCC Report No 43 (1998).

[183] *Various* v *The Daily Telegraph*, PCC Report No 43 (1998).

[184] *Bright* v *Daily Mail*, PCC Report No 44 (1999).

[185] *PCC* v *Daily Mirror*, PCC Report No 63 (2003).

[186] *Bradley* v *The Sunday Times*, PCC Report No 50 (2000); *Barlow* v *The Daily Telegraph*, PCC Report No 47 (1999).

[187] See, e.g., *PCC* v *Daily Mirror*, PCC Report No 63 (2003); *Bright* v *Daily Mail*, PCC Report No 44 (1999). It should be noted that it seems odd to consider necessity from the perspective of the payee rather than simply inquiring, as is the approach in some adjudications, as to whether the newspaper needed to make the payment in order to secure the material.

[188] *PCC* v *The Sun*, PCC Report No 54 (2001); *Bradley* v *The Sunday Times*, PCC Report No 50 (2000); *Barlow* v *The Daily Telegraph*, PCC Report No 47 (1999).

[189] *Bright* v *Daily Mail*, PCC Report No 44 (1999).

[190] *Barlow* v *The Daily Telegraph*, PCC Report No 47 (1999).

[191] *Cupit* v *News of the World*, PCC Report No 50 (2000).

[192] Ibid.

[193] *Various* v *The Daily Telegraph*, PCC Report No 43 (1998), 5.2.

Extract 2.3.18
Various v *The Daily Telegraph*, PCC Report No 43 (1998)

1. THE COMPLAINTS

1.0 The Commission considered three sets of complaints under Clause 16 . . . of the Code of Practice, which prohibits payments by newspapers or magazines for stories to convicted or confessed criminals, except where publication of such stories is in the public interest.

1.1 The first set of complaints related to the serialisation by *The Times* of the book *Cries Unheard* by Gitta Sereny about the child killer Mary Bell. Serialisation took place from 29 April to 1 May 1998.

1.2 The second set of complaints related to articles in *The Mirror* and *The Express* setting out the story of Deborah Parry and Lucille [McLauchlan], both convicted of a killing in Saudi Arabia but released from prison there following a Royal Pardon. These articles were published in the week beginning 20 May 1998. For ease, these complaints are referred to throughout the first part of this adjudication as the nurses.

1.3 The third set of complaints related to the serialisation by *The Daily Telegraph* of a book, *The Informer*, by convicted IRA terrorist Sean O'Callaghan. The serialisation began on 16 May 1998 . . .

3. WAS THERE A PUBLIC INTEREST JUSTIFICATION?

3.0 **Mary Bell and *The Times*.** The Commission found the newspaper's public interest arguments in the case of the serialisation of *Cries Unheard* to be compelling. The newspaper summed up that public interest as something that runs like a spine through [Gitta Sereny's book] and was the reason Sereny felt impelled to return to the case she covered at the time of the trial. Does the criminal justice system do real justice to such damaged children? If not, how can it be improved?

3.1 Many specific issues of public interest were raised by the newspaper. They included: the circumstances in which a child who grew up in surroundings of depravity came to be a murderer; the connection between Bell's own crime and the abuse to which she herself was subjected; and the first authoritative account of how the penal system deals with child criminals. Indeed, the editor had summed up the public interest justification in a way the Commission found highly cogent: Only by trying to understand what could conceivably have driven an 11 year old girl to kill two small boys . . . can we come any closer to stopping these crimes.

3.2 The Commission also noted that the newspaper was only serialising the work – and an argument of freedom of expression, and the public interest attaching to that, therefore also arose. The material had already been put into the public domain – as a result of the willing co-operation of Mary Bell herself – and what she had to say was original material of relevance to a wide range of issues relating to crime and punishment. As such the public – not just those who would buy her book – had a right to access the material. As the newspaper said, *Cries Unheard* publishes information which should be put in the public domain for no more specific reason than that it is better for important facts to be available for dissection and discussion than for them to remain hidden.

3.3 The Commission noted that a recent review of the book, by Mary Margaret McCabe of the Department of Philosophy at Kings College London, had summed up the issue extremely well. Should this book have [been] published? The answer is a firm yes . . . The doubt it provokes, both about this case and how we should deal with it, is a vital component of our reaching [a] proper understanding of how we live our family lives, and of how our institutions might correct them (17 July 1998).

3.4 **Parry and *The Express*, [McLauchlan] and *The Mirror*.** In both cases, it was not for the Commission to make any finding or pass any judgement on the allegations that had been made about the Saudi justice system. The Commission's role was only to decide whether there was any public interest in newspapers promoting a debate about it.

3.5 Against that background, the Commission found the newspapers' public interest justifications in both these cases to be substantial.

3.6 In the case of Lucille [McLauchlan], the newspaper published evidence that she had allegedly been tortured and sexually assaulted after her arrest by the Saudi police. She had, apparently, been denied access to British Embassy staff and to proper legal representation in advance of a trial in private without a jury and without being allowed to give evidence on her own behalf. Independent experts had analysed her confession and concluded that it was not genuine – as she had always maintained. An independent organisation, Fair Trials Abroad, had been unequivocal in its criticism of the alleged conduct of the police, and made clear its view that the convictions ought not to be sustained. The newspaper believed that the combination of these factors showed that the entire process was carried out by what it described as a primitive court dispensing barbaric justice. The articles, they said, would go some way to prevent such miscarriages of justice in the future and encourage the Saudi government to examine and reform its judicial system. The Commission also noted that the Prime Minister and Foreign Secretary had been instrumental in the sentences being commuted – which itself added a substantial element of public interest to the entire story.

3.7 In the case of Deborah Parry, the newspaper said that it was the nurse's family which had convinced it that . . . the story should be told. There had, the paper said, been a miscarriage of justice. They, too, noted that her story was a warning to other people thinking they might make easy money working in the Middle East. The money that had been given to her, the paper said, would be used almost entirely to pursue this line of public interest: it would be spent on legal costs to assist her in clearing her name; the newspaper would continue to assist her in this.

3.8 Having regard to all the matters set out above, the Commission took the view that the newspapers had an abundant public interest justification.

3.9 First, the British Government itself had been involved in the case – arguing for the commutation of the nurses' sentences and their release. This was therefore a matter of legitimate public interest and debate: indeed, the Government would not have become involved otherwise. To argue that there was no public interest would – in effect – be to say that the public had no right to understand the circumstances of a high profile case involving British citizens abroad, with which their Government was closely involved.

3.10 Second – again emphasising the point that it was not a matter for the Commission to make any judgement whatever about Saudi justice – the Commission noted that 30,000 British citizens currently work in Saudi Arabia. Many thousands of others are no doubt contemplating doing so. Allegations had been made about the way in which justice was dispensed in the country – and it could not be argued that there was no public interest in airing these, whether or not they were well founded. Newspapers have a legitimate role in scrutinising justice in this country, and every other one where British citizens reside. They were fulfilling that role in this case.

3.11 Third, as with the case of Mary Bell, the Commission noted that there was an important argument of freedom of expression and the public interest attaching to the story. The two nurses had a right to give their account – especially against a background in which other newspapers were putting the other side of the story. This was particularly important as the nurses had been convicted following a closed trial – in which their side of the story was never heard by the British public.

3.12 **Sean O'Callaghan and *The Daily Telegraph*.** The newspaper provided the Commission with a strong public interest justification. The book they were serialising provided, they said, a unique inside account – such as no other book or court testimony has ever provided – of the inner workings, thinking and strategy and tactics of the IRA. The newspaper had said that it was proud to provide this account because of the service to truth that Sean O'Callaghan had performed. Everyone in the British Isles, they added, needed to understand how the most important terrorist organisation in Western Europe worked – and the threat to democracy which the fascism of Sinn Fein posed.

3.13 The Commission agreed with the newspaper that there was a very strong public interest justification in serialising the book. For the first time, an informer had thrown the spotlight onto the workings of a terrorist organisation that had been responsible for many deaths throughout the United Kingdom. The book was an invaluable work – and deserved the wide audience that serialisation gave it.

Questions for discussion

1. Does it make sense to consider the profit motive as relevant to necessity? Is it relevant to the public interest?
2. Do you think it is ever in the public interest to allow criminals (or their associates) to profit from their crimes?

Selected further reading

The Leveson Inquiry, An Inquiry into the Culture, Practices and Ethics of the Press (HC 2012–13, 780). This report provides a comprehensive overview of the history of self-regulation of the press, a critical analysis of the operation of the PCC and proposals for reform.

3 Broadcasting structure and regulation

3.1 INTRODUCTION

In addition to obligations imposed by the general law, broadcasting has been, and continues to be, subject to special regulatory obligations and restrictions (see Chapter 1, Section 1.3). Licences to broadcast have been required while obligations are imposed upon broadcasters concerning the type and content of programmes and commercial content. These are restrictions and obligations that would be regarded as intolerable if imposed upon the press, yet are generally accepted as necessary for broadcasting. Chapter 1 examined the justifications for this differential treatment. This chapter describes the regulatory framework for broadcasting activities in the United Kingdom, both public and private. The term 'broadcasting' has varied in meaning over time. New technologies have changed the way in which television and radio services are delivered and regulation has had to adapt to those changes, with the result that content services, such as on-demand audiovisual services may now be regulated in ways once confined to broadcasting. Section 3.2 will outline the types of services now regulated like broadcasting.

The changes in the way television and radio services can be accessed and the increasing number of services available have called into question the continued viability of the traditional justifications for broadcast regulation. However, regulation has remained, and in fact extended, its reach to cover some on-demand services (see also Chapter 5), although the regulation of the latter differs from the regulation of the more traditional services. Hence, recalling the justifications for regulation discussed in Chapter 1 (see especially Extract 1.3.2), the model and/or extent of regulation of certain services will reflect, for example, the likelihood that they may have a more limited influence on the audience. This chapter will examine regulation of the various audio and audiovisual services.

3.2 MEDIA MARKETS AND TECHNOLOGY

Before the proliferation of technologies available for delivery of content services, it was relatively easy to identify what was broadcasting and to isolate it for regulation. 'Broadcasting' was understood to refer to the delivery of television and radio services via wireless technology. It also encompassed the idea that the service was a one-to-many service which was 'pushed-at' its audience. The viewer or listener could access the service, if they had the appropriate receiving equipment, in other words, a television or radio, but had no control over when programmes were watched or listened to. Programmes were available according to a schedule decided by the broadcaster. Apart from switching off the receiving equipment, the viewer or listener had no ability to control the material received. Similarly, the broadcaster had no technological means to control who received the service – services were delivered free-to-air. One can see how this might have influenced certain aspects of broadcasting regulation. With the introduction of the delivery of services by cable and satellite in the 1980s, the notion of what was 'broadcasting' became more flexible as the Broadcasting Act 1990 regulatory scheme incorporated delivery of television and radio services regardless of the technical means of transmission. In this way the touch point for regulation becomes the service being provided rather than the means of delivery. So 'broadcasting' can now be seen as a term which has a broader meaning, although the Broadcasting Acts 1990 and 1996 (which still have regulatory relevance) retain some references which adhere to the traditional meaning of 'broadcasting'. For example, section 202(1) of the Broadcasting Act 1990 refers to a 'broadcast' as meaning 'broadcast by wireless technology' (see also section 405(1) of the Communications Act 2003). Since that time, advances in digital technology have given the public much greater control over the television and radio content they can receive and when they receive it. On-demand, catch-up services and digital devices represent a break away from the characteristics of the early model of broadcasting because they do not require delivery of programmes at scheduled times; they allow non-simultaneous viewing, and are more akin to a one-to-one, pulled model of delivery. Almost a quarter of UK Internet users (more than in the United States) access television content weekly via the Internet using catch-up services such as BBC iPlayer.[1] On-demand services are now a standard part of the broadcasters' output with scope for interactivity growing.

Extract 3.2.1
Department for Culture, Media and Sport, *DCMS Digital Strategy: becoming digital by default* (December 2012), http://www.dcms.gov.uk/images/publications/ DCMS_Digital_Strategy.pdf (accessed 27 December 2012), para 4.3

4.3 Broadcasters

DCMS are responsible for broadcasting policy and look after the government's relationship with the broadcasters – but those broadcasters are completely independent. They are absolute market-leaders in the development of digital services, fundamentally influencing the way that the public interact with the media. When DCMS set the purpose and remit for Channel 4 and S4C (the Welsh fourth channel), and negotiated the Royal Charter that establishes the BBC, we ensured that they included digital aims.

The BBC has as one of its six public purposes 'delivering to the public the benefit of emerging communications technologies and services'. BBC iPlayer has been a true game-changer in the way the public digest media content. The BBC released performance figures in October 2012 showing that iPlayer programme requests reached 213 million in that month, breaking the 200 million mark for the first time. It is also now quick and easy to pay for your TV licence online.

Channel 4's public service remit states that they must demonstrate 'innovation, experiment and creativity in form and content of programmes'. The remit was updated by the 2010 Digital Economy Act, requiring Channel 4 to broadcast or distribute 'relevant media content by means of a range of different types of electronic communications networks'. Building on the success of the hugely popular 4OD, they are now looking to introduce more digital innovations. They have developed a viewer relationship strategy, whereby they ask viewers to register so that they can communicate with them directly and in a more targeted way. So far they have 6 million registered users, with 1 in 3 16–24 year olds registered.

S4C have created a group to agree a way forward on digital media. This recommended redefining the channel's core purpose of providing 'television services' to include 'a range of different media', establishing a detailed digital strategy and investing in online content through the S4C digital fund.

---

[1] Ofcom, *International Communications Market Report 2012* (13 December 2012), http://stakeholders.ofcom.org.uk/binaries/research/cmr/cmr12/icmr/ICMR-2012.pdf (accessed 19 December 2012), para 3.1.5.

Digital technology has also significantly affected the broadcasting landscape in the United Kingdom. Until the late 1990s, television and radio broadcasters relied on analogue technology to deliver programmes to the public. The introduction of digital technology increased channel capacity. This means that digital technology not only provides a better quality of sound and picture but it also allows more services to be provided. In 2008 a digital switchover programme commenced in the United Kingdom. The transition from analogue to digital was completed in October 2012. From that point it is only possible to access television broadcast services if one has equipment that allows digital reception. The transfer from analogue to digital has been a complex process because it affected all forms of the more usual ways of receiving television – terrestrial (generally, understood as wireless), cable and satellite. Because of the importance of the public having access to communication services, as discussed in Chapter 1, the transition to digital had to be carefully staged with assistance for certain groups within the community to acquire the necessary equipment. Radio is also available in digital technology but take-up has been slower. The government has stated its intention to plan for a digital radio switchover by 2015, but this will depend upon take-up of digital radio services. However, it will not set a timetable for switchover until certain criteria are met: namely, 50 per cent of all listening is digital; national digital coverage is comparable to FM; and, local digital services reach 90 per cent of the population and all major roads. Even a definite intention of having a switchover is not yet clear, although the government has indicated it will make a decision by the end of 2013.[2] While digital radio listening is growing, it still only accounts for 29.5 per cent of all listening time.[3]

3.3 REGULATOR AND SOURCES OF LAW

The regulator for broadcasting (and all UK electronic communications and, since 2011, postal services) is the Office of Communications (Ofcom), an independent statutory regulator.[4] Ofcom is responsible for licensing and regulating all UK commercial radio and television services. It also has regulatory responsibility for some aspects of the BBC's licence fee-funded services, and through co-regulatory arrangements with the Advertising Standards Authority (see Chapter 6) and the Authority for Television on Demand (ATVOD) (see Section 3.11 below) has regulatory oversight of these bodies and enforcement powers in relation to the areas under co-regulation. Ofcom's powers and duties were formally vested in December 2003 and its establishment was part of a major regulatory reshaping of the communications sector. Prior to the establishment of Ofcom, the broadcasting sector was answerable to a number of regulatory authorities, causing some confusion and regulatory tension. In relation to radio and television services, Ofcom will be primarily responsible for licensing, competition and economic regulation and content regulation. The Communications Act 2003 sets out Ofcom's powers and duties. Underpinning these specific duties are two general duties: 'to further the interests of citizens in relation to communications matters' and 'to further the interests of consumers in relevant markets, where appropriate by promoting competition' (section 3(1)). Section 3 goes on to prescribe a set of more specific duties, for example to secure a wide range of

[2] Department for Culture, Media and Sport, *Digital Radio Action Plan, version 7* (October 2012), http://www.culture.gov.uk/images/publications/Digital_Radio_Action_Plan_Version_7.pdf (accessed 19 December 2012).
[3] Ofcom, *The Communications Market: Digital Radio Report* (17 October 2012), http://stakeholders.ofcom.org.uk/binaries/research/radio-research/drr-2012/2012_DRR.pdf (accessed 19 December 2012), 16.
[4] Ofcom was established under the Office of Communications Act 2002.

television and radio services, providing high quality and calculated to appeal to a variety of tastes and interests (section 3(2)(c)).

The establishment of Ofcom also heralded a preference for a lighter touch style of regulation. Thus in carrying out its duties, Ofcom must ensure that regulatory activities are 'transparent, accountable, proportionate, consistent and targeted only at cases in which action is needed' (section 3(3)(a)). Ofcom is also required to have regard to the desirability of promoting effective forms of self-regulation (section 3(4)(c)). Ofcom is guided by a set of regulatory principles which include operating with a bias against intervention, an intention to seek the least intrusive regulatory mechanisms to achieve its policy objectives, and to intervene to achieve a public policy goal only when markets cannot.[5] Ofcom also has a statutory duty to keep its functions under review to ensure that its regulation is not imposing unnecessary burdens (section 6(1)). The main statute governing broadcasting is the Communications Act 2003. However, two earlier statutes, as amended by the Communications Act 2003, remain relevant: the Broadcasting Act 1990 and the Broadcasting Act 1996, and it is necessary to refer to these Acts for significant aspects of the regulatory regime such as licensing.

3.4 THE PUBLIC SERVICE BROADCASTING CONCEPT – AN EVOLVING POLICY

An important influence on the way in which broadcasting policy and regulations has developed and continued in the United Kingdom has been the adherence to public service broadcasting (PSB). The concept was developed in the early days of the British Broadcasting Corporation (BBC) but applied also to the private commercial broadcasting – television and radio – sector. The United Kingdom differs from other European countries in having a long broadcasting tradition offering public and private services. Until around 1990, both sectors were regulated in very much the same way with similar responsibilities. PSB still forms the primary obligation of BBC broadcasting. Even now that the private broadcasting sector is less bound by this concept, its influence can still be felt.

Extract 3.4.1
L. Hitchens, *Broadcasting Pluralism and Diversity: a comparative study of policy and regulation* (Oxford: Hart Publishing, 2006), 142–3 (some footnotes omitted)

. . . The idea of broadcasting as a public service was developed by the first director-general of the BBC, Lord (as he was to become) Reith, and taken up in the first Royal Charter. One aspect of Reith's ideas was national coverage: 'broadcasting could and should serve everybody in the community who wished to 'listen'.[6] National coverage relates closely to that aspect of media freedom which recognizes the rights of viewers and listeners to be able to receive programming, and ideas and opinions. Reith believed that national coverage meant that the greatest number of homes should be reached, a radical idea at the time.[7] [. . . There] was no precise definition of public service broadcasting, and different elements might be stressed over others depending upon the context, but, certainly, the concept embraced expectations of quality and diverse programming.
[. . .]

---

[5] See, for example, Ofcom, *Annual Report and Accounts for the period 1 April 2011 to 31 March 2012* (HC 237, 2012), 38.
[6] A. Briggs, *The History of Broadcasting in the United Kingdom*, Vol. 1: *The Birth of Broadcasting* (Oxford: Oxford University Press, 1961), 236.
[7] Ibid.

The BBC maintained its monopoly status until the early 1950s, when commercial television was introduced. Although there had been concerns about the BBC's monopoly, there were also concerns about the impact commercial television would have on broadcasting quality, particularly in the light of the perceived US experience.[8] . . .

Although the public service concept has a direct relevance to broadcasting pluralism, it is not clear that this was a consciously sought outcome. Sendall has suggested that the commercial regulatory framework was not just a response to the problem of finding a balance between the dangers of commercialism and the maintenance of the traditions of public service broadcasting, but that it stemmed also from a generally held belief that television was a particularly potent '. . . means of influencing minds'.[9] Although this concern about influence probably had more to do with a fear of broadcasting and a desire to retain control of this 'mass voice', understandable in the wake of the Second World War and the experience of fascist regimes, a drive to contain undue influence and control can all the same be seen as having a bearing on diversity.[10] The arrangement which enabled the commercial sector to undertake a public service mandate was changed drastically with the 1990 reforms, which saw the end of the comfortable duopoly, and the introduction of greater reliance on market forces and competition. Although the commercial sector could no longer be viewed as a public service broadcaster in the way it had traditionally been, particularly with regard to investment in programming, many content-related rules were retained.

Despite radical reforms to the broadcasting and communications environment, the 2003 reforms have retained a commitment to public service broadcasting. . . .

The [Communications Act 2003] includes explicit statutory reference to public service broadcasting [section 264(4)] and identifies the public service broadcasters as the BBC and Channels Three, Four, Five and S4C (a Welsh language public broadcaster). Each public service broadcaster also has a specific public service remit in addition to the general public service broadcasting responsibilities. With the exception of the BBC, public service principles apply only to television, although commercial radio retains some obligations in relation to programme remits. The legislation's reference to the purposes of public service broadcasting, or more precisely, public service television broadcasting, makes clear that the concern is with the provision of a wide range of programmes catering to a variety of interests, and with programmes that meet standards of quality, professionalism and editorial integrity. Greater detail is given in section 264(6) which sets out the manner in which those purposes would be taken to be fulfilled . . .

Extract 3.4.2
Communications Act 2003, section 264(4) and (6)

(4) The purposes of public service television broadcasting in the United Kingdom are—

(a) the provision of relevant television services which secure that programmes dealing with a wide range of subject-matters are made available for viewing;

(b) the provision of relevant television services in a manner which (having regard to the days on which they are shown and the times of day at which they are shown) is likely to meet the needs and satisfy the interests of as many different audiences as practicable;

(c) the provision of relevant television services which (taken together and having regard to the same matters) are properly balanced, so far as their nature and subject-matters are concerned, for meeting the needs and satisfying the interests of the available audiences; and

---

[8] B. Sendall, *Independent Television in Britain*, vol 1: *Origin and Foundation, 1946–62* (London: Macmillan Press, 1982), 4 and 15.

[9] Ibid., 34.

[10] See R. Craufurd-Smith, *Broadcasting Law and Fundamental Rights* (Oxford: Clarendon Press, 1997), chs 1 and 2.

(d) the provision of relevant television services which (taken together) maintain high general standards with respect to the programmes included in them, and, in particular with respect to —

   (i)   the contents of the programmes;

   (ii) the quality of the programme making; and

   (iii) the professional skill and editorial integrity applied in the making of the programmes.

(6) A manner of fulfilling the purposes of public service television broadcasting in the United Kingdom is compatible with this subsection if it ensures —

(a) that the relevant television services (taken together) comprise a public service for the dissemination of information and for the provision of education and entertainment;

(b) that cultural activity in the United Kingdom, and its diversity, are reflected, supported and stimulated by the representation in those services (taken together) of drama, comedy and music, by the inclusion of feature films in those services and by the treatment of other visual and performing arts;

(c) that those services (taken together) provide, to the extent that is appropriate for facilitating civic understanding and fair and well-informed debate on news and current affairs, a comprehensive and authoritative coverage of news and current affairs in, and in the different parts of, the United Kingdom and from around the world;

(d) that those services (taken together) satisfy a wide range of different sporting and other leisure interests;

(e) that those services (taken together) include what appears to Ofcom to be a suitable quantity and range of programmes on educational matters, of programmes of an educational nature and of other programmes of educative value;

(f) that those services (taken together) include what appears to Ofcom to be a suitable quantity and range of programmes dealing with each of the following, science, religion and other beliefs, social issues, matters of international significance or interest and matters of specialist interest;

(g) that the programmes included in those services that deal with religion and other beliefs include —

   (i)   programmes providing news and other information about different religions and other beliefs;

   (ii) programmes about the history of different religions and other beliefs; and

   (iii) programmes showing acts of worship and other ceremonies and practices (including some showing acts of worship and other ceremonies in their entirety);

(h) that those services (taken together) include what appears to Ofcom to be a suitable quantity and range of high quality and original programmes for children and young people;

(i) that those services (taken together) include what appears to Ofcom to be a sufficient quantity of programmes that reflect the lives and concerns of different communities and cultural interests and traditions within the United Kingdom, and locally in different parts of the United Kingdom;

(j) that those services (taken together), so far as they include programmes made in the United Kingdom, include what appears to Ofcom to be an appropriate range and proportion of programmes made outside the M25 area.

Section 264 also requires Ofcom to carry out periodic reviews of the state of public service broadcasting (see section 264(3)). In carrying out these reviews, Ofcom must also be mindful of the costs of providing PSB and the sources of income available to meet those costs (section 264(7)). These reviews, and the annual statements of programme policy by the public service television licensees (see Section 3.7 below), reveal that commitment to certain programme areas has declined, for example the coverage of children's programmes on

Channel 3.[11] Despite the policy commitment to PSB, the digital multichannel, multiplatform environment will create uncertainty for its continuation. Ofcom has noted that although the five public service broadcasters and their portfolio channels (the additional digital channels offered, for example BBC Three and ITV2) enjoy 73.5 per cent of total viewing in multichannel homes, a share which has increased, the share of viewing hours enjoyed by the five main public service channels has declined to 53.2 per cent.[12] In a report on options for licensing renewals for Channel 3 and Channel 5, Ofcom reviewed the current uncertainties for the maintenance of PSB.

Extract 3.4.3

Ofcom, *Licensing of Channel 3 and Channel 5: A report to the Secretary of State under section 229 of the Communications Act 2003* (23 May 2012), http://stakeholders. ofcom.org.uk/broadcasting/tv/c3-c5-licensing (accessed 27 December 2012), paras 1.7–1.15 [some confidential references in the report are redacted]

1.7 Licence commitments are currently focused on meeting public service purposes in a small number of core programming genres regarded by audiences as the most important (in particular news and current affairs). In return, the licensees receive specific benefits. These include the right to appropriate prominence on Electronic Programme Guides (EPGs) as well as access to spectrum that enables them to make their services available to 98.5% of the UK population on the digital terrestrial platform.

1.8 Despite significant changes in technology and evolving consumer consumption patterns, the commercial public service broadcasters (PSBs) have continued to play a key role in delivering public service programming and providing opportunities for the UK content production industry. Both Channel 3 and Channel 5 exceeded their respective production and programming obligations between 2007 and 2010, the last year for which full data is available.

1.9 For the Channel 3 licensees, this contribution is also reflected by:

- collective spending on original content second only to the BBC, of which around 40% has been sourced from independent producers in recent years;
- the provision of competition for the BBC in relation to universally accessible UK television news; and
- plurality in nations and regions news coverage.

1.10 In comparison, delivery by Channel 5 is more modest, in part a reflection of the more limited range of PSB benefits it receives. Furthermore, between 2007 and 2010 spend by Channel 5 declined by 49% from £122m to £62m. Within this context, however, we note that Channel 5's own provisional figures indicate that its investment in new programming increased to £[✂]m in 2011. We also note that its most popular news bulletin receives an audience broadly comparable in size with *Channel 4 News*.

1.11 The background to our present assessment of licence renewal is very different from the analogue environment in which the Channel 3 licences were first awarded in 1991. At that time, new businesses were created effectively to serve licences which offered privileged access to mass audiences across the UK. Companies competed vigorously to secure this advantage.

1.12 Within the current digital framework, the licences represent a set of assets among others to companies that, in most cases, have media interests far beyond the public service broadcasting licences which they operate. The pressures that changes in digital technology have placed on this long-standing broadcasting model are likely to continue over the next licence period.

---

[11] See, for example, Ofcom, *Ofcom Statement on the delivery of public service programmes by ITV Network* (1 April 2010), http://stakeholders.ofcom.org.uk/broadcasting/tv/itv-kids-2010 (accessed 13 January 2013).

[12] Ofcom, *The Communications Market Report* (18 July 2012), http://stakeholders.ofcom.org.uk/market-data-research/market-data/communications-market-reports/cmr12/uk/ (accessed 26 September 2012), para 2.3.1.

1.13 Set against this environment, the Channel 3 and Channel 5 licensees have argued to us that the benefits they receive in return for PSB status have declined significantly as digital switchover has progressed and choice for viewers has grown. Nevertheless, the licensees maintain that, in broad terms and with some amendments, their existing public service obligations could continue to be sustainable during the next licence period.

1.14 Given uncertainty around future changes in technology and viewer consumption patterns, some of the Channel 3 and Channel 5 licensees have made it clear to us that they cannot be sure that their commercial imperatives and obligations to fulfil public service remits will remain aligned throughout the next licence period. Channel 5, in particular, has argued that amendments to certain PSB obligations may be necessary. Equally, all licensees have stated that they consider a contribution beyond existing levels is not possible.

1.15 The lack of clarity faced by the licensees about market developments and their impact up to 2024 is a matter that we have noted within this report. We also note that the existing licensees do not acknowledge any value in intangible factors linked to PSB status. We consider that there are benefits to the licence holders arising from certain elements – including the additional media coverage PSB programme schedules receive and viewer awareness of channel brands. Although they are difficult to quantify, we consider the potential loss of these benefits could represent a risk to an incumbent broadcaster. Nevertheless, taken as a whole, it is our assessment that the licensees have sought to present proposals for public service delivery that are realistic, sustainable and commensurate with current levels of delivery.

Source: © Ofcom copyright 2006–11.

Questions for discussion
1. Does the PSB concept have a continued relevance in a multichannel multiplatform environment?
2. Notice in Extract 3.4.3 the awareness that PSB obligations have been able to be secured because of certain benefits enjoyed by the broadcasters. Are there other ways in which the PSB goal could be secured?

3.5 PUBLIC BROADCASTING

(a) Introduction

The major public broadcaster in the United Kingdom is the BBC. The BBC also represents the major embodiment of the PSB concept, especially since it applies to all services it offers: television, radio and online. There are other public broadcasters although they have more minor roles. The Welsh Channel, known as S4C (Sianel Pedwar Cymru), commenced in 1982, offering a major proportion of its programmes in Welsh. S4C has a traditional public service mandate that requires it to broadcast programming that is high quality and diverse (Schedule 12, para 3, Communications Act 2003). As part of its public service remit, the majority of its programmes must be in Welsh, and the majority of programmes broadcast during the peak evening period must also be in Welsh. Programmes not broadcast in Welsh were expected to be programmes broadcast on Channel 4, although S4C now broadcasts entirely in the Welsh language. S4C commissions Welsh language programmes. S4C is governed by the Welsh Authority (usually referred to as the 'S4C Authority') and the Authority is responsible for ensuring that S4C meets its statutory responsibilities.[13]

---

[13] The Authority is established under section 56 of and Schedule 6 to the Broadcasting Act 1990, but its functions are now set out in section 204 of the Communications Act 2003.

Although the Authority is accountable for the output of S4C, it does not directly commission programmes or make editorial decisions, leaving these functions to day-to-day management. The third public broadcaster is the Gaelic Media Service (Seirbheisnam Meadhanan Gàidhlig). The service was originally established under section 183 of the Broadcasting Act 1990 and renamed, with an expanded remit, by section 208(1) of the Communications Act 2003. Its members are appointed by Ofcom, subject to the approval of the Secretary of State and Scottish ministers (section 183A, Broadcasting Act 1990[14]), and the Service is regulated by Ofcom. Funded by the Scottish government,[15] its remit is to secure the broadcast or transmission of a '. . . wide and diverse range of high quality programmes in Gaelic . . . so as to be available to persons in Scotland' (section 183(3B)). The service can finance and/or make or commission programmes in Gaelic (section 183(4A)). The service operates under the name 'MG Alba' and in partnership with the BBC operates a digital Gaelic channel, 'BBC Alba'.[16] The focus of Section 3.5 of this chapter will be on the BBC.

The BBC began radio broadcasting in 1922 under a licence granted by the government. Although it operated as a monopoly it was established as a private company, known as the British Broadcasting Company. Its shares were owned by British wireless manufacturing companies for whom the broadcasting company was a necessary means of facilitating the sale of the new technology and their radio equipment.[17] In 1927, it became a public corporation, established under royal charter and renamed the British Broadcasting Corporation, the name it retains today. The changed structure came about as a result of recommendations from the Crawford Committee that broadcasting should not be left to a commercial entity.[18] The BBC continues to operate under a royal charter although there have been changes in the way it is structured and governed. The concept of 'public broadcasting' should not be confused with the idea of state broadcasting. Indeed, if the public broadcaster is to fulfil its public service mandate, it will be crucial for it to be free not just of commercial pressures, but also of state control and influence. Accordingly, the manner in which the public broadcaster is structured and financed, and the terms under which it operates, will be significant.

(b) The structure of the BBC

The BBC is established under a royal charter that is supplemented by an agreement made between the Secretary of State (currently, the Secretary of State for Culture, Media and Sport) and the BBC. These constitutional documents set out the mandate, structure and operational aspects of the BBC. They were last renewed in 2006: *Royal Charter for the continuance of the British Broadcasting Corporation* (the Charter)[19] and *Agreement Between Her Majesty's Secretary of State for Culture, Media and Sport and the British Broadcasting Corporation* (the Agreement).[20] The Charter and Agreement commenced operation in January 2007 and are to continue until 31 December 2016. Each time the constitutional documents of the BBC are renewed there is an opportunity to reconsider the role and structure of the public broadcaster. It is a period in which the BBC might also feel vulnerable with a

---

[14] Amended by the Scotland Act 2012, section 17(4).

[15] Section 183(1) of the Broadcasting Act 1990, as amended by the Scotland Act 2012, section 17(2).

[16] BBC Alba is operated under a service licence issued by the BBC Trust. The governance structure for BBC Alba partnership is complex, for further information see: http://www.mgalba.com/about/corporate/alba-partnership.html?lang=en (accessed 19 December 2012).

[17] R.H. Coase, *British Broadcasting: A Study in Monopoly* (London: Longmans, Green & Co, 1950), 15–16.

[18] T. Gibbons, *Regulating the Media* (London: Sweet & Maxwell, 2nd edn, 1998), 57.

[19] Cm 6925, October 2006.

[20] Cm 6872, July 2006.

chilling effect on its editorial decision-making. In the lead-up to the current Charter and Agreement there was an expectation that the BBC might lose its autonomy.

Extract 3.5.1
T. Gibbons and P. Humphreys, *Audiovisual Regulation under Pressure: Comparative cases from North America and Europe* (London: Routledge, 2012), 95–6 (references omitted)

In the 2000s, the BBC engaged in major policy initiatives to assert its relevance and importance in the new digital era. When [Gavin] Davies took over as Chairman of the BBC in 2001, with an agenda to modernise in the way his report [a report on BBC funding, 1999] had indicated, one of his earliest challenges was to ward off a proposal that the BBC should be brought entirely within the new Ofcom remit. However, the BBC's self-confidence received a serious setback in 2004, following severe criticisms of its standards of journalism and its management and governance, in the wake of its broadcast of Andrew Gilligan's story about the government's dossier on the likely existence of weapons of mass destruction in Iraq. [The criticisms were made in the Hutton Report, a judicial inquiry established by the government following the death of David Kelly, a government-employed weapons expert who was named as the source of the information in the BBC report.] Davies and the director-general, Greg Dyke, resigned and the BBC conducted a major review of its practices. The Hutton Report put the BBC on the back foot, making it more vulnerable to government pressure, and leading to a general sense that its structure needed reform. At the same time, the Hutton Report's conclusions were widely regarded as being harsh and, not only could the government not be seen to be vindictive, it did not appear to have any wish to discipline the BBC.

Source: Copyright © 2012 Routledge. Reproduced by permission of Taylor & Francis Books UK.

The previous charter and agreement, which were settled in 1996, provided more detail about the BBC's role, governance structure and obligations than previous versions, and this trend has continued. The current constitutional documents also differ in their attempt to provide a much more detailed iteration of the BBC's public service role. The Charter also introduced a new governance structure. The Charter, granted under Crown prerogative, sets outs the objects and overall structure and functions of the BBC, while the Agreement is more concerned with the operational aspects. Relevant legislation, such as the Communications Act 2003, also now cover in much greater detail the responsibilities of the public broadcaster, as will be apparent in Chapter 4, while Ofcom also has a greater regulatory role to play in relation to the BBC. An important provision in the Charter declares the independence of the BBC, but the way in which the BBC is structured and governed could affect that independence or perception of independence. Indeed, the very renewal process might impact on that independence or the sense of it.

Extract 3.5.2
Department for Culture, Media and Sport, *Royal Charter for the continuance of the British Broadcasting Corporation* (Cm 6925, October 2006), article 6

1. The BBC shall be independent in all matters concerning the content of its output, the times and manner in which this is supplied, and in the management of its affairs.
2. Paragraph (1) is subject to any provision made by or under this Charter or any Framework Agreement or otherwise by law.

Prior to the current Charter, the corporation comprised 12 members, known as the BBC governors. The governors were appointed by the government and were responsible for ensuring that the BBC achieved its objects, although in practice operational matters, including programming decisions, were left to the director-general, a full-time executive of the BBC, and the professional staff. The current Charter has established a new structure and makes clearer the roles within this function, also exhorting the BBC to have regard to '. . . such general guidance concerning the management of the affairs of public bodies . . .' and '. . . to generally accepted principles of corporate governance . . .' (article 11). The new structure comprises a BBC Trust and an Executive Board, and the members of these two bodies are the members of the Corporation (article 1(2)). The Charter sets out the composition and roles of these two bodies, and their relationship. The use of descriptive and explanatory language in a formal legal document is also interesting to note.

Extract 3.5.3
Department for Culture, Media and Sport, *Royal Charter for the continuance of the British Broadcasting Corporation* (Cm 6925, October 2006), articles 7–9, 12

7. Introduction

Within the BBC, there shall be a BBC Trust and an Executive Board of the BBC. These two bodies shall each play important, but different, roles within the BBC. In summary, the main roles of the Trust are in setting the overall strategic direction of the BBC, including its priorities, and in exercising a general oversight of the work of the Executive Board. The Trust will perform these roles in the public interest, particularly the interest of licence fee payers. The Executive Board has responsibility for delivering the BBC's services in accordance with the priorities set by the Trust and for all aspects of operational management, except that of the Trust's resources. Further details of the respective functions of the Trust and Executive Board are set out below and may also be addressed in a Framework Agreement.

8. Trust and Executive Board to act separately

As described in article 1(2), the Corporation that is the BBC shall comprise all the members of the BBC Trust and the Executive Board. This reflects the importance of both the Trust and the Board, and the status and standing which their respective members are to enjoy. However, all the functions of the Corporation shall be exercised through either the Trust or the Board in accordance with the provisions set out in this Charter and any Framework Agreement. The members of the Trust and the members of the Board shall never act together as a single corporate body.

9. Relationship between the Trust and the Executive Board

(1) The Trust must maintain its independence of the Executive Board.
(2) The Trust shall be the sovereign body within the BBC, in the sense that wherever it has a function under this Charter or any Framework Agreement, it may always fully exercise that function as it sees fit and require the Executive Board to act in ways which respect and are compatible with how the Trust has seen fit to exercise that function. In particular, where the Executive Board has operational responsibility for activities which are subject to a Trust function of approval, supervision, review or enforcement, any decision of the Trust in exercise of such a function shall be final within the BBC. (Of course, in certain areas, the activity in question may also be subject to regulation by external bodies, such as Ofcom.)
(3) However, the Trust must not exercise or seek to exercise the functions of the Executive Board.

12. Legal nature of the Trust

The word 'trust' is used in the name of the BBC Trust in a colloquial sense, to suggest a body which discharges a public trust as guardian of the public interest. The word is not used in its technical legal sense, and it is not intended to imply that the members of the Trust are to be treated as trustees of property or to be subject to the law relating to trusts or trustees.

The Charter sets out the role and functions of the Trust and its general duties (articles 22–4). The Trust must adopt and publish protocols that provide further detail on the manner in which it will carry out its functions and on its relationship with the Executive Board (article 25). While the protocols themselves offer a means of transparency, the Trust is specifically required to take into account the views of licence fee payers and to consult publicly before adopting a protocol (article 26) and to ensure that the considerations and reasons behind important decisions are made public (article 27).

As can be seen in the following extract, it is clear why the language of 'trust' is being used to describe the role of this governing organ of the BBC.

Extract 3.5.4
Department for Culture, Media and Sport, *Royal Charter for the continuance of the British Broadcasting Corporation* (Cm 6925, October 2006), articles 22–3

22. The Trust is the guardian of the licence fee revenue and the public interest in the BBC. The Trust has the ultimate responsibility, subject to the provisions of this Charter, for—

(a) the BBC's stewardship of the licence fee revenue and its other resources;
(b) upholding the public interest within the BBC, particularly the interests of licence fee payers; and
(c) securing the effective promotion of the Public Purposes.

23. In exercising all its functions, the Trust must act in the public interest and, in particular, it must—

(a) represent the interests of licence fee payers;
(b) secure that the independence of the BBC is maintained;
(c) carefully and appropriately assess the views of licence fee payers;
(d) exercise rigorous stewardship of public money;
(e) have regard to the competitive impact of the BBC's activities on the wider market; and
(f) ensure that the BBC observes high standards of openness and transparency.

Article 24(1) sets out the general high level functions of the BBC Trust whilst article 24(2) identifies the specific functions.

Extract 3.5.5
Department for Culture, Media and Sport, *Royal Charter for the continuance of the British Broadcasting Corporation* (Cm 6925, October 2006), article 24(1)

(1) The Trust has the general function of—

(a) setting the overall strategic direction for the BBC within the framework set by this Charter and any Framework Agreement;
(b) approving high-level strategy and budgets in respect of the BBC's services and activities in the UK and overseas; and
(c) assessing the performance of the Executive Board in delivering the BBC's services and activities and holding the Executive Board to account for its performance.

Articles 28 to 31 deal with the composition and appointment of the Executive Board, which consists of executive and non-executive members. The director-general, who is the chief executive officer and editor-in-chief of the BBC (article 40), is always a member of the Executive Board (article 30(1)) and may be its Chairman (article 40(2)). The functions of the Executive Board are set out in article 38 and they illustrate the Board's responsibility for the actual delivery of the BBC's services and editorial role.

Extract 3.5.6

Department for Culture, Media and Sport, *Royal Charter for the continuance of the British Broadcasting Corporation* **(Cm 6925, October 2006), article 38(1)**

(1) The Executive Board is the executive body of the BBC and is responsible for—

(a) the delivery of the BBC's services in accordance with the priorities set by purpose remits and the framework set by service licences and any other strategies;

(b) the direction of the BBC's editorial and creative output;

(c) the operational management of the BBC (except the BBC Trust Unit);

(d) ensuring compliance with all legal and regulatory requirements placed upon the BBC (including the initial handling of complaints about the BBC) except to the extent that they relate to the affairs of the Trust or the BBC Trust Unit;

(e) ensuring compliance with requirements placed upon the Executive Board by the Trust (for example, through Protocols or the Trust's statement of policy on fair trading);

. . .

(g) appointing, and holding to account, the management of the BBC and its subsidiaries;

(h) the conduct of the BBC's operational financial affairs (except those relating directly to the affairs of the Trust and the BBC Trust Unit) in a manner best designed to ensure value for money; . . .

. . .

Questions for discussion

1. Article 6 (Extract 3.5.2) declares the independence of the BBC. Review the provisions of the Charter that relate to the appointment of the Trust members and their terms of office. What impact might these processes have on the BBC's independence?

2. Review the rest of the Charter and the Agreement. Are there other provisions which could compromise the independence of the BBC?

3. It has been suggested that the process of Charter renewal could have an impact on the BBC's willingness to assert its independence. What strengths might a royal charter offer in preserving the BBC's independence? What other forms could be used for the establishment of the BBC and what would be their strengths and weaknesses?[21]

(c) The public purposes of the BBC

Clause 11 of the Agreement identifies the services designated as the UK public services and to which the public service responsibilities of the BBC will apply. The BBC's public service responsibilities have always been linked with the traditional mantra of 'inform, entertain and educate' and this remains the case. However, there is also a noticeable difference in the way the responsibilities are set out with the specification of a set of public purposes as the BBC's main object.

---

[21] Department for Culture, Media and Sport, *Review of the BBC's Royal Charter: A strong BBC, independent of government* (March 2005), http://news.bbc.co.uk/2/shared/bsp/hi/pdfs/02_03_05_bbcgreen.pdf (accessed 19 December 2012), 54–7.

Extract 3.5.7
Department for Culture, Media and Sport, *Royal Charter for the continuance of the British Broadcasting Corporation* **(Cm 6925, October 2006), articles 3(1) and (2), 4 and 5(1)–(2)**

3. The BBC's public nature and its objects

(1) The BBC exists to serve the public interest.
(2) The BBC's main object is the promotion of its Public Purposes.

4. The public purposes

The Public Purposes of the BBC are as follows—

(a) sustaining citizenship and civil society;
(b) promoting education and learning;
(c) stimulating creativity and cultural excellence;
(d) representing the UK, its nations, regions and communities;
(e) bringing the UK to the world and the world to the UK;
(f) in promoting its other purposes, helping to deliver to the public the benefit of emerging communications technologies and services and, in addition, taking a leading role in the switchover to digital television.

5. How the BBC promotes its Public Purposes: the BBC's mission to inform, educate and entertain

(1) The BBC's main activities should be the promotion of its Public Purposes through the provision of output which consists of information, education and entertainment, supplied by means of—

(a) television, radio and online services;
(b) similar or related services which make output generally available and which may be in forms or by means of technologies which either have not previously been used by the BBC or which have yet to be developed.

(2) The BBC may also carry out other activities which directly or indirectly promote the Public Purposes, but such activities should be peripheral, subordinate or ancillary to its main activities. Overall, such peripheral, subordinate or ancillary activities of the BBC should bear a proper sense of proportion to the BBC's main activities, and each of them should be appropriate to be carried on by the BBC alongside its main activities.

At first glance it might be difficult to see how these public purposes reveal what the BBC should be doing in relation to broadcasting.[22] They are more a statement of values, providing the value context for the BBC as it develops and delivers its media services. However, article 5 links this back to the delivery of broadcasting services and to the traditional public service mission to 'inform, educate and entertain'. The Agreement elaborates on the public purposes. The Charter and the Agreement also require the BBC to develop purpose remits setting out priorities and means of judging performance (article 24(2)(a) and (b), Charter, and clause 5, Agreement). Clauses 6–10 set out the matters the Trust must take into account in developing and reviewing the remits, and elaborate on each of the public purposes.

---

[22] Although this section on the BBC will generally refer to 'broadcasting', it should be remembered that the public service mandate of the BBC covers its television, radio and online services. Thus references in this section to 'broadcasting' should be taken to include online services also, unless the context indicates otherwise.

Questions for discussion
1. In relation to each of the public purposes, try to identify the activities of the BBC which might be said to be in fulfilment of each public purpose. 2. Article 5 (Extract 3.5.7) does not provide much detail on how the BBC should promote its public purposes? Why is that? What difficulties might arise if the Charter was to be more detailed?

In addition to the public purposes, the Agreement also explicitly confirms three core features of the PSB concept: universality, access, and quality. Article 15 reminds the BBC that it must also have regard to the purposes of PSB as set out in section 264(4) of the Communications Act 2003.

Extract 3.5.8
Agreement Between Her Majesty's Secretary of State for Culture, Media and Sport and the British Broadcasting Corporation (Cm 6872, July 2006), clauses 12–14

12(1) The BBC must do all that is reasonably practicable to ensure that viewers, listeners and other users (as the case may be) are able to access the UK Public Services that are intended for them, or elements of their content, in a range of convenient and cost effective ways which are available or might become available in the future. These could include (for example) broadcasting, streaming or making content available on-demand, whether by terrestrial, satellite, cable or broadband networks (fixed or wireless) or via the internet.

. . .

13(1) The BBC must not charge any person, either directly or indirectly, in respect of the reception in the UK, by any means, of—

(a) the UK Public Services;

(b) any assistance . . . provided for disabled people . . . ;

. . .

(2) For the purposes of paragraph (1), the television licence fee is not to be regarded as a charge for the reception of any UK Public Service.

. . .

14(1) The content of the UK Public Services taken as a whole must be high quality, challenging, original, innovative and engaging.

(2) Every programme included in the UK Public Broadcasting Services must exhibit at least one of those characteristics. In relation to the other UK Public Services, each item of content must exhibit at least one of those characteristics.

(d) Funding

Since its inception, the BBC has been funded by licence fee. This is payable by anyone in possession of a television receiver and it is an offence to install or use a television receiver without the licence.[23] The term 'television receiver' includes more than the traditional television set, applying to any device, such as a computer or mobile phone, which is capable of receiving a television programme service as broadcast (in other words, the

---

[23] Communications Act 2003, section 363. Initially, the fee applied to radio sets, but radios have been exempt since 1971.

programmes are being received at the same time as they are broadcast to the public).[24] Although the BBC undertakes commercial activities (clauses 68–74, Agreement), its major source of funding remains the licence fee (see Extract 3.5.9). The BBC can use the licence fee income to fund any of its activities, except any of its commercial activities, or any service aimed primarily at audiences outside the United Kingdom (clause 75(2)). In 2011, the Agreement was amended to require the BBC to take on additional responsibilities, including funding of the World Service (from April 2014). The World Service was previously funded by direct government grant, but will be funded from the licence fee.[25] Accordingly, clause 75 has been amended to exclude the World Service from the prohibition on the licence fee being used for services aimed at non-UK audiences.

The manner in which a public broadcaster is funded may also be relevant to its independence. The licence fee as a form of funding has some disadvantages, but it also has some strengths by creating a greater measure of distance from government interference. The following extract reviews different funding models and their strengths and weaknesses.

Extract 3.5.9
Department for Culture, Media and Sport, *Review of the BBC's Royal Charter: A strong BBC, independent of government* (March 2005), http://webarchive. nationalarchives.gov.uk/+/http://www.bbccharterreview.org.uk/have_your_say/ green_paper/bbc_cr_greenpaper.pdf (accessed 12 September 2012), 58–61 (footnotes omitted)

4. Funding

What people think

- The licence fee is widely considered to be the best – or the 'least worst' – way to pay for the BBC for the next Charter, although there is some support for other options, particularly in combination with the licence fee.
- The public's view of the value for money delivered by the BBC is equivocal – with 46% saying it delivered fairly good or very good value for money, compared to 33% taking the opposite view.
- There is strong support for the BBC's independence from Government and from commercial pressures.
- The way the licence fee is set and collected raised issues about fairness (particularly for those on low incomes) and efficiency (using significant public money to chase evaders).
- Some proposals were put forward for different ways to distribute the licence fee to other broadcasters and production companies.

. . .

The licence fee and the arguments made against it

4.1 At present, the BBC receives most of its funding from the TV licence fee (currently £121.00 per household per year). Licence fee income in 2003/4 was around £2.8 billion (£408 million of which came from the Department for Work and Pensions to compensate the BBC for free TV

---

[24] The Communications (Television Licensing) Regulations 2004 (SI 2004/692), reg 9.
[25] See Department for Culture, Media and Sport, *Agreement Between Her Majesty's Secretary of State for Culture, Media and Sport and the British Broadcasting Corporation dated 30 June 2006* (Cm 8002, 11 February 2011), clause 2(1) and *Agreement Between Her Majesty's Secretary of State for Culture, Media and Sport and the British Broadcasting Corporation dated 30 June 2006* (Cm 8170, 13 September 2011). The new arrangements also required the BBC to enter into a partnership with S4C and to provide funding for that service out of the licence fee.

licences given to over 75s). It supplements that income with the contribution made to its public services by its commercial services (which contributed profits of around £38.5 million in 2003/4) and some direct Government funding – around £220 million from the Foreign and Commonwealth Office – that pays for the World Service.

4.2 A significant minority of respondents to our public consultation argued for the abolition of the licence fee, and there are a number of arguments made against the principle of the licence fee as it exists today:

- It is a regressive form of taxation – everyone pays the same flat charge, regardless of their income, the number of televisions they own or the extent to which they watch television in general and BBC services in particular.
- The unfairness of the flat rate charge is intensifying as the number of TV channels increases and the BBC's overall audience share decreases.
- The BBC uses the income it receives from TV viewers to pay for its other services, in radio and new media, and its non-programming activities.
- The costs of collection and evasion are high (£300 million annually – £150 million for collection, £150 million for evasion) and enforcement is often perceived to be draconian especially where evaders are criminalised and those who fail to pay their fines are occasionally imprisoned.

4.3 It is also argued in some quarters that the licence fee will become more difficult to sustain in future as technology develops, for three main reasons:

- As digital take-up increases, audiences for BBC services may fall significantly, reducing public support for a universal charge.
- Subscription and on-demand payment systems will be developed for use across all forms of television, making it possible for viewers to be charged only for those programmes or services they want to watch.
- TV viewing may no longer be confined to TV sets, but could take place via computer terminals or mobile phones. A licence fee based on TV ownership could therefore become redundant.

. . .

Government funding

4.5 Government funding could be considered fairer than the licence fee in that it would be progressive – each individual would in effect only contribute according to his or her income. This would make the BBC an area of Government spending like any other public service. The objections to this arrangement are made on the grounds that the BBC is a public service like no other, and it is feared that direct Government funding might threaten both:

- the BBC's independence – if the Government held the purse strings; and
- its stability and security – were the BBC to be subject to reviews of its funding through the biennial Government Spending Review process.

[. . .]

Advertising and sponsorship

4.7 The case for allowing advertising on the BBC is a difficult one to make. There was quite vehement opposition expressed to the idea of advertising on the BBC in the course of our public consultation and research. 60% say it interferes with their enjoyment of programmes (31% disagree). The lack of advertising is therefore felt to be a key distinguishing characteristic of the BBC – it was the third most frequent value spontaneously attributed to the BBC by contributors to our quantitative research.

4.8 The BBC would certainly attract advertisers if it were allowed to, particularly to its mainstream services. However, modelling of the advertising market suggests that the effect of such a move would be to push down prices (since the total amount of money spent on advertising would not rise significantly but many more ad 'spots' would become available). This would almost certainly reduce the income of both the BBC and the existing ad-funded broadcasters (including other public service broadcasters, such as ITV and Channel 4).

4.9 Advertising would also create conflicting incentives for the BBC – the requirement to fulfil public purposes would have to be weighed against the need to generate revenue. The character of programming might drift towards the middle ground of taste as a result. Ofcom has pointed out that such a conflict of incentives already exists for ITV1, Channel 4 and Five, and that it will be increasingly difficult to regulate in future as commercial competition intensifies. 52% of those we surveyed said they thought the BBC would lose its independence if it relied on advertising or sponsorship.

4.10 The long-term trends in the TV advertising market are anyway uncertain. New digital technology – particularly PVRs – increasingly allows audiences to skip through advertising breaks. It may be unwise to increase the dependency of public service broadcasting on advertising revenue at a time of such uncertainty.

4.11 There are probably fewer concerns about allowing the BBC to take sponsorship for some programmes. There would still be some questions to answer, however, about a potential conflict of incentives and the commercial impact of such a move. Viewers and listeners may feel it detracted from their experience of the BBC if commercial messages were attached to their favourite programmes – although our research suggests they would prefer it to advertising. And sponsorship alone would never deliver sufficient income to sustain the BBC without some additional source of funding.

Subscription

4.12 The BBC's own 'willingness to pay' research suggests that some people are willing to pay significant amounts for access to BBC services – 42% say £20 per month and 19% say £30 per month. If services were put together in differently priced packages, with premium programmes available at different prices depending, for example, on their newness or exclusivity, audiences would have more freedom of choice and some argue that the BBC might retain a sustainable level of funding.

4.13 This sort of model would raise significant issues of principle. The chief argument against subscription as a funding method is that it would undermine the principle of universal access – BBC content would no longer be free at the point of use. It can be argued in response that the existing licence fee is anyway a form of 'compulsory subscription'. Services are only 'free' once a bulk licence fee has been paid. But if people could choose not to subscribe then prices might have to rise for those who carried on paying, and some low-income viewers and listeners who did want to subscribe might well be priced out of the market for BBC content. If that content were not universally available, its potential benefit to society would be reduced.

4.14 In the short term, there are also significant practical problems. In mainstream radio, no subscription facility exists, nor does one look likely to be widely available for some time. While a TV subscription service could function in satellite and cable homes, for most terrestrial viewers (including most digital terrestrial or Freeview homes) there is presently no way of controlling access to individual channels. New subscription technology (code-protected cards for 'conditional access') of the sort used in satellite and cable homes would need to be included in most, if not all, digital terrestrial equipment before any subscription system could function for the BBC.

Despite the strengths of the licence fee, Gibbons and Humphreys illustrate how vulnerable the broadcaster can be to changes in licence fee policy.

Extract 3.5.10

T. Gibbons and P. Humphreys, *Audiovisual Regulation under Pressure: Comparative cases from North America and Europe* (London: Routledge, 2012), 101–2, (references omitted)

. . . So far, successive UK governments have periodically granted the BBC licence settlements that have been comparatively generous, certainly compared to the French case. This has allowed the BBC to launch its range of new media services. However, the last New Labour licence fee settlement in 2007 was considerably less than the BBC had said it needed, necessitating some painful cuts and sparking a degree of public controversy. . . .

Under the new Conservative–Liberal Democrat Coalition, elected in 2010, there has been a notable shift in political mood and it is clear that the BBC will have to reduce its scale of operations. The early indications were that the Corporation would have to extract more value for money rather than seek further public subsidies, and that online content needed 'clearer red lines' to allow competitors, dependent on private revenue, to survive. The BBC responded with a Strategy Review, promising greater emphasis on quality, its traditional mission to inform, educate, and entertain, improved efficiency and the need to 'leave space for the market'. That strategy will have to be radically revisited in the light of a sudden and controversial licence fee settlement imposed in October 2010. As part of the government's comprehensive spending review in the aftermath of the 2008 recession, it approached the BBC and asked it to accept responsibility for general government funding of free licences for the over-75s and for the Foreign Office's subsidy of broadcasting the BBC World Service and BBC monitoring (which surveys other countries' broadcasting). The BBC did put up some resistance but, following rather hasty negotiations, it agreed a new set of arrangements. While it has not taken responsibility for the free licence fees, it has done so for the Foreign Office services, and it has also entered a form of partnership with S4C . . . whereby most of S4C's funding will come from the licence fee. While the ring-fenced digitalisation element of the licence fee will continue, it will be devoted to broadband roll-out after the digital switchover, and the BBC will be required to provide some funding to support the provision of local television. The licence fee will be set at £145.50 until 31 March 2017, with a government 'guarantee' of no additional obligations being placed on the BBC and/or licence fee revenues during that period, except by mutual agreement.

As the House of Commons Culture, Media and Sport Committee has noted in a very critical report [in 2011], the implications of this settlement for the BBC are serious. Quite apart from the unseemly haste and lack of accountability in the process, the BBC appears to have breached its own 'red-line' in resisting the top-slicing of its income, since none of the Foreign Office activities, S4C, local commercial television or broadband can be considered core BBC interests. The BBC argues that they are closer to those core interests than the proposed alternative of subsidising pensioners' licence fees, that they largely represent a logical focus on programme production, and that the overall settlement brings stability for the remainder of its ten-year Charter period. But, to make provision for all this, the BBC will inevitably have to cut its core services. The irony of this scenario is that, in the quest for plurality of PSB, the BBC is being expected to finance some of the other services that are considered necessary to complement its own service. For those who consider that the BBC has grown to excess, with expansive programme agendas to fill the new channels that it has chosen to create, and 'bloated' salaries for performers and executives, the requirement for further efficiency will be welcomed. But, if plurality of PSB is to continue as the UK's principal policy tool, the underlying problem is not the BBC but the need for sufficient finance to maintain diversity of PSB content . . .

Income generated through commercial activities can be used to support the BBC's public purposes. The BBC cannot operate commercial activities directly, only through commercial subsidiaries (clause 68, Agreement). The BBC does not have an entirely free hand in the choice of commercial activity. Pursuant to clause 69(1), a commercial activity must meet the following criteria:

- fit with the BBC's public purpose activities;
- exhibit commercial efficiency;
- not jeopardise the good reputation of the BBC or the value of the BBC brand; and
- comply with fair trading guidelines (see clause 67(1)(a)) and avoid distorting the market.

Questions for discussion

1. Do you agree with the government's view (Extract 3.5.9) that the licence fee does provide greater independence for the BBC?
2. Is the licence fee a sustainable funding model in the multiplatform environment?

(e) Accountability

As noted earlier, the BBC is required under the Charter to have regard to the views of the licence fee payers and to establish audience councils 'to bring the diverse perspectives of licence fee payers to bear on the work of the Trust' (article 39(1)). Article 23(f) also requires the BBC in exercising all of its functions to ensure that it 'observes high standards of openness and transparency'. Although the BBC, through the Trust, retains a significant self-governing role, the broadcaster is nevertheless subject to a complex portfolio of responsibilities designed to render it accountable, with varying degrees of formality. Ofcom also has a role to play. In pursuit of its obligation to be open and transparent, the BBC publishes information on a variety of matters including operational matters such as salary and expense disclosures, annual work plans, board meeting minutes and information about complaints and responses. Clause 21 of the Agreement requires the Executive Board to publish annual statements of programme policy in relation to each of the BBC public broadcasting services – television and radio. The statements must indicate how that service will contribute to the BBC's public service remit in the forthcoming year. In preparing these statements, the BBC is required to have regard to any guidance given by Ofcom regarding the preparation of statements of programme policy (which must also be completed by the licensed public service broadcasters), pursuant to section 266 of the Communications Act 2003, or reports prepared by Ofcom, including on the fulfilment of the public service remit by broadcasters, pursuant to section 264 (clause 21(3)).

The charter renewal process, which led to the Charter and Agreement, introduced several new accountability measures. These new measures see further engagement with external bodies. With respect to one measure, the value for money examination, the National Audit Office has a role to play, while the new public value test provides a role for Ofcom. Only the remaining new measure, service licences, is left to the BBC Trust alone to oversee. It was noted earlier that under the Charter, the Trust is the guardian of the licence fee revenue and the public interest (Extract 3.5.4). Pursuant to clause 79(1) of the Agreement, the Trust must examine the value for money achieved by the BBC in relation to the licence fee income. The process has to be agreed with the Auditor General and the reviews are conducted by the National Audit Office or other independent experts. Since this requirement was introduced there have been about 15 reviews, covering a wide variety of topics such as financial management, processes for management of sports rights, efficiency of radio production, and on-air and on-screen talent costs.[26]

Under article 24(2)(c) of the Charter, the Trust has the power to issue service licences for BBC public services and is responsible for reviewing performance under the licences (clauses 16–20, Agreement). Before issuing a service licence, the BBC must consult publicly (clause 19). The BBC has issued service licences for each of its public services.[27] Related to the service licence concept is the public value test (the Agreement, clauses 23–33). The Agreement recognises that the BBC must have flexibility to modify its public services in order '. . . to respond to changes in technology, culture, market conditions, public expectations and views, etc.' (clause 23(1)). However, any significant proposal for change must be subject to the scrutiny of the public value test (clause 23(2)). A change here includes a proposal to start a new service or to discontinue a service (clause 25(1)). The introduction of the service licence model and the public value test were seen by the government as part of a 'triple lock' of accountability and a means of measuring the Executive's performance and accountability to the Trust, and of judging the Trust's effectiveness.

Extract 3.5.11
Department for Culture, Media and Sport, *A public service for all: the BBC in the digital age* (Cm 6763, March 2006), http://webarchive.nationalarchives.gov.uk/+/ http://www.bbccharterreview.org.uk/have_your_say/white_paper/bbc_whitepaper_ march06.pdf (accessed 1 January 2013), 3 and para 3.1.11

There will also be a new 'triple lock' system to ensure the highest standards in everything the BBC produces – through its TV, radio and new media services. Firstly, every service will be run according to a new, detailed service licence. It will set out what the key characteristics of the service should be, how it helps meet the BBC's purposes and what the public can expect from it.

Secondly, the content produced for each of these channels will have to be demonstrably right for the BBC. To ensure this, there will be new criteria of quality, originality, innovation, challenge and engagement to help meet the concerns about ratings chasing by the Corporation.

And lastly, there needs to be a mechanism to allow scrutiny of BBC proposals to vary service licences to accommodate changes in technology or public taste. So, in future, any significantly changed or new BBC service will have to undergo detailed scrutiny via a Public Value Test to determine how it will serve the public interest, and to weigh that against any impact on the market. This will include a rigorous market impact assessment provided by Ofcom. The test is intended to help balance the benefits of public service broadcasting with the health of the wider media market.

. . .

3.1.11 The characteristics [quality, originality etc.] are broad enough to allow the BBC to provide a wide range of programming of appeal to its whole audience. However, in combination with the purposes and service licences, they will also provide the Trust with powerful mechanisms for holding the Executive to account – and, in turn, there will be clear standards against which the Trust's effectiveness can be judged.

---

[26] Full details of the reviews and the reports can be accessed at: http://www.bbc.co.uk/bbctrust/our_work/ value_for_money/ (accessed 1 January 2013).

[27] Details of each licence can be accessed at: http://www.bbc.co.uk/bbctrust/our_work/services/television/ service_licences.html (accessed 1 January 2013).

Since the commencement of the Charter, the BBC has issued two new television service licences – BBC Alba and BBC HD – both subject to the public value test.[28] On the one hand, the requirement for the BBC Trust to issue service licences may seem rather artificial given that it is the BBC itself which will monitor performance. Although the Trust can recommend that a service be discontinued under clause 20(4), the consequences of this are unclear. It would presumably not prevent a new service being proposed by the BBC Executive to replace the unsatisfactory service. On the other hand, the service licences, with clear statements of aims and objectives and characteristics of the service, and the reviews do presumably provide a more transparent means of judging whether a service and the BBC generally are meeting their responsibilities.

A vexed area for BBC accountability is parliamentary scrutiny, and it is in the course of parliamentary debates that members of Parliament will often express frustration at what they perceive to be the lack of BBC accountability. There is a fine line to be drawn between what is legitimate inquiry and what amounts to interference in day-to-day broadcasting decisions. In November 2012, the BBC director-general resigned following the broadcast of an item on *Newsnight*, which wrongly accused a former senior politician of child sexual abuse. As editor-in-chief, the director-general took responsibility for the journalistic failings which led to the broadcast item. Shortly thereafter, the question of parliamentary oversight of the BBC was debated in Parliament. The extract provides a good example of the line which must be drawn between legitimate inquiry and interference, and arguably the difficulty in drawing that line.

Extract 3.5.12
House of Commons Debates, *Hansard*, 554 (5 December 2012), cols 307WH–314WH

DAVID MORRIS (MORECAMBE AND LUNESDALE) (CON):

. . . I am grateful to have this opportunity to bring this debate to the Chamber. It comes at a time when many people up and down the country are thinking and talking about media regulation. It also comes against a backdrop of shocking allegations, first against commercial media outlets and then against our own public service broadcaster. 2012 has been a dire year for the BBC, and the recent child abuse allegations levelled against BBC stars has been described as 'the worst crisis to hit the corporation for 50 years'.

None of us knows the full details of what has happened, and I have no desire to dwell on the allegations, but we do know that the BBC – like many nationalised institutions – lacks accountability to the public. I believe that we, as Members of Parliament, should now force the BBC to become more accountable.

When I was first elected, I wrote a series of parliamentary questions about the BBC and took them to the Table Office, only to learn that we MPs do not have the power to scrutinise the BBC. We have the right to ask about the property portfolio of the Church of England through Church Commissioners questions, but not the right to ask questions about our national state broadcaster. That must change.

I have no problem with the BBC Trust being the governing body of the BBC, but I believe that there must be some oversight by MPs. It has often been said in this House, and in wider public debate, that transparency and accountability improve public services. I believe that applies to the BBC as much as it does to any other state institution. In this debate, therefore, I am calling for several things. The first is that the director-general's appointment should be confirmed by the

---

[28] For an example of where the public value test resulted in a decision by the Trust to refuse to approve a new local video service see: http://www.bbc.co.uk/bbctrust/governance/tools_we_use/new_services/pvt/local_video_proposal.html (accessed 1 January 2013).

House of Commons. Clearly we would have to devise a system to do that. Perhaps it could be done by a vote of the whole House, or through a special panel or committee. I am agnostic about the system, but I think the principle is vital. The director-general is an important public figure who wields huge power in this country, and it must be the duty of Parliament to ensure that the candidate is the right choice for both the BBC and the country, while the BBC has to accept that this appointment is one the most significant public sector appointments, and act accordingly.

Secondly, MPs should have the right to table parliamentary questions to the BBC and the BBC should have a duty to answer them. I do not mind if those answers are only written answers; the important thing is that we can bring in greater openness. Obviously, answering questions would have a cost associated with it, but I believe that that cost is a small price to pay for greater accountability.

Thirdly, the Select Committee on Culture, Media and Sport should have regular insight into the actions of both the BBC and the BBC Trust. That should be formalised into a system, rather than meetings being held on an ad hoc basis. I believe that those three proposals, implemented together, would restore public confidence in the BBC, and as a result the BBC, Parliament and the media environment would all be enhanced.

. . .

THE PARLIAMENTARY UNDER-SECRETARY OF STATE FOR CULTURE, MEDIA AND SPORT (MR EDWARD VAIZEY):

. . .

The BBC is a hugely important global institution, and its value to the UK not only as a content creator of the highest calibre but as a promoter of the UK's values and culture cannot and should not be underestimated. In the context of recent events, which I will come to in a minute, it would be all too easy to forget the positive impact that the BBC has on a daily basis. [. . .]

. . .

MR VAIZEY: . . .

I want to make clear this Government's firm commitment to the long-standing principle, which is of the utmost importance, that the BBC must be independent of Government and of political intervention. The political independence of the media is a live subject both in the House and outside, so it is important to reiterate that principle. The political independence of all media is key to any healthy democracy, and the Government must always ensure that such independence is secured and, where possible, strengthened. Independence, however, does not mean that the BBC, or indeed any broadcaster, should be unaccountable for its actions. Because of the unique way in which it is funded and owned, the BBC should be accountable, and primarily to licence fee payers.

. . .

We have recently reinforced the oversight of the BBC. During the last licence fee settlement we introduced new mechanisms to further strengthen the BBC's financial accountability, and the National Audit Office is now empowered to conduct a value-for-money review of the BBC

. . .

JOHN MCDONNELL (HAYES AND HARLINGTON) (LAB):

I think that many Members from across the House have welcomed the National Audit Office's involvement, but there seems to be a disconnect between the audit that goes on at that office and the Trust having a role in ensuring that there is some financial accountability. There seems to be a lack of expertise on the Trust's board with which to translate the audit information, or the understanding of it, into action.

I will give a brief example. The National Union of Journalists has, over the past week or two, pointed out that the cuts in the number of journalists and the outsourcing that have taken place have resulted in some of the BBC's recent failings. In comparison, however, BBC management have collected £3 million in car allowances – even if they do not drive – £2 million in private health care and £4.7 million in golden goodbyes. The information provided by audit does not seem to be translated by the Trust into actions to control management expenditure.

MR VAIZEY:

I hear what the hon. Gentleman says about the expertise of the BBC Trust. The way of dodging his point would be to say that that is a matter for the Trust. It would not be right for me to interfere or to comment on appointments to the Trust. The appointment process is independent and ensures that members of the Trust are appointed without political interference. The chairman of the Trust is appointed by the Secretary of State and the appointment is approved by the Prime Minister, but the hon. Gentleman should perhaps contact the chairman of the trust to raise his concerns and to explain why he feels that the trust is not doing enough to examine the BBC's finances.

. . .

MR VAIZEY: . . .

Returning to parliamentary scrutiny, which is at the heart of the debate, the BBC charter sets out two mechanisms under which the appointment of the director-general can be made. It can be made by the BBC Trust, whereby the director-general shall also operate as chairman of the executive board, or by the chairman of the executive board, if that role is held by a non-executive appointed by the trust. At this time, we see little benefit of either the Government or Parliament having a role, whether through consultation or ratification, in the appointment of the director-general. Indeed, such a proposal has the potential to make the most important appointment at the BBC – a position that, as we know only too well from recent events, crucially includes the role of editor-in-chief – political, which could undermine the principles of an independent BBC.

That is not to say that Parliament should not have overview of a public institution as important as the BBC. Of course, we entirely support the right of Parliament to question the decisions made by the BBC and the trust, including in debates such as this one. In the past three months, senior BBC figures have appeared before at least two parliamentary Committees.

Finally, we recognise that it is necessary to put this debate in the context of recent events at the BBC, and most importantly of how the BBC responds to the significant loss of public confidence. We have been clear that the primary objective of the BBC Trust at this time must be to rebuild the public's trust in the BBC, and I know that [chairman] Lord Patten agrees. To that end, we have set out three things we believe the BBC Trust needs to achieve.

First, the immediate task must be to address the failings in the editorial process, particularly at 'Newsnight', in order to restore public confidence. The trust needs to act swiftly to ensure that the management and leadership issues are resolved and that the failings cannot be repeated. It is clear from what the interim director-general has said that the BBC is looking seriously at what went wrong, where responsibility lies and how to address the matter in the long term, and the Government welcome that.

Secondly, the trust must ensure that a strong and stable executive board is in place to manage the BBC. To that end, we welcome the appointment of Tony Hall as director-general of the BBC . . .

Thirdly, we must not lose sight of the inquiries into what is at the heart of these events. None of the developments in recent days should overshadow the investigations into the alleged horrendous abuse of children in institutions across our country. It is vital that the BBC responds correctly and decisively to the Pollard inquiry into the decision to drop the 'Newsnight' item on Savile, and to the Smith inquiry on Savile's abuses and the culture and practices of the BBC. We must wait until those investigations have concluded and consideration has been given to their findings. At this time, however, we see no evidence that suggests that greater oversight of the BBC by Parliament would have had any impact on recent events. Even if that case could be made, we must balance any benefits of such oversight against the impact on the BBC's independence.

. . .

Questions for discussion

1. As this brief overview has shown, the BBC is subject to a wide range of tools designed to ensure it is accountable. Is this necessary? Could accountability be achieved in a less complex manner?
2. What negative consequences might arise from these accountability tools?
3. Given the extent to which the BBC is now accountable to external bodies, would a better solution be to transfer governance of the BBC to Ofcom?

3.6 PRELIMINARY LICENSING REQUIREMENTS FOR INDEPENDENT TELEVISION AND RADIO SERVICES

It is a criminal offence to offer a television or radio service unless a licence has been granted (sections 13 and 97, Broadcasting Act 1990). The reference in the legislation to 'independent' services is a reference to private or commercial broadcasting services. Although the requirements imposed upon the licence holders will differ according to the nature of the service, and the process for obtaining a licence may differ, all services are subject to certain preliminary requirements. These 'pre-vetting' tests essentially focus on who may hold (and retain) a licence. These three tests are set out in sections 3(3) and 5(1) (for television) and sections 86(4) and 88 (for radio) of the Broadcasting Act 1990.[29] First, the holder of a licence must be a fit and proper person. Second, certain persons may be disqualified from holding a licence. Disqualification may arise because of activity or affiliation (Schedule 2, Part II, Broadcasting Act 1990). For example, religious bodies and advertising agencies are disqualified persons, although disqualification may not apply to every type of licence. Third, media ownership and control rules will prevent some persons from holding licences or restrict the number of licences which can be held (Communications Act 2003, Schedule 14). These rules are examined in Chapter 7.

Ofcom has an ongoing obligation to be satisfied that a licensee is fit and proper. In 2010, Ofcom determined that Bang Media (London) Ltd and Bang Channels Ltd were not fit and proper persons to hold a licence following numerous licence breaches and their licences were revoked (see Extract 4.6.3).[30] In 2012 Ofcom ruled that British Sky Broadcasting Limited remained a fit and proper person to continue to hold licences under the Broadcasting Acts 1990 and 1996. Its assessment was made following the alleged wrongdoing (phone hacking practices) which took place at certain newspapers owned by News Group Newspapers Limited. In the following extract, Ofcom explains why the alleged wrongdoing of the newspapers was relevant to fitness and propriety under the Broadcasting Acts.

---

[29] Other services, such as digital multiplexes and programme services, are subject to the same requirements: see Broadcasting Act 1996, sections 3(3) and 5(1) (television) and sections 42(2) and 44(1) (radio).

[30] One of Ofcom's predecessors, the Radio Authority, also found that the majority shareholder of a company which held four local radio licences was not fit and proper following rape and indecent assault convictions: Radio Authority, *Radio Authority agrees transfer of control of licences held by Owen Oyston* (News Release 28/98, 9 April 1998).

Extract 3.6.1

Ofcom, *Decision under section 3(3) of the Broadcasting Act 1990 and section 3(3) of the Broadcasting Act 1996: Licences held by British Sky Broadcasting Limited* (20 September 2012), http://stakeholders.ofcom.org.uk/binaries/broadcast/tv-ops/ fit-proper/bskyb-final.pdf (accessed 2 January 2013), paras 8–12

8. We consider that wrongdoing of the kind alleged to have taken place at the newspapers owned by NGN [News Group Newspapers Ltd] is in principle capable of being relevant to the fitness and propriety of a broadcaster, notwithstanding the fact that such wrongdoing was not related to the performance of broadcasting functions. If a broadcaster's fitness and propriety were measured only by reference to its performance or conduct as a broadcaster, this would mean that very serious wrongdoing by the licensee or those who controlled or influenced it, whatever its nature or gravity, was no impediment to the grant or retention of a licence, as long as the wrongdoing was unrelated to the licensee's broadcasting activities. We do not consider that this can be right. Ofcom is responsible for protecting public confidence in broadcasting and the public interest in there being an appropriately rigorous regulatory regime, through its powers and duties under the statutory scheme established by Parliament.

9. To date, there is no evidence that Sky was directly or indirectly involved in any of the wrongdoing either admitted or alleged to have taken place at *News of the World* ('NOTW') or *The Sun*. Sky has admitted to some instances of email hacking in two cases unrelated to the cases alleged to have taken place at NGN. Ofcom is currently considering these issues under the Broadcasting Code.

10. In contrast to some other UK regulatory regimes, Ofcom does not have any statutory responsibility for declaring individuals 'fit and proper' (unless they are broadcast licensees themselves). The behaviour of persons (individuals or corporations) other than Sky can only be relevant to an assessment of Sky if such persons' relationship to Sky is such that Sky's fitness and propriety is affected by their character and conduct. Since Sky is a non-natural person, its fitness and propriety may be judged by reference to the conduct and character of any individual or individuals who exert influence over it. The conduct and character of any director, of any shareholder with a significant holding, and of any other person able to exert influence over the company are therefore relevant in principle to Ofcom's assessment.

11. Ofcom has therefore considered whether any such person, exercising a requisite degree of control over Sky, such that he, she or it exerts influence, has been implicated in, or tainted by, alleged or admitted wrongdoing or criminality at newspapers owned by NGN, in a way, or to an extent, which raises questions about Sky's ongoing fitness and propriety. For these purposes, Ofcom considers that the following individuals' and entity's character and conduct are in principle relevant, because they stand in a relationship to Sky of material influence or control such that they are able to exert influence over it:

(a) James Murdoch's conduct and character are relevant because:
   (i)   he is a director of the parent company, British Sky Broadcasting Group plc ('Sky plc'), which exercises complete control over Sky;
   (ii) he is a director of News Corporation, which owns around 40% of the issued shares of Sky plc; and
   (iii) the Murdoch family trust owns approximately 38% of the Class B stock of News Corporation, which owns around 40% of the issued shares of Sky plc.

(b) Rupert Murdoch's conduct and character are relevant because:
   (i)   he is Chairman and CEO of News Corporation, which owns around 40% of the issued shares of Sky plc; and
   (ii) his family trust owns approximately 38% of the Class B stock of News Corporation, which owns around 40% of the issued shares of Sky plc.

(c) News Corporation's corporate conduct and character are relevant, in light of News Corporation's approximate 40% shareholding in Sky plc.

12. In considering whether Sky remains fit and proper to hold broadcasting licences, Ofcom has therefore had regard to evidence relating to the conduct or character of these persons, and to the extent of influence which they exert over Sky.

Questions for discussion

1. What is the relevance of a 'fitness and propriety' test to broadcast licensing?
2. Is such a test still tenable in a multiplatform media environment?

3.7 COMMERCIAL PUBLIC SERVICE TELEVISION BROADCASTING

(a) Introduction

Commercial television services can be classified as services which have PSB obligations and those which do not. The traditional television broadcasting services, Channels 3, 4 and 5 represent the first category. In the latter are services such as television licensable content services and digital television programme services. Public service television (PST) broadcasting is examined in this section, the other services are examined in Section 3.8.

Until the introduction of cable television in the early 1980s, television broadcasting in the United Kingdom followed a largely unchanging pattern. The private television sector, the Independent Television Association (ITV), relied upon advertising revenue. To enable it to pursue a PSB mandate it faced no competition from other commercial television services, nor did it have to compete with the BBC for advertising revenue. When Channel 4 commenced broadcasting in 1992, ITV's position remained secure because it controlled the sale of Channel 4's advertising. The 'comfortable duopoly', as it was termed, continued until the Broadcasting Act 1990 introduced a new regulatory structure and permitted new services. The Communications Act 2003 further changed the media and regulatory environment and the role of PSB. Although the days of the comfortable duopoly and the sense of the commercial broadcaster having BBC-like obligations are long past, some private, commercial services are still designated as PST broadcasters. These are Channel 3 (or, as it is popularly known, ITV), Channel 5 and Channel 4.

(b) Channel 3

Channel 3 has inherited the structure that was in place when ITV was established in 1956. Hence, although intended as a nationwide service (section 14, Broadcasting Act 1990), it is actually delivered via 15 regional services plus one national breakfast service, GMTV Ltd. This structure means that ITV operates as a network and there are regulatory arrangements in place to manage the supply and distribution of programming between the licensees (see Chapter 8). After BBC1, Channel 3 has the highest audience share of all UK channels (17 per cent, BBC1, 21 per cent). This is significantly ahead of Channel 5 (5 per cent) and Channel 4 (6 per cent).[31]

---

[31] Ofcom, *Licensing of Channel 3 and Channel 5: A report to the Secretary of State under section 229 of the Communications Act 2003* (23 May 2012), http://stakeholders.ofcom.org.uk/binaries/broadcast/tv-ops/c3_c5_licensing.pdf (accessed 27 December 2012), para 3.22.

The Broadcasting Act 1990 introduced a system of competitive tendering for the Channel 3 licence to replace the former practice of largely discretionary allocation of programme contracts. The new system was consistent with the then government's policy approach which favoured market-based processes and objective allocation.[32] However, the process was not only based on price because financial viability and quality thresholds had to be met, and there was scope for the highest cash bid to be bypassed in the case of 'exceptional circumstances', such as the quality of the proposed service. Aside from these discretionary factors, the auction system did not prove to be a reliable indicator of the market value of the licences with bids ranging from £2,000 to £43 million. The low bids were the result of some incumbent franchise (the then name for the 'licences') holders rightly predicting that they would face no competition.[33] The Channel 3 licences were renewed in 2002, but the then regulator, the Independent Television Commission, elected not to repeat the competitive tendering process, instead setting a fee based in part on its assessment of the market value of each licence. The auction process has not been repeated. Under the Communications Act 2003 the Channel 3 licensees were offered digital licences as replacements for the analogue licences as part of the digital switchover (section 215). These licences expire at the end of the 2014. However, following a report by Ofcom, pursuant to section 229, the Secretary of State has agreed to Ofcom instituting a process to renew the licences for a further ten years.[34] The report and the Secretary of State's decision apply also to the renewal of Channel 5. Under section 230 the Secretary of State could, but in this instance has elected not to, block the renewal process which would mean that the licences would have to be offered for re-auction. The effect of this decision means that the government is currently committed to PSB continuing in the commercial sector, although whether this will be sustainable for another ten years remains an open question.

The commercial PST broadcasters have a specific public service remit. Channel 3's public service remit is set out in section 265(2)(a) of the Communications Act 2003 and the licensees are required under section 266 to prepare a statement of programme policy annually and to review their own performance.

Extract 3.7.1
Communications Act 2003, sections 265(2)(a) and 266(1) and (2)

265(2) The public service remit—

(a) for every Channel 3 service . . .

is the provision of high quality and diverse programming.

266(1) The regulatory regime for every licensed public service channel includes a condition requiring the provider of the channel—

(a) as soon as practicable after the coming into force of this section and subsequently at annual intervals, to prepare a statement of programme policy; and

(b) to monitor his own performance in the carrying out of the proposals contained in the statements made in pursuance of the condition.

---

[32] Home Office, *Broadcasting in the '90s: Competition, choice and quality – the Government's plans for broadcasting legislation* (Cm 517, 1988), para 6.17.

[33] For a discussion of the auction see E.M. Barendt, *Broadcasting Law: A Comparative Study* (Oxford: Oxford University Press, 1993), 89–91.

[34] Letter from the Rt Hon Maria Miller, Secretary of State to Ed Richards, Chief Executive, Ofcom (16 November 2012). See also: Ofcom, note 31 above.

(2) The condition must require every statement of programme policy prepared in accordance with the condition to set out the proposals of the provider of the channel for securing that, during the following year—

(a) the public service remit for the channel will be fulfilled; and

(b) the duties imposed on the provider by virtue of sections 277 to 296 will be performed.

The public service remit relates back to the section 264 PST broadcasting purposes. However, Channel 3 (and the other commercial PST broadcasters) also have additional specific obligations, some of which are common to Channels 3, 5 and 4 and some which apply to specific channels. Section 278 requires an appropriate proportion of broadcast time to be given to original productions, with a split between peak viewing periods and other periods. An original production is one which is commissioned with a view to their first showing in the United Kingdom on a licensed PST channel.[35] This is an obligation which applies to Channels 3, 5 and 4 but the quota, which is set by Ofcom, differs for each broadcaster.[36] Thus for Channel 3, which has the highest obligation, the quota is 65 per cent of the overall schedule and 85 per cent quota for programming in peak period. The qualifying programming can include sports and factual programmes as well as drama and arts. Ofcom sees the rationale for this obligation as '[t]o stabilise investment in the UK creative economy and encourage production of content which reflects and strengthens our cultural identity at a UK level.'[37] In a recent report, Ofcom has noted the types of programming which are increasing and those which are decreasing.

Extract 3.7.2

Ofcom, *Licensing of Channel 3 and Channel 5: A report to the Secretary of State under section 229 of the Communications Act 2003* (23 May 2012), http://stakeholders.ofcom.org.uk/broadcasting/tv/c3-c5-licensing (accessed 27 December 2012), paras 3.31, 3.34–3.36 (some confidential references in the report are redacted)

3.30 [. . . The] Channel 3 licensees have consistently exceeded their obligations, with original programming accounting for 97% of content in peak time and 82% of the network's overall schedule.

3.34 However, the breadth of Channel 3 programming has shifted in recent years as the network has looked to increase the proportion of its schedule based on factual output, particularly during daytime. Between 2006 and 2010, factual programming – which predominantly consists of talk based formats such as *The Jeremy Kyle Show*, *Loose Women* and *The Alan Titchmarsh Show* – grew by 53% from 1,729 hours in 2006 to 2,653 hours in 2010.

3.35 Conversely, despite maintaining investment in event programming like *Downton Abbey* with significant resale value, the amount of drama (including soap operas) aired by the network declined from 649 hours in 2006 to 464 hours in 2010 [✕].

3.36 This shift has, however, broadly been positively received by viewers. The proportion of viewers surveyed by Ofcom who considered that Channel 3 showed 'well made, high quality programmes' increased by 4% to 67% between 2007 and 2010.

Source: © Ofcom copyright 2006–11.

---

[35] Broadcasting (Original Productions) Order 2004 (SI 2004/1652), article 3.

[36] The specific public service requirements for Channels 3, 5 and 4 can be found in their licence conditions. The licences can be accessed on the Ofcom website: http://licensing.ofcom.org.uk/tv-broadcast-licences/current-licensees/?a=0 (accessed 5 January 2013).

[37] Ofcom, note 31 above, page 17, figure 6.

All of the commercial PST broadcasters have an identical obligation to ensure that not less than 25 per cent of qualifying original programming is allocated to independent productions (section 277).[38] Ofcom has reported that Channel 3 regularly exceeds this quota.[39]

Regional programming is another obligation imposed upon the PST channels, although the obligations vary slightly and Channel 3 has an additional obligation. Pursuant to section 286 (and section 288, for Channel 4), Ofcom must set licence conditions to ensure that a suitable proportion of programmes are made outside the area bounded by the M25 (the M25 orbital motorway) area. Ofcom must also be satisfied that the programmes cover a suitable range and that the production is spread across a suitable range of production centres. It is for Ofcom to determine the quota for each of the channels and the following extract illustrates the necessity for Ofcom to be flexible in its approach.

> **Extract 3.7.3**
> **Ofcom, *Licensing of Channel 3 and Channel 5: A report to the Secretary of State under section 229 of the Communications Act 2003* (23 May 2012), http://stakeholders.ofcom.org.uk/broadcasting/tv/c3-c5-licensing (accessed 27 December 2012), paras 3.40–3.42**
>
> 3.40 The quotas for Channel 3 licensees increased in 2005 from 33% by volume and 40% by expenditure to 50% by both volume and spend. This was in response to a concern that output on the PSB channels could not adequately reflect the full cultural diversity of the UK when (at the time) less than 40% of programming was produced outside London.
>
> 3.41 However, it subsequently became clear that meeting the revised quota had imposed a significant cost on the Channel 3 network. We also concluded that the requirement, which had been met by long-running shows including quiz and other studio-based programming, had not delivered the additional diversity on screen which, in part, it had been intended to achieve. Accordingly, in 2009 Ofcom cut the quota to 35% by spend and volume.
>
> 3.42 The percentage of qualifying Channel 3 programmes made outside London consequently fell from 50% to 39% by value and 50% to 44% by volume between 2008 and 2010. Despite this, the percentage of viewers surveyed by Ofcom who considered that the channel's entertainment and factual programming featured 'people from different parts of the UK' increased by 5% between 2007 and 2010 to 57%.
>
> Source: © Ofcom copyright 2006–11.

In addition, section 287 requires Channel 3 to broadcast an appropriate amount of regional news and non-news programming.

> **Extract 3.7.4**
> **Communications Act 2003, section 287(1)**
>
> (1) The regulatory regime for every regional Channel 3 service includes the conditions that Ofcom consider appropriate for securing—
>   (a) that what appears to Ofcom, in the case of that service, to be a sufficient amount of time is given in the programmes included in the service to what appears to them to be a suitable range of programmes (including regional news programmes) which are of particular interest to persons living within the area for which the service is provided;

---

[38] For meaning of 'independent' see Broadcasting (Independent Productions) Order 1991 (SI 1991/1408), amended by Broadcasting (Independent Productions) Amendment Order 2003 (SI 2003/1672).
[39] Ofcom, note 31 above, para 3.38.

(b) that the regional programmes included in the service are of high quality;
(c) that what appears to Ofcom, in the case of that service, to be a suitable proportion of the regional programmes included in the service consists of programmes made in that area;
(d) that the regional news programmes included in the service are broadcast for viewing at intervals throughout the period for which the service is provided and, in particular, at peak viewing times;
(e) that what appears to Ofcom, in the case of that service, to be a suitable proportion of the other regional programmes that are included in the service consists of programmes broadcast for viewing—
  (i)   at peak viewing times; and
  (ii) at times immediately preceding or following those times.

Each PST channel will also have obligations to deliver news and current affairs of high quality and covering national and international affairs (section 279(1), Communications Act 2003). Each Channel 3 licensee is required to deliver 365 hours of national and international news each year, of which 125 must be broadcast in peak hours, and 43 hours of current affairs per calendar year, of which 35 hours must be shown in peak-time. The Channel 3 licensees are also required to make arrangements for an appointed news provider capable of delivering a national news services (section 280, Communications Act 2003, and see section 283). Independent Television News (ITN) was established in the early 1950s and has been the provider for ITV national news since the ITV service commenced. ITN also delivers news for Channels 5 and 4.

Questions for discussion

1. How do the requirements of original programming relate (if at all) to the PSB concept?
2. What might the rationale be for a requirement to include independent productions?
3. Extract 3.7.3 shows Ofcom's flexibility in setting regional quotas. How does this flexibility align with Ofcom's duties under sections 3 and 6 of the Communications Act 2003?

(c) Channel 5

Channel 5, like Channel 3, is intended to be a mainstream terrestrial commercial service and it has similar, although lighter obligations.

Extract 3.7.5
Ofcom, *Licensing of Channel 3 and Channel 5: A report to the Secretary of State under section 229 of the Communications Act 2003* (23 May 2012), http://stakeholders.ofcom.org.uk/broadcasting/tv/c3-c5-licensing (accessed 27 December 2012), para 3.52

Channel 5, like the Channel 3 services, has a public service remit to provide 'a range of high quality and diverse programming'. Spectrum limitations at the time of its launch in 1997 meant that it was only available to 70% of UK households, although this differential has largely disappeared through digital switchover. However, Channel 5 still receives fewer benefits than the Channel 3 and Channel 4 licensees, such as their licence to operate Multiplex 2, and Channel 5 has operated with a more limited set of programme obligations to reflect this.

Source: © Ofcom copyright 2006–11.

Unlike Channel 3, the Channel 5 service consists of one licence rather than a regional network. It commenced transmission in 1997. The initial licence award used the competitive tendering process and was something of a fraught process requiring two rounds and resulting in judicial review.[40] Channel 5's licence is due to expire at the end of 2014, but like Channel 3, the Secretary of State has agreed to the commencement of a renewal process licence for a further 10 years (see Section 3.7(b) above). Channel 5 has the same public service remit as Channel 3, namely the provision of a high quality and diverse programming (section 265(2)(b), Communications Act 2003). As with Channel 3, Channel 5 also has specific obligations but because the service differs, as explained in Extract 3.7.5, one can see a difference also in the quantitative obligations imposed. Thus, Channel 5's obligation in relation to original production requires the service to include only 50 per cent original programming overall and 40 per cent in peak time. Ofcom initially set this obligation higher.

Extract 3.7.6
Ofcom, *Licensing of Channel 3 and Channel 5: A report to the Secretary of State under section 229 of the Communications Act 2003* (23 May 2012), http://stakeholders.ofcom.org.uk/broadcasting/tv/c3-c5-licensing (accessed 27 December 2012), paras 3.58–3.59 and 3.64

3.58 From 2003, Channel 5 was required to ensure that at least 50% of its programming content qualified as original programming, and to increase this to 60% by 2009. In our first PSB review in 2005 we concluded that this obligation would be unsustainable given the limited benefits of PSB status which the channel received, and set the quota at 55%. In 2009, the quota was reduced to 50%, in line with the minimum EU wide requirements for European content. Channel 5's peak-time obligations were reduced at the same time to 40% from the 42% set in 2003. Channel 5 has consistently met these obligations . . .

3.59 Channel 5's investment in original programming is significantly lower than that of the other commercial PSBs. Between 2006 and 2010, its spend on first-run originations fell by 49% to £62m, compared to £321m at Channel 4 (a 25% reduction since 2006) and £760m for Channel 3 (down 12% over the same period).

3.64 Finally, as noted above, the statutory definition of original programming covers repeats. In 2010, 59% of Channel 5's original programming was made up of repeats, compared to 25% for ITV plc and 51% of Channel 4's content. In particular, repeats accounted for 92% of the children's programming shown by Channel 5 in 2010, compared with 73% in 2005.

Source: © Ofcom copyright 2006–11.

However, because Channel 5 operates more as a publisher than an in-house producer, it generally exceeds the requirement to have 25 per cent of its original programming allocated to independent productions.[41] Channel 5's obligations in relation to regional are also significantly lower than Channel 3; 10 per cent of programming expenditure and 10 per cent of programming hours must be regionally produced. Channel 5 must broadcast not less than 260 hours per year of news, of which 100 hours must be broadcast during peak viewing times, and not less than 130 hours of current affairs programming, of which 10 hours must be broadcast in peak period. Unusually, the current affairs obligation is set higher than Channel 3, although it usually manages to exceed this target mainly because of a morning phone-in programme, *The Wright Stuff*.[42]

---

[40] R v *Independent Television Commission, ex parte Virgin* [1996] EMLR 318. For further information see Gibbons, n 18 above, 167–8.
[41] Ofcom, n 31 above, para 3.66.
[42] Ibid., para 3.57.

(d) Channel 4

The structure of Channel 4 falls somewhere between that of a public broadcaster and a private commercial service. It is publicly owned, operates as a not-for-profit corporation, and is funded through advertising sponsorship revenue. It also differs from the other services considered in this chapter because it is specifically prohibited from making its own programmes under section 295 of the Communications Act 2003. It is, therefore, a publisher of programmes rather than a producer. Channel 4 commenced transmission in 1982. Under the Broadcasting Act 1990, it became a statutory corporation, Channel 4 Corporation Limited (C4C), whose directors are appointed by Ofcom, subject to the approval of the Secretary of State (section 23(4)). C4C is licensed by Ofcom to ensure the continued provision of Channel 4 (section 24). Its current licence expires at the end of 2014 (section 231(6), Communications Act 2003).

The public service remit of Channel 4 is quite different from the remits of Channels 3 and 5.

Extract 3.7.7
Communications Act 2003, section 265(3)

(3) The public service remit for Channel 4 is the provision of a broad range of high quality and diverse programming which, in particular—

   (a) demonstrates innovation, experiment and creativity in the form and content of programmes;

   (b) appeals to the tastes and interests of a culturally diverse society;

   (c) makes a significant contribution to meeting the need for the licensed public service channels to include programmes of an educational nature and other programmes of educative value; and

   (d) exhibits a distinctive character.

Following amendments by the Digital Economy Act 2010, Channel 4's responsibilities have been broadened to move away from a television-centric remit to one which encompasses digital media. This is not only an acknowledgement of the current multiplatform environment but also an attempt to future-proof the service should the balance shift away from the television platform.[43]

Extract 3.7.8
Communications Act 2003, section 198A(1)–(6)

(1) C4C must participate in—

   (a) the making of a broad range of relevant media content of high quality that, taken as a whole, appeals to the tastes and interests of a culturally diverse society,

   (b) the making of high quality films intended to be shown to the general public at the cinema in the United Kingdom, and

   (c) the broadcasting and distribution of such content and films.

(2) C4C must, in particular, participate in—

   (a) the making of relevant media content that consists of news and current affairs,

   (b) the making of relevant media content that appeals to the tastes and interests of older children and young adults,

---

[43] Department for Business, Innovation and Skills & Department for Culture, Media and Sport, *Digital Britain, Final Report* (Cm 7650, 2009), para 45.

    (c) the broadcasting or distribution by means of electronic communications networks of feature films that reflect cultural activity in the United Kingdom (including third party films), and

    (d) the broadcasting or distribution of relevant media content by means of a range of different types of electronic communications networks.

(3) In performing their duties under subsections (1) and (2) C4C must—

    (a) promote measures intended to secure that people are well-informed and motivated to participate in society in a variety of ways, and

    (b) contribute towards the fulfilment of the public service objectives (as defined in section 264A).

(4) In performing their duties under subsections (1) to (3) C4C must—

    (a) support the development of people with creative talent, in particular—

        (i)   people at the beginning of their careers in relevant media content or films, and

        (ii) people involved in the making of innovative content and films,

    (b) support and stimulate well-informed debate on a wide range of issues, including by providing access to information and views from around the world and by challenging established views,

    (c) promote alternative views and new perspectives, and

    (d) provide access to material that is intended to inspire people to make changes in their lives.

(5) In performing those duties C4C must have regard to the desirability of—

    (a) working with cultural organisations,

    (b) encouraging innovation in the means by which relevant media content is broadcast or distributed, and

    (c) promoting access to and awareness of services provided in digital form.

(6) In this section—

'participate in' includes invest in or otherwise procure;

'relevant media content' means material, other than advertisements, which is included in any of the following services that are available to members of the public in all or part of the United Kingdom—

    (a) television programme services, additional television services or digital additional television services,

    (b) on-demand programme services, or

    (c) other services provided by means of the internet where there is a person who exercises editorial control over the material included in the service;

and a film is a 'third party film' if C4C did not participate in making it.

In relation to these new responsibilities, C4C must prepare a statement of media content policy alongside its statement of programme policy (section 198B, Communications Act 2003), which will be reviewed by Ofcom (section 198C).

    Channel 4 also has additional responsibilities in relation to education. Under section 296 of the Communications Act 2003 Channel 4's licence includes conditions to secure a suitable proportion of programming suitable for schools. In an indication of the influence of the move away from a television-centric approach, Ofcom agreed in 2010 to reduce this quota to a nominal level to reflect Channel 4's change to a focus on developing interactive online educational content.[44] With regard to the quantitative public service obligations, Channel 4's obligations are similar to those imposed upon Channels 3 and 5, although differing in level.

---

[44] Channel 4, *Statement of Programming Policy 2010* available at: http://www.channel4.com/media/documents/corporate/programme-policy/2010.pdf (accessed 5 January 2013), 1. Other statements and annual reports can also be found online.

Aside from the 25 per cent independent production quota imposed uniformly, Channel 4's licence requires it to include at least 56 per cent of original programming in its television service and at least 70 per cent in peak viewing time. Channel 4 is also subject to regional production quotas (section 288) and is obliged to ensure that at least 35 per cent of all programmes hours and 35 per cent of programme expenditure is in respect of programmes produced outside the M25 area. Channel 4 must broadcast not less than 208 hours per calendar year of news during peak viewing times, and not less than 208 hours of current affairs programming, of which 80 hours must be broadcast in peak period. Channel 4 has reported meeting all of its quota obligations, although Ofcom has expressed concern about falling audiences for Channel 4 television news and a lack of audience engagement by audiences with the online delivery of educational content. These concerns may be indicative of the pressures faced by traditional broadcasters trying to expand digital content services and reach new audiences or retain old audiences.[45]

Questions for discussion

1. Why has the government not expanded the obligations of Channel 3 and 5 in the same way as it has done for Channel 4 in relation to digital media?
2. What is the significance of the wording of the obligation in section 265(3)(c) (see Extract 3.7.7)? (Refer also to Ofcom's responsibilities under section 264 (see Section 3.4 above).)

3.8 COMMERCIAL TELEVISION SERVICES

There is a range of licences available for the non-public service television sector.[46] For these services licensing processes and ongoing obligations are usually more straightforward, reflecting the fact that these services are likely to offer niche content and may be more discretionary in their reach, for example, subscription services. Nevertheless they will have to comply with a minimum set of standards (examined in Chapter 4) and satisfy the preliminary licensing requirements discussed in Section 3.6 above.

(a) Television licensable content services

Television licensable content services (TLCS) were introduced by the Communications Act 2003 (sections 232–240) to replace licensable programme service licences (for programmes carried via cable networks) and satellite television service licences issued under the Broadcasting Act 1990. Essentially, a TLCS is a service consisting of conventional television programmes or electronic programme guides, available to the public (whether free-to-air or by subscription) and delivered via satellite, electronic communications network (such as cable or the Internet), or radio multiplex (section 232). However, it is also important to be aware of what it is not (section 233). Licensing is straightforward: applications can be

---

[45] Channel Four Television Corporation, *Channel Four Television Corporation Report and Financial Statements 2011 Incorporating the Statement of Media Content Policy* (2012), 200 and Letter from Ofcom to Lord Burns and David Abraham, 11 May 2012, http://stakeholders.ofcom.org.uk/binaries/broadcast/tv-ops/c4/c4-letter-2012.pdf (accessed 6 January 2013).

[46] Two types of licences will not be examined. A restricted television service licence under section 42A, Broadcasting Act 1990, is issued for a specific event or location; a digital television advanced service licence is generally issued for stand-alone data or text services, such as electronic programme guides (section 24, Broadcasting Act 1996).

made at any time and licences will usually be issued within 25 working days.[47] Licences are awarded per service and continue until revoked or surrendered (section 235(6)). Ofcom's scope for refusing to grant a licence is limited. It may only refuse a licence if the applicant fails to meet the preliminary licensing requirements (section 235(3)(a)–(b)). In addition, Ofcom must be satisfied that the service is unlikely to be involved in contraventions of the programme and advertising standards (section 235(3)(c), see also Chapters 4 and 6).

Although there is only one form of TLCS licence, Ofcom has classified three different types of service which can be provided under a TLCS licence: editorial, teleshopping or self-promotional.[48] This is because the quantitative rules on advertising, as set out in the *Code on the Scheduling of Television Advertising* (see Chapter 6, Section 6.5(c)) will vary according to the type of service offered. The type of service will also affect the licence fee.

Questions for discussion

1. How would you summarise the type of service which would fall within the definition of a TLCS?
2. Review the exclusions in section 233. What is the legislation concerned to exclude from licensing?
3. To what extent is the concept of a TLCS linked to the technology via which the service might be conveyed?

(b) Digital television programme service

A digital television programme service (DTPS) is linked to a specific platform: digital terrestrial television multiplexes. A DTPS is a service consisting of conventional television programmes, available to the general public (section 1(4), Broadcasting Act 1996). However, 'qualifying services' are not required to be licensed. This is a reference to the conventional television services such as the BBC and Channel 3 that are carried via the multiplexes, originally as part of the digital switchover (section 2(2)). Like the TLCS, the licensing process is straightforward. Applications can be made at any time, and Ofcom can only refuse a licence on grounds similar to the TLCS (section 18(4)) and licences continue until surrendered or revoked (section 19(1)). Again, like TLCS, Ofcom requires the type of service – editorial, teleshopping and self-promotional – to be specified.

One difference, however, from TLCS licensing is that it is the provider of the DTPS which is licensed rather than the actual service. This means that one licence may cover one or more services.

Extract 3.8.1
Communications Act 2003, section 362(2)

[A provider of the service is] the person with general control over which programmes and other services and facilities are comprised in the service (whether or not he has control of the content of individual programmes or of the broadcasting or distribution of the service).

---

[47] Ofcom, *Television Licensable Content Services, guidance notes for licence applicants* (5 July 2011), http://licensing.ofcom.org.uk/binaries/tv/tlcs_guidance.pdf (accessed 26 September 2012), para 13. Licences can also only be granted if the service is within the UK jurisdiction: see Chapter 5.
[48] Ibid., paras 27–9.

(c) Local digital television programme services

In 2012 the government legislated to introduce local television.[49] The legislative framework establishes a new multiplex service for local television, which initially offers 21 local television services with a planned later tranche of around 24 licences, with only one licence permitted per location. The local television licences are in the form of local digital television programme services (L-DTPS) licences with specific obligations to broadcast local content. Ofcom issued the first L-DTPS licences in September 2012 and it is expected that the first services will be aired by autumn 2013. With the move to broadband services and the 'demise' of old media business models, it might be considered curious that the government has chosen this time to introduce a more traditionally structured and delivered television service. The government explained its rationale and its choice of technology in its Local Media Action Plan issued in June 2011:

Extract 3.8.2
Department for Culture, Media and Sport, *Local Media Action Plan* (19 January 2011), http://www.culture.gov.uk/images/consultations/ConDoc-Local_Media_Action_Plan_190111.pdf (accessed 2 October 2012), 6–7 (footnotes omitted)

Despite significant technological changes, television remains the main platform for the consumption of news. But while television in the UK provides international, national and regional news, it has struggled to provide truly local content. The Government believes that now is the right time to address this gap and wishes to see an increase in local TV content with more locally-focused perspectives.

As the Government seeks to decentralise power from Westminster and give people a greater say in how their communities are run, the Government wants to see a strong local media sector that has plurality in platform and voice. Local press and local radio are well-established in the marketplace and hold direct experience of delivering local content to local audiences. Local websites provide even more locally targeted information and offer links to other media platforms. However, local television does not currently have any strong foothold in the UK and given the right conditions, the Government believes that local TV services can take an active role in local as well as national democracy. In the nations (Scotland, Wales and Northern Ireland), local or nations-based news is particularly important as part of devolution. Local TV can be a tool to hold local institutions to account and encourage local political engagement. It provides viewers with information about where they live and issues that affect them, all from a local perspective.

Technological change continues to have a massive impact on the media markets and our daily lives. Internet protocol television (IPTV) is the latest technical development which will provide video on demand and connect the television set to the internet. This will allow audiences to receive television services in a seamless way whether these are distributed through traditional broadcasting technologies such as roof top aerials (digital terrestrial), cable or satellite and those distributed via fixed broadband or wireless. Nicholas Shott [who undertook a viability study of local television] said that in the long term, local TV looked set to be delivered through IPTV technology. The Government agrees that IPTV is likely to become the distribution means for local TV services as well as other TV services as it has the scope to be far more local and targeted at individual localities in a way that distribution via television masts cannot.

However, it is uncertain when IPTV will be sufficiently well-established and widely in use; accordingly the Government proposes to facilitate a transitional phase for local television by putting in place a new framework that will allow existing and new entrants an opportunity to provide local services on mainstream television . . .

---

[49] See section 244, Communications Act 2003 and the Local Digital Television Programme Services Order 2012 (SI 2012/292).

The government was especially concerned to ensure commercial viability of local television.[50] The services are permitted to carry advertising, but are prohibited from charging for the service. In addition, two other strategies have been adopted. First, L-DTPS will be encouraged to develop networking arrangements with each other in order to enable content to be developed, share costs and co-ordinate national advertising sales.[51] The second strategy was developed as part of the BBC's licence fee settlement in 2010. As a means of providing revenue to the L-DTPS during the start-up period, the BBC is to provide start-up capital of up to 25 million pounds to assist the development of local television infrastructure and up to 15 million pounds, over three years, to acquire local content for BBC use from the L-DTPS licensees.[52]

To be an L-DPTS, the service must meet the criteria set out in article 3 of the Local Digital Television Programme Services Order 2012 (LDTPSO). Ofcom has some discretion over the length of a L-DTPS licence, up to a maximum of 12 years (article 10, LDTPSO), and it has determined that the licences should be granted for up to 12 years in order to coincide with the multiplex licence which will have a term of 12 years.[53]

Extract 3.8.3
The Local Digital Television Programme Services Order 2012 (SI 2012/292), article 3

(1) A local digital television programme service is a digital programme service of the following description—

    (a) it is provided in digital form with a view to its being included in a television multiplex service; and

    (b) it falls within paragraphs (2) and (5).

(2) A service falls within this paragraph if it is a service in relation to which all of the following conditions are satisfied—

    (a) it is intended for reception only within a particular area or locality;

    (b) its provision meets, or would meet, the needs of the area or locality where it is received;

    (c) its provision is or would be likely to broaden the range of television programmes available for viewing by persons living or working in that area or locality; and

    (d) its provision is or would be likely to increase the number and range of the programmes about that area or locality that are available for such viewing, or to increase the number of programmes made in that area or locality that would be so available.

(3) A service is to be taken for the purposes of paragraph (2) to meet the needs of an area or locality if, and only if—

    (a) its provision brings social or economic benefits to that area or locality, or to different categories of persons living or working in that area or locality; or

    (b) it caters for the tastes, interests and needs of some or all of the different descriptions of persons living or working in the area or locality (including, in particular, tastes, interests and needs that are of special relevance in the light of the descriptions of persons who do so live and work).

(4) In paragraphs (2) and (3) the references to persons living or working in an area or locality include a reference to persons undergoing education or training in that area or locality.

---

[50] Department for Culture, Media and Sport, *Local Media Action Plan* (19 January 2011), http://www.culture.gov.uk/images/consultations/ConDoc-Local_Media_Action_Plan_190111.pdf (accessed 2 October 2012), para 2.4.

[51] Ibid., para 2.7.

[52] Ibid., para 2.4.

[53] Ofcom, Licensing Local Television, Statement (10 May 2012), http://stakeholders.ofcom.org.uk/consultations/local-tv/statement (accessed 2 October 2012), para 1.40.

(5) A service falls within this paragraph if it includes or would include a range of programmes which—

    (a) facilitate civic understanding and fair and well-informed debate through coverage of local news and current affairs;

    (b) reflect the lives and concerns of communities and cultural interests and traditions in that area or locality; and

    (c) include content that informs, educates and entertains and is not otherwise available through a digital television programme service which is available across the United Kingdom.

The government has opted for a 'beauty contest' type of licensing process for these licences – in other words, the licence is on a merits basis, having regard to the matters set out in article 9 (LDTPSO). Ofcom has emphasised the importance of local news on these services.[54]

3.9 COMMERCIAL RADIO SERVICES

(a) Introduction

Unlike commercial television, the commercial radio sector is not bound by PSB obligations. Only the BBC offers public service radio. This was not always so. When local commercial radio services began broadcasting in 1972, they were expected to meet PSB obligations, but by the late 1980s there was pressure for relaxation. In a government green paper reviewing the future development of commercial radio broadcasting, the financial sustainability of the industry and its ability to match the BBC in programming were questioned.

> **Extract 3.9.1**
> ***Radio: Choices and Opportunities, Green Paper* (Cm 92, 1987), para 2.7**
>
> The financial pressure on [Independent Local Radio] has been reflected in programmes. The drama and education output has been limited. The need for economies in stations has had implications for the coverage of local news . . . But, is it still sensible to expect each small independent local radio station to provide a microcosm of the public service broadcasting output of four BBC national networks?

The Broadcasting Act 1990 introduced significant relaxation of radio industry regulation.[55] Local and national commercial radio services have remained the pattern and analogue radio services are likely to dominate the radio market for some time (see Section 3.2 above).

(b) Analogue commercial radio – national services

The 1990 reforms introduced national commercial radio services. There are only three services – one FM and two AM – because spectrum options are more limited, although

---

[54] Ibid., para 1.46.
[55] Two types of licences will not be examined. A restricted radio licence (section 245(4)(c), Communications Act 2003) is licensed under the Broadcasting Act 1990 (section 104) for a specific event or location. A digital advanced sound service licence is generally issued for stand-alone data or text services (section 63, Broadcasting Act 1996).

these services are now being simulcast in digital. The Broadcasting Act 1990 is quite specific about the type of national radio services that can be licensed.

Extract 3.9.2
Broadcasting Act 1990, section 85(2)(a)

(2) Ofcom shall do all that they can to secure the provision within the United Kingdom of—

    (a) a diversity of national services each catering for tastes and interests different from those catered for by the others and of which—

        (i) one is a service the greater part of which consists in the broadcasting of spoken material, and

        (ii) another is a service which consists wholly or mainly, in the broadcasting of music which, in the opinion of Ofcom, is not pop music . . .

Classic FM began broadcasting in September 1992 and meets the 'not pop music' category. The 'spoken word' service was originally launched in 1995 as Talk Back UK and was relaunched in 2000 as talkSPORT. The third national service commenced in 1995, as Virgin Radio; following a sale the service is now broadcast as Absolute Radio. As with television, a competitive tendering process was used for the award of licences (sections 98–100, Broadcasting Act 1990), but the process has not been used since. The licences were initially awarded for a term of eight years. They were renewed in 1999/2000 for a further term of eight years. As an incentive to digital simulcast, the Digital Economy Act 2010 amended the Broadcasting Act 1990 to permit a further renewal period of seven years (section 103B, Broadcasting Act 1990).[56]

Questions for discussion

1. PSB obligations have been retained for television but not for radio. Given that programming costs can be expected to be much higher for television compared with radio, why might radio otherwise find it difficult to maintain such obligations?
2. Section 85(2)(a) of the Broadcasting Act 1990 specifies the type of services to be offered on national commercial radio. Why might this have been seen as necessary? Is it an appropriate form of intervention?

(c) Analogue commercial radio – local services

There are approximately 296 local commercial radio services licensed across the United Kingdom; the majority (242) are broadcast via FM transmission. This makes local commercial radio the largest of the radio sectors, although the audience size varies considerably from service to service. There has been considerable consolidation in the radio industry. Global Radio holds 24.2 per cent of all analogue licences while the second largest group, the Bauer Radio Group, holds 14 per cent. The consolidation has also resulted in extensive programme sharing between the services.[57] The licensing process for local services does not follow the same competitive bid process of the national regime. In exercising its discretion, Ofcom will have regard to a range of matters.

---

[56] See also section 103A, Broadcasting Act 1990.
[57] Ofcom, note 12 above, paras 3.2.3 and 3.2.5.

Extract 3.9.3
Broadcasting Act 1990, section 105

Where Ofcom have published a notice under section 104(1), they shall, in determining whether, or to whom, to grant the local licence in question, have regard to the following matters, namely—

(a) the ability of each of the applicants for the licence to maintain, throughout the period for which the licence would be in force, the service which he proposes to provide;

(b) the extent to which any such proposed service would cater for the tastes and interests of persons living in the area or locality for which the service would be provided, and, where it is proposed to cater for any particular tastes and interests of such persons, the extent to which the service would cater for those tastes and interests;

(c) the extent to which any such proposed service would broaden the range of programmes available by way of local services to persons living in the area or locality for which it would be provided, and, in particular, the extent to which the service would cater for tastes and interests different from those already catered for by local services provided for that area or locality; and

(d) the extent to which there is evidence that, amongst persons living in that area or locality, there is a demand for, or support for, the provision of the proposed service.

Despite this discretionary process, Ofcom adopts a scoring system as a guide – but not a definitive guide – for the award. Points between '0 and 10' are awarded against each of the statutory criteria, but no overall total score is provided. Ofcom's guidance emphasises that the licensing committee might well decide to award the licence to an applicant without the highest scores. Similarly, while all the statutory criteria have to be taken into account, Ofcom may view one or more as having greater weight given the licence on offer.[58] Licences were initially granted for a period of eight years (section 86(3)(a), Broadcasting Act 1990). Provided that a digital service is also offered, a licence can be renewed for a term of 12 years (section 104A) and a further renewal of seven years (section 104AA).

Not surprisingly, 'localness' is an important theme of local radio provision and Ofcom has a statutory obligation to secure that local services provide an appropriate amount of local material and locally made programmes under section 314 of the Communications Act 2003. However, the maintenance of a locally focused, locally made regime has been under pressure in an uncertain broadcasting environment. The localness obligation was amended by the Digital Economy Act 2010 to alleviate the burden it imposed regarding the costs of locally made programming.[59] Under Ofcom's redrafted localism guidelines, licensees can request changes to their licence formats to permit programme-sharing within approved areas. Requests can also be made to co-locate programming with stations outside approved areas. In considering such requests, Ofcom is likely to take into account the size of the stations, cultural affinity and financial viability.[60] Section 106 of the Broadcasting Act 1990 also permits licensees to request other changes to a station's format provided that the character of the service does not significantly change.[61]

---

[58] See Ofcom, *Scoring system for Ofcom's assessment of commercial radio licence applications* at http://licensing.ofcom.org.uk/radio-broadcast-licensing/analogue-radio/apply-for-licence/how-to-apply/scoring/ (accessed 9 October 2012).

[59] Ofcom, Statement on commercial radio localness regulation (15 April 2010), http://stakeholders.ofcom.org.uk/consultations/radio/statement/ (accessed 3 January 2013), paras 1.1, 1.10 and 1.12.

[60] Ibid., 40–1.

[61] Section 106 also applies to national radio services. In the case of local services, Ofcom may need to conduct a public consultation: section 106ZA.

Extract 3.9.4
Broadcasting Act 1990, section 106(1A)

(1A) Conditions included in a licence . . . may provide that Ofcom may consent to a departure from the character of the licensed service if, and only if, they are satisfied—

  (a) that the departure would not substantially alter the character of the service;

  (b) that the departure would not narrow the range of programmes available by way of relevant independent radio services to persons living in the area or locality for which the service is licensed to be provided;

  (c) that, in the case of a local licence, the departure would be conducive to the maintenance or promotion of fair and effective competition in that area or locality;

  (d) that, in the case of a local licence, there is evidence that, amongst persons living in that area or locality, there is a significant demand for, or significant support for, the change that would result from the departure; or

  (e) that, in the case of a local licence—

    (i) the departure would result from programmes included in the licensed service ceasing to be made at premises in the area or locality for which the service is provided, but

    (ii) those programmes would continue to be made wholly or partly at premises within the approved area (as defined in section 314 of the Communications Act 2003 (local content and character of services)).

Ofcom has discretion as to whether to approve a change, even if the statutory grounds are satisfied. In exercising that discretion, Ofcom takes into account a range of matters such as the significance of the original format in the initial award of licence; the extent of the impact of change on the service's character; time elapsed since the licence was awarded; the avoidance of 'format creep'; and, whether the station broadcasts on AM or FM.[62] Ofcom is aware that AM services, because of technical quality, are at a disadvantage in maintaining audiences. 'Format creep' indicates Ofcom's concern that small format changes may over time amount to a substantial alteration to the character of the service so it will look at a change request in the context of any other changes which have been approved for that service. When one considers the matters informing Ofcom's discretion, it is apparent that there is a balancing of factors such as the desirability of maintaining the service's character in question, responding to changes over time, and also being alive to the economic imperatives which may be pushing the changes.

Questions for discussion

1. What factors might have contributed to the government's decision not to use a competitive bidding process for the award of local licences?

2. To what extent do the regulatory arrangements for local commercial radio suggest that PSB concepts are still influential? Is this still the case after the Digital Economy Act 2010 amendments?

---

[62] Ofcom, *The Regulation of Format Changes*, http://stakeholders.ofcom.org.uk/broadcasting/radio/formats-content/changes/ (accessed 3 January 2013).

(d) Community radio

Community radio was introduced by section 262 of the Communications Act 2003 and implemented pursuant to the Community Radio Order 2004.[63] For these purposes 'community' has a broader meaning than simply a geographical area.

Extract 3.9.5
Community Radio Order 2004 (SI 2004/1944), articles 2(1)–(3) and 3

2 (1) In this Order—

. . .

'community' means—

    (a) the persons who live or work or undergo education or training in a particular area or locality, or

    (b) persons who (whether or not they fall within paragraph (a)) have one or more interests or characteristics in common;

. . .

'social enterprise' means a business which has as its primary objective the support of one or more projects of a social nature (rather than the production of a financial profit);
'social gain' has the meaning given by paragraph (2).

(2) In relation to a community radio service, 'social gain' means the achievement, in respect of individuals or groups of individuals in the community that the service is intended to serve, or in respect of other members of the public, of the following objectives—

    (a) the provision of sound broadcasting services to individuals who are otherwise underserved by such services,

    (b) the facilitation of discussion and the expression of opinion,

    (c) the provision (whether by means of programmes included in the service or otherwise) of education or training to individuals not employed by the person providing the service, and

    (d) the better understanding of the particular community and the strengthening of links within it,

and may also include the achievement of other objectives of a social nature and, in particular, those mentioned in paragraph (3).

(3) Those objectives are—

    (a) the delivery of services provided by local authorities and other services of a social nature and the increasing, and wider dissemination, of knowledge about those services and about local amenities;

    (b) the promotion of economic development and of social enterprises;

    (c) the promotion of employment;

    (d) the provision of opportunities for the gaining of work experience;

    (e) the promotion of social inclusion;

    (f) the promotion of cultural and linguistic diversity;

    (g) the promotion of civic participation and volunteering.

3 (1) It is a characteristic of community radio services that they are local services provided primarily—

(a) for the good of members of the public, or of particular communities, and

(b) in order to deliver social gain, rather than primarily for commercial reasons or for the financial or other material gain of the individuals involved in providing the service.

---

[63] SI 2004/1944 and amended by the Community Radio Amendment Order 2010 (SI 2010/118).

(2) It is a characteristic of every community radio service that it is intended primarily to serve one or more communities (whether or not it also serves other members of the public).

(3) It is a characteristic of every community radio service that the person providing the service—

(a) does not do so in order to make a financial profit by so doing, and

(b) uses any profit that is produced in the provision of the service wholly and exclusively for securing or improving the future provision of the service, or for the delivery of social gain to members of the public or the community that the service is intended to serve.

(4) It is a characteristic of every community radio service that members of the community it is intended to serve are given opportunities to participate in the operation and management of the service.

(5) It is a characteristic of every community radio service that, in respect of the provision of that service, the person providing the service makes himself accountable to the community that the service is intended to serve.

The first community radio licences were awarded in 2005. Two hundred and fifty-four licences have been granted, and, although some have been handed back, by end May 2012 there were 198 community radio stations broadcasting, the majority being transmitted on FM.[64] The two major sources of revenue for community radio are grants (for example from Community Radio Fund and local authorities) (33 per cent) and on-air advertising and sponsorship (26 per cent), although interestingly, those services targeting ethnic communities receive most of their income from on-air advertising and sponsorship, and at 43 per cent, well above the average for the sector. While donations across the sector form only 13 per cent of income, stations catering for religious communities receive 36 per cent.[65] Community radio licences cannot be applied for on an 'ad hoc' basis, only when Ofcom announces a licensing round. These rounds are organised by regions across the United Kingdom. It is not expected that a licence applicant should cover the whole area; the applicant will specify the location and community for the service. The licensing model is an adaptation of the local radio licensing process, and licences are awarded on a merits-basis, having regard to the statutory selection criteria (section 105, Broadcasting Act 1990, as amended by the Community Radio Order 2004 (CRO 2004), Schedule, para 5).

Aside from the statutory selection criteria, Ofcom must also have regard to the potential impact of a community station on the economic viability of any other local (non-community) radio service (section 105(3), Broadcasting Act 1990, as amended by the CRO 2004, Schedule, para 5(2)) in deciding whether to award the licence. Two further measures aimed at protecting local radio apply. First, a community radio licensee is limited in the amount of income derived from advertising and sponsorship. Ofcom is required to specify as a licence condition the permitted amount of advertising and sponsorship revenue (up to 50 per cent) (section 105(4)(c) and (6), Broadcasting Act 1990, as amended by the CRO 2004). Second, where a community radio station overlaps with a local commercial service and has a potential audience of up to 150,000 persons (15 years and above), the community station is prohibited from earning advertising and sponsorship revenue (section 105(4)(b), Broadcasting Act 1990, as amended by the CRO 2004). Licences are granted for five years (section 86(3), Broadcasting Act 1990, as amended by the CRO 2004, Schedule, para 2), with the possibility of one renewal of five years (section 253A, Communications Act 2003).

---

[64] Ofcom, note 12 above, para 3.2.5.

[65] Ibid., para 3.2.6. The Community Radio Fund is administered by Ofcom, funded by the government, and provides support to community radio operators: section 359, Communications Act 2003.

Questions for discussion
1. Are community radio services intended to be the equivalent of local television services?
2. Does the regime for community radio also show the influence of the PSB concept?

(e) Radio licensable content services

As with TLCS, radio licensable content services (RLCS) were introduced to replace licences for radio services carried by satellite and cable. Sections 247 and 248 of the Communications Act 2003 set out what is and what is not an RLCS, following a similar pattern to the definition of TLCS. As with TLCS, licences are awarded per service, the licensing process is straightforward and can be made at any time (section 250). Again, as with TLCS, licences are granted for an indefinite period until revoked or surrendered (section 86(1)(a), Broadcasting Act 1990). Unlike TLCS, there is only one form of licence.

(f) Digital sound programme services

Digital sound programme services (DSPS) also follow a similar pattern to DTPS: in other words, they are services that will be carried via a digital radio multiplex. However, DSPS are divided into national and local services and will be delivered via national and local multiplexes respectively (section 60(1), Broadcasting Act 1996). Again, the licensing process is straightforward (section 60) and licences will be held until revoked or surrendered (section 61(1)). Licences are granted to the provider of the service (see Extract 3.8.1). This means that more than one service can be attached to a licence although separate licences must be obtained for national and local DSPS (section 60(2), Broadcasting Act 1996).

3.10 DIGITAL MULTIPLEXES

(a) Introduction

Multiplex licences were developed when digital broadcasting was introduced. Because digital technology increased the number of channels that could be transmitted, multiplexes were used to carry a number of channels – using spectrum capacity, which may previously have permitted only one channel to be carried. Multiplexes are therefore primarily concerned with the technical delivery of terrestrial digital television and sound services, and this is reflected in the licensing process.

(b) Television multiplexes

Before the complete switchover to digital technology, the free-to-air broadcasters were required to simulcast their services in analogue and digital form to ensure that the public was not denied access to communications while digital was in its infancy. As part of this simulcasting obligation, three multiplexes were allocated: Multiplex 1 to the BBC; Multiplex 2 to carry Channels 3 and 4; and, Multiplex A for Channels 5 and S4C. This enabled the analogue services to be transmitted in digital, with some capacity for new digital services. Multiplex 2 and Multiplex A are licensed under the Broadcasting Act 1996.

Multiplex 1 is not licensed, but it does hold a licence (as do the other multiplex licensees) under the Wireless Telegraphy Act 2006 in relation to the allocation of spectrum. There are three other multiplexes (B, C and D) and initially these were allocated through a competitive merits-based process under sections 7 and 8 of the Broadcasting Act 1996 to assist the development of digital television broadcasting. The first licensee tried to run a pay digital terrestrial service but failed. Subsequently, the licences were awarded to a joint venture of the BBC, Channels 3 and 5, BSkyB and Arqiva Services Limited (a major network provider). The joint venture, Freeview, which offered a relatively inexpensive digital set-top box, commenced operation in 2002 and played a significant role in expanding digital take-up.[66] Although the matters to be taken into account in determining the award of a licence are concerned with technical matters, there are broader concerns as well, consistent with the public service traditions of broadcasting regulation in the United Kingdom. For example, section 8(2)(d) requires Ofcom to consider whether the proposed services to be carried on the multiplex will appeal to a variety of tastes and interests. The services referred to here are separately licensed as DTPS (see Section 3.8(b) above).

(c) Local television multiplex

Provision for a local television multiplex has been made to enable the distribution of the new L-DTPS (Section 3.8(c) above). One multiplex service is intended to cover the whole of the United Kingdom. The licensing process in Part I of the Broadcasting Act 1996, save as modified by the LDTPSO, applies to the local television multiplex as it did to the television multiplex licences. One difference, however, is that under section 8(2)(d), Ofcom is to have regard not to whether the services will appeal to a variety of tastes and interests but to 'proposals by the applicant for promoting local digital television programmes services'.

(d) Radio multiplexes

As explained in section 3.9 above, radio services are still provided in a mix of analogue and digital formats so that some services will be simulcast. Nevertheless, the radio multiplex regulatory process is similar to the television multiplex process. Radio multiplexes are regulated under Part II of the Broadcasting Act 1996. National radio multiplexes (sections 46–47) and local radio multiplexes (sections 50–51) are licensed. There are two operating national radio multiplexes. One is allocated to the BBC and the other, Digital One, broadcasts the three national commercial radio services as well as other digital only services. In recognition of the more extensive network of local commercial radio, there are 46 local radio multiplexes carrying simulcast and digital-only services.[67]

3.11 VIDEO ON-DEMAND SERVICES

Implementation of the EU Audiovisual Media Services Directive (see Chapter 5) has required the introduction of a regulatory regime for video on-demand programme services (ODPS). Essentially, this regime covers non-linear, television-like programme services.

---

[66] See L. Hitchens, *Broadcasting Pluralism and Diversity; A Comparative Study of Policy and Regulation* (Oxford: Hart Publishing, 2006), 16.
[67] Ofcom, note 12 above, para 3.2.5.

Such services are not required to be licensed. A system of notification operates, and the services are subject to regulation concerning harmful content, advertising, sponsorship and product placement (see Chapters 4 and 6). Section 368A of the Communications Act 2003 determines what services will fall under this regulatory regime.

Extract 3.11.1
Communications Act 2003, section 368A(1)–(4)

(1) For the purposes of this Act, a service is an 'on-demand programme service' if—

    (a) its principal purpose is the provision of programmes the form and content of which are comparable to the form and content of programmes normally included in television programme services;

    (b) access to it is on-demand;

    (c) there is a person who has editorial responsibility for it;

    (d) it is made available by that person for use by members of the public; and . . .

    (e) that person is under the jurisdiction of the United Kingdom for the purposes of the Audiovisual Media Services Directive.

(2) Access to a service is on-demand if—

    (a) the service enables the user to view, at a time chosen by the user, programmes selected by the user from among the programmes included in the service; and

    (b) the programmes viewed by the user are received by the user by means of an electronic communications network (whether before or after the user has selected which programmes to view).

(3) For the purposes of subsection (2)(a), the fact that a programme may be viewed only within a period specified by the provider of the service does not prevent the time at which it is viewed being one chosen by the user.

(4) A person has editorial responsibility for a service if that person has general control—

    (a) over what programmes are included in the range of programmes offered to users; and

    (b) over the manner in which the programmes are organised in that range;

and the person need not have control of the content of individual programmes or of the broadcasting or distribution of the service (see also section 368R(6)).

The regulatory regime relies on a co-regulation model. Ofcom has the power under section 368B to designate a body as the regulatory authority. Ofcom designated the Association for Television Video on Demand as the regulatory authority. The Association, which has now been renamed the Authority for Television on Demand (ATVOD), was, prior to the designation, an industry self-regulatory body representing cable and Internet service providers.[68] The designation commenced in March 2010 and was reviewed in 2012. The designation (amended) will continue for ten years.[69] ADTVOD's duties are set out in section 368C, and it also has enforcement powers in relation to any breach of the notification requirements under section 368BA (section 368BB).

Services falling within section 368A cannot be provided unless they have given advance notification to ATVOD under section 368BA(1). Notification must also be given if there are any significant differences to the service or the service ceases (section 368BA(2)). ATVOD is empowered under section 368BB to take action where it determines that there

---

[68] For a detailed analysis of the co-regulatory scheme see D. Mac Síthigh, 'Co-regulation; video-on-demand and the legal status of audio-visual Media' (2011) 2(1) *International Journal of Digital Television* 49–66.

[69] Ofcom, *Review of the Ofcom Designation of the Authority for Television on Demand – Statement* (15 August 2012), http://stakeholders.ofcom.org.uk/broadcasting/tv/video-on-demand/ (accessed 22 October 2012).

is a breach of section 368BA. In making such a determination it must have acted on reasonable grounds and provided the provider with an opportunity to make representations (section 368BB(2)). Following such a determination, ATVOD can issue an enforcement notice or impose a penalty. The enforcement notification provides an opportunity for the contravention to be remedied (section 368BB(3)). Section 368BB has perhaps provided ATVOD with the greatest challenge, because under this enforcement power ATVOD is making determinations about what is and what is not within the scope of this regulatory regime: in other words, what is an ODPS. It has exposed also the on-going regulatory challenge, referred to in this chapter (and see also Chapters 1 and 9), namely how to justify the special regulation of broadcasting when the traditional forms of electronic and print media are converging. In early 2011, ATVOD made a determination that a service offered by the *Sun* newspaper on its website was an ODPS.[70] This was one of a number of determinations made by ATVOD in relation to newspaper and magazine websites.[71] News Group Newspapers Limited, the proprietor of the *Sun*, successfully appealed to Ofcom. As a result of Ofcom's decision, ATVOD withdrew nine other determinations that it had made concerning similar websites.

Extract 3.11.2

Ofcom, *Appeal by News Group Newspapers Limited against a notice of determination by ATVOD that the provider of the service 'Sun Video' has contravened section 368BA of the Communications Act 2003* (December 2011), http://www.atvod.co.uk/uploads/files/Ofcom_Decision_-_SUN_VIDEO_211211.pdf (accessed 10 January 2013), paras 48–9, 68–74, 91, 94 and 96 (footnotes omitted)

48. In light of this consideration, Ofcom has decided that the reasons and evidence ATVOD relied upon in its Determination were not sufficient for it to decide that the Video section of the *Sun*'s website was an ODPS. In addition, Ofcom considers that, in the Determination, too much focus was placed on the 'Sun Video' section of the *Sun*'s website . . .

49. Further, Ofcom view, applying the statutory scheme, and taking account of the reasoning and evidence relied upon by ATVOD, together with the evidence it subsequently provided to Ofcom, the evidence (and submissions) from News Group and the evidence found by Ofcom, is that the Video section of the *Sun*'s website was not a service having the principal purpose of providing audio visual material. Ofcom's Decision that the relevant section was not an ODPS should, therefore, be substituted for ATVOD's.

. . .

68. Applying the statutory scheme, the approach that should be taken [. . .] is to consider the whole of what is provided: in this case the written content and audio visual material on the *Sun* website. The question to consider is whether there is anything amongst that material which is a service whose *principal purpose* is the provision of *TV-like* programmes. In other words, it is only possible to define the scope of a service, and whether it could be an ODPS, by identifying the principal purpose(s) of what is provided (and any ancillary purposes).

69. It is also necessary to take a step back and, having regard to the AVMS Directive, consider whether:

a. the material is likely to compete for the same audience as (linear) television broadcasts; and

b. the nature of the material, and the means of access to it, would lead users reasonably to expect regulatory protection within the scope of the Directive.

---

[70] ATVOD, *Scope Determination, Sun Video* (11 February 2011), http://www.atvod.co.uk/regulated-services/scope-determinations/sun-video (accessed 22 October 2012).

[71] See http://www.atvod.co.uk/regulated-services/scope-determinations.

70. The key provision for present purposes is sub-section 368A(1)(a). As far as that subsection can be broken down into constituent parts, there are two such parts that might be described as:

a. 'the principal purpose part;' and
b. 'the comparability part.'

71. These two parts of the statutory definition should be applied to what is provided as a whole. Ofcom has identified characteristics that could be considered when applying the first of them . . . That is, characteristics of a service more likely to have the required *principal purpose*. It is not necessary, in light of the decision Ofcom has made, to consider characteristics relevant to the *comparability part* . . .

72. Where audio visual material is provided amongst other things, the *principal purpose part* of the statutory definition means it is necessary to ask whether, considering what is provided as a whole, any of the audio visual material:

a. comprises something that in its own right is a 'service' whose 'principal purpose' is the provision of that material; or
b. is ancillary to the provision of some other service.

. . .

73. If the answer to (a) is in the affirmative, it is necessary to apply the *comparability part* of the statutory definition. That is a question of whether, taken as a whole, the audio visual material comprising the service is comparable in form and content to the form and content of programmes normally included in television programme services.

74. Applying this to the *Sun*'s website, the appropriate approach was to have begun by considering whether there was anything on it that was a service whose principal purpose was providing audio visual material. Having made that assessment, it may have been that what was provided was more than one service, each with its own principal purpose. For example, one having the principal purpose of providing an electronic version of the *Sun* newspaper, *and* another whose principal purpose was providing audio visual material. The *comparability part* of the statutory definition of an ODPS should then have been applied to the latter. It may have been an ODPS.

. . .

91. Accordingly, in assessing the application of section 368A(1)(a) to the audio visual material on the *Sun*'s website, the appropriate approach was for ATVOD to have considered the website as a whole, to determine whether any of the audio visual material on the site comprised a service having the principal purpose of providing that material.

. . .

94. The Determination suggests that ATVOD placed too much focus on the 'Sun Video' section of the *Sun*'s website. It suggests ATVOD considered that section of the website, and certain material in it, without looking enough at the whole of what was provided on the site.

. . .

96. ATVOD's Determination therefore demonstrates a consideration of the Video section and part of its relationship with other content on the site. However, it does not go further and show ATVOD's consideration of the other and, in this context, key dimensions of the appropriate analysis of the site. That is, consideration of the other parts of the site, principally the written content of the electronic version of the *Sun* newspaper, their purpose(s) and presentation, their relationship with the audio visual material in the Video section and their effect on what should properly be regard as the *principal purpose* of the service(s) News Group provided on the *Sun*'s website.

Questions for discussion

1. If ATVOD's determination had been upheld, what would have been the implications for regulation of the print media websites? Would it have provided consistency in terms of the matters regulated having regard to the other types of activities carried on by the print media?
2. Does Ofcom's decision mean that no print media websites will be classified as ODPS?

Selected further reading

Broadcasting regulation generally

E.M. Barendt, *Broadcasting Law: A Comparative Study* (Oxford: Oxford University Press (1993) is a comparative study of radio and television regulation in the United Kingdom, France, Italy, Germany and the United States. Although no longer a description of current regulation, it is an excellent discussion of the principles informing regulation and the different approaches across jurisdictions.

R. Craufurd-Smith, *Broadcasting Law and Fundamental Rights* (Oxford: Oxford University Press, 1997) examines the role of judicial intervention in broadcasting with special regard to broadcasting licensing and ownership. The book considers the European Courts of Justice and Human Rights, as well as the United Kingdom, France and Italy. The review in chapter 1 of the historical foundations for broadcasting regulation is especially useful.

D. Goldberg, T. Prosser and S. Verhulst (eds), *Regulating the Changing Media: A Comparative Study* (Oxford: Clarendon Press, 1998) is a broad comparative study of media developments and regulatory responses. The descriptions of the law should not be relied upon as statements of the current laws, but the study provides a useful examination of regulatory principles, especially chapter 1, the overview chapter.

M. Feintuck and M. Varney, *Media Regulation, Public Interest and the Law* (Edinburgh: Edinburgh University Press, 2nd edn, 2006) is an exploration of the rationales for regulation of media with a particular focus on the meaning of 'public interest'. The main focus of the book is the United Kingdom although there is some reference to other jurisdictions.

T. Gibbons and P. Humphreys, *Audiovisual Regulation under Pressure: Comparative Cases from North America and Europe* (London: Routledge, 2012) is a study of policy pressures on regulation such as deregulation and the preferencing of market objectives over cultural and democratic objectives. Chapter 5 focuses on the United Kingdom.

L. Hitchens, 'Approaches to broadcasting regulation: Australia and United Kingdom compared' (1997) 17(1) *Legal Studies* 40–64 compares regulatory models for broadcasting in these two jurisdictions. It offers a study of the policy and regulatory approach of the UK Broadcasting Act 1990.

D. Mac Síthigh, 'Co-regulation, video-on-demand and the legal status of audio-visual media' (2011) 2(1) *International Journal of Digital Television* 49–66 provides a very thorough account of the regulatory map for media, including video on-demand and the regulatory challenges posed by the Audiovisual Media Services Directive.

T. Prosser, *Law and the Regulators* (Oxford: Oxford University Press, 1997). An examination of the role of regulators in applying the law. Chapter 10 focuses on television broadcasting.

Communications Act 2003 and Ofcom

M. Feintuck, 'Walking the high-wire: the UK's draft communications bill' (2003) 9(1) *European Public Law* **105–24** offers a discussion of the policy proposals for the Communications Act 2003.

T. Gibbons, 'Competition policy and regulatory style: issues for Ofcom' (2005) 7(5) *Info* **42–51** offers a critique of Ofcom's regulatory style especially in relation to its mandate regarding public service broadcasting.

S. Livingstone, P. Lunt and L. Miller, 'Citizens and consumers: discursive debates during and after the Communications Act 2003' (2007) 29(4) *Media Culture and Society*, **613–38** reviews the parliamentary debates and subsequent implementation by Ofcom of the responsibility to have regard to the consumer and citizen interests in the regulation of communications.

P. Smith, 'The politics of UK television policy: the making of Ofcom' (2006) 28(6) *Media Culture and Society* **929–40** argues that the politics of UK television policy from the nineties were a significant influence on the design of Ofcom, which in turn represented a policy shift in relation to broadcasting policy objectives.

BBC and public service broadcasting generally

E.M. Barendt, 'Legal aspects of BBC Charter renewal' (1994) 65(1) *Political Quarterly* **20–8** offers a succinct analysis of the importance of choice of legal structure to protect the independence of the BBC.

G. Born and T. Prosser, 'Culture and consumerism: citizenship, public service broadcasting and the BBC's fair trading obligations' (2001) 64(5) *Modern Law Review* **657–87** examines the commercial pressures and accountability measures imposed upon the BBC and the implications for public service broadcasting.

R.H. Coase, *British Broadcasting: A Study in Monopoly* (London: Longmans, Green & Co., 1950) is one of the first scholarly analyses of broadcasting. Coase, an economist, examines how broadcasting came to be organised as a monopoly.

T. Gibbons, 'The future of public service content in the United Kingdom' (2009) 1 *Journal of Media Law* **1–14** examines options for the funding of public service content.

Ofcom, *Ofcom Review of Public Service Broadcasting: Phase 1* (April 2004). All public service broadcasting reviews can be accessed at http://stakeholders.ofcom.org.uk/ broadcasting/reviews-investigations/public-service-broadcasting/).

These Ofcom reviews of public service broadcasting are prepared in response to Ofcom's regulatory responsibility to review public service broadcasting every five years and to make recommendations for its maintenance and strengthening. They provide useful analyses of the media environment and the challenges for the continued provision of public service content.

Ofcom, *Ofcom Review of Public Service Broadcasting: Phase 2 – Meeting the Digital Challenge* (September 2004).

Ofcom, *Ofcom Review of Public Service Broadcasting: Phase 3 – Competition for Quality* (February 2005).

Ofcom, *Second Public Service Broadcasting Review: Phase 1 – the Digital Opportunity* (April 2008).

Ofcom, *Second Public Service Broadcasting Review: Phase 2 – Preparing for the Digital Future* (September 2008).

M. Starks, 'Can the BBC Live to 100? Public service broadcasting after digital switchover (2011) 2(2) *International Journal of Digital Television* 181–200 examines the future of the public broadcaster in the context of a digital media environment.

Commercial broadcasting

N. Lewis, 'IBA Programme contract awards' [1975] *Public Law* 317–40 provides a useful description and analysis of how commercial broadcasting was organised prior to the introduction of licensing under the UK Broadcasting Act 1990.

T. Prosser, *Law and the Regulators* (Oxford: Oxford University Press, 1997), 241–67 offers a discussion of the UK Broadcasting Act 1990 system of allocating broadcasting licences.

Digital and new media services

S. Lax, 'Digital radio switchover: the UK experience' (2011) 2(2) *International Journal of Digital Television* 145–60 examines the role of industry and policy-makers in the development of digital radio and the likelihood of digital radio replacing the analogue service.

P. Smith, 'The politics of UK television policy: the case of digital switchover in the United Kingdom' (2011) 2(1) *International Journal of Digital Television* 31–47 argues that the politics of UK television policy from the 1990s were a significant influence on the design of Ofcom, which in turn represented a policy shift in relation to broadcasting policy objectives.

4 Programme regulation

4.1 INTRODUCTION

Some broadcast programming obligations were examined in Chapter 3. Those obligations relate to the public service remits of the public broadcasters and the licensed public service television (PST) providers. In general, those obligations might be thought of as positive programming requirements. It was also seen in Chapter 3 that services, such as local commercial radio, are required to have regard to the local character of the service in order to meet the requirements of a local radio licence. This, too, will have an effect on programme format, and, hence, the content broadcast. In this chapter, the focus is on programme rules or standards which must be observed by all television and radio services licensed by Ofcom, as well as the services provided by the BBC (although there will be some exceptions in the case of BBC services) and S4C. In general, these programme rules could be viewed as negative requirements because they often dictate what the broadcaster must not do. The focus of this chapter will be on these programme standards, although content regulation of video-on-demand services will also be briefly covered. Content regulation for these services is under the supervision of ATVOD pursuant to co-regulatory arrangements with Ofcom. In relation to radio and television broadcasting, Ofcom has responsibility for developing and reviewing programme standards, as well as enforcement (section 319(1), Communications Act 2003). Section 319 sets out the standards objectives and Ofcom's responsibilities. In the following extract the standards relating to advertising have been omitted (see Chapter 6, Section 6.5).

Extract 4.1.1
Communications Act 2003, section 319

(1) [*Omitted*].

(2) The standards objectives are—

    (a) that persons under the age of eighteen are protected;

    (b) that material likely to encourage or to incite the commission of crime or to lead to disorder is not included in television and radio services;

    (c) that news included in television and radio services is presented with due impartiality and that the impartiality requirements of section 320 are complied with;

    (d) that news included in television and radio services is reported with due accuracy;

    (e) that the proper degree of responsibility is exercised with respect to the content of programmes which are religious programmes;

    (f) that generally accepted standards are applied to the contents of television and radio services so as to provide adequate protection for members of the public from the inclusion in such services of offensive and harmful material;

    (fa)–(k) [*Omitted*];

    (l) that there is no use of techniques which exploit the possibility of conveying a message to viewers or listeners, or of otherwise influencing their minds, without their being aware, or fully aware, of what has occurred.

(3) [*Omitted*].

(4) In setting or revising any standards under this section, Ofcom must have regard, in particular and to such extent as appears to them to be relevant to the securing of the standards objectives, to each of the following matters—

   (a) the degree of harm or offence likely to be caused by the inclusion of any particular sort of material in programmes generally, or in programmes of a particular description;

   (b) the likely size and composition of the potential audience for programmes included in television and radio services generally, or in television and radio services of a particular description;

   (c) the likely expectation of the audience as to the nature of a programme's content and the extent to which the nature of a programme's content can be brought to the attention of potential members of the audience;

   (d) the likelihood of persons who are unaware of the nature of a programme's content being unintentionally exposed, by their own actions, to that content;

   (e) the desirability of securing that the content of services identifies when there is a change affecting the nature of a service that is being watched or listened to, and, in particular, a change that is relevant to the application of the standards set under this section; and

   (f) the desirability of maintaining the independence of editorial control programme content.

(5) [*Omitted*].

(6) Standards set to secure the standards objective specified in subsection (2)(e) shall, in particular, contain provision designed to secure that religious programmes do not involve—

   (a) any improper exploitation of any susceptibilities of the audience for such a programme; or

   (b) any abusive treatment of the religious views and beliefs of those belonging to a particular religion or religious denomination.

(7)–(9) [*Omitted*].

Section 319(3) requires the standards to be contained in a code. The code developed by Ofcom is known as the Ofcom Broadcasting Code (the Broadcasting Code),[1] and will be the focus of this chapter, although advertising rules are covered in Chapter 6. Each licensed service is required under a licence condition to observe the Broadcasting Code (section 325, Communications Act 2003) while the BBC is obliged pursuant to clause 46 of the BBC Agreement to observe the programme standards.[2] In addition, under section 107 of the Broadcasting Act 1996, Ofcom must, from time to time, develop and review a code in connection with the avoidance of unjust or unfair treatment in programmes or any unwarranted infringement of privacy in relation to the obtaining of material which is included in programmes. Although incorporated into the Broadcasting Code, these provisions are usually referred to separately as the Fairness Code. Licensed broadcasters are required to observe the Fairness Code pursuant to section 326 of the Communications Act 2003. The BBC is also bound to observe the Fairness Code (clause 45, BBC Agreement) and S4C under Schedule 12, paragraph 17 of the Communications Act 2003. The reference to a separate fairness code relates to regulatory arrangements in place before the establishment of Ofcom. The Fairness Code was supervised by the Broadcasting Standards Commission. The Broadcasting Standards Commission had specific programme

---

[1] The latest version of the Broadcasting Code came into effect on 28 February 2011. It can be accessed in full at the Ofcom website: http://stakeholders.ofcom.org.uk/broadcasting/broadcast-codes/broadcast-code/. Previous versions of the Code can also be accessed.

[2] S4C is also regulated by Ofcom and required to observe the Broadcasting Code: Communications Act 2003, Sch 12, para 12.

regulatory responsibilities, such as fairness and privacy, for radio and television.[3] As well as the Commission, there were two other main regulatory authorities for broadcasting: the Independent Television Commission and the Radio Authority. These bodies also had responsibility for aspects of programme regulation. This multiplicity of regulatory authorities and the potential for overlap and inconsistent outcomes was a cause of concern for the industry and the regulatory authorities.[4] With the establishment of a single regulator, Ofcom, the regulatory position has been simplified.

As can be seen from section 319 (and section 107, Broadcasting Act 1996), the Broadcasting Code covers a range of concerns relevant to television and radio content. Ofcom notes that

> . . . the Code has also been drafted in the light of the Human Rights Act 1998 and the European Convention on Human Rights ('the Convention'). In particular, the right to freedom of expression, as expressed in Article 10 of the Convention, encompasses the audience's right to receive creative material, information and ideas without interference but subject to restrictions prescribed by law and necessary in a democratic society.[5]

As discussed in Chapter 1, regulation of the media may be necessary in order to ensure that the public has access to certain content, for example, news; but what about those aspects of the Broadcasting Code more concerned with protecting the public from harmful and offensive material? It may be more difficult to justify some of these provisions in light of the Human Rights Act 1998 (HRA), especially since similar material may be available over the Internet and possibly without any regulatory supervision.[6] Justifying and maintaining content regulation of the type examined in this chapter will be an ongoing challenge. The Government considered this issue in the white paper that led to the Communications Act 2003 in relation to content regulation of harmful and offensive material.

Extract 4.1.2
Department of Trade and Industry and Department of Media, Culture and Sport,
A New Future for Communications **(Cm 5010, 2000), paras 6.3, 6.3.1–6.3.2**

6.3 Maintaining acceptable content standards

- Building on the bedrock of the general protections provided in law, we shall establish a high level set of principles and objectives for the regulation of content across all electronic communications.
- Taking full account of the differences between services and people's expectations of them, Ofcom will be responsible for maintaining content standards in the electronic media. It will develop Codes underpinned by statute for the most pervasive broadcast services, and work with industry to ensure effective co- and self-regulatory approaches to protection for other services, such as the Internet, where they are more appropriate.

6.3.1 Research shows that viewers and listeners continue to have strong views on what is, and is not, acceptable in communications content: they wish to see some continuing regulation of

---

[3] The Broadcasting Standards Commission was established in 1996, a merger of two other regulatory bodies: the Broadcasting Standards Council (established in 1988), which was responsible for complaints concerning the portrayal of sexual or violent conduct, and the Broadcasting Complaints Commission, which had been established in 1981 to deal with fairness and privacy complaints.

[4] Department of Trade and Industry (DTI) and Department of Media, Culture and Sport (DMCS), *A New Future for Communications* (Cm 5010, 2000), para 8.3.1.

[5] Ofcom, Broadcasting Code (2011), 2.

[6] See H. Fenwick and G. Phillipson, *Media Freedom under the Human Rights Act* (Oxford: OUP, 2006), 607–12 and ch 11 generally. See also I. Hare, 'Insulting politicians on the radio' (2012) 4(1) *Journal of Media Law* 29–34.

standards. It also demonstrates, however, that viewers and listeners have different expectations about the acceptability of content provided to them in different ways or circumstances.

6.3.2 Technological changes and the increasing convergence of different systems, such as the Internet and broadcasting, are challenging the framework within which people have traditionally formed these expectations. But this will not necessarily lead to all services looking the same or expectations of all media becoming the same. Some media are particularly powerful and differences in expectations, power, context of use and intrusiveness of different services remain. An approach which sought to impose the same rules on all media despite these differences might have to adopt the standards of the medium where regulation was hardest to enforce and least justified, which, today, is the Internet. Or it would require a level of intervention in the Internet which may not only be impractical, but would disproportionately infringe free speech and access to information which people have actively and knowingly sought. Neither approach would be right.

Questions for discussion

1. Recalling the discussion of broadcasting regulation justifications (see Chapter 1, Section 1.3), what justifications do you consider are in play in the government's justification for continued regulation of certain types of content (Extract 4.1.2)?
2. What justifications are reflected in the standards set out in section 319 (Extract 4.1.1)?
3. What is section 319(4) trying to address? Is it also indicative of the, or any of the, justifications?

4.2 BROADCASTING PROGRAMME STANDARDS

(a) Introduction

The Broadcasting Code covers all of the standards that must be addressed under section 319 and the Fairness Code obligations. Ofcom has also published guidance notes in relation to Broadcasting Code obligations. The current Broadcasting Code came into force on 28 February 2011 and only applies to programmes broadcast after that date. It followed a review, consistent with Ofcom's statutory obligation to review and revise the Code from time to time (section 319(1)). The most significant changes have been to the advertising and sponsorship rules (referred to as 'commercial references in programming' in the Broadcasting Code) following the government's decision to permit product placement (see Chapter 6, Section 6.5(d)). Although the BBC will be subject, with some exceptions (impartiality being the main one), to the Broadcasting Code and Ofcom's regulatory supervision, the public broadcaster also has in place a detailed set of editorial guidelines, covering a range of matters similar to the Broadcasting Code.[7] It will not be possible to cover all aspects of the programme standards in detail (and the focus will be on the Broadcasting Code), however the websites of Ofcom and the BBC provide good sources of information, including full details of the rules, guidance and investigations of complaints.[8]

Each section of the Broadcasting Code deals with a specific standard and within each section Ofcom lays down principles (to understand the nature of the standard and its objective, and the application of the rules), definitions ('meanings'), and rules. In determining whether there have been breaches of the Broadcasting Code, Ofcom will look to the provider

---

[7] See http://www.bbc.co.uk/editorialguidelines/.
[8] See http://stakeholders.ofcom.org.uk/broadcasting/ and http://www.bbc.co.uk/bbctrust/governance/complaints_framework/.

of the service who will be '. . . the person with general control over which programmes and other services and facilities are comprised in the service (whether or not he has control of the content of individual programmes or of the broadcasting or distribution of the service)' (section 362(2), Communications Act 2003). Ofcom considers that 'general control is wider than editorial control because it includes control over services and facilities to which access is provided (for example through the inclusion in the main service of a link or facility to interactive features) and over which the broadcaster may not have editorial control' (Broadcasting Code, p. 3). In the 12 months ending 31 March 2012, Ofcom closed a total of 7,551 cases (representing 21,772 complaints). Of these, 7,263 cases (21,484 complaints) were in relation to content standards, and a total of 288 complaints related to fairness and privacy.[9]

(b) Harm and offence

Section two of the Broadcasting Code is concerned with content that might be harmful and/or offensive. Section one covers the protection of persons under the age of eighteen, although section two will also be relevant to under-eighteens, as well as to adults. The particular statutory standards section two addresses are section 319(2)(a)(f) and (l). The general principle applying to the section two rules is stated in the Broadcasting Code as 'To ensure that generally accepted standards are applied to the content of television and radio services so as to provide adequate protection for members of the public from the inclusion in such services of harmful and/or offensive material'. The rules cover a range of different matters, indicating a broad understanding of what might cause harm or offence. For example: avoiding materially misleading audiences in factual programmes (rule 2.2); portrayal of material which is violent, dangerous, discriminatory, or depicts seriously antisocial behaviour or suicide (rules 2.3–2.5); demonstrations of exorcism or occult practices (rules 2.6–2.8); and, broadcasting of demonstrations of hypnotic or subliminal techniques (rule 2.9). There are also provisions designed to ensure that television viewers with photosensitive epilepsy are not affected by a broadcast which might contain, for example, flashing lights (rule 2.12), that audiences are not confused into believing that simulated news (as part of drama or documentary programme, for example) is genuine news (rule 2.10); and that broadcast competitions and voting are conducted fairly (rules 2.13–2.16).[10]

[9] Ofcom, *Annual Report & Accounts for the period 1 April 2011 to 31 March 2012* (HC 237, 2012), 112–13. Individual complaints are assigned to cases, and a case may consist of one or more complaints about the same programme or issue. Fairness and privacy complaints are normally made by individuals or organisations as the complaint is about their unfair treatment or infringement of privacy, and so do not need to be combined into cases. In the period being examined, Ofcom changed its procedures for dealing with complaints. The figures given here have been totalled across the old and new procedures.

[10] The rules concerning the conduct of competitions were amended following a code review in 2009. This followed a series of investigations conducted by Ofcom over several years which established serious compliance failings concerning the conduct of broadcast competitions and voting. The broadcasters who had committed these compliance failures included the BBC and the PST channels as well as commercial radio services. The compliance failures also concerned competitions and voting requiring audience payment, for example, through the use of premium rate telephony services, and the code review also dealt with this issue, now covered in sections nine and ten of the Broadcasting Code (see Chapter 6). The investigations led to the highest financial penalties ever ordered by Ofcom (see Section 4.6(c) below). For information about the code review, see Ofcom, *Broadcasting Code Review: proposals on revising the Broadcasting Code* (15 June 2009), http://stakeholders. ofcom.org.uk/binaries/consultations/bcode09/summary/main.pdf and *Broadcasting Code Review: statement on the Ofcom Broadcasting Code* (16 December 2009), http://stakeholders.ofcom.org.uk/binaries/consultations/ bcode09/statement/statement.pdf. For general information about the investigations, see Letter from E. Richards to The Rt Hon James Purnell (19 December 2007), http://stakeholders.ofcom.org.uk/binaries/broadcast/ reviews-investigations/prs/prsletter.pdf. See also R. Ayre, *Report of an inquiry into television broadcasters' use of premium rate telephone services in programmes* (June 2007), http://stakeholders.ofcom.org.uk/binaries/ broadcast/reviews-investigations/prs/report.pdf (all accessed 31 October 2012). The sanctions decisions can also be found at: http://stakeholders.ofcom.org.uk/enforcement/content-sanctions-adjudications.

Prior to the Communications Act 2003, the Broadcasting Act 1990 programme rules referred to content which might offend 'good taste and decency'. This phrase is no longer used: the Communications Act 2003 refers now to 'generally accepted standards'. The Broadcasting Code rules address the need to observe 'generally accepted standards' and the importance of context in making programming decisions. The Ofcom guidance seeks to elaborate on the term.

Extract 4.2.1
Ofcom, Broadcasting Code (28 February 2011), rules 2.1 and 2.3

Generally accepted standards

2.1 Generally accepted standards must be applied to the contents of television and radio services so as to provide adequate protection for members of the public from the inclusion in such services of harmful and/or offensive material.

. . .

2.3 In applying generally accepted standards broadcasters must ensure that material which may cause offence is justified by the context (see meaning of 'context' below). Such material may include, but is not limited to, offensive language, violence, sex, sexual violence, humiliation, distress, violation of human dignity, discriminatory treatment or language (for example on the grounds of age, disability, gender, race, religion, beliefs and sexual orientation). Appropriate information should also be broadcast where it would assist in avoiding or minimising offence.

Meaning of 'context':

Context includes (but is not limited to):

- the editorial content of the programme, programmes or series;
- the service on which the material is broadcast;
- the time of broadcast;
- what other programmes are scheduled before and after the programme or programmes concerned;
- the degree of harm or offence likely to be caused by the inclusion of any particular sort of material in programmes generally or programmes of a particular description; the likely size and composition of the potential audience and likely expectation of the audience;
- the extent to which the nature of the content can be brought to the attention of the potential audience for example by giving information; and
- the effect of the material on viewers or listeners who may come across it unawares.

Source: © Ofcom copyright 2006–11.

Extract 4.2.2
Ofcom, Guidance Notes, Section 2: Harm and Offence (23 July 2012), re rules 2.1 and 2.3

Rule 2.1 Generally accepted standards

We recognise that some programming may include material that has the potential to be harmful or offensive. This puts a responsibility on the broadcaster to take steps to provide adequate protection for the audience. The criteria outlined in the meaning of 'context' give an indication of what this may involve. Ofcom regularly publishes complaints bulletins which provide information on matters members of the public have found harmful or offensive and Ofcom's decision in those cases.

Broadcasters and the public view and listen to material measured against a background of generally accepted standards. Ofcom licenses an increasing number of satellite and cable channels, who broadcast solely to non-UK countries where different standards may apply. The understanding of what is 'generally accepted standards' should be underpinned by relevant research.

Generally accepted standards will change over time and will also vary according to the context (as set out under Rule 2.3 of the Broadcasting Code).

Generally accepted standards also apply where programmes invite viewers or listeners to participate in them. Broadcasters should ensure that they take all due care to avoid disadvantaging any viewer or listener who votes, enters a competition, takes part in a poll or otherwise interacts with a programme by participating in some way . . .

Rule 2.3 Context and information

Offensive language

It should be noted that audience expectations and composition vary between television and radio and each medium has different listening/viewing patterns. Broadcasters should know their audiences.

The use of language (including offensive language) is constantly developing. Whether language is offensive depends on a number of factors. Language is more likely to be offensive, if it is contrary to audience expectations. Sensitivities can vary according to generation and communities/cultures.

Offensive material (including offensive language) must be justified by the context. . . .

Broadcasters should be aware that there are areas of offensive language and material which are particularly sensitive.

Racist terms and material should be avoided unless their inclusion can be justified by the editorial of the programme. Broadcasters should take particular portrayal of culturally diverse matters and should avoid stereotyping unless editorially justified. When considering such matters, broadcasters should take into account the possible effects programmes may have on particular sections of the community.

Source: © Ofcom copyright 2006–11.

It is not clear whether the rules and/or the guidance add much clarity, and there will be clearly different views about what is acceptable and what is not, and in what circumstances. Ofcom has tried to deal with this in the Broadcasting Code and the guidance note, but there is little elaboration on what are the accepted standards, although, as shown in Extract 4.2.3, Ofcom and broadcasters have carried out some research on these issues.[11] Extract 4.2.3 concerns a rule designed to protect under-18s but it provides a useful insight into how Ofcom approaches matters, such as language and whether it offends generally accepted standards. The decision concerned rule 1.6 which refers to material broadcast after the 'watershed'. The 'watershed' occurs at 21.00 hours and applies only to television.[12] Material that is not suitable for children should not in general be shown before 21.00 (or after 05.30) (see Broadcasting Code, rule 1.4). However, the watershed is not a rigid divide between child-suitable and child-unsuitable material; some judgement must be exercised in relation to the type of adult material being broadcast immediately after the watershed.

[11] See also references to research in Ofcom, *Guidance Notes, Section 2: Harm and Offence* (23 July 2012).
[12] However, radio broadcasters are required to have regard to times when children are most likely to be listening to the radio, for example the school run or at breakfast: rule 1.5.

Extract 4.2.3
Ofcom, 'Big Brother', *Broadcast Bulletin 196* **(19 December 2011), 31**
Big Brother, Channel 5, 23 and 30 September 2011, 21:00

Introduction

A complainant alerted Ofcom to the broadcast of the words 'fuck' and 'fucking' in the opening sequence in an episode of this well-known reality show broadcast on 23 September 2011. Ofcom noted a similar incident in the eviction show broadcast the following week.

Both episodes began at 21:00 with clips of notable events in the Big Brother house from the previous week. Each pre-title sequence contained two instances of the word 'fuck' or 'fucking'. In the case of the episode transmitted on 23 September 2011, Ofcom noted the word 'fucking' was broadcast at 11 seconds and again 16 seconds after the 21:00 watershed. On 30 September, the word 'fuck' was broadcast 18 seconds and the word 'fucking' 31 seconds after the watershed.

. . .

[In its response, Channel 5 argued that the language was editorially justified, viewers were familiar with the format, and there had been appropriate warnings.]

Decision

. . .

Rule 1.6 is not prescriptive. It does not stipulate a certain set time after the watershed when broadcasters may start to transmit the most offensive language. What constitutes an 'unduly abrupt' transition to more adult material depends on the context: for example, factors such as the editorial content of the programme, the time it is broadcast and the expectations of the audience. Clearly however, bearing in mind that there is an absolute prohibition on the most offensive language immediately before 21:00 (Rule 1.14), a broadcaster would need very strong reasons to justify starting to broadcast the most offensive language in the period immediately after the 21:00 watershed.

Ofcom noted that the episode broadcast on 23 September featured housemate Rebeckah saying 'are you fucking crackers?' 11 seconds after the watershed and less than six seconds into the programme. The second use of 'fucking' was 16 seconds after the watershed. The episode on broadcast 30 September featured housemate Harry shouting 'stay the fuck out of other people's business' 18 seconds after the watershed, and another housemate used 'fucking' 31 seconds after the watershed. We therefore did not accept Channel 5's argument that 'the programmes did not include strong language "immediately" after the watershed'.

Ofcom therefore went on to consider whether there was sufficient editorial justification for broadcasting this strong language repeatedly within the 31 seconds after the watershed. We acknowledged that the programmes' pre-title sequences served as reminders about the preceding weeks' notable events. We also recognised Channel 5's aim to reflect accurately both the tension between contestants and the different personalities in the house.

Ofcom's research, however, confirms that the word 'fuck' and its derivatives are regarded as examples of the most offensive language with the capacity to cause a considerable degree of offence. [See Ofcom, *Audience attitudes towards offensive language on television and radio*, August 2010 http://stakeholders.ofcom.org.uk/binaries/research/tv-research/offensive-lang.pdf] . . . In Ofcom's opinion most viewers of *Big Brother* do not expect examples of the most offensive language in a pre-recorded sequence during the first 31 seconds of the programme after the watershed, particularly when broadcast on a public service channel like Channel 5.

Ofcom noted that viewers of *Big Brother* do expect some degree of offensive language and that there was a warning of strong language immediately before these programmes started. We noted Channel 5's argument that the preceding programmes (*The Gadget Show* on

23 September 2011 and *Ultimate Police Interceptors* on 30 September 2011) were unlikely to attract a high child audience. Audience figures do bear this out. On 23 September, there were 82,000 4–15 year olds watching *The Gadget Show*. However, this figure rose significantly to 155,000 during *Big Brother*. Likewise, on 30 September, 55,000 4–15 years olds watched *Ultimate Police Interceptors*. This figure rose sharply to 168,000 during *Big Brother*. Therefore, Ofcom considered that in cases like this – where a programme broadcast after the watershed attracts more child viewers than the preceding programme – it is especially important for a broadcaster to apply Rule 1.6 to ensure people under eighteen are appropriately protected.

Channel 5 also argued that it was necessary to include the strong language unedited in the pre-title sequences to ensure viewers were not misled and voting patterns influenced. Ofcom disagreed. Voting did not close until much later in the programme after the broadcast had featured several other longer clips of events in the house which reflected more accurately the personalities and tensions there. Ofcom did not consider that any examples of the most offensive language needed to be included in the pre-title sequences to ensure viewers were not misled in relation to the voting.

. . .

Taking the above factors into account, Ofcom did not consider there was sufficient editorial justification to include repeated use of the most offensive language in these programmes so soon after the watershed. The two uses of the word 'fuck' or 'fucking' in each programme in the period directly after the watershed did, in Ofcom's view, constitute an 'unduly abrupt' transition to more adult material at the watershed. Rule 1.6 was therefore breached.

Source: © Ofcom copyright 2006–11.

Questions for discussion

1. In addition to proximity to the watershed, what other factors were relevant to Ofcom's decision?
2. Was it relevant that the programme was broadcast on a public service channel? If so, why should this be relevant?
3. With regard to the type of matters covered under the Broadcasting Code section two, would it be feasible for the rules to be drafted with any greater precision? If not, does this indicate that this is an area which should not be subject to regulation?

Rule 2.3 refers also to the context in which the potentially harmful or offensive matter occurs. The context will be relevant to whether or not the material was justified. In 2005 Ofcom had to decide whether a BBC broadcast of an opera, *Jerry Springer: the Opera* was offensive. Ofcom received 8,860 complaints (4,264 of which were part of an email campaign) about the broadcast (as well as 7,941 complaints prior to transmission). As Ofcom noted: '[t]he level was unprecedented for Ofcom or any previous broadcasting regulator and appears to have been the first large scale Internet campaign to Ofcom on any broadcasting issue'.[13] The broadcast also particularly offended members of the Christian community. Ofcom had to apply the standards code of one of its regulatory predecessors, the Broadcasting Standards Commission. The code covered issues similar to the Broadcasting Code and, for the purposes of this decision, required Ofcom to consider complaints about scheduling and offensive material. Complaints were also made that the programme offended religious sensibilities; a separate provision of the Broadcasting

---

[13] Ofcom, 'Jerry Springer: The Opera', *Broadcast Bulletin 34* (9 May 2005), 13. Ofcom also received 210 contacts in support of the broadcast.

Standards Commission code. In making its decision, Ofcom also took into account its statutory duties under the Communications Act: 'The Act also requires Ofcom – to the extent it appears relevant – to apply standards regarding "harm and offence" in a manner that "best guarantees an appropriate level of freedom of expression".'[14]

Extract 4.2.4
Ofcom, 'Jerry Springer: the Opera', *Broadcast Bulletin 34* (9 May 2005), 12
BBC2, 8 January 2005, 22:00

(a) Summary

Ofcom recognises that a large number of people were deeply offended by the transmission of *Jerry Springer: The Opera*. Nevertheless, it is Ofcom's view that the show was an important work and commentary on modern television.

In assessing these complaints, and in line with our statutory duties, Ofcom has sought to achieve the appropriate balance between, on the one hand, the standards set in the Code (ex-BSC Code on Standards) and the need to apply those standards to give adequate protection from harmful and offensive material, and on the other hand the need to guarantee an appropriate level of freedom of expression. Freedom of expression is particularly important in the context of artistic works, beliefs, philosophy and argument.

Ofcom appreciated that the representation of religious figures was offensive to some people. Their main concern arose from the depictions of figures at the heart of the complainants' religious beliefs. However, the show addressed moral issues in the context of a contemporary setting and contained a strong message. The show's effect was to satirise modern fame and the culture of celebrity. The images that caused the most offence were part of a 'dream' sequence serving as a metaphor for the fictional Jerry Springer and his chat show. In Ofcom's view, these were not meant to be faithful or accurate depictions of religious figures, but a product of the lead character's imagination. Even as he lay dying, the fictional Jerry Springer still saw his life through the lens of his confessional show.

The programme as broadcast was not only clearly labelled and signposted, but was preceded by programmes which aimed to put the whole show in context. As always with matters of offence, the context is key. Whilst the show clearly had the potential to offend and indeed the intention to shock it was set in a very clear context as a comment on modern television. The strongest and most offensive language occurred well after the watershed: at 2230 onwards, with the most challenging material after 2300.

. . .

(b) Introduction

Jerry Springer: The Opera was a televised performance of the West End stage production based on Jerry Springer's television show. The US programme is a 'reality-based' talk show which features members of the public discussing their emotional and personal lives. It is highly charged emotionally and regularly features strong language, violent behaviour and revelations of an extreme or shocking nature.

In the Opera, Jerry, the host, is shot at the end of the first act. In the second act, as he is dying, he imagines he is in Hell and forced to present a special show in which Satan wishes to confront figures from the Bible. In the same way as a 'dysfunctional' family in the actual television show might behave, these figures tackle the fundamental issues that divide them. The fictional Springer, dying, reflects on the meaning of life and death and the part he has played in the world. Adam and Eve, Jesus, Mary and God are all introduced as characters in his imagination in this context.

. . .

---

[14] Ofcom, 'Jerry Springer: The Opera', *Broadcast Bulletin 34* (9 May 2005), 14.

Exceptionally on this occasion, Ofcom decided that it would be appropriate in all the circumstances for *Jerry Springer: The Opera* to be considered at the highest level within Ofcom, by Ofcom's Content Board. This was because: it had already been considered at the highest level within the BBC; there was a need to avoid delay; the strength of feeling on the part of complainants; the general public interest; the high profile nature of the programme; and the fact that it had provoked strong emotions.

. . .

Decision

[. . .]

(c) Respect and dignity

. . .

Ofcom recognises that a great number of complainants felt that the Opera denigrated the Christian religion. Complainants clearly felt that the programme mocked their strongly held beliefs.

However, in Ofcom's view, serious thought had been given to the material, its production and its transmission. The subject of the Opera was '*The Jerry Springer Show*' and the society it reflects. The show was created as a caricature of television. Importantly, in Ofcom's view the Opera did not gratuitously humiliate individuals or any groups and in particular the Christian community. Its target was television and fame.

(d) Swearing and offensive language

[T]he programme was appropriately scheduled well after the watershed (as required by the Code) and the strongest language was transmitted after 2230. However, the Opera as broadcast also pointed up the absurdities of excessive swearing in many of the songs and exchanges – rendering them on occasions meaningless and ridiculous. The most extreme language was directed at the character of Satan. This was a programme that satirised modern day 'confessional shows' where such language is common place. The Opera was a parody of such programming and as such, the language was to be expected and could be understood in such a context.

Furthermore, . . . the information and warnings available to any potential viewer should have given sufficient indication of the likely content of the programme.

(e) Offences against religious sensibilities

Many complainants accused the BBC of committing the crime of blasphemy.

However, criminal law is not a matter for Ofcom but for the courts . . .

. . .

In considering offence against religious sensibilities, Ofcom took into account the clear context of the Opera. The fictional Jerry Springer lay dying in a delusional state. As he hallucinated, this character was asked to pitch Jesus against the Devil in his own confessional talk show. This 'dream' sequence was emphasised by the fact that the same actors, who played guests on his show in the first act, played the characters in the second act. What resulted was a cartoon, full of grotesque images, which challenged the audience's views about morality and the human condition. The production made clear that all the characters in the second act were the product of the fictional Springer's imagination: his concepts of Satan, God, Jesus and the others and modelled on the guests in his show.

In addition to this was the blatant use of *The Jerry Springer Show* format. The characters throughout behaved as people do on the show, using strong language and violence in a highly emotional manner. In light of this, Ofcom did not believe that the characters represented were, in the context of this piece, conveyed as faithful or accurate representations of religious figures, but were characterisations of the show's participants.

. . .

Questions for discussion

1. In the *Big Brother* determination there was only one complainant, in contrast to the *Jerry Springer* matter. Should that be relevant? Should it be relevant to a determination of 'generally accepted standards'?
2. What is the significance of a particular group within the community being offended? Do you think that Ofcom gave sufficient regard to this in determining the *Jerry Springer* matter?
3. Context was important in Ofcom's consideration of this matter. What limits might there be on an argument that the context justified the programme material? (For another example of the role of context in considering a potential breach of rule 2.3, see Extract 4.2.7.)
4. If this matter had arisen under the current Broadcasting Code, what rules would Ofcom apply?

(c) Impartiality and accuracy

Impartiality requirements, given their particular association with information and opinion, highlight the dilemma, explored in Chapter 1, where restrictions are imposed upon broadcasting which are not imposed on the print media or Internet content. With the decline of spectrum scarcity it may be increasingly difficult to justify such restrictions, although, as suggested in Chapter 1, they may be consistent with the view that media freedom is an instrumental freedom. This still does not address the problem of inconsistent treatment between the different modes of content delivery, although as Fenwick and Phillipson point out: 'In the UK control over broadcasting on grounds of . . . political content . . . is an accepted feature of the regulatory regime for private and public sector broadcasting'.[15]

The standards objectives set out in section 319 (Extract 4.1.1) include a requirement that television and radio news be presented with due impartiality and reported with due accuracy. Although the focus of the rules tends to be on impartiality, one can see why accurate reporting will be important to impartial presentation. Section 320 imposes additional requirements, known as the 'special impartiality requirements'. While section 319 refers only to news programmes, section 320 has a broader reach. Significantly, section 320 prescribes different responsibilities depending upon the nature of the service. The main requirements under section 320 are:

- The providers of all radio and television services (other than a restricted radio service) must not air their own views or opinions in programmes on those services on matters of political or industrial controversy or relating to current public policy (section 320(1)(a)).
- All television services, national radio services and national digital sound programme services must observe due impartiality on matters of political or industrial controversy or relating to current public policy (section 320(1)(b)). This obligation can be satisfied by reference to a series of programmes taken as a whole (section 320(4)(a)).

---

[15] Fenwick and Phillipson, note 6 above, 994.

- Local radio services, local digital sound programme services and radio licensable content services must not give undue prominence to the views and opinions of particular persons or bodies on matters of political or industrial controversy or relating to current public policy (section 320(1)(c)). This obligation can be satisfied by taking into account all programmes included in the service and considering them as a whole (section 320(4)(b)).

Section 5 of the Broadcasting Code covers the impartiality and accuracy obligations for broadcasters, with the exception of BBC licence fee-funded services, which are regulated by the BBC Trust. Although the Communications Act 2003 led to greater regulatory supervision of the BBC by Ofcom, it was considered important that this area remained under BBC supervision because it was so closely tied to the editorial independence of the BBC and the Trust's responsibility to secure that independence.[16] In the same way, the Trust also takes responsibility for supervision of the BBC's obligations in relation to election and referendum broadcasting (see Section 4.4). It might be questioned whether this is really necessary. Although, as discussed in Chapter 3, maintaining the independence of the BBC and its structure is important if it is to function as a public broadcaster, Ofcom is an independent statutory regulatory authority and as such should be expected to carry out its functions with fairness and transparency.

The impartiality obligation is qualified by the use of the word 'due'.

Extract 4.2.5

Ofcom, Broadcasting Code (28 February 2011), Section Five: Due Impartiality and Due Accuracy and Undue Prominence of Views and Opinions, 23

Meaning of 'due impartiality':

'Due' is an important qualification to the concept of impartiality. Impartiality itself means not favouring one side over another. 'Due' means adequate or appropriate to the subject and nature of the programme. So 'due impartiality' does not mean an equal division of time has to be given to every view, or that every argument and every facet of every argument has to be represented. The approach to due impartiality may vary according to the nature of the subject, the type of programme and channel, the likely expectation of the audience as to content, and the extent to which the content and approach is signalled to the audience. Context, as defined in Section Two: Harm and Offence of the Code, is important.

Source: © Ofcom copyright 2006–11.

Questions for discussion

1. Why are broadcasters under an obligation to act with 'due impartiality' instead of with 'impartiality'? What practical difference will it have on programme makers?
2. Can you identify some subjects or scenarios where the 'due' qualification may be especially relevant?
3. What are the practical differences between the different obligations under the 'special impartiality requirements' (section 320(1))? Why have different obligations been imposed according to the nature of the service?

The Broadcasting Code impartiality and accuracy rules are fairly straightforward, requiring news to be reported with due accuracy and presented with due impartiality (rule 5.1). Significant mistakes in news should normally be acknowledged and corrected on air quickly

[16] DTI and DCMS, note 4 above, para 5.6.4.

(rule 5.2). A further rule proscribes the use of politicians as newsreaders, interviewers or reporters in any news programme, unless editorially, and exceptionally, justified. In such a case the political allegiance of the politician must be disclosed to the audience (rule 5.3). Rules 5.4–5.12 address the special impartiality requirements and elaborate in some detail what must be done to ensure compliance. Hence, the rules address series of programmes or editorially linked programmes (rules 5.5–5.6) and personal view programmes (rules 5.9–5.10). In matters of major political or industrial controversy or current public policy, impartiality must be preserved in each programme or in clearly linked and timely programmes (rule 5.11). Rule 5.12 emphasises the importance in relation to major matters of providing '. . . an appropriately wide range of significant views'. Ofcom's guidance states that these two rules '. . . are necessary because of the nature of the subject matter concerned: it is of a significant level of importance and is likely to be of the moment'.[17] The Broadcasting Code provides a definition of 'matters of political or industrial controversy and current public policy'.

> **Extract 4.2.6**
> **Ofcom, Broadcasting Code (28 February 2011), Section Five: Due Impartiality and Due Accuracy and Undue Prominence of Views and Opinions, 24**
>
> Matters of political or industrial controversy are political or industrial issues on which politicians, industry and/or the media are in debate. Matters relating to current public policy need not be the subject of debate but relate to a policy under discussion or already decided by a local, regional or national government or by bodies mandated by those public bodies to make policy on their behalf, for example non-governmental organisations, relevant European institutions, etc.
>
> Source: © Ofcom copyright 2006–11.

A preliminary step for Ofcom, in considering whether a breach of the special impartiality requirements has occurred, will be to determine whether the subject matter of the programme is a matter of political or industrial controversy or current public policy. In Extract 4.2.7 below, Channel 4 argued that a documentary it had broadcast, *Sri Lanka's Killing Fields*, was not such a programme because it dealt with a subject (alleged war crimes in Sri Lanka) in respect of which 'there is no political controversy in the UK Parliament and public policy on the international community's role . . . is settled policy at the UK Parliament'. However, Ofcom rejected this argument determining that it was not necessary for a matter to be a matter of political controversy in the UK Parliament nor was it the case that, if the UK Parliament had a settled policy, the matter ceased to be a 'matter of current public policy'. Ofcom also observed that even though the documentary examined allegations and concerns similar to the findings of a UN Panel Report (published two months prior to the broadcast) on the matter, that fact did not remove it from being a matter of political controversy. Accordingly, section 5 of the Broadcasting Code applied. Ofcom received 118 complaints about the programme and investigated potential code breaches of impartiality, misleading material and offensiveness. The extract is useful in showing how Ofcom balances freedom of expression rights and the responsibility of a licensee in ensuring impartiality. The licensee, Channel 4, was found not to be in breach on any of the counts considered. In the extract the 'misleading material' complaint is not included. The decision also illustrates how Ofcom approaches potentially offensive material (under the section 2, Harm and Offence, Broadcasting Code) in this type of programme, and the importance of context.

---

[17] Ofcom, *Guidance Notes, Section 5: Due impartiality and due accuracy and undue prominence of views and opinions* (16 December 2009), 4.

Extract 4.2.7
Ofcom, *Sri Lanka's Killing Fields*, Broadcast Bulletin 192 (24 October 2011), 45
[footnotes omitted]
Channel 4, 14 June 2011, 23:05

Introduction

. . .

Sri Lanka's Killing Fields was a documentary which focused on: the conclusions of the UN report by the Secretary-General's Panel of Experts on Accountability in Sri Lanka ('UN Panel Report') into the Sri Lankan civil war in 2008/2009; the actions and policies of the armed forces of the Sri Lankan government and of the Tamil Tigers ('LTTE') towards the civilian population at this time; and the call, by the survivors of the conflict, on the international community to investigate the potential war crimes set out in the programme. The information about potential war crimes presented in the programme, which supported the UN Panel Report findings, was drawn from a dossier of evidence including film (such as mobile phone footage), photographs and eye witness accounts collected by Channel 4 in the previous two years.

. . .

Decision

Due impartiality

Rule 5.5 of the Code states: 'Due impartiality on matters of political or industrial controversy and matter relating to current public policy must be preserved on the part of any person providing a service.'

When interpreting due impartiality, Ofcom must take into account the broadcaster's and audience's right to freedom of expression . . .

The broadcaster's right to freedom of expression is therefore not absolute. In carrying out its duties, Ofcom must balance the right to freedom of expression on one hand, with the requirement in the Code to preserve 'due impartiality' on matters relating to political or industrial controversy or matters relating to current public policy. Ofcom recognises that this requirement acts to limit, to some extent, freedom of expression. This is because its application necessarily requires broadcasters to ensure that neither side of a debate relating to matters of political or industrial controversy and matters relating to current public policy is unduly favoured.

. . .

It is important to note that the broadcasting of highly critical comments concerning the policies and actions of any state or government (such as happened here concerning the Sri Lankan Government's military forces) is not in itself a breach of the Code. It is, in fact, essential that current affairs programmes are able to explore and examine such issues and take a position even if that position is highly critical.

However, it is the responsibility of the broadcaster, when the subject matter of the programme raises a matter of political controversy, to ensure that 'due' impartiality is maintained. Under the Code, the term 'due' means adequate or appropriate to the subject matter. Therefore 'due' impartiality' does not mean an equal division of time has to be given to every view, or that every argument and every facet of the argument has to be represented. Due impartiality may be preserved in a number of ways and it is an editorial decision for the broadcaster as to how it ensures due impartiality is maintained.

In this case, Ofcom noted that:

- Channel 4 did seek to include the viewpoints of the Sri Lankan Government and produced evidence that it had put all of the significant allegations included in the programme to them for a response in advance of the programme. As the Sri Lankan Government chose not to respond in full, Channel 4 could only broadcast the limited statement provided;

- the programme included – when the relevant evidence was presented – several official statements previously made by the Sri Lankan Government regarding the events in the final stage of the civil war. The narration at various points referred to the Government's official position. The programme also included clips of Government officials setting out that position stating for example that: there had been 'zero civilian casualties'; it was engaged in a 'humanitarian rescue operation'; all the civilians inside the no fire zones were rescued by government forces; and, that the first video of an execution shown in the programme was a fake. The programme also explicitly referred to the Sri Lankan Government's rejection of the UN Panel Report;
- the subject matter of this documentary was clearly presented as being about the final stages of the Sri Lankan civil war, and in particular, the serious effects on many in the civilian population of the offensive of the Sri Lankan Government against the LTTE-held areas of Sri Lanka. It was never intended to be an analysis of the entire conflict or the actions of the LTTE and Sri Lankan Government during the duration of the civil war as a whole. Consequently, the programme was only required to maintain due impartiality of the specific subject matter presented . . .

Ofcom therefore concluded that overall Channel 4 preserved due impartiality in its examination of the Sri Lankan Government's actions and policies during its offensive and there was no breach of Rule 5.5.

. . .

Offensive material

Rule 2.3 of the Code states: 'In applying generally accepted standards broadcasters must ensure that material which may cause offence is justified by the context'.

Ofcom acknowledges that some viewers may have been very offended by the graphic images depicting executions of bound prisoners, mutilated corpses, the maltreatment of women and the victims of bombings included in this programme.

The Code requires Ofcom to consider the context in which the content was presented in order to assess if this considerable potential offence was justified by the context. . . . Given the brutal nature of the images shown and the level of potential offence which may have been generated by these images, Ofcom considered that Channel 4 had to ensure a correspondingly high level of contextual justification.

With reference to the editorial content, Ofcom noted that the broadcast was presented as a serious documentary investigating important issues that had only recently before been the subject of the UN Panel Report and that it commenced very late in the schedule at 23:05 when viewers understand that they should expect more adult material.

Nonetheless, the strength of the images broadcast required in Ofcom's view, clear guidance to viewers about what they may expect to view. Ofcom noted that the broadcaster clearly set out from before the start of the programme that the content included disturbing images . . .

Further warnings followed during each advertising break: . . .

In addition, presenter Jon Snow gave further onscreen warnings both during his introduction . . . and immediately before particularly disturbing images were shown . . .

In Ofcom's view these warnings were explicit and helped provide viewers with the information to decide if they wished to continue to view.

Ofcom also considered the nature of the channel on which this programme was broadcast and audience expectations. Channel 4 has a unique public service remit to provide programming that is challenging, diverse and likely to provoke debate. Consequently, the broadcaster has a history of broadcasting very challenging material from war zones (including graphic footage) and seeking out the voices and views of those who may not be represented. The images included in this programme, whilst brutal and shocking, would not have exceeded the expectations of the audience for this Channel 4 documentary scheduled well after the watershed with very clear warnings about the nature of the content.

Source: © Ofcom copyright 2006–11.

In the following extract, the licensee was found to be in breach of rule 5.5. Section 5 applied because the issues discussed in the programme – the policies and actions of the Indian government towards the Sikh community in India and elsewhere – were matters of interest to the Sikh community and therefore matters of political controversy and relating to current public policy. The extract shows the degree of responsibility that will have to be exercised in making a programme and seeking out 'alternative views' where section 5 applies. The approach taken by the programme makers in this decision can be contrasted with those of the Channel 4 decision. The decision also highlights the difficulties that services broadcasting to particular communities of interest may have in observing the impartiality obligations. And, indeed, at the end of this decision, Ofcom refers to a pattern of breaches by the licensee.

Extract 4.2.8
Ofcom, *Sikh Channel Youth Show*, Broadcast Bulletin 211 (13 August 2012), 6
[footnotes omitted]
In Breach Sikh Channel Youth Show, Sikh Channel, 26 April 2012, 22:00

Introduction

The Sikh Channel is in the religious section of the Sky Electronic Programme Guide ('EPG'), and is aimed at the Sikh community in the UK. The *Sikh Channel Youth Show* was a weekly live programme broadcast in Punjabi. The licence for the Sikh Channel is held by TV Legal Limited ('TV Legal' or 'the Licensee'). This programme consisted of live discussion, with a presenter and guest and an audience broadcast from a Sikh Gurdwara [place of worship].

The discussion touched on a range of subjects of interest to the Sikh community and various reported actions taken by the Indian Government towards the Sikh community in India, including Operation Blue Star [an Indian military action].

A viewer alerted Ofcom to the programme, stating that the broadcast contained 'inflammatory' content about the Indian Government and 'no alternative views' concerning the Sikh community in India . . .

Decision

. . .

It is not part of Ofcom's remit to question or investigate the validity of the political views expressed in a case like the current one, but to require the broadcaster to comply with the relevant rules in the Code. The Code does not prohibit broadcasters from discussing any controversial subject or including any particular point of view in a programme. To do so would be an unacceptable restriction on a broadcaster's freedom of expression.

. . .

In this case, Ofcom considered that the programme included a number of viewpoints, but all of them were: either critical of the Indian state's policy and actions in relation to its treatment to the Sikh community in India; or could be interpreted as arguing the case for an independent homeland for the Sikh community in India. For example, within the programme, the Indian Government was accused, variously: of committing '*genocide*' against the Sikh community; '*malign*[ing] *the Sikh community outside of India*'; and putting the Punjab under '*occupation*'. In addition, there were views expressed demanding an independent homeland for the Sikh community in India, because, for example, the Sikhs '*don't have a future in the Indian State*', and '*Sikhism cannot survive* [in India] *in its present form, and in its truest form, within India as it stands*'.

We considered that the programme did not contain any alternative views, which could be reasonably and adequately classed as: supportive of, or which sought to explain, the policy and actions of the Indian State in relation to the Sikh community within India, and in particular, the Punjab; or supportive of the arguments against an independent homeland for the Sikh community within India. Therefore, this programme when considered alone gave a one-sided view on these matters of political controversy and current public policy.

Ofcom recognises that there may be a number of ways that broadcasters can ensure that alternative viewpoints are included within its programming. For example, they could: summarise within the programme what those alternative points of view are; or include interviewees to express alternative views. In this case, however, the programme did not provide any alternative views on these matters of political controversy and current public policy. Further, and importantly, the broadcaster did not provide any evidence of alternative views on these issues in any series of programmes taken as a whole (i.e. more than one programme in the same service, editorially linked, dealing with the same or related issues within an appropriate period and aimed at a like audience).

In reaching our decision, we took account of the representations made by TV Legal. First, we noted the Licensee's representation that it is a 'small community funded channel'. Ofcom points out in response that, irrespective of the size of any holder of an Ofcom television service licensee, it must comply with the Code, including the due impartiality requirements in Section Five.

Second, we noted the Licensee's submission that the programme's producers contacted various organisations, including 'Indian Government affiliates' to participate in the programme. However, the various organisations contacted either did not respond or said they would not be able to attend. Merely by attempting to obtain the participation within the programme of an organisation to provide an alternative viewpoint, the broadcaster did not discharge its obligations under Section Five of the Code.

. . .

Source: © Ofcom copyright 2006–11.

Questions for discussion

1. What due diligence will be required of a broadcaster in presenting a programme like the one considered in Extract 4.2.7?
2. Identify all the relevant contextual matters which determined whether or not the (Extract 4.2.7) programme was offensive.
3. How might the (Extract 4.2.7) programme have been different if the broadcaster was not under any obligation to preserve due impartiality? Would it have mattered?
4. The special impartiality rules apply to a wide range of television services. Given the multichannel environment is there a case for restricting the application of these rules, for example, to apply only to PST services and national radio services? Many broadcasters now place additional material relevant to a programme on the station's website. Should this practice influence the 'due impartiality' approach?

In contrast with the Broadcasting Code, the BBC Editorial Guidelines are highly detailed containing rules, requirements for approvals from more senior management on certain matters ('mandatory referrals'), principles and practice guidance. Section 3 covers accuracy and section 4, impartiality. The introduction to section 4 illustrates how central impartiality is to the role of the BBC.

Extract 4.2.9
BBC, *Editorial Guidelines* (2010), Section 4.1: Introduction [footnotes omitted]

Impartiality lies at the heart of public service and is the core of the BBC's commitment to its audiences. It applies to all our output and services – television, radio, online, and in our international services and commercial magazines. We must be inclusive, considering the broad perspective and ensuring the existence of a range of views is appropriately reflected.

The Agreement accompanying the BBC Charter requires us to do all we can to ensure controversial subjects are treated with due impartiality in our news and other output dealing with matters of public policy or political or industrial controversy. But we go further than that, applying due impartiality to all subjects. However, its requirements will vary.

The term 'due' means that the impartiality must be adequate and appropriate to the output, taking account of the subject and nature of the content, the likely audience expectation and any signposting that may influence that expectation.

Due impartiality is often more than a simple matter of 'balance' between opposing viewpoints. Equally, it does not require absolute neutrality on every issue or detachment from fundamental democratic principles.

The BBC Agreement forbids our output from expressing the opinion of the BBC on current affairs or matters of public policy, other than broadcasting or the provision of online services.

The external activities of staff, presenters and others who contribute to our output can also affect the BBC's reputation for impartiality. Consequently, this section should be read in conjunction with Section 15: Conflicts of Interest.

Source: © 2010 BBC.

The BBC's approach to its impartiality obligations can have broader consequences. In 2009, the BBC rejected a request by the Disasters Emergency Committee (DEC) to broadcast an appeal for humanitarian assistance for Gaza residents. The DEC represented at least 13 UK aid agencies and it ran appeals annually across a range of humanitarian situations. The BBC Director-General took the view that, because the Israeli–Palestinian conflict was deeply divisive, to broadcast the appeal could adversely affect the BBC's reputation for impartiality. The BBC had not always broadcast these appeal requests from the DEC, but this decision was subject to criticism. However, the BBC Trust upheld the decision to refuse the appeal request.[18]

For the past five years or so the BBC has been undertaking reviews of its treatment of impartiality with specific subject areas. These have followed on from its first review, published in 2007, *From Seesaw to Wagon Wheel: Safeguarding Impartiality in the 21st Century*.[19] Other reviews have considered BBC business coverage, news coverage across the four nations, science coverage and reporting on the 'Arab Spring'.[20] In October 2012, the BBC announced the commencement of a new impartiality review, on this occasion into the BBC's breadth of opinion. In other words, to what extent does the BBC output

---

[18] BBC Trust, *Determination of an appeal against the decision of the Director-General not to broadcast the DEC Gaza Crisis Appeal* (February 2009), http://downloads.bbc.co.uk/bbctrust/assets/files/pdf/appeals/gaza/decision.pdf (accessed 21 November 2012). See also M. Feintuck, 'Impartiality in News Coverage: the present and the future' in M. Amos, J. Harrison and L. Woods (eds), *Freedom of Expression and the Media* (Leiden: Martinus Nijhoff Publishers, 2012), 73 at 78–81.

[19] June 2007, http://downloads.bbc.co.uk/bbctrust/assets/files/pdf/review_report_research/impartiality_21century/report.pdf (accessed 31 October 2012). The report is also useful for understanding the history of impartiality obligations within the BBC.

[20] Reports of these reviews can be accessed from the BBC website at http://www.bbc.co.uk/bbctrust/our_work/editorial_standards/impartiality.html (accessed 31 October 2012).

reflect a range of voices and viewpoints?[21] The most recent impartiality review focused on the BBC coverage of the 'Arab Spring'.[22] A feature of the 'Arab Spring' events was the role played by social media and user-generated content (UGC).[23] The review was generally positive about the BBC coverage, although it indicated some weaknesses. The report is perhaps more useful in illustrating the challenge for the BBC (and other broadcasters) of preserving impartiality when trying to cover complex, dynamic political situations in a context incorporating UGC, multiple media platforms, and 24/7 news cycles.

Questions for discussion

1. Is it necessary that the BBC retain responsibility for supervision of impartiality obligations to maintain BBC independence or might BBC independence and accountability be better served by being subject to Ofcom jurisdiction?
2. Is there a risk that BBC responsibilities for self-regulation might actually have a chilling effect on its output?

4.3 BROADCASTING FAIRNESS AND PRIVACY STANDARDS

The fairness and privacy standards operate differently from other programme standards because the former are concerned less with standards compliance, and more with the impact of a programme on individuals or organisations who may have participated in or been directly affected by the programme content. Section 7 of the Broadcasting Code covers fairness, and section 8, privacy. Ofcom has direct regulatory authority over the BBC for these standards. In addition to principles and rules, sections 7 and 8 contain 'practices to be followed'. Whether these practices have been followed will be relevant to an investigation of possible breach of the fairness and privacy provisions but will not be decisive: '[f]ollowing these practices will not necessarily avoid a breach of this section of the Code (Rule 7.1). *However, failure to follow these practises* [sic.] *will only constitute a breach where it results in unfairness to an individual or organisation in the programme.* Importantly, the Code does not and cannot seek to set out all the "practices to be followed" in order to avoid unfair treatment.'[24] During the period 1 June 2011 to 31 March 2012, a total of 288 Fairness and Privacy complaints were received. Of these, 22 were upheld.[25]

(a) Fairness

There is only one fairness rule. Rule 7.1 states that 'Broadcasters must avoid unjust or unfair treatment of individuals or organisations in programmes.' The statement of the rule is followed by a series of practices, grouped together in the following categories: 'dealing fairly with contributors and obtaining informed consent'; 'opportunity to contribute and

---

[21] BBC, *Trust sets out planned approach for review of BBC's 'breadth of opinion'* (10 October 2012), http://www.bbc.co.uk/bbctrust/news/press_releases/2012/breadth_of_opinion.html (accessed 31 October 2012).

[22] BBC Trust, *A BBC Trust report on the impartiality and accuracy of the BBC's coverage of the events known as the 'Arab Spring'* (June 2012), http://downloads.bbc.co.uk/bbctrust/assets/files/pdf/our_work/arabspring_impartiality/arab_spring.pdf (accessed 31 October 2012).

[23] The 2007 impartiality report also considered the impact of new technologies and the changed relationship between broadcaster and audience: note 19 above, 5.

[24] Ofcom, Broadcasting Code (28 February 2011), 33. A similar statement is made in relation to section 8, privacy at 37.

[25] Ofcom, *Annual Report and Accounts for the period 1 April 2011 to 31 March 2012* (HC 237, 2012), 113.

proper consideration of facts'; and, 'deception, set-ups and "wind-up" calls'. It is likely that many of the fairness issues will arise in relation to news reporting and investigative journalism. There may be pressures upon the journalist of time and the nature of the subject matter being investigated, making errors in editing more likely, for example, or exacerbating the difficulty of obtaining the necessary consents. However, a failure to exercise fairness in reporting may have serious reputational consequences for the person who is the subject of unfair treatment. Practice 7.3 sets out a variety of steps which should be undertaken to ensure informed consent is obtained. However, the Code also recognises that '[i]t may be fair to withhold all or some of this information where it is justified in the public interest or under other provisions of this section [section 7] of the Code'. The Code provides examples of 'public interest': '. . . revealing or detecting crime, protecting public health or safety, exposing misleading claims made by individuals or organisations or disclosing incompetence that affects the public'.[26] These examples are given in section 8 of the Code to explain when the public interest may outweigh the right to privacy and justify an infringement of privacy. However, section 7 makes clear this explanation applies to section 7, although it seems that the 'public interest justification' is raised more often in privacy complaints than in complaints of fairness. In the following determination, Ofcom had to consider whether the public interest justified Channel 4's decision not to obtain consent from the mother of a child, nor to provide the mother with an opportunity to respond to the material to be broadcast. The mother had also argued that her child's privacy was unwarrantably infringed, a claim not upheld. The programme had concerned the issue of failing standards in British secondary schools and the reporter (a qualified teacher) had worked undercover as a supply teacher, filming covertly. The child in question had been filmed throwing a pencil and replying 'no' to a question asked by the teacher. The child's face had been pixelated. The determination required Ofcom to apply the Fairness Code of the former regulator, the Broadcasting Standards Commission; however, the provisions are essentially the same as the fairness and privacy provisions of the Broadcasting Code. The extract shows Ofcom's response to the complaint about lack of consent and consideration of public interest. The mother's complaint about lack of opportunity to respond (not extracted) was also rejected by Ofcom.

Extract 4.3.1
Ofcom, 'Complaint by Ms V on behalf of her daughter (a Minor)' *Dispatches,*
Channel 4, 7 July 2005, Broadcast Bulletin 77 (29 January 2007), 15

. . .

Decision

. . .

The Committee took account of [. . . practice 7.14] of the Fairness Code under which broadcasters should not normally obtain or seek information or pictures through deception, except where the disclosure is reasonably believed to serve an overriding public interest and the material cannot reasonably be obtained by any other means. . . .

The [Fairness] Committee considered whether Channel 4 had reasonable grounds for believing that it served an overriding public interest to obtain the pictures taken at Mrs V's daughter's school by surreptitious filming without consent, bearing in mind the particular vulnerabilities of children. The Committee noted Channel 4's response, that prior to filming, the programme makers had research evidence that the secondary school state education system was suffering

[26] Ofcom, Broadcasting Code (28 February 2011), 38.

from chronic disruption by misbehaving children in the classroom, and that teachers were at best unable to control it and at worst colluding to hide its impact from school inspectors. The Committee considered that these grounds were reasonable and they supported Channel 4's view that, given the nature of the research evidence on severe failures in the education system, it would serve an overriding public interest to obtain the pictures by surreptitious filming. Furthermore, it was the Committee's view that such material could not have been obtained had consent been sought from the school and parents, and that the programme could not have portrayed a true picture of the school. The material was at the heart of the investigation, showing the reality of disruption in the classroom was, in the Committee's view, in the public interest and could only be obtained by surreptitious recording.

. . .

The Committee accepted that the nature of this subject depended on obtaining relevant footage through the use of surreptitious recording and in the Committee's view it would not have been possible to obtain the material by any other means. Therefore, in view of the overriding public interest in the alleged failures, the Committee considered that the use of deception in gathering the material was proportionate.

Source: © Ofcom copyright 2006–11.

Questions for discussion

1. What other factors contributed to Ofcom's determination that the broadcaster's actions were justified in the public interest?
2. What is the relationship between freedom of expression and public interest justification?

Practice 7.11 requires a person, normally, to be given an opportunity to respond where wrongdoing or incompetence is alleged or other serious allegations are made. As a result of a broadcast of a news item by ITV News, the then Chief Constable of South Yorkshire Police, Mr Meredydd Hughes, complained that he had been treated unfairly.[27] The news item dealt with Anti-Social Behaviour Orders and used sections of an interview with Mr Hughes broadcast on a previous occasion. Ofcom did not uphold a complaint that he was not given an opportunity to respond. Although practice 7.11 was relevant, Ofcom considered that it was not necessary in this instance as the broadcaster already had available Mr Hughes' comments in relation to anti-social behaviour and the police response. In re-using material, broadcasters must ensure that the re-use does not create unfairness (practice 7.8). Ofcom emphasised the broadcaster's editorial freedom to use and edit footage, including footage that may have been filmed for another occasion. However, the way in which Mr Hughes' earlier interview had been edited, and taken out of context, created the impression that he was saying that anti-social behaviour was unimportant, and had created unfairness. It is perhaps curious that in re-using and editing previous footage, Ofcom did not consider that an opportunity to respond was necessary, given that the editing essentially created a new set of serious allegations.

(b) Privacy

As with the fairness code, the privacy code (section 8) contains one rule (and one principle) and a series of practices to be followed. The practices to be followed are grouped around

---

[27] Ofcom, 'Complaint by Mr Meredydd Hughes, ITV News, ITV1, 21 January 2010' *Broadcast Bulletin 176* (21 February 2011), 14. The determination is applying an earlier version of the Code but the provisions under consideration are the same.

various circumstances: 'private lives, public places and legitimate expectation of privacy'; 'consent'; 'gathering information, sound or images and the re-use of material'; 'suffering and distress'; and, 'people under sixteen and vulnerable people'.

Ofcom recognises that difficult judgements may have to be made by the broadcaster in situations, such as major disasters, which may warrant immediate filming.

Extract 4.3.2
Ofcom, Broadcasting Code (28 February 2011), Foreword, 37

. . . The Broadcasting Act 1996 (as amended) requires Ofcom to consider complaints about unwarranted infringements of privacy in a programme or in connection with the obtaining of material included in a programme. This may call for some difficult on-the-spot judgments about whether privacy is unwarrantably infringed by filming or recording, especially when reporting on emergency situations . . . We recognise that there may be a strong public interest in reporting on an emergency situation as it occurs and we understand there may be pressures on broadcasters at the scene of a disaster or emergency that may make it difficult to judge at the time whether filming or recording is an unwarrantable infringement of privacy. These are factors Ofcom will take into account when adjudicating on complaints . . .

Source: © Ofcom copyright 2006–11.

As seen in relation to fairness, public interest may also justify an infringement of privacy.

Extract 4.3.3
Ofcom, Broadcasting Code (28 February 2011), rule 8.1

Any infringement of privacy in programmes, or in connection with obtaining material included in the programmes, must be warranted.

Meaning of 'warranted':

In this section 'warranted' has a particular meaning. It means that where broadcasters wish to justify an infringement of privacy as warranted, they should be able to demonstrate why in the particular circumstances of the case, it is warranted. If the reason is that it is in the public interest, then the broadcaster should be able to demonstrate that the public interest outweighs the right to privacy. Examples of public interest would include revealing or detecting crime, protecting public health or safety, exposing misleading claims made by individuals or organisations or disclosing incompetence that affects the public.

Source: © Ofcom copyright 2006–11.

Determining whether a person has a legitimate expectation to privacy may also be difficult and will depend upon a range of circumstances. The Ofcom Section 8 Guidance Note accepts that privacy is least likely to be infringed in a public place, although this will also depend upon the circumstances. A recent determination concerned the filming of a woman, Mrs Geddes, riding her mobility scooter in a suburban area where the 'secret millionaire' was going to live. Mrs Geddes, and only a back view, was only briefly captured on film, with no other identifying information used such as name and address. Ofcom considered that because Mrs Geddes was filmed on a public street and was not engaged in any activity which could be said to be sensitive or private there was nothing to give rise to a legitimate expectation of privacy.[28] Without special circumstances it is unlikely that the ordinary citizen, accidentally caught up in filming, will have any entitlement to complain.

[28] Ofcom, 'Complaint by Mrs Sandra Geddes', *Broadcast Bulletin 215* (8 October 2012), 16. Can be accessed at http://stakeholders.ofcom.org.uk/binaries/enforcement/broadcast-bulletins/obb215/obb215.pdf (accessed 31 October 2012).

However, Extract 4.3.4, another recent determination, illustrates how careful broadcasters must be with using information, which might be thought to be scene-setting for the news commentary; in this case filming someone viewing a Facebook page.

Extract 4.3.4
Ofcom, 'Complaint by Miss F', *Broadcast Bulletin 213* **(10 September 2012), 75**
[footnotes omitted]

Summary

Ofcom has upheld this complaint by Miss F of unwarranted infringement of privacy in the programme as broadcast.

On 12 February 2012, Central News broadcast an item concerning the medical consequences for women who had had Poly Implant Prosthèse (PIP) breast implants. A contributor to the programme, Miss Brown, was interviewed and she spoke about the Facebook group she had set up in light of the anxiety that many of the women who had PIP implants were feeling. Miss Brown was filmed while viewing a Facebook page in the programme. While she did so, the Facebook page briefly showed posts made by Miss F. Following the broadcast of the programme, Miss F complained to Ofcom that her privacy was unwarrantably infringed in the broadcast of the programme.

Ofcom found that Miss F did have a legitimate expectation that her posts, which indicated that she had had breast implants, would not be broadcast in the programme. While Ofcom took into account the broadcaster's right to freedom of expression and the fact that the infringement was limited, Ofcom considered that on balance in these particular circumstances, the broadcaster's right to freedom of expression did not outweigh Miss F's expectation of privacy.

. . .

Decision

. . .

Ofcom noted that as the reporter explained that Miss Brown had set up a Facebook group for other women, a shot was shown on screen for approximately five seconds of the post made by Miss F which included a small photograph of her with two other women. In this first shot the text of the first post would not have been legible to the normal viewer, but if the image was paused it was legible. If paused, the text did identify that Miss F had undergone implant surgery. It was not clear from the footage shown exactly what the post had said, although Ofcom observed that Miss F's full name and words '*transform*' and '*PIP*' were visible. The footage showed the webpage being scrolled to the top of the page which had the title '*PIP implants through Transform Support Group*' and '*Closed group*'. Ofcom also noted that the footage of Miss F's posts was shown in the programme without her having given her consent.

Ofcom took into account that the group was 'closed' – which means that only members of a particular group are able to view posts and material that appear on the page in question. Therefore Miss F would not have expected people outside that group to be able to view her posts, by them being broadcast to a wider audience without her consent. It was a reasonable assumption for viewers watching this material to make from the material shown in the context of the report that Miss F had undergone implant surgery. Ofcom considers that information confirming that an individual has undergone cosmetic surgery is normally medical information which is sensitive and personal in nature. Therefore, this type of information would usually attract a significant legitimate expectation of privacy.

Ofcom noted that Miss F had placed material confirming that she had PIP implants on other forums. For example, on 14 January 2012, Miss F posted on the PIP Implant Forum and on 16 January 2012 she posted a comment in relation to a request from a broadcaster who was doing some research on PIP implants. However, Ofcom noted that these posts were not readily available on the internet without entering particular search terms and conducting further research. Further, the posts were confined to members of groups who had a common interest in the issue of PIP implants and were limited to the Facebook community. Ofcom therefore did not agree with ITV that this meant that the information was in the public domain and that therefore Miss F did not have a legitimate expectation of privacy. Rather, when taking all these factors into consideration, Ofcom took the view that Miss F would not have expected information pertaining to medical surgery she had had to be disclosed to a group outside of this community and then broadcast to a wider audience. Consequently, Ofcom's view was that Miss F did have a legitimate expectation of privacy which was only marginally limited by the posts that she made on other forums <u>and</u> on Facebook.

Ofcom further observed that: in the first shots Miss F's post appeared on screen for no more than five seconds in duration in total, and that her name was only clearly legible for around two seconds. In the shot at the end of the report her name was clearly legible for around one second. Ofcom also took into account that Miss F was not the subject of the report and that showing her posts was incidental. It also took into account that, although the text of posts shown on screen containing sensitive personal information would not have been legible to the normal viewer, if the image were paused some text was legible. In these circumstances, Ofcom's view was that the infringement of her privacy was limited to some extent.

. . .

Ofcom considered the particular justification put forward by ITV for including the posts made by Miss F in its news programme. Ofcom noted that the news report voiced concerns, principally raised by Miss Brown, that not enough was '*being done to help patients worried for their health*'. Ofcom took into account that there was considerable interest in these events because of the medical implications for the thousands of women who had PIP implants and therefore considered that there was a public interest in general terms in the subject of the report. Although incidental, Miss F's posts were relevant to the report in that they illustrated that Miss Brown had set up a Facebook group to help women who had PIP implants and Miss F was one of the many people who had joined this group. Ofcom considered that the brief footage of Miss F's Facebook post was used as a visual device to illustrate the fact that Miss Brown had '*now set up a Facebook support group for other women in the same position*'.

While Ofcom noted the public interest in the subject matter of the news item and ITV's submission that the footage complained of was fleeting and incidental, it did not consider on balance that there was any public interest which warranted infringing Miss F's privacy, by disclosing that she had undergone a breast implant procedure.

. . .

Questions for discussion

1. Review the 'Mrs Geddes' decision. Does it give any indication of when someone filmed in a public place may be said to have a legitimate expectation of privacy?
2. What was the real legitimate expectation in the matter concerning Ms F? What will be the effect of the information being available elsewhere?
3. Why did the public interest not outweigh the privacy interest in the matter concerning Ms F?

Although, section 8, like section 7, is designed to provide individuals or organisations who may be affected by a programme with recourse, this may not prevent others responding to a programme. This was the case with a BBC Radio 2 broadcast of *The Russell Brand Show* in 2008.[29] Ofcom received 1,939 complaints while the BBC received 42,851 complaints, although many of these complaints occurred after extensive press coverage. In fact, the BBC received only two complaints immediately after the first broadcast.[30] The complaints concerned the nature of the material broadcast as well as the possibility that very private information may have been revealed without consent. In addition to these public complaints, Andrew Sachs complained to the BBC that his privacy had been infringed by the broadcast.[31] Ofcom considered complaints of harm and offence (rules 2.1 and 2.3) and an infringement of rule 8.1.[32] The complaints concerned two broadcasts of *The Russell Brand Show* on 18 and 25 October 2008. The programme was broadcast weekly on a Saturday night and was '. . . comedic in tone', often containing adult humour (para 1.2). The programme was usually co-hosted with a guest presenter. Jonathan Ross was the co-host for the 18 October broadcast. This broadcast was pre-recorded and had been scheduled to include a telephone interview with actor, Andrew Sachs, although he was unavailable when the programme contacted him. As a result Brand and Ross made several telephone calls to Sachs, leaving '. . . a series of lewd messages' on his answerphone. 'During these calls both Brand and Ross referred to Georgina Baillie [Sachs' granddaughter], stating that Brand had had a sexual relationship with her. In the first phone call, while Brand was leaving a message on Andrew Sachs' answerphone, Ross shouted out: "He fucked your granddaughter". Ross and Brand continued to make further references to the sexual relationship between Baillie and Brand within the programme. This ended with Brand singing an improvised song – allegedly intended by him to be an apology to Sachs' (paras 1.4–1.5). Further references to the sexual relationship were made on the programme broadcast live on 25 October 2008 and the improvised song was replayed. The BBC acknowledged that it had breached the harm and offence provisions and infringed without justification the privacy of Sachs and his granddaughter. In addition to the failure of editorial judgement, there were compliance failures, and, by replaying parts of the first broadcast, the initial errors were compounded (para 1.9). The BBC also acknowledged a conflict of interest had arisen because a BBC producer, who would normally have had day-to-day responsibility for the show, had been loaned out to the independent production company (partly owned by Russell Brand) producing *The Russell Brand Show*. Ofcom considered that this posed problems for risk management: '. . . although the greatest compliance risk in the series lay in what Russell Brand would say on the air, part of the risk management had effectively been ceded to those working for him. It would appear that the interests of the presenter had been given greater priority than the BBC's risk management systems' (para 1.15). Ofcom found that the broadcasts had breached harm and offence provisions and constituted an unjustifiable infringement of privacy. A financial penalty of £150,000 was imposed on the BBC for these breaches (see Section 4.6(c) below).

---

[29] Ofcom, 'The Russell Brand Show', *Broadcast Bulletin 131* (6 April 2009), 4. Full adjudication can be accessed: http://www2.ofcom.org.uk/tv/obb/ocsc_adjud/BBCRadio2TheRussellBrandShow.pdf (accessed 31 October 2012).

[30] Ibid., paras 4.1–4.2.

[31] Mr Sachs' agent made the complaint to the BBC. The letter of complaint was later copied to Ofcom. The BBC tried to argue that Ofcom could not impose a sanction given that no complaint had been made to Ofcom directly but this was rejected by Ofcom: ibid., para 10.19.

[32] Ofcom was applying an earlier version of the Broadcasting Code but the substance of the rules was the same.

Extract 4.3.5

Ofcom Content Sanctions Committee, 'British Broadcasting Corporation ("BBC"), *The Russell Brand Show*, **BBC Radio 2, 18 and 25 October 2008',** *Broadcast Bulletin 131* **(6 April 2009), 4 [footnotes omitted]**

. . .

1.14 In deciding this case, Ofcom recognises the paramount importance that is attached to freedom of expression in the broadcasting environment. In particular, broadcasters must be permitted to enjoy the creative freedom to explore issues and ideas without undue interference. Comedy in particular has a tradition of challenging and even deliberately flouting boundaries of taste. Whilst such programming must have room for innovation and creativity, it does not have unlimited licence. Individual performers and presenters may sometimes overstep the line. However, it is the responsibility of broadcasters operating in creative environments to have robust systems in place and apply them so as to ensure compliance with the Code, and specifically in this case so that individuals and members of the public are provided adequate protection from offensive and harmful material and unwarranted infringements of privacy.

1.15 Creative risk is therefore part of the BBC's public service role but so is risk management.

. . . [The following paragraphs consider whether there had been an infringement of rule 8.1 in relation to the 18 October broadcast. A similar finding was reached in relation to the 25 October broadcast [not extracted].]

. . .

5.7 Ofcom first considered whether Mr Sachs and Ms Baillie had a legitimate expectation of privacy in relation to the comments broadcast in this programme. Ofcom considered that all of these remarks were likely to be regarded as relating to matters of a highly personal, intimate and sensitive nature, including details of Ms Baillie's sex life. The comments were unambiguous and were disclosed in the context of a programme in which Ms Baillie and Mr Sachs were named and therefore clearly identifiable. In these circumstances Ofcom considered that Mr Sachs and Ms Baillie did have a legitimate expectation of privacy in relation to the broadcast of the remarks in this programme.

5.8 In light of the above, Ofcom then considered whether Mr Sachs and Ms Baillie's privacy was infringed in the broadcast. Ofcom took account of the requirement in Practice 8.6 of the Code . . . Ofcom also noted the guidelines in Practice 7.3 of the Code regarding the obtaining of consent, for example whether Mr Sachs and Ms Baillie had been told the nature and purpose of the programme, whether Mr Sachs was made aware of any significant changes to the programme as it developed and whether he was given any clear information about whether he would have been able to effect any changes to the programme.

5.9 Ofcom noted from the BBC's representations that the BBC had admitted that the necessary informed consent was not obtained from either Mr Sachs or Ms Baillie.

5.10 It was Ofcom's view that the broadcast of this material which was of such a personal, intimate and sensitive nature, in which both Mr Sachs and Ms Baillie were named and in the absence of informed consent, did result in an infringement of their privacy in the programme as broadcast.

5.11 Ofcom then considered whether the infringement of privacy was warranted. Ofcom was not satisfied that there was any public interest in the broadcast of such personal, intimate and sensitive information and for this reason the infringement of privacy was therefore unwarranted. Ofcom noted from the BBC's representations that it accepted that this infringement of privacy was unwarranted. Further, the BBC admitted that the principles expressed in Section 8 of the Code were neither properly considered nor properly applied as regards this broadcast.

. . .

While the Russell Brand matter did not raise public interest considerations, a programme, *Dispatches*, broadcast by Channel 4 concerning the conditions in privately owned 'houses of multiple occupancy' provided to local authorities for the housing of the homeless did.[33] Here one of the landlords featured in the programme was filmed secretly discussing repairs with a local authority representative. Ofcom, having accepted that the complainant, Mr Adedeji, had a legitimate expectation to privacy, considered whether the covert filming was warranted in the public interest. Ofcom concluded that the surreptitious filming was justified because there was a public interest in revealing the poor standards of the accommodation and the cursory attitude of the local authorities towards inspection of the facilities.[34]

Questions for discussion

1. What expectation of privacy was infringed in relation to Mr Sachs?
2. Did Ofcom have jurisdiction to deal with the privacy matter concerning the Russell Brand Show?
3. Comparing the matters affecting the Russell Brand Show and the Dispatches programme (having reviewed the determination), will there be any circumstances in which a programme with a purpose or format similar to the Russell Brand Show could argue that the invasion of privacy was warranted? Having regard to freedom of expression rights, should some latitude be given for creative risk?
4. Does Ofcom's decision in the *Dispatches* matter give an indication of the circumstances in which public interest won't be sufficient to justify an invasion of privacy?

4.4 POLITICAL AND ELECTION BROADCASTING

(a) Introduction

The obligation to ensure due impartiality has already been considered. The rules on political and election broadcasting bear a relationship to this obligation because they aim to preserve a balance between the political parties and to avoid the promotion of any one political party, and hence viewpoint. The extent to which political and election broadcasting should take place is a difficult and sensitive matter. The pervasiveness of broadcasting makes it an attractive medium for politicians to put across their message, and political parties will no doubt be tempted to try for as much access as possible to radio and television outlets. Equally, broadcasters may be sensitive to such pressures, and may wish to resist pressures for access in order to preserve their independence and the balance of their output.

It is important to be clear about the meaning of political broadcasts. Programmes such as news, current affairs and others touching upon political issues will be under the control of broadcasters and will have to comply with the Broadcasting Code, especially the rules on impartiality. Such programmes are not political broadcasts. Further, party political

---

[33] Ofcom, 'Complaint by Mr Yinka Adedeji, Dispatches: Landlords from Hell, Channel 4, 5 December 2011', *Broadcast Bulletin 207* (11 June 2012), 83, can be accessed at http://stakeholders.ofcom.org.uk/binaries/enforcement/broadcast-bulletins/obb207/obb207.pdf (accessed 31 October 2012).

[34] Ibid., 94–5.

and election broadcasts must be distinguished from political advertisements. Although modern party political and election broadcasts may have presentational styles more usually associated with advertising, paid political broadcasting is banned in the UK (see Chapter 6, Section 6.7). The focus in this section is on the provisions made to allow the political parties to broadcast messages during an election campaign and at other times. Although the tendency, for example, in the legislation, is to refer to 'party political broadcasts', this term is usually used to refer to party political and election broadcasts. These two types of broadcasts need to be distinguished because different rules and policies will apply. In this chapter, they will be referred to separately where necessary, but otherwise will be referred to as 'party political broadcasts'. Once again this is an area which illustrates the differences between press and broadcasting regulation; the former not being under the constraints such as those considered here. These days many political parties and politicians use social media to reach the public – another realm not constrained by the type of regulatory restrictions examined in this chapter. Does this mean that, here, too, the continued special regulation of broadcasting is becoming strained and even more difficult to justify, especially if it is seen to limit the public's access to political information and ideas. On the other hand, one could view the regulatory arrangements for political and election broadcasting as enabling, rather than restricting, political speech. The arrangements in place seek to ensure that there is access for party political voices, which will not be dependent upon money or 'friendly' media. Too, the regulatory arrangements apply to the most pervasive of the broadcasting outlets thereby enabling the widest possible access for speaker and audience. Nevertheless, even accepting that it is important for political parties to have access to broadcasting outlets, difficult questions may remain to be resolved about which parties should have access and how much access should be permitted.

The regulatory arrangements for political and election broadcasting comprise some specific access opportunities as well as more generalised opportunities. Section 333 of the Communications Act 2003 requires Ofcom to ensure that the licensed PST broadcasters and the national radio broadcasters are required to include in their services party political and election broadcasts and referendum campaign broadcasts. These obligations extend only to registered political parties and designated referendum organisations.[35] Pursuant to section 333 Ofcom has developed a set of rules, *Ofcom Rules on Party Political and Referendum Broadcasts* (25 February 2010) laying down minimum requirements, but leaving the broadcasters free to offer additional allocations. These are considered in more detail in the following sections. In addition, section 6 of the Broadcasting Code, 'Elections and Referendums', deals with the broadcasters' impartiality responsibilities during these periods. Section 6 does not apply to BBC licence fee-funded services.[36] Clause 48 of the BBC Agreement requires the BBC to carry party political and referendum campaign broadcasts although decisions regarding which BBC services will carry the broadcasts, allocation, length and frequency, and so forth are left to the BBC Trust. An interesting aspect of this area of broadcast regulation is that the broadcasters with responsibilities for airing party political broadcasts have tended to work together, now through the Broadcasters' Liaison Group (BLG), to reach a consensus on allocation of broadcasts. The Electoral Commission is a member of the BLG. Pursuant to section 333(5) of the Communications Act 2003, Ofcom is required to take into account the views of the Commission in determining rules for political broadcasts. The BBC has a similar obligation (section 11(3), Political

---

[35] See also sections 37, 108 and 127 of the Political Parties, Elections and Referendums Act 2000.
[36] Section 4 of the Editorial Guidelines, 'Impartiality' also covers elections and referendums.

Parties, Elections and Referendums Act 2000). The S4C Authority is required to have regard to the Electoral Commission's views and the ruled developed by Ofcom (Communications Act 2003, Schedule 12, para 18(5)). In 2003, the Electoral Commission published a report on Party Political Broadcasting following a review in which it concluded that party political broadcasts remained an important direct campaigning tool.[37] Having regard to the dramatic change in the number and nature of broadcasting outlets, it questioned whether it was appropriate that only a small range of broadcasters were obliged to carry party political broadcasts, and recommended that the obligation should be expanded to include any television or radio channel achieving a certain audience reach and share threshold.[38] It also recommended that Ofcom should regulate all broadcasters who had obligations to carry party political broadcasts and that the BLG should have a statutory basis.[39]

Questions for discussion

1. To what extent does the ban on paid political advertising drive the regulatory arrangements for allocating time for political and election broadcasts?
2. Given that political parties are not subject to the same type of restrictions in relation to access to the press or the social media, what arguments can be presented to justify still the restrictions regarding the broadcast media?
3. Are the recommendations of the Electoral Commission regarding who should have the obligation to carry broadcasts desirable? Are they still relevant given the advances since 2003 in Internet and social media communications?

(b) Party political and election broadcasts and referendums

The Ofcom Rules on Party Political and Referendum Broadcasts (Ofcom Party Political Rules) set down the minimum requirements to be followed by those licensees who are subject to the section 333 provisions.[40] A licensee can offer more, although such arrangements would have to be in compliance with a broadcaster's due impartiality responsibilities. The general obligations with regard to party political, party election and referendum campaign broadcasts are set out in rules 7 to 9 of the Ofcom Party Political Rules. Notice that outside of elections and referendums, the obligation to carry party political broadcasts is limited to set occasions, such as the Queen's Speech, Budget and party conferences, and will apply only to major political parties which Ofcom defines currently as 'the Conservative Party, the Labour Party and the Liberal Democrats and, in Scotland and Wales respectively, the Scottish National Party ("SNP") and Plaid Cymru. The major parties in Northern Ireland are: the Democratic Unionist Party, Sinn Fein, the Social Democratic & Labour Party and the Ulster Unionist Party' (rule 11). In relation to these other political events, the major parties are offered one broadcast in relation to each event (rule 9).

---

[37] The Electoral Commission, *Party Political Broadcasting: Report and recommendations* (January 2003), http://www.electoralcommission.org.uk/__data/assets/electoral_commission_pdf_file/0018/16047/Finalversion_7607-6718__E__N__S__W__.pdf (accessed 6 November 2012), 13. This report was published when the Communications Act was still at Bill stage.

[38] Ibid., 25–7.

[39] Ibid., 22.

[40] The BBC and the S4C Authority have also developed policies dealing with similar matters. For the BBC, see: http://www.bbc.co.uk/bbctrust/our_work/editorial_standards/party_political_broadcasts.html and for S4C: http://www.s4c.co.uk/abouts4c/authority/e_plansandpolicies.shtml (accessed 6 November 2012).

Probably the most sensitive time for broadcasters will be during election campaigns and here the rules are more detailed, although broadcasters will still be called upon to exercise judgement and discretion as can be seen in the following extract of the Ofcom Party Political Rules. Although the responsibility for such decisions will remain with the broadcaster, through the Broadcasters' Liaison Group, the broadcasters, including the BBC and S4C, and working also with the Electoral Commission, try to ensure a consistent approach.

Extract 4.4.1
Ofcom, *Rules on Party Political and Referendum Broadcasts* (25 February 2010), rules 12–17

Allocation of broadcasts

Party Election Broadcasts ('PEBs')

12. Before a General Election, and in the case of other elections where appropriate, each major party (referred to in Rule 11) should be offered a series of two or more PEBs, the length of a series offered to a particular party being determined by the Licensee. This includes the SNP and Plaid Cymru on Channel 4 and Five. In every case, the number of PEBs should be determined having regard to the circumstances of a particular election, the nation in which it is held, and the individual party's past and/or current electoral support in that nation (see Rule 15).

13. Other registered parties should qualify for a PEB if they are contesting one sixth or more of the seats up for election in the case of first-past-the-post, multi-constituency elections such as a General Election. For proportional representation systems of election (such as the European Parliamentary Elections), the minimum qualifying requirement for the allocation of one PEB should be adapted appropriately, reasonably and fairly for each election, according to criteria which have regard to the particular system of voting, the number of seats available for election, the number of constituencies/regions, and the number of candidates nominated by the party.

14. Licensees should consider making additional allocations of PEBs to other registered parties (which satisfy the criteria at Rule 13) if evidence of their past and/or current electoral support at a particular election or in a relevant nation/electoral area means it would be appropriate to do so. In this regard, Licensees should consider whether other registered parties should qualify for a series of PEBs and/or peak-time scheduling, as major parties do.

15. In determining allocations of PEBs at elections, the four nations of the UK should be considered separately.

16. In accordance with Rules 7 to 9, parties which qualify for at least one PEB in one of the nations of England, Scotland, Wales or Northern Ireland will be offered PEBs on the Channel 3 licensee in the appropriate regions of those nations.

17. Parties which qualify for a PEB in all three nations of England, Scotland and Wales will additionally be offered a PEB on Channel 4 (at General Elections), Five (at General Elections and European Elections) and the UK-wide analogue radio services (at General Elections) (provided these broadcasters are carrying the relevant series of broadcasts; see Rules 7–9).

Source: © Ofcom copyright 2006–11.

The political parties and designated organisations are offered a choice of broadcast lengths: 2'40", 3'40" or 4'40" for television and up to 2'30" for radio (rule 20). There are also rules about the scheduling of broadcasts (rules 21–22). For example, party election broadcasts, on behalf of the major parties, must be carried during peak time (6pm to 10.30pm).

As can be observed from rules 12 to 17, only registered parties can expect to be allocated party election broadcasts, but not all registered parties may qualify for allocation of a party election broadcast (rules 13 and 14). This means that it may be very difficult for smaller, minority and new political parties to have the same type of access to the public as the major and larger minority parties. Even parties meeting the rule 13 criteria, may find it difficult to establish the evidence of past or current electoral support under rule 14. In the 2009 European parliamentary elections, Ofcom dealt with two disputes concerning allocations of party election broadcasts.[41] The determination of these disputes shows the careful judgements to be made by a broadcaster, or Ofcom in a dispute, about 'electoral support'. The rules were slightly different to the current version of the Ofcom Party Political Rules, but not significantly for these purposes. The Traditional Unionist Voice Party (TUV) unsuccessfully complained to Ofcom about its allocation of only one party election broadcast by the Channel 3 Northern Ireland broadcaster, UTV, asserting that it should have been allocated three broadcasts as had the major parties in Northern Ireland. In the second dispute, the UK Independence Party in Wales (UKIP Wales) also complained about an allocation of only one party election broadcast. The complaint was based on the fact that the Welsh Liberal Democrats had been allocated three broadcasts, although that party had received fewer votes than UKIP Wales in the 2004 European parliamentary elections. In this determination, Ofcom upheld the complaint although it was prepared to allocate only one extra broadcast. In both matters, the main issue for Ofcom was the application of the criterion of electoral support (see rule 14). Because of procedural flaws in the way that both the matters had first been dealt with by the broadcasters, Ofcom considered the complaints by re-applying the criteria used by the broadcasters.

Extract 4.4.2
Ofcom, Letter to Mr Allister, concerning Ofcom Election Committee's Determination of the TUV's Party Election Broadcast Dispute with UTV, 1 May 2009, 2, 5–6

You made clear in your referral letter and subsequent correspondence that you disputed the allocation of one PEB to the TUV. Your primary position was that UTV should have allocated three PEBs to the TUV, equal to the number allocated to the major parties of Northern Ireland, and specifically to the other currently sitting MEPs. In particular, you submitted that it was not reasonable or rational for UTV to allocate the TUV with one PEB, when the alliance Party had been granted two.

. . .

The Committee's decision

. . . For the reasons set out below, the Committee reached the view that it was appropriate on the evidence to grant the TUV one PEB.

First, whilst the Committee noted the submission . . . that electors in Northern Ireland vote for individual candidates and not for parties on a party list system, you were originally elected for a major party in Northern Ireland (i.e. the DUP) and will be standing on behalf of a different party, the TUV, for the first time in this election. So whilst you personally may have topped the European Parliamentary Elections in 2004, the Committee considered that you are likely to have benefited from particularly strong support because you were the candidate for the DUP at that election, and cannot necessarily rely on a comparable level of support at this election in June 2009.

Second, the Committee weighed the relevant evidence of the result in the Dromore local by-election in February 2008, being the only election which the TUV polled 19.6% of the total first preference votes . . . However, in the Committee's view, it is not possible to extrapolate the

---

[41] Disputes about allocations are considered by Ofcom's Election Committee applying Ofcom's *Procedures for Determination of Disputes under Ofcom's Rules on Party Political and Referendum Broadcasts* (25 February 2010).

extent of support which the TUV currently enjoys (or has recently enjoyed) across the whole of Northern Ireland purely from the result of a single local council by-election . . .

. . . In this respect, the Committee noted UTV's statement that they would be prepared to reconsider their allocation decision if provided with evidence of a 'credible opinion poll or some other reliable measure' to show substantial levels of current national support; yet you did not provide any evidence of this nature to the Committee for it to take into account . . .

Thirdly, the Committee carefully considered your specific comparison with the Alliance Party's performance in the Dromore by-election (and other subsequent elections). However, in the Committee's view, it is relevant to the differential allocation of PEBs to the Alliance Party that . . . this party is recognised as a medium-sized party, with seven Members of the Legislative Assembly ('MLAs') and 34 local councillors elected for that party, which has consistently contested elections . . .

In considering this last point, the Committee appreciated that the specific issue is the level of past or current support for the TUV among electors, rather than among elected representatives. Nevertheless, the Committee considered that this was a relevant consideration in the comparison of the TUV's overall support with that of the Alliance Party.

Source: © Ofcom copyright 2006–11.

Extract 4.4.3
Ofcom, Letter to Mr Bufton, UK Independence Party Wales, concerning Ofcom Election Committee's Determination of the UKIP Wales's Party Election Broadcast Dispute with ITV, 21 May 2009, 2, 4, 5

[. . . You] complained that the UKIP Wales was entitled to be allocated the same number of PEBs as the Welsh Liberal Democrats (i.e. three) on the basis that UKIP Wales received more votes than the Welsh Liberal Democrats in the European Parliamentary Elections in 2004 . . .

The Committee's decision

. . .

In the Committee's view, it was implicit in ITV's letter that it considered that UKIP Wales satisfied the minimum discretionary requirement for one PEB . . . because it had decided to allocate a single PEB to UKIP Wales for this election.

Furthermore, the Committee considered that the reference in ITV's letter of 15 May 2009 to UKIP Wales not having 'enjoyed substantial levels of past and/or current support in Wales' suggested that ITV had also applied an additional specific criterion against which ITV had considered whether UKIP Wales should be granted further PEBs by comparison with the Liberal Democrats . . .

In determining whether UKIP met the threshold for this additional criterion of 'substantial levels of past and/or current support in Wales', the Committee considered that the particular evidence of UKIP Wales's past performance in the 2004 European election (where it polled 10.5% of the vote and actually received more votes than the Liberal Democrats) did show substantial levels of past support in Wales sufficient to grant more than one PEB to UKIP Wales in this election.

The Committee then considered whether it was appropriate to grant UKIP two more PEBs as you requested by further reference to UKIP's performance in the 2004 European Elections, giving UKIP Wales parity with the Welsh Liberal Democrats. In the Committee's view, this would give undue weight to UKIP's performance in that one particular election. The Committee considered it should look at that result in the overall context of UKIP Wales's performance in other more recent elections in Wales . . . in which UKIP Wales polled significantly less of the vote than the Liberal Democrats and the other major parties.

On that basis, the Committee decided it was fair and appropriate to grant UKIP Wales one more PEB.

Source: © Ofcom copyright 2006–11.

Although the broadcasters have discretion to offer more than what is required, they will still have to bear in mind their own impartiality obligations. Further, they may be reluctant to offer more broadcast time for political broadcasts for fear that the viewing or listening audience may be irritated by too many broadcasts. The difficulty arises also in the approach a broadcaster should adopt to determine which of these other political parties should be offered party political broadcasts and the degree of access. As just seen, even the Ofcom rules will require a broadcaster to make complex decisions during the allocation process. The two disputes just examined concerned established, but not major, parties. What criteria should a broadcaster take into account when there has been no opportunity to demonstrate electoral support? In relation to broadcasters' obligations to exercise due impartiality during elections, Ofcom addressed this issue in the process of developing guidance for broadcasters during the first elections to be held (in 2012) for the Police and Crime Commissioners posts across England and Wales: *Ofcom Code Guidance for broadcast coverage of the 2012 Police and Crime Commissioner Elections* (2012). The guidance is intended to help broadcasters comply with their obligations under the Broadcasting Code, especially sections 5 and 6. In its draft guidance, Ofcom suggested a range of factors that broadcasters could take into account in determining evidence of support including positive mentions in news outlets, public expressions of support, and social media support.[42] However, the Electoral Commission had concerns.

Extract 4.4.4
Letter from A. Robertson, The Electoral Commission, to A. Baxter, Ofcom (3 September 2012)

We have some concerns, however, about the stipulation in paragraph 2.25 that one of the factors which might be used to assess current levels of support could be 'previous experience of candidates that may make them serious candidates for the role'. We understand the motivation behind this suggestion, but it would in our view entail broadcasters making a value-judgment about what constitutes a 'serious candidate' and it is difficult to think of how this assessment could be made objective.

All candidates already have to meet certain requirements to stand – including securing the signatures of 100 registered voters from the police area supporting the nomination – so an alternative would be simply to treat all candidates equally until there is objective evidence of current support.

Source: © Ofcom copyright 2006–11.

In its response, Ofcom recognised the concerns of the Electoral Commission and also broadcasters' concerns that it was not appropriate to specify criteria and reworded the guidance so that there would be greater reliance on objective and measurable means of support.[43]

---

[42] Ofcom, *Guidance for broadcast coverage of the 2012 Police and Crime Commissioner Elections*, Consultation (26 July 2012), http://stakeholders.ofcom.org.uk/consultations/2012-police-elections/ (accessed 7 November 2012), para 2.25.

[43] Ofcom, *Guidance for broadcast coverage of the 2012 Police and Crime Commissioner Elections*, Statement (28 September 2012), http://stakeholders.ofcom.org.uk/binaries/consultations/2012-police-elections/statement/statement.pdf (accessed 7 November 2012), paras 2.52–2.53.

Questions for discussion

1. Extracts 4.4.2 and 4.4.3 demonstrate that allocation decisions can be quite complex and will often have to be made within a short space of time. Is the approach a satisfactory way of providing access given the prohibition on paid political advertising?
2. Extract 4.4.4 similarly shows the complexity involved in allocating broadcast time. Given the ubiquity of social media forms of communication, are these allocation processes still relevant?
3. Given the prohibition on political advertising, are these rules actually limiting freedom of communication?

The BBC has followed a similar approach to the allocation of party political broadcasts, although, in December 2011, the BBC Trust launched a consultation in which it proposed that the offer of party political broadcasts should be severed from specific political events and offered instead on a 'seasonal' basis in autumn, winter and spring.[44] The proposal envisaged removing the Budget broadcasts, although it would be open to a party to schedule their broadcast during that period. The reasoning for this proposed change can be seen in the following extract.

Extract 4.4.5
BBC Trust, *Consultation on draft party political broadcasts policy* (December 2011), 4

Why are we proposing this change?

The existing system for scheduling PPBs follows historic practice and does not take into account changes to the political environment over the years, such as the televising of parliament and progress of devolution.

Now the Welsh Assembly and Scottish Parliament are established, it is not obvious why there should be a different number of PPBs throughout the year in different parts of the UK.

We recognise that there is a different context in Northern Ireland that justifies differential treatment. This lies in the fact that the political structure in Northern Ireland is different from the rest of the UK (which could give rise to some impartiality issues) and that the different timing of devolution in Northern Ireland has meant the practice of PPBs only began relatively recently.

We also recognise that for some political parties, especially in Northern Ireland, PPBs may present a financial difficulty and that too could give rise to impartiality issues.

. . .

Linking PPBs with events has meant parties being offered fewer PPBs in years (such as 2011) when there was no Queen's Speech, as well as uncertainty over timing. The government's decision to move the Queen's Speech to 'Spring' means this is no longer appropriate, as it is likely, most years, to fall either just before or just after the beginning of an election period, when PPBs cannot be broadcast (because that is when Party Election Broadcasts are scheduled).

The Trust is of the provisional view that current practice behind Budget broadcasts is also outdated. The BBC has no obligation under its Charter or Agreement to offer a Budget broadcast and believes it no longer serves the audience for the intended purpose. The broadcasts originated when there was neither TV nor radio available from the chamber of the House of Commons and the Budget broadcast was the only way in which the Chancellor could be seen and heard communicating directly to the public the content of the budget . . . It is the Trust's provisional view that in a devolved UK, allocating separate PPBs which are broadcast by nation is fairer and more consistent than the current system for the Budget broadcast . . .

Source: © 2011 BBC.

---

[44] BBC Trust, *Consultation on Draft Party Political Broadcasts Policy* (December 2011), 3. For Northern Ireland the proposal was to retain the current practice (one party political broadcast during September to March) or introducing two in that period.

Questions for discussion

1. If these new arrangements were to be adopted, might they impose more complexity for the BBC in ensuring that it meets its impartiality obligations?
2. Given that paid political advertising is prohibited, should the BBC be concerned, as it was in the case of Northern Ireland parties, with the fact that financial constraints might limit the scope for taking up these party political broadcasts?

In February 2012, the BBC announced that following consultation it would adopt its proposed new system of party political broadcasts allocation.[45] However, it chose to retain the current arrangements for Northern Ireland, noting that there was no widespread demand for increasing the number of broadcasts. It referred to a submission of the Electoral Commission which had also noted the financial difficulties for some parties of increased broadcasts and the potential risk that might have for impartial treatment of the political parties.[46] Ofcom also launched a review of the Ofcom Party Political Rules in late 2012. As a consequence of the BBC's decision, Ofcom also proposed a move to seasonal broadcasts.[47]

(c) Impartiality

Section 5 of the Broadcasting Code will apply to licensed broadcasters during election periods and referendums. This is emphasised in rule 6.1 of section 6, a section devoted to elections and referendums and applicable to licensed broadcasters. Broadcasters will have to be especially careful that programmes they air to discuss election or referendum-related matters, such as debates, do not infringe the impartiality rules. Ensuring balance may mean that they cannot broadcast some matters. During the 2005 General Election, Bloomberg TV broadcast live coverage of the Labour Party's launch of its business manifesto. The broadcast included long interviews with various senior members of the Labour Party, including then Prime Minister, Tony Blair, who also faced critical questioning from the press and invited audience. The event took place at Bloomberg's auditorium. Bloomberg had offered the same coverage to the Conservative and Liberal Democrat parties, but they had declined. Ofcom found that Bloomberg, while not deliberately biased, had breached its impartiality obligations. Although Bloomberg had approached other parties, this was not sufficient to discharge these obligations: what mattered was what was transmitted.[48]

---

[45] BBC Trust, *Consultation on Party Political Broadcasts: Outcome of Consultation* (February 2012), 4.

[46] Ibid., 5–6.

[47] Ofcom, *A review of the Ofcom rules on party political and referendum broadcasts and Proposed Ofcom Guidance for broadcast coverage of elections*, Consultation (19 November 2012), http://stakeholders.ofcom.org.uk/consultations/party-political-referendum-rules/ (accessed 20 November 2012). The consultation also includes consideration of local television carrying party political broadcasts.

[48] Ofcom Content Sanctions Committee, *Bloomberg LP* (25 November 2005).

Questions for discussion

1. Ofcom emphasised that the test for impartiality was based on transmission, not other efforts. It also noted that Bloomberg was a niche channel with a specialised audience (the business community) and the programme was unlikely to have been seen outside this audience. Is this a sensible response? Would it be feasible in relation to niche channels, for example, to make clear the efforts re invitations and then broadcast?

2. In a multichannel environment is it appropriate that the public should actually be denied access to information and opinion as Ofcom is suggesting in circumstances such as these?

Rules 6.2 and 6.3 emphasise that due weight must be given to the coverage of the major parties during an election period and to designated organisations during a referendum period. However, 'broadcasters must also consider giving appropriate coverage to other parties and independent candidates with significant views and perspectives' (rule 6.2). A similar obligation applies for referendums (rule 6.3). Broadcasters are also restricted in the broadcasting of other (non-political) programmes in which a candidate may appear. Unless the programme was planned or scheduled prior to the election or referendum period, no such programmes can be broadcast (rule 6.7). The BBC also covers obligations of impartiality during elections and referendums in the Editorial Guidelines (sections 4.4.24–4.4.28 and 10) and separate guidelines are issued for each election campaign. Both the Broadcasting Code and the Editorial Guidelines permit impartiality to be achieved over a range of programmes, although obviously the time frame may be tighter.

Extract 4.4.6
BBC, Editorial Guidelines, section 10.4.18

The way in which due impartiality is achieved between parties will vary, depending upon the format, output and platform. It may be done in a single item, a single programme, a series of programmes or items, or over the course of the campaign as a whole. But programme makers and content producers must take responsibility for achieving due impartiality in their own output and not rely on other BBC content or services to redress any imbalance for them.

However, on some occasions, the programme itself may be regarded of such significance that impartiality cannot be achieved. In 1995, during a Scottish local election period, the BBC planned to broadcast an interview with the then Prime Minister, John Major, on *Panorama*. The broadcast would have occurred three days before the election. The interdict (injunction), which prevented the broadcast in Scotland until the close of the polls, was obtained only a few hours before the programme was due to be broadcast.[49]

Source: © 2010 BBC.

The following discussion by Munro provides a good overview of the issues.

---

[49] An appeal was dismissed only half an hour before the programme was due to be broadcast. The following day, leave to appeal to the House of Lords was refused: *Houston v British Broadcasting Corporation* 1995 SLT 1305.

Extract 4.4.7
C. Munro, 'The Banned Broadcasting Corporation' [1995] *New Law Journal* 518, 519–20 [footnotes omitted]

The circumstances

. . . For the pursuers, it was argued that an extended interview with the party leader on the BBC's flagship current affairs programme would give the Conservatives an advantage, when corresponding opportunities had not been made available to Messrs Blair and Ashdown. For the defenders, counsel tried to deny that a searching interview need be viewed as advantageous, and tried to deny that the subject matter would be very relevant to local elections, whereas the pursuers had argued that it was naïve to suggest that British political issues and local political issues were separable.

More generally, it was argued for the BBC that it was the *totality* of political coverage which fell to be considered, and that over time or over a series of programmes they would treat the political parties with due impartiality, as was always their aim.

However, the issue was crucially sharpened by the proximity of the local elections being held in Scotland on April 6, a few weeks ahead of elections in England . . .

Significantly, the BBC also appeared to have failed to make arrangements to afford equal or reasonable prominence to other party leaders in the run-up to the election . . .

Comment

Some caution is advisable, in case too much weight is given to the *Panorama* decision, which was, after all, only argued on an interim interdict basis, and hurriedly at that. That said, it needs to be remembered that applications for interim interdicts or injunctions are very important in practice, because matters often need not or do not proceed beyond that stage.

So far as the media are concerned, restraints on publications are erosions of their freedom, even when the ban is temporary rather than permanent . . .

. . . One wonders if the Court of Session did not act rather precipitately in banning a single television programme of uncertain influence when, apart from other considerations, there was still a period of two clear days in which perceived imbalances or partiality might have been redressed. In the result, the courts have cast themselves in the role of censors, and their actions have formed an unattractive precedent. It is understandable that Mr Tony Hall (the BBC's Managing Director of News and Current Affairs) should regard the decision as an 'objector's charter', and that Mr Michael Grade (the chief executive of Channel 4) should fear that 'we are all going to be in the courts forever'.

The suggestion that some margin of discretion may be applicable is arguably reflected in a matter that arose in the context of the 1997 General Election. During that campaign there was discussion about the possibility of a televised debate between the main party leaders. There were difficulties in reaching agreement about what would be fair between the parties, so the debate did not proceed.[50] However, before this became clear, the Scottish National Party, fearing that their party leader would not be included, commenced proceedings for an interdict to prevent the debate on the ground that it would infringe the impartiality rules. The application was dismissed by the Court of Session on the ground that the matter was hypothetical since no arrangements for the debate had been concluded. However, the Court did consider the responsibilities of impartiality.

[50] C. Munro, 'The 1997 General Election and Media Law' (1997) 2(5) *Communications Law* 166, 167.

Extract 4.4.8
Scottish National Party v Scottish Television plc and another, 15 April 1997, LEXIS
(Court of Session, Outer House)

LORD EASSIE:

It might also be said indeed that an interview with one political spokesman must by definition involve partiality and that where several viewpoints obtain, a programme which gives scope to only some of them, will, in isolation, also be partial. For that very practical reason also it is in my view plain that in judging whether a licensee is observing due impartiality, particularly in the context of political broadcasting in an election campaign, it is the generality or entirety of the broadcasting output in the relevant field to which one must look, rather than to a single programme in isolation.

While the approach of the Court appears to be a practical one, it may limit the scope for parties to challenge decisions taken by broadcasters. As Munro has commented:

> Once it is accepted that the obligation to preserve 'due impartiality' can only properly be judged across a range of programmes and over time, then there will in any event be difficulties in abstracting any particular programme or programmes, because there may always be others to put in the equation or additional or balancing programmes to be taken into account.[51]

Source: Reproduced by permission of Reed Elsevier (UK) Limited trading as LexisNexis. Copyright © 1997 LexisNexis.

Questions for discussion

1. Do you agree with Munro that the Court acted precipitately?
2. Should it be a relevant consideration for the Court as Munro seems to suggest that the influence of the programme might be uncertain?
3. If the circumstances of the *Panorama* interview arose today, would such a ban be effective? How would a Court today be likely to decide?
4. Comparing the *Scottish National Party* and the *Panorama* cases, do they suggest that it may be easier to establish a case the nearer one comes to the election date?

Another factor broadcasters may have to consider in trying to preserve impartiality during election and referendum periods over a range of programmes is the position of the devolved nations. During the 2010 General Election campaign the Plaid Cymru party complained to Ofcom about its exclusion from the 'First Election Debate' broadcast on the ITV network across the United Kingdom.[52] The debate had included the three major parties of the United Kingdom, the Conservative Party, the Labour Party, and the Liberal Democrats. Plaid Cymru argued that its exclusion meant that due impartiality had failed to be preserved and that for Welsh viewers the debate presented the election as a 'three horse race' whereas in Wales there were four major parties contesting the election.[53] Ofcom determined that the rules of impartiality did not require every party to be represented, rather only those parties which could properly be considered 'major parties across the UK as a whole'. The debate provided the public across the UK with an opportunity to hear from leaders who had a realistic prospect of forming the next UK government.[54] Further, Ofcom considered it relevant that the broadcaster notified

[51] Ibid., 168.
[52] Ofcom, *Decision of the Election Committee on a Due Impartiality Complaint Brought by the Plaid Cymru in relation to the 'First Election Debate', ITV1, 15 April 2010* (28 April 2010).
[53] Ibid., 2.
[54] Ibid., 6.

the audience in the devolved nations that there would be televised debates of the major parties in those nations, debating issues relevant to the devolved nations. The First Election Debate and the devolved debates were in Ofcom's view editorially linked within an appropriate time frame.[55]

The requirements of due impartiality are also emphasised in relation to coverage of a constituency (or 'electoral area' for local government elections) during elections (rules 6.8–6.10). Once nominations have closed, a report or discussion on a constituency must include the names of all the candidates (rule 6.11). Although the broadcaster must extend an invitation to all candidates, their refusal to appear will not prevent the broadcast proceeding. This is a change to the previous rules whereby the refusal of one candidate to appear effectively prevented the broadcast being aired.[56] The practical effect of the rule was that broadcasters rarely interviewed any of the candidates.[57] This former rule often had unintended consequences. For example, in one general election a broadcaster had to abandon plans to follow the progress of black candidates across the country because of a concern that other candidates could veto their appearance.[58] The former rule provides a good example of how rules designed to ensure balance could perversely have a chilling effect on debate. Although broadcasters are no longer hamstrung by this virtual veto, they will still have to keep in mind their impartiality obligations. The *Guidance Notes, Section 6: Elections and Referendums*, illustrate the type of considerations a broadcaster will have to take into account, for example when profiling candidates or constituencies.

(d) Referendum broadcasts and impartiality

Section 333 of the Communications Act 2003 requires broadcasters to include coverage of referendum campaigns. Prior to the 2003 Act, there were no specific obligations regarding referendum coverage, although in practice the broadcasters allocated time. However, this invoked their impartiality obligations and potentially created some difficulty if the political parties were likely all to favour a particular position. In the 1979 referendum on Scottish devolution, the approach to allocation of broadcast time was challenged. The then equivalent of Channel 3 (and the BBC, although they were not a party to the proceedings) had allocated one political broadcast to each of the four main Scottish political parties using an approach similar to that used for election broadcasts. However, this was likely to result in three broadcasts advocating a 'yes' vote and only one 'no' vote broadcast. The petitioners successfully argued that the broadcaster had failed in its statutory duty to maintain a proper balance.[59]

Legislative provisions and Ofcom's rules should now minimise the difficulties that arose in *Wilson*. Pursuant to section 127(1) of the Political Parties, Elections and Referendums Act 2000 referendum broadcasts can only be allocated to organisations designated under section 108 of the 2000 Act. Designated organisations are organisations which are permitted participants (section 105). Permitted participants are individuals or bodies who are recognised as referendum campaigners. A participant designated by the Electoral Commission will be recognised as the lead campaigner for one of the outcomes of the referendum, for example for the 'yes' outcome or for the 'no' outcome. The Electoral

---

[55] Ibid., 7–8.
[56] This rule was required because of section 93 of the Representation of the People Act 1983, which has now been repealed.
[57] Ofcom, *Guidance Notes, Section 6: Elections and Referendums* (16 December 2009), 1.
[58] *Press Gazette*, 30 August 1996, 14.
[59] *Wilson* v *Independent Broadcasting Authority* 1979 SLT 279.

Commission must designate an organisation for each outcome or not at all (section 108(2)). These provisions should make it easier for broadcasters allocating broadcast time since the 'designated organisation' model severs the direct link between political parties and referendum positions, and the Ofcom rules make clear that the allocation of broadcasts will be equal for each designated organisation (rule 19). However, it is theoretically possible that there may be no designated organisation. Unless the Electoral Commission can designate an organisation for each of the possible referendum outcomes, it is not permitted to make any designation. This would mean that no one would be entitled to a referendum campaign broadcast and it may mean that broadcasters providing coverage of the referendum might face an even more sensitive role in meeting impartiality obligations. Whether or not there are designated organisations, rule 6.3 makes clear that broadcasters will have to exercise their judgement in coverage of referendums, and where there are designated organisations may not be able to rely simply on coverage of them.

Extract 4.4.9
Ofcom, Broadcasting Code (28 February 2011), rule 6.3

Due weight must be given to designated organisations in coverage during the referendum period. Broadcasters must also consider giving appropriate coverage to other permitted participants with significant views and perspectives.

Source: © Ofcom copyright 2006–11.

Questions for discussion

1.   Do the new arrangements mean that broadcasters will no longer have to concern themselves with the issues raised in *Wilson*?
2.   If a referendum is held at the same time as an election, what difficulties might arise for broadcasters in relation to their obligations to preserve 'due impartiality'?

(e) Content of party political and election broadcasts

While broadcasters are under obligations to ensure impartiality, the political parties and designated organisations are naturally free to promote their own views during political broadcasts. However, these broadcasts must comply with other programme standards as well as the general law. This can present difficulties for the broadcaster who will be responsible for the broadcast as transmitted. During the 2001 General Election, a registered party, opposed to abortion, the ProLife Alliance, was allocated a party election broadcast. The video it submitted for broadcast was refused transmission by the BBC (and other broadcasters) on the grounds that the video, because of its graphic imagery of aborted foetuses, would infringe taste and decency programme requirements. (This would now come under the harm and offence provisions of the Broadcasting Code.) ProLife had applied for a judicial review of the decision which was refused but allowed on appeal. However, the BBC successfully appealed to the House of Lords.[60] The House of Lords held, by a majority, that the BBC's decision had been lawful because it was applying programme rules which it was required to apply to political broadcasts as well as to its own programmes, and the BBC had not acted in a discriminatory, unreasonable or arbitrary manner.

[60] *R (ProLife Alliance)* v *British Broadcasting Corporation* [2004] 1 AC 185.

However, the decision has been criticised for its failure to give due weight to the party's freedom of expression rights.[61] Barendt has suggested that the Law Lords '. . . should have decided that the HRA establishes a right to freedom of political expression, the exercise of which can rarely be limited on the grounds of offensiveness'.[62]

Questions for discussion

1. Leaving aside the approach taken by the House of Lords, is it appropriate for rules such as those in the 'harm and offence' category to be applicable to party political broadcasts? Should 'context' have a greater role to play?
2. If the ProLife Alliance party political broadcast had been transmitted via the Internet, would there have been any regulatory consequences?

Political broadcasting is another area where regulatory strain can be seen. At a meeting of the BLG in 2010, it was noted that parties were publishing their party political broadcasts on their own website, sometimes prior to the broadcast: '. . . even if parties put up their PEBs on their websites before they have been broadcast, the broadcasters still have a right to not broadcast them if they are problematic and do not meet the rules/law on compliance'.[63]

4.5 REGULATION OF VIDEO ON-DEMAND PROGRAMME SERVICES

The Audiovisual Media Services Directive means that on-demand services will also have to comply with content standards, and, under the co-regulatory arrangements discussed earlier (see Chapter 3, Section 3.11), ATVOD has regulatory responsibility for developing and determining compliance with the content standards. Standards relating to advertising are the responsibility of the Advertising Standards Authority, although ATVOD is responsible for sponsorship and product placement rules (see Chapter 6, Section 6.6). The content standards under the jurisdiction of the ATVOD are set out in section 368E of the Communications Act 2003. ATVOD has developed a code, Rules & Guidance (Statutory Rules and Non-Binding Guidance for Providers of On-Demand Programme Services (ODPS)) (ODPS Code).[64] The ODPS Code rules essentially replicate the language of section 368E: rule 10 deals with material which may be likely to incite hatred and rule 11 with the protection of under-18s from harmful material. In relation to rule 11, the guidance given by ATVOD is quite extensive and is of interest in the way that it picks up on government intended policy concerning sexually explicit material, even though it is not part of the regulatory framework. It has been argued that the precautionary approach '. . . risked driving legitimate ODPS providers of "adult" content offshore, depriving UK citizens of the protection of UK regulation'.[65]

---

[61] E. Barendt, 'Free Speech and Abortion' [2003] *PL* 580–91.
[62] Ibid., 591. See also Hare, note 6 above, who suggests that the courts have distanced themselves from the deference shown to broadcasters in the *ProLife* decision: at 32.
[63] Broadcasters' Liaison Group (BLG) Meeting, *Notes of conclusions and action points* (2 September 2010), http://www.broadcastersliaisongroup.org.uk/docs/Meeting_2_Sep_2010.pdf (accessed 19 October 2012), 2.
[64] Edition 2.0, 3 May 2012.
[65] Ofcom, *Review of the Ofcom Designation of the Authority for Television on Demand* (15 August 2012), http://stakeholders.ofcom.org.uk/binaries/consultations/on-demand/statement/statement.pdf (accessed 22 October 2012), para 5.15. The argument was made by an ODPS provider of adult content.

Questions for discussion

1. Do you see any difficulties with ATVOD adopting an approach which reflects government policy?
2. Why should the precautionary approach drive legitimate ODPS providers offshore?

ATVOD assumed regulatory responsibility for dealing with complaints in relation to the Code in September 2010. Since that time, the vast majority of complaints have been in relation to rule 11 and, in most cases, the issue, once the content has been determined as harmful, has been the question of access and protection of under-18s.

Extract 4.5.1
ATVOD, *Determination that the Provider of the On Demand Programme Service 'English Milf' was in breach of Rule 11*, 2 July 2012, 1, 4, 6–7

. . . English Milf is a website on-demand adult programme service, notified to ATVOD as having been available since April 26 2012. The service provider describes its content as 'Adult oriented video files and photo sets'.

. . .

Since much of the content available on the service appeared to be equivalent to that rated 'R18' by the BBFC [British Board of Film Classification] its provision falls within the scope of Rule 11. Specifically, ATVOD was satisfied that the content met the high statutory test of material which might seriously impair, and that ATVOD's precautionary approach meant an effective Content Access Control system was essential.

ATVOD therefore examined how a consumer might access the material and what access controls were in place.

. . .

Determination

While ATVOD acknowledges the action that has been undertaken to date to obscure R18 level detail from images in front of the paywall, this does not affect the finding that a breach has occurred. ATVOD does not consider a tick box system to constitute effective age verification, as it is easily penetrated by those under eighteen.

. . .

ATVOD notes the service provider's assertion that payment processors cannot differentiate debit and credit cards. It is the service provider's responsibility to ensure that R18 level content is made available in a manner which secures that persons under eighteen will not normally see or hear it. If the service provider cannot do this then the R18 level content should be removed. It is not the responsibility of the regulator to find technical solutions for commercial service providers. In any case, ATVOD does not accept the claim that an effective CAC System is not practicable, as other service providers have found satisfactory solutions.

To date most cases have resulted in ATVOD accepting changes to the service, although some services have subsequently closed rather than make the service compliant. However, ATVOD is also mindful of the limits of its remit in relation to content. In 2011 it considered a complaint in relation to an ODPS provided by Channel 4, 4OD, regarding a feature film, *Mr Woodcock*, which had caused considerable distress to the complainant viewer.

Extract 4.5.2
ATVOD, *Determination of ATVOD on a complaint that the On Demand Programme Service 4OD included unsuitable or harmful content. Complaint AT126WSPBY (Mr Woodcock)*, 29 March 2012, 1–4

. . .

The service

. . . Channel 4 Television is the provider of this service, which offers content derived from Channel 4, More 4 and E4 under the 4OD and Film4 On Demand brands. Programming is described as 'Catch-up' – approx 50 hrs/week made up primarily of peak content which has been transmitted between 6pm and 11pm; 'Archive' – a maximum of 600 hours at any one time taken from Channel 4's back catalogue and a pay-per-view feature film service.

. . . The complainant had viewed a feature film on a TalkTalk TV set top box.

The complaint

. . .

The complainant referred to having suffered abuse as a child (physical abuse and being terrorised) in the 1950's and 1960's which had resulted in enduring anxiety and depression. The complainant's life had been ruined by the abuse.

The complainant had accessed the film as a pay-per-view 'rather hoping it was a film about an abuser getting his come-uppance.' Instead, in the complainant's view, the film poured scorn on the abused, suggesting they should 'embrace their past'. The complainant described the film as offensive to someone who had been abused and the experience of viewing the film subject to the complaint as 'like being raped psychologically', and urged its withdrawal.

. . .

Investigation and consideration

It was recognised that viewing the film had clearly caused significant distress and offence to the complainant. It was also noted that 4OD had provided an adequate level of information to viewers in advance of their accessing the film.

However, it was further noted that ATVOD is not empowered to enforce any standards in relation to content which might cause offence and distress *per se*, or to exercise any restraint over the provision of such material on demand. Rather, ATVOD's review of the VOD content complained of is limited to compliance with the statutory requirements (likely to incite hatred and serious impairment to under 18's as referred to above), neither of which is relevant to this complaint. ATVOD therefore determines that there has been no breach of the rules.

i) Material likely to incite hatred (ATVOD Rule 10)

This is a very high and specific test of programme content, and one which is very rarely contravened by any audio visual material in the UK. The sub-committee noted that as none of the content of the film alluded to race, sex, religion or nationality there could be no question of the film inciting hatred. There could therefore be no breach of Rule 10.

ii) Protection of the under-18's

While the complainant is not under the age of 18, and was not complaining of children being able to access the film, it was felt that the film and the complaint should be considered in the light of Rule 11, which is concerned with *'material which might seriously impair the physical, mental or moral development of persons under the age of eighteen'*. Protection of young people against potential harm from such material – generally hard-core pornography – is secured by use of robust access controls.

[. . .]

[T]he BBFC classification of *Mr. Woodcock* is '12'. It is very hard to envisage how a film so classified could simultaneously be held to *seriously impair* the moral, mental or physical development of minors (in general).

. . .

While the film may not be to everyone's taste, it is a comedy: it is hard to see any serious message about the real world which could affect children's development. Unless one takes the view that comedic treatment is not permissible for such subject matter, it cannot be held to condone or trivialise psychological or physical abuse . . .

The test is not whether even a vulnerable minor who has been abused would be further victimised or distressed by the film. It is whether development of persons under 18 would be seriously impaired.

. . .

In the period 1 January 2011 to 31 December 2011, ATVOD received 493 complaints, of which 339 were referred to the service provider initially and were not subsequently referred to ATVOD, while 154 were referred to ATVOD. Of the 154 complaints, 153 were closed after an initial assessment because they were considered 'out of remit', because they did not relate to an ODPS or the issue did not relate to a matter within ATVOD's jurisdiction. Only one case was subject to a full investigation during that period and the complaint was upheld.[66]

4.6 ENFORCEMENT PROCEDURES AND SANCTIONS

(a) Introduction

Although broadcasters and specialist regulatory authorities will be responsible for ensuring compliance with the standards reviewed in this chapter, Ofcom may also have a role in the enforcement process and the imposition of sanctions. Ofcom's authority may arise through direct regulatory responsibility, for example as regulator of licensed broadcasting services, or because it has regulatory authority over the BBC for certain aspects of content. In other cases, Ofcom's responsibility will be the product of co-regulatory arrangements such as those with ATVOD, or in the case of advertising with the Advertising Standards Authority (see Chapter 6, Section 6.5). This section reviews the enforcement procedures and approaches towards the imposition of sanctions.

(b) Ofcom and broadcasting services

Ofcom is responsible for ensuring that standards are in place to provide protection for the public and secure compliance with the content and fairness and privacy standards. Given the number of complaints received each year it would not be feasible for Ofcom to carry out a full investigation in relation to every complaint received. For example, during the period 1 April 2011 to 31 March 2012, Ofcom received around 24,400 complaints about content standards.[67] Nevertheless the potential impact of sanctions means that

---

[66] ATVOD, *Review of the Designation ATVOD Submission, Annex B: Report to Ofcom for the period 1 January–31 December 2011* (30 May 2012), http://stakeholders.ofcom.org.uk/binaries/broadcast/tv-ops/responses/atvod_responses/annexB.pdf (accessed 21 November 2012), para 4.8. ATVOD's handling of complaints, such as *Mr Woodcock*, was relevant to Ofcom's review of ATVOD.

[67] Ofcom, *Annual Report and Accounts for the period 1 April 2011 to 31 March 2012*, 112.

Ofcom must exercise procedural fairness. Ofcom has a statutory duty to establish procedures for the handling and resolution of complaints (section 325(2), Communications Act 2003) and has published its procedures: *Procedures for Investigating Breaches of Content Standards for Television and Radio* (1 June 2011) (Content Standards Procedures).[68] Ofcom has also published procedures for dealing with infringements of the fairness and privacy codes: *Procedures for the Consideration and Adjudication of Fairness & Privacy Complaints* (1 June 2011) (Fairness and Privacy Procedures).[69]

In relation to the consideration of breaches of content standards, Ofcom may initiate its own investigation as well as entertain complaints from any person or body (Content Standards Procedures, paras 1.6–1.7). Complainants are encouraged to follow the complaints procedures provided by the broadcaster before complaining to Ofcom. Simultaneous complaints can be lodged, but Ofcom will not usually proceed until the broadcaster has had an opportunity to resolve the matter (para 1.16). If a broadcaster fails to respond or the complainant is not satisfied, then the complaint can proceed to Ofcom. The requirement that the complainant should first try to resolve the matter with the broadcaster might seem a sensible way to manage the volume of complaints, many of which may not disclose a code matter. However, it means, and subject to any processes the broadcaster may have in place to ensure independence, the complainant has to take the complaint to the very body about whom they are complaining. The Code rules are not dealing with individual harms (in contrast to the Fairness and Privacy Codes), but with the impact of programmes on a broader constituency and the public interest in the standards being observed. It is always open to Ofcom to investigate if it considers the matter serious enough and it will probably do so. However, the requirement to try to resolve the matter first with the broadcaster is a reflection of Ofcom's statutory responsibility to minimise unnecessary regulatory intervention (see Chapter 3, Section 3.3).

Ofcom manages the volume of complaints by first conducting a preliminary review to determine whether the complaint (or complaints) raises substantive issues under the Broadcasting Code to warrant an investigation (Content Standards Procedures, para 1.18). Ofcom will then consider whether there may have been a breach of the Broadcasting Code (para 1.20). Where Ofcom considers that a breach is sufficiently serious to warrant the imposition of a sanction, it will then apply its *Procedures for the Consideration of Statutory Sanctions in Breaches of Broadcast Licences* (1 June 2011), considered in Section 4.6(c) below.

When dealing with Fairness and Privacy Complaints, Ofcom will only consider complaints made by 'the person affected' (which can include organisations) or a person authorised to make the complaint on their behalf (Fairness and Privacy Procedures, para 1.6). As with content standards complaints, the complainant should attempt to resolve the matter first with the broadcaster (para 1.7). It will be remembered that in the *Russell Brand Show* matter, the issue of whether a proper complaint had been made was raised (see Section 4.3(b) above). Ofcom's Fairness and Privacy Procedures address this and Ofcom will only consider complaints submitted through 'the completion of Ofcom's Fairness and Privacy Complaint form', but this stricture is qualified 'Ofcom will normally . . .' (para 1.8). In exceptional circumstances, Ofcom may consider fairness or privacy matters in the absence of a complaint, if it considers that the protection of the public warrants such a path (para 1.5).

---

[68] Available at http://stakeholders.ofcom.org.uk/broadcasting/guidance/complaints-sanctions/standards/ (accessed 22 October 2012).

[69] Available at http://stakeholders.ofcom.org.uk/broadcasting/guidance/complaints-sanctions/fairness/ (accessed 22 October 2012).

(c) Ofcom and sanctions

Ofcom's sanctioning role will arise not only in relation to matters which it has directly determined, but also through the co-regulatory arrangements. Although the type of sanctions which can be imposed are similar, Ofcom has separate procedures for the co-regulation sanctions (see Section 4.6(e) below). Only the more serious breaches will be likely to attract sanctions.

Extract 4.6.1
Ofcom, *Procedures for the consideration of statutory sanctions in breaches of broadcast licences* (1 June 2011), paras 1.10–1.11 [footnotes omitted]

1.10 The imposition of a sanction against a broadcaster is a serious matter. Ofcom may, following due process, impose a sanction if it considers that a broadcaster has seriously, deliberately, repeatedly, or recklessly breached a relevant requirement.

1.11 The sanctions available to Ofcom include a decision to:

- issue a direction not to repeat a programme or advertisement;
- issue a direction to broadcast a correction or a statement of Ofcom's findings which may be required to be in such form, and to be included in programmes at such times, as Ofcom may determine;
- impose a financial penalty;
- shorten or suspend a licence (only applicable in certain cases) and/or
- revoke a licence (not applicable to the BBC, S4C or Channel 4).

Financial penalty

In most cases the maximum financial penalty for commercial television or radio licensees is £250,000 or 5% of the broadcaster's 'Qualifying Revenue', whichever is the greater.

For licensed Public Service Broadcasters the maximum financial penalty payable is 5% of the broadcaster's 'Qualifying Revenue'. For the BBC or S4C, the maximum financial penalty payable is £250,000.

Source: © Ofcom copyright 2006–11.

Ofcom's *Procedures for the Consideration of Statutory Sanctions in Breaches of Broadcast Licences* (1 June 2011) (Sanctions Procedures) set out the process Ofcom will follow when deciding whether or not to impose a sanction.[70] However, when dealing with a breach of the content or the fairness and privacy standards by a licensed service, it may proceed to impose a direction upon the broadcaster without invoking the Sanctions Procedures (Content Standards Procedures, paras 1.34–1.35 and Fairness and Privacy Procedures, para 1.32).

In place of the former Sanctions Committee, two executive members of the Ofcom senior executive and a non-executive member of the Ofcom Content Board make sanction decisions. Ofcom will write to the broadcaster, if it considers a sanction may be appropriate, setting out, inter alia, Ofcom's preliminary views as to the type and level of sanction and the matters it has taken into account in reaching that view. The broadcaster will be invited to make representations before Ofcom makes its final decision (Sanctions Procedures, paras 1.17–1.20). Financial penalty decisions will be made in accordance with the Ofcom Penalty Guidelines while revocation of licences will follow the statutory

---

[70] Available at http://stakeholders.ofcom.org.uk/broadcasting/guidance/complaints-sanctions/procedures-statutory-sanctions/.

provisions for revocation where applicable (Sanctions Procedures, paras 1.25–1.26).[71] Ofcom is required by section 392(1) of the Communications Act 2003 to publish a statement of the guidelines to be followed in imposing penalties.

Extract 4.6.2
Ofcom, *Penalty Guidelines* (13 June 2011), paras 3–4, 6, 8, 10

3. Ofcom will consider all the circumstances of the case in the round in order to determine the appropriate and proportionate amount of any penalty. The central objective of imposing a penalty is deterrence. The amount of any penalty must be sufficient to ensure that it will act as an effective incentive to compliance, having regard to the seriousness of the infringement.

4. The factors taken into account in each case will vary, depending on what is relevant. Some examples of potentially relevant factors are:

- the degree of harm, whether actual or potential, caused by the contravention, including any increased cost incurred by consumers or other market participants;
- the duration of the contravention;
- any gain (financial or otherwise) made by the regulated body in breach (or any connected body) as a result of the contravention;
- any steps taken for remedying the consequences of the contravention;
- whether the regulated body in breach has a history of contraventions (repeated contraventions may lead to significantly increased penalties);
- whether in all the circumstances appropriate steps had been taken by the regulated body to prevent the contravention;
- the extent to which the contravention occurred intentionally or recklessly, including the extent to which senior management knew, or ought to have known, that a contravention was occurring or would occur;
- whether the contravention in question continued, or timely and effective steps were taken to end it, once the regulated body became aware of it; and
- the extent to which the level of penalty is proportionate, taking into account the size and turnover of the regulated body.

6. Ofcom will have regard to any relevant precedents set by previous cases, but may depart from them depending on the facts and the context of each case.

8. Ofcom may increase the penalty where the regulated body in breach has failed to cooperate fully with our investigation.

10. Ofcom will have regard to any representations made to us by the regulated body in breach.

Source: © Ofcom copyright 2006–11.

In the Russell Brand matter (see Section 4.3(b) above) Ofcom imposed a financial penalty on the BBC of £150,000. Press TV was licensed as a television licensable content service. Ofcom determined that it had breached rules 7.1 and 8.1 of the Broadcasting Code following its broadcast of an interview with Mr Maziar Bahari, who was then a prisoner in Iran, detained on suspicion of spying and facing the possibility of a death sentence. Ofcom held an oral hearing and in its decision reviewed the basis for imposing a statutory sanction and a financial penalty and imposed a penalty of

---

[71] Ofcom, *Penalty Guidelines* (13 June 2011). Available at http://www.ofcom.org.uk/about/policies-and-guidelines/penalty-guidelines/ (accessed 26 October 2012).

£100,000.[72] Shortly after this sanction was imposed, Ofcom revoked Press TV's licence on the ground that it was not satisfied that the licence holder was the person who was in general control of the television service as required by section 362(2) of the Communications Act 2003. The licensee was Press TV, based in London, but during the sanctions hearing it appeared that editorial control may have been with Press TV International (based in Tehran). Press TV did not respond to Ofcom's communications on the matter and Ofcom revoked the licence in January 2012.[73]

Questions for discussion

1. Review the Russell Brand sanctions decision. What factors in the Sanctions and Penalty Guidelines were particularly relevant to the decision to impose a financial penalty, and the level?
2. Review the *Press TV* sanctions decision. What different factors influenced the Press TV determination and the amount of the financial penalty?
3. Public broadcasters are subject to a lesser penalty than commercial broadcasters because it is considered that a heavy financial penalty will adversely affect the availability of licence fee payers' money for programme making. Is the commercial situation necessarily so different, especially in the case of PST?

Ofcom has been willing to impose very heavy financial penalties, even on the mainstream public and public service broadcasters. Following a lengthy investigation into ITV, Channels 4 and 5, commercial radio and the BBC concerning the conduct of viewer and listener competitions, fines of around £10 million were imposed across the sector and new Broadcasting Code rules were drafted.[74] By contrast, licence revocation seems more likely to be imposed on the niche services than the mainstream terrestrial broadcasters. In 2010, Ofcom revoked four licences – three television licensable content services and one digital television programme service – held by the Bang Media group, for repeated breaches of the Broadcasting Code in relation to the provisions dealing with harm and offence and the protection of under-18s (and breaches of advertising rules). Given the repeated breaches and failure to demonstrate an intention to meet regulatory responsibilities, Ofcom determined that it was no longer satisfied that the licensees were fit and proper persons to hold the licences under sections 3(3)(b) of the Broadcasting Act 1990 and 3(3)(b) of the Broadcasting Act 1996 (see Chapter 3, Section 3.6).

---

[72] Ofcom, *Decision by the Broadcasting Sanctions Committee, Press TV Limited*, for breaches of the Ofcom Broadcasting Code (1 December 2011, BSC 68(11)). This and the Russell Brand sanctions decisions are too long to extract sensibly but they can be viewed at http://stakeholders.ofcom.org.uk/binaries/enforcement/content-sanctions-adjudications/press-tv.pdf (accessed 26 October 2012) and http://www2.ofcom.org.uk/tv/obb/ocsc_adjud/BBCRadio2TheRussellBrandShow.pdf (accessed 23 October 2012), respectively.

[73] Ofcom, *Revocation, Provider of the Service Press TV Limited*. The financial penalty was not paid and Press TV had indicated that it was unwilling to pay.

[74] The sanctions adjudications can be found in full on the Ofcom website, Broadcasting Sanctions Adjudications at http://stakeholders.ofcom.org.uk/enforcement/content-sanctions-adjudications/?a=0. Summaries of the determinations and the financial penalties can also be found at Ofcom, *Annual Report and Accounts for the period 1 April 2007 to 31 March 2008*, 20–1 and *Annual Report and Accounts for the period 1 April 2008 to 31 March 2009*, 20.

Extract 4.6.3
Ofcom, *Bang Media (London) Ltd and Bang Channels Ltd: Notice of Revocation of Licences*, Statement (25 November 2010), paras 1.36–1.38

Revocation

1.36 In Ofcom's view, the numerous and repeated breaches of the relevant standards codes and Condition 11 by the Licensees over an extended period of time, despite formal breach findings, the imposition of a statutory sanction, and the provision by Ofcom of various guidance, demonstrated a disregard for their licence obligations, including their obligation to comply with the Code, and for the regulatory regime as a whole. By providing guidance to the industry and to the Licensees, as well as making numerous breach findings and imposing a financial penalty, Ofcom provided ample opportunity for the Licensees to ensure that they were aware that such material was considered unacceptable for broadcast. However, such material continued to be broadcast, and has persisted since sending the Licensees the notice of proposed revocation, resulting in the further nine breach findings relating to material broadcast between 9 November 2010 and 16 November 2010. This pattern of similar breaches by the Licensees, in particular the frequency and degree of repetition over such a short period of time, is unprecedented.

1.37 The actions of the Licensees demonstrated that the imposition of financial penalties would have been highly unlikely to result in the Licensees ensuring compliance with the provisions of the Code in the future. The financial penalty of £157,250 which was imposed on the Licensees on 29 July 2010 was immediately followed by three further breaches of the Broadcasting Code and a further nine similar breaches of the BCAP Code have been recorded since the issue of the notice of intention to revoke on 2 November 2010. The penalty has therefore clearly failed to have the required deterrent effect. Indeed, the penalty remains unpaid and Ofcom is pursuing this as a separate matter. In Ofcom's view, imposing further financial penalties under section 237 of the [2003] Act would therefore be unlikely to safeguard against further breaches, taking into account the conduct of the Licensees over this period, and would not therefore be an effective remedy.

1.38 Indeed, Ofcom has evidence that the Licensees are continuing to breach the direction to cease broadcasting despite the Licensees' representations that new compliance systems will be put in place and that those responsible for the lack of compliance in the past have been removed from their positions. The Licensees' representations did not provide any substantial proposals for improving compliance with the relevant codes in the future. Ofcom cannot therefore be satisfied with any level of certainty in those circumstances that sufficient changes have been made to the structure of the Licensees and their compliance arrangements that further serious repeated breaches of the licensing regime will not occur.

Source: © Ofcom copyright 2006–11.

Questions for discussion

1. The breaches by the mainstream broadcasters in relation to the conduct of competitions were found to be repeated, and were regarded as serious failures of trust. What, and having regard to Extract 4.6.3, would be needed before revocation was ordered?

2. What other factors might come into play regarding revocation of a mainstream broadcaster compared with a pay television service?

(d) Public broadcasting

Although Ofcom will have a role to play in relation to BBC public services and BBC licensed services, the BBC is responsible for dealing with complaints in relation to those content matters not covered by the Ofcom Broadcasting Code.[75] In addition, the BBC has formal processes for dealing with all complaints received in relation to its Editorial Guidelines and/or the Broadcasting Code. The BBC Trust has overall responsibility for determining the complaints framework, although BBC management (the Executive) considers complaints in the first instance.[76] The Trust steps in to consider appeals from complainants who remain dissatisfied with the Executive's response, although the Trust will only step in if the complaint raises a matter of substance.[77] The current framework protocol was published in June 2012 following a review of the complaints framework commenced in 2011. The review was intended to improve complaints processes to ensure simpler, faster and more streamlined, consistent and transparent processes. It was also conducted in the context of a huge increase in the number of complaints received by the BBC: over 123,000 in 2007–8 to approximately 240,000 in 2010–11.[78] It should be remembered that the BBC complaints framework covers all BBC services including BBC publications and websites.

The relevant set of procedures for dealing with editorial complaints concerning BBC content is *BBC Complaints Framework, Procedure no 1: Editorial complaints and appeals procedure* (26 June 2012) (Editorial Complaints Procedure).[79] The BBC understands an editorial complaint to be a complaint about any BBC content that has allegedly failed to follow the Editorial Guidelines (para 1.1). Essentially the complaints process has three stages, with dissatisfied complainants progressing from the Executive, through to the Editorial Complaints Unit and the BBC Trust.[80] The Trust is not obliged to consider every appeal request and will only consider appeals that raise matters of substance. Normally, a 'matter of substance' will mean that the Trust considers that there is a reasonable prospect that it will find a breach of the Editorial Guidelines (paras 5.8 and 5.10). It is interesting to observe the extent to which, in determining its process, the Trust must have regard to matters not directly relevant to the matter in hand but related more to its public broadcaster role.

---

[75] For details of the S4C complaints procedures, see http://www.s4c.co.uk/e_complaint_procedure.shtml#ID3.

[76] See BBC Trust, *BBC Protocol E3 – Complaints Framework* (26 June 2012), www.bbc.co.uk/bbctrust/governance/complaints_framework (accessed 26 October 2012). The complaints framework also covers other types of complaints, in addition to editorial complaints, such as complaints about television licensing, fair trading and any general complaints. Associated with the complaints framework protocol are sets of procedures covering each type of complaint, including procedure 1 for editorial complaints. The complaints framework and procedures can be viewed at http://www.bbc.co.uk/bbctrust/governance/complaints_framework/ (accessed 26 October 2012).

[77] Ibid., para 2.4.

[78] BBC Trust, *Trust Review of BBC Complaints Framework: Conclusions* (May 2012), http://downloads.bbc.co.uk/bbctrust/assets/files/pdf/our_work/complaints_framework/2012/complaints_framework_review.pdf (accessed 26 October 2012), 1–2.

[79] *BBC Complaints Framework, Procedure no 5: party political broadcast, party election broadcast and referendum campaign broadcast complaints procedure* (26 June 2012) deals with complaints relating to party political broadcasts.

[80] The procedures also cover, with some variations, complaints by persons directly affected by BBC content (called 'first party complaints') with respect to unfair treatment or unwarranted invasions of privacy. There are also time limits in which complaints must be made. The BBC won't investigate some complaints, for example if they are vexatious or gratuitously abusive or offensive.

Extract 4.6.4
**BBC Trust, *BBC Trust Committee Terms of Reference: Editorial Standards
Committee* (December 2011), para 5.20**

... It is up to the Trust to decide which approach is appropriate, proportionate and cost-
effective in relation to your appeal, and in making that decision it will take account of all relevant
circumstances, including its role as the final arbiter in appropriate cases, its duty to exercise
rigorous stewardship of public money, and its duty to hold the BBC Executive to account for the
BBC's compliance with applicable regulatory requirements and the general law.

Source: © 2011 BBC.

The full BBC Trust does not hear appeals, only a committee of the Trust, the Editorial
Standards Committee, comprising normally five trustees. If an appeal is upheld, the BBC
Trust may:

(a) make an apology to the appellant;
(b) require the Executive to take remedial action to guard against the conduct happening
     again, and/or consider the appropriate disciplinary action;
(c) publish its findings; and/or
(d) require an on-air apology or correction (para 5.22).

Considering the number of complaints the BBC receives each year, the number actually
dealt with at appeal stage is relatively low. For the period 1 April 2011 to 31 March 2012,
the Editorial Standards Committee received 240 requests for appeal and agreed to hear 77,
rejecting the remainder on the ground that they did not have a reasonable prospect of
success. Of the 77 appeals, three were upheld, 23 were partially upheld and 51 were not
upheld.[81]

(e) Video on-demand programme services

ATVOD has primary responsibility for dealing with compliance failures and enforcement
and Ofcom has back-up statutory powers for certain sanctions. Pursuant to section 368C
of the Communications Act 2003, ATVOD must ensure that every provider complies with
the requirements of section 368D, which, in turn require compliance with sections 368E
to 368H (content and advertising rules). When determining a section 368D contravention,
ATVOD must ensure there are adequate grounds for believing that a contravention has
occurred and provide an opportunity for the ODPS provider to make representations
(section 368I(2)). ATVOD has published its procedure for dealing with complaints,
Procedure for Complaints about Editorial Content on VOD Services (Edition 1.2, 25 June
2012). Although members of the public can make complaints to ATVOD directly, it is
expected that they will have first tried to resolve the complaint with the ODPS provider,
although ATVOD can take action directly if it considers that a serious breach may have
taken place (paras 9–10). If the matter concerns material which may be likely to encourage
or incite the commission of a crime or lead to disorder, the complainant should go directly
to ATVOD (para 8). In such situations, ATVOD will refer the matter to Ofcom without
reference to the service provider so that Ofcom can take the action necessary to suspend
or restrict access to the service (para 34).

---

[81] BBC, *Annual Report and Accounts 2011/12* (July 2012), 1–19.

Once ATVOD becomes involved it will make a preliminary assessment and if it decides that the complaint raises potential compliance issues warranting further investigation, ATVOD Executive will investigate, and a sub-committee of the Board will consider and determine the complaint (para 19). The complainant and service provider can request a review by the full ATVOD board, less the members involved in the initial decision. In the case of a breach, ATVOD can issue an enforcement notification pursuant to section 368I. ATVOD had been required to consult with Ofcom prior to issuing a notification, but this requirement was removed following the 2012 review and renewal of ATVOD's designation.[82] An enforcement notification may require the provider to cease or to restrict access to a programme or programmes (or advertisement); to modify an advertisement; to provide additional information to users of the service; to publish a correction, and/or to publish a statement of ATVOD's findings. Alternatively, or if the breach continues, ATVOD may refer the matter to Ofcom for imposition of a financial penalty (section 368J) or suspension of the service (section 368K). A financial penalty cannot exceed five per cent of the provider's qualifying revenue or £250,000, whichever is the greater (section 368J(1)). Ofcom has procedures in place for dealing with sanctions.[83]

In the period 1 April 2011 to 31 March 2012, ATVOD received 602 complaints.[84] Of these, 206 were referred to the Authority because the complainant was dissatisfied with the response, and of these 204 were ruled out of remit after an initial assessment either because the service was not an ODPS or the complaint did not raise a breach of the statutory requirements. Of these one was upheld (the service subsequently ceased to operate) and one was found not to be in breach.

Selected further reading

Programme regulation, general

L. Hitchens, *Broadcasting Pluralism and Diversity: A Comparative Study in Policy and Regulation* (Oxford: Hart Publishing, 2006). Chapter 4 examines the role of programme regulation, in the United Kingdom, the United States and Australia, as an instrument in the promotion of media diversity.

H. Fenwick and G. Phillipson, *Media Freedom under the Human Rights Act* (Oxford: OUP, 2006) examines the impact of the Human Rights Act 1998 protection of freedom of expression on media regulation. Chapters 10, 11 and 20 are relevant to the aspects of programme regulation considered in this chapter.

Harm and offence

E. Barendt, 'Free speech and abortion' [2003] *Public Law* 580–91 examines judicial approaches to the freedom of political expression regarding party election broadcasts that may contain offensive material.

I. Hare, 'Insulting politicians on the radio' (2012) 4(1) *Journal of Media Law* 29–34 examines a judicial review challenge on the grounds of freedom of expression to an Ofcom decision.

---

[82] Ofcom, *Review of the Ofcom Designation of the Authority for Television on Demand*, Statement (15 August 2012), http://stakeholders.ofcom.org.uk/binaries/consultations/on-demand/statement/statement.pdf (accessed 22 October 2012), 28.

[83] Ofcom, *Procedures for the consideration of statutory sanctions arising in the context of on-demand programme services* (15 August 2012).

[84] ATVOD, *Annual Report 2011/12*, 12. These complaints may have also been for advertising/sponsorship breaches.

Political broadcasting and/or impartiality

S. Barnett, ' "Imposition or empowerment": freedom of speech, broadcasting and impartiality' in M. Amos, J. Harrison and L. Woods (eds), *Freedom of Expression and the Media* (Leiden: Martinus Nijhoff Publishers, 2012), 45–71. This provides a critical analysis of the role of impartiality and rules in broadcasting.

M. Feintuck, 'Impartiality in news coverage: the present and the future' in M. Amos, J. Harrison and L. Woods (eds), *Freedom of Expression and the Media* (Leiden: Martinus Nijhoff Publishers, 2012), 73–95 explores the difficulty of putting UK impartiality rules in practice.

I. Katsirea, 'Judicial review of party broadcasts in Germany and the United Kingdom' (2009) 2 *Journal of Media Law* 269–87 examines the scope for editorial control of party political broadcasts by regulatory authorities comparing the United Kingdom and Germany.

C. Munro, 'The Banned Broadcasting Corporation' [1995] *New Law Journal* 518 reviews a Scottish judicial decision to prohibit the BBC broadcasting an interview with the then Prime Minister during an election period.

On-demand services

D. Mac Síthigh, 'Co-regulation, video-on-demand and the legal status of audio-visual media' (2011) 2(1) *International Journal of Digital Television* 49–66 provides a very thorough account of the regulatory map for media, including video on-demand and the regulatory challenges posed by the Audiovisual Media Services Directive.

R. Craufurd-Smith, 'Determining regulatory competence for audiovisual media services in the European Union' (2011) 3(2) *Journal of Media Law* 263–85 examines the complexity of determining who has regulatory competence for the regulation of audiovisual media service providers under the directive.

5 European media law

5.1 INTRODUCTION

The locus of power in relation to media regulation has traditionally rested with the nation state. Although the printed press in many European countries had by the end of the nineteenth century freed itself from draconian sedition and libel laws, licensing regimes and stamp duties, the new forms of communication that developed in the first half of the twentieth century – film, radio and television – were met, for a variety of political and social reasons, with rapid assertions of state or government control. Of these 'new media', radio and television posed particular challenges for nation states, in that broadcasting signals cannot be contained within national borders. In Europe, many countries exist in close proximity and frequently share a common language: Germany, Austria and Switzerland are obvious examples. As a result, radio and subsequently television services broadcast from one country were often received in neighbouring countries. These technical overspills were largely incidental to the broadcaster's main focus of coverage and did not create major difficulties; indeed some countries benefited by establishing co-operation agreements enabling greater access to programme material.[1]

The development of cable and satellite technology made it easier for broadcasters to target foreign audiences and related commercial revenues. This form of broadcasting raised a number of questions. Who should be responsible for regulating the broadcast and its content? Was the receiving country free to prevent transmission of a foreign broadcasting service, particularly if it infringed national rules on content or advertising? As satellite broadcasting developed, and viewers started to receive services directly through their own receiving dishes, it was also apparent that governments might find it difficult to enforce regulation even where they considered it desirable or necessary.[2]

Within Europe, there is the potential to resolve these difficulties collaboratively through initiatives co-ordinated by one or both of two regional organisations: the Council of Europe, established in 1949, and the European Union (EU), which dates back to the European Economic Community (EEC), founded in 1957. This chapter examines the competence of these two organisations in the media field and how they have sought to facilitate the development of a European-wide market in audiovisual services.

Given their overlapping remits and membership, it was perhaps inevitable that there would be controversy over which organisation should take forward specific media initiatives. The Council of Europe, with its particular focus on protecting human rights, enhancing democratic government and promoting cultural co-operation, coupled with its wide membership base (currently 47 states, including Russia and Turkey), would seem a logical choice. The Council of Europe oversees the drafting and adoption of conventions, binding on those member states that sign and ratify them, of which the most important is

---

[1] F.W. Hondius, 'Regulating Transfrontier Television – The Strasbourg Option' (1988) 8 *Yearbook of European Law* 141, at 146.

[2] See, for example, Case 52/79 *Procureur du Roi* v *Marc JVC Debauve and Others* [1980] ECR 833, where the Belgian government did not enforce a copyright law that was being breached by cable operators, in part because it was aware that viewers were able to receive the protected content directly.

undoubtedly the 1950 European Convention for the Protection of Human Rights and Fundamental Freedoms (ECHR). In addition, its political organs, the Committee of Ministers and Parliamentary Assembly, have issued a range of non-binding recommendations and declarations relating to the mass media.[3]

The EU, with its narrower membership base (28 states with Croatia) and historic focus on economic integration, appears at first sight a less suitable forum for co-ordinating domestic media law and policy. On the other hand, EU law offers considerable advantages in terms of its effectiveness and the consistency of its implementation across the Member States. Key articles in the Treaty on the Functioning of the European Union (TFEU), particularly those relating to the free movement of goods, services, establishment and persons, can be enforced directly in domestic courts. EU binding secondary law takes the form of regulations, directives and decisions, of which directives must be implemented within a given time by the Member States in their domestic legal systems. Non-binding explanatory or advisory measures take the form of recommendations or opinions.

In reality, recourse to the Council of Europe or EU has never been a simple 'either/or' and both organisations have produced a range of legal instruments relating to the operation of communications networks, intellectual property rights, and the content and funding of media services.[4] This chapter focuses on the creation of an integrated European market for audiovisual services, but it is important to bear in mind that this is just one aspect of a wide range of media-related activities undertaken by the two institutions.

5.2 THE COUNCIL OF EUROPE – JURISDICTION

The aims of the Council of Europe are established in its founding statute, set out below.

Extract 5.2.1
Statute of the Council of Europe, London, 5 May 1949, ETS no 1, art 1

Article 1

a. The aim of the Council of Europe is to achieve a greater unity between its members for the purpose of safeguarding and realising the ideals and principles which are their common heritage and facilitating their economic and social progress.
b. This aim shall be pursued through the organs of the Council by discussion of questions of common concern and by agreements and common action in economic, social, cultural, scientific, legal and administrative matters and in the maintenance and further realisation of human rights and fundamental freedoms.

Source: © Council of Europe.

The Council of Europe has engaged with the media sector in two main ways. First, the ECHR has played an important role in clarifying the legitimate limits of state intervention in the media sector, with particular reference to article 10 ECHR (see Extract 1.2.1). Second, the Council has itself co-ordinated a number of important international agreements and soft law measures relating to the media.

As discussed in Chapter 1, the right to freedom of expression is not an unqualified right. As cross border broadcasting became more common, a key question for Member

---

[3] S. Nicoltchev and T. McGonagle (eds), *Freedom of Expression and the Media: Standard Setting by the Committee of Ministers of the Council of Europe* (European Audiovisual Observatory, Strasbourg 2011).
[4] See O. Castendyk, E.J. Dommering, A. Scheuer, *European Media Law* (Kluwer Law, Netherlands, 2008).

States was whether it was lawful under article 10 ECHR to impede the transmission, or to regulate the content of, foreign broadcasts and, if so, on what grounds. *Groppera Radio* was the first of a number of cases in which the ECtHR was called to consider exactly this question. A Swiss radio company, via a subsidiary, had intentionally broadcast radio programmes consisting mainly of light music and advertising from Italy into Switzerland. The programmes could be received directly over the air and were also relayed by cable companies within Switzerland. The purpose in setting up the station had been to evade the Swiss state broadcasting monopoly. The Swiss government prohibited cable operators from relaying programmes that did not comply with the relevant international radio and telecommunication laws, including those designed to ensure the orderly use of radio frequencies. The applicants challenged the prohibition before the ECHR arguing that it infringed their right to 'impart information and ideas . . . regardless of frontiers' under article 10.

Extract 5.2.2
Groppera Radio AG and Others v *Switzerland* (1990) 12 EHRR 321, at 337, 338–9, 340, 342–3 (footnotes omitted)

[T]he Court considers that both broadcasting of programmes over the air and cable retransmission of such programmes are covered by the right enshrined in the first two sentences of Article 10(1), without there being any need to draw distinctions according to the content of the programmes . . . [Having held that there was an interference by a public authority with the exercise of the Article 10 right, the Court had to consider whether that interference was justified. The answer to this turned on how the third sentence of Article 10(1) (entitling states to require licensing of broadcasting) was to be understood, and its relationship to Article 10(2).]

The insertion of the sentence in issue, at an advanced stage of the preparatory work on the Convention, was clearly due to technical or practical considerations such as the limited number of available frequencies and the major capital investment required for building transmitters. It also reflected a political concern on the part of several States, namely that broadcasting should be the preserve of the State. Since then, changed views and technical progress, particularly the appearance of cable transmission, have resulted in the abolition of State monopolies in many European countries and the establishment of private radio stations – often local ones – in addition to the public services. Furthermore, national licensing systems are required not only for the orderly regulation of broadcasting enterprises at the national level but also in large part to give effect to international rules . . .

The object and purpose of the third sentence of Article 10(1) and the scope of its application must however be considered in the context of the article as a whole and in particular in relation to the requirements of paragraph (2).

. . .

The Court observes that Article 19 of the 1966 International Covenant on Civil and Political Rights[5] does not include a provision corresponding to the third sentence of Article 10(1). The negotiating history of Article 19 shows that the inclusion of such a provision in that Article had been proposed with a view to the licensing not of the information imparted but rather of the technical means of broadcasting in order to prevent chaos in the use of frequencies. However, its inclusion was opposed on the ground that it might be utilised to hamper free expression, and it was decided that such a provision was not necessary because licensing in the sense intended was deemed to be covered by the reference to 'public order' in paragraph (3) of the Article.

---

[5] Which guarantees the rights to hold opinions without interference and freedom of expression, subject to limited specified exceptions

This supports the conclusion that the purpose of the third sentence of Article 10(1) of the Convention is to make it clear that States are permitted to control by a licensing system the way in which broadcasting is organised in their territories, particularly in its technical aspects. It does not, however, provide that licensing measures shall not otherwise be subject to the requirements of paragraph 2, for that would lead to a result contrary to the object and purpose of Article 10 taken as a whole.

The sentence in question accordingly applies in the instant case in as much as it permits the orderly control of broadcasting in Switzerland . . .

In sum, the interference was in accordance with the third sentence of paragraph 10(1); it remains to be determined whether it also satisfied the conditions in paragraph (2) . . .

Legitimate aim

The Government contended that the impugned interference pursued two aims recognised by the Convention.

The first of these was the 'prevention of disorder' in telecommunications . . .

The Government submitted, secondly, that the interference complained of was for the 'protection of the . . . rights of others', as it was designed to ensure pluralism, in particular of information, by allowing a fair allocation of frequencies internationally and nationally. This applied both to foreign radio stations, whose programmes had been lawfully retransmitted by cable . . .

. . .

The Court finds that the interference in issue pursued both the aims relied on, which were fully compatible with Article 10(2) namely the protection of the international telecommunications order and the protection of the rights of others.

'Necessary in a democratic society'

The applicants submitted that the ban affecting them did not answer a pressing social need; in particular, it went beyond the requirements of the aims being pursued. It was tantamount to censorship or jamming.

The Government stated that it had no other recourse seeing that its representations to the Italian authorities continued to be fruitless . . .

According to the Court's settled case law, the Contracting States enjoy a certain margin of appreciation in assessing whether and to what extent an interference is necessary, but this margin goes hand in hand with European supervision covering both the legislation and the decisions applying it; when carrying out that supervision, the Court must ascertain whether the measures taken at national level are justifiable in principle and proportionate.

In order to verify that the interference was not excessive in the instant case, the requirements of protecting the international telecommunications order as well as the rights of others must be weighed against the interest of the applicants and others in the retransmission of [the] . . . programmes by cable. The Court reiterates, firstly, that once the 1983 Ordinance had come into force, most Swiss cable companies ceased retransmitting the programmes in question. Moreover, the Swiss authorities never jammed the broadcasts . . . although they made approaches to Italy and the International Telecommunications Union. Thirdly, the impugned ban was imposed on a company incorporated under Swiss law . . . whose subscribers all lived on Swiss territory and continued to receive the programmes of several other stations. Lastly and above all, the procedure chosen could well appear necessary in order to prevent evasion of the law; it was not a form of censorship directed against the content or tendencies of the programmes concerned, but a measure taken against a station which the authorities of the respondent State could reasonably hold to be in reality a Swiss station operating from the other side of the border in order to circumvent the statutory telecommunications system in force in Switzerland.

> ## Questions for discussion
>
> 1. Would the Court have taken a different approach if the Swiss government had jammed the broadcasts?
> 2. What would the Court's reaction have been if the Swiss government had banned, say, the advertising content of the broadcasts?

In *Autronic AG* v *Switzerland*[6] the Court emphasised that article 10 ECHR applied not only to content but also to the means of transmission or reception of the broadcast. In this case, the Swiss government was not justified in prohibiting reception by a dish aerial of satellite broadcasts received in unencoded form. The continuing importance of the principle established in *Autronic* is illustrated by the more recent ruling in *Khurshid Mustafa and Tarzibachi* v *Sweden*.[7] In *Khurshid Mustafa* the ECtHR held that the state's enforcement of a private tenancy agreement that prevented an Iraqi family positioning a satellite antenna outside their rented flat, contravened article 10 ECHR. The arguments of the landlord that this was for safety and aesthetic reasons were not found to be convincing and the importance for the family of access to foreign programmes that reflected their own culture, in their own language, was emphasised.

The early *Groppera* and *Autronic* decisions were significant because they reminded European governments that they would have to be able to justify any laws that restricted transfrontier broadcasting. It was also apparent that this case-by-case approach was unlikely to be a satisfactory way of resolving all the difficulties arising from the growth of cross-border radio and television services. As a result, the Council of Europe initiated discussions with a view to establishing a common framework for European broadcasting. This led to the adoption in 1989 of the European Convention on Transfrontier Television (the Television Convention). In the following extract, the relationship between the right to freedom of expression and the Television Convention is described.

Extract 5.2.3
Hondius, F., 'Regulating transfrontier television – The Strasbourg option' (1988) *Yearbook of European Law* 141, at 148 and 159–60 (footnotes omitted)

In the Council of Europe, the existence of frontiers between States is accepted as a reality. Television, and in particular satellite broadcasting, can help to enhance the free flow of information and ideas across those frontiers and, as it stated in Article 10 . . . 'regardless of frontiers'.

The purpose of the Convention is to achieve a framework for the transfrontier circulation of television programmes. It does not seek to regulate the broadcasting activities, policies and structures of the Member States. It remains for every country to determine these in accordance with its own traditions. Nor does the Convention seek to impinge on the independence and autonomy of the broadcasters. Rather, it sets out a number of basic standards, notably on the rights of viewers, the duties of States, programming standards, advertising, and sponsorship. Under article 4, parties to the Convention guarantee the non-restriction of the retransmission of programme services conforming to these standards, it being understood that in any case there may be no interference with the transmission and direct reception of programme services, whether conforming or not. The latter principle follows from article 10 of the European Human Rights Convention.

Source: Hondius F., 'Regulating Transfrontier Television – The Strasbourg Option' (1988) Yearbook of European Law 141, pp. 148 and 159–160. By permission of Oxford University Press. © Oxford University Press.

---

[6] (1990) 12 EHRR 485.
[7] App. no 23883/06, *Khurshid Mustafa and Tarzibachi* v *Sweden* (2011) 52 EHRR 24.

5.3 EUROPEAN UNION – JURISDICTION

EU competence in the media field has proved to be considerably more controversial. The founding European Economic Community (EEC) Treaty of 1957 did not specifically provide for EEC intervention in the media sector and this remains the case today under the two current EU treaties, which came into force in December 2009: the Treaty on European Union (TEU) and the Treaty on the Functioning of the European Union (TFEU).[8] These treaties build on and replace the Treaty on European Union and the European Community (EC) Treaty adopted in 1992, which in turn superseded the original EEC Treaty. The TEU and TFEU have not only changed the name of the European Community to European Union, they have also altered the numbering of the Treaty articles. Where the excerpts refer to articles in the previous EEC or EC Treaties or Treaty on European Union, reference is also made to the equivalent article numbers in the current TEU or TFEU.

Despite there being no explicit competence relating to the media in the EEC Treaty, the EEC's mandate to establish a common market, ensuring free movement of goods, services, establishment and persons throughout the Member States, made it inevitable that, with increasing cross-border trade, the media sector would be seen as a legitimate subject for European oversight. The first case in which the European Court of Justice (ECJ, now referred to as the Court of Justice) had to consider the relationship between EU law and broadcasting was the 1974 case of *Italy* v *Sacchi* (extracted below). Sacchi was the owner of a cable undertaking which received and retransmitted television programmes. Sacchi had refused to pay the licence fee, required from those operating receiving equipment. The Italian government had granted to Radio Audizione Italiana (RAI) a monopoly on television broadcasting and commercial television advertising and the licence fee was used to fund this operation. As a defence to proceedings brought for failure to pay the licence fee, Sacchi argued that this monopoly restricted the reception in Italy of foreign programmes and advertisements, and, therefore, prevented the free movement of goods. The ECJ rejected this argument but, importantly, decided that broadcasting was covered by the EEC Treaty provisions on services.

Extract 5.3.1
Case 155/73, *Italy* v *Sacchi* [1974] ECR 409, at paras 6–7

6. In the absence of express provision to the contrary in the Treaty, a television signal must, by reason of its nature, be regarded as provision of services.

Although it is not ruled out that services normally provided for remuneration may come under the provisions relating to free movement of goods, such is however the case . . . only insofar as they are governed by such provisions.

It follows that the transmission of television signals, including those in the nature of advertisements, comes, as such, within the rules of the Treaty relating to services.

7. On the other hand, trade in material, sound recordings, films, apparatus and other products used for the diffusion of television signals are subject to the rules relating to freedom of movement for goods.

Source: © European Union, 1995–2013.

Under EU law, many media products are thus classified as services, though the sale of certain material products, such as printed books, newspapers or magazines, as well as

---

[8] The consolidated texts of the TEU and TFEU are available at [2010] OJ C83/1.

compact or digital video discs continues to be covered by the rules relating to goods.[9] On the other hand, access to online versions of newspapers or magazines, where no material product is relayed, is covered by the rules on services.[10] The guarantees of free movement for goods, establishment and services, as currently provided for in the TFEU, are set out below.

Extract 5.3.2
TFEU, arts 34, 49, 56 and 57

Article 34

Quantitative restrictions on imports and all measures having equivalent effect shall be prohibited between Member States.

Article 49

Within the framework of the provisions set out below, restrictions on the freedom of establishment of nationals of a Member State in the territory of another Member State shall be prohibited. Such prohibition shall also apply to restrictions on the setting-up of agencies, branches or subsidiaries by nationals of any member State established in the territory of any Member State . . .

Article 56

Within the framework of the provisions set out below, restrictions on freedom to provide services within the Union shall be prohibited in respect of nationals of Member States who are established in a State of the Community other than that of the person for whom the services are intended . . .

Article 57

Services shall be considered to be 'services' within the meaning of the Treaties where they are normally provided for remuneration, in so far as they are not governed by the provisions relating to freedom of movement for goods, capital and persons.

Source: © European Union, 1995–2013.

Sacchi helped to clarify the application of the fundamental freedoms in the Treaty to a range of media goods and services but it still left many questions unanswered regarding the degree of latitude that EU law affords states when regulating the media on policy grounds. Where domestic measures directly discriminate against foreign products, states can only rely on the specific derogations set out in article 36 TFEU in relation to goods and article 52 TFEU in relation to establishment and services. Both articles identify public policy, public security and public health concerns as legitimate reasons for restrictions, although article 36 also mentions public morality; the health and life of animals or plants; the protection of national treasures and the protection of industrial or commercial property. These exceptions are construed narrowly and any restrictions must be shown to be proportionate to the stated ends.

The application of these principles is illustrated by the case of *Bond van Adverteerders*, excerpted below, which concerned Dutch rules designed to limit the impact of foreign satellite services on the carefully regulated Netherlands broadcasting system. The Netherlands

---

[9] See, for example, Case C-368/95, *Vereinigte Familiapress Zeitungsverlags-und vertriebs GmbH v Heinrich Bauer Verlag* [1997] ECR I-3689, relating to the sale of newspapers.

[10] More controversial is the case where electronic versions of books or articles are downloaded onto the purchaser's computer to be retained for future use: is the consumer buying a good or a service? The sale of ebooks, for instance, have been treated as electronic services for VAT purposes, which places them at a disadvantage compared to traditional books where reduced VAT rates are allowed: see I. Griffiths, 'Amazon to be Stripped of Tax Advantage on Sale of Ebooks', *The Guardian*, 24 October 2012.

sought to ensure that the different political, cultural and social strands in Dutch society all obtained airtime and, to facilitate this, a public foundation (STER) was given sole rights to arrange television advertising and distribute the revenues among a diverse range of broadcasters. The domestic advertising rules were, however, very strict and to circumvent them, broadcasters established themselves in Luxembourg, where the rules were more relaxed, and transmitted their services back to the Netherlands by satellite. In response, the Netherlands prohibited cable companies from relaying advertising, as well as programmes subtitled in Dutch, contained in foreign satellite services. The Dutch advertisers argued that this restricted their freedom to provide services protected by EEC law.

The ECJ held that the prohibitions were indeed contrary to what is now article 56 TFEU and were discriminatory: domestic channels could carry advertising aimed at the domestic audience, albeit allocated by STER, while foreign broadcasters could not. The ECJ then turned to consider whether such discriminatory measures could be justified under what is now article 52 TFEU (previously art 56 TEEC).

Extract 5.3.3
Case 352/85, *Bond van Adverteerders and Others* v *The Netherlands* [1988] ECR 2085, at 2135–6

It must be pointed out that economic aims, such as that of securing for a national public foundation all the revenue from advertising intended especially for the public of the Member State in question, cannot constitute grounds of public policy within the meaning of Article 56 [now 52] of the Treaty.

However, the Netherlands Government has stated that, in the final analysis, the prohibitions of advertising and subtitling have a non-economic objective, namely that of maintaining the non-commercial and, thereby, pluralistic nature of the Netherlands broadcasting system . . .

It is sufficient to observe in that regard that the measures taken by virtue of that article must not be disproportionate to the intended objective. As an exception to a fundamental principle of the Treaty, Article 56 [now 52] of the Treaty must be interpreted in such a way that its effects are limited to that which is necessary in order to protect the interests which it seeks to safeguard.

The Netherlands Government itself admits that there are less restrictive, non-discriminatory ways of achieving the intended objectives. For instance, broadcasters of commercial programmes established in other Member States could be given a choice between complying with objective restrictions on the transmission of advertising, such as a prohibition on advertising certain products or on certain days and limiting the duration or the frequency of advertisements – restrictions also imposed on national broadcasters – or, if they did not wish to comply, refraining from transmitting advertising intended especially for the public in the Netherlands.

. . .

It must therefore be held that [the] prohibitions of advertising and subtitling . . . cannot be justified on grounds of public policy under article 56 [now 52] of the Treaty.

It is not only directly discriminatory rules that impede the free flow of goods and services across borders. Rules that apply without distinction to foreign and domestic products, such as a requirement that broadcasts be in a certain language or a limit on advertising to a given number of minutes an hour, can also impede access to other countries' markets. The Court of Justice has held that where such 'indistinctly applicable' measures are liable to 'prohibit, impede or render less advantageous' the provision of services by a provider in another Member State they fall within the scope of article 56 TFEU.[11] The Court has similarly interpreted article 34 TFEU as applying to indistinctly applicable restrictions relating to goods.[12] Member States are, however, allowed considerable latitude to justify such indistinctly applicable measures, beyond the limited considerations set out in articles 36 and 52 TFEU discussed above. The protection of cultural or linguistic diversity,[13] public morality and the protection of children,[14] have, for instance, all been considered legitimate policy objectives. Such measures must, however, be suitable for attaining the specified objective and not go beyond what is necessary to attain it.[15]

In the aftermath of *Sacchi* and *Bond van Adverteerders*, commercial broadcasters made increasing use of EU law to challenge both discriminatory and indistinctly applicable domestic regulations and the problems these cases brought to light both for the EU and the Member States created a powerful impetus for co-ordination and clarification at the European level.

Before turning to consider how the Council of Europe and EU addressed these impediments to the free movement of broadcasting services in Europe, it is necessary to note that there are a number of other potential Treaty bases for EU action in the media field. These include the competition articles 101–109 TFEU, considered in more detail in Chapter 8, the provisions relating to external action under part five of the TFEU, which allow the EU to negotiate international trade and aid agreements in the media field, and the specific article on culture, now article 167 TFEU, introduced by the Maastricht Treaty in 1992.

Extract 5.3.4
TFEU, article 167 (formerly 151 TEC)

1. The Union shall contribute to the flowering of the cultures of the Member States, while respecting their national and regional diversity and at the same time bringing the common cultural heritage to the fore.

2. Action by the Union shall be aimed at encouraging cooperation between Member States and, if necessary, supporting and supplementing their action in the following areas:

   • improvement of the knowledge and dissemination of the culture and history of the European peoples;

   • conservation and safeguarding of cultural heritage of European significance;

   • non-commercial cultural exchanges;

   • artistic and literary creation, including in the audiovisual sector.

3. The Community and the Member States shall foster cooperation with third countries and the competent international organisations in the sphere of culture, in particular the Council of Europe.

4. The Union shall take cultural aspects into account in its action under other provisions of this Treaty, in particular in order to respect and to promote the diversity of its cultures.

---

[11] Case C-250/06, *United Pan-Europe Communications Belgium SA and Others* v *Belgium* [2007] ECR I-11135, para 29.

[12] In order to keep review within manageable bounds, non-discriminatory selling arrangements that affect the sale of goods, such as promotional offers, are not covered by art 34: Joined Cases 267/91–268/91, *Keck and Mithouard* [1993] ECR I-6097. Such rules may, however, be covered by the rules on services, for instance, where they affect the sale of advertising. More recent case law also suggests that non-discriminatory rules that significantly impede market access are covered by art 34. See, for example, case C-108/09, Ker-Optika [2010] ECR I-12213.

[13] Case 222/07, *Unión de Televisiones Comerciales Asociadas (UTECA)* v *Administración General del Estado* [2009] ECJ I-1407.

[14] Case C-244/06, *Dynamic Medien Vertriebs GmbH* v *Avides Media AG* [2008] ECR I-505.

[15] For a recent application of these principles, see Case C-250/06, *United Pan-Europe Communications Belgium SA and Others* v *Belgium* [2007] ECR I-11135, paras 42–4 and 46.

5. In order to contribute to the achievement of the objectives referred to in this Article:
    *   the European Parliament and the Council acting in accordance with the ordinary legislative procedure and after consulting the Committee of the Regions, shall adopt incentive measures, excluding any harmonisation of the laws and regulations of the Member States.
    *   the Council, on a proposal from the Commission, shall adopt recommendations.

. . .

Despite the specific mention of the audiovisual sector in paragraph two, article 167 TFEU has to date had limited impact on the media sector. The explicit prohibition in the fifth and final paragraph of the article on introducing harmonising measures in the cultural field means that it has primarily been used as a basis for establishing funding programmes designed to support various cultural projects.[16] Separate EU funding initiatives for the media sector have been introduced not on the basis of article 167 TFEU but with reference to the articles on vocational training and industry in articles 166 and 157 TFEU.[17] Article 167(4) TFEU was, however, explicitly identified as a point of reference in recital 6 of the Audiovisual Media Services Directive, discussed further below, and serves to remind the EU that cultural matters cannot be disregarded in pursuit of a competitive internal market.[18] A greater focus on cultural issues is apparent in recent Commission policy documents, such as its 2007 communication on a *European agenda for culture in a globalizing world*,[19] and the EU played an active part in the negotiations leading to the adoption in 2005 of the UNESCO Convention on the Protection and Promotion of the Diversity of Cultural Expressions, which it ratified in 2006.[20]

Unlike the Council of Europe, the EU does not have general competence to protect human rights, though specific rights, such as the right to equal treatment, are included in the body of the TFEU (see arts 18–19 TFEU). Rather, the EU institutions and Member States, when acting within the field of EU law, must comply with the binding provisions in the Charter of Fundamental Rights, which now has 'treaty status' (art 6.1 TFEU), as well as international guarantees, notably those in the ECHR, and the constitutional traditions of the Member States relating to human rights (art 6.3 TEU). States that fail to conform to basic EU values may be subject to sanctions under art 7 TEU. Human rights are thus an important constraint on EU action rather than a distinct basis for action in their own right.

Questions for discussion

1. Which, if any, media goods and services would you classify as 'cultural' and why?
2. Should the TFEU be amended to include a specific article relating to the media? If so, what should it say?

---

[16] See Decision no 1855/2006/EC, European Parliament and Council, establishing the Culture Programme (2007 to 2013), OJ L 372/1 and Communication from the Commission, *Creative Europe – A new framework programme for the cultural and creative sectors* (2014–2020), COM (2011) 786/2.

[17] See, for example, the MEDIA Programme 2007 [2006] OJ L 327/12.

[18] Codified in Directive 2010/13/EU, on the co-ordination of certain provisions laid down by law, regulation or administrative action in Member States concerning the provision of audiovisual media services (Audiovisual Media Services Directive) [2010] OJ L95/1.

[19] COM (2007) 242 final.

[20] See C.B. Graber, 'The UNESCO Convention on Cultural Diversity: A Counterbalance to the WTO?' (2006) 9/3 *Journal of International Economic Law* 553–74.

5.4 INITIAL DEVELOPMENT OF AUDIOVISUAL POLICY AT THE EUROPEAN LEVEL

Within the Council of Europe, early legislative initiatives focused on ensuring that broadcasters could in principle transmit their services in other member states but also sought to ensure that domestic regulatory systems were not deliberately circumvented by 'pirate' broadcasters operating outside national territories, such as Radio Caroline, located on a boat.[21] These were supplemented by a number of soft law provisions, notably the 1984 Committee of Ministers' recommendation on the use of satellite capacity for television and radio broadcasting, which presaged many of the key elements of the 1989 Television Convention in establishing jurisdictional criteria and basic content standards.[22]

The development of EU policy can be traced back to 1982 and the Hahn Report on radio and television broadcasting.[23] The Report,[24] adopted unanimously by the European Parliament, underlined the importance of information to the process of European integration. The response to the Hahn Report was twofold. On the one hand, measures were taken to support the development of a number of pan-European satellite television channels, which, it was believed, would help to foster a sense of European identity.[25] These channels did not, however, prove popular with Europe's citizens, who found the foreign content alienating.[26] Though other collaborative ventures such as Euronews and the more recent Franco-German cultural station Arte have survived in a competitive environment, the 'cultural discount' that hampers reception of foreign content remains a significant challenge for the development of pan-European television.

The second, and more practical, response was to propose agreement of a set of programme standards and jurisdictional rules that would pave the way for a 'single broadcasting area'. This idea was explored by the European Commission (the Commission) in its 'Television Without Frontiers' Green Paper.[27]

> **Extract 5.4.1**
>
> **European Commission, *Television Without Frontiers, Green Paper on the establishment of the Common Market for broadcasting, especially by satellite and cable*, Summary, Communication from the Commission to the Council, COM (84) 300 final/2, paras 4–7**
>
> 4. The Commission considers that action needs to be taken at the present time in the broadcasting field because of the importance of its effect, already considerable and steadily growing, on the process of European integration. This effect, actual and potential, is not only economic in character but also social, cultural and political.

---

[21] European Agreement on the Protection of Television Broadcasts, 22 June 1960 (ETS no 34); European Agreement for the Prevention of Broadcasts transmitted from Stations outside National Territories, 22 January 1965 (ETS no 53).

[22] Recommendation No R (84) 22 of the Committee of Ministers on the use of satellite capacity for television and radio broadcasting.

[23] R. Wallace and D. Goldberg, 'The EEC Directive on television broadcasting' (1989) 9 *Yearbook of European Law* 175. See generally for history of the development of Community audiovisual policy: R. Collins, *Broadcasting and Audio-visual Policy in the European Single Market* (London: John Libbey, 1994) and A. Littoz-Monnet, *The European Union and Culture: Between Economic Regulation and Cultural Policy* (Manchester University Press, 2007), ch 4.

[24] European Parliament, *Report drawn up on behalf of the Committee on Youth, Culture, Education, Information and Sport on radio and television broadcasting in the European Community*, Working Documents, 1981–82, Doc 1–1013/81.

[25] Collins, n 22 above, ch 3.

[26] Ibid.

[27] COM (84) 300 final.

5. Certainly broadcasting is a strategic sector of the Community's service economy, particularly as technical change increases the scope and availability of programmes and associated services including new information and communications services which will create many opportunities for innovation and employment. It constitutes one of the main factors accelerating the transition to an economy that will in large part be based on ready access to information and to rapid methods of communication. One of the principle [sic] components in the development of the infrastructure necessary for a modern information and communications network will be cable and satellite systems dedicated in substantial part to the broadcasting of a wide variety of programmes. The considerable investment in infrastructure and programme industries will be the more easily and rapidly found if, from the outset, those providing the new services can count on access to a single broadcasting area corresponding to the European Community as a whole.

6. But, equally clearly, broadcasting cannot be approached in exclusively technical and economic terms, even if its economic dimension is necessarily the starting point for policy making in an Economic Community. More fundamentally, broadcasting is a powerful medium for the communication of all kinds of information, ideas and opinion. It thereby influences the attitudes of almost all Community citizens, and provides the means by which they can influence the attitudes of others . . .

7. . . . In this context, emphasis has been placed on the need to respect the European Convention on Human Rights and Fundamental Freedoms and, in particular, its provision the right to freedom of expression . . .

Source: © European Union, 1995–2013.

It can be seen from this extract that although the Commission's concerns were not purely economic there was a strong emphasis on broadcasting's economic and industrial importance. In particular, the need to improve Europe's competitiveness with regard to the USA was an important motivating factor. The Commission concluded that harmonisation was required and could be taken forward under what is now article 52 TFEU. Questions remained, however, as to how exacting the set standards should be and which media and regulatory fields should be covered.

When seeking to co-ordinate diverse domestic rules a number of regulatory strategies are possible. First, minimum standards can be set, with which all providers must comply. States remain free, however, to impose higher standards and can exclude goods or services from other countries that do not conform to these more exacting requirements. Second, high uniform standards can be fixed in a given field. Compliance with these standards guarantees free movement across all participating states, which are not allowed to impose higher standards on their own or foreign providers. Third, minimum standards can be set at a level that states consider sufficient to guarantee free movement. States are required to ensure that domestic providers comply with these standards and can also impose higher standards on domestic operators. They must, however, allow in goods and services that comply with the rules imposed by the state of origin of the service, even if these are less exacting than their own.

Although the first approach can assist free movement by generally ramping-up standards at the bottom end it does not guarantee it, while uniform standards under the second option are difficult to agree at an international level given the cultural and constitutional differences among states. The third approach is more feasible politically and affords states residual freedom to maintain more exacting rules for their own broadcasters in line with domestic expectations.[28] This was the approach adopted in the 1989 Television Without Frontiers

---

[28] For discussion of some of the limitations of this approach, see Littoz-Monnet, n 22, above.

Directive (TWFD) and, with some modification, also in the Television Convention, which applies to those domestic broadcasts that can be received in another state party.

Although some EEC Member States, including the UK, had reservations about the need for legislation,[29] a proposal for a directive was put forward in 1986.[30] At the same time the Council of Europe was engaged in preparations for its broadcasting convention, and there was a degree of rivalry over which instrument should be settled first.[31] At a European Council meeting in December 1988,[32] however, it was agreed that the Television Convention should be adopted first as it had a wider constituency and this took place on 5 May 1989.[33] The TWFD followed on 3 October 1989.[34] Article 27(1) of the Television Convention governs the relationship between the two measures and provides that signatories to the Convention which are also EU Member States are to comply with EU law, thereby affording the Convention a residual status.

The scope of the two instruments was at this stage broadly similar, in that they both covered advertising, protection of minors, the right of reply and promotion of European programming, though the Convention was rather more extensive. Initial proposals to include radio and copyright issues were ultimately dropped.[35] In 1997 the Directive, and in 1998 the Convention, were amended, primarily to clarify the rules relating to jurisdiction, though changes or additions were also made regarding public access to events of major importance, sponsorship, tele-shopping and child protection.[36]

The two measures thus appeared to be developing in parallel but in 2007 the TWFD was radically amended to take into account the impact of convergence on the delivery of television services.[37] The Directive was renamed the Audiovisual Media Services Directive (AVMSD) and Member States were required to implement its provisions by the end of 2009. Once again, the Council of Europe moved to adapt the Television Convention but, at a late stage in the negotiations, the Commission objected to EU Member States agreeing the amending protocol on the basis that competence in the field now rested exclusively with the EU.[38] Moreover, the EU indicated that it would not itself seek to become a party

[29] Ibid., and T. Gibbons and P. Humphreys, *Audiovisual Regulation Under Pressure: Comparative Cases from North America and Europe* (Abingdon Routledge, 2012), 138–9.

[30] Proposal for a Council Directive on the co-ordination of certain provisions laid down by law, regulation or administrative action in Member States concerning the pursuit of broadcasting activities, COM (86) 146/2 final.

[31] For accounts see Hondius, n 1 above and Schwartz, 'The EEC Directive on "Television without Frontiers"' (1988) 21 *Revue Belge de Droit International* 329.

[32] B. de Witte, 'The European content requirement in the EC Television Directive – five years after' in E.M. Barendt (ed.), *The Yearbook of Media and Entertainment Law 1995* (Oxford University Press, 1995), 101, 104.

[33] European Treaty Series (ETS), no 132.

[34] Council Directive 89/552/EEC of 3 October 1989 on the co-ordination of certain provisions laid down by law, regulation or administrative action in Member States concerning the pursuit of television broadcasting activities [1989] OJ L298/23.

[35] Copyright proved too complex a matter on which to reach agreement at this stage and a separate Directive 93/83/EEC of 27 September 1993 on the co-ordination of certain rules concerning copyright and rights related to copyright applicable to satellite broadcasting and cable retransmission [1993] OJ L248/15 was eventually enacted to deal with the copyright aspects of transfrontier broadcasting.

[36] Directive 97/36/EC amending Council Directive 89/552/EEC on the co-ordination of certain provisions laid down by law, regulation or administrative action in Member States concerning the pursuit of television broadcasting activities [1997] OJ L202/60 and Protocol amending the European Convention on Transfrontier Television, ETS No 171, October 1998.

[37] Codified in Directive 2010/13/EU, on the co-ordination of certain provisions laid down by law, regulation or administrative action in Member States concerning the provision of audiovisual media services (Audiovisual Media Services Directive) [2010] OJ L95/1.

[38] See details published by the Standing Committee on Transfrontier Television (T-TT) at: http://www.coe.int/t/dghl/standardsetting/media/T-TT/default_en.asp.

on the basis that this could prejudice its ability to develop audiovisual policy in the future.[39] The review of the Convention was thus discontinued and there is consequently a significant difference in scope between the two measures, with the AVMSD alone applicable to on-demand television services.

The following sections focus on the AVMSD, as the more advanced measure in the field, but, as noted at the end of this chapter, there are already calls for the Directive itself to be revised.

5.5 WHY WAS THE AVMSD ADOPTED?

The digitisation of audiovisual content coupled with growing public access to the Internet over personal computers began to make online transmission of radio and television services viable. The TWFD only applied (as does the current Television Convention) to 'television broadcasting', understood as the electronic transmission of television programmes intended for simultaneous reception by the public.[40] New audiovisual services offered on an 'on-demand' basis, where consumers could choose when to watch specific programmes, consequently fell outside the reach of the Directive. In many instances these services were covered by the Electronic Commerce Directive,[41] which applies to services 'provided at a distance by electronic means and at the individual request of a recipient of services' (art 1(2)). The Electronic Commerce Directive imposes a relatively limited range of content obligations, largely designed to ensure that consumers know whom to contact if they wish to complain about a service; it also serves to protect intermediaries, such as Internet service providers, who relay services for others and thus exercise little, if any, editorial control over content, from legal liability.

The results of this regulatory matrix began to look increasingly arbitrary, with television broadcasters subject to strict content regulations under the TWFD while companies providing the same content on an on-demand basis over the Internet were largely free from EU controls. Member States, however, remained competent to impose more exacting requirements on domestic service providers and to regulate incoming on-demand services on a range of general interest grounds under articles 1.6 and 3.4 of the Electronic Commerce Directive.[42] Signal compression and the availability of additional spectrum also led to the development of 'near-video-on-demand' services, involving the repeated broadcasting of films or other programmes at short intervals of fifteen minutes or so, creating a service that approximated, from the consumer's perspective, an on-demand service. Should such services be categorised as broadcasting or on-demand services?

This issue was considered in the *Mediakabel* case, where the providers of a near-video-on-demand service sought to evade the European content requirements in the TWFD, discussed further at section 5.10 below, by arguing that they were not providing a broadcast service and thus fell outside the scope of the Directive.

---

[39] Ibid. See D. Mac Síthigh. 'Death of a Convention: Competition between the Council of Europe and European Union in the Regulation of Broadcasting' (2013) 5/1 *Journal of Media Law* 133–55.
[40] See art 1(a) TWF Directive and art 2(c) Television Convention.
[41] Directive 2000/31/EC on certain legal aspects of information society services, in particular electronic commerce, in the Internal Market [2000] OJ L1781.
[42] Ibid.

Extract 5.5.1

Case C-89/04, *Mediakabel BV v Commissariaat voor de Media* [2005] ECR I-4891, paras 19, 28–32, 39 and 49

19. Directive 98/34 and the Directive on electronic commerce have a purpose different from that of Directive 89/552. They lay down the Community legal framework applicable only to information society services referred to in Article 1(2) of Directive 98/34, that is, any services provided at a distance by electronic means and at the individual request of a recipient of services. Directive 98/34 provides expressly in that provision that it does 'not apply to . . . television broadcasting services covered by point (a) of Article 1 of Directive 89/552'.

. . .

28. A service constitutes 'television broadcasting' if it consists of initial transmission of television programmes intended for reception by the public.

29. First, the Court notes that the manner in which images are transmitted is not a determining factor in that assessment, as evidenced by the use in Article 1(a) of Directive 89/552 of the terms 'by wire or over the air, including that by satellite, in unencoded or encoded form'. The Court has thus held that transmission by cable comes within the scope of that directive, even though cable distribution was not very widespread at the time when Directive 89/552 was adopted (see Case C-11/95 *Commission v Belgium* [1996] ECR I-4115, paragraphs 15 to 25).

30. Next, the service in question must consist of the transmission of television programmes intended for reception by the public, that is, an indeterminate number of potential television viewers, to whom the same images are transmitted simultaneously.

31. Lastly, the exclusion of 'communication services . . . on individual demand' from the concept of 'television broadcasting' means that, conversely, the latter concept covers services which are not supplied on individual demand. The requirement that the television programmes must be 'intended for reception by the public' in order to come within that concept supports this analysis.

32. Thus, a pay-per-view television service, even one which is accessible to a limited number of subscribers, but which comprises only programmes selected by the broadcaster and is broadcast at times set by the broadcaster, cannot be regarded as being provided on individual demand. Consequently, it comes within the concept of 'television broadcasting'. The fact that the images in such a service are accessible using a personal code is not relevant in this respect, because the subscribing public all receive the broadcast at the same time.

. . .

39. Such a service is thus not commanded individually by an isolated recipient who has free choice of programmes in an interactive setting. It must be considered to be a near-video on-demand service, provided on a 'point to multipoint' basis and not 'at the individual request of a recipient of services'.

. . .

49. The scope of application of legislation cannot be made contingent on possible adverse consequences it may have for traders to whom the Community legislature intended it to apply. In addition, a narrow interpretation of the concept of 'television broadcasting service', which would have the effect of excluding a service such as that at issue in the main proceedings from the scope of application of the directive, would jeopardise the objectives pursued by it and therefore cannot be accepted.

Source: © European Union, 1995–2013.

The near-video-on-demand service provided by Mediakabel was thus required to comply with the European content requirements in the TWFD, while true video-on-demand services could include as little or as much European content as their editors wished, subject to any applicable domestic regulations. The AVMSD was consequently introduced to level the regulatory playing field, tilted against traditional television broadcasters, by bringing true video-on-demand services within the scope of the Directive.

The AVMSD had two further objectives. First, by harmonising content regulations for on-demand services in fields such as advertising, child protection and hate speech, the Directive prevented barriers being erected, as a result of divergent domestic regulations, to the developing European 'on-demand' market. Second, certain rules in the TWFD were considered to be in need of updating in the light of market developments: for example, the broadcast advertising rules were relaxed somewhat and the way opened to include product placement in certain categories of programme.[43]

5.6   SCOPE AND STRUCTURE OF THE AVMSD

The AVMSD applies to 'audiovisual media services', which fall into three distinct categories: 'television broadcasts', 'on-demand audiovisual media services' and 'audiovisual commercial communications'. This chapter focuses on the first two of these, which are further explained in article 1.1 AVMSD set out below.

Extract 5.6.1
Directive 2010/13/EU, on the co-ordination of certain provisions laid down by law, regulation or administrative action in Member States concerning the provision of audiovisual media services (Audiovisual Media Services Directive) [2010] OJ L95/1, art 1.1

Article 1.1

(a) 'audiovisual media service' means:
  (i)   a service as defined by Articles 56 and 57 of the Treaty on the Functioning of the European Union which is under the editorial responsibility of a media service provider and the principal purpose of which is the provision of programmes, in order to inform, entertain or educate, to the general public by electronic communications networks within the meaning of point (a) of Article 2 of Directive 2002/21/EC. Such an audiovisual media service is either a television broadcast as defined in point (e) of this paragraph or an on-demand audiovisual media service as defined in point (g) of this paragraph;
  (ii) audiovisual commercial communication;

(b) 'programme' means a set of moving images with or without sound constituting an individual item within a schedule or a catalogue established by a media service provider and the form and content of which are comparable to the form and content of television broadcasting. Examples of programmes include feature-length films, sports events, situation comedies, documentaries, children's programmes and original drama;

(c) 'editorial responsibility' means the exercise of effective control both over the selection of the programmes and over their organisation either in a chronological schedule, in the case of television broadcasts, or in a catalogue, in the case of on-demand audiovisual media services. Editorial responsibility does not necessarily imply any legal liability under national law for the content or the services provided;

(d) 'media service provider' means the natural or legal person who has editorial responsibility for the choice of the audiovisual content of the audiovisual media service and determines the manner in which it is organised;

---

[43] Discussed further in Chapter 6.

(e) 'television broadcasting' or 'television broadcast' (i.e. a linear audiovisual media service) means an audiovisual media service provided by a media service provider for simultaneous viewing of programmes on the basis of a programme schedule;

(f) 'broadcaster' means a media service provider of television 'broadcasts';

(g) 'on-demand audiovisual media service' (i.e. a non-linear audiovisual media service) means an audiovisual media service provided by a media service provider for the viewing of programmes at the moment chosen by the user and at his individual request on the basis of a catalogue of programmes selected by the media service provider . . .

Source: © European Union, 1995–2013.

As noted above, a key objective underpinning the Directive was to level the playing field between 'linear' television broadcasters and broadly equivalent 'non-linear' on-demand services. Defining these broadly equivalent services has not proved, however, to be entirely unproblematic and, even with additional guidance from the non-binding recitals to the Directive, some uncertainties regarding the outer reaches of the Directive remain. The requirement in article 1.1(b) that there be moving images, for example, clearly excludes radio and purely text-based services, while recital 28 confirms that the Directive was not intended to cover 'electronic versions of newspapers and magazines'. Increasingly, however, online newspapers and magazines include video content, some of which may be similar to that available in on-demand or broadcast television. Where this is merely incidental to other types of content, recital 22 confirms that the site should not fall within the scope of the Directive, but it is possible to imagine cases where the video content begins to dominate or is combined by the newspaper into something approximating a television programme, rendering the application of the Directive more plausible.

The framers of the Directive also sought to exclude private correspondence, such as email, amateur websites and sites created to allow the posting and exchange of user-generated content (recitals 21 and 22). Here, too, the provisions in article 1 render application of the AVMSD to such sites unlikely. Thus, to be caught by the Directive, services must engage in or be linked to some form of economic activity; they must be 'television like', competing for television audiences in circumstances where a viewer would expect a similar level of regulatory oversight (recital 24); and the provider must intend to offer the service 'to the public'. The Directive consequently applies to the 'mass media', defined as those services that 'could have a clear impact on a significant proportion of the general public' (recital 21). Few video-blogs or sites relying on user-generated content have this profile, although a site such as YouTube that earns significant revenues from advertising and attracts hundreds of millions of viewers for its most popular videos, could, if located within the EU, potentially be caught.[44] Although user-generated content tends to be rather different in style and subject matter from standard television fare, television services are themselves beginning to evolve in response to online developments, experimenting, for example, with short or composite programmes, so that a dynamic approach to what is 'television like' is called for (recital 24).

Finally, the provider of the audiovisual media service must have 'editorial control' over the choice and organisation of the content transmitted. Companies that merely transmit programmes for third parties, with no control over what is relayed, are not covered. This is a further reason why services such as YouTube, where the content is reviewed reactively

---

[44] YouTube is established in the United States and does not fall within the jurisdiction of EU Member States according to the criteria discussed in Section 5.7 below. Subsidiaries may, however, be caught.

only after it has been posted by the user to the site, are generally thought not to be caught by the Directive, though recital 25 affords Member States some discretion in determining such matters.[45] These observations serve as an additional reminder that what is considered to constitute an audiovisual media service may evolve over time as domestic regulators seek to apply the Directive to concrete situations and co-ordinate their actions at the European level, with reference to the Contact Committee established in article 29.

Although on-demand services were brought within the scope of the AVMSD in order to level the regulatory playing field with broadcasters, certain differences between on-demand and broadcast services were thought to warrant some continuing variation in the applicable rules. Three main reasons were put forward for differential regulation.[46] First, viewers were considered to exercise more control over on-demand than broadcast services: broadcast programmes are potentially accessible as soon as the television is switched on while an on-demand service requires more conscious selection, involving a number of clicks of the television remote control or computer mouse to locate. Second, broadcast services, with their established audience base and wide reach, were considered potentially more influential than on-demand services. Third, the EU sought to avoid imposing unduly onerous restrictions on an industry that was at an early stage of development. As a result, broadcasters remain subject to a rather more expansive, and in some cases more exacting, set of regulations than those applicable to on-demand services.

The AVMSD thus establishes a basic tier of standards that apply to all audiovisual media service providers. These require the provision of consumer information regarding the service provider and relevant regulatory authority; prohibit hate speech; establish minimum requirements for commercial speech, sponsorship and product placement; require services to be accessible to those with disabilities; and control the exhibition of films made for the cinema. A second group of measures apply solely to on-demand services and concern child protection and the promotion of European programming. These provisions modify parallel provisions that apply to broadcast services, in part to reflect the different way in which such services are accessed. The third, and final, group of substantive provisions apply solely to broadcast services and concern access to events of major social importance and short news reports; quotas for European and independently produced programmes; advertising and tele-shopping; the protection of minors and the right of reply. The provisions relating to child protection and hate speech, European programme quotas and the right of reply are considered in more detail below, while the advertising provisions and those relating to major events are addressed in Chapters 6 and 8, respectively.

Questions for discussion

1. Were the reasons given for imposing more exacting requirements on broadcast than on-demand services convincing? Are they now?
2. What arguments are there for including or excluding services such as YouTube from the scope of the AVMSD?

---

[45] For discussion, see P. Valcke and K. Lefever, *Media Law in the European Union* (Alphen aan den Rijn: Wolters Kluwer, 2012), 65.
[46] See recital 58 and R. Craufurd-Smith, 'Media convergence and the regulation of audiovisual content: is the European Community's Audiovisual Media Services Directive fit for purpose?' (2007) 60 *Current Legal Problems* 238–77 at 250–4.

5.7 ESTABLISHING JURISDICTION UNDER THE AVMSD

The AVMSD is a minimum harmonising directive with the country of origin principle 'at its core' (recital 33). This approach, previously established in the TWFD, is now set out in articles 2, 3 and 4 of the Directive.

Extract 5.7.1

Directive 2010/13/EU, on the co-ordination of certain provisions laid down by law, regulation or administrative action in Member States concerning the provision of audiovisual media services (Audiovisual Media Services Directive) [2010] OJ L95/1, arts 2–4

Article 2

1. Each Member State shall ensure that all audiovisual media services transmitted by media service providers under its jurisdiction comply with the rules of the system of law applicable to audiovisual media services intended for the public in that Member State.

. . .

Article 3

1. Member States shall ensure freedom of reception and shall not restrict retransmissions on their territory of audiovisual media services from other Member States for reasons which fall within the fields coordinated by this Directive.

. . .

Article 4

1. Member States shall remain free to require media service providers under their jurisdiction to comply with more detailed or stricter rules in the fields coordinated by this Directive provided that such rules are in compliance with Union law.

Source: © European Union, 1995–2013.

The AVMSD thus establishes a single European market for audiovisual services. Once a service complies with the rules of its 'home state' it should be able to circulate freely within the EU, even in states that have imposed more exacting standards on their own providers.[47] The far-reaching implications of the Directive were not immediately understood when first formulated in the TWFD. Belgium, for example, sought to maintain a system of review over foreign broadcasts on the basis that some states might not enforce the Directive effectively. The ECJ was clear, however, that this was no longer an option.

Extract 5.7.2

Case C-11/95, *Commission of the European Communities* v *Kingdom of Belgium* [1996] ECR I-4115, at paras 30, 31, 34 and 36

30. . . . [T]he Belgian Government maintains that it is apparent from the recitals in the preamble to the directive, and from Article 2(1) thereof, that a television programme may circulate freely throughout the Community only if it complies with the programme applicable law of the originating State, including the provisions of the directive. It necessarily follows from that principle that the receiving Member State must be able to verify whether foreign television broadcasters applying for authorization to retransmit their programmes in the territory of the French Community

---

[47] A limited range of audiovisual media services, intended solely for reception in third countries (art 2.6 AVMSD) and broadcasts intended solely for local audiences (art 18 AVMSD), are excluded from the scope of the Directive on the basis that they do not have an EU dimension.

of Belgium comply with the law of the originating State and are justified in calling for the application of Article 2(2) [now art 3.1 AVMSD] of the directive.

31. Having regard to the system whereby Directive 89/552 divides obligations between the Member States from which programmes emanate and the Member States receiving them, those arguments cannot be accepted.

. . .

34. It follows, first, that it is solely for the Member State from which television broadcasts emanate to monitor the application of the law of the originating Member State applying to such broadcasts and to ensure compliance with Directive 89/552, and, second, that the receiving Member State is not authorized to exercise its own control in that regard.

. . .

36. Only in the circumstances provided for in the second sentence of Article 2(2) [now art 3.2 AVMSD] . . . may the receiving Member State exceptionally suspend retransmission of televised broadcasts, on the conditions laid down by that provision. Moreover, if a Member State considers that another Member State has failed to fulfil its obligations under the directive, it may, as the Commission has rightly observed, bring Treaty infringement proceedings . . . or request the Commission itself to take action against that Member State.

Source: © European Union, 1995–2013.

As *Commission* v *Belgium* illustrates, fixing jurisdiction is of central importance because, save for the limited exceptions noted in paragraph 36 and discussed in more detail at Section 5.8 below, states are responsible for enforcing the terms of the Directive, and can impose more exacting requirements, only in relation to *domestic* service providers. The AVMSD establishes a cascading hierarchy of criteria designed to ensure that jurisdiction can be clearly determined: where one criterion fails to provide an answer, further criteria come into play.

Extract 5.7.3
Directive 2010/13/EU, on the co-ordination of certain provisions laid down by law, regulation or administrative action in Member States concerning the provision of audiovisual media services (Audiovisual Media Services Directive) [2010] OJ L95/1, art 2.3

2.3. For the purposes of this Directive, a media service provider shall be deemed to be established in a Member State in the following cases:

(a) the media service provider has its head office in that Member State and the editorial decisions about the audiovisual media service are taken in that Member State;

(b) if a media service provider has its head office in one Member State but editorial decisions on the audiovisual media service are taken in another Member State, it shall be deemed to be established in the Member State where a significant part of the workforce involved in the pursuit of the audiovisual media service activity operates. If a significant part of the workforce involved in the pursuit of the audiovisual media service activity operates in each of those Member States, the media service provider shall be deemed to be established in the Member State where it has its head office. If a significant part of the workforce involved in the pursuit of the audiovisual media service activity operates in neither of those Member States, the media service provider shall be deemed to be established in the Member State where it first began its activity in accordance with the law of that Member State, provided that it maintains a stable and effective link with the economy of that Member State;

(c) if a media service provider has its head office in a Member State but decisions on the audiovisual media service are taken in a third country, or vice versa, it shall be deemed to be established in the Member State concerned, provided that a significant part of the workforce involved in the pursuit of the audiovisual media service activity operates in that Member State.

2.4. Media service providers to whom the provisions of paragraph 3 are not applicable shall be deemed to be under the jurisdiction of a Member State in the following cases:

(a) they use a satellite up-link situated in that Member State;
(b) although they do not use a satellite up-link situated in that Member State, they use satellite capacity appertaining to that Member State.

Source: © European Union, 1995–2013.

If all else fails, the basic provisions relating to establishment developed by the Court of Justice are to be applied (art 2.5). Though this detailed list looks as though it should resolve all possible uncertainties, questions concerning the location of the head office as well as the meaning of terms such as 'editorial control' and 'significant part of the workforce' indicate that this is not necessarily so, as is explained in the following extract that considers similar provisions contained in the TWFD.

Extract 5.7.4
Jackie Harrison and Lorna Woods, *European Broadcasting Law and Policy* (Cambridge University Press, 2007) at 185–6

. . . paragraph 3b [now 2.3(b)] recognizes that there may be more complicated corporate structures than the one mentioned in paragraph 3a [now 2.3(a)]. This is evidenced by the separation of the criteria of 'head office' and 'editorial decisions on programme schedules' now 'editorial decisions on the audiovisual media service'. Whilst this distinction is aimed at making the case for jurisdiction more clear cut, it actually obscures the issue . . .

    We still need to identify the level of autonomy ascribed to the notion of editorial decision-making. This may vary widely between different broadcasters, particularly depending on where and how an individual broadcaster sources its content. The same content and scheduling may be broadcast to different member states, changed only in relation to dubbing or subtitling, meaning the local offices, in practice, have little autonomy. By contrast, it may be possible for branch offices or subsidiaries to have a greater degree of control over scheduling . . .

Note also that art 2.3(c) refers merely to 'decisions' and not 'editorial decisions', which could be read as all encompassing. These questions become even more complex to answer when one considers who should be included in the relevant workforce – does this, for example, extend to those involved in dubbing or subtitling programmes – and the development of interactive and new-media services?

    The system of home state control established by the AVMSD only applies to matters that 'fall within the fields co-ordinated by' the Directive. This has raised some tricky questions as to whether particular domestic rules fall within the scope of the Directive or not. It is now, however, clear that states remain free to apply general laws that are not television specific, for instance on matters such as consumer protection or obscenity, provided this does not prevent the actual transmission of the television service. The issue was initially considered in *KO* v *De Agostini*, where the ECJ held that Sweden could fine firms advertising beauty products and detergents under consumer protection rules where the advertisements suggested unwarranted skin-care and environmental benefits respectively. The Swedish measures did not directly restrict the retransmission of the satellite broadcasts, though had the potential to undercut their advertising base.[48]

---

[48] Joined Cases C-34/95, *Konsumentombudsmannen (KO)* v *De Agostini (Svenska) Förlag AB* and C35 and 36/95, *KO* v *TV-Shop I Sverige AB* [1997] ECR I-3843.

Similar issues arose in the case of *Mesopotamia Broadcast A/S METV and Roj TV S/A*. Mesopotamia broadcast the Roj TV channel from Denmark into Germany. Denmark concluded that Roj TV's pro-Kurdish stance and apparent support for Kurdish groups engaged in armed conflict with Turkey did not breach the AVMSD rules, particularly those relating to hate speech. Germany, with significant numbers of both Kurdish and Turkish residents, considered that it could exacerbate tensions among these groups and undermine international understanding. It therefore took action to prevent Roj TV engaging in any production or fund-raising activity in Germany but did not seek to prevent reception within Germany of the Danish-based service. The key finding by the Court of Justice is set out below, mirroring that in *KO* v *De Agostini*.

Extract 5.7.5
Cases C-244/10 and C-245/10, *Mesopotamia Broadcast A/S METV and Roj TV A/S* v *Bundesrepublik Deutschland*, 22 September 2011, not yet reported, paras 52–3

52. The German Government stated . . . that, although, by the decision of the Federal Interior Ministry of 13 June 2008, all the activities of the broadcaster at issue in the main proceedings were prohibited in Germany, that Member State was unable to prevent any repercussions in Germany of television broadcasts made abroad. Thus, the reception and private use of Roj TV's programme is not prohibited and remains in fact possible in practice. In particular, that Member State stated that while it does not prevent retransmissions on its territory from Denmark of television programmes made by that broadcaster, all activities organised by Roj TV or for the benefit of the latter in the Federal Republic of Germany are illegal on account of the prohibition on activity imposed by the decision of the Federal Interior Ministry of 13 June 2008. Therefore, the production of broadcasts and the organisation of events consisting in screening Roj TV's broadcasts in a public place, in particular in a stadium, and the sympathy actions taking place in Germany are prohibited.

53. Measures such as those mentioned in the previous paragraph do not, in principle, constitute an obstacle to retransmission per se, but it is for the referring court to determine the actual effects which follow from the prohibition at issue . . .

Source: © European Union, 1995–2013.

Questions for discussion

1. Why should a non-EU based television company be under the jurisdiction of a Member State where it uses the satellite capacity of that Member State but not where it uses a video hosting service located in that state to distribute similar content?

2. To what extent could rulings such as *De Agostini* and *Roj TV* undermine the single market in television services established in the AVMSD?

5.8 DEROGATIONS TO THE COUNTRY OF ORIGIN PRINCIPLE

Although the country of origin principle is central to the operation of the AVMSD, certain derogations are allowed in relation to the transmission of harmful content where the normal procedures for review could prove to be unduly slow. In relation to broadcast services, article 3.2 allows a state to take action against a service coming from another Member

State that 'manifestly, seriously and gravely' infringes the provisions on child protection or hate speech (see further Section 5.9 below). Article 3.4 allows states to restrict incoming on-demand services on public policy, public health, public security and consumer protection grounds. The country of origin and Commission must be notified before any action is taken, though in exceptional cases relating to on-demand services these requirements may be waived (art 3.5).

Derogations are also possible in the context of 'forum shopping', where broadcasters establish themselves in one country in order to avoid the stricter rules in another. This has been a long-standing problem for Member States as the *Bond van Adverteerders* case discussed at Extract 5.3.3 above illustrates. In the subsequent *TV10* ruling, however, the ECJ held that a Member State could act against a service that was 'entirely or principally directed at its territory' where the broadcaster had established itself abroad in order to avoid the stricter rules in the receiving state.[49] *TV10* related to circumstances pre-dating the coming into force of the TWFD and it was not certain whether the circumvention principle remained applicable after 1989. Member State concerns were underlined by the 1997 case of *VT4*, in which the ECJ held that the mere fact that a UK broadcaster, VT4, aimed all its broadcasts and advertisements exclusively at the Flemish public in Belgium did not mean that VT4 could not be considered to be established in the UK.[50] The Court went on to note that 'the Treaty does not prohibit an undertaking from exercising the freedom to provide services if it does not offer services in the Member State in which it is established' (para 22). *VT4* suggested that broadcasters could locate wherever they wished in the EU, encouraging a process of deregulatory competition among states.

These developments, in particular the establishment of television companies in London to take advantage of the UK's light-touch approach to regulating satellite broadcasts, are discussed in the extract below.

Extract 5.8.1

Thomas Gibbons and Peter Humphreys, *Audiovisual Regulation Under Pressure: Comparative Cases from North America and Europe* (Abingdon: Routledge, 2012) at 140

Nordahl Svendsen refers to these [UK based] channels as being typically US channels and 're-flagged channels', taking the analogy from 'international shipping practices where a ship from a particular country gets itself re-flagged as though from another country in order to get around some rules that would otherwise constrain operators'.[i] Our research suggests that this may be exaggerated (many of the international channels licensed by Ofcom were not US ones, and a large number catered to UK ethnic minorities). However, it is beyond question that some channels located themselves in London in order to avoid their target country's stricter rules. Other countries with channels deliberately targeting other European countries were Luxembourg . . . Wallonia . . . and also Germany. . . . As will be seen this led to demands mainly from small countries – to tighten up the country of origin rule . . .'

Source: Copyright © 2012 Routledge. Reproduced by permission of Taylor & Francis Books UK.

[i] E. Nordahl Svendsen, 'From sovereignty to liberalization. Media policy in small European countries' in G. Ferrell Lowe and C.S. Nissen (eds), *Small Among Giants: Television Broadcasting in Smaller Countries* (Göteborg: Nordicom, 2011).

---

[49] Case C23/93, *TV10* v *Commissariaat Voor de Media* [1994] ECR I-4795, para 20.
[50] Case C-56/96 *VT4 Ltd* v *Vlaamse Gemeenschap* [1997] ECR I-3143.

The TWFD was thus amended in 1997 to include a new recital 14, confirming the right of states to take action against broadcasters deliberately evading domestic rules, now further developed in article 4.2 AVMSD. This establishes a two-stage procedure for resolving cases involving television broadcasting. The first stage involves discussions among the countries of origin and reception, potentially leading to the country of origin requesting the broadcaster concerned to comply with the rules of the receiving state. Where this proves ineffective and the broadcaster has chosen its location 'in order to circumvent' the stricter rules of the receiving state, the latter state may then take 'appropriate measures' against the service.

Proving a subjective intention to circumvent the rules of the receiving state is likely to be difficult and it has been suggested that this should be inferred from the objective factual arrangements, leaving it to the broadcaster to then put forward a convincing alternative explanation for its choice of location.[51] Before taking such measures, however, the state must notify the Commission and the host state of its intentions (art 4.4) and cannot proceed further where the Commission, within three months from notification, concludes that this would be incompatible with EU law (art 4.5). These procedural requirements are characteristic of the AVMSD, which repeatedly places domestic action within a framework of EU supervision.

There are no parallel provisions relating to on-demand services. Article 3.4 AVMSD may, however, allow states to take action where one of the public interest grounds listed in that article is at stake but this list is not all encompassing and does not, for example, include cultural concerns. These could arise where an on-demand service seeks to evade domestic rules, such as a tax intended to help fund film production, an approach adopted by France and Spain.[52] In this context, the receiving Member State may have to fall back on the general circumvention principle identified in cases such as *TV10* if it wishes to restrict access to the service.

5.9 CONTENT REQUIREMENTS I: THE PROTECTION OF MINORS AND HATE SPEECH

The article on hate speech in the AVMSD applies to all audiovisual media services, while the child protection measures differ slightly depending on whether the service is offered on a broadcast or on-demand basis. The relevant articles in the Directive are set out below.

Extract 5.9.1
Directive 2010/13/EU, on the co-ordination of certain provisions laid down by law, regulation or administrative action in Member States concerning the provision of audiovisual media services (Audiovisual Media Services Directive) [2010] OJ L95/1, arts 6, 12 and 27

Article 6

Member States shall ensure by appropriate means that audiovisual media services provided by media service providers under their jurisdiction do not contain any incitement to hatred based on race, sex, religion or nationality.

---

[51] See discussion in R. Craufurd-Smith, 'Determining regulatory competence for audiovisual media services in the European Union' (2011) 3/2 *Journal of Media Law* 263–85 at 274–8.
[52] Ibid., 281.

Article 12

Member States shall take appropriate measures to ensure that on-demand audiovisual media services provided by media service providers under their jurisdiction which might seriously impair the physical, mental or moral development of minors are only made available in such a way as to ensure that minors will not normally hear or see such on-demand audiovisual media services.

Article 27

1. Member States shall take appropriate measures to ensure that television broadcasts by broadcasters under their jurisdiction do not include any programmes which might seriously impair the physical, mental or moral development of minors, in particular programmes that involve pornography or gratuitous violence.

2. The measures provided for in paragraph 1 shall also extend to other programmes which are likely to impair the physical, mental or moral development of minors, except where it is ensured, by selecting the time of the broadcast or by any technical measure, that minors in the area of transmission will not normally hear or see such broadcasts.

3. In addition, when such programmes are broadcast in unencoded form Member States shall ensure that they are preceded by an acoustic warning or are identified by the presence of a visual symbol throughout their duration.

Source: © European Union, 1995–2013.

The objective behind the AVMSD was to establish threshold requirements that all services must meet. In areas such as hate speech and child protection, however, constitutional, social and cultural factors have a strong influence on what each state considers acceptable or harmful, which renders agreement difficult. For this reason, the AVMSD provisions are here very open-ended and a key question is whether they should be understood as establishing uniform 'European-wide' standards or as permitting each Member State to determine what is acceptable. This has been a live issue in the context of child protection measures but has also been raised more recently in the context of hate speech in the *Roj-TV* case (see Extract 5.7.5 above).

In the child protection field, these questions were initially explored with reference to article 22 TWFD, the comparable provision to article 27 AVMSD. The article identifies two categories of content: content where there is a low risk of serious harm (now art 27.1 AVMSD) and content where there is a high risk of some, but not serious, harm (art 27.2 AVMSD). Content of the former type is prohibited, while the latter type is permissible provided effective steps are taken to ensure that children will not normally hear or see it, such as late night scheduling or encryption. States have varied in their application of these provisions. The European Commission has noted, for example, that 'there is a wide gap between the Nordic countries, which are tough on violent material but easy-going where sexually explicit material is concerned, and the Latin countries, tough on sex but less so on violence', although the *TV1000* case discussed below reveals differences even among Nordic countries on sexual matters.[53]

Given that this is one area where Member States are allowed to take direct action against foreign broadcasts under article 3(2) AVMSD (previously art 2(2) TWFD, discussed at Section 5.8 above), these differences become highly relevant and are likely to cause disputes between states. Article 3(2) AVMSD enables states to suspend or take other measures to impede transmission of broadcasts that 'manifestly, seriously and gravely'

---

[53] European Commission, *Green Paper on the Protection of Minors and Human Dignity in Audiovisual dn Information Services*, COM (96) 483 final, annex 3.II.1.

infringe articles 27(1) or (2) AVMSD, as well as the hate speech provisions in article 6 AVMSD.[54] Once again, article 3(2) sets out certain notification and procedural requirements and if the Commission decides within two months from being notified of the proposed measures that they infringe EU law, the Member State is required, as a matter of urgency, to bring them to an end.

Key questions relating to the interpretation of these provisions were raised in the 1998 *TV1000* case, which concerned Sweden and Norway. Sweden was then a member of the EC but Norway, a member of the European Free Trade Area (EFTA) was not, so the case was referred to the EFTA court. The EFTA court was asked to interpret the child protection provisions in the TWFD, which applied to the EFTA countries and governed the relations between the parties.[55] A Swedish-based broadcaster, TV1000, had been transmitting an encrypted, pornographic channel, FilmMax, into Norway. Sweden considered the channel to be a category two case, acceptable provided children could not normally see it, while Norway considered that the channel's content could seriously harm children, a category one case, and prohibited its relay over cable networks in Norway. The question for the EFTA Court was whether the Directive established a common European standard relating to child protection and, if so, whether Norway or Sweden was correct in its categorisation of the service. Alternatively, was it solely for Sweden, as the country of origin, to determine the extent of harm that exposure to the service might cause children?

Extract 5.9.2

Case E-8/97, *TV 1000 Sverige AB* v *Norway*, EFTA Court Report 1998, p. 68 at paras 24 and 26

24. The reference in Article 2(2)(a) of the Directive [now 3.2 AVMSD] to a television broadcast infringing Article 22 [now 27 AVMSD] must be understood as being a reference to the criterion that it 'might seriously impair the physical, mental or moral development of minors'. The Court notes that, as pointed out by *inter alia* the EFTA Surveillance Authority and the Commission of the European Communities, the provision does not purport to lay down any standards for what might have such detrimental effects, leaving it up to the Member States to define these terms, as well as the term 'pornography', in accordance with their national legislation and moral standards. This applies equally to the transmitting State, pursuant to Article 22, with regard to broadcasts under its jurisdiction and to the receiving State exercising its powers under Article 2(2), second sentence, cf. Article 22.

. . .

26. Protection of minors is a legitimate goal of each of the Contracting Parties to the EEA Agreement. The protection of the mental and moral development of minors forms an important part of the protection of public morality, an area where it is not possible to determine a uniform European conception, as the requirements of morals vary, depending on time and place (see the *Handyside* judgment of the European Court of Human Rights of 7 December 1976, Series A Vol. 24). This approach has been confirmed by the ECJ (see Case 121/85 *Conegate* v *HM Customs and Excise* [1986] ECR 1007). In that judgment, the ECJ observed that a Member State is permitted by the EC Treaty to make its own assessment relating to public morality within its territory. Nevertheless, a State is guilty of arbitrary discrimination if it seeks to prohibit the importation of goods or services that could be made and marketed lawfully within its territory.

Source: © EFTA Secretariat, 2011.

---

[54] In the UK, Ofcom has power to refer to the Secretary of State certain objectionable foreign services. The Secretary of State can then issue a proscription order prohibiting the inclusion of the service in multiplex services or cable packages: see sections 329–332 of the Communications Act 2003.

[55] R. Craufurd-Smith, 'Sex and violence in the internal market: the impact of European Community law on television programme standards' (1998) 3/2 *Contemporary Issues in Law* 135–53.

The EFTA Court thus confirmed that *both* the transmitting and receiving state could make their own determinations as to the potential impact of the service on the physical, mental and moral development of children. The EFTA ruling is not, however, binding on the Court of Justice and there is still to be a determinative ruling on this issue at the EU level.

In relation to on-demand services a more relaxed approach is taken in article 12 AVMSD. Rather than prohibit content that *might seriously harm* children, states are merely required to ensure that children will 'not normally hear or see' it. There are no restrictions on content that is likely to merely impair child development. On the other hand, states appear to retain a residual capacity to control non-domestic on-demand EU services on public policy grounds under article 3.4 AVMSD, which explicitly extends to the 'protection of minors'. Recourse to article 3.4 is overseen, however, by the Commission and it is questionable whether the Commission would accept the legitimacy of measures taken against seriously harmful content that is effectively encrypted or content that is potentially less harmful but freely accessible. Recital 60 makes reference to the use of personal identification numbers, filtering systems and labelling as mechanisms that can be used to help protect children and the EU has itself supported the development of such mechanisms through its various 'safer internet' programmes.[56]

It is apparent from the *Mesopotamia Broadcast* case, discussed at Section 5.7 above, that similar tensions can arise in the field of hate speech, with states differing in their approach to the balance to be struck between freedom of expression and the protection of human dignity. Unlike the EFTA Court in *TV1000*, however, the Court of Justice in this context seems to be developing a common European approach to hate speech within the terms of the Directive.

Extract 5.9.3

Cases C-244/10 and C-245/10, *Mesopotamia Broadcast A/S METV and Roj TV A/S* v *Bundesrepublik Deutschland*, 22 September 2011, not yet reported, paras 38–45

38. . . . it must be observed, first, that the Directive does not contain any definition of the terms referred to in Article 22a [now art 6 AVMSD] thereof.

39. Furthermore, and as stated in point 63 of the Advocate General's opinion, the drafting history of Directives 89/552 and 97/36 does not contain any relevant information relating to the scope of the concept of 'incitement to hatred', and confirms that the European legislature intended to lay down, in Article 22a of the Directive, a ground for prohibition based on public order considerations which would be distinct from the grounds relating particularly to the protection of minors.

40. It follows that the scope of Article 22a of the Directive must be determined by considering the usual meaning in everyday language of the terms used in that article, while also taking into account the context in which they occur and the purposes of the rules of which they are part (see, Case C336/03 *easyCar* [2005] ECR I1947, paragraph 21 and the case-law cited).

41. As regards the words 'incitation' and 'hatred', it must be observed that they refer, first, to an action intended to direct specific behaviour and, second, a feeling of animosity or rejection with regard to a group of persons.

42. Thus, the Directive, by using the concept 'incitement to hatred', is designed to forestall any ideology which fails to respect human values, in particular initiatives which attempt to justify violence by terrorist acts against a particular group of persons.

---

[56] Currently Decision no 1351/2008/EC establishing a multiannual Community programme on protecting children using the Internet and other communication technologies [2008] OJ L348/118.

43. As regards the infringement of the principles of international understanding, as stated in paragraph 25 of the present judgment, Mesopotamia Broadcast and Roj TV, according to the referring court, play a role in stirring up violent confrontations between persons of Turkish and Kurdish origin in Turkey and in exacerbating the tensions between Turks and Kurds living in Germany, thereby infringing the principles of international understanding.

44. Consequently, it must be held that such behaviour is covered by the concept of 'incitement to hatred'.

45. Therefore, as the Advocate General observed in points 88 and 89 of his Opinion, compliance with the rule of public order laid down in Article 22a of the Directive must be verified by the authorities of the Member State which have jurisdiction over the broadcaster concerned, irrespective of the presence in that Member State of the ethnic or cultural communities concerned. The application of the prohibition laid down in Article 22a does not depend on the potential effects of the broadcast in question in the Member State of origin or in one Member State in particular, but only on the combination of the two conditions stipulated in that article, namely incitement to hatred and grounds of race, sex, religion or nationality.

Source: © European Union, 1995–2013.

Questions for discussion

1. Should, in your opinion, the approach to child protection differ depending on whether the service is provided on an on-demand or broadcast basis?
2. To what extent does it make sense to characterise the AVMSD as a harmonising measure in the fields of child protection and hate speech? Is harmonisation here realistic or even desirable?

5.10 CONTENT REQUIREMENTS II: SUPPORT FOR EUROPEAN CONTENT

Some of the most controversial provisions in the TWFD were those designed to promote the European film and television industries. These have been retained and extended in the AVMSD and require states to ensure that broadcasters allocate, where practicable, 10 per cent of their transmission time to programmes produced by independent producers (art 17); that audiovisual media service providers within their jurisdiction do not undermine the cinema release of films by co-terminous distribution on other platforms (art 8); and that audiovisual media service providers comply, where practicable, with European programme quotas (arts 1(n), 1(2)–(4), 13 and 16). This section focuses on what is arguably the most problematic of these provisions, the European quotas, set out below.

Extract 5.10.1
Directive 2010/13/EU, on the co-ordination of certain provisions laid down by law, regulation or administrative action in Member States concerning the provision of audiovisual media services (Audiovisual Media Services Directive) [2010] OJ L95/1, arts 1, 13 and 16

Article 1

(n) 'European works' means the following:
(i) works originating in Member States;
(ii) works originating in European third States party to the European Convention on Transfrontier Television of the Council of Europe and fulfilling the conditions of paragraph 3;

(iii) works co-produced within the framework of agreements related to the audiovisual sector concluded between the Union and third countries and fulfilling the conditions defined in each of those agreements.

3. The works referred to in points (n)(i) and (ii) of paragraph 1 are works mainly made with authors and workers residing in one or more of the States referred to in those provisions provided that they comply with one of the following three conditions:

(i)   they are made by one or more producers established in one or more of those States;

(ii) the production of the works is supervised and actually controlled by one or more producers established in one or more of those States;

(iii) the contribution of co-producers of those States to the total co-production costs is preponderant and the co-production is not controlled by one or more producers established outside those States.

4. Works that are not European works within the meaning of point (n) of paragraph 1 but that are produced within the framework of bilateral co-production agreements concluded between Member States and third countries shall be deemed to be European works provided that the co-producers from the Union supply a majority share of the total cost of production and that the production is not controlled by one or more producers established outside the territory of the Member States.

Article 13

1. Member States shall ensure that on-demand audiovisual media services provided by media service providers under their jurisdiction promote, where practicable and by appropriate means, the production of and access to European works. Such promotion could relate, inter alia, to the financial contribution made by such services to the production and rights acquisition of European works or to the share and/or prominence of European works in the catalogue of programmes offered by the on-demand audiovisual media service . . .

Article 16

1. Member States shall ensure, where practicable and by appropriate means, that broadcasters reserve for European works a majority proportion of their transmission time, excluding the time allotted to news, sports events, games, advertising, teletext services and teleshopping. This proportion, having regard to the broadcaster's informational, educational, cultural and entertainment responsibilities to its viewing public, should be achieved progressively, on the basis of suitable criteria.

Source: © European Union, 1995–2013.

The 'quota' for on-demand providers is notably less exacting than that for broadcasters. Because of the element of consumer selection, it is difficult for on-demand services to ensure that a minimum proportion of transmission time is given over to European programmes. There are thus no specified numerical limits and Member States appear to be adopting different combinations of techniques, along the lines suggested in article 13, to promote European content in this context.[57]

The quotas have both industrial and cultural rationales, in each case linked to the dominant presence of US films and television programmes in Europe. US content has proved extremely popular across Europe, whereas, in relation to European content, Europe's television markets have remained fragmented along cultural and linguistic lines, with comparatively little internal exchange of programming. In 2010, for example, European broadcasters spent around 69 per cent of their total acquisitions budget on US content but

---

[57] Commission, *First Report on the Application of Articles 13, 16 and 17 of Directive 2010/13/EU for the period 2009–2010*, COM (2012) 522 final, at 5.

only 14 per cent on programmes from other European countries.[58] There is a strong economic logic behind these figures. The production costs of a US television programme are generally recouped from sales within the large, integrated US market before it is sold abroad. Content can thus be sold to foreign broadcasters at a fraction of the production cost, creating an unbeatable combination of high production values and relatively cheap prices. A one-hour television drama costing 2 million US dollars to produce, for example, might be sold for a mere 15,000 dollars in Austria or 75,000 dollars in the UK.[59] Without an incentive for broadcasters to continue to include European content there is a risk that European production could go into terminal decline, with serious cultural and economic implications.

Despite these concerns, the European quota polarised opinions when originally proposed. The UK, Germany and Denmark were all strongly opposed on the basis that it constituted an unwarranted form of protectionism and incursion into domestic cultural policies; France, on the other hand, supported by the Commission and European Parliament, pressed hard for its inclusion in binding form.[60] The result was a messy political comprise that is still reflected in the wording of the quota provisions detailed above.

Questions for discussion

1. What aspects of the drafting of articles 13 and 16 render their legal enforceability doubtful?
2. What determines whether a programme is European or not? To what extent does article 1 indicate that the European quotas are more concerned with industrial rather than cultural policy goals?

Not only was the European quota adopted in a highly qualified form, its effectiveness in addressing the underlying industrial and cultural concerns has been questioned.[61] Article 16 AVMSD, for example, apart from excluding certain programme genres, does not specify the type of programming that is to satisfy the quota obligation. Thus, broadcasters might be tempted to concentrate on the more inexpensive 'flow' type of programmes, for example, studio discussion programmes, which have only a very short shelf life, and, therefore, do not contribute to the development of a library of programmes that can be rebroadcast or sold. For this, 'stock' programmes, such as fiction series, are required, but these are more expensive to produce, particularly when compared with American products. The quota does nothing to encourage this type of programming, yet it is stock programmes that are necessary for the development of programme catalogues, a need recognised early on by the Commission.[62] Nor do the quotas encourage the exchange of European content, building a European market, in that they can be met by transmission of domestic programmes. In the Commission's most recent report on the implementation

---

[58] Attentional, Gide Loyrette Nouel, Headway International, Oliver and Ohlbaum, *Study on the implementation of the provisions of the Audiovisual Media Services Directive concerning the promotion of European works in audiovisual media services*, 13 December 2011, 107 at: http://ec.europa.eu/avpolicy/info_centre/library/studies/index_en.htm.

[59] P.S. Grant and C. Wood, *Blockbusters and Trade Wars: Popular Culture in a Globalized World* (Vancouver: Douglas and McIntyre Ltd, 2004), 129–31.

[60] B. de Witte, 'The European content requirement in the EC Television Directive – Five Years After' in E.M. Barendt (ed), *The Yearbook of Media and Entertainment Law 1995* (Oxford University Press, 1995), 101–2, 104, 106–7; I. Katsirea, 'Why the European broadcasting quota should be abolished' (2003) 28 *E.L. Rev.* 190–209 at 191.

[61] See J. Harrison and L. Woods, *European Broadcasting Law and Policy* (Cambridge University Press, 2007), ch 11.

[62] Commission of the European Communities, *Strategy Options to Strengthen the European Programme Industry in the Context of the Audiovisual Policy of the European Union*, Green Paper, COM (94) 96 final, p. 8.

of the quotas it was noted that only 8.1 per cent of European works on broadcast channels were non-domestic.[63] This suggests that inclusion of a 'non-domestic' element in the quota could have positive effects.[64]

Similarly, as a tool of cultural policy, article 16 has its limits. The article is silent on transmission times. Broadcasters may be tempted to transmit European works at less popular viewing times, in order to leave the prime viewing periods free for productions likely to gain a wider audience. Moreover, by virtue of article 1.3, works are categorised as 'European' essentially on the basis of the residency of the authors and workers and country of establishment of the producer/s. However, nationality and location alone will not ensure that programmes are produced that reflect European or national identity. This, of course, illustrates the inherent difficulty of trying to introduce measures that will promote a certain type of programming. Although both the Court of Justice and ECHR have accepted that cultural policy measures and the promotion of pluralism constitute legitimate grounds for restricting freedom of expression, any such measures must be proportionate (see Extracts 5.3.3 and 5.2.2 above). Were the EU to define in more detail the type of content to be included there would be a greater risk that the quotas would be held to be illegitimate as more restrictive of the service providers' freedom of speech. As they stand now, however, the quota requirements are at best a crude instrument of cultural policy.

A number of further questions regarding the legality of the European quotas have arisen. On the one hand, it has been suggested that the EEC had no competence to introduce such measures, since they did not facilitate the creation of an internal market in audiovisual services,[65] and, on the other, that the quota is incompatible with the EU's international trade obligations. The European broadcast quota has, however, been in force for well over 20 years and was extended to on-demand services in the AVMS without legal challenge. As a result, the first of these concerns appears less significant today. In relation to the latter, the quota was strongly contested by the US when it was introduced, who argued that it acted as a barrier to free trade under the General Agreement on Tariffs and Trade (GATT). When the General Agreement on Trade in Services (GATS) was agreed in 1994, the then European Community and its Member States made reservations to the 'Most Favoured Nation' principle, which requires states to afford similarly favourable terms to all trading partners. The European Community also refrained from making any commitments in relation to market access and national treatment under GATS. This approach has been maintained to date and serves to shield the quotas from challenge under GATS, where there is no explicit derogation for cultural services.[66] To underline the special status of cultural goods and services the EU also supported adoption of the 2005 UNESCO Convention on Cultural Diversity, which, though not superseding state commitments under GATT or GATS, nevertheless emphasises the importance of state measures to support cultural creation and innovation.[67]

Question for discussion

1.   How would your redraft the European quotas, if at all, to address their weaknesses?

---

[63] European Commission (2012), *First Report on the Promotion of European Works*, n 57 above, p. 9.
[64] See Harrison and Woods (2007), n 61 above at pp. 252–3.
[65] For detailed analysis, see Katsirea, n 61 above.
[66] Gibbons and Humphreys (2012), n 28, pp. 148–51.
[67] See, in particular, Articles 20–21 of the 2005 Convention and discussion by Gibbons and Humphreys (2012) n 28, pp. 148–51, and Graber (2006) n 19, both above.

Despite concerns over the validity and effectiveness of the European quotas, they have become a firm component of the EU's audiovisual policy. Articles 13.2 and 16.3 require Member States to report regularly to the Commission on their implementation of the quotas and although the data on on-demand services is still too limited to draw firm conclusions it is clear that, overall, European content on broadcast channels is holding up, with an average of 64.3 per cent in 2010.[68] On the other hand, the extent of European content varies significantly, with the average share of transmission time ranging from 47.4 per cent (Slovenia and UK) to 81 per cent (Hungary) in 2010. Three countries, including the UK, did not reach the 50 per cent quota.[69] The detailed returns for the UK indicate that a substantial number of satellite and cable channels include little, if any, European content.[70] Among the reasons given were the small scale of the channel concerned; difficulty finding European programmes or finding programmes at competitive prices; and the fact that certain companies are subsidiaries of companies based in non-member countries, which broadcast programmes mostly from the parents' own stock.[71] It is clear from this that without further exchange of programming among the Member States the expansion of television services across Europe will continue to suck in programmes from abroad, largely to the benefit of producers in the US.

5.11 CONTENT REQUIREMENTS III: RIGHT OF REPLY

Article 28 AVMSD provides a right of reply to natural or legal persons in relation to content in a broadcast television programme. There must be no unreasonable terms or conditions hindering the exercise of the right of reply, and it must be transmitted within a reasonable time, and at a time and in a manner appropriate to the offending broadcast. There is no comparable provision relating to on-demand services.

Extract 5.11.1
Directive 2010/13/EU, on the co-ordination of certain provisions laid down by law, regulation or administrative action in Member States concerning the provision of audiovisual media services (Audiovisual Media Services Directive) [2010] OJ L95/1, art 28

Article 28

1. Without prejudice to other provisions adopted by the Member States under civil, administrative or criminal law, any natural or legal person, regardless of nationality, whose legitimate interests, in particular reputation and good name, have been damaged by an assertion of incorrect facts in a television programme must have a right of reply or equivalent remedies. Member States shall ensure that the actual exercise of the right of reply or equivalent remedies is not hindered by the imposition of unreasonable terms or conditions. The reply shall be transmitted within a reasonable time subsequent to the request being substantiated and at a time and in a manner appropriate to the broadcast to which the request refers.

2. A right of reply or equivalent remedies shall exist in relation to all broadcasters under the jurisdiction of a Member State.

. . .

Source: © European Union, 1995–2013.

---

[68] European Commission (2012), *First Report on the Promotion of European Works*, n 57 at p. 12.
[69] Ibid., at p. 10.
[70] European Commission Staff Working Document, *Promotion of European Works in EU Scheduled and On-demand Audiovisual Media Services, part II*, COM (2012) 522 final, at pp. 150–72.
[71] Ibid., at p. 170.

Questions for discussion

1. Do the provisions relating to a right of reply in section 6 of the BBC's Editorial Guidelines (http://www.bbc.co.uk/guidelines/editorialguidelines/guidelines/) and to fairness in section 7 of the Ofcom Broadcasting Code (http://stakeholders.ofcom.org.uk/broadcasting/broadcast-codes/) amount to a right of reply within the terms of the Directive?
2. Should a right of reply be introduced for on-demand audiovisual services?

5.12 THE FUTURE OF EUROPEAN MEDIA REGULATION?

It is apparent that the AVMSD is not the last word on EU audiovisual regulation. With the advent of connected TVs, allowing access to the full range of services available on the Internet, the distinctions between broadcast, on-demand and other types of audiovisual content are wearing increasingly thin. At time of writing, the Commission had initiated two consultations on whether additional rules are needed to ensure the independence of media regulatory bodies and to implement the findings of the High Level Group on Media Freedom and Pluralism, which suggested, among other things, that there should be further harmonisation at EU level in areas such as defamation and data protection.[72] With an increasingly interconnected media environment the logic of the internal market appears compelling, raising the question: what space can, and should now, be left for domestic media law and policy?

Selected further reading

For a historical perspective

R. Collins, *Broadcasting and Audiovisual Policy in the European Single Market* **(John Libbey, 1994)** explores the tensions between liberals and 'dirigistes' in the early development of EU media policy.

For an overview of the field and key issues

O. Castendyk, E. Dommering and A. Scheuer (eds), *European Media Law* (Alphen aan den Rijn: Kluwer Law International, 2008).

T. Gibbons and P. Humphreys, *Audiovisual Regulation under Pressure: Comparative Cases from North America and Europe* **(Routledge, 2012),** chs 1, 7 and 8, focusing on the interaction between domestic law and policy and the EU and the position of smaller Member States.

A. Harcourt, *The European Union and the Regulation of Media Markets* **(Manchester University Press, 2005).**

P. Humphreys, 'EU audio-visual policy, cultural diversity and the future of public service broadcasting' in J. Harrison and B. Wessels, *Mediating Europe: New Media, Mass Communications and the European Public Sphere* (Berghan Books, 2009), 183–212.

P. Keller, *European and International Media Law, Liberal Democracy, Trade and the New Media* **(Oxford, 2011)** explores the underlying philosophy and objectives behind European media law, with reference to both the EU and the Council of Europe as well other international organisations such as UNESCO and the WTO.

---

[72] European Commission, Public Consultations on Media Issues, 22 March 2013 at: https://ec.europa.eu/digital-agenda/en/public-consultations-media-issues. For discussion of the High Level Group, see Chapter 7.6(b).

P. Valcke and K. Lefever, *Media Law in the European Union* (Wolters Kluwer, 2012). A short but detailed, clear overview of the field.

D. Ward, *The European Union Democratic Deficit and the Public Sphere: An Evaluation of EU Media Policy* (IOS Press, 2002) provides a balanced and thoughtful critique of the development of EU policies relating to the media, with specific emphasis on the place of the media in supporting citizenship and democracy.

L. Woods and J. Harrison, *European Broadcasting Law and Policy* (Cambridge University Press, 2007). This leading textbook contains a wealth of material relating to the development of EU media law up to consideration of the AVMSD with a clear explanation of underlying policy issues and technical concerns.

In relation to specific aspects of the TWFD and AVMSD, including the European quotas

S. Broughton Micova, 'Content Quotas: What and Whom are they Protecting?' in K. Donders, C. Pauwels and J. Loisen (eds), *Private Television in Western Europe. Content, Markets, Policies* (Palgrave Macmillan, 2013), ch 17. This explores the impact of the quotas on a small state with an economically weak media system, Macedonia, and concludes that the quotas can help to protect national cultures, with even low quality quota content capable of supporting the national language or local music.

R. Craufurd-Smith, 'Determining regulatory competence for audiovisual media services in the European Union' (2011) 3/2 *Journal of Media Law* 263–85, focuses on whether the AVMSD can be said to be a harmonising directive and the problem of forum shopping.

A. Herold, 'The new audiovisual media services directive' in C. Pauwels, H. Kalimo, K. Donders and B. Van Rompuy (eds), *Rethinking European Media and Communications Policy* (VUB Press, 2009) offers a helpful overview of the changes made in the AVMSD.

H. Lutz, 'The distinction between linear and non-linear services in the new proposal for an audiovisual media directive' (2006) *Computer and Telecommunications Law Review* 141–4. This offers a short and penetrating critique of the distinction between linear and on-demand services in the AVMSD.

M. Burri-Nenova, 'Cultural diversity and the EC audiovisual media services directive: beyond the handsome rhetoric' (2007) 44/6 *Common Market Law Review* 1689–725, questions whether the EU went far enough in supporting cultural production in the AVMSD.

P. Valcke and D. Stevens, 'Graduated regulation of "regulatable" content and the European audiovisual media services directive. One small step for the industry and one giant leap for the legislator?' (2007) 24 *Telematics Inform* 285–302 provides a clear explanation of the differential approach to regulation in the AVMSD.

B. De Witte, 'The European content requirement in the EC television directive', 1 *The Yearbook of Media and Entertainment Law* (Oxford University Press, 1995), 101–27. This provides an early critique of the European quotas with commentary on their compatibility with fundamental human rights and WTO law.

I. Katsirea, *Public Broadcasting and European Law. A Comparative Examination of Public Service Obligations in Six Member States* (Wolters Kluwer, 2008). Chapter 13, contains a critical commentary on the EU quota and considers its legal basis and application.

For a broader focus on EU cultural policies

E. Psychogiopoulou, *The Integration of Cultural Considerations in EU Law and Policies* (Martinus Nijhoff Publishers, 2008) provides a wide-ranging and detailed account of the influence of cultural concerns on EU law and policy in fields such as the internal market and competition law.

6 Advertising regulation

6.1 INTRODUCTION

Advertising has an important role within the media because it is a significant revenue source for both broadcasting and the press. Generally, the press is funded by a combination of advertising revenue and newspaper sales. Private broadcasting channels have been primarily funded by advertising, thereby enabling their programme services to be delivered free to the viewer.[1] Although, with the development of satellite and cable services, subscription has emerged as a source of funding television, advertising revenue is presently still the major funding source for broadcasters, and even subscription services usually rely on a combination of advertising and subscription revenue. Commercial radio broadcasting has also depended on advertising for revenue, while the Internet now takes an increasingly large share of advertising revenue.[2]

While the general law governs all advertisements,[3] the specific regulation of advertising depends upon whether it appears in the broadcast or non-broadcast sector. To some extent regulation of advertising has reflected a pattern similar to the regulation of press editorial content and broadcasting programmes. As was seen in earlier chapters, press and broadcasting are regulated quite differently. Press advertising (as well as cinema, video, Internet, magazines, direct mail and so forth) is controlled mainly through a self-regulatory system by the Advertising Standards Authority (the ASA). Broadcast advertising is subject to some specific legislative control administered by Ofcom, but in 2004 it delegated much of its authority over advertising to the ASA, while retaining the ultimate back-stop power to apply sanctions in extreme cases.[4]

Several issues arise concerning the relationship between advertising and the media. Clearly advertisers have an incentive to place as much advertising as they can, and the non-broadcast media are free to accept as much as they wish, subject only to constraints such as how much advertising readers will tolerate. Roughly 45 per cent of space in UK newspapers is taken up by advertising.[5] However, in the case of television, there are strict limits on the amount and frequency of advertising. Although radio is not subject to such limits, licensees might find themselves in breach of their licences if they were to broadcast an undue amount of advertising, so that the nature of their service changed. The advertising rules imposed on broadcasters can be seen as a reflection of the familiar justifications for broadcasting regulation (Chapter 1, Section 1.3); they can be justified as necessary to protect the interests of viewers and the rights of the directors of drama, films and other

---

[1] The Peacock Committee found that advertising revenue provided about 95 per cent of the income of commercial television companies and most of the income of local radio stations: *Report of the Committee of Financing the BBC*, Cmnd 9824 (1986), para 80.

[2] In 2007 the Internet is estimated to have received about 16 per cent of total advertising expenditure: J. Curran and J. Seaton, *Power without Responsibility* (London: Routledge, 7th edn, 2010), 270.

[3] This includes the law of contract, intellectual property law, and various statutory regulations, including the Consumer Protection from Unfair Trading Regulations 2008 (discussed in Section 6.5).

[4] See Section 6.5.

[5] *Power without Responsibility* (n 2 above), Table 7.2. In the USA, the comparable figure is 65 per cent: see C.E. Baker, *Advertising and a Democratic Press* (Princeton, NJ: Princeton University Press, 1995), 45.

programmes in having their works shown relatively free of advertising interruptions. Advertisers, despite their importance to broadcast funding, cannot have unlimited access, and they are subject to restrictions on the amount of advertising, what can be advertised and how it can be advertised.

Advertising may exercise a significant impact on media content. As far as newspapers are concerned, editors (or press owners) may choose to avoid offending advertisers on whose financial support their paper depends; further, they may avoid taking radical political positions which will alienate readers, and thereby lose some of the potential buyers of advertised products and services.[6] Edwin Baker concluded in his magisterial study of the impact of advertising on the media: 'Advertisers "pay" the media to obtain the audience they desire, providing a strong incentive for the media to shape content to appeal to this "desired" audience.'[7] The importance of advertising support was shown most dramatically in the UK, when Rupert Murdoch decided in July 2011 to close the *News of the World* in the wake of advertisers' response to the phone-hacking scandal involving the paper.[8]

The influence of advertisers is even clearer in the case of television. As an American advertising agent has explained: 'The networks are in the business not of delivering programmes, that's not their business. The networks' business is to deliver audiences.'[9] Advertisers have an interest in reaching as many viewers or listeners as possible during any given advertising slot, while broadcast companies, in the interests of being able to charge higher advertising rates, have an incentive to present programming which will deliver the largest possible audience to the advertisers. These interests can have an effect on programme quality and diversity. To some extent, this risk is compensated for by the structure of broadcasting; for example, the BBC is a public broadcaster, not dependent upon advertising, and therefore able to provide diversified and minority programming (see Chapter 3). Commercial broadcasters cannot simply succumb to advertisers' pressure, as they also have to meet certain programme standards. Finally, the advertising rules examined in this chapter also try to limit the temptation of broadcasters to cater for advertisers' needs.

However, the impact of advertising on the quality and range of programming remains a serious concern. With growing competition for audiences and advertising, broadcasters are under great pressure to produce programming aimed at a mass audience. This pressure has become more marked in recent years, partly because the Internet has drawn an increasing share of overall advertising revenue, and partly because of the economic recession which has led to a decline in this revenue. These factors have led in turn to pressure on regulators to relax advertising rules; the amount of permitted advertising in peak hours was increased recently (see Section 6.5). In the following extract, the Peacock Committee, which was established in 1985 to examine BBC financing, but which also looked more widely at broadcast financing, discusses these concerns.

---

[6] Ibid., ch 2.
[7] Ibid., 66.
[8] See the report in *The Guardian*, 7 July 2011: http://www.guardian.co.uk/media/2011/jul/07/news-of-the-world-rupert-murdoch (accessed 13 November 2012).
[9] Quoted in J.G. Blumler, 'Television in the United States: funding sources and programme consequences': report prepared for the Peacock Committee on Financing the BBC, Cmnd 9824 (1986).

Extract 6.1.1
Report of the Committee on Financing the BBC, Cmnd 9824 (1986), para 421

Under an advertising-supported broadcasting system, broadcasters are effectively attracting an audience by their programmes that will also be an audience to advertisers. An advertising-supported system will lead to programme diversity only to the extent that different advertisers are willing to pay to associate their messages with different programmes. The important point from an efficiency perspective is that there is no reason why the value of programmes to advertisers should correspond to the value attached to the programmes by viewers and listeners. In fact, the value to advertisers and the value to the audience of a particular programme may well differ markedly. The reason for this is that under an advertising-supported system, people can only express their preferences either by watching or not watching a particular programme, whereas the value to all viewers is measured by their aggregate willingness to pay which measures the intensity of their preferences . . . In the broadcasting case, advertisers can bid for the service of supplying a message to a particular size and type of audience, but the audience has no way of bidding for programme services apart from watching or not watching a programme. The commercial viability of a programme in an advertising system means that the programme must generate a sufficiently large audience to induce advertisers to pay enough to cover the cost of showing the programme. This may lead to programmes being shown because they are popular numerically, even though programmes that are less popular numerically but more intensely demanded are not shown.

Questions for discussion

1. Is the Committee's analysis valid now, when viewers may choose between (at least) 50 channels?
2. Many of the new broadcasting services are special-interest services; does this alter the Committee's analysis?

The next section of this chapter is concerned with the general impact on advertising regulation of the right to freedom of expression guaranteed by the ECHR, art 10, now incorporated into UK law (see Chapter 1, Section 1.2). Section 6.3 examines the organisation and procedures of the Advertising Standards Authority (ASA), the organisation which determines complaints against all forms of non-broadcast advertising, and since 2004 has examined complaints against the contents, though not the general scheduling (and a few other matters), of broadcast advertising on television and radio. The ASA also considers complaints against advertising on video on-demand (VOD) under arrangements introduced in 2010.[10] This chapter examines the regulation of non-broadcast advertising in Section 6.4 and broadcast advertising in Section 6.5, while also considering in the latter the impact of European regulation, most recently the Audiovisual Media Services Directive (AVMSD), on advertising restrictions. There is a brief discussion of the regulation of advertising on VOD in Section 6.6. The final section of the chapter discusses the ban on the broadcast of political advertising in UK law, in particular the question whether the ban is compatible with the right to freedom of expression.

---

[10] ASA Annual Report 2010, 13.

6.2 THE IMPACT OF FREEDOM OF EXPRESSION ON ADVERTISING REGULATION

What impact does the European Convention on Human Rights, now incorporated into English law, have on advertising regulation? There are at least two important legal questions in this context. First, is commercial advertising covered by article 10 of the Convention in the same way as political speech and discussion of public or social affairs? Second, there is the question how far advertising regulation may be regarded as a necessary restriction on the exercise of free commercial expression, imposed, say, to protect the interests of viewers in relatively uninterrupted programmes? In *Casado Coca* a lawyer challenged a ban on advertising his service as a violation of article 10 of the Convention. It was argued by the Spanish government that advertising which served only the advertiser's private interests, and not the public interest, was not protected by article 10.

Extract 6.2.1

Casado Coca v *Spain* (1994) 18 EHRR 1, at 20, 23–4 and 25 (European Court of Human Rights) (some footnotes omitted)

The Court would first point out that Article 10 guarantees freedom of expression to 'everyone'. No distinction is made in it according to whether the type of aim pursued is profit-making or not.[i]

In its *Barthold v Germany* judgment of 25 March 1985[ii] the Court left open the question whether commercial advertising as such came within the scope of the guarantees under Article 10, but its later case law provides guidance on this matter. Article 10 does not apply solely to certain types of information or ideas or forms of expression,[iii] in particular those of a political nature; it also encompasses artistic expression, information of a commercial nature as the Commission rightly pointed out – and even light music and commercial transmitted by cable.[iv]

In the instant case the impugned notices merely gave the applicant's name, profession, address and telephone number. They were clearly published with the aim of advertising, but they provided persons requiring legal assistance with information that was of definite use and likely to facilitate their access to justice.

. . . The applicant contended that the . . . [prohibition] was not 'necessary in a democratic society', because it constituted a disproportionate interference with his right to impart commercial information, a right which members of the Bar, like other citizens, were guaranteed under Article 10. He added that such a restriction was permissible only if it reflected a freely and democratically accepted willingness to exercise self-restraint; that was not so in the instant case.

. . .

Under the Court's case law, the States parties to the Convention have a certain margin of appreciation in assessing the necessity of an interference, but this margin is subject to European supervision as regards both the relevant rules and the decisions applying them.[v] Such a margin of appreciation is particularly essential in the complex and fluctuating area of unfair competition.[vi] The same applies to advertising. In the instant case, the Court's task is therefore confined to ascertaining whether the measures taken at national level are justifiable in principle and proportionate.[vii]

For the citizen, advertising is a means of discovering the characteristics of goods and services offered to him. Nevertheless, it may sometimes be restricted, especially to prevent unfair competition and untruthful or misleading advertising. In some contexts, the publication of even objective, truthful advertisements might be restricted in order to ensure respect for the rights of others or owing to the special circumstances of particular business activities and professions. Any such restrictions must, however, be closely scrutinised by the Court, which must weigh the requirements of those particular features against the advertising in question . . .

In the present case, [the] Court notes that . . . [the] rules allowed advertising in certain cases – namely when a practice was being set up or when there was a change in its membership, address or telephone number – and under certain conditions. The ban was therefore not an absolute one.

. . .

The wide range of regulations and the different rates of change in the Council of Europe's Member States indicate the complexity of the issue. Because of their direct, continuous contact with their members, the Bar authorities and the country's courts are in a better position than an international court to determine how, at a given time, the right balance can be struck between the various interests involved, namely the requirements of the proper administration of justice, the dignity of the profession, the right of everyone to receive information about legal assistance and affording members of the Bar the possibility of advertising their practices.

In view of the above, the Court holds that at the material time – 1982/83 – the relevant authorities' reaction could not be considered unreasonable and disproportionate to the aim pursued.

[i] See *mutatis mutandis*, *Autronic AG* v *Switzerland* (A/178); (1990) 12 EHRR 485, para. 47. [See Chapter 5, Section 5.2.]

[ii] (1985) 7 EHRR 383, para. 42.

[iii] See *Markt Intern. Verlag Gmbh and Klaus Beermann* v *Germany*, Series A, No 165; (1990) 12 EHRR 161, para. 26.

[iv] See *Groppera Radio AG* v *Switzerland* (A/193); (1990) 12 EHRR 321, paras 54–5.

[v] See, *inter alia*, Markt Intern. Verlag, note 13 above, para. 33.

[vi] Ibid.

[vii] Ibid., and see, *inter alia*, Barthold, note 12 above, para. 55.

In a number of cases, however, the Court has upheld challenges to bans on commercial speech. In addition to the *Barthold* decision mentioned in *Casado Coca*, it held incompatible with ECHR, art 10, an injunction granted by Swiss courts to stop a scientist criticising in journal articles microwave ovens as dangerous to health,[11] while in *Stambuk* v *Germany* it upheld a challenge to decisions of disciplinary courts penalising a medical practitioner for giving press interviews in which he indicated he had a 100 per cent success rate with his laser treatment to correct defective vision.[12] The Court emphasised that the advertising had been placed in the context of a press article, and could not be regarded as misleading advertising – which could legitimately be restricted.[13]

It is clear from the Court's jurisprudence that advertising in the context of a press or journal feature and broadcast political advertising (see Section 6.7) is covered, and may well be strongly protected, under the Convention. There does not seem to be any case, however, concerned directly with the compatibility of restrictions on pure commercial advertising in newspapers or on the broadcast media with the Convention right to freedom of expression. It is unlikely that the Strasbourg Court would hold that article 10 does not cover such advertising at all, but it would almost certainly uphold restrictions on, say, misleading or unsubstantiated claims as necessary to protect the rights of consumers, and would probably uphold limits on the scheduling and duration of television commercials (see Section 6.5) as necessary to protect the interest of viewers. Moreover, it is implicit in the important ruling of the Court in *Informationsverein* v *Austria* (see Extract 1.2.4) that states are entitled to take necessary steps to protect programme quality; that argument

[11] *Hertel* v *Switzerland* (1998) 28 EHRR 534.

[12] (2003) 37 EHRR 845.

[13] Ibid., paras 46–9.

could be used to justify proportionate restrictions on the quantity of television commercials. The Supreme Court of Canada has ruled that a ban on broadcasting advertisements targeted at children under the age of 13 is a justified restriction on the exercise of free commercial expression;[14] it would be surprising if the Strasbourg Court did not reach the same conclusion in a comparable case.

Questions for discussion

1. UK law now bans all forms of advertising for tobacco products (Tobacco Advertising and Promotions Act 2002). Could this ban be challenged under ECHR, art 10?
2. Do you agree with the view that limits on the scheduling (for example, no interruption of news programmes) of commercials, or on their duration (no longer than, say, two minutes) are compatible with freedom of expression?

6.3 THE ADVERTISING STANDARDS AUTHORITY

(a) General

The ASA's primary concern is to ensure industry observance of the separate Codes of Advertising for broadcast and for non-broadcast advertising drawn up by the two Committees of Advertising Practice (see Sections 6.4 and 6.5). The ASA was established in 1962 by the advertising industry largely to stave off the threat of statutory regulation, arising from a report of the Molony Committee on Consumer Protection, which had criticised the voluntary system then operating.[15]

The Council of the ASA is the body which takes the final decision on complaints about advertising, determining whether or not there has been a breach of the Codes. Its present Chair is Lord Smith of Finsbury, who had been Secretary of State for Culture, Media and Sport. There are 13 other members, 8 of whom are lay, in that they are not drawn from the advertising industry or the media; 11 of them adjudicate complaints arising under either the non-broadcasting or the broadcasting advertising codes, while the other two are concerned exclusively with one or other category of complaint. They are appointed by the Chairman, rather than by an independent Appointments Commission as with the PCC (see Chapter 2).

The ASA does not receive any public money, but is financed by the advertising industry itself so as to ensure that it is independent of both government and industry pressure. Collected by the Advertising Standards Board of Finance (ASBOF) and the Broadcast Advertising Standards Board of Finance (BASBOF), there is a 0.1 per cent levy on the cost of buying advertising space and a 0.2 per cent levy on some direct mail advertising. These levies also finance the copy advice service operated by the Committee of Advertising Practice (CAP) (see Section 6.4) which gives pre-publication advice on press and other non-broadcast advertisements. In the year ending 31 December 2010, there was a total income of just under £6,700,000 and expenditure of about £6,870,000.[16]

Complaints may be made within three months of the first appearance of the advertisement by anyone, whether or not they are personally offended or affected by it, or by a competitor

---

[14] *Irwin Toy* v *Attorney General for Quebec* [1989] 1 SCR 927.
[15] Cmnd 1781 (1962).
[16] For the detailed figures, see ASA Annual Report 2010, 36–7.

of the advertiser. Complaints from members of the public represent about 95 per cent of the complaints received. In 2011, the ASA received a record 31,458 complaints concerning 22,397 advertisements.[17] This was a significant increase from the number in earlier years, and is attributable to the assuming of jurisdiction in March 2011 over advertisers' claims on their own websites. Individual consumers may complain anonymously, but a competitor or other person with a direct interest in the resolution of the complaint must consent to being named before the ASA will consider it. Complaints are resolved quickly, generally within a few days or weeks;[18] decisions are drafted by the staff of the ASA under the direction of a Senior Management Team, but formally taken by its Council. As with the PCC, speed is of the essence, and there is no opportunity for the complainant or the advertiser to give oral evidence.

(b) Jurisdiction

There may occasionally be an argument whether the ASA has jurisdiction to consider a complaint about the contents of an 'advertisement', because, for example, the publisher regards the material as part of the editorial content of a newspaper or magazine. This sort of dispute should not arise in the broadcasting context, as it is a fundamental principle that advertising must be kept clearly separate and distinguishable from programmes (see Section 6.5(b)). However, difficulties may arise, as the *Charles Robertson* case illustrates, in the context of the print media. The applicant operated a number of stores in Cornwall and Devon, and advertised in various local newspapers. Its chairman wrote an 'editorial column', alongside this advertising; it expressed political and social views, which the ASA ruled, after receiving complaints, were racist and offensive. The applicant argued that the ASA had no jurisdiction because the column was not an advertisement, an argument rejected by Moses J. In his view that argument was separate from any contention that the column was covered by the right to freedom of expression under ECHR, art 10, which would have to be considered once the HRA came into force.[19]

Extract 6.3.1
R v Advertising Standards Authority, ex parte Charles Robertson (Developments) Ltd
[2000] EMLR 463, 475–6

MOSES J:

It is undisputed that on each of the pages in issue, advertisements for the products of Trago Mills Shopping Centres were displayed. The real question is, therefore, whether the columns were part of those advertisements. To resolve that question it is not necessary to define an advertisement . . .

. . .

I accept that the concept of promotion is inherent within the concept of an advertisement. That which plays no part in the promotion of a product, however widely 'product' is defined, cannot be said to be part of the advertisement. I reject the argument that the connection can only lie in content. The visual impact may be of equal or greater importance . . .

---

[17] ASA Annual Report 2011, 37.
[18] The length of time depends on whether there is an informal investigation, conducted within 35 days or a more formal investigation where all parties are invited to comment and advertisers are called on to justify their claims, which may take up to 85 days, or in more complex cases up to 20 weeks: see ASA Annual Report 2011, 38–9.
[19] The HRA came into force in October 2000, a year after the decision in this case.

> The question of whether material is part of an advertisement seems to me a paradigm of an issue as to which there can be no clear-cut test and as to which different decision-makers may legitimately reach different conclusions . . . [I]t was for the ASA to decide whether the columns formed part of the advertisements on the pages in issue . . .
>
> . . .
>
> I am satisfied that the ASA exercised jurisdiction because it believed that the columns formed part of the advertisement for the products of Trago Mills Shopping Centres and not merely because the columns were paid for by the applicant. I should only add that if I am wrong and the decision was not for the ASA but for the court, I believe that the visual impact of the column and its position demonstrates that it was part of the advertisement for Trago Mills Shopping Centres' products. It played a significant part in their promotion . . .

Print columns or features of this kind – generally known as 'advertorials' – may therefore come under the ASA's jurisdiction, even when they express political views. There is no equivalent jurisdiction over comparable broadcast material; commercial spots cannot be used for political advertising which is strictly forbidden by statute (see Section 6.7). Since 1999 the ASA has had no jurisdiction over political party advertising. The present provision in the CAP Code is set out in the following extract:

Extract 6.3.2
The UK Code of Non-broadcast Advertising, Sales Promotion and Direct Marketing on Non-Broadcast Advertising (12th edn, 2010), Rule 7

7.1 Claims in marketing communications, whenever published or distributed, whose principal function is to influence voters in a local, regional, national or international election or referendum are exempt from the Code.

7.2 Marketing communications by central or local Government, as distinct from those concerning party policy, are subject to the Code.

Source: © Committee of Advertising Practice (CAP).

This provision was introduced in the Code, following the controversy over a Conservative Party advertisement in 1996, showing a picture of Tony Blair, then Leader of the Opposition, with demonic looking eyes, and with the caption, 'New Labour, new danger'. Complaints against this advertisement were partly upheld.[20] However, complaints may still be made against claims made by government departments, as distinct from political party advertising; for example, in 2010 the ASA upheld complaints that press advertisements by the Department of Energy and Climate Change exaggerated the impact of extreme weather conditions.[21]

Questions for discussion

1. Do you agree with the decision in *ex parte Charles Robertson* that 'advertorials' are subject to the ASA? Could the decision to uphold the complaint now be challenged under the HRA?
2. Is it right totally to exclude political party advertising, etc., from the ASA? Why should government advertising be regulated in the same way as commercial advertising?

---

[20] ASA Annual Report 1996, 1.
[21] ASA Annual Report 2010, 24.

(c) Control of ASA decisions

There is no formal appeal from a decision of the ASA, though complainant, the advertiser, and (with regard to broadcast advertising complaints) the broadcaster may ask for it to be reviewed by an Independent Reviewer (now Sir Hayden Phillips)[22] within 21 days of the decision. He will only conduct a review if the request establishes that there was a substantial flaw in the adjudication or shows new relevant evidence. The Reviewer makes a recommendation to the ASA, and its Council then takes the final decision. Sometimes this procedure does lead to the reversal of an earlier decision, as in the *Gypsies* complaint decided in October 2012 (see Extract 6.4.6). In 2011, the Reviewer received 60 requests for reconsideration of an ASA Council adjudication, the vast majority of them relating to non-broadcast advertisements.

Alternatively, the ASA is subject to judicial review. That was established by the Divisional Court in *ex parte The Insurance Service*,[23] when Glidewell LJ held that the ASA exercised a public function, which would have to be discharged by, say, the Director General of Fair Trading, if it did not exist. It was irrelevant that it had no powers under statute or at common law. This decision was followed by the Court in *ex parte Matthias Rath*, where the applicant challenged decisions of the ASA and the Independent Reviewer on a number of grounds, in particular that the decision of the former restricted its right to claim in advertising material that it had been responsible for a change in government policy (identified as MLX 249), and so restricted its freedom of political expression. The ASA had found this claim, as well as others, unsubstantiated. The applicant argued that the Codes applied by the ASA were not 'prescribed by law', as required by ECHR, art 10(2).

Extract 6.3.3
R v Advertising Standards Authority, ex parte Matthias Rath BV **[2001] EMLR 22, paras 19, 26–8**

TURNER J:
19. In my judgment, the position is clear. Given the material which was already before the Council of the ASA when it made its decision which the claimants wished to be reviewed by the Independent Reviewer, it was not incumbent on him to do more than to say that the new material did not cause him to embark on a review. In short, the claimants had only themselves to thank that there were no translations of the testimonials available when the Council made its adjudication, the Independent Reviewer's comments on this were factual. The other material upon which the claimants now rely, was in large part, if not in whole before the Council at the time of its adjudication. There was not in respect of this so-called new evidence anything new which should have persuaded the Independent Reviewer that the original decision was flawed or that there was new evidence which he should review. Nor yet was there any need for him to have said more than he had.

. . .

26. In my judgment, the application for permission to bring proceedings for judicial review has to fail . . . The reasons can be shortly stated. I entertain no doubt that the Code of Practice, which has an underpinning of subordinate legislation and which is readily accessible is 'prescribed by law'. In the absence of a self-regulatory code, which met the implicit approval of the Director General of Fair Trading, direct action could have been taken under the Regulations,[24] albeit they

---

[22] Previously Permanent Secretary to the Lord Chancellor's Department.
[23] *R v Advertising Standards Authority Ltd, ex parte The Insurance Service plc* (1990) 2 Admin Law Reports 77.
[24] See Section 6.4 below.

are less specific than the elaborate provisions of the Code of Practice. The Code of Practice is readily accessible and its provisions are sufficiently clear and precise to enable any person who is minded to place advertisements to know within what limits they are likely to prove acceptable and will also know what are the consequences if he were to infringe its provisions. In these circumstances, given the statutory underpinning, albeit short of direct statutory effect, the Code of Practice meets the purposive intentions of Article 10.2. An intending advertiser, moreover, can readily discover how to frame his advertisement without infringing the Code's provisions and will also know the consequences if he does not comply with them. Moreover, the advertisements themselves were explicitly concerned with matters of health as a consequence the requirement that the challenged rulings were 'necessary for the protection of health', in the sense that the advertisements were capable of conveying misleading information, was fully met.

27. The applicant did not address any argument to the effect that if the Code complied with the Article 10.2 limitation of being prescribed by law, its provisions were not reasonably necessary in a democratic society. This was eminently a wise decision.

28. It remains to consider the first defendants' submission to the effect that what the claimants were seeking to protect was not the right to assert that they had been effective in obtaining the withdrawal of the proposed MLX249, as constituting an expression of political opinion, but their reputation. Such an objective was plainly outside the protection afforded by Article 10.1. It is quicker to dispose of the claimants' argument in relation to expression of political opinion first. On a proper reading of the claim that the claimants' had been effective in obtaining the withdrawal or abandonment of the proposed MLX249, the claim was not one which asserted any political opinion. It was a claim based on the proposition that the claimants had been effective in persuading the Government, or the relevant governmental agency to change its mind. I have not been persuaded that such an activity, even if the underlying factual proposition had been proved (which it has not), was the expression of political opinion. It was an attempt to persuade a governmental agency to change its mind. As to the right to freedom of expression it has been said

> The nature of the expression which is restrained or interfered with by the state will determine the strength and the cogency of the justification for the interference required by the court. Accordingly, where the interference is with political speech rather than commercial or artistic speech, the court generally requires the strongest reasons to justify the impediments to free speech.

See *Lester and Pannick* Human Rights Law and Practice §4.10.8. In my judgment, the public interest is served by the publication of the ASA monthly report, one of the objects of which is to notify the media world of advertising which is not of an acceptable standard. In the instances of which the claimants complain the ASA was clearly entitled to reach the conclusions which it did. There is, after all, no challenge mounted by these proceedings to the substance of the Authority's rulings.

The courts are reluctant to interfere with advertising decisions, partly because they prefer to respect the judgments of specialist bodies such as the PCC (see Chapter 2), broadcasting authorities (Chapter 4), and the ASA, but also because commercial speech is less strongly protected than political discourse. It is only when the ASA has failed to take any account, for example, of an advertiser's representations, as in the *Insurance Service* case, that a court will quash its decision. Nor will they intervene to stop the publication of an ASA adjudication pending resolution of an application for judicial review to challenge its validity.[25]

---

[25] *R v ASA, ex parte Vernons Organisation Ltd* [1992] 1 WLR 1289, Laws J.

Questions for discussion

1. Compare the arrangements for reviewing ASA adjudications with those for reviewing decisions taken by the PCC. Should a formal appeal procedure be instituted for challenging ASA adjudications?
2. What were the reasons given by Turner J in *Matthias Rath* for holding that the ASA Codes are 'prescribed by law'? Is it enough that the scheme is underpinned by subordinate legislation (see the discussion in Section 6.4 of the Consumer Protection from Unfair Trading Regulations 2008)?

6.4 REGULATION OF NON-BROADCAST ADVERTISING

(a) Background

The Committee of Advertising Practice (CAP) drafts and revises the Code for non-broadcast advertising. It consists of representatives of members of the CAP: advertising bodies such as the Advertising Association, the Cinema Advertising Association, the Direct Marketing Association, and the Internet Marketing Bureau, newspaper and publisher organisations such as the Newspaper Society and the Professional Publishers' Association, and one or two other institutions, such as Royal Mail (which may allow or withdraw discounts on direct mail advertising). Therefore, unlike the ASA, it is an exclusively trade body, although not composed entirely of advertising agency representatives. Like the ASA, however, it is funded by levies on advertisers collected through the Advertising Standards Board of Finance.

(b) The Non-Broadcast Advertising Code

(i) Introduction

The present 12th edition of the Non-Broadcast Code on Advertising, Sales Promotion and Direct Marketing (CAP Code) came into force in September 2010. It applies to all advertising in print media – newspapers, magazines, journals and leaflets – as well as in posters, cinema, video and DVD, non-broadcast electronic media, including online advertisements, and direct marketing. It does not, however, apply to classified personal advertisements, advertising by telephone, or, as already noted, political party advertising.[26] Nor, of course, does it apply to broadcast advertising, covered by the separate Broadcast Advertising Code discussed in Section 6.5.

The CAP Code contains a number of general provisions, the most important of which are discussed here, and also some particular rules pertinent to particular products and services, for example, medicines and medical products, financial products and services, food and food supplements, alcohol, and products related to motoring.

The general principles which all advertisers should follow are set out in Rule 1 of the CAP Code, set out in Extract 6.4.1.

---

[26] For further details see the Scope of the Code, available at http://www.cap.org.uk/Advertising-Codes/Non-broadcast-HTML.aspx (accessed 13 November 2012).

Extract 6.4.1
The UK Code of Non-broadcast Advertising, Sales Promotion and Direct Marketing, 12th edition, 2010, Rule 01 Compliance

1.1 Marketing communications should be legal, decent, honest and truthful.

1.2 Marketing communications must reflect the spirit, not merely the letter, of the Code.

1.3 Marketing communications must be prepared with a sense of responsibility to consumers and to society.

1.4 Marketers must comply with all general rules and with relevant sector-specific rules.

1.5 No marketing communication should bring advertising into disrepute.

1.6 Marketing communications must respect the principles of fair competition generally accepted in business.

1.7 Any unreasonable delay in responding to the ASA's enquiries will normally be considered a breach of the Code.

1.7.1 The full name and geographical business address of the marketer must be given to the ASA or CAP without delay if requested.

1.8 Marketing communications must comply with the Code. Primary responsibility for observing the Code falls on marketers. Others involved in preparing or publishing marketing communications, such as agencies, publishers and other service suppliers, also accept an obligation to abide by the Code.

1.9 Marketers should deal fairly with consumers.

Legality

1.10 Marketers have primary responsibility for ensuring that their marketing communications are legal. Marketing communications should comply with the law and should not incite anyone to break it.

1.10.1 Marketers must not state or imply that a product can legally be sold if it cannot.

Source: © Committee of Advertising Practice (CAP).

The principle that advertising should be legal, decent, honest and truthful has been a key feature of the Code since it was first drafted in the 1960s. The other principles supplement it. It is important to note that marketing communications – the term now used to cover all forms of non-broadcast advertising – should reflect the spirit of the Code, not merely its strict terms; a similar principle has been found in the Press Complaints Commission Code. These Codes are not interpreted literally, as is often the case with statutes.

Marketing communications should be clearly identifiable as such, and the character of 'advertorials' as marketing communications should be made clear by identifying them as 'advertisement features'.[27] Application of this rule should remove the difficulty which led to the *Charles Robertson* case discussed earlier (Extract 6.3.1).

(ii) Misleading advertising

An important set of rules in the CAP Code concern misleading advertising. They cover much the most frequent ground of complaint against non-broadcast marketing communications.[28] It is also a particularly complex area, largely because it is also governed by detailed statutory regulations, the Consumer Protection from Unfair Trading Regulations 2008, which the

---

[27] CAP Code, Rule 02.4.
[28] In 2011 well over half the total 22,397 cases concerned misleading advertising on non-broadcasting media (13,502 cases): ASA Annual Report 2011, 39.

ASA takes into account when ruling on a complaint of misleading advertising. The principal provisions of the CAP Code are set out in Extract 6.4.2.

Extract 6.4.2

The UK Code of Non-broadcast Advertising, Sales Promotion and Direct Marketing, 12th edition, Rule 03 Misleading Advertising

3.1 Marketing communications must not materially mislead or be likely to do so.

3.2 Obvious exaggerations ('puffery') and claims that the average consumer who sees the marketing communication is unlikely to take literally are allowed provided they do not materially mislead.

3.3 Marketing communications must not mislead the consumer by omitting material information. They must not mislead by hiding material information or presenting it in an unclear, unintelligible, ambiguous or untimely manner.

Material information is information that the consumer needs to make informed decisions in relation to a product. Whether the omission or presentation of material information is likely to mislead the consumer depends on the context, the medium and, if the medium of the marketing communication is constrained by time or space, the measures that the marketer takes to make that information available to the consumer by other means.

3.4 For marketing communications that quote prices for advertised products, material information [for the purposes of Rule 3.3] includes:

3.4.1 the main characteristics of the product

3.4.2 the identity (for example, a trading name) and geographical address of the marketer and any other trader on whose behalf the marketer is acting

3.4.3 the price of the advertised product, including taxes, or, if the nature of the product is such that the price cannot be calculated in advance, the manner in which the price is calculated

3.4.4 delivery charges

3.4.5 the arrangements for payment, delivery, performance or complaint handling, if those differ from the arrangements that consumers are likely to reasonably expect

3.4.6 that consumers have the right to withdraw or cancel, if they have that right (see Rule 3.55).

3.5 Marketing communications must not materially mislead by omitting the identity of the marketer.

[*Provisions omitted.*]

3.6 Subjective claims must not mislead the consumer; marketing communications must not imply that expressions of opinion are objective claims.

Substantiation

3.7 Before distributing or submitting a marketing communication for publication, marketers must hold documentary evidence to prove claims that consumers are likely to regard as objective and that are capable of objective substantiation. The ASA may regard claims as misleading in the absence of adequate substantiation.

3.8 Claims for the content of non-fiction publications should not exaggerate the value, accuracy, scientific validity or practical usefulness of the product. Marketers must ensure that claims that have not been independently substantiated but are based merely on the content of a publication do not mislead consumers.

[*Further provisions omitted.*]

Source: © Committee of Advertising Practice (CAP).

A number of points should be emphasised. Application of these provisions depends on an understanding of the meaning of the advertisement within the context of its publication and of its likely impact on consumers. The notion of an 'average consumer' (see Rule 3.2) is itself problematic, particularly when advertisements are targeted at vulnerable groups, for example, young people, lower income groups or the infirm. It is, in any case, far from clear how an 'average consumer' understands claims that a type of food, for example, yoghurt, is 'low fat' or 'fat free'.[29] Rule 3.7 requires advertisers to be in a position to justify factually objective claims about their products or services with documentary evidence. The Divisional Court has upheld an ASA decision, enforcing this requirement against an advertisement for a soft drink, claiming that it 'does not encourage tooth decay'.[30] The more categorical or absolute a claim was, 'the greater the degree of substantiation' required.[31] It was appropriate for the ASA to consider whether this absolute claim had been substantiated.

The misleading advertising rules are well illustrated by an ASA decision upholding complaints that a Procter & Gamble advertisement for an eye illuminator was likely to mislead, although it also ruled that it was not socially irresponsible (see now Rule 1.3 in Extract 6.4.1 above).

Extract 6.4.3
ASA Adjudication of 16 December 2009: Procter & Gamble (Health and Beauty Care) Ltd

Ad

A magazine ad for the Olay Definity eye illuminator featured an image of the model Twiggy. A testimonial adjacent to her stated 'Olay is my secret to brighter-looking eyes!' Further text stated 'Because younger-looking eyes never go out of fashion. Olay Definity eye illuminator. Reduces the look of wrinkles and dark circles for brighter, younger-looking eyes.'

Background

We received identical complaints about a magazine ad for the Olay Definity eye illuminator from over 700 members of the public who complained via a website campaign. Their complaints were forwarded to the ASA by Jo Swinson MP. We also received a complaint from a member of the public who contacted us directly. All the complainants challenged whether the ad was misleading because they believed the image of Twiggy had been digitally re-touched; the people who complained as part of Jo Swinson's campaign also complained that the ad was socially irresponsible.

Issue

1. Many complainants, who had forwarded their complaints to Jo Swinson MP as part of a website campaign, objected that the ad was misleading and socially irresponsible. They believed the image of Twiggy had been digitally retouched and the use of post-production techniques could have a negative impact on people's perceptions of their own body image.

2. One complainant, who contacted the ASA directly, objected that the ad was misleading, because it implied that Twiggy's appearance in the ad was achieved solely through the use of Olay Definity rather than with the assistance of photographic post-production.

---

[29] See the discussion in A. Durant, *Meaning in the Media* (Cambridge: CUP, 2010), ch 10, esp. 192–6.
[30] *R (On the Application of Smith Kline Beecham Ltd) v ASA* [2001] EMLR 23.
[31] Ibid., para 32, per Hunt J.

Response

1. & 2. Procter and Gamble Ltd (P&G) said that Twiggy was a beautiful woman who had been chosen to appear in a number of high profile advertising campaigns, including theirs . . .

P&G said that, in the photo shoot for the Olay Definity campaign, Twiggy's hair and make-up were done by professional hair and make-up artists. They said it was entirely routine practice to choose beautiful women as models and use cosmetics, hair styling and lighting to show them at their best. They said it was also routine practice to use post-production techniques to correct for lighting and other minor photographic deficiencies before publishing the final shots as part of an advertising campaign.

P&G said that, in July 2009, when the ad was questioned in the media, they reviewed the post-production used in the ad and concluded there had been some minor retouching around Twiggy's eyes which was inconsistent with their own policies. They said they withdrew that ad and replaced it with one in which there had been no post-production work in the eye area.

P&G said the ad for Definity eye illuminator had been placed in magazines read by more mature women to whom Twiggy would be likely to appeal. They said they did not accept that there was any likelihood of that ad, regardless of any post-production retouching, having a negative impact on people's perceptions of their own body image, or being in any way socially irresponsible.

Assessment

1. & 2. Upheld

The ASA noted the original ad seen by the complainants had been withdrawn and replaced with one that did not have re-touching around Twiggy's eyes. We acknowledged that advertisers were keen to present their products in their most positive light using techniques such as post-production enhancement and the re-touching of images. However, we considered that the post-production re-touching of this ad, specifically in the eye area, could give consumers a misleading impression of the effect the product could achieve. We considered that the combination of references to 'younger-looking eyes', including the claim 'Reduces the look of wrinkles and dark circles for brighter, young-looking eyes', and post-production re-touching of Twiggy's image around the eye area was likely to mislead.

Notwithstanding that, we considered that consumers were likely to expect a degree of glamour in images for beauty products and would therefore expect Twiggy to have been professionally styled and made-up for the photo shoot, and to have been photographed professionally. We also noted the ad appeared in a magazine that targeted mature women and considered that readers of Good Housekeeping magazine and the Sunday Times Style Supplement would understand that the ad set out to associate the well-known mature female model with a brand, and would not infer that Twiggy's appearance in the ad was achieved solely through the use of Olay Definity. We concluded that, in the context of an ad that featured a mature model likely to appeal to women of an older age group, the image was unlikely to have a negative impact on perceptions of body image among the target audience and was not socially irresponsible.

The ad breached CAP Code clause 7.1 (Misleading advertising).

We also investigated the ad under 2.2 (Social responsibility) but did not find it in breach.

Source: © Advertising Standards Authority (ASA).

In a completely different context, misleading advertising complaints about a poster with the headline 'EXPERIENCE ISRAEL' and with a map showing Gaza and the West Bank were upheld, as it implied that these areas were recognised as part of Israel,[32] as were complaints against a magazine advertisement promoting travel to Palestine; it suggested misleadingly that Palestine was a recognised country and that areas such as Jerusalem were in that country.[33]

---

[32] ASA Annual Report 2009, 17.
[33] ASA Annual Report 2011, 19.

(iii) Harm and offence

Claims that advertisements harm or cause offence are the second most common ground of complaint against press and other non-broadcast advertisements, although there are more complaints on these grounds in the broadcasting context, where they outnumber the number of complaints against misleading commercials. The rules in the CAP Code have to strike a balance between commercial free speech and the protection of individuals and groups against serious offence. They take account of the fact that some people may find material very offensive, while others consider it completely harmless or even humorous.

Extract 6.4.4
The UK Code of Non-broadcast Advertising, Sales Promotion and Direct Marketing, 12th edition, Rule 04 Harm and Offence

4.1 Marketing communications must not contain anything that is likely to cause serious or widespread offence. Particular care must be taken to avoid causing offence on the grounds of race, religion, gender, sexual orientation, disability or age. Compliance will be judged on the context, medium, audience, product and prevailing standards. Marketing communications may be distasteful without necessarily breaching this rule. Marketers are urged to consider public sensitivities before using potentially offensive material. The fact that a product is offensive to some people is not grounds for finding a marketing communication in breach of the Code.

4.2 Marketing communications must not cause fear or distress without justifiable reason; if it can be justified, the fear or distress should not be excessive. Marketers must not use a shocking claim or image merely to attract attention.

4.3 References to anyone who is dead must be handled with particular care to avoid causing offence or distress.

4.4 Marketing communications must contain nothing that is likely to condone or encourage violence or anti-social behaviour.

4.5 Marketing communications, especially those addressed to or depicting a child, must not condone or encourage an unsafe practice (see Section 5 of the CAP Code: Children).

4.6 Marketing communications must not encourage consumers to drink and drive . . .

[Provision omitted.]

Source: © Committee of Advertising Practice (CAP).

Naturally, the application by the ASA of this provision, and of similarly worded clauses in earlier editions of the Code, has given rise to controversial decisions. In one difficult case the ASA seems to have rejected complaints brought by dentists against a poster picturing the face of a black man next to the headline 'Scared?' and stating in smaller print below, 'You should be. He's a dentist', only because the CAP had earlier vetted the advertisement and advised that it was unlikely it would be ruled offensive. The ASA thought that some people would have found the poster seriously offensive as negatively stereotyping black people, although others would have accepted it as challenging these stereotypes. A sexually suggestive poster advertisement featuring a naked Sophie Dahl was found offensive, but the ASA dismissed complaints against the same material in a magazine because that was targeted at a particular group of readers likely to find it acceptable.[34]

In an illuminating commentary on ASA rulings written in 1997, Colin Munro suggested that there may be some inconsistency of approach on gender grounds.

---

[34] Yves St Laurent Beate Ltd, ASA Annual Report 1999–2000 and also in Annual Report 2011.

Extract 6.4.5
C. Munro, 'Self-regulation in the media' [1997] *Public Law* **6, at 11**

Pity the poor adjudicators who must pick their way through these considerations and counter-considerations [referring to the wording of the decency clause]. In 1995 billboard advertisements for Club 18–30 ('Beaver Espana', 'You get two weeks for being drunk and disorderly' and 'Girls, can we interest you in a package holiday?', the last displayed above a photograph of a man with a prominent bulge in his boxer shorts), notwithstanding their humour, were condemned by the A.S.A. as 'offensive' and 'irresponsible in advocating sexual and alcoholic excess'. There had been several hundred complaints received, but others regarded the verdicts as hypocritical. It is sometimes difficult to find a thread of consistency between the decisions. Complaints about Wonderbra advertisements ('Hello boys', 'We've been apart too long') were dismissed, while a proposed advertisement for underpants which featured a genitally well endowed male ('The Loin King') was disapproved on the ground that it treated the male body like a piece of meat.

In a recent ruling, the ASA after an Independent Review (see Section 6.3(c) above) reconsidered its own earlier decision which had rejected 372 complaints against four posters for the Channel 4 documentary, *Big Fat Gypsy Weddings*. It took advice from the Equality and Human Rights Commission which pointed to research showing the racial stereotyping suffered by members of the Gypsies and Travellers community as a result of sensational media reporting. The extract shows why the ASA upheld two complaints that two posters were offensive and irresponsible.

Extract 6.4.6
Adjudication on Channel 4, 3 October 2012

a. The first poster featured a close-up of a young boy looking directly at the camera. Large text across the ad stated 'BIGGER. FATTER. GYPSIER'.
b. The second poster showed a man leading a horse across a field. Caravans were visible behind a fence in the background. Large text across the ad stated 'BIGGER. FATTER. GYPSIER'.
c. The third poster showed two young women wearing low-cut bra tops. Large text across the ad stated 'BIGGER. FATTER. GYPSIER'.
d. The fourth poster showed three young girls dressed for their first Holy Communion standing in front of a caravan. Large text across the ad stated 'BIGGER. FATTER. GYPSIER'.

. . .

Upheld in relation to ads (a) and (c)

We understood that the first series had experienced high viewing figures and was widely covered in the press and we considered that references to it were likely to be recognisable beyond just its television audience. We considered that many who were familiar with the programme might well interpret the strap-line to mean that the second series being advertised offered even more examples of Gypsy and Traveller life, however, we considered that many readers would not share that interpretation and that many were likely to infer from the word 'Gypsier' that the depictions in the individual ads were highly typical of the Gypsy and Traveller community.

In relation to ad (a) we noted that the boy in the image was shown in close-up and had his lips pursed in a manner that we considered was likely to be seen as aggressive. We considered that negative image, when combined with the strap-line which suggested that such behaviour was 'GYPSIER', would be interpreted by many members of the Gypsy and Traveller communities and some of the wider public to mean that aggressive behaviour was typical of the younger members of the Gypsy and Traveller community. We considered that implication was likely to cause serious offence to some members of those communities while endorsing the prejudicial view that young Gypsies and Travellers were aggressive. We therefore concluded that ad (a) was offensive and irresponsible.

In relation to ad (b) we understood that the man featured was a key contributor both to the series and other entertainment programmes and would therefore be recognisable to a number of readers. We noted that he was leading a horse across a field and that caravans were visible in the background and we understood these were representative of the community in which he lived. We considered that image, when combined with the strap-line, was suggestive that horses and caravans were highly representative of the Gypsy and Traveller community. Although we understood that many Gypsies and Travellers, for example Settled Travellers, might not like the suggestion that caravans and horses were typical of their lives, we did not consider that it was likely to cause them either serious or widespread offence, or endorse prejudice.

We understood that the photo in ad (c) was an accurate depiction of how the young women had chosen to dress for the occasion at which they had been photographed and we considered that it was clear that they were dressed for a night out. However, we noted that they were heavily made-up and wearing low cut tops and we considered that, when combined with the strap-line and in particular the word 'GYPSIER', the ad implied that appearance was highly representative of the Gypsy and Traveller community in a way that irresponsibly endorsed that prejudicial view and was likely to cause serious offence to the Gypsy and Traveller community.

In relation to ad (d) we noted that the girls were dressed and made-up for their First Holy Communion and we considered that their heavy make-up and elaborate dresses might appear unusual to those who did not understand the reason for them being dressed in that way. However, although we considered that some Gypsies and Travellers might find distasteful the suggestion that their presentation was 'GYPSIER', we did not consider that the ad was likely to cause them serious or widespread offence, or endorse prejudice.

On this point ads (a) and (c) breached CAP Code (Edition 12) rules 1.3 (Social responsibility) and 4.1 (Harm and offence). We also investigated ads (b) and (d) under these Code rules, but did not find them in breach.

The ASA also considered that the first advertisement (a) was likely to harm children from Gypsy communities in breach of Rule 5 of the Code (see below), while the third poster (c) depicted a young girl, 15 years old when the photo was taken, in a sexualised way and was therefore harmful to children. However, it dismissed complaints against the other two posters.

(iv) Children

As the *Gypsies* adjudication shows, there are special provisions protecting children, defined as persons under the age of 16. Rule 5.1 provides that advertising 'addressed to, targeted directly at or featuring children must contain nothing that is likely to result in their physical, mental or moral harm'. Other rules protect children from advertising exploiting their credulity or vulnerability or putting them under unfair pressure to buy products or respond to charitable appeals.[35]

(v) Privacy

Rule 6 of the Code protects personal privacy from unfair or offensive infringements, with particularly strong protection for members of the Royal Family.

---

[35] ASA Code, Rules 5.2–5.4.

Extract 6.4.7

The UK Code of Non-broadcast Advertising, Sales Promotion and Direct Marketing, 12th edition, 2010, Rule 06 Privacy

6.1 Marketers must not unfairly portray or refer to anyone in an adverse or offensive way unless that person has given the marketer written permission to allow it. Marketers are urged to obtain written permission before:

- referring to or portraying a member of the public or his or her identifiable possessions; the use of a crowd scene or a general public location may be acceptable without permission
- referring to a person with a public profile; references that accurately reflect the contents of a book, an article or a film might be acceptable without permission
- implying any personal approval of the advertised product; marketers should recognise that those who do not want to be associated with the product could have a legal claim.

Prior permission might not be needed if the marketing communication contains nothing that is inconsistent with the position or views of the featured person.

6.2 Members of the Royal Family should not normally be shown or mentioned in a marketing communication without their prior permission but an incidental reference unconnected with the advertised product, or a reference to material such as a book, article or film about a member of the Royal Family, may be acceptable.

It is unclear whether these provisions, the substance of which has not changed since 1999, offer adequate protection to public figures, where the advertiser has not obtained written permission before using their image in a marketing communication. In one well-known case, when an advertisement in *The Times* attributed a quotation to Peter Mandelson, the ASA accepted the argument that the advertisement was a 'humorous and entertaining play on words linking a [football] match to speculation about Peter Mandelson's sexuality', and so dismissed complaints that it was offensive or invaded the prominent politician's privacy.[36] It would now perhaps be open for the ASA to uphold a comparable complaint on the ground that prior permission should have been obtained in these circumstances.

Another set of privacy rules is contained in CAP Code, Rule 10, Database Practice. Marketers are required to comply with data protection legislation, supplemented by the Code provisions. Among the rules are those prohibiting marketers from sending persistent and unwanted advertising communications by telephone, fax, post or email, and requiring electronic advertising to supply a valid email address, so the customer can opt out of further commercial communications.[37]

Questions for discussion

1. What do you think are the main problems for the ASA in applying Rule 3 of the Code on misleading marketing communications? Do you agree with its decision in the Olay eye illuminator case?
2. How relevant is the character of the target audience to determining whether an advertisement, say, in a magazine with predominantly 20–35 year old readers is offensive or harmful?
3. Do you agree with the ASA adjudication on the BIGGER, FATTER, GYPSIER posters?
4. Do the provisions in Rule 6 of the Code provide adequate protection for the privacy of politicians and other public figures?

---

[36] ASA Monthly Report April 1999. The ad showed an exchange between Gordon Brown and Mandelson, in which in reply to the former's question, 'Do you fancy Laudrup for tonight?', Mandelson replied, 'Yes, I think he should get an outing.'

[37] CAP Code, Rules 10.4 and 10.6.

(c) Sanctions

The ASA cannot usually use the law to enforce its adjudications. It must in the first place rely on the co-operation of the marketer to withdraw a communication which has been found to break the CAP Code. However, it can use a range of informal sanctions, which almost certainly make it a more effective regulatory body than the PCC has been for the editorial content of newspapers and magazines (see Chapter 2). These sanctions are discussed in full in the section of the CAP Code entitled 'How the system works'. First, there is the sanction of adverse publicity – on the ASA website, in the press and in radio news bulletins which report every month on significant breaches of the Codes. Second, the CAP may issue Ad Alerts to its members, advising press and other members not to provide space for offending marketing communications; Internet websites may be asked to remove links to offending material. Further, trading privileges conferred by advertising associations on its members may be removed, and the Royal Mail may withdraw from advertisers found in breach of the Code the discounts it provides for the bulk mailing of marketing communications.

The ASA and CAP may require persistent offenders to have their material pre-vetted before distribution by the CAP Copy Advice team. (The team offers on a voluntary basis free advice within 24 hours on particular advertisements.[38]) There is a special pre-vetting regime for offending posters. Mandatory pre-vetting may be required, if the ASA adjudicates against a poster on the grounds of serious or widespread offence or of social irresponsibility. If it is believed that the advertiser either is incapable of complying with the Code or seems to have deliberately flouted it with the intention of generating publicity, the poster industry members of CAP and the CAP Senior Management Team will compel the advertiser to check future posters with the CAP Copy Advice team for a fixed period (usually two years).

In one set of circumstances, however, the ASA may have recourse to a legal remedy. It can refer advertisers responsible for misleading marketing communication in breach of Rule 3 of the Code (see above) to the Office of Fair Trading (OFT). It has recourse to this legal back-stop only occasionally, although in each of the last three Annual Reports reference is made to the use of this power in the case of material of Ryanair,[39] First Class Trading Ltd (a business promising paid work in modelling and entertainment industries),[40] and Groupon (My City Deal Ltd).[41] Under statutory regulations, the OFT may apply to the courts for an injunction to enforce the ban on distributing misleading and unfair advertising. In exercising this power, the OFT (and other bodies with authority to enforce the ban) 'shall have regard to the desirability of encouraging control of unfair commercial practices by such established means as it considers appropriate having regard to all the circumstances of the particular case'.[42] The ASA is regarded as an 'established means' for the control of unfair commercial practices, so the OFT should encourage the system of informal self-regulation of advertising practice in which the Authority plays such an important role.

This position has been recognised by the courts. In a case arising under the earlier Misleading Advertising Regulations, the Director General of Fair Trading (now the OFT)

---

[38] In 2011, a paid for Express Copy Advice service was launched, in which advice is provided within four hours: ASA Annual Report 2011, 22.

[39] ASA Annual Report 2009, 5.

[40] ASA Annual Report 2010, 8.

[41] ASA Annual Report 2011, 12.

[42] Consumer Protection from Unfair Trading Regulations 2008, SI 2008/1277, reg 19(4). These regulations implement EU Directive 2005/29/EC, and replace the earlier Control of Misleading Advertisements Regulations 1988, SI 1988/915. Also see Business Protection from Misleading Marketing Regulations 2008, SI 2008/1276, reg 13(4).

applied for an injunction to stop the continued publication of advertising for a slimming aid which the ASA had ruled to be misleading.

Extract 6.4.8
***Director General of Fair Trading* v *Tobyward Ltd and Another* [1989] 2 All ER 266, 270–1**

HOFFMANN J:

'Misleading', as I have said, is defined in the regulations as involving two elements: first, that the advertisement deceives or is likely to deceive the persons to whom it is addressed and, second, that it is likely to affect their economic behaviour. In my judgment in this context there is little difficulty about applying the concept of deception. An advertisement must be likely to deceive the persons to whom it is addressed if it makes false claims on behalf of the product. It is true that many people read advertisements with a certain degree of scepticism. For the purposes of applying the regulations, however, it must be assumed that there may be people who will believe what the advertisers tell them, and in those circumstances the making of a false claim is likely to deceive. Having regard to the evidence . . . there is in my judgment a strong prima facie case that these advertisements were likely to deceive in each of the six respects of which complaint is made. The other element, namely that the advertisement is likely to affect the economic behaviour of the persons to whom it is addressed, means in this context no more than that it must make it likely that they will buy the product. As that was no doubt the intention of the advertisement, it is reasonable to draw the inference that it would have such a result. I am therefore satisfied that the court has jurisdiction under reg 6 to make an injunction in this case.

The making of the injunction is, however, a matter of discretion, and I must consider whether in this case it would be appropriate to do so. There are two reasons why I think I should. First, the regulations contemplate that there will only be intervention by the director when the voluntary system has failed.[43] It is in my judgment desirable and in accordance with the public interest to which I must have regard that the courts should support the principle of self-regulation. I think that advertisers would be more inclined to accept the rulings of their self-regulatory bodies if it were generally known that in cases in which their procedures had been exhausted and the advertiser was still publishing an advertisement which appeared to the court to be prima facie misleading an injunction would ordinarily be granted. The respondents did offer undertakings to the director which could not have been enforced by any legal process other than the making of an application such as this for an injunction. But they were in terms which the director thought to be inadequate . . .

Second, in my view the interests of consumers require the protection of an injunction pending trial of the action. It does not seem to me that the respondents could complain of any legitimate interference with their business if they were restrained from making claims of the kind to which the director is here taking objection.

Source: © Advertising Standards Authority (ASA).

Questions for discussion

1. How do the range of extra-legal sanctions for breach of the CAP Code compare to those for breach of the PCC Code, discussed in Chapter 2?
2. How important is it that in some cases the ASA can refer the matter to the OFT for it to take enforcement proceedings?
3. Should the power to refer the continued use of misleading marketing communications be extended to cover infringements of other provisions of the Code, e.g., Rule 4 on harm and offence?

---

[43] Under the Control of Misleading Advertisements Regulations, reg 4(3) the Director might require the complainant to satisfy him that the 'established means' for dealing with the complaint have not resolved it adequately.

6.5 REGULATION OF BROADCAST ADVERTISING

(a) Introduction

Broadcast advertising, particularly on television, has sometimes been regarded with suspicion, because it has been thought unduly to influence consumer choices.[44] Moreover, if its quantity were unregulated, it might interfere with viewers' enjoyment as well as prejudicing the moral right of film and drama directors not to have their work subjected to derogatory treatment.[45] Further, there is a fear that advertisers, particularly the sponsors of a single drama or series, may exercise an undesirable influence on the scheduling or content of programmes, so that challenging or other material of minority appeal is never, or only rarely, shown. For all these reasons, broadcast advertising has always been relatively tightly regulated since the inception of commercial television in 1955.

The current regulatory position is more complicated than it is for non-broadcast advertising. Under the Communications Act 2003, Ofcom is required to set and revise standards for advertising in codes, although the only detailed rules in the statute concern the ban on political advertising considered in the final section of this chapter. Under section 319 of the Communications Act, Ofcom must ensure that the inclusion of misleading, harmful and offensive advertising in radio and television services is prevented, that international obligations in this context are respected, that there is no unsuitable sponsorship, and finally that there is no undue discrimination between advertisers wanting to show commercials.[46] However, in 2004, with government approval, Ofcom delegated its powers with respect to the content of broadcast advertising to the Broadcast Committee on Advertising Practice (BCAP) and the ASA, while retaining authority over the scheduling and duration of advertisements on television, and over sponsorship and product placement.

The detailed arrangements for the delegation of regulatory authority over broadcast advertising were set out in a Memorandum of Understanding between Ofcom on the one hand, and the ASA, BCAP and the Broadcast Advertising Board of Finance on the other.[47] The legal basis is an Order[48] made under the Deregulation and Contracting Out Act 1994, which allows public authorities such as Ofcom to transfer their functions to other organisations. The BCAP has been given the responsibility for setting, monitoring and revising Codes regulating the content of broadcast advertisements, while the ASA assumed responsibility for considering complaints, as it does under the CAP Code for non-broadcast adverts. Ofcom, however, has retained responsibility for political advertising and for sponsorship (and now product placement), as these are matters closely connected with ensuring broadcasters' independence from commercial pressure. It has also kept authority over the general rules concerned with the scheduling, duration and frequency of commercials, although the CAP Code contains detailed rules about the scheduling of *particular* advertisements, primarily to protect children. This complex division of responsibility between Ofcom and the specialist advertising authorities makes exposition of this area of law difficult. A further complication is that two other bodies,

---

[44] *Power without Responsibility* (n 2 above), 167–8.

[45] Copyright, Designs and Patents Act 1988, s 50.

[46] Communications Act 2003, s 319(2)(h)–(k).

[47] For discussion of the negotiations leading to the delegation, see A Brown, 'Advertising regulation and co-regulation: the challenge of change' (2006) 26 *Economic Affairs* 31. Andrew Brown was chair of the CAP (and later the BCAP) from 1999 until 2010.

[48] Contracting Out (Functions relating to Broadcast Advertising) and Specification of Relevant Functions Order 2004, SI 2004/1975.

Clearcast (for television) and the Radio Advertising Clearance Centre (RACC) pre-vet commercials before transmission; their decisions are taken into account by the ASA when it considers complaints against commercials, but are not binding on it.

Broadcasting licensees are required as a condition of their licence to comply with any directions given by Ofcom or by authorities to which Ofcom has delegated powers. In the first place it is for the ASA to notify the broadcaster and Clearcast (or the RACC) of its ruling, and to instruct the former not to broadcast the advertisement again. However, in cases of serious breach or of continued broadcast of offending commercials, the ASA may refer the matter to Ofcom for it to consider further action. The ASA itself may not fine a broadcaster; that power remains the prerogative of Ofcom.

Although Ofcom has kept responsibility for the more important constraints on broadcasters' freedom to show commercials, the discussion begins with a description of the BCAP Code, many provisions of which are similar to those in the CAP Code which have just been considered. This section of the chapter continues with a discussion of the Ofcom rules on sponsorship and product placement and on the scheduling of commercials; it also considers briefly the significance of the advertising provisions in the EU Audiovisual Media Services Directive (AVMSD), which lay down minimum standards with which UK broadcast advertising regulation must comply.[49] As already mentioned, the ban on broadcast political advertising is considered below in Section 6.7.

(b) The BCAP Code

(i) Introduction

The BCAP consists of representatives of advertising associations, the principal commercial broadcasting organisations (ITV plc, Channel 4 Corporation, Channel 5 and BSkyB), and Clearcast and the RACC. It has the same chair as the CAP – now James Best, previously a member of the ASA and chairman of an advertising agency. Since September 2010 there has been one Broadcasting Code, replacing four codes, including a separate code for radio advertising.

Like the CAP Code, the broadcasting code contains general provisions, and others concerned with particular types of advertisement, for example, charitable appeals or advertising by religious bodies, or commercials for particular products such as alcohol, medicines, foods and food supplements, and financial services and products. Rule 10 sets out a list of prohibited advertisements, including those for all tobacco products, guns and gun clubs, prostitution and sexual massage parlours, and on television (but not radio) escort agencies.

Many of the general provisions are comparable to those in the CAP Code for non-broadcast advertising. Rule 2, for example, provides that commercials must be clearly distinct from programme content, and in particular that they should not feature people currently and regularly presenting news or current affairs programmes. Rule 3 on misleading advertising is similar to the equivalent provision in the CAP Code (see Section 6.4(b)(ii) above); in an interesting ruling where the meaning of the advertisement was in dispute, the ASA decided that the claim that 'Two-way action Deep Relief gel contains prescription strength ibuprofen' implied that it contained ibuprofen normally available only on prescription, and so was misleading.[50] Privacy rules provide that living people

---

[49] Now Directive 2010/13/EU of 10 March 2010; for full treatment of the AVMSD, see Chapter 5 above.
[50] Adjudication of 26 January 2011, available at ASA website: www.asa.org.uk.

should not generally be referred to in commercials without permission; the limited exceptions to this rule for television apply only where the reference is neither defamatory nor offensive.[51]

(ii) Offensive advertising, the protection of children and scheduling

Offensive and harmful advertising provides the most frequent ground of complaint to the ASA in the broadcasting context; in 2010 there were over 8,000 complaints of offensive advertising, and in 2011 there were 5,567 complaints on that ground. Rule 4 sets out the relevant rules.

Extract 6.5.1
BCAP Code, Rule 04, Harm and Offence

4.1 Advertisements must contain nothing that could cause physical, mental, moral or social harm to persons under the age of 18.

4.2 Advertisements must not cause serious or widespread offence against generally accepted moral, social or cultural standards.

4.3 Advertisements must not exploit the special trust that persons under the age of 18 place in parents, guardians, teachers or other persons.

4.4 Advertisements must not include material that is likely to condone or encourage behaviour that prejudices health or safety.

4.5 Radio only – Advertisements must not include sounds that are likely to create a safety hazard, for example, to those listening to the radio while driving.

4.6 Television only – Advertisements must not include visual effects or techniques that are likely to affect adversely members of the audience with photosensitive epilepsy (see Ofcom's Guidance Note for Licensees on Flashing Images and Regular Patterns in Television).

4.7 Television only – Advertisements must not be excessively noisy or strident. The maximum subjective loudness of advertisements must be consistent and in line with the maximum loudness of programmes and junction material.

. . .

4.8 Advertisements must not condone or encourage harmful discriminatory behaviour or treatment. Advertisements must not prejudice respect for human dignity.

4.9 Advertisements must not condone or encourage violence, crime, disorder or anti-social behaviour.

4.10 Advertisements must not distress the audience without justifiable reason. Advertisements must not exploit the audience's fears or superstitions.

4.11 Television only – Animals must not be harmed or distressed as a result of the production of an advertisement.

4.12 Advertisements must not condone or encourage behaviour grossly prejudicial to the protection of the environment.

The ASA has dismissed complaints against commercials which it considers humorous rather than offensive, as in the case of the HomePride advertisement for an oven cleaner with the line, 'So easy, even a man can do it.'[52] It also rejected over 1,000 complaints against

---

[51] BCAP Code, Rule 6.
[52] It also dismissed a complaint against an ad for an air freshener with a child saying, 'Mummy, I want to poo at Paul's house': ASA Annual Report 2009, 17.

a TV advertisement for Marie Stopes International on the grounds that it was misleading, harmful and offensive. (It should be noted that the advertisement was by a charity, not by a commercial company.) The next extract is concerned with the ASA treatment of the complaints on the grounds of offensiveness.

Extract 6.5.2
ASA Adjudication on Marie Stopes International, 4 August 2010

Ad

Three women were featured in a TV ad for Marie Stopes International (MSI), a not-for-profit organisation which provided sexual and reproductive healthcare advice, information and services. First, a woman waiting at a bus stop, looking down the road, with the onscreen text 'Jenny Evans is late'; then, a woman in a park with her two small children, with the text 'Katie Simmons is late'; and finally, a woman in a café, with the text 'Shareen Butler is late'. A female voiceover said: 'If you're late for your period, you could be pregnant. If you're pregnant and not sure what to do, Marie Stopes International can help.' The end caption carried the text 'Are you late?', a phone number, and the website address.

Issue

Complainants included members of the public, GPs, people who offered counselling, MPs and other representatives, and MPs who forwarded their constituents' concerns.

The complainants objected that the ad was misleading, offensive and harmful and queried its compliance with specific Code rules.

1. Viewers objected that the ad was offensive because:

- it promoted abortion;
- of their religious beliefs;
- it trivialised the difficult decision faced by women experiencing an unwanted pregnancy;
- decisions about the life of an unborn child were being equated to decisions about consumer goods;
- it would be distressing to those women who had taken the decision to have an abortion;
- it did not take into account the views of the father;
- it was sexist towards women by implying that the pregnancy was solely the woman's responsibility; and
- by featuring a mother with her small children, it suggested that the life of an unborn child was less important than a woman's existing children.

. . .

Assessment

1. Not upheld

The ASA acknowledged that the issue of abortion was controversial and distasteful to some, and that the complainants had strong personal and religious objections to the advertising of abortion services, or services that gave advice about abortion. We also noted that many complainants regarded the advertisers as advocates of abortion and therefore interpreted the ad as a promotion of abortion. However, the ad was for an advice service for women dealing with an unplanned pregnancy, and stated that MSI could help women who were 'pregnant and not sure what to do'. We understood that MSI provided a wide range of advisory and health services and advised on all options during consultations with clients. We noted that the ad did not focus on any one particular service offered by MSI and did not mention abortion. We therefore considered it was an ad for a general pregnancy advice service for women who wished to learn about and discuss their options, which might include, but were not limited to, abortion.

> We understood that post-conception decisions could be very difficult, but considered the ad dealt with the issue of possible pregnancy in an understated way and was not sensationalist. The women featured in the ad looked deep in thought, and we did not therefore consider that the ad trivialised the dilemma of an unplanned pregnancy. Whilst the ad featured three women, we did not consider that it suggested that only the woman would be affected, or that she should take any decisions alone. We did not consider that the ad focussed on or advocated any particular choice or course of action over another, or put forward any assumptions about what the women would or should do. Whilst we recognised that any reminder of a difficult time, such as an unplanned pregnancy, could evoke a response in someone directly affected, we considered that the ad was unlikely to cause serious or widespread offence on that basis.
>
> On this point, we investigated the ad under CAP (Broadcast) TV Advertising Standards Code rules 6.1 (Offence), 6.6 (Harmful or negative stereotypes) and 11.3.4 (Charities – Ethical responsibility) but did not find it in breach.

Source: © Advertising Standards Authority (ASA).

Offensiveness complaints are sometimes coupled with complaints under the scheduling rules, now Rule 32 of the BCAP Code. The general principle underlying that rule is that broadcasters should take special care when scheduling advertisements that might be unsuitable for children or for an audience for religious programmes or for broadcast around sensitive programmes or news items, perhaps dealing with a disaster or tragic event. Timing restrictions should be applied to advertisements, the content of which might harm or distress children of particular ages;[53] in that context the 9 pm watershed in the Ofcom Programme Code may be particularly relevant (see Chapter 4, Section 4.2(b)). The specific rules for the protection of children, now in Rule 5 of the BCAP Code, should also be taken into account. For their purpose a child is defined as a person under 16. Advertisements should not condone, encourage or feature unreasonable conduct that could be dangerous for children to emulate, or condone or encourage practices harmful to their health.[54] Commercials condoning or encouraging bullying, or depicting children in a sexual way are banned.[55] An advertisement must not take advantage of children's 'inexperience, credulity, or sense of loyalty',[56] or directly exhort them to buy a product or encourage them to ask parents or others to buy them.[57]

Some particular scheduling rules should be noted.

Extract 6.5.3
The UK Code of Non-broadcast Advertising, Sales Promotion and Direct Marketing, Rule 32 Scheduling, rules 32.5–32.11

Under-16s

32.5 These products may not be advertised in or adjacent to programmes commissioned for, principally directed at or likely to appeal particularly to audiences below the age of 16:

32.5.1 food or drink products that are assessed as high in fat, salt or sugar (HFSS) in accordance with the nutrient profiling scheme published by the Food Standards Agency (FSA) on 6 December 2005 . . .

32.5.2 matches

---

[53] Rule 32.3.
[54] Rules 5.2 and 5.3.
[55] Rules 5.4 and 5.5.
[56] Rule 5.7.
[57] Rule 5.9.

32.5.3 trailers for films or videos carrying an 18-certificate or 15-certificate (that does not preclude the scheduling in or adjacent to children's programmes of an advertisement containing brief extracts from such a film if those are used in connection with a promotional offer, derived from the film, for other types of product, subject to content).

Under-10s

32.6 These products may not be advertised in or adjacent to programmes commissioned for, principally directed at or likely to appeal particularly to children below the age of 10:

32.6.1 sanitary protection products

32.6.2 condoms.

Administering medicines, vitamins or food supplements to children

32.7 Advertisements in which children are shown having a medicine, vitamin or other food supplement administered to them must not be broadcast before 9.00 p.m.

Children's Merchandise, Endorsements and Appearances by Persons

. . .

32.8 Advertisements for merchandise based on a children's programme must not be broadcast in the two hours before or after episodes or editions of that programme. The ASA and BCAP reserve the right to require a wider separation around some programmes, including a prohibition of any advertisement while a programme series is running.

32.9 Advertisements in which persons (including puppets) who appear regularly in any children's programme on any UK television channel present or endorse products of special interest to children must not be broadcast before 9.00 p.m.

32.10 To maintain a distinction between programmes and advertisements that is clear to a child audience, and to minimise any risk of confusion between the two, advertisements featuring a well-known personality or performer, or a person who takes a leading role in or whose appearance is central to a children's programme, must not be scheduled in breaks in or adjacent to that programme . . . [*Some qualifications to this Rule are omitted.*]

32.11 Advertisements containing appearances by persons in extracts from a children's programme must not be broadcast in the two hours before or after an episode or edition of the relevant programme.

Source: © Committee of Advertising Practice (CAP).

The ban in Rule 32.5.1 on advertising HFSS foods in children's programmes has an interesting provenance. Health professionals had campaigned for a total ban on such advertising, or at least a ban on it before the 9 pm watershed, but any ban was resisted both by the producers of 'junk foods' who preferred industry self-regulation and by the commercial channels which feared the loss of advertising revenue. The solution adopted represents a compromise struck by Ofcom after it had commissioned a number of expert reports on the links between advertising and the rise in obesity. The ban appears to have been effective in limiting the exposure of children to junk food advertising, but an unfortunate consequence has been that ITV has felt unable to provide as much children's programming as its quota required.

The application of the comparable scheduling rules in an earlier television advertising code were considered in 2008, when 840 complaints were made against charitable advertisements in a Dr Barnardo's campaign, which many viewers found upsetting and unsuitable for broadcast at times when children were likely to be watching. The ASA rejected the complaints. It noted that Clearcast, when pre-vetting the advertisements, had required them to be shown after 9 pm, and further that Barnardo's had made a particular point of showing them away from programmes after 9 pm, which were likely to attract a large audience of children. With regard to the complaints that the advertisements were distressing to adult viewers, particularly those who had been abused as children, the ASA concluded that their aim was to raise awareness of child abuse in the home, not to glorify it, and that under the Code charity appeals were allowed greater latitude in the depiction of violence than conventional commercials.

Questions for discussion

1. What are the advantages and disadvantages of the co-regulatory system for advertising control over broadcast commercials introduced in 2004?
2. Why are there relatively so many complaints against broadcast advertisements on the grounds of offence or harm?
3. Do you agree with the ASA resolution of the complaints against the Marie Stopes International advertisement?

(c) Ofcom general rules and Code on the Scheduling of Advertisements

General rules for the regulation of television advertising are set out now in Section 9 of the Ofcom Broadcasting Code, 'Commercial References in Television Programming'. They are designed to reflect five fundamental principles, notably that broadcasters maintain editorial independence and control over their programmes, and that there is a clear distinction between editorial content and advertising. Other rules prohibit surreptitious advertising, where an intended reference to a commercial product, service or trade mark is not made clear to viewers, and the promotion of such products and services. Programming should not give undue prominence to a product, etc. Charitable appeals are allowed, provided that they meet certain conditions: viewers must be told the purpose of the appeal and how much money it raises. Advertising by churches and other religious bodies has not been banned since 1990, and the Ofcom Code does not impose any specific limits on such advertising.

Ofcom has kept authority over the general rules for the scheduling of advertisements; it was not delegated to the specialist advertising authorities, although, as just explained, the BCAP does contain rules concerning the scheduling of particular advertisements. The Ofcom rules are concerned with the frequency and duration of advertisements. The present rules implement the requirements of the AVMSD, although for the principal commercial channels, identified in the Ofcom Code as 'public service channels', the rules are stricter than the advertising rules in the EU Directive. The Ofcom Code incorporates some general rules in the AVMSD – that advertising must be readily recognisable and distinguishable from programme content, and that advertising inserted during programmes should not prejudice the integrity of the programme and take account of its nature and duration – but adds specific rules about the number and duration of permitted advertising breaks. The Directive imposes a general rule that the proportion of advertising time within a given clock hour is not to exceed 20 per cent, as well as a general ban on the interruption of religious services and a limit on the commercials to be broadcast during films, news programmes and children's programmes; the Ofcom Code supplements these rules with more specific provisions.

Extract 6.5.4

Ofcom Code on the Scheduling of Advertisements (2011), Rules 4–8, 11–16

4. Subject to paragraphs 5 to 8 below, time devoted to television advertising and teleshopping spots on any channel in any one hour must not exceed 12 minutes. In addition:

a) on public service channels time devoted to television advertising and teleshopping spots must not exceed: i) an average of 7 minutes per hour for every hour of transmission time across the broadcasting day; and ii) subject to (i) above, an average of 8 minutes an hour between 6 p.m. and 11 p.m.;

b) on other channels time devoted to television advertising and teleshopping spots must not exceed an average of 12 minutes of television advertising and teleshopping spots for every hour of transmission across the broadcasting day, of which no more than 9 minutes may be television advertising.

5. During programmes broadcast by the national Channel 3 licensee, the amount of time permitted for television advertising and teleshopping spots between 6 a.m. to 9.25 a.m. may be averaged across the week.

6. Channels exclusively comprised of teleshopping and advertising are not subject to the limits on advertising and teleshopping spots set out in paragraph 4(b) above.

7. Channels exclusively comprised of self-promotional content are not subject to the limits on advertising set out in paragraph 4(b) . . . On those channels comprising both self-promotional and other content, the self-promotional content will be treated as advertising, and will be subject to the limits on advertising set out in paragraph 4(b).

8. Teleshopping windows must be at least 15 minutes long: a) on public service channels, teleshopping windows may be scheduled only between midnight and 6am; and b) on other channels, there are no limits on the number or scheduling of teleshopping windows.

. . .

Identification of advertising and teleshopping breaks

11. Broadcasters must ensure that television advertising and teleshopping is readily recognisable and distinguishable from editorial content and kept distinct from other parts of the programme service. This shall be done by optical (including spatial) means; acoustic signals may also be used as well.

Advertising and teleshopping breaks during programmes

12. Where television advertising or teleshopping is inserted during programmes, television broadcasters must ensure that the integrity of the programme is not prejudiced, having regard to the nature and duration of the programme, and where natural breaks occur.

13. To avoid excessive abruptness, transition between live coverage of Parliamentary proceedings and advertising should take place where natural breaks occur via a programme presenter in sound or vision. Programme directors/editors must have the discretion to reschedule or cancel breaks to avoid artificial interruptions in live proceedings. Breaks should be dropped altogether where this would be incompatible with editorial responsibility, for example in coverage of matters of great gravity or emotional sensitivity.

14. Breaks during programmes on public service channels may not exceed 3 minutes 0 seconds, of which advertisements may not exceed 3 minutes 30 seconds.

Scheduling restrictions

15. Isolated television advertising and teleshopping spots, other than in the transmission of sports events, shall remain the exception . . .

16. Restrictions apply when inserting advertising breaks during the following programmes:

a) films and news programmes may only include one advertising or teleshopping break for each scheduled period of at least 30 minutes;

b) children's programmes (other than schools programmes) with a scheduled duration of 30 minutes or less may not include an advertising or teleshopping break. Such programmes with a scheduled duration of longer than 30 minutes may have one break for each scheduled period of at least 30 minutes. Breaks are not permitted within schools programmes, but may be scheduled between programmes;

c) programmes including a religious service may not include advertising or teleshopping breaks during the service;

d) broadcasts of a formal Royal ceremony may not include advertising or teleshopping breaks during the ceremony;

e) broadcasts of live Parliamentary proceedings may not include advertising and teleshopping breaks in programmes of a scheduled duration of 30 minutes or less;

f) in programmes of live events, more breaks may be taken than are indicated in Tables 1 and 2 [not reproduced here], provided that:

   i) the timing of the event and its constituent parts are outside the control of the programme provider; and

   ii) there would not be sufficient time within the number of permitted breaks which are also natural breaks to schedule the permitted amount of advertising.

g) live programme feeds from an overseas broadcaster may take the break pattern of the originating broadcaster. The broadcaster retransmitting the feed from the UK remains responsible for ensuring compliance with other relevant parts of this Code and the Television Advertising Standards Code.

17. With the exceptions described in paragraph 16 above, the number of internal breaks permitted in programmes on public service channels is set out in Table 1; the number permitted in programmes on other channels is set out in Table 2. For every additional 20-minute period beyond that set out in the tables, a further break is permitted.

Source: © Ofcom copyright 2006–11.

Under Table 1, one advertising break is allowed in programmes of 21–44 minutes' duration, with two permitted in programmes of 45–54 minutes, and three in programmes of 55–65 minutes. One additional break is then allowed every 20 minutes. The limits for programmes set out in Table 2 are more generous for shorter programmes on non-public service channels, for example, those of BSkyB.

Questions for discussion

1. Does it make sense to permit teleshopping channels and windows, when there are (relatively) strict limits on the frequency and duration of advertising and teleshopping spots?

2. In general, are the limits imposed by Ofcom on the frequency and duration of advertising spots too strict, or not strict enough?

3. Is it right to allow more advertising in peak viewing hours (see Rule 4 (a)(ii) above)?

(d) The rules on product placement and sponsorship

(i) Product placement

Until recently product placement – the inclusion of, or reference to, a commercial product, service or trade mark in a programme in return for payment to the broadcaster – has been prohibited in the UK, as it has been in other European countries; it has been regarded as a form of surreptitious advertising – advertising concealed from the audience. However, it was a common practice in US films and television programmes, so one argument for relaxing the total ban was to achieve a level playing field with regard to the financial support for European and US audiovisual works for television. Another important factor has been the decline in general advertising revenue for television, compelling broadcasters to look for other forms of commercial revenue.

It has been difficult to know how to treat a form of covert advertising, regarded in principle as undesirable, but reluctantly accepted for pragmatic reasons. This dilemma is reflected in a remarkable schizophrenic provision in the EU Directive. Article 11.2 of the AVMSD states that product placement is prohibited, but Article 11.3 provides that by way of derogation from this ban, it shall be admissible in specified cases, unless a Member State decides otherwise. It is admissible in films, sports and light entertainment programmes (but not for children's programmes), or where there is no payment, but only the provision of goods or services free of charge with a view to inclusion in the programme – the phenomenon known as 'prop placement'. Programmes with product placement must meet further requirements, in particular that the editorial independence of the programme provider is not affected, and that viewers are clearly informed of the existence of the placement.

Like all EU states (with the exception of Denmark), the UK now allows product placement. The step was taken with some misgiving, but was considered necessary to protect the competitiveness of UK programme makers in relation to those in other EU states which permitted it. The changes were made by regulations, amending provisions in the Communications Act 2003, which might have been applied to ban the practice. It inserts a new Schedule 11A into the Act which defines 'product placement' and related terms, and which prohibits the practice in specified circumstances.

Extract 6.5.5

Communications Act 2003, Schedule 11A, paras 1–6, inserted by Audiovisual Media Services Directive (Product Placement) Regulations 2010, SI 2010/831

1.—(1) In this Part 'product placement', in relation to a programme included in a television programme service, means the inclusion in the programme of, or of a reference to, a product, service or trade mark, where the inclusion—

(a) is for a commercial purpose;

(b) is in return for the making of any payment, or the giving of other valuable consideration, to any relevant provider or any person connected with a relevant provider; and

(c) is not prop placement.

(2) 'Prop placement', in relation to such a programme, means the inclusion in the programme of, or of a reference to, a product, service or trade mark where—

(a) the provision of the product, service or trade mark has no significant value; and

(b) no relevant provider, or person connected with a relevant provider, has received any payment or other valuable consideration in relation to its inclusion in, or the reference to it in, the programme, disregarding the costs saved by including the product, service or trade mark, or a reference to it, in the programme.

2. The product placement requirements are—

(a) that the product placement does not fall within any of paragraphs 3 to 6;

(b) that all of the conditions in paragraph 7 are met; and

(c) that, where paragraph 8 applies, the condition in that paragraph is also met.

Prohibitions of product placement

3.—(1) Product placement falls within this paragraph if it is in a children's programme.

(2) In sub-paragraph (1) 'children's programme' means a programme made—
  (a) for a television programme service or for an on-demand programme service, and
  (b) for viewing primarily by persons under the age of sixteen.

4. Product placement falls within this paragraph if it is—

(a) of cigarettes or other tobacco products;
(b) by or on behalf of an undertaking whose principal activity is the manufacture or sale of cigarettes or other tobacco products; or
(c) of prescription-only medicines.

5. Product placement of alcoholic drinks falls within this paragraph if—

(a) it is aimed specifically at persons under the age of eighteen; or
(b) it encourages immoderate consumption of such drinks.

6.—(1) Product placement falls within this paragraph if it is in a programme to which this paragraph applies and—
  (a) the programme is a religious, consumer affairs or current affairs programme;
  (b) the product placement is of anything within sub-paragraph (2); or
  (c) the product placement is otherwise unsuitable.

(2) The following are within this sub-paragraph—
  (a) electronic or smokeless cigarettes, cigarette lighters, cigarette papers or pipes intended for smoking;
  (b) medicinal products;
  (c) alcoholic drinks;
  (d) infant formulae or follow-on formulae;
  (e) a food or drink high in fat, salt or sugar;
  (f) gambling services.

(3) This paragraph applies to—
  (a) a programme that has been produced or commissioned by the provider of the television programme service in which it is included, or by a person connected with that provider, and that is not a film made for cinema; and
  (b) a programme that has been produced or commissioned by any other person with a view to its first showing taking place in a television programme service which is provided by a person under the jurisdiction of the United Kingdom for the purposes of the Audiovisual Media Services Directive.

Paragraph 7 of the Schedule outlines the genres of programmes in which product placement is permitted – films, series made for television (or other audiovisual media services), sports and light entertainment programmes – and also outlines a number of general rules, for example, that the placement must not influence the content and scheduling of a programme in a way which affects editorial independence, and that references to the products must not be unduly prominent. There must be a clear signalling of product placement at the beginning and end of a programme in which the placement appears, in the case of programmes produced or commissioned by the broadcaster (as distinct from, say, an imported film): Schedule 11A, para 8. These rules follow those in the EU Directive, although the UK provisions are stricter in banning product placement for alcoholic drinks, gambling, and HFSS foods and drinks. Indeed, the ban on product placement for HFSS food goes further than the advertising rule, for it applies to all programmes, not solely to children's programmes. The rules in Schedule 11A are also set out more informally in Rule 9 of the Ofcom Broadcasting Code.

Under Schedule 11A and the Ofcom Code a distinction is drawn between product placement and prop placement; the latter practice is defined as the inclusion in a programme of, or reference to, a product, service or trade mark where the provision has no significant value, and where no relevant provider has received any payment or other valuable consideration in relation to the provision. It is unclear whether the terms 'significant value' and 'valuable consideration' should be understood purely in monetary terms. If that is so, a clear reference to a brand of (non-alcoholic) drink or chocolate would be understood as prop placement, and so might be unregulated, although it would be extremely valuable to its provider in marketing terms. On the other hand, the provision of a product of 'significant value' is subject to the product placement rules, even though no money changes hands.

On the other hand, prop placement of the kind discussed in the previous paragraph might be covered by the general ban on surreptitious advertising. That covers commercial references intended by the broadcaster to amount to advertising. Advertising is likely to be considered intentional, if the broadcaster is paid for it or receives some other valuable consideration for making the reference. In the absence of payment, it will be hard to show that the reference was intentional, rather than incidental. There are indeed difficulties in distinguishing product placement (permitted in certain genres of programme, subject to certain conditions) and prop placement (generally permitted) from surreptitious advertising (banned if it is intentional). In summary, the tolerance of product placement is understandable from a commercial perspective, but bristles with legal problems.

(ii) Sponsorship

Rule 9 of the Ofcom Broadcasting Code also sets out principles and rules governing programme sponsorship, defined as programming that has some or all of its costs met by a sponsor. The rules are designed to preserve editorial independence and to ensure that sponsorship arrangements are transparent. So news and current affairs programmes must not be sponsored; prohibited advertisers, for example, of tobacco products, may not sponsor programmes; and a sponsor must not influence the content or scheduling of the programme. Sponsorship must be clearly identified by credits, making clear the identity of the sponsor and any association between it and the sponsored content; the credits must be broadcast at the start of, and/or during the intervals of, and/or at the end of the programme, although the usual practice seems to be to show them at all these stages. Credits should not be used to advertise the sponsor's goods or services, but solely to identify it. However, of course any reference to the sponsor inevitably draws viewers' attention to its goods, etc., so this rule might be considered somewhat futile.

These rules implement Ofcom's obligation under the Communications Act 2003 to set standards which prevent unsuitable sponsorship, and the requirement of the EU AVMSD. As with its product placement provisions, the AVMSD sponsorship rules apply to all audiovisual media services, so they cover video on-demand, as well as television broadcasting. Member States may choose to ban the showing of a sponsorship logo during children's and religious programmes and documentaries, but this power has not been implemented in the Ofcom Code; its terms do, however, reflect the other sponsorship provisions in the EU Directive.

Questions for discussion

1. Was it right to relax the restrictions on product placement? How can it be distinguished from surreptitious advertising which is banned by the Ofcom Code?
2. Why is product placement prohibited in certain genres of programmes, but allowed in others?
3. Are the restrictions on sponsorship sufficient to protect broadcasters from commercial pressures?

(e) Advertising on radio

Radio advertising is regulated by Rule 10 of the Ofcom Broadcasting Code, supplemented by the BCAP Code which has a few separate rules for radio. However, radio presents relatively few complaints compared to television (or indeed some other media). In 2011, some 709 complaints were made in respect of radio, compared to 11,245 in respect of television. Radio advertising is lightly regulated; there are no limits on the frequency or duration of advertisements, equivalent to those in the Ofcom Scheduling Code (see Extract 6.5.4 above). Programmes associated with any commercial arrangement, including sponsorship and the provision of competition prizes or premium rate telephone services, must be appropriately signalled, so the arrangement is clear to listeners, and spot advertisements must be clearly separate from programming. No commercial references are permitted in or around news bulletins, or in children's programming. However, there are no specific rules about sponsorship, although it is covered by the prohibition of commercial arrangements with a party banned from advertising on radio under Rule 10 of the BCAP Code, for example, a party advertising tobacco products, guns or sexual massage parlours. However, a specific rule governs charitable appeals, more common on radio than on television. A charitable appeal must be broadcast free of charge and must not contain any commercial reference.

(f) Sanctions

As outlined earlier (see Section 6.5(a) above), the authority to apply sanctions for breach of the advertising rules is divided between Ofcom and the ASA. The statutory authority to issue a direction requiring a broadcasting licensee not to show a particular advertisement, or to direct the exclusion of descriptions of advert and methods of advertising has been delegated to the ASA. However, the authority to apply the more serious sanctions under the broadcasting legislation, for example, to direct the broadcast of a correction or apology, to impose a fine, or in extreme cases even to revoke a broadcasting licence has been retained by Ofcom. These powers have been exercised on occasion by Ofcom, as they were under earlier broadcasting legislation by its predecessor, the Independent Television Commission. In 1994, Granada, a Channel 3 licensee, was fined £500,000 for giving undue prominence to a product and for breach of the current sponsorship code. In 2004 1,360 complaints against Auction world's shopping channel for misleading commercials and failure to meet delivery promises led to a reference to Ofcom, which revoked the channel's licence.

The crucial point is that serious, legally enforceable sanctions may be imposed on broadcasters as an alternative to, or to supplement, the directions of the ASA. Consequently, enforcement of advertising regulation in the broadcast context is more effective than it is in the non-broadcasting media context, where the ASA generally has recourse only to a range of informal sanctions; it has no legal authority to direct a newspaper or magazine not to publish an offending advertisement, let alone to fine it. (For misleading broadcast commercials, as for such advertisements in the print media or on hoardings, a reference may be made to the OFT for it to consider action under the consumer protection regulations.) The availability of sanctions against broadcasters, coupled with the fact that all broadcast advertisements are previewed either by Clearcast or the RACC, should mean that advertising restrictions are strictly observed; but the number of complaints to the ASA, particularly for offensive commercials, seems to show that this is not the case.

(g) UK advertising regulation and the AVMSD

It has already been pointed out that in many respects the terms of advertising regulation in the Ofcom and BCAP Codes have been drafted to comply with the requirements of EU Directives, now the AVMSD.[58] The UK rules, for example, on product placement and sponsorship have been significantly shaped by the need to comply with the standards set out in this Directive, which applies to all audiovisual media services (television and video on demand) but not to radio. Member States are free under Article 4 of the Directive to require audiovisual media services 'under their jurisdiction to comply with more detailed or stricter rules in the fields co-ordinated by [the] Directive', provided those rules comply with EU law.[59] The Ofcom Code on the Scheduling of Advertising takes advantage of this freedom by providing more detailed, and in some respects stricter, rules for the frequency of advertising than those prescribed by the Directive.

The question which arose in *De Agostini* was whether a Member State could act in relation to broadcasts from another Member State, which did not comply with national laws on misleading advertising and on advertising directed at children. The case primarily concerned advertisements placed by Swedish companies on two television channels: TV3, a satellite service licensed in, and broadcast from, the UK, to Sweden; and TV4, a broadcaster operating within Sweden. The advertisements were for a children's magazine, each issue of which contained a model dinosaur part which could be collected. Under Swedish broadcasting law advertising directed at children younger than 12 was prohibited. The advertisements were also alleged to be in breach of the Marketing Practices Act, Swedish legislation dealing with unfair and misleading advertising.

Extract 6.5.6
Joined Cases C-34–36/95 Konsumentombudsmannen (KO) v De Agostini (Svenska) Forlag AB and TV-Shop I Sverige AB **[1997] ECR I-3843, at 3888–9 and 3894–5 (footnotes omitted)**

[*laws on misleading advertising*]

. . .

Although the Directive provides that the Member States are to ensure freedom of reception and are not to impede retransmission on their territory of television broadcasts coming from other Member States on grounds relating to television advertising and sponsorship, it does not have the effect of excluding completely and automatically the application of rules other than those specifically concerning the broadcasting and distribution of programmes.

---

[58] The background to, and terms of, this Directive are fully discussed in Chapter 5.
[59] The ECJ had confirmed in Case C-412/93, *Leclerc-Siplec* v *TFI Publicité SA and Another* [1995] 3 CMLR 422 that Member States were entitled to impose stricter rules on advertising for broadcasters within their jurisdiction. France was entitled to ban advertisements for goods distributors to protect the regional press.

Thus the Directive does not in principle preclude application of national rules with the general aim of consumer protection provided that they do not involve secondary control of television broadcasts in addition to the control which the broadcasting Member State must carry out.

Consequently, where a Member State's legislation such as that in question . . . which, for the purpose of protecting consumers, provides for a system of prohibitions and restraining orders to be imposed on advertisers, enforceable by financial penalties, application of such legislation to television broadcasts from other Member States cannot be considered to constitute an obstacle prohibited by the Directive.

According to . . . [the advertisers] and the Commission, the principle that broadcasts are to be controlled by the State having jurisdiction over the broadcaster would be seriously undermined in both its purpose and effect if the Directive were held to be inapplicable to advertisers. They argue that a restriction relating to advertising has an impact on television broadcasts, even if the restriction concerns only advertising.

In response to that objection, it is sufficient to observe that Council Directive 84/450 relating to . . . misleading advertising, which provides in particular in Article 4(1) that Member States are to ensure that adequate and effective means exist for the control of misleading advertising in the interests of consumers as well as competitors and the general public, could be robbed of its substance in the field of television advertising if the receiving Member State were deprived of all possibility of adopting measures against an advertiser and that this would be in contradiction with the express intention of the Community legislature . . .

It follows from the foregoing that the Directive does not preclude a Member State from taking, pursuant to general legislation on protection of consumers against misleading advertising, measures against an advertiser in relation to television advertising broadcast from another Member State, provided that those measures do not prevent the retransmission, as such, in its territory of television broadcasts coming from that other Member State.

[prohibition on advertising aimed at children]

Application of such a domestic provision to advertising broadcast by a television broadcaster established in the same State cannot be contrary to the Directive since Article 3(1) of that provision [now AVMS Directive, art 4] does not contain any restriction as regards the interests which the Member States may take into consideration when laying down more strict rules for television broadcasters established in their territory. However, the situation is not the same where television broadcasters established in another Member State are concerned.

. . . [t]he Directive contains a set of provisions specifically devoted to the protection of minors in relation to television programmes in general and television advertising in particular.

The broadcasting State must ensure that those provisions are complied with.

This certainly does not have the effect of prohibiting application of legislation of the receiving State designed to protect consumers or minors in general, provided that its application does not prevent retransmission, as such, in its territory of broadcasts from another Member State.

However, the receiving Member State may no longer, under any circumstances, apply provisions specifically designed to control the content of television advertising with regard to minors.

If provisions of the receiving State regulating the content of television broadcasts for reasons relating to the protection of minors against advertising were applied to broadcasts from other Member States, this would add a secondary control to the control which the broadcasting Member State must exercise under the Directive.

It follows that the Directive is to be interpreted as precluding the application to television broadcasts from other Member States of a provision of a domestic broadcasting law which provides that advertisements broadcast in commercial breaks on television must not be designed to attract the attention of children under 12 years of age.

In short, the principle that in those areas of audiovisual media services law now regulated by the AVMSD, Member States must not restrict the retransmission of services from other Member States,[60] covers advertising regulation to protect children; but this principle does not apply to domestic rules on unfair and misleading advertising, since this field is not 'co-ordinated' by the AVMSD.[61] However, the power to apply its own advertising rules does not allow the state to ban the retransmission of programmes emanating from other Member States.

Questions for discussion

1. Will the decision in *De Agostini* satisfy those Member States who want stricter laws on advertising?
2. What action can a Member State take in respect of misleading advertising broadcast from another Member State?
3. If the rules in Rule 32 of the BCAP Code (see Extract 6.5.3 above) were applied to advertising in programmes broadcasting from, say, France, could this be challenged as infringing the AVMSD?

6.6 REGULATION OF VIDEO ON-DEMAND ADVERTISING

Many of the advertising rules in the AVMSD apply to all audiovisual services, including video on-demand (VOD) as well as to traditional television broadcasting. This is the case with the general rules banning surreptitious advertising and requiring advertising to be readily recognisable, as well as the specific bans on advertising tobacco products, medicines available on prescription, and on advertising causing physical or moral harm to minors.[62] The sponsorship and product placement provisions also apply to all audiovisual services,[63] but the rules on the scheduling and frequency of commercials do not.[64]

On-demand programme services (ODPS), such as VOD, are now regulated in the UK by amendments to the Communications Act 2003, made by the Audiovisual Media Services Regulations 2009.[65] The providers of ODPS must comply with detailed rules on advertising, sponsorship and product placement set out in the amendments; they implement the terms of the AVMS Directive, and replicate in similar terms the provisions in legislation (see for example Extract 6.5.5) and the Ofcom Broadcasting Code. Under the amended Communications Act,[66] Ofcom may designate other bodies as the appropriate regulatory authority, although Ofcom itself may act concurrently with that body, and may confer only limited regulatory powers. It has designated the CAP and ASA as appropriate regulatory authorities for the content of advertisements on ODPS, putting on a formal basis the previous self-regulatory arrangements.[67] The contents rules are set out in Rule 30

---

[60] AVMSD, art 3, discussed in Chapter 5 above.
[61] For discussion of the *De Agostini* case, see R. Craufurd-Smith 'Sex and violence in the internal market: the impact of European Community Law on television programme standards' [1998] *Contemporary Issues in Law* 135, 147–8.
[62] AVMSD, art 9.
[63] Ibid., arts 10–11.
[64] Ibid., arts 19–26 which apply only to television broadcasting and teleshopping channels.
[65] SI 2009/2979, inserting into the Communications Act 2003, ss 368A–368R.
[66] Section 368B.
[67] ASA Annual Report 2010, 13. In 2011, there were 119 complaints against adverts on VOD, compared with 11, 245 for broadcasting and 10,123 for the Internet: Annual Report, 2011, 41.

in Appendix 2 of the CAP Code. It is perhaps a legacy of these previous arrangements that ODPS is regulated by the CAP Code for non-broadcast advertising, rather than by the BCAP Code governing broadcast advertising; one might have expected that on-demand programme services, which are comparable to programmes normally included in television schedules, would be regulated by the latter Code.

On the other hand, the regulatory authority over sponsorship and product placement has been transferred to ATVOD (see Chapter 4, Section 4.5).[68] ATVOD rules 12 and 13 concern respectively sponsorship and product placement, replicating in less formal language the terms of the amended Communications Act 2003. Like the CAP (and BCAP) ATVOD may direct broadcasters in breach of these rules to stop the infringing practice, but it has no power to fine, let alone impose a more serious sanction on offending licensees.

Questions for discussion

1.   Are the arrangements for regulating advertising, etc. on VOD too complex?
2.   What are the advantages and disadvantages of these arrangements?

6.7 THE BAN ON BROADCAST POLITICAL ADVERTISING

(a) The statutory ban

UK broadcasting legislation has always banned the broadcast of political advertising, while making provision for the allocation of free political and election broadcasts to the political parties.[69] The ban extends, as will be explained shortly, to all forms of political advertising, not only to that by political parties. It is considered necessary to prevent the distortion of politics which would be brought about by the greater resources of rich parties and pressure groups able to buy much more advertising time than smaller groups could afford. Its defenders point to the USA, where candidates and pressure groups spend vast amounts of money on election advertising (and time and energy on raising this money); the super rich, such as Mitt Romney, can use their own wealth to increase their chances of election to high office by saturation advertising on television.[70]

Critics of the ban make a number of points.[71] First, it precludes the acceptance by a broadcaster of all advertisements 'directed towards a political end', defined in the Communications Act 2003 as including influence on the policies or decisions of national or local government, or influence on public opinion on any matter of public controversy. So an environmental pressure group cannot pay for an advertisement on radio or television, even in reply to the regular commercials of car manufacturers or air lines. One point, therefore, is that the ban discriminates between commercial advertisements (allowed) and political and social activist advertising (prohibited). Second, the ban discriminates between the different media, for there are no legal limits on the amount of political advertising which can be carried by newspapers and magazines; sometimes, however, this point is made in support of the ban on broadcasting political advertisements

---

[68] For details of these arrangements, see the ATVOD Rules available on its website (accessed 10 November 2012): http://www.atvod.co.uk/uploads/files/ATVOD_Rules_and_Guidance_Ed_2.0_May_2012.pdf.

[69] See Chapter 4, Section 4.4 for election broadcasts.

[70] For a defence of the UK position, see J. Rowbottom, *Democracy Distorted* (Cambridge: CUP, 2010), 202–5.

[71] See in particular, A. Scott, '"A monstrous and unjustifiable infringement"? Political expression and the broadcasting ban on advocacy advertising' (2003) 66 *Modern Law Review* 224.

– pressure groups remain free to pay for adverts in the press. However, they cannot advertise on the media which reaches most people – television. The third point is that the ban disproportionately restricts freedom of political expression, which is usually strongly protected, but in this context is less well protected than commercial speech.

For all these reasons the European Court of Human Rights has upheld challenges to bans on political advertising: see the discussion in Section 6.7(b). However, the prohibition has been kept in the Communications Act 2003, although when the Bill was introduced, the Secretary of State for Culture, Media and Sport was unable, in light of the Strasbourg Court decision in the *VgT* case (see Extract 6.7.1 below) to state its compatibility with the ECHR.[72] However, the ban has been supported by a number of bodies, notably the Joint Committee of the House of Lords and House of Commons on Human Rights when considering the draft Communications Bill,[73] and by the Electoral Commission when reviewing the arrangements for party political broadcasts.[74]

Under the Act, an advertisement infringes the ban on political advertising if it is inserted by, or for, a body whose objects are wholly or mainly of a political nature, or is directed to a political end, or has a connection with an industrial dispute.[75] The Communications Act 2003, Section 321 defines political objects and ends extremely broadly to include influencing the outcome of elections or the policies or decisions of government, local, regional or national, or of bodies with public functions, or bringing about changes in the law.[76] It is immaterial whether the influencing concerns the policies, etc., of governments in the UK or elsewhere; it covers both. Influencing public opinion on any matter which, in the UK, is a matter of public controversy is also treated as political.[77] The ban does not, however, apply to advertisements of a public service nature by, or for, government departments or to party political broadcasts.[78] These rules are implemented by the BCAP Code, which replicates in less formal language the terms of the Communications Act.[79]

(b) Strasbourg jurisprudence

In 1994 the applicant, a Swiss association dedicated to the protection of animals, was refused permission to broadcast, in reaction to meat industry commercials, a short advertisement protesting against methods of pig farming and ending with the message, '. . . eat less meat, for the sake of your health, the animals, and the environment'. The decision of the broadcasting authorities was upheld by the courts in Switzerland, so the applicant took the case to the European Court of Human Rights, arguing that the refusal to broadcast its commercial infringed ECHR, art 10. The European Court, in one of its most radical decisions on the scope of article 10, upheld the application. It found that the association's message was not a conventional commercial, but rather reflected a controversial view, which the Swiss authorities themselves had treated as political. So they did not enjoy the

[72] Under HRA 1998, s 19 the Minister in charge of a Bill must certify that it is compatible with the ECHR, or that although he cannot make such a statement, the government wishes to proceed with the Bill.
[73] 19th Report of Session 2001–2, HL 149, HC 1102, para 301.
[74] *Report and Recommendations on Party Political Broadcasting* (2003), 15–17.
[75] Section 321(2). The meaning of 'wholly or mainly of a political nature' was considered by the Court of Appeal in *R v Radio Authority, ex parte Bull* [1998] QB 294, when it upheld a ban on radio advertisements by Amnesty International (British Section).
[76] Section 321(3).
[77] Section 321(3)(f).
[78] Section 321(7).
[79] BCAP Code, Rule 7.

wide margin of appreciation which was accorded national courts and other bodies in respect of commercial speech (see Section 6.2).[80]

Extract 6.7.1
***VgT Verein gegen Tierfabriken* v *Switzerland (VgT)* (2002) 34 EHRR 4, paras 74–7**

74. In the present case, the contested measure, namely the prohibition of political advertising as provided in section 18(5) of the Federal Radio and Television Act, was applied only to radio and television broadcasts, and not to other media such as the press. The Federal Court explained in this respect in its judgment of 20 August 1997 that television had a stronger effect on the public on account of its dissemination and immediacy. In the Court's opinion, however, while the domestic authorities may have had valid reasons for this differential treatment, a prohibition of political advertising which applies only to certain media, and not to others, does not appear to be of a particularly pressing nature.

75. Moreover, it has not been argued that the applicant association itself constituted a powerful financial group which, with its proposed commercial, aimed at endangering the independence of the broadcaster; at unduly influencing public opinion or at endangering equality of opportunity among the different forces of society. Indeed, rather than abusing a competitive advantage, all the applicant association intended to do with its commercial was to participate in an ongoing general debate on animal protection and the rearing of animals. The Court cannot exclude that a prohibition of 'political advertising' may be compatible with the requirements of Article 10 of the Convention in certain situations. Nevertheless, the reasons must be 'relevant' and 'sufficient' in respect of the particular interference with the rights under Article 10. In the present case, the Federal Court, in its judgment of 20 August 1997, discussed at length the general reasons which justified a prohibition of 'political advertising'. In the Court's opinion, however, the domestic authorities have not demonstrated in a 'relevant and sufficient' manner why the grounds generally advanced in support of the prohibition of political advertising also served to justify the interference in the particular circumstances of the applicant association's case.

76. The domestic authorities did not adduce the disturbing nature of any particular sequence, or of any particular words, of the commercial as a ground for refusing to broadcast it. It therefore mattered little that the pictures and words employed in the commercial at issue may have appeared provocative or even disagreeable.

77. In so far as the Government pointed out that there were various other possibilities to broadcast the information at issue, the Court observes that the applicant association, aiming at reaching the entire Swiss public, had no other means than the national television programmes of the Swiss Radio and Television Company at its disposal, since these programmes were the only ones broadcast throughout Switzerland. The Commercial Television Company was the sole instance responsible for the broadcasting of commercials within these national programmes. Private regional television channels and foreign television stations cannot be received throughout Switzerland.

. . .

The implications of the ruling in *VgT* were unclear. Some of the remarks in paragraph 75 suggested that in other situations – perhaps during an election campaign – a ban on political advertising might be upheld. Further, in *Murphy* v *Ireland* the European Court did uphold the application of the total ban in Ireland on religious and political advertising to a radio advertisement by the Irish Faith Centre for showing a video at the Centre during the week before Easter. In upholding the refusal to show the advertisement, the Court

---

[80] *VgT* (2002) 34 EHRR 4, paras 70–1.

referred to the immediate, invasive and powerful impact of the broadcasting media, and the fact that larger churches and religious organisations would be able to purchase a substantial amount of advertising time.[81] It also accepted the government's argument that it would be difficult for it to apply fairly a selective approach to religious advertising by filtering out unacceptable or excessive religious commercials; in contrast a blanket ban was easy to apply.[82] The *VgT* decision was distinguished on the ground that it concerned political speech on a matter of public interest, while state authorities enjoy a wider margin of appreciation when deciding what restrictions are necessary on religious expression and advertising.[83] Interestingly, there is no restriction in the UK on broadcasting an advertisement similar to that in *Murphy*.

The Strasbourg Court has affirmed its ruling in *VgT*. The animal rights association returned to the Court when the Swiss authorities persisted in their refusal to allow a showing of its commercial. In 2009 a Grand Chamber of the Court ruled that Switzerland had again infringed ECHR, art 10.[84] It treated the refusal as a prior restraint on speech, calling for most careful scrutiny (see Chapter 1, Section 1.6), and robustly, and correctly, dismissed the argument that the unpleasant character of the commercial – in the eyes of some consumers and meat traders – could justify it. It has also re-affirmed this approach in the Norwegian *Pensioners Party* case,[85] when a broadcaster was fined after it had transmitted before local and regional elections three short commercials by a small political party representing pensioners' interests. The European Court held that the application to the party of the complete ban in Norway on political advertising infringed ECHR, art 10. The Court accepted the argument that it might be justifiable to restrict political expression, including the broadcast of political advertising, to prevent the distortion of democratic debate, but that argument could not be applied here; the Pensioners Party was a small one, which enjoyed little coverage in news programmes. The ban was intended to prevent distortion of debate by wealthy groups, not small parties like the applicant in this case.[86] It was also perhaps relevant that there is no system of free election broadcasting in Norway, as there is in the UK, so the effect of the advertising ban was to deprive the Pensioners Party of any opportunity to put across its political message.

(c) The *ADI* case

The compatibility of the UK ban on all broadcast political advertising with the right to freedom of political expression was challenged in the *ADI* case. Animal Defenders International sought to bring about changes in the law concerning the treatment of animals, and to influence public and political opinion to achieve that goal. It prepared an advertisement for broadcast, showing a young girl playing with a primate in a cage, with a voice-over protesting about the ill-treatment of primates, and inviting the public to send £10 for an information pack. The advert was submitted for clearance by the Broadcast Advertising Clearance Centre (now Clearcast), which rejected it as political. The Divisional

---

[81] *Murphy* v *Ireland* (2004) 38 EHRR 13, para 74.

[82] Ibid., para 77.

[83] For a critical discussion of this decision, see A. Geddis, 'You Can't Say "God" on the Radio: Freedom of Expression, Religious Advertising and the Broadcast Media after *Murphy* v *Ireland*' (2004) 9 *European Human Rights Law Review* 181.

[84] *VgT Verein gegen Tierfabriken* v *Switzerland* (2011) 52 EHRR 8.

[85] *TV Vest and Rogaland Pensjonparti* v *Norway* (2009) 48 EHRR 51.

[86] Ibid., paras 72–3.

Court after a lengthy consideration of the arguments dismissed the application by ADI for a declaration that the ban on political advertising in the Communications Act 2003 was incompatible with the Convention right to freedom of expression guaranteed by the HRA (see Chapter 1, Section 1.2 above).[87] It distinguished *VgT*, the authority of which had been weakened, in its view, by the later decision in *Murphy*; *VgT* concerned the application on the facts of the Swiss ban to a particular advertisement, while ADI was challenging the statutory ban as a whole. The Court did not consider that a selective ban on political advertising – confined to election periods or to political parties, but permitting commercials by pressure groups – was a practicable alternative; it might, for instance, encourage, political parties to use associated groups to advertise their message.[88] ADI appealed unsuccessfully to the House of Lords.

Extract 6.7.2
R (on the application of Animal Defenders International) **v** *Secretary of State for Culture, Media and Sport* **[2008] UKHL 15, [2008] 1 AC 1312, paras 28–34**

LORD BINGHAM:

28. The fundamental rationale of the democratic process is that if competing views, opinions and policies are publicly debated and exposed to public scrutiny the good will over time drive out the bad and the true prevail over the false. It must be assumed that, given time, the public will make a sound choice when, in the course of the democratic process, it has the right to choose. But it is highly desirable that the playing field of debate should be so far as practicable level. This is achieved where, in public discussion, differing views are expressed, contradicted, answered and debated. It is the duty of broadcasters to achieve this object in an impartial way by presenting balanced programmes in which all lawful views may be ventilated. It is not achieved if political parties can, in proportion to their resources, buy unlimited opportunities to advertise in the most effective media, so that elections become little more than an auction. Nor is it achieved if well-endowed interests which are not political parties are able to use the power of the purse to give enhanced prominence to views which may be true or false, attractive to progressive minds or unattractive, beneficial or injurious. The risk is that objects which are essentially political may come to be accepted by the public not because they are shown in public debate to be right but because, by dint of constant repetition, the public has been conditioned to accept them. The rights of others which a restriction on the exercise of the right to free expression may properly be designed to protect must, in my judgment, include a right to be protected against the potential mischief of partial political advertising.

29. I do not think the full strength of this argument was deployed in *VgT*. And in that case the applicant was seeking to respond, with a wholly inoffensive advertisement, to commercials broadcast by the meat industry. In the present case also the proposed advertisement is wholly inoffensive, and one may be sympathetic to the appellant's aims or some of them. But the issue must be tested with reference to objects with which one may not be sympathetic. Hypothetical examples spring readily to mind: adverts by well-endowed multi-national companies seeking to thwart or delay action on climate change; adverts by wealthy groups seeking to ban abortion; or, if not among member states of the Council of Europe, adverts by so-called patriotic groups supporting the right of the citizen to bear arms. Parliament was entitled to regard the risk of such adverts as a real danger, none the less so because legislation has up to now prevented its occurrence.

---

[87] [2006] EWHC 3069; [2007] EMLR 6.
[88] Ibid., paras 79–80, per Auld LJ, and paras 109–11, per Ouseley J.

30. The question necessarily arises why there is a pressing social need for a blanket prohibition of political advertising on television and radio when no such prohibition applies to the press, the cinema and all other media of communication. The answer is found in the greater immediacy and impact of television and radio advertising. This was recognised by the European Court in *Jersild* v *Denmark* (1994) 19 EHRR 1, para 31, and again in *Murphy* [in paras 74 and 78], although the court appeared to discount the point somewhat in para 74 of its judgment in *VgT*. Here, the chief executive of the appellant in her evidence has described television and radio as 'the most influential advertising option' and stated that 'Moving images are an enormously effective way of getting across evidence of social and environmental problems, and giving the public the chance to participate in change'. Plainly, this application is made precisely because television and radio are judged to be the most effective advertising media. I share the view of Ouseley J in para 90 of his judgment 'that it is not really a matter of serious debate but that the broadcast media is more pervasive and potent than any other form of media'.

31. Since, in principle, no restriction may be wider than is necessary to promote the legitimate object which it exists to serve, it is necessary to ask whether any restriction on political advertising less absolute than that laid down in sections 319 and 321 would suffice to meet the mischief in question. The possibility suggests itself of regulating political advertising by time or frequency or expenditure or by the nature and quality of the adverts in question. It is, I think, unnecessary to explore this possibility in detail, for four main reasons. First, Mr Fordham for the appellant has not, clearly advisedly, advanced such an argument although, as I understand, he did so below. Secondly, it is difficult to see how any system of rationing or capping could be devised which could not be circumvented, as, for instance, by the formation of small and apparently independent groups pursuing very similar political objects. In its judgment in *Murphy*, para 77, the European Court recognised the difficulty of invigilating religious adverts fairly, objectively and coherently on a case by case basis and exactly the same difficulty would arise here, perhaps even more embarrassingly. It is hard to think that any such system would not accord excessive discretion to officials, and give rise to many legal challenges. Thirdly, the important duty of broadcasters to present a fair, balanced and reasonably comprehensive cross-section of public opinion on the issues of the day across the range of their programmes, hard as it is to discharge in any event, would be rendered even harder to discharge if account had to be taken of what might well be a considerable volume of political advertising. Fourthly, despite an express request by the Joint Human Rights Committee to consider compromise solutions, the government judged that no fair and workable compromise solution could be found which would address the problem, a judgment which Parliament accepted. I see no reason to challenge that judgment.

32. While television and radio are, as noted above, the preferred media for advertising, it is not irrelevant that all other media are open to the appellant: newspapers and magazines, direct mailshots, billboards, public meetings and marches. The appellant may also contribute to broadcast programmes and radio phone-ins. The European Court attached little weight to this consideration in *VgT*, paras 74, 77, but did so in *Murphy*, para 74. In my opinion, this is a factor of some weight . . .

33. The weight to be accorded to the judgment of Parliament depends on the circumstances and the subject matter. In the present context it should in my opinion be given great weight, for three main reasons. First, it is reasonable to expect that our democratically-elected politicians will be peculiarly sensitive to the measures necessary to safeguard the integrity of our democracy. It cannot be supposed that others, including judges, will be more so. Secondly, Parliament has resolved, uniquely since the 1998 Act came into force in October 2000, that the prohibition of political advertising on television and radio may possibly, although improbably, infringe article 10 but has nonetheless resolved to proceed under section 19(1)(b) of the Act.

It has done so, while properly recognising the interpretative supremacy of the European Court, because of the importance which it attaches to maintenance of this prohibition. The judgment of Parliament on such an issue should not be lightly overridden. Thirdly, legislation cannot be framed so as to address particular cases. It must lay down general rules: [authorities omitted.] A general rule means that a line must be drawn, and it is for Parliament to decide where. The drawing of a line inevitably means that hard cases will arise falling on the wrong side of it, but that should not be held to invalidate the rule if, judged in the round, it is beneficial.

34. If, as in *VgT*, a body with aims similar to those of the applicant in that case or the appellant in this had grounds for wishing to counter the effect of commercial advertising bearing on an issue of public controversy, it would have strong grounds for seeking an opportunity to put its case in the ordinary course of broadcast programmes. The broadcaster, discharging its duty of impartiality, could not ignore such a request. But that is not this case. A question of compatibility might arise if a body whose objects were wholly or mainly of a political nature sought to broadcast an advertisement unrelated to its objects, or if an advertisement were rejected as of a political nature or directed towards political ends when it did not fall within section 321(3)(a), (b), (c), (d), (e) or (g) but only within section 321(3)(f). But the present is not such a case. The appellant's proposed advertisement was, as one would expect, consistent with its objects and, as the appellant's chief executive makes plain in her evidence, its object is to persuade Parliament to legislate. If such a limited challenge were to arise, there might well be scope for resort to section 3 of the 1998 Act, agreed to be inappropriate in the present case.

Baroness Hale drew attention to the dominance of advertising in the USA, and the impact there of the absence of limits on the expenditure of pressure groups. In her view, the case concerned not just limits on freedom of expression, but the appropriate balance between that freedom and voter equality.[89]

ADI has taken its case to the European Court of Human Rights. The Grand Chamber rejected the application and upheld the UK ban by a 9–8 majority.

Questions for discussion

1. Are you persuaded by the arguments of Lord Bingham for the UK absolute ban on broadcast political advertising?
2. Can the *ADI* case be distinguished from *VgT*?
3. Would it be possible to amend the UK ban to allow pressure group advertising, for example in circumstances comparable to those in *VgT*, but to preclude the distortion of democratic debate by saturation television advertising by wealthy individuals, parties and pressure groups?

---

[89] Paragraphs 47–9.

Selected further reading

Commercial speech and advertising

C.E. Baker, *Advertising and a Democratic Press* (Princeton, NJ: Princeton University Press, 1995) examines the influence of advertising on the media, and the constitutionality of advertising regulation in the USA.

C. Munro, 'The value of commercial speech' (2003) 62 *Cambridge Law Journal* 134–58 discusses the European and US approaches to commercial speech, and doubts whether it is sensible to classify 'commercial' speech as a distinct category.

R. Shiner, *Freedom of Commercial Expression* (Oxford: OUP, 2003) provides a critique of Canadian, European, and US jurisprudence on commercial speech.

W. Skouris (ed.), *Advertising and Constitutional Rights in Europe* (Baden-Baden: Nomos, 1994) is a comparative study of the constitutional position of advertising in European countries.

Advertising regulation

Advertising Standards Authority Annual Reports, the CAP and BCAP Codes, adjudications of complaints, and other information available at **www.asa.org.uk.**

T. Gibbons and I. Katsirea, 'Commercial influences on programme content; the German and UK approaches to transposing EU rules on product placement' (2012) 4 *Journal of Media Law* 159–88 compares the German and UK implementation of the product placement rules in the EU AVMS Directive.

L. Hitchens, *Broadcasting Pluralism and Diversity* (Oxford and Portland, OR: Hart, 2006), 190–203 discusses the regulation of broadcast advertising in the UK, USA and Australia.

P. Lunt and S. Livingstone, *Media Regulation* (London: Sage, 2012). Chapter 7 discusses Ofcom decision to regulate advertisements for high fat, etc., foods.

C. Munro, 'Self-regulation in the media' [1997] *Public Law* 6–17 compares advertising self-regulation with press content self-regulation by the PCC.

Political advertising

J. Rowbottom, *Democracy Distorted* (Cambridge, CUP: 2010). Chapter 7 discusses advertising within the context of media regulation to ensure fair democratic politics.

A. Scott, '"A monstrous and unjustifiable infringement"? Political expression and the the broadcasting ban on advocacy advertising' (2003) 66 *Modern Law Review*, 224–44 is a sustained critique of the UK ban on broadcast political advertising.

7 Media ownership and plurality

7.1 INTRODUCTION

Although the preceding chapters have described the regulatory rules that structure the provision of audiovisual services, there is a specific aspect of these rules that attracts considerable regulatory attention and warrants further examination, namely the extent to which individuals and companies should be allowed to own and/or control the media. There are essentially two concerns here. On the one hand, regulators wish to ensure that media companies, like other companies operating in the commercial sector, do not engage in any unfair competitive behaviour. Anti-competitive practices are controlled by general competition rules, which, within Europe, can be enforced at the domestic or European Union levels. The operation of these rules is considered in more detail in the following chapter. The second concern is that ownership concentration can unduly limit the number of independent sources of information or lead to particular individuals or companies wielding undue social and political power.

The UK has introduced specific measures to address the latter of these two sets of concerns and promote what is often referred to as 'media pluralism'. Initially, different regulatory approaches were employed in the press and broadcasting fields. In the press sector, provision was made for the plurality implications of major newspaper mergers to be assessed on a case by case basis but primary reliance was placed on the operation of the competition rules to keep the print market open. In the audiovisual sector, fixed ownership limits were introduced, coupled with restrictions on broadcasting licences being awarded to certain categories of individual or organisation where there could be a conflict of interest between the strategic interests of the licensee and the broader democratic or social interests that underpin state regulation in the field. These measures were supplemented by a range of content controls and quotas designed to maintain programme diversity. Over time, however, the UK has removed most of the fixed ownership limits in the audiovisual sector and the structural controls employed to promote media pluralism are now very similar for both the press and audiovisual media.

This chapter focuses on specific media ownership rules in the UK and the scope for European intervention to promote media pluralism. Two questions are central to the matters covered in this chapter. First, can media specific ownership rules still be justified in light of technological developments or should we now rely simply on the operation of general competition rules to regulate the structure of media markets? Second, are the media specific ownership rules that remain in place in the UK credible and effective and, if not, what, if anything, should be put in their place?

7.2 WHY INTRODUCE SECTOR-SPECIFIC MEDIA OWNERSHIP RULES?

Four main rationales for specific regulation of media ownership are usually mentioned: first, to ensure that the media provide a forum for the exchange of diverse information and ideas, thus facilitating the operation of the democratic process and individual self-determination;

second, to prevent specific media owners exerting excessive social or political influence; third, to ensure that the media continue to investigate and evaluate the actions of those who do wield political, economic or social power, thus performing their 'watchdog function'; and, fourth, to preserve cultural and linguistic diversity. These rationales receive careful and sophisticated elaboration in the work of C. Edwin Baker.

Extract 7.2.1

C.E. Baker, *Media Concentration and Democracy. Why Ownership Matters* (Cambridge University Press, 2007), 7 and 16

The media, like elections, constitute a crucial sluice between public opinion formation and state 'will formation'. The mass media, like elections, serve to mediate between the public and the government. For this reason, a country is democratic only to the extent that the media, as well as elections, are structurally egalitarian and politically salient.

The best institutional interpretation of this democratic vision of the public sphere is, I suggest, an egalitarian distribution of control, most obviously meaning ownership, of the mass media. The basic standard for democracy would then be a very wide dispersal of power and ubiquitous opportunities to present preferences, views, visions. This is a *democratic distribution principle* [original emphasis] for communicative power . . .

In any local, state, or national community, concentrated media ownership creates the possibility of an individual decision maker exercising enormous, unequal and hence undemocratic, largely unchecked, potentially irresponsible power. History exhibits countless instances of abuse of concentrated communicative power in this and other countries at either local or national levels. Historical stories, however, are not crucial here. Even if this power were seldom if ever exercised, the democratic safeguard value amounts to an assertion that *no democracy should risk the danger* [original emphasis].

Matthew Gentzkow and Jesse Shapiro have identified three mechanisms by which increasing the number of independently-owned firms in specific media markets can reduce bias or distortion in the coverage of news. First, in helping to defeat government attempts at manipulation; second, in defeating attempts by media firms themselves to suppress or distort information consequent on political or commercial interests; and, third, through stimulating firms to invest in the provision of timely and accurate coverage.

Extract 7.2.2

Gentzkow M. and Shapiro J.M., Competition and truth in the market for news, *Journal of Economic Perspectives* (JEP), Vol. 22 No. 2, Spring 2008, pp. 133–154.

Independence

. . . The oldest and most frequently discussed objection to handing control of the media to a small number of firms is that those firms will be captured by the government. Even in countries where the press is protected by strong constitutional guarantees of independence, the state has many levers by which to influence it. In the case of CBS, a phone call was sufficient to delay broadcast of the Abu Ghraib photographs. To suppress the Pentagon Papers, the Nixon administration used legal action premised on its special powers in the domain of national security. Governments can also dispense with legality and explicitly bribe the media . . .

In the end, competition played a pivotal role in the resolution of the Pentagon Papers case. The *New York Times* had originally obtained the documents from Daniel Ellsberg, an MIT researcher best known to economists for demonstrating a famous violation of expected utility theory (Ellsberg, 1961). When Ellsberg learned of the injunction against the *Times*, he contacted the three major television networks and offered them the documents. All three refused to make them public, presumably fearing similar legal action. Ellsberg then offered the documents to the *Washington Post,* which agreed to publish them. Thus, no sooner had the administration succeeded in silencing the *Times*, than the *Post* picked up printing where it had left off . . .

Diversity

. . . If a firm knows that some consumers will learn the truth from its competitors, the costs of pursuing an ideological agenda by suppressing or distorting information are increased, because it becomes more likely that such actions will be exposed. Firms that compete head-to-head in markets are especially likely to try to expose such information, since they benefit directly from undermining their competitor's reputation. Of course, this mechanism will only operate if firms value a reputation for reporting the truth . . .

Investment

. . . Reputation provides one way to understand why firms continue to invest in getting scoops and why competition can strengthen this incentive. A fundamental feature of information goods is that by definition their content cannot be known until they are consumed. Information is the quintessential experience good . . . This means that consumers' *expectations* [emphasis added] about the timeliness, comprehensiveness, and accuracy of news coverage (not to mention its entertainment value) are the key drivers of sales. Competition allows consumers to judge quality more accurately because they can benchmark one firm's reporting against the other. It can therefore strengthen firms' incentives to invest in high-quality reports.

There are, therefore, economic as well as political grounds for being wary of undue media concentration. In particular, large media corporations are inevitably concerned with the bottom line, the size of shareholder dividends and directors' pay and may thus be insufficiently committed to the production of quality, even ethical, journalism. Powerful corporations, subject to limited competition, will be tempted to cut their expenditure on journalists and original reporting and rely instead on third party content, such as press releases or news agency copy. In 2007, for example, in order to cut costs, the *Pasadena Now* news website hired reporters in India to provide local news coverage relating to California City, though, as Eric Schwartz has noted, at least the firm actually hired reporters.[1] Concentration can thus lead to attractive economic dividends for owners and key personnel but negative externalities for the rest of society.

The importance of a media sector that offers diverse content and is able to hold power to account is widely accepted in democratic countries but the need to impose specific ownership limits in order to achieve these goals is hotly disputed. Such rules are increasingly challenged on the basis that they are both ineffective and no longer required. In some instances, concentration may actually enhance media quality and diversity. Where, for example, a specific media market is generating limited revenues it may be better for one company to operate than two, to avoid unduly fragmenting available resources. Technological developments, notably the Internet, now allow individuals and companies to access a vast, international communications network at relatively low cost. Citizens no longer need to own a printing press or broadcasting licence to engage in a national, if not international, debate. Are there now so many different views and ideas being published on the Internet that we can simply stop worrying about media ownership concentration

[1] E.C. Schwartz, *Conflict of Interest: How Media Pluralism Protects Democracy and Human Rights*, ProQuest LLC 2010, UMI dissertation publishing no 3423027. Available at: http://gradworks.umi.com/3423027.pdf, p 35.

altogether? As the following extract indicates there may be other technological or structural features of media markets that push them in an oligopolistic direction.

Extract 7.2.3
P. Seabright and H. Weeds, 'Competition and market power in broadcasting: where are the rents?' in P. Seabright and J. Von Hagen (eds), *The Economic Regulation of Broadcasting Markets* **(Cambridge University Press, 2007), 47–80 at 50**

With digital transmission, however, spectrum constraints on the number of channels are effectively removed and scarcity rents are eliminated. Existing transmission capacity is sufficient to meet demands (at current and anticipated future levels) and there is a strong incentive to utilise spare capacity that militates against using access to transmission as a barrier to entry.

This discussion would seem to imply that following digitisation, barriers to entry are eliminated and competition concerns fall away . . . [but] Alongside the growth in multi-channel television, the price of key broadcasting content – for example the right to televise live Premier League football matches in the UK – has increased dramatically . . . if key content rights are scarce, these, rather than transmission capacity, accrue scarcity rents and become potential sources of market power.

Questions for discussion

1. Are 'new media' a substitute for, or a complement to, 'old media'?
2. Given technological developments, is it necessary to retain specific media ownership controls in addition to general competition rules?

7.3 THE EVOLUTION OF MEDIA-PLURALITY CONTROLS IN THE UK

(a) UK control of ownership concentration in the print and broadcasting sectors prior to the Communications Act 2003

Until the 2003 Communications Act the printed press and broadcast media were subject to distinct ownership regimes. In the newspaper sector, controls were introduced in 1965 and subsequently enforced through the Fair Trading Act 1973. Section 58 of the 1973 Act required the approval of the Secretary of State for mergers involving newspapers with a combined circulation of 500,000 copies. The Secretary of State was required to obtain a report on any public interest implications of the merger from the Monopolies and Mergers Commission (MMC) (replaced by the Competition Commission (CC) in 1999) prior to making a decision but this was not required where the newspaper to be taken over was failing, small scale or would not be continued as a separate concern. It was on the 'failing firm' basis that the relevant Secretary of State for Trade and Industry, John Biffen, controversially decided not to refer News International's proposed purchase of *The Times* and the *Sunday Times* to the MMC in 1981. Given consolidation in the industry, the effectiveness of the Act has been questioned: of the 50 newspaper cases referred to the MMC and CC since 1973, there were adverse findings (in relation to all or part of the transfer in question) in ten cases and, of these, editorial issues relating to freedom of expression and the accurate presentation of news were considered relevant in only five.[2] A number of these cases did, however, expressly address plurality concerns, as when the merger between the Northern Irish *Belfast Telegraph*

---

[2] DTI, *Enterprise Act 2002: Public Interest Intervention in Media Mergers*, Guidance Document (May 2004), para 5.4.

and *News Letter*, which supported Protestant and Unionist views respectively, was blocked on the basis that this would lead to the loss of a distinctive Unionist viewpoint, the merged enterprise being expected to move to the middle ground.[3]

In the audiovisual sector the 1990 Broadcasting Act introduced a complex set of provisions that both restricted certain types of individual or organisation, for instance political organisations and advertising agencies that might have an interest in suppressing specific information, from owning broadcasting licences and established fixed limits on the accumulation of certain media interests. Thus, the Act limited the number of national and regional radio or television broadcasting licences that could be awarded to a particular firm, sometimes referred to as 'mono-media restrictions'. It also restricted the 'cross-holding' of interests in different media sectors. Thus, companies with national newspaper interests were restricted from holding more than a 20 per cent stake in companies with national television or radio interests and local newspapers were similarly constrained in relation to television and radio services transmitted in their circulation area. These restrictions did not, however, extend to satellite services, allowing Rupert Murdoch to develop his Sky satellite television platform alongside his growing newspaper interests. Concerns about the rigidity of the 1990 regime and the position of News International in both print and television sectors were factors that led the government to set up its review of media ownership controls in 1994. In May 1995 the government published its policy paper, *Media Ownership: The Government's Proposals*.

Extract 7.3.1
Department of National Heritage, *Media Ownership: The Government's Proposals*, Cm 2872 (1995), para 6.1

6.1 The Government believes that the existing structure of media ownership regulation, relying as it does on prohibitions which reinforce the traditional segmentation of the media market, is insufficiently flexible to allow media companies to exploit to the full the opportunities offered by the new technologies, particularly in view of the expansion of media services which will follow the introduction of digital broadcasting. The Government recognises that these technologies are making the traditional segmentation of the market increasingly anachronistic and that media businesses need to be able to regard the provision of media services as a single activity. This Government therefore believes that media ownership regulation needs to evolve to reflect these changes in the shape of the industry . . .

The government considered replacing the existing mono and cross-media restrictions in the 1990 Broadcasting Act with limits based on a company's overall market share. This would have involved making an initial assessment of a company's audience shares in the print, television and radio markets respectively, the shares would then have been weighted according to the degree of influence ascribed to each media sector and then added together to give an overall figure. Those with ownership shares exceeding certain limits would have been required to reduce their holdings. The underlying complexities of this system, in particular the question of how to weight the various media sectors, led the government to step back from such a radical move. As a result the 1996 Act kept in place key elements of the 1990 regime, though it did modify the existing concentration controls to combine market share and accumulation limits in specific sectors and brought digital television within the scope of the regulations.

---

[3] Ibid., para 5.13.

(b) The Communications Act 2003 and the Media Ownership (Radio and Cross-media) Order 2011

There was thus scope, when the New Labour government was elected in 1997, to initiate a more far-reaching reform of media ownership rules in line with technological developments. In particular, the government noted that the earlier broadcasting Acts had failed to address the communications sector as a whole and had not attempted to 'bring the regulation of newspaper ownership into line with that of the other media'.[4] A recurrent argument used by those pressing the government to deregulate further was that competition law on its own could now be relied on to ensure a sufficient plurality of media owners and services.

Extract 7.3.2
House of Commons Library Research Paper no 02/68, accompanying the draft Communications Bill 2002, pp 13–14

The prevailing orthodoxy is that competitive forces, supplemented by competition law, are the most desirable way of ensuring that markets work well and efficiently for business and consumers. Under this view, the opposite pole of competition is regulation, which is seen as an alternative or supplementary force to control the workings of uncompetitive or immature markets so as to prevent undesirable outcomes. As those markets are opened up to competition, or mature, then the expectation is that regulatory controls will give way to ordinary competition controls. This, for example, is the pattern that the telecoms market has taken in the twenty years since privatisation . . . There are those who argue that competition law would be sufficient in itself to control the newspaper and broadcasting sector, and that special controls on media ownership are unnecessary . . .

However, the economic objectives underlying the application of competition rules differ from the democratic, social and cultural objectives that underpin media pluralism rules. Competition rules, as discussed further in Chapter 8, are primarily concerned to ensure that markets remain open and contestable in order to enhance economic efficiency, innovation and consumer choice. This is not to say that the two regimes cannot be mutually supportive, rather, they are not complete substitutes, being founded on different concerns, employing different tests and usually implemented by different institutions. Although the government favoured greater reliance on competition, it recognised in its 2001 consultation paper on media ownership that there remained a case for specific regulation.

Extract 7.3.3
Department of Culture, Media and Sport, *Consultation on Media Ownership Rules* (2001), para 110

. . . although competition law is an important part of regulation, it is not designed to deliver diversity and plurality in the media. Competition rules can address issues of concentration, efficiency and choice, and will tend to encourage dispersed ownership and new entry . . . However, they cannot guarantee any of it. Competition law cannot therefore provide the certainty we need that a significant number of different media voices will continue to be heard, or that prospective new entrants to the market will be able to add their voice. Moreover, it cannot directly address concerns over editorial freedom or community voice.

---

[4] Department of Culture Media and Sport, *Consultation on Media Ownership Rules* (2001), para 3.4.

The same document underlined the government's commitment to finding a 'middle ground' that would 'safeguard both competition and democracy'.

Extract 7.3.4
Department of Culture Media and Sport, *Consultation on Media Ownership Rules* **(2001), paras 1.2–1.11**

1.2 The current ownership rules are being overtaken by a changing media landscape. In devising new, forward-looking legislation, we have two main aims. We want to encourage competition and economic growth, by being as deregulatory as possible. However, we must also allow the media to continue to perform its vital role in democratic society, as a forum for public debate and opinion.

1.3 We want to ensure that citizens receive a diverse range of content from a plurality of sources. The terms 'plurality' and 'diversity' are sometimes used interchangeably, but they are quite distinct concepts. Diversity refers to the variety of different programmes, publications and services that are available, whereas plurality is about the choice people can make between different providers of those services. Both are key to the quality of service and the range of news and opinion we as citizens receive from the media. They are, however, delivered by different means.

1.4 Since *diversity* is about the availability of a wide range of content, it has traditionally been maintained through content regulation, rather than ownership controls. . . . In New Zealand, research suggests that an almost completely deregulated market has led to a significant decline in the quality and diversity of programming. We therefore continue to believe that content regulation is essential.

. . .

1.6 With *plurality* it is not content but the source of that content that matters – the company controlling it, the 'voice' behind it. We want a plurality of voices, giving the citizen access to a variety of views that, in a competitive market, maintain their own balance. We need regulation that is specifically directed to ensure such plurality. That is why we have imposed rules on media ownership.

. . .

1.8 Whilst the need for a plurality of media sources remains clear, we are committed to a deregulatory approach to media markets. From a commercial point of view, further liberalisation would benefit existing companies and potential new investors, providing for further consolidation, greater efficiency, more scope for investment, and a more significant international presence. Growth and investment provide opportunities for innovation, and this should result in new, improved and cheaper products for the consumer. Proponents of a freer market suggest that only through deregulation can choice and diversity really flourish. A competitive market should also contribute to the health of the national economy.

. . .

1.11 The Government's task is to find a middle ground that safeguards both competition and democracy, re-aligning ownership rules to adapt to the new market that is emerging. In other words, we should act to encourage a dynamic market whilst at the same time guaranteeing plurality, diversity and quality for the consumer.

Examination of the media ownership rules in Schedule 14 to the Communications Act 2003 support the view that the primary motivation behind this part of the Act was deregulatory and that deregulation was considered compatible with maintaining, or even enhancing, media pluralism. In particular, the Act removed all specific restrictions on the accumulation of television and analogue radio licences at the national level, rendering it possible for one company to own both the Channel 3 and 5 television licences. Channel 3, previously known as ITV, currently brings together 15 regional licence holders who together provide a networked national service with regional opt-outs. The Communications Act removed all remaining restrictions on consolidation among the holders of the Channel 3 regional television licences, opening the door to the merger of Granada and Carlton in 2004 and the formation of ITV plc, which holds all but three of the 15 regional licences.

The impact of the Communications Act 2003 was less far-reaching in relation to the radio and cross-media ownership rules. It maintained restrictions on the accumulation of local radio licences and digital radio multiplexes at both local and national levels. The three existing local cross-media ownership rules, which addressed consolidation between regional Channel 3 licence holders and local newspapers; local radio and local newspaper or regional Channel 3 interests; and combinations of local radio, local newspaper and regional Channel 3 interests, were all retained. At the national level, the Act now allows the cross-media accumulation of interests in national newspapers and Channel 5, but kept in place a key restriction on combining national newspaper interests with a Channel 3 licence. It is this provision that serves to block any attempt by News International, the company that groups together the UK newspaper interests of Rupert Murdoch, to gain control of the Channel 3 television service.

Extract 7.3.5
Communications Act 2003, Schedule 14, Media Ownership Rules, Part 1,
Channel 3 Services

Ban on newspaper proprietors holding Channel 3 licences

1 (1) A person is not to hold a licence to provide a Channel 3 service if—

  (a) he runs a national newspaper which for the time being has a national market share of 20 per cent or more; or

  (b) he runs national newspapers which for the time being together have a national market share of 20 per cent or more.

(2) A person is not to hold a licence to provide a regional Channel 3 service if—

  (a) he runs a local newspaper which for the time being has a local market share of 20 per cent or more in the coverage area of the service; or

  (b) he runs local newspapers which for the time being together have a local market share of 20 per cent or more in that coverage area.

(3) For the purposes of this paragraph, where there is a licence to provide a Channel 3 service, each of the following shall be treated as holding that licence—

  (a) the actual licence holder; and

  (b) every person connected with the actual licence holder.

Restrictions on participation

2 (1) A person who is—

  (a) the proprietor of a national newspaper which for the time being has a national market share of 20 per cent or more, or

  (b) the proprietor of national newspapers which for the time being together have a national market share of 20 per cent or more, is not to be a participant with more than a 20 per cent interest in a body corporate which is the holder of a licence to provide a Channel 3 service.

(2) A person who is the holder of a licence to provide a Channel 3 service is not to be a participant with more than a 20 per cent interest in a body corporate which is a relevant national newspaper proprietor.

(3) A body corporate is not to be a participant with more than a 20 per cent interest in a body corporate which holds a licence to provide a Channel 3 service if the first body corporate is one in which a relevant national newspaper proprietor is a participant with more than a 20 per cent interest.

(4) A restriction imposed by this paragraph on participation in a body corporate which is the holder of a Channel 3 licence applies equally to participation in a body corporate which controls the holder of such a licence.

(5) Any restriction on participation imposed by this paragraph—

  (a) on the proprietor of a newspaper, or
  (b) on the holder of a licence,
  is to apply as if he and every person connected with him were one person.

(6) In this paragraph 'a relevant national newspaper proprietor' means a person who runs—

  (a) a national newspaper which for the time being has a national market share of 20 per cent or more; or
  (b) national newspapers which for the time being together have a national market share of 20 per cent or more.

The Communications Act 2003 requires Ofcom to report on the operation of the media ownership rules every three years. In its 2009 review, Ofcom recommended that all remaining concentration limits should be removed save the national cross-ownership rule set out above and the cross-ownership restriction on combining local radio, local newspaper and regional Channel 3 interests.[5] Removal of this latter provision was considered a potential threat to media pluralism. The government enthusiastically took up these proposals but went further in also favouring removal of the local radio/press/television cross-ownership limit and referred the matter back to Ofcom for reconsideration. Ofcom concluded the matter was ultimately a policy decision for government to take and when the Media Ownership (Radio and Cross-Media) Order 2011 (SI 2011/1503), was adopted all three local cross-media ownership restrictions were removed. The following impact assessment gives a good indication of the government's priorities.

Extract 7.3.6
Department of Culture, Media and Sport, Impact Assessment, The Media Ownership (Radio and Cross-Media) Order 2011, IA No: DCMS 010, 9 February 2011, p 1

The principal objective of the proposed order for full deregulation at the local level is 'to promote a strong and secure local media industry' as set out in *The Coalition: our programme for government*. We believe that securing the long term economic sustainability of the local media and the provision of high quality commercial news and content is likely to require greater consolidation within local markets which will allow local media companies, radio and newspapers, greater opportunities and flexibility to merge and reduce the high fixed costs, such as premises and staffing, which are characteristic of local media business. We believe such reduction will help to counter-balance the failing income of local advertising, which is increasingly being delivered via the internet.

---

[5] Ofcom, Report to the Secretary of State (Culture, Media and Sport) on the Media Ownership Rules (17 November 2009), para 1.44.

Question for discussion

1. How might consolidation among print, radio and television interests at the local level enhance or degrade media pluralism?

(c) Deregulation or re-regulation? The Communications Act 2003 and the 'Media-plurality Test'

The New Labour government had initially envisaged a two-step approach to controlling media ownership. First, a limited set of media specific ownership rules would be kept in place to protect media plurality. These would comprise the radio and cross-media ownership rules discussed above, together with the restrictions on certain categories of owner, such as local authorities, political organisations and advertising authorities, obtaining broadcasting licences, contained in Schedule 2 to the Broadcasting Act 1990. Even here, however, the government pushed for relaxation and the Communications Act, when enacted, removed the prohibition on foreign (non-EU) ownership of broadcasting licences on the basis that this would encourage inward investment, and opened the way for religious organisations to hold certain types of, notably local, licences.

Second, concentration concerns not addressed by these media specific provisions would be dealt with through application of the general competition rules, discussed in Chapter 8 below. Whether competition law provided an adequate safety net for any outstanding media plurality concerns was, however, widely questioned, notably by the Joint Committee on the Draft Communications Bill, chaired by the film maker Lord Puttnam. The Committee pressed for the introduction of a third strand of protection: an overarching 'media-plurality test' to be applied on a case by case basis where there was consolidation in press and broadcasting markets.[6] What was thus envisaged was a modified and expanded version of the existing controls applicable in the newspaper field. This was reluctantly taken up by the government and the Communications Act 2003 amended the Enterprise 2002 to include a series of media-plurality considerations that could be brought into play in the event of significant media mergers. Given the application of these provisions to print and broadcast mergers, the existing newspaper controls set up under the Fair Trading Act 1973 were abolished.

Interestingly, although the Communications Act 2003 extended the scope of the plurality review from the print to broadcasting sectors it did not address existing concerns over the effectiveness of the previous newspaper regime. And in enhancing ministerial discretion as to whether or not to refer a merger for investigation the new procedure increased, rather than reduced, the scope for political considerations to come into play. The Enterprise Act 2002, as amended, enables but does not require the Secretary of State to issue an 'intervention notice' when they consider that an impending media merger could raise media pluralism concerns. To be applicable, the company being taken over must have a turnover in excess of £70 million or the merger must lead to the creation or enhancement of a 25 per cent share of supply of the relevant goods or services across the UK or a substantial part of it for the firms involved. In the context of media mergers it is also enough for one of the companies to already have a 25 per cent share of supply.

---

[6] Joint Committee on the Draft Communications Bill, Report, Draft Communications Bill, HL 169-I and HC 876-I (25 July 2002).

The intervention notice triggers an initial investigation by the OFT into any competition aspects and by Ofcom into the stated media-plurality concerns. On the basis of the OFT and Ofcom reports, together with any representations made as a result of further consultations, the Secretary of State will decide whether to refer the matter to the Competition Commission for a more detailed examination, to accept behavioural or other modifications designed to address any concerns raised, or to allow the merger to proceed. Where the matter is referred on to the Competition Commission, the Secretary of State will consider the Commission's report and any further representations before deciding whether or not to allow the merger and, if to allow it, on what terms. He or she is under no obligation to follow the Competition Commission's advice on the plurality issues, though is so bound regarding any competition points. An aggrieved party can seek review of the Secretary of State's decision before the Competition Appeal Tribunal (CAT) and rulings of the CAT can be appealed, provided leave is granted, to the Court of Appeal in England or Court of Session in Scotland.

The importance of the media public interest test has been further enhanced by passage of the Media Ownership (Radio and Cross-Media) Order 2011, which, as noted, removed all remaining restrictions on media accumulations at the local level. The public interest criteria are set out in section 58 of the Act and differ depending on whether the merger involves just newspaper publishers or broadcasters.

Extract 7.3.7
Enterprise Act 2002, section 58

[in relation to newspapers the public interest considerations are:]

58(2A) The need for—

(a) accurate presentation of news; and
(b) free expression of opinion;

. . . [and]

58(2B) The need for, to the extent that it is reasonable and practicable, a sufficient plurality of views in newspapers in each market for newspapers in the United Kingdom or a part of the United Kingdom . . .

[In relation to broadcasting and newspaper/broadcast cross-media mergers the considerations are:]

58(2C) . . .

(a) the need, in relation to every different audience in the United Kingdom or in a particular area or locality of the United Kingdom, for there to be a sufficient plurality of persons with control of the media enterprises serving that audience;
(b) the need for the availability throughout the United Kingdom of a wide range of broadcasting which (taken as a whole) is both of high quality and calculated to appeal to a wide variety of tastes and interests; and
(c) the need for persons carrying on media enterprises, and for those with control of such enterprises, to have a genuine commitment to the attainment in relation to broadcasting of the standards objectives set out in section 319 of the Communications Act 2003.

The Secretary of State was at pains to reassure industry when these provisions were introduced that they would not generally be used where specific ownership restrictions were retained or in areas where there had not previously been controls, for example, in relation to mergers between satellite and cable television services. The measures were thus primarily designed to constrain the deregulatory impact of the Communications Act 2003, not introduce new controls. As the following extract illustrates, however, the Secretary of State did not altogether exclude a re-regulatory dimension to the operation of the Enterprise Act provisions.

Extract 7.3.8
Department of Trade and Industry, Enterprise Act 2002 Public Interest Intervention in Media Mergers. Guidance on the operation of the public interest merger provisions relating to newspaper and other media mergers (May 2004), para 8.8

In exceptional circumstances, the Secretary of State may consider it necessary to intervene in mergers in areas where there continue to be media ownership rules or where there have never been such rules. The Secretary of State will only consider intervening in such a merger where she believes that it may give rise to serious public interest concerns in relation to any of the three considerations. During Parliamentary debate of these provisions, Ministers suggested that these might include circumstances where a large number of news or educational channels would be coming under single control, or if someone were to take over all the music channels. The Secretary of State may consider intervention if a prospective new entrant to local radio ownership has not shown a genuine commitment to broadcasting standards in other media or countries. The Secretary of State is not currently aware of any other types of cases in which exceptional circumstances might arise.

Only three intervention notices have been issued to date, in all cases based on section 58(2C) of the Act, which focuses on the need for a 'sufficient plurality of owners'. The first case concerned the 2006 purchase by satellite broadcaster British Sky Broadcasting ('Sky') of a 17.9 per cent shareholding in terrestrial television broadcaster ITV (the '*Sky/ITV*' case). Because the previous cross-ownership restrictions had kicked in where there were shares of 20 per cent or more Sky might reasonably have expected, under the guidelines set out above, that no review would take place. The case thus underlined the fact that the media-plurality provisions could have a distinct re-regulatory effect, extending controls into areas not previously covered.

The case also revealed the substantive and procedural complexities of the process. It took more than three years to conclude and Ofcom, the CC, the Secretary of State, the CAT and the Court of Appeal all considered the plurality issue.[7] Although the merger was ultimately found not to threaten media plurality, divestiture by Sky of the bulk of the ITV shares was ordered on competition grounds, discussed further in Chapter 8. The divergent conclusions reached in relation to the 'sufficiency of plurality' by the various organisations involved were in part influenced by the different emphases they placed on the importance of maintaining content diversity and controlling undue media power, though the case was also complicated by a number of presumptions introduced by the 2002 Act, notably the presumption in section 58A(5) that media enterprises under common ownership or control, understood as extending to the ability to materially influence corporate policy, should be treated as 'under the control of only one person'. The different approaches are illustrated by the following extracts taken from the CC report and CAT opinion respectively.

---

[7] Key documents can be located at http://webarchive.nationalarchives.gov.uk/+/http://www.berr.gov.uk/policies/business-law/competition-matters/mergers/mergers-with-a-public-interest/broadcasting-and-cross-media-mergers.

Extract 7.3.9

Competition Commission, Acquisition by British Sky Broadcasting Group Plc of 17.9 per cent of the Shares in ITV Plc, Report sent to Secretary of State (BERR) (14 December 2007), paras 5.61–5.63 and 5.75

5.61 Paragraph 5.15 sets out our view that we should undertake a qualitative assessment of the impact of the acquisition on the sufficiency of the plurality of persons with control of media enterprises, taking into account the nature and extent of any control acquired by BSkyB over ITV and the implications of the acquisition for the range of information and views made available to audiences for news.

5.62 We looked at the impact of the acquisition on the control of media enterprises serving audiences for news. The acquisition creates a link of control between BSkyB and ITV, and hence between Sky News and ITN (see Section 4). Sky News and ITN are two of the three significant providers of television news programming, together with the BBC. ITN provides news programming to both ITV and Channel 4 and Sky News provides news programming to both BSkyB and Five. Sky News and ITN therefore provide news programming to four of the five channel providers with significant audience shares for television news. The largest shareholder in BSkyB is News International, the ultimate parent company of which is News Corporation. Looking at cross-media audiences, the acquisition also creates a link of control between the second largest channel provider of television news (ITV) and the largest provider of newspapers (News International), again through News Corporation.

5.63 Nevertheless, we noted that the acquisition does not bring ITV and BSkyB under common ownership. Rather, the degree of control which BSkyB exercises over ITV is limited to an ability materially to influence matters of policy. That ability may be treated under the Act as control for the purposes of establishing jurisdiction, but it does not equate in practice to full control or ownership.

. . .

5.75 Given the extent of the influence conferred on BSkyB by its acquisition of a 17.9 per cent shareholding in ITV, we conclude that the regulatory mechanisms, combined with a strong culture of editorial independence within television news production, are likely to be effective in preventing any prejudice to the independence of ITV news. We do not therefore expect BSkyB's ability materially to influence ITV to have an adverse effect on the plurality of news relative to the position absent the acquisition. We therefore concluded that the acquisition would not materially affect the sufficiency of plurality of persons with control of media enterprises servicing audiences for news.

Extract 7.3.10

Paragraphs 262 and 263 of Competition Appeal Tribunal's judgment [2008] CAT 25 of 29 September 2008, Case: 1095/4/8/08 (British Sky Broadcasting Group plc v (1) Competition Commission (2) The Secretary of State) and Case: 1096/4/8/08 (Virgin Media, Inc v (1) Competition Commission (2) Secretary of State for Business, Enterprise and Regulatory Reform)

262. We consider that the aspects of the legislation which impose a constraint upon the plurality assessment are explicable in the light of the importance and sensitivity of ensuring structural media plurality. First, the nature of media plurality – what Mr Gordon referred to as its 'fragility' – is such that once lost, it may be very difficult or indeed impossible to restore. Second, as is common ground, media plurality is important for our society . . .

263. Third, though an increase in the level of control from one type of control to another (for instance, from material influence over policy to *de facto* control) may be caught by the merger

control provisions and subject to a further assessment, not all increases in shareholding and not all increases in the level of control or influence generally would necessarily be so caught. The degree of control exercised over media enterprises may change after the Commission's assessment without triggering a new investigation. This may justify a precautionary approach to the assessment of the sufficiency of plurality of ownership of media enterprises, which is more concerned with the structure of the market and of ownership of the relevant media enterprises rather than the precise level and degree of control capable of being exercised at any given point in time. There may be a creeping increase in influence over time.

Although the CC's approach was overruled by the CAT it was ultimately endorsed by the Court of Appeal.

The second of the cases that have arisen to date in which the Secretary of State has raised an intervention notice under the Enterprise Act 2002 concerned the bid by News Corporation ('News Corp') to purchase 61 per cent of the shares in Sky (the 'News Corp/ Sky' case). Since News Corp already owned a 39 per cent holding, this would have given it complete control of the company. News Corp, through its subsidiary News International, currently publishes the *Sun*, *The Times* and the *Sunday Times* newspapers in the UK and, until its recent closure as a result of the phone-hacking scandal, the *News of the World* – now replaced by the *Sun on Sunday*. Consolidation would thus have brought together two major players from the print and audiovisual sectors. The evaluation of the merger was, however, itself engulfed by the phone-hacking dispute and in July 2011 News Corp withdrew its bid.[8]

Although there was no definitive ruling on the case at this point, Ofcom had completed its provisional report on the proposed acquisition and concluded that in bringing together the second and fourth largest provider of news in the UK the merger could 'be expected to operate against the public interest'.[9] News Corp then proposed spinning-off Sky's dedicated news service, Sky News, into a separate company in order to address the plurality concerns raised by Ofcom. News Corp would have owned a 39 per cent holding in the separate news provider, the same interest it currently holds in Sky, enabling it to argue that the proposed merger would have no impact on the plurality of available news sources. It was these proposals that the Secretary of State was examining when the bid was withdrawn. Despite the takeover being ultimately aborted, the case raised a number of troubling questions about the effectiveness and robustness of the UK media-plurality rules and in October 2011 the Secretary of State, Jeremy Hunt, sought advice from Ofcom as to how media plurality might best be measured with a view to possible reform.[10]

The third case involved consolidation at the local radio level, with Global Radio acquiring a number of local radio stations owned by the Guardian Media Group (GMG).[11] The Global and GMG services overlapped in ten areas and in these areas the number of independent providers therefore went down by one. In the North Wales area this left just two local radio operators, the BBC and Global. OFCOM was asked to advise the Secretary of State on the acquisition and, following its earlier guidance, it sought to measure the availability and consumption of news and current affairs services pre and post the sale, taking into account

---

[8] Key documents can be located at www.culture.gov.uk/news/news_stories/7738.aspx.

[9] Ofcom, Report on public interest test on the proposed acquisition of British Sky broadcasting Group plc by News Corporation (31 December 2010), para 1.57.

[10] Ofcom, Measuring media plurality, Ofcom's advice to the Secretary of State for Culture, Olympics, Media and Sport (19 June 2012).

[11] Ofcom, Report on public interest test on the acquisition of Guardian Media Group's radio stations (Real and Smooth) by Global Radio (11 October 2012).

the impact of different delivery platforms.[12] OFCOM concluded that the consolidation was unlikely to have a significant effect on plurality. In particular, it considered local television and newspaper services to be adequate alternative sources to local radio, bringing the number of available sources across platforms in North Wales to seven. This view was bolstered by the response to its impact survey, which indicated that the number of people who regarded television to be their main source of information about local affairs was much greater than that for radio. In addition, Global undertook to provide additional news content in the North Wales area. On the basis of OFCOM's initial advice the Secretary of State decided not to pursue the plurality enquiry further.

Questions for discussion

1. Has the Communications Act 2003 successfully realised the New Labour government's projected 'middle ground', where both democracy and competition are adequately protected?
2. In the Sky/ITV case, which opinion do you prefer – that of the CC or CAT – and why?
3. Does it matter if there is just one commercial provider of local radio if there is also a number of local newspapers and television stations?

7.4 PROCEDURAL REFORM?

The concerns raised in relation to the existing media-plurality test are both procedural and substantive. Procedurally, it is debatable whether the power to decide whether to initiate (and ultimately determine) a media plurality investigation should be vested in a government minister, given governments' interest in maintaining positive press coverage and fear of antagonising powerful media companies. The Secretary of State initially responsible for the News Corp/Sky investigation was Vince Cable, but in December 2010 oversight of the case was transferred to Jeremy Hunt after Dr Cable stated to an undercover reporter that he had 'declared war' on Rupert Murdoch. The position of Jeremy Hunt was then itself brought into question by the scale and nature of his contacts, and those of his special adviser, Adam Smith, with the News Corporation lobbyist Frédéric Michel.[13] Where, as in this context, the outcome of a case is likely to be of direct interest to a particular political party or politician it would seem prudent and desirable to place the decision in the hands of an independent body, insulated from political influence. On the other hand, given the importance of the policy issues involved, Vince Cable has argued that the final decision in such cases should continue to rest with a government minister. A further procedural question is whether the process can be streamlined in order to simplify and reduce the time taken for review.

Question for discussion

1. What role, if any, should Ministers, the Competition Commission and/or Ofcom play in assessing the plurality implications of media mergers?

---

[12] Ofcom, Report on Global acquisition of GMG, n 11, Table 1, p 8.
[13] See, for example, BBC, 'Hunt and Michel text correspondence read out at Leveson', 31 May 2012. Available at: http://www.bbc.co.uk/news/uk-18286137.

7.5 SUBSTANTIVE REFORM: HOW TO MEASURE PLURALITY IN PRACTICE

Substantively, the questions raised are even more complex. In particular, what should we measure and how and when should we measure it? Each of these issues is considered in turn below.

(a) What should be measured – media sectors, digital intermediaries, genres?

In relation to what we should measure, it is necessary to consider the impact of convergence on what and how content is now delivered; whether we should extend our scrutiny to new intermediaries and aggregators; and whether some content genres are more relevant than others from a plurality perspective.

Increasingly, citizens obtain their information from diverse sources, including online and on-demand sources, whereas the media-plurality provisions in the Enterprise Act 2002 relate solely to newspapers and broadcast services. Although section 58 of the Act makes reference to the potentially broader 'media enterprises', section 58A(1) confirms that a media enterprise must 'consist in or involve' broadcasting. Print, radio or television companies operating on a solely online basis are not, therefore, caught by these provisions regardless of their significance in the market. But bringing these measures up-to-date by including online services raises difficult questions regarding which online providers should be categorised as 'media enterprises' and whether it is practically feasible to bring organisations located abroad, yet which offer services to the UK, within the scope of domestic constraints. Traditionally, media ownership controls have focused on those companies that publish and assume editorial responsibility for their own distinct newspaper or radio or television channel. Online, however, there has gradually been developing a category of increasingly important digital intermediaries. This category includes companies that act as aggregators of third party content, such as YouTube, that provide search facilities, such as Google, or networking sites, such as Facebook. These companies themselves may play very little, if any, role in content production but still exert a powerful influence over what information individuals access online. When assessing measures to promote media pluralism we need, therefore, to keep in mind the various production, distribution and sales activities, sometimes referred to as the 'value chain', involved in bringing creative content to the ultimate consumer.

In a 2012 report on digital intermediaries, Robin Foster suggests that we should be cautious about extending existing media-plurality regulations to such organisations in that 'they do not yet match the power or impact of today's front-page headlines of editorials'.[14] However, he notes that such organisations could well become more influential in the future, particularly if they combine with existing news producing organisations, and their impact on citizens' access to a plural media environment, both positive and negative, could be part of a more general system of media-plurality reviews undertaken by Ofcom.

---

[14] R. Foster, 'News plurality in a digital world', report for the Reuters Institute for the Study of Journalism (July 2012), 41.

Extract 7.5.1

R. Foster, 'News plurality in a digital world', report for the Reuters Institute for the Study of Journalism (July 2012), 49

In carrying out its assessment, Ofcom could examine indicators of consumption and impact, such as:

- the share of news consumed via intermediaries collectively and via any single intermediary;
- the extent to which users can easily switch between intermediaries or choose other ways of accessing news;
- levels of user satisfaction and trust associated with intermediaries;
- the extent to which intermediaries provide access to a sufficiently wide range of news, in an easily accessible format;
- the extent to which intermediaries enable easy access to sources of impartial news and other news deemed to be of public interest.

The conclusions of such reviews would indicate whether any measures needed to be introduced to help secure desired plurality outcomes.

A further question that arises in part from convergence is whether, for plurality purposes, we should now treat radio, audiovisual and text-based sources as all part of a single market for news. All these services can now be relayed online and an integrated market approach has been adopted by countries such as Italy. Alternatively, should each media sector continue to be treated as distinct, given subtle differences in how information is selected and presented within each medium?

Extract 7.5.2

Ofcom, Measuring media plurality, Ofcom's advice to the Secretary of State for Culture, Olympics, Media and Sport (19 June 2012), 12

4.3 Platforms play different roles in people's lives – such as delivering an immersive audio-visual experience, breaking news, detailed analysis, and providing space for hearing and contributing to the debate. Therefore TV, Radio, Newspapers, Online should not be seen as direct substitutes; rather, they complement each other in many ways.

4.4 Our qualitative consumer research highlighted the main characteristics of each platform, as follows:

- TV is a powerful platform because it is immersive and can show consumers the news as it unfolds, lending realism – 'the camera doesn't lie'. Furthermore, TV has a regulatory obligation to be impartial. Viewers perceive TV as providing a level of transparency, which in turn lends the platform trust and credibility.
- Radio is a convenient medium for news that can be listened to whilst doing something else. The phone-in/debate feature of some stations/programmes helps to make news and current affairs accessible and relevant, offering listeners the opportunity to engage and debate.
- Newspapers provide space for in-depth analysis, and reflection on events, helping citizens understand issues. Newspapers may be less relevant than other platforms for up-to-the-minute news, although they do still play an important investigative function in breaking stories. Most newspapers have clear and distinct editorial positions and the tabloids in particular are seen as partial and headline-grabbing. They also offer broader entertainment than news alone.
- Internet is growing in popularity as a source of news. Among users, the internet is felt to provide the ultimate convenience which drives use. It also allows users to tailor consumption to their own news interests. Within online, social media is becoming a valuable source for breaking news in its 'word-of-mouth' role, as many users learn of breaking news through friends' posts. It also offers a space for citizens to contribute to the story or debate with others.

The conclusions reached by Ofcom suggest that continuing differentiation among the various media remains credible, with television still the most used and important source. Although note OFCOM's willingness in the Global Radio case to treat local news provision on different platforms as substitutable.[15]

A final question is whether we should continue to distinguish not only between different media but also different genres? In the media-plurality cases raised in the UK to date all the actors involved focused on providers of news and current affairs programming, arguably the type of content that is most important for democratic purposes. But should a broader perspective be taken? Countries such as Germany and Italy, which also have in place specific regimes to protect media pluralism, do not draw content-based distinctions of this type. The following extracts taken from Ofcom's June 2012 report and Craig Arnott's commentary on the ITV/Sky case, discussed above, illustrate diverging views on the issue, with Arnott arguing for more, rather than less, differentiation.

Extract 7.5.3
Ofcom, Measuring media plurality, Ofcom's advice to the Secretary of State for Culture, Olympics, Media and Sport (19 June 2012), 9

3.11 A variety of genres are potentially relevant to media plurality, and it is important to provide clarity as to which of these are included within the scope of any review process. In their plurality reviews to date, Ofcom and other regulatory authorities have focused on news and current affairs but are not required by the current regulatory framework to do so.[16]

3.13 There are arguments for broadening this scope:

- Respondents to our Invitation to Comment highlighted other relevant content types. The BBC said '*drama, comedy and factual formats can play a role, alongside news and current affairs, in helping condition the political discourse. These genres contribute to the way we see ourselves as a society*' [original emphasis]. But the BBC concluded by recognising that news and current affairs were likely to be the focus of our work.

- We note from our research into international case studies, a number of jurisdictions (such as Germany, France, Norway) carry out their analyses on media content in the broadest sense and do not attempt to measure or regulate particular genres.

3.14 However, we remain of the view that news and current affairs play the primary role in delivering the public policy goals set out earlier.

- The unrestricted dissemination of a diverse range of information, opinions and arguments about the day's news and events provides the greatest potential to inform citizens and ensure an effective democratic process.

- From a consumer's perspective, news ranks highest in both societal and personal importance. Current affairs also plays an important role in providing consumers with information and analysis and therefore in the development of public opinion . . .

Source: © Ofcom copyright 2006–11.

Ofcom also noted that news was a readily identifiable genre and that this could be particularly important from a practical perspective were online sources to be included in any future analysis.

---

[15] See Ofcom, Report on Global acquisition of GMG, n 11, above.

[16] The definition of 'newspapers' presupposes some news content, but 'media enterprise' includes all broadcast licensees. The Secretary of State's *Guidance on the operation of the public interest merger provisions relating to newspaper and other media mergers* (May 2004) suggests intervention on public interest grounds in relation to mergers involving education or music channels (para 8.8).

Extract 7.5.4
Craig Arnott, 'Media mergers and the meaning of sufficient plurality: A tale of two acts' (2010) 2/2 *The Journal of Media Law* 245–75 at 269–70

There is a significant literature on the blurring of lines between news and entertainment in mass media societies, and although I cannot investigate that here, it could form the subject of investigation in a review of media plurality, and it is further reason not to privilege the place of news over other programming.

The argument of this article suggests that it is precisely such a privileging of one audience that the legislation [s. 58(2C)(a) of the Enterprise Act 2002] forbids . . . It is the very distinctness of one audience that precludes another from being a substitute for it. News could easily have been identified as having an exclusive role in the media plurality test, as it is identified expressly, for instance in section 58(2A), but it was not. Recall also that the DCMS Consultation and the Joint Committee Report both referred to the breadth of the concept of plurality and expressly said that news was only one category of consideration, certain a very important one, but one among other styles of programming that contribute to 'cultural vitality and experience'. Lord Puttnam has stressed this point in his comments since:

. . . The public demand for media plurality extended right across the programme genres: drama, entertainment, documentary, children's, comedy, arts and current affairs'.[17]

Questions for discussion

1. Do you agree with Ofcom that the focus of any media-plurality test should be on news and current affairs content?
2. From a democratic or cultural perspective does it matter who provides us with drama or comedy programmes?

(b) How and when should media plurality be measured?

In relation to how best to evaluate, from a plurality perspective, the scale of an organisation's media interests, different forms of measurement or 'metrics' have been suggested. Ofcom has identified three different types of measure: those that focus on *availability, consumption* and *impact*.[18] The first of these 'captures the number of providers available at the point of consumption', with the greater the number of available sources the greater the potential level of plurality in the market. But availability is not a sufficient indicator of media power and influence. A company may provide multiple services but be less influential than the provider of a single source that commands most of the audience and is widely trusted. Consumption metrics seek to address this point by looking at the demand side, how individuals actually consume the media services that are available, rather than simply the supply side. The situation is rendered complicated, however, by the diversity of measurements employed to evaluate consumption in the different media sectors.

---

[17] D. Puttnam, 'Lessons from the First Communications Act' in T. Gardam and D. Levy (eds), *The Price of Plurality: Choice, Diversity and Broadcasting Institutions in the Digital Age* (Reuters Institute for the Study of Journalism, 2008) at 36.
[18] Ofcom, 'Measuring media plurality', Ofcom's advice to the Secretary of State for Culture, Olympics, Media and Sport (19 June 2012) at 18.

Extract 7.5.5
Ofcom, Measuring media plurality, Ofcom's advice to the Secretary of State for Culture, Olympics, Media and Sport (19 June 2012), 19–20

- Volume of consumption – often expressed as a 'share' of total consumption – this captures the level of consumption, typically in a manner that depends on the nature of the content being consumed. For TV and radio, the primary focus is minutes of viewing or listening. For newspapers, the key volume measure is time spent reading. For online, the key measures may be page hits, or dwell time. It is not meaningful to combine volume measures for different platforms . . . and thus generate a cross-platform picture of share, unless grounded in a common methodology and unit of consumption.

Source: © Ofcom copyright 2006–11.

An alternative consumption metric is share of *revenue*, though the link between revenue and an outlet's capacity to influence the public is by no means clear. In particular, the value to advertisers of access to a particular audience may bear little relation to the influence of the programme or column in which the advertisement is inserted on *its* audience. Similarly *reach*, which measures the percentage of people exposed to a service over a specific period of time, is unlikely on its own to be an adequate measure of influence: many people, for example, may briefly tune into a particular service but pay it little attention. Supplementary consideration of the duration ('volume') of exposure and the extent to which other sources are accessed, 'multi-sourcing', help to provide a better picture of influence.

Consumption measures are particularly problematic where a global or cross-media approach is adopted. This is because we then need to decide whether or not to weight different media according to their degree of influence. But our knowledge of how people use and are influenced by the media is not sufficiently developed to enable weighting of this kind to be implemented with confidence: is, for example, reading a newspaper for five minutes more or less influential than listening to the news on the radio for a similar period? Moreover, specific products *within* media sectors can be more or less influential, and *specific individuals* attach very different weights to particular print or audiovisual services. Weighting thus tends to be arbitrary, and can expose regulators to legal challenge. Attempts by the Federal Communications Commission (FCC) in the United States to develop a 'diversity index' to assess levels of concentration in specific markets was, for example, struck down in the first *Prometheus Radio Project* case in part because 'its decision to count the Internet as a source of viewpoint diversity, while discounting cable, was not rational.'[19]

Ofcom, in the context of its NewsCorp/Sky investigation, suggested a new 'share of reference' metric, explained in the extract below, which appeared to dispense with the need for weighting of this type.

Extract 7.5.6
R. Craufurd-Smith and D. Tambini, 'Measuring media plurality in the United Kingdom: policy choices and regulatory challenges' (2012) 4/1 *The Journal of Media Law* 35–63, at 48

. . . Ofcom developed a novel 'share of reference' approach. This involved a survey of 2,018 adults, who were asked to indicate from a list which news sources they used on a regular basis (weekly for daily sources, monthly for weekly sources). They were also asked to indicate which

---

[19] *Prometheus Radio Project* v *FCC*, 373 F 3d 372 (3d Cir 2004) at D.2.

of these they regarded as their 'main source of news'.[20] The sources ranged across all platforms and included an 'other' category, which identified a wide range of international and regional media as well as online search engines and websites. Ofcom used the regular use data to determine for each provider or title, first, its overall 'influence', by calculating the number of references it received as a proportion of the total number made, and, secondly, its reach, by calculating what proportion of those surveyed accessed it on a weekly basis.[21]

Ofcom's approach consequently enabled it to adopt a cross-platform analysis, without artificial weighting, based on what individuals actually said they consumed. The approach can accommodate new and evolving forms of media use and enabled Ofcom to focus on its target content, news, though other genres could similarly be identified. Ofcom also configured its share of reference data from the perspective of wholesale and retail provision.[22] This is an important distinction in that many news channels and services rely on information provided wholesale by third parties and thus contribute little, in qualitative terms, to media pluralism.

Ofcom's analysis thus looked both to exposure, through reported regular use, but also to individual assessments of importance through its 'main source' question. Consumption measures that address exposure can only ever be indirect indicators of influence and the final type of measurement identified by Ofcom thus seeks to directly assess 'impact'.

Extract 7.5.7
R. Craufurd-Smith and D. Tambini, 'Measuring media plurality in the United Kingdom: policy choices and regulatory challenges' (2012) 4/1 *Journal of Media Law* 35–63, at 50–1 (some notes removed)

In relation to opinion-forming power, subjective assessments of influence obtained through consumer surveys are potentially the most relevant form of measurement. But the process by which the media influence consumers remains controversial and individuals inevitably interpret media messages in different ways. Moreover, consumers may have only limited understanding of how they have in fact been influenced by media exposure: they may, for example, over-emphasise the impact of sources with which they agree and downplay those with which they disagree, even though the latter help to shape how they categorise issues or see the world. Napoli has identified two criteria that may provide the basis for more objective measurement, namely *recall* and *attitude change*.[23] Audience recall can be measured relatively easily, and is already being recorded by some companies for advertising purposes, but assessing how individual attitudes or behaviour has been affected by media exposure, particularly outside the advertising context where a change in purchasing behaviour can be identified, remains difficult. Even when dealing with clearly identifiable decisions, such as voting preferences, it is difficult to disentangle the effect of media exposure from other sources of influence.

It seems, then, that there is currently no one simple and reliable way of measuring media plurality and media influence. For this reason, Ofcom has suggested regular monitoring of media markets using a 'basket' of the metrics identified above. Consideration would thus be given to the number of providers, outlet reach and share of consumption, user multi-sourcing and self-reported impact, together with other contextual factors such as

[20] OFCOM, Report on public interest test on the proposed acquisition of BSkyB Group plc by News Corporation (31 December 2010), 96.

[21] OFCOM, Report on public interest test on the proposed acquisition of BSkyB Group plc by News Corporation (31 December 2010), Annex 1.

[22] OFCOM, Report on public interest test on the proposed acquisition of BSkyB Group plc by News Corporation (31 December 2010), para 4.14.

[23] P. Napoli, *Audience Evolution: New Technologies and the Transformation of Media Audiences* (Columbia University Press, 2011), 91.

background content requirements and internal governance processes. Ofcom's proposal is that such reports would be produced every four or five years.[24]

Questions for discussion

1. Does regular monitoring replace the need for specific case-by-case oversight of media mergers?
2. What are the advantages and disadvantages of Ofcom's suggested multi-metric approach?
3. Which criteria would you use to decide when media concentration has become excessive from a plurality perspective?

7.6 MEDIA PLURALISM: THE EUROPEAN DIMENSION

The discussion of whether Internet sources should be included in any future system of plurality review in the UK highlights the international implications of domestic regulations in this field. Increasingly, services are provided on a cross-border basis and where states seek to control foreign services on plurality grounds they potentially run up against not only the guarantees of freedom of expression and access to information contained in domestic constitutions but also international and regional treaties. Some consideration has already been given to these provisions in Chapters 1 and 5 but it is worth spending a little time here also to underline their present and potential importance. From a European perspective it is particularly important to bear in mind the role of the Council of Europe and European Convention on Human Rights in establishing certain threshold requirements as well as the evolving engagement of the EU with plurality concerns.

(a) The Council of Europe

In early rulings of the ECtHR, such as *Informationsverein Lentia and Others* v *Austria* (1993) 17 EHRR 93, state regulations to promote media pluralism were seen as restrictions on freedom of expression and thus potentially suspect. Such restrictions could, however, be justified as being in the general interest if shown to be proportionate. More recently, the Court has come to underline that article 10 of the ECHR imposes positive duties on states to protect media pluralism not merely negative duties not to interfere with, or censor, the speech of others. This is illustrated in the following case of *Centro Europa 7* in which Centro Europa 7 challenged the refusal of the Italian regulatory authorities to award it the necessary radio frequencies to transmit its service.

Extract 7.6.1
***Centro Europa 7 S.R.L. and Di Stefano v Italy*, Application no 38433/09, 7 June 2012, paras 133–4**

133. A situation whereby a powerful economic or political group in society is permitted to obtain a position of dominance over the audiovisual media and thereby exercise pressure on broadcasters and eventually curtail their editorial freedom undermines the fundamental role of freedom of expression in a democratic society as enshrined in Article 10 of the Convention, in particular where it serves to impart information and ideas of general interest, which the public is

---

[24] Ofcom, Measuring media plurality, Ofcom's advice to the Secretary of State for Culture, Olympics, Media and Sport (19 June 2012), para 5.65.

moreover entitled to receive (see *VgTVerein gegen Tierfabriken* v *Switzerland*, no. 24699/94, §§73 and 75, ECHR 2001-VI; see also *De Geillustreerde* v *the Netherlands*, no. 5178/71, Commission decision of 6 July 1976, §86, Decisions and Reports 8, p. 13). This is true also where the position of dominance is held by a State or public broadcaster. Thus, the Court has held that, because of its restrictive nature, a licensing regime which allows the public broadcaster a monopoly over the available frequencies cannot be justified unless it can be demonstrated that there is a pressing need for it (see *Informationsverein Lentia and Others*, cited above, §39).

134. The Court observes that in such a sensitive sector as the audiovisual media, in addition to its negative duty of non-interference the State has a positive obligation to put in place an appropriate legislative and administrative framework to guarantee effective pluralism (see paragraph 130 above). This is especially desirable when, as in the present case, the national audiovisual system is characterised by a duopoly.

With this in mind, it should be noted that in Recommendation CM/Rec(2007)2 on media pluralism and diversity of media content (see paragraph 72 above) the Committee of Ministers reaffirmed that 'in order to protect and actively promote the pluralistic expressions of ideas and opinions as well as cultural diversity, member states should adapt the existing regulatory frameworks, particularly with regard to media ownership, and adopt any regulatory and financial measures called for in order to guarantee media transparency and structural pluralism as well as diversity of the content distributed'.

Source: © Council of Europe.

As this extract also indicates, the Council of Europe, with its broad remit in the media field, has passed a number of recommendations and declarations which emphasise the importance of media pluralism, including Recommendation CM/Rec(2007)2 on media pluralism and diversity of media content, noted in the extract above. This latter document emphasises the importance of regulatory independence from political influence, the desirability of ensuring that media ownership is fully transparent, and the role that public service broadcasters and not-for-profit media organisations can play in enhancing media diversity.

Although the Council of Europe has produced a wealth of informed and detailed guidance as to how state parties can enhance freedom of expression and media pluralism, its recommendations and declarations are soft law measures that can simply be ignored by the states concerned. For this reason, lobby groups and civil society organisations within EU Member States have begun to focus more heavily on the EU, because of the Union's ability to pass binding directives and regulations.

(b) The European Union

As discussed in Chapter 5, the media sector is not expressly mentioned in the competences of the EU set out in articles 3–6 of the Treaty on the Functioning of the European Union, and EU competence to enact legislation in the field has proved extremely controversial. Even if the EU were to be held to have competence, many would still argue that, given the economic, demographic and linguistic diversity of domestic media markets and local political sensitivities, this is a matter best left to domestic regulation. But not all states have risen to the challenge and pressure on the EU institutions for action has come particularly from civil society organisations in states such as Italy where political and corporate influence in the media sector is considerable. An initial draft of a directive setting upper media ownership limits was put forward by the European Commission in 1996. The proposal was based on the internal market provisions in the Treaty, with domestic ownership restrictions seen as potential barriers to the free movement of goods and services and freedom of establishment.

Extract 7.6.2

G. Doyle, 'From "pluralism" to "ownership": Europe's emergent policy on media concentrations navigates the doldrums' (1997) (3) *Journal of Information Law and Technology*, http://elj.warwick.ac.uk/jilt/commsreg/97_3doyl/

In spite of the obstacles and objections to the advancement of a pan-European media ownership policy, DG XV [then responsible for the internal market] managed to take a small step forward in July 1996 with the first draft of a possible EC Directive on Media Pluralism.

The Commission's proposals involved a 30 per cent upper limit on monomedia ownership for radio and television broadcasters in their own transmission areas. In addition, the draft Directive suggested an upper limit for total media ownership – i.e. ownership of television, radio and/or newspapers – of 10 per cent of the market in which a supplier is operating. All market shares would be based on audience measures . . . The proposed derogations would allow member states to exclude public service broadcasters from these upper limits, if they so wish.

Despite modifications to allow some flexibility to account for domestic variations, the level of opposition to the draft meant that it was not approved by the College of Commissioners and thus never formally entered the legislative process. The failure to even propose the directive has cast a long shadow over EU action in the field but, with growing recognition of the scale of media ownership consolidation both within and across Member States, the pressure for action has once again begun to build.

In 2007 the Commission initiated a 'three step' approach to addressing media pluralism. The first step was to publish a staff working document exploring the degree of protection afforded media pluralism in the Member States (SEC(2007)32). The second step involved commissioning an independent study into indicators for media pluralism in the various Member States, which was formally published in July 2009. This was intended as a tool that could be used to assess risks to media pluralism in the Member States and render the process of regular monitoring more robust. It ultimately put forward 166 indicators that can be used to assess the risks to media pluralism in a given country.[25]

Extract 7.6.3

P. Valcke, R. Picard, M. Sükösd, B. Klimkiewicz, B. Petkovit, C. dal Zotto and R. Kerremans, 'The European media pluralism monitor: bridging law. Economics and media studies as a first step towards risk-based regulation in media markets' (2010) 2/1 *Journal of Media Law* 85–113, at 88–9

In its terms of references for the study on indicators for media pluralism . . . the Commission therefore stipulated that the tool would have to cover pertinent legal, socio-cultural and economic factors, combining three sets of indicators: a first set, measuring the presence and effectiveness of policies and legal instruments that support pluralism in Member States; a second set to measure the range of media available to citizens in different Member States in the light of socio-demographic factors such as geographic location, social class, age and gender, and to define different types of media markets from an end-user perspective; and a third set to assess the range and diversity of media, looking at the supply side and economic performance of the media, such as the number of media companies and concentration and profitability ratios. These indicators, drawn from law, economics and social science would have to be placed within a risk-based framework . . . At the same time, it was stressed that the Commission's intention is not to regulate, but to monitor and create the necessary tools for comparison and increased transparency, enabling a more concrete and rationalised debate on media pluralism.

[25] The report and monitor can be located at: http://ec.europa.eu/information_society/media_taskforce/doc/pluralism/study/final_report_09.pdf.

Following on from the study on indicators, the Commission stated that the third step would be to report and consult further with a view to determining whether, and, if so, what action at the EU level might be warranted. To this end it convened a High Level Group of Experts ('HLG') to advise on how best media freedom might be protected and promoted in Europe, with a wide-ranging remit covering issues such as media accountability, professional ethics and the impact of digitisation.[26] The HLG reported in January 2013 and suggested that, in light of the growing importance of the status of EU citizenship and human rights within the EU legal order, a rather more robust view of EU competence in the field should be taken. The basis for this is set out in the excerpt below.

Extract 7.6.4
High Level Group on Media Freedom and Pluralism, Report 'A free and pluralistic media to sustain European democracy', 19–20, available at: http://ec.europa.eu/ information_society/media_taskforce/doc/pluralism/hlg/hlg_final_report.pdf

EU competences with respect to media freedom and pluralism have been already partly recognised and exercised in the area of the internal market, in particular free movement provisions. Certain national policies that restrict media pluralism and/or violate media freedom are naturally bound to also hinder the exercise of free movement to that Member State by media companies or journalists . . . This reasoning can be extended to the rights arising from European citizenship, in particular the right to move and reside freely in the territory of the Member States.[27] It is arguable that a case of systematic restriction of media freedom and pluralism in a Member State must be considered as having 'the effect of depriving citizens of the Union of the genuine enjoyment of the substance of the rights conferred by virtue of their status as citizens of the Union'.[28] The legal argumentation for this is contested, but it is worth noting that it is there . . .

The second ground for EU action is the intimate relationship between a free, open and pluralist media space at the national level and the exercise of democracy at the European level. The democratic legitimacy of the European Union is achieved in different ways, but a core component is representative democracy at the EU level, as required by Article 10 TEU. This is realised, in the first place, by the right granted, by the same provision, to all European citizens to participate in the elections to the European Parliament. This fundamental right would be compromised in any Member State where media freedoms are curtailed or media pluralism compromised, for this would deprive citizens of their right to form informed opinions . . .

The protection of the right to vote in European elections, however, is not the only dimension of EU democracy required by the Treaties. It also requires an open, free, informed and plural political debate that supports such elections, as well as the permanent accountability of the European Parliament and other EU institutions to the citizens . . . Seen in this light, the democratic requirements of participation and representation stated in the Treaties give authority to the Union to act at a national level, whenever the challenges to media freedom and pluralism are serious enough to put into question the very democratic legitimacy of the Union.

This, as is well recognised, does not mean that the Union has a general jurisdiction over state measures susceptible of impacting on media freedom and pluralism. Its competence and jurisdiction must remain within the framework of the arguments advanced above. The threshold for potential intervention is high, yet such power to act at the EU level must exist, in order to protect those EU rights to which media freedom and pluralism are instrumental.

Source: © European Union, 1995–2013.

---

[26] Its September 2011 terms of reference are detailed at: http://ec.europa.eu/information_society/media_taskforce/doc/pluralism/hlg/hlg_tor.pdf.

[27] Consolidated Version of the Treaty on the Functioning of the European Union, Article 20, para 2a).

[28] Judgment of the Court of Justice of the European Union of 8 March 2011, C-34/09, *Gerardo Ruiz Zambrano* v *Office national de l'emploi*, not yet published, para 42.

Although the HLG was not in favour of setting 'arbitrary quantitative thresholds for the desirable level of pluralism, which could not avoid being grossly subjective, as well as impossible to apply uniformly across the whole of the EU' (ibid., 37), it has proposed a wide range of EU initiatives designed to promote the protection of media pluralism, including requiring European and national competition authorities to take into account media pluralism in the enforcement of competition rules; regular 'pro-active' monitoring of the state of pluralism in the various media sectors by national competition authorities and the EU; and an over-arching monitoring role relating to media pluralism in the EU for the European fundamental rights agency (recommendations 2, 7 and 8). Whether the Member States have sufficient political appetite to take forward the HLG's proposals is an open question but, with a growing consensus that media pluralism does, indeed, fall within the EU's mandate, it seems likely that the EU will continue to be a target for those who feel that media pluralism can no longer be entrusted simply to the Member States.

Questions for discussion

1. When are challenges to media pluralism at the national level serious enough to bring into question the democratic legitimacy of the EU?
2. Should the EU require competition authorities to take into account media pluralism considerations when adjudicating on media cases – what modifications to their usual practices might this entail?

Selected further reading

C.E. Baker, *Media Concentration and Democracy: Why Ownership Matters* **(Cambridge University Press, 2007)** provides a clear and detailed explanation of why states may need to intervene to support media pluralism.

R. Collins and M. Cave, **'Media pluralism and the overlapping instruments needed to achieve it' (2013) 37** *Telecommunications Policy* **311–20** is an up-to-date review of the various techniques that can be used to assess and promote media pluralism.

P.S. Grant and C. Wood, *Blockbusters and Trade Wars: Popular Culture in a Globalized World* **(Douglas and McIntyre, 2004), ch 12.** The book focuses on the international dominance of the US film and television industry and mechanisms to support indigenous production.

D. Freedman, *The Politics of Media Policy* **(Polity Press, 2008),** especially at ch 8, which includes a helpful review of the various industry and other influences on policy development in the UK.

E.S. Herman and R.W. McChesney, *The Global Media: The New Missionaries of Corporate Capitalism* **(Continuum, 1997)** is an early and influential exploration of the implications of media consolidation at the international level.

House of Lords Select Committee on Communications, Inquiry into Media Plurality, at: http://www.parliament.uk/business/committees/committees-a-z/lords-select/ communications-committee/inquiries/parliament-2010/media-plurality/. The website provides access to a wealth of written submissions and oral contributions on the subject of potential options for regulating media plurality in the UK and the role of the EU.

P. Iosifidis, *Global Media and Communication Policy* (Palgrave Macmillan, 2011).

L. Hitchens, *Broadcasting Pluralism and Diversity, A Comparative Study of Policy and Regulation* (Hart Publishing, 2006), especially at ch 1–3.

N. Just, 'Measuring media concentration and diversity: new approaches and instruments in Europe and the United States' (2009) 31 *Media Culture and Society* 97 explores how states such as Germany and the UK are experimenting with different regulatory techniques to promote media pluralism.

K. Karppinen, *Rethinking Media Pluralism: A Critique of Theories and Policy Discourses* (Fordham University Press, 2013).

Ofcom, *Measuring Media Plurality, Ofcom's advice to the Secretary of State for Culture, Olympics, Media and Sport*, 19 June 2012.

E.C. Schwartz, *Conflicts of Interest: How Media Pluralism Protects Democracy and Human Rights* (2010). Available at: http://gradworks.umi.com/3423027.pdf.

On EU perspectives

Centre for Media Pluralism and Media Freedom, *European Union Competencies in Respect of Media Freedom and Pluralism*, RSCAS Policy Paper 2013/01, contains a range of expert papers considering the economics of media markets and the legal framework for EU intervention to support media pluralism in the Member States.

High Level Group on Media Freedom and Pluralism, *A Free and Pluralistic Media to Sustain European Democracy*, January 2013. Available at: http://ec.europa.eu/digital-agenda/en/high-level-group-media-freedom-and-pluralism.

P. Valcke, R. Picard, M. Sükösd, B. Klimkiewicz, B. Petkovic, C. dal Zotto and R. Kerremans, 'The European media pluralism monitor: bridging law, economics and media studies as a first step towards risk-based regulation in media markets' (2010) 2/1 *Journal of Media Law* 85–113. This provides a clear explanation of the objectives and potential operation of the monitor.

8 Competition law

8.1 INTRODUCTION

Alongside the specific media ownership controls designed to promote pluralism and diversity, considered in more detail in Chapter 7, competition law plays an essential role in ensuring that media markets remain open and contestable in order to enhance consumer welfare. Competitive markets help to keep prices down and encourage producers to act efficiently and innovate, leading to improved products and greater consumer choice. However, there will always be a temptation for some firms to distort or destroy competition for their own advantage. Practices that can harm competition include:

i)   mergers that reduce the pool of competitors or that enable the merged firm to foreclose access to certain markets;

ii) agreements between firms to restrict competition, for instance by fixing prices or other terms of trade;

iii) abusive behaviour by a firm with a dominant position in the market, for instance, a refusal to allow access to an essential distribution network or key content; and

iv) public measures, such as state subsidies, that distort the market and advantage particular firms.[1]

Media markets have proved to be particularly susceptible to such distortions and instances of each of these practices are discussed in turn in the sections below.

In order to understand the impact of an agreement or practice on competitors it is necessary to identify the various product (good or service) and geographic (sale or distribution area) markets involved. In determining what should be included within a given market, competition authorities apply a test of substitutability: a good or service that would be bought in substitution for another, if not available, will generally be considered part of the same market.[2] The delimitation of the market is of central importance in all competition cases. The broader the definition given to the market, the less likely it is that a specific agreement or practice will be considered to restrict competition, there being a greater likelihood that competitors will have access to alternative sources of supply or distribution platforms. Defining the market in the media sector has become more problematic with the development of new digital services. As markets evolve, goods or services that were previously seen as distinct may begin to be substitutes. Regulatory authorities have, for example, been called to determine whether online and printed newspapers or free to air and on-demand television services are part of the same markets.[3]

Constraints on competition can arise at different stages of the 'value' or 'supply chains', which map out the complex web of commercial relations underpinning the development, and ultimate exploitation, of media goods and services. In the following extract Ofcom explains the basic structure of one particular value chain, that for pay-TV.

---

[1] R. Whish and D. Bailey, *Competition Law* (7th edn) (Oxford University Press, Oxford 2012), ch. 1.
[2] Ibid., 29–53.
[3] See discussion of the *Kent Messenger* and *NewsCorp/Telepiú* cases at Section 8.2 below.

Extract 8.1.1
Ofcom, Competition issues in premium pay-TV movies. Proposed reference to the Competition Commission, 31 March 2010, para 3.8

3.8 . . . the supply chain for the UK broadcasting industry consists of four layers:

- Content production, for example creating and recording content which can be broadcast.
- Wholesale channel provision, which is the aggregation of content to bundle into channels. This could include acquiring rights to broadcast content or licensing content from other providers.
- Wholesale platform service provision, which is the provision of services to enable retailers to restrict the supply of content to consumers [eg encryption technology], or providing Electronic Programme Guide ('EPG') services to broadcasters.
- Retail service provision, includes the bundling of channels into packages to retail to consumers.

Source: © Ofcom copyright 2006–11.

There will also be links with a number of other service providers, such as commercial advertisers, engaged in related markets.

Restraints on competition can arise from action at the 'horizontal' level, involving firms operating in the same market, or from 'vertical' consolidation or agreements between firms operating at different levels in the supply chain. An early case illustrating both horizontal collusion and abuses stemming from vertical integration is *United States* v *Paramount Pictures, Inc.*, decided by the US Supreme Court in 1948.[4] The case concerned the five major US film studios, which were at that point involved in film production, distribution and exhibition. In particular, the studios owned numerous cinemas across the country, in some cases jointly. By preferring their own cinemas and engaging in distribution deals that limited competition, notably through requiring block purchases of films and fixing admission prices, the studios were able to maintain their stranglehold of the industry. The Supreme Court held these practices to be unlawful under the antitrust rules contained in the 1890 Sherman Act. In particular, it indicated that vertical integration involving not just joint ownership of cinemas but also ownership by a single studio could contravene the Act as being designed to restrict and suppress competition.[5]

Not all forms of collusion or concentration are damaging for the consumer, however, and some can lead to market efficiencies or innovation. Derogations are thus provided in the various competition rules that require the relevant regulatory bodies to determine whether specific benefits stemming from the proposed activities are likely to outweigh the long term structural impact on the market in question.

Within the UK, the main competition rules are contained in the Enterprise Act 2002 and the Competition Act 1998. In addition, the communications regulator, Ofcom, has certain powers to oversee competition in the communications sector under the Communications Act 2003.[6] Where there is a European dimension to the agreement or practice EU competition rules come into play, contained in articles 101–109 TFEU and the 2004 Merger Regulation.[7] The law in this field tends to develop incrementally on a case by case basis, but there has been statutory intervention where concerns are deemed to merit a more structured response. Sections 2–4 of this chapter explore how domestic and EU competition rules have been used to tackle anti-competitive behaviour by media firms;

---

[4] *United States* v *Paramount Pictures*, Inc, 334 U.S. 131 (1948).
[5] Ibid., 334.
[6] Section 316 of the Communications Act 2003.
[7] Regulation 139/2004, On the Control of Concentrations Between Undertakings (2004) OJ L 24/1.

section 5 discusses a number of areas where legislative intervention was felt to be necessary; while the final section 6 considers the impact of EU state aid rules on public support for public service media organisations.

Question for discussion

1. Which activities would you include in the value chain for an online newspaper? How do the various links relate to each other and other potential markets?

8.2 MEDIA MERGERS

Mergers among media firms can constrain competition in various ways: where the firms are active in the same market, the merger may enable them to raise prices or reduce output or quality; where they are active at different stages of the supply chain they may be able to block competitors' access to key content, networks or related facilities. These twin concerns, ensuring access to premium content and transmission networks, lie behind many of the cases considered in this chapter.

In the UK, the Office of Fair Trading (OFT) has to date had powers under Part 3 of the Enterprise Act 2002 to consider 'relevant mergers', which arise where two or more enterprises cease to be distinct enterprises and the turnover or share of supply in the UK exceeds certain thresholds.[8] The relevant consideration for the OFT is whether the merger will result in a 'substantial lessening of competition' (SLC).[9] In relation to local media mergers, the OFT can seek advice from Ofcom as to market conditions.[10] Where the OFT considers that a proposed merger could result in a SLC it can agree undertakings with the firms to address its concerns.[11] Where it is not possible to agree such terms the OFT will generally refer the merger on to the Competition Commission (CC) for an in-depth second stage review.[12] Review of the CC's subsequent decision can be sought before the Competition Appeal Tribunal (CAT), with appeal on a point of law to the Court of Appeal, where permission is granted.

The Enterprise and Regulatory Reform Act 2013 has sought to strengthen and rationalise competition control in the UK. A new single competition regulator, the Competition and Markets Authority (CMA), will replace the OFT and Competition Commission from April 2014. In relation to mergers the two stage process will, however, remain in place, with the CMA carrying out both initial and second stage reviews where this is considered necessary.

The UK competition authorities do not have competence in relation to mergers that have a Community dimension, These are governed by Regulation 139/2004 ('Merger Regulation').[13] For a merger to have a Community dimension the turnover of the companies involved must exceed certain financial thresholds set out in article 1 of the

---

[8] The turnover in the UK of the firm being taken over must exceed £70 million or, as a result of the transaction, a single company would gain a 25 per cent share of supply of goods or services in the UK (or a substantial part thereof): s 23 Enterprise Act 2002.

[9] See sections 22(1) and 33(1) Enterprise Act 2002.

[10] OFT, *Mergers – Jurisdictional and Procedural Guidance*, June 2009, para 6.15.

[11] Section 33 Enterprise Act 2002, especially at 33(3)(b) and s 73.

[12] The OFT is not required to do so where one of the conditions in s 33(2) of the Enterprise Act 2002 is met, which includes the situation where the customer benefits from the merger outweigh the substantial lessening of competition concerned and any adverse effects arising therefrom.

[13] Regulation 139/2004, On the Control of Concentrations Between Undertakings (2004) OJ L 24/1.

Merger Regulation. Community level mergers must be notified in advance to the European Commission, which assesses whether the merger 'significantly impedes effective competition within the common market or a substantial part of it'.[14] Although the turnover thresholds are high, many media firms have global ambitions and a number of media mergers are referred to the Commission each year. The EU is, however, solely concerned with the competition aspects of a merger, which explains why the UK authorities remain competent to consider the public interest aspects of even large scale media mergers under section 58 of the Enterprise Act 2002.[15]

At the UK level, most cases are resolved at the preliminary stage by the OFT but a few, such as the purchase by BSkyB of a 17 per cent share in ITV, are referred on to the CC.[16] A practical example of the operation of these provisions is provided by the Kent Messenger (KM) reference of 2011. KM sought to acquire a portfolio of seven local papers owned by Northcliffe Media (NM).[17] These papers were distributed in areas where KM also offered newspapers or other media services and the merger would have led to a monopoly in the local weekly newspaper market in six local areas. The OFT concluded that it created a realistic possibility of a substantial lessening of competition.[18] Ofcom, however, in its market report for the OFT, emphasised the financially precarious position of many local newspapers and noted that, absent the merger, some of the NM titles might close.[19] The merger could also lead to a rationalisation of costs and place the titles on a sounder commercial basis. The OFT did not, however, regard these potential benefits to be sufficiently well established and therefore referred the matter on to the CC for a full second stage review.[20]

The case highlights the significant administrative and financial costs that competition law assessments entail for the companies involved. In light of the reference to the CC, KM withdrew its bid, claiming that it could not afford to pursue the case further. Absent the merger, three of the NM papers subsequently closed, suggesting that Ofcom's concerns were well founded.[21] One of the failed NM papers was, however, replaced by a new paper, launched by KM.[22]

At the EU level, merger cases have touched on all aspects of the media industry, from recorded music to satellite broadcasting.[23] Two cases, *NewsCorp/Telepiú* and *News Corp/BSkyB* illustrate some of the concerns that can arise where mergers take place involving media consolidation at horizontal and vertical levels.[24] *NewsCorp/Telepiú* decided in April 2003, involved a merger between two competing Italian satellite pay-TV broadcasters,

[14] Ibid., article 2(2).
[15] Regulation 139/2004, On the Control of Concentrations Between Undertakings (2004) OJ L 24/1, art 21(4), and see further discussion in Chapter 7.
[16] OFT, *Acquisition by British Sky Broadcasting Group plc of a 17.9 per cent stake in ITV plc. Report to the Secretary of State for Trade and Industry*, 27 April 2007.
[17] ME/5121/11, *Anticipated acquisition of seven local weekly newspaper titles by Kent Messenger Limited from Northcliffe Media Limited*.
[18] Ibid., paras 52 and 142.
[19] Ofcom, *Proposed acquisition by Kent Messenger Group of seven newspaper titles from Northcliffe Media. Local Media Assessment*, 2 September 2011.
[20] Ibid., para 154.
[21] P. Linford, 'Now KM Group launches replacement for axed *Northcliffe Weekly*', *Hold the Front Page.uk*, 7 December 2011.
[22] Ibid.
[23] For details see the European Commission competition website regarding media issues at: http://ec.europa.eu/competition/sectors/media/overview_en.html.
[24] COMP/M.2876 – *Newscorp/Telepiú* (2004) OJ L110/73 and COMP/M.5932 – *News Corp/BSkyB*, 21 December 2010.

Telepiú and Stream, and was designed to give News Corporation ultimate control of the new company. Both broadcasters were badly affected by the spiralling cost of popular film and sports rights and were losing money, with Stream in a precarious financial position. In determining the relevant product market, the Commission concluded that, though there was some interaction between free-to-air and pay-TV channels, they were not in competition.[25] In particular, the business models were quite different with pay-TV being subscription based, while free-TV was mainly advertiser or publicly funded. Free-to-air services were therefore considered unlikely to constrain any anti-competitive tendencies arising from the merger.

In relation to these tendencies, the Commission was particularly concerned at the merged company's 'unparalleled' holding of premium film and sports rights, which, as key drivers of the pay-TV market, could prevent the development of alternative services on digital terrestrial or cable platforms.[26] In relation to infrastructure, the merged company was expected to adopt News Corporation's proprietary conditional access system. Conditional access systems control subscriber access, usually through encryption and decryption of the relevant signal, and are operated by means of a decoder or set-top box. News Corporation's system was thus likely to become the standard for satellite broadcasting in Italy, creating the risk that competing providers of satellite services might be prevented from using it, in effect shutting them out of the market. These concerns were addressed by a raft of undertakings made by News Corporation, key aspects of which are detailed below.

Extract 8.2.1
Case COMP/M.2876 – *Newscorp/Telepiú*, at paras 229, 231–4, 236 and 257

229. As regards access to contents, the scope and duration of exclusivity rights held by the combined platform will be extensively reduced to allow such rights to be contested on a frequent (in the case of [direct to home] DTH rights) or permanent (in the case of non-DTH rights) basis. Furthermore, premium contents to be broadcast via DTH by the combined platform will be made fully available to non-DTH platforms at wholesale prices via the wholesale offer. In addition Newscorp will not acquire, through future contracts or re-negotiations of the terms of the existing contracts, any protection or black-out right with respect to DTH.

. . .

231. Newscorp has also undertaken to waive exclusivity and other protection rights for non-DTH transmission for football and other sport events. This will allow operators competing on other means of transmission (for example, cable, Internet and UMTS) to have direct and immediate access to premium sport contents.

232. As regards movie rights, Newscorp has undertaken to waive exclusivity and other protection rights for non-DTH transmission. This will allow operators competing on other means of transmission (for example, cable, Internet and UMTS) to have direct and immediate access to premium movie contents . . .

233. As regards football rights, the limitation of the duration of future exclusive contracts for DTH transmission with football teams to two years and the unilateral termination right granted to football right owners are effective undertakings, in that they will make premium football contents contestable on the market at regular intervals.

---

[25] Ibid., paras 40–7.
[26] COMP/M.2876 – *Newscorp/Telepiú* (2004) OJ L110/73, para 182.

234. As regards movie rights, a limitation on the duration of future exclusive contracts for DTH transmission will be applied to output deals concluded by the combined platform and the Studios (both Hollywood majors and Italian film producers). The duration of future output deals with studios will not exceed three years.

. . .

236. As regards movie rights, Newscorp has undertaken not to acquire exclusivity and other rights for non-DTH means of transmission. This will allow operators competing on other platforms (for example, cable, Internet and UMTS) to have direct access to premium movie contents.

. . .

257. Access to the platform and to technical services necessary to operate are instrumental in ensuring that intra-platform competition is actually possible. The undertakings submitted by Newscorp go a long way in providing accessibility to the combined platform with a view to allowing effective competition to be achieved.

By limiting the extent and duration of the film and sports rights that the new company could obtain, requiring it to make its channels available to competitors on a wholesale basis, and controlling access to its conditional access system, the Commission sought to keep open the possibility of pay-TV services developing on digital terrestrial and cable platforms, even though competition in the satellite market would effectively come to an end.[27] On the basis of these (time-limited) undertakings, the Commission approved the merger.[28]

News Corporation faced less opposition from the Commission in relation to its proposed take-over of UK satellite pay-TV broadcaster BSkyB, being given clearance for the merger, without commitments, in December 2010.[29] As discussed in Chapter 7, the merger was highly controversial in the UK on plurality grounds and News Corporation ultimately withdrew its bid. The competition concerns in this case arose primarily from vertical, as opposed to horizontal, integration, in that BSkyB purchased programming, digital equipment, encryption and set-top box technology, as well as advertising services, from News Corporation.[30] The merger had the potential, therefore, to influence News Corporation's willingness to make such services available to BSkyB's competitors in the future. The Commission concluded that the merged company would not be in a position to prevent BSkyB's competitors gaining access to premium films or television programming, in that News Corporation was just one among a number of potential suppliers; it also noted that, at least in the UK, BSkyB was already required to make its technical satellite platform available to other pay-TV providers on fair, reasonable and non-discriminatory terms to other pay-TV providers and had an incentive to enhance rather than reduce the range of services it carried.[31]

The case also illustrates a specific competition concern, bundling, that can arise where a company supplies a range of goods or services. Bundling involves the sale of products in a composite package, enticing through rebates, or alternatively forcing, customers to buy services they would not otherwise have bought as part of the package. Bundling can

---

[27] A rival pay-TV channel distributed via digital terrestrial television was in fact established by Mediaset.
[28] Just before the undertakings came to an end in 2011 they were varied to allow Sky Italia (the merged company) to obtain a digital terrestrial multiplex licence, provided the services offered were free-to-air for a period of five years: European Commission 'Mergers: Commission allows Sky Italia to participate in allocation of digital terrestrial TV frequencies, subject to conditions', Press Release IP/10/983, 20 July 2010.
[29] Case no. COMP/M.5932 – News Corp/BSkyB, 21 December 2010.
[30] Ibid., paras 20 and 122.
[31] Ibid., paras 147 and 163–8. See further discussion of the investigations carried out by Ofcom and the CC in relation to BSkyB's position in the pay-TV market at Section 8.4 below.

arise at the wholesale level, as in the *Paramount* case discussed in the introduction, or, as envisaged here, at the retail level.[32] In the *News Corp/BSkyB* investigation it was suggested that the merged company might offer a mixed bundle of subscriptions relating to News Corporation's print or online newspapers and BSkyB's popular pay-TV content, making it difficult for stand-alone newspapers to compete.[33] In order to find 'conglomerate leveraging' of this kind, the Commission stated that the merged entity would need to hold a significant degree of market power and noted that bundling would be more likely where the goods were complementary.[34] As can be seen from the extract below, the Commission concluded, on considering these and other factors, that even if the merged company did engage in bundling this would be unlikely to affect consumers' choice of newspaper.

Extract 8.2.2
Case no. COMP/M.5932 – *News Corp/BSkyB*, 21 December 2010, at paras 226 and 229–31

226. The notifying party submits that BSkyB does not hold any significant degree of market power in the provision of audiovisual content to end-users in the UK and/or Ireland, and that absent dominance, bundling cannot have any anti-competitive effect. The Commission does not share this view and considers that BSkyB has a strong position in the market for the retail supply of pay-TV in the UK, with a market share raising a presumption of dominance . . .

. . .

229. The result of the market investigation was inconclusive as to whether, and to what extent, TV and newspapers are complementary goods or not . . .

230. Furthermore, the market investigation confirmed that the UK has historically had low newspaper subscription rates (around 6% of overall circulation) . . . [and as a result the newspaper/ TV bundle] may not be sufficiently appealing to customers as subscriptions are currently not the distribution channel through which the vast majority of them buy their newspapers, even though customers are generally given a substantial discount (between 25 and 30%) in case of subscriptions.

231. The market investigation also confirmed that out of the factors motivating readers to purchase a particular newspaper, price is not the first factor, and only one out of several important factors . . . The perceived political stance of a newspaper, family heritage, social-economic factors and the type of content are more important factors. The Commission therefore also considers that creating a bundled subscription . . . at an attractive price may not guarantee either that customers will switch in a significant manner away from their usual newspapers in order to start reading News Corp's newspapers, just because they are cheaper.

Taking into account the evolving nature of the news market, the Commission also considered whether the merged entity would be able to bundle its pay-TV services with subscriptions to online news services or newspaper applications on tablets or e-readers. In relation to the former, it concluded that even if bundling occurred it would not lead readers to stop consulting other online services and, in relation to the latter, given the early stage of development of these markets and the different power relations involved, it concluded that the merged entity was unlikely to be able to engage in bundling.[35]

---

[32] Bundling has also arisen as a concern in relation to the sale of sports rights in the UK, on which see Extract 8.3.2 below.
[33] Case no. COMP/M.5932 – *News Corp/BSkyB*, 21 December 2010, para 219.
[34] Case no. COMP/M.5932 – *News Corp/BSkyB*, 21 December 2010, para 225.
[35] Ibid., at paras 233–56.

Questions for discussion

1. What would have happened to the provision of pay-tv services in Italy if the Commission had not approved the merger in *Newscorp/Telepiú*? Could the Commission have addressed any concerns relating to the competitiveness of the pay-TV market by other means?
2. Under what circumstances *could* the bundling of News Corporation's newspapers with BSkyB's television content be problematic from a competition perspective?

8.3 ANTI-COMPETITIVE AGREEMENTS

Market constraints in the media sector are often the result of horizontal or vertical agreements between companies. As Whish and Bailey note

> [t]he mysteries of some aspects of competition policy should never be allowed to obscure the most simple fact of all: that competitors are meant to compete with one another for the business of their customers, and not to cooperate with one another to distort the process of competition.[36]

Both domestic and EU rules may be applicable in this context. Domestic law is set out in section 2 of the Competition Act 1998, while EU law in the form of article 101 TFEU comes into play where the agreement affects trade between Member States. Given that article 101 TFEU is directly effective within the Member States, the OFT or Ofcom (in relation to the specific sectors it regulates) may be required to apply both EU and domestic law.[37] The European Commission retains competence in relation to article 101, however, and there may be instances where a case is better resolved in this forum.[38] The domestic and EU provisions are very similar and, for this reason, article 101 TFEU alone is detailed below.

Extract 8.3.1
Treaty on the Functioning of the European Union, article 101(1)–(3)

Article 101

1. The following shall be prohibited as incompatible with the internal market: all agreements between undertakings, decisions by associations of undertakings and concerted practices which may affect trade between Member States and which have as their object or effect the prevention, restriction or distortion of competition within the internal market, and in particular those which:

   (a) directly or indirectly fix purchase or selling prices or any other trading conditions;
   (b) limit or control production, markets, technical development, or investment;
   (c) share markets or sources of supply;
   (d) apply dissimilar conditions to equivalent transactions with other trading parties, thereby placing them at a competitive disadvantage;

---

[36] R. Whish and D. Bailey, *Competition Law* (7th edn) (Oxford University Press, Oxford 2012), 513.

[37] Domestic law must not, however, undermine EU law, on which see R. Whish and D. Bailey, *Competition Law*, at 77; European Commission, *Guidelines on the application of Article [101(3)TFEU]* (2004) OJ C101/8, para 14. From April 2014 the powers of the OFT in this field will be transferred to the new Competition and Markets Authority.

[38] Chapter III, Council Regulation (EC) 1/2003, on the implementation of the rules on competition laid down in Articles 81 and 82 of the Treaty (2003) OJ L1/1, which also sets out the relationship between the Commission and national regulatory authorities.

(e) make the conclusion of contracts subject to acceptance by the other parties of supplementary obligations which, by their nature or according to commercial usage, have no connection with the subject of such contracts.

2. Any agreements or decisions prohibited pursuant to this Article shall be automatically void.

3. The provisions of paragraph 1 may, however, be declared inapplicable in the case of:

   — any agreement or category of agreements between undertakings,
   — any decision or category of decisions by associations of undertakings,
   — any concerted practice or category of concerted practices,

   which contributes to improving the production or distribution of goods or to promoting technical or economic progress, while allowing consumers a fair share of the resulting benefit, and which does not:

   (a) impose on the undertakings concerned restrictions which are not indispensable to the attainment of these objectives;
   (b) afford such undertakings the possibility of eliminating competition in respect of a substantial part of the products in question.

Source: © European Union, 1995–2013.

As is indicated by paragraph 1, collusive agreements often involve attempts to fix prices, control supply or divide-up markets. A recent case involving the sale of e-books provides an example of apparent collusion at both horizontal and vertical levels in a new and evolving media market.[39] Investigations by the European Commission led it to provisionally conclude that five major e-book publishers, including Harper Collins and Simon and Schuster, had acted together to maintain the price of e-books. The collusion was triggered by the pricing policy of major online retailer, Amazon, which had been selling e-books at, or below, wholesale prices. This, in turn, was likely to depress the amount that the publishers could charge other competing retailers such as Apple. To address this, the publishers agreed to move from a wholesale model, where the retailer determines the retail price, to an agency model, where the publisher retains control. Each of the publishers entered into agency contracts with Apple, which included a 'most favoured nation' (MFN) clause providing that they would match, on Apple's iBookstore, any low prices at which their titles were offered on competing retail outlets.[40] The effect of the MFN clause was to deter the publishers from using the wholesale model with other firms, such as Amazon, where they would not be able to control the retail price, and move to an agency model. Though the publishers did not accept the Commission's provisional findings, they were prepared to make significant modifications to their behaviour in order to avoid potential sanction. In particular, they terminated their agency contracts with Apple and agreed that, for a period of five years, they would not adopt MFN clauses or, for two years, seek to restrict e-book retailers offering discounts or promotions.[41]

The e-book case illustrates the continuing importance of content in driving new services. Some of the most valuable, although least enduring, rights in the media field are the television rights to key sporting events, especially football. As recognised in the *Newscorp/Telepiù* case, discussed above, the attractiveness of sport to both advertisers and subscribers creates the risk that ownership of the most popular rights will enable one,

[39] Case COMP/39.847, *E-Books*, (2013) OJ C73/17.
[40] For a rather similar attempt by the US film studios to align prices in their contracts with pay-TV operators using an MFN clause see European Commission, 'Commission closes investigation into contracts of six Hollywood studios with European pay-TVs', RAPID Press Release IP/04/1314, 26 October 2004.
[41] Case COMP/39.847, *E-Books*, (2013) OJ C73/17, paras 16–25.

or a group of companies, to shut out competitors and foreclose new markets. Though consolidation and hoarding of rights can result from the actions of purchasers, access to the rights and the shape of the market is also heavily influenced by the actions of the vendors.[42] The European Commission considered this issue in a cluster of cases concerned with the joint selling of media rights by national and international football associations. Key principles were established in the initial *UEFA Champions League* case, which influenced subsequent decisions, including that relating to the sale of media rights for the English Premier League.[43]

The restriction on competition in these cases is caused by the participating clubs agreeing to cede their media rights to a centralised association – UEFA or the Premier League – for exploitation on their behalf. Rather than competing against each other to sell their rights individually, they co-operate by creating a single point of sale. In the *UEFA* case, the Commission had first to determine whether the agreements restricted competition. UEFA argued for a wide product market, embracing a variety of sport and entertainment programmes: firms unable to purchase the rights to the Champions League could still buy other sport or entertainment programmes and would not be disadvantaged by the agreements.

Extract 8.3.2
COMP/C.2-37.398, *Joint selling of the commercial rights of the UEFA Champions League* (2003) OJ L291/25 at paras 55–6, 63 and 73–4

55. UEFA submits that although the UEFA Champions League is a very important sport event, it does not constitute a separate relevant product market. UEFA argues that it is part of a much wider market with a large number of sports events in addition to the UEFA Champions League, which allow broadcasters, sponsors and suppliers to achieve the same commercial objective, such as the national club football leagues. In addition, there are other prestigious and quality sports events on the market. Furthermore, non-sport content, in particular, popular films, soap operas and comedy shows can also attract very sizeable audiences . . . UEFA also submits that the free-TV market and the pay-TV market constitute distinct relevant product markets.

. . .

56. The Commission considers that the following markets are relevant to an assessment of the effects of the joint selling arrangements:

(a) the upstream markets for the sale and acquisition of free-TV, pay-TV and pay-per-view rights;

(b) the downstream markets on which TV broadcasters compete for advertising revenue depending on audience rates, and for pay-TV/pay-per-view subscribers;

(c) the upstream markets for wireless/3G/UMTS rights, Internet rights and video-on-demand rights, which are emerging new media markets at both the upstream and downstream levels that parallel the development of the markets in the pay-TV sector;

(d) the markets for the other commercial rights namely sponsorship, suppliership and licensing.

. . .

---

[42] Though beyond the scope of this chapter it is worth noting that concerns have also been raised in relation to joint purchasing, in particular regarding the European Broadcasting Union Eurovision system, discussed by K. Lefever, *New Media and Sport, International legal Aspects* (Springer, TMC Asser Press, the Hague, 2012), ch. 10.

[43] COMP/C.2-37.398, *Joint selling of the commercial rights of the UEFA Champions League* (2003) OJ L291/25 and Case COMP/38.173, *Joint selling of the media rights to the FA Premier League* (summary) (2008) OJ C7/18.

63. In the present case, the Commission also considers that the relevant product market can appropriately be defined as the market for the acquisition of TV broadcasting rights of football events played regularly throughout every year. This definition would in practice mainly include national First and Second division and cup events as well as the UEFA Champions League and UEFA Cup. The TV rights of football events create a particular brand image for a TV channel and allow the broadcaster to reach a particular audience at the retail level that cannot be reached by other programmes. In pay-TV football is a main driver of the sale of subscriptions. As regards free TV, football attracts a particular consumer demographic and hence advertising, which cannot be attracted with other types of programming.

. . .

73. Not all types of viewers are of equal value to broadcasters (and advertisers). Some people watch more TV than others do. People have different spending powers and patterns. Amongst the most sought-after viewers are men with an above-average spending power and who are in the age groups of 16 to 20 and 35 to 40, because those groups are generally considered to have a less fixed spending pattern compared to older people. They are therefore more likely to try new products and services.

74. The Commission's investigation of the situation in the Member States has shown that football, which is a mass attractive sport with high viewing figures, is the programme which seems to be the most effective tool to address this particular group of the population. Two thirds of the viewers are male and in the appropriate age groups.

Source: © European Union, 1995–2013.

The Commission thus adopted a narrow product market definition. It also found that the joint selling arrangements restricted competition among the clubs. It remained open, however, for UEFA to argue for an exemption on the basis of article 101(3) TFEU (extract 8.3.1 above) and the Commission was in principle willing to accept that the arrangements could contribute to improving the production and distribution of goods.[44] In particular, broadcasters benefited from a quality, branded product. Moreover, the single point of sale meant they did not need to negotiate separately with each club, and could plan their schedules, knowing they would have access to a specific number of games spread across the tournament. The Commission also accepted that the solidarity system inherent in the scheme, involving a degree of redistribution from richer to poorer clubs, could also be said to stimulate the development of the sport. The problem for UEFA was that the system initially notified allowed the rights to be sold in a highly concentrated manner: free-TV and pay-TV rights were offered for sale in a single bundle to a single broadcaster per territory for several years in a row, thereby helping to entrench the position of a specific broadcaster in each market. In addition, certain categories of new media rights were unexploited.

To address these concerns, UEFA agreed to 'unbundle' the rights, limit their duration and ensure that unused rights could be exploited, particularly in relation to new and evolving markets.[45] For example, the broadcasting rights were to be broken up into two main and a further subsidiary packages, potentially enabling more broadcasters to show part of the tournament. Both UEFA and the clubs were to be allowed to exploit certain internet and wireless rights, the clubs limited to club-branded products, thus creating scope for new services to develop. In addition, the contracts were generally to extend for no more than three seasons. On this basis, the Commission was prepared to exempt the agreements.

[44] COMP/C.2-37.398, *Joint selling of the commercial rights of the UEFA Champions League* (2003) OJ L291/25 at paras 136–65.
[45] COMP/C.2-37.398, *Joint selling of the commercial rights of the UEFA Champions League* (2003) OJ L291/25 paras 25–54.

Similar concerns were raised in relation to the joint selling of the rights to English Premier League games, the Commission finally agreeing modified terms for the 2007/8 season onwards.[46] These terms included a guarantee that rights would be awarded on a technologically neutral basis, regardless of means of distribution, and allowed the purchasers to decide whether to exploit the rights on a free-to-air, pay-TV or subscription basis. Unlike the agreed terms in UEFA, it also included a 'single buyer rule', which provided that all six live audiovisual rights should not be sold to the same purchaser.

In regulating the sale of media rights to football in this way the Commission hoped to keep open, if not enhance, competition in media markets and to ensure that new services could be developed. But how successful has this strategy been in practice and what are its implications for the ultimate consumer, the football fan? The following extract discusses the impact of the Premier League commitments on the development of the pay-tv market in the UK.

Extract 8.3.4
K. Lefever, *New Media and Sport, International Legal Aspects* (TMC Asser Press/Springer, The Hague, 2012) at p. 145, some footnotes omitted

However, it is debatable whether the inclusion of the 'no single buyer' commitment, regardless of the underlying rationale, has in fact substantially broadened the offer of sports on television in the UK. A recent interim report on pay-television in the UK of Ofcom demonstrates the limited practical effects of the European Commission's action on consumers' choice and pricing.[i] With the help of this remedy, in 2006, BSkyB won four of the six live packages and Setanta won the other two live packages. The outcome of the 2009 auction was that BSkyB won the rights to five of the six available packages, which is the maximum available to a single bidder. Only a few months after the auction the FAPL announced that Setanta had been unable to meet its financial obligations, and that the existing license agreement would be terminated. A couple of days later, Setanta went into administration and ceased its operations in the UK market. By the end of June 2009, the FAPL announced that ESPN had won the rights previously belonging to Setanta. ESPN's UK sports channel will be distributed on Sky's pay-television platform. As indicated by Van Rompuy, although this remedy did facilitate the entry of a new pay-television operator, Setanta, into the market, the greater competition for the live Premier League matches could not be maintained.[ii]

[i] Ofcom (2009) *Pay TV Phase Three Document: Proposed Remedies* at paras 2.51–2.55.
[ii] B. Van Rompuy (2009) 'Fair access to exclusive sports rights still a long shot in UK pay TV market' (2009) 14/4 *Commun. L.* 118–22 at 119.

The most recent sale of the Premier League media rights for the three seasons from 2013–14 brought in a record sum in excess of £3 billion, with Sky gaining rights to transmit 116 games and British Telecom (BT) the remaining 38.[47] ESPN was unable to retain it toe-hold in the market. Despite Van Rompuy's prognosis, it appears that there remains competition for the rights with new players, such as BT, prepared to bid for discrete packages in order to build an admittedly subsidiary pay-tv presence.

Question for discussion

1. Who has benefited most from the Commission's intervention in the sale of premium sports rights – rights holders, broadcasters, or consumers – and why?

---

[46] Case COMP/38.173, *Joint selling of the media rights to the FA Premier League* (summary) (2008) OJ C7/18.
[47] C. Sale, 'Forget the financial crisis – BT joins the Premier League party and football lands an incredible £3BILLION', *Mail Online*, 13 June 2012. Available at: http://www.dailymail.co.uk/sport/football/article-2158825/Premier-League-sell-TV-rights-3-billion-BT-Sky.html#ixzz2QXFDXWPk.

Although the joint selling cases may have increased costs for football fans in the UK by requiring them to take out multiple subscriptions in order to watch all Premier League games, EU competition rules have also enabled consumers to look beyond domestic providers and purchase cheaper decoder cards for sports channels broadcast in other European countries. This was the scenario explored in a cluster of cases involving the purchase by a number of UK pub owners and licensees of satellite decoders for foreign sports channels (for ease of reference referred to here as the 'Murphy' case).[48] One such channel was provided by the Greek company, NOVA, which held the rights to distribute Premier League games in Greece. Although NOVA's licence with the League required it not to distribute decoders for its service outside Greece, these decoders were being marketed by distributors such as QC Leisure in the UK at considerably lower prices than a subscription to Sky's sports channels, which cover Premier League games in the UK. The Premier League brought actions against the publicans and distributors of the decoders in the English courts, which then referred a number of questions of EU law to the Court of Justice. In particular, the courts sought guidance as to whether the restrictions on the distribution of decoders in the licensing agreements contravened the competition rules in article 101 TFEU.

Extract 8.3.5
Joined cases C-403/08 and C-429/08, *Football Association Premier League Ltd.* *and Others* v *QC Leisure and Others* and *Murphy* v *Media Protection Services Ltd.*, [2012] All ER (EC) 629; (2011) 1 CMLR 29, also available at the Curia website at http://curia.europa.eu/, paras 137–9 and 142

137. As regards licence agreements in respect of intellectual property rights, it is apparent from the Court's case-law that the mere fact that the right holder has granted to a sole licensee the exclusive right to broadcast protected subject-matter from a Member State, and consequently to prohibit its transmission by others, during a specified period is not sufficient to justify the finding that such an agreement has an anti-competitive object (see, to this effect, Case 262/81 *Coditel and Others* ('*Coditel II*') [1982] ECR3381, paragraph 15).

138. That being so, and in accordance with Article 1(2)(b) of the Satellite Broadcasting Directive, a right holder may in principle grant to a sole licensee the exclusive right to broadcast protected subject-matter by satellite, during a specified period, from a single Member State of broadcast or from a number of Member States.

139. None the less, regarding the territorial limitations upon exercise of such a right, it is to be pointed out that, in accordance with the Court's case-law, an agreement which might tend to restore the divisions between national markets is liable to frustrate the Treaty's objective of achieving the integration of those markets through the establishment of a single market. Thus, agreements which are aimed at partitioning national markets according to national borders or make the interpenetration of national markets more difficult must be regarded, in principle, as agreements whose object is to restrict competition within the meaning of Article 101(1) TFEU (see, by analogy, in the field of medicinal products, Joined Cases C-468/06 to C-478/06 *Sot. Lélos kai Sia and Others* [2008] ECR I-7139, paragraph 65, and *GlaxoSmithKline Services and Others* v *Commission and Others*, paragraphs 59 and 61).

. . .

---

[48] Key cases in the saga include: *Murphy* v *Media Protection Services Ltd*, [2007] EWHC 3091 (Admin); [2008] 1 WLR 1869; joined cases C-403/08 and C-429/08, *Football Association Premier League Ltd and Others* v *QC Leisure and Others* and *Murphy* v *Media Protection Services Ltd.*, [2012] All ER (EC) 629; (2011) 1 CMLR 29 and *Football Association Premier League Ltd.* v *QC Leisure* [2012] EWCA Civ 1708. For discussion of the competition aspects see S. Pibworth, 'The *Murphy* Judgment: Not Quite Full Time for Football Broadcasting Rights' (2012) 8/2 *The Competition Law Review* 209–216.

142. Such clauses prohibit the broadcasters from effecting any cross-border provision of services that relates to those matches, which enables each broadcaster to be granted absolute territorial exclusivity in the area covered by its licence and, thus, all competition between broadcasters in the field of those services to be eliminated.

Source: © European Union, 1995–2013.

Although copyright afforded the Premier League considerable control over the way in which it marketed its rights, the League could not employ those rights to partition markets along national lines and prevent the sale by NOVA of decoders giving access to its services abroad. Nor could such a restriction be justified under article 101(3) TFEU and was thus null and void.[49] The Court also concluded that domestic restrictions on the sale of foreign decoders would infringe the Treaty free movement rules.[50] Additional arguments by the Premier League that the communication to the public of foreign satellite services in the pubs infringed certain of their copyrights under sections 19 and 20 of the Copyright Designs and Patents Act 1988 also proved unsuccessful when the issue returned to the English courts. The Court of Appeal ruled in *Football Association Premier League Ltd.* v *QC Leisure* that there was a clear defence in section 72(1)(c) of the Act to such a claim, the UK having failed to properly implement EU law on this matter.[51]

Question for discussion

1. What is the long-term impact of *Murphy* likely to be on the way in which premium sport and film rights are sold in Europe?[52]

8.4 ABUSE OF A DOMINANT POSITION

A powerful player in the market may be able to restrict competition without having to enter into agreements with other firms. As we have seen, in the media context, control over distribution networks, access technology, such as set-top-boxes, or key content can all be used to exclude or marginalise rival firms.[53] In the UK these concerns are addressed by section 18 of the Competition Act 1998, which prohibits 'any conduct on the part of one or more undertakings which amounts to an abuse of a dominant position' where it affects trade in the UK. Where the activity in question affects trade between Member States, EU law is applicable in the form of article 102 TFEU. Within the UK, both domestic and EU provisions can once again be enforced by the OFT (from 2014 the CMA) and Ofcom, with the European Commission also retaining competence in relation to article

---

[49] Joined cases C-403/08 and C-429/08, *Football Association Premier League Ltd and Others* v *QC Leisure and Others* and *Murphy* v *Media Protection Services Ltd.*, [2012] All ER (EC) 629; (2011) 1 CMLR 29, para 145 with reference back to paras 105–124.

[50] Joined cases C-403/08 and C-429/08, *Football Association Premier League Ltd and Others* v *QC Leisure and Others* and *Murphy* v *Media Protection Services Ltd.*, [2012] All ER (EC) 629; (2011) 1 CMLR 29, para 125.

[51] *Football Association Premier League Ltd.* v *QC Leisure* [2012] EWCA Civ 1708.

[52] Helpful analysis is provided by A. Kaburakis, J. Lindholm and R. Rodenberg, 'British Pubs, Decoder Cards, and the Future of Intellectual Property Licensing After Murphy', (2012) 18/2 *Columbia Journal of International Law* 307–22.

[53] See, for examples, case 7/97, *Oscar Bronner GmbH & Co. KG* v *Mediaprint Zeitungs- und Zeitschriftenverlag GmbH & Co. KG, Mediaprint Zeitungsvertriebsgesellschaft mbH & Co. KG and Mediaprint Anzeigengesellschaft mbH & Co. KG.* [1998] ECR I-7791; case COMP/JV.37, *BSkyB/Kirch Pay TV*, paras 78–80; and case T-201/04, *Microsoft* v *Commission* [2007] ECR II-3601.

102 TFEU.[54] Although the terms of section 18 of the Competition Act and article 102 TFEU are similar, it remains open for the domestic regulator, in this context, to interpret domestic law more restrictively than EU law.[55]

Extract 8.4.1
Article 102, Treaty of the Functioning of the European Union

Article 102

Any abuse by one or more undertakings of a dominant position within the internal market or in a substantial part of it shall be prohibited as incompatible with the internal market in so far as it may affect trade between Member States.

   Such abuse may, in particular, consist in:

(a) directly or indirectly imposing unfair purchase or selling prices or other unfair trading conditions;

(b) limiting production, markets or technical development to the prejudice of consumers;

(c) applying dissimilar conditions to equivalent transactions with other trading parties, thereby placing them at a competitive disadvantage;

(d) making the conclusion of contracts subject to acceptance by the other parties of supplementary obligations which, by their nature or according to commercial usage, have no connection with the subject of such contracts.

Source: © European Union, 1995–2013.

Article 102 TFEU can address some of the concerns discussed previously in this chapter by enabling a company to obtain access to a competitor's network, facilities or intellectual property rights. Such claims are, however, inherently controversial in that the addressee has often attained its market position through hard work and innovation and it would consequently be unfair to allow others to free ride on this investment. On the other hand, certain media markets display 'winner-take-all' characteristics that make it difficult for new firms to get a foothold, even on a small scale. These competing concerns can be identified in two early article 102 TFEU cases, *Magill* and *Oscar Bronner*.[56] The first involved the refusal by three television broadcasters to make their programme listings available to Magill. At that time, each broadcaster produced a magazine giving details of their programmes for the forthcoming week but there was no comprehensive weekly guide collating information on all available channels. Magill wished to provide such a guide. Although the listings were protected by copyright, the ECJ held that the broadcasters' refusal to supply constituted an abuse of a dominant position. The broadcasters were the sole potential source of this information and their actions prevented the development of a new product, for which there was potential consumer demand.[57]

---

[54] Council Regulation (EC) 1/2003, on the implementation of the rules on competition laid down in Articles 81 and 82 of the Treaty (2003) OJ L1/1.

[55] For discussion see R. Whish and D. Bailey, *Competition Law* at 77 and note cases no: 1156-1159/8/3/10, *British Sky Broadcasting Limited, Virgin Media, Inc, The Football Association Premier League Limited, British Telecommunications Plc* v *Office of Communications*, [2012] CAT 20 at paras 18–19, discussed further in the section below.

[56] Joined cases C-241/91P and C-242/91P, *Radio Telefis Eireann (RTE) and Independent Television Publications Ltd (ITP)* v *Commission of the European Communities* [1995] ECR I-743.

[57] Ibid., paras 53–54. See also case T-201/04, *Microsoft* v *Commission* [2007] ECR II-3601, where the refusal of Microsoft to provide competitors with interoperability information was found capable of restricting future technical development, at para 647.

The second case, *Oscar Bronner*, concerned access to a distribution network.[58] Oscar Bronner produced the daily newspaper *Der Standard* and wished to use the home-delivery system that its bigger rival, Mediaprint, had developed for its own daily papers. Mediaprint refused. The ECJ held that to be successful Oscar Bronner would have to show that the home delivery scheme was indispensable for it to carry out its business, there being no possible substitutes. The Court concluded that there were indeed other methods of distributing its newspaper, for instance through shops, kiosks, or by post and, unlike *Magill*, there were not here any technical, legal or even economic obstacles to creating an alternative distribution network. It was not enough that Oscar Bronner would find it difficult to establish a similar system or that it was inconvenient for it not to be able to use Mediaprint's service.

In the UK, concerns over market power have focused on the pay-TV market and BSkyB's pivotal position within it. BSkyB's strength in the field is in part due to its extensive holding of attractive sport and film rights. After a three-year investigation, Ofcom decided to address these concerns by imposing on BSkyB wholesale supply obligations relating to two of its sports channels.[59] In relation to film, Ofcom requested the CC, under its powers in the Enterprise Act 2002, to investigate further the impact of BSkyB's movie rights on the pay-TV market. Ofcom set out its approach in its Pay TV statement, extracted below.

Extract 8.4.2
Ofcom, *Pay TV Statement*, 31 March 2010 at: http://stakeholders.ofcom.org.uk/ binaries/consultations/third_paytv/statement/paytv_statement.pdf, paras 1.5–1.8

1.5 For many years Sky has held the exclusive rights to broadcast first-run Hollywood movies and many of the most sought-after premium sports. We have now concluded that Sky has market power in the wholesale of certain channels including this content. However, the position differs between sport and movies:

- Sky's position in sport arises from the unique ability of broadcast TV to reach a large live audience, and Sky's control of the live broadcast rights for many of the most important sports. This is unlikely to change in the next few years.
- The position in movies is more complex, since there are a variety of ways consumers can purchase movies content, and the importance of linear channels is starting to reduce. Looking forward, we expect video-on-demand to become increasingly important. However Sky controls not only all the major linear channel movie rights, but also all of the rights that would be required to develop a subscription video-on-demand service for first-run Hollywood movies.

1.6 Sky exploits its market power by limiting the wholesale distribution of its premium channels, with the effect of restricting competition from retailers on other platforms. This is prejudicial to fair and effective competition, reducing consumer choice and holding back innovation by companies other than Sky. In the case of movies the fact that Sky also owns but barely uses the subscription video-on-demand rights denies competitors the opportunity to develop innovative services.

---

[58] Case 7/97, *Oscar Bronner GmbH & Co. KG v Mediaprint Zeitungs- und Zeitschriftenverlag GmbH & Co. KG, Mediaprint Zeitungsvertriebsgesellschaft mbH & Co. KG and Mediaprint Anzeigengesellschaft mbH & Co. KG.* [1998] ECR I-7791.

[59] Ofcom relied here on its competition powers under 316 of the Communications Act 2003, which enables it to insert into the licences it grants conditions to ensure 'fair and effective competition'.

1.7 We have decided that we should use our powers under section 316 of the Communications Act to ensure fair and effective competition by requiring Sky to offer the most important sports channels – Sky Sports 1 and Sky Sports 2 – to retailers on other platforms:

- Given that we cannot expect commercial agreement between Sky and other retailers, we have set a price for standard-definition versions of these channels at a level that should allow an efficient competitor to match Sky's retail prices.

  . . .

- We have set a wholesale price for each of Sky Sports 1 and 2, when sold on a standalone basis, which is 23.4% below the current wholesale price to cable operators. Most consumers currently buy packages which include both channels, and the wholesale price for the service bundle which applies in those circumstances has been reduced by 10.5%.

  . . .

- We have not set a price for high-definition versions of Sky Sports 1 and 2. We have accepted Sky's argument that high-definition services are a relatively recent innovation, and that pricing flexibility will help promote future innovation. We instead require Sky to offer contractual terms for supply of these channels on a fair, reasonable and non-discriminatory basis.

  . . .

1.8 We have decided it would not be appropriate to impose a similar obligation on Sky's movies channels. We have concerns over restricted distribution of movies channels, but our main forward looking concern relates to the sale of video-on-demand rights. We cannot adequately address this concern under section 316 (which relates primarily to linear channels). Instead we believe we should make a reference to the Competition Commission under the Enterprise Act 2002, and as required by statute, we are consulting on that proposed decision.

Source: © Ofcom copyright 2006–11.

The wholesale scheme was immediately challenged by BSkyB and, though implemented, was overturned on appeal by the CAT in August 2012.[60] The CAT did not consider that there was sufficient evidence that BSkyB had been blocking wholesale access to its sports channels for strategic reasons, though it acknowledged that BSkyB preferred to retain control.[61] In particular, it concluded that Ofcom had misinterpreted the nature of the negotiations that BSkyB had undertaken with potential retailers regarding access to its sports channels. August 2012 proved to be a generally good month for BSkyB in that the CC also finalised its investigation into the market for movie rights, concluding that no modifications were required to BSkyB's holdings or the use it made of its rights.[62] The CC found that although BSkyB held the rights to the movies of all six Hollywood studios for the first subscription pay-TV window, this did not enable it to distort competition. In coming to this conclusion, the CC placed particular emphasis on the rapid nature of developments in the market, reflected in the following quote from the Chairman of the Inquiry.

---

[60] Cases no: 1156-1159/8/3/10, *British Sky Broadcasting Limited, Virgin Media, Inc., The Football Association Premier League Limited, British Telecommunications Plc v Office of Communications*, [2012] CAT 20.
[61] Ibid., paras 27–31.
[62] Competition Commission, *Movies on Pay-TV Market Investigation. A Report on the Supply and Acquisition of Subscription Pay-TV Movie Rights and Services*, 2 August 2012. Available at: http://www.competition-commission.org.uk/assets/competitioncommission/docs/2010/movies-on-pay-tv/main_report.pdf.

Extract 8.4.3
Comments by Laura Carstensen, Chairman of the CC Inquiry Group, 2 August 2012, available at: http://www.competition-commission.org.uk/media-centre/latest-news/2012/Aug/cc-confirms-views-in-pay-tv-movies

We have seen significant change in pay-TV movie services in the course of our inquiry and have considered the implications of these developments carefully in reaching our final views. It is clear that consumers now have a much greater choice than they had a couple of years ago when our investigation began. LOVEFILM and Netflix are proving attractive to many consumers, which reinforces our view that consumers care about range and price as well as having access to the recent content of major studios; and the launch of Sky Movies on Now TV, which ends the requirement to buy Sky Movies alongside a basic pay-TV subscription, is a further significant development. Overall, we do not believe that Sky's position with regard to first pay movie content is driving subscribers' choice of pay-TV provider.

Question for discussion

1. What sort of market developments led the CC to conclude that Sky's portfolio of movie rights did not enable it to engage in anti-competitive practices? Were they right?

8.5 LEGISLATIVE RESPONSES

Case by case resolution may not be the best way to deal with certain inherent risks or systemic problems that arise in a given market. Where this is so, legislation can set standards and pre-empt future problems. Two examples of legislation designed to address specific competition concerns in the media field are discussed briefly below, that relating to listed events and conditional access systems.

(a) Listed events

The financial strength of pay-TV companies creates the risk that content considered socially or culturally important may only be available to those sections of society that can afford a pay for it. For this reason, countries such as the UK have introduced legislation designed to ensure that coverage of key 'listed events' remains, wherever possible, on free-to-air television. The listed events provisions are set out in sections 98–101 of the Broadcasting Act 1996, as amended.[63] The Act establishes two categories of provider: those offering services free to the ultimate consumer and accessible by 95 per cent of the UK population (currently the BBC, Channels 3, 4, and 5) and all other providers. Except where authorised by Ofcom, a provider in one of the categories cannot include a live listed event in their service unless a provider in the other category has also acquired the right to live coverage of that event. The provisions are thus designed to prevent exclusivity and ensure that free-to-air broadcasters have the opportunity to purchase certain rights considered socially important.

---

[63] The operation of the system is explained in Ofcom's *Code on Sports and Other Listed and Designated Events*, 2 September 2008. Available at: http://stakeholders.ofcom.org.uk/broadcasting/broadcast-codes/code-sports-events/.

The listed events covered by these provisions are drawn up by the Secretary of State and are included in what is now referred to as Group A. Group B events are those that must not be transmitted live on an exclusive basis unless provision has been made for secondary coverage in the form of highlights.[64] Both of these are detailed below.

Extract 8.5.1

Sports events protected under Part IV of the Broadcasting Act 1996, available at: http://stakeholders.ofcom.org.uk/binaries/broadcast/other-codes/listed_events.pdf

Group A (Full live coverage protected)

The Olympic Games
The FIFA World Cup Finals Tournament
The European Football Championship Finals Tournament
The FA Cup Final
The Scottish FA Cup Final (in Scotland)
The Grand National
The Derby
The Wimbledon Tennis Finals
The Rugby League Challenge Cup Final
The Rugby World Cup Final

Group B (Secondary coverage protected)

Cricket Test Matches played in England
Non-Finals play in the Wimbledon Tournament
All Other Matches in the Rugby World Cup Finals Tournament
Six Nations Rugby Tournament Matches Involving Home Countries
The Commonwealth Games
The World Athletics Championship
The Cricket World Cup – the Final, Semi-finals and Matches Involving Home Nations' Teams
The Ryder Cup
The Open Golf Championship

Source: © Ofcom copyright 2006–11.

Because rules of this type restrict the way in which rights are sold across Europe they also raise questions of EU law. Article 14 of the Audiovisual Media Services Directive (AVMSD) confirms, however, that Member States may take measures to guarantee free-to-air transmission of 'events of major importance to society' and goes further in requiring that Member States ensure that broadcasters within their jurisdiction do not undermine the systems of protection established in other countries.[65] Thus, in *R v Independent Television Commission (ITC), ex parte TV Danmark 1 Ltd*, the House of Lords held that it was legitimate for the ITC to refuse to allow UK broadcaster, TV Danmark 1, to transmit to its subscribers in Denmark, on an exclusive basis, certain football matches involving the Danish team that had been listed by Denmark.[66]

---

[64] Ibid., para 1.18.
[65] Directive 2010/13/EU, Audiovisual Media Services Directive (AVMSD) (2010) OJ L95/1. Provision is also made in article 15 AVMSD for broadcasters to be able to include short news reports of events of high interest, on which see case C-283/11, *Sky Österreich GmbH v Österreichischer Rundfunk*, 22 January 2013, nyr.
[66] R. Craufurd-Smith and B. Böttcher, 'Football and Fundamental Rights: Regulating Access to Major Sporting Events on Television' (2002) 8/1 *European Public Law* 107–32.

Member States are required to notify their lists to the European Commission, which, having checked that there has been no manifest error, arranges their publication in the EU *Official Journal*.[67] The approval by the Commission of the UK list, which includes all World Cup and European Championship games, and the Belgian lists, which include all final stage World Cup games, was challenged by FIFA and UEFA on the basis that not all games in these tournaments could be classified as 'events of major importance' and that the overbroad lists constituted an infringement of the associations' property rights.[68] In February 2011, the General Court dismissed these claims, in part because it is difficult for states to establish at the start of a tournament which of the games will ultimately prove to be of major interest but also because even 'non-prime' matches appeared capable of attracting significant audiences.[69] Given the financial stakes, it is not surprising that the case was appealed on to the Court of Justice, which, though disagreeing with the General Court that the World Cup should be considered a single event, held that the Commission had received sufficient information to conclude there was no 'manifest error' in the designation of all final stage matches.[70]

Questions for discussion

1. Which criteria would you use to determine whether an event is 'of major importance for society' within the terms of Article 14 of the AVMSD?
2. Why is the protection offered by inclusion in Group B of the UK list not sufficient for the events in Group A?

(b) Access to conditional access systems and associated services

Conditional access systems perform an important role in enabling pay-TV companies to ensure that only subscribers gain access to their channels. But, as the extract below explains, they can also be used to exclude competitors from the market.

Extract 8.5.2
P. Valcke and K. Lefever, *Media Law in the European Union* (Wolters Kluwer, Alphen aan den Rijn, 2012), pp. 110–12

Subscribers using a specific conditional access system are unlikely to invest in a second set-top box to watch broadcasts that use a different system. Accordingly, the operator of a conditional access system that is used by a large proportion of the viewing population may constitute a 'gatekeeper' for television broadcasters to reach viewers, particularly if it is part of a vertically integrated broadcaster. Therefore, there is a risk that a vertically integrated broadcaster that is the operator of a conditional access system could take advantage of its position to prevent market entry by competing broadcasters. Therefore specific *ex ante* regulation is needed beyond the application of competition rules to prevent dominant providers of conditional access systems from abusing their market power.

The 2002 EU Conditional Access Directive, as amended, is just such a regulation and key provisions are set out below.[71]

---

[67] Article 14(2), Directive 2010/13/EU, Audiovisual Media Services Directive (AVMSD) (2010) OJ L95/1.
[68] Cases T-385/07, T-55/08 and T-68/08, *FIFA* and *UEFA* v *Commission* [2011] ECR II-205.
[69] Ibid.
[70] Case C-204/11P, *FIFA* v *Commission* judgment 18 July 2013, nyr.
[71] Directive 2002/19/EC, on access to, and interconnection of, electronic communications networks and associated facilities (2002) OJ L108/7, amended by Directive 2009/140/EC (2009) OJ L 337/37.

Extract 8.5.3
Directive 2002/19/EC, on access to, and interconnection of, electronic communications networks and associated facilities, (2002) OJ L108/7, Annex I, Part I(b)

Part I . . .

In relation to conditional access to digital television and radio services broadcast to viewers and listeners in the Community, irrespective of the means of transmission, Member States must ensure . . . that the following conditions apply:

. . .

(b) all operators of conditional access services, irrespective of the means of transmission, who provide access services to digital television and radio services and whose access services broadcasters depend on to reach any group of potential viewers or listeners are to:

- offer to all broadcasters, on a fair, reasonable and non-discriminatory basis compatible with Community competition law, technical services enabling the broadcasters' digitally-transmitted services to be received by viewers or listeners authorised by means of decoders administered by the service operators, and comply with Community competition law,
- keep separate financial accounts regarding their activity as conditional access providers.

Source: © European Union, 1995–2013.

It should be noted that these provisions only apply to providers of digital television and radio broadcast services and do not, therefore, cover on-demand services. They were implemented in the UK by section 45 of the Communications Act 2003, which enables Ofcom to impose 'access related' conditions on certain operators such as BSkyB that provide technical services.[72] Under the Access Directive national regulatory authorities may also take measures to ensure that digital radio and television broadcasting services can obtain access to electronic programme guides (EPGs) on fair, reasonable and non-discriminatory terms.[73] The Ofcom code on EPG listings seeks to ensure that fair competition is maintained by, among other things, requiring those providing access to an EPG to refrain from giving undue prominence to channels with which they are connected and to publish, and comply with, an objectively justifiable method of allocating listings.[74]

8.6 STATE AID

State aid is prohibited solely by EU law and is designed to prevent states giving their own companies an advantage when in competition with providers from other EU countries. The provisions are contained in articles 107–9 TFEU and require states to notify any plans to grant new aid or alter existing aid to the European Commission prior to its adoption. Systems of aid that pre-date a state's membership of the EU are kept under review. States will be required to terminate or modify unlawful aid and repayment of unlawful aid will usually be demanded. Initial investigation and decisions in such cases are made by the European Commission.

---

[72] See P. Valcke and K. Lefever, *Media Law in the European Union* (Wolters Kluwer, Alphen aan den Rijn, 2012), 112.
[73] Directive 2002/19/EC, on access to, and interconnection of, electronic communications networks and associated facilities (2002) OJ L108/7, article 5(1)(b) and Annex 1, Part II. The Directive was amended by Directive 2009/140/EC (2009) OJ L337/37. A consolidated version is available on the EUR-Lex website.
[74] Ofcom, *Code of Practice on Electronic Programme Guides*, paras 14–16.

In Europe, aid for the media sector has primarily been provided to assist with broadband and digital terrestrial development, for film production and public service broadcasting.[75] States tend to consider such funding a matter for domestic policy and have strongly opposed EU intervention in these areas. On the other hand, it may be difficult for commercial media companies to compete with companies that receive significant public funds. In particular, there is a risk that state-funded companies will cross-subsidise commercial ventures; inflate the prices for 'up-stream' products, such as programme rights; or move into and foreclose developing markets. This section focuses, by way of illustration, on public service broadcasting, where the controversy over state aid has been greatest. The key provision is contained in article 107 TFEU.

Extract 8.6.1
Treaty on the Functioning of the European Union, article 107

Article 107

1. Save as otherwise provided in the Treaties, any aid granted by a Member State or through State resources in any form whatsoever which distorts or threatens to distort competition by favouring certain undertakings or the production of certain goods shall, in so far as it affects trade between Member States, be incompatible with the internal market.

. . .

3. The following may be considered to be compatible with the internal market:

. . .

c)   aid to facilitate the development of certain economic activities or of certain economic areas, where such aid does not adversely affect trading conditions to an extent contrary to the common interest;

d)   aid to promote culture and heritage conservation where such aid does not affect trading conditions and competition in the Union to an extent that is contrary to the common interest;

. . .

Source: © European Union, 1995–2013.

Three key aspects of the first paragraph should be noted. First, it applies to *any* aid, whatever its form: tax breaks, low interest loans, free accommodation or use of spectrum, as well as more orthodox subsidies such as financial grants, are all potentially covered. Second, the aid must be granted through *state resources*. Third, it must *distort competition*.

Aid for public service broadcasting takes various forms but is often obtained through a licence fee, levied on users or the public more generally, and collected by, or transferred to, the broadcaster concerned. It has been argued that funding of this type is not state aid because it is not paid for out of state resources but is instead composed of payments made by viewers to receive the service. Alternatively, even if the aid is derived from state resources, it constitutes payment for the provision of a public service, like education or health care, and thus does not distort competition.

The first of these arguments has met with little success as the following extract illustrates, though countries such as Germany remain reluctant to accept that the licence fee constitutes

---

[75] See Commission, *EU Guidelines for the application of state aid rules in relation to the rapid deployment of broadband networks* (2013) OJ C25/1; R. Craufurd-Smith, 'Balancing Culture and Competition: State Support for Film and Television in European Community Law' (2007–8) *Cambridge Yearbook of European Legal Studies* 35–67; J. Broche, O. Chatterjee, I. Orssich and N. Tosics, 'State Aid for Films: A Policy in Motion?' (2007) 27/1 *Competition Policy Newsletter* 44–8; and I. Katsirea, *Public Broadcasting and European Law, A Comparative Examination of Public Service Obligations in Six Member States* (Wolters Kluwer, New York, Netherlands, 2008).

state aid. The case involved two Commission decisions relating to two Danish public broadcasters, funded by a mixture of licence fees and advertising. In the first of these decisions the Commission had ordered TV2/Danmark to repay 628.2 million Danish kroner, considered to be illegal state aid. This was challenged before the then Court of First Instance by TV2 and the Danish State, which questioned the Commission's finding that the licence fee revenues, as well as the advertising, could be considered state resources.

Extract 8.6.2

Joined cases T-309/04, T-317/04, T-329/04 and T-336/04, *TV 2/Danmark A/S and Others* v *Commission of the European Communities* [2008] ECR II-2935, paras 158–9

158. As regards, first, the licence fee, it emerges from the contested decision – and is not seriously disputed – that the amount is determined by the Danish authorities (recital 22); that the obligation to pay the licence fee does not arise from a contractual relationship between TV2 and the person liable to pay, but simply from the ownership of a television or radio receiver (recitals 22 and 59); that, where necessary, the licence fee is collected in accordance with the rules on the collection of personal taxes (recital 23); and, lastly, that it is the Danish authorities who determine TV2's share of the income from licence fees (recital 59).

159. It follows from the above that licence fee resources are available to and under the control of the Danish authorities and that they therefore constitute State resources.

Source: © European Union, 1995–2013.

The Court also held that the Commission had failed to explain why it classified advertising revenue as a state resource and ordered the decision to be annulled in this regard.

The success of the second argument, that payment for public broadcasting does not distort competition because it is merely payment for a public service, depends on whether the state can meet the four criteria established in the *Altmark* case, extracted below. The case concerned German subsidies intended to maintain the provision of certain public bus services.

Extract 8.6.3

Case C280/00 *Altmark Trans and Regierungspräsidium Magdeburg* [2003] ECR I7747, paras 89–90 and 92–3

89. First, the recipient undertaking must actually have public service obligations to discharge, and the obligations must be clearly defined. . . .

90. Second, the parameters on the basis of which the compensation is calculated must be established in advance in an objective and transparent manner . . .

. . .

92. Third, the compensation cannot exceed what is necessary to cover all or part of the costs incurred in the discharge of public service obligations, taking into account the relevant receipts and a reasonable profit for discharging those obligations . . .

93. Fourth, where the undertaking which is to discharge public service obligations, in a specific case, is not chosen pursuant to a public procurement procedure which would allow for the selection of the tenderer capable of providing those services at the least cost to the community, the level of compensation needed must be determined on the basis of an analysis of the costs which a typical undertaking, well run and adequately provided with means of transport so as to be able to meet the necessary public service requirements, would have incurred in discharging those obligations, taking into account the relevant receipts and a reasonable profit for discharging the obligations.

Source: © European Union, 1995–2013.

Questions for discussion

> ## Questions for discussion
>
> 1. Does the present system for funding the BBC meet the four *Altmark* criteria?
> 2. If the UK were to establish a fund to assist the production of public service programming that all broadcasters could bid for, would this constitute state aid?

Most financial assistance provided by the state for public service broadcasting is likely, therefore, to be considered state aid. There are, however, two derogations to the state aid provisions that are potentially applicable in this context. The first is contained in article 107(3)(d) (see Extract 8.6.1 above) and concerns aid to promote culture. The Commission appears, however, to have taken a rather narrow interpretation of this provision, and in *Kinderkanal and Phoenix* it held that two thematic television channels, one for children and one concerned with current affairs, did not fall within the cultural derogation.[76] Culture was to be interpreted in 'a generally accepted sense and not extended beyond', leading one to conclude that this might be considered to relate to, for instance, the arts or civilisation.[77]

The second derogation that has been applied in the context of public service broadcasting is contained in article 106(2) TFEU, set out below.

> **Extract 8.6.4**
> **Treaty on the Functioning of the European Union, (2010) OJ C83/1, article 106(2)**
>
> **Article 106**
>
> . . .
>
> 2. Undertakings entrusted with the operation of services of general economic interest or having the character of a revenue-producing monopoly shall be subject to the rules contained in the Treaties, in particular to the rules on competition, in so far as the application of such rules does not obstruct the performance, in law or in fact, of the particular tasks assigned to them. The development of trade must not be affected to such an extent as would be contrary to the interests of the Union.
>
> Source: © European Union, 1995–2013.

Services of general economic interest (SGEIs) include economic activities that are subject to public service obligations and thus extend to public service broadcasting. Article 106 does not, however, automatically exempt such services, rather it seeks to strike a balance between public interest considerations and the effective operation of media markets. This scope for appraisal on the part of the Commission raised concerns, first, that a 'reactive' approach to public interest programming might be adopted, including only those programme genres not provided by commercial broadcasters, and, secondly, that 'new', for instance online or mobile, services might not be considered SGEIs.

The Member States responded by formally asserting their competence to determine the remit and funding of public service broadcasting in the 1997 Amsterdam Protocol, attached to the EC Treaty, though the Protocol also recognises that such funding should not affect competition contrary to the public interest.

---

[76] Ibid.
[77] State aid NN 70/98, *Kinderkanal/Phoenix*, para 6.2.

Extract 8.6.5

Protocol 29, On the system of Public Broadcasting in the Member States, TFEU (2012) OJ C326/1 at 312

THE HIGH CONTRACTING PARTIES, CONSIDERING that the system of public broadcasting in the Member States is directly related to the democratic, social and cultural needs of each society and to the need to preserve media pluralism, HAVE AGREED UPON the following interpretive provisions, which shall be annexed to the Treaty on European Union and to the Treaty on the Functioning of the European Union:

> The provisions of the Treaties shall be without prejudice to the competence of Member States to provide for the funding of public service broadcasting and in so far as such funding is granted to broadcasting organisations for the fulfilment of the public service remit as conferred, defined and organised by each Member State, and in so far as such funding does not affect trading conditions and competition in the Union to an extent which would be contrary to the common interest, while the realisation of the remit of that public service shall be taken into account.

Source: © European Union, 1995–2013.

In practice, the fears of the Member States have proved largely, though not entirely, unfounded. EU law has ultimately had more of an impact on the *processes* by which aid is awarded and the *internal operation and accountability* of public service organisations than the remit and development of public service provision in the media sector, a matter still primarily in the hands of the Member States.

The Commission set out guidelines regarding its approach to SGEIs in the broadcasting field in two communications in 2001 and 2009 respectively.[78] Both confirm that Member States can adopt a broad approach to the public service remit, including commercially attractive content such as entertainment and sport. The role of the Commission is here solely to check for 'manifest errors' of assessment.[79] Where a broad definition is adopted, qualitative requirements should, however, be established.[80] The application of these principles is illustrated once again by the *TV2/Danmark* case discussed above, which also involved a challenge to the Commission's acceptance of the wide remit for TV2.

Extract 8.6.6

Joined cases T-309/04, T-317/04, T-329/04 and T-336/04, *TV 2/Danmark A/S and Others v Commission of the European Communities* [2008] ECR II-2935, paras 115 and 117

115. In recital 84 of the contested decision, the Commission stated that 'TV2 is obliged by [Danish] law to provide as a public service "through television, radio, Internet and the like, a wide range of programmes and services comprising news coverage, general information, education, art and entertainment"'. In that recital, the Commission referred to recital 15 of the contested decision, in which reference is made to the Danish Law as providing that '[TV2's broadcasting] range shall aim to provide quality, versatility and diversity', that '[i]n the planning of programmes, freedom of information and of expression shall be a primary concern ...' and that 'in addition, particular emphasis shall be placed on Danish language and culture'.

---

[78] Commission *Communication on the application of state aid rules to public service broadcasting* [2001] OJ C320/05 and Commission *Communication on the application of state aid rules to public service broadcasting* [2009] OJ C257/ 1.

[79] Commission *Communication on the application of state aid rules to public service broadcasting* [2001] OJ C320/05, paras 13 and 36, and Commission *Communication on the application of state aid rules to public service broadcasting* [2009] OJ C257/ 1, paras 3–49.

[80] Commission *Communication on the application of state aid rules to public service broadcasting* [2009] OJ C257/1, para 40.

. . .

117. The Court of First Instance finds that the Commission is not mistaken in its assessment. Admittedly, the definition chosen by the Danish authorities is broad since, being essentially qualitative, it leaves the broadcaster free to establish its own range of programmes. None the less, it cannot be called imprecise, as alleged by the applicants. On the contrary, TV2's mandate is perfectly clear and precise: to offer the entire Danish population varied television programming which aims to provide quality, versatility and diversity.

Nor was the position affected by the fact that certain of TV2's programmes were similar to those offered by its commercial rivals. The Court held that TV2 was subject to a legal mandate to provide those programmes, whereas the commercial broadcasters were not. The latitude afforded states is not absolute, however, and in its decision relating to the funding of German public broadcasters ARD and ZDF the Commission indicated that the time allocated for certain popular genres such as sport should not be excessive, though in that case a 10 per cent limit to airtime for sport was considered acceptable.[81]

The Commission has also confirmed that the public service remit may include 'audiovisual services *on all distribution platforms*'.[82] This does not, however, go quite as far as confirming that they may diversify into text-based services, an issue on which European countries have adopted different approaches. In the UK, for example, the BBC has developed a range of text-based services whereas in Germany strict controls have been placed on the provision by the public broadcasters of 'press like services' that are not linked to specific programmes.[83]

Where EU law has been much more constraining has been in relation to the practical organisation and operation of public service broadcasting.[84] Thus, the public service remit must be clearly specified in advance, there must be a clear separation between commercial and public service activities with separate accounts, funding must be strictly proportionate to the public service commitments and financial reserves are to be limited, with proper auditing in place.[85] The Commission has also indicated that some form of public value test should be adopted for new services, involving wide consultation and an assessment of the impact of the proposed service on competitors.[86] Although these are essentially structural requirements they could ultimately have an impact on the way in which public service media develop and the nature of their services in the future.[87] The broad thrust of the EU's intervention in this field, rendering public service broadcasters more transparent and accountable, though traumatic for certain Member States, is not without merit as the concluding extract by Karen Donders indicates.

---

[81] State aid E 3/2005, *Financing of Public Service Broadcasting in Germany*, para 292.
[82] Commission *Communication on the application of state aid rules to public service broadcasting* [2009] OJ C257/1, para 40, emphasis added.
[83] K. Donders, *Public Service Media and Policy in Europe* (Palgrave Macmillan, Basingstoke, 2012), ch 9, especially at 137.
[84] R. Craufurd-Smith, 'Balancing Culture and Competition: State Support for Film and Television in European Community Law' (2007–8) *Cambridge Yearbook of European Legal Studies* 35–67.
[85] Commission *Communication on the application of state aid rules to public service broadcasting* [2009] OJ C257/1.
[86] Ibid., para 88.
[87] For details of the public value test applied by the BBC Trust in the UK, under which Ofcom provides advice on any market implications, see the BBC Trust website at: http://www.bbc.co.uk/bbctrust/governance/tools_we_use/public_value_tests.html.

Extract 8.6.7

K. Donders, *Public Service Media and Policy in Europe* (Palgrave Macmillan, Basingstoke, 2012) 197–8

. . . MS [member states] and other stakeholders have to live with the idea of European intervention in the area of PSB. Although resistance can be necessary during negotiations, one should realise that public broadcasting and competition goals are not always in opposition. A number of competition principles have furthered good governance practices in public broadcasting. MS should embrace the opportunities of state aid control in order to review and adapt their public broadcasting policies if necessary.

Selected further reading

For a general overview of the principles of competition law

R. Whish and D. Bailey, *Competition Law* (7th edn) (Oxford, 2011). An authoritative text covering all aspects of the field.

The following publications explore the specific nature of the economics of media markets and their underlying value chains

G. Doyle, *Understanding Media Economics* (2nd edn) (Sage, 2013).

P. Seabright and J. von Hagen, *The Economic Regulation of Broadcasting Markets. Evolving Technology and Challenges for Policy* (Cambridge University Press, 2007). A helpful collection of essays that explore, among other things, the economics of public service broadcasting, advertising and the relationship between competition law and sector-specific regulation.

J.C. Ulin, *The Business of Media Distribution, Monetizing Film, TV and Video Content in an Online World* (Elsevier, 2010). A clear overview of the film and television industries in the US.

The following publications offer insights into competition law as it applies to the media sector

L. Garzaniti and M. O'Regan (eds), *Telecommunications, Broadcasting and the Internet. EU Competition Law and Regulation* (3rd edn) (Thomson Sweet and Maxwell, 2010).

P.S. Grant and C. Wood, *Blockbusters and Trade Wars. Popular Culture in a Globalized World* (Douglas and McIntyre, 2004), ch 12.

L. Hitchens, *Broadcasting Pluralism and Diversity, A Comparative Study of Policy and Regulation* (Hart Publishing, 2006), ch 5.

M. Wheeler, 'Supranational regulation: the EU Competition Directorate and the European audio-visual marketplace' in J. Harrison and B. Wessels, *Mediating Europe: New Media, Mass Communications and the European Public Sphere* (Berghahn Books, 2009), 262–85.

For competition concerns that have arisen in relation to new digital intermediaries and, in particular, search engines

R.H. Bork and J.G. Sidak, 'What does the Chicago School teach about Internet search and the antitrust treatment of Google?' (2012) 8/4 *Journal of Competition Law and Economics* 663–700. This argues that the operation of Google's search services enhance consumer welfare and should not be seen as anti-competitive.

T. Vecchi, J. Vidal and V. Fallenius, 'The Microsoft/Yahoo! Search Business Case' (2010) 2 *Competition Policy Newsletter* 41–8. This provides a very clear explanation of the nature of search operations and the implications of merger law in this field.

For an examination of whether EU competition law can accommodate broader social and cultural considerations

E. Psychogiopoulou, *The Integration of Cultural Considerations in EU Law and Policies* (Martinus Nijhoff Publishers, 2008), ch 5.

Competition law and premium content

Competition Commission, *Movies on Pay-TV Market Investigation. A Report on the Supply and Acquisition of Subscription Pay-TV Movie Rights and Services*, 2 August 2012. Available at: http://www.competition-commission.org.uk/assets/ competitioncommission/docs/2010/movies-on-pay-tv/main_report.pdf provides a key overview of how premium movie rights are sold and the role of the US majors.

R. Craufurd-Smith and B. Boettcher, 'Football and fundamental rights: regulating access to major sporting events on television' (2002) 8 *European Public Law* 107–33. This discusses consideration of the TWFD provisions in the UK courts.

K. Lefever and B. van Rompuy, 'Ensuring access to sports content: 10 years of EU intervention: time to celebrate?' (2009) 1/2 *Journal of Media Law* 243–68, considers the application of EU competition law to both joint buying and selling of sports rights and the listed event rules in the AVMSD.

K. Lefever, *New Media and Sport. International Legal Aspects* (Springer, TMS Asser Press 2012). This contains a wide-ranging and accessible examination of the social as well as competition law issues at stake in the regulation of access to sports rights. The book contains examples drawn from domestic and EU law.

Ofcom, *Pay TV Statement*, 31 March 2010. Available at: http://stakeholders.ofcom.org. uk/binaries/consultations/third_paytv/statement/paytv_statement.pdf, provides an extensive analysis of how sports rights help to shape media markets, with specific reference to the UK.

On the application of EU state aid law

R. Craufurd-Smith, 'Balancing culture and competition: state support for film and television in European Community law' (2007–8), 10 *The Cambridge Yearbook of European Legal Studies* 35–67. This compares the approach of the European Commission to state aid cases relating to film and television, noting that procedural as opposed to substantive rules appear to be increasingly important in the latter context.

K. Donders and H. Moe (eds) *Exporting the Public Value Test: The Regulation of Public Broadcasters' New Media Services Across Europe* (Nordicom, 2011). This contains a range of comparative articles exploring the impact of EU state aid rules on public service broadcasters across Europe.

K. Donders, *Public Service Media and Policy in Europe* (Palgrave Macmillan, 2012). A leading overview of EU state aid rules and the media sector, highlighting both some of the potential advantages and drawbacks of EU intervention in the field.

W. Schulz, 'The legal framework for public service broadcasting after the German state aid case: Procrustean bed or hammock?' (2009) 1/2 *Journal of Media Law* 219–42. This focuses on the controversial application of EU state aid rules in Germany.

L. Repa and N. Tosics, 'Commission and Germany agree on better control for the use of state aid in the broadcasting sector' (2009) 1 *Competition Policy Newsletter* 97–9. This provides a helpful overview of the key Commission decision relating to aid for public service broadcasters in Germany.

9 Convergence

9.1 INTRODUCTION

One of the recurring themes of this book has been the differences in approach to press and broadcasting regulation. The justifications for this were canvassed in Chapter 1, Section 1.3. While the press has been largely regulated by the general law, radio and television have been subjected to close regulatory control on matters such as who can broadcast and what can be broadcast, in other words structural and content regulation (Chapters 2, 3 and 4). Spectrum scarcity was one of the reasons put forward for this special treatment, as was impact.

The model of telecommunications regulation differed from that for broadcasting. Regulation of telecommunications adopted what is known as a common carrier model. The carrier simply acts as a distributor of all messages received and does not exercise any control over content. Unlike broadcasting, legal control over content is essentially a matter for the general law. Telecommunications services, previously provided by a public monopoly and regulated by a distinct telecoms regulator, are now offered by private operators in an increasingly competitive market regulated by Ofcom. Separate regulation of the broadcasting and telecommunications sectors initially made sense because there seemed to be little overlap between the two industries: broadcasting relayed sound and, in the case of television, also images from one point to many points simultaneously (point-to-multipoint communication) while telecommunications provided the opportunity for one-to-one communication via mainly voice telephony services (point-to-point communication). A third sector, which initially seemed far removed from broadcasting, was the computing industry. The computing industry was treated like any other industry, subject to regulation by the general law.

These three sectors developed separately and were treated by the law separately. This established pattern was, however, challenged by the adoption, during the latter part of the twentieth century, of digital technology in the print and broadcasting sectors, resulting in a process commonly referred to as 'convergence'. Until the introduction of digital television in the UK in 1998, radio and television programmes were transmitted using analogue technology. Digital technology means that sound and pictures are converted into digital bits (a series of noughts and ones) and then reconverted by receivers into the final service for consumers. The most immediate impact of digital technology on the UK broadcasting market was to increase the number of services that could be provided as well as to improve picture and sound quality. A more significant consequence, however, was that broadcasting came to share a transmission technology with telecommunications and computing. As a result of these developments it is now possible for a specific network, linked to a single receiver, such as a television set, personal computer or mobile phone, to deliver a range of video, audio and text services, both public and private. Ithiel de Sola Pool was among the first to explore the importance of these developments in his ground-breaking book *Technologies of Freedom* in 1983.

Extract 9.1.1
Ithiel de Sola Pool, *Technologies of Freedom: On Free Speech in an Electronic Age* (Harvard University Press, 1983), p. 23

Once upon a time companies that published newspapers, magazines and books did very little else; their involvement with other media was slight. They reviewed plays and movies, they utilized telephones and telegraphs, they reported on the electrical industry but before about 1920 they had limited ties with any of those industries. The situation is changing, and with implications adverse to freedom.

A process called the 'convergence of modes' is blurring the lines between media, even between point-to-point communications, such as the post, telephone and telegraph, and mass communications, such as the press, radio and television. A single physical means – be it wires, cables or airwaves – may carry services that in the past were provided in separate ways. Conversely, a service that was provided in the past by any one medium – be it broadcasting, the press or telephone – can now be provided in several different physical ways. So the one-to-one relationship that used to exist between a medium and its use is eroding. That is what is meant by the convergence of modes.

De Sola Pool feared that convergence would gradually erode the 'dykes' that had previously restrained governments from exerting control over the print media. A more up-to-date explanation of convergence is contained in the European Commission Green Paper, *Preparing for a Fully Converged Audiovisual World*, published in April 2013.

Extract 9.1.2
European Commission, *Green Paper: Preparing for a Fully Converged Audiovisual World: Growth, Creation and Values*, COM (2013) 231 final, p. 3

Convergence can be understood as the progressive merger of traditional broadcast services and the internet. This results in viewing possibilities extending from TV sets with added internet connectivity, through set-top boxes delivering video content 'over-the-top' (OTT)[i] to audiovisual media services provided via PCs, laptops or tablets and other mobile devices. Consumers use tablets or smartphones while simultaneously watching TV, for instance to find out more about what they are watching or to interact with friends or with the TV programme itself.

Lines are blurring quickly between the familiar twentieth-century consumption patterns of linear broadcasting received by TV sets versus on-demand services delivered to computers. Moreover, with every smartphone enabling converged production as well as consumption, there might be a future shift from 'lean-back' consumption to active participation.

It is expected that connectable TVs will move from 40.4 million devices at the end of 2012 to a presence in a majority of EU TV households by 2016.[ii]

Source: © European Union, 1995–2013.

[i] Over-the-top players provide audiovisual content online without themselves being electronic communications services and network providers.
[ii] I H S *Screen Digest*.

Although consumer hardware continues to be tailored to accommodate the different ways in which individuals wish to access communication services – smart phones are small and compact for ease of carriage on the move; wide-screen televisions allow viewers to become immersed in a film or football match in the comfort of their homes – each piece of equipment increasingly offers access to a similar but increasing range of distinct services. Technological development is thus facilitating processes of divergence as well as convergence, which are arguably two sides of the same evolutionary coin.[1]

Our focus so far has been on *technological convergence*, but there are other possible forms of convergence in the media field. Although there is no inevitability that technological convergence will lead to *convergence in the services relayed*, it is apparent that traditional media, such as the printed press, have diversified their content online, taking advantage of the opportunity to include video and interactive features. The 'press' thus begins to incorporate aspects more often associated with television. Similarly, broadcasters, such as the BBC, have launched text-based websites incorporating their own video feeds. Content that combines different media in this way is sometime referred to as 'multimedia' or new media content.[2] Although the medium may not be determinative of the message, it is clearly influential and, as discussed in section 9.2 below, the interactive and networked nature of modern communications systems has not only influenced the look and feel of established media but has also led to an explosion of new media services, much of it user-generated. Alongside technological and content convergence, there is also the potential for *industry convergence*, as firms seek to obtain economies of scope by expanding into closely related markets.

These developments raise fundamental questions as to whether existing regulatory goals and structures are coherent and remain appropriate in this new media environment. Should there, for example, be greater convergence in standards for text and video content, now that both can be relayed and combined with such ease over the Internet? Furthermore, if standards do still need to be maintained, who should develop them and which regulatory techniques are likely to be most effective in ensuring their realisation? Do we need convergence among regulators as well as in the standards that are applied?

These questions are not new. Policy makers have been grappling with the implications of convergence from its inception and have already developed measures to address some of the concerns arising from it.[3] For example, the EU and Member States have adopted rules on access to conditional access systems and the ranking of channels on electronic programme guides (see Chapter 8, Section 8.5(b)); while the EU broadcasting regulations were extended to on-demand television services in the Audiovisual Media Services Directive (AVMSD) (discussed in greater detail in Chapter 5). However, these initiatives merely mark the start, rather than the end, of regulatory adaptation. Both the European Commission in its Green Paper on *Preparing for a Fully Converged Audiovisual World* and the House of Lords Select Committee on Communications in its report on *Media Convergence* have sought to consider the challenges and opportunities posed by convergence today, key parts of which are set out below.

---

[1] H. Jenkins, *Convergence Culture. Where Old and New Media Collide* (New York University Press, New York, 2006), 10.

[2] D. Tambini, D. Leonardi and C. Marsden, *Codifying Cyberspace. Communications Self-Regulation in the Age of Internet Convergence* (Routledge, Abingdon, 2008), 33.

[3] For an early policy paper on the field see European Commission, *Green Paper on the Convergence of the Telecommunications, Media and Information Technology Sectors, and the Implications for Regulation: Towards an Information Society Approach*, COM (97) 623.

Extract 9.1.3
European Commission, Green Paper: *Preparing for a Fully Converged Audiovisual World: Growth, Creation and Values*, **COM (2013) 231 final, pp. 3–4**

The Commission's vision is to seize the opportunity of this changing technological environment to ensure the widest possible access to European diversified content for all Europeans and the widest choice of high quality offers. The technological ability to deliver content to be legally accessible to viewers throughout the EU could also incentivise market players to create new types of content. The need for private economic actors to further innovate and for policy makers to ensure the right framework conditions, and to reflect on possible public policy responses, results in the following questions:

- How to transform the process of convergence in a larger European market into economic growth and business innovation in Europe . . . ?
- What are the implications of convergence for values such as media pluralism, cultural diversity, and the protection of consumers, including specific groups such as minors . . . ?

Source: © European Union, 1995–2013.

The main areas addressed by the Commission in its paper were summarised in an accompanying policy brief, detailed below.

Extract 9.1.4
European Commission, 'Internet on TV, TV on Internet: European Commission seeks views on rapidly converging audiovisual world', RAPID IP/13/358, 24 April 2014

The Green Paper adopted by the Commission today invites stakeholders and the wider public to share their views . . . on issues such as:

The rules of the game. Fostering the right conditions for dynamic EU businesses to deal with international (especially US) competition; especially given that competing players may be subject to different rules.

Protecting European values (including media freedom) and user interests (e.g. protecting children, accessibility for users with disabilities). Do people expect higher protection for TV programmes than for internet content; and where is the line to be drawn?

Single market and standards. Seemingly, some devices do not work the same way across Member States. How can we promote the right technological environment?

Financing. How will convergence and changing consumer behaviour influence how films, TV shows and other content is financed? How are different actors in the new value-chain contributing?

Openness and media pluralism. Should pre-defined filtering mechanisms, for example in search engines, be subject to public intervention? Are the existing practices relating to premium content – for example, major sport events and successful recently released films – at wholesale level affecting market access and sustainable business operations? Are platforms sufficiently open?

This new reality is already being discussed in several EU countries and in the European Parliament. Views differ on how to respond. Some parties call for immediate changes to rules and regulations; some remain satisfied with the status quo for the time being, while others point to self and co-regulation. The Green Paper does not pre-suppose any action, but in following up, the Commission might explore regulatory and policy responses, including self-regulation.

Source: © European Union, 1995–2013.

Extract 9.1.5
House of Lords Select Committee on Communications, *Media Convergence*,
27 March 2013, HL Paper 154, paras 4–8

4. . . . In a converged world . . . the clear boundaries between media are breaking down, new methods of consumption are undermining traditional regulatory approaches, and public expectations are changing. Among some of the questions posed by these changes are:

    What standards, if any, will the public expect to be applied in future to different media, and what tools are available to ensure they are delivered?

    How can we continue to secure wide availability of high quality content made in the UK, including accurate and trustworthy news and information?

    How can we secure healthy and competitive media markets which contribute to the public interest?

5. The proposals for responding to media convergence that we heard over the course of this inquiry varied in their radicalism and urgency. These differences emerged particularly strongly in the specific recommendations witnesses made for regulatory reform. Some believed that a sweeping response is required now, some believed that we needed to begin planning for reform, while others believed that we should adopt a 'wait-and-see' approach . . .

6. While it might be tempting to strike a 'wait-and-see' posture, it has become clear to us that whether audiences are aware or not, new technologies and behaviours are evolving more quickly than regulatory protections and than many people suggest. To a great extent, different media and media platforms do still exist, and audiences have some cherished expectations linked to them, but there are important changes taking place which require a policy response. At present, we do not see the need for a complete overhaul of the regulatory architecture overnight; indeed, we would counsel against this. But in our view it is imperative that a new, proportionate, approach is fashioned which is capable of gradually responding to this more complex world, which audiences can trust, and which may involve new priorities and changes to the assumptions underpinning the current policy stance.

7. Over four months, we heard a wide range of evidence and proposals, falling broadly under three themes:

    Content standards
    (i)   consumer trust and confidence;
    (ii) access to content via the internet;

    Content creation
    (i)   safeguarding public service content;

    Competition
    (i)   an effective competition regime for a converged world.

8. As the inquiry progressed, complex issues around content standards rose to prominence. Nevertheless, we continue to believe that the other two broad issues are of equal relevance. As content regulation becomes more complex, so it will be even more important to design effective 'positive' public service intervention to secure high quality content from the UK's public service providers, which will help set industry-wide standards. Alongside this, well regulated and effective competition – with more open markets and lower barriers to entry – should encourage innovation and deliver value and choice for consumers.

Source: Contains Parliamentary information licensed under the Open Parliament Licence v1.0.

Questions for discussion

1. Why might traditional regulatory techniques no longer be effective in a converged environment?

2. Have the European Commission and House of Lords Select Committee identified similar issues arising from convergence? To what extent do they see convergence as a challenge or an opportunity – and for whom?

9.2 CHARACTERISTICS OF THE CONVERGENT MEDIA ENVIRONMENT

Before exploring how our approach to regulation may need to adapt to these developments it is necessary to briefly consider how media markets are being affected by convergence. A number of important characteristics have been identified in the literature and are set out below.

(a) Networked communications

A communication network has been defined as

> any set of interconnected points (persons or places) that enable the transmission and exchange of information between them. For the most part, mass communication is a network that connects very many receivers to one source, while new media technologies usually provide interactive connections of several different kinds.[4]

The distribution networks that characterised the 'legacy' print and broadcast media reinforced the top-down, one-to-many nature of twentieth-century mass communications. They were also largely located within states or linguistic regions, facilitating state control. By contrast, the Internet is configured to facilitate the development of non-hierarchical, decentralised and interactive communication networks, originally developed to provide the US with an alternative communication system in the face of nuclear attack.[5] Its reach is global.

Extract 9.2.1
R. Wacks, 'Privacy in cyberspace: personal information, free speech, and the Internet' in P. Birks (ed.), *Privacy and Loyalty* (Clarendon Press, 1997), pp. 93 and 95–6

The Internet has no physical existence. A huge network, it interconnects innumerable smaller groups of linked computer networks. It is a network of networks. Many networks are linked to other networks, which are in turn connected to other networks, so that each computer in any network can communicate with computers on any other network in the system. This global web of linked networks and computers is the Internet . . .

This mosaic of computers and computer networks – some owned by government and public institutions, some by non-profit organisations, and some privately owned, is a decentralised, unrestricted global medium of communications – or what the science-fiction writer, William Gibson, called 'cyberspace' – that links individuals, institutions, corporations and governments around the world. It permits the tens of millions of people with access to the Internet to exchange ideas, software, images, literature, sound or simple e-mail. These communications are almost instantaneous, and can be directed either to specific individuals, to a group of individuals interested in a particular subject, or to the world as a whole.

. . . It would seem that no entity – academic, corporate, governmental, or non-profit-making – controls, or indeed runs, the Internet. It functions solely as a result of the fact that hundreds of thousands of separate operators of computers and computer networks independently decided to use a common data transfer protocol to exchange communications and information with other computers . . .

Source: PRIVACY AND LOYALTY edited by Peter Briks (1997) Ch. 4 "Privacy in Cyberspace: Personal Information, Free Speech, and the Internet" by Raymond Wacks pp. 93–112. Excerpts from pp. 93, 95 & 96. By permission of Oxford University Press.

---

[4] D. McQuail, *McQuail's Mass Communication Theory* (6th edn) (Sage, London 2010), 16.
[5] Ibid.

The Internet has had a profound effect on the production, output and economics of today's media, leading to what Yochai Benkler has termed the 'networked information economy'.[6] It also poses particular challenges and opportunities for regulators. As Raymond Wacks suggests in the extract above, the decentralised configuration of the Internet means that it is often possible for users to 'route around' state restrictions designed, for example, to protect copyright or protect children. However, there may also be specific nodes in the networks or gatekeepers, such as Internet service providers, that states can target to enforce standards or censor content. Where these are controlled by private parties there is a risk of anti-competitive behaviour or private constraints on speech. Our very reliance on the Internet makes the potential for such wide-scale censorship particularly troubling. Both aspects are discussed in the extract below, which uses Wikileaks and Internet controls imposed by the Egyptian state in 2011 as examples.

Extract 9.2.2
A. Guadamuz, *Networks, Complexity and Internet Regulation. Scale-Free Law* (Edward Elgar, Cheltenham, 2011), pp. 211–14, footnotes omitted

On November 28 2010, the whistleblowing site Wikileaks began releasing some of the more than 250,000 diplomatic cables from USA embassies around the world, in a coordinated exercise with five major international newspapers, but the bulk of the release was conducted through the Wikileaks website. The cables contained embarrassing details both to the United States and to various governments around the world, and in some cases, even some sensitive data that has sparked political unrest on various fronts.

From the very beginning, there were calls from numerous parties within the United States to try to shut down Wikileaks. What followed was almost a textbook case study on Internet resilience, and just how difficult it is to police the Internet.

. . .

If you wanted to reach Wikileaks with your Internet browser of choice (then identified as www.wikileaks.org), you had to know its address, or you could enter 'wikileaks' into a search engine. The result would be that the Domain Name System [DNS] would translate wikileaks.org into a computer IP address, and would direct your browser to the server hosting that content.

The actual Wikileaks website was housed in several hosting services, mostly in Sweden and France, but they had also bought hosting space in the cloud computing web services offered by Amazon.com. The wikileaks.org domain name was assigned by Californian domain name registrar EveryDNS.net, which also provided free DNS services for the site. By 1 December 2010, just a couple of days after the initial leaks, Amazon had dropped the service alleging breach of its Terms of Use, and EveryDNS.net had revoked the DNS registration alleging damage to its servers from coordinated cyber-attacks. By the end of that week, several payment systems which took donations for Wikileaks (including Visa, MasterCard and PayPal) had also dropped the organization. Bereft of hosting, routing and monetary channels, one would have thought that Wikileaks would simply be forced to disappear.

. . .

However, as it has been repeatedly stated . . . there is something at which the Internet is really good at (sic), it takes censorship as an attack to its infrastructure and re-routes services to avoid the affected area. Because the site was still being hosted in a computer linked to the Internet, it was still possible to access the content via an IP address despite the fact that writing [Wikileaks.org] into a browser would take you nowhere. Similarly, several mirrors[i] and new DNS registrations started popping up everywhere – social media services were used to retransmit the

---

[6] Y. Benkler, *The Wealth of Networks. How Social Production Transforms Markets and Freedom* (Yale University Press, New Haven, CT, 2006), 3.

latest IP addresses as they became available . . . Moreover, Wikileaks made available an encrypted torrent file through Pirate Bay which allegedly contained all of the cables as a manner of online insurance against complete disconnection. In short, this was Internet resilience at its best.

. . .

Here is where the second story comes into play. Right after the Wikileaks Cablegate scandal (and some have suggested because of it), the Arab world erupted in civil unrest . . . When the conflict reached Egypt in January 2011, a large part of the protests were coordinated using the Internet . . . What is certain is that the Egyptian government considered that the Internet posed a threat to their interests, so they did something that had never been done before to such extent: they shut down the Internet.

On January 27 2011, at around 10.30 GMT, the entire Egyptian Internet was disconnected from the rest of the world.[ii] This was possible because Egypt, just as many other countries in the Middle East, has a national firewall consisting of an extra layer of Internet servers that intermediate all traffic in and out of the country through servers running the adequately named Border Gateway Protocol (BGP). Egyptian authorities managed to shut down simultaneously 3,500 BGP routes into the country, which meant that 90 percent of all traffic in and out of the country could not get through . . .

What the Egyptian case illustrates is an excellent example of the dual nature of Internet architecture. At the larger scale, the Web is a scale-free network, entirely distributed and remarkably robust. At the national level, the Internet is increasingly centralized, and therefore more likely to suffer from large cascading local failures. The more centralized the system, the easier it is to regulate.

This is therefore the conundrum currently presented to regulators around the world . . . It is possible to control the Internet, but to do so it must stop being decentralized. Higher levels of centrality allow for more control, but this . . . translates into a less open system.

[i] In Internet architecture terms, a mirror is an exact copy of another site.
[ii] C. Williams, 'How Egypt shut down the Internet', the *Telegraph* (28 January 2011), http://goo.gl/j5PTU.

The Egyptian case provides a good example of the role that network design can play in determining who can speak and on what basis. Architecture or software code was identified by Lawrence Lessig as an increasingly important 'modality' by which communication systems can be regulated, alongside law, social norms and the market.[7]

(b) Disruption to established business models

Digitisation and widespread access to the Internet has stimulated new producers, new products and new ways of accessing content. This has destabilised both the funding and mode of operation of the mainstream media, particularly for the print press.[8] With many more television channels, websites and apps from which to choose, audiences are fragmenting along with revenues. A survey for the Reuters Institute in April 2012 found that 82 per cent of those surveyed in the UK had accessed news online in the last week, predominantly from their computer or mobile phone but increasingly from tablets.[9] Social networks such as Facebook and Twitter play an increasingly important role in alerting people to news items and enabling an exchange of views, while search engines continue to be widely deployed to find news online. Only 4 per cent of those surveyed, however, had ever paid for digital news content. Some of the opportunities and challenges of this new environment are summarised by Rodney Benson in the extract below.

[7] L. Lessig, *Code 2.0* (Basic Book, 2006).
[8] Reuters Institute for the Study of Journalism, *Digital News Report 2012*, July 2012, 12.
[9] Ibid.

Extract 9.2.3

R. Benson, 'Futures of the news: international considerations and further reflections'
in N. Fenton (ed.) *New Media, Old News: Journalism and Democracy in the Digital Age* (Sage, London, 2010), 188

[Benson starts by detailing] the kinds of communication practices that online media uniquely afford: archiving capabilities that increase depth of coverage, multimedia formats that draw readers into complex topics, easy access to a multiplicity of voices and viewpoints outside the mainstream, and opportunities for ordinary citizens to ask questions of political and cultural elites via chat rooms and forums or even to create vast activist networks . . .

[Then proceeds to identify concerns leading to] a strong dose of 'techno-pessimism': the dramatic decline of newspaper circulation and advertising revenues, due at least in part to the flight of classified advertising to the internet; the sharp increase in online media audiences accompanied by the failure to find a way to make online media pay for itself, even as the parent media companies often remain quite profitable; the fragmentation of news audiences across multiple media outlets, both offline and online; massive newsroom layoffs and cost-cutting, with especially deep cutbacks in foreign and investigative reporting, and greater job insecurity for those who remain; and finally, intensifying time pressures on journalists to produce news 'content' across multiple media platforms, contributing to the increasing homogenization of content . . . and the use of pre-packaged 'news' provided by public relations professionals.

Source: © Sage Publishing.

The picture Benson paints is a troubling one, but it would be wrong to see old and new media as inevitably in opposition. Indeed, new media are more often than not old media in different guise, with some of the most popular online news sites provided by mainstream media. Trust in, and familiarity with, certain brands continues to shape news consumption.[10] Although traditional media have found it difficult to establish similar market shares online to those offline, operators such as the BBC have been remarkably successful in adapting to the online environment, with 58 per cent of those surveyed for Reuters stating that they had accessed the BBC News website in the previous week.[11] A few publications, such as the *Guardian* and *Telegraph*, have managed to increase their market share online, particularly through the development of tablet apps.[12] As Rasmus Neilsen notes:

> The *New York Times*, through its printed paper, its website, its mobile and tablet apps, its international edition (the *International Herald Tribune*), an international weekly supplement printed in 36 countries, and a syndication of content by two dozen newspapers around the world, reaches a combined audience far larger than the readership of the printed paper itself at any time before in its illustrious history.[13]

The challenge is to convert this diverse consumer base into concrete revenues.

Online services are thus frequently used to supplement or redistribute rather than replace existing mainstream media. In particular, broadcast television continues to maintain a strong presence in the market, particularly for older generations.[14] A recent study on public access to foreign news by Sambrook, Terrington and Levy found that coverage of a news item on broadcast television could stimulate further online interest, underlining the continuing agenda setting role and journalistic capabilities of established media.[15]

[10] Reuters Institute for the Study of Journalism, *Digital News Report 2012*, Oxford, July 2012, 16.
[11] Reuters Institute for the Study of Journalism, *Digital News Report 2012*, Oxford, July 2012, 14.
[12] Reuters Institute for the Study of Journalism, *Digital News Report 2012*, Oxford, July 2012, 16.
[13] R.K. Neilsen, *Ten Years That Shook the Media World, Big Questions and Big Trends in International Media Developments*, Reuters Institute for the Study of Journalism, October 2012, 17.
[14] Reuters Institute for the Study of Journalism, *Digital News Report 2012*, July 2012, 24.
[15] R. Sambrook, S. Terrington, and D.A.L. Levy, *The Public Appetite for Foreign News on TV and Online*, Reuters Institute for the Study of Journalism, Oxford, April 2013, 44.

Changes to the way products are stored and distributed also influence what it is viable to produce. The Internet enables a consumer base to be built-up over time and space, encouraging on-demand services to specialise in, or extend their catalogues to, niche or untested products that rarely feature on commercial broadcast television services. This phenomenon is sometimes referred to as the 'long tail' after the distinctive curve in graphs that depict markets of this type – the end, or 'tail', of the curve being long and low relative to the head, indicating small but consistent sales over time.[16] Despite the economic difficulties currently being encountered by both established and new media, the online environment enables a richer range of content to be made available and, as discussed further in the section below, for new operators to enter the market.

Question for discussion

1. Should states intervene to assist traditional media in this transitional phase? Should they assist the development of new media?

(c) Democratisation of the communications space

The Internet has broken the stranglehold of the traditional media and their owners over the flow of information to the public. The falling cost of personal computers and Internet access means that individuals and organisations, previously excluded from the field of mass communications, can now supplement, or comment on, the material that the established news organisations choose to publish. This fundamental change is reflected in the following extract by Yochai Benkler.

Extract 9.2.4
Y. Benkler, *The Wealth of Networks: How social production transforms markets and freedom* (Yale University Press, New Haven, 2006), pp. 30 and 32–3

The Internet . . . is the first modern communications medium that expands its reach by decentralizing the capital structure of production and distribution of information, culture, and knowledge. Much of the physical capital that embeds most of the intelligence in the network is widely diffused and owned by the end users . . . This basic change in the material conditions of information and cultural production and distribution have substantial effects on how we come to know the world we occupy and the alternative courses of action open to us as individuals and as social actors.

. . . Any person who has information can connect with any other person who wants it, and anyone who wants to make it mean something in some context, can do so. The high capital costs that were a prerequisite to gathering, working, and communicating information, knowledge, and culture, have now been widely distributed in society. The entry barriers they posed no longer offers a condensation point for the large organizations that once dominated the information environment. Instead, emerging models of information and cultural production, radically decentralized and based on emergent patterns of cooperation and sharing, but also of simple coordinate coexistence, are beginning to take on an ever-larger role in how we produce meaning – information, knowledge, and culture – in the networked information economy.

---

[16] C. Anderson, *The Long Tail. How Endless Choice is Creating Unlimited Demand* (Random House Business Books, London, 2006).

The rise of participatory journalism is not, however, without its risks.[17] Detractors have been quick to point out that the professionalism, editorial control, and research resources that characterise at least a proportion of the mainstream media cannot generally be replicated by amateur publishers and that user-generated content can be inaccurate, malicious and in some cases seriously harmful.[18] Moreover, commercial interests inevitably seek to gain control over successful forms of public interaction, such as Twitter, and in so doing may distort the communicative process.[19] It is also suggested that the open Internet has led to information overload and that, with greater choice, individuals will select only sources that confirm their existing opinions, leading to social polarisation and prejudice.[20]

Extract 9.2.5
R. Foster, *News Plurality in a Digital World*, Reuters Institute for the Study of Journalism, Oxford, July 2012, p. 22

More worrying from the plurality perspective is the contention that, through the filtering of stories via friends, or via the personalization of search, digital media encourages people to remain within their own comfort zone. Eli Pariser[i] uses the term 'filter bubble' to describe this phenomenon – in which search engines and social networks use algorithms and personal data to select only content which matches existing tastes and preferences. The risk, some have suggested, is that people access only those news stories in their direct field of interest, and read only those opinions with which they are familiar and agree. As a result they get less exposure to conflicting viewpoints and become closed to new ideas, subjects and information. Tim Berners-Lee[ii] warns that social networks like Facebook constitute one of the 'several threats to the Web's universality', arguing that such sites create 'closed silos of content' that may threaten the Internet's original open status.

    Others have disputed Pariser's findings, arguing that personalization still works in a very crude way, and does not prevent users seeking a wide range of voices. And to the casual observer it is hard to believe that the scope for searching and finding news offered by digital media can be any less mind-broadening than the much narrower range of news and comment available from some traditional newspapers.

[i] E. Pariser, *The Filter Bubble: What the Internet is Hiding From You* (Penguin Press, 2011).
[ii] T. Berners-Lee, 'Long live the web', *Scientific American*, 22 November 2010.

The significance of these concerns is thus disputed. In particular, Foster cites evidence that the average online news reader in 2011 visited 5.2 sites compared with the average newspaper reader who read only two newspapers, indicating that online users may in fact be exposed to more sources.[21]

(d) New power relations

Convergence opens up new opportunities for companies and individuals to participate in media markets, as producers, service providers, and consumers. However, it has also led to a shift in power relations, with intermediaries such as search engines, news aggregators,

---

[17] For an overview and critique of these concerns see Y. Benkler, *The Wealth of Networks. How Social Production Transforms Markets and Freedom* (Yale University Press, New Haven, CT, 2006), 253–7.
[18] A. Keen, *The Cult of the Amateur. How Today's Internet is Killing our Culture and Assaulting our Economy* (Nicolas Brearley Publishing, London, 2007).
[19] D. Murthy, *Twitter. Social Communication in the Twitter Age* (Polity, Cambridge, 2013).
[20] C.R. Sunstein, *Republic.com 2.0* (Princeton University Press, Princeton, 2007).
[21] R. Foster, *News Plurality in a Digital World*, Reuters Institute for the Study of Journalism, Oxford, July 2012, 20.

social media and digital app stores gaining greater influence over market developments. Although these intermediaries can have a positive effect on media plurality, pointing consumers to a wider range of sources, they may also be able to marginalise content providers that are not prepared to agree to their terms or favour services with which they have commercial links.

Extract 9.2.6
R. Foster, *News Plurality in a Digital World*, Reuters Institute for the Study of Journalism, Oxford, July 2012, p. 27

In the context of the general debate about news plurality, there are arguably four broad and interrelated aspects of the conduct of digital intermediaries which could be of public concern, reflecting their hybrid nature.

- The first is the extent to which these intermediaries each or collectively are becoming bottlenecks for the distribution of news. The larger their role in the overall news distribution market, or a particular part of it, the more they have the potential to exercise control over the way in which users access news and news suppliers reach their audiences.
- The second is the extent to which these intermediaries commission, select, promote and make other (editorial-like) judgements about the news content they make available to users, potentially influencing the news agenda . . .
- The third is the role they play in shaping the future economic models for news provision . . .
- The fourth is the extent to which, based on the above, they themselves have the capacity, and incentive, to influence the political agenda . . .

A fifth and slightly different concern . . . is connected with the increasingly important and pervasive role which – at least some – digital intermediaries play in the everyday lives of their individual users.

Related concerns have arisen with regard to Internet service providers (ISPs), which play an even more fundamental role in connecting individuals to the Internet. Broadband capacity is not limitless and, with increasing amounts of information-rich data being relayed, ISPs adopt various 'traffic management' policies to deal with the resultant congestion. This has led to heated debates worldwide, notably in the US and within the EU, as to the desirability of regulatory intervention to preserve 'Net neutrality'.[22] Net neutrality focuses on a range of practices by ISPs that either discriminate among content providers or block access to specific content or services, raising censorship concerns.[23] In particular, neutrality can be compromised where ISPs guarantee quicker and more reliable transmission to firms willing to pay an additional fee, thereby making access to their websites more attractive to consumers.[24] Prioritising content in this way may be efficient, but it can also result in access to other free or public content being degraded with long-term implications for the innovative and open nature of the Internet. More troublingly, certain ISPs block access to content provided by competitors or certain high bandwidth applications. A study for the European Commission revealed that around 20 per cent of mobile broadband users

---

[22] For details of EU policy see European Commission, *Communication on The Open Internet and Net Neutrality in Europe*, COM (2011) 222 final, European Commission, *Declaration on New Neutrality*, (2009) OJ C308/2; in relation to the UK see Ofcom, *Traffic Management and 'Net Neutrality', A Discussion Document*, 24 June 2010, Ofcom, *Ofcom's Approach to Net Neutrality*, 24 November 2011; and for a review of developments in the USA, see A. Packard, *Digital Media Law* (2nd edn) (Wiley-Blackwell, 2013), 86.

[23] See for helpful discussion of different dimensions A. Packard, *Digital Media Law* (2nd edn) (Wiley-Blackwell, 2013), 80–6 and C.T. Marsden, *Net Neutrality, Towards a Co-Regulatory Solution* (Bloomsbury Academic, 2010).

[24] J. Scott, 'The mobile side of net neutrality', 19 June 2012, *ComputerWeekly.com* at: http://www.computerweekly.com/news/2240158314/The-mobile-side-of-net-neutrality.

in the EU have contracts that allow their ISP to restrict services such as the Internet telecommunications service Skype or peer-to-peer file sharing.[25]

In response to these concerns, the EU has established minimum transparency requirements to help individuals assess the likely quality of the services open to them, sought to facilitate switching among providers, and authorised national regulators to establish basic quality standards where they deem these to be necessary.[26] Moreover, national telecoms regulatory authorities are required to promote 'the ability of end users to access and distribute information or run applications and services of their choice'.[27] More recently, the European Commission has consulted on whether further steps are needed to enhance consumer information, assist switching among ISPs, and to control certain forms of traffic management.[28] The relevance of EU intervention for domestic policy is noted in Ofcom's stated approach to net neutrality in the extract below.

Extract 9.2.7
Ofcom, *Ofcom's Approach to Net Neutrality*, 24 November 2011, at http://stakeholders.ofcom.org.uk/binaries/consultations/net-neutrality/statement/statement.pdf, paras 1.3–1.6

1.3 The appropriateness of different approaches to traffic management is at the heart of the Net Neutrality debate. Given the controversial nature of this debate, it is important to bear in mind that traffic management is often beneficial. It is commonly used for example to protect safety-critical traffic such as calls to the emergency services. The question is not whether traffic management is acceptable in principle, but whether particular approaches to traffic management cause concern.

1.4 It is possible to identify two broad forms of internet traffic management:

- 'Best-efforts' internet access, under which network operators attempt to convey all traffic on more or less equal terms. This results in an 'open internet' with no specific services being hindered or blocked, although some may need to be managed during times of congestion.
- Managed services, under which network operators prioritise certain traffic according to the value they ascribe to it. An example may be the prioritisation of a high quality IPTV [Internet Protocol Television] service over other traffic. This amounts to a form of discrimination, but one that is normally efficiency enhancing.

1.5 Our approach to traffic management recognises the benefits associated with both types of service, and seeks for them to co-exist. Our overall aim is to ensure that consumers and citizens continue to benefit from both innovation in services and investment in networks.

1.6 The tools available to achieve this have recently changed, due to revisions in the EU framework and corresponding UK law. These changes enable regulators to enhance consumer protection, by requiring greater transparency as to the use of traffic management by network operators, and to protect the quality of 'best-efforts' internet access by setting a minimum quality of service . . .

Source: © Ofcom copyright 2006–11.

---

[25] BEREC, *A view of traffic management and other practices resulting in restrictions to the open Internet in Europe*, BoR (12) 30, 29 May 2012, 8.

[26] Rules relating to transparency, to facilitate switching among providers, and authorising the establishment of minimum quality of service standards are included in arts 21, 30 and 22 respectively of Directive 2002/22/EC on universal service and users' rights relating to electronic communications networks and services (2002) OJ L108/51, as amended by Directive 2009/136/EC (2009) OJ L337/11.

[27] Article 8(4) of Directive 2002/21/EC of the European Parliament and the Council of 7 March 2002 on a common regulatory framework for electronic communications networks and services (2002) OJ L108/33 as amended by Directive 2009/140/EC (2009) OJ L337/37.

[28] European Commission, 'Digital Agenda: Commission opens public consultation on preservation of the open internet (net neutrality)', RAPID IP/12/817, 23 July 2012. In light of the consultation new proposals are to be put forward, on which see N. Kroes, 'The EU, safeguarding the open internet for all', SPEECH/13/498, 04/06/2013.

In relation to transparency, Ofcom confirmed the importance of consumers having access to clear information about the speed of available services, as well as ISPs' traffic management and blocking policies, but placed considerable reliance on ISPs themselves to establish acceptable standards through self-regulatory initiatives. It also considered there to be adequate network capacity for 'best efforts' access to the open Internet and thus concluded there was currently no need to introduce minimum quality of service requirements. Ofcom did, however, note the ongoing importance of this issue and undertook to keep the situation under review.[29]

ISPs' traffic management policies could have significant financial implications for public service broadcasters, which now transmit large amounts of video data on an on-demand basis; similarly the existing protection public service broadcasters enjoy in terms of access to platforms and electronic programme guides may also need to be revisited in the light of technological developments.[30] Manufacturers of connected televisions, for example, can configure the 'home' page on the initial screen so that it navigates viewers to content the manufacturer has selected, making it more difficult for specific providers to reach their target audience and bypassing controls introduced, for example, in relation to electronic programme guides. New configurations of power can also lead to other familiar problems such as bundling, discussed in the extract below.

Extract 9.2.8
House of Lords Select Committee on Communications, *Media Convergence*, 27 March 2013, HL Paper 154, paras 189–91

189. Some concern has been expressed that ISPs and bundled service providers may abuse their control of audience's internet access to their own advantage. Convergence has resulted in people often buying bundles or a range of services (telephony, broadband, TV) from the same supplier. While landline and broadband packages remain the most popular type of bundle, 19% of UK homes have a triple-play bundle of fixed voice, broadband and multichannel TV (up 3% on 2011).[i]

190. The reason this is considered an issue arises from the fact that, even though the triple-play bundle presents a single proposition to the consumer, its constituent elements (broadband, telephony, and premium TV content) are regulated in different ways, and different treatment of competition issues in the broadcasting and telecoms sectors, it is argued, may risk distorting competition for retail bundles of services.

191. An additional concern was expressed over the effectiveness of competition in the market for premium content (sports and in particular first-window pay TV movies), particularly as market power here may be used to attract customers to bundled services where other elements of the bundle are subject to different competition. Again, some witnesses argued for new powers to be awarded to Ofcom to investigate and/or intervene in this market.

Source: Contains Parliamentary information licensed under the Open Parliament Licence v1.0.

[i] Ofcom, *Communications Market Report 2012*, July 2012, 4. Available online: http://stakeholders.ofcom. org.uk/binaries/research/cmr/cmr12/CMR_UK_2012.pdf.

Questions for discussion

1. Which, if any, online news sources do you access and why? Do you yourself contribute to the publication, dissemination or discussion of news items online?
2. Which of the regulatory challenges posed by convergence are novel and which are familiar problems arising in a different context?

[29] Ofcom, *Ofcom's Approach to Net Neutrality*, 24 November 2011, at http://stakeholders.ofcom.org.uk/binaries/consultations/net-neutrality/statement/statement.pdf.
[30] See Chapter 8, Section 8.5(b).

9.3 THE IMPACT OF CONVERGENCE ON MEDIA REGULATION IN THE FUTURE

Convergence has been gradually undermining the established framework for media regulation in the UK. It is tempting to suggest that because of convergence and the likely abundance of programme outlets, a case need no longer be made for regulation of the media along traditional lines. However, as Gibbons argues in the extract below, that would be to confuse the reasons for specialised regulation of the media with the means of delivery. What we have to keep in mind are the reasons why media goods and services are special and, therefore, require special regulation.

Extract 9.3.1
T. Gibbons, *Regulating the Media*, 2nd edn (Sweet & Maxwell, 1998), pp. 301–2

The development and adoption of new, especially digital, technology may raise the possibility that media regulation will no longer be necessary in the middle to long term, but that depends on characterising media products as purely commercial and without political and social significance. While it is true that the media are primarily concerned with entertainment, they also provide a major resource for communication and cannot be wholly shaped by market mechanisms. Indeed, it is the potentially *mediating* character of the media which makes them important and distinguishes them from simple information services. Newspapers, radio and television do more than convey ideas in a neutral way; they are part of our culture and provide a means of obtaining and presenting knowledge and engaging in political activity. As a result of their ability to select information and order priorities, they have a profound influence on the way we think about the world. Furthermore, it is doubtful whether information services can be completely neutral about the way they package material and make it available to consumers; they also select and shape what they convey. There is, therefore, a public interest in activities which are mediating, one which denies the mediators complete control over their goals and practices.

That is not to say that new forms of media will have no implications for media regulation, but the issue is one of re-regulation, rather than de-regulation,[i] the need to tailor regulation to fit the values which are sought to be promoted. Here a functional approach is required, one which does not depend on technology or forms of delivery, but which recognises the nature of the service being provided and the character of the audience receiving it. The early justification for regulating broadcasting, that it was *broad-casting*, rests on the belief that material which is transmitted to a universal audience, both in terms of geographic reach and personal profile, requires special treatment. The reason is that the audience has no effective control over the scheduling and content of the material received. For universal programming, then, there will always be a need for sensitivity to audience membership, regardless of the public service or commercial quality of the content. To the extent that programming is made available in progressively segmented forms, either by 'narrow-casting' or subscription, the case for content regulation becomes correspondingly weaker,[ii] although there will continue to be a public interest in the overall provision of media output.

[i] See W. Hoffman-Reim, *Regulating Media: The Licensing and Supervision of Broadcasting in Six Countries* (Guildford Press, 1996); P. Humphreys, *Media and Media Policy in Western Europe* (1996); T. Prosser, *Law and the Regulators* (1997), ch 10. See also Culture, Media and Sport Select Committee, *Fourth Report: The Multi-Media Revolution*, v 1 (1997–99) HC 520–1, para 116.

[ii] See J. Balkin, 'Media filters, the v-chip and the foundations of broadcast regulation' (1996) 45 *Duke Law Journal* 1131–75.

Convergence does not mean, therefore, that the social and economic objectives that underpinned regulation in the past cease to be relevant, but it does require us to rethink how we seek to realise, or indeed whether we still need to intervene to realise, these objectives. In particular, Gibbons suggests that services should not be regulated differently simply because they are relayed by different technical means, an approach referred to as 'technological neutrality'. Thus, a television programme should, in principle, be regulated in the same way whether it is broadcast over the airwaves or streamed over the Internet. On the other hand, Gibbons is also clear that technology does make a difference. The more protective broadcasting standards, developed with a universal audience in mind, may not be appropriate in an environment where individuals can choose what to access and when to access it. In the following section we consider in more detail how standards might be regulated in the future, before going on to examine who should regulate and the different regulatory techniques that are being employed in this new environment.

Question for consideration

1. Why should the media not be regulated in the same way as other products, for instance, food?

(a) Content standards in the context of convergence

At present there are eight main regulatory regimes relating to media content, key characteristics of which are indicated briefly below (for more detail see Chapters 2, 3 and 4).[31] The first, and most exacting, is that applicable to broadcast television and radio, centred on the Ofcom Broadcasting Code and BBC Editorial Guidelines. These codes broadly seek to *protect the audience*, particularly vulnerable members such as children, from offensive as well as harmful content, for instance, programmes containing pornography or details of suicide techniques. They also seek to *protect third parties* from invasive or unfair investigative techniques and inaccurate reporting. Requirements of accuracy and impartiality in news and current affairs programmes also pursue *wider social and political objectives*, in this case to support informed personal and political decisions, as do the rules prohibiting broadcasters from making payments to criminals for their stories or to witnesses at certain points of the trial process. Alongside these largely negative code provisions, a range of positive content obligations have been imposed by statute or agreement, primarily on public service broadcasters, which pursue social and political, as well as industrial, objectives.

The second regime, applicable to the printed and online press, is currently set out in the PCC Editor's Code of Practice, to be replaced under the new system of press regulation post-Leveson. The PCC Code (and it is anticipated its successor will adopt a similar approach) focuses almost entirely on *protecting third parties* from damaging reports, for instance articles that are inaccurate or prejudicial on grounds of race, colour, sexual orientation or other attributes, as well as from inappropriate investigative techniques, particularly in the field of privacy. Wider *social concerns* are reflected, as in the broadcasting codes, in the provisions on payments to witnesses and criminals. Importantly, the Code does not contain rules designed to protect readers from harm or offence, nor does it impose an obligation of impartiality or positive content requirements.

The third regime relates to on-demand 'television-like' services and is overseen by ATVOD. The ATVOD guidelines contain limited rules designed to *protect third parties and children*

---

[31] For a schematic overview see House of Lords Select Committee on Communications, *Media Convergence*, 27 March 2013, HL Paper 154, 12.

from specific forms of harm, namely hate speech and exposure to violent or pornographic content respectively, as well as provisions relating to sponsorship and product placement. The fourth regime covers other video, audio or text material relayed over the Internet. In this context, the general law is primarily applicable, though the Electronic Commerce (EC Directive) Regulations 2002 protects intermediaries, such as Internet service providers, from legal liability for third-party content which they relay, cache or host, where they have no knowledge of what that content comprises.[32] In addition to these four regimes, there are also specific self- and co-regulatory regimes applicable to advertising, video games, cinema and video recordings, and premium rate phone services.[33]

As will be apparent, this regulatory patchwork results in a variable and highly uneven application of content standards, determined both by the mode of delivery and the nature of the provider. For example, save in relation to child protection and hate speech, the negative standards designed to protect audiences, third parties and society more generally in relation to broadcast services cease to apply where video content is relayed on an on-demand basis. However, where the same video content is included in the website of a newspaper, at least on an ancillary basis,[34] it will be subject to the rules on accuracy and protection of third parties contained in the PCC Code (and likely its replacement). Positive obligations are only operative in the broadcasting context and regulatory controls relating to radio largely disappear online.

This disparate framework has a number of very apparent drawbacks. First, it is likely to confuse consumers. Particularly with the advent of connected televisions, offering access to both the Internet and broadcast services, audiences will find it difficult to tell which regulatory regime applies and the standards that are in operation. Second, third-party redress varies depending on the medium, the nature of the provider and substantive concern. Thus, in both the broadcast and press contexts, an individual damaged by inaccurate or intrusive reporting has access to an alternative process for resolving disputes, while no such recourse is available in relation to other on-demand content. In this latter context the individual has only the expensive and time-consuming option of commencing legal proceedings for defamation or privacy. Third, it discriminates among media services depending on their mode of transmission (broadcast or on-demand) or origin (newspaper/magazine or other media organisation), leading to potential distortions of the market. These observations suggest that there is a strong case for rendering the present regulatory framework more coherent.

When considering how this might be taken forward we need to keep in mind the various types of regulatory measures, both positive and negative, discussed above. In an on-demand environment, audiences can be empowered to take more responsibility for their consumption, rendering a one-size-fits-all approach to matters such as offence and decency inappropriate. For such a regulatory shift to be acceptable, however, individuals must have access to meaningful information about available content and effective control devices, such as filters, as well as the knowledge to apply them. On the other hand, it is not apparent why the application of rules designed to protect audiences and third parties from harm, as opposed to offence, should vary depending on type of medium or its delivery.

---

[32] Electronic Commerce (EC Directive) Regulations 2002, statutory instrument no 2013 of 2002, at regulations 17–20. In addition, s 5 of the Defamation Act 2013 protects the operator of a website from a defamation action where the operator can show that they did not post the content at issue on their website and the complainant is able to identify who did post it. On the other hand, ISPs are increasingly expected to address potential illegal activities by users, particularly copyright infringement, on which see the Digital Economy Act 2010.

[33] These are detailed in D. Mac Síthigh, 'Co-regulation, video-on-demand and the legal status of audio-visual media' (2011) 2(1) *International Journal of Digital Television*, 49–66.

[34] See Extract 3.11.2.

More controversially, it could also be desirable for providers of on-demand services to take over at least some of the positive obligations previously imposed on broadcasters, particularly in the field of content production. This approach was endorsed in the AVMSD but has not been carried through in relation to on-demand services in the UK.[35]

Whether the regulation of a particular sector is considered to be out of step with that applicable to others will depend, of course, on which sectors are considered to be comparable. The ATVOD and PCC regimes undoubtedly fall short of that applicable to broadcast content, but impose additional constraints beyond those applicable to other types of online content. Are we therefore to conclude that they are over or under protective? Medium specific regulation also appears an increasingly blunt instrument given the different types of communication that can be relayed in any given format. Finer distinctions may thus be required both within and across media, to take into account the varying expectations and degrees of tolerance that apply in different contexts, for example, on social network sites or a comment section attached to an online mainstream news service.[36]

Faced with the increasingly incoherent and confusing nature of domestic regulation, the House of Lords Select Committee on Communications has suggested a new framework. It proposes that the existing regime for public service broadcasting should be retained, with other broadcast services, such as those provided by satellite broadcaster BSkyB, grouped together with on-demand television-like services to create a second unified regime. A third area would be covered by the future press regulator. A fourth area, referred to as the 'open Internet', would apply to all other Internet content. The Committee envisages that Ofcom and digital intermediaries, such as Internet service providers, could play a greater role in monitoring services and co-ordinating self-regulatory initiatives to protect the public in this fourth domain. The Committee did not consider these reforms to require immediate implementation but recognised that, with the advent of connected-TVs they could be needed in the near future. They thus suggested that provision be made for their introduction in the next Communications Act.

Extract 9.3.2
House of Lords Select Committee on Communications, *Media Convergence*,
27 March 2013, HL Paper 154, paras 58, 63 and 65–8

58. The most straightforward area in the framework requires no regulatory or legislative change. It contains the public service broadcasters. In this area we suggest that comprehensive regulation and enforcement of the Broadcasting Code should be retained.

. . .

63. The second category in our suggested framework establishes a new regulatory area. Overseen by a single body, this area would contain TV-like content providers irrespective of their platform as well as broadcasters without PSB status.

. . .

65. First, this area responds directly to trends set in motion by convergence. As TV and TV-like content merge within audiences' decision making, the confusion generated by their obligatory

---

[35] Article 13 of the AVMSD extended the European content quotas, in modified form, to on-demand services, Directive 2010/13/EU (2010) OJ L95/1.

[36] See, for a context-aware approach, the interim guidelines for prosecuting cases involving social media, published by the Crown Prosecution Service in England, discussed at: http://www.cps.gov.uk/consultations/social_media_consultation_index.html.

adherence to different standards codes will reach a point at which the disparity must be addressed. In the absence of change, there will be a detriment to audiences' ability to form expectations of the content standards they can rely on . . . Accordingly, at a certain point, the sensible course of action will be to establish a regulatory area for content inherently similar from the perspective of the audience, and to move the relevant providers into it. This will include TV-like providers and those TV broadcasters not captured by the first regulatory area by virtue of their PSB status.

66. Second, establishing this area responds to the risk that the existing framework might inhibit content providers from exploiting the opportunities for innovation and growth brought about by convergence . . . Hybrid on-demand and linear services, interactive TV services such as Sesame Street Kinect available over Internet-connected Xbox consoles, streamed hyper-local news services, next generation YouTube services: all and more would be covered by the new content framework. Bringing providers of all these services into a single regulatory area and establishing over time parity between their standards codes will help remove barriers to innovation and the development of services with potentially significant benefit to UK citizens.

67. Third, this new regulatory area responds to the changing role of audiovisual content. This is very different from the one it played when extensive standards regulation was warranted on the basis of the scarcity of spectrum, the resulting power of broadcasters and the special influence of their TV content. Audio-visual content in a more converged world will in time move closer in nature to all other published media content, and the standards framework should adjust to reflect this change.

68. Last but not least, an important aim of establishing this regulatory area, in line with Ofcom's duties as set out in the Communications Act 2003, would be to reduce regulatory costs.

Source: Contains Parliamentary information licensed under the Open Parliament Licence v1.0.

The Committee suggested that a new co-regulatory system be introduced for the combined broadcast/on-demand television sector, with general principles set by the designated co-regulator and a detailed code established by the industry itself.[37] The Committee was not prepared to speculate as to the content of any future code but considered it likely that this would 'ultimately be less detailed than Ofcom's Broadcasting Code', but could 'be greater in scope than ATVOD's current rules for on-demand services'.[38] It did, however, recommend that impartiality requirements be removed from non-PSB broadcasters to bring them into line with the current regulatory regime for non-broadcast news and current affairs (paras 114–16).[39]

Questions for discussion
1. Which rules, if any, would you include in a code of conduct for a converged television regulator?
2. Is audience confusion a sufficient ground for removing impartiality requirements from non-PSB broadcasters? If implemented, what impact do you consider this proposal would have on the diversity of news and current affairs services in the UK?[40]
3. Is the Committee's proposal likely to be deregulatory or re-regulatory or both?

[37] For further discussion of co- and self-regulation see the next section below.
[38] House of Lords Select Committee on Communications, *Media Convergence*, 27 March 2013, HL Paper 154, para 73.
[39] For a helpful overview of the arguments for and against retaining impartiality requirements see R. Sambrook, *Delivering Trust: Impartiality and Objectivity in the Digital Age*, Reuters Institute for the Study of Journalism, Oxford, July 2012.
[40] Ibid.

The new regulatory framework proposed by the House of Lords Communications Committee relies heavily on the concept of 'television-like' services, developed by the EU in the Audiovisual Media Services Directive (AVMSD) and carried over into ATVOD's remit in the UK.[41] Key criteria employed to determine whether a programme is 'television-like', notably 'whether it is comparable in form and content to programmes normally included in television programme services' or 'competes for the same audience as TV broadcasts',[42] leave considerable margin for appreciation and it is questionable whether factors such as the style or structure of a programme should play such a crucial role in determining whether regulatory obligations to protect the audience or third parties apply. An alternative, simplified, regulatory framework can be envisaged, one which enforces certain standards uniformly across video, audio and text content. The Committee did, in fact, take a step in this direction by suggesting a *genre-based* approach to regulation, whereby news and current affairs content provided by all non-PSB providers, video as well as text, should be regulated by the new press regulator (para 118). This would not, however, reduce the overall number of regulators and would subject non-PSB television providers to two different regulators in relation to different aspects of their service, potentially creating a new set of boundary disputes.

Lara Fielden has proposed a more radical response to convergence, which focuses on the intensity of the regulatory obligations rather than the medium. Her scheme involves four tiers of regulation, equally open to providers of text-, audio- and video-based services.[43] The first, most demanding, 'public service tier', incorporates both impartiality requirements and the standards currently contained in the Ofcom Code. Public service audiovisual providers would be required to be part of this tier but adherence would be optional for all other operators. The second, voluntary, 'ethical private content tier', would be somewhat more exacting than the present press regime, but less so than the existing broadcast one. The third 'baseline private content tier' would maintain the minimum requirements set out in the AVMSD and would thus be compulsory for the services covered by that directive, although optional for other operators. A final fourth tier would apply to operators not caught by, or opting-in to, the other three tiers, where the general law alone would apply. Operators falling within each of the three key tiers of regulation would be able to employ standard marks to inform the public as to the type of service they offered and Fielden proposes a number of incentives for service providers to commit to tiers one and two, such as prominence on electronic programme guides. One of the advantages of this scheme is that it would also be open to bloggers and amateur publishers who could buy into one or other of the tiers in order to benefit from the quality mark and related advantages.

Extract 9.3.3

L. Fielden, *Regulating for Trust in Journalism: Standards regulation in the age of blended media* (Reuters Institute for the Study of Journalism, Oxford, 2011), pp. 126–7

The approach proposed invites commercial providers to consider the advantages of independent regulation, of association with similarly regulated content producers and thereby attracting advertising associations. It invites bloggers and other new media participants to benefit from

---

[41] For more details see Extracts 3.11.1 and 3.11.2 and Chapter 5.
[42] See Extract 3.11.1.
[43] L. Fielden, *Regulating for Trust in Journalism. Standards Regulation in the Age of Blended Media* (Reuters Institute for the Study of Journalism, Oxford, 2011).

accreditation through regulatory affiliation; broadcasters to benefit from associated EPG ranking; consumers to engage with a framework that is responsive to complaints, providing a place for informal resolution as well as more formal sanctions for breaches of the codes associated with each tier; citizens to be provided with an informed basis on which to base media expectations and engagement; regulators to resolve current areas of confusion and inconsistency; and forthcoming legislation to promote a coherent and transparent approach to media regulation.

Questions for discussion

1. Would implementation of Lara Fielden's proposed converged regulatory scheme weaken the independence of the press?
2. Which standards do you think should, or should not, vary depending on whether a service contains text or video content?
3. Should standards vary depending on the size of the audience or the professional or amateur status of the publisher?[44]

(b) Convergent regulators?

During much of the last century, media regulators tended to be highly specialised. There were specific regulators for each media sector and content, carriage and competition issues were often addressed by different bodies. This compartmentalisation was inevitably challenged by convergence. At first glance, the notion of a single regulator appears attractive, bringing together all regulatory functions for all aspects of communications, while avoiding the difficulties of defining the remit for sector-specific regulators. However, with a single regulator the need for a clear separation of functions and identification of objectives become particularly important, failing which there is the risk that specific concerns or interests will be inappropriately downgraded or even ignored. The question whether it is desirable to consolidate regulatory functions in this way was widely discussed prior to the passage of the Communications Act in 2003 and opposing views, written at the time, can be seen in the following two extracts.

Extract 9.3.4
R. Collins and C. Murroni, *New Media New Policies* (Polity Press, 1996), pp. 173–5

On balance, we find arguments for fewer regulators compelling, and argue for a single regulator in the communications sector. Media and communications are becoming increasingly interconnected and it is less troublesome to conceive of them as an interconnected whole than as a series of discrete phenomena. Although content regulation and the regulation of markets are different tasks, they are not necessarily best done by separate bodies. Indeed, the ITC and Radio Authority now regulate both structure and content. Each regulatory task is more efficiently discharged because both are done by the same body. The leverage which accrues from structural and carriage regulation assists enforcement of content regulation. Carriage and structural regulatory decisions, such as those concerning diversity of outlets, are influenced by considerations of content. To regulate concentration of ownership effectively, both the individual and the aggregate UK media and communication markets must be considered together. Consumers will be better served by one stop regulatory shopping . . .

---

[44] See J. Rowbottom, 'Media Freedom and Political Debate in the Digital Era' (2006) 69 *Modern Law Review* 489–513.

What is required is a single regulator – we suggest 'Ofcom' – applying common content guidelines and codes with different standards of severity and exactitude for different media and types of communication. For communications that can be consumed involuntarily, i.e. public media (posters on street, advertising sites and free-to-air radio and television), content codes will apply with greater severity than with media that are unlikely to be consumed involuntarily.

Extract 9.3.5
T. Gibbons, *Regulating the Media*, 2nd edn (Sweet & Maxwell, 1998), p. 304 (footnotes omitted)

Problems in deciding the appropriate scope of regulation may lead to the conclusion that the establishment of a single, 'super' regulator would be the most effective solution. The advantages would be that regulatory policy could be co-ordinated in one body and regulatory compliance would be made easier. However, there are strong arguments against such a move. It would be a delusion to believe that the existence of one regulator would remove any conflict between regulatory objectives. Instead, such conflict would be hidden from public gaze and become a matter of office politics rather than democratic debate. There would be a real risk that economic arguments would prevail, given the liberalising trends in the industry. There would also be a rather extreme concentration of power in one regulator for an industry which is so important to democratic aims. Both considerations suggest that it would be much healthier to have more than one regulator, with each defending its own corner through public and Parliamentary discussion. To create a single regulator would actually serve to pre-empt such debate, since it would not be policy-neutral.

The concerns identified by Gibbons have not been entirely allayed in practice, as the next extract explains.

Extract 9.3.6
P. Lunt, S. Livingstone and B. Brevini, 'Changing regimes of regulation: implications for public service broadcasting' in G. Ferrell Lowe and J. Steemers (eds) *Regaining the Initiative for Public Service Media* (Nordicom, 2012), pp. 113–28 at pp. 116–17 (some footnotes omitted)

As an institution, Ofcom could establish a unified approach to regulation across the sector (notwithstanding that areas such as advertising, film and the internet were excluded), having sufficient scope and capacity to meet the challenges of an increasingly global, converged media landscape. While such a unified approach was much called for, given the confusion caused by multiple regulators . . . one might understandably express caution about what is thereby lost – the ability of smaller scale, targeted regulators to be 'fine tuned' to their specific domains, even resulting in different positions on key value debates in media and communications policy.

Notably, Ofcom's statutory duties prioritised furthering the interests of both citizens and consumers, thereby combining competition and consumer protection with social and cultural aspects of media and communications policy in a manner that might be regarded as either ambitious or problematic.[i] Indeed, this particular combination of priorities generated concerns that Ofcom would tend to favour market competition at the expense of public policy and citizen-related aims, including the management of PSB.[ii] After observing its early days, Gibbons argued that this bias led Ofcom subtly to renegotiate its statutory duties by casting social and cultural issues in economic language, explaining them using economic metaphors.[iii] One example is Ofcom's interpretation of the BBC's importance as a PSB provider as a monopoly problem, sidelinig the diversity of PSB content produced by the BBC (and, even, the competitive processes within the BBC).

. . . As things have turned out, much of Ofcom's work has indeed been devoted to competition policy, structural issues in the communications market, consumer protection and technical issues such as digitisation and spectrum allocation.

[i] S. Livingstone, P. Lunt and L. Miller, 'Citizens and consumers: discursive debates during and after the Communications Act 2003, (2007) 29/4 *Media, Culture and Society* 613–38.
[ii] S. Harvey, 'Ofcom: the reluctant regulator' in J. Petley and G. Williams (eds) *The Media in Contemporary Britain* (Palgrave Macmillian, 2011) and N. Just, 'Measuring media concentration and diversity: new approaches and instruments in Europe and the US' (2009) 31/1 *Media, Culture and Society* 97–117.
[iii] T. Gibbons, 'Competition policy and regulatory style: issues for Ofcom' (2005) 7/5 *Info: the Journal of Policy, Regulation and Strategy for Telecommunications* 42–51.

Despite the Communications Act 2003 replacing five regulatory bodies, including the Radio Authority and ITC, with a single communications regulator, Ofcom, a significant number of media regulators continue to operate: it has been estimated, for example, that there are around 17 regulatory bodies in the UK concerned with media content.[45] Although the proposals put forward by the House of Lords Committee on Communications, discussed above, would retain distinct regulatory bodies for press-based and audiovisual services, with some overlap in areas such as news and current affairs, Lara Fielden's scheme would divide regulators according to the intensity of the regulatory standards they applied.

Whether or not there is further consolidation among media regulators in the UK there is clearly a need for co-ordination among existing regulators at both domestic and international, particularly European, levels, in order to promote coherent approaches.[46] At present this takes place through organisations such as the European Platform for Regulatory Authorities (EPRA), which brings together 53 media authorities in Europe for regular discussions, and through more specific forms of co-ordination, such as that undertaken by means of the Contact Committee, provided for by article 20 of the AVMSD, which seeks to ensure that Member States adopt a consistent approach to implementation of that directive.[47]

Questions for discussion

1. Do you find the arguments in favour of a single regulator convincing?
2. Why might convergence lead to a multiplication of regulatory bodies rather than a reduction?

(c) Regulatory strategies in a convergent media environment

Convergence brings into question not only regulatory standards and regulatory structures but also regulatory strategies and techniques. Established forms of 'command and control' regulation can quickly become outdated or unenforceable in a rapidly evolving, increasingly international, environment. As a result, emphasis is now placed on a range of integrated co- and self-regulatory initiatives by a variety of state, industry and civil society actors. Key regulatory options are explained, together with some of their respective advantages and disadvantages, in the extract below, taken from a study prepared by Ofcom.

---

[45] See D. Mac Síthigh, 'Co-regulation, video-on-demand and the legal status of audio-visual media' (2011) 2(1) *International Journal of Digital Television* 49–66.
[46] See House of Lords Select Committee on Communications, *Media Convergence*, 27 March 2013, HL Paper 154, para 92.
[47] Article 29, Directive 2010/13/EU, (2010) OJ L95/1.

Extract 9.3.7
Ofcom, *Identifying Appropriate Regulatory Solutions: principles for analysing self- and co-regulation. Statement*. 10 December 2008, pp. 7–11

2.1 Three broad approaches can be used to secure policy objectives that are not met by the markets: industry self-regulation; co-regulation, and statutory regulation.

. . .

No regulation

2.4 Regulation, in all its forms, aims to secure public objectives where these are not being delivered by the markets on their own. In many areas intervention is not necessary, for example where:

- desired outcomes are delivered by competitive markets (e.g. increased choice and reduced prices);
- all companies delivering a product or service have incentives to address citizen and consumer needs through best practice and corporate policies; and
- regulatory activity would fail to achieve desired outcomes due to the nature of the issue, and where emphasis needs to shift to empowering consumers to benefit from new services and protect themselves from harm.

. . .

Self-regulation

2.7 We define self-regulation as a situation in which industry administers a regulatory solution to address citizen or consumer issues without formal oversight from government or regulator. In particular, there are usually no explicit legal backstops in relation to issues administered by a scheme to guarantee enforcement.

2.8 It is often considered that self-regulation may present a more flexible, targeted and less costly option than statutory regulation, and that it benefits from industry expertise. Several respondents to our consultation also noted that it promotes a sense of ownership and responsibility, encouraging the industry to resolve the issue.

2.9 The Mobile Broadband Group suggested that self-regulation has further benefits compared with formal regulation in that it: allows more organisations to take part; is more conducive to innovation and competition; encourages companies to take risks in adhering to high standards; can provide low entry point for regulation that builds over time; and makes participants answerable for their own action.

2.10 We agree that in many cases self-regulation can offer an effective option, however, this needs to be considered on a case by case basis. Broadly, the success of self-regulation depends on whether industry incentives are aligned with the interests of citizens and consumers . . . [a]lso, in some cases, an industry-led scheme may be more costly to run than if the same task were performed by a regulator in-house.

. . .

Co-regulation

2.14 Co-regulation combines elements of self- and statutory regulation, with the industry and public authorities administering a solution in a variety of combinations. The aim is to harness the benefits of self-regulation in circumstances where regulatory oversight is required for some elements of the solution, with the government or regulator usually retaining some backstop powers.

2.15 In our consultation we referred to the Dutch NICAM (Nederlands Instituut voor de Classificatie van Audiovisuele Media) scheme for audiovisual media classification as a positive example of co-regulation. NICAM is widely known, adopted and respected . . . As we indicated above, we recognise that self- or co-regulation may at times be more costly to run than if they were undertaken by a regulator; but it may still be desirable to benefit from industry's experience and commitment.

. . .

2.19 We believe that different roles are appropriate for a regulator in different cases.

Where industry incentives to act are sufficiently strong, the regulator's role may be limited, for example, by a form of back-stop powers. In other cases a more direct involvement may be required, with only some parts of the solution delegated to the industry. Decisions on the split of responsibilities should be based on the analysis of the specific issue at hand . . .

. . .

Statutory regulation

2.21 State intervention has two main forms: direct obligations imposed by legislation or government regulations, or the direct enforcement of general legal requirements by a sectoral regulator. Statutory regulation may be particularly effective in certain market conditions, for example, where:

- one large player commands significant market power and where self-regulation would not be effective;
- the issue at hand is unlikely to affect companies' commercial success or their reputations; or
- the structure of the industry (e.g. a large number of diverse players with different interests) does not lend itself to a co-ordinated industry response.

2.22 In addition, as BT pointed out in its response, statutory regulation can in some cases be more predictable and therefore more attractive for the regulated companies.

2.23 However, statutory regulation may also have disadvantages. As a number of stakeholders highlighted, it may in some circumstances be inflexible or too slow to react, and may lack the benefit of industry expertise. It may be over-prescriptive and result in disproportionate costs, eventually borne by consumers in the form of higher service or product prices.

Source: © Ofcom copyright 2006–11.

Ofcom thus considered each technique to have distinct advantages and disadvantages. It also noted that co- and self-regulatory systems could be very diverse, tailored to specific market conditions and the objectives at hand. As noted above, social norms and values, market incentives and 'architecture' comprising software code can all be used to shape industry behaviour and consumer options, with or without direct input from the law.[48] Less directional forms of state intervention such as subsidies, tax incentives and disclosure requirements can all be deployed to nudge behaviour in particular directions.[49]

In particular, states are increasingly focussing their attention on intermediaries, notably ISPs, which act as gateways to the Internet. Digital intermediaries are now, for example, expected to play a key role in protecting children and preventing copyright infringement and their potential liability for continuing to publish certain forms of harmful content, once notified of its existence, means that there is a strong incentive for them to co-operate with industry watchdogs, such as the Internet Watch Foundation, to

---

[48] L. Lessig, *Code and other Laws of Cyberspace* (Basic Books, 1999).
[49] C.R. Sunstein, 'Private broadcasters and the public interest: notes towards a "third way"', University of Chicago, Law School, Chicago John M. Olin, *Law and Economic Working Paper Series*, No 65 at: http://www. law.uchicago.edu/Publications/Working/index.html.

block sites that contain material such as child pornography.[50] But this also creates a risk that firms will over-regulate in order to simplify procedures and cut potential administrative costs, leading to undesirable censorship. Where this happens it may be difficult to get the site reinstated and consumers may well be unaware that particular sites have been blocked in this way.

Alongside the more structured forms of co-regulation there are also many experiments with private or community forms of control, variously introduced to protect the reputation of the firm involved or to prevent potential legal disputes.[51] YouTube, for example, has its own code of conduct for those who post content to its site and relies on the community of users to flag-up content that contravenes these rules, which is then removed:

Extract 9.3.8
YouTube, *Community Guidelines* (accessed 2 May 2013). Available at:
http://www.youtube.com/t/community_guidelines?gl=GB&hl=en-GB

- YouTube is not for pornography or sexually explicit content. If this describes your video, even if it's a video of yourself, don't post it on YouTube. In addition, please be advised that we work closely with law enforcement and we report child exploitation. Please read our Safety Tips and stay safe on YouTube.
- Don't post videos showing things like animal abuse, drug abuse or bomb making.
- Graphic or gratuitous violence is not allowed. If your video shows someone getting hurt, attacked or humiliated, don't post it.
- YouTube is not a shock site. Don't post gory videos of accidents, dead bodies or similar things.
- Respect copyright. Only upload videos that you made or that you are authorised to use. This means don't upload videos you didn't make, or use content in your videos to which someone else owns the copyright, such as music tracks, snippets of copyrighted programmes or videos made by other users, without the requisite authorisations. Read our Copyright Tips for more information.
- We encourage free speech and defend everyone's right to express unpopular points of view. But we do not permit hate speech (speech which attacks or demeans a group based on race or ethnic origin, religion, disability, gender, age, veteran status and sexual orientation/gender identity).
- There is zero tolerance of predatory behaviour, stalking, threats, harassment, invading privacy or the revealing of other members' personal information. Anyone caught doing these things may be permanently banned from YouTube.
- Everyone hates spam. Do not create misleading descriptions, tags, titles or thumbnails in order to increase views. It's not OK to post large amounts of untargeted, unwanted or repetitive content, including comments and private messages.

Although these private forms of control or direction can be effective, flexible and responsive to consumer demands they also raise concerns over democratic legitimacy, accountability, and compliance with fundamental rights. Who is involved in setting the standards, whose interests do they serve, who applies them and can decisions taken be challenged, if necessary in court? These issues are explored in the following extract.

---

[50] See A. Murray, *Information Technology Law: the Law and Society* (Oxford, 2010) for a brief discussion of intermediary liability and potential censorship concerns at 70–3 and, for more recent developments, the Digital Economy Act 2010.

[51] See discussion in House of Lords Select Committee on Communications, *Media Convergence* HL Paper 154, 27 March 2013, at 35–40. For a critical assessment of private standard setting in the US see A. Bartow, 'Bad Samaritan, Barnes v Yahoo! and Section 230 ISP immunity' in H. Travis (ed) *Cyberspace Law, Censorship and Regulation of the Internet* (Routledge, 2013).

Extract 9.3.9
D. Tambini, D. Leonardi and C. Marsden, *Codifying Cyberspace: communications self-regulation in the age of internet convergence* (Routledge, 2008) pp. 284–5

We have identified the possibility of a clash between the freedom-of-expression rights such as they are laid out in Article 10 of the ECHR, and the limitations on speech imposed by self-regulatory bodies. We acknowledge the tension that there is between the expediency and advantages offered by an industry self-regulating versus the need to take the limits imposed by the contractual and voluntary self-regulatory bodies seriously whenever they engage speech rights. We have tried to move the debate to the legal arena, beyond arguments of the left that believes self-regulation privatises censorship and that of the right that self-regulation means less government.

Once we see that self-regulation and freedom of speech need not necessarily be in opposition, a more constructive policy debate on the components that make up a self- or a co-regulatory regime can take place. From our analysis it emerges that self-regulatory bodies have the technical expertise which seems particularly relevant in a field in which there is fast technological change. Efficiency reasons justify regulatory decisions being taken at lower levels and in a decentralised manner, with courts being able to examine the correctness of the decision-making process in cases of complaints, thus ensuring that the protection of the law has opportunities to become effective. Procedural considerations are of great relevance. Regulatory decisions are strengthened by transparency in decision making and stakeholder participation. Curbs on free speech are justifiable when, for example, the balance of rights as set out in Article 10 is accomplished by bodies not only following, but where they are seen to be following, impartial and legitimate procedures.

Questions for discussion

1. Identify examples of both self- and co-regulation in operation in the media field in the UK today. Do they meet the procedural requirements for legitimacy identified by Tambini *et al.* in the extract above?
2. If your YouTube post is taken down by the company what redress, if any, do you have?

If the rationale for removing a layer of protective regulation is that individuals can increasingly tailor consumption to their own sensitivities, whether in relation to sex, violence, strong language, horror or some other concern, then it is imperative that they have the means and knowledge to protect themselves. In particular, there must be reliable and readily understandable content information; provision made for appropriate filtering or control mechanisms; and more general information about how to search for, select, and evaluate what is available. This has raised the profile of media literacy as a policy objective at domestic and international levels. The EU, for example, has developed wide-ranging recommendations that go beyond mere consumer protection and which emphasise the need to empower individuals, of all ages and backgrounds, to engage actively with digital society as consumers, citizens and publishers in their own right.[52] Article 33 of the AVMSD also requires the Commission to make three-yearly reports to the European Parliament, Council and European Economic and Social Committee concerning the implementation

---

[52] See Commission Recommendation 2009/625/EC of 20 August 2009 on media literacy in the digital environment for a more competitive audiovisual and content industry and an inclusive knowledge society, (2009) OJ L227/9. Ofcom and EU media literacy initiatives are reviewed by P. Lunt and S. Livingstone in *Media Regulation, Governance and the Interests of Citizens and Consumers* (Sage 2012), ch 6.

of the Directive and any changes that may be necessary in light of, among other things, levels of media literacy in the Member States.[53]

In the non-linear environment, the positive programme requirements that promoted exposure to diverse content are likely to be retained solely for public service media and, with greater choice, audience exposure may be limited, rather than enhanced (see Extract 9.2.5 above). As companies increasingly tailor content to the user's profile the opportunity for serendipitous encounters with novel content may be curtailed. This has led Natali Helberger to suggest that we need to develop policies designed to break the path dependencies and technical constraints that militate against exposure to diverse content and provide consumers with the skills needed to assess the quality of the information they receive and the commercial or other motivations that lie behind it.[54]

Extract 9. 3.10
N. Helberger, 'Exposure diversity as a policy goal' (2012) 4/1 *Journal of Media Law* pp. 65–92 at 74–5

While the amount of content is growing, there is only a limited amount of time and attention that users are willing and able to invest. A study of the German audience's use of EPGs found that many users respond to increased digital channel variety with 'simplification strategies'. They concentrate on what they know and appreciate, and, interestingly, they are convinced that there is a great probability that the odd additional channel will add little new.[i] Findings like these suggest the importance of the availability of effective mechanisms to help people cope with the digital abundance, and support them in making diverse choices.

'Choice intermediaries' or 'information guides' have traditionally been an important tool for users to manage the media offering. Traditional examples are offline programme guides and EPGs. These are increasingly accompanied by, or are making way for, newer phenomena such as search engines, social networks and applications, but also personalisation services and 'targeted broadcasting' . . . They help users to manage the abundance of content, define their preferences and set their consumption agenda . . . Ultimately, these choice intermediaries or information regimes might help users to enjoy a more diverse media diet, although it is important to note that the decisions of these gatekeepers follow their own logic and (economic) preferences.[ii] As a result, the diversity of the programming that ultimately reaches users via choice intermediaries can be very different from the kind of diversity that traditional broadcasters deliver, or that media policy makers and academics would like the audience to enjoy.

The fact that the audience responds to abundant choice with restrictive coping strategies highlights the importance of education and media literacy. Some see here the most serious challenge for future diversity policies . . . Such policies would need to stimulate the viewer's appetite and demand for diverse fare. More than that, they would also need to teach people how to find and choose a diverse media diet. This is because, with the increased choice, the process of accessing and consuming media content has become more complex. Exposure to media diversity is thus increasingly also a matter of possessing the rights skills to find the relevant information.[iii]

i B. Stark, 'Elektronische Programführer aud Nutzersicht' in U. Haserbrink, H.-D. Schröder and B. Stark (eds), *Elektronische Programmführung im digitalen Fernsehen, Nutzerstudie und Marktanalyse* (Schriftenreihe der Landesmedienanstalten No 40, Vistas, 2008).

ii N. Helberger, 'Diversity by design' (2011) 1 *Journal of Information Policy* 441.

iii E. Hargittai, 'The digital divide and what to do about it' (2003) 24, www.eszter.com/research/pubs/hargittai-digitaldivide.pdf.

---

[53] Directive 2010/13/EU, (2010) OJ L95/1.
[54] See also the proposals by R. Foster in *News Plurality in a Digital World*, Reuters Institute for the Study of Journalism, Oxford, July 2012.

Questions for consideration
1. What would you include in a media literacy course? 2. What additional information, or 'metadata', would help individuals evaluate news and current affairs content? Consider the Media Standards Trust transparency initiative at: http://mediastandardstrust.org/projects/transparency-initiative/.

9.4 THE EUROPEAN DIMENSION

Convergence poses challenges for regulators at both the domestic and international levels and important studies, guidelines and regulatory measures have been adopted at both the Council of Europe and European Union levels. At Council of Europe level, although amendment to the Transfrontier Television Convention was stalled as a result of EU legal concerns (see further Chapter 5), the Committee of Ministers and Parliamentary Assembly have passed a range of advisory declarations, recommendations and resolutions on matters directly related to convergence, including Internet governance, the openness of the Internet and Net neutrality, the protection of freedom of expression on private websites, online protection of children and human rights issues arising from the operation of search engines and social media.[55] The European Court of Human Rights has drawn on certain of these in underlining the continuing importance of human rights and freedom of expression online. In *Yildirim* v *Turkey*, for example, the Court held that the wholesale blocking of Google sites by Turkey contravened article 10 of the ECHR.[56]

The EU in its development of the law in this area is also guided by fundamental human rights, including freedom of expression set out in article 11 of the Charter of Fundamental Rights of the EU.[57] It has shown a longstanding commitment to the principle of 'technological neutrality' and the AVMSD, discussed in greater depth in Chapter 5, was an initial response to the impact of convergence in the audiovisual sector. The European Commission's most recent *Green Paper: preparing for a fully converged audiovisual world: growth, creation and values* specifically asks whether there is a 'need to adapt the definition of AVMS providers and/or the scope of the AVMSD, in order to make those currently outside subject to part or all of the obligations of the AVMSD' or whether there are other ways to protect core values.[58] The EU has also been active in studying and promoting alternative approaches to state regulation, in particular co- and self-regulation, in supporting

[55] See, for instance, Parliamentary Assembly Resolution 1877 (2012) on *The protection of freedom of expression and information on the Internet and online media*, 25 April 2012; Declaration by the Committee of Ministers on *Internet governance principles*, 21 September 2011; Recommendation CM/Rec(2011)8 of the Committee of Ministers on *The protection and promotion of the universality, integrity and openness of the Internet*, 21 September 2011; Declaration of the Committee of Ministers on *The protection of freedom of expression and freedom of assembly and association with regard to privately operated Internet platforms and online service providers*, 7 December 2011; Recommendation CM/Rec(2012)3 of the Committee of Ministers on *The protection of human rights with regard to search engines*, 4 April 2012; Declaration of the Committee of Ministers *On network neutrality*, 29 September 2010.

[56] App No 311/10, *Yildirim* v *Turkey*, judgment of 18 December 2012. For a general overview see European Court of Human Rights Research Division, Internet: Case Law of the European Court of Human Rights, Council of Europe, 2011, at: http://www.echr.coe.int/NR/rdonlyres/E3B11782-7E42-418B-AC04-A29BEDC0400F/0/RAPPORT_RECHERCHE_internet_Freedom_Expression_EN.pdf.

[57] See, for instance, case C-70/10, *Scarlet Extended SA* v *Société Belge des auteurs, compositeurs et éditeurs SCRL*, 24 November 2011, not yet reported.

[58] European Commission, *Green Paper: Preparing for a Fully Converged Audiovisual World: Growth, Creation and Values*, COM (2013) 231 final, at 12.

the protection of children online, and, as noted above, in developing media literacy policies.[59] EU measures relating to access to conditional access systems, electronic programme guides and Net neutrality, as well as the application of its general competition rules, have helped to maintain an open and contestable media environment.[60]

EU law is thus an essential consideration when exploring regulatory options for the UK. The UK cannot lawfully reduce standards for on-demand audiovisual or broadcast services below those set out in the AVMSD, which could bring into question the House of Lords Select Committee proposal for a lightening of the standards applicable to non-public service broadcasters. Attempts to impose higher standards than those set out in the AVMSD on foreign on-demand audiovisual media services could also be problematic, in that the UK would have to convince the Commission that such measures pursued a legitimate aim and were proportionate.[61] The Committee was thus correct in its understanding that any domestic response to convergence would need to be co-ordinated with developments at the EU level in mind.[62]

9.5 CONCLUSION

Henry Jenkins has argued that convergence should not be seen primarily as a technological process but rather a cultural one, encouraging consumers to 'seek out new information and make connections among dispersed media content'.[63] Through collaboration, individuals can create alternative sources of power that have the potential to influence 'the ways religion, education, law, politics, advertising, and even the military operate'.[64] It is for this reason that the regulatory responses to media convergence – whether we intervene and if so, how we intervene – are of such central importance today and in the future. In the final extract in this chapter, Jonathan Zittrain warns against a complacent belief that the Internet will inevitably continue to be as open and empowering as it has been, at least in most democratic states, over the past 30 years.

Extract 9.5.1
J. Zittrain, *The Future of the Internet and How to Stop It* (Yale University Press, 2008) pp. 245–6

Today's consumer information technology is careening at breakneck pace, and most see no need to begin steering it. Our technologists are complacent because the ongoing success of the generative Net has taken place without central tending – the payoffs of the procrastination principle. Rank-and-file Internet users enjoy its benefits while seeing its operation as a mystery, something they could not hope to effect. They boot their PCs each day and expect them more or less to work, and they access Wikipedia and expect it more or less to be accurate.

But our Net technologies are experiencing the first true shock waves from their generative successes. The state of the hacking arts is advancing. Web sites can be compromised in an

[59] 'For more details see in particular the European Commission audiovisual website at: http://ec.europa.eu/avpolicy/index_en.htm, which provides links to the Safer Internet Programme and media literacy initiatives.

[60] See s 8.5(b) and 9.2(d).

[61] Article 3(4), Directive 2010/13/EU, (2010) OJ L95/1.

[62] House of Lords Select Committee on Communications, *Media Convergence*, 27 March 2013, HL Paper 154, paras 89–91.

[63] H. Jenkins, *Convergence Culture. Where Old and New Media Collide* (New York University Press, New York, 2006), at 3.

[64] H. Jenkins, *Convergence Culture. Where Old and New Media Collide* (New York University Press, New York, 2006), at 4.

instant, and many visitors will then come away with an infected PC simply for having surfed there. Without a new cadre of good hackers unafraid to take ownership of the challenges posed by their malicious siblings and create the tools needed to help non-hackers keep the Net on a constructive trajectory, the most direct solutions will be lockdown that cuts short the Net experiment, deprives us of its fruits, and facilitates a form of governmental control that upends a balance between citizens and sovereign . . .

The deciding factor in whether our current infrastructure can endure will be the sum of the perceptions and actions of its users. There are roles for traditional state sovereigns, pan-state organizations, and formal multistakeholder regimes to play. They can help reinforce the conditions necessary for generative blooming, and they can also step in – with all the confusion and difficulty that notoriously attends regulation of a generative space – when mere generosity of spirit among people of goodwill cannot resolve a conflict. But such generosity of spirit is a society's powerful first line of moderation.

Our fortuitous starting point is a generative device in tens of millions of hands on a neutral Net. To maintain it, the users of those devices must experience the Net as something with which they identify and to which they belong. We must use the generativity of the Net to engage a constituency that will protect and nurture it. That constituency may be drawn from the ranks of a new generation able to see that technology is not simply a video game designed by someone else, and that content is not simply what is provided through a TiVo or iPhone.

Source: Extract from The Future of the Internet and How to Stop It by Jonathan Zittrain reprinted by permission of Peters Fraser & Dunlop (www.petersfraserdunlop.com) on behalf of Jonathan Zittrain.

Selected further reading

On the 'generative potential' of the Internet and its limitations

Y. Benkler, *The Wealth of Networks: How Social Production Transforms Markets and Freedom* (Yale University Press, New, 2006).

H. Jenkins, *Convergence Culture. Where Old and New Media Collide* (New York University Press, 2006).

D. Murthy, *Twitter. Social Communication in the Twitter Age* (Polity, Cambridge, 2013).

C.R. Sunstein, *Republic.com 2.0* (Princeton University Press, Princeton, 2007).

J. Zittrain, *The Future of the Internet and How to Stop It* (Yale University Press, 2008).

On new power relations

M. Castells, *Communication Power* (Oxford, 2009).

R. Foster, *News Plurality in a Digital World* (Reuters Institute for the Study of Journalism, Oxford, July 2012).

C.T. Marsden, *Net Neutrality, Towards a Co-Regulatory Solution* (Bloomsbury Academic, 2010).

N. van Eijk, 'Search engines, the new bottleneck for content access' in B. Preissel, J. Haucap and P. Curwen (eds), *Telecommunication Markets*: *Drivers and Impediments* (Springer Physica-Verlag HD, 2009), 141–56.

On evolving economic models and their impact on news production

S. Allan, *Online News* (Open University Press, 2006).

C. Anderson, *The Long Tail. How Endless Choice is Creating Unlimited Demand* (Random House Business Books, London, 2006).

N. Fenton (ed.), *New Media, Old News* (Sage, 2010).

A. Keen, *The Cult of the Amateur. How Today's Internet is Killing our Culture and Assaulting our Economy* (Nicolas Brearley Publishing, London, 2007).

R.K. Neilsen, *Ten Years That Shook the Media World. Big Questions and Big Trends in International Media Developments*, Reuters Institute for the Study of Journalism, October 2012.

Reuters Institute for the Study of Journalism, *Digital News Report 2012*, Oxford, July 2012.

On regulatory techniques

J. Black, 'Decentring regulation: understanding the role of regulation and self-regulation in a "post-regulatory" world' (2001) 54 *Current Legal Problems* 103.

R. Collins, 'Internet governance in the UK' (2006) 28/3 *Media, Culture and Society* 337–58.

L. Fielden, *Regulating for Trust in Journalism. Standards Regulation in the Age of Blended Media* (Reuters Institute for the Study of Journalism, Oxford, 2011).

L. Lessig, *Code and Other Laws of Cyberspace* (Basic Books, 1999).

L. Lessig, *Code Version 2.0* (Basic Books, 2006).

P. Lunt and S. Livingstone, *Media Regulation, Governance and the Interests of Citizens and Consumers* (Sage, 2012).

C. Marsden, *Internet Co-regulation. European Law, Regulatory Governance and Legitimacy in Cyberspace* (Cambridge, 2011).

A. Murray, *Information Technology Law. The Law and Society* (Oxford University Press, 2010), chapter 4.

A. Murray and C. Scott, 'Controlling the new media: hybrid responses to new forms of power' (2002) 65 *Modern Law Review* 491–516.

S. Nikoltchev (ed.), *Co-Regulation of the Media in Europe* (European Audiovisual Observatory, 2003).

D. Tambini, D. Leonardi and C. Marsden, *Codifying Cyberspace. Communications Self-Regulation in the Age of Internet Convergence* (Routledge, Abingdon, 2008).

10 Defamation

10.1 INTRODUCTION

Perhaps more than any other area of the law, the protection of reputation through the tort of defamation has a significant impact on the day-to-day activities of the media. Indeed, even the *threat* of potential liability has been shown to have a 'chilling-effect' on the media's decision-making about what to publish.[1] The modern law of defamation has sought to balance the right to reputation and the right to freedom of speech through a complex array of defamation defences (discussed in Section 10.4). An enduring criticism of the tort, however, is that it favours the protection of reputation over the right to freedom of speech. Further, while it is true that greater weight is now given to freedom of speech as a result of the Human Rights Act 1998 and the influence of article 10(1) of the European Convention on the development of the common law of defamation, the threat of civil liability under the tort continues to place considerable restrictions on media freedom.[2]

A number of features of the law of defamation (and litigation) mean that it is of particular concern to media organisations. First, it is relatively easy for a claimant to establish the requirements of the tort: as discussed in Section 10.3, the tort of defamation is established as soon as the defendant publishes defamatory allegations concerning the claimant. This formulation means that a claimant is not required to prove that the published allegations are false (this is presumed). Rather, to avoid liability, the burden rests on the publisher either to prove that the allegations are true (known as 'justification') or to establish one of the other alternative defences (see Section 10.4). This disparity in evidentiary burdens has meant that the tort is often seen as being 'claimant-friendly' or as having a bias in favour of protecting reputation over freedom of expression. Second, media organisations are particularly troubled by the risk that the jury (or judge, if the matter is heard without a jury) will award a successful claimant substantial damages. Jury decisions are notoriously unpredictable;[3] it may be impossible to foresee whether it will believe the plaintiff or the press (or other defendant). While the use of juries in defamation trials has substantially declined in recent years, it nevertheless remains true that the quantum of damages for defamation generally remains high. Third is the presumption of damage. Defamation is actionable per se, which means that the claimant does not have to prove any actual harm or loss. Rather, it is presumed that injury will result from the publication of words defamatory of the claimant. Fourth, it is often said that defamation is a 'strict liability tort' – in other words, a defendant need not intend for the material to be defamatory in order to be liable, and it is even immaterial whether the defendant was aware that it referred to the claimant.[4] Liability, instead, turns simply on the defendant's responsibility for the publication of the defamatory matter.

Over the last few years there has been an intense scrutiny of the operation of libel law in the UK. At least initially, this was driven by the national press and by two influential

---

[1] See Eric Barendt *et al.*, *Libel and the Media: The Chilling Effect* (Oxford University Press, 1997).
[2] Prosecutions for criminal libel have been abolished: see Coroners and Justice Act 2009, cl 29, s 73.
[3] Clause 11 of the Defamation Bill proposes to introduce a presumption of trial without jury in defamation cases.
[4] See *Slim v Daily Telegraph Ltd* [1968] 2 QB 157, 172 (per Diplock LJ).

lobby groups, Index on Censorship and English PEN, who managed to spearhead an effective campaign for libel reform, arguing that the existing legal regime placed a disproportionate and anti-democratic burden on freedom of speech. The subject of libel reform has also been considered in a series of recent official inquiries and consultations.[5] The debate has centred around, to a greater or lesser degree, three perceived 'problems' with English libel law: the cause of action (in particular, the burden of proof) as well as complex and inadequate defences; the claimed prevalence of so-called 'libel tourism' (where supposedly undeserving foreign claimants sue foreign defendants under domestic law in the domestic courts); and, lastly, procedure and costs issues involved in libel litigation. Reform advocates have also taken advantage of a number of high profile cases as evidence of the 'chilling effect' of libel law on the media's freedom to publish,[6] including *BCA* v *Singh*[7] (where science writer, Simon Singh, was sued by the British Chiropractic Association for questioning the effectiveness of chiropractic techniques) and *Mahfouz* v *Ehrenfeld*[8] (where Sheikh Khalid bin Mahfouz obtained summary judgment against Rachel Ehrenfeld over the publication of her book, 23 copies of which were published in the UK and which contained allegations that Mahfouz was funding terrorism). In May 2010, as part of the Coalition Agreement, the government made a commitment to libel reform. At around the same time, Lord Lester introduced a Bill into the House of Lords to reform some of the perceived substantive problems with libel law. This bill was superseded by the coalition government's own Defamation Bill, published in draft form in March 2011. Following public consultation[9] and consideration by the Joint Committee on the Draft Defamation Bill,[10] a revised Bill was introduced into the House of Commons on 10 May 2012. At the time of writing, the Bill had reached its third reading in the House of Commons and was set to enter the Committee stage in the House of Lords.[11]

The amendments proposed by the Defamation Bill are, in many respects, moderate. In the name of clarity and certainty, some of the clauses simply seek to codify the existing common law – see clause 2 (truth) and clause 4 (responsible publication on matter of public interest). Clause 1 (serious harm threshold) might also be relegated to this category. It has been argued that such codification, at least in the short term, could have the effect of promoting expensive litigation to resolve lingering uncertainty as to whether, and to what extent, the new law departs from existing common law standards. According to Mullis and Scott, for example, '[i]n the absence of any substantive change, the risks of codification arguably outweigh prospective gains.'[12] Other clauses, however, are likely to have greater

---

[5] See, e.g., Media and Sport Committee, *Press Standards, Privacy and Libel: Second Report of Session 2009–2010* (HC 2009–10, 362-I); Ministry of Justice, *Controlling Costs in Defamation Proceedings* (CP4/09, 24 February 2009); Ministry of Justice, *Controlling Costs in Defamation Proceedings: Reducing Conditional Fee Agreement Success Fees* (CP1/2010, 19 January 2010); Ministry of Justice, *Defamation and the Internet: The Multiple Publication Rule* (CP20/09, 16 September 2009); Ministry of Justice, *Report of the Libel Working Group* (23 March 2010); Ministry of Justice, *Draft Defamation Bill: Consultation* (Cm 8020, 2011); Joint Committee on the Draft Defamation Bill, *First Report – Draft Defamation Bill* (2011–2012, HL 203, HC 930-I).

[6] English PEN and Index on Censorship, *Free Speech is Not for Sale* (2009). Available at http://www.libelreform.org/reports/LibelDoc_LowRes.pdf.

[7] *British Chiropractic Association* v *Singh* [2011] 1 WLR 133; *British Chiropractic Association* v *Singh* [2009] EWHC 1101 (QB).

[8] [2005] EWHC 1156 (QB).

[9] Ministry of Justice, *Draft Defamation Bill: Consultation* (Cm 8020, 2011).

[10] Joint Committee on the Draft Defamation Bill, *First Report – Draft Defamation Bill* (2011–12, HL 203, HC 930-I).

[11] The Defamation Act 2013 (c.26) was passed on 25 April 2013 with some changes that are not reflected in this chapter.

[12] Alastair Mullis and Andrew Scott, 'Worth the Candle? The Government's Draft Defamation Bill' (2011) 3(1) *Journal of Media Law* 1, 2.

substantive effect – see clause 3 (honest opinion), clause 7 (absolute and qualified privilege), and clause 8 (single publication rule), amongst others. While some of the changes proposed in the Bill are sensible and should be encouraged, it has been suggested that others appear to miss the mark by paying too little attention to the right to reputation, now protected as a free-standing right under article 8 (right to private life) of the European Convention (see section 2).[13] Further consideration is given to each of the proposed clauses of the Bill at appropriate places throughout this chapter. It should also be noted, however, that while the Bill purports to deal with the effect of substantive libel law on freedom of speech, an equally important (if not greater) cause of libel law's chilling effect arises not from problems with substantive law but from issues of procedure and costs.[14]

At the outset of this chapter it is important to point out that the distinction between libel and slander is of no relevance to the media. It is a libel to publish defamatory allegations in a *permanent* form; a verbal publication amounts to slander. Under the Defamation Act 1952, however, broadcast statements are to be treated as publication in permanent form.[15] Defamation actions against the media are, therefore, for libel, rather than for slander; as a consequence, the terms 'defamation' and 'libel' are used interchangeably in this chapter.

10.2 THE RIGHT TO REPUTATION AND FREEDOM OF EXPRESSION

The relationship between the right to reputation and the right to freedom of expression under the jurisprudence of the European Court of Human Rights (ECtHR) has advanced dramatically in recent years.[16] Under article 10, the right to freedom of expression is subject to restrictions necessary in a democratic society for 'the protection of the reputation and rights of others', as set out in article 10(2). The overall approach is that freedom of expression is the starting point and any restrictions must be narrowly construed. Prior to the 1980s, however, the Court did not appear to recognise the full impact of criminal and civil libel laws on freedom of expression, despite the special significance and broad scope that the Court had given to that fundamental right in its decisions.[17] Even where the

---

[13] See, e.g., Alastair Mullis and Andrew Scott, 'Reframing Libel: Taking (All) Rights Serious and Where it Leads' (2011) 63(1) *Northern Ireland Legal Quarterly* 3; Gavin Phillipson, 'The "global pariah", the Defamation Bill and the Human Rights Act' (2012) 63(1) *Northern Ireland Legal Quarterly* 149.

[14] It is extremely expensive to bring and defend libel claims. Much of the 'chilling effect' on media speech is said to arise from claimant lawyers acting under conditional fee agreements (CFAs), whereby a 'success' fee of up to 100 per cent is charged to the losing side. Losing defendants also face the prospect of having to pay a claimant's 'after-the-event' (ATE) insurance premiums (this insurance protects an unsuccessful claimant from having to pay the defendant's costs in defending an action). The ECtHR has found that, at least when used by wealthy claimants, the recovery of success fees under CFAs constitutes a disproportionate interference with article 10 (freedom of expression): see *MGN Ltd v United Kingdom* (2011) 53 EHRR 5. Under the Legal Aid, Sentencing and Punishing of Offenders Act 2012, which implements broader civil procedure reforms recommended by Lord Justice Jackson and will come into force in April 2013, success fees and ATE insurance premiums will cease to be recoverable inter-parties. However, the government announced on 12 December 2012 that the reforms will not come into force for defamation and privacy claims until a new regime of costs protection (protection against paying an opponent's costs) is introduced for such proceedings. This follows recommendations made by Lord Justice Leveson in his *Inquiry into the Culture, Practices and Ethics of the Press* (HC 780-I, November 2012).

[15] Section 1. In *Youssoupoff* (Extract 10.3.5) two members of the Court of Appeal held that spoken words in a film amounted to libel.

[16] For comprehensive coverage of the article 10 jurisprudence, see Helen Fenwick and Gavin Phillipson, *Media Freedom under the Human Rights Act* (Oxford University Press, 2006) 1054–70.

[17] See, e.g., *Handyside v United Kingdom* (1976) 1 EHRR 737.

impact was acknowledged, the Court appeared reluctant at first to find that national libel laws were in breach of article 10.[18]

Beginning with the important case of *Lingens v Austria*[19] in the mid-1980s, however, the Court's approach changed quite dramatically; the Court became much more willing to find that national defamation laws offended article 10. A number of general principles can be deduced from the Court's jurisprudence in determining whether the restrictions imposed by the law of defamation are necessary 'for the protection of the reputation or rights of others'. First, the Court has regard to the important role of the media and the press as a 'public watchdog'. It is recognised that, while the media must not 'overstep the bounds set . . . for the "protection of the reputation of others", it is nevertheless incumbent on it to impart information and ideas on political issues just as on those in other areas of public interest'.[20] In fulfilling its function, the media will also be permitted 'recourse to a degree of exaggeration, or even provocation'.[21]

Second, the subject-matter of the speech will be a significant factor. Greater protection is given to political and public interest speech over, for example, artistic or commercial speech. This means that a state's margin of appreciation in imposing limitations on such speech for the protection of reputation will be correspondingly narrow. It is important to note that, while the Court has not been willing to draw a *per se* distinction between strictly 'political speech' and broader 'public interest' speech in assessing the latitude of permissible restrictions,[22] it has held that 'the limits of acceptable criticism are wider as regards a politician . . . than regards an individual'.[23] This is not to suggest that politicians do not have the right to protect their reputations;[24] rather, the greater latitude given to the free discussion of politicians arises from the particular importance that the Convention attaches to the freedom of political debate in a democracy.[25] Nevertheless, restrictions imposed by libel law on broader public interest speech are also subject to particularly close scrutiny.[26]

Third, particular latitude is given to the making of value judgements. This is because '[t]he existence of facts can be demonstrated, whereas the truth of value-judgements is not susceptible of proof'.[27] Value judgements, however, will be considered excessive where they are not supported by 'a sufficient actual basis'.[28]

---

[18] The 'margin of appreciation', or latitude, given to national laws to restrict defamatory speech has been said to be 'extraordinarily wide': see Ian Loveland, *Political Libels: A Comparative Study* (Hart Publishing, 2000) 107; see also Helen Fenwick and Gavin Phillipson, *Media Freedom Under the Human Rights Act* (Oxford University Press, 2006) 1055.

[19] (1986) 8 EHRR 407.

[20] See, e.g., *Bladet Tromsø v Norway* (2000) 29 EHRR 125, 59.

[21] *De Haes and Gijsels v Belgium* (1997) 25 EHRR 1, 46; *Oberschlick v Austria* (1995) 19 EHRR 389, 38.

[22] See, e.g., *Thorgeirson v Iceland* (1992) 14 EHRR 843, 64.

[23] *Lingens v Austria* (1986) 8 EHRR 407, 42.

[24] Ibid.

[25] See ibid., 42 ('freedom of political debate is at the very core of the concept of a democratic society which prevails throughout the Convention'); Barendt, 223. For other cases where speech critical of the conduct of politicians has received robust protection, see: *Oberschlick v Austria (No 1)* (1995) 19 EHRR 389; *Oberschlick v Austria (No 2)* (1998) 25 EHRR 357; *Castells v Spain* (1992) 14 EHRR 445; *Schwabe v Austria* (European Court of Human Rights, Application No 13704/88, 28 August 1992).

[26] See, e.g., *De Haes and Gijsels v Belgium* (1997) 25 EHRR 1 (allegations, made against judges, concerning child welfare and the administration of justice); *Thoma v Luxembourg* (2003) 36 EHRR 21 (corruption by government officials); *Thorgeirson v Iceland* (1992) 14 EHRR 843 (allegations of police violence); *Bladet Tromsø v Norway* (2000) 29 EHRR 125 (allegations that seal hunters breached regulations and engaged in animal cruelty); *Bergens Tidende v Norway* (2001) 31 EHRR 16 (allegation regarding a plastic surgeon).

[27] *Lingens v Austria* (1986) 8 EHRR 407, 46; *Pedersen and Badsgaard v Denmark* (2006) 42 EHRR 24, 76.

[28] See, e.g., *Lindon, Otchakovsky-Laurens and July v France* (2008) 46 EHRR 35, 55; *Pedersen and Badsgaard v Denmark* (2006) 42 EHRR 24, 76; *De Haes and Gijsels v Belgium* (1997) 25 EHRR 1, 47.

Fourth, where the media cannot prove the truth of factual allegations, the Court will have regard to standards of journalistic conduct. Thus, in line with the 'duties and responsibilities' inherent in the exercise of freedom of speech under article 10, the Court will consider whether the journalist was 'acting in good faith in order to provide accurate and reliable information in accordance with the ethics of journalism',[29] with a particular emphasis on the steps taken to verify factual allegations. Any such verification must be 'proportionate to the nature and degree' of the factual allegations published.[30] In *Pedersen and Badsgaard* v *Denmark*,[31] for example, it was not a breach of article 10 for the domestic courts to uphold a libel action against two television journalists who alleged that the Chief Superintendent had suppressed important evidence in a murder case. This had, according to the programme that was broadcast, resulted in a miscarriage of justice. The Court found that, unlike politicians, civil servants do not 'knowingly lay themselves open to close scrutiny';[32] thus, although subject to wide limits of acceptable criticism, the Chief Superintendent was not on 'an equal footing with politicians when it came to public discussion of his actions'.[33] Importantly, however, there was no breach of article 10 because the producers of the programme had fallen short of acceptable journalistic standards by failing to take adequate steps to verify the factual basis upon which the allegations were based.[34] In *De Haes and Gijsels* v *Belgium*, on the other hand, it was found to be a breach of article 10 to impose criminal libel sanctions in relation to the publication of newspaper articles that alleged that judges had granted custody to a father suspected of abusing his children and that they were influenced in their decision because he was a member of the legal profession. The articles, according to the Court, addressed important matters of public concern; moreover, the information published 'was based on thorough research into the allegations . . . and on the opinions of several experts'.[35] Thus, the applicants in the case could not be accused of 'having failed in their professional obligations by publishing what they had learned about the case'.[36]

Only in special circumstances, depending on the nature and degree of the defamation and the apparent reliability of the journalist's sources, will the media be relieved of the obligation to verify the factual allegations it publishes.[37] One such case is *Bladet Tromsø* v *Norway*,[38] where the Court found that holding a newspaper liable for failing to verify allegations contained in an unpublished government report regarding inhumane methods used by seal hunters was a breach of article 10. Taking into account all of the circumstances of the case, including the genuine public interest in the controversy over seal hunting and the reputational interests of the seal hunters, the Court found that 'the paper could reasonably rely on the official . . . report, without being required to carry out its own research into the accuracy of the facts reported'.[39] A similar result was reached in *Thoma* v *Luxembourg*.[40] In that case, the applicant read out on a national radio station a quotation

[29] *Bladet Tromsø* v *Norway* (2000) 29 EHRR 125, 65. See also, *Pedersen and Badsgaard* v *Denmark* (2006) 42 EHRR 24, 78.
[30] *Pedersen and Badsgaard* v *Denmark* (2006) 42 EHRR 24, 78.
[31] Ibid.
[32] Ibid., 66.
[33] Ibid.
[34] Ibid., 82.
[35] *De Haes and Gijsels* v *Belgium* (1997) 25 EHRR 1, 39.
[36] *De Haes and Gijsels* v *Belgium* (1997) 25 EHRR 1, 39.
[37] *Bladet Tromsø* v *Norway* (2000) 29 EHRR 125, 66; *Pedersen and Badsgaard* v *Denmark* (2006) 42 EHRR 24, 78.
[38] (2000) 29 EHRR 125.
[39] Ibid., 72.
[40] (2003) 36 EHRR 21.

taken from an article originally published in *Tageblatt*, a Luxembourg daily newspaper, which alleged that members of the Forestry Commission were corrupt. The broadcaster did not adopt or endorse the allegations. Fifty-four forest wardens and nine forestry engineers subsequently brought defamation actions against the applicant, claiming that the broadcaster had quoted the allegations 'without in any way toning them down, correcting them or commenting on them "the slightest bit critically"'.[41] Each claim was upheld by the Luxembourg domestic courts, with the Court of Cassation finding liability on the basis that 'the applicant had not formally distanced himself from the quoted text and was [therefore] deemed to have adopted the allegation it contained'.[42] The ECtHR found this a disproportionate interference with article 10. In particular, it held that the discussion was one of genuine public interest and that a 'general requirement for journalists systematically and formally to distance themselves from the content of a quotation that might insult or provoke others or damage their reputation was not reconcilable with the press's role of providing information on current events, opinions and ideas'.[43] Furthermore, it was held that the broadcaster had clearly indicated when he was beginning and ending a quote, and had also asked a third party, on air, whether he thought the quoted allegations were true.[44] The upshot of this case is that, depending on all the circumstances, liability for reporting allegations made by another person in the context of a discussion on a matter of public interest – otherwise known as reportage – may not be a proportionate interference with article 10. Reportage, in the context of domestic law, is discussed further in Chapter 10, Section 10.4(c)(v).

Under the article 10 jurisprudence just discussed, the right to reputation is treated as a narrowly construed exception to the right to freedom of expression; in other words, there is no question of balancing two competing Convention rights. This has now changed, however, with the Court's recognition, first noted in *Radio France* v *France*,[45] that reputation is a stand-alone interest protected under article 8 of the Convention as an aspect of the right to private life.[46] A consequence of this development is that the right to reputation is not – at least in certain circumstances – to be treated as a mere exception to freedom of speech; rather, the Convention now requires that a fair balance be struck between reputation and freedom of speech as *equally competing interests*.[47] A further consequence, in light of the positive obligation on the state to provide remedies for breaches of the privacy between private individuals,[48] is that defamation claimants who are unsuccessful in the domestic courts can now apply to the ECtHR to complain that their article 8 rights have been breached.[49] (Previous to this, all applications to the ECtHR arising from domestic defamation decisions were brought by unsuccessful defamation *defendants* who claimed that the decisions of the national courts were in violation of article 10.)

---

[41] *Thoma* v *Luxembourg* (2003) 36 EHRR 21, 17.

[42] Ibid., 50.

[43] Ibid., 64.

[44] Ibid.

[45] (2005) 40 EHRR 29, 31; see also *Chauvy* v *France* (2005) 41 EHRR 29, 70; *Cumpana and Mazare* v *Romania* (2005) 41 EHRR 14, 91.

[46] This is despite the fact that there was a deliberate decision not to explicitly include reputation within the terms of art 8: see Geoffrey Robertson and Andrew Nicol, *Media Law* (Penguin Books, 5th edn, 2008) 66–8.

[47] *Chauvy* v *France* (2005) 41 EHRR 29, 70; *Lindon* v *France* (2008) 46 EHRR 35 (concurring opinion of Judge Loucaides).

[48] See Chapter 11, Section 11.3.

[49] The first such case under art 8, albeit unsuccessful, was *White* v *Sweden* (2008) 46 EHRR 3.

Pfeifer v *Austria*[50] is one such case. Pfeifer, the applicant, had many years earlier been critical of the neo-Nazi political stance of a third party, P, who later committed suicide. A letter published in *Zur Zeit*, a right-wing magazine, repeated allegations made in an earlier article published in the same magazine that Pfeifer's criticisms of P had sparked a manhunt that led P to take his own life. Pfeifer brought defamation proceedings against the magazine's publishing company. The Vienna Court of Appeal found in favour of the magazine on the basis that the 'impugned letter contained a value judgment which relied on a sufficient factual basis'.[51] The value judgement was not 'excessive', even though the comment proceeded from 'a strongly ideological point of view'.[52] The ECtHR upheld Pfeifer's application on the basis that the approach of the Austrian courts violated Pfeifer's rights under article 8 of the Convention. The Court reiterated that a person's right to reputation is 'encompassed by article 8 as being part of the right to respect for private life' and further explained that:

> a person's reputation, even if that person is criticised in the context of a public debate, forms part of his or her personal identity and psychological integrity and therefore also falls within the scope of his or her 'private life'.[53]

The question, according to the Court, is to determine whether a 'fair balance' has been achieved between the applicant's article 8 right to the protection of reputation and the right of the press to freedom of expression under article 10.[54] Despite recognising that there is 'little scope' under article 10(2) to limit political speech or debate on questions of public interest, it was held that the Austrian courts had not protected the applicant against 'excessive criticism'.[55] In particular, the Court was not satisfied with the assessment that the statements at issue were value judgements.[56]

More recent cases, however, have indicated that article 8 does not provide protection for reputation in all circumstances. Thus, in *Karakó* v *Hungary*,[57] the Court reiterated that the protection of private life in article 8 is focused on ensuring personal integrity[58] and that this is unrelated to the protection of reputation:

> Concerning the question whether or not the notion of 'private life' should be extended to include reputation as well, the Court notes that the references to personal integrity ... reflect a clear distinction ... between personal integrity and reputation, the two being protected in different legal ways. In the legislation of several Member States, reputation has traditionally been protected by the law of defamation as a matter related primarily to financial interests or social status.

> For the Court, personal integrity rights falling within the ambit of art 8 are unrelated to the external evaluation of the individual, whereas in matters of reputation, that evaluation is decisive: one may lose the esteem of society – perhaps rightly so – but not one's integrity, which remains inalienable. In the Court's case law, reputation has only been deemed to be an independent right sporadically ... and mostly when the factual allegations were of such a seriously offensive nature that their publication had an inevitable direct effect on the applicant's private life.[59]

---

[50] (2009) 48 EHRR 8.
[51] Ibid., 20.
[52] Ibid.
[53] Ibid., 35.
[54] Ibid., 38.
[55] Ibid., 44.
[56] Ibid., 47–8.
[57] (2011) 52 EHRR 36.
[58] Ibid., 20.
[59] Ibid., 22–3.

The application was brought by a politician who was criticised by an opponent of not acting in the interests of his electorate. The Court rejected that there had been a violation of article 8 when the domestic courts refused to entertain that the opponent had committed criminal libel. The publication in question did not, according to the Court, constitute 'a serious interference' with the private life of the application so as to 'undermine his personal integrity';[60] rather, it was the 'applicant's reputation alone which was at stake'.[61] As article 8 was not engaged, the Court turned to consider whether the protection of the applicant's reputation *would have* been a legitimate exception to freedom of expression under article 10(2). It found that, in the circumstances, any such restriction would have been disproportionate.[62] Thus, the approach of the domestic courts was consistent with article 10. In line with *Karakó*, subsequent cases – including the Grand Chamber in *Axel Springer AG* v *Germany* – have confirmed that an 'attack on a person's reputation must attain a certain level of seriousness and in a manner causing prejudice to personal enjoyment of the right to respect for private life'[63] before article 8 is implicated. In such circumstances, the analysis will involve striking a fair balance between articles 8 and 10. However, where reputation alone is concerned, the analysis will focus on reputation as a strictly construed exception to freedom of expression under article 10(2).

The recognition of reputation as a right protected under article 8 (albeit much less extensively than first thought) may require a recalibration of England's domestic law to take greater account of reputational interests, as pointed out by Tugendhat J in *Terry* v *Persons Unknown*.[64] It may warrant, for example, reconsideration of the long-standing rule in *Bonnard* v *Perryman*,[65] which currently imposes an almost insurmountable hurdle in obtaining interim injunctions in defamation cases (see Section 10.5(a)); or, as specifically raised by Tugendhat J in *Terry*, those seeking to rely on the truth defence (justification) – at common law a complete defence based on 'truth alone' – may be required to establish that the publication of the true but damaging material was in the public interest.[66] One area where the article 8 protection of reputation has already had an influence on domestic jurisprudence is in the area of the *Reynolds* public interest defence (see Section 10.4(c)(iv)). It can no longer be the case, as suggested by Lord Nicholls when he originally formulated the defence, that any 'lingering doubts should be resolved in favour of publication';[67] nor can any priority be given to freedom of expression in the application of the '*Reynolds* factors'. Rather, the Court of Appeal in *Flood* v *Times Newspapers Ltd* has confirmed that this understanding of *Reynolds* would be contrary to the balancing exercise required under the Convention: 'articles 8 and 10 have equal weight'.[68] It is also important to bear in mind that any libel reform proposals to make the law more free speech 'friendly', including the government's Defamation Bill currently before Parliament, will have to equally comply with article 8.

---

[60] Ibid., 23.
[61] Ibid.
[62] Ibid., 24–8.
[63] *Axel Springer AG* v *Germany* (2012) 55 EHRR 6, 83; *A* v *Norway* (European Court of Human Rights, Application No 28070/06, 9 April 2009).
[64] *Terry* v *Persons Unknown* [2010] EWHC 119 (QB), 79–80 (per Mr Justice Tugendhat).
[65] [1891] 2 Ch 269.
[66] *Terry* v *Persons Unknown* [2010] EWHC 119 (QB) 80.
[67] *Reynolds* v *Times Newspapers Ltd* [2001] 2 AC 127, 205.
[68] *Flood* v *Times Newspapers Ltd* [2011] 1 WLR 153, 20, where the Court of Appeal agreed with Tugendhat J at trial (*Flood* v *Times Newspapers Ltd* [2009] EWHC 2375 (QB) that Lord Nicholls' statement that '[a]ny lingering doubts should be resolved in favour of publication' can no longer stand as good law: at 145–6.

> ### Questions for discussion
> 1. Do you agree that reputation should be protected under article 8?
> 2. What is the meaning given to the concept of 'reputation' by the Court in *Karakó*?
> 3. Is it satisfactory that there are some circumstances where reputation is protected under article 8 and others where it is not? Is the seriousness threshold set out in *Karakó* satisfactory?

10.3 LIABILITY FOR DEFAMATION

For a defendant to be liable for defamation, they must have published to a third party matter which is defamatory of the claimant. It is often said, therefore, that the tort has three basic 'elements' that must be satisfied:

1. Defamatory meaning;
2. Identification of the claimant; and
3. Publication.

It is not necessary that defamatory matter be published in the form of written or spoken words. Defamatory meaning, for example, can be conveyed through photographs and pictures, human gestures and facial expressions, cartoons, as well as through artistic works such as sculpture and statue.[69] Even the act of burning an effigy of a person has been held to have the capacity to convey defamatory meaning.[70]

(a) Defamatory meaning

(i) Meaning: general principles

The law draws a distinction between defamatory allegations, for which the claimant may sue in libel, and remarks that, however offensive or abusive, are not actionable. In principle, a claimant should be able to bring an action only for those allegations which infringe the right to reputation; that is, the right each individual enjoys to protect the esteem in which he is held in the community.[71] The media would be placed in an intolerable position if an action could be brought in respect of any irritating newspaper article or item on radio or television.

In order to determine whether a publication has defamatory meaning in the required sense, the judge and the jury have distinct roles.[72] The judge is required to answer two question of law: (1) whether the matter is capable of conveying the meaning complained of by the claimant and, if so, (2) whether such meaning is capable of being defamatory. The purpose of this exercise is to act as a 'judicial filter'[73] by ruling out meanings being put to the jury which 'can only emerge as the product of some strained, or forced, or

---

[69] For a useful summary of the different forms that defamatory matter can take see Gatley 3.1–3.5.
[70] *Eyre* v *Garlick* (1878) 42 JP 68.
[71] For a discussion of why the law protects the right to reputation, see Robert C. Post, 'The Social Foundations of Defamation Law: Reputation and the Constitution' (1986) 74 *California Law Review* 691. See also Lawrence McNamara, *Reputation and Defamation* (Oxford University Press, 2007); David Rolph, *Reputation, Celebrity and Defamation Law* (Ashgate, 2008).
[72] *Jones* v *Skelton* [1963] 3 All ER 952, 958 (per Lord Morris).
[73] *John Fairfax Publications Pty Ltd* v *Rivkin* (2003) 201 ALR 77, 96 (per Kirby J). On the role of the judge in this regard, see also *Mapp* v *News Group Newspapers Ltd* [1998] QB 520 (CA); *Lewis* v *Daily Telegraph* [1964] AC 234, 271 (per Lord Hodson).

utterly unreasonable interpretation'.[74] The task is approached by the judge as a matter of impression, with the governing test being one of reasonableness:[75] any meaning which a jury could not reasonably find established must be struck out.

If these questions are answered in the affirmative by the judge and the matter is held to be reasonably capable of conveying the defamatory imputations complained of by the claimant, the jury is required to answer two questions of fact: (1) whether the matter *in fact* gives rise to the imputations complained of and, if so, (2) whether such imputations *in fact* convey a defamatory meaning. Where the matter is reasonably capable of bearing several meanings – for example, one defamatory and one not – it is up to the jury to determine which of the two meanings is the 'correct' meaning.[76] In other words, the jury must arrive at a single meaning for the purposes of defamation law, even if the reality is that the meaning of the matter might reasonably differ between recipients. This is known as the 'single meaning rule'[77] and, as pointed out by Lord Diplock, 'is what makes the meaning ascribed to words for the purposes of the tort of libel so artificial.'[78]

Both questions of capacity (law) and both questions of fact are determined by reference to how the ordinary, reasonable reader/listener/viewer would understand the matter. Meaning is therefore determined according to an objective rather than a subjective standard. This means that it does not matter what the publisher intended the publication to mean;[79] nor does it matter what meaning the actual recipients derived from the publication.[80]

The attributes of the ordinary, reasonable reader have been usefully summarised by Hunt J in *Farquhar* v *Bottom* (citations omitted):

> I must proceed upon the basis that the ordinary, reasonable reader is a person of fair, average intelligence; who is neither perverse; nor morbid or suspicious of mind; nor avid for scandal . . . This ordinary reasonable reader does not, we are told, live in an ivory tower. He can, and does, read between the lines, in the light of his general knowledge and experience of worldly affairs. It is important to bear in mind that the ordinary reasonable reader is a layman, not a lawyer, and that his capacity for implication is much greater than that of the lawyer.[81]

In applying the standard of the ordinary, reasonable reader, they will be taken to have read the publication in context and as a whole. This is because a comment which would appear to mean one thing in isolation can take on an entirely different meaning when encountered in context.

The medium of publication will also be relevant to determining meaning. Whereas the ordinary, reasonable reader of a book or newspaper, for example, will have the opportunity to closely analyse the text, the viewer of a television broadcast will often only have a limited opportunity to scrutinise the language used with any degree of precision.[82] This means that for publications which are considered ephemeral, such as television and radio programmes, the assessment as to meaning will often be much more a matter of overall

---

[74] *Jones* v *Skelton* [1963] 3 All ER 952, 958 (per Lord Morris).
[75] *Jeynes* v *News Magazine Ltd* [2008] EWCA Civ 130, 14 (per Sir Anthony Clarke MR).
[76] See *Slim* v *Daily Telegraph Ltd* [1968] 2 QB 157; *Charleston* v *News Group Newspapers Ltd* [1995] 2 AC 65.
[77] For a recent discussion of the history of the 'single meaning rule' see *Ajinomoto Sweeteners Europe SAS* v *Asda Stores Limited* [2011] QB 497 (per Sedley J).
[78] *Slim* v *Daily Telegraph Ltd* [1968] 2 QB 157, 172.
[79] *Berkoff* v *Burchill* [1996] 4 All ER 1008, 1018.
[80] See *Hough* v *London Express Newspaper Ltd* [1940] 2 KB 507 (CA).
[81] *Farquhar* v *Bottom* [1980] 2 NSWLR 380, 386.
[82] *Skuse* v *Granada Television* [1996] EMLR 278 (CA) 286; *Amalgamated Television Services Pty Ltd* v *Marsden* (1998) 43 NSWLR 158, 165–6; *Hinduja* v *Asia TV Limited* [1998] EMLR 516.

impression when compared to the assessment of text-based publications. Consequently, a greater degree of latitude will be given to the range of meanings that are capable of being conveyed.[83]

In addition to the medium, the broader nature of the publication will be taken into account. For example, the ordinary, reasonable reader might expect a particularly high level of accuracy and attention to detail in a book or in a broadsheet newspaper.[84] Furthermore, the reader of a book might be expected to read it with a greater degree of attention than the reader of a newspaper.[85] On the other hand, the ordinary, reasonable reader of a sensational publication (such as a tabloid newspaper) may be less likely to read with care[86] and may be taken to expect a lesser degree of accuracy.[87] As such, the reader of this type of publication will be taken to engage in a 'certain amount of loose thinking'.[88] By contrast, the reader of the *Law Society Gazette* might be expected to be less prone to such 'loose thinking'.[89]

In the context of satire, jest or vulgar abuse, it might be that the ordinary, reasonable recipient would not take the meaning seriously and therefore it may not be capable of being defamatory of the claimant. In *John* v *Guardian News and Media Ltd*,[90] for example, a spoof of Sir Elton John's diary published in the 'Weekend' lift-out section of the *Guardian* was not capable of bearing a defamatory meaning because the ordinary, reasonable reader would take the allegations not as serious but as an 'attempt at humour'. The reader would have expected any such allegations, if serious, to have appeared in the 'news' section of the paper. A similar approach might also be adopted in relation to certain Internet publications, particularly user-generated posts on bulletin boards and forums.[91]

The case of *Charleston* v *News Group* demonstrates the importance of assessing the publication as a whole, including the prominence given to the allegedly defamatory allegations. In a report on a new computer game, the *News of the World* published photos of the faces of two actors, who were stars in the well-known soap opera, *Neighbours*; their faces were superimposed on the bodies of other persons engaged in pornographic poses. While the photos and headline suggested the actors had willingly engaged in the poses, the captions and full text made it plain that this was an illusion.

Extract 10.3.1

Charleston v _News Group Newspapers Ltd_ [1995] 2 AC 65 (HL) 73–4

LORD NICHOLLS OF BIRKENHEAD:

My Lords, newspapers get thicker and thicker. The 'News of the World' published on 15 March 1992 contained 64 pages. Everybody reads selectively, scanning the headlines and turning the pages. One reader, whose interest has been quickened by an eye-catching headline or picture, will pause and read an article. Another reader, with different interests or less time, will read the headline and pass on, leaving the article unread. What if a headline, taken alone or with an attached picture, is defamatory, but the text of the article removes the defamatory imputation? That is the question of law raised by this appeal.

---

[83] *Amalgamated Television Services Pty Ltd* v *Marsden* (1998) 43 NSWLR 158, 165–6.
[84] See *Lewis* v *Daily Telegraph* [1964] AC 234, 265; *Al-Fayed* v *Telegraph Group Ltd* [2002] EWHC 1631 (QB).
[85] *Amalgamated Television Services Pty Ltd* v *Marsden* (1998) 43 NSWLR 158, 165.
[86] *Morgan* v *Odhams Press Ltd* [1971] 1 WLR 1239, 1254 (per Lord Morris), 1269 (per Lord Pearson).
[87] *Morgan* v *Odhams Press Ltd* [1971] 1 WLR 1239, 1270 (per Lord Pearson).
[88] *Amalgamated Television Services Pty Ltd* v *Marsden* (1998) 43 NSWLR 158, 165.
[89] *Rees* v *Law Society Gazette* (Unreported, Gray J, 2003).
[90] [2008] EWHC 3066 (QB).
[91] See, e.g., *Clift* v *Clarke* [2011] EWHC 1164 (QB); *Smith* v *ADVFN Plc* [2008] EWHC 1797 (QB).

At first sight one would expect the law to recognise that some newspaper readers will have seen only the banner headline and glanced at the picture. They will not have read the text of the accompanying article. In the minds of these readers, the reputation of the person who is the subject of the defamatory headline and picture will have suffered. He has been defamed to these readers. The newspaper could have no cause for complaint if it were held liable accordingly. It has chosen, for its own purposes, to produce a headline which is defamatory. It cannot be heard to say that the article must be read as a whole when it knows that not all readers will read the whole article.

To anyone unversed in the law of defamation that, I venture to think, would appear to be the common sense of the matter. Long ago, however, the law of defamation headed firmly in a different direction. The law adopts a single standard for determining whether a newspaper article is defamatory: the ordinary reader of that newspaper. I leave aside cases where some readers may have special knowledge of facts which would cause them to give the words a different meaning.

In principle this is a crude yardstick, because readers of mass circulation newspapers vary enormously in the way they read articles and the way they interpret what they read. It is, indeed, in this very consideration that the law finds justification for its single standard. The consequence is that, in the case of some publications, there may be many readers who understand in a defamatory sense words which, by the single standard of the ordinary reader, were not defamatory.

In respect of those readers a plaintiff has no remedy. The converse is equally true. So a newspaper may find itself paying damages for libel assessed by reference to a readership many of whose members did not read the words in a defamatory sense.

I do not see how, consistently with this single standard, it is possible to carve the readership of one article into different groups: those who will have read only the headlines, and those who will have read further. The question, defamatory or no, must always be answered by reference to the response of the ordinary reader to the publication.

This is not to say that words in the text of an article will always be efficacious to cure a defamatory headline. It all depends on the context, one element in which is the layout of the article. Those who print defamatory headlines are playing with fire. The ordinary reader might not be expected to notice curative words tucked away further down in the article. The more so, if the words are on a continuation page to which a reader is directed. The standard of the ordinary reader gives a jury adequate scope to return a verdict meeting the justice of the case.

The present case is well on the other side of the borderline. The ordinary reader could not have failed to read the captions accompanying the pictures. These made clear that the plaintiffs' faces had been superimposed on other actors' bodies. The plaintiffs had not themselves been indulging in the activities shown in the pictures. The ordinary reader would see at once that the headlines and pictures could not be taken at their face value. And the reader's eye needed to travel no further than the 'victims' caption to the smaller photographs, and to the second sentence, at the top of the article, to find confirmation that the plaintiffs were 'unwitting' stars in the sordid computer game.

Accordingly, when the ordinary reader put down the 'News of the World' on 15 March 1992, he or she would have thought none the worse of the two actors who are well known for their roles in the 'Neighbours' television serial. The ordinary reader might have thought worse of the producers of the pornographic computer game, and of the 'News of the World,' but that is a different matter. In agreement with my noble and learned friend, Lord Bridge of Harwich, I, too, would dismiss this appeal.

Question for discussion

1. Do you think it is appropriate to take the ordinary, reasonable reader as having read the whole of a publication? Was it unfair to the claimants in *Charleston*?

As *Charleston* v *News Group Newspapers Ltd* demonstrates, the requirement to consider the matter as a whole means that a claimant is not entitled to isolate and rely solely on the defamatory part of the publication. An article which neutralises the defamatory 'sting' by sufficiently explaining it away will not be considered to carry a defamatory meaning. This is known as 'the bane and the antidote'.[92] However, it will be a 'rare occasion'[93] and only in the 'clearest of cases'[94] that the antidote will be sufficient to extinguish the defamatory part of a publication.

While the publication must be considered as a whole in determining defamatory meaning, this does not extend to other articles within a newspaper or magazine.[95] An exception to this rule, however, might arise where one article refers to another article in the same edition of a newspaper[96] or where a single item is published over a number of parts, such as the serialisation of a book in a newspaper or a television series.[97] What, however, of an Internet website? How does one define the scope of a publication on a website for the purpose of assessing meaning? Is a claimant or a defendant, for example, able to rely on the whole website as the relevant 'publication'? Or does each page constitute a separate publication? In relation to non-Internet publications, Simpson J in *Phelps* v *Nationwide News Pty Ltd*[98] said that there is 'no rigid dividing line, no categoric test that can be applied to the determination of the boundaries' between a single publication and a 'composite' publication.[99] Relevant factors will include whether one article invites the reader to read the other,[100] as well as the 'diversity of the content'.[101] Only a handful of cases have sought to define the scope of website publications. In *Buddhist Society of Western Australia Inc* v *Bristile Ltd*,[102] it was held that separate pages on a website were to be treated as separate publications where their form, purpose and 'substantive identity' were sufficiently different.[103] In relation to the facts in question, the court said that the page was 'drafted as a discrete written communication unconnected in form or by reference to its content to any other document'.[104] A similar conclusion was reached in the case of *Kermode* v *Fairfax Media Publications Pty Ltd*,[105] despite the fact that the article in question included a hyperlink embedded under the words 'Find out how Reg Kermode got to the top, and read the documents which put him there'.[106] That page, in turn, linked to further pages that the defendant contended should also be read as a part of the publication. The court concluded that even though some readers might pursue the hyperlinks, it did not follow that the material should be read as a single publication.[107]

---

[92] *Chalmers* v *Payne* (1835) 2 Cr M & R 156, 159. See also *Charleston* v *News Group Newspapers Ltd* [1995] 2 AC 65; *Jameel* v *Times Newspapers Ltd* [2004] EWCA Civ 983; *Mark* v *Associated Newspapers Ltd* [2002] EWCA Civ 772; *Cruise* v *Express Newspapers* [1999] QB 931.

[93] *Morosi* v *Broadcasting Station 2GB Pty Ltd* [1980] 2 NSWLR 418n.

[94] *Mitchell* v *Faber and Faber Ltd* [1998] EMLR 807, 815.

[95] *Cruise* v *Express Newspapers* [1999] QB 931.

[96] *Thornton* v *Stephen* (1837) 2 Mood & R 45; 174 ER 209; *Phelps* v *Nationwide News Pty Ltd* [2001] NSWSC 130 (9 March 2001).

[97] See, e.g., *Burrows* v *Knightley* (1987) 10 NSWLR 651.

[98] [2001] NSWSC 130 (9 March 2001).

[99] Ibid., 10.

[100] Ibid., 24.

[101] Ibid., 25.

[102] [2000] WASCA 210 (9 August 2000).

[103] Ibid., 10.

[104] Ibid.

[105] [2009] NSWSC 1263 (23 November 2009).

[106] Ibid., 4.

[107] Ibid., 19.

More recently, however, an English case has reached the opposite conclusion. In *Budu v The British Broadcasting Corporation*,[108] three articles had been accessible from the defendant's website for a period of weeks, after which they were automatically archived. The three articles each contained links to the other two. The Court upheld the defendant's argument that the reader of such an article will have read all three. Sharp J said that it 'stretches credulity to suppose that [the] notional reader, who has only obtained access to the articles at all, because he is interested enough to do a search using the Claimant's name, would read say, the second and not the third articles.'[109]

Question for discussion

1. How do you think the boundaries of a publication on a website should be determined for the purposes of defamation law?

(ii) Natural and ordinary meaning

In establishing meaning, a claimant will usually rely on the natural and ordinary meaning of the matter. This is the meaning given to the matter by an ordinary, reasonable recipient 'in light of his or her general knowledge and experience'.[110] This includes the literal meaning of the matter as well as any 'indirect' meaning that may arise by implication or by inference. Such implications or inferences are called 'false' or 'popular' innuendo because they are meanings which do not arise expressly from the matter but nor do they rely upon the recipient having specialised knowledge.

Extract 10.3.2
***Lewis v Daily Telegraph* [1964] AC 234 (HL) 258–60**

An article in the *Daily Telegraph* stated: 'Officers of the City of London Fraud Squad are inquiring into the affairs of Rubber Improvement, Ltd . . . The investigations were requested after criticisms of the chairman's statement and the accounts by a shareholder at the recent company meeting.' The plaintiffs, the Rubber Improvement company and its chairman, Lewis, argued that the meaning of this article was that their affairs were conducted fraudulently or, at least, that the police suspected fraud.

LORD REID:
The gist of the two paragraphs is that the police, the City Fraud Squad, were inquiring into the appellants' affairs. There is no doubt that in actions for libel the question is what the words would convey to the ordinary man: it is not one of construction in the legal sense. The ordinary man does not live in an ivory tower and he is not inhibited by a knowledge of the rules of construction. So he can and does read between the lines in the light of his general knowledge and experience of worldly affairs. I leave aside questions of innuendo where the reader has some special knowledge which might lead him to attribute a meaning to the words not apparent to those who do not have that knowledge. That only arises indirectly in this case . . .

What the ordinary man would infer without special knowledge has generally been called the natural and ordinary meaning of the words. But that expression is rather misleading in that it conceals the fact that there are two elements in it. Sometimes it is not necessary to go beyond the words themselves, as where the plaintiff has been called a thief or a murderer. But more

---

[108] [2010] EWHC 616 (QB).
[109] [2010] EWHC 616 (QB,) 32. See also *Dee v Telegraph Media Group Ltd* [2010] EWHC 924 (QB).
[110] *Lewis v Daily Telegraph* [1964] AC 234, 258.

often the sting is not so much in the words themselves as in what the ordinary man will infer from them, and that is also regarded as part of their natural and ordinary meaning. Here there would be nothing libellous in saying that an inquiry into the appellants' affairs was proceeding: the inquiry might be by a statistician or other expert. The sting is in inferences drawn from the fact that it is the fraud squad which is making the inquiry. What those inferences should be is ultimately a question for the jury, but the trial judge has an important duty to perform.

. . .

Generally the controversy is whether the words are capable of having a libellous meaning at all, and undoubtedly it is the judge's duty to rule on that. I shall have to deal later with the test which he must apply. Here the controversy is in a different form. The respondents admit that their words were libellous, although I am still in some doubt as to what is the admitted libellous meaning. But they sought and seek a ruling that these words are not capable of having the particular meaning which the appellants attribute to them. I think that they are entitled to such a ruling and that the test must be the same as that applied in deciding whether the words are capable of having any libellous meaning . . .

In this case it is, I think, sufficient to put the test in this way. Ordinary men and women have different temperaments and outlooks. Some are unusually suspicious and some are unusually naïve. One must try to envisage people between these two extremes and see what is the most damaging meaning they would put on the words in question. So let me suppose a number of ordinary people discussing one of these paragraphs which they had read in the newspaper. No doubt one of them might say – 'Oh, if the fraud squad are after these people you can take it they are guilty.' But I would expect the others to turn on him, if he did say that, with such remarks as:

> Be fair. This is not a police state. No doubt their affairs are in a mess or the police would not be interested. But that could be because Lewis or the cashier has been very stupid or careless. We really must not jump to conclusions. The police are fair and know their job and we shall know soon enough if there is anything in it. Wait till we see if they charge him. I wouldn't trust him until this is cleared up, but it is another thing to condemn him unheard.
>
> . . .

What the ordinary man, not avid for scandal, would read into the words complained of must be a matter of impression. I can only say that I do not think that he would infer guilt of fraud merely because an inquiry is on foot. And, if that is so, then it is the duty of the trial judge to direct the jury that it is for them to determine the meaning of the paragraph but that they must not hold it to impute guilt of fraud because as a matter of law the paragraph is not capable of having that meaning. So there was here, in my opinion, misdirection of the two juries sufficiently serious to require that there must be new trials.

(iii) True innuendo meanings

Alternatively, it is open to a claimant to argue that a defamatory meaning arises not from the natural and ordinary meaning of the matter but rather from the meaning that the publication would have for an ordinary, reasonable recipient with knowledge of special extrinsic facts (called a 'true innuendo' meaning).[111] To say, for example, that 'A has slept with B', may not give rise to a defamatory meaning on the natural and ordinary interpretation of those words. However, it will be otherwise where an ordinary reasonable recipient has knowledge that A is married to C. Thus, the true innuendo meaning is that

---

[111] It should be noted that a true innuendo meaning gives rise to a cause of action separate from a cause of action arising from the natural and ordinary meaning of the material: see *Grubb* v *Bristol United Press Ltd* [1963] 1 QB 309, 327 (per Pearce LJ).

A has committed adultery with B.[112] Another example often given is that of a man entering a brothel.[113] To say that 'X entered a building at 12 Anderson Street' may be innocuous on its natural and ordinary meaning. However, the meaning will be very different for a recipient with knowledge that a brothel operates from that address. It is important to note that a claimant wishing to rely on a true innuendo must specify the defamatory meaning upon which he or she relies as well as the relevant extrinsic facts.[114] While the claimant is not required to prove that any recipient understood the matter in the pleaded defamatory sense,[115] the claimant is required to prove that at least one recipient of the matter had knowledge of the relevant extrinsic facts and that he or she had such knowledge at the time the matter was published.[116]

In *Cassidy* v *Daily Mirror*, a photograph was published in the defendant's newspaper of Mr Cassidy, who was also known as Mr Corrigan, and an unnamed woman. The following inscription accompanied the photograph: 'Mr M Corrigan, the race horse owner, and Miss X [name omitted by the court], whose engagement has been announced.' The publication was not defamatory in its natural and ordinary meaning; however, Mrs Cassidy, Mr Cassidy's wife, argued that it was defamatory of her, when read by an ordinary reasonable person attributed with knowledge that she claimed to be his wife.

Extract 10.3.3
***Cassidy* v *Daily Mirror Newspapers* [1929] 2 KB 331**

RUSSELL LJ:

. . .

(351) The plaintiff sued the defendants for damages for libel, alleging that the photograph and words bore a meaning defamatory of the plaintiff – namely, that the plaintiff was not lawfully married to her husband, but had lived with him as his mistress, pretending to her friends to be a respectable married woman. The judge, being of opinion that the photograph and words were capable of bearing a meaning defamatory of the plaintiff, left it to the jury to decide whether they were in fact defamatory of the plaintiff. The jury returned a verdict for the plaintiff for 500l.

. . .

The defendants contend that the published matter is not, on the face of it, defamatory at all either of the plaintiff or of any one else. That must I think be conceded. Nevertheless words may be published with reference to such circumstances, and to such persons knowing the circumstances, as to convey a meaning which would not be attributable to them in different circumstances: see per Lord Blackburn in *Capital and Counties Bank* v *Henty*. So too, I think, words may be published with reference to such circumstances, and to such persons, knowing the circumstances, as to suggest an inference in regard to someone not in terms mentioned in the statement, which (352) would not be involved by the publication of the same words either in different circumstances or to persons ignorant of the particular circumstances which occasion the inference.

The first thing to consider in this case is this question: Can the published matter be reasonably construed as a statement that Mr Corrigan is an unmarried man? For myself I would answer that the published matter may not only reasonably be so construed, but must necessarily be so construed. I discard as too far fetched the suggestion that it might refer to the announcement of an engagement made by a married man either in anticipation of a divorce or with a view to

---

[112] See, e.g., *Cornes* v *Ten Group Pty Ltd* [2011] SASC 104 (5 July 2011).
[113] *Lewis* v *Daily Telegraph* [1964] AC 234, 278.
[114] *Grubb* v *Bristol United Press Ltd* [1963] 1 QB 309, 327; *Lewis* v *Daily Telegraph* [1964] AC 234.
[115] *Radio 2UE Sydney Pty Ltd* v *Chesterton* (2009) 238 CLR 460, 51; *Hough* v *London Express Newspaper Ltd* [1940] 2 KB 507 (CA); *Tolley* v *J S Fry & Sons Ltd* [1931] AC 333.
[116] *Grappelli* v *Derek Block (Holdings) Ltd* [1981] 1 WLR 822.

seduction. If then the published matter is a statement that AB is an unmarried man, can AB's wife successfully complain of that as a statement defamatory of her? This must depend upon (1) whether the statement that AB is an unmarried man is capable of being defamatory of AB's wife, and (2) whether the statement is in fact defamatory of AB's wife. McCardie J came to the conclusion that in the present case the published matter was capable of being defamatory of the plaintiff. I can see no reason for differing from that view. The Lord Chancellor in *E Hulton & Co* v *Jones* used the following language, which seems appropriate to the present case:

> Libel . . . consists in using language which others, knowing the circumstances, would reasonably think to be defamatory of the person complaining of and injured by it. A person charged with libel cannot defend himself by showing that he intended in his own breast not to defame, or that he intended not to defame the plaintiff, if in fact he did both.

Applying those words to a statement (which for this purpose must be false) that AB is an unmarried man, is it a reasonable view that people who have known a lady who has called and is calling herself the wife of AB might think the statement to be defamatory of the lady? In my opinion the view is an eminently reasonable one. Whether, being capable of a defamatory meaning, the statement was in the circumstances of the particular (353) case defamatory of the plaintiff, is another question. That is a question of fact for the jury to answer according to their view of the evidence adduced.

It was argued by the appellants that no liability attaches to the publisher of a statement which is not on the face of it defamatory, but which only becomes defamatory in the light of outside facts, unless those facts are known both to the person who publishes the statement and to the persons to whom it is published. For this proposition reliance was placed upon the views expressed in Henty's case by Brett LJ in the Court of Appeal. So far as concerns knowledge on the part of the persons to whom the statement is published, no difficulty presents itself. If the defamatory meaning only arises from a knowledge of outside facts, and the persons to whom the statement is published are ignorant of those facts, those persons could not reasonably attach a defamatory meaning to the statement.

So far as concerns knowledge on the part of the person by whom the statement is published, I feel difficulty in supporting the proposition . . . (354) Liability for libel does not depend on the intention of the defamer; but on the fact of defamation. If you once reach the conclusion that the published matter in the present case amounts to or involves a statement that Mr Corrigan is an unmarried man, then in my opinion those persons who knew the circumstances might reasonably consider the statement defamatory of the plaintiff. The statement being capable of a meaning defamatory to the plaintiff, it was for the jury upon the evidence adduced to decide whether the plaintiff had been libelled or not.

It was said that it would be a great hardship on the defendants if they were made liable in consequence of a statement innocent on its face and published by them in good faith. The answer to this appeal for sympathy seems to be to point out that, in stating to the world that Mr Corrigan was an unmarried man (for that construction is the foundation of their liability), they in fact stated that which was false. From a business point of view no doubt it may pay them not to spend time or money in making inquiries, or verifying statements before publication; but if they had not made a false statement they would not now be suffering in damages. They are paying a price for their methods of business.

. . .

(355) When all is said and done, the defendants have published to the world the statement that Mr Corrigan was, on February 21, 1928, an unmarried man. That statement was in fact false, and has been found by the jury to be defamatory of the plaintiff, and to have caused her damage. There is ample evidence to support the findings, unless we can say that the published matter was incapable of being defamatory of the plaintiff. This I am not prepared to do.

For these reasons I agree with Scrutton LJ that the appeal fails.

> ### Questions for discussion
>
> 1. Natural and ordinary meaning will include what types of meanings?
> 2. When will a claimant rely on a 'true innuendo' meaning? What was the true innuendo meaning in *Cassidy* v *Daily Mirror Newspapers*?

(iv) Definitions of defamatory

Once the meaning of the publication has been ascertained, the question then arises as to whether that meaning is defamatory. The law of defamation, of course, seeks to provide redress for the harm caused to a person's reputation. However, it is one of the peculiarities of this area of law that there is no single, accepted (or even coherent) test for whether the matter in question is defamatory. Rather, given the difficulties in finding a complete definition of reputation, there are a number of judicially accepted tests used to determine whether reputation is likely to be adversely affected by what was published.[117]

The following extract from *Thornton* v *Telegraph Media Group Ltd* sets out the various tests that have been accepted. However, it is important to note three important points at the outset. First, the publication of the matter need not have an actual negative effect on the claimant's reputation; rather, it is sufficient if the matter has the *tendency* to have such an effect.[118] Second, in judging such tendency, the ordinary, reasonable reader is taken to be 'right-thinking' and to have a uniform moral and social standard, meaning that sectional attitudes cannot be taken into account.[119] For example, it is not libellous to suggest that someone has reported a crime to the police or otherwise behaved with propriety, even though as a result many colleagues or friends might think less highly of him. In *Byrne* v *Deane*,[120] for example, the majority of the Court of Appeal ruled that a member of a golf club could not sue in libel in respect of the allegation that he had reported the club to the police for keeping illegal gaming machines on the premises. Third, it is now accepted, following the decision of *Thornton* v *Telegraph Media Group Ltd*,[121] that each of the accepted tests for defamation will only be satisfied where a threshold of seriousness is met.[122] It should be pointed out that, in addition, a defendant may seek to have a defamation action struck out as an abuse of process – known as '*Jameel* abuse' – on the basis that a 'real and substantial tort' has not been committed, either because the defamation is trivial or because it has only been published to a limited number of recipients.[123]

---

[117] For a useful analysis of the relationship between the concept of reputation and the law of defamation see: David Rolph, *Reputation, Celebrity and Defamation Law* (Ashgate, 2008).

[118] See, e.g., *Morgan* v *Odhams Press Ltd* [1971] 1 WLR 1239, 1253; *Hough* v *London Express Newspaper Ltd* [1940] 2 KB 507 (CA) 515.

[119] *Tolley* v *JS Fry & Sons Ltd* [1930] 1 KB 467.

[120] [1937] 1 KB 818.

[121] [2010] EWHC 1414 (QB).

[122] The 'threshold of seriousness' is inherent in the 'hatred, contempt, ridicule' and 'shun and avoid' tests; in relation to the broader 'lower in the estimation of others' test, the defamation must have a tendency to affect the claimant 'in an adverse manner': see *Thornton* v *Telegraph Media Group* [2010] EWHC 1414 (QB) 50–95 (per Tugendhat J).

[123] See, e.g., *Dow Jones* v *Jameel* [2005] QB 946.

Extract 10.3.4
***Thornton* v *Telegraph Media Group Ltd* [2011] 1 WLR 1985**

MR JUSTICE TUGENDHAT:

What is defamatory?

28. In *Berkoff* v *Burchill* [1996] 4 All ER 1008 Neill LJ set out some of the definitions . . . The following is the list given in *Berkoff* . . . [A]ll the emphasis is added. The emphasis in bold type relates to the tendency or likelihood of damage that must be demonstrated. The underlining relates to the effect upon the publishees, and through them upon the claimant, that must be demonstrated:

> I am not aware of any entirely satisfactory definition of the word 'defamatory'. It may be convenient, however, to collect together some of the definitions which have been used and approved in the past.

1. . . . The classic definition is that given by Lord Wensleydale (then Parke B) in *Parmiter* v *Coupland* (1840) 6 M & W 105 at 108, 151 ER 340 at 341–2. He said that in cases of libel it was for the judge to give a legal definition of the offence which he defined as being: 'A publication, without justification or lawful excuse, which is calculated to injure the reputation of another, by exposing him to *hatred, contempt, or ridicule* . . .' It is to be noted that in *Tournier* v *National Provincial Union Bank of England Ltd* [1924] 1 KB 461 at 477, [1923] All ER Rep 550 at 557 Scrutton LJ said that he did not think that this 'ancient formula' was sufficient in all cases, because words might damage the reputation of a man as a business man which no one would connect with hatred, ridicule or contempt . . .

. . .

3. . . . In *Sim* v *Stretch* [1936] 2 All ER 1237 at 1240 Lord Atkin expressed the view that the definition in *Parmiter* v *Coupland* was probably too narrow and that the question was complicated by having to consider the person or class of persons whose reaction to the publication provided the relevant test. He concluded this passage in his speech: '. . . after collating the opinions of many authorities I propose in the present case the test: would the words tend to *lower the plaintiff in the estimation of right-thinking members of society generally?*'

4. . . . [B]oth Scrutton and Atkin LJJ in *Tournier's* case drew attention to words which damage the reputation of a man as a business man. In *Drummond-Jackson* v *British Medical Association* [1970] 1 All ER 1094, [1970] 1 WLR 688 the Court of Appeal was concerned with an article in a medical journal which, it was suggested, impugned the plaintiff's reputation as a dentist. Lord Pearson said:

> . . . words may be defamatory of a trader or business man or professional man, although they do not impute any moral fault or defect of personal character. They [can] be defamatory of him if they impute lack of qualification, knowledge, skill, capacity, judgment or efficiency in the conduct of his trade or business or professional activity . . .

(See [1970] 1 All ER 1094 at 1104, [1970] 1 WLR 688 at 698–9.) It is therefore necessary in some cases to consider the occupation of the plaintiff.

5. . . . In *Youssoupoff* v *Metro-Goldwyn-Mayer Pictures Ltd* (1934) 50 TLR 581 at 587 Slesser LJ expanded the *Parmiter* v *Coupland* definition to include words which cause a person to be shunned or avoided.

. . .

A possible ordering of defamation cases

33. There can be derived from the authorities referred to above at least some systematic ordering of the varieties of defamation along the following lines:

i)   There are two main varieties of each of the torts of libel and slander: (A) personal defamation, where there are imputations as to the character or attributes of an individual and (B) business or professional defamation, where the imputation is as to an attribute of an individual, a corporation, a trade union, a charity, or similar body, and that imputation is as to the way the profession or business is conducted. These varieties are not mutually exclusive: the same words may carry both varieties of imputation. By contrast, if the imputation is as to the product of the business or profession, then it will be the tort of malicious falsehood, not defamation, to which the claimant must look for any remedy.

ii) Personal defamation comes in a number of sub-varieties including:

    a) Imputations as to what is 'illegal, mischievous, or sinful' in Pollock CB's phrase (in *Clay* v *Roberts* (1863), 8 LT 397, cited in *Sim* v *Stretch*). This would perhaps now be expressed as what is illegal, or unethical or immoral, or socially harmful, but will now cover imputations which are less serious than that (see definitions (1), (3) . . .);

    b) Imputations as to something which is not voluntary, or the result of the claimant's conscious act or choice, but rather a misfortune for which no direct moral responsibility can be placed upon the claimant (such as disease – definition (5));

    c) Imputations which ridicule the claimant (definition (1) and *Berkoff*).

iii) Business or professional defamation also comes in a number of sub-varieties (definition (4) and the examples given in *Derbyshire County Council* v *Times Newspapers Ltd* [1993] AC 534 discussed below under the heading Business Defamation):

    a) Imputations upon a person, firm or other body who provides goods or services that the goods or services are below a required standard in some respect which is likely to cause adverse consequences to the customer, patient or client. In these cases there may be only a limited role for the opinion or attitude of right-thinking members of society, because the required standard will usually be one that is set by the professional body or a regulatory authority;

    b) Imputations upon a person, firm or body which may deter other people from providing any financial support that may be needed, or from accepting employment, or otherwise dealing with them. In these cases there may be more of a role for the opinion or attitude of right-thinking members of society.

34. In addition to these varieties, there is a distinction between sub-varieties of business defamation in which:

(a) The action is brought by an individual, where damage may include injury to feelings, and

(b) The action is brought by a corporation, where damage cannot include injury to feelings.

35. For the purposes of this judgment it is not necessary to consider defamation by ridicule. Nor is it necessary to consider defamation by definition (5), that is, where words impute a personal attribute which will cause others to treat the subject less favourably, but an attribute which is involuntary and attracts no moral discredit, such as disease or other misfortune. Cases that come within this definition are now likely to be brought under misuse of private information, although that will not necessarily or always be the case. So the definition still has a role to play.

Business defamation

. . .

37. Definition (4) is derived from *Tournier* and *Drummond-Jackson* . . . It envisages a claim for libel succeeding which may not involve any adverse reflection upon the personal qualities of a claimant. In commenting on this meaning the editors of Gatley [on Libel and Slander] at para 2.1 say this:

> Without suggesting that there is a separate tort of 'business defamation', as a practical matter it has been thought necessary where the words denigrate the claimant's business or professional capacity to recognise that the words may be defamatory even though they in no way reflect on the *character* of the claimant. It may be that those 'community standards' of 'right-thinking people' of which the jury is the ultimate guardian have less of a role in these cases and it has been suggested that the correct

approach is to ask whether the tendency of the words is to convey to the reader that the claimant's fitness or competence falls short of what are generally necessary for the business or profession (see *Radio 2UE Sydney* v *Chesterton* [2008] NSWCA 66 at [19]*).

38. There is a further reason why cases of business defamation require separate consideration, whether or not there is a separate tort of 'business defamation'. What is at stake in a defamation reflecting on a person's character is now likely to be recognised as engaging that person's rights under Art 8. On the other hand, if an alleged defamation engages only a person's professional attributes, then what is at stake is less likely to engage their rights under Art 8, but may engage only their commercial or property rights (which are Convention rights, if at all, under Art 1 of the First Protocol) . . . However, neither party advanced submissions to me on the basis of Art 8. So it is not necessary to consider that aspect of the matter further.

. . .

* Author's note: the NSW Court of Appeal decision in *Radio 2UE* v *Chesterton* [2008] NSWCA 66 (17 April 2008), cited in *Thornton*, was subsequently overturned by the High Court of Australia (*Radio 2UE Sydney Pty Ltd* v *Chesterton* (2009) 238 CLR 460), where it was held that general community standards apply equally to personal as well as to business defamation.

In order to discourage trivial and unfounded claims, clause 1 of the Defamation Bill proposes a statutory threshold of 'serious harm': '[a] statement is not defamatory unless its publication has caused or is likely to cause serious harm to the reputation of the claimant.' It is said to raise the bar 'for bringing a claim so that only cases involving serious harm to the claimant's reputation can be brought.'[124] In explaining the clause, reference is made in the Explanatory Memorandum to the 'threshold of seriousness' in *Thornton* and to the existing possibility of striking out a claim on the basis of a '*Jameel* abuse'.

Questions for discussion

1. Is it satisfactory that there is no single test for defamation?
2. What are the main tests for defamation?
3. What distinction is drawn in *Thornton* between personal defamation and business defamation? Do the same standards apply to each?
4. Does the seriousness threshold in *Thornton* mean that article 8 (see Section 10.2) will always be engaged in defamation cases? Why/why not?
5. Would it be compatible with article 8 to 'raise the bar' above the test of seriousness in *Thornton*, as proposed by clause 1 of the Defamation Bill?
6. How would clause 1 apply in a '*Jameel* abuse' type scenario where the allegation is of a relatively serious nature, and therefore meets the 'threshold of seriousness', but is published only to a limited audience? What effect do you think clause 1 is intended to have?

In the *Youssoupoff* case, the plaintiff was a Russian princess who claimed that she had been libelled in the film, *Rasputin, the Mad Monk*, produced by the defendants, inasmuch as it suggested that Princess Natasha, a character in the film identifiable as the plaintiff, had been seduced or raped by Rasputin.

---

[124] Explanatory Notes, Defamation Bill 2012–13 (HL Bill 41, 21 September 2012) 12. See also HC Deb 12 June 2012, vol 546, col 180 ('nudging the threshold up by a modest extent').

Extract 10.3.5
Youssoupoff v MGM Pictures Ltd **(1934) 50 TLR 581 (CA) 587**

SLESSER LJ:

I, for myself, cannot see that from the plaintiff's point of view it matters in the least whether this libel suggests that she has been seduced or ravished. The question whether she is or is not the more or the less moral seems to me immaterial in considering this question whether she has been defamed and for this reason, that, as has been frequently pointed out in libel, not only is the matter defamatory if it brings the plaintiff into hatred, ridicule, or contempt by reason of some moral discredit on her part, but also if it tends to make the plaintiff be shunned and avoided and that without any moral discredit on her part. It is for that reason that persons who have been alleged to have been insane, or to be suffering from certain diseases, and other cases where no direct moral responsibility could be placed upon them, have been held to be entitled to bring an action to protect their reputation and their honour.

One may, I think, take judicial notice of the fact that a lady of whom it has been said that she has been ravished, albeit against her will, has suffered in social reputation and in opportunities of receiving respectful consideration from the world. It is to shut one's eyes to realities to make these nice distinctions, but in this case I see no reason to suppose that this jury did come to a conclusion on this film that the imaginary lady depicted in the film, the Princess Natasha, was ravished and not seduced. I have looked at the pictures carefully, I have read the language, and it seems to me perfectly consistent with either view, and to assume at the outset that this film does represent a ravishment and not a seduction seems to me itself to assume that which the jury might have refused to assume at all.

Questions for discussion

1. What test for defamation was used in *Youssoupoff*? How would it be decided today?
2. What types of allegations would cause a person to be 'shunned or avoided'?

In the *Berkoff* case the issue was whether two reviews in the *Sunday Times*, written by Julie Burchill, intimating that the actor and director Steven Birkoff was 'hideously ugly' were capable of being defamatory. The majority of the Court of Appeal held that they were.[125]

Extract 10.3.6
Berkoff v Burchill **[1997] EMLR 139 (CA) 151, 153**

NEILL LJ:

It may be that in some contexts the words 'hideously ugly' could not be understood in a defamatory sense, but one has to consider the words in the surroundings in which they appear . . .

It is trite law that the meaning of words in a libel action is determined by the reaction of the ordinary reader and not by the intention of the publisher, but the perceived intention of the publisher may colour the meaning. In the present case it would in my view be open to a jury to conclude that in the context the remarks about Mr Berkoff gave the impression that he was not merely physically unattractive in appearance but actually repulsive. It seems to me that to say this of someone in the public eye who makes his living, in part at least, as an actor,

---

[125] Phillips LJ held the jury should decide whether the words so exposed the plaintiff to ridicule that they damaged his reputation. Compare *Norman v Future Publishing* [1999] EMLR 325, where the Court of Appeal held the attribution of vulgar and undignified language to the opera singer, Jessye Norman, was not capable, in the context of the whole article, of bearing a defamatory meaning.

is capable of lowering his standing in the estimation of the public and of making him an object of ridicule.

MILLETT LJ:

The line between mockery and defamation may sometimes be difficult to draw. When it is it should be left to the jury to draw it . . . A decision that it is an actionable wrong to describe a man as 'hideously ugly' would be an unwarranted restriction on free speech. And if a bald statement to this effect would not be capable of being defamatory, I do not see how a humorously exaggerated observation to the like effect could be. People must be allowed to poke fun at one another without fear of litigation. It is one thing to ridicule a man; it is another to expose him to ridicule. Miss Burchill made a cheap joke at Mr Berkoff's expense; she may thereby have demeaned herself, but I not believe that she defamed Mr Berkoff.

Questions for discussion

1. Would you have agreed with the majority in *Berkoff* or with Millett LJ?
2. Consider the arguments for and against judicial reluctance to withdraw issues from the jury.

(b) Identification

It is not sufficient for the claimant to prove that the publication contains a defamatory meaning; the claimant must show that the defamatory allegations were made about him or her – that is, that the words were 'of and concerning' the claimant.[126] The test is whether the ordinary reasonable person would identify the plaintiff as being the person referred to.[127] In most cases, identification will be easily established where the claimant is identified by name.[128] However, such direct identification is not required. Where the claimant is not directly identified, the question is whether the ordinary reader would understand the allegations as referring to the claimant. This would be satisfied, for example, where the publication refers to the Prime Minister. In other cases, identification will only be able to be established by arguing that an ordinary reasonable reader with special knowledge of extrinsic facts would be able to identify the person referred to as the claimant. This is based on the same principle as a 'true innuendo' meaning discussed above (see Section 10.3(a)(iii)).[129]

A publisher need not intend to refer to the claimant in order to attract liability. This can result in some unintended consequences for a publisher where the intention is to refer to X but it inadvertently defames someone else of the same name.[130] This will be the case even where the publisher intends to refer to a fictional person.[131] In *Hulton* v *Jones*, the *Sunday Chronicle* in publishing a sketch about English holiday-makers enjoying themselves in Dieppe, referred to an 'Artemus Jones with a woman who is not his wife, who must be,

---

[126] *Knupffer* v *London Express Newspaper Ltd* [1944] AC 116.
[127] *Morgan* v *Odhams Press Ltd* [1971] 1 WLR 1239.
[128] Direct reference by name, however, will not be sufficient if the name is particularly common: see *Dow Jones & Co Inc* v *Jameel* [2005] EWCA Civ 75, 45.
[129] However, it is considered a 'reference innuendo' rather than a 'meaning innuendo': *Baturina* v *Times Newspapers Ltd* [2011] EWCA Civ 308, 20–31.
[130] *Lee* v *Wilson and Mackinnon* (1934) 51 CLR 276.
[131] For a discussion of the impact of libel law on writers of fiction, see Eric Barendt, 'Defamation and Fiction' in Michael Freeman and Andrew Lewis (eds), *Law and Literature* (Oxford University Press, 1999) 481.

you know – the other thing!' The paper argued, rather disingenuously,[132] that it had never heard of Artemus Jones, the plaintiff, a sober Welsh barrister.

Extract 10.3.7
***Hulton* v *Jones* [1910] AC 20 (HL) 24**

LORD LOREBURN LC:

If the intention of the writer be immaterial in considering whether the matter written is defamatory, I do not see why it need be relevant in considering whether it is defamatory of the plaintiff. The writing, according to the old form, must be malicious, and it must be of and concerning the plaintiff. Just as the defendant could not excuse himself from malice by proving that he wrote it in the most benevolent spirit, so he cannot shew that the libel was not of and concerning the plaintiff by proving that he never heard of the plaintiff. His intention in both respects equally is inferred from what he did. His remedy is to abstain from defamatory words.

It is suggested that there was a misdirection by the learned judge in this case. I see none. He lays down in his summing up the law as follows:

> The real point upon which your verdict must turn is, ought or ought not sensible and reasonable people reading this article to think that it was a mere imaginary person such as I have said – Tom Jones, Mr Pecksniff as a humbug, Mr Stiggins, or any of that sort of names that one reads of in literature used as types? If you think any reasonable person would think that, it is not actionable at all. If, on the other hand, you do not think that, but think that people would suppose it to mean some real person – those who did not know the plaintiff of course would not know who the real person was, but those who did know of the existence of the plaintiff would think that it was the plaintiff – then the action is maintainable, subject to such damages as you think under all the circumstances are fair and right to give to the plaintiff.

In short, there is liability if a newspaper, however innocently, publishes material which reasonable readers may link to someone they know.[133] Writers and broadcasters must, therefore, be precise in their description of a suspect or offender in order to minimise the risk of a libel action by another person of the same name. The difficulties faced by the media were made plain by the Court of Appeal in the *Newstead* case; a newspaper had published an account of a bigamy trial, stating that 'Harold Newstead, 30-year-old Camberwell man, who was jailed for nine months, liked having two wives at once'. That was true of a Camberwell barman of that name, but not of the claimant, a hairdresser of the same name who also lived in Camberwell.

Extract 10.3.8
***Newstead* v *London Express Newspapers Ltd* [1940] 1 KB 377 (CA) 388**

SIR WILFRID GREENE MR:

After giving careful consideration to the matter, I am unable to hold that the fact that defamatory words are true of A, makes it as a matter of law impossible for them to be defamatory of B, which was in substance the main argument on behalf of the appellants. At first sight this looks as though it would lead to great hardship. But the hardships are in practice not so serious as might appear, at any rate in the case of statements which are ex facie defamatory. Persons who make statements of this character may not unreasonably be expected, when describing the person of whom they are made, to identify that person so closely as to make it very unlikely that a judge would hold them to be reasonably capable of referring to someone else, or that a jury would hold that they did so refer. This is particularly so in the case of statements which purport to deal with

---

[132] It is clear that the writer of the sketch knew and disliked Jones, who had previously worked for the paper: see Paul Mitchell, 'Artemus Jones and the Press Club' (1999) 20 *Journal of Legal History* 64.
[133] But the media may rely on the offer of amends defence: see Section 10.4(d).

actual facts. If there is a risk of coincidence it ought, I think, in reason to be borne not by the innocent party to whom the words are held to refer, but by the party who puts them into circulation. In matters of fiction, there is no doubt more room for hardship. Even in the case of matters of fact it is no doubt possible to construct imaginary facts which would lead to hardship. There may also be hardship if words, not on their faces defamatory, are true of A, but are reasonably understood by some as referring to B, and as applied to B are defamatory. But such cases must be rare. The law as I understand it is well settled, and can only be altered by legislation.

The decision in *Newstead* can be compared to Morland J's decision in *O'Shea* v *MGN Ltd and Free4Internet.net Ltd*. In that case, an advertisement for pornographic services used a photograph of a woman said to be identical to the claimant.

Extract 10.3.9
***O'Shea* v *MGN Ltd and Free4Internet.net Ltd* [2001] EMLR 40**

MR JUSTICE MORLAND:

. . .

28. In view of the weight of the highest authority I must conclude that at Common Law the strict liability principle applies notwithstanding the novelty of facts in this case nor am I able to say that it would be unreasonable for a hypothetical sensible reader who knows the special facts to be proved in this case to infer that the advertisement referred to the claimant.

29. I now consider the impact of Article 10 of the Convention bearing in mind Section 12(4) of the Human Rights Act 1998 that I 'must have particular regard to the importance of the Convention right to freedom of expression'.

. . .

37. The second defendants' advertisement published by the 1st defendants will have been regarded by many as squalid and degrading to women but distasteful though it may be, it is not unlawful and in accordance with European Law is a form of expression protected by Article 10.

38. I have to consider the application of Article 10(2) of the Convention. As in my judgment the strict liability principle is a restriction of the exercise of the freedom of expression, I must answer the question whether in the factual circumstances of this case that restriction is necessary in a democratic society for the protection of the reputation of others such as the claimant.

. . .

41. Photography and filming play a major role in modern journalism in newspapers, magazines and television in getting the message across.

42. Pictures are necessary, effective, and telling adjuncts to a story.

43. It would impose an impossible burden on a publisher if he were required to check if the true picture of someone resembled someone else who because of the context of the picture was defamed. Examples are legion:- unlawful violence in street protest demonstrations, looting, hooliganism at football matches, people apparently leaving or entering Court with criminal defendants and investigative journalism into drug dealing, corruption, child abuse and prostitution.

44. Whereas theoretically the existence of the real Artemus Jones and the second Harold Newstead, a 30-year-old Camberwell man, could have been discovered, it would be impossible to discover whether a 'look-alike' or 'spit and image' of the photograph of a real person existed.

45. The fact that in over a century no claim has been made in respect of a libel in respect of a 'look-alike' picture is an indication that there is no pressing social need for the application of the strict liability principle for the protection of the reputation of the 'look-alike'.

46. If someone were deliberately to publish a defamatory article or broadcast a defamatory film not naming the victim but using a 'look-alike' picture of a person, perhaps a celebrity, so that those who know that person would identify that person from the 'look-alike' picture, that person would have a remedy, the tort of malicious falsehood. That in my judgment would provide sufficient protection of reputation.

47. In conclusion my judgment is that the strict liability principle should not cover the 'look-alike' situation. To allow it to do so would be an unjustifiable interference with the vital right of freedom of expression disproportionate to the legitimate aim of protecting the reputations of 'look-alikes' and contrary to Article 10 of the Convention.

48. While I have every sympathy for the claimant and her family at the embarrassment caused by the pornographic advertisement and the 'look-alike' photograph, in my judgment her claim as a matter of law has no realistic prospect of success nor should it have.

It should be noted that in *Baturina v Times Newspapers Ltd*[134] the Court of Appeal sought to narrowly interpret Morland J's decision in *O'Shea v MGN Ltd* as 'a small extension of the *Reynolds* defence'[135] (see Section 10.4(c)(iv)) and suggested that, in any event, it should not be applied to a case where 'a newspaper publishes an untrue story, and the publisher is unable to raise a *Reynolds* defence'.[136]

A group cannot sue in libel to protect its collective reputation. The media are free to say that 'all politicians are corrupt' and 'lawyers are greedy', because no individual can show that the allegations implicate him. But in some circumstances an individual member may be able to sue in defamation for an attack on that group. *Knupffer* is the leading case on this aspect of the law. A newspaper article was published about the activities of a pro-Nazi group in the Soviet Union, which was described as a 'minute body professing a pure Fascist ideology'.[137]

Extract 10.3.10
***Knupffer* v *London Express Newspaper Ltd* [1944] AC 116 (HL) 124–5**

LORD PORTER:
No doubt, it is true to say that a class cannot be defamed as a class, nor can an individual be defamed by a general reference to the class to which he belongs . . . Nevertheless, the words or the words combined with the relevant circumstances may be shown to refer to some person or persons individually . . .

. . .

The question whether the words refer in fact to the plaintiff or plaintiffs is a matter for the jury or for a judge sitting as a judge of fact, but as a prior question it has always to be ascertained whether there is any evidence on which a conclusion that they do so refer could reasonably be reached. In deciding this question the size of the class, the generality of the charge and the extravagance of the accusation may all be elements to be taken into consideration, but none of them is conclusive. Each case must be considered according to its own circumstances. I can imagine it being said that each member of a body, however large, was defamed where the libel consisted in the assertion that no one of the members of a community was elected as a member unless he had committed a murder.

. . .

---

[134] [2011] EWCA Civ 308.
[135] Ibid., 29.
[136] Ibid., 30.
[137] *Knupffer* v *London Express Newspaper Ltd* [1944] AC 116.

Whatever the tribunal, the first question is: Are the words in conjunction with the relevant circumstances reasonably capable of being understood to apply to the plaintiff? In the present case that question must, I think, be answered in the negative. It is true that the appellant was and is a member of a body on which very grave reflections have been cast, that he is the representative of that body in England, and that there are only twenty-four members of it in this country, but the newspaper article makes no reference to England. It confines itself to allegations about 'a minute body' 'established in France and the United States'. Minute, no doubt, its membership of 2,000 is when compared with the vast population of Russia, but in itself it forms a considerable body. Out of that body there was nothing to point to the appellant, nor indeed to any individual in this country. Nor do I think the appellant's case is improved by the allegations of his friends that 'their minds turned to' him when they read the article. Apart from the vagueness of the question, I can see no justification for an inference that he was the person aimed at. If it could be said, as it is conceded it could not, that each member of the body, wherever resident, could claim to be defamed, some case might be made on behalf of the appellant as one of its members, but as the evidence stands I see nothing to point to him in contra-distinction to the rest. Indeed, inasmuch as he is a member of the English group, he is the less likely to be referred to. I agree that the appeal should be dismissed.

The risks run by newspapers in this context are highlighted by two actions brought by police officers. In one of them, 10 CID officers stationed in Banbury successfully brought an action in respect of reported allegations of rape and violence by unnamed officers stationed there. There were only 12 CID officers at this station; had there been, say, a hundred, it would have been impossible for the plaintiffs to show the libel identified them. In the second case, the Court of Appeal held an action brought by 10 officers could proceed when the *Police Review* disclosed that a police dog-handler was resigning from the force because of anti-semitism on the part of his colleagues. There were only 27 dog-handlers in the particular dog-handling section so the plaintiffs could claim to be individually identifiable by readers of the journal.[138]

Questions for discussion

1. Do you think the principle established in *Hulton* v *Jones* and the *Newstead* case is right? Would it be fairer to require the claimant to show that the media had been negligent in making defamatory allegations about him?
2. Do you agree with the approach of Moreland J in *O'Shea* v *MGN Ltd*?

(c) Publication

(i) General principles

Essential to the tort of defamation is the publication of the defamatory matter. The publication requirement will be satisfied where the matter is communicated to at least one person other than the claimant[139] in a form capable of being understood by that person.[140] It is important to note that each communication of defamatory matter gives rise to a separate publication and, hence, a separate cause of action.[141] This is known as the 'multiple

---

[138] *Aiken* v *Police Review Publishing Co* (Unreported, Court of Appeal (Civil Division), 12 April 1995).

[139] *Pullman* v *Walter Hill & Co* [1891] 1 QB 524, 527 (Lord Esher MR).

[140] For example, matter in a foreign language will not be considered to be published until it has been communicated to a recipient who understands that language: *Jones* v *Davers* (1596) Cro Eliz 496; 78 ER 747.

[141] *Duke of Brunswick* v *Harmer* (1849) 14 QB 185; *Pullman* v *Walter Hill & Co* [1891] 1 QB 525.

publication rule'. In practical terms, this rule means that the limitation period[142] begins to run each time the matter is communicated, regardless of when it was originally 'published'. This, of course, raises particular concerns for the operators of archives. In the case of *Duke of Brunswick v Harmer*,[143] for example, the Duke had been defamed in an edition of a journal that had been printed 17 years prior. The communication of the archived article to his servant, who the Duke himself had sent to retrieve the article, was held to constitute a fresh cause of action. This was despite the fact that an action in relation to the original cause of action was statute barred.

Concern over the application of the multiple publication rule to archives has been magnified by the growing availability of Internet media content, mainly due to the ease with which archival material can be accessed in the online environment. This was the subject of litigation in *Loutchansky v Times Newspapers Ltd [No 2]*.[144] In that case, the claimant brought an action against Times Newspapers Ltd, as well as the editor of *The Times* and two journalists, over two articles published in the newspaper. A further action was instituted regarding the continued publication of those same articles online more than one year after they were uploaded by the newspaper. Due to this lapse in time, the respondent sought to argue that the claimant was statute barred in bringing the second action in relation to the Internet publications. In particular, it was contended that an otherwise conventional application of the multiple publication rule in bringing about a fresh cause of action would be in breach of article 10.

Extract 10.3.11
***Loutchansky v Times Newspapers Ltd [No 2]* [2002] QB 783**

LORD PHILLIPS MR:

. . .

54. The argument before the judge turned on how [the provisions of the Limitation of Actions Act] should be applied in the case of publication on the Internet. The amendment sought by the defendants was designed to enable them to advance the case that the limitation period would begin to run as soon as the allegedly defamatory article was first posted on the website and that subsequent occasions upon which the website was accessed did not give rise to separate causes of action, each with its individual limitation period. As stated, the judge refused leave to amend because he considered that this argument was unsustainable . . .

55. Lord Lester . . . accepted that the amendment that the defendants sought to plead would only succeed if the Court were prepared to make new law. He submitted, however, that this area of the common law had developed to suit traditional hard copy publication and was inimical to modern conditions. He urged that the law should develop to reflect those conditions and to accommodate the requirements of the Human Rights Act 1998 and the [European Convention of Human Rights].

. . .

62. . . . Why do the defendants suggest that that law should be changed? The answer appears from the following passage in their skeleton argument:

> The difficulties which [the multiple publication] rule poses for the new technology of the internet, and in particular for website publication by newspapers of back numbers, are obvious. Above all, every day during which a back number remains on a website potentially gives rise to a new publication of that issue,

---

[142] In England and Wales the limitation period is currently one year from the date of publication of the libel or slander: Limitations Act 1980, s 4A.
[143] *Duke of Brunswick v Harmer* (1948) 14 QB 185.
[144] [2002] QB 783.

and therefore a new cause of action, whether by actual accessing of a defamatory article by an internet user, or (as the claimant argued was open to it) by reliance on an inference that someone must have accessed the article. The continuous and indefinite nature of that publication has the consequence that section 4A of the Limitation Act 1980 (which provides for a one-year limitation period in cases of libel and slander) is rendered nugatory, and that the maintainer of the website is liable to be indefinitely exposed to repeated claims in defamation. If it is accepted that there is a social utility in the technological advances which enable newspapers to provide an internet archive of back numbers which the general public can access immediately and without difficulty or expense, instead of having to buy a back number (if available) or visit a library which maintains a collection of newspaper back numbers, then the law as it had developed to suit traditional hard copy publication is now inimical to modern conditions, and (as has always been the strength of the common law) must evolve to reflect those conditions. As is developed below, it must evolve also to accommodate the requirements of the European Convention and of the Human Rights Act 1998.

63. How is it that the defendants suggest that the law should evolve? They focus on the provision of section 4A of the Limitation Act 1980 . . . that no action shall be brought after the expiration of one year from the date on which *the cause of action accrued.* They contend that the words italicised should be interpreted to mean *the date of the initial publication.*

. . .

67. . . . Section 4A of the Limitation Act 1980 . . . imposes an unusually short limitation period in defamation cases. The object of this is to ensure that defamation claims are initiated promptly. If claims are brought within a year of the initial publication, the defendants will be able to marshal any available defence and data available. Lord Lester argued that these benefits will be defeated if, long after the initial publication, a claimant can base a claim on access by a single person to a copy of the publication in question.

68. This was always true of documents in an archive or a library, as the *Duke of Brunswick* case . . . demonstrates. Lord Lester argued, however, that the position was much more acute where archives were provided on a website and thus very much more readily accessible.

. . .

71. Maintaining an archive of past press publications was a valuable public service. If a newspaper defendant which maintained a website of back numbers was to be indefinitely vulnerable to claims in defamation for years and even decades after the initial hard copy and Internet publication, such a rule was bound to have an effect on the preparedness of the media to maintain such websites, and thus to limit freedom of expression.

. . .

Our conclusion

73. . . . The defendants' submissions recognise that if they are to establish that the claims in the second action were time-barred they must, when applying section 4A, displace the rule in the *Duke of Brunswick* . . . and replace it by the American single publication rule. They must also establish that, under that rule, placing a publication on their website constitutes a single publication that occurs at the time it is placed on the website regardless of the period during which it remains there. The latter is by no means clear, but it is at least arguable. In our judgment the crucial question in relation to this part of the appeal is whether the defendants have made good their assertion that the rule in the *Duke of Brunswick* is in conflict with article 10 of the Human Rights Convention because it has a chilling effect upon the freedom of expression that goes beyond what is necessary and proportionate in a democratic society for the protection of the reputation of others.

74. We do not accept that the rule in the *Duke of Brunswick* case imposes a restriction on the readiness to maintain and provide access to archives that amounts to a disproportionate restriction on freedom of expression. We accept that the maintenance of archives, whether in

hard copy or on the Internet, has a social utility, but consider that the maintenance of archives is a comparatively insignificant aspect of freedom of expression. Archive material is stale news and its publication cannot rank in importance with the dissemination of contemporary material. Nor do we believe that the law of defamation need inhibit the responsible maintenance of archives. Where it is known that archive material is or may be defamatory, the attachment of an appropriate notice warning against treating it as the truth will normally remove any sting from the material.

. . .

76. The change in the law of defamation for which the appellants contend is a radical one. In our judgment they have failed to make out their case that such a change is required. The Internet Single Publication appeal is therefore dismissed.

An application on the part of *The Times* to the ECtHR that the decision in *Loutchansky* was a breach of article 10 of the European Convention (freedom of expression) was subsequently rejected.[145] The ECtHR held, however, that the case might be otherwise if there had been 'a significant lapse of time' between the original publication and the subsequent publication for which the defendant was being held liable.[146]

As pointed out in the above extract from *Loutchansky* v *Times Newspapers*, an alternative to the multiple publication rule would be to adopt the 'single publication rule' as it is applied in most states of the United States of America.[147] A key feature of this rule is that a single cause of action accrues at the date of the first publication of the matter, with the effect that there is a single date of publication for limitation purposes. This alternative to the multiple publication rule was canvassed by the Law Commission in 2002[148] and again by the Ministry of Justice in 2009.[149] A variation of the single publication rule has more recently been adopted in clause 8 of the government's draft Defamation Bill.

Extract 10.3.12
Defamation Bill

Clause 8 Single publication rule

1. This section applies if a person –

    (a) publishes a statement to the public (the first publication), and
    (b) subsequently publishes (whether or not to the public) that statement or a statement which is substantially the same.

2. In subsection (1) 'publication to the public' includes publication to a section of the public.

3. For the purposes of section 4A of the Limitation Act 1980 (time limit for actions for defamation etc.) any cause of action against the person for defamation in respect of the subsequent publication is to be treated as having accrued on the date of the first publication.

---

[145] *Times Newspapers Limited (Nos 1 and 2)* v *United Kingdom* (European Court of Human Rights, Application Nos 3002/03 and 23676/03, 10 March 2009).

[146] For a discussion of this aspect of the case see *Budu* v *British Broadcasting Corporation* [2010] EWHC 616 (QB) 112–15.

[147] See, e.g., Matthew Collins, *The Law of Defamation and the Internet* (Oxford University Press, 3rd edn, 2010) 30.16–30.19.

[148] Law Commission, *Defamation and the Internet: A Preliminary Investigation* (Law Com No 2, 2002). Available at: http://www.justice.gov.uk/lawcommission/docs/Defamation_and_the_Internet_Scoping.pdf.

[149] See Ministry of Justice, *Report of the Libel Working Group* (23 March 2010), 21; see also Ministry of Justice, *Defamation and the Internet: the Multiple Publication Rule* (CP20/09, 16 September 2009).

4. This section does not apply in relation to the subsequent publication if the manner of that publication is materially different from the manner for the first publication.

5. In determining whether the manner of a subsequent publication is materially different from the manner of the first publication, the matters to which the court may have regard include (amongst other matters) –

   (a) the level of prominence that a statement is given;
   (b) the extent of the subsequent publication.

. . .

Question for discussion

1. Do you agree with the 'single publication rule' set out in clause 8 of the Defamation Bill?
2. Does clause 8 technically impose a 'single cause of action', or does it achieve its purpose in another way? Why/how?

(ii) Cross-jurisdictional publications and forum shopping

Publication of defamatory material occurs at the place where the defamatory matter is received.[150] In turn, the place of publication is the place where the tort is committed. This, combined with the multiple publication rule, means that a single media item may give rise to claims in tort in all of the different jurisdictions where it is read, viewed or heard, regardless of where it originated. For example, an English tort will be committed every time a publication originating in a foreign jurisdiction, such as the US, is viewed in England.[151] This has particular relevance for international media organisations that distribute their content to recipients in multiple jurisdictions (e.g., book publishers or international news producers) and, as a result, are required to consider the defamation laws of each of the jurisdictions in which their content is published. It also raises particular concerns in relation to material uploaded onto the Internet. Thus, the High Court of Australia in *Dow Jones v Gutnick*,[152] in rejecting the adoption of a 'single publication rule' in relation to Internet content, held that a tort is committed in each of the jurisdictions where the defamatory material is *downloaded* rather than the place where the servers are located or place from where the material was uploaded.

The apparent willingness of English courts to accept jurisdiction where there has been limited local publication, along with the application of relatively 'claimant friendly' common law standards to resolve such disputes,[153] has meant that England is often said to be the jurisdiction of choice for claimants wishing to pursue 'international libels'. Under the European Union's Regulation on Jurisdiction, Recognition and Enforcement of Judgements (Brussels I),[154] English courts must accept jurisdiction if the defendant is domiciled in England, irrespective of where the material originated or where the claimant is domiciled.[155] English courts must also accept jurisdiction under the Regulation if the defendant is

---

[150] *Bata v Bata* [1948] WN 366 (CA); *Berezovsky v Michaels* [2000] UKHL 25.
[151] *Berezovsky v Michaels* [2000] UKHL 25.
[152] (2002) 210 CLR 575.
[153] Common law choice of law rules apply to defamation. This means that the law of the place of the tort (England) will apply to the resolution of the dispute. Defamation is explicitly excluded from *Rome II Regulation, Regulation (EC) No 864/2007* [2007] OJ L 199/40, art 1(2)(g).
[154] *Regulation (EC) No 44/2001* [2001] OJ L 12/1.
[155] *Owusu v Jackson* (C-281/02) [2005] ECR I-553.

domiciled in another EU Member State *and* the material was published to *any* extent in England; but under this option the claim will be limited to damages suffered in England.[156] In the more recent case of *eDate Advertising GmbH* v *X* and *Olivier Martinez* v *MGN Ltd*,[157] however, the Grand Chamber of the ECJ held that, where Internet publications are concerned, a claim for all of the damage can also be brought in the place where the claimant has their 'centre of interests'.[158] This will be the place where the claimant resides or where they pursue their professional activities.[159] On the other hand, where a defendant is not domiciled in a Member State – for example, where the defendant resides in the US but the material has been published in England – Brussels I is not applicable and the usual rules of personal jurisdiction will apply. This requires that a 'real and substantial tort' be committed within the jurisdiction, judged by reference to the claimant's local reputation and the extent of the publication within the jurisdiction.[160]

Forum shopping in the libel context is considered particularly open to criticism when pursued by foreign claimants suing over publications originating with a foreign publisher – known otherwise as 'libel tourism'. Critics of this variety of forum shopping claim that it imposes significant burdens on freedom of speech (especially where it is used to circumvent more stringent free speech standards in the publisher's home jurisdiction) or that it is an inappropriate use of English court resources. On the other hand, it has been suggested that there is no reason why a foreign claimant should not be able to sue in England in order to vindicate their English reputation.[161] Still others argue that much of the concern over libel tourism is anecdotal and is not supported empirically when one considers the number of cases that can be characterised as 'libel tourism' cases.

Clause 9 of the Defamation Bill is intended to combat the 'problem' of libel tourism.

Extract 10.3.13
Defamation Bill

Clause 9 Action against a person not domiciled in the UK or a Member State etc.

1. This section applies to an action for defamation against a person who is not domiciled –

    (a) in the United Kingdom;
    (b) in another Member State; or
    (c) in a state which is for the time being a contracting party to the Lugano Convention.

2. A court does not have jurisdiction to hear and determine an action to which this section applies unless the court is satisfied that, of all the places in which the statement complained of has been published, England and Wales is clearly the most appropriate place in which to bring an action in respect of the statement.

. . .

---

[156] *Shevill* v *Press Alliance* (C-68/93) [1995] ECR I-415.
[157] (Court of Justice of the European Union, C-509/09 and C-161/10, 25 October 2011). Although a privacy case, the rule would apply equally in the defamation context.
[158] *eDate Advertising GmbH* v *X* and *Olivier Martinez* v *MGN Ltd* (Court of Justice of the European Union, C-509/09 and C-161/10, 25 October 2011), 48.
[159] Ibid., 49.
[160] See, e.g., *Berezovsky* v *Michaels* [2000] UKHL 25; *Dow Jones* v *Jameel* [2005] QB 946. Where a real and substantial tort has not occurred within the jurisdiction, a defendant may apply to have service set aside or a stay of proceedings on the basis of *forum non conveniens*. Alternatively, a defendant who has already submitted to the jurisdiction may be able to have the case struck out as an abuse of process on the basis that no real and substantial tort has been committed (now known as a '*Jameel* abuse').
[161] See, e.g., Lord Hoffmann, 'Libel Tourism' (Speech delivered at the Dame Ann Ebsworth Memorial Lecture, Inner Temple Hall, London, 6 February 2010).

Question for discussion

1. Is libel tourism a concern? Should measures be adopted to prevent foreign claimants suing foreign defendants in the English courts and, if so, do you think the solution proposed in clause 9 of the Defamation Bill is appropriate?

(iii) Liability for publication: who can be sued?

Any person who has 'participated in, secured or authorised'[162] the communication of the defamatory matter will be liable, provided he or she intended to make the publication or was negligent as to publication occurring.[163] For the media, this means that the claimant may sue the author of a libellous newspaper or magazine article as well as the editor, proprietor and printer. Disseminators of defamatory publications will also be liable, such as newsagents, newsstand operators, libraries and archives (however, such 'secondary publishers' may avoid liability by showing that they did not know that the publication contained defamatory matter and that they had exercised reasonable care – see Section 10.4(e)). Similarly, in the case of television and radio, a broadcasting company is liable for anything said in the course of a studio discussion or phone-in programme, along with the programme's producer as well as the person who actually spoke the impugned words. Importantly, where more than one person is responsible for a publication, each joint tortfeasor may be sued individually for all of the damage caused by the publication.

In certain circumstances, a defendant may also be liable where they fail to remove defamatory matter posted by another on property under the defendant's control.[164] In *Byrne v Deane*,[165] the proprietors of a golf club were liable for failing to remove a defamatory notice from a bulletin board. While the notice had been posted anonymously, Greer LJ held that by allowing the material to remain on the board, with the knowledge that it would be read by others, an inference could be properly drawn that the proprietors were 'consenting parties to its continued presence',[166] and hence, were 'taking part in the publication of it'.[167] Such an inference, however, will not be drawn where the removal of the matter would require 'very great trouble and expense.'[168]

A person who repeats a defamatory comment made by another will be liable for such repetition; repeating a libel constitutes a fresh publication and gives rise to a separate cause of action.[169] This will be the case even where it is made clear on the face of the republication that the allegation originated with someone else – for example, through use of the words 'X said that P . . .'.[170] The potential liability for republication, of course, has particular relevance for the media in their daily business of reporting newsworthy allegations made

---

[162] Gatley, 6.4.

[163] See, e.g., *Pullman v Hill* [1891] 1 QB 524. The question of intention to publish is different from that of intention to defame. In order to be liable, a defendant need not intend that the published words be defamatory of the claimant: *Cassidy v Daily Mirror* [1929] 2 KB 331 (Extract 10.3.3). It is in this sense that defamation is considered to be a strict liability tort. Thus, '[t]here is no liability for intentionally defamatory matter published accidentally, unlike accidentally defamatory matter published intentionally': Carolyn Sappideen and Prue Vines (eds), *Fleming's: The Law of Torts* (Thomson Reuters, 10th edn, 2011) 631.

[164] *Byrne v Deane* [1937] 1 KB 818, 838 (per Greer LJ).

[165] [1937] 1 KB 818.

[166] Ibid., 838.

[167] Ibid., 830.

[168] Ibid., 838.

[169] See, e.g., *Lewis v Daily Telegraph Ltd* [1964] AC 234, 260; *Stern v Piper* [1997] QB 123 (CA); *Charman v Orion Publishing Ltd* [2007] EWCA Civ 972.

[170] *Lewis v Walter* (1821) 4 B & Ald 605, 106 ER 1058; see Gatley, 6.32.

by others. It should be noted, however, that media organisations may be able to take advantage of the so-called 'reportage defence' in reporting the making of allegations (see Section 10.4(c)(v); see also discussion of the 'repetition rule': Section 10.4(a)).

In addition to liability on the part of the republisher, the original publisher of defamatory matter may also be liable for its repetition.[171] Such liability is dependent upon whether (1) the defendant authorised (expressly or impliedly), secured or participated in its republication[172] or (2) republication was a 'reasonably foreseeable consequence of the original publication'.[173] Where an interviewee defames someone in the course of an interview given to the media, they will, generally speaking, be considered to have authorised the republication of the defamation or, alternatively, such republication will be considered to be a natural and probable consequence of the original publication. In *Sims* v *Wran*, for example, it was held that a natural and probable consequence of a politician giving a statement at a press conference would be its repetition in the media.[174] The same has been held where a defendant gives a statement to a reporter[175] or issues a press release.[176] In *McManus* v *Beckham*,[177] a singer and wife of a well-known footballer advised customers in a memorabilia shop that a signed photograph of her husband was a fake. The shop owners sought to hold the defendant liable for damage to their business suffered as a result of the widespread repetition of the allegations in the press. It was held by the Court of Appeal that a strike out order should not have been issued by the trial judge in relation to the repetition and that the claimant's particulars that the defendant was a well-known celebrity who courted publicity and knew, or ought reasonably to have foreseen, that her remarks would be repeated by the media should stand.[178]

Clause 10 of the Defamation Bill seeks to limit liability to authors, editors and publishers. This is to prevent the threat of liability being imposed on non-primary publishers.

Extract 10.3.14
Defamation Bill

Clause 10 Action against a person who was not the author, editor etc.

1. A court does not have jurisdiction to hear and determine an action for defamation brought against a person who was not the author, editor or publisher of the statement complained of unless the court is satisfied that it is not reasonably practicable for an action to be brought against the author, editor or publisher.
2. In this section 'author', 'editor' and 'publisher' have the same meaning as in section 1 of the Defamation Act 1996.[179]

---

[171] In such a situation, the claimant may elect to sue the defendant either (1) for separate causes of action arising from the original publication and the repetition or (2) for the cause of action arising from the original publication but seek to claim for the damage caused by its repetition: *Sims* v *Wran* [1984] 1 NSWLR 317, 320. The latter option will, of course, be the only course where the repetition does not amount to, for whatever reason, to a separate libel: see, e.g., *Slipper* v *BBC* [1991] 1 QB 283 (CA).
[172] Mullis in Carter-Ruck on Libel and Privacy, 5.28.
[173] Ibid., 5.31, citing *McManus* v *Beckham* [2002] EWCA Civ 939. An original publisher will also be liable for republication where there was a moral, legal or social duty on the part of the recipient to republish to a third party: see Mullis in Carter-Ruck on Libel and Privacy, 5.34.
[174] [1984] 1 NSWLR 317.
[175] *Richards* v *New South Wales* [2004] VSC 198 (24 May 2004).
[176] *Kirby-Harris* v *Baxter* [1995] EMLR 516 (CA).
[177] [2002] EWCA Civ 939.
[178] It should be noted that the court in *McManus* v *Beckham* [2002] EWCA Civ 939 at 33 expressed caution about using the language of reasonable foreseeability alone in directing the jury.
[179] Extracted at 10.4.16.

> ## Questions for discussion
>
> 1. Do you think responsibility for publication should be limited to authors, editors and publishers, as proposed by clause 10 of the Defamation Bill?
> 2. Do you think clause 10 is necessary to achieve this, or do subordinate publishers currently receive adequate protection through the innocent dissemination defence?

(iv) Liability for Internet publication

In the Internet intermediary context, it was held in *Bunt* v *Tilley* that an Internet service provider (ISP) acting as a mere conduit for the publication of defamatory matter will not be considered, in the absence of knowledge, to be a publisher.[180] Eady J held that for an ISP to be responsible 'there must be knowing involvement in the process of publication of *the relevant words*';[181] playing merely a 'passive' role in the communication of the matter will not be enough.[182] In contrast, in the case of *Godfrey* v *Demon Internet Ltd*, decided prior to *Bunt* v *Tilley*, Morland J found that an ISP was responsible as a publisher of defamatory material hosted on its online bulletin board service; in this sense, the ISP was much more than a mere conduit.[183] While the defendant on the facts had been put on notice that the defamatory material was being hosted on its servers and had refused to remove it, Morland J indicated that the defendant would nevertheless be liable for hosting defamatory content even in the absence of knowledge.[184] In *Metropolitan International Schools Ltd* v *Designtechnica Corp*[185], Eady J applied his own reasoning in *Bunt* v *Tilley* in finding that Google could not be considered to have published defamatory material appearing on a search results page where the material is generated by an automated search engine.[186] Nor, it appeared, will a search engine operator be treated as having published the pages to which it links, although the court did not consider this point directly.

More recently, the question of Internet intermediary liability – including the approach of Eady J in the decisions just described – was considered by the Court of Appeal in the case of *Tamiz* v *Google Inc.*[187] The claimant brought proceedings against Google Inc. regarding comments appearing in response to a blog post that was hosted on Google Inc.'s servers as part of its 'Blogger.com' service. Despite receiving notification of the comments, Eady J held that Google Inc. was not to be regarded either as a publisher or to have authorised publication. A significant factor, according to Eady J, was that Google was 'not required to take any positive step, technically, in the process of continuing the accessibility of the offending material'.[188] Hence, applying and expanding upon his reasoning in *Bunt* v *Tilley*,

---

[180] See, e.g., *Bunt* v *Tilley* [2006] EWHC 407 (QB). For a full discussion of the law relating to publication and Internet intermediaries, see Matthew Collins, *The Law of Defamation and the Internet* (Oxford University Press, 3rd edn, 2011) 6.36–6.56.

[181] *Bunt* v *Tiley* [2006] EWHC 407 (QB) [23] (emphasis added).

[182] Ibid.

[183] Contrary to Eady J's later decision in *Bunt* v *Tilley*, however, Morland J held that a mere conduit would also be a publisher: see *Godfrey* v *Demon Internet Ltd* [2001] QB 201, 212.

[184] See, e.g., *Godfrey* v *Demon Internet Ltd* [2001] QB 201, 207. An ISP without knowledge, however, would be able to rely on defences under s 1 of the Defamation Act 1996 and the Electronic Commerce (EC Directive) Regulations 2002 (see Extracts 10.4.16 and 10.4.17).

[185] [2009] EMLR 27.

[186] Cf. *Trkulja* v *Google* [2012] VSC 533 (12 November 2012) (where Beach J refused to interfere with a jury's verdict that Google was the publisher of its search results page).

[187] [2012] EWHC 449 (QB).

[188] Ibid., 39.

his Honour found that Google's role as a platform provider was 'a purely passive one'.[189] Tamiz appealed to the Court of Appeal.

Extract 10.3.15
Tamiz v *Google* **[2013] EWCA Civ 68**

Whether Google Inc was a publisher of the comments

. . .

16. . . . [T]he judge noted *inter alia* that it was virtually impossible for Google Inc to exercise editorial control over the content of the blogs it hosts, which in the aggregate contain more than half a trillion words, with 250,000 new words added every minute. He referred to the submission that it would be unrealistic to attribute responsibility for publication of material on any particular blog to Google Inc, whether before or after notification of a complaint. He also referred to the importance of striving to achieve consistency in decisions in the face of rapidly developing technology, and to paying proper regard to the values enshrined in the ECHR. He said that the fact that an entity in Google Inc's position had been notified of a complaint did not immediately convert its status or role into that of a publisher. If Google Inc's status before notification of a complaint was that of a provider or a facilitator, it was not easy to see why that role should be expanded thereafter into that of a person who authorised or acquiesced in publication. Google Inc claimed to remain as neutral in the process after notification as it was before. It might be true that it had the technical capability of taking down blogs or comments on its platform, yet that was not by any means the same as saying that it had become an author or authoriser of the publication:

> It is no doubt often true that the owner of a wall which has been festooned, overnight, with defamatory graffiti could acquire scaffolding and have it all deleted with whitewash. That is not necessarily to say, however, that the unfortunate owner must, unless and until this has been accomplished, be classified as a publisher.

. . .

17. The judge went on at 39 to attach significance to the evidence that Google Inc was not required to take any positive step, technically, in the process of continuing the accessibility of the offending material: he said that its role as a platform provider was 'a purely passive one'. The situation was thus in his view closely analogous to that described in *Bunt* v *Tilley* [2007] 1 WLR 1243, and in striving to achieve consistency in the court's decision-making he would rule that Google Inc was not liable at common law as a publisher . . .

18. *Bunt* v *Tilley* concerned internet service providers (ISPs) who were not alleged to have *hosted* any website relevant to the claims. The issue was whether they could be liable simply in respect of defamatory material communicated via the services they provided . . .

19. At 36 he held that an ISP which performs no more than a passive role in facilitating postings on the internet cannot be deemed to be a publisher at common law. A telephone company or other passive medium of communication, such as an ISP, is not analogous to someone in the position of a distributor, who might at common law be treated as having published so as to need a defence . . .

20. In *Metropolitan International Schools Ltd* v *Designtechnica Corpn* [2011] 1 WLR 1743 Eady J applied a similar analysis in relation to defamatory comments which, having been posted on a website, appeared as a 'snippet' of information when an Internet search was carried out under the claimant's name on Google Inc's search engine. The judge said that for a person to be fixed at common law with responsibility for publishing defamatory words, there needed to be a mental element, as summarised in *Bunt* v *Tilley*. He held that the search in issue was performed automatically and involved no input from Google Inc, which had not authorised or caused the

---

[189] Ibid.

snippet to appear on the user's screen in any meaningful sense but had merely by the provision of its search service played the role of a facilitator. As to the position once Google Inc had been informed of the defamatory content of the snippet, the judge said that a person can be liable for the publication of libel by acquiescence, that is to say by permitting publication to continue when he or she has the power to prevent it. He drew a distinction between a search engine and someone hosting a website, pointing to the greater difficulty of ensuring that offending words do not appear on a search snippet. Google Inc's 'take-down' procedure might not have operated as rapidly as the claimant would wish, but it did not follow as a matter of law that between notification and take-down Google Inc became liable as a publisher of the offending material. While efforts were being made to achieve a take-down in relation to a particular URL it was hardly possible to fix Google Inc with liability on the basis of authorisation, approval or acquiescence. On the facts of the case, he believed it unrealistic to attribute responsibility for publication to Google Inc . . .

21. At the forefront of the appellant's submissions to this court was an elaborate attack on *Bunt* v *Tilley* as applied in *Metropolitan International Schools Ltd* and the present case. Mr Busuttil submitted that the reasoning in *Bunt* v *Tilley* erroneously conflated a number of different threads of law. What Eady J said about the need for 'knowing involvement in the process of publication of *the relevant words*' is at odds with the principle of strict liability for publication, irrespective of knowledge of the defamatory words. Further, in certain circumstances a person may be or become involved in publishing defamatory material by omission, by failing or forbearing to take a step that ought to have been taken, or by remaining passive . . .

. . .

23. I do not find it necessary to address the full detail of Mr Busuttil's criticisms of *Bunt* v *Tilley*. I am not persuaded that Eady J fell into any fundamental error of analysis or reached the wrong conclusion in relation to the kind of internet service under consideration in that case. For the reasons set out below, however, I respectfully differ from Eady J's view that the present case is so closely analogous to *Bunt* v *Tilley* as to call for the same conclusion. In my view the judge was wrong to regard Google Inc's role in respect of Blogger blogs as a purely passive one and to attach the significance he did to the absence of any positive steps by Google Inc in relation to continued publication of the comments in issue . . .

24. By the Blogger service Google Inc provides a platform for blogs, together with design tools and, if required, a URL; it also provides a related service to enable the display of remunerative advertisements on a blog. It makes the Blogger service available on terms of its own choice and it can readily remove or block access to any blog that does not comply with those terms (a point of distinction with the search engine under consideration in *Metropolitan International Schools Ltd*, as the judge himself noted in that case) . . .

25. By the provision of that service Google Inc plainly facilitates publication of the blogs (including the comments posted on them). Its involvement is not such, however, as to make it a primary publisher of the blogs. It does not create the blogs or have any prior knowledge of, or effective control over, their content. It is not in a position comparable to that of the author or editor of a defamatory article. Nor is it in a position comparable to that of the corporate proprietor of a newspaper in which a defamatory article is printed. Such a corporation may be liable as a primary publisher by reason of the involvement of its employees or agents in the publication. But there is no relationship of employment or agency between Google Inc and the bloggers or those posting comments on the blogs: such people are plainly independent of Google Inc and do not act in any sense on its behalf or in its name. The appellant's reliance on principles of vicarious liability or agency in this context is misplaced . . .

26. I am also very doubtful about the argument that Google Inc's role is that of a secondary publisher, facilitating publication in a manner analogous to a distributor. In any event it seems to me that such an argument can get nowhere in relation to the period prior to notification of the

complaint. There is a long established line of authority that a person involved only in dissemination is not to be treated as a publisher unless he knew or ought by the exercise of reasonable care to have known that the publication was likely to be defamatory: *Emmens* v *Pottle* (1885) 16 QBD 354, 357–358; *Vizetelly* v *Mudie's Select Library Ltd* [1900] 2 QB 170, 177–180; *Bottomley* v *FW Woolworth and Co Ltd* (1932) 48 TLR 521 . . . Since it cannot be said that Google Inc either knew or ought reasonably to have known of the defamatory comments prior to notification of the appellant's complaint, that line of authority tells against viewing Google Inc as a secondary publisher prior to such notification. Moreover, even if it were to be so regarded, it would have an unassailable defence during that period under section 1 of the 1996 Act . . .

27. In relation to the position *after* notification of the complaint, however, additional considerations arise, and it is in relation to this period that I take a different view from that of Eady J on the issue of publication. I am led to do so primarily by the decision of the Court of Appeal in *Byrne* v *Deane* [1937] 1 KB 818 . . .

. . .

30. *Byrne* v *Deane* was considered in *Godfrey* v *Demon Internet Ltd* [2001] QB 201 . . .

31. More directly in point is *Davison* v *Habeeb and Others* [2011] EWHC 3031 (QB), which concerned defamatory material posted on a blog hosted by Google Inc itself. HHJ Parkes QC, sitting as a deputy judge of the High Court, considered it arguable that Google Inc was a publisher from the outset, subject to the defence under section 1 of the 1996 Act, but he also relied on *Byrne* v *Deane* as an alternative strand in the reasoning that led him to conclude that there was an arguable case against Google Inc . . .

. . .

33. In the present case, Eady J referred at 32–33 to *Godfrey* v *Demon Internet Ltd* and to *Davison* v *Habeeb*, observing that the position may well be fact sensitive: liability may turn upon the extent to which the relevant ISP has knowledge of the words complained of, and of their illegality or potential illegality, and/or on the extent to which it has control over publication. In relation to Blogger he said nothing about HHJ Parkes QC's analogy with the provision of a gigantic notice board on which others post comments. Instead, he drew an analogy with ownership of a wall on which various people choose to inscribe graffiti, for which the owner is not responsible (see 16 above). I have to say that I find the notice board analogy far more apposite and useful than the graffiti analogy. The provision of a platform for the blogs is equivalent to the provision of a notice board; and Google Inc goes further than this by providing tools to help a blogger design the layout of his part of the notice board and by providing a service that enables a blogger to display advertisements alongside the notices on his part of the notice board. Most importantly, it makes the notice board available to bloggers on terms of its own choice and it can readily remove or block access to any notice that does not comply with those terms . . .

34. Those features bring the case in my view within the scope of the reasoning in *Byrne* v *Deane*. Thus, if Google Inc allows defamatory material to remain on a Blogger blog after it has been notified of the presence of that material, it might be inferred to have associated itself with, or to have made itself responsible for, the continued presence of that material on the blog and thereby to have become a publisher of the material . . .

Questions for discussion

1. Do you prefer the reasoning of Eady J or the Court of Appeal in *Tamiz* v *Google Inc*?
2. Can the Court of Appeal's reasoning in *Tamiz* v *Google Inc*, where Google was put on notice of the offending material, be reconciled with Eady J's decision in *Metropolitan International Schools*? Why/why not?

A further issue in the Internet context relates to whether hyperlinking to defamatory content constitutes publication of such content.[190] Under general principles, one would have thought that a defendant who links to another's site containing defamatory material would be considered to have participated in its publication.[191] Thus, by analogy, it has been held that a defendant 'may be liable for republishing by reference to a statement originally published on another occasion by himself or another'.[192] However, in *Crookes v Newton*,[193] the Supreme Court of Canada disagreed. In that case, Newton owned and operated a website that focused on free speech and the Internet in Canada. It contained a number of hyperlinks that linked to websites said to be defamatory of the plaintiff, Crookes.

Extract 10.3.16
***Crookes* v *Newton* [2011] 3 SCR 269**

ABELLA J:

26. A reference to other content is fundamentally different from other acts involved in publication. Referencing on its own does not involve exerting *control* over the content. Communicating something is very different from merely communicating that something exists or where it exists. The former involves dissemination of the content, and suggests control over both the content and whether the content will reach an audience at all, while the latter does not. Even where the goal of the person referring to a defamatory publication is to expand that publication's audience, his or her participation is merely ancillary to that of the initial publisher: with or without the reference, the allegedly defamatory information has already been made available to the public by the initial publisher or publishers' acts. These features of references distinguish them from acts in the publication process like creating or posting the defamatory publication, and from repetition.

27. Hyperlinks are, in essence, references. By clicking on the link, readers are directed to other sources. Hyperlinks may be inserted with or without the knowledge of the operator of the site containing the secondary article. Because the content of the secondary article is often produced by someone other than the person who inserted the hyperlink in the primary article, the content on the other end of the link can be changed at any time by whoever controls the secondary page. Although the primary author controls whether there is a hyperlink and what article that word or phrase is linked to, inserting a hyperlink gives the primary author no control over the content in the secondary article to which he or she has linked.

. . .

29. Although the person selecting the content to which he or she wants to link might *facilitate* the transfer of information (a traditional hallmark of publication), it is equally clear that when a person follows a link they are leaving one source and moving to another. In my view, then, it is the actual creator or poster of the defamatory words in the secondary material who is publishing the libel when a person follows a hyperlink to that content. The ease with which the referenced content can be accessed does not change the fact that, by hyperlinking, an individual is referring the reader to other content . . .

30. Hyperlinks thus share the same relationship with the content to which they refer as do references. Both communicate that something exists, but do not, by themselves, communicate

---

[190] For a detailed discussion of defamation liability for hyperlinking see Matthew Collins, *Defamation and the Internet* (Oxford University Press, 3rd edn, 2010) 5.42–5.62. The matter was recently raised in *McGrath* v *Dawkins* [2012] EWHC B3 (QB) where it was said (at 26) that 'the law on liability for hyperlinks is in a state of some uncertainty at present' and may well be 'fact-sensitive'.
[191] Gatley 6.34.
[192] See *Buchanan* v *Jennings* [2005] 1 AC 115, 12.
[193] [2011] 3 SCR 269.

its content. And they both require some act on the part of a third party before he or she gains access to the content. The fact that access to that content is far easier with hyperlinks than with footnotes does not change the reality that a hyperlink, by itself, is content neutral – it expresses no opinion, nor does it have any control over, the content to which it refers.

31. This interpretation of the publication rule better accords with our Court's recent jurisprudence on defamation law. This Court has recognized that what is at stake in an action for defamation is not only an individual's interest in protecting his or her reputation, but also the public's interest in protecting freedom of expression: *Hill* v *Church of Scientology of Toronto*, [1995] 2 SCR 1130.

. . .

36. The Internet cannot, in short, provide access to information without hyperlinks. Limiting their usefulness by subjecting them to the traditional publication rule would have the effect of seriously restricting the flow of information and, as a result, freedom of expression. The potential 'chill' in how the Internet functions could be devastating, since primary article authors would unlikely want to risk liability for linking to another article over whose changeable content they have no control. Given the core significance of the role of hyperlinking to the Internet, we risk impairing its whole functioning.

. . .

42. . . . Only when a hyperlinker presents content from the hyperlinked material in a way that actually repeats the defamatory content, should that content be considered to be 'published' by the hyperlinker. Such an approach promotes expression and respects the realities of the Internet, while creating little or no limitations to a plaintiff's ability to vindicate his or her reputation. While a mere reference to another source should not fall under the wide breadth of the traditional publication rule, the rule itself and the limits of the one writer/any act/one reader paradigm may deserve further scrutiny in the future.

[Abella J dismissed the appeal.]

THE CHIEF JUSTICE AND FISH J:

46. We have read the reasons of Deschamps J and Abella J. While we agree in large part with the reasons of Abella J, we respectfully propose a different formulation of the test for when a hyperlink reference in a text constitutes publication of defamatory matter to which it links.

. . .

48. Abella J concludes that '[o]nly when a hyperlinker presents content from the hyperlinked material in a way that actually repeats the defamatory content, should that content be considered to be "published" by the hyperlinker' (para 42). In our view, the combined text and hyperlink may amount to publication of defamatory material in the hyperlink in some circumstances. Publication of a defamatory statement via a hyperlink should be found if the text indicates *adoption or endorsement of the content of the hyperlinked text*. If the text communicates agreement with the content linked to, then the hyperlinker should be liable for the defamatory content. The defendant must adopt or endorse the defamatory words or material; a mere general reference to a web site is not enough. Thus, defendants linking approvingly to an innocent web site that later becomes defamatory would not be liable.

49. Finding publication in adoption or endorsement of the defamatory material in a web site is consistent with the general law of defamation. In *Hill* v *Church of Scientology of Toronto*, [1995] 2 SCR 1130, at para 176, this Court held:

> If one person writes a libel, another repeats it, and a third approves what is written, they all have made the defamatory libel. Both the person who originally utters the defamatory statement, and the individual who expresses agreement with it, are liable for the injury.

50. In sum, in our view, a hyperlink should constitute publication if, read contextually, the text that includes the hyperlink constitutes adoption or endorsement of the specific content it links to.

51. It is true that the traditional publication rule does not require the publisher to approve of the material published; he or she must merely communicate that material to a third party. However, the proposed adoption or endorsement standard for references is conceptually different. A mere reference without any adoption or endorsement remains that – a content neutral reference. Adoption or endorsement of the content accessible by a link in the text can be understood to actually incorporate the defamatory content into the text. Thus the content of the text comes to include the defamatory content accessed via hyperlink. The hyperlink, combined with the surrounding words and context, ceases to be a mere reference and the content to which it refers becomes part of the published text itself.

[The Chief Justice and Fish J dismissed the appeal.]

DESCHAMPS J:

55. . . . [P]ublication has two components: (1) an act that makes the defamatory information available to a third party in a comprehensible form, and (2) the receipt of the information by a third party in such a way that it is understood.

. . .

58. To create a specifically Canadian exception for references, which has the effect of excluding hyperlinks from the scope of the publication rule, is in my view an inadequate solution to the novel issues raised by the Internet. On the one hand, this blanket exclusion exaggerates the difference between references and other acts of publication. On the other hand, it treats all references, from footnotes to hyperlinks, alike. In so doing, it disregards the fact that references vary greatly in how they make defamatory information available to third parties and, consequently, in the harm they can cause to people's reputations.

59. A more nuanced approach to revising the publication rule, and one that can be applied effectively to new media, would be for the Court to hold that in Canadian law, a reference to defamatory content can satisfy the requirements of the first component of publication if it makes the defamatory information *readily available* to a third party in a comprehensible form. In addition, the Court should make it clear that not every act, but only *deliberate* acts, can lead to liability for defamation.

. . .

61. . . . With respect, a shortcoming in [Abella J's] approach is that she fails to consider the law of defamation generally, and instead focusses narrowly on one aspect of the rules governing publication. The result is problematically one-sided, as individuals who suffer harm to their reputations are left with no recourse against those who perpetuate defamatory information.

[Deschamp J dismissed the appeal, finding that Crookes could not establish the second component of publication – i.e., that the links had actually resulted in the defamatory content being viewed].

Questions for discussion

1. Do you agree that hyperlinking should constitute publication of the matter being linked to?
2. Do you prefer the reasoning of Abella J, or the reasoning of the Chief Justice and Fish J?

(d) Who can sue in defamation?

(i) Natural persons and corporations

Any person, natural or legal, may bring an action for libel. Companies (including banks)[194] and partnerships are entitled to sue; trade unions, on the other hand, cannot sue in their own name, since they are not treated as having legal personality.[195] (However, their officers may bring an action, so in practice this disability does not much matter.) Nor can a dead person sue, or for that matter be sued. It may be in bad taste to criticise the dead, let alone defame them, but they are fair game for the media.

While a corporation has standing to sue, it is clear that it is impossible for it to be injured in its feelings. A corporation, therefore, can only sue for compensation of economic loss (either loss of income or damage to its goodwill). However, there is no requirement for a corporation to prove this loss as special damage; rather, a corporation is entitled to the presumption of damage in relation to such harm. This was recently reaffirmed by a 3–2 majority of the House of Lords in the case of *Jameel* v *Wall Street Journal Europe Sprl*,[196] where it was found that it was not a violation of article 10 of the European Convention to afford corporations the presumption of damage. Mohammed Jameel and the company of which he was president brought an action against the Wall Street Journal Europe Sprl over an article that alleged that the company's bank accounts were being monitored in order to prevent them from being used to fund terrorism.

Extract 10.3.17
***Jameel* v *Wall Street Journal Europe Sprl* [2007] 1 AC 359**

LORD BINGHAM:

18. . . . The newspaper in this case relies on article 10 to contend that a domestic rule entitling a trading corporation to sue in libel when it can prove no financial loss is an unreasonable restraint on the right to publish protected by article 10 . . .

19. This is not an unattractive argument, and it would be persuasive if, in such a case, excessive, punitive or exemplary damages were awarded. But the damages awarded to the second claimant in this case were not excessive, and the argument encounters three problems of principle. First, as the text of article 10 itself makes plain, the right guaranteed by the article is not unqualified. The right may be circumscribed by restrictions prescribed by law and necessary and proportionate if directed to certain ends, one of which is the protection of the reputation or rights of others. Thus a national libel law may, consistently with article 10, restrain the publication of defamatory material . . .

20. Secondly, the national rule here in question, pertaining to the recovery of damages by a trading corporation which proves no financial loss, has been the subject of challenge before the European Commission and Court in the context of libel proceedings brought by two corporate plaintiffs against two individual defendants. In *S and M* v *United Kingdom* (1993) 18 EHRR CD 172, 173, the challenge to the rule was somewhat oblique and the Commission made the points summarised in para 19 above. In *Steel and Morris* v *United Kingdom* (2005) 41 EHRR 403 the challenge was direct: see para 31 (a) and (b), p 419. The Court accepted that the domestic rule was as stated in *Derbyshire* (para 40) but held (para 94) that:

---

[194] *Jameel* v *Wall Street Journal Europe Sprl* [2007] 1 AC 359.
[195] *EETPU* v *Times Newspapers* [1980] QB 585. However, the correctness of this view has been subject to doubt: see Gatley 8.23.
[196] [2007] 1 AC 359.

The state therefore enjoys a margin of appreciation as to the means it provides under domestic law to enable a company to challenge the truth, and limit the damage, of allegations which risk harming its reputation.

The Court cited and echoed observations in an earlier decision, *Märkt Intern and Beerman* v *Germany* (1989) 12 EHRR 161, paras 33–38. Thus the Court did not hold the current rule to be necessarily inconsistent with article 10: it was a matter for the judgment of the national authorities.

21. Thirdly, the weight placed by the newspaper on the chilling effect of the existing rule is in my opinion exaggerated. Among the arguments it advances is that the rule is unnecessary since, it is said, defamation of a company involves defamation of directors and individuals who are free to sue as personal plaintiffs. I very much doubt if this is always so, although in some cases it will be. But, to the extent that it is so, I question whether the possibility of a claim by the company will add significantly to the chilling effect of a claim by the individuals.

22. I would accordingly answer this question in the negative . . .

Revision of the current law

. . .

24. The tort of defamation exists to afford redress for unjustified injury to reputation. By a successful action the injured reputation is vindicated. The ordinary means of vindication is by the verdict of a judge or jury and an award of damages. Most plaintiffs are individuals, who are not required to prove that they have suffered financial loss or even that any particular person has thought the worse of them as a result of the publication complained of. I do not understand this rule to be criticised. Thus the question arises whether a corporation with a commercial reputation within the jurisdiction should be subject to a different rule . . .

25. There are of course many defamatory things which can be said about individuals (for example, about their sexual proclivities) which could not be said about corporations. But it is not at all hard to think of statements seriously injurious to the general commercial reputation of trading and charitable corporations: that an arms company has routinely bribed officials of foreign governments to secure contracts; that an oil company has wilfully and unnecessarily damaged the environment; that an international humanitarian agency has wrongfully succumbed to government pressure; that a retailer has knowingly exploited child labour; and so on. The leading figures in such corporations may be understood to be personally implicated, but not, in my opinion, necessarily so. Should the corporation be entitled to sue in its own right only if it can prove financial loss? I do not think so, for two main reasons . . .

26. First, the good name of a company, as that of an individual, is a thing of value. A damaging libel may lower its standing in the eyes of the public and even its own staff, make people less ready to deal with it, less willing or less proud to work for it. If this were not so, corporations would not go to the lengths they do to protect and burnish their corporate images. I find nothing repugnant in the notion that this is a value which the law should protect. Nor do I think it an adequate answer that the corporation can itself seek to answer the defamatory statement by press release or public statement, since protestations of innocence by the impugned party necessarily carry less weight with the public than the prompt issue of proceedings which culminate in a favourable verdict by judge or jury. Secondly, I do not accept that a publication, if truly damaging to a corporation's commercial reputation, will result in provable financial loss, since the more prompt and public a company's issue of proceedings, and the more diligent its pursuit of a claim, the less the chance that financial loss will actually accrue . . .

27. I do not on balance consider that the existing rule should be changed, provided always that where a trading corporation has suffered no actual financial loss any damages awarded should be kept strictly within modest bounds.

Questions for discussion

1. Should corporations have standing to sue in defamation? What are the arguments for and against?
2. Do you agree with the common law position that it is not possible to defame the dead? What arguments can be made for allowing an action for defamation of the dead? Does a deceased person have a reputation to protect?

(ii) Public authorities

In *Derbyshire County Council* v *Times Newspapers Ltd*,[197] the House of Lords established the important principle that a local government authority does not have standing to sue for defamation. The Derbyshire City Council, a local authority, brought an action in respect of allegations about the propriety of some investments made for its superannuation fund.

Extract 10.3.18
***Derbyshire County Council* v *Times Newspapers* [1993] AC 534 (HL) 547–9**

LORD KEITH:

There are . . . features of a local authority which may be regarded as distinguishing it from other types of corporation, whether trading or non-trading. The most important of these features is that it is a governmental body. Further, it is a democratically elected body, the electoral process nowadays being conducted almost exclusively on party political lines. It is of the highest public importance that a democratically elected governmental body, or indeed any governmental body, should be open to uninhibited public criticism. The threat of a civil action for defamation must inevitably have an inhibiting effect on freedom of speech. In *City of Chicago* v *Tribune Co* (1923) 139 NE 86 the Supreme Court of Illinois held that the city could not maintain an action of damages for libel. Thompson CJ said, at p 90:

> The fundamental right of freedom of speech is involved in this litigation, and not merely the right of liberty of the press. If this action can be maintained against a newspaper it can be maintained against every private citizen who ventures to criticise the ministers who are temporarily conducting the affairs of his government. Where any person by speech or writing seeks to persuade others to violate existing law or to overthrow by force or other unlawful means the existing government, he may be punished . . . but all other utterances or publications against the government must be considered absolutely privileged. While in the early history of the struggle for freedom of speech the restrictions were enforced by criminal prosecutions, it is clear that a civil action is as great, if not a greater, restriction than a criminal prosecution. If the right to criticise the government is a privilege which, with the exceptions above enumerated, cannot be restricted, then all civil as well as criminal actions are forbidden. A despotic or corrupt government can more easily stifle opposition by a series of civil actions than by criminal prosecutions . . .

These propositions were endorsed by the Supreme Court of the United States in *New York Times Co* v *Sullivan* (1964) 376 US 254, 277. While these decisions were related most directly to the provisions of the American Constitution concerned with securing freedom of speech, the public interest considerations which underlaid them are no less valid in this country. What has been described as 'the chilling effect' induced by the threat of civil actions for libel is very important. Quite often the facts which would justify a defamatory publication are known to be true, but admissible evidence capable of proving those facts is not available. This may prevent the publication of matters which it is very desirable to make public. In *Hector* v *Attorney-General of Antigua and Barbuda* [1990] 2 AC 312 the Judicial Committee of the Privy Council held that

---

[197] [1993] AC 534.

a statutory provision which made the printing or distribution of any false statement likely to undermine public confidence in the conduct of public affairs a criminal offence contravened the provisions of the constitution protecting freedom of speech.

. . .

It is of some significance to observe that a number of departments of central government in the United Kingdom are statutorily created corporations, including the Secretaries of State for Defence, Education and Science, Energy, Environment and Social Services. If a local authority can sue for libel there would appear to be no reason in logic for holding that any of these departments (apart from two which are made corporations only for the purpose of holding land) was not also entitled to sue. But as is shown by the decision in *Attorney-General* v *Guardian Newspapers Ltd (No 2)* [1990] 1 AC 109, a case concerned with confidentiality, there are rights available to private citizens which institutions of central government are not in a position to exercise unless they can show that it is the public interest to do so. The same applies, in my opinion, to local authorities. In both cases I regard it as right for this House to lay down that not only is there no public interest favouring the right of organs of government, whether central or local, to sue for libel, but that it is contrary to the public interest that they should have it. It is contrary to the public interest because to admit such actions would place an undesirable fetter on freedom of speech.

While the precise scope of the *Derbyshire* principle remains to be tested, later cases have extended it to deny the capacity of unelected public corporations[198] and political parties[199] to bring libel actions. However, as Lord Keith made plain in *Derbyshire*, an individual whose reputation is damaged by the allegations remains free to bring an action.[200]

Questions for discussion

1. What are the reasons given in *Derbyshire* for denying local government authorities the right to sue for defamation? Do you agree?
2. How far should the principle in *Derbyshire* extend? To what other entities should it apply?

(iii) Public officials and public figures

Under the common law, public officials and public figures are not denied standing to sue for defamation and are held to the same burdens as regular claimants in establishing that a libel has been committed. The position is different in the United States. In the landmark case of *New York Times Inc* v *Sullivan*, the United States Supreme Court held that a public official can only succeed in a libel action if he or she can establish that the matter was published with 'actual malice' – that is, that the defendant knew the allegations were false or was reckless as to their truth. It was also subsequently held that the claimant bears the burden of proving the falsity of the charges, in addition to fault, in order to recover damages.[201]

---

[198] *British Coal Corpn* v *NUM* (Unreported, 28 June 1996).
[199] *Goldsmith* v *Bhoyrul* [1998] QB 459.
[200] [1993] AC 534, 550. See also *McLaughlin* v *London Borough of Lambeth* [2010] EWHC 2726 (QB).
[201] *Philadelphia Newspapers, Inc* v *Hepps*, 475 US 767 (1986).

Extract 10.3.19
New York Times Inc v Sullivan, 376 US 254 (1964)

(267) Under Alabama law as applied in this case, a publication is 'libelous per se' if the words 'tend to injure a person in his reputation' or to 'bring (him) into public contempt'; the trial court stated that the standard was met if the words are such as to 'injure him in his public office, or impute misconduct to him in his office, or want of official integrity, or want of fidelity to a public trust.' . . . Once 'libel per se' has been established, the defendant has no defense as to stated facts unless he can persuade the jury that they were true in all their particulars. His privilege of 'fair comment' for expressions of opinion depends on the truth of the facts upon which the comment is based. Unless he can discharge the burden of proving truth, general damages are presumed, and may be awarded without proof of pecuniary injury . . .

(268) The question before us is whether this rule of liability, as applied to an action brought by a public official against critics of his official conduct, abridges the freedom of speech and of the press that is guaranteed by the First and Fourteenth Amendments.

. . .

(269) . . . The general proposition that freedom of expression upon public questions is secured by the First Amendment has long been settled by our decisions . . .

(270) . . . Thus we consider this case against the background of a profound national commitment to the principle that debate on public issues should be uninhibited, robust, and wide-open, and that it may well include vehement, caustic, and sometimes unpleasantly sharp attacks on government and public officials.

(271) . . . Authoritative interpretations of the First Amendment guarantees have consistently refused to recognize an exception for any test of truth – whether administered by judges, juries, or administrative officials – and especially one that puts the burden of proving truth on the speaker. The constitutional protection does not turn upon 'the truth, popularity, or social utility of the ideas and beliefs which are offered.' . . . That erroneous statement is inevitable in free debate, and that it must be protected if the freedoms of expression (272) are to have the 'breathing space' that they 'need to survive,' . . . was also recognized by the Court of Appeals for the District of Columbia Circuit in *Sweeney* v *Patterson*, 76 US App DC 23, 24, 128 F 2d 457, 458 (1942), cert. denied, 317 US 678, 63 S Ct 160, 87 L Ed 544. Judge Edgerton spoke for a unanimous court which affirmed the dismissal of a Congressman's libel suit based upon a newspaper article charging him with anti-Semitism in opposing a judicial appointment. He said:

> Cases which impose liability for erroneous reports of the political conduct of officials reflect the obsolete doctrine that the governed must not criticize their governors. The interest of the public here outweighs the interest of the appellant or any other individual. The protection of the public requires not merely discussion, but information. Political conduct and views which some respectable people approve, and others condemn, are constantly imputed to Congressmen. Errors of fact, particularly in regard to a man's mental states and processes, are inevitable. Whatever is added to the field of libel is taken from the field of free debate.

. . .

(278) The state rule of law is not saved by its allowance of the defense of truth. A defense for erroneous statements honestly made is no less essential here than was the requirement of proof of guilty knowledge which, in *Smith* v *California*, 361 US 147, 80 S Ct 215, 4 L Ed 2d 205, we held indispensable to a valid conviction of a bookseller for possessing obscene writings for sale. We said:

> For if the bookseller is criminally liable without knowledge of the contents, he will tend to restrict the books he sells to those he has inspected; and thus the State will have imposed a restriction upon the distribution of constitutionally protected as well as obscene literature. And the bookseller's burden would become the public's burden, for by restricting him the public's access to reading matter would be restricted. [H]is timidity in the face of his absolute criminal liability, thus would tend to restrict the public's access

to forms of the printed word which the State could not constitutionally (279) suppress directly. The bookseller's self-censorship, compelled by the State, would be a censorship affecting the whole public, hardly less virulent for being privately administered. Through it, the distribution of all books, both obscene and not obscene, would be impeded.

A rule compelling the critic of official conduct to guarantee the truth of all his factual assertions – and to do so on pain of libel judgements virtually unlimited in amount – leads to a comparable 'self-censorship.' Allowance of the defense of truth, with the burden of proving it on the defendant, does not mean that only false speech will be deterred. Even courts accepting this defense as an adequate safeguard have recognized the difficulties of adducing legal proofs that the alleged libel was true in all its factual particulars. . . . Under such a rule, would-be critics of official conduct may be deterred from voicing their criticism, even though it is believed to be true and even though it is in fact true, because of doubt whether it can be proved in court or fear of the expense of having to do so. They tend to make only statements which 'steer far wider of the unlawful zone.' The rule thus dampens the vigor and limits the variety of public debate. It is inconsistent with the First and Fourteenth Amendments.

The constitutional guarantees require, we think, a federal rule that prohibits a public official from recovering damages for a defamatory falsehood relating to his official conduct unless he proves that the statement was made (280) with 'actual malice' – that is, with knowledge that it was false or with reckless disregard of whether it was false or not.

The actual malice standard established in *New York Times* v *Sullivan* for public officials was extended to 'public figures' in *Curtis Publishing Co* v *Butts*.[202] The suggestion that English law should adopt the actual malice standard for public officials/figures was rejected by the Faulks Committee in its review of libel law in 1975, and also by a Supreme Court Committee on Defamation Practice and Procedure under the chairmanship of Neill LJ in 1991. Instead, freedom of expression concerns arising from the various burdens under the common law have been dealt with through the recognition by the House of Lords of the *Reynolds* 'public interest' defence (see Section 10.4(c)(iv)).

Questions for discussion

1. Is the principle in *New York Times* v *Sullivan* sound?
2. Does it strike an appropriate balance between freedom of speech and the right to reputation? Would it survive scrutiny under article 8 of the European Convention on Human Rights?

10.4 DEFENCES

(a) Justification

Truth, otherwise known as 'justification', provides a complete defence to a defamatory publication at common law. A defendant is required to prove, on the balance of probabilities, that the defamatory matter is substantially true as a matter of fact. Minor inaccuracies will not preclude a successful defence of justification; nor will it be denied to a publisher who has acted with malice in making the publication.[203]

---

[202] 388 US 130 (1967).
[203] There is one exception to this rule: under the Rehabilitation of Offenders Act 1974, s 8(5), the media cannot plead the truth of a reference to a 'spent' conviction as a defence to a libel action, if it was made maliciously.

It should be noted that at common law a publisher will only have a defence of justification to a defamatory publication if he or she can prove the substantial truth of each defamatory imputation that is alleged to arise from the publication. It will not be sufficient if he or she can only justify some of them – otherwise known as 'partial justification'.[204] However, where a claimant relies on multiple 'separate and distinct' imputations, partial justification will provide, in certain circumstances, a complete defence by virtue of section 5 of the Defamation Act 1952.

Extract 10.4.1
Defamation Act 1952

Section 5

In an action for libel or slander in respect of words containing two or more distinct charges against the plaintiff, a defence of justification shall not fail by reason only that the truth of every charge is not proved if the words not proved to be true do not materially injure the plaintiff's reputation having regard to the truth of the remaining charges.

The meaning which must be proved to be true by the defendant is the natural and ordinary meaning of the words, or, where relevant, any true innuendo meaning that is pleaded by the claimant. The meaning of the words, however, is a matter for the jury (or judge, where the matter is tried without a jury). This means that it is open to a defendant to prove the substantial truth of a meaning different from that contended for by the claimant. Provided the jury accepts the defendant's contended meaning as the correct meaning of the words, and provided the defendant can establish the truth of that meaning, he or she will have a valid defence. For example, a claimant may argue that a publication means that he or she is *guilty* of a particular offence, whereas the defendant might argue that it means that he or she is *reasonably suspected* as having committed the offence and may seek to prove the truth of that meaning. This is known as a 'Lucas-Box' defence meaning.[205] Alternatively, a defendant may be able to rely upon what is known as a 'Polly Peck' defence meaning.[206] Where a publication gives rise to two or more 'non-separate and distinct' allegations, the defendant may be able to establish that the allegations, in their context, have a 'common sting'. If the defendant can establish the substantial truth of the common sting he or she will have a complete defence. For example, imagine an article alleges that the claimant had affairs with three different women: X, Y and Z. The claimant may choose to sue on allegation X, which is untrue, but not Y and Z, which are true. While unable to prove the truth of X, the defendant could argue that the three allegations, in context, convey the common sting (a higher level or more abstract meaning) that the claimant is an adulterer. In turn, even though the defendant cannot prove the truth of allegation X, he or she will have a complete defence by proving the substantial truth of the common sting by reference to the truth of allegations Y and Z.[207]

As mentioned above (Section 10.3(c)(iii)), the media are responsible for the republication of an allegation and cannot escape liability on the basis that the allegation was originally made by someone else. Nor, under the so-called 'repetition rule', can a defendant seek to justify an allegation by proving that the original publisher in fact *made* the allegation;

---

[204] Partial justification, however, will be relevant to mitigation of damages.
[205] *Lucas-Box* v *News Group Newspapers Ltd* [1986] 1 WLR 147.
[206] *Polly Peck (Holdings)* v *Trelford* [1986] QB 1000.
[207] See, e.g., *Khashoggi* v *IPC Magazines* [1986] 3 All ER 577.

rather, the republisher is required to prove the truth of the *substance* of the allegation.[208] This is the case even where the defendant believes the allegation to be true and names his or her source.[209] The effect of the repetition rule is to limit the circulation by the media of gossip and rumour in circumstances where the substance of the allegations themselves cannot be substantiated. (However, media reports of allegations made in court or legislative proceedings or at public meetings may be covered by the defence of qualified privilege; alternatively, the media may be able to rely on the doctrine of reportage – see Section 10.4(c)(v)).

For reasons of clarity and accessibility, the Defamation Bill seeks to abolish the common law defence of justification and replace it with a statutory defence of substantial truth. It also replaces section 5 of the Defamation Act 1952.

Extract 10.4.2
Defamation Bill

Clause 2 Truth

1. It is a defence to an action for defamation for the defendant to show that the imputation conveyed by the statement complained of is substantially true.
2. Subsection (3) applies in an action for defamation if the statement complained of conveys two or more distinct imputations.
3. If one or more of the imputations is not shown to be substantially true, the defence under this section does not fail if, having regard to the imputations which are shown to be substantially true, the imputations which are not shown to be substantially true do not seriously harm the claimant's reputation.

. . .

Questions for discussion

1. What is the difference between a Polly Peck and a Lucas-Box plea?
2. How does clause 2 of the Defamation Bill differ, if at all, from the extant law?

(b) Fair/honest comment

The common law defence of fair comment, now called 'honest comment',[210] enables the media to express their opinion on matters of public interest. The defence is consistent with the balance to be struck under the Convention between the right to reputation under article 8 and freedom of expression under article 10.[211] Strasbourg has consistently held that wide latitude should be given to the making of 'value judgements' under article 10 because, unlike statements of fact, such judgements are not susceptible to proof.[212]

The defence will be available where the defendant can prove:

1. the matter in respect of which the comment is made is a matter of public interest;
2. the statement in issue is comment and not fact;

---

[208] See *Watkin* v *Hall* (1867-68) LR 3 QB 396 (QB); *Stern* v *Piper* [1997] QB 123 (CA); *Shah* v *Standard Chartered Bank* [1999] QB 241 (CA).
[209] *Roberts* v *Gable* [2008] QB 502, 55.
[210] *Spiller* v *Joseph* [2011] 1 AC 852, 117.
[211] Ibid., 74–9.
[212] See, e.g., *Sorguc* v *Turkey* (European Court of Human Rights, Application No 17089/03, 23 June 2009).

3.   the comment is based on facts which are true or published on an occasion of privilege;
4.   the comment is fair/pertinent.

The defence will be defeated where the defendant makes the comment maliciously. The onus of proving malice rests with the claimant.

A classic statement of the defence is to be found in a summing-up to the jury by Diplock J. A prominent Labour politician sued a newspaper for alleging that he was insincere in expressing political hostility to Germany when he was chairman of a company which marketed German cars.

Extract 10.4.3
Silkin v Beaverbrook Newspapers Ltd **[1958] 1 WLR 743 (QB) 746–7**

DIPLOCK J:

Let us look a little more closely at the way in which the law balances the rights of the public man, on the one hand, and the rights of the public, on the other, in matters of freedom of speech. In the first place, every man, whether he is in public life or not, is entitled not to have lies told about him; and by that is meant that one is not entitled to make statements of fact about a person which are untrue and which redound to his discredit, that is to say, tend to lower him in the estimation of right-thinking men.

The first point, therefore, is that you should not misstate the material facts on which you are commenting. That is common sense and it is the common law. In a great many libel actions one of the matters which the jury have to consider is whether the facts are materially misstated . . .

[His Lordship said that the second and very important requirement was that the subject of the comment should be a matter of public interest. In the present case the plaintiff's attitude to Germany and the Germans was a matter of public interest, not a mere matter of private interest, and his Lordship so directed the jury. He continued:] What are the limits of the right of comment? Quite rightly they are very wide. First of all, who is entitled to comment? The answer to that is 'everyone'. A newspaper reporter or a newspaper editor has exactly the same rights, neither more nor less, than every other citizen, and the test is no different whether the comment appears in a Sunday newspaper with an enormous circulation, or in a letter from a private person to a friend or, subject to some technical difficulties with which you need not be concerned, is said to an acquaintance in a train or in a public-house. So in deciding whether this was fair comment or not, you dismiss from your minds the fact that it was published in a newspaper, and you will not, I am sure, be influenced in any way by any prejudice you may have for or against newspapers any more than you will be influenced in any way by any prejudice which you may have for or against Lord Silkin's politics. Those are matters which you will, I am sure, all of you, dismiss from your minds.

I have been referring, and counsel in their speeches to you have been referring, to fair comment, because that is the technical name which is given to this defence, or, as I should prefer to say, which is given to the right of every citizen to comment on matters of public interest. But the expression 'fair comment' is a little misleading. It may give you the impression that you, the jury, have to decide whether you agree with the comment, whether you think it is fair. If that were the question you had to decide, you realize that the limits of freedom which the law allows would be greatly curtailed. People are entitled to hold and to express freely on matters of public interest strong views, views which some of you, or indeed all of you, may think are exaggerated, obstinate or prejudiced, provided – and this is the important thing – that they are views which they honestly hold. The basis of our public life is that the crank, the enthusiast, may say what he honestly thinks just as much as the reasonable man or woman who sits on a jury, and it would be a sad day for freedom of speech in this country if a jury were to apply the test of whether it agrees with the comment instead of applying the true test: was this an opinion, however exaggerated, obstinate or prejudiced, which was honestly held by the writer?

(i) Matter of public interest

As the following extract shows, the courts have taken a broad view of 'public interest' for the purposes of the defence of fair/honest comment.

Extract 10.4.4
***London Artists Ltd v Littler* (1969) 2 QB 375 (CA) 391**

LORD DENNING MR:
There is no definition in the books as to what is a matter of public interest. All we are given is a list of examples, coupled with a statement that it is for the judge and not for the jury. I would not myself confine it within narrow limits. Whenever a matter is such as to affect people at large, so that they may be legitimately interested in, or concerned at, what is going on; or what may happen to them or to others; then it is a matter of public interest on which everyone is entitled to make fair comment . . . Here the public are legitimately interested. Many people are interested in what happens in the theatre. The stars welcome publicity. They want to be put at the top of the bill. Producers wish it too. They like the house to be full. The comings and goings of performers are noticed everywhere. When three top stars and a satellite all give notice to leave at the same time – thus putting a successful play in peril – it is to my mind a matter of public interest in which everyone, press and all, are entitled to comment freely.

(ii) Distinguishing comment and fact

The fair/honest comment defence will only be established where the defamatory imputation is an expression of opinion rather than an allegation of fact. It is not always easy to characterise a statement as one or the other. As a general rule, a fact is something which is subject to verification; a comment, on the other hand, is characterised as 'a deduction, inference, conclusion, criticism, remark [or] observation'.[213] Relevant factors in drawing a distinction in any particular case include the language or words used and the context in which they appear. It was held by a majority of the House of Lords in *Telnikoff* v *Matusevitch*,[214] however, that it is not permissible to go beyond the context of the defamatory publication itself. The claimant in that case had written an article in the *Daily Telegraph* criticising the BBC Russian Service for its recruitment policies. The defendant published a letter in response in the same newspaper a few days later, where it was suggested (in paragraphs 6 and 7) that the claimant's article in effect demanded a blood test for employment in the Russian Service and the dismissal of non-Russian staff. In other words, the defendant accused the claimant of racialism. When looked at in isolation, the relevant paragraphs were capable of being read as allegations of fact; however, if looked at in the context of the claimant's earlier article, the paragraphs were capable of being understood as comment. In finding that the letter had to be considered on its own, Lord Keith said:

> The matter cannot turn on the likelihood or otherwise of readers of the letter having read the article. In some cases many readers of a criticism of some subject matter may be familiar with that subject matter but in other cases very few may be, for example where that subject matter is a speech delivered to a limited audience. The principle must be the same in either case.[215]

Lord Ackner, dissenting, argued that the majority decision posed real difficulties for the publication of readers' letters and reviews of plays and films. Editors might feel it prudent

---

[213] *Clarke* v *Norton* [1910] VLR 494 (7 November 1910) 499.
[214] [1992] 2 AC 343.
[215] Ibid., 352.

to set out substantial extracts from the original material for any opinion on its merits to be treated as comment, rather than a statement of fact.[216]

The difficulty in deciding whether an imputation is one of fact or comment is confounded by the recognition that, depending on the context, a statement of fact inferred or deducted from other facts stated or referred to in the publication can be protected as comment.[217] Courts, however, have been reluctant to extend this to objectively verifiable facts.[218] For example, imputations concerning the state of a person's mind might be considered comment because, although fact, such matters are generally unverifiable,[219] whereas an imputation that there are reasonable grounds for suspicion of guilt is subject to proof and therefore is verifiable and cannot constitute comment.[220] The case of *British Chiropractic Association v Singh*[221] demonstrates the problems inherent, philosophically and practically, in drawing a line between unverifiable fact and verifiable fact. In that case, Simon Singh, the science writer, wrote a comment piece published in the *Guardian* that criticised chiropractic techniques. He argued that there was 'not a jot of evidence' that such techniques worked to cure many of the ailments that were often claimed it could cure. Moreover, Singh claimed that the British Chiropractic Association 'happily promotes bogus treatments'. Eady J at first instance found that this was a clear allegation of verifiable fact and struck out the defendant's fair comment defence.[222] Singh appealed to the Court of Appeal.

Extract 10.4.5
British Chiropractic Association v Singh **[2011] 1 WLR 133**

LORD JUDGE, LORD CHIEF JUSTICE:

17. One error which in Ms Page's submission affects Eady J's decision on meaning is that . . . he treats 'verifiable fact' as antithetical to comment, so that any assertion which ranks as the former cannot qualify as the latter. This, it is submitted, is a false dichotomy. It led the judge to postulate the resultant issue as 'whether those responsible for the claims put out by the BCA were well aware at the time that there was simply no evidence to support them'. This, he held, was 'a matter of verifiable fact' . . .

18. It seems to us that there is force in Ms Page's critique – not necessarily because fact and comment are not readily divisible (that is a philosophical question which we do not have to decide), but because the subject matter of Dr Singh's article was an area of epidemiology in which the relationship of primary fact to secondary fact, and of both to permissible inference, is heavily and legitimately contested. The issue posed by the judge is in reality two distinct issues: first, was there any evidence to support the material claims? And secondly, if there was not, did the BCA's personnel know this? If, as Dr Singh has contended throughout, the first issue is one of opinion and not of fact, the second issue ceases to matter.

19. In our judgment Eady J, notwithstanding his very great experience, has erred both in conflating these two elements of the claim and, more particularly, in treating the first of them as an issue of verifiable fact.

. . .

---

[216] Ibid., 361.
[217] *O'Brien v Marquis of Salisbury* (1889) 54 JP 215.
[218] See comments by the Supreme Court in *Spiller v Joseph* [2011] 1 AC 852, 114.
[219] *Branson v Bower* [2001] EWCA Civ 791.
[220] *Hamilton v Clifford* [2004] EWHC 1542 (QB).
[221] [2011] 1 WLR 133.
[222] *British Chiropractic Association v Singh* [2009] EWHC 1101 (QB).

22. One has only to contemplate this prospect to conclude that something is amiss. It is one thing to defame somebody in terms which can only be defended by proving their truth, even if this ineluctably casts the court in the role of historian or investigative journalist. It is another thing to evaluate published material as giving no evidential support to a claim and, on the basis of this evaluation, to denounce as irresponsible those who make the claim. Recent years have seen a small number of high-profile libel cases in which the courts, however reluctantly, have had to discharge the first of these functions. But these have been precisely cases in which the defendant has made a clear assertion of highly damaging fact, and must prove its truth or lose . . .

23. The present case is not in this class: the material words, however one represents or paraphrases their meaning, are in our judgment expressions of opinion. The opinion may be mistaken, but to allow the party which has been denounced on the basis of it to compel its author to prove in court what he has asserted by way of argument is to invite the court to become an Orwellian ministry of truth . . .

. . .

26. What 'evidence' signifies depends heavily on context. To a literalist, any primary fact – for example, that following chiropractic intervention a patient's condition improved – may be evidence of a secondary fact, here that chiropractic works. To anyone (and not only a scientist) concerned with the establishment of dependable generalisations about cause and effect, such primary information is as worthless as evidence of the secondary fact as its converse would be. The same may equally well be true of data considerably more complex than in the facile example we have given: whether it is or not is what scientific opinion is there to debate. If in the course of the debate the view is expressed that there is not a jot of evidence for one deduction or another, the natural meaning is that there is no worthwhile or reliable evidence for it. That is as much a value judgment as a contrary viewpoint would be.

27. The pleadings in the present case usefully illustrate this. Dr Singh's defence includes, in para 8(25), a survey of controlled clinical trials on the efficacy of chiropractic in treating infantile colic, none of which, he contends, affords objective support for the BCA's claim. The BCA, in para 9(23) of its reply, relies (among other studies) on a 1989 observational study of 316 children, of which it is said:

> This . . . measured the number of hours each child spent in crying. It showed a reduction in crying time from 5.2 hours each day to 0.65 hours each day at 14 days. This was a very substantial improvement. There was no control group. However, the study constitutes evidence.

One need go no further in order to see how value-laden the word 'evidence' is in the present context, let alone to envisage the examination and cross-examination of witnesses called to testify about it, and about the dozens of other reports cited by one side or the other . . .

33. . . . [W]e consider that the judge erred in his approach to the need for justification by treating the statement that there was not a jot of evidence to support the BCA's claims as an assertion of fact. It was in our judgment a statement of opinion, and one backed by reasons.

. . .

[The appeal was allowed.]

One issue of particular contention is the extent to which the defendant must set out in the publication, either explicitly or implicitly, the facts upon which his or her comment is based. Where the subject matter of the comment has been submitted to the public domain (as in the case of a book, play or film, etc.) or where the comment is based on a matter of notoriety, there will be no need to set out the particular facts, provided the 'subject-matter [is] indicated with sufficient clarity'.[223] In *Kemsley* v *Foot*, for instance, the defendants

---

[223] *Kemsley* v *Foot* [1952] AC 345, 357.

sought to defend, by way of fair comment, an article published under the headline 'Lower than Kemsley', which was critical of the conduct of a newspaper published by Lord Beaverbrook. Lord Kemsley, the newspaper proprietor, objected to the article and sued. The House of Lords held that it was at least arguable that the headline implied the fact that Lord Kemsley is the proprietor 'in control of a number of known newspapers and that the conduct of those newspapers is in question'. Thus, the defendant was entitled to make the argument: 'We have pointed to your press. It is widely read. Your readers will and the public generally can know at what our criticism is directed. It is not bare comment; it is comment on a well-known matter, much better known, indeed, than a newly printed book or a once-performed play.'[224]

Until recently, however, the position was less clear where the facts had not been submitted to the public domain, or where they were not notorious or well-known in the sense recognised in *Kemsley* v *Foot*. On one view, setting out the relevant 'factual substratum' upon which the comment is based is a factor going to whether the ordinary reasonable reader would identify the imputation as one of comment as distinct from one of fact.[225] A more burdensome view, as expressed by Lord Nicholls in *Tse Wai Chun* v *Cheng*, is that the facts must be sufficiently indicated so that the recipient can judge for himself the extent to which the comment is well founded.[226] This issue was resolved by the UK Supreme Court in the case of *Spiller* v *Joseph*.[227] The defendant sought to defend on the basis of fair comment an allegation that the claimants, members of musical group 'The Gillettes', were 'grossly unprofessional and untrustworthy'. The question was whether the defendant had sufficiently referred to the fact that the claimants had breached their contract with the defendant as the material fact upon which the comment was based.

Extract 10.4.6
Spiller v Joseph **[2011] 1 AC 852**

LORD PHILLIPS:

. . .

96. I can summarise the position as follows. Where, expressly or by implication, general criticism is made of a play, a book, an organ of the press or a notorious course of conduct in the public domain, the defendant is likely to wish in his defence to identify particular aspects of the matter in question by way of explanation of precisely what it was that led him to make his comment. These particular aspects will be relevant to establishing the pertinence of his comment and to rebutting any question of malice, should this be in issue. Lord Porter's speech [in *Kemsley* v *Foot*] indicates that the comment does not have to refer to these particular aspects specifically . . .

97. Can Lord Nicholls' fourth proposition in *Tse Wai Chun* v *Cheng* [2001] EMLR 777, [2000] HKCFA 35, para 19 be reconciled with these propositions? The passage in *Odgers on Libel and Slander*, 6th ed (1929), p. 166 that was cited with approval by Lord Porter . . . suggested that where conduct is identified by a clear reference the defendant thereby enables his readers to judge for themselves how far his opinion is well founded. As Lord Ackner pointed out, however, in *Telnikoff* v *Matusevitch* [1992] 2 AC 343, 361, it is fallacious to suggest that readers will be able to form their own view of the validity of the criticism of a matter merely because in the past it was placed in the public domain. Readers of the Tribune who did not read the Kemsley Press could no doubt have gained access to a representative sample of this, but this will not

---

[224] Ibid., 357.
[225] See, e.g., *Lowe* v *Associated Newspapers Ltd* [2007] QB 580, 55–7; *Kemsley* v *Foot* [1952] AC 345, 356.
[226] [2000] HKCFA 35, 19, [2001] EMLR 31.
[227] [2011] 1 AC 852.

be possible where the criticism is of an ephemeral matter such as a concert, or the single performance of a play, or a football match, all of which can give rise to general criticism that is protected by the defence of fair comment . . .

98. For these reasons I do not consider that Lord Nicholls' fourth proposition in *Cheng* can be reconciled with *Kemsley* v *Foot* . . . There is no case in which a defence of fair comment has failed on the ground that the comment did not identify the subject matter on which it was based with sufficient particularity to enable the reader to form his own view as to its validity. For these reasons, where adverse comment is made generally or generically on matters that are in the public domain I do not consider that it is a prerequisite of the defence of fair comment that the readers should be in a position to evaluate the comment for themselves . . .

99. What of a case where the subject matter of the comment is not within the public domain, but is known only to the commentator or to a small circle of which he is one? Today the internet has made it possible for the man in the street to make public comment about others in a manner that did not exist when the principles of the law of fair comment were developed, and millions take advantage of that opportunity. Where the comments that they make are derogatory it will often be impossible for other readers to evaluate them without detailed information about the facts that have given rise to the comments. Frequently these will not be set out. If Lord Nicholls' fourth proposition is to apply the defence of fair comment will be robbed of much of its efficacy . . .

100. The cases have none the less emphasised repeatedly the requirement that the comment should identify the subject matter on which it is based . . . If the requirement that the comment should identify the subject matter on which it is based is not imposed in order to enable the reader of the comment to form his own view of its validity, what is the object of the requirement? Bingham LJ in *Brent Walker Group plc* v *Time Out Ltd* [1991] 2 QB 33, 44 said that the true facts must be 'stated or sufficiently indicated' – sufficiently for what? . . .

101. There are a number of reasons why the subject matter of the comment must be identified by the comment, at least in general terms. The underlying justification for the creation of the fair comment exception was the desirability that a person should be entitled to express his view freely about a matter of public interest. That remains a justification for the defence, albeit that the concept of public interest has been greatly widened. If the subject matter of the comment is not apparent from the comment this justification for the defence will be lacking. The defamatory comment will be wholly unfocussed . . .

102. It is a requirement of the defence that it should be based on facts that are true. This requirement is better enforced if the comment has to identify, at least in general terms, the matters on which it is based. The same is true of the requirement that the defendant's comment should be honestly founded on facts that are true . . .

103. More fundamentally, even if it is not practicable to require that those reading criticism should be able to evaluate the criticism, it may be thought desirable that the commentator should be required to identify at least the general nature of the facts that have led him to make the criticism. If he states that a barrister is 'a disgrace to his profession' he should make it clear whether this is because he does not deal honestly with the court, or does not read his papers thoroughly, or refuses to accept legally aided work, or is constantly late for court, or wears dirty collars and bands . . .

104. Such considerations are, I believe, what Mr Caldecott had in mind when submitting that a defendant's comments must have identified the subject matter of his criticism if he is to be able to advance a defence of fair comment. If so, it is a submission that I would endorse. I do not consider that Lord Nicholls was correct to require that the comment must identify the matters on which it is based with sufficient particularity to enable the reader to judge for himself whether it was well founded. The comment must, however, identify at least in general terms what it is that has led the commentator to make the comment, so that the reader can understand what the

comment is about and the commentator can, if challenged, explain by giving particulars of the subject matter of his comment why he expressed the views that he did. A fair balance must be struck between allowing a critic the freedom to express himself as he will and requiring him to identify to his readers why it is that he is making the criticism.

Conclusion

. . .

105. For the reasons that I have given I would endorse Lord Nicholls' summary of the elements of fair comment . . . save that I would re-write the fourth proposition: 'Next the comment must explicitly or implicitly indicate, at least in general terms, the facts on which it is based.'

(iii) Based on true facts or facts published on an occasion of privilege

While it is now established that it is sufficient that the facts upon which the comment is based be set out only in general terms in the publication itself, the defendant is nevertheless required to particularise the facts upon which the comment is based. This will be relevant to establishing that the comment was fair and, where necessary, to rebut any question of malice.[228] Such facts must have existed and been known to the defendant,[229] at least in general terms, at the time the comment was made[230] and must have been instrumental in forming the opinion expressed.[231] Moreover, such facts necessary to support the opinion must be proved by the defendant to be true or must have been published on a privileged occasion.

At common law, where the defendant sets out in the publication the facts relied on in support of the comment, he or she will be required to establish the substantial truth of all such facts.[232] Any misstatement of fact (including any relevant omission) will result in the defence being defeated.[233] This has been modified by section 6 of the Defamation Act 1952.

Extract 10.4.7
Defamation Act 1952

Section 6

In an action for libel or slander in respect of words consisting partly of allegations of fact and partly of expression of opinion, a defence of fair comment shall not fail by reason only that the truth of every allegation of fact is not proved if the expression of opinion is fair comment having regard to such of the facts alleged or referred to in the words complained of as are proved.

However, where the facts relied on by the defendant in support of the comment are contained in the defendant's particulars rather than expressed in the publication itself, there is no requirement that all such factual allegations be proven to be true. All that is required is that those facts which can be proved true are 'sufficient to support the comment so as to make it fair'.[234] While the differential treatment between facts stated in the publication and facts stated in the defendant's particulars has been subject to legitimate criticism, the distinction appeared to be endorsed by the UK Supreme Court in *Spiller* v *Joseph*.[235]

---

[228] Ibid., 96.
[229] *Cohen* v *Daily Telegraph Ltd* [1968] 1 WLR 916, 918.
[230] *Lowe* v *Associated Newspapers Ltd* [2007] QB 580.
[231] *Spiller* v *Joseph* [2011] 1 AC 852, 95.
[232] *Digby* v *Financial News Ltd* [1907] 1 KB 502.
[233] *Branson* v *Bower* [2002] QB 737, 37.
[234] *Kemsley* v *Foot* [1952] AC 345, 358.
[235] [2011] 1 AC 852, 114.

(iv) Fairness

The 'fairness' (or 'pertinence')[236] element requires showing that, objectively speaking, the comment was one 'which could have been made by an honest person, however prejudiced he might be, and however exaggerated or obstinate his views'.[237] The question is not whether a reasonable person would arrive at such views.

The comment must also be germane to the subject-matter being criticised. Thus, it has been said that '[c]riticism cannot be used as a cloak for mere invective, nor for personal imputations not arising out of the subject-matter or not based on fact'.[238]

(v) Malice

The defence of honest opinion will be defeated if the claimant can establish that the defendant did not honestly believe the comment that he or she made. However, unlike the rebuttal of a defence of qualified privilege (see Section 10.4(c)(vi)), malice will not be established where the defendant was motivated by 'spite, animosity, intent to injure, intent to arouse controversy or other motivations' in making the comment.[239]

(vi) Defamation Bill

Clause 3 of the Defamation Bill repeals the common law of honest comment and replaces it with a statutory defence. The goal is to 'retain the broad principles of the current common law defence . . . but avoid the complexities which have arisen in the case law'[240] – particularly in relation to the question of the degree to which the facts underlying the opinion need to be expressed or referred to in the material itself. The defence, if enacted, will broadly reiterate the common law but, importantly, will dispense with the requirement that the comment be on a matter of public interest.[241] It should also be noted that the Explanatory Memorandum makes it clear that inferences of fact expressed as opinion will be covered by the new defence.[242]

Extract 10.4.8
Defamation Bill

Clause 3 Honest opinion

1. It is a defence to an action for defamation for the defendant to show that the following conditions are met.

2. The first condition is that the statement complained of was a statement of opinion.

3. The second condition is that the statement complained of indicated, whether in general or specific terms, the basis of the opinion.

4. The third condition is that an honest person could have held the opinion on the basis of –

   (a) any fact which existed at the time the statement complained of was published;
   (b) anything asserted to be a fact in a privileged statement published before the statement complained of.

[236] Ibid., 6.
[237] *Tse Wai Chun v Cheng* [2000] HKCFA 86, 20, as endorsed by the Supreme Court in *Spiller v Joseph* [2011] 1 AC 852, 105.
[238] *McQuire v Western Morning News Co* [1903] 2 KB 100, 109.
[239] *Tse Wai Chun v Cheng* [2000] HKCFA 86, 79.
[240] Explanatory Notes, Defamation Bill 2012–13 (HL Bill 41, 21 September 2012) 22.
[241] For criticism of this aspect of the proposal, see Gavin Phillipson, 'The "global pariah", the Defamation Bill and the Human Rights Act' (2012) 63(1) *Northern Ireland Legal Quarterly* 149, 176–80.
[242] Explanatory Notes, Defamation Bill 2012–13 (HL Bill 41, 21 September 2012) 21.

5. The defence is defeated if the claimant shows that the defendant did not hold the opinion.
6. Subsection (5) does not apply in a case where the statement complained of was published by the defendant but made by another person ('the author'); and in such a case the defence is defeated if the claimant shows that the defendant knew or ought to have known that the author did not hold the opinion.

. . .

Questions for discussion

1. What are some of the problems in distinguishing fact from comment? Is the distinction always clear?
2. When should statements of fact be capable of being defended under honest comment?
3. Is the requirement that comment have a sufficient factual basis too onerous? Why/ why not?
4. Do you agree with the public interest element of the defence?
5. Do you think the honest comment defence would be useful to the media?
6. How does the 'honest opinion' defence in clause 3 differ from the 'honest comment' defence under the common law?
7. Do you envisage any problems arising from the proposal in clause 3 of the Defamation Bill to dispense with the public interest requirement? If enacted, will this be compatible with the Convention?

(c) Absolute and qualified privilege

The defence of honest comment does not protect defamatory statements of fact. Nevertheless, there are times where it is in the public interest that people enjoy the freedom to make allegations of fact without the fear of liability. Thus, it is a defence to defamation to show that a statement was made on a privileged occasion. Privilege may be absolute or qualified. The former provides a complete defence; it is immaterial whether the defendant was malicious. In contrast, proof of malice will defeat qualified privilege. Furthermore, unlike fair comment, the facts need not be true where a defence of privilege is raised and it is immaterial whether the defendant made the statement carelessly.[243]

As set out in the following sections, some privileges are recognised by common law, while others have been conferred by statute.

(i) Absolute privilege

Perhaps the best known absolute privilege, the immunity of Members of Parliament from liability for anything said or written during the course of parliamentary proceedings, was conferred by article 9 of the Bill of Rights 1689.[244] It provides '[t]hat the freedom of speech and debates or proceedings in Parliament ought not to be impeached or questioned in any court or place out of Parliament.'

---

[243] But there may be liability for the tort of negligent misstatement if a reference covered by qualified privilege is given carelessly: *Spring* v *Guardian Assurance Plc* [1995] 2 AC 296. It is unclear whether this decision might undermine the effectiveness of qualified privilege for the media.

[244] Article 9. The privilege may be waived to enable evidence to be given of parliamentary proceedings in the course of a libel action brought by an MP: Defamation Act 1996, s 13, removing the difficulty highlighted by *Allason* v *Haines and Another* [1996] EMLR 143.

At common law, absolute privilege also protects the making of statements during the course of court proceedings, and section 14 of the Defamation Act 1996 extends absolute privilege to fair and accurate reports of certain court proceedings provided they are published contemporaneously with the proceedings (otherwise entitled to qualified protection at common law).[245] A fair and accurate report need not be verbatim;[246] it may be a summary or an abridged report provided it gives an accurate and correct impression of what transpired.[247] A fair and accurate report must also be impartial.[248]

Extract 10.4.9
Defamation Act 1996

Section 14 Reports of court proceedings absolutely privileged

1. A fair and accurate report of proceedings in public before a court to which this section applies, if published contemporaneously with the proceedings, is absolutely privileged.

2. A report of proceedings which by an order of the court, or as a consequence of any statutory provision, is required to be postponed shall be treated as published contemporaneously if it is published as soon as practicable after publication is permitted.

3. This section applies to –
   a. any court in the United Kingdom,
   b. the European Court of Justice or any court attached to that court,
   c. the European Court of Human Rights, and
   d. any international criminal tribunal established by the Security Council of the United Nations or by an international agreement to which the United Kingdom is a party.

In paragraph (a) 'court' includes any tribunal or body exercising the judicial power of the State.

(ii) Qualified privilege – reports

At common law, fair and accurate reports of court and parliamentary proceedings are protected by qualified privilege. The protection covers the reporting of the proceedings of domestic courts, as well as the proceedings of international courts where such proceedings would be of 'legitimate and proper interests for English readers, and the reasonable man in England will wish to read it or hear about it'.[249]

The common law is supplemented by section 15 of the Defamation Act 1996. A list of reports or statements which receive the automatic protection of qualified privilege is contained in Part I of Schedule 1. Part II of Schedule 1, on the other hand, contains a list of reports or statements that receive the protection of qualified privilege 'subject to explanation or contradiction'.

Extract 10.4.10
Defamation Act 1996

Section 15, and Schedule 1, paras 1–12

15.—(1) The publication of any report or other statement mentioned in Schedule 1 to this Act is privileged unless the publication is shown to be made with malice, subject as follows.

---

[245] Clause 7(1) of the Defamation Bill would extend this, if enacted, to cover reports of 'any court established under the law of a country or territory outside of the United Kingdom.'
[246] *Lewis v Levy* (1858) EB & E 537, 120 ER 610.
[247] *Andrews v Chapman* (1853) 3 C & K 286, 175 ER 558.
[248] *Grech v Odhams Press* [1958] 2 QB 275 (CA).
[249] *Webb v Times Publishing Co* [1960] 2 QB 535, 570.

(2) In defamation proceedings in respect of the publication of a report or other statement mentioned in Part II of that Schedule, there is no defence under this section if the plaintiff shows that the defendant—

(a) was requested by him to publish in a suitable manner a reasonable letter or statement by way of explanation or contradiction, and

(b) refused or neglected to do so.

For this purpose 'in a suitable manner' means in the same manner as the publication complained of or in a manner that is adequate and reasonable in the circumstances.

(3) This section does not apply to the publication to the public, or a section of the public, of matter which is not of public concern and the publication of which is not for the public benefit.

(4) Nothing in this section shall be construed—

(a) as protecting the publication of matter the publication of which is prohibited by law, or

(b) as limiting or abridging any privilege subsisting apart from this section.

Schedule 1
Qualified privilege

Part I
Statements having qualified privilege without explanation or contradiction

1. A fair and accurate report of proceedings in public of a legislature anywhere in the world.
2. A fair and accurate report of proceedings in public before a court anywhere in the world.
3. A fair and accurate report of proceedings in public of a person appointed to hold a public inquiry by a government or legislature anywhere in the world.
4. A fair and accurate report of proceedings in public anywhere in the world of an international organisation or an international conference.
5. A fair and accurate copy of or extract from any register or other document required by law to be open to public inspection.
6. A notice or advertisement published by or on the authority of a court, or of a judge or officer of a court, anywhere in the world.
7. A fair and accurate copy of or extract from matter published by or on the authority of a government or legislature anywhere in the world.
8. A fair and accurate copy of or extract from matter published anywhere in the world by an international organisation or an international conference.

Part II
Statements privileged subject to explanation or contradiction

9.—(1) A fair and accurate copy of or extract from a notice or other matter issued for the information of the public by or on behalf of—

(a) a legislature in any member State or the European Parliament;

(b) the government of any member State, or any authority performing governmental functions in any member State or part of a member State, or the European Commission;

(c) an international organisation or international conference.

(2) In this paragraph 'governmental functions' includes police functions.

10. A fair and accurate copy of or extract from a document made available by a court in any member State or the European Court of Justice (or any court attached to that court), or by a judge or officer of any such court.

11. (1) A fair and accurate report of proceedings at any public meeting or sitting in the United Kingdom of—

(a) a local authority or local authority committee;

(b) a justice or justices of the peace acting otherwise than as a court exercising judicial authority;

(c) a commission, tribunal, committee or person appointed for the purposes of any inquiry by any statutory provision, by Her Majesty or by a Minister of the Crown or a Northern Ireland Department;

(d) a person appointed by a local authority to hold a local inquiry in pursuance of any statutory provision;

(e) any other tribunal, board, committee or body constituted by or under, and exercising functions under, any statutory provision.

(2) [*Omitted*]

(3) [*Omitted*]

12.—(1) A fair and accurate report of proceedings at any public meeting held in a member State.

(2) In this paragraph a 'public meeting' means a meeting bona fide and lawfully held for a lawful purpose and for the furtherance or discussion of a matter of public concern, whether admission to the meeting is general or restricted.

. . .

The meaning of a 'fair and accurate report of proceedings at any public meeting' was considered by the House of Lords in *McCartan Turkington Breen* v *Times Newspapers Ltd*. A press conference had been organised by an informal committee established to advocate for the release and vindication of Private Lee Clegg, who had been convicted of committing serious criminal offences and had been sentenced to life imprisonment. The press conference was held at a private residence and members of the press were invited to attend. A press release was made available to all of those in attendance, which was briefly referred to at the meeting but had not been read out. A journalist in attendance wrote an article for the *Times*, which reported that members of the committee had expressed criticism of the claimants, a firm of solicitors who had acted for Private Clegg. The firm sued the proprietor of the newspaper for defamation. The trial judge and the Court of Appeal rejected the defence of qualified privilege on the basis that the meeting was not public. This was on the basis of the so-called 'nexus test': '[w]hat makes a meeting a public meeting as opposed to a private or non-public meeting is the absence of any particular nexus between those organising the meeting and those taking part.'[250] The House of Lords disagreed. Lord Bingham, with whom the remainder of the House agreed, held that a meeting is public 'if those who organise it or arrange it open it to the public or, by issuing a general invitation to the press, manifest an intention or desire that the proceedings of the meeting should be communicated to a wider public'.[251] Thus, a meeting which is not open to all members of the public will not necessarily fall outside the definition of a 'public meeting'.[252] Lord Bingham, on the facts, concluded:

> Everything points towards the public character of the press conference in issue here. The object was to stimulate public pressure to rectify what the Committee as promoters of the conference saw as a grave miscarriage of justice, and publicity was the essence of the exercise. A general invitation to attend was issued to the press. While the attendance of other members of the public was not solicited, nor was admission denied to anyone, journalist or non-journalist. Both journalists and other members of the public in fact attended in significant numbers. A public meeting need not involve participation, or the opportunity for participation, by those attending it, but here the

---

[250] Cited in *McCartan Turkington Breen* v *Times Newspapers Ltd* [2001] 2 AC 277, 287.
[251] *McCartan Turkington Breen* v *Times Newspapers Ltd* [2001] 2 AC 277, 292.
[252] Ibid.

opportunity to ask questions and make statements was extended to those attending. Save that the meeting was held at [a private residence], there was nothing whatever private about it.[253]

A second point considered in the case was whether including in the article a passage from the press release not read aloud at the meeting constituted a 'report of proceedings' of a public meeting. Lord Bingham thought that it did. Considering that it has become general practice to reduce materials to writing for the purpose of proceedings and that it was clear that the press release was 'treated by the committee as read even though not read aloud', the press release formed part of proceedings.[254] The test, according to Lord Bingham, is whether, 'assuming the meeting to have been public, the contents of the written press release formed part of the materials communicated at the meeting to those attending'.[255]

(iii) Duty and interest qualified privilege

Common law qualified privilege covers communications made by a person with a duty or interest – legal, social or moral – in making it to a person who has a reciprocal interest in receiving it. Although the circumstances in which such a reciprocal duty and interest will be found are not closed, some well-established categories include, for example, statements made in the context of employment[256] and credit references,[257] and those made in the course of criminal investigations[258] or in volunteering information on a crime.[259] Whether or not an occasion is privileged will turn on all the circumstances of the case, including the nature, status and source of the material published.[260] While common law duty and interest qualified privilege is said to be recognised for the 'common convenience and welfare of society', the English courts up until the late twentieth century resisted finding that widespread media publications could be protected by duty-interest qualified privilege. Instead, the defence was overwhelmingly confined to communications of a private nature or those made to more limited audiences.[261] Other than in exceptional cases, media publishers were generally not seen as having a duty to publish nor the public an interest in receiving widespread publications. This position was broadly true even in the case of material concerning political figures and other material directly relevant to the democratic process.

One exception to the traditional common law stance is where the media is publishing a reply to an attack. Where A is defamed by B, A's reply will be protected by qualified privilege provided it is 'a proportionate response which [is] appropriate both in terms of subject matter and scale of publication'.[262] Where B's original attack was published in the media, the qualified privilege protecting A's retort will also extend to the media who publish it (called a 'derivative privilege'):

---

[253] Ibid., note that clause 7(5) the Defamation Bill, if enacted, would extend qualified privilege to a 'fair and accurate report of proceedings at a press conference held anywhere in the world for the discussion of a matter of public interest'.
[254] *McCartan Turkington Breen* v *Times Newspapers Ltd* [2001] 2 AC 277, 293.
[255] Ibid.
[256] *Fountain* v *Boodle* (1842) 3 QB 5.
[257] *Waller* v *Loch* (1881) 7 QBD 619.
[258] *Kine* v *Sewell* (1838) 3 M & W 297, 150 ER 1157. Note, however, that answers to police inquiries may fall within absolute privilege: see *Taylor* v *Director of the Serious Fraud Office* [1999] 2 AC 177.
[259] *Hasselblad (GB)* v *Orbinson* [1985] QB 475.
[260] *London Association for Protection of Trade* v *Greenlands Ltd* [1916] 2 AC 15, 23.
[261] *Chapman* v *Ellesmere* [1932] 2 KB 431 (CA).
[262] *Hamilton* v *Clifford* [2004] EWHC 1542 (QB), 65.

The rationale for the derivative privilege is that a privilege to reply to an attack addressed to the public at large would be of no avail to the person who was the object of the attack if the means of exercising it were not also protected.[263]

The media will maintain this privilege even if it instigates the story,[264] provided it does not include material gratuitous to the attack and reply.[265]

(iv) Reynolds qualified privilege

It was not until the case of *Reynolds v Times Newspapers Ltd* that the House of Lords was willing to extend common law duty and interest qualified privilege to widespread publications made in the public interest.[266] By the time *Reynolds* was decided a number of factors had coalesced so as to make the common law's traditional stance untenable. Academic criticism of the status quo certainly played its part, but other factors were also at play. Greater protection for media speech, for example, had recently been acknowledged by courts in comparable jurisdictions,[267] and the House of Lords itself had recently shown more awareness of the free speech implications of political libels by denying local authorities the right to sue for defamation.[268] Equally important to the decision was the desire to ensure that the common law was 'developed and applied' consistently with article 10 of the Convention. In particular, there was legitimate concern about the 'chilling effect' that the existing law was having on public interest speech – especially as a result of the high evidentiary burdens that the common law imposed on media defendants in proving the truth of the allegations that they publish.

The claim was brought against the *Sunday Times* by Albert Reynolds, the former Taoiseach of the Republic of Ireland. The article alleged that Reynolds had misled the Dáil (House of Representatives) of the Irish Parliament and a number of his colleagues by suppressing vital information concerning the appointment of the then Attorney-General as President of the High Court. The newspaper argued, akin to the actual malice standard recognised in *New York Times v Sullivan*, that common law qualified privilege should automatically extend to the media's discussion of political matters, unless the claimant could prove that the publication was made with actual malice (i.e., recklessness) or that it was unreasonable. This was rejected by the Court of Appeal[269] as well as the House of Lords[270] on the basis that it was both too narrow and too broad: on the one hand, it gave too much protection to freedom of speech over the right to reputation and, on the other hand, it too narrowly focused on political speech over other forms of public interest speech. On appeal to the House of Lords, the 'generic' privilege for political speech was also rejected; the House, however, recognised a broader form of qualified privilege for the publication of material in the 'public interest'.

---

[263] *Chesterton v Radio 2UE Sydney Pty Ltd* [2010] NSWSC 982 (1 September 2010) 16.

[264] *Loveday v Sun Newspapers Ltd* (1937) 59 CLR 503.

[265] *Radio 2UE Sydney Pty Ltd v Parker* (1992) 29 NSWLR 448.

[266] [2001] 2 AC 127.

[267] See, for example, the qualified privilege for political speech in Australia, established in *Lange v Australian Broadcasting Corporation* (1997) 189 CLR 520, and similar developments in New Zealand (*Lange v Atkinson* [1998] 3 NZLR 424, later affirmed in *Lange v Atkinson* [2000] 3 NZLR 385) and South Africa (*National Media Ltd v Bogoshi* [1998] ZASCA 94). For a discussion of these changes, see Adrienne Stone and George Williams, 'Freedom of Speech and Defamation: Developments in the Common Law World' (2000) 26 *Monash University Law Review* 362.

[268] See, e.g., *Derbyshire County Council v Times Newspapers Ltd* [1993] AC 534.

[269] *Reynolds v Times Newspapers Ltd* [2001] 2 AC 127, 178.

[270] Ibid., 204–5.

Extract 10.4.11
Reynolds v *Times Newspapers Ltd* **[2001] 2 AC 127**

LORD NICHOLLS:

(200) . . . My starting point is freedom of expression. The high importance of freedom to impart and receive information and ideas has been stated so often and so eloquently that this point calls for no elaboration in this case . . .

Likewise, there is no need to elaborate on the importance of the role discharged by the media in the expression and communication of information and comment on political matters. It is through the mass media that most people today obtain their information on political matters. Without freedom of expression by the media, freedom of expression would be a hollow concept . . .

Reputation is an integral and important part of the dignity of the individual. It also forms the basis of many decisions in a democratic society which are fundamental to its well-being: whom to employ or work for, whom to promote, whom to do business with or to vote for. Once besmirched by an unfounded allegation in a national newspaper, a reputation can be damaged for ever, especially if there is no opportunity to vindicate one's reputation. When this happens, society as well as the individual is the loser. For it should not be supposed that protection of reputation is a matter of importance only to the affected individual and his family. Protection of reputation is conducive to the public good. It is in the public interest that the reputation of public figures should not be debased falsely. In the political field, in order to make an informed choice, the electorate needs to be able to identify the good as well as the bad . . .

The crux of this appeal, therefore, lies in identifying the restrictions which are fairly and reasonably necessary for the protection of reputation . . .

(203) For the newspaper, Lord Lester's fallback position was that qualified privilege should be available for political discussion unless the plaintiff proved the newspaper failed to exercise reasonable care. One difficulty with this suggestion is that it would seem to leave a newspaper open to publish a serious allegation which it had been wholly unable to verify. Depending on the circumstances, that might be most unsatisfactory . . .

I have been more troubled by Lord Lester's suggested shift in the burden of proof. Placing the burden of proof on the plaintiff would be a reminder that the starting point today is freedom of expression and limitations on this freedom are exceptions. That has attraction. But if this shift of the onus were applied generally, it would turn the law of qualified privilege upside down. The repercussions of such a far-reaching change were not canvassed before your Lordships. If this change were applied only to political information, the distinction would lack a coherent rationale. . . . On balance I favour leaving the onus in its traditional place, on him who asserts the privilege, for two practical reasons. A newspaper will know much more of the facts leading up to publication. The burden of proof will seldom, if ever, be decisive on this issue . . .

(204) My conclusion is that the established common law approach to misstatements of fact remains essentially sound. The common law should not develop 'political information' as a new 'subject matter' category of qualified privilege, whereby the publication of all such information would attract qualified privilege, whatever the circumstances. That would not provide adequate protection for reputation. Moreover, it would be unsound in principle to distinguish political discussion from discussion of other matters of serious public concern. The elasticity of the common law principle enables interference with freedom of speech to be confined to what is necessary in the circumstances of the case. This elasticity enables the court to give appropriate weight, in today's conditions, to the importance of freedom of expression by the media on all matters of public concern.

(205) Depending on the circumstances, the matters to be taken into account include the following. The comments are illustrative only. 1. The seriousness of the allegation. The more

serious the charge, the more the public is misinformed and the individual harmed, if the allegation is not true. 2. The nature of the information, and the extent to which the subject matter is a matter of public concern. 3. The source of the information. Some informants have no direct knowledge of the events. Some have their own axes to grind, or are being paid for their stories. 4. The steps taken to verify the information. 5. The status of the information. The allegation may have already been the subject of an investigation which commands respect. 6. The urgency of the matter. News is often a perishable commodity. 7. Whether comment was sought from the plaintiff. He may have information others do not possess or have not disclosed. An approach to the plaintiff will not always be necessary. 8. Whether the article contained the gist of the plaintiff's side of the story. 9. The tone of the article. A newspaper can raise queries or call for an investigation. It need not adopt allegations as statements of fact. 10. The circumstances of the publication, including the timing.

This list is not exhaustive. The weight to be given to these and any other relevant factors will vary from case to case. Any disputes of primary fact will be a matter for the jury, if there is one. The decision on whether, having regard to the admitted or proved facts, the publication was subject to qualified privilege is a matter for the judge. This is the established practice and seems sound. A balancing operation is better carried out by a judge in a reasoned judgment than by a jury. Over time, a valuable corpus of case law will be built up.

In general, a newspaper's unwillingness to disclose the identity of its sources should not weigh against it. Further, it should always be remembered that journalists act without the benefit of the clear light of hindsight. Matters which are obvious in retrospect may have been far from clear in the heat of the moment. Above all, the court should have particular regard to the importance of freedom of expression. The press discharges vital functions as a bloodhound as well as a watchdog. The court should be slow to conclude that a publication was not in the public interest and, therefore, the public had no right to know, especially when the information is in the field of political discussion. Any lingering doubts should be resolved in favour of publication.

Broadly speaking, the effect of *Reynolds* privilege is that a newspaper is free to publish false and defamatory allegations to the world at large provided they are on a topic of public interest and the newspaper can establish, to the court's satisfaction, that it acted according to the conduct expected of a responsible journalist. Once this is established, and as long as the newspaper has not acted with malice, the claimant loses all possible avenues of redress for published untruths. Although a claimant is deprived of his or her right to an unsullied reputation, this is balanced against the burden placed on the publisher to show that it acted responsibly ('the price journalists pay in return for the privilege').[271]

At the time, commentators generally viewed *Reynolds* as a 'marked liberalisation'[272] of libel law. This newly found media freedom, however, proved to be, for the most part, elusive in practice. The restrictive interpretation of the defence by the lower courts meant that it seldom succeeded. In fact, prior to 2006 the defence had been successfully argued in only 3 of 20 cases where it was pleaded.[273] In the cases that failed the responsible journalism standard, publishers were found, contrary to the *Reynolds* factors, to have relied on sources that were unreliable,[274] to have not taken reasonable steps to verify the allegations,[275] or to

---

[271] *Bonnick* v *Morris* [2003] 1 AC 300, 309.

[272] Kevin Williams, 'Defaming Politicians: The Not So Common Law' (2000) 63 *Modern Law Review* 748, 754.

[273] See Andrew Scott, 'The Same River Twice? *Jameel* v *Wall Street Journal Europe*' (2007) 12(2) *Communications Law* 52. If the 'reportage' cases are excluded, the defence succeeded in only one case: *GKR Karate Ltd* v *Yorkshire Post Newspapers Ltd (No 2)* [2000] EMLR 410.

[274] *Gilbert* v *MGN* [2000] EMLR 680.

[275] Ibid; *Armstrong* v *Times Newspapers Ltd* [2004] EWCA 2928 (Ch); *Galloway* v *The Telegraphic Group* [2005] EMLR 7.

have not given a claimant a meaningful opportunity to comment on the allegations prior to publication.[276] Only the neutral reporting of an allegation[277] (see Section 10.4(c)(v) below) or, possibly, the reporting of time sensitive material would excuse the failure to delay publication in order to get a comment from the claimant or to more closely verify the facts.[278] Conversely, adopting allegations as fact, especially in a sensational and repeated manner, inevitably saw the defence fail.[279] On the general approach of the lower courts, one commentator has suggested that in dismissing the defence the judges 'applied a dollop of hindsight, finding something which they, as a responsible editor or journalist, would have done differently'.[280] Furthermore, the judges treated the *Reynolds* factors as a checklist or series of hurdles to be overcome before finding that the defendant acted responsibly, rather than considering the totality of the circumstances of the publication.

The House of Lords sought to put an end to this trend in the case of *Jameel* v *Wall Street Journal Europe Sprl*,[281] where it explicitly rejected that the *Reynolds* factors should operate as a checklist. Importantly, the court said that, while these factors may provide guidance to the court's analysis, and while the standard is an objective standard to be determined by the court, greater attention and weight should be given to the professional and editorial judgement of journalists in determining whether a defendant has met the responsible journalism standard. The facts of *Jameel* v *Wall Street Journal* are set out above (see Section 10.3(d)(i)).

Extract 10.4.12
Jameel v *Wall Street Journal Europe Sprl* [2007] 1 AC 359

LORD BINGHAM:

28. The decision of the House in *Reynolds* v *Times Newspapers Ltd* [2001] 2 AC 127 built on the traditional foundations of qualified privilege but carried the law forward in a way which gave much greater weight than the earlier law had done to the value of informed public debate of significant public issues. Both these aspects are, I think, important in understanding the decision.

. . .

30. I do not understand the House to have rejected the duty/interest approach . . . But Lord Nicholls . . . considered that matters relating to the nature and source of the information were matters to be taken into account in determining whether the duty-interest test was satisfied or, as he preferred to say 'in a simpler and more direct way, whether the public was entitled to know the particular information'.

. . .

32. Qualified privilege as a live issue only arises where a statement is defamatory and untrue. It was in this context, and assuming the matter to be one of public interest, that Lord Nicholls proposed, at p 202, a test of responsible journalism, a test repeated in *Bonnick* v *Morris* [2003] 1 AC 300, 309. The rationale of this test is, as I understand, that there is no duty to publish and

---

[276] *Jameel* v *Wall Street Journal Europe Sprl (No 2)* [2004] EMLR 11; *Jameel* v *Wall Street Journal Europe Sprl (No 3)* [2005] EMLR 17.
[277] *Al-Fagih* v *HH Saudi Research & Marketing (UK) Ltd* [2001] EWCA Civ 1634; *Roberts* v *Gable* [2008] QB 502.
[278] This will depend on the gravity of the allegations and the tone of the article: see *Grobbelaar* v *News Group Newspapers Ltd* [2001] 2 All ER 437, citing (at 45) urgency as the reason for finding *Reynolds* privilege in *GKR Karate Ltd* v *Yorkshire Post Newspapers Ltd (No 2)* [2000] EMLR 410.
[279] *Gilbert* v *MGN* [2000] EMLR 680; *Grobbelaar* v *News Group Newspapers Ltd* [2001] 2 All ER 437.
[280] David Hooper, 'The Importance of the *Jameel* case' (2007) 18(2) *Entertainment Law Review* 62.
[281] [2007] 1 AC 359.

the public have no interest to read material which the publisher has not taken reasonable steps to verify. As Lord Hobhouse observed with characteristic pungency, at p 238, 'No public interest is served by publishing or communicating misinformation'. But the publisher is protected if he has taken such steps as a responsible journalist would take to try and ensure that what is published is accurate and fit for publication . . .

33. Lord Nicholls . . . listed certain matters which might be taken into account in deciding whether the test of responsible journalism was satisfied. He intended these as pointers which might be more or less indicative, depending on the circumstances of a particular case, and not, I feel sure, as a series of hurdles to be negotiated by a publisher before he could successfully rely on qualified privilege. Lord Nicholls recognised, at pp 202–203, inevitably as I think, that it had to be a body other than the publisher, namely the court, which decided whether a publication was protected by qualified privilege. But this does not mean that the editorial decisions and judgements made at the time, without the knowledge of falsity which is a benefit of hindsight, are irrelevant. Weight should ordinarily be given to the professional judgment of an editor or journalist in the absence of some indication that it was made in a casual, cavalier, slipshod or careless manner.

34. Some misunderstanding may perhaps have been engendered by Lord Nicholls's references, at pp 195, 197, to 'the particular information'. It is of course true that the defence of qualified privilege must be considered with reference to the particular publication complained of as defamatory, and where a whole article or story is complained of no difficulty arises. But difficulty can arise where the complaint relates to one particular ingredient of a composite story, since it is then open to a plaintiff to contend, as in the present case, that the article could have been published without inclusion of the particular ingredient complained of. This may, in some instances, be a valid point. But consideration should be given to the thrust of the article which the publisher has published. If the thrust of the article is true, and the public interest condition is satisfied, the inclusion of an inaccurate fact may not have the same appearance of irresponsibility as it might if the whole thrust of the article is untrue . . .

35. These principles must be applied to the present case. As recorded in para 8, the Court of Appeal upheld the judge's denial of *Reynolds* privilege on a single ground, discounting the jury's negative findings concerning Mr Dorsey's sources: that the newspaper had failed to delay publication of the respondents' names without waiting long enough for the respondents to comment. This seems to me, with respect, to be a very narrow ground on which to deny the privilege, and the ruling subverts the liberalising intention of the *Reynolds* decision. The subject matter was of great public interest, in the strictest sense. The article was written by an experienced specialist reporter and approved by senior staff on the newspaper and *The Wall Street Journal* who themselves sought to verify its contents. The article was unsensational in tone and (apparently) factual in content. The respondents' response was sought, although at a late stage, and the newspaper's inability to obtain a comment recorded. It is very unlikely that a comment, if obtained, would have been revealing, since even if the respondents' accounts were being monitored it was unlikely that they would know. It might be thought that this was the sort of neutral, investigative journalism which *Reynolds* privilege exists to protect. I would accordingly allow the appeal and set aside the Court of Appeal judgment . . .

I am in much more doubt than my noble and learned friends what the consequence of that decision should be. The House has not, like the judge and the jury, heard the witnesses and seen the case develop day after day. It has read no more than a small sample of the evidence. It seems to me a large step for the House, thus disadvantaged, to hold that the publication was privileged, and I am not sure that counsel for the newspaper sought such a ruling. But I find myself in a minority, and it serves no useful purpose to do more than express my doubt.

LORD HOFFMANN:

43. The newspaper's principal defence was based on *Reynolds* v *Times Newspapers Ltd* [2001] 2 AC 127. It is called in the trade '*Reynolds* privilege' but the use of the term privilege, although historically accurate, may be misleading. A defence of privilege in the usual sense is available when the defamatory statement was published on a privileged occasion and can be defeated only by showing that the privilege was abused.

. . .

46. Although Lord Nicholls uses the word 'privilege', it is clearly not being used in the old sense. It is the material which is privileged, not the occasion on which it is published. There is no question of the privilege being defeated by proof of malice because the propriety of the conduct of the defendant is built into the conditions under which the material is privileged. The burden is upon the defendant to prove that those conditions are satisfied. I therefore agree with the opinion of the Court of Appeal in *Loutchansky* v *Times Newspapers Ltd (Nos 2–5)* [2002] QB 783, 806 that '*Reynolds* privilege' is 'a different jurisprudential creature from the traditional form of privilege from which it sprang.' It might more appropriately be called the *Reynolds* public interest defence rather than privilege.

47. In *Reynolds* itself, the publication failed by a very considerable margin to satisfy the conditions for the new defence. The House was therefore able to deal with those conditions only in very general terms. Lord Nicholls offered guidance in the form of a non-exhaustive, illustrative list of matters which, depending on the circumstances, might be relevant. 'Over time', he said, at p 205, 'a valuable corpus of case law will be built up.' This case, in my opinion, illustrates the circumstances in which the defence should be available.

Applying *Reynolds*

(a) The public interest of the material

48. The first question is whether the subject matter of the article was a matter of public interest. In answering this question, I think that one should consider the article as a whole and not isolate the defamatory statement . . .

50. In answering the question of public interest, I do not think it helpful to apply the classic test for the existence of a privileged occasion and ask whether there was a duty to communicate the information and an interest in receiving it. The *Reynolds* defence was developed from the traditional form of privilege by a generalisation that in matters of public interest, there can be said to be a professional duty on the part of journalists to impart the information and an interest in the public in receiving it. The House having made this generalisation, it should in my opinion be regarded as a proposition of law and not decided each time as a question of fact. If the publication is in the public interest, the duty and interest are taken to exist. The *Reynolds* defence is very different from the privilege discussed by the Court of Appeal in *Blackshaw* v *Lord* [1984] QB 1, where it was contemplated that in exceptional circumstances there could be a privileged occasion in the classic sense, arising out of a duty to communicate information to the public generally and a corresponding interest in receiving it . . .

(b) Inclusion of the defamatory statement

51. If the article as a whole concerned a matter of public interest, the next question is whether the inclusion of the defamatory statement was justifiable. The fact that the material was of public interest does not allow the newspaper to drag in damaging allegations which serve no public purpose. They must be part of the story. And the more serious the allegation, the more important it is that it should make a real contribution to the public interest element in the article. But whereas the question of whether the story as a whole was a matter of public interest must be decided by the judge without regard to what the editor's view may have been, the question of whether the defamatory statement should have been included is often a matter

of how the story should have been presented. And on that question, allowance must be made for editorial judgment. If the article as a whole is in the public interest, opinions may reasonably differ over which details are needed to convey the general message. The fact that the judge, with the advantage of leisure and hindsight, might have made a different editorial decision should not destroy the defence. That would make the publication of articles which are, *ex hypothesi*, in the public interest, too risky and would discourage investigative reporting.

. . .

(c) Responsible journalism

53. If the publication, including the defamatory statement, passes the public interest test, the inquiry then shifts to whether the steps taken to gather and publish the information were responsible and fair . . .

56. In *Reynolds*, Lord Nicholls gave his well-known non-exhaustive list of ten matters which should in suitable cases be taken into account. They are not tests which the publication has to pass. In the hands of a judge hostile to the spirit of *Reynolds*, they can become ten hurdles at any of which the defence may fail. That is how Eady J treated them. The defence, he said, can be sustained only after 'the closest and most rigorous scrutiny' by the application of what he called 'Lord Nicholls's ten tests'. But that, in my opinion, is not what Lord Nicholls meant. As he said in *Bonnick*, at p 309, the standard of conduct required of the newspaper must be applied in a practical and flexible manner. It must have regard to practical realities.

57. Instead, Eady J rigidly applied the old law. Building upon some obiter remarks of Lord Cooke of Thorndon in *McCartan Turkington Breen* v *Times Newspapers Ltd* [2001] 2 AC 277, 301 to which he referred seven times in the course of his judgment (the case was actually about statutory privilege), the judge insisted that *Reynolds* had changed nothing. It was not in his opinion sufficient that the article concerned a matter of public interest and was the product of responsible journalism. It was still necessary to show, in the words of Parke B in *Toogood* v *Spyring* (1834) 1 CM & R 181, 193, that the newspaper was under a social or moral duty to communicate to the public at large not merely the general message of the article (the Saudis were co-operating with the United States Treasury) but the particular defamatory statement that accounts associated with the claimants were being monitored. A 'useful cross-check', he suggested, was 'whether the journalists concerned might be the subject of legitimate criticism if they withheld the *ex hypothesi* false allegations.' In my opinion this approach, equating a responsible journalist reporting on matters of public interest with an employer who has a moral duty to include in his reference the fact that his former employee was regularly drunk on duty, is quite unrealistic. Its use by Eady J on two previous occasions had already been criticised by the Court of Appeal in *Loutchansky* v *Times Newspapers Ltd (Nos 2–5)* [2002] QB 783, 811 at para 49. In my opinion it is unnecessary and positively misleading to go back to the old law on classic privilege. It is the principle stated in *Reynolds* and encapsulated by Lord Nicholls in *Bonnick* which should be applied. On this question I have had the advantage of reading in draft the opinion of my noble and learned friend, Baroness Hale of Richmond, and wholeheartedly concur in her remarks . . .

BARONESS HALE:

146. It should by now be entirely clear that the *Reynolds* defence is a 'different jurisprudential creature' from the law of privilege, although it is a natural development of that law. It springs from the general obligation of the press, media and other publishers to communicate important information upon matters of general public interest and the general right of the public to receive such information. It is not helpful to analyse the particular case in terms of a specific duty and a specific right to know. That can, as experience since *Reynolds* has shown, very easily lead to a narrow and rigid approach which defeats its object. In truth, it is a defence of publication in the public interest . . .

147. This does not mean a free-for-all to publish without being damned. The public only have a right to be told if two conditions are fulfilled. First, there must be a real public interest in communicating and receiving the information. This is, as we all know, very different from saying that it is information which interests the public – the most vapid tittle-tattle about the activities of footballers' wives and girlfriends interests large sections of the public but no-one could claim any real public interest in our being told all about it . . .

. . .

149. Secondly, the publisher must have taken the care that a responsible publisher would take to verify the information published. The actual steps taken will vary with the nature and sources of the information. But one would normally expect that the source or sources were ones which the publisher had good reason to think reliable, that the publisher himself believed the information to be true, and that he had done what he could to check it. We are frequently told that 'fact checking' has gone out of fashion with the media. But a publisher who is to avoid the risk of liability if the information cannot later be proved to be true would be well advised to do it. Part of this is, of course, taking reasonable steps to contact the people named for their comments . . .

The Supreme Court has more recently considered *Reynolds* privilege in *Flood* v *Times Newspapers Ltd*.[282] The newspaper published an article in June 2006 alleging that the claimant, Gary Flood, a Detective Sergeant (DS) in the Extradition Unit of the Metropolitan Police Service (MPS), was under investigation for having taken £20,000 in bribes from a security company, ISC, to provide it sensitive information on the Kremlin's attempts to extradite to Russia opponents of the Russian government. The events leading up to the newspaper article unfolded as follows. The journalist, Michael Gillard, and two colleagues, had been investigating the allegations since December 2005; they had four sources, including an ISC insider, and had been provided documentary evidence. The ISC insider speculated, but could not confirm, that the person involved in the bribery, referred to as 'Noah' in the documentary evidence, was DS Flood. The Directorate of Professional Standards (DPS) of the MPS had been provided with information about the alleged bribery by the ISC insider; however, the DPS did not appear to be investigating the matter or taking the allegations seriously. Following an attempt by Gillard to speak directly to the claimant, the MPS Press Office contacted Gillard and, following a series of exchanges, issued a brief statement on 18 April 2006 that a current investigation was being conducted 'into allegations that a serving office made unauthorised disclosures of information to another individual in exchange for money'. A few days later, DS Flood was removed from the Extradition Unit. Following further investigation by Gillard, the newspaper article was published. Subsequent to this, however, the formal investigation by the DPS cleared DS Flood of any wrongdoing; thus, as the allegations contained in the article could not be justified, the newspaper sought to rely on *Reynolds* privilege.

At trial, Tugendhat J found that allegations of police corruption were in the public interest and that the journalists had been justified in naming Flood as the officer under investigation. Tugendhat J noted that the 'basis for the allegation was weak' – the journalists had no actual evidence that Flood was the officer in question or even that ISC had been in receipt of any confidential information. However, the fact that the police had obtained a search warrant to search Flood's home and were carrying out an investigation indicated that there was sufficient evidence.[283] The Court of Appeal overturned Tugendhat J's decision. It was accepted by the claimant that, by virtue of

---

[282] [2012] 2 WLR 760.
[283] *Flood* v *Times Newspapers Ltd* [2009] EWHC 2375 (QB) 203.

section 15 of the Defamation Act 1952, the newspaper could report the press release by the MPS and that this extended to naming DS Flood as the relevant officer.[284] The issue, instead, was whether the newspaper's publication of the specific allegations themselves were protected by *Reynolds* privilege. The Court of Appeal held that, considering the seriousness of the allegations, the journalists had not taken sufficient steps to verify their accuracy. Rather, they were 'unsubstantiated unchecked accusations . . . coupled with speculation'.[285] Moreover, the Court of Appeal drew a distinction between the facts in *Jameel*, where *Reynolds* privilege succeeded, and the facts at issue in *Flood*.[286] The Court of Appeal said that the newspaper article in *Jameel* merely reported an allegation that the Saudi Arabian Monetary Authority was cooperating with terrorism investigations by monitoring bank accounts to prevent them from being used 'wittingly or unwittingly' to funnel terrorist funds. It did not go further and report, for example, that there was evidence that the claimant's accounts were being used to funnel funds for terrorism. Hence, there was no need to take steps to verify such allegations. In *Flood*, on the other hand, the newspaper reported that DS Flood was the subject of an investigation *as well as* details of the precise allegations; in fact, 'the allegations *were* the whole story'.[287]

The Supreme Court allowed the appeal and restored the trial judge's findings. Lord Phillips held that 'responsible journalism' required that the journalists should have been satisfied on reasonable grounds that, as a result of their investigations, the facts supporting the allegations were true and that 'there was a serious possibility that Sergeant Flood had been guilty of the corruption of which he was suspected'.[288] On the facts, according to Lord Phillips, the supporting facts *were* true (there was reliable documentary evidence that cash payments totalling £20,000 had been made by ISC to a person named 'Noah') and that the journalists could not be faulted in failing to take further steps to verify such facts. Moreover, it was not unreasonable for the journalists to assume that the actions of the DPS in obtaining and executing a search warrant of DS Flood's house and removing him from service in the Extradition Unit were the result of information provided by the ISC insider; hence it was a 'natural inference . . . that the accusations made against Sergeant Flood might be well founded.'[289]

Questions for discussion

1. Do you agree with the responsible journalism standard set out in *Reynolds*? Does it provide sufficient certainty to the media?
2. What might be some of the difficulties faced by the media in relying on *Reynolds* privilege?
3. What happens when a journalist refuses to reveal his or her sources? Does it make it difficult to rely on *Reynolds* privilege?

---

[284] *Flood v Times Newspapers Ltd* [2011] 1 WLR 153, 25. Note that the claimant's concession that the newspaper was entitled to name DS Flood was withdrawn when the matter went to the Supreme Court: see *Flood v Times Newspapers Ltd* [2012] 2 WLR 760, 53.
[285] *Flood v Times Newspapers Ltd* [2011] 1 WLR 153, 73.
[286] Ibid., 61 (per Lord Neuberger MR), 97–105 (per Moore-Bick LJ). This distinction was also accepted by the Supreme Court: see *Flood v Times Newspapers Ltd* [2012] 2 WLR 760, 75–8.
[287] *Flood v Times Newspapers Ltd* [2011] 1 WLR 153, 100 (per Moore-Bick LJ), 66 (per Lord Neuberger MR).
[288] *Flood v Times Newspapers Ltd* [2012] 2 WLR 760, 81.
[289] Ibid., [95].

(v) Doctrine of reportage

A 'special example' of *Reynolds* qualified privilege, first recognised in the case of *Al-Fagih v HH Saudi Research & Marketing (UK) Ltd*,[290] is the 'reportage doctrine'.[291] Reportage essentially provides a defence for the republication of allegations originally made by someone else in the context of a dispute or controversy of public interest.[292] A key feature of the defence is that as long as the allegations are neutrally reported, there is no obligation on the publisher, as is usually required under *Reynolds* privilege, to take steps to verify them; nor is there an obligation to seek comment from the claimant. The nature of the defence, and its relationship to 'classic *Reynolds*'[293] privilege was considered by the Court of Appeal in *Roberts* v *Gable*.[294] In that case, an anti-fascist magazine neutrally reported allegations that were being cast back and forth between members of the far-right British National Party in the context of an ongoing political dispute. The magazine reported allegations of theft and violence that had been made against two BNP members, brothers Christopher and Barry Roberts.

Extract 10.4.13
Roberts v Gable [2008] QB 502

LORD JUSTICE WARD:

Reportage

33. The pleaded defence is that the article did not allege that either of the claimants was guilty of criminal conduct. It described the allegations being made by both groups of suppo.rters against each other to illustrate the enmity between rival groups struggling for political leadership of the British National Party. It is a defence of what is now becoming known as *reportage*. This appeal has given this Court the opportunity to explore the nature and extent of that defence and its place in the libel law landscape.

[Ward LJ reviewed domestic and international authority on the reportage doctrine.]

Where have we arrived so far?

53. What can be learnt so far from this review of the authorities is that the journalist has a good defence to a claim for libel if what he publishes, even without an attempt to verify its truth, amounts to *reportage*, the best description of which gleaned from these cases is that it is the neutral reporting without adoption or embellishment or subscribing to any belief in its truth of attributed allegations of both sides of a political and possibly some other kind of dispute. Mr Tomlinson objects that this is vague and wide and constitutes an unprincipled extension to freedom of expression. His objections can only be met by placing *reportage* in its proper place in the legal landscape. To do so one must answer these questions:

1. Why is the reporter of *reportage* free from the responsibility of verifying the information and why does the well-established repetition rule not require the journalist to justify the truth of what he is reporting?
2. Do the *Reynolds* rules apply to *reportage*?
3. What then is the proper approach to the *reportage* defence?

---

[290] [2001] EWCA Civ 1634.
[291] *Al-Fagih v HH Saudi Research and Marketing (UK) Ltd* [2001] EWCA Civ 1634. For commentary critical of the defence, see Godwin Busuttil, 'Reportage: A Not Entirely Neutral Report' (2009) 20 *Entertainment Law Review* 44; Jason Bosland, 'Republication of Defamation under the Doctrine of Reportage – The Evolution of Common Law Qualified Privilege in England and Wales' (2011) 31(1) *Oxford Journal of Legal Studies* 89.
[292] Repeating allegations would usually give rise to liability on the part of the republisher: see Section 10.3(c)(iii).
[293] As it was referred to by Eady J in *Prince Radu of Hohenzollern v Houston* [2007] EWHC 2735 (QB) 26.
[294] [2008] QB 502.

Reportage and the repetition rule

. . .

54. The repetition rule is well-established and has an important place in libel law . . .

59. . . . [T]he repetition rule and *reportage* are not in conflict with each other. The former is concerned with justification, the latter with privilege. A true case of *reportage* may give the journalist a complete defence of qualified privilege. If the journalist does not establish the defence then the repetition rule applies and the journalist has to prove the truth of the defamatory words.

. . .

Reportage and *Reynolds'* qualified privilege

. . .

60. Once *reportage* is seen as a defence of qualified privilege, its place in the legal landscape is clear. It is, as was conceded in the *Al-Fagih* case . . . a form of, or a special example of, *Reynolds'* qualified privilege, a special kind of responsible journalism but with distinctive features of its own. It cannot be a defence *sui generis* because the *Reynolds* case . . . is clear authority that whilst the categories of privilege are not closed, the underlying rationale justifying the defence is the public policy demand for there to be a duty to impart the information and an interest in receiving it . . . If the case for a generic qualified privilege for political speech had to be rejected, so too the case for a generic qualified privilege for *reportage* must be dismissed.

The proper approach to the reportage defence

61. Thus it seems to me that the following matters must be taken into account when considering whether there is a defence on the ground of *reportage*.

1. The information must be in the public interest.

2. Since the public cannot have an interest in receiving misinformation which is destructive of the democratic society (see Lord Hobhouse . . . in the *Reynolds* case, at p 238), the publisher will not normally be protected unless he has taken reasonable steps to verify the truth and accuracy of what is published: see, also in the *Reynolds* case, Lord Nicholls's factor 4 at p 205 b, and Lord Cooke, at p 225, and in the *Jameel* case . . . Lord Bingham . . . at para 12 and Baroness Hale, at para 149. This is where *reportage* parts company with *Reynolds*. In a true case of *reportage* there is no need to take steps to ensure the accuracy of the published information.

3. The question which perplexed me is why that important factor can be disregarded. The answer lies in what I see as the defining characteristic of *reportage* . . . To qualify as *reportage* the report, judging the thrust of it as a whole, must have the effect of reporting, not the truth of the statements, but the fact that they were made. Those familiar with the circumstances in which hearsay evidence can be admitted will be familiar with the distinction . . . If upon a proper construction of the thrust of the article the defamatory material is attributed to another and is not being put forward as true, then a responsible journalist would not need to take steps to verify its accuracy. He is absolved from that responsibility because he is simply reporting in a neutral fashion the fact that it has been said without adopting the truth.

. . .

5. This protection will be lost if the journalist adopts the report and makes it his own or if he fails to report the story in a fair, disinterested and neutral way. Once that protection is lost, he must then show, if he can, that it was a piece of responsible journalism even though he did not check the accuracy of his report.

6. To justify the attack on the claimant's reputation the publication must always meet the standards of responsible journalism as that concept has developed from the *Reynolds* case, . . . the burden being on the defendants . . . All the circumstances of the case and

> the 10 factors listed by Lord Nicholls adjusted as may be necessary for the special nature of *reportage* must be considered in order to reach the necessary conclusion that this was the product of responsible journalism.
>
> 7. The seriousness of the allegation (Lord Nicholls's factor 1) is obviously relevant for the harm it does to reputation if the charges are untrue. Ordinarily it makes verification all the more important . . . There is, however, no reason in principle why *reportage* must be confined to scandal-mongering as Mr Tomlinson submits. Here equally serious allegations were being levelled at both sides of this dispute. In line with factor 2, the criminality of the actions bears upon the public interest which is the critical question: does the public have the right to know the fact that these allegations were being made one against the other? . . . All the circumstances of the case are brought into play to find the answer but if it is affirmative, then *reportage* must be allowed to protect the journalist who, not having adopted the allegation, takes no steps to verify his story.
>
> . . .
>
> 9. The urgency is relevant, see factor 5, in the sense that fine editorial judgements taken as the presses are about to roll may command a more sympathetic review than decisions to publish with the luxury of time to reflect and public interest can wane with the passage of time . . . Public interest is circumscribed as much by events as by time and every story must be judged on its merits at the moment of publication.

It has been argued by Bosland, one of the authors of the current book, that the reportage defence sits uncomfortably as a particular application, or 'species', of *Reynolds* privilege.[295] One reason put forward for this is that *Reynolds* privilege and reportage are treated in the court's process of analysis as separate defences. More importantly, however, it is argued that the locus of the public interest is different in *Reynolds* and reportage cases. In a classic *Reynolds* case, the public interest is in the truth, or potential truth, of the allegations; hence, the responsible journalism standard aims to ensure that journalists are as accurate as possible in the allegations that they report. Lord Bingham made this clear in *Jameel*:

> The rationale of [the responsible journalism] test is, as I understand, that there is no duty to publish and the public have no interest to read material which the publisher had not taken reasonable steps to verify . . .[296]

In a reportage case, on the other hand, the public interest is not in the truth or potential truth of the allegations themselves, but in the *fact that they have been made.*[297] This distinction was recently confirmed by the Supreme Court in *Flood v Times Newspaper Ltd*:[298] the public interest that justifies publication in the reportage context is 'knowing that the allegations [have] been made, it [does] not turn on the content or the truth of those allegations'. If this is the defining feature of reportage, it explains why journalists are relieved of the obligation to satisfy the usual markers of responsible journalism set out by Lord Nicholls in *Reynolds*, such as taking steps to verify the allegations, seeking comment from the claimant or ensuring that the source is reliable (although they will be required to act responsibly in verifying that the allegations have, in fact, been made).[299]

One of the consequences of treating reportage as a species of broader *Reynolds* privilege, according to Bosland, is that this key distinction is sometimes lost in the case law and by

---

[295] Jason Bosland, 'Republication of Defamation under the Doctrine of Reportage – The Evolution of Common Law Qualified Privilege in England and Wales' (2011) 31(1) *Oxford Journal of Legal Studies* 89.

[296] *Jameel* v *Wall Street Journal Europe Sprl* [2007] 1 AC 359, 149.

[297] Ibid., 92.

[298] [2012] 2 WLR 760, 34–5.

[299] On this latter point, see Eric Barendt, 'Balancing Freedom of Expression and the Right to Reputation: Reflections on *Reynolds* and Reportage' (2012) 63(1) *Northern Ireland Legal Quarterly* 59, 73.

commentators.[300] This has created 'uncertainty and confusion' as to the availability of the defence and an 'overestimation as to its potential breadth'.[301] Concerns have been expressed, for example, that the defence could amount to a 'general privilege to report 'matters of public concern'.[302] In order to avoid such misunderstanding, Bosland argues that the courts should directly engage with the critical question as to when and why the public will have an interest in the fact that allegations have been made and that such analysis should be used to establish the express contours of the defence. Based on jurisprudence under the analogous 'neutral reportage' defence recognised in some states of the US, he suggests that there are only two 'scenarios' where it is possible for public interest to arise from the fact that allegations *have been made* separate from the allegations themselves. (Barendt, also an author of the current book, has questioned, on the other hand, whether it is possible for there to be public interest in the fact that allegations have been made which is 'entirely divorced from their nature of subject-matter').[303]

The first scenario suggested by Bosland is where the very fact of the dispute itself is in the public interest – such as where there is a dispute between two political or community leaders. The public interest here is not based on the truth or falsity of the allegation being cast back and forth; rather it is based on the fact that such leaders are in dispute (i.e., that they are party to a dysfunctional relationship). The second situation is where the statement can be said to be in the public interest due to the *status of the original speaker* – for example, where the statement is made by a political leader or some other public figure. Some speakers are so important that it is in the public interest that anything they say should be able to be freely reported. Interestingly, under this scenario there might be particular public interest in the fact that the speaker has made false allegations rather than true or potentially true allegations. In other words, reporting that such allegations have been made might be valued more for what it says about the original speaker than the subject. Because the public interest might arise from the fact that the person has made *false* allegations, the truth or falsity of the allegations may not necessarily be irrelevant. This leaves open the possibility that it might be in the public interest to republish attributed allegations which the republisher knows or suspects to be false. Baroness Hale in *Jameel* warned that in such circumstances, the publisher 'would be well advised to make this clear'.[304] Such an obligation, however, creates a tension because it would appear to be at odds with the requirement of neutrality under the defence.

Questions for discussion

1. What are the requirements of reportage?
2. Do you agree or disagree with Bosland that reportage sits uncomfortably as an application of *Reynolds*? Why/why not?
3. Can you think of additional scenarios where there would be public interest in reporting the fact that allegations have been made?

---

[300] See, e.g., *Galloway v The Daily Telegraph Group* [2006] EWCA Civ 17, where the Court focused on the public interest in the allegations of fact contained in the 'Baghdad documents' rather than the fact that the allegation had been made. According to the Court (at 48) '[i]f the documents had been published without comment or further allegations of fact Mr Galloway could have no complaint since, in so far as they contained statements or allegations of fact it was in the public interest for *The Daily Telegraph* to publish them . . . Such publication would be *reportage*.'

[301] Jason Bosland, 'Republication of Defamation under the Doctrine of Reportage – The Evolution of Common Law Qualified Privilege in England and Wales' (2011) 31(1) *Oxford Journal of Legal Studies* 89, 103.

[302] Gatley 540.

[303] Eric Barendt, 'Balancing Freedom of Expression and the Right to Reputation: Reflections on Reynolds and Reportage' (2012) 63(1) *Northern Ireland Legal Quarterly* 59, 73.

[304] *Jameel v Wall Street Journal Europe Sprl* [2007] 1 AC 359, 149.

(vi) Malice

Qualified privilege can be defeated where a statement is made with 'express malice'. The concept, considered in this context to be a 'term of art', was authoritatively explored by Lord Diplock in *Horrocks* v *Lowe*.

Extract 10.4.14
***Horrocks* v *Lowe* [1975] AC 135 (HL) 149–50**

LORD DIPLOCK:
My Lords, as a general rule English law gives effect to the ninth commandment that a man shall not speak evil falsely of his neighbour. It supplies a temporal sanction: if he cannot prove that defamatory matter which he published was true, he is liable in damages to whomever he has defamed, except where the publication is oral only, causes no damage and falls outside the categories of slander actionable per se. The public interest that the law should provide an effective means whereby a man can vindicate his reputation against calumny has nevertheless to be accommodated to the competing public interest in permitting men to communicate frankly and freely with one another about matters in respect of which the law recognises that they have a duty to perform or an interest to protect in doing so. What is published in good faith on matters of these kinds is published on a privileged occasion. It is not actionable even though it be defamatory and turns out to be untrue. With some exceptions which are irrelevant to the instant appeal, the privilege is not absolute but qualified. It is lost if the occasion which gives rise to it is misused. For in all cases of qualified privilege there is some special reason of public policy why the law accords immunity from suit – the existence of some public or private duty, whether legal or moral, on the part of the maker of the defamatory statement which justifies his communicating it or of some interest of his own which he is entitled to protect by doing so. If he uses the occasion for some other reason he loses the protection of the privilege.

So, the motive with which the defendant on a privileged occasion made a statement defamatory of the plaintiff becomes crucial. The protection might, however, be illusory if the onus lay on him to prove that he was actuated solely by a sense of the relevant duty or a desire to protect the relevant interest. So he is entitled to be protected by the privilege unless some other dominant and improper motive on his part is proved. 'Express malice' is the term of art descriptive of such a motive. Broadly speaking, it means malice in the popular sense of a desire to injure the person who is defamed and this is generally the motive which the plaintiff sets out to prove. But to destroy the privilege the desire to injure must be the dominant motive for the defamatory publication; knowledge that it will have that effect is not enough if the defendant is nevertheless acting in accordance with a sense of duty or in bona fide protection of his own legitimate interests.

The motive with which a person published defamatory matter can only be inferred from what he did or said or knew. If it be proved that he did not believe that what he published was true this is generally conclusive evidence of express malice, for no sense of duty or desire to protect his own legitimate interests can justify a man in telling deliberate and injurious falsehoods about another, save in the exceptional case where a person may be under a duty to pass on, without endorsing, defamatory reports made by some other person.

Apart from those exceptional cases, what is required on the part of the defamer to entitle him to the protection of the privilege is positive belief in the truth of what he published or, as it is generally though tautologously termed, 'honest belief.' If he publishes untrue defamatory matter recklessly, without considering or caring whether it be true or not, he is in this, as in other branches of the law, treated as if he knew it to be false. But indifference to the truth of what he publishes is not to be equated with carelessness, impulsiveness or irrationality in arriving at a positive belief that it is true. The freedom of speech protected by the law of qualified privilege may be availed of by all sorts and conditions of men. In affording to them immunity from suit if they have acted in good faith in compliance with a legal or moral duty or in protection of a legitimate interest the law must take them as it finds them. In ordinary life it is rare indeed for people to form their beliefs by a process of logical deduction from facts ascertained by a rigorous search for all available evidence and a judicious assessment of its probative value. In greater or in less degree according to their temperaments, their training, their intelligence, they are swayed by prejudice, rely on intuition instead of reasoning, leap to conclusions on inadequate evidence and fail to recognise the cogency of material which might cast doubt on the validity of the conclusions they reach. But despite the imperfection of the mental process by which the belief is arrived at it may still be 'honest,' that is, a positive belief that the conclusions they have reached are true. The law demands no more.

Even a positive belief in the truth of what is published on a privileged occasion – which is presumed unless the contrary is proved – may not be sufficient to negative express malice if it can be proved that the defendant misused the occasion for some purpose other than that for which the privilege is accorded by the law. The commonest case is where the dominant motive which actuates the defendant is not a desire to perform the relevant duty or to protect the relevant interest, but to give vent to his personal spite or ill will towards the person he defames. If this be proved, then even positive belief in the truth of what is published will not enable the defamer to avail himself of the protection of the privilege to which he would otherwise have been entitled. There may be instances of improper motives which destroy the privilege apart from personal spite. A defendant's dominant motive may have been to obtain some private advantage unconnected with the duty or the interest which constitutes the reason for the privilege. If so, he loses the benefit of the privilege despite his positive belief that what he said or wrote was true.

Judges and juries should, however, be very slow to draw the inference that a defendant was so far actuated by improper motives as to deprive him of the protection of the privilege unless they are satisfied that he did not believe that what he said or wrote was true or that he was indifferent to its truth or falsity.

An interesting question, yet unresolved, is whether *Reynolds* privilege – and, indeed, reportage – can ever be defeated by showing malice. It has certainly been recognised by the courts that *Reynolds* privilege leaves 'little scope . . . for any subsequent finding of malice'.[305] This is because the assessment of the *Reynolds* factors necessarily requires the Court to consider the publisher's motives and knowledge of the truth: matters typically considered at the malice stage. *Reynolds* would not arise, for example, where the defendant was recklessly indifferent to the truth or, arguably, had a dominant motive of injuring the claimant.[306] On the latter, the Court of Appeal in *Loutchansky* v *Times Newspapers Ltd*, said the following:

> it may be doubted whether in truth there remains room for such a principle in a case of *Reynolds* privilege. Once the publication of a particular article is held to be in the public interest on the basis of the public's right to know, can the privilege really be lost because the journalist (or editor?) had the dominant motive of injuring the claimant rather than fulfilling his journalistic duty? It is a surprising thought.[307]

This approach to malice in the *Reynolds* context has the procedural implication that the burden of proof surrounding the 'reasonableness' of the publication – involving the sort of questions traditionally going to whether the defendant abused the privilege – has effectively been transferred from the claimant to the defendant.

---

[305] *Loutchansky* v *Times Newspapers Ltd (Nos 2–5)* [2002] QB 783, 33.
[306] Ibid., 34.
[307] *Loutchansky* v *Times Newspapers Ltd (Nos 2–5)* [2002] QB 783, 34.

It is suggested that malice in the reportage context *may* be treated slightly differently; it may be that, if there is scope for malice, that the defendant's disregard for the truth may not be enough to establish it. Thus, if the defence applies such that a reporter can legitimately report that an identified source has made an allegation that the reporter knows or suspects to be false (because the fact that *it has been said* is in the public interest), then under the reasoning in *Horrocks* v *Lowe*, evidence of the defendant's actual knowledge or reckless disregard for the truth of the substance of the allegation should not constitute malice: the defendant would simply not be acting outside the scope of the privilege.[308] If the defence does indeed apply to such known falsehoods, it would appear to leave open the possibility that, unlike *Reynolds*, malice could be proven on the basis that the defendant's dominant motive was to injure the claimant. This was certainly contemplated by the Court of Appeal in *Al-Fagih*[309] and subsequently left open in *Loutchansky* v *Times Newspapers Ltd.*[310]

Questions for discussion

1. Is there scope for the application of malice in the *Reynolds* context?
2. Is it right that actual knowledge of falsity, or reckless disregard for falsity, may not constitute malice in the reportage context?

(vii) Defamation Bill: proposed reforms to the law of absolute and qualified privilege

The Defamation Bill contains a number of reforms to the law of absolute and qualified privilege. Clause 7 extends the protection of absolute and qualified privilege under the Defamation Act 1996, including a new defence of qualified privilege for the report of proceedings of 'a scientific or academic conference held anywhere in the world'.[311] Clause 4 replaces *Reynolds* qualified privilege with a statutory defence. Like many of the other proposed changes, clause 4 is based on the common law but is designed make the law clearer and more accessible. The existing case law under *Reynolds* would 'constitute a helpful (albeit not binding) guide to interpreting how the new statutory defence should be applied'.[312] Clause 6 provides a new defence for the publication of defamation comments in peer-reviewed scientific and academic journals.

Extract 10.4.15
Defamation Bill

Clause 4 Responsible publication on matter of public interest

1. It is a defence to an action for defamation for the defendant to show that –

   (a) the statement complained of was, or formed part of, a statement on a matter of public interest; and

   (b) the defendant acted responsibly in publishing the statement complained of.

---

[308] Certainly, it was suggested in *Al-Fagih* v *HH Saudi Research & Marketing (UK) Ltd* [2001] EWCA Civ 1634 (at 55) that failure to verify in the reportage context would not be evidence of recklessness; see also *Loutchansky* v *Times Newspapers Ltd (Nos 2–5)* [2002] QB 783, 34.

[309] *Al-Fagih* v *HH Saudi Research & Marketing (UK) Ltd* [2001] EWCA Civ 1634, 55.

[310] *Loutchansky* v *Times Newspapers Ltd (Nos 2–5)* [2002] QB 783, 34.

[311] See cl 7(9).

[312] Explanatory Notes, Defamation Bill 2012–13 (HL Bill 41, 21 September 2012), 37.

2. Subject to subsections (3) and (4), in determining for the purposes of this section whether a defendant acted responsibly in publishing a statement the matters to which the court may have regard include (amongst other matters) –
   (a) the nature of the publication and its context;
   (b) the seriousness of the imputation conveyed by the statement;
   (c) the relevance of the imputation conveyed by the statement to the matter of public interest concerned;
   (d) the importance of the matter of public interest concerned;
   (e) the information the defendant had before publishing the statement and what the defendant knew about the reliability of that information;
   (f) whether the defendant sought the claimant's views on the statement before publishing it and whether an account of any views the claimant expressed was published with the statement;
   (g) whether the defendant took any other steps to verify the truth of the imputation conveyed by the statement;
   (h) the timing of the statement's publication;
   (i) the tone of the statement.
3. Subsection (4) applies in relation to the defence under this section if the statement complained of was, or formed part of, an accurate and impartial account of a dispute to which the claimant was a party.
4. In determining for the purposes of this section whether the defendant acted responsibly in publishing the statement complained of, the court must disregard any omission of the defendant to take steps to verify the truth of the imputation conveyed by it.

. . .

Clause 6 Peer-reviewed statement in scientific or academic journal

1. The publication of a statement in a scientific or academic journal is privileged if the following conditions are met.
2. The first condition is that the statement relates to a scientific or academic matter.
3. The second condition is that before the statement was published in the journal an independent review of the statement's scientific or academic merit was carried out by –
   (a) the editor of the journal, and
   (b) one or more persons with expertise in the scientific or academic matter concerned.
4. Where the publication of a statement in a scientific or academic journal is privileged by virtue of subsection (1), the publication in the same journal of any assessment of the statement's scientific or academic merit is also privileged if –
   (a) the assessment was written by one or more of the persons who carried out the independent review of the statement; and
   (b) the assessment was written in the course of that review.
5. Where the publication of a statement or assessment is privileged by virtue of this section, the publication of a fair and accurate copy of, extract from or summary of the statement or assessment is also privileged.
6. A publication is not privileged by virtue of this section if it is shown to be made with malice.

. . .

Questions for discussion
1. Will clause 4 bring greater clarity to the law? Will it make it more accessible?
2. How is reportage accommodated in clause 4? Is it appropriate in light of the commentary on reportage (above, Section 10.4(c)(v))?
3. What role does malice play in clause 4?

(d) Offer of amends

The Defamation Act 1996 provides that where a defendant makes an offer of amends he or she may have a valid defence. An offer to make amends is an offer to publish a suitable correction and sufficient apology in a reasonable manner, and to pay compensation to be agreed by the parties or assessed by the court.[313] It is valuable to newspapers which realise they have got the facts wrong and are prepared to make amends. If the claimant accepts an offer of amends, he may not bring defamation proceedings, but is only entitled to enforce the offer. In default of agreement, compensation is to be determined by a judge, not a jury, on the same principles as damages in libel proceedings.[314] But if the claimant considers the media knew or 'had reason to believe' its allegations were false, it can decline the offer and sue for damages in the usual way.[315]

(e) Innocent dissemination

The common law provides a defence of 'innocent dissemination' for 'subordinate distributors' where it can be established: (1) that they did not know the publication was defamatory; (2) that they did not know that the publication was likely to be defamatory; and (3) that such lack of awareness was not due to any negligence on their part. This defence has been held to apply to newspaper and magazine vendors[316] and libraries.[317]

The common law defence of innocent dissemination has now been modernised by the Defamation Act 1996.

Extract 10.4.16
Defamation Act 1996

Section 1

1.—(1) In defamation proceedings a person has a defence if he shows that—

(a) he was not the author, editor or publisher of the statement complained of,
(b) he took reasonable care in relation to its publication, and
(c) he did not know, and had no reason to believe, that what he did caused or contributed to the publication of a defamatory statement.

(2) For this purpose 'author', 'editor' and 'publisher' have the following meanings, which are further explained in subsection (3)—

'author' means the originator of the statement, but does not include a person who did not intend that his statement be published at all;

'editor' means a person having editorial or equivalent responsibility for the content of the statement or the decision to publish it; and

'publisher' means a commercial publisher, that is, a person whose business is issuing material to the public, or a section of the public, who issues material containing the statement in the course of that business.

(3) A person shall not be considered the author, editor or publisher of a statement if he is only involved—

---

[313] Defamation Act 1996, s 2.
[314] Ibid., s 3.
[315] Ibid., s 4. Note that the claimant must prove the defendant knew the allegations were false and defamatory.
[316] *Emmens* v *Pottle* (1885) 16 QBD 354.
[317] *Vizetelly* v *Mudie's Select Library Ltd* [1900] 2 QB 170 (CA).

(a) in printing, producing, distributing or selling printed material containing the statement;
(b) in processing, making copies of, distributing, exhibiting or selling a film or sound recording (as defined in Part I of the Copyright, Designs and Patents Act 1988) containing the statement;
(c) in processing, making copies of, distributing or selling any electronic medium in or on which the statement is recorded, or in operating or providing any equipment, system or service by means of which the statement is retrieved, copied, distributed or made available in electronic form;
(d) as the broadcaster of a live programme containing the statement in circumstances in which he has no effective control over the maker of the statement;
(e) as the operator of or provider of access to a communications system by means of which the statement is transmitted, or made available, by a person over whom he has no effective control.

In a case not within paragraphs (a) to (e) the court may have regard to those provisions by way of analogy in deciding whether a person is to be considered the author, editor or publisher of a statement.

(4) Employees or agents of an author, editor or publisher are in the same position as their employer or principal to the extent that they are responsible for the content of the statement or the decision to publish it.

(5) In determining for the purposes of this section whether a person took reasonable care, or had reason to believe that what he did caused or contributed to the publication of a defamatory statement, regard shall be had to—

(a) the extent of his responsibility for the content of the statement or the decision to publish it,
(b) the nature or circumstances of the publication, and
(c) the previous conduct or character of the author, editor or publisher.
. . .

The range of persons who may take advantage of the defence are not defined in positive terms, but rather negatively: they must not be 'authors', 'editors', or 'publishers'. The definition of a 'publisher', of course, is narrower than at common law.

The Electronic Commerce (EC Directive) Regulations 2002, which came into force on 21 August 2001, provides Internet intermediaries with specific exemptions from liability for 'damages or for any pecuniary remedy or for any criminal sanctions'. This clearly includes liability for defamation. The Regulation applies to 'information society services', which is defined in reg 2(1) as 'any service normally provided for remuneration, at a distance, by electronic means and at the individual request of a recipient of services'. The Regulation distinguishes between mere conduits, caching services and hosting services in defining the boundaries of the exemption.

Extract 10.4.17
Electronic Commerce (EC Directive) Regulations 2002

Mere conduit

17.—(1) Where an information society service is provided which consists of the transmission in a communication network of information provided by a recipient of the service or the provision of access to a communication network, the service provider (if he otherwise would) shall not be liable for damages or for any other pecuniary remedy or for any criminal sanction as a result of that transmission where the service provider—

(a) did not initiate the transmission;
(b) did not select the receiver of the transmission; and
(c) did not select or modify the information contained in the transmission.

(2) The acts of transmission and of provision of access referred to in paragraph (1) include the automatic, intermediate and transient storage of the information transmitted where:

(a) this takes place for the sole purpose of carrying out the transmission in the communication network, and

(b) the information is not stored for any period longer than is reasonably necessary for the transmission.

[*Section 18 omitted*].

Hosting

19. Where an information society service is provided which consists of the storage of information provided by a recipient of the service, the service provider (if he otherwise would) shall not be liable for damages or for any other pecuniary remedy or for any criminal sanction as a result of that storage where—

(a) the service provider—
   (i) does not have actual knowledge of unlawful activity or information and, where a claim for damages is made, is not aware of facts or circumstances from which it would have been apparent to the service provider that the activity or information was unlawful; or
   (ii) upon obtaining such knowledge or awareness, acts expeditiously to remove or to disable access to the information, and

(b) the recipient of the service was not acting under the authority or the control of the service provider.

Clause 5 of the Defamation Bill introduces a new defence for the operators of websites.

Extract 10.4.18
Defamation Bill

Clause 5 Operators of websites

1. This section applies where an action for defamation is brought against the operator of a website in respect of a statement posted on the website.

2. It is a defence for the operator to show that it was not the operator who posted the statement on the website.

3. The defence is defeated if the claimant shows that –

(a) it was not possible for the claimant to identify the person who posted the statement;
(b) the claimant gave the operator a notice of complaint in relation to the statement; and
(c) the operator failed to respond to the notice of complaint in accordance with any provision contained in regulations.

. . .

5. Regulations may –

(a) make provision as to the action required to be taken by an operator of a website in response to a notice of complaint . . .
(b) make provision specifying a time limit for the taking of any such action;
(c) make provision conferring on the court a discretion to treat action taken after the expiry of the time limit as having been taken before the expiry . . .

. . .

10. The defence under this section is not defeated by reason only of the fact that the operator of the website moderates the statements posted on it by others.

Questions for discussion

1. Does the Defamation Act 1996, section 1 provide a defence for (a) the publisher of occasional pamphlets, for example a student union; (b) a radio station broadcasting a live interview; (c) an Internet service provider?
2. What has the Electronic Commerce Directive added to the protection afforded to intermediaries under section 1 of the Defamation Act 1996?
3. What would clause 5 of the Defamation Bill add to the extant law? Would it be useful for the media?

10.5 REMEDIES

(a) Injunctions

While permanent injunctions to restrain publication are sometimes granted, the courts are very reluctant to grant interim (formerly, interlocutory) injunctions to restrain publication of an alleged libel before trial. This is an aspect of the hostility to prior restraints on the media, discussed in Chapter 1. The application of this principle to libel law is known as the rule in *Bonnard* v *Perryman*.

Extract 10.5.1
Bonnard v Perryman **[1891] 2 Ch 269 (CA) 284**

LORD COLERIDGE CJ:
But it is obvious that the subject-matter of an action for defamation is so special as to require exceptional caution in exercising the jurisdiction to interfere by injunction before the trial of an action to prevent an anticipated wrong. The right of free speech is one which it is for the public interest that individuals should possess, and, indeed, that they should exercise without impediment, so long as no wrongful act is done; and, unless an alleged libel is untrue, there is no wrong committed; but, on the contrary, often a very wholesome act is performed in the publication and repetition of an alleged libel. Until it is clear that an alleged libel is untrue, it is not clear that any right at all has been infringed; and the importance of leaving free speech unfettered is a strong reason in cases of libel for dealing most cautiously and warily with the granting of interim injunctions. We entirely approve of, and desire to adopt as our own, the language of Lord Esher, MR, in *Coulson* v *Coulson* – 'To justify the Court in granting an interim injunction it must come to a decision upon the question of libel or no libel, before the jury have decided whether it was a libel or not. Therefore the jurisdiction was of a delicate nature. It ought only to be exercised in the clearest cases, where any jury would say that the matter complained of was libellous, and where, if the jury did not so find, the Court would set aside the verdict as unreasonable'. In the particular case before us, indeed, the libellous character of the publication is beyond dispute, but the effect of it upon the Defendant can be finally disposed of only by a jury, and we cannot feel sure that the defence of justification is one which, on the facts which may be before them, the jury may find to be wholly unfounded; nor can we tell what may be the damages recoverable. Moreover, the decision at the hearing may turn upon the question of the general character of the Plaintiffs; and this is a point which can rarely be investigated satisfactorily upon affidavit before the trial – on which further it is not desirable that the Court should express an opinion before the trial.

Defendants may even claim the protection of the *Bonnard* v *Perryman* rule when they publish the libel out of self-interest or vindictiveness.[318] It should be noted that a potential anomaly is raised by the strict application of the *Bonnard* v *Perryman* rule in the defamation context and the willingness of the courts to grant interim injunctions in so-called 'false light' privacy cases. This is explored further in Chapter 13.

The Court of Appeal in *Greene* v *Associated Newspapers*[319] held that the rule in *Bonnard* v *Perryman* is unaffected by the introduction of the Human Rights Act 1998. In that case it was argued that the rule was incompatible with section 12(3) of the Act, which provides that relief which would restrain publication before trial is not to be granted 'unless the court is satisfied that the applicant is likely to establish that publication should not be allowed.' The court said: '[i]n a section of an Act of Parliament which is expressly concerned with the protection of freedom of expression and not with undermining it, Parliament cannot be interpreted as having abrogated the rule in *Bonnard* v *Perryman* by a sidewind.' It was argued in the alternative that, contrary to section 6 of the Act, a court applying the rule would be acting incompatibly with the right to reputation protected under article 8.

Extract 10.5.2
Greene v *Associated Newspapers Ltd* **[2005] QB 972**

71. Mr Spearman [for the appellant] argued that a rights-based approach requires a careful balancing at every stage of every case between the competing rights . . .

72. Mr Caldecott, who appeared for the defendants, submitted that it is at the trial of a defamation action that English law shows itself appropriately solicitous of the claimant's right to a fair reputation. At the trial the burden lies on defendants to prove that their defamatory statement was true, or that it represented fair comment on a matter of public interest, or that it was made on an occasion that attracted privilege. If they fail to do so, they have to pay the penalty for infringing the claimant's right, and the claimant thereby sees his/her reputation vindicated in a very public way. Even if the case is settled before trial, rules of court uniquely allow a statement to be made in open court by way of vindication.

73. At the pre-trial stage, he argued, the position is different. As Stuart-Smith LJ said in *Lonrho* v *Fayed* [1993] 1 WLR 1489, 1502:

> [N]o one has a right to a reputation which is unmerited. Accordingly one can only suffer an injury to reputation if what is said is false. In defamation the falsity of the libel or slander is presumed; but justification is a complete defence.

74. If a claimant were able to stop a defendant from exercising its right under article 10 of the Convention merely by arguing on paper-based evidence that it was more likely than not that the defendant could not show that what it wished to say about the claimant was true, it would seriously weaken the effect of article 10. In *The Observer and The Guardian* v *UK* (1992) 14 EHRR 153 . . . the court at Strasbourg said, at para 60:

> [T]he dangers inherent in prior restraints are such that they call for the most careful scrutiny on the part of the Court. This is especially so as far as the press is concerned, for news is a perishable commodity and to delay its publication, even for a short period, may well deprive it of all its value and interest.

75. Scoops, as Mr Caldecott observed, are the lifeblood of the newspaper industry. He might have added that stale news is no news at all. If Mr Spearman was correct, people with a fair reputation they do not deserve could stifle public criticism by obtaining injunctions simply

---

[318] *Holley* v *Smyth* [1998] QB 726 (CA).
[319] [2005] QB 972.

because on necessarily incomplete information a court thought it more likely than not that they would defeat a defence of justification at the trial.

76. In our judgment Mr Caldecott's submissions are well-founded. As Sir John Donaldson MR observed in *Khashoggi* v *IPC Magazines Ltd*, once a claimant's right to a fair reputation is put in issue it is the function of the trial, and the duty of the jury, to determine whether he/she does have a right to be vindicated. One cannot speak sensibly of the violation of the right until it is established at the trial, and at the trial the rules of evidence will favour the claimant.

77. In the passage quoted at para 31 above the editors of the current edition of *Gatley on Libel and Slander* correctly refer to 'the usually impossible task of investigating summarily the merits of the defence of justification which is so often dependent on the credibility of witnesses and detailed consideration of documents'. The judicial authors of the rule in *Bonnard* v *Perryman* recognised this phenomenon when they created the rule in the first place. This court recognised it a generation ago when it refused to apply *American Cyanamid* principles in a defamation action. And in our judgment there is nothing in the Convention that requires the rule to be done away with.

Questions for discussion

1. Do you agree with the rule in *Bonnard* v *Perryman*?
2. Do you find the reasoning of the Court of Appeal in *Greene* v *Associated Newspapers* convincing? Why/why not?

(b) Damages

Damages are the principal remedy for libel. In contrast to continental European legal systems, there is no legally enforceable right of reply. Nor is there any right to have a libellous allegation corrected, though the publication of a correction, or statement by way of explanation or contradiction, may be required as part of an accepted offer of amends or as a condition for reliance on the qualified privilege defence: see Sections 10.4(d) and 10.4(c) above.

Libel damages may be classified in a number of ways. One distinction is between *general* and *special* damages. The latter compensate the plaintiff for any particular financial loss, for example cancellation of a contract, shown to have resulted from the publication. They are much less important than general damages, which are presumed to follow publication of the libel.[320] The claimant does not have to prove the particular respects in which it has damaged his reputation or injured his feelings.[321] General damages can be classified as *compensatory*, *aggravated* or *exemplary* (sometimes known as punitive) damages.

The subjective character of general damages – 'damages at large', as they are sometimes described – was emphasised by Lord Hailsham LC in *Broome* v *Cassell & Co*, a leading authority on the award of exemplary damages. *Sutcliffe* v *Pressdram* is notable for its exposition of the role of the jury in awarding damages; Nourse LJ also explains the distinction between 'aggravated' damages (really an element of compensatory damages) and exemplary damages.

---

[320] In contrast, damages must generally be proved in the case of slander.
[321] See Eric Barendt, 'What is the Point of Libel Law?' (1999) 52 *Current Legal Problems* 110.

Extract 10.5.3
Broome v *Cassell & Co* [1972] AC 1027 (HL) 1071

LORD HAILSHAM OF ST MARYLEBONE LC:

In actions of defamation and in any other actions where damages for loss of reputation are involved, the principle of restitutio in integrum has necessarily an even more highly subjective element. Such actions involve a money award which may put the plaintiff in a purely financial sense in a much stronger position than he was before the wrong. Not merely can he recover the estimated sum of his past and future losses, but, in case the libel, driven underground, emerges from its lurking place at some future date, he must be able to point to a sum awarded by a jury sufficient to convince a bystander of the baselessness of the charge. As Windeyer J well said in *Uren* v *John Fairfax & Sons Pty Ltd*, 117 CLR 115, 150:

> It seems to me that, properly speaking, a man defamed does not get compensation *for* his damaged reputation. He gets damages *because* he was injured in his reputation, that is simply because he was publicly defamed. For this reason, compensation by damages operates in two ways – as a vindication of the plaintiff to the public and as consolation to him for a wrong done. Compensation is here a solatium rather than a monetary recompense for harm measurable in money.

This is why it is not necessarily fair to compare awards of damages in this field with damages for personal injuries. Quite obviously, the award must include factors for injury to the feelings, the anxiety and uncertainty undergone in the litigation, the absence of apology, or the reaffirmation of the truth of the matters complained of, or the malice of the defendant. The bad conduct of the plaintiff himself may also enter into the matter, where he has provoked the libel, or where perhaps he has libelled the defendant in reply. What is awarded is thus a figure which cannot be arrived at by any purely objective computation. This is what is meant when the damages in defamation are described as being 'at large'.

Extract 10.5.4
Sutcliffe v *Pressdram Ltd* [1991] 1 QB 153 (CA) 182–184

NOURSE LJ:

When one turns to the matter of damages the primacy of the jury is seen to be even more firmly established. I do not know that it was ever doubted that the amount of the damages should be left to the jury. The rule received the unqualified support of Scrutton LJ in *Youssoupoff* v *Metro-Goldwyn-Mayer Pictures Ltd* (1934) 50 TLR 581, 584:

> The constitution has thought, and I think there is great advantage in it, that the damages to be paid by a person who says false things about his neighbour are best decided by a jury representing the public, who may state the view of the public as to the action of the man who makes false statements about his neighbour, the plaintiff.

This rule had nothing to do with the freedom of the press, being only an application of the general practice of the common law courts for the amount of the damages to be assessed by the jury and not by the judge. It may be that until recently the press were as content with the rule as was anyone else. But Mr Lightman, for the defendants, has said that the recent large awards of damages in libel cases against newspapers, in some of which at any rate no claim for exemplary damages has been made, have put the press in fear, perhaps even in despair, of the law. It is said that they have endangered the freedom of the press to investigate and report fearlessly on matters of public interest. That is without doubt a consideration of great importance, although it must be said that the value of any freedom cannot properly be estimated without asking whether there has been an acceptance of the responsibilities which go with it, an acceptance with which not every section of the press can justly be credited. Be that as it may, these recent large awards have raised an important question in the public mind. Ought damages in defamation cases to be assessed not by the jury but by the judge?

In most early systems of law injuries committed by the spoken or written word were treated as remediable not by compensation to the injured but by punishment of those who committed them; the substitution of public opprobrium for private revenge. It was therefore only natural in systems such as our own, where the civil action has been developed out of the criminal and has virtually replaced it, that juries should have tended to include a punitive, now called an 'exemplary', element in their awards of damages and, moreover, that judges should not have discouraged them from doing so. In the 18th century a similar tendency had been seen in the actions brought before Lord Camden, then Sir Charles Pratt CJ, in the Court of Common Pleas for trespass and false imprisonment arising out of the illegality of general warrants; see eg *Wilkes* v *Wood* (1763) Lofft 1 and *Huckle* v *Money* (1763) 2 Wils 205. For the greater part of this century (and I assume throughout the 19th century) it was thought to be the law that an award of general damages in defamation cases could include an exemplary element if the conduct of the defendant had been so wanton as to merit punishment. But in *Broome* v *Cassell & Co Ltd* [1972] AC 1027 the House of Lords, affirming and applying to defamation cases their earlier decision in *Rookes* v *Barnard* [1964] AC 1129 (an intimidation case), authoritatively held that exemplary damages can only be awarded in three instances, of which the only one with any practical relevance to defamation cases is where the defendant, either with knowledge of the tort or recklessly, decides to publish because the prospects of material advantage to him outweigh the prospects of material loss. In all other cases the damages may be compensatory only.

The rule having been settled at the highest level, it has ever since been loyally applied by judges at trial and in this court. But I cannot help thinking that the occasions on which exemplary damages are now claimed in defamation cases are rarer than the framers of the rule would have expected. More significantly, it is possible that they did not well appreciate the difficulties which its application would cause to juries, and perhaps to judges also. The difficulty most in point is that compensatory damages may include compensation for the natural injury to the plaintiff's feelings at having been written or spoken of in defamatory terms, injury which can be aggravated by the defendant's subsequent conduct. In *Broome* v *Cassell & Co Ltd* [1972] AC 1027, Lord Reid, speaking of the wide bracket within which an amount of compensation might reasonably fall and echoing the words of Pearson LJ in *McCarey* v *Associated Newspapers Ltd (No 2)* [1965] 2 QB 86, 104, said, at p 1085:

> It has long been recognised that in determining what sum within that bracket should be awarded, a jury, or other tribunal, is entitled to have regard to the conduct of the defendant. He may have behaved in a high-handed, malicious, insulting or oppressive manner in committing the tort or he or his counsel may at the trial have aggravated the injury by what they there said. That would justify going to the top of the bracket and awarding as damages the largest sum that could fairly be regarded as compensation.

There are statements to the same effect in the speeches of Lord Devlin in *Rookes* v *Barnard* [1964] AC 1129, 1221, and of Lord Hailsham of St Marylebone LC in *Broome* v *Cassell & Co Ltd* [1972] AC 1027, 1073, and of Lord Diplock, at p 1124. In a case where compensation for injury to the plaintiff's feelings, original or aggravated, is claimed, the attention of the jury may thus be directed towards the reprehensible conduct of the defendant. And however carefully the judge might seek to protect them against it, it would not be surprising if an element, even a large one, in their award exceeded a due consideration for the plaintiff's feelings and trespassed into punishment of the defendant's conduct.

The conduct of a defendant which may often be regarded as aggravating the injury to the plaintiff's feelings, so as to support a claim for 'aggravated' damages, includes a failure to make any or any sufficient apology and withdrawal; a repetition of the libel; conduct calculated to deter the plaintiff from proceeding; persistence, by way of a prolonged or hostile cross-examination of the plaintiff or in turgid speeches to the jury, in a plea of justification which is bound to fail; the general conduct either of the preliminaries or of the trial itself in a manner calculated to attract further wide publicity; and persecution of the plaintiff by other means. I think it likely that many of these misconducts were featured in many of the recent cases in which these large awards have been made. Nobody could say that the jury were not entitled to view them with abhorrence. Nobody could really blame the jury if, as representatives of the public and not as lawyers, they included an exemplary element in their award.

The size of jury awards has frequently been criticised, particularly by the media. The award of £1.5 million to Lord Aldington against the author and distributor of a pamphlet – alleging he had been responsible in 1945 for handing over Cossack prisoners of war to the Soviet authorities – led to an application to the European Court of Human Rights. It held unanimously that UK law did not afford adequate safeguards against disproportionately large awards; the award of such a large sum violated freedom of expression.[322] Since the enactment of the Courts and Legal Services Act 1990, the Court of Appeal now has much greater scope to change the amount awarded by a jury where it is excessive. Previously the Court of Appeal had to be satisfied that the award was 'divorced from reality'[323] before it would overturn it; now, the question is: '[c]ould a reasonable jury have thought that this award was necessary to compensate the plaintiff and to re-establish his reputation?'[324]

In the case of *Steele and Morris* v *United Kingdom*, however, the European Court of Human Rights held that article 10 had been violated by a disproportionately large award made against the applicants by the Court of Appeal. The applicants had defamed McDonald's, the famous fast food restaurant.

Extract 10.5.5
Steel and Morris v *United Kingdom* (2005) 41 EHRR 403

96. . . . [T]he Court considers that the size of the award of damages made against the two applicants may also have failed to strike the right balance. Under the Convention, an award of damages for defamation must bear a reasonable relationship of proportionality to the injury to reputation suffered (see *Tolstoy Miloslavsky* v *the United Kingdom*, judgment of 13 July 1995, Series A, No 316-B, §49). The Court notes on the one hand that the sums eventually awarded in the present case (GBP 36,000 in the case of the first applicant and GBP 40,000 in the case of the second applicant) although relatively moderate by contemporary standards in defamation cases in England and Wales, were very substantial when compared to the modest incomes and resources of the two applicants. While accepting, on the other hand, that the statements in the leaflet which were found to be untrue contained serious allegations, the Court observes that not only were the plaintiffs large and powerful corporate entities but that, in accordance with the principles of English law, they were not required to, and did not, establish that they had in fact suffered any financial loss as a result of the publication of the 'several thousand' copies of the leaflets found to have been distributed by the trial judge . . .

97. While it is true that no steps have to date been taken to enforce the damages award against either applicant, the fact remains that the substantial sums awarded against them have remained enforceable since the decision of the Court of Appeal. In these circumstances, the Court finds that the award of damages in the present case was disproportionate to the legitimate aim served.

[322] *Miloslavsky* v *United Kingdom* [1996] EMLR 152.
[323] *McCarey* v *Associated Newspapers Ltd (No 2)* [1965] 2 QB 86, 111.
[324] *Rantzen* v *Mirror Group Newspapers* [1994] QB 670 (CA) 692.

Jury awards have also been criticised as excessive in relation to awards in personal injury cases. In the *Rantzen* case,[325] the Court of Appeal held it would be inappropriate to refer juries to awards in previous libel actions or to awards for personal injuries. But it did permit them to be referred to awards made by the Court of Appeal. Subsequently in the *Elton John* case, it changed its approach.[326] The case arose from the publication of a feature in the *Sunday Mirror* alleging that the entertainer practised bizarre eating habits. The Master of the Rolls admitted that libel awards had given rise to justified criticism, though that was not the fault of juries, acting without adequate guidance from the courts. He agreed with *Rantzen*, in so far as it had held that juries should not for the time being be reminded of previous awards, which in the absence of direction from the judge would provide unreliable pointers, and in so far as it had held that reference could be made to awards made or approved by the Court of Appeal. But then his judgment took a more radical turn.

Extract 10.5.6
Elton John v MGN Ltd [1997] QB 586 (CA) 53–5, 57–8

SIR THOMAS BINGHAM MR:

In [*Rantzen*] the Court of Appeal essentially adopted the approach of Lord Hailsham LC in *Broome* v *Cassell & Co Ltd* [1972] AC 1027 in concluding that there was no satisfactory way in which conventional awards in actions for damages for personal injuries could be used to provide guidance for an award in an action for defamation. Much depends, as we now think, on what is meant by guidance: it is one thing to say (and we agree) that there can be no precise equiparation between a serious libel and (say) serious brain damage; but it is another to point out to a jury considering the award of damages for a serious libel that the maximum conventional award for pain and suffering and loss of amenity to a plaintiff suffering from very severe brain damage is about £125,000 and that this is something of which the jury may take account.

It is of interest that in the present case Drake J, who has much recent experience in this field, expressed some criticism of the existing rules. He observed, on 3 November 1993:

> Counsel made submissions on the extent to which it is proper to address the jury in speeches or in the summing up on the quantum of damages. I need only say that although I think the law is in need of change, I shall have regard to the guidelines given by the Court of Appeal in *Rantzen* v *Mirror Group Newspapers (1986) Ltd* [1994] QB 670. I shall therefore not make any comparison with awards in personal injury cases. I shall invite the jury to consider the purchasing power of any award they make.

It has often and rightly been said that there can be no precise correlation between a personal injury and a sum of money. The same is true, perhaps even more true, of injury to reputation. There is force in the argument that to permit reference in libel cases to conventional levels of award in personal injury cases is simply to admit yet another incommensurable into the field of consideration. There is also weight in the argument, often heard, that conventional levels of award in personal injury cases are too low, and therefore provide an uncertain guide. But these awards would not be relied on as any exact guide, and of course there can be no precise correlation between loss of a limb, or of sight, or quadriplegia, and damage to reputation. But if these personal injuries respectively command conventional awards of, at most, about

---

[325] *Rantzen* v *Mirror Group Newspapers* [1994] QB 670 (CA).
[326] The award of exemplary (or punitive) damages is controversial in principle; the defendant is punished on the civil burden of proof, and the plaintiff receives a windfall in terms of damages which go beyond what is appropriate to compensate him. The Law Commission has however proposed their retention: see Law Commission, *Aggravated, Exemplary and Restitutionary Damages* (Law Com No 247, 1997), Part V.

£52,000, £90,000 and £125,000 for pain and suffering and loss of amenity (of course excluding claims based on loss of earnings, the cost of care and other specific financial claims), juries may properly be asked to consider whether the injury to his reputation of which the plaintiff complains should fairly justify any greater compensation. The conventional compensatory scales in personal injury cases must be taken to represent fair compensation in such cases unless and until those scales are amended by the courts or by Parliament. It is in our view offensive to public opinion, and rightly so, that a defamation plaintiff should recover damages for injury to reputation greater, perhaps by a significant factor, than if that same plaintiff had been rendered a helpless cripple or an insensate vegetable. The time has in our view come when judges, and counsel, should be free to draw the attention of juries to these comparisons.

Reference to an appropriate award and an appropriate bracket

It has been the invariable practice in the past that neither counsel nor the judge may make any suggestion to the jury as what would be an appropriate award . . .

In *Sutcliffe* v *Pressdram* [1991] 1 QB 153 Russell LJ gave his reasons for rejecting the argument that counsel or the judge might be allowed to refer to figures. He approved the following passage in the summing up by Michael Davies J in that case, at p 190:

> Well, supposing I were to suggest a figure to you or a bracket. Supposing I were to say 'if she succeeds, what about giving her between so much and so much.' Well, there are two possibilities. One is that you would say that I was quite wrong and you would either give much more than I suggested or much less. Well now, can you imagine what would happen then? The party that did not like it: the plaintiff if you have given much less, or the defendant if you have given much more than I suggested, would be off to the Court of Appeal saying: 'Well, look at that jury, they were quite unreasonable. Here was this experienced judge suggesting a figure to them and they ignored it.' You can see readily how that would happen. Supposing you did give the figure or very close to the figure, that I suggested to you, well then you would have been wasting your time here on damages, you would simply be acting as a rubber stamp for me . . . So we look to you, as representatives of the public, applying the principles I have indicated, if you come to damages, to come to that figure.

We have come to the conclusion, however, that the reasons which have been given for prohibiting any reference to figures are unconvincing. Indeed, far from developing into an auction (and we do not see how it could), the process of mentioning figures would in our view induce a mood of realism on both sides.

In personal injury actions it is now commonplace for the advocates on both sides to address the judge in some detail on the quantum of the appropriate award. Any apprehension that the judge might receive a coded message as to the amount of any payment into court has not to our knowledge been realised. The judge is not in any way bound by the bracket suggested, but he finds it helpful as a check on his own provisional assessment. We can for our part see no reason why the parties' respective counsel in a libel action should not indicate to the jury the level of award which they respectively contend to be appropriate, nor why the judge in directing the jury should not give a similar indication. The plaintiff will not wish the jury to think that his main object is to make money rather than clear his name. The defendant will not wish to add insult to injury by underrating the seriousness of the libel. So we think the figures suggested by responsible counsel are likely to reflect the upper and lower bounds of a realistic bracket. The jury must, of course, make up their own mind and must be directed to do so. They will not be bound by the submission of counsel or the indication of the judge. If the jury make an award outside the upper or lower bounds of any bracket indicated and such award is the subject of appeal, real weight must be given to the possibility that their judgment is to be preferred to that of the judge.

. . .

The modest but important changes of practice described above would not in our view undermine the enduring constitutional position of the libel jury. Historically, the significance of the libel jury has lain not in their role of assessing damages, but in their role of deciding whether the publication complained of is a libel or [not]. The changes which we favour will, in our opinion, buttress the constitutional role of the libel jury by rendering their proceedings more rational and so more acceptable to public opinion.

Exemplary damages

. . .

We . . . consider that where exemplary damages are claimed the jury should in future receive some additional guidance to make it clear that before such damages can be awarded the jury must be satisfied that the publisher had no genuine belief in the truth of what he published. The publisher must have suspected that the words were untrue and have deliberately refrained from taking obvious steps which, if taken, would have turned suspicion into certainty.

. . .

Secondly, the publisher must have acted in the hope or expectation of material gain. It is well established that a publisher need not be shown to have made any precise or arithmetical calculation. But his unlawful conduct must have been motivated by mercenary considerations: the belief that he would be better off financially if he violated the plaintiff's rights than if he did not, and mere publication of a newspaper for profit is not enough.

. . .

We do not accept, as was argued, that in seeking to establish that the conditions for awarding exemplary damages have been met the plaintiff must satisfy the criminal rather than the civil standard of proof. But a jury should in our judgment be told that as the charge is grave, so should the proof be clear. An inference of reprehensible conduct and cynical calculation of mercenary advantage should not be lightly drawn . . .

It is plain on the authorities that it is only where the conditions for making an exemplary award are satisfied, and only when the sum awarded to the plaintiff as compensatory damages is not itself sufficient to punish the defendant, show that tort does not pay and deter others from acting similarly, that an award of exemplary damages should be added to the award of compensatory damages. Since the jury will not know, when making their decision, what costs order will be made, it would seem that no account can be taken of the costs burden which the unsuccessful defendant will have to bear, although this could in itself have a punitive and deterrent effect. It is clear that the means of the defendant are relevant to the assessment of damages. Also relevant are his degree of fault and the amount of any profit he may be shown actually to have made from his unlawful conduct.

. . .

The authorities give judges no help in directing juries on the quantum of exemplary damages. Since, however, such damages are analogous to a criminal penalty, and although paid to the plaintiff play no part in compensating him, principle requires that an award of exemplary damages should never exceed the minimum sum necessary to meet the public purpose underlying such damages, that of punishing the defendant, showing that tort does not pay and deterring others.

The Court of Appeal reduced the jury award of compensatory damages from £75,000 to £25,000, and exemplary damages from £275,000 to £75,000.

But the Court of Appeal is not always willing to interfere with jury awards. It dismissed an appeal from an award of £45,000 against the *Sunday Times* in respect of an article in its business section. The article wrongly alleged that the plaintiff was being sued for defaulting on a loan and was filing for bankruptcy.

Extract 10.5.7
Kiam v Neil (No 2) **[1996] EMLR 493 (CA) 507–508, 510**

BELDAM LJ:

It is, I think, necessary to bear in mind that Parliament has repeatedly declined to attenuate the right of a plaintiff who claims trial by jury in a libel action . . . Whilst it is tempting to think that the greater the guidance given by judges, the more rational the jury's conclusion is likely to be, it seems to me that if the failure of the jury to keep its award within bounds indicated by a judge gives rise merely to the possibility that their judgment is to be preferred to that of the judge, the court may appear to preserve only the semblance of a right which Parliament has repeatedly affirmed.

. . .

Unless the Times establishes that the award . . . is out of proportion, this court would not be entitled to substitute its own assessment nor would it be sensible to accede to [counsel for The Times] invitation to lay down guidelines for this or similar cases.

. . .

[W]as an award of £45,000 excessive in the sense that it exceeded the sum which a jury could reasonably have regarded as proportional to the injury done to Mr Kiam? The jury were entitled to have regard to the fact that the Times publication was irresponsible. No effort was made to check its accuracy . . . The jury could properly take into account the prominence of Mr Kiam's reputation when deciding what figure was required to vindicate it. They were also entitled to take account of the fact that it struck at the core of his life's achievement and personality and that . . . it had had a prolonged and significant effect on him personally. Judged by the criteria of reasonableness and proportionality, I do not find an award of £45,000 for a widespread, grave and irresponsible assertion of insolvency against a prominent entrepreneur to be excessive and would dismiss the appeal.

It is therefore unclear how far the *Elton John* decision marks a radical step in controlling jury awards.

It is often said that one of the limitations of the remedy of damages is that it is not particularly well suited to restoring a successful claimant's reputation.[327] Discursive remedies – such as an apology, correction or declaration – are much better suited to achieving vindication. The Defamation Bill, under clause 12, proposes to give the power to the court to order that a summary of the court's judgment be published by the defendant. In addition, clause 13 proposes to confer on the court the power to order the removal of defamatory statements from websites.

Extract 10.5.8
Defamation Bill

Clause 12 Power of court to order a summary of its judgment to be published

1. Where a court gives judgment for the claimant in an action for defamation the court may order the defendant to publish a summary of the judgment.
2. The wording of any summary and the time, manner, form and place of its publication are to be for the parties to agree.
3. If the parties cannot agree on the wording, the wording is to be settled by the court.
4. If the parties cannot agree on the time, manner, form or place of publication, the court may give such directions as to those matters as it considers reasonable and practicable in the circumstances.
5. . . .

---

[327] See, e.g., Alastair Mullis and Andrew Scott, 'Reframing Libel: Taking (All) Rights Seriously and Where It Leads' (2012) 63(1) *Northern Ireland Legal Quarterly* 5, 17.

Clause 13 Order for removal of defamatory statement from website

1. Where a court gives judgment for the claimant in an action for defamation the court may order the operator of a website on which the defamatory statement is posted to remove the statement.
2. . . .

Questions for discussion

1. Are the principles in the *Elton John* decision satisfactory?
2. Should the jury assess damages in libel cases?
3. Do you agree with the remedies proposed in clauses 12 and 13 of the Defamation Bill?
4. Will clause 12 be effective in providing vindication to a claimant?
5. Should damages in defamation be subject to a statutory cap? Why/why not?

Selected further reading

Matthew Collins, *The Law of Defamation and the Internet* **(Oxford University Press, 3rd edn, 2010).** This book provides a comprehensive treatment of all aspects of the law of defamation and its application in the context of Internet publications.

Helen Fenwick and Gavin Phillipson, *Media Freedom under the Human Rights Act* **(Oxford University Press, 2006).** This book is useful for understanding the Convention and Strasbourg's article 10 case law, and the impact that the Human Rights Act has had on English domestic law. Its coverage of domestic defamation law focuses mainly on *Reynolds* privilege.

Andrew T. Kenyon, *Defamation: Comparative Law and Practice* **(UCL Press, 2006).** This book provides insight into issues to do with defamatory meaning, defences and litigation practice. It is also comparative, covering aspects of US, UK and Australian law.

Lawrence McNamara, *Reputation and Defamation* **(Oxford University Press, 2007).** This book considers the concept of reputation, including its history and application in libel jurisprudence. It offers a theory of reputation by which to critique the law and proposes a new legal framework.

Patrick Milmo *et al.* **(eds),** *Gatley on Libel and Slander* **(Sweet & Maxwell, 11th edn, 2008).** This is the leading treatise on black-letter defamation law and also provides substantial treatment of procedural issues in defamation litigation.

Alistair Mullis and Cameron Doley (eds), *Carter-Ruck on Libel and Privacy* **(LexisNexis, 6th edn, 2011).** A useful and in-depth book on black-letter defamation law. It is a very good alternative to *Gatley*.

David Rolph, *Reputation, Celebrity and Defamation Law* **(Ashgate Press, 2008).** This book provides an historical and sociological analysis of the concept of reputation in defamation law and how it responds to various cultural and technological changes over time. It focuses, in particular, on the contemporary impact of celebrity on how reputation is understood by the law.

11 Privacy and breach of confidence

11.1 INTRODUCTION

The law in relation to the protection of privacy has undergone significant development since the Human Rights Act (HRA) came into force in 2000. Traditionally, the common law resisted recognising a freestanding right to privacy. Privacy, instead, received 'de facto' protection through a range of other legal claims – most notably through the equitable action of breach of confidence but also defamation,[1] malicious falsehood,[2] nuisance and trespass. Technically speaking this is still the case even today. Despite the existence of the HRA and the impact of article 8 (the right to respect for private life) of the European Convention on Human Rights on the development of the common law, the House of Lords in *Wainwright* v *Home Office* confirmed that a general tort of invasion of privacy is not recognised by the common law.[3] Rather, the right to privacy enshrined in article 8 has been given effect in domestic law through the extension of existing causes of action – in particular through a 'new' cause of action developed out of the pre-existing law of breach of confidence, now called 'misuse of private information'.

This chapter explores the protection of personal privacy as it relates to the activities of the media. Section 11.2 considers the concept of privacy and the justifications for its legal protection; Section 11.3 explores the right to privacy under article 8 of the European Convention and the Strasbourg jurisprudence; Section 11.4 provides a comprehensive treatment of privacy developments in the UK following the HRA, focusing on misuse of private information; Sections 11.5, 11.6 and 11.7 consider, respectively, the protection of personal privacy under the Data Protection Act 1998, the Protection from Harassment Act 1997, and the Ofcom Broadcasting Code. The self-regulation of the press under the Press Complaints Commission (PCC) Editors' Code of Practice and the PCC adjudication process in relation to privacy complaints is considered in Chapter 2.

11.2 WHAT IS PRIVACY AND WHY PROTECT IT?

It is often said that privacy can 'mean different things to different people'.[4] Thus, a definition of privacy remains elusive. For one, the understanding of privacy as a concept is socially and culturally specific; it 'cannot be understood independently from society'.[5] This, of course, can lead to different legal outcomes across jurisdictions. According to James Whitman, for example:

> American privacy law is a body caught in the gravitational orbit of liberty values, while European law is caught in the orbit of dignity. There are certainly times when the two bodies of law approach each other more or less nearly. Yet they are consistently pulled in different directions, and the

---

[1] See, e.g., *Tolley* v *JS Fry & Sons Ltd* [1931] AC 333.
[2] See, e.g., *Kaye* v *Robertson* [1991] FSR 62.
[3] [2004] 2 AC 406.
[4] Moreham in *The Law of Privacy and the Media*, 2.01; David Rolph, Vitins and Judith Bannister, *Media Law: Cases, Materials and Commentary* (Oxford University Press, 2010) 509; J. Thomas McCarthy, *The Rights of Publicity and Privacy* (West, 2nd edn, 2012), 5.50.
[5] Daniel Solove, 'A taxonomy of privacy' (2006) 154(3) *University of Pennsylvania Law Review* 477, 484.

consequence is that these two legal orders really do meaningfully differ: continental Europeans are consistently more drawn to problems touching on public dignity, while Americans are consistently more drawn to problems touching on the depredations of the state.[6]

However, even within individual legal regimes the problem of defining the concept of privacy persists. As noted by Ruth Gavison, the first definitional problem relates to the status of *privacy*: 'is privacy a situation, a right, a claim, a form of control, a value?'[7] It is probably legitimate to conceive of privacy as being all of these things, depending on why the question is being asked. If, however, it is suggested that privacy is something worthy of protection in the form of legal rights, this begs the question as to the characteristic of the 'thing' sought to be protected, and also the justifications for protection and what the appropriate legal response should be.

The literature on the difficulties in defining the essential characteristic of privacy is extensive.[8] What makes something – a fact, a situation, a physical place, a story, a communication or the body – part of someone's privacy or private life and, therefore, an appropriate object of legal protection? On the one hand, it might be considered useful to conceptualise a single unifying theory to define the concept of privacy. Richard Bruyer, for example, has called for the articulation of a 'common denominator', or 'common value inherent in all privacy cases'.[9] Others, however, have dismissed both the possibility and the utility of such an approach.[10]

Extract 11.2.1
Daniel Solove, 'A Taxonomy of Privacy' (2006) 154(3) *University of Pennsylvania Law Review* **477–564 (footnotes omitted)**

(480) . . . Often, privacy problems are merely stated in knee-jerk form: 'That violates my privacy!' When we contemplate an invasion of privacy – such as having our personal information gathered by companies in databases – we instinctively recoil. Many discussions of privacy appeal to people's fears and anxieties. What commentators often fail to do, however, is translate those instincts into a reasoned, well-articulated account of why privacy problems are harmful. When people claim that privacy should be protected, it is unclear precisely what they mean. This lack of clarity creates a difficulty when making policy or resolving a case because lawmakers and judges cannot easily articulate the privacy harm . . .

Many commentators have spoken of privacy as a unitary concept with a uniform value, which is unvarying across different situations. In contrast, I have argued that privacy violations involve a variety of types of harmful or problematic activities. Consider the following examples of activities typically referred to as privacy violations: (481)

---

[6] James Whitman, 'The Two Western Cultures of Privacy: Dignity Versus Liberty' (2004) 113 *Yale Law Journal* 1151, 1163.

[7] Ruth Gavison, 'Privacy and the Limits of the Law' (1980) 89(3) *Yale Law Journal* 421, 424.

[8] See, e.g., Robert C. Post, 'Three Concepts of Privacy' (2001) 89 *Georgetown Law Journal* 2087; Daniel J. Solove, 'Conceptualizing Privacy' (2002) 90 *California Law Review* 1087; James Whitman, 'The Two Western Cultures of Privacy: Dignity Versus Liberty' (2004) 113 *Yale Law Journal* 1151; Richard B. Bruyer, 'Privacy: A Review and Critique of the Literature' (2006) 43 *Alberta Law Review* 553; Ruth Gavison, 'Privacy and the Limits of the Law' (1980) 89(3) *Yale Law Journal* 421; Daniel Solove, 'A Taxonomy of Privacy' (2006) 154(3) *University of Pennsylvania Law Review* 477; Raymond Wacks, 'The Poverty of Privacy' (1980) 96 *Law Quarterly Review* 73.

[9] Richard B. Bruyer, 'Privacy: A Review and Critique of the Literature' (2006) 43 *Alberta Law Review* 553, 576.

[10] See, e.g., Daniel J. Solove, 'A Taxonomy of Privacy' (2006) 154(3) *University of Pennsylvania Law Review* 477; Robert C. Post, 'Three Concepts of Privacy' (2001) 89 *Georgetown Law Journal* 2087. See also Australian Law Reform Commission, *For Your Information: Australian Privacy Law and Practice*, Report No 108 (2008) 142–50.

- A newspaper reports the name of a rape victim.
- Reporters deceitfully gain entry to a person's home and secretly photograph and record the person.
- New X-ray devices can see through people's clothing, amounting to what some call a 'virtual strip-search.'
- The government uses a thermal sensor device to detect heat patterns in a person's home.
- A company markets a list of five million elderly incontinent women.
- Despite promising not to sell its members' personal information to others, a company does so anyway.

These violations are clearly not the same . . . Courts and policymakers frequently have a singular view of privacy in mind when they assess whether or not an activity violates privacy. As a result, they either conflate distinct privacy problems despite significant differences or fail to recognize a problem entirely. Privacy problems are frequently misconstrued or inconsistently recognized in the law. The concept of 'privacy' is far too vague to guide adjudication and lawmaking. How can privacy be addressed in a manner that is non-reductive and contextual, yet simultaneously useful in deciding cases and making sense of the multitude of privacy problems we face?

Source: Copyright © University of Pennsylvania Law School, 1945.

In the absence of a 'common denominator' to illuminate privacy in all contexts, it may be best to view 'privacy' as an umbrella term to describe a series or bundle of rights that arise from broader interests in human dignity and autonomy. The central problem with this approach, of course, is that it suffers from arbitrariness. Why might some interests be protected in the form of a right to privacy and not others?

Despite this limitation, it nevertheless remains that the concepts of individual autonomy and human dignity can be used to explain some of the 'core' interests that might be recognised as falling within the scope of privacy.[11] Those interests are usually said to include, inter alia, informational privacy, bodily privacy, territorial privacy and privacy of communications.[12] The fundamental requirements of individual autonomy are that individuals should be afforded self-determination as to how they live their lives and that they have the right to be left alone. Such a conception of individual autonomy can justify the protection of aspects of a person's bodily privacy, territorial privacy and privacy of communications – for example, the right to prevent trespass, covert photography or harassment. Individual autonomy may also justify granting the individual the right to choose what information can be published about them (the main focus of this chapter). Similarly, the principle of human dignity requires recognition of and respect for the inherent value of all human beings. It may, therefore, be considered an affront to human dignity to violate a person's information privacy (for example, to publish personal information about them), or to behave in a manner contrary to any one of the other core privacy interests.

The first recognition of the *legal* protection of the right to privacy can be traced to a well-known 1890 article by Samuel Warren and Louis Brandeis, *A Right to Privacy*. This article is said to have been instrumental in the development of the law of privacy in the United States and has certainly been influential in many other jurisdictions around the world.

[11] Scott in *Carter-Ruck on Libel and Privacy*, 18.2–18.3; Moreham in *The Law of Privacy and the Media*. See also Lord Hoffmann in *Campbell v MGN Ltd* [2004] 2 AC 457, 50, where it was said that private information was 'something worth protecting as an aspect of human autonomy and dignity'.

[12] See Australian Law Reform Commission, *For Your Information: Australian Privacy Law and Practice* (Report 108) 142; Moreham in *The Law of Privacy and the Media*, 2.08–2.23.

Extract 11.2.2
Samuel D Warren and Louis D Brandeis, 'The Right to Privacy' (1890) 4 *Harvard Law Review* 193, 196

Of the desirability – indeed of the necessity – of some such protection, there can, it is believed, be no doubt. The press is overstepping in every direction the obvious bounds of propriety and of decency. Gossip is no longer the resource of the idle and of the vicious, but has become a trade, which is pursued with industry as well as effrontery. To satisfy a prurient taste the details of sexual relations are spread broadcast in the columns of the daily papers. To occupy the indolent, column upon column is filled with idle gossip, which can only be procured by intrusion upon the domestic circle. The intensity and complexity of life, attendant upon advancing civilization, have rendered necessary some retreat from the world, and man, under the refining influence of culture, has become more sensitive to publicity, so that solitude and privacy have become more essential to the individual; but modern enterprise and invention have, through invasions upon his privacy, subjected him to mental pain and distress, far greater than could be inflicted by mere bodily injury. Nor is the harm wrought by such invasions confined to the suffering of those who may be made the subjects of journalistic or other enterprise. In this, as in other branches of commerce, the supply creates the demand. Each crop of unseemly gossip, thus harvested, becomes the seed of more, and, in direct proportion to its circulation, results in a lowering of social standards and of morality. Even gossip, apparently harmless, when widely and persistently circulated, is potent for evil. It both belittles and perverts. It belittles by inverting the relative importance of things, thus dwarfing the thoughts and aspirations of a people. When personal gossip attains the dignity of print, and crowds the space available for matters of real interest to the community, what wonder that the ignorant and thoughtless mistake its relative importance. Easy of comprehension, appealing to that weak side of human nature which is never wholly cast down by the misfortunes and frailties of our neighbours, no one can be surprised that it usurps the place of interest in brains capable of other things. Triviality destroys at once robustness of thought and delicacy of feeling. No enthusiasm can flourish, no generous impulse can survive under its blighting influence.

Questions for discussion

1. Do you agree that the concept of 'privacy' is difficult to define? Do you think a unified theory of privacy can be identified?
2. What are the values that appear to underpin the concern for privacy in the article by Warren and Brandeis?

11.3 ARTICLE 8 AND STRASBOURG JURISPRUDENCE

The right to respect for private life is guaranteed by article 8 of the European Convention on Human Rights.

Extract 11.3.1
Convention for the Protection of Human Rights and Fundamental Freedoms

Article 8

1. Everyone has the right to respect for his private and family life, his home and his correspondence.
2. There shall be no interference by a public authority with the exercise of this right except such as is in accordance with the law and is necessary in a democratic society in the interests of national security, public safety or the economic well-being of the country, for the prevention of disorder or crime, for the protection of health or morals, or for the protection of the rights and freedoms of others.

The European Court of Human Rights (ECtHR) has not provided an exhaustive definition of the meaning of 'private life'[13] and has warned against interpreting the right restrictively.[14] Nevertheless, it has held that article 8 concerns 'rights of central importance to the individual's identity, self-determination, physical and moral integrity, maintenance of relationships with others and a settled and secure place in the community'.[15] It has been held to include 'the right to privacy, the right to live, as far as one wishes, protected from publicity',[16] the right to enjoy private space free from outside interference and surveillance[17] and the right to a 'zone of interaction' – including in public – where an individual can develop relations with others.[18] The focus of article 8 on the underlying principle of personal autonomy further means that private life includes 'the ability to conduct one's life in a manner of one's own choosing', even where such choices appear to be 'physically or morally harmful'.[19] As pointed out by Clayton and Tomlinson, the 'general test as to whether the right to private life in article 8 is engaged is whether there is a "reasonable" or "legitimate" expectation of privacy'.[20]

It is now accepted that the activities of the media in collecting, storing and publishing personal information can result in a violation of article 8. Considering the reference to 'interference by a public authority' in article 8(2), it was not entirely clear until relatively recently that article 8 imposed a positive obligation on the state to provide a remedy for breach of privacy as between private individuals – even less whether it applied to the media. While the ECtHR had long suggested this to be the case,[21] it was not definitively confirmed until 2004 in *Von Hannover* v *Germany*.[22] In that case, Princess Caroline of Monaco sought to prevent the publication of photographs of her and her children engaged in everyday activities, such as horse riding, shopping and dining at a restaurant. She applied to the ECtHR when the German courts failed to provide her with a remedy. This case is important – not only in confirming that such a remedy is required, but also in its discussion of the scope of article 8 and how it is to be balanced with the media's competing right to freedom of expression under article 10.

Extract 11.3.2
***Von Hannover* v *Germany* (2005) 40 EHRR 1 (footnotes omitted)**

50. The Court reiterates that the concept of private life extends to aspects relating to personal identity, such as a person's name. Furthermore, private life, in the Court's view, includes a person's physical and psychological integrity; the guarantee afforded by Article 8 of the Convention is primarily intended to ensure the development, without outside interference, of

---

[13] For a comprehensive summary of the Strasbourg case law in this area, see Richard Clayton and Hugh Tomlinson, *The Law of Human Rights* (Oxford University Press, 2nd edn, 2009), 12.234–[]–12.302.
[14] *Peck* v *United Kingdom* (2003) 36 EHRR 41, 57.
[15] *Connors* v *United Kingdom* (2005) 40 EHRR 9, 82.
[16] *X* v *Iceland* (1976) 5 DR 86.
[17] See, e.g., *PG* v *United Kingdom* (2008) 46 EHRR 51; *Halford* v *United Kingdom* (1997) 24 EHRR 523.
[18] *Von Hannover* v *Germany* (2005) 40 EHRR 1, 50; *Von Hannover* v *Germany* (*No 2*) (2012) 55 EHRR 15, 95.
[19] *Pretty* v *United Kingdom* (2002) 35 EHRR 1, 62.
[20] Richard Clayton and Hugh Tomlinson, *The Law of Human Rights* (Oxford University Press, 2nd edn, 2009), 12.264, citing *Halford* v *United Kingdom* (1997) 24 EHRR 523, 65; *PG* v *United Kingdom* (2008) 46 EHRR 51, 57; *Von Hannover* v *Germany* (2005) 40 EHRR 1, 51.
[21] See, e.g., *X & Y* v *Netherlands* (1986) 8 EHRR 235, 23; *Earl Spencer* v *United Kingdom* (1998) 25 EHRR CD 105; *G* v *United Kingdom* (2001) 33 EHRR 1. *Peck* v *United Kingdom* (2003) 36 EHRR 41 indicated that media intrusion into private life may constitute a breach of article 8; however, in that case the defendant was not a media entity but a local council who had released footage to the media.
[22] (2005) 40 EHRR 1.

the personality of each individual in his relations with other human beings. There is therefore a zone of interaction of a person with others, even in a public context, which may fall within the scope of 'private life'.

51. The Court has also indicated that, in certain circumstances, a person has a 'legitimate expectation' of protection and respect for his or her private life. Accordingly, it has held in a case concerning the interception of telephone calls on business premises that the applicant 'would have had a reasonable expectation of privacy for such calls'.

52. As regards photos, with a view to defining the scope of the protection afforded by Article 8 against arbitrary interference by public authorities, the Commission had regard to whether the photographs related to private or public matters and whether the material thus obtained was envisaged for a limited use or was likely to be made available to the general public.

53. In the present case there is no doubt that the publication by various German magazines of photos of the applicant in her daily life either on her own or with other people falls within the scope of her private life.

. . .

(b) The general principles governing the protection of private life and the freedom of expression

56. In the present case the applicant did not complain of an action by the State, but rather of the lack of adequate State protection of her private life and her image.

57. The Court reiterates that although the object of Article 8 is essentially that of protecting the individual against arbitrary interference by the public authorities, it does not merely compel the State to abstain from such interference: in addition to this primarily negative undertaking, there may be positive obligations inherent in an effective respect for private or family life. These obligations may involve the adoption of measures designed to secure respect for private life even in the sphere of the relations of individuals between themselves. That also applies to the protection of a person's picture against abuse by others.

The boundary between the State's positive and negative obligations under this provision does not lend itself to precise definition. The applicable principles are, nonetheless, similar. In both contexts regard must be had to the fair balance that has to be struck between the competing interests of the individual and of the community as a whole; and in both contexts the State enjoys a certain margin of appreciation.

58. That protection of private life has to be balanced against the freedom of expression guaranteed by Article 10 of the Convention. In that context the Court reiterates that the freedom of expression constitutes one of the essential foundations of a democratic society. Subject to paragraph 2 of Article 10, it is applicable not only to 'information' or 'ideas' that are favourably received or regarded as inoffensive or as a matter of indifference, but also to those that offend, shock or disturb. Such are the demands of that pluralism, tolerance and broadmindedness without which there is no 'democratic society'. In that connection the press plays an essential role in a democratic society . . .

59. Although freedom of expression also extends to the publication of photos, this is an area in which the protection of the rights and reputation of others takes on particular importance. The present case does not concern the dissemination of 'ideas', but of images containing very personal or even intimate 'information' about an individual. Furthermore, photos appearing in the tabloid press are often taken in a climate of continual harassment which induces in the person concerned a very strong sense of intrusion into their private life or even of persecution.

60. In the cases in which the Court has had to balance the protection of private life against the freedom of expression it has always stressed the contribution made by photos or articles in the press to a debate of general interest . . .

(c) Application of these general principles by the Court

61. The Court points out at the outset that in the present case the photos of the applicant in the various German magazines show her in scenes from her daily life, thus engaged in activities of a purely private nature such as practising sport, out walking, leaving a restaurant or on holiday. The photos, in which the applicant appears sometimes alone and sometimes in company, illustrate a series of articles with such anodyne titles as 'Pure happiness', 'Caroline . . . a woman returning to life', 'Out and about with Princess Caroline in Paris' and 'The kiss. Or: they are not hiding anymore . . .'.

62. The Court also notes that the applicant, as a member of the Prince of Monaco's family, represents the ruling family at certain cultural or charitable events. However, she does not exercise any function within or on behalf of the State of Monaco or one of its institutions.

63. The Court considers that a fundamental distinction needs to be made between reporting facts – even controversial ones – capable of contributing to a debate in a democratic society relating to politicians in the exercise of their functions, for example, and reporting details of the private life of an individual who, moreover, as in this case, does not exercise official functions. While in the former case the press exercises its vital role of 'watchdog' in a democracy by contributing to 'impart[ing] information and ideas on matters of public interest' it does not do so in the latter case.

64. Similarly, although the public has a right to be informed, which is an essential right in a democratic society that, in certain special circumstances, can even extend to aspects of the private life of public figures, particularly where politicians are concerned, this is not the case here. The situation here does not come within the sphere of any political or public debate because the published photos and accompanying commentaries relate exclusively to details of the applicant's private life.

65. As in other similar cases it has examined, the Court considers that the publication of the photos and articles in question, of which the sole purpose was to satisfy the curiosity of a particular readership regarding the details of the applicant's private life, cannot be deemed to contribute to any debate of general interest to society despite the applicant being known to the public.

66. In these conditions freedom of expression calls for a narrower interpretation.

67. In that connection the Court also takes account of the resolution of the Parliamentary Assembly of the Council of Europe on the right to privacy, which stresses the 'one-sided interpretation of the right to freedom of expression' by certain media which attempt to justify an infringement of the rights protected by Article 8 of the Convention by claiming that 'their readers are entitled to know everything about public figures'.

68. The Court finds another point to be of importance: even though, strictly speaking, the present application concerns only the publication of the photos and articles by various German magazines, the context in which these photos were taken – without the applicant's knowledge or consent – and the harassment endured by many public figures in their daily lives cannot be fully disregarded. In the present case this point is illustrated in particularly striking fashion by the photos taken of the applicant at the Monte Carlo Beach Club tripping over an obstacle and falling down. It appears that these photos were taken secretly at a distance of several hundred metres, probably from a neighbouring house, whereas journalists' and photographers' access to the club was strictly regulated.

69. The Court reiterates the fundamental importance of protecting private life from the point of view of the development of every human being's personality. That protection – as stated above – extends beyond the private family circle and also includes a social dimension. The Court considers that anyone, even if they are known to the general public, must be able to enjoy a 'legitimate expectation' of protection of and respect for their private life.

70. Furthermore, increased vigilance in protecting private life is necessary to contend with new communication technologies which make it possible to store and reproduce personal data. This also applies to the systematic taking of specific photos and their dissemination to a broad section of the public.

71. Lastly, the Court reiterates that the Convention is intended to guarantee not rights that are theoretical or illusory but rights that are practical and effective.

. . .

(d) Conclusion

76. As the Court has stated above, it considers that the decisive factor in balancing the protection of private life against freedom of expression should lie in the contribution that the published photos and articles make to a debate of general interest. It is clear in the instant case that they made no such contribution since the applicant exercises no official function and the photos and articles related exclusively to details of her private life.

77. Furthermore, the Court considers that the public does not have a legitimate interest in knowing where the applicant is and how she behaves generally in her private life even if she appears in places that cannot always be described as secluded and despite the fact that she is well known to the public. Even if such a public interest exists, as does a commercial interest of the magazines in publishing these photos and these articles, in the instant case those interests must, in the Court's view, yield to the applicant's right to the effective protection of her private life.

78. Lastly, in the Court's opinion the criteria established by the domestic courts were not sufficient to ensure the effective protection of the applicant's private life and she should, in the circumstances of the case, have had a 'legitimate expectation' of protection of her private life.

79. Having regard to all the foregoing factors, and despite the margin of appreciation afforded to the State in this area, the Court considers that the German courts did not strike a fair balance between the competing interests.

80. There has therefore been a breach of Article 8 of the Convention.

Questions for discussion

1. What did the court view as coming within the scope of 'private life'? Do you find the explanation given by the Court to be satisfactory?
2. What particular factors do you think the Court relied on in finding that Princess Caroline's right to private life had been infringed?
3. How did the Court reconcile the right to privacy with the right to freedom of expression?

In a more recent case brought by Princess Caroline and her husband, *Von Hannover* v *Germany (No 2)*, the Grand Chamber set out the criteria relevant to balancing the right to privacy under article 8 and the right to freedom of expression under article 10. In that case, two separate magazines had published a series of photographs of the applicants going about their private affairs while on holiday. The German courts refused an injunction preventing further publication of one of the photographs on the basis that publication was justified because it was legitimately included as part of a public interest story on the ailing health of her father, Prince Rainier III, the reigning monarch of Monaco. Princess Caroline and her husband applied to the ECtHR.

Extract 11.3.3
Von Hannover v Germany (No 2) (2012) 55 EHRR 15

The criteria relevant for the balancing exercise

108. Where the right to freedom of expression is being balanced against the right to respect for private life, the criteria laid down in the case law that are relevant to the present case are set out below.

Contribution to a debate of general interest

109. An initial essential criterion is the contribution made by photos or articles in the press to a debate of general interest (see *Von Hannover*, cited above, [60] . . .). The definition of what constitutes a subject of general interest will depend on the circumstances of the case. The Court nevertheless considers it useful to point out that it has recognised the existence of such an interest not only where the publication concerned political issues or crimes . . . but also where it concerned sporting issues or performing artists . . .

How well known is the person concerned and what is the subject of the report?

110. The role or function of the person concerned and the nature of the activities that are the subject of the report and/or photo constitute another important criterion, related to the preceding one. In that connection a distinction has to be made between private individuals and persons acting in a public context, as political figures or public figures. Accordingly, whilst a private individual unknown to the public may claim particular protection of his or her right to private life, the same is not true of public figures . . . A fundamental distinction needs to be made between reporting facts capable of contributing to a debate in a democratic society, relating to politicians in the exercise of their official functions for example, and reporting details of the private life of an individual who does not exercise such functions . . .

While in the former case the press exercises its role of 'public watchdog' in a democracy by imparting information and ideas on matters of public interest, that role appears less important in the latter case. Similarly, although in certain special circumstances the public's right to be informed can even extend to aspects of the private life of public figures, particularly where politicians are concerned, this will not be the case – despite the person concerned being well known to the public – where the published photos and accompanying commentaries relate exclusively to details of the person's private life and have the sole aim of satisfying public curiosity in that respect (see *Von Hannover*, cited above, [65] . . .). In the latter case, freedom of expression calls for a narrower interpretation . . .

Prior conduct of the person concerned

111. The conduct of the person concerned prior to publication of the report or the fact that the photo and the related information have already appeared in an earlier publication are also factors to be taken into consideration. . . . However, the mere fact of having cooperated with the press on previous occasions cannot serve as an argument for depriving the party concerned of all protection against publication of the photo at issue . . .

Content, form and consequences of the publication

112. The way in which the photo or report are published and the manner in which the person concerned is represented in the photo or report may also be factors to be taken into consideration . . . The extent to which the report and photo have been disseminated may also be an important factor, depending on whether the newspaper is a national or local one, and has a large or a limited circulation . . .

Circumstances in which the photos were taken

113. Lastly, the Court has already held that the context and circumstances in which the published photos were taken cannot be disregarded. In that connection regard must be had to

whether the person photographed gave their consent to the taking of the photos and their publication . . . or whether this was done without their knowledge or by subterfuge or other illicit means. . . . Regard must also be had to the nature or seriousness of the intrusion and the consequences of publication of the photo for the person concerned . . . For a private individual, unknown to the public, the publication of a photo may amount to a more substantial interference than a written article . . .

Application of the principles to the present case

117. . . . The Federal Constitutional Court, for its part, observed that the Federal Court of Justice had accepted that the reigning prince of Monaco's illness could be regarded as a matter of general interest and that the press was therefore entitled to report on how the prince's children reconciled their obligations of family solidarity with the legitimate needs of their private life, among which was the desire to go on holiday. It also confirmed that there was a sufficiently close link between the photo and the event described in the article.

118. The Court observes that the fact that the Federal Court of Justice assessed the information value of the photo in question in the light of the accompanying article cannot be criticised under the Convention . . . Regarding the characterisation of Prince Rainier's illness as an event of contemporary society, the Court is of the opinion that, having regard to the reasons advanced by the German courts, that interpretation cannot be considered unreasonable . . . It is worth mentioning in this connection that the Federal Court of Justice upheld the injunction forbidding publication of two other photos showing the applicants in similar circumstances, precisely on the grounds that they were being published for entertainment purposes alone . . . The Court can therefore accept that the photos in question, considered in the light of the accompanying articles, did contribute, at least to some degree, to a debate of general interest . . .

120. Admittedly, the Federal Court of Justice based its reasoning on the premise that the applicants were well-known public figures who particularly attracted public attention, without going into their reasons for reaching that conclusion. The Court considers, nonetheless, that irrespective of the question whether and to what extent the first applicant assumes official functions on behalf of the Principality of Monaco, it cannot be claimed that the applicants, who are undeniably very well known, are ordinary private individuals. They must, on the contrary, be regarded as public figures . . .

121. The Federal Court of Justice then examined the question whether the photos had been taken in circumstances unfavourable to the applicants. The Government submitted that the fact that the photos had been taken without the applicants' knowledge did not necessarily mean that they had been taken surreptitiously in conditions unfavourable to the applicants. The latter, for their part, alleged that the photos had been taken in a climate of general harassment with which they were constantly confronted.

122. The Court observes that the Federal Court of Justice concluded that the applicants had not adduced evidence of unfavourable circumstances in that connection and that there was nothing to indicate that the photos had been taken surreptitiously or by equivalent secret means such as to render their publication illegal . . .

123. The Court observes that, according to the case law of the German courts, the circumstances in which photos have been taken constitutes one of the factors that are normally examined when the competing interests are balanced against each other. In the present case it can be seen from the decisions of the national courts that this factor did not require a more thorough examination as the applicants did not put forward any relevant arguments and there were no particular circumstances justifying an injunction against publishing the photos. The Court notes, moreover, as pointed out by the Federal Court of Justice, that the photos of the applicants in the middle of a street in St Moritz in winter were not in themselves offensive to the point of justifying their prohibition.

Conclusion

124. The Court observes that, in accordance with their case law, the national courts carefully balanced the right of the publishing companies to freedom of expression against the right of the applicants to respect for their private life. In doing so, they attached fundamental importance to the question whether the photos, considered in the light of the accompanying articles, had contributed to a debate of general interest. They also examined the circumstances in which the photos had been taken.

. . .

126. In those circumstances, and having regard to the margin of appreciation enjoyed by the national courts when balancing competing interests, the Court concludes that the latter have not failed to comply with their positive obligations under Article 8 of the Convention. Accordingly, there has not been a violation of that provision.

Questions for discussion

1. Is *Von Hannover* v *Germany (No 2)* consistent with *Von Hannover (No 1)*?
2. What significance did the ECtHR give to the public figure status of the applicants?
3. Do you find it convincing that the photograph contributed to a 'debate of general interest'?

11.4 THE PROTECTION OF PRIVACY UNDER ENGLISH LAW

(a) Breach of confidence

The lack of protection of a general privacy tort under English law was acutely felt in the case of *Kaye* v *Robertson*,[23] a case decided prior to the introduction of the Human Rights Act. In that case, a well-known actor, Gordon Kaye, was involved in a car accident and suffered serious head injuries. While in hospital, a journalist and a photographer from the *Sunday Sport* publication entered Kaye's private room without permission, interviewed him and took photographs. An injunction was sought to restrain the publication of the photographs and any story that Kaye had posed for them or that he had granted an interview. Medical evidence was admitted to the effect that Kaye was in no fit condition for an interview and that notices were posted at the entrance of the private ward asking visitors to see a member of staff. While a limited injunction was granted to prevent the publication of a story that Kaye consented to the interview, the Court of Appeal was incapable of providing a remedy on the basis of invasion of privacy. This was a situation which each of the judges expressly regretted.[24]

Despite the absence of a stand-alone privacy tort, the equitable action for breach of confidence did provide an adequate remedy in certain cases. The decision in *Prince Albert* v *Strange*[25] is regarded as the seminal authority in this area of the law. In that case, Queen Victoria and Prince Albert sought to restrain the publication of etchings drawn by them as well as a catalogue of their works. The defendant had obtained the drawings from an employee of the printers to whom they had been given in confidence by the Queen and

---

[23] [1991] FSR 62.
[24] Ibid., 66 (per Glidewell LJ), 70 (per Bingham LJ), 71 (per Leggatt LJ).
[25] (1849) 2 De G & Sm 652, 64 ER 293.

Prince Albert for the purpose of private publication. In restraining publication, the Court was clearly concerned with protecting the claimants' privacy, even though the relief was based on breach of confidence and property.[26]

Since the case of *Prince Albert* v *Strange*, a three-part test has been used to establish claims under breach of confidence:

> First, the information itself . . . must 'have the necessary quality of confidence about it'. Secondly, that information must have been imparted in circumstances importing an obligation of confidence. Thirdly, there must be an unauthorised use of that information to the detriment of the party communicating it.[27]

It is clear from the second element that breach of confidence, at least in its traditional sense, is focused on preventing the misuse of *relationships* involving confidences and not the protection of confidential or private information *per se*.[28] As a result, an action could only be established where the information was imparted from A to B in the context where equity would recognise an obligation of confidence (i.e., a confidential relationship) or where there was an express or implied agreement as to confidentiality – although the obligation would extend to third parties who obtained the confidential information with knowledge (actual or constructive) that such information was subject to a pre-existing obligation of confidence.[29]

Even prior to the introduction of the Human Rights Act, however, it was clear that the courts were increasingly willing to protect privacy interests through breach of confidence by expanding the circumstances in which they would recognise the existence of a duty of confidence.[30] Not only were the courts prepared to find that a pre-existing relationship between the parties was 'not the determining factor',[31] a duty of confidence could arise even in the absence of a communication between the parties. Thus, as suggested in the following extract from Lord Goff's judgment in *Attorney General* v *Guardian Newspaper (No 2)* ('*Spycatcher Case*'),[32] an obligation may arise where a stranger receives information in circumstances where it is obvious that it is confidential.[33] This would extend even to

---

[26] See, e.g., (1849) 1 Mac & G 25, 41 ER 1171, 1179 (per Lord Cottenham LC) ('In the present case, where privacy is the right invaded, postponing the injunction would be equivalent to denying it altogether.'); (1849) 2 De G & Sm 652, 64 ER 293, 313 (per Knight Bruce V-C) ('[I]t is an intrusion – . . . an intrusion not alone in breach of conventional rules, but offensive to that inbred sense of propriety natural to every man – if intrusion, indeed, fitly describes a sordid spying into the privacy of domestic life').

[27] *Coco* v *A N Clark (Engineers) Ltd* [1969] RPC 41, 47–8, approved by the House of Lords in *Attorney General* v *Guardian Newspapers (No 2)* [1990] 1 AC 109, 268.

[28] See *Campbell* v *MGN Ltd* [2004] 2 AC 457, 44 (per Lord Hoffmann) ('Breach of confidence was an equitable remedy and equity traditionally fastens on the conscience of one party to enforce equitable duties which arise out of his relationship with the other. So the action did not depend upon the personal nature of the information or extent of publication but upon *whether a confidential relationship existed between the person who imparted the information and the person who received it*' (emphasis added)).

[29] See *Attorney General* v *Guardian Newspapers (No 2)* [1990] 1 AC 109, 268 (per Lord Griffiths); *Campbell* v *MGN Ltd* [2004] 2 AC 457, 44 (per Lord Hoffmann).

[30] See, e.g., *Attorney General* v *Guardian Newspapers (No 2)* [1990] 1 AC 109, 255 (per Lord Keith): 'In other cases there may be no financial detriment to the confider, since the breach of confidence involves no more than an invasion of personal privacy . . . The right to personal privacy is clearly one which the law should in this field seek to protect.' See also: *Prince Albert* v *Strange* (1849) 2 De G & Sm 652, 64 ER 293; *Pollard* v *Photographic Co* (1889) 40 Ch D 345; *Argyll* v *Argyll* [1967] Ch 302; *Stephens* v *Avery* [1988] Ch 449; *Barrymore* v *News Group Newspapers Ltd* [1997] FSR 600. For a full discussion of these cases, see Aplin *et al.*, 6.54–6.73.

[31] See, e.g., *Stephens* v *Avery* [1988] Ch 449, 456.

[32] [1990] 1 AC 109.

[33] Cf *Gurry on Breach of Confidence*, where it is suggested (at 7.148) that the dictum of Lord Goff in *Attorney General* v *Guardian Newspapers (No 2)* has been 'overstated' and has been 'imbued . . . with more significance' by appellate courts because of the introduction of the HRA.

the situation where obviously private information was obtained by surreptitious means. For example, as noted by Lord Justice Law in *Hellewell* v *Chief Constable of Derbyshire*, relying on Lord Goff's judgment in the *Spycatcher Case*, 'if someone with a telephoto lens were to take from a distance and with no authority a picture of another engaged in some private act, his subsequent disclosure of the photograph would . . . surely amount to a breach of confidence'.[34]

Extract 11.4.1
Attorney General v Guardian Newspapers (No 2) [1990] 1 AC 109

LORD GOFF OF CHIEVELEY:
I start with the broad general principle (which I do not intend in any way to be definitive) that a duty of confidence arises when confidential information comes to the knowledge of a person (the confidant) in circumstances where he has notice, or is held to have agreed, that the information is confidential, with the effect that it would be just in all the circumstances that he should be precluded from disclosing the information to others. I have used the word 'notice' advisedly, in order to avoid the (here unnecessary) question of the extent to which actual knowledge is necessary; though I of course understand knowledge to include circumstances where the confidant has deliberately closed his eyes to the obvious. The existence of this broad general principle reflects the fact that there is such a public interest in the maintenance of confidences, that the law will provide remedies for their protection.

   I realise that, in the vast majority of cases, in particular those concerned with trade secrets, the duty of confidence will arise from a transaction or relationship between the parties – often a contract, in which event the duty may arise by reason of either an express or an implied term of that contract. It is in such cases as these that the expressions 'confider' and 'confidant' are perhaps most aptly employed. But it is well settled that a duty of confidence may arise in equity independently of such cases; and I have expressed the circumstances in which the duty arises in broad terms, not merely to embrace those cases where a third party receives information from a person who is under a duty of confidence in respect of it, knowing that it has been disclosed by that person to him in breach of his duty of confidence, but also to include certain situations, beloved of law teachers – where an obviously confidential document is wafted by an electric fan out of a window into a crowded street, or where an obviously confidential document, such as a private diary, is dropped in a public place, and is then picked up by a passer-by. I also have in mind the situations where secrets of importance to national security come into the possession of members of the public – a point to which I shall refer in a moment. I have however deliberately avoided the fundamental question whether, contract apart, the duty lies simply 'in the notion of an obligation of conscience arising from the circumstances in or through which the information was communicated or obtained' (see *Moorgate Tobacco Co Ltd* v *Philip Morris Ltd (No 2)* (1984) 156 CLR 414, 437 per Deane J, and see also *Seager* v *Copydex Ltd* [1967] 1 WLR 923, 931 per Lord Denning MR), or whether confidential information may also be regarded as property (as to which see Dr Francis Gurry's valuable monograph on *Breach of Confidence* (1984), pp 46–56 and Professor Birks' *An Introduction to the Law of Restitution* (1985), pp 343–44). I would also, like Megarry J in *Coco* v *A N Clark (Engineers) Ltd* [1969] RPC 41, p 48, wish to keep open the question whether detriment to the plaintiff is an essential ingredient of an action for breach of confidence. Obviously, detriment or potential detriment to the plaintiff will nearly always form part of his case; but this may not always be necessary. Some possible cases where there need be no detriment are mentioned in the judgment of Megarry J to which I have just referred (at p 48), and in *Gurry on Breach of Confidence* (1984) at pp 407–8. In the present case the point is immaterial, since it is established that in cases of Government secrets the Crown has to establish not only that the information is confidential, but also that publication

---

[34] [1995] 1 WLR 804, 807.

would be to its 'detriment' in the sense that the public interest requires that it should not be published. That the word 'detriment' should be extended so far as to include such a case perhaps indicates that everything depends upon how wide a meaning can be given to the word 'detriment' in this context.

To this broad general principle, there are three limiting principles to which I wish to refer. The first limiting principle (which is rather an expression of the scope of the duty) is highly relevant to this appeal. It is that the principle of confidentiality only applies to information to the extent that it is confidential. In particular, once it has entered what is usually called the public domain (which means no more than that the information in question is so generally accessible that, in all the circumstances, it cannot be regarded as confidential) then, as a general rule, the principle of confidentiality can have no application to it. I shall revert to this limiting principle at a later stage.

The second limiting principle is that the duty of confidence applies neither to useless information, nor to trivia. There is no need for me to develop this point.

The third limiting principle is of far greater importance. It is that, although the basis of the law's protection of confidence is that there is a public interest that confidences should be preserved and protected by the law, nevertheless that public interest may be outweighed by some other countervailing public interest which favours disclosure. This limitation may apply, as the learned judge pointed out, to all types of confidential information. It is this limiting principle which may require a court to carry out a balancing operation, weighing the public interest in maintaining confidence against a countervailing public interest favouring disclosure.

The apparent 'expansion' of breach of confidence raised the question as to whether a duty of confidence could be imposed on the basis of the obviously confidential (or private) nature of the information alone, or whether 'there still had to be something *over and above the quality of the information itself* in order to put the hypothetical reasonable person on notice that he or she was assuming an obligation of confidentiality'.[35] In other words, had the second element of the traditional cause of action been conflated with the first? As explained in the following section, this debate was resolved in the landmark decision of *Campbell* v *MGN Ltd*,[36] where the House of Lords confirmed that, at least in the personal privacy context, a 'duty of confidence' will arise where there is a 'reasonable expectation of privacy' irrespective of the circumstances in which the information is received,[37] and that the focus of the cause of action in this context was now on the protection of *private* information rather than the protection of confidences.

(b) Human Rights Act 1998 and misuse of private information

The development recognised in *Campbell* v *MGN Ltd* was motivated by the introduction of the HRA. Under the HRA, it is unlawful for a public authority, including a court,[38] to act in a way which is incompatible with a Convention right,[39] including article 8.[40] As explained in Section 11.3 (above), article 8 imposes an obligation on the state to provide a remedy for breach of privacy as between private parties. Therefore, in the absence of

---

[35] Fenwick and Phillipson, 730 (emphasis in original).
[36] [2004] 2 AC 457.
[37] Of the lower courts, it was Butler-Sloss P's judgment in *Venables* v *News Group Newspapers Ltd* [2001] Fam 430 which first recognised that a court may grant an injunction based on the 'private' nature of the information itself rather than the circumstances in which it was obtained: see, e.g., discussion of the significance of *Venables* by the Court of Appeal in *Douglas* v *Hello!* [2006] QB 125, 68–9.
[38] Human Rights Act 1998, s 6(3)(a).
[39] Ibid., s 6(1).
[40] Ibid., s 1(a).

Parliament stepping in and providing a statutory cause of action for invasion of privacy or the like, the courts have been required to develop the common law in order to provide such a remedy. The precise way in which the courts were to achieve this was, at least initially, uncertain. It was decided early on, however, that the HRA does not require 'the creation of a free standing cause of action based directly upon the articles of the Convention'.[41] Rather, the obligation on the courts is to 'act compatibly with Convention rights in adjudicating upon *existing* common law causes of action'.[42] That view was confirmed by the House of Lords in *Campbell v MGN Ltd*, where Lord Nicholls held that 'the values enshrined in Articles 8 and 10 are now part of the cause of action for breach of confidence'.[43] To accommodate these interests, the court recognised a new 'variant' of breach of confidence called 'misuse of private information'.[44]

In February 2001 a number of articles were published in the *Mirror* newspaper concerning Naomi Campbell, the famous fashion model, and her battle with drug addiction. The first article, headed 'Naomi: I am a drug addict', revealed that Campbell had been attending Narcotics Anonymous and provided various details about her treatment, including the frequency with which she attended and the way in which she was treated there. The article, which was generally supportive of Campbell, was accompanied by several photographs showing her on the street as she was leaving an NA meeting. Campbell commenced proceedings against MGN Ltd, the publisher of the *Mirror*. The newspaper responded by publishing a series of further articles which were highly critical of Campbell in a number of respects.

Five categories of private information were said to have been disclosed in the first article:

1. the fact of Miss Campbell's drug addiction;
2. the fact that she was receiving treatment;
3. the fact that she was receiving treatment at Narcotics Anonymous;
4. the details of the treatment – how long she had been attending meetings, how often she went, how she was treated within the sessions themselves, the extent of her commitment, and the nature of her entrance on the specific occasion; and
5. the visual portrayal of her leaving a specific meeting with other addicts.[45]

Campbell conceded that she could not rely on the information in categories (1) and (2) in light of her repeated denials in public that she did not take drugs: '[b]y repeatedly making these assertions in public Miss Campbell could no longer have a reasonable expectation that this aspect of her life should be private.'[46] At trial, Moreland J found in favour of Campbell, awarding her £2,500 plus £1,000 in aggravated damages. MGN then succeeded on appeal. It was held by the Court of Appeal that since the newspaper was entitled to publish the information that Campbell was a drug addict and that she was receiving treatment, publication of the additional details, including the photograph, did not add to the intrusion and 'were a legitimate, if not an essential, part of the journalistic package designed to demonstrate that Miss Campbell had been deceiving the public when she said that she did not take drugs'.[47] Campbell appealed to the House of Lords.

---

[41] *Venables v News Group Newspapers Ltd* [2001] Fam 430, 27.
[42] Ibid. (emphasis added). See also *Douglas v Hello! Ltd* [2001] QB 967 (CA); *Theakston v MGN Ltd* [2002] EWHC 137 (QB); *A v B plc and C* [2003] QB 195.
[43] [2004] 2 AC 457, 17; see also 133 (per Baroness Hale).
[44] *Campbell v MGN Ltd* [2004] 2 AC 457.
[45] Ibid., 23 (per Lord Nicholls).
[46] Ibid., 24.
[47] Ibid., 62.

Extract 11.4.2
Campbell v MGN Ltd **[2004] 2 AC 457**

LORD NICHOLLS:

. . .

Breach of confidence: misuse of private information

. . .

12. The present case concerns one aspect of invasion of privacy: wrongful disclosure of private information. The case involves the familiar competition between freedom of expression and respect for an individual's privacy. Both are vitally important rights. Neither has precedence over the other. The importance of freedom of expression has been stressed often and eloquently, the importance of privacy less so. But it, too, lies at the heart of liberty in a modern state. A proper degree of privacy is essential for the well-being and development of an individual. And restraints imposed on government to pry into the lives of the citizen go to the essence of a democratic state . . .

13. The common law or, more precisely, courts of equity have long afforded protection to the wrongful use of private information by means of the cause of action which became known as breach of confidence. A breach of confidence was restrained as a form of unconscionable conduct, akin to a breach of trust. Today this nomenclature is misleading. The breach of confidence label harks back to the time when the cause of action was based on improper use of information disclosed by one person to another in confidence. To attract protection the information had to be of a confidential nature. But the gist of the cause of action was that information of this character had been disclosed by one person to another in circumstances 'importing an obligation of confidence' even though no contract of non-disclosure existed: see the classic exposition by Megarry J in *Coco v A N Clark (Engineers) Ltd* [1969] RPC 41, 47–48. The confidence referred to in the phrase 'breach of confidence' was the confidence arising out of a confidential relationship.

14. This cause of action has now firmly shaken off the limiting constraint of the need for an initial confidential relationship. In doing so it has changed its nature. In this country this development was recognised clearly in the judgment of Lord Goff of Chieveley in *Attorney General v Guardian Newspapers Ltd (No 2)* [1990] 1 AC 109, 281. Now the law imposes a 'duty of confidence' whenever a person receives information he knows or ought to know is fairly and reasonably to be regarded as confidential. Even this formulation is awkward. The continuing use of the phrase 'duty of confidence' and the description of the information as 'confidential' is not altogether comfortable. Information about an individual's private life would not, in ordinary usage, be called 'confidential'. The more natural description today is that such information is private. The essence of the tort is better encapsulated now as misuse of private information.

. . .

17. The time has come to recognise that the values enshrined in articles 8 and 10 are now part of the cause of action for breach of confidence. As Lord Woolf CJ has said, the courts have been able to achieve this result by absorbing the rights protected by articles 8 and 10 into this cause of action: *A v B plc* [2003] QB 195, 202, para 4. Further, it should now be recognised that for this purpose these values are of general application. The values embodied in articles 8 and 10 are as much applicable in disputes between individuals or between an individual and a non-governmental body such as a newspaper as they are in disputes between individuals and a public authority.

. . .

19. In . . . giving effect to the values protected by article 8, courts will often be aided by adopting the structure of article 8 in the same way as they now habitually apply the Strasbourg court's

approach to article 10 when resolving questions concerning freedom of expression. Articles 8 and 10 call for a more explicit analysis of competing considerations than the three traditional requirements of the cause of action for breach of confidence identified in *Coco v A N Clark (Engineers) Ltd* [1969] RPC 41.

20. I should take this a little further on one point. Article 8(1) recognises the need to respect private and family life. Article 8(2) recognises there are occasions when intrusion into private and family life may be justified. One of these is where the intrusion is necessary for the protection of the rights and freedoms of others. Article 10(1) recognises the importance of freedom of expression. But article 10(2), like article 8(2), recognises there are occasions when protection of the rights of others may make it necessary for freedom of expression to give way. When both these articles are engaged a difficult question of proportionality may arise. This question is distinct from the initial question of whether the published information engaged article 8 at all by being within the sphere of the complainant's private or family life.

21. Accordingly, in deciding what was the ambit of an individual's 'private life' in particular circumstances courts need to be on guard against using as a touchstone a test which brings into account considerations which should more properly be considered at the later stage of proportionality. Essentially the touchstone of private life is whether in respect of the disclosed facts the person in question had a reasonable expectation of privacy.

. . .

BARONESS HALE:

. . .

132. Neither party to this appeal has challenged the basic principles which have emerged . . . in the wake of the Human Rights Act 1998. The 1998 Act does not create any new cause of action between private persons. But if there is a relevant cause of action applicable, the court as a public authority must act compatibly with both parties' Convention rights. In a case such as this, the relevant vehicle will usually be the action for breach of confidence . . .

134. . . . How does the scope of the action for breach of confidence accommodate the article 8 rights of individuals? . . . The position we have reached is that the exercise of balancing article 8 and article 10 may begin when the person publishing the information knows or ought to know that there is a reasonable expectation that the information in question will be kept confidential . . .

137. It should be emphasised that the 'reasonable expectation of privacy' is a threshold test which brings the balancing exercise into play. It is not the end of the story. Once the information is identified as 'private' in this way, the court must balance the claimant's interest in keeping the information private against the countervailing interest of the recipient in publishing it. Very often, it can be expected that the countervailing rights of the recipient will prevail.

138. The parties agree that neither right takes precedence over the other. This is consistent with Resolution 1165 (1998) of the Parliamentary Assembly of the Council of Europe, para 11:

> The Assembly reaffirms the importance of everyone's right to privacy, and of the right to freedom of expression, as fundamental to a democratic society. These rights are neither absolute nor in any hierarchical order, since they are of equal value.

139. Each right has the same structure. Article 8(1) states that 'Everyone has the right to respect for his private and family life, his home and his correspondence'. Article 10(1) states that

> Everyone has the right to freedom of expression. This right shall include freedom to hold opinions and to receive and impart information and ideas without interference by public authority and regardless of frontiers . . .

Unlike the article 8 right, however, it is accepted in article 10(2) that the exercise of this right 'carries with it duties and responsibilities'. Both rights are qualified. They may respectively be interfered with or restricted provided that three conditions are fulfilled: (a) The interference or restriction must be 'in accordance with the law'; it must have a basis in national law which conforms to the Convention standards of legality. (b) It must pursue one of the legitimate aims set out in each article. Article 8(2) provides for 'the protection of the rights and freedoms of others'. Article 10(2) provides for 'the protection of the reputation or rights of others' and for 'preventing the disclosure of information received in confidence'. The rights referred to may either be rights protected under the national law or, as in this case, other Convention rights. (c) Above all, the interference or restriction must be 'necessary in a democratic society'; it must meet a 'pressing social need' and be no greater than is proportionate to the legitimate aim pursued; the reasons given for it must be both 'relevant' and 'sufficient' for this purpose.

140. The application of the proportionality test is more straightforward when only one Convention right is in play: the question then is whether the private right claimed offers sufficient justification for the degree of interference with the fundamental right. It is much less straightforward when two Convention rights are in play, and the proportionality of interfering with one has to be balanced against the proportionality of restricting the other. As each is a fundamental right, there is evidently a 'pressing social need' to protect it. The Convention jurisprudence offers us little help with this . . . In the national court, the problem of balancing two rights of equal importance arises most acutely in the context of disputes between private persons.

141. Both parties accepted the basic approach of the Court of Appeal in *In re S* [2004] Fam 43, 72–73, paras 54–60. This involves looking first at the comparative importance of the actual rights being claimed in the individual case; then at the justifications for interfering with or restricting each of those rights; and applying the proportionality test to each. The parties in this case differed about whether the trial judge or the Court of Appeal had done this, the appellant arguing that the Court of Appeal had assumed primacy for the article 10 right while the respondent argued that the trial judge had assumed primacy for the article 8 right.

As pointed out by Lord Hoffmann, the House of Lords was unanimous on the state of the law but divided on its application to the facts at hand.[48] The majority (Lord Hope, Baroness Hale and Lord Carswell) found in favour of Campbell. The information in categories (3) and (4), being health information, was clearly private in nature[49] and the newspaper was not justified in publishing it.[50] There was no public interest in knowing the additional details of Campbell's treatment; it was not, for example, information relevant to a public figure's capacity to fulfil their public role,[51] nor were any 'political or democratic values at stake'.[52] The same conclusion was reached in relation to the photograph. Under normal circumstances, taking and publishing a photograph of a person on a public street going about their daily business would not give rise to a reasonable expectation of privacy. According to the majority, however, the photograph of Campbell was different. It was taken surreptitiously with a view to publication with the article;[53] moreover, it showed her arriving at or leaving an NA meeting, disclosed where the meeting was being held and, when considered with the article, 'added to the impact' of what the words conveyed.[54]

The minority, comprised of Lord Nicholls and Lord Hoffmann, disagreed. Considering the information that could be published (categories (1) and (2)), their honours held that

---

[48] Ibid., 36.
[49] Ibid., 95 (per Lord Hope), 144–7 (per Baroness Hale), [165] (per Lord Carswell).
[50] Ibid., 112–24 (per Lord Hope), 148–57 (per Baroness Hale), 168–70 (per Lord Carswell).
[51] Ibid., 157.
[52] Ibid., 117.
[53] Ibid., 123 (per Lord Hope).
[54] Ibid., 154–5 (per Baroness Hale).

Campbell did not have a legitimate expectation of privacy in relation to the remainder.[55] The fact that she was receiving treatment at NA and details of the treatment did not add to the information which the newspaper was allowed to publish; even if it did, the newspaper's interest in freedom of expression meant that it was entitled to publish the additional details to 'add colour and conviction' to its reporting.[56] As to the photographs, they were found not to show private information beyond that in the article itself.[57] They contained nothing 'untoward' and 'there was nothing undignified or distrait about her appearance'.[58]

> ## Question for discussion
>
> 1.   Do you prefer the reasoning of the majority or the minority in *Campbell* v *MGN Ltd*?

Despite emerging as an 'extension' of traditional breach of confidence, the cause of action for the misuse of private information is now considered separate and distinct. As explained by Lord Nicholls in *Douglas* v *Hello! Ltd*:

> As the law has developed breach of confidence, or misuse of confidential information, now covers two distinct causes of action, protecting two different interests: privacy and secret ('confidential') information. It is important to keep these two distinct. In some instances information may qualify for protection both on grounds of privacy and confidentiality. In other instances information may be in the public domain, and not qualify for protection as confidential, and yet qualify for protection on the grounds of privacy. Privacy can be invaded by further publication of information or photographs already disclosed to the public. Conversely, and obviously, a trade secret may be protected as confidential information even though no question of personal privacy is involved.[59]

A further important distinction to draw is that misuse of private information will always engage article 8, whereas a claim under traditional breach of confidence (i.e., trade secrets) may not.[60] Moreover, despite the methodology employed in some of the cases decided prior to *Campbell* – where, as argued by Phillipson, the courts had 'a noticeable tendency to gravitate back towards confidentiality principles'[61] – the shift to a 'rights-based' analysis has meant that the authorities on traditional breach of confidence 'are largely of historic interest only'.[62]

In absorbing articles 8 and 10 into the cause of action,[63] the House of Lords in *Campbell* v *MGN* introduced a 'new methodology' for resolving claims for the misuse of private information.[64] The proper approach now involves two stages of analysis. The first stage is a 'threshold test'[65] as to whether or not article 8 is engaged by the publication of the

---

[55] Ibid., 26–7 (per Lord Nicholls).
[56] Ibid., 28 (per Lord Nicholls), 59–71 (per Lord Hoffmann).
[57] Ibid., 30–1 (per Lord Nicholls), 76 (per Lord Hoffmann).
[58] Ibid., 31 (per Lord Nicholls).
[59] *Douglas* v *Hello! Ltd* [2008] 1 AC 1, 255.
[60] Ibid., 48 (per Lord Hoffmann).
[61] Gavin Phillipson, 'Transforming Breach of Confidence? Towards a Common Law Right of Privacy under the Human Rights Act' (2003) 66 *Modern Law Review* 726, 731; see also Fenwick and Phillipson 735–8.
[62] *A* v *B plc and C* [2003] QB 195, 9 (per LCJ Woolf).
[63] See *Campbell* v *MGN Ltd* [2004] 2 AC 457, 17; *McKennitt* v *Ash* [2006] EWCA Civ 1714, 11. This 'new' cause of action is sometimes labelled a 'tort' (see Lord Nicholls in *Campbell* v *MGN Ltd* [2004] 2 AC 457, 14); however, its precise juridical basis remains unsettled: see Warby, Speker and Hirst in *The Law of Privacy and the Media*, 5.06. Whether the cause of action is a tort or arises in equity may be important for a number of reasons, including available remedies, jurisdiction and applicable law. It is beyond the scope of this chapter to deal with this issue in detail.
[64] *Re S (A Child)* [2005] 1 AC 593, 23 (per Lord Steyn).
[65] See *Campbell* v *MGN* [2004] 2 AC 457, 137 (per Baroness Hale).

information. The second stage (the 'ultimate balancing test'[66]) is concerned with balancing the competing interests of privacy and freedom of expression in order to determine which interest should prevail.

(c) First stage: reasonable expectation of privacy

Whether or not the claimant has a reasonable expectation of privacy in relation to the particular information is a question of fact to be judged objectively by reference to all the circumstances of the case.[67] The most important, sometimes determinative, factors will be the nature of the information or activity itself, or the way in which the information is stored.[68] Other factors, however, may also be relevant. The Court of Appeal in *Murray v Express Newspapers plc* set out a non-exhaustive list of further considerations that may be relevant:

> [The Court must take into account] all the circumstances of the case. They include the attributes of the claimant, the nature of the activity in which the claimant was engaged, the place at which it was happening, the nature and purpose of the intrusion, the absence of consent and whether it was known or could be inferred, the effect on the claimant and the circumstances in which and the purposes for which the information came into the hands of the publisher.[69]

It is clear that there will only be a reasonable expectation of privacy in relation to information which is personal to the claimant and which he or she did not intend to disclose.[70] Examples of recognised categories of potentially private information include:[71] health and medical information;[72] gender identification[73] and sexual orientation;[74] details of personal, intimate and sexual relationships[75] as well as information conveyed in the context of such relationships;[76] personal appearance and image[77]; information about a person's home and home life;[78] political opinions[79] and religious beliefs;[80] personal financial and business information;[81] grief and

---

[66] *Re S (A Child)* [2005] 1 AC 593, 17.
[67] *Murray v Express Newspapers plc* [2009] Ch 481, 36.
[68] See, e.g., *Douglas v Hello!* [2006] QB 125, 83.
[69] *Murray v Express Newspapers plc* [2009] Ch 481, 36.
[70] See, e.g., *Douglas v Hello!* [2006] QB 125, 83.
[71] For a detailed treatment of categories of private information, see Scott in *Carter-Ruck on Libel and Privacy*, 587–647; Warby, Speker and Hirst in *The Law of Privacy and the Media*, 5.28–5.79.
[72] See, e.g., *Campbell v MGN Ltd* [2004] 2 AC 457, 57.
[73] *Goodwin v United Kingdom* (2002) 35 EHRR 18; *Chief Constable of West Yorkshire v A* [2005] 1 AC 51, 37–40 (per Baroness Hale).
[74] *Lustig-Prean v United Kingdom* (2000) 29 EHRR 548; *Smith v United Kingdom* (1999) 29 EHRR 493; *KA and AD v Belgium* (European Court of Human Rights, Application Nos 42758/98 and 45558/99, 17 February 2005); *Applause Store Productions Ltd v Raphael* [2008] EWHC 1781 (QB). Cf. *Trimingham v Associated Newspapers Ltd* [2012] EWHC 1296 (QB).
[75] See, e.g., *Mosley v News Group Newspapers Ltd* [2008] EWHC 1777 (QB); *Applause Store Productions Ltd v Raphael* [2008] EWHC 1781 (QB); *McKennitt v Ash* [2005] EWHC 3003 (QB); *T (by her litigation friend the Official Solicitor) v BBC* [2007] EWHC 1683 (QB), (family relationship).
[76] *McKennitt v Ash* [2005] EWHC 3003 (QB); *Browne v Associated Newspapers Ltd* [2008] QB 103; *HRH Prince of Wales v Associated Newspapers Ltd* [2006] EWCA Civ 1776.
[77] *Von Hannover v Germany* (2005) 40 EHRR 1; *Douglas v Hello!* [2006] QB 125; *Murray v Express Newspapers plc* [2009] Ch 481.
[78] *Beckham v MGN Ltd* (HC, Stanley Burnton J, 23 June 2001); (QBD, Eady J, 28 June 2001); *Archer v Williams* [2003] EWHC 1670 (QB); *McKennitt v Ash* [2005] EWHC 3003 (QB); *Green Corns Ltd v CLA Verley Group Ltd* [2005] EWHC 958 (QB).
[79] *HRH Prince of Wales v Associated Newspapers Ltd* [2006] EWCA Civ 1776; *Applause Store Productions Ltd v Raphael* [2008] EWHC 1781 (QB).
[80] *Applause Store Productions Ltd v Raphael* [2008] EWHC 1781 (QB).
[81] *Browne v Associated Newspapers Ltd* [2007] EWHC 202 (QB); *McKennitt v Ash* [2005] EWHC 3003 (QB).

emotional distress;[82] information contained in personal and business correspondence and records;[83] and, in certain circumstances, identity.[84] A reasonable expectation of privacy may also arise by virtue of the circumstances in which the information is imparted to another individual.[85] The protection of information about personal relationships, and the protection of personal identity and image, are explored in detail in the following sections. It is important to note, however, that article 8 will only be engaged where the intrusion (or threatened intrusion) is of a certain level of seriousness.[86]

(i) Personal relationships

Information regarding personal relationships – especially sexual relationships[87] – will often be the subject of legitimate claims to privacy. The fact of a relationship,[88] intimate details of a relationship and information conveyed between the parties during the course of a relationship may all form information over which a person may have a legitimate expectation of privacy. Depending on the circumstances, however, a distinction is sometimes drawn between the 'bare fact' of sexual relationships and the more private details of such relationships.[89]

In relation to details of sexual relationships, the early decisions that followed the introduction of the HRA tended to apply traditional breach of confidence principles by focusing on the obligation of confidence arising from the relationship rather than the private nature of the relationship itself.[90] Thus, as stated by the Court of Appeal in *A v B plc*, 'the more stable the relationship the greater will be the significance which is attached to it'.[91] In that case, a well-known footballer, Gary Flitcroft, sought an injunction to prevent the disclosure in a newspaper of the fact of two extramarital affairs that he had had with separate women, both of whom sold their story to the newspaper. The Court of Appeal overturned the decision of the trial judge to grant an injunction on the basis that,

> [q]uite apart from the recognition which the law gives to the status of marriage, there is a significant difference in our judgment between the confidentiality which attaches to what is intended to be a permanent relationship and that which attaches to the category of relationships which A was involved with here.[92]

---

[82] *Peck v United Kingdom* (2003) 36 EHRR 41; *McKennitt v Ash* [2005] EWHC 3003 (QB);

[83] *Halford v UK* (1997) 24 EHRR 523 (telephone); *Copland v UK* (2007) 45 EHRR 37 (emails); *Archer v Williams* [2003] EWHC 1670 (QB), (diaries); *HRH Prince of Wales v Associated Newspapers Ltd* [2006] EWCA Civ 1776 (letters).

[84] See, e.g., *Venables v News Group Newspapers Ltd* [2001] Fam 430; *X and Y v News Group Newspapers and MGN Ltd* [2003] FSR 850; *Carr v News Group Newspapers Ltd* [2005] EWHC 971 (QB); *Green Corns Ltd v CLA Verley Group Ltd* [2005] EWHC 958 (QB), (identity of youths living in charity housing). Cf. *Author of a Blog v Times Newspapers Ltd* [2009] EMLR 22.

[85] See, e.g., *McKennitt v Ash* [2005] EWHC 3003 (QB), 59–60.

[86] *Wood v Commissioner of Police for the Metropolis* [2009] EWCA Civ 414, 22–5; *Ferdinand v MGN Ltd* [2011] EWHC 2454 (QB), 54; *McKennitt v Ash* [2006] EWCA Civ 1714, 13.

[87] See, e.g., *Ferdinand v MGN Ltd* [2011] EWHC 2454 (QB), where Eady J said (at 56) '[s]exual behaviour in private is part of the core aspects of individual autonomy which article 8 is intended to protect'.

[88] See, e.g., *CC v AB* [2006] EWHC 3083 (QB); *ASG v GSA* [2009] EWCA Civ 1574; *ETK v News Group Newspapers Ltd* [2011] EWCA Civ 439, 11.

[89] See, e.g., *Browne v Associated Newspapers Ltd* [2007] EWHC 202 (QB); *Terry v Persons Unknown* [2010] EWHC 119 (QB), 68–9; *Ntuli v Donald* [2010] EWCA Civ 1276, 38; *Hutcheson v News Group Newspapers Ltd* [2011] EWCA Civ 808, [8]–[10]; *Goodwin v NGN Ltd* [2011] EWHC 1437 (QB), 93–104; *SKA v CRH & Persons Unknown* [2012] EWHC 766 (QB), 26.

[90] Gavin Phillipson, 'Transforming Breach of Confidence? Towards a Common Law Right of Privacy under the Human Rights Act' (2003) 66 *Modern Law Review* 726.

[91] *A v B plc and C* [2003] QB 195, 11(xi).

[92] Ibid., 43.

This conclusion was reached despite the fact that the Court of Appeal held that breach of confidence had a 'new strength and breadth' as a result of absorbing the right to privacy into the action and that,[93] as a consequence, traditional authorities on breach of confidence were to be 'largely of historic interest only'.[94]

A similar approach can be seen in the case of *Theakston* v *MGN Ltd*.[95] Jamie Theakston, a television and radio personality, sought to restrain the publication of an article in the *Sunday People* disclosing the fact that he had visited a Mayfair brothel and engaged the services of three prostitutes, as well as details relating to the sexual activities which took place. Theakston also sought to restrain the publication of photographs of him partaking in sexual activities with the prostitutes. Ouseley J held that sexual activity in transitory relationships was entitled to less protection than sexual activity in more stable relationships, such as marriage. Referring to the facts at hand, his honour found '[i]f this sexual activity in that fleeting relationship in this location were invested with confidentiality, the concept of confidentiality would become all embracing for all physical intimacy'.[96] The same conclusion was reached in relation to the details of the sexual activity that took place. Considering their particularly intrusive nature, however, Ouseley J held that Theakston was entitled to prevent the publication of the photographs.

The conservative approach applied in *A* v *B plc* and *Theakston* v *MGN Ltd* to the protection of the fact and details of intimate relationships has since been abandoned, largely due to the House of Lords' decision in *Campbell* v *MGN Ltd*. In fact, it is widely agreed that both *A* v *B plc* and *Theakston* v *MGN Ltd* would now be decided differently. The new approach was first adopted in *CC* v *AB*.[97] In that case, the claimant had been in an adulterous relationship with the defendant's wife; the defendant wished to sell the story of the affair to the media and reveal details of it on the Internet.

Extract 11.4.3
CC v AB [2006] EWHC 3083 (QB)

EADY J:

25. Judges need to be wary about giving the impression that they are ventilating, while affording or refusing legal redress, some personal moral or social views, and especially at a time when society is far less homogeneous than in the past. At one time, when there was, or was perceived to be, a commonly accepted standard in such matters as sexual morality, it may have been acceptable for the courts to give effect to that standard in exercising discretion or in interpreting legal rights and obligations. Now, however, there is a strong argument for not holding forth about adultery, or attaching greater inherent worth to a relationship which has been formalised by marriage than to any other relationship.

. . .

27. With such a wide range of differing views in society, perhaps more than for many generations, one must guard against allowing legal judgments to be coloured by personal attitudes. Even among judges, there is no doubt a wide range of opinion. It is all the more important, therefore, that the outcome of a particular case should not be determined by the judge's personal views or, as it used to be said, by 'the length of the Chancellor's foot'. There is a risk that with greater emphasis on applying an 'intense focus' to the particular facts, with the room this leaves for the

---

[93] Ibid., 4.
[94] Ibid., 9.
[95] [2002] EWHC 137 (QB).
[96] Ibid., 63.
[97] [2006] EWHC 3083 (QB).

making of individual judgments, differing outcomes on what may seem to be broadly comparable facts may be interpreted by onlookers as being explicable on the basis of arbitrary personal differences between the judges. That is plainly undesirable because it would undermine faith in the rule of law, but the danger has to be recognised as inherent in the 'new methodology' of balancing Convention rights.

. . .

30. I have come to the conclusion that there can be no rule of 'generality' that an adulterer can *never* obtain an injunction to restrain the publication of matters relating to his adulterous relationship; or, to put it another way, even an adulterous relationship may attract, at least in certain respects, a legitimate expectation of privacy. That being so, there is no rule which exempts a 'wronged' husband from restraint automatically, by virtue of his status, although in any given situation there may be particular respects in which his right to free speech should be accorded greater priority.

31. It follows that the Claimant's Article 8 rights are engaged once there is a threat to publish, to the world at large (whether for payment or otherwise), the fact of his sexual relationship and the details of how it was conducted.

. . .

39. Sometimes . . . the court will recognise a legitimate expectation of privacy, not on the basis of the means by which the information was imparted, but rather because of the nature of the information itself. Quite often, for a variety of reasons, people prefer to conduct sexual relationships, at least temporarily, on a secret basis. They would appear to be entitled to do so and, until they choose to 'go public', to enjoy a legitimate expectation of privacy *vis à vis* the world at large. That is to say, such information is capable of being regarded as confidential.

It was made even more clear in the case of *Mosley v News Group Newspapers Ltd*[98] that information regarding sexual encounters, howsoever conducted, will be the subject of a legitimate expectation of privacy. Max Mosley, the then President of the Federation Internationale de l'Automobile (the FIA), sued the *News of the World* in relation to an article published by the newspaper under the headline 'F1 BOSS HAS SICK NAZI ORGY WITH 5 HOOKERS' and under the subheading 'Son of Hitler-loving fascist in sex shame'. The article described Mosley's participation in a sadomasochistic sex party with five prostitutes, one of whom (Woman E) had sold her story to the newspaper, and was accompanied by a series of still photographs. Mosley also sued over an article which appeared on the *News of the World* website, similar in terms to the newspaper article but which was also accompanied by video footage of the event. Mosley did not dispute the truth that he participated in the alleged activities; however, he did dispute that it involved a 'Nazi' role-play. Eady J refused an interim injunction in relation to the video on the basis that such an order would 'serve no useful purpose' due to the wide availability of the footage.[99] Following the refusal to grant an injunction, a further article about the event appeared on the front page of the *News of the World*. Despite the fact that he was denied an interim injunction, Mosley proceeded to trial to seek damages.

---

[98] [2008] EWHC 1777 (QB).
[99] See *Mosley v News Group Newspapers Ltd* [2008] EWHC 687 (QB).

Extract 11.4.4
***Mosley* v *News Group Newspapers Ltd* [2008] EWHC 1777 (QB)**

EADY J:

Was there a reasonable expectation of privacy or a duty of confidence?

98. In deciding whether there was at stage one a reasonable expectation of privacy generalisations are perhaps best avoided, just as at stage two, and the question must be addressed in the light of all the circumstances of the particular case: see, e.g., *Murray* v *Big Pictures* [2008] EWCA Civ 446 at [35]–[39]. Nevertheless, one is usually on safe ground in concluding that anyone indulging in sexual activity is entitled to a degree of privacy – especially if it is on private property and between consenting adults (paid or unpaid).

. . .

99. There is now a considerable body of jurisprudence in Strasbourg and elsewhere which recognises that sexual activity engages the rights protected by Article 8. As was noted long ago in *Dudgeon* v *UK* (1981) 4 EHRR 149, there must exist particularly serious reasons before interferences on the part of public authorities can be legitimate for the purposes of Article 8(2) because sexual behaviour 'concerns a most intimate aspect of private life' . . .

. . .

100. There are many statements to similar effect, the more lofty of which do not necessarily withstand rigorous analysis. The precise meaning is not always apparent. Nevertheless, the underlying sentiments are readily understood in everyday language; namely, that people's sex lives are to be regarded as essentially their own business – provided at least that the participants are genuinely consenting adults and there is no question of exploiting the young or vulnerable.

. . .

101. More recently, in *Tammer* v *Estonia* (2003) 37 EHRR 43 it was held that criminal penalties imposed in respect of the reporting of a sexual relationship could not be said to violate Article 10 – notwithstanding that the persons concerned were the Prime Minister and a political aide. However broadly one defines the term, it has been recognised in this jurisdiction also that 'public figures' are entitled to a private personal life. The notion of privacy covers not only sexual activities but personal relationships more generally.

. . .

109. An argument has been pleaded also to the effect that the Claimant forfeited any expectation of privacy partly because of the numbers involved; that is to say, with so many participants it should not be regarded as private. This was coupled with reliance upon the fact that he liked to record these gatherings on video, with the consent of all those present, so as to have a 'memento'. That can be safely rejected . . .

Questions for discussion

1. When should the bare fact of a relationship be subject to a reasonable expectation of privacy?
2. Should a distinction be drawn between transitory and more permanent relationships? Why/why not?

(ii) *Disclosure of information imparted in the course of confidential or private relationships*

In addition to facts relating to sexual relationships, information disclosed during the *course of* personal relationships can also be the subject of privacy claims. These relationships would often have given rise to an obligation of confidence under traditional breach of confidence. While the mere fact that information has been imparted in the context of an intimate relationship is not in and of itself enough to give rise to a legitimate expectation of privacy,[100] the context of any such relationship will be a relevant, often weighty, consideration.

However, cases involving the disclosure of private information in the context of personal, sexual, and even business, relationships highlight the existence of a complicated, and somewhat unresolved, relationship between 'old fashioned' breach of confidence and the 'new' action for misuse of private information.[101] It is obvious that where the information in question does not engage article 8 but satisfies the requirement of confidentiality (for example, trade secret cases), breach of confidence will continue to provide a cause of action. The statement of Lord Nicholls (quoted above) in *Douglas v Hello! Ltd* makes this clear.[102] What, however, of the situation where the requirements of traditional breach of confidence are established *and* the information engages article 8? Is the Court required to apply the new methodology to such a case, or does breach of confidence continue to operate as a separate cause of action concurrent to misuse of private information? It appears that a number of different approaches have been adopted in the cases to date.

In *McKennitt v Ash*, the defendant, Ash, was a former friend of Canadian folk singer, Loreena McKennitt. Following a falling out with McKennitt, Ash published a book about their relationship, called *Travels with Loreena McKennitt: My Life as a Friend*. McKennitt sought a declaration that the publication of the book constituted a breach of confidence and/or the breach of the terms of a confidentiality agreement,[103] as well as an injunction to prevent its further publication. There were said to be five categories of 'confidential information' at issue: McKennitt's personal and sexual relationships; information about her feelings, particularly McKennitt's grief following the death of her fiancé in a boating accident in 1998; information relating to McKennitt's health and diet; information about her emotional vulnerability; and details regarding a dispute between McKennitt, and Ash and her partner, regarding a property deal.[104] It was considered relevant to the case that McKennitt had always sought to guard her private life. At trial, Eady J found in favour of McKennitt on some of the claims but not others.[105] On appeal, Buxton LJ held that the fact of any pre-existing relationship between the parties is a relevant consideration in determining whether the claimant has a reasonable expectation of privacy,[106] and that private information may be 'doubly private' when it is 'imparted in the context of a relationship of confidence'.[107]

The relationship between breach of confidence and misuse of private information was further considered in *Browne v Associated Newspapers Ltd*.[108] In that case, the *Mail on Sunday* wished to publish an article disclosing certain information about Lord Browne of Madingley, the then Group Chief Executive of British Petroleum. The information had

---

[100] See, e.g., *Browne v Associated Newspapers* [2008] QB 103, 29.

[101] For a thorough analysis of the relationship between breach of confidence and misuse of private information, see Aplin *et al.* 7.143–7.159.

[102] *Douglas v Hello! Ltd* [2008] 1 AC 1, 255.

[103] It was held at trial, and upheld by the Court of Appeal, that this confidentiality agreement did not add to the equitable obligations of confidence that Ash owed McKennitt by reason of their close relationship: see *McKennitt v Ash* [2006] EWCA Civ 1714, 43.

[104] *McKennitt v Ash* [2005] EWHC 3003 (QB), 11.

[105] *McKennitt v Ash* [2005] EWHC 3003 (QB).

[106] *McKennitt v Ash* [2006] EWCA Civ 1714, 15.

[107] Ibid., 23.

[108] [2008] QB 103.

been provided to the newspaper by Lord Browne's former domestic partner, Jeff Chevalier (JC), and included the following five categories of subject matter: (a) BP strategy; (b) Lord Browne's misuse of BP resources and manpower to assist Mr Chevalier; (c) the 'bare fact' of the relationship between Mr Chevalier and Lord Browne; (d) that Lord Browne discussed confidential BP matters with and disclosed confidential documents to Mr Chevalier; and (e) details of Lord Browne's relationships with colleagues at BP. Eady J held that categories (a) and (e) were subject to a reasonable expectation of privacy – not because the information was inherently private but because 'of the circumstances of communication and the nature of the relationship'.[109] In relation to the remaining categories, however, Lord Browne did not have a legitimate expectation of privacy.

Eady J appeared to agree that business information would not, in and of itself, engage article 8.[110] However, his Honour said that such information may receive protection where it is disclosed in the context of personal relationships or in the domestic environment:

> For example, one would expect most people from time to time to come home from work and to feel free to unburden themselves about the horrors of the day – whether to a wife, husband, lover, mistress or partner (homosexual or otherwise). People feel free in the privacy of their own homes to have a moan about colleagues or employers. What puts such communications, potentially, under the protection of the law is that revelations of such information would infringe the reasonable expectation people have that intimate and uninhibited discussions in a domestic environment will be respected. . . . It is not the subject-matter which determines the issue in those cases, but the circumstances in which the opinions or information may be imparted.[111]

Eady J also found that personal information disclosed during the course of a dinner party would engage article 8, as would matters relating to domestic financial arrangements and decisions about private investment strategies.[112] Lord Browne appealed to the Court of Appeal.

Extract 11.4.5
Browne v Associated Newspapers Ltd **[2008] QB 103**

SIR ANTHONY CLARKE MR (delivering the judgment of the Court):

24. The first question under article 8 is whether in respect of the disclosed facts the claimant has a reasonable expectation of privacy in the particular circumstances of the case. That is the relevant question whether there was a previous confidential relationship between the parties or not . . .

25. In *McKennitt* at [15] . . . Buxton LJ said that in the case where there is no pre-existing relationship of confidence, as in *Campbell* v *MGN*, *Douglas* v *Hello!* and *von Hannover* v *Germany* (2005) 40 EHRR 1, the primary focus is on the nature of the information. In a case like this, where there is a previous relationship of confidence, the focus is different.

26. The cases make it clear that, in answering the question whether in respect of the disclosed facts the claimant has a reasonable expectation of privacy in the particular circumstances of the case the nature of any relationship between the relevant persons or parties is of considerable potential importance . . .

27. The issue between the parties in this appeal centers on the relevance of the nature of the information which it is sought to publish. Ms Sharp QC submits that the mere fact that the parties had a pre-existing relationship, such as marriage or a relationship of friendship, as in *McKennitt*,

---

[109] *Browne* v *Associated Newspapers Ltd* [2007] EWHC 202, 57.
[110] Ibid., 33–42.
[111] Ibid., 45–6.
[112] Ibid., 59.

or an intimate and sexual relationship, such as that between the claimant and JC, does not create a reasonable expectation of privacy in relation to all information learned or activities witnessed during the relationship . . .

29. . . . [W]e accept Ms Sharp's submission that the *mere* fact that the information was imparted in the course of a relationship of confidence does not satisfy Lord Nicholls' test of 'expectation of privacy'. An example would be a husband telling his wife that Oxford or Cambridge won the boat race in a particular year. However, the relationship may be of considerable importance in answering the question whether there was an expectation of privacy. . . .

31. In our judgment, the cases support the conclusion that the relationship between the relevant persons or parties is of considerable importance in answering Lord Nicholls' question, namely whether there was a reasonable expectation of privacy. In answering that question there are a number of potentially relevant questions, depending upon the circumstances. They include whether the person concerned (here JC) received information which he knew or ought reasonably to have known was fairly and reasonably to be regarded as confidential or private.

32. There was some discussion in the course of the argument as to whether it was sufficient for the claimant to show that there was a relationship of confidence and whether, once such a relationship is shown, all information obtained in the course of the relationship is confidential without regard to the nature of the information. In our judgment, the answer to those questions is no. That is clear, for example from Lord Nicholls' formulation of the test, namely whether *in respect of the disclosed facts* the claimant has a reasonable expectation of privacy – our emphasis. As we see it, the test must be applied to each item of information communicated to or learned by the person concerned in the course of the relationship.

33. The nature of the relationship is of considerable importance. For example, the mere fact that the piece of information can be regarded as trivial does not seem to us to be decisive against answering Lord Nicholls' question in the affirmative . . . [I]t may or may not be. We agree with the general proposition advanced by Ms Sharp that the question whether any particular piece of information qualifies as private and the claimant has a reasonable expectation of privacy in respect of it, requires a detailed examination of all the circumstances on a case by case basis. The circumstances include the nature of the information itself and the circumstances in which it has been imparted or obtained . . .

34. Ms Sharp submits that there is no authority for the proposition that information relating to business activities will be characterised as private merely because it is communicated or learned in a domestic environment, or in the course of a personal relationship. We accept that that is so but, again, it appears to us that all depends upon the circumstances of the particular case. The judge suggested at [33] that as a matter of first impression the characterisation of business information as private would appear inconsistent with the policy objectives behind article 8, namely that this is a human right concerned with protecting personal integrity, dignity and domestic life. We are not sure that that is quite right because it seems to us that business information passed by a company director to his sexual partner could readily be held to be information which the latter knew or ought reasonably to have known was fairly and reasonably to be regarded as confidential or private and in respect of which the former had a reasonable expectation of privacy. However, it seems to us that the judge recognised that that was or might be so . . .

36. In short, each case must be decided on its own facts and the judge was correct to say, as he did . . . that, without entering into a preliminary inquiry as to whether any particular piece of information should be allocated a 'business' or a 'personal' characterisation, the question to ask, in relation to each of the categories individually, was whether there was a reasonable expectation of privacy.

[The Court found that the trial judge had correctly approached the task of determining whether Lord Browne had a reasonable expectation of privacy in relation to the five categories of information and dismissed the appeal.]

It appears from *McKennitt* v *Ash* and *Browne* v *Associated Newspapers Ltd* that the courts will apply the 'new methodology' to cases involving breach of confidence where it is argued that article 8 is engaged. That is, the courts will treat the presence of a confidential relationship as a relevant, often weighty, factor in establishing that a reasonable expectation of privacy exists – with the result that even information which is not 'inherently private' may be analysed according to the new methodology.

A different approach, however, was taken in *Associated Newspapers* v *HRH Prince of Wales*.[113] The claimant, the Prince of Wales, sought summary judgment against the newspaper defendant for publishing extracts of his private journal which it had obtained from one of the claimant's former employees in breach of confidence. The journal, handwritten by the claimant, contained 'impressions and reflections on his visit to Hong Kong' in 1997.

Extract 11.4.6
Associated Newspapers Ltd v HRH Prince of Wales [2006] EWCA Civ 1776

LORD PHILLIPS (delivering the judgment of the Court):

27. Many of the recent decisions in this area of the law involve situations where information has been published that has not involved the breach of a relationship of confidence. In such circumstances the issue has been whether the information was of a private nature, so that its disclosure interfered with Article 8 rights and, if so, how the tension between Article 8 and Article 10 should be resolved.

. . .

28. This action is not concerned, however, with a claim for breach of privacy that involves an extension of the old law of breach of confidence. There is an issue in this case as to whether the information disclosed was private so as to engage Article 8 and there is an obvious overlap between this question and the question of whether the information was capable of being the subject of a duty of confidence under the old law. Assuming that it was, there are in this action all the elements of a claim for breach of confidence under that law. The information was disclosed in breach of a well recognised relationship of confidence, that which exists between master and servant. Furthermore, the disclosure was in breach of an express contractual duty of confidentiality. The Newspaper was aware that the journals were disclosed in breach of confidence.

. . .

35. In many cases it will be perfectly obvious that information is both confidential and of a private nature. This is such a case. The Journal set out the personal views and impressions of Prince Charles. They were set out in a journal in his own hand. They were seen by his staff, who were under an express contractual obligation to treat their content as confidential. They were sent to selected recipients under cover of a letter signed by Prince Charles in an envelope marked 'private and confidential'. The journals were paradigm examples of confidential documents. They also satisfied each of the tests of confidential and private documents to which we have referred above.

36. It is not easy in this case, as in many others, when concluding that information is private to identify the extent to which this is because of the nature of the information, the form in which it is conveyed and the fact that the person disclosing it was in a confidential relationship with the person to whom it relates. Usually, as here, these factors form an interdependent amalgam

---

[113] As pointed out in the latest edition of *Gurry on Breach of Confidence*: see Aplin *et al.*, 7.153.

of circumstances. If, however, one strips out the fact of breach of a confidential relationship, and assumes that a copy of the Journal had been brought to the Newspaper by someone who had found it dropped in the street, we consider that its form and content would clearly have constituted it private information entitled to the protection of Article 8(1) as qualified by Article 8(2).

. . .

The impact of Article 10 on an action for breach of confidence

. . .

48. We do not believe that Lord Hoffman [sic] [in *Campbell* v *MGN Ltd*] intended to suggest that the fact that information has been disclosed in breach of the duties of good faith that arise in a relationship of trust and confidence is irrelevant when considering the balance between the requirements of Article 8 and Article 10. In that case the press had been informed of Ms Campbell's treatment as a result of a breach of confidence, either on the part of a fellow participant at meetings of Narcotics Anonymous or on the part of one of her staff or entourage. But the House of Lords did not have to consider the extent to which this weighed in the balance to be struck between Article 8 and Article 10 rights. It was common ground that, had Ms Campbell not herself put her experience of drugs into the public domain, all the information published would have constituted an interference with her Article 8 rights which was not justified by Article 10 considerations.

. . .

65. . . . Whether a publication, or threatened publication, involves a breach of a relationship of confidence, an interference with privacy or both, it is necessary to consider whether these matters justify the interference with Article 10 rights that will be involved if the publication is made the subject of a judicial sanction. A balance has to be struck. Where no breach of a confidential relationship is involved, that balance will be between Article 8 and Article 10 rights and will usually involve weighing the nature and consequences of the breach of privacy against the public interest, if any, in the disclosure of private information.

66. What is the position where the disclosure relates to 'information received in confidence'? The authors of *The Law of Privacy and the Media* in their Second Supplement at 6.111 express the view that it would be surprising if this consideration was ignored. We agree. It is a factor that Article 10(2) recognises is, of itself, capable of justifying restrictions on freedom of expression.

67. There is an important public interest in the observance of duties of confidence. Those who engage employees, or who enter into other relationships that carry with them a duty of confidence, ought to be able to be confident that they can disclose, without risk of wider publication, information that it is legitimate for them to wish to keep confidential. Before the Human Rights Act came into force the circumstances in which the public interest in publication overrode a duty of confidence were very limited. The issue was whether exceptional circumstances justified disregarding the confidentiality that would otherwise prevail. Today the test is different. It is whether a fetter of the right of freedom of expression is, in the particular circumstances, 'necessary in a democratic society'. It is a test of proportionality. But a significant element to be weighed in the balance is the importance in a democratic society of upholding duties of confidence that are created between individuals. It is not enough to justify publication that the information in question is a matter of public interest. To take an extreme example, the content of a budget speech is a matter of great public interest. But if a disloyal typist were to seek to sell a copy to a newspaper in advance of the delivery of the speech in Parliament, there can surely be no doubt that the newspaper would be in breach of duty if it purchased and published the speech.

68. For these reasons, the test to be applied when considering whether it is necessary to restrict freedom of expression in order to prevent disclosure of information received in confidence is not simply whether the information is a matter of public interest but whether, in all the circumstances, it is in the public interest that the duty of confidence should be breached. The court will need to consider whether, having regard to the nature of the information and all the relevant circumstances, it is legitimate for the owner of the information to seek to keep it confidential or whether it is in the public interest that the information should be made public.

69. In applying the test of proportionality, the nature of the relationship that gives rise to the duty of confidentiality may be important. Different views have been expressed as to whether the fact that there is an express contractual obligation of confidence affects the weight to be attached to the duty of confidentiality. In *Campbell* v *Frisbee* [2002] EWCA Civ 1374 . . . at paragraph 22 this court drew attention to this conflict of view, and commented:

> We consider that it is arguable that a duty of confidentiality that has been expressly assumed under contract carries more weight, when balanced against the right of freedom of expression, than a duty of confidence that is not buttressed by express agreement.

We adhere to this view. But the extent to which a contract adds to the weight of duty of confidence arising out of a confidential relationship will depend upon the facts of the individual case.

[Appeal dismissed].

Questions for discussion

1. What is the approach of the Court of Appeal in *Associated Newspapers Ltd* v *HRH Prince of Wales* to the relationship between traditional breach of confidence and misuse of private information?
2. Can the approach in *Associated Newspapers Ltd* v *HRH Prince of Wales* be reconciled with the approach in *Lord Browne* v *Associated Newspapers Ltd* and *McKennitt* v *Ash*?
3. Which approach is to be preferred and why?

In other cases where article 8 is engaged, courts have treated 'old fashioned' breach of confidence and misuse of private information as causes of action that continue to operate concurrently. In *Tchenguiz* v *Imerman*,[114] the claimant shared office space and a computer server with his wife's two brothers. The claimant and his wife were in the process of divorcing. In order to prevent the claimant from concealing his assets from his wife, one of the brothers accessed the server and copied information and documents. Some of the documents were given to the wife's solicitor. The claimant sought, and was granted, an injunction to restrain the defendants from communication or disclosing to third parties any information contained in the documents. The defendants appealed. The Court of Appeal concluded that there had been an 'invasion of privacy in an underhand way and on an indiscriminate scale';[115] however, it also spoke in terms of breach of confidence, concluding that 'there is no real doubt but that the defendants have substantially breached Mr Imerman's rights of confidence'.[116] Despite ambiguity in the use of terminology in the case, the authors of *Gurry on Breach of Confidence* are of the view that the Court of

[114] [2010] EWCA Civ 908.
[115] *Tchenguiz* v *Imerman* [2010] EWCA Civ 908, 144.
[116] Ibid., 141.

Appeal found that both breach of confidence *and* misuse of private information had been made out, 'with the discussion of Articles 8 and 10 being largely implicit'.[117]

A much clearer example of breach of confidence and misuse of private information being applied concurrently is evident in the decision of Eady J in *Mosley v News Group Newspapers Ltd*. In that case, Eady J characterised the claim as one 'partly founded, as in *McKennitt v Ash* . . . upon ". . . old fashioned breach of confidence by way of conduct inconsistent with a pre-existing relationship, rather than simply of the purloining of private information"'.[118] His Honour went on to consider the action under both traditional breach of confidence and under misuse of private information, where he ultimately concluded that he would be 'prepared to hold that Woman E had committed an "old fashioned breach of confidence" *as well as* a violation of the Article 8 rights of all those involved'.[119]

(iii) Personal image

The depiction of a person by photographic or audiovisual means has been held to be especially capable of interfering with a person's right to private life under article 8. The European Court of Human Rights held in *Von Hannover v Germany* (extracted above at 11.3.2) that Princess Caroline's article 8 rights were engaged when photographs of her participating in everyday activities outside of her official duties were published by the media. Considering the nature of the activities and the fact that they were conducted in public, it has been suggested that the decision in *Von Hannover* stands for the proposition that photographs of individuals 'will always involve the conveyance of "private" information in circumstances where the subject is not engaged in some demonstrably official, public activity'.[120] This is said to be tantamount to an 'image right'.[121] An alternative to this 'absolutist' view of *Von Hannover v Germany* has been offered by Fenwick and Phillipson. They suggest that the judgment can be viewed in the context of the persistent harassment that was faced by Princess Caroline as she tried to go about her private life.[122] Indeed, this view would appear to be supported by the ECtHR's explicit regard for the 'context in which these photographs were taken – without the applicant's knowledge or consent – and the harassment endured by many public figures in their daily lives'.[123]

The absolutist view, however, might be said to better reflect the state of Strasbourg jurisprudence following more recent cases – especially *Von Hannover v Germany (No 2)*[124] (the facts of the case are set out at Extract 11.3.3), a further case brought in the ECtHR by Princess Caroline and her husband. As the following extract shows, the Court emphasised in its discussion of article 8 the importance of the right to the protection of one's image.

---

[117] Aplin *et al.*, 7.155.
[118] *Mosley v News Groups Newspapers Ltd* [2008] EWHC 1777 (QB), 5.
[119] Ibid., 108 (emphasis added).
[120] Scott in *Carter-Ruck on Libel and Privacy*, 19.67.
[121] Ibid.
[122] Fenwick and Phillipson, 680–3; *John v Associated Newspapers Ltd* [2006] EMLR 722, 16. Cf. *McKennitt v Ash* [2006] EWCA Civ 1714, 39–42; *Murray v Express Newspapers Ltd plc* [2007] EWHC 1908 (Ch) 48–9.
[123] *Von Hannover v Germany* (2005) 40 EHRR 1, 68.
[124] *Von Hannover v Germany (No 2)* (2012) 55 EHRR 15. See also *Sciacca v Italy* (2006) 43 EHRR 20 (regarding publication of a photograph taken in a public place). The mere taking of photographs has also been held to violate art 8: see *Reklos and Davourlis v Greece* [2009] EMLR 16.

Extract 11.4.7
Von Hannover v Germany (No 2) (2012) 55 EHRR 15

(b) General principles

(i) Concerning private life

95. The Court reiterates that the concept of private life extends to aspects relating to personal identity, such as a person's name, photo, or physical and moral integrity; the guarantee afforded by Article 8 of the Convention is primarily intended to ensure the development, without outside interference, of the personality of each individual in his relations with other human beings. There is thus a zone of interaction of a person with others, even in a public context, which may fall within the scope of private life. Publication of a photo may thus intrude upon a person's private life even where that person is a public figure . . .

96. Regarding photos, the Court has stated that a person's image constitutes one of the chief attributes of his or her personality, as it reveals the person's unique characteristics and distinguishes the person from his or her peers. The right to the protection of one's image is thus one of the essential components of personal development. It mainly presupposes the individual's right to control the use of that image, including the right to refuse publication thereof . . .

97. The Court also reiterates that, in certain circumstances, even where a person is known to the general public, he or she may rely on a 'legitimate expectation' of protection of and respect for his or her private life.

The Grand Chamber held that the German courts complied with article 8 on the particular facts of the case because it was open for them to find, in balancing the applicant's right to private life and the publishers' right to freedom of expression, that the photographs contributed to a debate or matter of general interest. Importantly, it is clear from the Grand Chamber's judgment that the applicant's article 8 rights were *engaged* by simply publishing, without permission or consent, photographs of the applicants going about their daily lives (even if, on the facts, their privacy rights were trumped by the media's right to freedom of expression). Moreover, while it was acknowledged that the circumstances in which photographs are taken is a relevant criterion in the balancing exercise,[125] there was no suggestion that it constitutes a necessary factor in finding that a photograph taken of a public figure in a public place will engage article 8.

Whatever the correct interpretation of the Strasbourg jurisprudence,[126] it is clear that photographs and video recordings are treated by the domestic courts, rightly or wrongly, as having the unique capacity to violate privacy to a greater degree than other forms of communication, such as a written or verbal description of private facts. As stated by the Court of Appeal in *Douglas* v *Hello!*, where surreptitiously obtained photographs of the wedding of actors Michael Douglas and Catherine Zeta Jones were published by *Hello!* magazine in breach of their privacy:

> Special considerations attach to photographs in the field of privacy. They are not merely a method of conveying information that is an alternative to verbal description. They enable the person viewing the photograph to act as a spectator, in some circumstances voyeur would be the more appropriate noun, of whatever it is that the photograph depicts. As a means of invading privacy, a photograph is particularly intrusive.[127]

---

[125] *Von Hannover* v *Germany (No 2) (2012)* 55 EHRR 15, 113. See Extract 11.3.3.
[126] Taking an absolute view, Scott argues that Strasbourg decisions are inconsistent with the domestic approach: see Scott in *Carter-Ruck on Libel and Privacy*, 19.79–19.84.
[127] *Douglas* v *Hello! Ltd* [2006] QB 125, 84.

Similarly, in *Theakston* v *MGN Ltd* (discussed above in Section 11.4(c)(i)), Ouseley J was willing to issue an injunction to prevent the publication of photographs of the applicant engaged in sexual activity with a number of prostitutes, but not a written description of the event. He said that photographs are 'particularly intrusive' and that they would violate the applicant's privacy in a 'peculiarly humiliating and damaging way'.[128]

Lord Hoffmann in *Campbell* v *MGN Ltd* also gave special significance to photographs:

> a photograph is in principle information no different from any other information. It may be a move vivid form of information than the written word . . . that has to be taken into account in deciding whether its publication infringes the right to privacy of personal information. The publication of a photograph cannot necessarily be justified by saying that one would be entitled to publish a verbal description of the scene . . . but the principles by which one decides whether or not the publication of a photograph is an unjustified invasion of the privacy of personal information are in my opinion the same as those [for written material].[129]

The majority in that case found that the publication of the photographs of Naomi Campbell arriving at or leaving a Narcotics Anonymous meeting engaged her article 8 rights, despite the fact that she was photographed on a public street. *Campbell* made it clear that there is no clear-cut distinction between photographs taken in a public as opposed to private place. However, as pointed out by Baroness Hale:

> If this had been, and had been presented as, a picture of Naomi Campbell going about her business in a public street, there could have been no complaint. She makes a substantial part of her living out of being photographed looking stunning in designer clothing. Readers will obviously be interested to see how she looks if and when she pops out to the shops for a bottle of milk. There is nothing essentially private about that information nor can it be expected to damage her private life.[130]

While acknowledging that no 'right to one's own image' was recognised under English law and that 'the mere fact of covert photography is [not] sufficient to make the information contained in the photograph confidential', Baroness Hale found that the photographs in question were different in that they added to the impact and substance of the words conveyed regarding Campbell's treatment for drug addiction.[131]

In *Murray* v *Express Newspapers plc*,[132] the Court of Appeal held that article 8 was engaged by the publication of anodyne photographs taken by covert means of a child being pushed along a public street. In that case, J.K. Rowling, the author of the famous Harry Potter series of books, and her husband, brought proceedings on behalf of their son, David, to prevent the publication of photographs of him on a family outing to a café located close to their home. The trial judge initially rejected the claim on the basis that 'routine acts such as the visit to the shop or the ride on the bus should not attract any reasonable expectation of privacy'.[133] The Murrays appealed.

[128] [2002] EWHC 137 (QB), 78.
[129] *Campbell* v *MGN Ltd* [2004] 2 AC 457, 72.
[130] Ibid., 154. This, it has been suggested, is out of step with *Von Hannover* v *Germany*: see Scott in *Carter-Ruck on Libel and Privacy*, 19.79–19.84.
[131] *Campbell* v *MGN Ltd* [2004] 2 AC 457, 154–5.
[132] [2009] Ch 481.
[133] *Murray* v *Express Newspapers plc* [2007] EWHC 1908 (Ch) 65.

Extract 11.4.8
SIR ANTHONY CLARKE MR (giving the opinion of the Court):

Discussion

45. We have reached a different conclusion from that of the judge. In our opinion it is at least arguable that David had a reasonable expectation of privacy. The fact that he is a child is in our view of greater significance than the judge thought. The courts have recognised the importance of the rights of children in many different contexts and so too has the international community . . . More specifically, clause 6 of the Press Complaints Commission Editors' Code of Practice contains this sentence under the heading Children:

> v) Editors must not use the fame, notoriety or position of the parent or guardian as sole justification for publishing details of a child's private life.

There is also a publication called The Editors' Codebook, which refers to the Code and to the above statement. Although it is true that the Codebook states . . . in a section headed 'Intrusion' that the Press Complaints Commission has ruled that the mere publication of a child's image cannot breach the Code when it is taken in a public place and is unaccompanied by any private details or materials which might embarrass or inconvenience the child, which is particularly unlikely in the case of babies or very young children, it seems to us that everything must depend on the circumstances.

46. So, for example, in *Tugendhat and Christie* on *The Law of Privacy and the Media* the authors note at paragraph 13.128 (in connection with a complaint made by Mr and Mrs Blair) that the PCC has stated that:

> the acid test to be applied by newspapers in writing about the children of public figures who are not famous in their own right (unlike the Royal Princes) is whether a newspaper would write such a story if it was about an ordinary person.

It seems to us to be at least arguable that a similar approach should be adopted to photographs. If a child of parents who are not in the public eye could reasonably expect not to have photographs of him published in the media, so too should the child of a famous parent. In our opinion it is at least arguable that a child of 'ordinary' parents could reasonably expect that the press would not target him and publish photographs of him. The same is true of David, especially since on the alleged facts here the Photograph would not have been taken or published if he had not been the son of J.K. Rowling.

47. Neither *Campbell* nor *Von Hannover* is a case about a child. There is no authoritative case in England of a child being targeted as David was here . . .

54. . . . [A]s we read [the trial judge's reasoning], he focuses on the taking of the Photograph. As we indicated earlier, it is our opinion that the focus should not be on the taking of a photograph in the street, but on its publication. In the absence of distress or the like caused when the photograph is taken, the mere taking of a photograph in the street may well be entirely unobjectionable. We do not therefore accept, as the judge appears to suggest . . . that, if the claimant succeeds in this action, the courts will have created an image right.

55. We recognise that there may well be circumstances in which there will be no reasonable expectation of privacy, even after *Von Hannover*. However, as we see it all will (as ever) depend upon the facts of the particular case. The judge suggests that a distinction can be drawn between a child (or an adult) engaged in family and sporting activities and something as simple as a walk down a street or a visit to the grocer's to buy the milk. This is on the basis that the first type of activity is clearly part of a person's private recreation time intended to be enjoyed in the company of family and friends and that, on the test deployed in *Von Hannover*, publicity of such activities is intrusive and can adversely affect the exercise of such social activities. We agree with the judge that that is indeed the basis of the ECtHR's approach but we do not

agree that it is possible to draw a clear distinction in principle between the two kinds of activity. Thus, an expedition to a café of the kind which occurred here seems to us to be at least arguably part of each member of the family's recreation time intended to be enjoyed by them and such that publicity of it is intrusive and such as adversely to affect such activities in the future.

56. We do not share the predisposition identified by the judge . . . that routine acts such as a visit to a shop or a ride on a bus should not attract any reasonable expectation of privacy. All depends upon the circumstances. The position of an adult may be very different from that of a child. In this appeal we are concerned only with the question whether David, as a small child, had a reasonable expectation of privacy, not with the question whether his parents would have had such an expectation. Moreover, we are concerned with the context of this case, which was not for example a single photograph taken of David which was for some reason subsequently published.

57. It seems to us that, subject to the facts of the particular case, the law should indeed protect children from intrusive media attention, at any rate to the extent of holding that a child has a reasonable expectation that he or she will not be targeted in order to obtain photographs in a public place for publication which the person who took or procured the taking of the photographs knew would be objected to on behalf of the child. That is the context in which the photographs of David were taken.

. . .

60. The context of *Von Hannover* was . . . different from this but we have little doubt that, if the assumed facts of this case were to be considered by the ECtHR, the Court would hold that David had a reasonable expectation of privacy and it seems to us to be more likely than not that, on the assumed facts, it would hold that the article 8/10 balance would come down in favour of David. We would add that there is nothing in the Strasbourg cases since *Von Hannover* which in our opinion leads to any other conclusion: see e.g. *Reklos and Davourlis* v *Greece*, petition no 1234/05, 6 September 2007.

61. In these circumstances, the judge was in our judgment wrong to strike out David's claim on the ground that he had no arguable case that he had a reasonable expectation of privacy. Understandably, the judge did not consider whether, if article 8 was engaged, David had an arguable case that the balance should be struck in his favour. In our opinion David has an arguable case on both points and his parents should be permitted to take his claim to trial on his behalf.

Questions for discussion

1. Can the law established in *Von Hannover* v *Germany (No 1)* and *Von Hannover* v *Germany (No 2)* be reconciled with domestic decisions?
2. Do you agree that photographs have the potential to be more invasive than verbal or written descriptions of private information?

(d) Factors going against a reasonable expectation of privacy: limiting factors

Even where information is found to be confidential or private on the basis of its nature or the manner in which it is kept or obtained, its publication may be nevertheless held not to engage article 8. This will be the case where the person does not have a *reasonable* expectation of privacy in relation to the information because: (1) consent has been given to the publication of the information; (2) the claimant is a public figure and the private information is relevant to that role; (3) the claimant has previously courted publicity in relation to that private information; (4) the information is already in the public domain; or (5) the information is trivial. In considering such 'limiting factors' it is important to bear in mind Lord Nicholls' warning in *Campbell* v *MGN Ltd* regarding factors that might 'more properly be considered at the later stage of proportionality'[134] rather than at the threshold stage of whether the claimant has a reasonable expectation of privacy.

(i) Consent

A claimant will not have a reasonable expectation of privacy where he or she has consented to the publication of the information in question.[135] Consent can be express or implied and may be given in writing, orally, or by conduct; however, mere acquiescence will not be sufficient.[136] Furthermore, where media publications are concerned, it will be necessary that consent was given for not only the precise information and form of publication but also the extent of the publication.

(ii) 'Public figure' status of the claimant

The mere fact that a person is a public figure will not, in and of itself, deprive that person of a reasonable expectation of privacy.[137] This is clear from the House of Lords' decision in *Campbell* v *MGN Ltd*, where Naomi Campbell's notoriety did not preclude her from asserting her right to privacy.[138] However, as mentioned above, the attributes of the claimant will be relevant to determining whether he or she has a reasonable expectation of privacy; one such attribute may be the claimant's public figure status. Thus, in the recent case of *Spelman* v *Express Newspapers*, Tugendhat J placed significant weight on the claimant's status as a professional sportsperson in finding that he had no reasonable expectation of privacy in relation to health information (later revealed by the media to be steroid abuse).[139] The important point about this case is that it appears, in order for status to be a relevant factor, that a close nexus must exist between the nature of the claimant's public figure status and the nature of the private information in question. The case is also significant because the claimant was a 17 year old boy as well as the child of a prominent MP.

Extract 11.4.9
***Spelman* v *Express Newspapers* [2012] EWHC 355 (QB)**

66. Mr Dean [for the claimant] submits that the critical attribute of the Claimant is that he is just 17. Ms Michalos [for the defendant] submits that that is less critical than it might be, because he will be 18 in less than a year. And she submits that his critical attribute is that he is a sportsman who has played, and who aspires to play, at national and international level.

---

[134] *Campbell* v *MGN Ltd* [2004] 2 AC 457, 21 (Lord Nicholls). See also *Murray* v *Express Newspapers plc* [2009] ch. 481, 26.

[135] For a thorough analysis of consent, see Warby in *The Law of Privacy and the Media*, 12.05–12.23; Scott in *Carter-Ruck on Libel and Privacy*, 19.74–19.75.

[136] Scott in *Carter-Ruck on Libel and Privacy*, 19.72.

[137] In the early cases that followed the introduction of the HRA, courts were willing to acknowledge that public figures had private lives; however, it also appeared to be accepted that such public figures should have a lesser expectation regarding their privacy: see, e.g., *A* v *B plc and C* [2003] QB 195, 11(xii).

[138] *Campbell* v *MGN Ltd* [2004] AC 457, 57 (per Lord Hoffmann), 120 (per Lord Hope). See also *Von Hannover* v *Germany* (2005) 40 EHRR 1, 72–5; *Von Hannover* v *Germany (No 2)* (2012) 55 EHRR 15, 95 (extracted at 11.4.7).

[139] *Spelman* v *Express Newspapers* [2012] EWHC 355 (QB), 69–71, where it was said that the status of a person as a sportsperson will result in a 'diminution of the reasonable expectation of privacy' in relation to health information.

. . .

67. Children (other than heirs to a throne) rarely appear as public figures in politics. But in sport and the performing arts they appear very frequently. Some athletes win an Olympic Gold Medal or a Tennis Championship while aged 16 or under. Some sports are dominated by competitors under 18. Even in sports where peak performance is reached in a person's 20s or 30s, it is necessary for aspiring performers to start their dedication to the sport as children. Much the same is true in many of the performing arts. Children can be world class performing artists, and performing artists often are children.

. . .

68. The material benefits to those few children who succeed at the highest level can be fabulous. But these benefits may come at a high price. It is a matter of common knowledge that the effort to achieve the highest honours in sport can damage a person's health and family life, and lead to an early death, or even to a life of misery when careers end early and in disappointment. But the price in terms of health and happiness may be paid even by the less successful performers (being the overwhelming majority, of course) without their ever obtaining the material or other significant benefits.

. . .

69. It is to these matters that I understand Mr Morgan to be referring when he speaks of the public interest. But it seems to me that Ms Michalos is right to submit these are matters which are relevant at the earlier stage of the inquiry, namely as to the extent of the Claimant's reasonable expectation of privacy. As Ms Michalos submits, those engaged in sport at the national and international level are subject to many requirements which are not imposed on other members of the public. Matters relating to their health have to be disclosed and monitored, and they may have little if any control over the extent to which such information is disseminated. It is a condition of participating in high level sport that the participant gives up control over many aspects of private life. There is no, or at best a low, expectation of privacy if an issue of health relates to the ability of the person to participate in the very public activity of national and international sport.

. . .

70. The diminution of the reasonable expectation of privacy in the world of participants in public sports and performing arts cannot be confined only to those who achieve the highest levels. They reach the highest level by ascending from the lower levels. The restriction on what might otherwise be a reasonable expectation of privacy may well apply to those who aim for the highest level, even if they do not achieve it, or can no longer expect to achieve it.

. . .

71. What the Claimant describes in his witness statement about the general circumstances of his life is what any informed observer would expect, even though such things are not so often talked about. Before his injury he spent 30 to 40 hours each week in training. This is time he spent in addition to the time devoted to preparing for his school exams. So he had little social life with his contemporaries outside his sport. If he cannot train, he loses both the main interest in his life, and most of his friends at the same time, because they are boys who train as he does.

. . .

72. In my judgment Ms Michalos is clearly right on the relevance of the Claimant being a child. The fact that the Claimant is a child is of limited support for a claim for an expectation of privacy, for both the reasons she gives. He is nearly 18. And even if he were still under 16, as he was when he first played for England, his status as an international player means that discussion of his sporting life, and the effect that it may have upon him, is discussion that contributes to a debate of general interest about a person who is to be regarded as exercising a public function.

Questions for discussion

1. Should the claimant's 'public figure' status be relevant to the threshold test, or should it only be considered in terms of the importance of the speech in question?
2. What limits do you think should be placed on a public figure's reasonable expectation of privacy?

(iii) Prior publicity by the claimant

While the issue of consent will arise relatively infrequently, it is expected that it will more often be the case that a claimant will not have a reasonable expectation of privacy due to the fact that they have engaged in previous public discussion or have courted publicity in relation to the particular area of their private life.[140] Prior to the introduction of the 'new methodology', some courts seemed willing to take the view that deliberately seeking publicity would result in the wholesale deprivation of rights under breach of confidence,[141] even where there was a tenuous link between the subject matter of the prior disclosure and the confidential facts at hand.[142] It is now recognised that this approach is inconsistent with article 8. As noted by Lindsay J in *Douglas v Hello! Ltd*: 'to hold that those who have sought *any* publicity lose all protection would be to repeal article 8's application to very many of those who are likely most to need it.'[143]

Even if a person has given publicity to a particular 'area' of their private life, it does not mean that they will lose their right to privacy in relation to that general area.[144] In *X and Y v Persons Unknown*[145] a married couple obtained an injunction to restrain the publication of facts relating to the state of their marriage. Several media organisations applied to have the injunction discharged, arguing that the claimants had lost any reasonable expectation of privacy due to media attention that they had drawn to their relationship.

Extract 11.4.10
***X and Y v Persons Unknown* [2006] EWHC 2783 (QB)**

EADY J:

24. Mr Spearman suggests that by their own conduct they have exhibited a willingness to forego the privacy to which they would be *prima facie* entitled; that they have, in effect, drawn public attention to their relationship and through interviews and comments made in the public domain offered a running commentary upon it. This is partly a question of fact and partly of evaluation upon the facts established by evidence. A considerable number of newspaper articles has been introduced, with a view to making good Mr Spearman's proposition. They had not been placed before me on the original application.

---

[140] For a detailed discussion, see Scott in *Carter-Ruck on Libel and Privacy*, 19.113–19.130.
[141] See, e.g., *Woodward v Hutchins* [1977] 1 WLR 760. Rather than constituting a 'waiver', this case is best explained on the basis that publication was justified in the public interest in order to 'correct' a false image fostered by the claimant(s): see, e.g., comments by Lindsay LJ in *Douglas v Hello! Ltd* [2003] EWHC 786 (Ch) 225. Even so, *Woodward v Hutchins* has been subject to judicial and academic criticism and should be treated with caution: see Warby in *The Law of Privacy and the Media*, 12.27.
[142] Scott in *Carter-Ruck on Libel and Privacy*, 19.115.
[143] [2003] EWHC 786 (Ch) 225.
[144] See *McKennitt v Ash* [2006] EWCA Civ 1714, 53–5; *X and Y v Persons Unknown* [2006] EWHC 2783 (QB), 65]. Cf. *Douglas v Hello! Ltd* [2003] EWHC 786 (Ch), where Lindsay J said (at 255) 'I would accept that a claimant who has himself publicised a certain area of his private life (for example his sexual proclivities and activity) might well lose the protection otherwise available to him *in that area* or, possibly, even more generally' (emphasis in original).
[145] [2006] EWHC 2783 (QB).

25. It is necessary to note that, by reason of her profession as a model, X is constantly the subject of media attention and enterprising journalists are anxious to find out as much as they can about her to put before their readers – much of which can fairly be categorised as trivial or tittle-tattle. There is no question of it being required to contribute to an ongoing 'public debate' of the kind contemplated in *Von Hannover* v *Germany*, or for the purpose of revealing (say) criminal misconduct or anti-social behaviour.

. . .

27. It is necessary to distinguish in this context between the concept of being in the public eye and that of being a publicity seeker – although inevitably the two will sometimes overlap.

28. In the present context, that distinction can be of some importance. It by no means follows that an individual who is photographed and described in print, and about whom information or speculation is published regarding his or her private life, must have so behaved as to forfeit or waive the entitlement to privacy with regard to (say) intimate personal relationships or the conduct of a private life generally. Close attention may need to be paid as to how such information came into the public domain and as to its limits. Some well known people are prepared to go along with 'lifestyle' pieces which reveal, for example, their likes and dislikes, and how they spend their spare time, without wishing to cross boundaries into personal relationships. Others, on the other hand, will be less fastidious and take the view that any publicity is good publicity, being prepared to reveal any titbit to attract attention to themselves or to make money. There is no hard and fast rule, since the general proposition has to be recognised that even well known people are entitled to some private life: see e.g. the observations in *A* v *B plc* [2003] QB 195 at 208. The court will in every case have to examine the specific evidence and make an evaluation (on which, inevitably, there may be room for differing opinions).

29. There is a significant volume of material in the papers about X. That is clear from the evidence, and Mr Spearman has highlighted those articles which he regards as best making his case. I am quite satisfied, in the light of X's evidence in particular, and the other material before me which I find consistent with it, that X is not a person who willingly sets out for self-promotion to live her private life in the public eye. Yet she is under contractual obligations to those whose products or services she promotes to give interviews from time to time. That is an important part of the context in which the Court has to reach its conclusion.

. . .

35. People often give bland answers in response to enquiries as to how things are going in their lives, which do not constitute a 'waiver' of Convention rights. To take an obvious example, if a journalist asks how a celebrity is and she replies 'Very well, thank you', that can be hardly said to open up her health to journalistic probing or exposure when she subsequently develops a serious illness.

36. Similarly, if someone asks 'How's married life treating you?' and the response is 'Fine', that does not mean that the public is entitled to a ring-side seat when stresses and strains emerge (as happens in most relationships from time to time). It is disingenuous to pretend otherwise. Ordinary polite 'chit chat' of this kind is qualitatively different from volunteering to release private information for public consumption.

37. To give bland responses when things are going well is very different from having to be subjected to an intrusive investigation of the individual pathology of marital breakdown – still less of every tiff, disagreement or quarrel . . . The circumstances of marital breakdown or tension are likely, beneath the surface, to be individual and specific to the people concerned. They will be generally unknowable by others without the revelation of what is in the nature of things private information by one party or the other. Naturally, if there are public rows, or recriminations in the media as sometimes happens, the situation will be rather different. But that is not so here. It is easy to give obvious examples, but in real life most cases would fall somewhere in

between such extremes. Obviously, however, the reasons for a breakdown in a relationship can only be protected if they have remained private.

38. This reasoning suggests that a distinction is to be drawn between matters which are naturally accessible to outsiders and those which are known only to the protagonists. So, if the parties are separated and are living at different addresses, it is difficult to see that this bare fact is one as to which there could be a reasonable expectation of privacy. If two people are no longer regarded by acquaintances as an 'item', that fact is a matter of public perception. That is to be distinguished, however, from private incompatibilities or disputes which may have contributed to the breakdown. Accordingly, in most (one can never say 'all') circumstances, if a separation has occurred between two people, it will not be appropriate to cast an injunction so widely that mention of the mere fact of separation itself is prohibited.

. . .

42. It is becoming increasingly common for media defendants to carry out what used to be called a 'cuttings' search in these cases. . . . The object is obviously to demonstrate, or at least give the impression, that the individual concerned has forfeited rights to privacy or confidentiality and become, to all intents and purposes, public property . . .

48. . . . Each situation must be judged according to the circumstances of the case. For example, it should be assessed objectively, and without having to determine the claimant's state of mind, whether it is any longer reasonable for there to be an expectation of privacy in respect of material in the public domain (and that will include material which the claimant has revealed).

. . .

65. Also, even where a claimant has chosen to put personal information into the public domain, it does not necessarily entail that the media is free to publish any other details relating to the same subject-matter. Individuals appear to be permitted some degree of control over how much information is released: *Douglas* v *Hello! Ltd* [2005] EWCA Civ 595; [2005] EMLR 609.

Given the fact specific nature of the analysis,[146] the decisions have varied as to the degree to which the private facts in question need to coincide with those that have been given prior publicity by the claimant.[147] Some cases have found that there need not be a direct correlation. In *Theakston* v *MGN Ltd*[148] (discussed in Section 11.4(c)(i) above), for example, Ouseley J was willing to accept the argument that Jamie Theakston had lost his right to complain about publication of the fact that he visited a Mayfair brothel because he had, in the past, willingly discussed intimate aspects of his sex life and personal relationships with the media, and had not previously objected to others publicly discussing such matters. This prior publicity, however, did not undermine his right to privacy in relation to the details of the activities that took place or the accompanying photographs.

A similar, although much less liberal, approach was adopted in *A* v *B*.[149] In that case, A sought an injunction to prevent the publication in a magazine of matters relating to his drug addiction, including specific facts about his drug taking and his behaviour at the time. Counsel for the media defendants sought to argue that the claimant did not have a reasonable expectation of privacy due to the fact that he had previously spoken publicly about his battle with drugs.

---

[146] *X and Y* v *Persons Unknown* [2006] EWHC 2783 (QB), 28, 48.
[147] See, e.g., discussion by Scott in *Carter-Ruck on Libel and Privacy*, [19.117]–[19.129].
[148] [2002] EWHC 137 (QB).
[149] [2005] EWHC 1651 (QB).

Extract 11.4.11
A v *B* [2005] EWHC 1651 (QB)

EADY J:

16. An important consideration when assessing the background of this case is that the Claimant has himself made public through the media a great deal of information that might usually be considered as falling within the protection afforded to private or personal information, including matters concerning B and the child of the marriage. Mr Caldecott [counsel for the media defendants] submits that this conduct is highly material to the question of whether the Claimant has a reasonable expectation of privacy in relation to any proposed publication touching upon the subject-matter in respect of which he has already revealed such information . . .

17. It was in this context that Mr Spearman [counsel for the claimant] drew my attention to two principles which seem to have emerged in the recent authorities:

i)   In the context of personal information . . . the fact that something has been published does not necessarily mean that further revelation cannot itself infringe the claimant's right to protect his privacy . . .
ii)   Where it is the claimant who has chosen to put personal information into the public domain, even though it may be such as to attract *prima facie* the protection of the law, it does not necessarily follow that it is open season for the media to publish any other information pertaining to the same subject-matter: see e.g. *Douglas* v *Hello!* [2005] EWCA Civ 595. Individuals are permitted some degree of control over how much they choose to reveal.

Those are important matters which I need to bear in mind.

. . .

21. Mr Caldecott . . . argued that the Claimant's own intimate revelations should be taken into account in determining whether it was reasonable for him to expect information of the relevant kind *still* to be protected . . .

23. It is consistent with European jurisprudence and with more recent decisions within this jurisdiction, such as *Douglas* v *Hello! Ltd* (cited above), to take into account the voluntary revelations on a case by case basis in determining whether any particular information is such that the claimant can any longer *reasonably* expect to keep it private. This question is likely to involve considerations such as whether, for example, the particular piece of information has itself already been published, whether similar instances of behaviour have already been out in the public domain, whether the claimant has made allegations involving other persons and, in particular, their personal lives so that it would be reasonable for such other persons to give another side of the story.

. . .

28. In the light of these statements, Mr Caldecott submits . . . [that] in identifying the scope of material within the public domain, once . . . a claimant has chosen to lift the veil on his personal affairs, the test will be 'zonal'; that is to say, the Court's characterisation of what is truly in the public domain will not be tied specifically to the details revealed in the past but rather focus upon the general area or zone of the claimant's personal life (e.g. drug addiction) which he has chosen to expose. Both these considerations are germane to the present case.

29. It so happens that A too, like Miss Campbell [in *Campbell* v *MGN Ltd*], has revealed information through press interviews about his drug addiction and his experiences in connection with that problem. One of the categories of information in respect of which he seeks to impose restraint upon the Defendants concerns drug-related incidents in the past similar to those about which he chose to make revelations. Mr Caldecott was prepared to concede, in principle, that a drug addict, or former addict, who has chosen to speak about his past experiences is not necessarily precluded thereafter, on a once for all basis, from seeking protection in respect of other experiences. Suppose he had chosen to speak about his addiction and the unpleasant

experiences he had suffered in the past, and recounted how he had overcome his addiction. If he were later to lapse, it would not necessarily follow that his new health problems would also automatically be open to media intrusion. On those hypothetical facts, his revelations would have related to a particular period in his life and would thus not cover the later lapse; nor, for that matter, would there be any question, on the facts I have posited, of the public being in any way misled by the information he had supplied.

30. Nevertheless, Mr Caldecott argues that on the facts of the present case the categories of information which his clients wish to be free to publish fall squarely within the area of A's earlier revelations; they are merely 'more of the same'. Moreover, if the Court were to prevent publication of the new information, notwithstanding the revelations on the earlier occasions, this would involve the application of 'altogether too fine a toothcomb'. All these factors are relevant, submits Mr Caldecott, at the threshold stage of determining to what extent there still remains a reasonable expectation on the Claimant's part of concealing information of this kind.

31. One has to recognise in this context that it is inherent in any communication of personal information to the public through the media that it may invite discussion. It would thus be unrealistic to confine future coverage to the precise details in the original revelations. People might wish to debate, for example, whether the revelations were accurate or whether they were so selective as to be misleading. It would be difficult to envisage circumstances in which this could be prevented on grounds of privacy.

. . .

37. In the letter of 14th June 2005, the same day on which his witness statement was signed, the Claimant's solicitors sent a letter marked 'extremely urgent' to the publishers' solicitors, in which they identified a list of concerns as to information which the Defendants might be about to publish. . . . Mr Caldecott addressed each of these in turn:

i) *The Claimant's 'frequent disappearances'*: The Claimant spoke extensively in earlier articles about his drug taking, where it took place, and consequent absences from his family. He also addressed the impact of these disappearances on them. Information was supplied about attendances for treatment, the identity of those treating him, and how he responded to it. Mr Caldecott made the following submissions:
   a) Drug taking in a social context could not sensibly be regarded as being personal or confidential information or as falling within the notion of marital confidence.
   b) The Claimant had already chosen to speak publicly about the impact of his drug related problems on his marriage.
   c) Information the Defendants wished to cover in the course of the article belonged to the same period of time about which the Claimant had apparently chosen to speak freely.
   d) The Claimant's position was to be contrasted to that adopted by Princess Caroline of Monaco (the subject of a recent case in the European Court of Human Rights: *Von Hannover* v *Germany* (2005) 40 EHRR 1) and by Mr and Mrs Michael Douglas, who had striven to keep the subject-matter of the relevant articles private. He could not thus expect reasonably to maintain the same degree of protection which the law would otherwise afford.

ii) *The details of a particular 'drug binge' in a specific location*: For the Defendants it was argued that this was not, as such, about the Claimant's addiction but about a 'specific and rather disgraceful episode of drug-taking'. It was merely a particular instance of his behaviour about which the Claimant had spoken in general terms.

iii) *'Details of paranoid fantasies' in particular locations*: The Defendants did wish to publish the fact that the Claimant had paranoid fantasies, but without any description of the fantasies themselves. Since the Claimant has publicly admitted large scale drug abuse, it would hardly come as a surprise to readers that he would be likely to suffer from such fantasies. It was accepted in argument, without any formal concession, that descriptions of his particular fantasies might be too intrusive.

iv) *The 'first relapse during the marriage' on a specific trip*: Reference was made to the *Evening Standard* article, in the light of which it was submitted that the Claimant could no longer have a reasonable expectation of privacy in relation to any similar 'chapter of drug-taking in the same historic period'.

v) *The allegation that the Claimant 'freebased and disappeared for several days at a time in different cities using [a pseudonym]' and visited a crack den*: The Defendants resist any restriction on a similar basis; namely, the information was confined to the same historic period and, furthermore, 'crack' is not so qualitatively different from cocaine as to be still covered by a reasonable expectation of privacy.

. . .

vii) *A promise made to his wife that he would 'stay clean' during his marriage*: The Defendants submit that this cannot be the subject of protection in the light of the fact that he had himself referred to private arrangements and promises made to his wife in connection with drug taking in the course of the earlier article. This could be categorised simply as 'more of the same'.

. . .

viii) *Certain problems the Claimant had with his trustees and to the use of his wife's funds*: The Defendants made clear there was no intention to refer to the trustees in the article; moreover, it was submitted that there could be no objection to B referring in the article to the Claimant having used some of her money. He himself had already chosen in one of the earlier articles to go into some detail as to his personal wealth.

. . .

x) *The subject of ancillary relief in the current matrimonial proceedings*: The Defendants will not be referring to the merits of the dispute but wish to reserve the right to identify in general terms the nature of the relief sought.

xi) *An allegation relating to the seizure of the Claimant's computer system*: This is said to be in the public domain, and the Defendants accordingly reserve their right to refer to it.

[Eady J held that the claimant had failed to establish that he had a reasonable expectation of privacy in relation to the relevant facts and refused to grant an interim injunction.]

In other cases, courts have insisted on greater correspondence between the prior disclosure and the specific facts in question. In *HRH Prince of Wales v Associated Newspapers Ltd*,[150] for example, an argument was made that the Prince of Wales did not have a reasonable expectation of privacy in relation to a journal recording his personal account of an official trip he took to Hong Kong due to the fact that he had 'courted public attention and [had] done so for views of the same or a similar kind to those contained in the Hong Kong journal'.[151] This argument was rejected by Blackburne J.

Extract 11.4.12
HRH Prince of Wales v Associated Newspapers Ltd **[2006] EWHC 522 (Ch)**

BLACKBURNE J:

106. The claimant, [according to counsel for the defendant], has made no secret of his views of the Chinese Government, his boycotting (as the defendant contends it to have been) of the 1999 Chinese Embassy banquet, his reception of the Dalai Lama, and his views on politicians as publicised in Mr Dimbleby's biography and on other matters of a political nature. Not only, said [counsel for the defendant], has the claimant never before brought proceedings or even complained to any newspaper on those occasions when his otherwise secret communications

---

[150] [2006] EWHC 522 (Ch).
[151] Ibid., 106.

with ministers have been leaked to the press but, according to the evidence of Mr Richard Kay, the Daily Mail's Royal Correspondent for seventeen years until 2003 and currently the Diary Editor of that newspaper, he has on at least one occasion, in September 2002, expressly authorised disclosure of an otherwise secret communication, namely a letter said to have been sent by the claimant to the then Lord Chancellor decrying the litigation culture in this country. As a result, the claimant has, it was submitted, 'opened up to legitimate public scrutiny' this 'zone' of his life and, having made these matters 'public property', cannot now claim a reasonable expectation of privacy in respect of the contents of a journal which covers similar matters.

. . .

115. In particular, I dissent from the view that, by speaking out publicly both in speeches and in published articles on issues which in the widest sense are political, the claimant has somehow forfeited any reasonable expectation of privacy in respect of such matters when committed to a handwritten journal not intended by the claimant to be open to public scrutiny. Were it otherwise no politician could ever have any reasonable expectation of privacy in a private diary in which he expresses political views. In this respect there is, to my mind, a world of difference between this case and the situation discussed in *A* v *B* [2005] EWHC 1651; [2005] EMLR 36 where by going public on some aspects of his private life – in that case it was the claimant's drug-taking – a person may no longer reasonably expect to maintain privacy, whatever his personal wishes, in respect of related matters. Whether in any case this is so and what in such circumstances the 'zone' is of the person's life that is thereby opened up to legitimate public scrutiny – matters which were discussed in *A* v *B* (at paragraph 28) – must turn on the particular facts of the case. This is not such a case.

An argument as to prior publicity was similarly rejected in *McKennitt* v *Ash*. The defendant in that case, Ash, sought to argue that 'once a person had revealed or discussed some information falling within a particular "zone" of their lives they had a greatly reduced expectation of privacy in relation to any other information that fell within that zone'.[152] She relied upon a number of articles where McKennitt had discussed the death of her fiancé and the water safety programme set up in his honour as justification for disclosing more personal information regarding McKennitt's grief and other aspects of her health. The trial judge, Eady J was quick to reject this argument; he said, 'there is in this context a significant difference between choosing to reveal aspects of private life with which one feels "comfortable" and yielding up to public scrutiny every detail of personal life, feelings, thoughts and foibles of character'.[153] The Court of Appeal agreed: 'with respect, the Judge seems to me to have been completely right. If information is my private property, it is for me to decide how much of it should be published. The "zone" argument completely undermines that reasonable expectation of privacy'.[154] Subsequence cases have interpreted *McKennitt* v *Ash* as an outright rejection of the zone argument.[155]

Questions for discussion

1. Where a person has given publicity to their private life, should they lose their right to privacy and, if so, to what extent?
2. Do you agree with the rejection of the 'zone' argument? Why/why not?

---

[152] *McKennitt* v *Ash* [2006] EWCA Civ 1714, 53.
[153] *McKennitt* v *Ash* [2005] EWHC 3003 (QB), 79.
[154] *McKennitt* v *Ash* [2006] EWCA Civ 1714, 55.
[155] *KGM* v *News Group Newspapers* [2010] EWHC 3145 (QB), 38; *Ferdinand* v *MGN Ltd* [2011] EWHC 2454 (QB), 56.

(iv) Public domain

In the context of traditional breach of confidence, information which is in the 'public domain' cannot be the subject of an obligation of confidence.[156] According to Lord Goff in *Spycatcher*, the public domain principle will apply where the information 'is so generally accessible that, in all the circumstances, it cannot be regarded as confidential'.[157] Whether this is the case is a matter of degree and will depend on the nature of the information at issue.[158] Confidentiality, however, will only be lost where the information is widely known as opposed to merely accessible.[159]

The public domain principle also applies to claims under misuse of private information, albeit in modified form.[160] Given the different nature of the interests protected by the action – privacy rather than confidentiality – the focus is much more on whether the repeated publication of information already in the public domain would cause the claimant further harm rather than whether the information has lost its secrecy.[161] This distinction between confidential information and private information was clearly made in the case of *Green Corns Ltd* v *Claverley Group*.[162] In that case, the claimant sought to restrain the publication of the addresses of housing for troubled youths. The defendant newspapers argued that the information was already in the public domain.

Extract 11.4.13
Green Corns Ltd v Claverley Group [2005] EWHC 958 (QB)

TUGENDHAT J:

72. Mr Caldecott QC's submissions have . . . been directed to public knowledge of the addresses . . . What it amounts to is that persons living in properties adjacent to the houses acquired by the applicant have learnt that the applicant is the new owner, and have sometimes also learnt in general terms about the purpose for which the houses have been bought and the sort of problems which may be suffered by children for whom the applicant cares.

. . .

76. Mr Caldecott QC relies on the passage from the judgment of Lord Goff in *Spycatcher* [1990] 1 AC 109 at p 282. He identified as one of the limiting principles of the law of confidentiality (as then understood) that:

> . . . once it (the information) has entered what is usually called the public domain (which means no more than that the information in question is so generally accessible that, in all the circumstances, it cannot be regarded as confidential) then, as a general rule, the principle of confidentiality can have no application to it.

. . .

---

[156] *Attorney General* v *Guardian Newspapers (No 2)* [1990] 1 AC 109, 282.
[157] Ibid., 282.
[158] *Douglas* v *Hello! Ltd* [2008] 1 AC 1, 48–9.
[159] *Stephens* v *Avery* [1988] Ch 449, 454–5.
[160] *Douglas* v *Hello!* [2006] QB 125, 105 (per Lord Phillips MR). Note, s 12(4) of the HRA also requires that the court 'have particular regard to . . . (a) the extent to which (i) the material has, or is about to, become available to the public' where the proceedings relate to 'journalistic, literary or artistic material'.
[161] *Green Corns Ltd* v *CLA Verley Group Ltd* [2005] EWHC 958 (QB), 69–81; *WB* v *H Bauer Publishing Ltd* [2002] EMLR 8; *CTB* v *News Group Newspapers Ltd* [2011] EWHC 1326 (QB). It should be noted that even prior to the introduction of the Human Rights Act and the recognition of misuse of private information as a stand-alone cause of action, courts were of the view that the degree of disclosure required to defeat a breach of confidence action was greater for private information than for commercial or trade secrets: see, e.g., *Attorney General* v *Guardian Newspapers (No 2)* [1990] 1 AC 109, 260 (per Lord Keith) and 287 (per Lord Goff).
[162] [2005] EWHC 958 (QB).

77. Mr Spearman QC submits that that must be read in context. The context was a claim for confidentiality in government secrets, which had already been published abroad. It made no sense to prevent publication in the UK, to those directly affected, when the information was already known to those who lived or travelled abroad. Lord Keith was careful to point to the different considerations that might apply where the information related to sensitive personal information, such as marital secrets. At p 260 he said that even where there were widespread publication abroad of such information, the subject could reasonably claim that publication of the same material at home would bring it to the attention of people otherwise unlikely to learn of it who were more closely interested in the subject's activities than the overseas readers . . .

78. There will be cases where personal information about a person (usually a celebrity) has been so widely published that a restraint upon repetition will serve no purpose, and an injunction will be refused on that account. It may be less likely that that will be so when the subject is not a celebrity. But in any event, it is not possible in a case about personal information simply to apply Lord Goff's test of whether the information is generally accessible, and to conclude that, if it is, then that is the end of the matter . . .

79. . . . In *WB* v *H Bauer Publishing Ltd* [2002] EMLR 8 at [25]–[26] Eady J referred to the words of Lord Keith in *Spycatcher* and to *R* v *Broadcasting Complaints Commission, ex parte Granada TV* [1995] EMLR 163. He said:

> It may be more difficult to establish that confidentiality has gone for all purposes, in the context of personal information, by virtue of its having come to the attention of certain readers or categories of readers.

80. In *Re X and Y (Children)* [2004] EMLR 607 paras 49, 66, 88–9, Munby J accepted submissions that that the repetition of information that has been placed in the public domain can be damaging to a child, and information in the public domain may be obscure so that republication could have a very significant effect, and items of information put separately into the public domain may, when republished together bring a story into the public domain in an entirely new way. He declined to include a public domain proviso in an order he granted and expressly decided to restrain republication of material already in the public domain, to give effect to compelling Art 8 rights of children.

81. I conclude that the information as to the addresses which is sought to be restrained is not in the public domain to the extent, or in the sense, that republication could have no significant effect, or that the information is not eligible for protection at all. The information as to the addresses linked with information as to the business of the applicant and thus to the likely disabilities and other characteristics of the occupants of the addresses brings together matters which together amount to new information which was previously accessible to the public only in a limited and theoretical sense. Publication or republication risks causing serious harm to the children and carers who occupy, or are to occupy, the addresses concerned. The extent to which the material has or is about to become available to the public is not, on the evidence of this case, a reason for withholding the injunction sought.

The court in *CTB* v *News Group Newspapers Ltd* was similarly unpersuaded that an interim injunction should be discharged on the basis that the information in question had entered the public domain. The claimant, Ryan Giggs, had conducted an extra-marital affair with former Big Brother contestant Imogen Thomas. An interim injunction was granted by Eady J against Thomas and News Group Newspapers to prevent the publication of the identity of Giggs in connection with the relationship. The identity of Giggs as the relevant person, however, had been widely circulated on the Internet, including on Twitter. News Group Newspapers sought to have the terms of the initial injunction varied to remove Giggs' anonymity.

Extract 11.4.14
CTB v News Group Newspapers Ltd [2011] EWHC 1326 (QB)

EADY J:

14. I turn next to Mr Spearman's application to vary the injunction and, in particular, so as to remove the anonymity of the Claimant. He says that many tens of thousands of people can, if they are sufficiently interested, find out who the Claimant is by making appropriate searches on the Internet, although it is fair to say that there was speculation about a number of possible candidates. Mr Spearman argues, as did Mr Kelvin MacKenzie in the radio programme of which I was supplied with a transcript, that in effect privacy injunctions (and no doubt other forms of injunction also) have ceased to serve any useful purpose in the age of the Internet. Not only can information be put out on various networks from within this jurisdiction, but it can obviously be done also by anyone who wishes in other jurisdictions.

15. Parliament may at some stage wish to change the law and make specific provision in the light of these developments, but in the meantime the courts are obliged to apply the law as it currently stands. The logical conclusion of Mr Spearman's argument is, perhaps, that the court should always refuse injunctive relief to applicants on the basis that, to a greater or lesser extent, the defendants or others may simply ignore its orders. It would not be right, however, for courts to ignore their responsibilities and to refuse relief in circumstances where it is properly sought . . .

18. Reference was made by Mr Spearman to the refusal of injunctive relief in yet another of his client's cases: *Mosley* v *News Group Newspapers Ltd* [2008] EWHC 687 (QB). It was there said:

> The court should guard against slipping into playing the role of King Canute. Even though an order may be desirable for the protection of privacy, and may be made in accordance with the principles currently being applied by the courts, there may come a point where it would simply serve no useful purpose and would merely be characterised, in the traditional terminology, as a *brutum fulmen*. It is inappropriate for the court to make vain gestures.

The circumstances here are rather different. In *Mosley*, I took the view that there was no point in granting an injunction because, even before the application was made, several hundred thousand people had seen the intimate video footage which NGN had put on line – conduct that was recently characterised by the European Court of Human Rights as a 'flagrant and unjustified intrusion': *Mosley* v *UK* (App. No. 48009/08), 10 May 2011 at [104]. In a real sense, therefore, it could be said that there was nothing left for the court to protect by an injunction.

19. Here, the Internet allegations prayed in aid by Mr Spearman took place after the order was made. Different policy considerations come into play when the court is invited to abandon the protection it has given a litigant on the basis of widespread attempts to render it ineffective. Furthermore, unlike the *Mosley* case, there is no doubt other information that Ms Thomas could yet publish, quite apart from this Claimant's identity, which is not yet in the public domain. The injunction thus continues to serve a useful purpose, from the Claimant's point of view, for that reason alone, since she is amenable to the jurisdiction of the court. Otherwise, he would not seek to maintain it.

20. Mr Spearman's application is therefore quite narrow. He seeks only to vary the injunction so as to permit the Claimant to be identified. The basis of this argument appears to be closely related to one of the 'limiting principles' explained by Lord Goff in *Att-Gen* v *Guardian Newspapers (No 2)* [1990] 1 AC 109, 282B-F, to the effect that the principle of confidentiality only applies to information to the extent that it is confidential . . . The law thus recognises that a time may come, at least in relation to state secrets or commercial confidentiality, when the information in question has become so widely available that there is really nothing left for the law to protect . . .

21. Yet even at the time of the *Spycatcher* litigation in the House of Lords, over 20 years ago, a distinction was being already flagged up between confidential information in the context of state or commercial secrets, on the one hand, and personal information on the other: *ibid.* at 260E-H and 287C-D.

22. Whereas it may be possible to a draw a bright line boundary as to commercial secrets between being public and private, that is not so easy, nor even generally appropriate, when it comes to publications infringing a person's rights under Article 8 of the European Convention on Human Rights and Fundamental Freedoms. As was explained in *Campbell* v *MGN Ltd* [2004] 2 AC 457, the law nowadays is required to protect information in respect of which there is a *reasonable* expectation of privacy and for so long as that position remains. What is 'reasonable' depends on the circumstances. It is a concept that is not susceptible in itself to bright line boundaries.

23. It is important always to remember that the modern law of privacy is not concerned solely with information or 'secrets': it is also concerned importantly with *intrusion*. That is one reason why it can be important to distinguish between the way the law approaches public domain arguments in relation to commercial or state secrets, for example, and that which is appropriate to personal information . . .

24. It is fairly obvious that wall-to-wall excoriation in national newspapers, whether tabloid or 'broadsheet', is likely to be significantly more intrusive and distressing for those concerned than the availability of information on the Internet or in foreign journals to those, however many, who take the trouble to look it up. Moreover, with each exposure of personal information or allegations, whether by way of visual images or verbally, there is a new intrusion and occasion for distress or embarrassment. Mr Tomlinson argues accordingly that 'the dam has not burst'. For so long as the court is in a position to prevent *some* of that intrusion and distress, depending upon the individual circumstances, it may be appropriate to maintain that degree of protection. The analogy with King Canute to some extent, therefore, breaks down.

25. It may be thought that the wish of NGN to publish more about this 'story', with a view to selling newspapers and perhaps achieving other commercial advantages, demonstrates that coverage has not yet reached saturation point. Had it done so, the story would no longer retain any interest. This factor tends, therefore, to confirm my impression that the court's attempts to protect the Claimant and his family have not yet become wholly futile.

26. In these circumstances, it seems to me that the right question for me to ask, in the light of *JIH* v *News Group Newspapers Ltd* [2011] 2 All ER 324 and *Re Guardian News and Media Ltd* [2010] UKSC 1, is whether there is a solid reason why the Claimant's identity should be generally revealed in the national media, such as to outweigh the legitimate interests of himself and his family in maintaining anonymity. The answer is as yet in the negative. They would be engulfed in a cruel and destructive media frenzy. Sadly, that may become unavoidable in the society in which we now live but, for the moment, in so far as I am being asked to sanction it, I decline to do so. On the other side, as I recorded in my judgment on 16 May, it has not been suggested that there is *any* legitimate public interest in publishing the story.

. . .

28. These are my reasons for rejecting the Defendant's application to vary the injunction.

Extract 11.4.15
***CTB* v *News Group Newspapers Ltd* [2011] EWHC 1334 (QB)**

TUGENDHAT J:

1. At about 1430 this afternoon Eady refused NGN's application to remove the anonymity he had granted to the claimant on 20 April. He said at para 23 ([2011] EWHC 1326 (QB)) that 'It is important always to remember that the modern law of privacy is not concerned solely with secrets: it is also concerned importantly with intrusion.' Intrusion in this sense includes harassment.

2. Very shortly afterwards a name was mentioned by Mr Hemming MP in the House of Commons in the course of a question which was interrupted by the Speaker. On that basis NGN asked me to hear a further application shortly after 5pm for the anonymity of the claimant to be removed. As the public now know, anyone who wanted to find out the name of the claimant could have learnt it many days ago. The reason is that it is has been repeated thousands of times on the internet. NGN now want to join in.

3. It is obvious that if the purpose of this injunction were to preserve a secret, it would have failed in its purpose. But in so far as its purpose is to prevent intrusion or harassment, it has not failed. The fact that tens of thousands of people have named the claimant on the internet confirms that the claimant and his family need protection from intrusion into their private and family life. The fact that a question has been asked in Parliament seems to me to increase, and not to diminish the strength of his case that he and his family need that protection. The order has not protected the claimant and his family from taunting on the internet. It is still effective to protect them from taunting and other intrusion and harassment in the print media.

Questions for discussion

1. Once private information has entered the public domain (especially on the Internet), do you see any point in the courts issuing an injunction to try to stop its further distribution?
2. What distinction did the Court in *CTB* v *News Group Newspapers Ltd* draw between the facts in that case and the situation in *Mosley* v *News Group Newspapers Ltd*? Do you agree?
3. What do the decisions in *CTB* v *News Group Newspapers Ltd* indicate about the nature of the privacy interests at stake?

Given the degree of intrusion said to be occasioned by the publication of a photograph depicting an aspect of a claimant's private life (see above Section 11.4(c)(iii)), there will be a reluctance to find that a photograph has entered the public domain. This will be the case following even widespread publication of the photograph or of a description of the private information contained therein.[163] This was explained by Lord Phillips in *Douglas* v *Hello!*[164]

Extract 11.4.16
***Douglas* v *Hello!* [2006] QB 125**

LORD PHILLIPS MR:

105. In general, however, once information is in the public domain, it will no longer be confidential or entitled to the protection of the law of confidence, though this may not always be true: see *Gilbert* v *Star Newspaper Company Limited* (1894) 51 TLR 4 and *Creation Records Limited* v *News Group Newspapers Ltd* [1997] EMLR 444 at p 456. The same may generally be true of private information of a personal nature. Once intimate personal information about a celebrity's private life has been widely published it may serve no useful purpose to prohibit further publication. The same will not necessarily be true of photographs. Insofar as a photograph does more than convey information and intrudes on privacy by enabling the viewer to focus on intimate personal detail, there will be a fresh intrusion of privacy when each additional viewer sees the photograph and even when one who has seen a previous publication of the photograph, is confronted by a

---

[163] See *D* v *L* [2003] EWCA Civ 1169, 23; *Campbell* v *MGN* [2004] 2 AC 457, 72.
[164] See also comments by Lord Nicholls in *Douglas* v *Hello! [No 3]* [2008] 1 AC 1, 72.

fresh publication of it. To take an example, if a film star were photographed, with the aid of a telephoto lens, lying naked by her private swimming pool, we question whether widespread publication of the photograph by a popular newspaper would provide a defence to a legal challenge to repeated publication on the ground that the information was in the public domain. There is thus a further important potential distinction between the law relating to private information and that relating to other types of confidential information.

106. Nor is it right to treat a photograph simply as a means of conveying factual information. A photograph can certainly capture every detail of a momentary event in a way which words cannot, but a photograph can do more than that. A personal photograph can portray, not necessarily accurately, the personality and the mood of the subject of the photograph. It is quite wrong to suppose that a person who authorises publication of selected personal photographs taken on a private occasion, will not reasonably feel distress at the publication of unauthorised photographs taken on the same occasion.

Even so, in *Mosley* v *News Group Newspapers Ltd*[165] (referred to in *CTB* v *News Group Newspaper Ltd*, above at Extract 11.4.14), Eady J was unwilling to grant an interim injunction to restrain the continued publication of footage of the claimant engaged in intimate sexual activity on the basis that the material was already in the public domain. Thus, his Honour found:

> In the circumstances now prevailing, as disclosed in the evidence before me, I have come to the conclusion that the material is so widely accessible that an order in the terms sought would make very little practical difference. One may express this conclusion either by saying that Mr Mosley no longer has any reasonable expectation of privacy in respect of this now widely familiar material or that, even if he has, it has entered the public domain to the extent that there is, in practical terms, no longer anything which the law can protect. The dam has effectively burst. I have, with some reluctance, come to the conclusion that although this material is intrusive and demeaning, and despite the fact that there is no legitimate public interest in its further publication, the granting of an order against this Respondent at the present juncture would merely be a futile gesture. Anyone who wishes to access the footage can easily do so, and there is no point in barring the *News of the World* from showing what is already available.[166]

This is an example of where even the most intimate information presented in a particularly invasive form may lose protection on the basis that it is so widely available that the claimant has lost any reasonable expectation of privacy.

(v) Trivial information

Lord Goff in *Spycatcher* held that a duty of confidence 'applies neither to useless information, nor to trivia'.[167] The principle is also applicable to misuse of private information cases – albeit, like the public domain principle discussed above, in a slightly adapted form. In most instances trivial information will not be regarded as private.[168] However, this will not always be the case.[169] Depending on the circumstance, even objectively trivial or anodyne information may attract a reasonable expectation of privacy – for example, where photographs are published of a child being pushed along in a stroller on a public street.[170]

---

[165] [2008] EWHC 687 (QB).
[166] *Mosley* v *News Group Newspapers Ltd* [2008] EWHC 687 (QB), 36.
[167] *Attorney General* v *Guardian Newspapers Ltd (No 2)* [1990] 1 AC 109, 282.
[168] See, e.g., *John* v *Express Newspapers* [2006] EWHC 1611 (QB).
[169] *McKennitt* v *Ash* [2005] EWHC 3003 (QB), 58.
[170] See, e.g., *Murray* v *Express Newspapers plc* [2009] Ch 481 (extracted at 11.4.8).

Conversely, the disclosure of certain types of information conventionally thought of as 'private' – such as medical information – may not be serious enough to warrant protection. The deciding factor appears to be whether the publication of the information would cause the victim harm. Thus, as pointed out by Lady Hale in *Campbell*:

> Not every statement about a person's health will carry the badge of confidentiality or risk doing harm to that person's physical or moral integrity. The privacy interest in the fact that a public figure has a cold or a broken leg is unlikely to be strong enough to justify restricting the press's freedom to report it. What harm could it possibly do?[171]

It should also be noted that, like the other limiting factors, the trivial nature of the information may militate against a finding that the claimant had a reasonable expectation of privacy or it may be relevant to the balancing exercise at the second stage.[172]

(e) Ultimate balancing test

Once it is established that the claimant has a reasonable expectation of privacy, the Court must proceed to the second stage – the 'ultimate balancing test'. Following *Campbell* v *MGN Ltd*, the appropriate approach was set out in *Re S (A Child)*:

> First, neither article has *as such* precedence over the other. Secondly, where the values under the two articles are in conflict, an intense focus on the comparative importance of the specific rights being claimed in the individual case is necessary. Thirdly, the justifications for interfering with or restricting each right must be taken into account. Finally, the proportionality test must be applied to each.[173]

In examining proportionality, the court must not deal in generalities;[174] rather, the court must undertake an 'intense focus' on the particular circumstances of the individual case.[175] However, given the nature of the analysis, it has been recognised that it is 'a process which may well lead different people to different conclusions'.[176]

Before turning to consider the factors relevant to the balancing exercise, it is important to outline the role of section 12(4) of the HRA in ensuring regard is had to the important principle of freedom of expression.

(i) Section 12(4) of the Human Rights Act

Misuse of private information cases against the media, which invariably affect the right to freedom of expression, will invoke the application of section 12(4) of the HRA (see Extract 1.2.5). Section 12(4) was introduced to ensure that adequate protection was given to the article 10 right to freedom of expression in the context of media speech.[177] It is clear, however, following the decision of Sedley LJ in *Douglas* v *Hello!*, that it does not – as the media had expected – give freedom of expression priority over other Convention rights. Rather, as article 10 is subject to exceptions, including for the 'protection of the . . . rights of others and the protection of information received in confidence', you cannot, in the

---

[171] *Campbell* v *MGN Ltd* [2004] 2 AC 457, 157.
[172] *McKennitt* v *Ash* [2005] EWHC 3003 (QB), 58.
[173] *Re S (A Child)* [2005] 1 AC 593, 17 (emphasis in original).
[174] *A Local Authority* v *W* [2006] 1 FLR 1, 53 (per Sir Mark Potter P).
[175] *Re S (A Child)* [2005] 1 AC 593, 17; *A Local Authority* v *W* [2006] 1 FLR 1, 53 (per Sir Mark Potter P).
[176] *Campbell* v *MGN Ltd* [2004] 2 AC 457, 168 (per Lord Carswell).
[177] See discussion in Fenwick and Phillipson, 125–7.

words of Sedley LJ, 'have particular regard to Article 10 without having equally particular regard at the very least to Article 8'.[178]

Relevant privacy codes referred to in section 12(4)(b) include the Ofcom Broadcasting Code (see 11.7.2) and the Press Complaints Commission Editors' Code of Practice (see Chapter 2). There are two points to note about the significance of such codes. First, compliance or non-compliance with a code will usually be decisive. Thus, a media organisation which 'flouts . . . [a code] is likely in those circumstances to have its claim to an entitlement to freedom of expression trumped by article 10(2) considerations of privacy'.[179] Second, while the text of any privacy code will be relevant, decisions made by those who administer the codes – such as the Press Complaints Commission or Ofcom – will have little, if any, bearing.[180]

(ii) The privacy interest and the degree of intrusion

Weighing in the balance against publication will be the nature of the information and the impact on the claimant of its disclosure. Details about a claimant's sex life and their financial and medical information are, of course, likely to be valued as highly private. Similarly, although not a 'trump card', private information regarding children will receive particularly weighty protection.[181] Thus, in the balancing exercise it is less likely that the scales will come down in favour of the publication with this type of information. Also relevant will be the form in which the information is presented and the level of detail revealed. As discussed above (Section 11.4(c)(iii)), the publication of private information in photographic or audiovisual form is often treated as being especially intrusive. Likewise, delving into intimate details as opposed to bare facts will add greater weight to the privacy interests at stake.[182]

The assessment of the impact of the intrusion will also be affected by the claimant's attitude to the disclosure of the private information in question. A claimant, for example, may have countenanced the disclosure of the same or similar information in the past[183] or may have been even willing to sell or trade such information for profit.[184] In such circumstances, depending on the nature of the information in question, the potential distress caused by disclosure is likely to be significantly weakened.

The privacy interests of third parties may also be relevant. In *CC v AB*, for example, the court took into consideration the interests of the claimant's wife and children, and the impact that publication of the claimant's affair and details of how it was conducted would have on their lives. Consideration was given, in particular, to the fragile mental state of the claimant's wife.[185] This will not be the case, however, where the claimant wants to prevent disclosure *to* such third parties. Moreover, evidence will usually be required for such third party interests to be taken into account. This, where practicable, will require that they 'speak for themselves'.[186]

---

[178] *Douglas v Hello! Ltd* [2001] QB 967, 133.
[179] Ibid., 94. For further discussion of the relevance of the codes, see Warby in *The Law of Privacy and the Media*, 12.138.
[180] *A v B plc and C* [2003] QB 195, 11 (xv).
[181] See, e.g., *Murray v Express Newspapers* [2009] Ch 481; *ETK v News Group Newspapers* [2011] EWCA Civ 439, 19.
[182] See, e.g., *Campbell v MGN Ltd* [2004] 2 AC 457; *Mosley v News Group Newspapers Ltd* [2008] EWHC 1777 (QB); *Terry v Persons Unknown* [2010] EWHC 119 (QB).
[183] *Theakston v MGN Ltd* [2002] EWHC 137 (QB).
[184] *Douglas v Hello! Ltd* [2006] QB 125.
[185] *CC v AB* [2006] EWHC 3083 (QB), 42–7; *ETK v News Group Newspapers* [2011] EWCA Civ 439, 14–22.
[186] *Terry v Persons Unknown* [2010] EWHC 119 (QB), 66.

In *ETK* v *News Group Newspapers Ltd*, the claimant, a male in the entertainment industry, sought an interim injunction to prevent the publication of the fact and details of a sexual relationship he had conducted with X, a colleague. Collins J held that the claimant's article 8 rights were engaged but, when balanced against the newspapers interest in freedom of expression, the latter prevailed. The claimant appealed to the Court of Appeal, arguing that Collins J did not give sufficient weight to the interests of X, or of his wife and children.

Extract 11.4.17
***ETK* v *News Group Newspapers Ltd* [2011] EWCA Civ 439**

WARD LJ:

18. Collins J may not have recognised the rights of the appellant's wife but he certainly did accept that the adverse effect on the children was relevant. Regrettably I cannot agree that the harmful effect on the children cannot tip the balance where the adverse publicity arises because of the way the children's father has behaved. The rights of children are not confined to their Article 8 rights. In *Neulinger* v *Switzerland* (2010) 28 EHRC 706 the Strasbourg court observed that:

> 131. The Convention cannot be interpreted in a vacuum but must be interpreted in harmony with the general principles of international law. Account should be taken . . . 'of any relevant rules of international law applicable in the relations between the parties' and in particular the rules concerning the international protection of human rights . . .

> 135. . . . there is currently a broad consensus – including in international law – in support of the idea that in all decisions concerning children, their best interests must be paramount.

. . .

19. . . . It is clear that the interests of children do not automatically take precedence over the Convention rights of others. It is clear also that, when in a case such as this the court is deciding where the balance lies between the Article 10 rights of the media and the Article 8 rights of those whose privacy would be invaded by publication, it should accord particular weight to the Article 8 rights of any children likely to be affected by the publication, if that would be likely to harm their interests. Where a tangible and objective public interest tends to favour publication, the balance may be difficult to strike. The force of the public interest will be highly material, and the interests of affected children cannot be treated as a trump card.

. . .

22. In my judgment the benefits to be achieved by publication in the interests of free speech are wholly outweighed by the harm that would be done through the interference with the rights to privacy of all those affected, especially where the rights of the children are in play.

[Laws and Moore-Bick LLJ agreed].

(iii) Article 10: freedom of expression

On the other side of the scales – in favour of publication – will be the media's right to freedom of expression. While, at least on a basic reading of article 10, the media has no greater claim to freedom of expression under article 10 than that of a private individual or non-media entity, the special role performed by the media in imparting information to the public in a democratic state has been recognised in both Strasbourg[187] and domestic

---

[187] See, e.g., *Lingens* v *Austria* (1986) 8 EHRR 407, 41; *Jersild* v *Denmark* (1994) 19 EHRR 1, 31; *Goodwin* v *United Kingdom* (1996) 22 EHRR 123, 39; *MGN* v *United Kingdom* [2011] ECHR 919, 141; *Mosley* v *United Kingdom* (2011) 53 EHRR 30, 112–13; *Von Hannover* v *Germany* (2012) 55 EHRR 15, 102; *Axel Springer AG* v *Germany* [2012] EMLR 15, 79–80.

jurisprudence.[188] Thus, the media is said to perform 'the vital role of watchdog' and, while it must not overstep the boundaries for the protection of reputation and privacy, it has a duty to impart to the public 'information and ideas on political issues just as on those in other areas of public interest'.[189] The safeguards provided by article 10, therefore, are of particular importance to media speech and the proportionality of any limitation thereof will be subject to particularly close scrutiny.[190]

The special role accorded to the media may be borne out in misuse of private information cases in a number of ways. First, the media are afforded latitude in determining the degree of intrusion justified and the way in which the story is presented.[191] The House of Lords was unanimous on this in *Campbell* v *MGN Ltd*. As stated by Lord Hope:

> The choice of language used to convey information and ideas, and decisions as to whether or not to accompany the printed word by the use of photographs, are pre-eminently editorial matters with which the court will not interfere. The respondents are also entitled to claim that they should be accorded a reasonable margin of appreciation in taking decisions as to what details needed to be included in the article to give it credibility. This is an essential part of the journalistic exercise.[192]

Similarly, according to Baroness Hale, 'newspaper editors often have to make their decisions at great speed and in difficult circumstances, so that to expect too minute an analysis of the position is in itself a restriction on their freedom of expression'.[193] While there was unanimous agreement in *Campbell* that journalistic latitude is essential to the proper recognition of freedom of expression, there was disagreement as to whether the newspaper on the facts acted reasonably within the scope of its discretion. Lord Nicholls and Lord Hoffmann were of the view that the publication of the additional details of Naomi Campbell's treatment for drug addiction (i.e., that she was attending Narcotics Anonymous and the frequency of her visits, how she was treated, etc.) as well as photographs of her leaving a meeting with other addicts, were justified because, essentially, they enhanced the story[194] and gave it credibility.[195] However, Baroness Hale, together with Lords Hope and Carswell, disagreed. Given that the right of the public to receive details about her treatment and the publication of the photographs were 'of a much lower order than the undoubted right to know that she was misleading the public' as to the fact of her addiction, the level of intrusion was not considered proportionate.[196]

Second, it has been suggested that, even in the absence of any specific public interest, there is intrinsic value in media speech and, accordingly, any restriction on press freedom must be subject to particularly close scrutiny.[197] It has further been suggested that the press should be afforded substantial latitude in its reporting in order to ensure the survival

---

[188] See, e.g., *Campbell* v *MGN Ltd* [2004] 2 AC 457, 106 citing with approval comments by Sedley LJ in *Douglas* v *Hello!* [2001] QB 967, 135.

[189] *Lingens* v *Austria* (1986) 8 EHRR 407, 41; *Axel Springer AG* v *Germany* [2012] EMLR 15, 79.

[190] See e.g., *Bergens Tidende* v *Norway* (2001) 31 EHRR 16, 48.

[191] *Campbell* v *MGN Ltd* [2004] 2 AC 457, 28 (per Lord Nicholls), 6–3 (per Lord Hoffmann), 112–13 (per Lord Hope), 143 (per Baroness Hale), 169 (per Lord Carswell); *Re Guardian News and Media Ltd* [2010] 2 AC 697, 63. See also *Jersild* v *Denmark* (1994) 19 EHRR 1; *Fressoz and Roire* v *France* (1999) 31 EHRR 28; *News Verlags GmbH & Co KG* v *Austria* (2000) 31 EHRR 246.

[192] [2004] 2 AC 457, 112.

[193] *Campbell* v *MGN Ltd* [2004] 2 AC 457, 143.

[194] Ibid., 28 (per Lord Nicholls), 77 (per Lord Hoffmann).

[195] Ibid., 77 (per Lord Hoffmann).

[196] Ibid., 117 (per Lord Hope), 152–7 (per Baroness Hale).

[197] *A* v *B plc and C* [2003] QB 195, [11(xii)]. Note also that the PCC Editors' Code of Practice provides that '[t]here is a public interest in freedom of expression itself': see Chapter 2.

of a sustainable press. In *A v B plc and C*, for example, Woolf CJ noted that '[t]he courts must not ignore the fact that if newspapers do not publish information which the public are interested in, there will be fewer newspapers published, which will not be in the public interest'.[198] Baroness Hale made a similar suggestion in *Campbell v MGN Ltd*:

> [o]ne reason why press freedom is so important is that we need newspapers to sell in order to ensure that we still have newspapers at all. It may be said that newspapers should be allowed considerable latitude in their intrusions into private grief so that they can maintain circulation.[199]

Her Ladyship seemed to suggest that such concerns would justify, without reference to a greater public interest, only trivial invasions of privacy. Nevertheless, there are legitimate reasons why arguments based *solely* on the intrinsic value of the press and its continued viability should be treated with caution. Andrew Scott, for example, convincingly suggests that '[i]t must be possible for media organisations to deliver diverting entertainment for their customers without trammelling the basic rights of individuals in the process. To suggest otherwise borders on the disingenuous'.[200]

The third point – although not yet resolved in the jurisprudence – is the extent to which a journalist's honest belief in the public interest quality of an intrusive publication should be taken into account in assessing whether article 10 should prevail. In other words, should there be a 'responsible journalism' defence for invasions of privacy? This issue is explored in more detail below (see Section 11.4(e)(vii)).

The weight given to the protection under article 10 of the defendant's right to freedom of expression, however, will predominantly turn on the degree to which the publication, or proposed publication, is in the public interest – that is, in the sense that it is 'capable of contributing to a debate in a democratic society'[201] or 'a debate of general interest'.[202] The differential treatment of different types of speech under article 10 is well-established in Strasbourg jurisprudence,[203] creating a 'hierarchy' of protected speech: political expression (broadly defined to include expression of legitimate public concern or public interest speech)[204] receives the widest protection, then artistic expression and then, finally, commercial speech. Thus, while nearly all forms of expression will fall within the scope of article 10, including 'banal and trivial' speech,[205] not all expression is considered to be of equal weight. The incorporation of article 10 into the substance of the cause of action has meant that this hierarchy has also been adopted at the domestic level. In *CC v AB*, for example, Eady J said: 'The communication of material to the world at large in which there is a genuine public interest is naturally to be rated more highly than the right to sell what is mere "tittle-tattle".'[206]

---

[198] *A v B plc and C* [2003] QB 195, [11(xii)]. See also discussion by the Joint Committee on Privacy and Injunctions, *Privacy and Injunctions* (Session 2010–2012, HL Paper 273 and HC 1443, 27 March 2012) 82–8; Eric Barendt, 'Privacy and Freedom of Speech' in Andrew T. Kenyon and Megan Richardson (eds) *New Dimensions in Privacy Law: International and Comparative Perspectives* (Cambridge University Press: Cambridge, 2006).

[199] *Campbell v MGN Ltd* [2004] 2 AC 457, 143.

[200] Scott in *Carter-Ruck on Libel and Privacy*, 20.36.

[201] *Von Hannover v Germany* (2005) 40 EHRR 1, 63.

[202] Ibid., 76; *McKennitt v Ash* [2005] EWHC 3003 (QB), [54]; *Ntuli v Donald* [2010] EWCA Civ 1276, 20; *Ferdinand v MGN Ltd* [2011] EWHC 2454 (QB), 62; *ETK v News Group Newspapers* [2011] EWCA Civ 439, 23.

[203] See, e.g., discussion in Fenwick and Phillipson, 50–72. Pursuant to s 2 of the HRA, such jurisprudence must be taken into account when domestic courts interpret the Convention rights (see *Cambell v MGN Ltd* [2004]) 2 AC 457, 106.

[204] See, e.g., *Sunday Times v United Kingdom* (1979) 2 EHRR 245, 66; *Thorgeirson v Iceland* (1992) 14 EHRR 843, 64. In the privacy context, see *Von Hannover v Germany* (2005) 40 EHRR 1 (Extract 11.3.2).

[205] *Ferdinand v MGN Ltd* [2011] EWHC 2454 (QB), 62.

[206] [2006] EWHC 3083 (QB), 36.

The distinction between different types of speech was considered by Baroness Hale in *Campbell* v *MGN Ltd*.

Extract 11.4.18
Campbell v *MGN Ltd* **[2004] 2 AC 457**

BARONESS HALE:

148. What was the nature of the freedom of expression which was being asserted on the other side? There are undoubtedly different types of speech, just as there are different types of private information, some of which are more deserving of protection in a democratic society than others. Top of the list is political speech. The free exchange of information and ideas on matters relevant to the organisation of the economic, social and political life of the country is crucial to any democracy. Without this, it can scarcely be called a democracy at all. This includes revealing information about public figures, especially those in elective office, which would otherwise be private but is relevant to their participation in public life. Intellectual and educational speech and expression are also important in a democracy, not least because they enable the development of individuals' potential to play a full part in society and in our democratic life. Artistic speech and expression is important for similar reasons, in fostering both individual originality and creativity and the free-thinking and dynamic society we so much value. No doubt there are other kinds of speech and expression for which similar claims can be made.

149. But it is difficult to make such claims on behalf of the publication with which we are concerned here. The political and social life of the community, and the intellectual, artistic or personal development of individuals, are not obviously assisted by poring over the intimate details of a fashion model's private life. However, there is one way in which the article could be said to be educational. The editor had considered running a highly critical piece, adding the new information to the not inconsiderable list of Miss Campbell's faults and follies detailed in the article, emphasising the lies and hypocrisy it revealed. Instead he chose to run a sympathetic piece, still listing her faults and follies, but setting them in the context of her now-revealed addiction and her even more important efforts to overcome it. Newspaper and magazines often carry such pieces and they may well have a beneficial educational effect.

Where the information contained in the publication is considered to be in the public interest, the respective interests protected by article 10 and article 8 are likely to be finely balanced. On the other hand, albeit receiving prima facie protection under article 10, expression devoid of public interest content – for example, mere 'tittle-tattle' or idle gossip – is more likely than not to be outweighed by a claimant's competing article 8 interests.[207]

In assessing the public interest, it has been established that 'what engages the interest of the public may not be material which engages the public interest'.[208] Rather, the 'public interest' is concerned with matters that are of legitimate concern to the public or affect the public at large.[209] Guidance as to the types of subject matter which fall within the scope of public interest speech can be gleaned from the existing case law (Strasbourg and domestic) where the concept has been considered, including in the context of defamation, breach of

---

[207] Fenwick and Phillipson, 780; Scott in *Carter-Ruck on Libel and Privacy*, 20.32.

[208] *Jameel* v *Wall Street Journal Europe Sprl* [2007] 1 AC 359, 31 (per Lord Bingham). See also 49 (per Lord Hoffmann) and 147 (per Baroness Hale); *Mosley* v *United Kingdom* (2011) 53 EHRR 30, [114].

[209] It should be noted that prior to the introduction of the HRA, the common law understanding of 'the public interest' was narrowly circumscribed: see Scott in *Carter-Ruck on Libel and Privacy*, 20.44; Warby in *The Law of Privacy and the Media*, 12.131.

confidence and copyright.[210] Relevant privacy codes, which must be taken into account according to section 12(4)(b) of the HRA, will also provide guidance.[211]

Generally speaking, however, there will be relatively few instances where the discussion of a matter of public interest will require the disclosure of personal or private information. Similarly, the discussion of a person's private life will rarely raise matters of public interest. In this sense – and despite the arguments often made by media interests to the contrary[212] – the collision of privacy and the right to freedom of speech on matters of public concern will occur relatively infrequently.[213] Due to the fact-intensive nature of the analysis, it is impossible to provide a definitive list of circumstances where such rights *will* collide, such that a claimant's privacy rights may be deferred to a publisher's interest in freedom of expression. Instead, the following sections provide a series of examples of the circumstances where media disclosure of private information may be expected to contribute to a debate on a matter of public interest.

Questions for discussion

1. When will it be in the public interest to reveal information about a person's private life? What situations do you envisage?
2. Do you think there is a public interest in freedom of expression itself? What about a public interest in supporting newspapers?
3. What degree of latitude do you think should be given to the media in assessing the balance between article 10 and article 8?

(iv) Criminality or exposure of wrongdoing/immorality

It is a long established principle of equity that, in the context of breach of confidence, there is 'no confidence as to the disclosure of iniquity'.[214] While, even prior to the introduction of the HRA, the defence had been extended to cover disclosures in the public interest rather than simply on the narrow grounds of iniquity,[215] the benefit of the public interest defence to media defendants was considered to be significantly limited. Courts were generally of the view that the public interest would best be served by exposure of the wrongdoing to the relevant authorities rather than to the public via the media.[216] Now, under the influence of the HRA, it is accepted that there is public interest in the media disclosure of wrongdoing, provided such disclosure is proportionate.[217] Indeed, such disclosure has been offered as

---

[210] For a comprehensive treatment, see Scott in *Carter-Ruck on Libel and Privacy*, 20.44–20.66.

[211] For example, para 3 of the PCC Editors' Code of Practice provides guidance on what constitutes the public interest (see Chapter 2).

[212] See, e.g., Paul Dacre, 'The Society of Editors Opening Lecture' (Speech delivered at the Society of Editors Conference, Bristol, 9 November 2008).

[213] See, e.g., comments by Lord Hoffmann in *Campbell* v *MGN Ltd* [2004] 2 AC 457, 474 [55–6]; *Mosley* v *United Kingdom* (2011) 53 EHRR 30, [114]. See also Sir David Eady, 'Injunctions and the Protection of Privacy' (2010) 29(4) *Civil Justice Quarterly* 411.

[214] *Gartside* v *Outram* (1856) 26 LJ Ch 113, 114 (per Sir William Page Wood VC).

[215] See, e.g., *Lion Laboratories* v *Evans* [1985] QB 526. See also discussion in *McKennitt* v *Ash* [2005] EWHC 3003 (QB), 94.

[216] *Francome* v *Mirror Group Newspapers Ltd* [1984] 2 All ER 408, 413 (per Sir John Donaldson MR).

[217] See, e.g., *X* v *Persons Unknown* [2006] EWHC 2783 (QB), 25; *Cream Holdings* v *Banerjee* [2005] 1 AC 253, [24]; *Campbell* v *MGN Ltd* [2004] 2 AC 457, 151, where Baroness Hale was of the view that 'the possession and use of illegal drugs is a criminal offence and a matter of serious public concern. The press must be free to expose the truth *and* put the record straight' (emphasis added); *Jockey Club* v *Buffham* [2003] QB 462, 46–8; *Theakston* v *MGN Ltd* [2002] EWHC 137 (QB), (where it was said by Ouseley J (at [69]) '[t]he free press is not confined to the role of a confidential police force; it is entitled to communicate directly with the public for the public to reach its own conclusion').

the quintessential example of widespread speech in the public interest.[218] Moreover, the PCC Editors' Code similarly provides that '[t]he public interest includes . . . detecting or exposing crime or serious impropriety'.[219]

The level of seriousness required to bring the disclosure of the impropriety, whether criminal or moral, within the public interest is uncertain. In *McKennitt* v *Ash*, Eady J considered that a 'very high degree of misbehaviour must be demonstrated'.[220] Without elaborating, however, the Court of Appeal thought that such a threshold may be set too high.[221] It is also clear that 'wrongdoing' is not confined to criminal behaviour; it may also relate to questions of decency and morality. Although a finding was not made on the issue, it was discussed by Tugendhat J in *Terry* v *Persons Unknown* (for the facts see Section 11.4(f)(ii) below).[222]

Extract 11.4.19
Terry v *Persons Unknown* [2010] EWHC 119 (QB)

TUGENDHAT J:

97. Mr Spearman submits that the level of social utility of the threatened speech is very low. He refers to the area of private life to which it relates, and to the fact it is not suggested that there has been any unlawful activity by [Terry]. He cites at length from Eady J's decision in *Mosley* [124]–[134]

. . .

99. Mr Spearman appeared to me to be submitting that conduct of one person in private must be unlawful, before another person should be permitted to criticise it in public. Otherwise the speech is not capable of contributing to a debate in a democratic society. Therefore I should attribute little value to the threatened speech in the present case when considering the balance between Art 8 and Art 10.

. . .

100. . . . I do not accept that the law has reached that point, or that Eady J was saying that it had. . . . Eady J was primarily directing his attention to the excesses of the defendant in that case . . . In *X* v *Persons Unknown* [25] Eady J gave as examples of a public interest speech 'for the purpose of revealing (say) criminal misconduct or antisocial behavior'. And in *Mosley* Eady J was giving a judgment after hearing submissions from the defendant.

. . .

104. There is much public debate as to what conduct is or is not socially harmful. Not all conduct that is socially harmful is unlawful, and there is often said to be much inconsistency in the law. For example, some commentators contrast the law on consumption of alcohol with that on other intoxicating substances. The fact that conduct is private and lawful is not, of itself, conclusive of the question whether or not it is in the public interest that it be discouraged. There is no suggestion that the conduct in question in the present case ought to be unlawful, or that any editor would ever suggest that it should be. But in a plural society there will be some who would suggest that it ought to be discouraged. That is why sponsors may be sensitive to the public image of those sportspersons whom they pay to promote their products. Freedom to live as one chooses is one of the most valuable freedoms. But so is the freedom to criticise

---

[218] See, e.g., *X & Y* v *Persons Unknown* [2006] EWHC 2783 (QB), 25.
[219] See Chapter 2.
[220] *McKennitt* v *Ash* [2005] EWHC 3003 (QB), 97.
[221] *McKennitt* v *Ash* [2006] EWCA Civ 1714, 69.
[222] The extracted passages received the support of the Court of Appeal in *Hutcheson* v *News Group Newspapers Ltd* [2011] EWCA Civ 808, 29; see also *Ferdinand* v *MGN Ltd* [2011] EWHC 2454, 63–4.

(within the limits of the law) the conduct of other members of society as being socially harmful, or wrong. Both the law, and what are, and are not, acceptable standards of lawful behaviour have changed very considerably over the years, particularly in the last half century or so. During that time these changes (or, as many people would say, this progress) have been achieved as a result of public discussion and criticism of those engaged in what were, at the time, lawful activities. The modern concept of public opinion emerged with the production of relatively cheap newspapers in the seventeenth century. Before that there was no medium through which public debate could be conducted. It is as a result of public discussion and debate, that public opinion develops.

Questions for discussion

1. Is there a public interest in the exposure of moral wrongdoing? If so, in what circumstances?
2. Is the exposure of a person's criminality to a widespread audience by the media justified, or should the matter be reported to the police?

(v) Public figures and role models

As already explained above (Section 11.4(d)(ii)), the mere fact that a person is a public figure does not deprive him or her of a reasonable expectation of privacy (although it may be relevant in some circumstances). This, however, is a different question from whether that right can be outweighed by any public interest that might arise from the disclosure of information pertaining to their private lives. In the cases that immediately followed the introduction of the HRA, the courts appeared to be much more sympathetic to the suggestion of the public's interest in the private lives of public figures.[223] This was the approach in the case of *A v B plc and C*, where Gary Flitcroft sought an injunction to prevent a newspaper from disclosing the fact that he had engaged in two extramarital affairs.

Extract 11.4.20
***A v B plc and C* [2003] QB 195**

LORD WOOLF CJ:

11. . . .

xii) . . . Even trivial facts relating to a public figure can be of great interest to readers and other observers of the media. Conduct which in the case of a private individual would not be the appropriate subject of comment can be the proper subject of comment in the case of a public figure. The public figure may hold a position where higher standards of conduct can be rightly expected by the public. The public figure may be a role model whose conduct could well be emulated by others. He may set the fashion. The higher the profile of the individual concerned the more likely that this will be the position. Whether you have courted publicity or not you may be a legitimate subject of public attention. If you have courted public attention then you have less ground to object to the intrusion which follows. In many of these situations it would be overstating the position to say that there is a public interest in the information being published. It would be more accurate to say that the public have an understandable and so a legitimate interest in being told the information. If this is the situation then it can be appropriately taken into account by a court when deciding on which side of the line a case falls . . .

[223] See *A v B plc and C* [2003] QB 195; *Theakston v MGN Ltd* [2002] EWHC 137 (QB).

43. . . .

vi) Again Jack J [the trial judge who granted the injunction] rejected any question of there being a public interest in B's proposed publications. Ignoring, as one must, the literary quality of what it was proposed to publish, it is not self-evident that how a well-known premiership football player, who has a position of responsibility within his club, chooses to spend his time off the football field does not have a modicum of public interest. Footballers are role models for young people and undesirable behaviour on their part can set an unfortunate example. While Jack J was right to say on the evidence which was before him that A had not courted publicity, the fact is that someone holding his position was inevitably a figure in whom a section of the public and the media would be interested.

In *Theakston* v *MGN Ltd*, Ouseley J took a similar approach by taking into account the 'role model' status of Jamie Theakston, the BBC television and radio presenter, in refusing an injunction to prevent a newspaper from publishing the fact and details of his visit to a Mayfair brothel (see above Section 11.4(c)(i)). It was found that there was a 'real element of public interest' in the fact that Theakston visited a brothel because his job as a television presenter meant that 'he will be seen as somebody whose lifestyle . . . is one which does not attract moral opprobrium'.[224]

A new approach, however, was first recognised by Lord Phillips MR in the Court of Appeal in *Campbell* v *MGN Ltd*, where it was held that the mere fact that someone is a public figure or a role model does not, in itself, make his or her private life fair game:

[W]e would observe that the fact that an individual has achieved prominence on the public stage does not mean that his private life can be laid bare by the media. We do not see why it should necessarily be in the public interest that an individual who has been adopted as a role model, without seeking this distinction, should be demonstrated to have feet of clay.[225]

Nevertheless, paragraph 6 of Resolution 1165 (1998) of the Parliamentary Assembly of the Council of Europe on the Right to Privacy[226] states that 'public figures must recognise that the position they occupy in society . . . automatically entails increased pressure on their privacy'. Public figures are defined in paragraph 7 as 'persons holding public office and/or using public resources and, more broadly speaking, all those who play a role in public life, whether in politics, the economy, the arts, the social sphere, sport or in any other domain'.

It was established in *Von Hannover* v *Germany*, however, that the publication of private information concerning a well-known person will only be justified if it contributes to a legitimate debate of general public interest – for example, the private conduct of a politician where such conduct affects the fulfilment of his or her public or official role.[227] The public interest may also extend to the discussion of sporting issues or matters concerning performing artists.[228] Conversely, the publication of private material, the sole purpose of which is to 'satisfy the curiosity of a particular readership' of a public figure's private life, 'cannot be deemed to contribute to any debate of general interest to society'.[229]

---

[224] *Theakston* v *MGN Ltd* [2002] EWCH 137 (QB), 69. For criticism of the reasoning in *Theakston* and *A* v *B plc and C*, see Gavin Phillipson, 'Judicial Reasoning in Breach of Confidence Cases under the Human Rights Act: Not Taking Privacy Seriously?' (2003) *European Human Rights Law Review* 54.

[225] *Campbell* v *MGN Ltd* [2003] QB 633, 41.

[226] Text adopted by the Assembly on 26 June 1998 (24th Sitting).

[227] *Von Hannover* v *Germany* (2005) 40 EHRR 1, 63; *Von Hannover* v *Germany (No 2)* (2012) 55 EHRR 15, 109; *Axel Springer AG* v *Germany* [2012] EMLR 15, 90.

[228] *Axel Springer AG* v *Germany* [2012] EMLR 15, 90.

[229] *Von Hannover* v *Germany* (2005) 40 EHRR 1, 65; *Von Hannover* v *Germany (No 2)* (2012) 55 EHRR 15, 110.

Certainly, the argument that Princess Caroline was a 'figure of contemporary society *par excellence*' was not sufficient to bring the disclosure under the mantle of the public interest. Although a member of the Monaco royal family, she did not perform an official function within the state; she did, however, occasionally represent the royal family and was involved in a number of charitable organisations. As Aplin *et al.* point out, the argument was not pursued that Princess Caroline, while not performing any official role, was nevertheless a role model.[230]

In *Von Hannover* v *Germany (No 2)*[231] (see Extract 11.3.3), on the other hand, the Grand Chamber found that the German courts did not violate Princess Caroline and her husband's article 8 rights by refusing to enjoin the publication of a photograph of the couple enjoying their holiday. The German Federal Court of Justice had found that the photograph, in the context of its publication, contributed to an article of general interest relating to the health of the then reigning sovereign of Monaco, Prince Rainier III, and the way in which his family, including Princess Caroline and her husband, were responding to his illness. This conclusion, according to the Grand Chamber, could not be considered unreasonable.[232] The key point to take away from this case, it is submitted, is not that it represents a 'rebalancing' of privacy and freedom of expression,[233] but rather that it clarifies that where a person is a public figure – as the applicants on the facts were found to be – even a relatively tenuous[234] or low level public interest in the private information might justify publication.

At the domestic level, the public interest in the private affairs of public figures – and role models in particular – was further considered by the Court of Appeal in *McKennitt* v *Ash*, where an attempt was made to reconcile *Von Hannover* v *Germany* with the earlier domestic decisions in *A* v *B plc and C* and *Theakston*.

Extract 11.4.21
McKennitt v Ash [2006] EWCA civ 1714

BUXTON LJ:

57. The first of these arguments involves consideration of two recent authorities, already introduced, *Von Hannover* and *A* v *B* [*plc and C*], to which I must now return.

Von Hannover

58. There is no doubt that the ECtHR has restated what was previously thought to be the rights and expectations of public figures with regard to their private lives. The court in its §58 recognised the important role of the press in dealing with matters of public interest, and the latitude in terms of mode of expression there provided. But a distinction was then drawn between a watchdog role in the democratic process and the reporting of private information about people who, although of interest to the public, were not public figures . . .

59. . . . If we follow in this case the guidance given by the English courts, that the content of the law of confidence is now to be found in articles 8 and 10 (see §10 above), then it seems

---

[230] Aplin *et al.*, 16.101–16.102.
[231] (2012) 55 EHRR 15.
[232] *Von Hannover* v *Germany (No 2)* (2012) 55 EHRR 15, 118.
[233] Cf. Elspeth Reid, 'Rebalancing Privacy and Freedom of Expression' (2012) 16(2) *Edinburgh Law Review* 253.
[234] Indeed, the connection between the photograph of Princess Caroline and her husband holidaying and the public interest in Prince Rainier's declining health and how it had impacted on his family has been described as 'strained': see Brid Jordan and Imogen Hurst, 'Privacy and the Princess – A Review of the Grand Chamber's Decisions in *Von Hannover* and *Axel Springer*' (2012) 23(4) *Entertainment Law Review* 108, 113.

inevitable that Ms Ash's case must fail. Even assuming that Ms McKennitt is a public figure in the relevant sense (which proposition I suspect the ECtHR would find surprising), there are no 'special circumstances' apart from the allegation of hypocrisy dealt with in the next section to justify or require the exposure of her private life. But the appellant argued that English courts could not follow or apply *Von Hannover* to the facts of the present case because we were bound by the contrary English authority of *A v B*. That effectively required Ms McKennitt's private affairs to be exposed to the world, hypocrite or not.

A v *B* [*plc and C*]

60. . . . The judgment of this court [in *A* v *B plc and C*] is notable for the detailed guidance that it contains as to how a court should address complaints about invasion of privacy by public or allegedly public figures.

. . .

62. The width of the rights given to the media by *A* v *B* [*plc and C*] cannot be reconciled with *Von Hannover*. Mr Price said that whether that was right or wrong, we had to apply *A* v *B* [*plc and C*], in the light of the rule of precedent laid down by the House of Lords in *Kay* v *Lambeth LBC* [2006] 2 WLR 570, in particular by Lord Bingham of Cornhill at §§43–45. Put shortly, the precedential rules of English domestic law apply to interpretations of Convention jurisprudence. Where, for instance, the Court of Appeal has ruled on the meaning or reach of a particular article of the Convention, a later division of the Court of Appeal cannot depart from that ruling simply on the basis that it is inconsistent with a later, or for that matter an earlier, decision of the ECtHR.

. . .

63. I would respectfully and fully agree with the importance of that rule. The alternative, as an earlier constitution of this court said, is chaos. But I do not think that the rule inhibits us in this case from applying *Von Hannover*. If the court in *A* v *B* had indeed ruled definitively on the content and application of article 10 then the position would be different; but that is what the court did not do. Having made the important observation that the content of the domestic law was now to be found in the balance between articles 8 and 10, the court then addressed the balancing exercise effectively in the former English domestic terms of breach of confidence. No Convention authority of any sort was even mentioned . . .

64. . . . [I]t seems clear that *A* v *B* [*plc and C*] cannot be read as any sort of binding authority on the content of articles 8 and 10. To find that content, therefore, we do have to look to *Von Hannover*. The terms of that judgment are very far away from the automatic limits placed on the privacy rights of public figures by *A* v *B* [*plc and C*].

. . .

65. But, in any event, even if we were to follow *A* v *B* [*plc and C*], the guidance that that case gives does not produce the outcome in our case that is sought by the appellant. First, as to the position of Ms McKennitt, she clearly does not fall within the first category mentioned by Lord Woolf, and 'hold a position where higher standards of conduct can be rightly expected by the public': that is no doubt the preserve of headmasters and clergymen, who according to taste may be joined by politicians, senior civil servants, surgeons and journalists. Second, although on one view Ms McKennitt comes within Lord Woolf's second class, of involuntary role models, I respectfully share the doubts of Lord Phillips, set out . . . above, as to the validity of that concept; and it would in any event seem difficult to include in the class a person such as Ms McKennitt, who has made such efforts not to hold herself out as someone whose life is an open book. Third, it is clear that Lord Woolf thought that role models were at risk, or most at risk, of having to put up with the reporting of *disreputable* conduct: such as was the conduct of claimant before him. Ms McKennitt does not fall into that category . . .

Questions for discussion

1. What are the qualifications Buxton LJ in *McKennitt* v *Ash* places on the argument that disclosure is in the public interest because of the claimant's position as a 'role model'?
2. Do you agree or disagree with the proposition that speech about a public figure or a role model can, in certain circumstances, be justified in the public interest? What circumstances do you think should be relevant?

As the authors of *Gurry on Breach of Confidence* point out, even where a public figure has voluntarily assumed the position of a public post or role model, any intrusion into their private life through the disclosure of private facts must contribute to a debate on a matter of legitimate public concern.[235] The public interest in such a case will most likely arise where the publication calls into question the person's fitness or suitability for the position they hold. A series of recent cases suggest that the courts are starting to give greater attention to the claimant's status as a public figure in finding that the publication of private facts is justified in the public interest. Much of this has relied on Lord Woolf's discussion of public figures in *A* v *B plc and C* (see Extract 11.4.20). Thus, in *Ferdinand* v *MGN Ltd*,[236] the claimant's position as an English football captain meant that he was held to a high standard on and off the field and that he had voluntarily assumed the position of a role model for young football followers. Thus, at least one factor in the finding that there was a public interest in publishing the information about the claimant's adultery was said to be that it called into question his fitness for the captaincy and, hence, his fitness as a role model.[237] The same conclusion was reached in *McClaren* v *News Group Newspapers Ltd*.[238] In that case, Steve McClaren, former manager of England's football team and current manager of a club in the Dutch football league, sought to prevent the publication of details of an extramarital affair. Lindblom J held that McClaren was 'undoubtedly a public figure' and therefore belonged to 'the category of those from whom the public could reasonably expect a higher standard of conduct'.[239] An additional factor justifying publication was that McClaren had freely given a previous interview to the media about a prior affair that he had conducted and had stated at the time that his marriage would survive.[240]

Questions for discussion

1. Do you think 'voluntary' role models should be treated different from 'involuntary' role models?
2. Do you agree with Lindblom J that the private life of Steven McClaren, the former manager of England's football team and the current manager of a Dutch football club, is a matter of genuine public interest?

---

[235] Aplin *et al.* [16.07–16.09].
[236] [2011] EWHC 2454 (QB).
[237] *Ferdinand* v *MGN Ltd* [2011] EWHC 2454 (QB), 87–98. See also discussion in *Mosley* v *MGN Ltd* [2008] EWHC 1777 (QB), 122.
[238] [2012] EWHC 2466 (QB).
[239] *McClaren* v *News Group Newspapers Ltd* [2012] EWHC 2466 (QB), 34.
[240] Ibid., 34.

(vi) Hypocrisy and correcting the record

As mentioned above (section 11.4(e)(ii)), the weight of a claimant's right to privacy in the balancing exercise may be affected by his or her attitude to the disclosure of the type of information in question. He or she, for example, may have consented to the publication of similar information in the past, or may even have sold private information for profit. In a similar vein, a media defendant's article 10 interests may be bolstered if there is an identifiable public interest in attempting to correct a past statement made by a claimant and/or to expose hypocrisy on his or her part.[241] As pointed out by Andrew Scott, a person may be exposed as a hypocrite in one of two ways: either where the claimant fails to meet 'normative prescriptions' of conduct that he or she expects of others, or where the claimant engages in the same conduct for which he or she has criticised third parties.[242]

In the early cases decided under the HRA, it was accepted that there was a public interest in correcting a false image created by a claimant. Thus, in *Theakston v MGN Ltd*, one of the factors that clearly influenced the decision of Ouseley J was that Theakston had sought to foster a favourable public image, including by revealing flattering personal details in the media. It was successfully argued that the information to be published would set the record straight.[243] A similar approach was adopted by the Court of Appeal in *Campbell v Frisbee*.[244] It should be noted, however, that both of these cases relied on *Woodward v Hutchins*,[245] now discredited in its support of a broad proposition that the media is justified in publishing any material contrary to the general image fostered by a claimant.[246] For this reason, both *Theakston v MGN Ltd* and *Campbell v Frisbee* should be treated with caution on this point. This, however, is not to say that a public interest argument on the basis of 'correcting the record' or exposure of hypocrisy is unavailable. Rather, as pointed out in *Tugendhat and Christie: The Law of Privacy and the Media*, it appears that the publication should focus on rebutting a '*particular* statement or other representations made'.[247]

In *Campbell v MGN Ltd*, for example, the press was justified in putting the record straight regarding the fact of the claimant's drug addiction (see Extract 11.4.2). The important point in that case was that the claimant had previously made specific statements through the press claiming that she was unlike other models who had succumbed to the temptation of illicit drug use. The claimant conceded that the press was entitled to publish the fact of her drug addiction in order to correct her previous false statements and this concession was clearly appropriate according to the Court of Appeal and the House of Lords. Thus Lord Nicholls approved the following passage from Lord Phillips MR in the Court of Appeal:[248]

> One principle, which has been recognised by the parties in this case, is that, where a public figure chooses to make untrue pronouncements about his or her private life, the press will normally be entitled to put the record straight.[249]

---

[241] On the public interest in 'putting the record straight', see John William Devine, 'Privacy and Hypocrisy' (2011) 3(2) *Journal of Media Law* 169, where it is argued (at 171) that 'the rationale behind [putting the record straight] appears to be not merely to ensure the accuracy of the public record. Rather, the rationale behind [putting the record straight] must be to expose a public figure's knowingly false or misleading pronouncements about his private life as not corresponding to reality.'

[242] Scott in *Carter-Ruck on Libel and Privacy*, 20.58.

[243] *Theakston v MGN Ltd* [2002] EWHC 137 (QB), 68.

[244] [2002] EWCA Civ 1374. In that case, it was held that it was at least arguable that the disclosure of the claimant's affair was justifiable in the public interest because she had promoted a false image of herself as stable: see discussion in Warby in *The Law of Privacy and the Media*, 12.163.

[245] [1977] 1 WLR 760. Caution, however, was expressed in *Campbell v Frisbee* [2002] EWCA Civ 1374, 34.

[246] See, e.g., *McKennitt v Ash* [2005] EWHC 3003 (QB), 101–5.

[247] Warby in *The Law of Privacy and the Media*, 12.164 (emphasis added).

[248] *Campbell v MGN Ltd* [2004] 2 AC 457, 24.

[249] *Campbell v MGN Ltd* [2003] QB 633, 43.

Similarly, in *Ferdinand v MGN Ltd* (see Section 11.4(e)(v)), a factor in finding that the publication was in the public interest was that it 'corrected' the claimant's previous declarations to the effect that he was a 'reformed character'. In his prior statements, contained in an interview published in *News of the World*, the claimant suggested that he was 'older, more mature, and, critically, in a stable family relationship with [his partner]'.[250] Thus, in addition to the claimant's position as a voluntary 'role model', the impugned article was justified in demonstrating that his self-projected image was false.[251]

Ferdinand v MGN Ltd can be contrasted with *McKennitt v Ash* (see Section 11.4(c)(ii) and Extract 11.4.21). In that case, the defendant, Ash, put forward a public interest argument on the basis that the private information disclosed in her book showed that the claimant, McKennitt, fell short of the standards, or list of 'compass points', published on the claimant's website. Eady J rejected Ash's arguments. It was found that such compass points merely represented her 'aspirations or ideals' and constituted a 'fragile pen on which to hang a public interest defence.'[252] His Honour further said:

> it is necessary to take note that, if [Ash's] argument is correct, any person in the public eye who chose to share his or her aspirations with fans, followers, admirers or the general public, would immediately become vulnerable to having every trivial detail in their private lives exposed to public scrutiny.[253]

The Court of Appeal agreed.[254]

It should also be noted that the PCC Editors' Code of Practice provides that the public interest includes '[p]reventing the public from being misled by an action or statement of an individual or organisation' (see Chapter 2).

Questions for discussion

1. Is there a public interest in setting the record straight? If so, what is the nature of that interest?
2. Should public figures always forfeit their privacy when they lie about particular aspects of their private lives?

(vii) Responsible journalism defence?

As already mentioned, journalists are granted a certain margin of appreciation as to how public interest stories are presented and the level of detail included. What happens, however, when a journalist is under a misapprehension as to the facts said to give rise to the public interest nature of the story? In *Mosley v News Group Newspapers Ltd*[255] (see facts at Section 11.4(c)(i)), Eady J raised the possibility that some degree of recognition should be given to the subjective views of the journalist and that there might be a role in the privacy context, as in defamation, for the concept of 'responsible journalism'.[256]

---

[250] *Ferdinand v MGN Ltd* [2011] EWHC 2454 (QB), 84.
[251] Ibid., 85.
[252] *McKennitt v Ash* [2005] EWHC 3003 (QB), 100.
[253] Ibid.
[254] *McKennitt v Ash* [2006] EWCA Civ 1714, 67–70.
[255] [2008] EWHC 1777 (QB).
[256] Note, the idea that invasions of privacy might be defended by defences analogous to qualified privilege in the context of defamation was recognised by Warren and Brandeis: Samuel D. Warren and Louis D. Brandeis, 'The Right to Privacy' (1890) 4 *Harvard Law Review* 193, 214–16.

Extract 11.4.22
Mosley v News Group Newspaper Ltd **[2008] EWHC 1777 (QB)**

EADY J:

136. I have decided that the only possible element of public interest here, in the different context of privacy, would be if the Nazi role-play and mockery of Holocaust victims were true. I have held that they were not. Does any weight need to 'be given to the professional judgment of [the] editor or journalist' to the contrary? Do I need to consider whether such judgments were 'made in a casual, cavalier, slipshod or careless manner'?

. . .

137. In the defamation context, it seems clear that it is for the court alone to decide 'whether the story as a whole was a matter of public interest', but there is scope for editorial judgment as to what details should be included within the story and as to how it is expressed (see e.g. also Lord Hoffmann at [51]). That distinction seems to be clear, although in individual cases the line may be difficult to draw. Here the situation is that the journalists' perception was, or may have been, that the story was about Nazi role-play. Even though I concluded that this was not the case, should some allowance be made for a different view on the matter? The answer is probably in the negative, because it is only the court's decision which counts on the central issue of public interest.

. . .

138. It might seem reasonable to allow in this context for some difference of opinion. I cannot believe that a journalist's sincere view on public interest, however irrationally arrived at, should be a complete answer. A decision on public interest must be capable of being tested by objectively recognised criteria. But it could be argued as a matter of policy that allowance should be made for a decision reached which falls within a range of reasonably possible conclusions. Little was said in submissions on this aspect of the case.

. . .

139. It would seem odd if the only determining factor was the decision reached by a judge after leisurely debate and careful legal submission – luxuries not available to a hard-pressed journalist as a story is breaking with deadlines to meet. Obviously, on the other hand, the courts could not possibly abdicate the responsibility for deciding issues of public interest and simply leave them to whatever decision the journalist happens to take. As Sir John Donaldson MR observed in *Francome* v *Mirror Group Newspapers Ltd* [1984] 1 WLR 892, 898, 'The media . . . are peculiarly vulnerable to the error of confusing the public interest with their own interest'.

. . .

140. Against this background, it would seem that there may yet be scope for paying regard to the concept of 'responsible journalism', which has been referred to over recent years in the context of public interest privilege in libel. There is an obvious analogy. This rather vague term has been illuminated and defined in such a way that it could now be regarded as approaching a legal term of art. It has to be assessed in the round, but there are certain guidelines which have been listed to assist in making a judgment: see e.g. Lord Nicholls' 10 non-exhaustive 'factors' in *Reynolds* v *Times Newspapers Ltd* [2001] 2 AC 127, 205.

. . .

141. There may be a case for saying, when 'public interest' has to be considered in the field of privacy, that a judge should enquire whether the relevant journalist's decision prior to publication was reached as a result of carrying out enquiries and checks consistent with 'responsible journalism'. In making a judgment about that, with the benefit of hindsight, a judge could no doubt have regard to considerations of that kind, as well as to the broad principles set out in the PCC Code as reflecting acceptable practice. Yet I must not disregard the remarks of Lord Phillips MR in *Campbell* [2003] QB 633 at [61] to the effect that the same test of public interest should *not* be applied in the 'two very different torts'.

> ## Question for discussion
>
> 1. Is there an 'obvious analogy' between responsible journalism in the libel context and the potential for such a principle in the privacy context? Are there any differences between the two causes of action to justify different approaches?

As explained by Eady J in *Mosley*, the availability of *Reynolds* privilege in the defamation context (see Chapter 10, Section 10.4(c)(iv)) is essentially an objective question for the Court to determine, with 'allowance for editorial judgment' as to the decision to include the impugned material in the story and as to the standards expected of a responsible journalist. The reasoning behind the suggestion that the subjective intention of the journalist may be required to play a greater role in the privacy context compared to the defamation context – whether under a *Reynolds*-style defence or otherwise – is not at all self-evident. The preferred approach, it is suggested, would be to follow, more or less, the objective methodology adopted under *Reynolds* privilege. Adopting Lord Hoffmann's three-stage formulation in *Jameel*, the first question would be to ask whether the story, without inquiring as to the truth or falsity of any factual claims, is on a topic of legitimate public interest.[257] If so, the second inquiry would be whether the private facts disclosed in the article form 'part of the story'.[258] In other words, are they relevant? A certain degree of latitude for journalistic discretion is required here. If this is satisfied, the third question would be whether the journalist acted responsibly in relation to the facts said to support the public interest aspect of the story (which may differ from the private facts themselves). This last requirement would differ from *Reynolds* privilege in the context of defamation, where the focus is on responsible journalism vis-à-vis the defamatory allegation(s) being sued upon. The distinction can be demonstrated by reference to facts in *Mosley* v *News Group Newspapers*. In that case, the private information related to Mosley's sex life, whereas the public interest argument was based on the allegation that the event involved a Nazi role play.

In *Terry* v *Persons Unknown*, Tugendhat J noted the uncertainty as to the 'extent to which, if at all, the belief of a person threatening to make a publication in the media is relevant on the issue of public interest'.[259] He noted, however, that it would be anomalous if the 'defence' under section 32 of the Data Protection Act (see Section 5 below), which requires the court to have regard to the fact that 'the data controller reasonably believes that . . . publication would be in the public interest', applied to a newspaper published online but the public interest 'defence' to misuse of private information did not.[260] Moreover, it was also highlighted as relevant by Tugendhat J that the subjective belief of a journalist is a factor under paragraph 3 of the Press Complaints Commission Editors' Code of Practice (see Chapter 2). A response to this argument, however, is correctly pointed out by Mark Warby QC – that to take account of the subjective beliefs of the publisher in privacy cases would 'give rise to [the further] anomalous distinction between the defences available in privacy and the *Reynolds* defence in defamation'.[261]

---

[257] *Jameel* v *Wall Street Journal Sprl* [2005] QB 904, 48–58.
[258] Ibid., 51.
[259] *Terry* v *Persons Unknown* [2010] EWHC 119 (QB), 70–1.
[260] Ibid., 73.
[261] Warby in *The Law of Privacy and the Media*, 12.215.

(f) Remedies for misuse of private information

The final remedies available to a claimant in an action for the misuse of private information may include a final (perpetual) injunction, damages, an account of profits, and an order directing the defendant to deliver up and/or destroy any material containing private information. However, in the privacy context, interim relief takes on special significance. This is because a claimant may see little benefit in pursuing a final remedy once the private information has been published. By that point, the damage will have already been done.[262] Rather, the preference for a claimant will be to *prevent* publication by applying to the court for an interim injunction, usually on a *quia timet* basis. Importantly, an interim injunction (called an 'interim non-disclosure order' in this context) will often act as a de facto final remedy. Thus, once an interim injunction is granted, a publisher will often undertake not to publish the story at all; on the other hand, where interim relief is refused, a claimant may choose to not pursue the matter to trial – they may decide that they are unlikely to be successful or they may not want to risk attracting further attention to the private information. As a result, few misuse of private information cases proceed to a full trial.[263]

(i) Interim injunctions

Prior to the introduction of the HRA, the courts followed the test set out in *American Cyanamid Co.* v *Ethicon Ltd*[264] in determining whether to grant or withhold interim relief. This required that the claimant establish, as a threshold matter, that there existed 'a serious question to be tried', otherwise known as the 'real prospect of success' test.[265] In addition, the claimant needed to establish that the balance of convenience – taking into account the respective harms likely to be suffered and whether damages would afford an adequate remedy – favoured the granting of the injunction to prevent publication. In the context of privacy claims, the 'threshold' test has now been altered as a result of section 12 of the HRA.

Section 12 applies when 'a court is considering whether to grant any relief which, if granted, might affect the exercise of the . . . right to freedom of expression.'[266] Under section 12(3), '[n]o such relief is to be granted so as to restrain publication before trial unless the court is satisfied that the applicant is likely to establish that publication should not be allowed.' The considerations set out in section 12(4) (see above section 11.4(e)(i) and Extract 1.2.5) also apply. The House of Lords in *Cream Holdings Ltd* v *Banerjee* considered whether the words 'likely to establish' in section 12(3) imposed a higher threshold test than that set out in *American Cyanamid*. The appellant argued that section 12(3) required the claimant to show that he or she was 'more likely than not' to succeed at trial. Lord Nicholls, with whom the court agreed, held that the word 'likely' could not be interpreted as imposing a 'single, rigid standard governing all applications for interim restraint orders'.[267] Rather, while the likelihood of success at trial is an 'essential element' in considering an application for interim relief, a flexible construction as to the degree of likelihood must be adopted. Such a flexible approach ensures that section 12(3) is 'Convention-compliant':

> [T]he [flexible approach] does not accord inappropriate weight to the Convention right of freedom of expression as compared with the right to respect for private life or other Convention rights. This

---

[262] See, e.g., *X & Y* v *Persons Unknown* [2006] EWHC 2783 (QB), 44.
[263] *Spelman* v *Express Newspapers* [2012] EWHC 355 (QB), 41.
[264] [1975] AC 396.
[265] *American Cyanamid Co* v *Ethicon Ltd* [1975] AC 396, 407–8.
[266] Human Rights Act 1998, s 12(1).
[267] *Cream Holdings Ltd* v *Banerjee* [2005] 1 AC 253, 22.

approach gives effect to the parliamentary intention that courts should have particular regard to the importance of the right to freedom of expression and at the same time it is sufficiently flexible in its application to give effect to countervailing Convention rights.[268]

In general, a claimant will be required to show that he or she will be 'more likely than not' to succeed at trial, taking into account the balance between competing Convention rights.[269] However, this will not always be the case. In some instances a lesser degree of likelihood will be sufficient – for example, where a short-lived interim injunction is granted pending proper consideration, or where the consequences of not granting the injunction would be especially severe.[270]

The impact of section 12(3), as interpreted in *Cream Holdings Ltd*, is that there is now a shift of focus in interim proceedings. Rather than the primary focus being on the 'balance of convenience', attention centres on the prospects of success at trial and is said to involve a 'pre-emptive determination of the merits of the case'.[271] Moreover, the burden of proof falls entirely on the claimant; thus, the claimant must persuade the judge that it is more likely than not that he or she has a reasonable expectation of privacy *and* that it is unlikely to be outweighed in the ultimate balancing exercise by the defendant's competing interests.[272] Any uncertainty in relation to the defendant's interests will be resolved against the granting of the injunction.

(ii) False private information, defamation and the rule in Bonnard v Perryman

It is not necessarily an obstacle to a claim based on misuse of private information or breach of confidence that the information in question is false.[273] In *McKennitt v Ash*, Eady J found that most of the information in Ash's book about the property dispute with McKennitt was false. Both Eady J at trial and the Court of Appeal held that this did not preclude McKennitt from relying on breach of confidence as the relevant cause of action to prevent its publication.[274] This, however, may not be the case where the false information is also defamatory and the claimant has argued breach of confidence or misuse of private information in order to avoid the requirements of the law of defamation, particularly the rule in *Bonnard v Perryman*[275] (see Extract 10.5.1) which severely curtails the ability to obtain interim injunctions in defamation cases.[276] A similar issue may also arise, of course, in relation to true information which is both private and defamatory.[277]

The relationship between breach of confidence/misuse of private information and defamation was considered by Tugendhat J in *Terry v Persons Unknown*.[278] In that case,

---

[268] Ibid., 23.

[269] Ibid., 22.

[270] Ibid., 16–19, 22.

[271] Scott in *Carter-Ruck on Libel and Privacy*, 21.22.

[272] *Browne v Associated Newspapers Ltd* [2008] QB 103, 43.

[273] See *McKennitt v Ash* [2006] EWCA Civ 1714, 78–80.

[274] *McKennitt v Ash* [2006] EWCA Civ 1714, 79 (Buxton LJ), 85–7 (Longmore LJ); [2005] EWHC 3003 (QB), 78]. See also *P, Q and R v Quigley* [2008] EWHC 1051 (QB). For criticism of this approach, see John Hartshorne, 'An Appropriate Remedy for the Publication of False Private Information' (2012) 4(1) *Journal of Media Law*, 93–115.

[275] [1891] 2 Ch 269 (CA).

[276] *McKennitt v Ash* [2006] EWCA Civ 1714, 79; *Browne v Associated Newspapers Ltd* [2007] EWHC 202 (QB), 23–30. For a useful analysis of the interlocutory injunctions in this context, see David Rolph, 'Irreconcilable Differences? Interlocutory Injunctions for Defamation and Privacy' (2012) 17(2) *Media & Arts Law Review*, 170.

[277] Note, an allegation can be true and defamatory; however, truth may be a defence to publication: see Chapter 10, Section 10.4(a).

[278] [2010] EWHC 119 (QB). See also *Spelman v Express Newspapers* [2012] EWHC 355 (QB), 57–65.

John Terry (LNS), a well-known footballer, brought an action in breach of confidence and misuse of private information to prevent the publication of four categories of information: (1) the fact of his relationship with a woman; (2) details of that relationship; (3) information leading to the identification of Terry or the woman; and (4) any photographic evidence of this information. Unlike the information regarding the property dispute in *McKennitt* v *Ash*, Terry admitted the truth of the information. Tugendhat J refused the interim injunction on the basis of a lack of evidence. His Honour also held that because Terry's case, on the evidence presented, was really about his reputation rather than his privacy, the interim injunction should be rejected on the basis of the rule in *Bonnard* v *Perryman*.

Extract 11.4.23
***Terry v Persons Unknown* [2010] EWHC 119 (QB)**

TUGENDHAT J:

74. I raised with Mr Spearman whether the facts LNS relies on in this case should not be regarded as constituting a cause of action in defamation . . .

77. Of course, LNS would not choose to sue in defamation because Mr Spearman recognises that any person or media intending to publish this story is likely to do so in words for which he will be able to say that he has a defence in law, under one or other of the defences available in defamation. If so, applying the rule in *Bonnard* v *Perryman*, no interim injunction could be granted.

78. The relationship between defamation and the new cause of action of misuse of private information is not yet clear. Breach of confidence was also a developing cause of action in and from the 1970s. Some remarks have been made, in cases in confidence and in conspiracy, about the relationship between those causes of action and defamation.

. . .

86. At p 344 Ralph Gibson LJ said [in *Gulf Oil (GB) Ltd* v *Page* [1987] Ch 327]:

> Although that principle, which is applied in defamation cases, is not directly applicable in its terms to a case where the basis of claim is conspiracy to inflict deliberate damage without any just cause, nevertheless it seems to me that that principle, namely the individual and the public interest in the right of free speech, is a matter of great importance in the consideration of the question whether in the exercise of the court's discretion an interlocutory injunction should be made and, if yes, what should be the extent of any restriction upon publication of any statement pending trial.

. . .

88. It appears to me, in particular from the judgement of Ralph Gibson LJ, that it is a matter for the court to decide whether the principle of free speech prevails or not, and that it does not depend solely upon the choice of the claimant as to his cause of action.

. . .

89. There have been a number of other references to the point in the interval, and in a number of cases injunctions have been refused on this basis, where the claim was brought in some cause of action other than defamation . . . The most recent observations of the Court of Appeal on this point are to be found in *McKennitt* v *Ash* [2006] EWCA Civ 1714 . . . At 79 Buxton LJ said:

> If it could be shown that a claim in breach of confidence was brought where the nub of the case was a complaint of the falsity of the allegations, and that that was done in order to avoid the rules of the tort of defamation, then objections could be raised in terms of abuse of process.

90. The reference to falsity in that passage is because the claimant in that case contested the truth of the book's allegations. The point would have had more force, not less, if the claimant admitted the truth of the allegations, and was attempting to protect an undeserved reputation

by recourse to the cause of action in misuse of private information, at least where there was a public interest in her not doing so.

. . .

95. On the evidence available to me now, I have reached the view that it is likely that the nub of LNS's complaint in this case is the protection of reputation, and not of any other aspect of LNS's private life. I note that in the evidence the most LNS is said to have expressed is 'grave concern over the possibility of intrusion into [LNS's] private life'. There is no mention of any personal distress. As to personal attributes, LNS appears to have a very robust personality, as one might expect of a leading professional sportsman. It does not seem likely to me that the concern expressed on [LNS's] behalf for the private lives of the other person and the interested persons is altruistic. This claim is essentially a business matter for LNS. That is why the assembling of the evidence has been put into the hands of the business partners and not of the solicitors. My present view is that the real basis for the concern of LNS is likely to be the impact of any adverse publicity upon the business of earning sponsorship and similar income.

96. Before leaving the topic of defamation, I note that it is only in limited classes of cases that the law of privacy gives rise to an overlap with the law of defamation. In broad terms the cases may be considered in at least four different groups. The first group of cases, where there is no overlap, is where the information cannot be said to be defamatory (e.g. *Douglas* v *Hello!*, and *Murray*). It is the law of confidence, privacy and harassment that are likely to govern such cases. There is a second group of cases where there is an overlap, but where it is unlikely that it could be said that protection of reputation is the nub of the claim. These are cases where the information would in the past have been said to be defamatory even though it related to matters which were involuntary e.g. disease. There was always a difficulty in fitting such cases into defamation, but it was done because of the absence of any alternative cause of action. There is a third group of cases where there is an overlap, but no inconsistency. These are cases where the information relates to conduct which is voluntary, and alleged to be seriously unlawful, even if it is personal (e.g. sexual or financial). The claimant is unlikely to succeed whether at an interim application or (if the allegation is proved) at trial, whether under the law of defamation or the law of privacy. The fourth group of cases, where it may make a difference which law governs, is where the information relates to conduct which is voluntary, discreditable, and personal (e.g. sexual or financial) but not unlawful (or not seriously so). In defamation, if the defendant can prove one of the libel defences, he will not have to establish any public interest (except in the case of *Reynolds* privilege, where the law does require consideration of the seriousness of the allegation, including from the point of view of the claimant). But if it is the claimant's choice alone that determines that the only cause of action which the court may take into account is misuse of private information, then the defendant cannot succeed unless he establishes that it comes within the public interest exception (or, perhaps, that he believes that it comes within that exception).

Questions for discussion

1. Do you think 'false private' information should be actionable under misuse of private information?

2. If the publication of private information satisfies the requirements of both defamation *and* misuse of private information, should the claimant be free to choose his or her cause of action, or should the court intervene and assess the 'nub' of the claimant's case?

3. What are the advantages to a claimant in relying on defamation as opposed to misuse of private information?

(iii) 'John Doe' interim injunctions and the 'Spycatcher' principle

On occasion, claimants have been permitted by the courts to obtain interim relief against 'persons unknown' – otherwise known as a 'John Doe' injunction.[279] This will arise where the claimant is uncertain as to the identity of the putative wrongdoer. The person or entity against whom such an injunction is granted is therefore defined not by reference to identity but by description. The granting of an injunction in such circumstances is an exception to section 12(2) of the HRA, which provides that a court is not to grant relief unless satisfied that (a) all practicable steps have been taken to notify the respondent, or (b) there are compelling reasons why such notification can be dispensed with.

When a John Doe interim injunction is granted, the claimant will be required to make 'some effort . . . to trace and serve the primary wrongdoer'.[280] However, this will not always be possible. The danger, therefore, is that the interim injunction will be left on foot and 'what is supposed to be a temporary holding injunction becomes a substitute for a full and fair adjudication'.[281] A further concern relates to the application of the *Spycatcher* principle in such circumstances. The *Spycatcher* principle[282] provides that an interim injunction granted against a defendant (identified or unidentified) will indirectly bind third parties upon whom notice of the injunction has been served, including third party media organisations.[283] Thus, seeking a John Doe order and serving it on a media organisation has been described as 'tantamount to permitting *ex parte* proceedings against the media';[284] indeed, it will often be the 'real value' in seeking such an order.[285] It is important to note, however, that where a claimant intends to serve an interim injunction on third party media organisations, advanced notice of the application and a realistic opportunity to be heard should normally be given to organisations that have shown an interest in publishing the information in question.[286] Even where such notice has not been given, it will be open to such organisations to apply to the court to have the interim injunction discharged or varied.[287] Nevertheless, the concern remains that, absent a return date[288] and unless a third party media organisation is 'prepared to take the risk in costs of applying to vary [the] order',[289] the interim injunction will potentially remain on foot in perpetuity. In the interests of active case management and to ensure that interim orders do not unduly

---

[279] See, e.g., *X & Y v Persons Unknown* [2006] EWHC 2783 (QB); *Terry v Persons Unknown* [2010] EWHC 119 (QB).

[280] *X & Y v Persons Unknown* [2006] EWHC 2783 (QB), 73–8.

[281] Ibid., 78.

[282] *Attorney-General v Newspaper Publishing plc* [1988], Ch. 333.

[283] The purpose of an interim injunction is to preserve the status quo in order to facilitate the administration of justice. Thus, the basis for third parties being bound is that acting contrary to an interim order would frustrate the administration of justice. A final injunction, on the other hand, is granted to protect a claimant's rights, and so is only binding on those against whom it is made. Losing the benefit of the *Spycatcher* principle is one of the reasons why claimants, once they have obtained an interim injunction, may be reluctant to proceed to full trial.

[284] Scott in *Carter-Ruck on Libel and Privacy*, 21.34.

[285] Committee on Super-Injunctions, *Report of the Committee on Super-Injunctions: Super-Injunctions, Anonymised Injunctions and Open Justice* (20 May 2010) 2.10.

[286] *X & Y v Persons Unknown* [2006] EWHC 2783 (QB), 18–20; *WER v REW* [2009] EWHC 1029 (QB), 15–18; *TUV v Person or Persons Unknown* [2010] EWHC 853 (QB), 26. See also Master of the Rolls, *Practice Guidance: Interim Non-Disclosure Orders*, 18–23.

[287] *X & Y v Persons Unknown* [2006] EWHC 2783 (QB), 73.

[288] On the importance of including a return date in such cases, see *Terry v Persons Unknown* [2010] EWHC 119 (QB), 134–6; *Goldsmith v BCD* [2011] EWHC 674 (QB), 30. Note also that in *JIH v News Group Newspapers Ltd* [2012] EWHC 2179 (QB), Tugendhat J discharged, on the motion of the court, a series of injunctions where 'the claimants were taking no steps, either to reach a final order by agreement, or to bring the cases to trial in accordance with the CPR' (at 4).

[289] *Terry v Persons Unknown* [2010] EWHC 119 (QB), 20.

restrict freedom of expression, Practice Guidance recently issued by the Master of the Rolls recommends that all interim non-disclosure orders now include a return date.[290]

(iv) Anonymity orders and other derogations from open justice

The principle of open justice requires that the media be free to describe what occurs during the course of judicial proceedings, including reporting the names of the parties and witnesses, the subject matter of the litigation and any of the evidence presented. Where a court finds in favour of a claimant in a misuse of private information case, however, publication of such details may undermine any order designed to protect the claimant's privacy.[291] Thus, in order to ensure the effectiveness of any relief granted, the court may adopt one of a number of strategies which derogate from the important principle of open justice. It may, for example, conduct the proceedings *in camera*,[292] refer to a claimant by an initial or pseudonym,[293] conceal the details of the private information from the public, redact any publicly available judgment,[294] place the details of the private information in a confidential schedule to the judgment, or seal the court file.[295] Furthermore, an order may include reporting restrictions in relation to various aspects of the case. Such an order may require, for example, that publicity given to the case be restricted to the contents of the judgment,[296] or it may require that publication of the identity of one or more of the parties,[297] or certain details regarding the private information, be prohibited.

In *Re Guardian News and Media Ltd* (see Extract 13.4.2) the Supreme Court affirmed the importance, as an aspect of freedom of speech, of being able to include the names of the parties in press reports of judicial proceedings.[298] Such reporting, according to Lord Rodger, is 'simply much more attractive to readers than stories about unidentified people'.[299] The Supreme Court, however, also affirmed the power of the court to make anonymity orders to protect the privacy interests of such parties. This requires a balancing of the various freedom of speech and privacy interests at stake.[300] In *JIH* v *News Group Newspapers Ltd*,[301] the Court of Appeal provided guidance on anonymity orders in the context of misuse of private information cases. JIH, a well-known sportsman, sought an injunction to prevent News Group Newspapers (NGN) publishing a story about a sexual relationship he had with ZZ, including the fact and details of the relationship. JIH and NGN negotiated an agreement pending trial of the matter. NGN agreed to submit to an injunction preventing it from publishing the material in question, that the identity of JIH

---

[290] Master of the Rolls, *Practice Guidance: Interim Non-Disclosure Orders*, 37–41.
[291] *Terry* v *Persons Unknown* [2010] EWHC 119 (QB), 108.
[292] See, e.g., *Spelman* v *Express Newspapers* [2012] EWHC 239 (QB); *ASG* v *GSA* [2009] EWCA Civ 1574; *AMM* v *HXW* [2010] EWHC 2457 (QB); *KJH* v *HGF* [2010] EWHC 3064 (QB); *MNB* v *News Group Newspapers Ltd* [2011] EWHC 528 (QB).
[293] See, e.g., *CVB* v *MGN Ltd* [2012] EWHC 1148 (QB).
[294] See, e.g., *X & Y* v *Persons Unknown* [2006] EWHC 2783 (QB), 30–4; *WER* v *REW* [2009] EWHC 1029 (QB), 19; *Spelman* v *Express Newspapers* [2012] EWHC 239 (QB).
[295] See, e.g., *DFT* v *TFD* [2010] EWHC 2335 (QB), 8; *Terry* v *Persons Unknown* [2010] EWHC 119 (QB), 23.
[296] *JIH* v *News Group Newspapers Ltd* [2011] EWCA Civ 42, 42; *Gray* v *UVW* [2010] EWHC 2367 (QB); *CDE* v *MGN Ltd* [2010] EWHC 3308 (QB); *KJH* v *HGF* [2010] EWHC 3064 (QB); *POI* v *Person Known as 'Lina'* [2011] EWHC 25 (QB); *MNB* v *News Group Newspapers Ltd* [2011] EWHC 528 (QB).
[297] See, e.g., *NEJ* v *Helen Wood* [2011] EWHC 1972 (QB); *Gray* v *UVW* [2010] EWHC 2367 (QB); *DFT* v *TFD* [2010] EWHC 2335 (QB); *XJA* v *News Group Newspapers Ltd* [2010] EWHC 3174 (QB); *STU* v *UVW* [2011] EWHC 3 EWCA Civ 439.
[298] [2010] 2 AC 697, 22.
[299] *Re Guardian News and Media Ltd* [2010] 2 AC 697, 63.
[300] Ibid., 43; *Ntuli* v *Donald* [2010] EWCA Civ 1276, 52.
[301] [2011] EWCA Civ 42.

should not be disclosed, and that the hearing of the application be in private and not subject to media reporting. Tugendhat J, however, had refused to make the order for anonymity.[302] JIH appealed to the Court of Appeal.

Extract 11.4.24
***JIH v News Group Newspapers Ltd* [2011] EWCA Civ 42**

THE MASTER OF THE ROLLS:

20. . . . In a case involving the grant of an injunction to restrain the publication of allegedly private information, it is, as I have indicated, rightly common ground that, where the court concludes that it is right to grant an injunction (whether on an interim or final basis) restraining the publication of private information, the court may then have to consider how far it is necessary to impose restrictions on the reporting of the proceedings in order not to deprive the injunction of its effect.

. . .

21. In a case such as this, where the protection sought by the claimant is an anonymity order or other restraint on publication of details of a case which are normally in the public domain, certain principles were identified by the Judge . . . [which] I would summarise as follows:

(1) The general rule is that the names of the parties to an action are included in orders and judgments of the court.
(2) There is no general exception for cases where private matters are in issue.
(3) An order for anonymity or any other order restraining the publication of the normally reportable details of a case is a derogation from the principle of open justice and an interference with the Article 10 rights of the public at large.
(4) Accordingly, where the court is asked to make any such order, it should only do so after closely scrutinising the application, and considering whether a degree of restraint on publication is necessary, and, if it is, whether there is any less restrictive or more acceptable alternative than that which is sought.
(5) Where the court is asked to restrain the publication of the names of the parties and/or the subject matter of the claim, on the ground that such restraint is necessary under Article 8, the question is whether there is sufficient general, public interest in publishing a report of the proceedings which identifies a party and/or the normally reportable details to justify any resulting curtailment of his right and his family's right to respect for their private and family life.
(6) On any such application, no special treatment should be accorded to public figures or celebrities: in principle, they are entitled to the same protection as others, no more and no less.
(7) An order for anonymity or for reporting restrictions should not be made simply because the parties consent: parties cannot waive the rights of the public.
(8) An anonymity order or any other order restraining publication made by a Judge at an interlocutory stage of an injunction application does not last for the duration of the proceedings but must be reviewed at the return date.
(9) Whether or not an anonymity order or an order restraining publication of normally reportable details is made, then, at least where a judgment is or would normally be given, a publicly available judgment should normally be given, and a copy of the consequential court order should also be publicly available, although some editing of the judgment or order may be necessary.
(10) Notice of any hearing should be given to the defendant unless there is a good reason not to do so, in which case the court should be told of the absence of notice and the reason for it, and should be satisfied that the reason is a good one.

[302] *JIH v News Groups Newspapers Ltd* [2010] EWHC 2818 (QB).

22. Where, as here, the basis for any claimed restriction on publication ultimately rests on a judicial assessment, it is therefore essential that (a) the judge is first satisfied that the facts and circumstances of the case are sufficiently strong to justify encroaching on the open justice rule by restricting the extent to which the proceedings can be reported, and (b) if so, the judge ensures that the restrictions on publication are fashioned so as to satisfy the need for the encroachment in a way which minimises the extent of any restrictions.

23. In the present case, as in many cases where the court grants an injunction restraining publication of information, the claimant's case as to why there is a need for restraints on publication of aspects of the proceedings themselves which can normally be published is simple and cogent. If the media could publish the name of the claimant and the substance of the information which he is seeking to exclude from the public domain (i.e. what would normally be information of absolutely central significance in any story about the case – who is seeking what), then the whole purpose of the injunction would be undermined, and the claimant's private life may be unlawfully exposed.

. . .

24. In the course of his judgment . . . Tugendhat J accepted the proposition advanced before him by Mr Tomlinson for JIH that:

> Where the court has accepted that the publication of private information should be restrained, if the court is to avoid disclosing the information in question it must proceed in one of two alternative ways:
> (1) If its public judgment or order directly or indirectly discloses the nature of the information in question then it should be anonymised;
> (2) If the claimant is named in the public judgment or order then the information should not be directly or indirectly identified.

. . .

25. While that is not an unfair assessment in the present case, in other cases the position will sometimes be a little less stark. However, in any case, it is plainly correct that, where the court permits the identity of the claimant to be revealed, it is hard to envisage circumstances where that would not mean that significantly less other information about the proceedings could be published than if the proceedings were anonymised. Thus, if the identity of JIH could be published in the context of the present proceedings, it would not be appropriate to permit the publication of even the relatively exiguous information . . . [T]he obvious corollary is that, if the claimant is accorded anonymisation, it will almost always be appropriate to permit more details of the proceedings to be published than if the claimant is identified.

Anonymity orders will only be made where 'strictly necessary'[303] and this will depend on the circumstances of the individual case.[304] Such an order will often be justified in cases involving an element of blackmail, where the interest of society in preventing and punishing blackmail is a factor taken into account in addition to the protection of the claimant's privacy.[305] An anonymity order may also be justified to reduce the risk of the so-called 'jigsaw' identification of the claimant.[306] The concern is that where information about the claimant has already been submitted to the public (during the course of the proceedings or

---

[303] *DFT v TFD* [2010] EWHC 2335 (QB), 30; *Ntuli v Donald* [2010] EWCA Civ 1276, 52–3; Master of the Rolls, *Practice Guidance: Interim Non-Disclosure Orders*, 10.

[304] *Ntuli v Donald* [2010] EWCA Civ 1276, 54; *Secretary of State for the Home Department v AP (No 2)* [2010] UKSC 26, 7.

[305] See, e.g., *AMM v HXW* [2010] EWHC 2457 (QB), 7–11; *DFT v TFD* [2010] EWHC 2335 (QB), 35.

[306] See, e.g., *OPQ v BJM* [2011] EWHC 1059 (QB), 4; *DFT v TFD* [2010] EWHC 2335 (QB); *JIH v News Group Newspapers Ltd* [2011] EWCA Civ 42, 40; *CDE v MGN Ltd* [2010] EWHC 3308 (QB), 74; *AMM v HXW* [2010] EWHC 2457 (QB), 41; *MNB v News Group Newspapers Ltd* [2011] EWHC 528 (QB), 32–42.

otherwise) it may be relatively easy to put together separate pieces of information that would, cumulatively, be capable of leading to their identification. A further factor in support of anonymity which has influenced a number of cases is the view, first expressed in *JIH* v *News Group Newspapers Ltd*,[307] that 'the public interest in open justice is better served by granting anonymity' where this would allow greater details of the case to appear in a publicly available judgment.[308]

On the other hand, it has been said that taking the opposite approach would avoid the potential problem of jigsaw identification. Thus, the view was taken in *Ntuli* v *Donald*[309] that publishing the claimant's name in a public judgment but redacting the private information may avoid the risk that the jigsaw identification of the claimant may result from the process of relating 'separate snippets' of the private information.[310] Of course, whether the risk of jigsaw identification is best allayed by making an anonymity order (as suggested in *JIH* v *News Group Newspapers Ltd*[311]) or by allowing publication of the claimant's identity but restricting the publication of the details of the private information (as suggested in *Ntuli* v *Donald*[312]) will vary depending on the particular circumstances of each case.

(v) Super-injunctions

On occasion, the courts have been asked to make a controversial type of interim injunction known as a 'super-injunction'. A super-injunction prevents a person from (1) publishing the confidential or private information *and* (2) publishing or informing others about the existence of the order and the proceedings.[313] In extreme cases, such an order may be made to protect against the 'jigsaw' identification of either the claimant's identity or the private information in question.[314] More usually, however, restrictions on the reporting of the fact of proceedings and the existence of the injunction will be granted on only a short-term basis to prevent the respondent being 'tipped-off' as to the proceedings prior to being served.[315] Thus, the need for a super-injunction will usually cease once the injunction has been served on the respondent and it is expected that such an order will expire at that time or at the return date.[316]

The use of such orders was the subject of criticism in a sustained media campaign, particularly by *The Guardian* and *The Independent*, between 2009 and 2011. The controversy erupted when two related companies, collectively referred to as Trafigura, obtained an interim injunction against *The Guardian* to prevent the publication of private information contained in a privileged company report.[317] The injunction included an anonymity order as well as an order – the 'super-injunction' – preventing the media from reporting that the

---

[307] [2011] EWCA Civ 42, 25.

[308] *ZAM* v *CFW* [2011] EWHC 476 (QB), 28. See also *NEJ* v *Wood* [2011] EWHC 1972 (QB), 26. Cf. *Spelman* v *Express Newspapers* [2012] EWHC 355 (QB), where the absence of an anonymity order limited the information that the court could disclose in a publicly available judgment.

[309] [2010] EWCA Civ 1276.

[310] *Ntuli* v *Donald* [2010] EWCA Civ 1276, 55.

[311] [2011] EWCA Civ 42, 40.

[312] See Extract 11.4.25.

[313] This was the definition given to a super-injunction by the Committee on Super-Injunctions, *Report of the Committee on Super-Injunctions: Super-Injunctions, Anonymised Injunctions and Open Justice* (20 May 2011) iv, 2.13.

[314] As argued in *DFT* v *TFD* [2010] EWHC 2335 (QB).

[315] *DFT* v *TFD* [2010] EWHC 2335 (QB); *Terry* v *Persons Unknown* [2010] EWHC 119 (QB), 138–9.

[316] *Terry* v *Persons Unknown* [2010] EWHC 119 (QB), 139.

[317] *RJW and SJW* v *Guardian News and Media Ltd and the Person or Persons* [2009] EWHC 2540 (QB). For a useful analysis of the Trafigura saga, see Sophie Matthiesson, 'Who's Afraid of the Limelight? The Trafigura and Terry Super-Injunctions, and the Subsequent Fallout' (2010) 2(2) *Journal of Media Law* 153.

injunction had been obtained. The concerns raised by such orders, of course, are that they severely curtail freedom of expression and constitute an extreme departure from the principle of open justice. Unfortunately, the term 'super-injunction' was largely misused in much of the media coverage to also including anonymity orders, resulting in significant exaggeration as to the frequency with which super-injunctions were being issued.[318]

It was nevertheless in light of the publicity given to the *Trafigura* case as well as to *Terry v Persons Unknown*[319] that the Master of the Rolls established a Committee on Super-Injunctions to conduct an inquiry into the use and application of super-injunctions and anonymity orders. The committee found that 'applicants now rarely apply for such orders and it is even rarer for them to be granted on anything other than an anti-tipping-off, short-terms basis'.[320] This was largely due to guidance that had been given in the meantime by the Court of Appeal in *Ntuli v Donald* (see Extract 11.4.25).[321] The committee also recommended that Practice Guidance be issued in relation to the procedure to be followed when applying for interim injunctions and the approach that should be taken to derogations from the principle of open justice, including the provision of a model order. Such guidance was issued by the Master of the Rolls in July 2011.[322]

In *Ntuli v Donald*, the Court of Appeal clarified the proper approach to be adopted in relation to applications for super-injunctions. The facts emerge sufficiently from the extract.

Extract 11.4.25
***Ntuli v Donald* [2010] EWCA Civ 1276**

LORD JUSTICE MAURICE KAY:

1. On 26 April 2010 Eady J granted an anonymised claimant an injunction restraining an anonymised defendant from doing specified but unpublishable things and further restraining the defendant and others from publishing the fact that the injunction had been sought and obtained. This type of relief has become known as a superinjunction. On this appeal the appellant/defendant seeks the discharge of the injunction in its entirety or, in the alternative, complains about its substantive terms. She also contends that the orders for anonymity and the non-disclosure of the application for and existence of the injunction were inappropriate. There is a cross-appeal whereby the respondent/claimant contends that the substantive injunction did not go far enough.

2. It will facilitate the writing and, indeed, reading of this judgment if I set out the result of the appeal and of the cross-appeal at the outset. It is that the substantive injunction will remain

---

[318] A particularly egregious example of the misunderstanding surrounded the Sir Fred Goodwin case. It was stated numerous times in Parliament (under privilege), and widely reported, that Goodwin had obtained a super-injunction to prevent him being referred to as a banker: see e.g., Afua Hirsch, 'Fred Goodwin gets superinjunction to stop him being called a banker', the *Guardian* (online), 10 March 2011, www.guardian.co.uk/business/2011/mar/10/fred-goodwin-superinjunction-banking. Goodwin, however, had not obtained a super-injunction but rather an anonymity order; and its terms prohibited him being identified as the claimant in the case, not Goodwin's position as a banker: see criticism of such misreporting by Tugendhat J in *Goodwin v News Group Newspapers Ltd* [2011] EWHC 1309 (QB), 9–11.

[319] [2010] EWHC 119 (QB), 24, 137–42 (where Tugendhat J granted a super-injunction on a short-term basis until he delivered his decision, at which time its continuation was refused).

[320] Committee on Super-Injunctions, *Report of the Committee on Super-Injunctions: Super-Injunctions, Anonymised Injunctions and Open Justice* (20 May 2011) iv.

[321] [2010] EWCA Civ 1276. This was referred to in Committee on Super-Injunctions, *Report of the Committee on Super-Injunctions: Super-Injunctions, Anonymised Injunctions and Open Justice* (20 May 2011), 2.29.

[322] Master of the Rolls, *Practice Guidance: Interim Non-Disclosure Orders*. Available at www.judiciary.gov.uk/Resources/JCO/Documents/Guidance/practice-guidance-civil-non-disclosure-orders-july2011.pdf.

but the order for anonymisation of the parties and the non-disclosure of the application for and the existence of the injunction will be discharged . . .

. . .

46. It seems that the only argument advanced on behalf of Mr Donald at the *ex parte* stage was that a superinjunction provision was necessary because, without one, the media might publicise the fact that 'a well-known popular musician' had obtained an injunction which prohibited the publication of (to put it neutrally) salacious details. This is unpersuasive because protection against personal identification could have been achieved by a simple anonymity order. Alternatively, the order could limit publicity to the fact that Mr Donald had obtained an injunction restraining Ms Ntuli from disclosing details of the relationship which existed between them.

. . .

47. Superinjunctions attract understandable controversy. Sometimes it is the product of more heat than light. Although the concept carries the nomenclature of novelty, there is much that is simply a reflection of general principles. The starting point is the principle of open justice, most notably expounded in *Scott* v *Scott* [1913] AC 417 . . .

48. Needless to say, it is not an absolute rule. As Lord Diplock said in *A-G* v *Leveller Magazine Ltd* [1979] AC 440 (at p. 450):

> . . . since the purpose of the general rule is to serve the ends of justice it may be necessary to depart from it where the nature or circumstances of the particular proceeding are such that the application of the general rule in its entirety would frustrate or render impracticable the administration of justice . . .

. . .

50. This line of authority (which includes numerous other examples) requires open justice to apply because it furthers the interests of justice unless a countervailing consideration overrides it in the interests of justice. There are well-known circumstances in which to insist upon open justice would itself create a greater injustice.

. . .

51. It is submitted on behalf of Mr Donald that this is such a case. Mr Sherborne seeks to fortify that submission by inviting us to dilute the test of necessity referred to in the earlier authorities on the basis that they preceded the Human Rights Act . . .

. . .

52. In my judgment, there is no need for a new approach. Indeed, it is significant that Article 6 of the ECHR itself prescribes a test of strict necessity in the context of publicity being permitted to be restricted in the interests of justice. However, as part of its consideration of all the circumstances of a case, a court will have regard to the respective and sometimes competing Convention rights of the parties. In *AP (No 2)*, this led Lord Rodger to formulate the question in these terms (at paragraph 7):

> . . . whether there is sufficient general, public interest in publishing a report of the proceedings which identifies [AP] to justify any resulting curtailment of his right and his family's right to respect for their private and family life.

53. There, anonymity was continued because the public interest in publication 'has to give way to the need to protect *AP* from the risk of violence' and the same public interest 'would not justify curtailing *AP*'s right to respect for his private and family life' (paragraph 18). Whilst this is not the language of 'necessity', it is not significantly different. Indeed, 'has to give way' is qualitatively similar to a necessity test. Necessity remains the test for the residual power to order a private hearing under the Civil Procedure Rules (CPR 39.2(3)(g)).

. . .

54. This is an essentially case-sensitive subject. Plainly Mr Donald is entitled to expect that the court will adopt procedures which ensure that any ultimate vindication of his Article 8 case is not undermined by the way in which the court has processed the interim applications and the trial itself. On the other hand, the principle of open justice requires that any restrictions are the least that can be imposed consistent with the protection to which Mr Donald is entitled. In my judgement, in view of the terms of the substantive injunction and the circumstances of this case, the appropriate restriction on publicity is one that limits reporting and publicity to what is contained in this judgment, together with any ancillary orders necessary to fortify such an order. I am simply unpersuaded that greater restriction is necessary at this stage. There is nothing in this judgment that is significantly invasive of Mr Donald's private or family life.

(vi) Prior notification and article 8

It is considered by some that the only adequate remedy for the misuse of private information is an injunction to restrain publication. Compensation in the form of an award of damages post-publication is a poor substitute because private information, once disclosed to the world, will have lost its private character forever. This is said to be particularly so in the age of the Internet and other digital communication technologies. The problem facing a claimant is that in order to seek a *quia timet* injunction to prevent publication, he or she must have notice that publication of the private information is about to occur. At law, however, a claimant has no right to be given prior notification of any such planned publication; nor are publishers legally obliged to make prospective claimants aware of a pending publication which may constitute a violation of privacy.[323] This was confirmed in *Mosley* v *United Kingdom*.[324] In that case, Max Mosley unsuccessfully argued that the United Kingdom was in violation of article 8 by failing to impose an obligation on *News of the World* to give him sufficient notice to enable him to obtain an interim injunction to restrain publication.[325] The ECtHR noted the wide margin of appreciation given to member states regarding positive protection under article 8 and that this did not require prior notification;[326] moreover, it was recognised that '*post facto* damages provide an adequate remedy for violations of article 8 rights arising from the publication by a newspaper of private information'.[327] It was also held, as a result of freedom of expression under article 10, that any prior notification requirement would need to include a public interest exception.[328] Even so, it was held that such a scheme was unlikely to be effective unless accompanied by sanctions of a 'punitively high level' in the event of a breach and that such sanctions had the potential to be in violation of article 10.[329]

Questions for discussion

1. Should the media be subject to an obligation of prior notification?
2. What problems might arise in the operation of such an obligation?

---

[323] The Joint Committee on Privacy and Injunctions recommended that a prior-notification requirement be included in the media regulator's code of conduct and taken into account when a court assesses damages: see Joint Committee on Privacy and Injunctions, *Privacy and Injunctions* (2010–2012, HL 273, HC 1443) 127; see also Culture, Media and Sports Committee, *Press Standards, Privacy and Libel* (HC 2009–10, 362-I) 40–57, 77–93.
[324] (2011) 53 EHRR 30.
[325] The facts of *Mosley* v *News Group Newspapers* [2008] EWHC 1777 are discussed at Section 4(c)(i).
[326] *Mosley* v *United Kingdom* (2011) 53 EHRR 30, 132.
[327] Ibid., 120.
[328] Ibid., 128.
[329] Ibid., 128–9. For a discussion of this case, see Kirsty Hughes, 'Privacy Injunctions – No Obligation to Notify Pre-Publication' (2011) 3(2) *Journal of Media Law* 179.

(vii) Final remedies

As mentioned above, most misuse of private information cases do not proceed to trial. When they do, the court may award a range of remedies, including a final injunction, damages or an account of profits.[330] It is important to note that section 12 of the HRA will be relevant to the court's assessment of each of these final remedies.

Although the award of a final injunction is an equitable remedy, and is therefore discretionary, a successful claimant will be granted an injunction in all but in exceptional circumstances.[331] A court, however, may be unwilling to grant an injunction where publication has already occurred, especially where the information is considered to have entered the public domain. In such circumstances, the court may be of the view that the only appropriate remedy is an award of damages or an account of profits.[332] Damages may be awarded for pecuniary loss as well as non-pecuniary loss. Damages for pecuniary loss may be calculated on the basis of any actual loss suffered by the claimant (i.e., loss of profit where he or she intended to exploit the private information) or may, in appropriate circumstances, be based on a reasonable licence fee that could have been charged for use of the private information. However, in most cases where the claimant did not intend to exploit the private information for commercial gain the award of damages will be for non-pecuniary loss, including for emotional distress, pain and suffering, and loss of dignity. The nature of non-pecuniary loss makes it difficult to assess, but an important factor to be taken into account will be whether the award is sufficient to provide vindication for the violation of the claimant's privacy.[333] Aggravated damages may also be awarded.

A particularly vexed question, referred to above in the discussion of prior notification (see Section 11.4(f)(vi)), is whether or not damages, in general, can ever provide an adequate remedy for non-pecuniary loss arising from the misuse of private information. Some are of the view that the only truly effective remedy in the area of privacy will be an interim injunction to prevent the publication of the private information in the first place. Damages post-publication, unlike in the defamation context, are inadequate because no amount of monetary compensation can return the information to its previously private state.[334] Others, however, have argued that damages can provide an adequate remedy, citing examples in other areas of law – for example, personal injury – where damages have been accepted as adequate even though such an award does not reverse the harm in question.[335] The ECtHR found in *Mosley* v *United Kingdom* that an award of damages was an adequate remedy for a violation of Article 8.[336] A similar view was taken in *Spelman* v *Express Newspapers*, where the court was considering the adequacy of damages in the context of assessing the question of balance of convenience in an application for an interim injunction (for the facts, see Section 11.4(d)(ii)).

---

[330] For a thorough review of final remedies for breach of confidence and misuse of private information, see Scott in *Carter-Ruck on Libel and Privacy*, 21.52–21.97; Aplin *et al.*, chs 18–20.

[331] See, e.g., Scott in *Carter-Ruck on Libel and Privacy*, 21.54. It should also be noted that the courts have, on occasion, awarded injunctions *contra mundum* – that is, against the world at large: see, e.g., *Venables* v *News Group Newspapers Ltd* [2001] Fam 430; *X (a woman formerly known as Mary Bell)* v *News Group Newspapers* [2003] EWHC 1101 (QB); *Carr* v *News Group Newspapers* [2005] EWHC 971 (QB); *OPQ* v *BJM & CJM* [2011] EWHC 1059 (QB).

[332] Scott in *Carter-Ruck on Libel and Privacy*, 21.55.

[333] Ibid., 21.79.

[334] See, e.g., discussion by Gavin Phillipson, 'Max Mosley Goes to Strasbourg: Article 8, Claimant Notification and Interim Injunctions' (2009) 1 *Journal of Media Law* 73; Barendt, 137.

[335] Andrew Scott, 'Prior Notification in Privacy Cases: A Reply to Professor Phillipson' (2010) 2(1) *Journal of Media Law* 49.

[336] *Mosley* v *United Kingdom* (2011) 53 EHRR 30, 120.

Extract 11.4.26
Spelman v *Express Newspapers* **[2012] EWHC 355 (QB)**

TUGENDHAT J:

109. Where the court finds, as I have, that a claimant has a good arguable case, then in deciding whether or not to grant an interim injunction, the court must go on to consider what is sometimes called the balance of convenience . . . For this, it is often important to consider to what extent damages, rather than an injunction, would provide an adequate remedy. In one sense damages are never an adequate remedy for a tort or for an interference with privacy. But the court law does not adopt as stark an approach as that.

. . .

110. In a case where the principle privacy interest at stake is the keeping of a secret, there is often a strong argument for saying that damages will not be an adequate remedy. Once a secret is known, that knowledge cannot be covered up.

. . .

111. However, there are privacy claims where the main issue at stake is intrusion, injury to feelings and other distress. In such case the position is less clear in relation to damages. The law commonly gives compensation for distress and injury to feelings, including in a libel action. The fact that a threatened defamatory publication would be highly distressing has never been considered a good reason for granting an injunction.

. . .

114. If a remedy in damages is to be an effective remedy, then the amount that the court may award must not be subject to too severe a limitation. Recent settlements in the much publicised phone hacking cases have been reported to be in sums far exceeding what in the past might have been thought to be available to be awarded by the courts. The sums awarded in the early cases such as *Campbell* were very low. But it can no longer be assumed that damages at those levels are the limit of the court's powers.

Questions for discussion

1. Do you agree that damages are an adequate remedy for privacy invasions? Why/ why not?
2. What does *Spelman* v *Express Newspapers* suggest about the calculation of the amount of damages?

11.5 DATA PROTECTION

The regime established under the Data Protection Act 1998 (DPA) implements the EU Data Protection Directive[337] and provides substantial protection regarding the 'processing' – including the collection, storage and use – of 'personal data'. The Act provides a specific exemption for information processed in the course of 'journalism'; however, as discussed in this section, the exemption will not always operate to exclude the media from the regime. In such circumstances, the DPA will provide, in some situations, a statutory cause of action that can be successfully argued alongside misuse of private information. This

---

[337] Council Directive 95/46/EC of 24 October 1995 on the protection of individuals with regard to the processing of personal data and on the free movement of such data [1995] OJ L281/31.

section provides a brief overview of the key provisions of the DPA – in particular, the operation of the exemption for activities conducted in the course of journalism.[338]

The DPA grants 'data subjects'[339] certain rights in relation to the processing of personal data and imposes obligations on 'data controllers'[340] in relation to the processing of personal data.[341] Of most relevance to the media, 'data' is defined in section 1(1) to include information which:

a. is being processed by means of equipment operating automatically in response to instructions given for that purpose,
b. is recorded with the intention that it should be processed by means of such equipment.

The definition of 'data' is clearly intended to target information which is processed using a computer or similar equipment, or information intended to be so processed.

Section 13 confers on an individual the right to seek compensation against a data controller for damage or distress caused by contravention of any of the requirements of the DPA. Compensation for distress, however, can only be claimed if (a) the individual also suffers damage (meaning financial loss)[342] or (b) if the data was processed for 'the special purposes'. Such 'special purposes' include for the purposes of journalism, as well as artistic and literary purposes.[343]

A data controller will contravene the DPA where the eight data protection principles set out in Schedule 1 are not complied with. The first of such principles is likely to be of most relevance to the media. It provides:

> Personal data shall be processed fairly and lawfully and, in particular, shall not be processed unless –
>
> (a) at least one of the conditions in Schedule 2 is met, and
> (b) in the case of sensitive personal data, at least one of the conditions in Schedule 3 is also met.

'Processing' of personal data is defined in section 1(1) to include 'obtaining, recording or holding the information or data or carrying out any operation or set of operations on the . . . data'. This includes the:

(a) organisation, adaptation or alteration of the information or data,
(b) retrieval, consultation or use of the information or data,
(c) disclosure of the information or data by transmission, dissemination or otherwise making available, or
(d) alignment, combination, blocking, erasure or destruction of the information or data.

---

[338] For a comprehensive treatment of the Data Protection Act 1998 and its operation in relation to the media, see Scott in *Carter-Ruck on Libel and Privacy*, ch 22. See also Rosemary Jay, *Data Protection Law and Practice* (Sweet and Maxwell, 3rd edn, 2007).

[339] Defined in s 1(1) as 'an individual who is the subject of personal data'.

[340] Defined in s 1(1) as 'a person who (either alone or jointly or in common with other persons) determines the purposes for which and the manner in which any personal data are, or are to be, processed'.

[341] 'Personal data' is defined in section 1(1) as 'data which relate to a living individual who can be identified (a) from those data, or (b) from those data and other information which is in the possession of, or is likely to come into the possession of, the data controller'. This has been interpreted to mean, 'in short . . . information that affects his privacy, whether in his personal or family life, business or professional capacity': see *Durant* v *Financial Services Association* [2003] EWCA Civ 1746, [28].

[342] *Johnson* v *Medical Defence Union* [2007] EWCA Civ 262, 72–8; *Campbell* v *MGN Ltd* [2002] EWHC 499 (QB), 123.

[343] Section 3.

In *Campbell* v *MGN Ltd* it was held that the publication of hard copies which 'reproduce data that has previously been processed by means of equipment operating automatically' will fall within the scope of 'processing'.[344]

'Sensitive personal data' is defined in section 2 to include:

(a) the racial or ethnic origin of the data subject,[345]
(b) his political opinions,
(c) his religious beliefs or other beliefs or a similar nature,
(d) whether he is a member of a trade union . . .
(e) his physical or mental health or condition,
(f) his sexual life,
(g) the commission or alleged commission by him of any offence, or
(h) any proceedings for any offence committed or alleged to have been committed by him, the disposal of such proceedings or the sentence of any court in such proceedings.

The conditions in Schedules 2 and 3 that have potential relevance for the media are set out in the following extract.

Extract 11.5.1
Data Protection Act 1998

SCHEDULE 2

Conditions relevant for purposes of the first principle: processing of any personal data

1 The data subject has given his consent to the processing.

. . .

6 (1) The processing is necessary for the purposes of legitimate interests pursued by the data controller or by the third party or parties to whom the data are disclosed, except where the processing is unwarranted in any particular case by reason of prejudice to the rights and freedoms or legitimate interests of the data subject.

SCHEDULE 3

Conditions relevant for purposes of the first principle: processing of sensitive personal data

1 The data subject has given his explicit consent to the processing of the personal data.

. . .

5 The information contained in the personal data has been made public as a result of steps deliberately taken by the data subject.

. . .

10 The personal data are processed in circumstances specified in an order made by the Secretary of State for the purposes of this paragraph.

[Pursuant to the immediately preceding paragraph, the Secretary of State made an order in 2000 to extend the list of conditions under Schedule 3 to include the following.][346]

1 (1) The processing—
(a) is in the substantial public interest;
(b) is necessary for the purposes of the prevention or detection of any unlawful act; and

---

[344] [2003] QB 633, 107.
[345] In *Murray* v *Express Newspapers plc* [2007] EWHC 1908 (Ch) it was held (at 80) that a photograph of a person, in that case a Caucasian child, can contain information about race or ethnicity.
[346] Data Protection (Processing of Sensitive Personal Data) Order 2000, SI 2000/417.

(c) must necessarily be carried out without the explicit consent of the data subject being sought so as not to prejudice those purposes.

(2) In this paragraph, 'act' includes a failure to act.

2 The processing—

(a) is in the substantial public interest;

(b) is necessary for the discharge of any function which is designed for protecting members of the public against-

    (i) dishonesty, malpractice, or other seriously improper conduct by, or the unfitness or incompetence of, any person, or

    (ii) mismanagement in the administration of, or failures in services provided by, any body or association; and

(c) must necessarily be carried out without the explicit consent of the data subject being sought so as not to prejudice the discharge of that function.

3 (1) The disclosure of personal data—

(a) is in the substantial public interest;

(b) is in connection with—

    (i) the commission by any person of any unlawful act (whether alleged or established),

    (ii) dishonesty, malpractice, or other seriously improper conduct by, or the unfitness or incompetence of, any person (whether alleged or established), or

    (iii) mismanagement in the administration of, or failures in services provided by, any body or association (whether alleged or established);

(c) is for the special purposes as defined in section 3 of the Act; and

(d) is made with a view to the publication of those data by any person and the data controller reasonably believes that such publication would be in the public interest.[347]

(2) In this paragraph, 'act' includes a failure to act.

In relation to paragraph 6 of Schedule 2, it was held in *Douglas v Hello! Ltd* that commercial publication in the form of a magazine was a relevant legitimate interest that the publisher, as a data controller, had in publishing the photographs of the claimants' wedding. However, Lindsay J held that *Hello!* failed to fulfil paragraph 6 because the publication of the photographs was unwarranted considering the prejudice to the rights of the claimants. According to Lindsay J, '[t]he provision is not, it seems, one that requires some general balance between freedom of expression and rights to privacy or confidence'; rather, 'any prejudice beyond the trivial would seem to suffice'.[348] In other cases, a balancing approach has been adopted.[349]

If the relevant conditions in schedules 2 or 3 have not been complied with, there is a 'defence' under section 13(3) for a data controller if he can 'prove that he had taken such care as in all the circumstances was reasonably required to comply with the requirement concerned'. In addition, the media may be able to rely upon the exemption contained in section 32.

---

[347] This condition was dismissed by Morland J at trial in *Campbell v MGN Ltd* [2002] EWHC 499 (QB), where he held (at 117) that '. . . disclosure of details of the claimant's therapy was not in the substantial public interest. Moreover the disclosure of that personal data was not in connection with the commission of drug offences but the claimant's efforts to avoid committing drug offences'.

[348] *Douglas v Hello! Ltd* [2003] EWHC 786 (Ch) 238.

[349] *Corporate Officer of the House of Commons v Information Commission, Leapman, Brooke and Thomas* [2008] EWHC 1084 (Admin); *Murray v Express Newspapers plc* [2007] EWHC 1908 (Ch).

Extract 11.5.2
Data Protection Act 1998

Section 32 Journalism, literature and art

(1) Personal data which are processed only for the special purposes are exempt from any provision to which this subsection relates if—

    (a) the processing is undertaken with a view to the publication by any person of any journalistic, literary or artistic material,

    (b) the data controller reasonably believes that, having regard in particular to the special importance of the public interest in freedom of expression, publication would be in the public interest, and

    (c) the data controller reasonably believes that, in all the circumstances, compliance with that provision is incompatible with the special purposes.

(2) Subsection (1) relates to the provisions of—

    (a) the data protection principles except the seventh data protection principle,

    . . .

(3) In considering for the purposes of subsection (1)(b) whether the belief of a data controller that publication would be in the public interest was or is a reasonable one, regard may be had to his compliance with any code of practice which—

    (a) is relevant to the publication in question, and

    (b) is designated by the Secretary of State by order for the purposes of this subsection.[350]

    . . .

(6) For the purposes of this Act 'publish', in relation to journalistic, literary or artistic material, means make available to the public or any section of the public.

Section 32 was considered in detail by the Court of Appeal in *Campbell* v *MGN Ltd*[351] (the facts are set out in Section 11.4(b)). At trial, Morland J dismissed the publisher's argument that section 32 applied. His Honour held that section 32 did not apply to the *act of publication*; rather, in light of the wording of the section and the weight of academic commentary, it was his view that it applied only to activities conducted *prior* to publication. This view was rejected by the Court of Appeal.

Extract 11.5.3
***Campbell v MGN Ltd* [2003] QB 633**

Does the s 32 exemption apply only up to the moment of publication?

. . .

121. . . . [W]e have reached the conclusion that, giving the provisions of the sub-sections their natural meaning and the only meaning that makes sense of them, they apply both before and after publication.

122. It seems to us that there are good reasons for sub-sections (1) to (3) to mean what they say. The overall scheme of the Directive and the Act appears aimed at the processing and retention of data over a sensible period. Thus the data controller is obliged to inform the data subject that personal data about the subject have been processed and the data subject is given

---

[350] The Press Complaints Commission and the BBC codes of conduct, along with the codes of conduct established by Ofcom's predecessors, have been designated by the Secretary of State: Data Protection (Designated Codes of Practice) (No 2) Order 2000, SI 2000/1864.
[351] [2003] QB 633.

rights, which include applying under s 14 for the rectification, blocking, erasure or destruction of the data on specified grounds. These provisions are not appropriate for the data processing which will normally be an incident of journalism.

123. This is because the definition of processing is so wide that it embraces the relatively ephemeral operations that will normally be carried out by way of the day-to-day tasks, involving the use of electronic equipment, such as the lap-top and the modern printing press, in translating information into the printed newspaper. The speed with which these operations have to be carried out if a newspaper is to publish news renders it impractical to comply with many of the data processing principles and the conditions in Schedules 2 and 3, including the requirement that the data subject has given his consent to the processing.

124. Furthermore, the requirements of the Act, in the absence of s 32, would impose restrictions on the media which would radically restrict the freedom of the press. Arguably, but in individual cases the argument would be likely to be intense, condition 6(1) of Schedule 2 might enable the lawful processing of personal data that was not sensitive, but the requirement to satisfy a condition in Schedule 3 would effectively preclude publication of any sensitive personal data, for the result would be a string of claims for distress under s 13. There would be no answer to these claims, even if the publication in question had manifestly been in the public interest. The facts of this case provide an illustration of this, for it seems to us that Miss Campbell could have invoked s 13 to seek compensation for the publication of the fact that she is a drug addict, if s 32 has the limited effect for which Mr White contended.

. . .

128. For the reasons we have given we have concluded that Morland J. erred in holding that the first three sub-sections of s 32 apply only to the period before publication. They are of general application.

Does the s 32 exemption apply to publication?

129. Because the exemption provided by s 32(1) depends upon the *processing* being undertaken *with a view to publication* the door was open to the argument advanced on behalf of Miss Campbell that the processing could not include the publication itself. The result of this argument is an absurdity. Exemption is provided in respect of all steps in the operation of processing up to publication on the ground that publication is reasonably believed to be in the public interest – yet no public interest defence is available to a claim for compensation founded on the publication itself. Much of the consideration that we have given to the previous issue underlines the absurdity of this result. We do not consider that the wording of s 32 compels such a result.

130. Under s 32(1) it is the *data* which is exempt from the provisions of the Act specified in sub-section (2). The Act only applies in relation to data. If, as we have held, the Act applies to publication, as part of the processing operation, it does so because the information published remains 'data', as defined by the Act. Where, by reason of s 32 the data becomes exempt as a result of the reasonable belief of the journalist that the publication *will be* in the public interest, the data remains subject to that exemption thereafter.

131. It follows that, contrary to the finding of Morland J., the appellants were entitled to invoke the provisions of s 32 in answer to Miss Campbell's claim.

Does the s 32 exemption apply on the facts of this case?

132. This question did not arise on Morland J.'s interpretation of s 32 and he did not deal with it. Before us the Appellants' submissions were succinct. S 32(1)(a) was plainly satisfied. S 32(1)(b) was also satisfied . . .

133. As to s 32(1)(c) the only condition of relevance was the obtaining of the consent, or the explicit consent, of Miss Campbell. Before publishing the first article Mr Morgan had approached

Miss Campbell's agent, Miss White, about the proposed publication. She had made it plain that there was no consent to the publication. In these circumstances, the public interest justified the publication of the article without Miss Campbell's consent.

134. For Miss Campbell, Mr White accepted that s 32(1)(a) was satisfied. As to s 32(1)(b), he submitted that it was not objectively reasonable for Mr Morgan to believe that publication of the matters complained of was in the public interest. In support of this submission he relied primarily on the arguments advanced in support of the contention that publication of the details of Miss Campbell's attendance at Narcotics Anonymous constituted a breach of confidence.

135. Mr White had a further point. Paragraph 3(ii) of the Press Complaints Commission Code of Practice provides that:

> The use of long lens photography to take pictures of people in private places without their consent is unacceptable.

The Judge had found that the covert photography of Miss Campbell emerging from the Narcotics Anonymous meeting was contrary to the letter and the spirit of the Code.

136. As to s 32(1)(c) Mr White submitted that there had been no necessity to publish the details of Miss Campbell's attendance at Narcotics Anonymous, or the photographs of her leaving the meeting, in order to put the record straight. It followed that Mr Morgan could not reasonably have believed it was incompatible with the purpose of journalism to refrain from publishing these details.

137. We have held earlier in this judgment that the details of Miss Campbell's attendance at Narcotics Anonymous was part of a journalistic package that it was reasonable to publish in the public interest. We do not consider that it would have been reasonably practicable to comply with the provisions of the data protection principles while at the same time making the publications in question. It follows that the Appellants have made good their contention that the three conditions of exemption under s 32 were satisfied.

138. For these reasons we find that there was no infringement by the Appellants of the Act.

In contrast, in *Douglas* v *Hello!*,[352] Lindsay J held that there was no evidence that the defendants reasonably believed that the publication of the photographs was in the public interest. His Honour stated that 'given the nature of the unauthorised photographs, the manner of their obtaining and that the *Hello!* defendants well knew that authorised photographs were shortly to be published by *OK!*', there was no basis upon which he could have concluded otherwise.[353]

It should be noted that in addition to potential civil actions that can arise from contravention of the requirements of the DPA, an offence in section 55 for obtaining or disclosing personal data will often be relevant to the media's newsgathering and publishing activities.

Extract 11.5.4
Data Protection Act 1998

Section 55 Unlawful obtaining etc. of personal data

(1) A person must not knowingly or recklessly, without the consent of the data controller –

   (a) obtain or disclose personal data or the information contained in personal data, or
   (b) procure the disclosure to another person of the information contained in personal data.

---

[352] [2003] EWHC 786 (Ch) 230–9.
[353] Ibid., 231.

(2) Subsection (1) does not apply to a person who shows –

    (a) that the obtaining, disclosing or procuring –

        (i) was necessary for the purpose of preventing or detecting crime . . .

    (b) that in the particular circumstances the obtaining, disclosing or procuring was justified as being in the public interest.

(3) A person who contravenes subsection (1) is guilty of an offence.

Questions for discussion

1. What benefit would a claimant obtain in relying on the DPA as opposed to misuse of private information? What would be the disadvantages?
2. Do you agree with the Court of Appeal's assessment of the wording of section 32?

11.6 HARASSMENT

The Protection from Harassment Act 1997 (PHA) also provides some measure of protection against media intrusions into privacy. While the PHA was introduced to prevent 'stalking' and similar types of conduct,[354] the range of activities that amount to 'harassment' are much wider. It has been held to extend to some of the more excessive media activities that intrude into the personal space and private lives of celebrities and public figures, particularly by the tabloid press and the paparazzi. Singers Amy Winehouse and Lily Allen, as well as actress Sienna Miller, for example, have each been able to secure court orders to restrain photographers from engaging in harassing behaviour, such as pursuing and photographing them in public places, either by car or on foot, confronting them as they enter or exit their homes, or besieging their homes for days on end.[355] More recently the mother of actor Hugh Grant's child, Ting Lan Hong, obtained an injunction to restrain harassing behaviour that she and her child had suffered at the hands of tabloid reporters and photographers who had repeatedly telephoned her and her friends, had followed her as she went about her daily business and had camped outside her home, preventing her from leaving.[356]

Extract 11.6.1
Protection from Harassment Act 1997

1 Prohibition of harassment

(1) A person must not pursue a course of conduct—

    (a) which amounts to harassment of another, and

    (b) which he knows or ought to know amounts to harassment of the other.

(1A) A person must not pursue a course of conduct—

    (a) which involves harassment of two or more persons, and

    (b) which he knows or ought to know involves harassment of those persons, and

---

[354] Moreham in *The Law of Privacy and the Media*, 447.

[355] For a summary of these cases, see Andrew Scott, 'Flash Flood or Slow Burn? Celebrities, Photographers and the Protection from Harassment Act' (2009) 14(4) *Media & Arts Law Review* 397. See also Mark Thomson and Nicola McCann, 'Harassment and the Media' (2009) 2 *Journal of Media Law* 149.

[356] *Ting Lan Hong* v *XYZ* [2011] EWHC 2995 (QB), see also *CC* v *AB* [2006] EWHC 3083 (QB).

(c)   by which he intends to persuade any person (whether or not one of those mentioned above)—
    (i)   not to do something that he is entitled or required to do, or
    (ii)   to do something that he is not under any obligation to do.[357]

(2)   For the purposes of this section, the person whose course of conduct is in question ought to know that it amounts to or involves harassment of another if a reasonable person in possession of the same information would think the course of conduct amounted to or involved harassment of the other.

(3)   Subsection (1) does not apply to a course of conduct if the person who pursued it shows—
    . . .
    (c)   that in the particular circumstances the pursuit of the course of conduct was reasonable.

Section 2 of the PHA makes it a criminal offence to pursue a course of conduct in breach of sections 1 and 1A.[358] Under section 3, on the other hand, the victim of such a breach or apprehended breach can pursue a civil action against a defendant. A court hearing such a claim can award damages for, inter alia, any anxiety caused by the harassment as well as any resulting financial loss.[359] A court may also issue an injunction to restrain any future harassing conduct.[360]

The requisite 'course of conduct' must involve conduct on two or more occasions or, where the harassment is by two or more persons under section 1A, one occasion will suffice,[361] and can include speech.[362] There must also be a 'consistent motive on a consistent course of conduct',[363] meaning that there must be some connection between the individual occasions of harassment.[364] Harassment itself is not defined in the PHA; however, under section 7(2) it is deemed to include conduct 'alarming the person or causing the person distress'.[365] In the absence of a clear statutory definition, the courts have established that harassment requires conduct which is 'oppressive and unreasonable' and which is calculated to produce the consequences (alarm or distress) set out in section 7(3).[366] This means that the consequences of the course of conduct must be sufficiently severe – certainly more than mere annoyance, irritation or upset[367] – before a defendant will be found liable for

---

[357] Note, the victim must be a person; however, the perpetrator may be a body corporate: *Majrowski v Guy's and St Thomas' NHS Trust* [2006] UKHL 34, 19.

[358] A second, more serious, criminal offence of putting a person in fear of violence is contained in section 4. This is likely to have little application in the media context. Note that in September 2012, the Director of Public Prosecutions published guidelines for prosecutors on cases affecting the media – including on decisions to charge journalists or those who interact with journalists: see Director of Public Prosecutions, *Guidelines for Prosecutors on Assessing the Public Interest in Cases Affecting the Media* (13 September 2012) Crown Prosecution Service www.cps.gov.uk/legal/d_to_g/.

[359] Protection from Harassment Act 1997, s 3(2). Damages are as of right: see *Majrowski v Guy's and St Thomas' NHS Trust* [2006] UKHL 34, 21–2.

[360] It is clear from sections 3(3) and 3(6) that a court may grant such an injunction: see *Majrowski v Guy's and St Thomas' NHS Trust* [2006] UKHL 34, 20.

[361] Protection from Harassment Act 1997, s 7(3).

[362] Ibid., s 7(4).

[363] *Tuppen and Singh v Microsoft Corporation Ltd* (QB, Douglas Brown J, 14 July 2000), 16, cited in Moreham in *The Law of Privacy and the Media*, 449.

[364] Ibid.

[365] This is inclusive not exhaustive and it is contemplated that conduct resulting in consequences other than alarm or distress might also be captured by the epithet. Alarm and distress, however, may be the 'baseline': see Scott in *Carter-Ruck on Libel and Slander*, 23.11.

[366] *Thomas v News Group Newspapers Ltd* [2001] EWCA Civ 1233, 30; *Majrowski v Guy's and St Thomas' NHS Trust* [2006] UKHL 34, 30.

[367] *Majrowski v Guy's and St Thomas' NHS Trust* [2006] UKHL 34, 30.

harassment, either criminally or civilly.[368] Whether conduct meets this severity threshold, of course, very much depends on the context in which the conduct occurs.[369] Whether the conduct constitutes harassment does not, however, depend on whether or not alarm or distress has, in fact, been experienced by the alleged victim;[370] nor must the alleged victim be aware of each instance of conduct said to constitute the harassment.[371] However, whether a person knew or ought to have known that his or her conduct would cause distress is to be judged by reference to what the person knew about the characteristics of the victim.[372]

There are at least two broad categories of conduct undertaken by the media which have the potential to amount to harassment: intrusive information gathering and the repeated publication of material.[373] The first category applies to the types of activities enjoined by Amy Winehouse, Sienna Miller and Lily Allen against errant journalists and photographers – for example, relentless pursuit and questioning, door-stopping, constant surveillance, entrapment and telephoning. An applicant, however, need not be a famous celebrity or public figure in order to seek relief under the PHA; moreover, an injunction will be imposed even where the media's interest in pursuing and publishing the material seemingly goes beyond idle celebrity gossip or tittle-tattle. In *AM v News Group Newspapers Ltd*,[374] for example, a landlord who rented his house to the wife of suspected terrorist Abu Qatada was able to obtain an injunction to prevent journalists and photographers from making contact with the applicant by any medium, from entering or approaching the applicant's address within 100 yards, and from harassing, pestering, threatening or otherwise interfering with any occupier or invitee within the house.

Harassment through repeated publication will also, in certain circumstances, be covered by the PHA. In *Thomas v News Group Newspapers*,[375] the Court of Appeal held that it was possible that repeated publication of a story concerning the victim in a newspaper could constitute harassment within the meaning of section 1. In that case, the alleged victim, a police worker, was subject to criticism in a series of articles, including readers' letters, published in *The Sun* regarding a complaint she had made about racist comments spoken in her presence by two police officers. The articles suggested that the respondent had only complained because of her race and therefore the complaint and the demotion of the officers in question was inappropriate. The newspaper's application to strike out the claim was refused at first instance; it then appealed to the Court of Appeal arguing that its conduct, in these circumstances, could not fall within the scope of the PHA in light of the HRA and the media's right to freedom of expression. In particular, it was argued that its conduct in publishing the articles should be considered to be 'reasonable' within the meaning of section 1(3)(c).

---

[368] See Moreham in *The Law of Privacy and the Media*, 450.
[369] *Conn v Sunderland City Council* [2007] EWCA Civ 1492, 12.
[370] *Majrowski v Guy's and St Thomas' NHS Trust* [2006] UKHL 34, 60 (per Baroness Hale).
[371] *Howlett v Holding* [2006] EWHC 41 (QB), 20.
[372] *Trimingham v Associated Newspapers Ltd* [2012] EWHC 1296 (QB), 89.
[373] For a detailed analysis of the application of the Protection from Harassment Act 1997 to the media, see Andrew Scott, 'Flash Flood or Slow Burn? Celebrities, Photographers and the Protection from Harassment Act' (2009) 14(4) *Media & Arts Law Review* 397; Scott in *Carter-Ruck on Libel and Privacy*, ch 23; Moreham in *The Law of Privacy and the Media*, 453–9.
[374] [2012] EWHC 308 (QB).
[375] [2001] EWCA Civ 1233.

Extract 11.6.2
Thomas v *News Group Newspapers Ltd* **[2001] EWCA Civ 1233**

LORD PHILLIPS MR:

15. . . . [T]he appellants concede that publication of press articles is, in law, capable of amounting to harassment albeit in only very rare circumstances. This is an important concession, but I consider that it is a concession rightly made. The suggestion [made at trial] that journalistic articles were implicitly outside the ambit of the 1997 Act was, in my view, unarguable. . . . The issue is whether it is arguable that the publications in question constituted 'harassment' having regard to the effect that the respondent alleges they had upon her.

. . .

24. Section 3 of the HRA requires the court, so far as it is possible to do so, to interpret and give effect to legislation in a manner which is compatible with Convention rights. Section 12 of the HRA emphasises the care which the court must take not to interfere with journalistic freedom unless satisfied that this is necessary according to the principles to which I have referred. Both these sections are important when considering the ambit of the criminal offence and the civil tort of harassment created by the 1997 Act in the context of publications by the media. Harassment must not be given an interpretation which restricts the right of freedom of expression, save in so far as this is necessary in order to achieve a legitimate aim. . . .

. . .

26. Both parties to this appeal recognise the importance of the right of freedom of expression and, in particular, press freedom. Both parties recognise that the duty to give effect to this right is an important consideration to any court when considering whether an offence or civil tort has been committed contrary to the 1997 Act.

The nature of harassment

. . .

30. The Act does not attempt to define the type of conduct that is capable of constituting harassment. 'Harassment' is, however, a word which has a meaning which is generally understood. It describes conduct targeted at an individual which is calculated to produce the consequences described in section 7 and which is oppressive and unreasonable. The practice of stalking is a prime example of such conduct.

31. The fact that conduct that is reasonable will not constitute harassment is clear from section 1(3)(c) of the Act. While that subsection places the burden of proof on the defendant, that does not absolve the claimant from pleading facts which are capable of amounting to harassment. Unless the claimant's pleading alleges conduct by the defendant which is, at least, arguably unreasonable, it is unlikely to set out a viable plea of harassment.

The nature of reasonable conduct

32. Whether conduct is reasonable will depend upon the circumstances of the particular case. When considering whether the conduct of the press in publishing articles is reasonable for the purposes of the 1997 Act, the answer does not turn upon whether opinions expressed in the articles are reasonably held. The question must be answered by reference to the right of the press to freedom of expression which has been so emphatically recognised by the jurisprudence both of Strasbourg and this country.

. . .

34. . . . In general, press criticism, even if robust, does not constitute unreasonable conduct and does not fall within the natural meaning of harassment. A pleading, which does no more than allege that the defendant newspaper has published a series of articles that have foreseeably

caused distress to an individual, will be susceptible to a strike-out on the ground that it discloses no arguable case of harassment.

. . .

35. It is common ground between the parties to this appeal, and properly so, that before press publications are capable of constituting harassment, they must be attended by some exceptional circumstance which justifies sanctions and the restriction on the freedom of expression that they involve. It is also common ground that such circumstances will be rare.

. . .

37. It is not necessary for this court to . . . attempt any categorisation of the types of abuse of freedom of the press which may amount to harassment. That is because the parties are agreed that the publication of press articles calculated to incite racial hatred of an individual provides an example of conduct which is capable of amounting to harassment under the 1997 Act . . .

. . .

38. This agreement between the parties reduces the central issue in this case to a relatively narrow one. It is Mr Pannick QC's case for the respondent that she pleaded an arguable case that the series of publications in The Sun were intended to provoke hostility on the part of its readers against her on the grounds of her race.

. . .

40. The substantive argument advanced by Mr Browne [for the appellant] is that the respondent's pleading does not raise even an arguable case of racism. Before the judge the appellants conceded that the tone of their publication was strident, aggressive and inflammatory, but they denied that it was racist.

. . .

49. When the three publications are considered together . . . I am satisfied that the respondent has pleaded an arguable case that the appellants harassed her by publishing racist criticism of her which was foreseeably likely to stimulate a racist reaction on the part of their readers and cause her distress.

. . .

50. Mr Browne argued that, if the test of whether a series of publications constitutes harassment is to turn on the question of whether the conduct of the publisher is reasonable, this test will lack the certainty that the Strasbourg court requires if it is to find that a restriction on freedom of expression is prescribed by law. On my analysis, the test requires the publisher to consider whether a proposed series of articles, which is likely to cause distress to an individual, will constitute an abuse of the freedom of press which the pressing social needs of a democratic society require should be curbed. This is a familiar test and not one which offends against Strasbourg's requirement of certainty.

51. For the reasons that I have given, I would dismiss the appeal.

A more recent claim of harassment as a result of repeated newspaper publication was rejected in *Trimingham* v *Associated Newspapers Ltd.*[376] Carina Trimingham was the press secretary of MP Christopher Huhne, with whom she had an affair. At the time, Huhne was married and Trimingham was living with her civil partner. Trimingham claimed that 65 articles, along with readers' comments, published by the defendant newspaper constituted a course of conduct amounting to harassment under the PHA. This was claimed to be by virtue of the fact that the articles made repeated reference to her appearance

---

[376] [2012] EWHC 1296 (QB).

and/or her sexuality (she was often described as 'bisexual' or as a 'former lesbian'). Tugendhat J made some important points about the operation of the PHA in light of the requirements of the HRA.

Extract 11.6.3
***Trimingham* v *Associated Newspapers Ltd* [2012] EWHCA 1296**

TUGENDHAT J:

48. Although passed before the HRA, the PHA is (like the law of libel and the Data Protection Act 1998) one of the many different laws of England that give effect to the obligation of the state to prevent interference with the right of individuals to protection of their private lives under ECHR Art 8 . . .

. . .

54. What I understand Lord Phillips [in *Thomas*] to be saying is that, for the court to comply with HRA s 3, it must hold that a course of conduct in the form of journalistic speech is reasonable under PHA s 1(3)(c) unless, in the particular circumstances of the case, the course of conduct is so unreasonable that it is necessary (in the sense of a pressing social need) and proportionate to prohibit or sanction the speech in pursuit of one of the aims listed in Art 10(2), including, in particular, for the protection of the rights of others under Art 8 . . .

55. . . . The court is required to follow the guidance of the House of Lords in *Re S (A Child)* . . . [as set out in Section 11.4(e) above]. PHA s 1(3)(c) requires the court apply that test to 'pursuit of the course of conduct'.

. . .

78. *Thomas* was a strike out application, not a trial . . . Lord Phillips did not have to explain the full implications of the requirement that the court interpret the PHA so that 'harassment must not be given an interpretation which restricts the right to freedom of expression'. In my judgment the points at which the court must give effect to that guidance include s 1(1) and (2) (what a reasonable person in possession of the relevant information would think would amount to harassment) . . .

Tugendhat J found, on a number of related bases, that the newspaper did not engage in a course of conduct amounting to harassment. First, his Honour found that there was no necessary causation between the alleged course of conduct (repeated publication about her appearance and sexuality) and the distress or damage said to be suffered by Trimingham. There was no doubt that Trimingham was distressed by the publications in question; such distress, however, arose from the focus of those publications on the circumstances surrounding her affair with Huhne rather than from references to her appearance or sexuality.[377] Second, in terms of section 1(2) of the PHA, Tugendhat J concluded that a reasonable person in the position of the defendant, with knowledge of the claimant's job as Huhne's press secretary and her past career as a journalist, would not think that publication of the material complained of would amount to harassment. Rather, such a reasonable person would consider Trimingham to be robust; in other words, 'that she was tough, a woman of strong character, not likely to be upset by comments or offensive language, a woman who was known to give as good as she got'.[378] Third, while the language about her appearance may have been upsetting, Tugendhat J did not accept that the defendant 'ought to have known that its conduct in relation to that language would be

---

[377] Ibid., 253–4.
[378] Ibid., 252.

sufficiently distressing to be considered oppressive or amount to harassment'.[379] In relation to the repeated references to Trimingham's sexuality, it was held that the terms 'bisexual' and 'lesbian' were not used, and would not be understood by a reasonable reader, in a pejorative sense.[380] Fourth, Tugendhat J found that the newspaper's conduct had been reasonable in the circumstances. Trimingham was considered by his Honour to be a 'public figure'; thus her role as Huhne's press secretary and her decision to have an affair which she knew would attract publicity meant that she could not be considered a private figure.[381] In light of this, his Honour held:

> [I]f an unusual event occurs involving sexual behaviour of a public figure, and one of the participants is homosexual, it is not of itself unreasonable for a newspaper to refer to that fact. Nor is it unreasonable to refer to those facts on as many occasions as the substance of the story is repeated and referred to explain subsequent events of public interest. And if a journalist is criticising a person for deceitful, unprofessional or immoral behaviour in a sexual and public context, it is not of itself unreasonable to refer to that person as homosexual if in fact they are, and it is their sexual conduct which is one of the factors giving rise to the newsworthy events.[382]

Moreover, Tugendhat J found that the defendant's conduct could not be considered unreasonable because Trimingham's article 8 rights in this regard were limited: not only was she not a private figure, but she had been open about her sexuality.[383] Furthermore, given that each of the articles reported a 'newsworthy event relating to Mr Huhne', in which Trimingham featured as a 'secondary character', the repetition of Trimingham's sexuality, even 65 times, did not amount to 'unreasonable' speech.[384]

Questions for discussion

1. Should the PHA apply to media publications? Why/why not?
2. Do you agree with the conclusion reached in *Trimingham* v *Associated Newspapers*?
3. What is the relationship between the HRA and the PHA?
4. Do you agree that the repeated reference to Trimingham's sexuality was not pejorative? Can this finding be reconciled with the decision in *Thomas* v *News Group Newspapers*?
5. Do you agree that Trimingham was a public figure? Should it be a factor in determining whether the conduct of the media was reasonable in the circumstances?

11.7 OFCOM BROADCASTING CODE

A complaint of invasion of privacy in the context of broadcasting may be made to Ofcom.[385] Ofcom has the duty to secure, in the case of all television and radio programmes, the application of standards for the adequate protection of privacy[386] and, in

---

[379] Ibid., 254.
[380] Ibid., 256.
[381] Ibid., 249.
[382] Ibid., 261.
[383] Ibid., 263.
[384] Ibid., 272.
[385] Ofcom is the successor to the previous regulators, the Independent Television Commission (ITC) and the Broadcasting Standards Commission (BSC), and was established under the Communications Act 2003.
[386] Communications Act 2003, s 3(2)(f)(ii). The securing of the application of appropriate standards for the protection of privacy must be 'in the manner that best guarantees an appropriate level of freedom of expression': Communications Act 2003, s 3(4)(g).

particular, is required to develop a code of conduct 'in connection with the avoidance of . . . unwarranted infringement of privacy in, or in connection with the obtaining of material included in' television and radio programmes.[387] The code directly binds independent television and radio broadcasters as part of their broadcasting licence conditions,[388] while the BBC is bound by a combination of the BBC Agreement and section 198 of the Communications Act 2003.[389]

In order to ensure compliance, Ofcom has the specific power to consider and adjudicate complaints in relation to violations of privacy under section 110 of the Broadcasting Act 1996.[390] A range of sanctions can be imposed for a breach, including: a direction to issue a correction or a statement of findings, or to not repeat the broadcast of the programme; the imposition of financial penalties or a shortening of the licence period; or the revocation of the licence.[391] Ofcom, however, does not have the power to award damages to a complainant,[392] nor can it issue an interim injunction to prevent an invasion of privacy by enjoining the broadcasting of material.

Extract 11.7.1
Broadcasting Act 1996

Section 110

1. . . . it shall be the duty of Ofcom to consider and adjudicate on complaints which are made to them . . . and relate—

. . .

(b) to unwarranted infringement of privacy in, or in connection with the obtaining of material included in, such programmes.[393]

3. In exercising their functions under subsection (1), Ofcom shall take into account any relevant provisions of the code maintained by them under section 107.

Complaints can only be made by a person or body of persons (including a corporation)[394] 'whose privacy was infringed', or a person authorised to make a complaint on his behalf.[395] Ofcom only has jurisdiction to consider a privacy complaint only where the programme, the making of which is alleged to have involved an infringement of privacy, is in fact broadcast.[396] However, it is immaterial whether the infringement occurred in the course of obtaining the material for broadcast or in the broadcast itself, provided it is at least closely linked to the obtaining of the material which is, in fact, broadcast.[397]

---

[387] Broadcasting Act 1996, s 107; Communications Act 2003, sch 1, para 14.

[388] Communications Act 2003, s 326.

[389] Prior to the introduction of the Communications Act 2003, the BBC was not subject to external regulation in relation to privacy. The BBC has established its own editorial guidelines regarding matters such as privacy: see BBC, *Editorial Guidelines* (2012), www.bbc.co.uk/guidelines/editorialguidelines/guidelines/.

[390] This role, previously conducted by the BSC, was transferred to Ofcom under the Communications Act 2003, sch 1, para 14. Note, Ofcom can only consider a complaint in relation to privacy if the conditions in ss 111 and 114 of the Broadcasting Act 1996 are satisfied: Broadcasting Act 1996, s 110.

[391] Communications Act 2003, ss 236–8.

[392] The lack of available remedies for a complainant has been said to be incompatible with article 8: see Fenwick and Phillipson, 862–4.

[393] This section applies to programmes broadcast by the BBC, Welsh Authority, and licensed commercial services: Broadcasting Act 1996, s 107(5).

[394] *R v Broadcasting Standards Commission, ex parte British Broadcasting Corporation* [2001] QB 885.

[395] Broadcasting Act 1996, s 111, and see definition of 'person affected' in s 130(1).

[396] *R v Broadcasting Complaints Commission, ex parte Barclay* [1997] EMLR 62, 65–6.

[397] Ibid., *R v Broadcasting Complaints Commission, ex parte British Broadcasting Corporation* [1993] EMLR 419.

The current privacy code, contained in Section Eight of the Ofcom Broadcasting Code, took effect on 28 February 2011. The following is a selected extract from the Code.

Extract 11.7.2
The Ofcom Broadcasting Code

Section Eight: Privacy

. . .

As well as containing a principle and a rule this section contains 'practices to be followed' by broadcasters when dealing with individuals or organisations participating or otherwise directly affected by programmes, or in the making of programmes. Following these practices will not necessarily avoid a breach of this section of the Code (Rule 8.1). However, failure to follow these practices will only constitute a breach where it results in an unwarranted infringement of privacy . . .

Principle

To ensure that broadcasters avoid any unwarranted infringement of privacy in programmes and in connection with obtaining material included in programmes.

Rule

8.1. Any infringement of privacy in programmes, or in connection with obtaining material included in programmes, must be warranted.

Meaning of 'warranted': In this section 'warranted' has a particular meaning. It means that where broadcasters wish to justify an infringement of privacy as warranted, they should be able to demonstrate why in the particular circumstances of the case, it is warranted. If the reason is that it is in the public interest, then the broadcaster should be able to demonstrate that the public interest outweighs the right to privacy . . .

Practices to be followed (8.2 to 8.22)

Private lives, public places and legitimate expectation of privacy

Meaning of 'legitimate expectation of privacy': Legitimate expectations of privacy will vary according to the place and nature of the information, activity or condition in question, the extent to which it is in the public domain (if at all) and whether the individual concerned is already in the public eye. There may be circumstances where people can reasonably expect privacy even in a public place. Some activities and conditions may be of such a private nature that filming or recording, even in a public place, could involve an infringement of privacy. People under investigation or in the public eye, and their immediate family and friends, retain the right to a private life, although private behaviour can raise issues of legitimate public interest.

8.2. Information which discloses the location of a person's home or family should not be revealed without permission, unless it is warranted.

8.3. When people are caught up in events which are covered by the news they still have a right to privacy in both the making and the broadcast of a programme, unless it is warranted to infringe it. This applies both to the time when these events are taking place and to any later programmes that revisit those events.

8.4. Broadcasters should ensure that words, images or actions filmed or recorded in, or broadcast from, a public place, are not so private that prior consent is required before broadcast from the individual or organisation concerned, unless broadcasting without their consent is warranted.

Consent

8.5. Any infringement of privacy in the making of a programme should be with the person's and/or organisation's consent or be otherwise warranted.

8.6. If the broadcast of a programme would infringe the privacy of a person or organisation, consent should be obtained before the relevant material is broadcast, unless the infringement of privacy is warranted. (Callers to phone-in shows are deemed to have given consent to the broadcast of their contribution.)

. . .

Gathering information, sound or images and the re-use of material

8.9. The means of obtaining material must be proportionate in all the circumstances and in particular to the subject matter of the programme.

. . .

8.13. Surreptitious filming or recording should only be used where it is warranted. Normally, it will only be warranted if:

- there is prima facie evidence of a story in the public interest; and
- there are reasonable grounds to suspect that further material evidence could be obtained; and
- it is necessary to the credibility and authenticity of the programme.

. . .

Meaning of 'surreptitious filming or recording': Surreptitious filming or recording includes the use of long lenses or recording devices, as well as leaving an unattended camera or recording device on private property without the full and informed consent of the occupiers or their agent. It may also include recording telephone conversations without the knowledge of the other party, or deliberately continuing a recording when the other party thinks that it has come to an end.

8.14. Material gained by surreptitious filming and recording should only be broadcast when it is warranted . . .

8.15. Surreptitious filming or recording, doorstepping or recorded 'wind-up' calls to obtain material for entertainment purposes may be warranted if it is intrinsic to the entertainment and does not amount to a significant infringement of privacy such as to cause significant annoyance, distress or embarrassment. The resulting material should not be broadcast without the consent of those involved. However if the individual and/or organisation is not identifiable in the programme then consent for broadcast will not be required.

Source: © Ofcom copyright 2006–11.

(a) Judicial review of Ofcom decisions

Ofcom's decisions are subject to judicial review. Moreover, Ofcom, as a public authority under the HRA, must not act incompatibly with a Convention right.[398] This means that Ofcom must interpret and apply Section Eight of the Broadcasting Code in accordance with article 8 and article 10. Courts, however, have evinced a general reluctance to interfere with determinations of Ofcom and its predecessors, the Broadcasting Standards Commission (BSC) and the Broadcasting Complaints Commission (BCC). This reluctance is evidenced in the case of *R* v *Broadcasting Complaints Commission, ex parte Granada Television Ltd.*[399] The BCC, the predecessor to the BSC, had held that two Granada programmes unwarrantably infringed privacy inasmuch as they included photographs of

---

[398] HRA, s 6(1). See *Gaunt, R (on the application of)* v *The Office of Communications* [2011] EWCA Civ 692 (where the aspect of the Code regarding offensive material was considered).
[399] [1995] EMLR 163. See also *R* v *Broadcasting Standards Commission, ex parte British Broadcasting Corporation* [2001] QB 885.

children who had died in tragic circumstances without warning their parents that this material would be included. The approach of the former BCC is now reflected in section 8.19 of the Broadcasting Code.

Extract 11.7.3

R v Broadcasting Complaints Commission, ex parte Granada Television Ltd **[1995] EMLR 163 (CA), 167–9**

BALCOMBE LJ:

It is a reasonable inference that another reason why Parliament did not provide a definition of privacy in the Act is because it considered it more appropriate that the difficult questions of fact and degree and value judgment, which are raised by the concept of an infringement of privacy, are best left to a specialist body, such as the BCC, whose members have experience of broadcasting. Two other factors are also relevant to the general approach to be adopted in the present case:

1. The only *legal* sanction which is attracted by a finding of unwarranted infringement of privacy is the duty to publish the finding . . . [T]he fact is that publication is the only legal sanction.
2. Parliament has not provided any right of appeal against the decisions of the BCC. This indicates a clear intention to leave to the BCC alone the determination of the difficult questions which I have mentioned above.

In the light of these considerations I accept the submission of Mr Pannick QC, counsel for the BCC, that the Court will be slow to overturn a finding of the BCC that the content of a broadcast is an unwarranted infringement of privacy . . .

Accordingly, unless on no interpretation of the word 'privacy' could the findings of the BCC be justified . . . there is no basis for the grant of judicial review.

With this general approach in mind I turn to a detailed consideration of Granada's two points.

Public domain

. . .

In my judgment it is clear that the fact that a matter has once been in the public domain cannot prevent its resurrection, possibly many years later, from being an infringement of privacy. Whether in such a case there is an unwarranted infringement of privacy is a matter of fact and degree and as such for the decision of the BCC with which the Court cannot interfere.

While this case was decided prior to the HRA entering into force, there is authority to indicate – albeit in slightly different contexts or under different parts of the Broadcasting Code – that courts will continue to be reluctant to depart from determinations made by Ofcom.[400]

---

[400] See, e.g., *R (on the application of Ford) v PCC* [2002] EMLR 5 (regarding a determination by the PCC of a privacy complaint under its privacy code); *R (on the application of ProLife Alliance) v BBC* [2004] 1 AC 185 (where the BBC refused to air a Party Election Broadcast on the basis that it offended the restriction on the broadcast of offensive material); *R (on the application of Gaunt) v Office of Communications* [2011] EWCA Civ 692 (where Ofcom found a radio broadcast licensee in breach of the restriction on offensive material under ss 2.1 and 2.3 of the Code). See also discussion in Fenwick and Phillipson, 864–9.

Selected further reading

Tanya Aplin *et al.*, *Gurry on Breach of Confidence: The Protection of Confidential Information* (Oxford University Press, 2nd edn, 2012). This title deals with both the law of breach of confidence and the action for misuse of private information. As well as being particularly thorough, it is also the most current treatment of the black letter law.

Helen Fenwick and Gavin Phillipson, *Media Freedom under the Human Rights Act* (Oxford University Press, 2006). This book is useful for understanding the Convention and Strasbourg jurisprudence and the impact that the Human Rights Act has had on the development of domestic privacy law.

Mark Warby QC *et al.* (eds), *Tugendhat and Christie: The Law of Privacy and the Media* (Oxford University Press, 2nd edn, 2011). This book focuses on the application of privacy laws in the context of media publications; it also has a particularly useful chapter on theories of privacy protection.

Cameron Doley and Alistair Mullis (eds), *Carter-Ruck on Libel and Privacy* (Lexis Nexis, 6th edn, 2010). This book (Chapters 18–24) provides a useful exposition of black letter privacy law; its value lies in the well-argued position that the author (Dr Andrew Scott) often takes in relation to particular doctrinal and theoretical issues that arise in the law of privacy.

12 Contempt of court

12.1 INTRODUCTION

At the beginning of 2011 England was gripped by the murder of an attractive young landscape architect, Joanna Yeates, whose body had been found in a wood near Bristol on Christmas Day 2010. The landlord of her flat, Chris Jefferies, was arrested a few days later. Tabloid media coverage of the case, and speculation on the Internet, was intense. The Attorney-General warned the media to be careful in their reporting and to avoid treatment which might prejudice eventual criminal proceedings. Subsequently Jefferies was released without charge, and another person arrested and prosecuted. The Attorney-General subsequently took proceedings for contempt of court against two tabloid newspapers, the *Daily Mirror* and the *Sun* in respect of their treatment of Jefferies (see Extract 12.2.5 for their outcome). The episode highlights the continuing importance of contempt of court law, particularly the branch of it which is concerned to avoid the risk of prejudice to legal proceedings from media publicity.

Contempt of court is a complex area of law.[1] Some of its varieties have little relevance for media law; for instance, it is a contempt to interrupt a trial or physically to prevent the parties or witnesses from attending proceedings. However, many types of contempt do typically involve the media. Indeed, for journalists and editors contempt of court is as significant a restraint on their freedom as that imposed by libel law. This chapter examines those parts of contempt law concerned to restrict media publications which may prejudice the fair conduct of legal proceedings. In this context, the freedom of the press and the broadcasting media is in conflict with the right of the parties to a fair trial. Both freedoms are fundamental rights guaranteed by the European Convention on Human Rights (ECHR): article 10 freedom of expression covers the media (see Chapter 1, Section 1.2), while article 6 guarantees the right to a 'fair and public hearing' (see Extract 13.2.3). Other instances of the conflict between these freedoms are considered in Chapter 13, where a number of restrictions on the freedom of the media to attend and report legal proceedings are discussed.

It used to be common to bring contempt proceedings for the abusive criticism of a judge, in particular when a publication suggested that he was biased. For example, the *New Statesman* was held guilty of this type of contempt, known as 'scandalising the court', when it doubted whether the birth control pioneer, Marie Stopes, could receive a fair hearing of her libel action from Mr Justice Avory, a Roman Catholic.[2] Frequent use of this type of contempt proceeding would constitute a significant fetter on the freedom of the media to discuss uninhibitedly the quality of the judiciary and the merits of their decisions.

It is now over 80 years since a successful contempt application for scandalising has been brought in England, though applications have been upheld in Commonwealth cases.[3] Clearly,

---

[1] The most authoritative work is D. Eady and A.T.H. Smith (eds), *Arlidge, Eady & Smith on Contempt*, 4th edn (London: Sweet & Maxwell, 2011).

[2] *R v New Statesman, ex parte DPP* (1928) 44 TLR 301 (DC).

[3] In both *Badry v DPP of Mauritius* [1983] 2 AC 297 and *Ahnee v DPP of Mauritius* [1999] 2 AC 294, the Privy Council upheld convictions for this variety of contempt, while imposing limits on its scope: see Robertson and Nicol, paras 7.053–55; Barendt, 316–22. For the most comprehensive treatment of this topic, see C. Walker, 'Scandalising in the eighties' (1985) 101 *Law Quarterly Review* 359.

good faith criticism, however abusive, has not been regarded as a contempt,[4] so the offence of scandalising the court became obsolescent. In this respect English law has been more protective of the freedom of the media to comment on the administration of justice than the European Court of Human Rights, which has sometimes declined to interfere with state court decisions convicting the media of libel of the judiciary or other offences comparable to this type of contempt of court.[5] At the end of 2012, the Law Commission recommended abolition of this form of contempt of court, and this has been done by section 33 of the Crime and Courts Bill 2012 for this purpose.[6]

The principal type of contempt considered in this chapter is the 'strict liability rule', under which a publication amounts to contempt if it creates a significant risk of prejudice to forthcoming legal proceedings. The leading common law authority in this area of law before its statutory reform in 1981 is the decision of the House of Lords in the famous *Sunday Times* thalidomide case.[7] The Attorney-General took proceedings against the newspaper which had proposed to publish an article suggesting that Distillers had not taken proper care before putting its drug on the market. While in the view of three members of the House there was no objection to an earlier article criticising Distillers for insisting on its legal rights, it was a contempt of court for the press to discuss the merits of the case and to suggest that Distillers had been negligent.[8] That amounted to 'trial by newspaper', and was, as Lord Reid put it, intrinsically 'objectionable.'[9]

The European Court of Human Rights held that the absolute rule formulated in the *Sunday Times* case was incompatible with the right to freedom of expression provided by article 10 of the ECHR (see Extract 1.2.2). Its approach in these cases is also shown in *Worm* v *Austria*. Worm, a journalist, had written an article to the effect that Hannes Androsch, a prominent politician and former finance minister, currently facing a trial for tax evasion, was guilty of the charges. The Court held that the conviction of Worm by the Austrian courts for the offence of discussing before judgment the outcome of legal proceedings in a manner capable of influencing that outcome was compatible with the right to freedom of expression.

Extract 12.1.1
Worm v Austria (1998) 25 EHRR 454, paras 50–1, 54

50. Restrictions on freedom of expression permitted by the second paragraph of Article 10 'for maintaining the authority and impartiality of the judiciary' do not entitle States to restrict all forms of public discussion on matters pending before the courts.

There is general recognition of the fact that the courts cannot operate in a vacuum. Whilst the courts are the forum for the determination of a person's guilt or innocence on a criminal charge . . . this does not mean that there can be no prior or contemporaneous discussion of the subject matter of criminal trials elsewhere, be it in specialised journals, in the general press or amongst the public at large (see, *mutatis mutandis*, the *Sunday Times* . . . judgment).

---

[4] See *Ambard* v *Attorney General for Trinidad & Tobago* [1936] AC 322 (PC), and *R* v *Metropolitan Police Commissioner, ex parte Blackburn* [1968] 2 QB 150 (CA).

[5] *Barford* v *Denmark* (1989) 13 EHRR 493; *Präger and Oberschlick* v *Austria* (1995) 21 EHRR 1. On the other hand, in *De Haes* v *Belgium* (1998) 25 EHRR 1 the Court held that it was a breach of art 10 for the state courts to have convicted journalists of libel for expressing the view that judges handling sensitive family cases were biased.

[6] Law Commission Report No 335, *Contempt of Court: Scandalising the Court*.

[7] *Attorney-General* v *Times Newspapers* [1974] AC 273.

[8] Lords Diplock and Simon would also have upheld the application on the ground that the article put public pressure on Distillers to abandon its right to have its liability determined by a court of law.

[9] See n 7, at 300.

Provided that it does not overstep the bounds imposed in the interests of the proper administration of justice, reporting, including comment, on court proceedings contributes to their publicity and is thus perfectly consonant with the requirement under Article 6 §1 of the Convention that hearings be public. Not only do the media have the task of imparting such information and ideas: the public also has a right to receive them (ibid.). This is all the more so where a public figure is involved, such as, in the present case, a former member of the Government. Such persons inevitably and knowingly lay themselves open to close scrutiny by both journalists and the public at large (see, among other authorities, the *Lingens* v. *Austria* judgment of 8 July 1986, Series A no.103, p. 26, §42). Accordingly, the limits of acceptable comment are wider as regards a politician as such than as regards a private individual (ibid.).

However, public figures are entitled to the enjoyment of the guarantees of a fair trial set out in Article 6, which in criminal proceedings include the right to an impartial tribunal, on the same basis as every other person. This must be borne in mind by journalists when commenting on pending criminal proceedings since the limits of permissible comment may not extend to statements which are likely to prejudice, whether intentionally or not, the chances of a person receiving a fair trial or to undermine the confidence of the public in the role of the courts in the administration of criminal justice.

51. The applicant was convicted of having attempted to exert prohibited influence on the outcome of the criminal proceedings concerning Mr Androsch . . .

. . . the Vienna Court of Appeal first considered whether the impugned article was objectively capable of influencing the outcome of the proceedings pending at the material time before the Vienna Regional Criminal Court.

It found that the applicant had commented unfavourably on the answers given by Mr Androsch at the trial and not merely carried out a critical psychological analysis, as held by the first-instance court. The court further considered that it could not be excluded that the members of Mr Androsch's trial court, more particularly the lay judges, might read the article . . .

The appellate court held that Mr Worm's long-standing involvement in the 'Causa Androsch' – he had been researching into the case since 1978 and had written more than a hundred articles about it – reinforced the impression gained from the wording of the article that he had written it with the intention of influencing the outcome of the proceedings. From the beginning, the applicant had been convinced that Mr Androsch had committed tax evasion and had stated so. In his article, he had not only criticised Mr Androsch; he had deliberately attempted to lead the reader to conclude that Mr Androsch was guilty of the charges against him and had predicted his conviction.

. . .

54. Having regard to the State's margin of appreciation, it was also in principle for the appellate court to evaluate the likelihood that at least the lay judges would read the article as it was to ascertain the applicant's criminal intent in publishing it. As to the latter point, the Court of Appeal pointed out that 'it can be inferred from the article that [the applicant] wished to usurp the position of the judges dealing with the case' . . . In this respect, to paraphrase the Court's words in its judgment in the *Sunday Times* (no.1) case (cited above), it cannot be excluded that the public's becoming accustomed to the regular spectacle of pseudo-trials in the news media might in the long run have nefarious consequences for the acceptance of the courts as the proper forum for the determination of a person's guilt or innocence on a criminal charge . . . For this reason, the fact that domestic law as interpreted by the Vienna Court of Appeal did not require an actual result of influence on the particular proceedings to be proved (see paragraph 18 above) does not detract from the justification for the interference on the ground of protecting the authority of the judiciary.

Questions for discussion

1. Why is 'trial by newspaper' wrong? What is the argument for a general rule prejudging issues in forthcoming cases? (Consider here the decisions of the European Court of Human Rights: Extracts 1.2.2 and 12.1.1 above.)
2. If it is wrong to prejudge issues in pending cases, is it less wrong to criticise a judge in abusive terms for his rulings?

12.2 THE STRICT LIABILITY RULE

(a) Introduction

The Contempt of Court Act 1981 (CCA) was enacted partly in order to bring UK law into line with the ruling of the European Court of Human Rights in the *Sunday Times* case, though it was also framed to implement recommendations of a committee which had reviewed contempt of court.[10] The legislative provisions reformulating the 'strict liability rule' are of fundamental importance; they have not been amended since their enactment.

Extract 12.2.1
Contempt of Court Act 1981, ss 1–3, 5, 7

1. In this Act 'the strict liability rule' means the rule of law whereby conduct may be treated as a contempt of court as tending to interfere with the course of justice in particular legal proceedings regardless of intent to do so.

2.—(1) The strict liability rule applies only in relation to publications, and for this purpose 'publication' includes any speech, writing, broadcast or other communication in whatever form, which is addressed to the public at large or any section of the public.

(2) The strict liability rule applies only to a publication which creates a substantial risk that the course of justice in the proceedings in question will be seriously impeded or prejudiced.

(3) The strict liability rule applies to a publication only if the proceedings in question are active within the meaning of this section at the time of the publication.

(4) Schedule 1 applies for determining the times at which proceedings are to be treated as active within the meaning of this section.

3.—(1) A person is not guilty of contempt of court under the strict liability rule as the publisher of any matter to which that rule applies if at the time of publication (having taken all reasonable care) he does not know and has no reason to suspect that relevant proceedings are active.

(2) A person is not guilty of contempt of court under the strict liability rule as the distributor of a publication containing any such matter if at the time of distribution (having taken all reasonable care) he does not know that it contains such matter and has no reason to suspect that it is likely to do so.

(3) The burden of proof of any fact tending to establish a defence afforded by this section to any person lies upon that person.

(4) [*Omitted*]

. . .

---

[10] Phillimore Committee on Contempt of Court, Cmnd 5794 (1974), paras 73–154.

5. A publication made as or as part of a discussion in good faith of public affairs or other matters of general public interest is not to be treated as a contempt of court under the strict liability rule if the risk of impediment or prejudice to particular legal proceedings is merely incidental to the discussion.

. . .

7. Proceedings for a contempt of court under the strict liability rule (other than Scottish proceedings) shall not be instituted except by or with the consent of the Attorney General or on the motion of a court having jurisdiction to deal with it.

These provisions make a number of important changes to the strict liability rule, which had penalised as a contempt of court any conduct, including a publication, which tended to prejudice the course of legal proceedings. First, the rule now applies only to 'active' proceedings: section 2(3). Criminal proceedings are active from the issue of an arrest warrant or from the time an arrest has been made until the sentence, acquittal or other verdict, while civil proceedings are active from the point when the case is set down for a hearing.[11] (The proceedings in the *Sunday Times* case were at any early stage – indeed, they had become dormant – so were not active; the strict liability rule could not, therefore, now have been applied to them.)[12] Second, only publications which create a *substantial* risk that proceedings will be *seriously* impeded or prejudiced are caught by the rule (section 2(2); it is not enough that they may tend to, or possibly, cause such prejudice. A third reform is made by the provision in section 5 to the effect that publication is not in contempt if the risk of prejudice created by it is merely incidental to a good faith discussion of public affairs: this is considered in the next subsection. Finally, proceedings for strict liability contempt may only be brought by or with the approval of the Attorney-General or by a court with authority to deal with them, the High Court: section 7, discussed below in Section 12.2(f).

(b) Contempt in the course of the discussion of public affairs

The Contempt of Court Act 1981 was intended to strike a better balance than the common law had done between freedom of expression, including press and media freedom, on the one hand, and on the other the rights of the parties, in particular the accused in criminal proceedings, to a fair trial. One important provision is section 5 of the legislation, although it should be noted that it does not provide for a full balancing of competing interests in freedom of expression and in the fair administration of justice.[13] However, the case from which the next extract is taken shows the value of section 5, although it is also important because the House of Lords laid down the principles for interpreting section 2(2) of the CCA in particular its requirement that the risk of prejudice to the proceedings must be 'substantial'. An article in the *Daily Mail*, written to support a pro-life candidate at a by-election, suggested that in the prevailing medical climate the chances of a physically handicapped baby surviving would be low, as 'someone would surely recommend letting her die of starvation, or otherwise disposing of her'. The trial of a doctor charged with murdering a Down's Syndrome baby had started two days before this publication. (He was later acquitted.)

---

[11] Schedule 1, paras 3–16.

[12] But see s 12.3 for discussion of the possibility that the newspaper article might have attracted liability for common law contempt.

[13] Compare the approach of the High Court of Australia in *Hinch v A-G (Victoria)* (1987) 164 CLR 15, and see S. Walker, 'Freedom of speech and contempt of court: the English and Australian approaches compared' (1991) 40 *ICLQ* 583.

Extract 12.2.2
Attorney-General v *English* [1983] 1 AC 116, at 141–4 (HL)

LORD DIPLOCK:

There is, of course, no question that the article in the 'Daily Mail' of which complaint is made by the Attorney-General was a 'publication' within the meaning of section 2 (1). That being so, it appears to have been accepted in the Divisional Court by both parties that the onus of proving that the article satisfied the conditions stated in section 2 (2) lay upon the Attorney-General and that, if he satisfied that onus, the onus lay upon the appellants to prove that it satisfied the conditions stated in section 5. For my part, I am unable to accept that this represents the effect of the relationship of section 5 to section 2 (2). Section 5 does not take the form of a proviso or an exception to section 2 (2). It stands on an equal footing with it. It does not set out exculpatory matter. Like section 2 (2) it states what publications shall not amount to contempt of court despite their tendency to interfere with the course of justice in particular legal proceedings.

For the publication to constitute a contempt of court under the strict liability rule, it must be shown that the publication satisfies the criterion for which section 2 (2) provides, viz., that it 'creates a substantial risk that the course of justice in the proceedings in question will be seriously impeded or prejudiced'. It is only if it falls within section 5 that anything more need be shown. So logically the first question always is: has the publication satisfied the criterion laid down by section 2 (2).

My Lords, the first thing to be observed about this criterion is that the risk that has to be assessed is that which was created by the publication of the allegedly offending matter at the time when it was published. The public policy that underlies the strict liability rule in contempt of court is deterrence. Trial by newspaper or, as it should be more compendiously expressed today, trial by the media, is not to be permitted in this country. That the risk that was created by the publication when it was actually published does not ultimately affect the outcome of the proceedings is, as Lord Goddard C.J. said in Reg. v Evening Standard Co. Ltd. [1954] 1 Q.B. 578, 582 'neither here nor there'. If there was a reasonable possibility that it might have done so if in the period subsequent to the publication the proceedings had not taken the course that in fact they did and Dr. Arthur was acquitted, the offence was complete. The true course of justice must not at any stage be put at risk.

Next for consideration is the concatenation in the subsection of the adjective 'substantial' and the adverb 'seriously', the former to describe the degree of risk, the latter to describe the degree of impediment or prejudice to the course of justice. 'Substantial' is hardly the most apt word to apply to 'risk' which is a noumenon. In combination I take the two words to be intended to exclude a risk that is only remote . . . If, as in the instant case and probably in most other criminal trials upon indictment, it is the outcome of the trial or the need to discharge the jury without proceeding to a verdict that is put at risk, there can be no question that that which in the course of justice is put at risk is as serious as anything could be.

My Lords, that Mr. Malcolm Muggeridge's article was capable of prejudicing the jury against Dr. Arthur at the early stage of his trial when it was published, seems to me to be clear. It suggested that it was a common practice among paediatricians to do that which Dr. Arthur was charged with having done, because they thought that it was justifiable in the interest of humanity even though it was against the law. At this stage of the trial the jury did not know what Dr. Arthur's defence was going to be; and whether at that time the risk of the jury's being influenced by their recollection of the article when they came eventually to consider their verdict appeared to be more than a remote one, was a matter which the judge before whom the trial was being conducted was in the best position to evaluate, even though his evaluation, although it should carry weight, would not be binding on the Divisional Court or on your Lordships. The judge thought at that stage of the trial that the risk was substantial, not remote. So, too, looking at the matter in retrospect, did the Divisional Court despite the fact that the risk had not turned into an actuality since Dr. Arthur had by then been acquitted. For my part I am not prepared to dissent from this evaluation. I consider that the publication of the article on the third day of what was to prove a lengthy trial satisfied the criterion for which section 2 (2) of the Act provides.

The article, however, fell also within the category dealt with in section 5. It was made, in undisputed good faith, as a discussion in itself of public affairs, viz., Mrs. Carr's candidature as an independent pro-life candidate in the North West Croydon by-election for which the polling day was in one week's time. It was also part of a wider discussion on a matter of general public interest that had been proceeding intermittently over the last three months, upon the moral justification of mercy killing and in particular of allowing newly born hopelessly handicapped babies to die. So it was for the Attorney-General to show that the risk of prejudice to the fair trial of Dr. Arthur, which I agree was created by the publication of the article at the stage the trial had reached when it was published, was not 'merely incidental' to the discussion of the matter with which the article dealt.

My Lords, any article published at the time when Dr. Arthur was being tried which asserted that it was a common practice among paediatricians to let severely physically or mentally handicapped new born babies die of starvation or otherwise dispose of them would (as, in common with the trial judge and the Divisional Court, I have already accepted) involve a substantial risk of prejudicing his fair trial. But an article supporting Mrs. Carr's candidature in the by-election as a pro-life candidate that contained no such assertion would depict her as tilting at imaginary wind-mills. One of the main planks of the policy for which she sought the suffrage of the electors was that these things did happen and ought to be stopped.

I have drawn attention to the passages principally relied upon by the Divisional Court as causing a risk of prejudice that was not 'merely incidental to the discussion'. The court described them as 'unnecessary' to the discussion and as 'accusations'. The test, however, is not whether an article could have been written as effectively without these passages or whether some other phraseology might have been substituted for them that could have reduced the risk of prejudicing Dr. Arthur's fair trial; it is whether the risk created by the words actually chosen by the author was 'merely incidental to the discussion', which I take to mean: no more than an incidental consequence of expounding its main theme . . .

My Lords, the article that is the subject of the instant case appears to me to be in nearly all respects the antithesis of the article which this House (pace a majority of the judges of the European Court of Human Rights) held to be a contempt of court in Attorney-General v Times Newspapers Ltd. [1974] A.C. 273. There the whole subject of the article was the pending civil actions against Distillers Co. (Biochemicals) Ltd. arising out of their having placed upon the market the new drug thalidomide, and the whole purpose of it was to put pressure upon that company in the lawful conduct of their defence in those actions. In the instant case, in contrast, there is in the article no mention at all of Dr. Arthur's trial. It may well be that many readers of the 'Daily Mail' who saw the article and had read also the previous day's report of Dr. Arthur's trial, and certainly if they were members of the jury at that trial, would think, 'that is the sort of thing that Dr. Arthur is being tried for; it appears to be something that quite a lot of doctors do'. But the risk of their thinking that and allowing it to prejudice their minds in favour of finding him guilty on evidence that did not justify such a finding seems to me to be properly described in ordinary English language as 'merely incidental' to any meaningful discussion of Mrs. Carr's election policy as a pro-life candidate in the by-election due to be held before Dr. Arthur's trial was likely to be concluded, or to any meaningful discussion of the wider matters of general public interest involved in the current controversy as to the justification of mercy killing. To hold otherwise would have prevented Mrs. Carr from putting forward and obtaining publicity for what was a main plank in her election programme and would have stifled all discussion in the press upon the wider controversy about mercy killing from the time that Dr. Arthur was charged in the magistrates' court in February 1981 until the date of his acquittal at the beginning of November of that year; for those are the dates between which, under section 2 (3) and Schedule 1, the legal proceedings against Dr. Arthur would be 'active' and so attract the strict liability rule.

Such gagging of bona fide public discussion in the press of controversial matters of general public interest, merely because there are in existence contemporaneous legal proceedings in which some particular instance of those controversial matters may be in issue, is what section 5 of the Contempt of Court Act 1981 was in my view intended to prevent. I would allow this appeal.

The application of section 5 is more problematic if the discussion, although of general public interest, makes specific reference to particular proceedings. The provision may apply, as was held by the House of Lords in *A-G v Times Newspapers*,[14] when it covered an article about the background of an intruder into the Queen's bedroom, discussing his relationship with a member of the royal household and matters of palace security. On the other hand, it was said that the provision should not cover the publication in the *Guardian Newspapers* case[15] (Extract 12.2.7 below) discussing the motives of an artist being tried at that time for the theft of body parts. More recently in the *Random House* case,[16] Tugendhat J declined to apply section 5, when he granted an injunction to stop the publication of a book with passages describing a large scale police investigation into a major terrorist plot; copies of the book had been sent to booksellers and some copies sold only a few days before the end of the trial of men charged with conspiracy to murder and other offences in connection with this plot. In his view the 'passages complained of discuss the very acts which led to the Trial . . . I am sure that these passages are not incidental to the discussion.'[17] These cases are hard to reconcile, and show that the application of the provision requires sensitive appreciation not only of the importance of the general discussion, but the nature of the risk it may pose for the criminal trial.

Questions for discussion

1. Did Lord Diplock's interpretation of 'substantial risk' mark any real change from the approach of the House of Lords in the *Sunday Times* case?
2. Should CCA section 5 be redrafted to allow a wider immunity from contempt proceedings for good faith discussion of public affairs?

(c) Substantial risk of serious prejudice

The scope of the strict liability rule has been considered in a number of cases. One question is whether the publication created a danger of *serious impediment* or *prejudice* to the course of justice in pending proceedings. In *A-G v Random House* Tugendhat J pointed out that 'impediment' and 'prejudice' are not identical. The latter term relates to the influence of the publication on the jury: does it create a real risk that it will be prejudiced against the accused? An impediment arises when the trial judge has to issue an extreme direction to the jury to avoid the risk of such prejudice or consider discharging it, because otherwise the failure to discharge would provide a ground for a convicted defendant's appeal.[18] However, the prejudice or impediment need not be so serious as to justify an actual stay of the proceedings and discharge of the jury or upholding an appeal against conviction: see Section 12.2(d) below.[19] Indeed, the courts have rarely been troubled by the question whether the prejudice was sufficiently *serious* to warrant a conviction for contempt of court. Much more consideration has been given to the question whether the publication in question created a *substantial* risk of impediment or prejudice to the course of justice in pending criminal proceedings. (In the *English* case, the proceedings were contemporaneous with the article.)

[14] The *Times*, 12 February 1983.
[15] *A-G v Guardian Newspapers* [1999] EMLR 904, 921 per Collins J.
[16] *A-G v Random House Group Ltd* [2009] EWHC 1727 (QB); [2010] EMLR 9.
[17] Ibid., para 94.
[18] [2010] EMLR 9; [2009] EWHC 1727 (QB), paras 19–24.
[19] See Simon Brown LJ in *A-G v Birmingham Post and Mail Ltd* [1998] 4 All ER 49 at 57, DC.

Two contrasting decisions show the courts' approach. In the first,[20] the Divisional Court was not persuaded that there had been a contempt when an early evening ITN news bulletin had reported that an Irishman arrested on suspicion of murder was a convicted IRA terrorist, and early editions of three national papers and a north of England regional paper had carried the story, referring to the suspect as an IRA fugitive. The report had not been broadcast in later ITN bulletins, nor had it been repeated in subsequent editions of the newspapers. The trial took place nine months later in London. Leggatt LJ emphasised that there was only a minimal risk that these unrepeated reports would have come to the attention of any member of the jury, and further that in view of the lapse of time before the trial – nine months – it was unlikely that he would have remembered them. The risk of prejudice to the trial was therefore remote. In contrast, the Divisional Court in *Hat Trick Productions* upheld contempt proceedings, when six months before the trial of the brothers, Kevin and Ian Maxwell, for pension fraud, remarks were made at the end of the programme, 'Have I Got News for You?', on BBC 2, suggesting the brothers' guilt.[21] Auld LJ admitted that six months was a long time before the trial and that memories of the broadcast might fade. However, the remarks were made by high profile speakers – Angus Deayton and Ian Hislop – and the programme had gone out on Friday night and been repeated on Saturday evening, with a combined audience of over 6 million people; the remarks were also highly prejudicial.[22] In the Court's view there was a substantial risk on these facts of serious prejudice to the trial of the Maxwells.

The *Mirror Group* case, from which the next extract is taken, concerned contempt proceedings against five national newspapers. A trial judge had earlier stayed proceedings against Geoffrey Knights on the charge of wounding with intent, on the ground that the pre-trial coverage in the five national newspapers of the incident, of Knights' character, and of his relationship with Gillian Taylforth, a well-known actress, made it impossible for him to have a fair trial. The reports had been published in April (shortly after the charge was brought) and May 1995, while the trial started at the end of September. The extract sets out the Court's statement of general principles, details of the article in the *Daily Mail*, and the Court's conclusions with regard to all the newspapers involved.

Extract 12.2.3
***Attorney-General v MGN Ltd and Others* [1997] 1 All ER 456, at 460–1, 466 (DC)**
(footnotes omitted)

SCHIEMANN LJ:

The principles governing the application of the strict liability rule
These are as follows and are not the subject of serious dispute.

(1) Each case must be decided on its own facts.
(2) The court will look at each publication separately and test matters as at the time of publication (see A-G v English [1982] 2 All ER 903 at 918, [1983] 1 AC 116 at 141 per Lord Diplock and A-G v Guardian Newspapers Ltd [1992] 3 All ER 38 at 48–49, [1992] 1 WLR 874 at 885); nevertheless, the mere fact that, by reason of earlier publications, there is already some risk of prejudice does not prevent a finding that the latest publication has created a further risk . . .

---

[20] *Attorney-General v ITN and others* [1995] 2 All ER 370.
[21] *Attorney-General v BBC, Hat Trick Productions* [1997] EMLR 76.
[22] At the end of the programme after the credits, a reference by Angus Deayton to the Maxwell brothers was highlighted by the following remarks of Ian Hislop: 'You're not going to leave in that bit about the Maxwell brothers being heartless scheming bastards?'

(3) The publication in question must create some risk that the course of justice in the proceedings in question will be impeded or prejudiced by that publication.

(4) That risk must be substantial.

(5) The substantial risk must be that the course of justice in the proceedings in question will not only be impeded or prejudiced but seriously so.

(6) The court will not convict of contempt unless it is sure that the publication has created this substantial risk of that serious effect on the course of justice.

(7) In making an assessment of whether the publication does create this substantial risk of that serious effect on the course of justice the following amongst other matters arise for consideration: (a) the likelihood of the publication coming to the attention of a potential juror; (b) the likely impact of the publication on an ordinary reader at the time of publication; and (c) the residual impact of the publication on a notional juror at the time of trial. It is this last matter which is crucial.

One must remember that in this, as in any exercise of risk assessment, a small risk multiplied by a small risk results in an even smaller risk.

(8) In making an assessment of the likelihood of the publication coming to the attention of a potential juror the court will consider amongst other matters: (a) whether the publication circulates in the area from which the jurors are likely to be drawn, and (b) how many copies circulated.

(9) In making an assessment of the likely impact of the publication on an ordinary reader at the time of publication the court will consider amongst other matters: (a) the prominence of the article in the publication, and (b) the novelty of the content of the article in the context of likely readers of that publication.

(10) In making an assessment of the residual impact of the publication on a notional juror at the time of trial the court will consider amongst other matters: (a) the length of time between publication and the likely date of trial (b) the focussing effect of listening over a prolonged period to evidence in a case, and (c) the likely effect of the judge's directions to a jury.

This last matter in particular has been the subject of extensive judicial comment in two different contexts: in the context of a trial or an appeal from a trial verdict and in the context of contempt proceedings. There have been many cases where, notwithstanding such prejudicial publications, the convictions have not been quashed. However, undoubtedly there have also been occasions where convictions have been quashed notwithstanding judicial directions to the jury to ignore prejudicial comments in the media.

. . .

The DAILY MAIL 13 May 1995

The article by Lynda Lee-Potter purports to be based on an interview given by Miss Taylforth in which she described the stormy and violent relationship between herself and Mr Knights. There were, in that article, references to the fact that he had previously been convicted of an offence of violence and in particular a reference to the evidence which he had given in the libel action when he had been asked about his previous convictions. Despite the fact that the article occupied two pages with large photographs of Miss Taylforth and Knights, the reference to the incident on the night of the 17–18 April was really only one short paragraph with no detail as to how Mr Davies had received his injuries. The inference, however, from the context of the remainder of the article is that Knights had caused them and caused them unlawfully.

Applying the principles set out earlier in this judgment we do not consider that this publication created a substantial risk that the course of justice in the proceedings would be seriously impeded or prejudiced.

Conclusion

There is no doubt that the so called 'news items' or 'articles', excluding for the moment the article on 13 May in the Daily Mail, were all written in typical graphic tabloid style. They include large banner headlines, large photographs of all three of those involved in the incident. There is a measure of exaggeration in the description of the injuries sustained by Mr Davies and the language used is undoubtedly emotive. However, all in all it is difficult to see how any one of the publications in April and May 1995 created any greater risk of serious prejudice than that which had already been created.

We are not called upon to rule upon the correctness of Judge Sanders' decision to stay the proceedings in front of him and nothing in this judgment should be taken as doing so. A consequence of the need in contempt proceedings, in which respondents face imprisonment or a fine, to be sure and to look at each publication separately and the need in trial proceedings to look at risk of prejudice created by the totality of publications can be that it is proper to stay proceedings on the ground of prejudice albeit that no individual is guilty of contempt. One may regret that situation or one may take the view that this is the best answer to a difficult problem. We are not called upon to express our view on that matter.

What however clearly follows from our findings is that each of these applications by the Attorney General is dismissed.

With the notable exception of the *Hat Trick Productions* case, the courts used to be reluctant to convict the media of strict liability contempt. This was perhaps best shown by the decision in *A-G v Guardian Newspapers* when the Divisional Court dismissed an application brought in respect of an article in the *Observer* discussing the motivation of an artist, Kelly, who had been charged with the theft of body parts used by him to make casts exhibited at an art fair.[23] The full-page article describing his personality as 'perverted' was published during the trial, but was read by only one juror; she promised not to mention it to other members of the jury and to disregard it when considering her verdict. No application to dismiss the juror, or to stay the trial and dismiss the whole jury was made (see Extract 12.2.6 below). The Court applied the strict liability rule in the light of the Convention right to freedom of expression and the ruling of the European Court in *Worm* (Extract 12.1.1), where it had been said that permissible comment may not extend to remarks likely to prejudice a fair trial. So one interpretation of this ruling is that the Divisional Court was raising the bar for upholding convictions under the strict liability rule; only publications *likely* to cause an impediment or prejudice may be convicted, not those which merely create a non-remote risk that this may occur.[24] However, that may read too much into this ruling; in any case it does not reflect the approach of the courts in some recent important cases.

In the *Random House* case,[25] it was held that publication of a book during a criminal trial which described the police investigations leading to the prosecution of the defendants at this trial created a substantial risk of a serious impediment to the course of these proceedings, if not of a serious prejudice to their outcome. Tugendhat J did not consider there was a real danger that any jurors would read the book and disregard the directions of the trial judge to consider only the evidence given in the proceedings, but he did rule that there was a real risk that the judge would discharge the jury, if the book were published

[23] [1999] EMLR 904.
[24] See Fenwick and Phillipson, 269–70.
[25] *A-G v Random House* [2009] EWHC 1727 (QB); [2010] EMLR 9.

freely, or that if he did not take that course, an appeal against a conviction would be brought. In either event there was a substantial risk of *impediment* to the course of justice.

In another recent case the Court considered the application of the strict liability rule to the online websites of two national papers, *Mail Online* and *Sun Online*. At the outset of a murder trial at Sheffield Crown Court the judge warned the jury 'to go on only the evidence you hear in this room . . .' and told it: 'Don't . . . consult the internet, if there is anything out there on it.' An article was published on *Mail Online* with a picture showing the defendant holding a pistol in his right hand with a finger on the trigger. Under the picture a caption read: 'Drink-fuelled attack: Ryan Ward was seen boasting about the incident on CCTV.' The picture remained on the site for nearly five hours. A similar photograph was shown on *Sun Online* for a longer period. There was no indication that any member of the jury had visited the Internet to find out any information about the case, so the judge rejected the defendant's application to discharge the jury and stay the trial.

Extract 12.2.4
A-G v Associated Newspapers [2011] EWHC 418 (Admin), [2011] EMLR 17,
paras 30–6, 41, 44, 50

MOSES LJ:

30. Both defendants rely upon the difficulty any reader would have in obtaining access to the photograph. It did not appear during the short time the article was heralded as recently published. Access would only be gained as a result of a deliberate decision to read the article, and not just the beginning of the article but as a result of scrolling down through the whole of the article. We reject any suggestion that a juror might have come across the photograph by chance; he would only have done so as a result of a deliberate decision to read the article about the trial online. The article could only be reached by taking a deliberate decision to scroll through the index of news items and click on the relevant article.

31. Since access to the photograph would be the result of a deliberate decision to read the whole of the article, it follows, contend both defendants, that any juror could only have seen the photograph by disobeying the judge's instruction, given before the photograph had been published, not to consult the internet, not to allow anyone to speak to them about the case and to rely only on the evidence they hear in court.

32. This contention gives rise to two distinct questions on which we need to focus: whether choosing to read the relevant article would amount to disobedience of the judge's instruction and, if it would, whether there was a substantial risk that the jurors would disobey. The jury was instructed not to consult the internet and not to seek information from outside the court. But the judge also told them, in his initial directions on 3 November . . . that the press would report the case, that they were free to do so but that the jury's view must be based on the evidence in court. These conventional and, we may add with respect, sensible instructions, created a blurring of the line between that which was, on the judge's instruction, prohibited and that which was permissible. The jury was not instructed to avoid any newspaper report about the case they were trying. Indeed, the likelihood was that, if they were in the habit of reading a newspaper, they would look at any report of the case they were trying.

33. If, then, they were in the habit of reading the news online, a reasonable juror, obedient to the instructions of the judge, might well regard reading the news online as being outwith the prohibition against 'consulting' the internet. The judge does use the expression 'don't go there' . . . But that was in the context of consulting or seeking information, not reading the news online. Once a juror regarded himself as being at liberty to read the news online, such a juror might well regard himself as being free to read about the case online. There was no prohibition against reading about the case in the newspapers. If he was permitted to do so in a newspaper, there would be

no reason to think he was not permitted to do so online. He would have no reason to think that the news would be carried online in a way different from that which appeared in the newspapers. A juror might well draw a distinction between reading about the case in a news item published online and consulting the internet or seeking information about the case on the internet. We are satisfied so that we are sure that a juror, conscientiously seeking to comply with the judge's instructions, would not have understood them to prohibit reading about the case in a contemporary news report online, published by well-known newspapers, the Mail and the Sun.

34. For those reasons, we reject the defendants' submission that, in assessing the likelihood that a juror would see the photograph, we should regard a juror's decision to read the article as a breach of the judge's prohibition.

35. The Attorney General also suggests that there was a substantial risk that someone other than a juror might have read a report of the case online, seen the photograph and communicated that fact to a member of the jury, in the knowledge that that juror was trying the case. It must be recalled that publication occurred on the first day of the trial. We are not satisfied so as to be sure that knowledge that a particular member of the jury was trying this particular case would have become known to the extent that someone else would have bothered to communicate the online news item, with the photograph, to that juror, even though such online information may be transmitted with ease and in an instant.

36. The next question, therefore, is whether, uninhibited by any prohibition, there was a substantial risk that a juror might read the news report and come across the photograph. We are sure that there was such a substantial risk. Jurors in the habit of reading a daily newspaper were likely to read about the case they were trying. Similarly, any juror in the habit of reading the news online was likely to choose to read an article about the case he or she was trying. The subsequent evidence of the number of 'hits', even assuming its accuracy (and the burden was on the Attorney to produce evidence to contradict it), does not undermine our assessment of the substantial risk that a juror would read the article online and see the photograph.

. . .

Serious prejudice: the impact of the photograph

41. Now that we have reached the conclusion that we are sure that there was a substantial risk that a juror would see the photograph, it is necessary to consider the impact of that photograph. Both defendants contend that the illustration of the accused with a gun was so remote from the factual issues in the case that the Attorney cannot prove that there was a substantial risk that a juror would be adversely influenced by it. We reject that submission. Visual images are designed for impact; that is why any editor would be keen to use them to add to the impact of the news story. The defence which Ward was running was self-defence. The image of the accused brandishing the pistol and apparently doing so in a brazen manner could not have failed to create an adverse impression of a young man who enjoyed demonstrating a propensity for violence. It was prejudicial in a manner directly relevant to the issues in the case.

. . . Serious prejudice: the ability of a jury to disregard extraneous material and obey directions

44. This conclusion gives rise to the final issue which we must consider, namely the effect of a judge's directions and the course of the trial on the impact of the photograph. Both defendants contend that even if there was a substantial risk that a juror would see the photograph, and even if the photograph was prejudicial, there was no substantial risk that it would have seriously impeded or prejudiced the trial . . . Any juror who had seen the photograph would not have been deflected from fairly reaching a just verdict but would have abided by the directions of judge to decide the case on the evidence heard and seen in court and on nothing else and would have focused on that evidence.

[In paragraphs 45–49 the Court considered, but rejected the argument that it would be wrong to convict for contempt of court, unless it decided that the prejudice was such as to justify halting the criminal trial or a successful appeal against conviction: this issue is discussed in Section 12.2(d) below.]

50. But we need not resolve the controversy for this reason. We are sure that . . . the photograph, published whilst the jury was hearing the case, created such prejudice that no juror, who saw it, could reasonably have been expected to put it out of his or her mind, however stringent the injunction to do so. If the judge had learnt that a juror or jurors had seen the photograph but had nevertheless chosen to continue the trial with the same panel, relying on directions to disregard it, we are sure that that would have given rise not only to a seriously arguable ground of appeal but one that would have succeeded.

The same general approach was taken by the Court in its disposition of the contempt application brought by the Attorney-General against two tabloid papers for their treatment of Christopher Jefferies, who had been arrested for the murder of Joanna Yeates in Bristol, but who had been subsequently released without charge. An article in the *Daily Mirror* suggested that Jefferies was a voyeur, and stated that he was a friend of a convicted paedophile and that the police regarded him as prime suspect for another unsolved murder committed in 1974 of a young woman whose body was found close to that of Miss Yeates. The article in the *Sun* alleged that Jefferies was a stalker with an unhealthy interest in young blonde women. It was an unusual case, because the article could not have had any impact on a trial of Jefferies, as there never was one. However, that made no difference to the treatment of the contempt application which was upheld by the Court.

Extract 12.2.5
Attorney-General v _MGN Ltd and News Group Ltd_ [2011] EWHC 2074 (Admin) 2074, [2012] EMLR 9, paras 17–21, 31–6

JUDGE LCJ:

17. Before the present applications can succeed it must be proved to the criminal standard and separately in relation to each defendant, that the individual publication or publications complained of created the risk specified in section 2(2) of the Act. That risk must be 'substantial', and therefore, neither remote nor theoretical. The risk however is directed to serious impediment or prejudice to the course of justice in the extant proceedings. In other words the question whether the risk to the course of justice is substantial must be assessed at the date of publication. On this basis the test is predictive.

18. One consequence of the legislation is that it is neither here nor there to the Attorney-General's applications that the proceedings against Mr Jefferies ceased to be 'active' within a short time of publication, or that in the result no criminal proceedings involving Mr Jefferies arising from the death of Miss Yeates will ever take place. This means that care is needed in the approach to be taken to the authorities which were decided when the issue (contempt or not) was considered and decided after the relevant criminal proceedings were concluded. In these authorities, while seeking to ascertain what it would have decided about the level of risk posed to the course of justice at the date when the publications took place, in reality the court was simultaneously looking back at the alleged consequences of the publications. None of these considerations arise here. Unusually we are being invited to focus attention on the question whether the criminal proceedings in which Mr Jefferies was involved at the date of the publication were at serious risk not only of being prejudiced but also impeded.

19. It was not suggested that we should consider any of the widespread media coverage of this tragic case before the arrest of Mr Jefferies. Any publicity before that date would not have fallen

within the ambit of the Act, which is confined to 'active' proceedings. And the application was approached on the basis that each publication should be looked at separately. (See *Attorney-General* v *MGN Limited* [1997] 1 All ER 456). This approach follows from the principle that where criminal allegations against more than one defendant are made the defendants cannot be lumped together. The case against each defendant must be considered separately from the cases of any other defendants. This is in marked contrast to submissions that are sometimes made at the start of the trial, that it should not proceed, or, after conviction, that it should not have been allowed to proceed, on the grounds of prejudicial publicity, when the trial judge or the Court of Appeal must make an assessment of the impact of the totality of media coverage, whether before or after any arrest. Whether the same approach should be adopted in contempt proceedings has been questioned. In February 1998 the National Heritage Committee recommended that section 2 of the Act should be strengthened 'so that it covers the collective or cumulative effect of pre-trial publicity in risking prejudicing a trial, as well as the effect of individual articles. This means that newspapers could not escape liability, as one case held they could, because a number of them had acted in a similar way and together had caused prejudice.'

20. Although it was stated in the House of Lords that the Government accepted this recommendation, no opportunity has yet been found for introducing it. Until legislation provides to the contrary, the case against each of these defendants must be treated separately. However where the same defendant is responsible for more than one publication there is no reason why the effect of each publication by the same defendant should not be considered as a whole.

21. In deference to the submissions by Mr Caplan and Miss Page, we immediately acknowledge many judicial observations about the responsible way in which juries can be trusted to perform their public duty. The connected feature is judicial understanding of what is described as the 'fade factor', that is, that what people read in their newspapers or watch on their television screens months before trial fades in the memory, and for that reason, too, the risk of conscious or even unconscious prejudice against the defendant will have dissipated when the trial takes place. The group of authorities gathered together in the written submissions by both sides represents the long standing confidence of the judiciary in the process of trial by jury.

. . .

31. In our judgment, as a matter of principle, the vilification of a suspect under arrest readily falls within the protective ambit of section 2(2) of the Act as a potential impediment to the course of justice. At the simplest level publication of such material may deter or discourage witnesses from coming forward and providing information helpful to the suspect, which may, (depending on the circumstances) help immediately to clear him of suspicion or enable his defence to be fully developed at trial. This may arise, for example, because witnesses may be reluctant to be associated with or perceived to be a supporter of the suspect, or, again, because they may begin to doubt whether information apparently favourable to the suspect could possibly be correct. Adverse publicity may impede the course of justice in a variety of different ways, but in the context we are now considering, it is not an answer that on the evidence actually available, the combination of the directions of the judge and the integrity of the jury would ensure a fair trial. The problem is that the evidence at trial may be incomplete just because its existence may never be known, or indeed may only come to light after conviction.

32. Our attention was drawn to article 10 of the European Convention on Human Rights. As is well understood this confirms the right to freedom of expression, and to receive and impart information and ideas without interference. It is however subject to express limitations and such restrictions as may be prescribed by law and necessary in a democratic society 'for the protection of . . . the rights of others' and 'for maintaining the authority and impartiality of the judiciary' which for present purposes includes the jury. The right to a fair trial is of course encapsulated in article 6 which declares the entitlement to a fair hearing. The 1981 Act represents the system provided in this jurisdiction to ensure that the right to a fair trial is protected. In the

present context any interference with the article 10 rights of the defendants depends on proof to the criminal standard that the publications in question have created a substantial risk of serious impediment or prejudice to the course of justice. This falls comfortably within the limitations acknowledged in the Convention itself.

33. With these considerations in mind we must return to the articles of which complaint is made. We begin by reminding ourselves of the passages in all three publications which purport to provide a measure of support for Mr Jefferies. We regard them as makeweight, and in the overall context of each article the observations supportive of Mr Jefferies do nothing to lessen the impact of the adverse reporting.

34. The material in the two publications of the Daily Mirror is extreme. True, it does not positively assert that Mr Jefferies was guilty of involvement in paedophile crimes, or the unsolved murdered many years earlier. It is submitted that the articles were unflattering, suggesting that he was an eccentric loner. So they were. But they went very much further. It was asserted, in effect directly, that his standard of behaviour, so far as sexual matters were concerned was unacceptable, and he was linked to both the paedophile offences and the much earlier murder offence. That indeed was the point of the articles. The juxtaposition of the photographs of two murdered women, together with the layout of the places where they died in proximity to Mr Jefferies home, was stark. And in the context of the murder of Miss Yeates herself, the second article implied that Mr Jefferies was in a particularly convenient position, as her landlord, to have gained access to her premises to commit a murder, according to the article, committed by an intruder. Taken on their own these articles would have provided Mr Jefferies with a serious argument that a fair trial would have been impossible. The argument would probably have been rejected on the familiar grounds of jury integrity and the fade factor. If he had been convicted, he would have argued on appeal that the trial was unfair because of this publicity. Again, we anticipate that any such appeal on this ground alone would have failed. We have no doubt, however, that these arguments would have been justified, and that the courts would have had to address them with care. To that extent the criminal justice process would have been held up and delayed.

35. As we have indicated, we are also concerned at a different additional aspect of this publicity, which is not one which has previously been subjected to any analysis in the authorities. As these articles vilified Mr Jefferies long before the fade factor could have begun to operate, the risks to the preparation of his defence would have been serious. Of course we expect witnesses to do their duty, and come forward, but we are also perfectly familiar with the fact that many do not, often when the Crown wishes them to do so. The impact of these articles on potential defence witnesses would have been extremely damaging to Mr Jefferies. In brief, reluctant witnesses would have been even more reluctant to come forward, and witnesses who might have been prepared to come forward may very well have assumed that anything helpful or supportive they might have said about Mr Jefferies could not be right.

36. In our judgment the two publications in the Daily Mirror created substantial risks to the course of justice. They constituted contempt under the strict liability rule.

[The Court also held that the vilification of Jefferies in the Sun amounted to a contempt of court, as it created 'a very serious risk that the preparation of his defence would be prejudiced'; the article would also have justified an abuse of process argument, had Jefferies been prosecuted for the murder: see para 37.]

These recent decisions show that the courts are now much more prepared to uphold an application to commit for contempt of court than they used to be. The strict liability rule remains a significant limit on the freedom of the media to cover police investigations; any media treatment which vilifies a suspect or which suggests any previous criminal record on his part, should be avoided, particularly in high profile cases.

Questions for discussion

1. What factors do the courts take into account in determining whether the risk of prejudice was substantial?
2. Is the decision in *BBC/Hat Trick Productions* compatible with the courts' approach in other cases where publication (or broadcast) occurred several months before the relevant trial?
3. Do you agree with the decision in the *Associated Newspapers* case? Was there really a substantial risk that the publication of a photograph on an online news website for a few hours would prejudice the trial?
4. On what grounds did the Court uphold the application for contempt of court in the *MGN/News Group* case?

(d) The strict liability rule and the stay of criminal trials

A contempt application under the strict liability rule may fail, even though the trial judge had earlier stayed the proceedings because extensive media publicity had made it impossible for the accused to have a fair trial: see the *MGN/Knights* case (Extract 12.2.3) Conversely, in the *BBC/Hat Trick Productions* case, the Divisional Court fined the respondents for contempt, although Phillips J had earlier refused to stay the Maxwell brothers' trial. The courts have usually emphasised that in contempt proceedings they are not bound by the decision of the trial judge or of the Court of Appeal on an appeal against an 'unsafe' conviction. The court form its own view on the distinct question whether the requirements for strict liability contempt have been met.[26]

These points were made by the Divisional Court in the *Birmingham Post* case,[27] when upholding a contempt application against a regional newspaper. It had inadvertently published, during the course of a murder trial, an article suggesting that the murder had been committed by members of a notorious criminal gang involved in drug dealing. Although none of the defendants was identified, the trial was halted and the jury discharged. (It commenced ten days later at a different venue, and the defendants were convicted.) Simon Brown LJ stated that CCA section 2(2) postulated a lesser degree of prejudice than would justify a stay or a successful appeal against conviction. So a decision in either of the latter circumstances should not be decisive for contempt proceedings. On the other hand it would be rare for a trial to be halted, or an appeal allowed, and contempt proceedings in these circumstances to fail. He added that his observations applied to cases where the prejudicial material was published during the course of the trial and where no other prejudicial publications complicated the issue, as they did in the *MGN/Knights* case (Extract 12.2.3). The newspaper was fined £20,000; the Court took into account that it was a first offence, committed by a regional paper with a circulation of 26,000, and that it was negligent, rather than reckless.

A somewhat different approach was taken in the *Guardian Newspapers* case where the trial judge had refused to stay the proceedings, when an article discussing the character of the motives of the accused was published in a Sunday newspaper during the course of the trial. The judges in the Divisional Court both disagreed with Simon Brown LJ when he had said in the *Birmingham Post* case that a lesser degree of prejudice was required for

---

[26] Pill LJ in *Attorney General v Morgan* [1998] EMLR 294, at 301 (DC).
[27] *Attorney General v Birmingham Post and Mail Ltd* [1998] 4 All ER 49.

a contempt conviction than for a successful appeal against conviction. This difference of approach is particularly clear in Sedley LJ's judgment.

Extract 12.2.6
A-G v *Guardian Newspapers Ltd* **[1999] EWHC Admin 730, [1999] EMLR 924–5, paras 68–73**

SEDLEY LJ:

68. This said, however, I respectfully share the concern expressed by Simon Brown LJ in Attorney-General v. Unger [1998] 1 Cr.App.R. 308, 318–9 and reiterated by him in Attorney-General v. Birmingham Post and Mail [1999] 1 WLR 361, 369, that the courts should not speak with a robust voice in criminal appeals and a sensitive one in contempt cases. Like Collins J I would be inclined to hold that this is not to be done by postulating different degrees of prejudice for the two purposes but by adopting a single standard and recognising that it will operate differently in the two contexts. The standard in both contexts is a substantial risk of prejudicing the fairness of a criminal trial. The self-evident difference is that the risk has ordinarily to be gauged prospectively in a contempt case (and therefore without regard to the outcome of the trial) but retrospectively in a criminal appeal (where ex hypothesi there has been a conviction).

69. One way, therefore, to ensure that the court speaks with a single voice is to test an accusation of contempt by assuming:

(a) that jurors have read the publication,
(b) that an application to discharge the jury has been made and refused,
(c) that the judge has given the jury a proper direction to disregard anything they have read,
(d) that a conviction was not inevitable, and
(e) that the jury have convicted.

70. If in such a situation an appeal on the ground of prejudice would not succeed, no more should the publisher be guilty of contempt. The prospective risk of serious prejudice cannot be any greater than the actual possibility, in the assumed situation, that it has occurred. By parity of reasoning, a case in which an appeal would in the assumed events succeed will ordinarily be a case where contempt is made out, provided always that the court is sure that the facts meet the test.

71. This formulation differs, I accept, from that of Simon Brown LJ in Unger: it looks to the existence of grounds for allowing or dismissing an appeal against conviction rather than for granting or refusing leave to appeal. This is because, the test on appeal being now the safety of the conviction (Criminal Appeal Act 1968, s.2(1), as amended by the Criminal Appeal Act 1995), any substantial risk (cf. s.2(2) of the 1981 Act) that a conviction has been contributed to by a prejudicial publication will ordinarily make it unsafe. To reduce this threshold to the leave stage, requiring only an arguable case of risk, may be to set the threshold of contempt unduly low, at a level where there is not a demonstrable risk of prejudice but only an arguable case of it.

72. The reason why I believe my test nevertheless to be consistent with Simon Brown LJ's view is that it makes the assumptions needed to produce parity between the two situations. Thus in the present case one asks: if the jurors had read the article but Judge Rivlin, though giving them a clear neutralising direction, had rejected an application to discharge them, would Mr. Kelly's conviction be unsafe? If the answer is no, then assuming (see assumption (d)) that it is not for some adventitious reason, I do not see how publication can be said to have prospectively carried any greater risk of prejudice.

73. It does not follow, of course, that the outcome of an appeal determines whether there has been a contempt of court. Those responsible for the publication will have played no part in the appeal. If the Attorney-General concludes that it is in the public interest to seek their committal, both sides are entitled to a hearing free of presumptions.

Recent judgments have, however, adopted the approach taken in the *Birmingham Post* case rather than that advocated by Sedley LJ.[28] Indeed, in the recent case emanating from the tabloid coverage of the Bristol murder investigation (see Extract 12.2.5) the Divisional Court said that the authority of Sedley LJ's formulation has now 'wholly evaporated'.[29] The usual approach is that taken in the *Associated Newspapers* decision (Extract 12.2.4), where Moses LJ explained that the question in contempt proceedings – whether the publication created a substantial risk of serious impediment or prejudice to the course of justice – is not the same as the question for the criminal appeal court whether the conviction was unsafe.[30] While the Court of Appeal looks back, the Divisional Court must look forward to assess the risk at the time of the publication of the material. Of course, it seems odd that an application for contempt may succeed when a judge has previously declined to stay a criminal trial or an appeal court has upheld a conviction as safe. However, this apparent difference of result is explicable, because the questions are different.

Questions for discussion

1. Does it make sense to hold a newspaper liable for contempt, even though the trial judge had earlier held that the prejudicial publicity would not render a conviction unsafe?
2. If the judge has stayed the criminal proceedings, will it generally follow that a contempt application will be successful?

(e) Remedies for infringement of the strict liability rule

The usual remedy for an infringement of the rule is an application to commit for a criminal contempt of court. If the application is upheld, the Court may impose a financial penalty, the level of which varies according to the seriousness of the contempt. In *Hat Trick Productions*, the contempt was serious, resulting from risk-taking, rather than carelessness. The respondents were each fined £10,000. A fine of £20,000 was imposed on the *Birmingham Post*, even though the Court found the newspaper had only been negligent and it was a first offence. However, a more critical view of the press conduct was taken in *Morgan*,[31] where the *News of the World* had published a sensational article detailing the involvement of its own reporter in the investigation of a massive forgery ring. Among other things the article revealed the criminal records of two persons alleged to be parties to a criminal conspiracy; their trial was halted, because of the possible impact of this publicity. In fining the company £50,000, Pill LJ took account of its means and the need to deter a contempt of court with such serious consequences.

A fine of £60,000 was imposed on Express Newspapers when the *Daily Star* named two Premiership footballers as suspects in connection with allegations of gang rape; they had not been identified at that time by the victim, so the publication created a substantial risk that the trial would be halted on the ground that her identification of the defendants might have been tainted by what she read in the press. The Court stressed that the newspaper had disregarded warnings by the Metropolitan Police and by the Attorney-General not

---

[28] In addition to the *Associated Newspapers* case, see *AG v Random House* [2009] EWHC 1727 (QB), paras 20–5.
[29] *Attorney-General v MGN Ltd and News Group* [2011 EWHC 2074 (Admin), para 28 per Judge, LCJ.
[30] [2011] EWHC 418 (Admin), para 48.
[31] *Attorney-General v Morgan* [1998] EMLR 294.

to name or identify the suspects.[32] Sentencing principles have been considered recently in *Attorney General* v *MGN Ltd*, where the Yorkshire edition of the *Daily Mirror* had published an article containing seriously prejudicial material about someone facing a trial for murder of a police officer in Bradford. As a result of the publication the trial was moved from Leeds to Newcastle. MGN had offered a full, though not immediate, apology for publication of the article.

Extract 12.2.7
Attorney-General v *MGN Ltd* **[2009] EWHC 1645 (Admin), paras 43–7**

RICHARDS LJ:

43. I do not propose to engage in an exercise of minute comparison with other cases . . . In general terms, however, it seems to me to be fair to say that, as is to be expected, the highest penalties are associated with contempts of court that result in aborted trials, postponed trials or permanent stays. I would also accept that account must be taken of the extent to which the contempt resulted in the throwing away of costs of the trial process, such costs not being recoverable prior to a change in the law in 2004.

44. One previous case to which it is right to draw particular attention is that of *Attorney-General* v *Mirror Group Newspapers Limited* [2002] EWHC 907. That was a case in which a fine of £75,000 was imposed on the same defendant in respect of articles in the Sunday Mirror which were published in breach of the strict liability rule. Mr Caldecott has drawn our attention to significant differences in that case. There was a deliberate editorial decision to publish an interview with the victim's father in the course of a trial of two Leeds United footballers charged with assaulting an Asian student. The articles were published at a very sensitive stage of the case when the jury was in retirement, and they raised issues of racial aggravation although the Crown had confirmed in court in the proceedings themselves that any suggestion of racial aggravation was not being pursued. The summary records that it was said that the gravity of the contempt was at the top end of the range of strict liability contempts, but there were mitigating factors, in particular the company's good record and its acceptance of the fact that it had erred. Moreover, a deterrent was not likely to be a significant factor in the case of a responsible newspaper with an excellent record.

45. The fact that such a serious contempt was committed only a few years ago by the same defendant is itself a factor to be borne in mind in the present case. Equally, however, I accept that the differences in that case are significant and that the points in favour of MGN to which the court referred in sentencing in that case should also be taken into account in the present context.

46. In broad terms the present case is a serious contempt, though not as serious as some of those that have occurred in the past. It arises from what appears to have been a single failure of a generally satisfactory vetting system. On the other hand, it is a failure that should not have occurred, especially given the nature of the article which was so obviously prejudicial, or potentially prejudicial, to the prospective trial of Mustaf Jama. Fortunately it did not, in the event, cause great or irreparable damage to the administration of justice. The court has received a full explanation and apology, and an assurance as to steps that have been taken to avoid repetition.

47. In all the circumstances, I take the view that an appropriate penalty would be to order the defendant, MGN, to pay a fine of £25,000. I would therefore so order in addition to the order as to costs which I have already mentioned. [The court ordered MGN to pay the Attorney-General's reasonable costs.]

---

[32] *Attorney-General* v *Express Newapapers* [2004] EWHC 2859 (Admin), [2005] EMLR 13, paras 22–4.

Following the heavy fine of £75,000 imposed on MGN in the case referred to in paragraph 44 of this judgment, legislation was amended to allow criminal courts to require a third party to pay all or part of the costs which were wasted as a result of 'serious misconduct', whether or not it amounted to a contempt of court.[33] The media may therefore in extreme cases be ordered to pay the costs of an aborted trial, which has been halted by the trial judge in view of prejudicial publicity; that might be an enormous sum, amounting to over £1 million. However, the power to order payment of these costs has not so far been exercised.[34] Further, the media are often required to pay the Attorney-General's costs in bringing contempt proceedings. For example, in the *Associated Newspapers* case (Extract 12.2.4 above), the defendants were required to pay costs of over £28,000, in addition to the fine of £15,000 imposed on each of them.[35]

The Attorney-General may apply for an injunction to stop the publication or distribution of material likely to prejudice legal proceedings. That course had been taken in the *Sunday Times* case under the common law before the reformulation of the strict liability rule in the Contempt of Court Act 1981. Recently, Tugendhat J granted the Attorney-General an injunction to stop the distribution of a book, passages in which referred to police operations leading to the trial of three men for serious terrorist offences. The application for an injunction was brought shortly after conclusion of evidence at the trial, when a few hundred copies of the book had been sold and many thousands had been sent to retailers in preparation for the publication date. After deciding that further publication of the book would create a substantial risk of serious prejudice to the current trial, the judge considered whether an injunction should be granted.

Extract 12.2.8
Attorney-General v Random House Group Ltd [2009] EWHC 1727 (QB), [2010] EMLR 9, paras 103–10

TUGENDHAT J:

[The judge had considered at paras 27–43 the principles on which interim injunctions may be granted, and said (at para 102) that the book was within the category of political expression – it discussed police operations – so it would be in the public interest for it to be published. Under HRA, s 12(4)(a)(ii) that factor had to be taken into account when determining whether it would be right to grant an injunction.]

103. Causing a publisher to recall a book (or any other publication) is always a major step to take. The costs will exceed by a very large measure the amount which the court might be expected to impose, following a committal for contempt, by way of fine in a case such as the present, assuming the facts were as I have set them out here. If the book had been sold out and no application made to the court for an injunction, it is for consideration whether the Attorney-General would have thought it in the public interest in this case to apply to commit for contempt of court. That would have depended upon all the circumstances, which may have included what happened at the Trial. It is in any case not a matter for this court, so I shall assume that the Attorney-General would have applied to commit. If she had, and depending on the circumstances, it seems to me that the court might have taken a lenient view in this case. It is unlikely that the financial consequences would have been as great as the evidence shows the consequences of this injunction have been and, if it is continued, will be in the future.

---

[33] Prosecution of Offenders Act 1985, s 19B, added by Courts Act 2003, s 93.
[34] See Arlidge, Eady and Smith (see n 1) para 14-148.
[35] *Attorney General v Associated Newspapers* [2011] EWHC 1894 (Admin).

104. I have considered what other measures might be to hand to address the risk which I have held to exist. A direction to the jury would not carry the weight that such directions usually carry, for reasons already discussed (para 85 above). The powers of the court under s.13 of the Juries Act have rarely been exercised in recent years. They should not be overlooked, but nor should the difficulties in exercising those powers. There may be cases where that would be the proportionate response. If so, there would be difficulties, except in those rare cases where an injunction is sought from a High Court Judge during a trial, as happened in the *HTV Cymru* case.[36] A circuit judge sitting in the Crown Court could not grant an injunction, and the judge of the High Court to whom the Attorney-General applied for an injunction cannot exercise the powers of the trial judge over the jury, nor require that any powers be exercised by him.

105. In my judgment the unique features of this case referred to at the start of this judgment put the case in a category of its own. It is important not to lose sight of what is at stake in the Trial. While I recall the finding that I have made as to the limited risk of prejudice that would be created in this case, what is at stake in the Trial makes it of the highest importance that the Trial be not seriously impeded.

106. The public interest in the Trial being fair could not be higher. If any of the accused is convicted on count 1, he will face the prospect of spending much if not all of the rest of his life in custody.

107. If any of the accused is innocent, and is nevertheless convicted, the scale of the injustice involved would be difficult to exaggerate. In addition, experience over the last 30 years shows that such injustice (on those occasions when it has occurred) has had a long lasting, and extremely adverse effect upon public confidence in the administration of justice. This is to the detriment of society as a whole.

108. On the other hand, if any of the accused did indeed take part in the conspiracy alleged in count 1, and if he is not convicted, or if his conviction has to be set aside on appeal and if he cannot be retried for a second time, the injustice and danger to the public is again difficult to exaggerate. In that event the lives of very many people may be put at risk.

109. In many cases less weight might be attached to the implications of any appeal and retrial that might follow if the jury were to be discharged, or any appeal against conviction succeeds. But in this case seven accused have been in custody for three years already, and there are three further accused (two in custody) whose trial is to follow the trial of these accused. If there is a retrial, they will have to wait for many more months before there is a verdict. Two juries have sat for many months in two separate trials. This places a very great strain on them and upon the administration of justice. There is not unlimited capacity in the criminal justice system. When one case is being tried, or retried, another case must be kept waiting. The cost to the public of each trial of the scale of the Trial runs into millions of pounds. The financial implications for the Publishers of a delay even as short as eight weeks are great. But they cannot be compared to the financial implications for the public at large of a delay to this trial, or an appeal. Even a trial of a single accused for a few days or weeks is expensive, but the administrative and financial implications of the trials of those accused of the airline plot is exceptional. The disparity of risk which exists between what the Publishers must suffer if this injunction is granted, and what the public must risk suffering if it is not, is beyond measurement, and is another unique feature of this case.

110. In my judgment, in the present case, for the reasons I have stated, it is necessary and proportionate that the injunction be granted.

There are remedies, other than applications for contempt of court or injunctions, to stop a publication, to deal with the dangers of prejudicial media publicity. Sometimes a judge may halt a criminal trial and discharge the jury, because he accepts the argument that, owing

---

[36] *Ex parte HTV Cymru (Wales) Ltd* [2002] EMLR 11, where Aikens J held that the Crown Court does have jurisdiction under the Senior Courts Act 1981 to grant injunctions to restrain contempt of court.

to massive pre-trial publicity, the accused is unable to receive a fair trial. This occurred, for instance, in the *MGN/Knights* case (Extract 12.2.3), in the *Birmingham Post* case and in *Morgan*. However, the trial judge may consider that a strong direction to the jury to consider the case on the basis only of the evidence in court and to exclude from its mind anything it may have read or heard in the press and other media, including the Net, is enough to ensure a fair trial, as in the *Guardian Newspapers* body parts case (Extract 12.2.6) and in the recent online news case (Extract 12.2.4) However, as that latter case shows, the direction may not be clear enough to remove a real risk of prejudice, and it certainly does not preclude the chance of a successful application – in that case against two tabloids in respect of their online news sites – for contempt of court.

Further, a convicted defendant may decide to appeal on the ground that the verdict of the jury was unsafe. In some circumstances the Court of Appeal has been prepared to accept an appeal on this ground. In *R v McCann*[37] the defendants, charged with conspiracy to murder Tom King, the Secretary of State for Ireland, had exercised their right not to give evidence; they argued that the announcement during the course of their trial of government proposals to modify that right had inevitably prejudiced its fairness. Television news bulletins had reported Tom King as saying that the proposals were aimed at terrorists, and had carried interviews with him and with Lord Denning, the former Master of the Rolls, who supported a change in the law. The trial judge had rejected arguments to halt the trial and discharge the jury. For the Court of Appeal Beldam LJ said that despite the two or three days' lapse of time between the broadcast interviews and the retirement of the jury to consider its verdict. He was left with the definite impression that the impact which the statements in the television interviews may have had on the fairness of the trial could not be overcome by any direction to the jury, and that the only way in which justice could be done and be obviously seen to be done was by discharging the jury and ordering a retrial.[38]

The appeal was allowed. The same approach was taken in the *Taylor* case. There had been saturation coverage in the press of the trial of two sisters for the murder of the wife of a man with whom one sister had had an affair before his marriage. The coverage included publication of a distorted photograph which gave the misleading impression that one sister had given the man an intimate kiss at his wedding to the murdered woman. McCowan LJ pointed out that it was unreasonable in these circumstances to expect defence counsel at the trial to have asked for the jury to be discharged; it would have entailed the defendants spending yet more time in custody.[39] Although the appeal was allowed, no proceedings for contempt of court were brought against the tabloids (see the discussion in Section 12.2(f) below).

Questions for discussion

1. Are the courts consistent in their decisions on the level of fines on the media for contempt of court? Are these fines heavy enough to deter the publication of prejudicial media publicity?
2. Do you agree with the grant of the injunction in the *Random House* case? Did the judge give adequate weight to the presumption against prior restraints?
3. Does the possibility of a successful appeal, as in *McCann* and *Taylor*, provide a satisfactory alternative remedy for prejudicial media publicity?

---

[37] (1991) 92 Cr App Rep 239.
[38] Ibid., at 253.
[39] *R v Taylor* (1994) 98 Cr App Rep 361, at 369 (CA).

(f) The role of the Attorney-General

Under section 7 of the Contempt of Court Act contempt proceedings in England may be brought only by the Attorney-General. The provision does allow for proceedings to be brought on the motion of a superior court, but in practice that jurisdiction is never used. If a trial judge considers a publication has endangered the fairness of the proceedings, he may refer the matter to the Attorney-General. The important point is that a contempt application cannot be brought by an aggrieved defendant or other party, or by concerned members of the public. Sometimes the Attorney-General has seemed surprisingly reluctant to bring contempt proceedings; no proceedings were brought subsequent to the *Taylor* decision, where the Court of Appeal had allowed the sisters' appeal after publication by tabloid papers of a mass of prejudicial material.[40] The Divisional Court then declined to review the Solicitor-General's decision to bring an application for contempt of court, so the sisters had no redress against the tabloids.[41]

This position is arguably very unsatisfactory.[42] There is a risk that the Attorney-General – a member of the government – may be nervous of bringing contempt proceedings against tabloid newspapers, on whose support political parties and governments rely. Even more clearly he may be reluctant to bring an application against a government colleague who may have given interviews to the media, explicitly or implicitly casting aspersions on the character of parties to legal proceedings or making other prejudicial remarks. There is some sign, however, that the present Attorney-General, Dominic Grieve, MP, is more likely than some of his predecessors to back up warnings to the media with contempt proceedings – as shown by the recent proceedings against two tabloid online news sites (Extract 12.2.4) and in the Chris Jefferies case (Extract 12.2.5). This is surely welcome. There is little point in contempt of court law unless it is enforced.

(g) Assessment and reform of the strict liability rule

The strict liability rule is open to a number of criticisms.[43] First, it does not appear to deal with cases where it is difficult to disentangle the impact of prejudicial material in one newspaper from a welter of adverse publicity in the press as a whole: see the *MGN/Knights* case (Extract 12.2.3). As long ago as 1997, a Committee of the House of Commons concluded that the strict liability rule should be strengthened to prevent a newspaper escaping liability for contempt of court because other newspapers had also contributed to the adverse publicity.[44] In these circumstances contempt of court law does not protect the rights of an accused to a fair trial, which can only be safeguarded by the trial judge deciding to halt the proceedings and discharge the jury, or by other drastic remedies such as postponing a trial or changing its venue.[45] Equally, too rigorous an application of the rule might disproportionately penalise the exercise of press freedom. It has been argued

---

[40] See text at n 39.

[41] *R v Solicitor General, ex parte Taylor*, The Times, 14 August 1995.

[42] See Fenwick and Phillipson, 252–7.

[43] The Law Commission Consultation Paper, *Contempt of Court* (no 209) issued in November 2012 canvasses a number of substantive and procedural reforms.

[44] 2nd Report of National Heritage Committee for 1996–7, *Press Activity Affecting Court Cases* (HC 86), paras 32–6.

[45] In the leading Canadian case, *Dagenais v Canadian Broadcasting Corpn* [1994] 3 SCR 835 the Supreme Court held that a ban on the broadcast of a television drama series which might prejudice a forthcoming trial could only be ordered if other remedies such as changing the venue of the trial or insulating the jury from the publicity would be ineffective.

that the requirement of a *substantial* risk of serious prejudice should be interpreted, in conformity with the requirements of the HRA guarantee of freedom of expression, to apply only to publications which are really likely to bring about that prejudice, rather than to any which creates a non-remote risk of that eventuality.[46] The general approach of the courts – affirmed recently in the *Associated News* online news case (Extract 12.2.4) – may penalise press freedom when it has been exercised without any actual impact on the course of justice. Judges are understandably concerned to deal with the risks of an impediment or prejudice to the course of legal proceedings. However, the consequence may be that the media are deterred from publishing any material which runs that risk, even if the general content has a real public interest. So the contempt of court laws may have an undesirable chilling effect on freedom of expression.[47]

Two more fundamental criticisms may be made of the strict liability rule. First, it can be questioned how much impact media publicity has on jurors. The assumptions underlying the rule is that they often do recall media reports and that these reports, particularly those suggesting the guilt of the defendant, may have an impact on their deliberations and verdict. Recent research, conducted by Professor Cheryl Thomas for the Ministry of Justice,[48] shows that in standard cases (those lasting less than two weeks with little media coverage), only 8 per cent of jurors had any recollection of pre-trial coverage, although in high profile cases (lasting two weeks or more with substantial media coverage) over a third of jurors recalled pre-trial reports. Her research confirmed what is known as the 'fade factor': prejudicial media publicity more than, say, about five or six months before the trial will have little residual impact on any member of the jury. The courts have recognised this factor in a number of cases, notably *ITN* and *Hat Trick Productions*, although it should be noted that in the latter it was not decisive – the broadcast as much as six months before the start of the trial was held to be in contempt of court. The fade factor is less crucial if the material is highly prejudicial, with explicit suggestions of the accused's guilt. Interestingly, Professor Thomas's study found that the vast majority of jurors in high profile cases who could recall the emphasis of the pre-trial media coverage remembered coverage suggesting the guilt of the defendant.[49] More general reports or fictional representations of the crime would be much less likely to have an impact.[50]

The second question is whether the courts place enough confidence in the ability of juries to follow the directions of the trial judge to exclude from their mind any media reports which they may have read and do recall. Courts hearing contempt applications do take into account the directions given by the trial judge (see *MGN/Knights,* Principle 10(c) and *Guardian Newspapers*) but these directions may not be enough to absolve the media from a finding of contempt of court (see *Hat Trick Productions*, and *Associated Newspapers* (Extract 12.2.4)). That is surely right. In many cases, a firm direction should be enough to obviate any risk of serious prejudice, but some publicity may be so prejudicial that jurors cannot be expected to exclude it altogether, however strong and clear the direction given by the judge. Professor Thomas found that in high profile cases a fifth of jurors found it

---

[46] See Fenwick and Phillipson, 275–9.

[47] For a vigorous statement of this case from an American perspective, see J.A. Brandwood, 'You say "fair trial" and I say "free press": British and American approaches to protecting defendants' rights in high profile trials' (2000) 75 *New York University Law Rev* 285, 303–15.

[48] *Are Juries Fair?* (Ministry of Justice Research Series 1/10), ch 3.4.

[49] Ibid., 42.

[50] T.M. Honess, S. Barker, E.A. Charman and M. Leiv, 'Empirical and legal perspectives on the impact of pre-trial publicity' [2002] *Criminal Law Rev*, 361–9 argue that an emotive story about the reasons for the defendant's conduct is particularly likely to have a prejudicial impact.

difficult to put media reports out of their mind. Moreover, the arguments for freedom of expression assume that speech may persuade and influence readers and listeners, so it is difficult to take seriously the view that prejudicial media publicity has little impact on jurors. In addition, of course, it may be immaterial whether jurors can recall the precise terms of the material they have looked at; features in the tabloids may create an imperceptible but general climate of hostility to an accused. In the light of these findings, the case for retaining the strict liability rule is powerful. Indeed, it should be strengthened to cope with a welter of prejudicial publicity, where it is difficult to isolate the role of a particular press article and hold that by itself it created a substantial risk of prejudice. Admittedly, there is always the risk of chilling some valuable media reporting, but that risk must be incurred if fair trial rights are to be safeguarded.

The most pressing problems now for the strict liability rule are brought about juror use of the Internet. Professor Thomas found that 12 per cent of jurors in high profile cases admitted to looking for information about the case on the Internet, despite having received directions from the judge not to do so.[51] Moreover, in both high profile and standard cases many more jurors saw reports on the Internet during the trial than actively looked for information. Jurors may, however, be deterred from searching, or looking at, the Net for information about the case, if they realise that they may be sentenced to six months imprisonment for disobedience to court directions.[52] Further, unless contempt proceedings are brought rigorously against websites and individual bloggers, it may become increasingly difficult to resist the argument of the traditional mass media that it is wrong to bring applications against them for breach of the strict liability rule, while bloggers and others are left unscathed. This is a new manifestation of a problem which has long existed in this area of law: national (or even continental) regulation cannot easily protect fair trial rights, which are threatened by satellite broadcasting and communications on the Internet which cross national boundaries instantaneously.[53]

Questions for discussion

1. Should the strict liability rule be reformulated, or applied differently, to give more weight to freedom of expression?
2. Does the strict liability rule wrongly assume that prejudicial media publicity influences the jury?
3. How should contempt of court law deal with the use by jurors of the Internet during the trial?

12.3 COMMON LAW CONTEMPT

The Contempt of Court Act 1981 is not an exhaustive code for the law of contempt, or even for that part of contempt law concerned to safeguard the administration of justice.

---

[51] More than 12 per cent may have done this, but were not willing to admit it: Thomas, 43.

[52] As happened in *Attorney General* v *Dallas* [2012] EWHC 156 (Admin). See the discussion in the Law Commission Consultation Paper (n 43), ch 4.

[53] For discussion, see C. Walker, 'Fundamental rights, fair trials, and the new audio-visual sector', (1996) 59 *Modern Law Rev* 517–39.

Extract 12.3.1
Contempt of Court Act 1981, section 6

6. Nothing in the foregoing provisions of this Act—

(a) prejudices any defence available at common law to a charge of contempt of court under the strict liability rule;

(b) implies that any publication is punishable as contempt of court under that rule which would not be so punishable apart from those provisions;

(c) restricts liability for contempt of court in respect of conduct intended to impede or prejudice the administration of justice.

Section 6(c) of the CCA 1981 may be significant for the media. In *Attorney General* v *News Group Newspapers*,[54] a tabloid offered to fund a private prosecution against a named doctor for rape, although the authorities had decided not to prosecute him for lack of evidence. As the doctor had not at that time been arrested and no warrant had been issued, proceedings were not 'active', and so the strict liability rule did not apply. The Divisional Court, however, held that under section 6(c) an application for common law contempt could be brought, even where the publication might prejudice only the outcome of proceedings which were not even imminent. The elements of common law contempt were further considered in the case from which the next extract is taken. An article in the *Sport* newspaper referred in lurid terms to the previous record of a man called Evans whom the police were looking for in connection with the disappearance of a schoolgirl. As in the *News Group* case. the strict liability rule did not apply.

Extract 12.3.2
***Attorney-General* v *Sport Newspapers Ltd* [1991] 1 WLR 1194, at 1207, 1209 (DC)**

BINGHAM LJ:

In my view section 6(c) was intended to preserve what was understood to be the existing law, that a publisher was liable in contempt for an intentionally prejudicial publication made at a time when proceedings were imminent. I cannot otherwise see what sensible purpose this provision could have been intended to serve.

. . .

If the question were at large, I would be much more hesitant whether that proposition could hold if proceedings were not imminent. *Attorney-General* v *News Group Newspapers Plc.* [1989] Q.B. 110 is, however, a very clear decision on the point, and in making it this court expressly recognised that it was extending the boundaries of contempt as previously understood. It is a decision with very serious implications in those cases, perhaps increasingly common, where reporters are concerned to highlight an alleged crime, to point an accusing finger at an identified culprit and to stimulate a demand for prosecution. It also has the effect of enlarging a quasi-criminal liability in a field very recently considered by Parliament . . . In a matter of this nature it is very highly desirable that the law should be clear so that it may be understood and observed. I am quite satisfied that we should not be justified in departing from the rule so recently and unambiguously laid down in this court.[55]

    Having heard the second respondent [the editor] give evidence, I think it is possible to reconstruct his state of mind at the time of publication. He said, as is obvious, that a newspaper is written for its readers, and I have no doubt that his main (although unadmitted) aim was to

---

[54] [1989] QB 110 (DC).
[55] Hodgson J disagreed on this point, but concurred with Bingham LJ that the respondent lacked the necessary intent.

publish a story of a kind which his readers could be expected to relish. According to him, his main aim was to alert the public to the danger of this violent and habitual sexual predator, which he felt the police had been wrong to conceal, and thereby perhaps increase the chance of his apprehension. I doubt if this concern was uppermost in the second respondent's mind, but I see no reason to doubt that it played a part in his thinking. I accept his evidence that he gave consideration to the police request not to reveal Evans' previous convictions, and also his evidence that he wondered whether the police were seeking to cover up their own failure to question a rather obvious local suspect before he slipped through the net . . . I accept the second respondent's evidence that at the date of publication he regarded the commencement of criminal proceedings against Evans as speculative and remote. With the benefit of hindsight, of course, we know that a warrant was issued shortly after publication and an arrest made shortly after that. But these facts were not known when the newspaper was published. At that time all that was known was that Evans had disappeared, with some reason to think he had gone abroad. There was nothing to suggest that he had been sighted or that the police were on his scent or that his early apprehension was expected. It was wholly uncertain whether he would be found and, if so, where or when, and uncertain when, if at all, proceedings might follow.

I have not found this factual issue easy to resolve, and I regard it as finely poised. But on balance I conclude that the applicant has not shown beyond reasonable doubt that at the date of publication the second respondent had the specific intention which must be proved against him. If proof of recklessness were enough, the answer might be different, but it is not. On the facts here I cannot be satisfied that the second respondent intended to prejudice the fair conduct of proceedings the very existence of which he regarded as speculative and remote. It follows that I would, on this ground, refuse this application against both respondents.

This ruling may mean that common law contempt will rarely be applied in these circumstances, for it will be difficult to prove the necessary intent to impede or prejudice justice. However, it is at least arguable that the article in the *Sunday Times* thalidomide case might now be held liable for common law contempt.[56] This would be very odd since an object of the CCA 1981 was to implement the decision of the European Court of Human Rights which had held the House of Lords' decision in that case incompatible with the ECHR. The strict liability rule would not apply, since the proceedings the article intended to influence were not 'active'. However, an application to commit for common law contempt would succeed on the facts of the *Sunday Times* case if the Attorney-General could prove the necessary intent.

Common law contempt may also be committed by the publication by one newspaper (or by a broadcaster or other media) of material, the publication of which by another media outlet has already been restrained by an injunction to prevent a breach of confidence. This variety of contempt prevented the *Sunday Times* and other newspapers from publishing extracts from *Spycatcher*, when the *Guardian* had been restrained from doing this by breach of confidence injunctions.[57] Lord Oliver, while concurring with the other Law Lords, thought the ruling had disturbing implications: it meant that someone seeking to stop the publication of allegedly confidential information,

> can effectively through the invocation of the law of contempt, restrain until the trial of the action, which may be two or three years ahead, publication not only by the defendant but by anyone else within the jurisdiction and thus stifle what may, in the end, turn out to be perfectly legitimate comment until it no longer has any importance or commands any public interest.[58]

[56] See text at nn 7–9.
[57] *Attorney-General* v *Times Newspapers Ltd* [1992] 1 AC 191 (HL).
[58] Ibid., at 226.

The leading case on this aspect of common law contempt is now *Attorney-General* v *Punch*, where the House of Lords, reversing the Court of Appeal, held that the editor of *Punch*, a famous literary magazine, had committed contempt when he published an article by David Shayler, a former member of the Security Service, about the Bishopsgate bomb in 1993. Shayler had been restrained by an interlocutory injunction, granted by Hooper J, from disclosing any information obtained by him in the course of his employment as a Security Service agent relating to its activities or to security and intelligence activities in general. The article in *Punch* disclosed material covered by this injunction and three pieces of information which had not previously been published, two of which concerned two suspects for the Bishopsgate bombing. The editor, James Steen, argued that he had not intended to publish material which would damage national security and so frustrate Hooper J's order. Lord Nicholls gave the leading speech in the House of Lords; like Lord Oliver in the *Spycatcher* case he also expressed concern about the implications of the decision for media freedom.

Extract 12.3.3

Attorney-General v *Punch* [2002] UKHL 50, [2003] 1 AC 1046, paras 43–4, 47–53, 61–3

LORD NICHOLLS:

43. When proceedings come before a court the plaintiff typically asserts that he has a legal right which has been or is about to be infringed by the defendant. The claim having come before the court, it is then for the court, not the parties to the proceedings or third parties, to determine the way justice is best administered in the proceedings. It is for the court to decide whether the plaintiff's asserted right needs and should have any, and if so what, interim protection. If the court orders that pending the trial the defendant shall not do certain acts the court thereby determines the manner in which, in this respect, the proceedings shall be conducted. This is the court's determination on what interim protection is needed and is appropriate. Third parties are required to respect this determination, as expressed in the court's order. The reason why the court grants interim protection is to protect the plaintiff's asserted right. But the manner in which this protection is afforded depends upon the terms of the interlocutory injunction. The purpose the court seeks to achieve by granting the interlocutory injunction is that, pending a decision by the court on the claims in the proceedings, the restrained acts shall not be done. Third parties are in contempt of court if they wilfully interfere with the administration of justice by thwarting the achievement of this purpose in those proceedings.

44. This is so, even if in the particular case, the injunction is drawn in seemingly over-wide terms. The remedy of the third party whose conduct is affected by the order is to apply to the court for the order to be varied. Furthermore, there will be no contempt unless the act done has some significant and adverse effect on the administration of justice in the proceedings. This tempers the rigour of the principle.

. . .

47. . . . I turn to consider the purpose of Hooper J's order. In my view, not only was the scope of the order clear, so also was its purpose; clear, indeed, beyond a peradventure. Self-evidently, the purpose of the judge in making the order was to preserve the confidentiality of the information specified in the order pending the trial so as to enable the court at trial to adjudicate effectively on the disputed issues of confidentiality arising in the action. This is apparent from merely reading the order. The Attorney General's claim for a permanent injunction might be defeated in advance of the trial if, before the trial, Mr Shayler was at liberty to put this information into the public domain. In other words, but to the same effect, the purpose of the court in making the order was to ensure that the court's decision on the claims in the

proceedings should not be pre-empted by Mr Shayler disclosing any of the information specified in the order before the trial.

48. This being the purpose of the injunction, the actus reus of contempt lies in thwarting this purpose by destruction of the confidentiality of the material which it was the purpose of the injunction to preserve.

49. As already stated, Mr Steen accepts that the publication of the offending magazine article constituted the actus reus of contempt. He is right to do so. He did an act which Hooper J's order prohibited Mr Shayler from doing. Publication of the information by 'Punch' was destructive in part of the purpose of Hooper J's order.

50. Although Mr Steen seems not to accept this, this is not a case where the conduct was inconsistent with the court's order in only a technical or trivial way. Disclosure of the three pieces of information mentioned above, not previously published, has had a significant and adverse effect on the trial of the action against Mr Shayler. Contrary to the court's object in granting the interlocutory injunction, the Attorney General's claim to keep these pieces of information confidential has now been thwarted in advance of the trial.

Mens rea: Mr Steen's intention

51. Before your Lordships' House the argument presented on behalf of Mr Steen was that it matters not whether the purpose of Hooper J's order was as set out above or as stated by Lord Phillips MR.[59] Either way, the Attorney General failed to prove that Mr Steen possessed the necessary mens rea. Mr Steen's evidence was that he thought the purpose of the order was to prevent damage to national security, it was not his intention to damage national security in any way, and he did not consider he was doing so. Before Silber J the Attorney General did not seek to challenge Mr Steen's evidence that when he published the article he did not believe it contained any damaging disclosures. Accordingly, so the argument runs, the Attorney General did not establish that Mr Steen intended to thwart the court's purpose in making the interlocutory injunction.

52. I am not impressed by this argument. The facts speak for themselves. Mr Steen is an intelligent man and experienced journalist. He knew that the action against Mr Shayler raised confidentiality issues relating wholly or primarily to national security. He must, inevitably, have appreciated that by publishing the article he was doing precisely what the order was intended to prevent, namely, pre-empting the court's decision on these confidentiality issues. That is knowing interference with the administration of justice.

53. I do not see how on this issue, which is the relevant issue, the admitted or proved facts are susceptible of any other interpretation. The judge was entitled so to conclude, even though these conclusions were not put in so many words to Mr Steen in the course of his cross-examination. No credible alternative conclusion regarding Mr Steen's relevant beliefs or intentions has been advanced on his behalf. Mr Steen may have thought the order was intended to protect national security, and that publication would not damage national security. He may have had, as he says, no intention of damaging national security. Those beliefs and intentions are not inconsistent with an intention to take it upon himself to make a decision which, as he knew, the court had reserved to itself. I have to say, however, that even on the basis of his stated beliefs and intentions Mr Steen's conduct was surprisingly irresponsible. He frankly admitted, as is obvious, that he was not qualified to assess whether disclosure of any particular information would damage national security. Despite this he proceeded to publish information whose disclosure was, as he knew, asserted by the Attorney General to be damaging to national security.

. . .

---

[59] Lord Phillips, MR, held that the purpose of the order was to prevent the disclosure of any material which arguably risked harm to national security, so that it was not a contempt for *Punch* to publish the article unless it intended to cause that harm: [2001] EWCA Civ 403, paras 100, 115–18.

61. The second matter I must mention . . . concerns the difficulty of drafting an interlocutory order in terms which are sufficiently certain but go no wider than is necessary to restrain disclosure of information in respect of which the Attorney General has an arguable case for confidentiality. In the present case the wide terms of Hooper J's order did not operate in a disproportionately restrictive manner so far as Punch Ltd and Mr Steen were concerned. They knowingly published previously unpublished material whose disclosure was, as they knew, asserted by the Attorney General to be damaging to national security.

62. This may not always be so. In particular, an interlocutory injunction in the wide form used in the present case may well in practice have a significant 'chilling' effect on the press and the media generally, inhibiting discussion and criticism of the Security Service. Parts of the media may well be discouraged from publishing even manifestly innocuous material which falls within the literal scope of the order. A newspaper may be unwilling to approach the Attorney General, the plaintiff in the action in which the order was made. An application to the court for a variation of the order may involve delay and expense. Even less attractive is the prospect of proceeding to publish without further ado, at the risk of having to face contempt proceedings and penal sanctions. The ability to defend such proceedings, on the basis that disclosure of the material had no adverse effect on the administration of justice, will not usually afford much consolation to a journalist.

63. This is not a satisfactory state of affairs. It is to be hoped that it may be possible to devise an improved form of words for interlocutory injunctions of this type which will give the Attorney General the protection he seeks in sufficiently certain terms but without being as all embracing as the order in the present case. It is to be hoped that the drafting difficulties may be capable of being overcome, at least to some extent. This is a matter for consideration by the Attorney General in the first instance. It is also a matter judges will wish to have in mind in future when asked to make interlocutory orders in this type of case.

This decision may fail to give due weight to the interest of freedom of expression and media freedom.[60] The House of Lords made no attempt to examine the proportionality of the restrictions imposed on these freedoms by common law contempt principles, under which any revelation of, say, security service activities will be penalised, no matter how great the legitimate public interest in their disclosure, merely because the publication was intended to frustrate the purpose of an earlier court order to keep such information confidential pending a full trial. The House of Lords did not examine the public interest in the article's revelations, although that might have provided *Punch* and its editor with a good defence to a civil action if they had been sued for breach of confidence. Freedom of expression arguments would, moreover, have been considered on the application for a permanent injunction. The decision in *Punch* suggests that freedom of expression arguments will not receive the same consideration in contempt of court applications.

Questions for discussion

1. Might the *Sunday Times* now be held liable for common law contempt for its press campaign against Distillers?
2. Do you agree with the decision of the House of Lords in *A-G v Punch*? Did Lord Nicholls do justice to the editor's arguments, or to freedom of expression?

---

[60] See Fenwick and Phillipson, 291–302.

12.4 POSTPONEMENT ORDERS

(a) Introduction

In a number of circumstances courts have power to ban or postpone the reporting of proceedings before them. Some of these powers are considered in Chapter 13, but the important power to order the postponement of reports on the ground that they might prejudice the administration of justice in legal proceeding is discussed here, because it is closely related to the strict liability rule.

> **Extract 12.4.1**
> **Contempt of Court Act 1981, section 4(1)–(2)**
>
> 4.—(1) Subject to this section a person is not guilty of contempt of court under the strict liability rule in respect of a fair and accurate report of legal proceedings held in public, published contemporaneously and in good faith.
>
> (2) In any such proceedings the court may, where it appears to be necessary for avoiding a substantial risk of prejudice to the administration of justice in those proceedings, or in any other proceedings pending or imminent, order that the publication of any report of the proceedings, or any part of the proceedings, be postponed for such period as the court thinks necessary for that purpose.

The effect of section 4(1) of the CCA 1981 is clear. The media is not liable for contempt of court under the strict liability rule, merely because a fair, accurate and contemporaneous report of legal proceedings might create a substantial risk of prejudice to their outcome (or that of other proceedings). However, section 4(2) gives the court power to order that reporting of proceedings be *postponed* in order to avoid such a risk. The provision puts what was considered to be a common law power of uncertain origin on a secure basis.[61] Indeed, it is now very doubtful whether this power ever existed. For in a case from the West Indies the Privy Council has ruled that any power to make orders binding on the public at large, including of course the media, must be conferred by statute and cannot be found in the common law.[62]

The statutory power may be exercised for a number of reasons, among them the need to prevent the reporting of evidence or legal arguments heard in the absence of the jury, or of the disclosure of evidence identifying a defendant who is likely to be involved in subsequent, related proceedings. A third common ground is that reporting may prejudice later trials involving the same or associated offences, by, for example, highlighting evidence which suggests the guilt of the defendants in those trials.[63] It is important to emphasise that the power is only to *postpone* the reporting of proceedings, or parts of them; the power cannot be exercised to ban *indefinitely* a report of the proceedings, or of particular evidence.[64]

---

[61] For leading common law cases, see *R v Clement* (1821) 4 B & Ald 218, and *R v Poulson, The Times*, 4 January 1974. The Phillimore Committee recommended that contemporaneous accurate court reporting should never attract contempt proceedings, without the qualification of the postponement power: Cmnd 5794 (1974), paras 134–41.

[62] *Independent Publishing Co v Attorney-General of Trinidad and Tobago* [2004] UKPC 26, [2005] 1 AC 190.

[63] See C. Walker, I. Cram and D. Hogarth, 'The reporting of Crown Court proceedings and the Contempt of Court Act 1981' (1992) 55 *Modern Law Rev* 647, at 658–60.

[64] *Re Times Newspapers Ltd* [2007] EWCA Crim 1925, [2008] 1 All ER 343, paras 12 and 21.

One legal question was whether it is a contempt of court merely to breach a postponement order or whether it must be shown that the breach would independently amount to contempt. Another difficulty was whether a court is entitled to order the postponement of the reporting of *all* the proceedings, even though only some *part* of them concerned sensitive matters, the reporting of which might create a substantial risk of prejudice. Answers to these questions were provided by the Court of Appeal in one of the first cases on the statutory power. In *R v Horsham Justices, ex parte Farquharson*,[65] the Court of Appeal upheld an application for judicial review to challenge a wide blanket order made by magistrates postponing the reporting of proceedings to commit the defendants to trial for arms offences; the magistrates should consider a more limited order, confined to the reporting of evidence which might lead to sensational reporting and which would therefore prejudice the course of the eventual trial. Further, the Court of Appeal ruled by a majority, with Lord Denning, MR, dissenting on this point, that an infringement of a postponement order was itself a contempt of court.

The Court of Appeal subsequently issued a Practice Direction in 1982 which was revised and consolidated with later orders in 2002.

Extract 12.4.2
Practice Direction (Criminal Proceedings: Consolidation) [2002] 1 WLR 2870, para 1.3.2

It is necessary to keep a permanent record of such [postponement] orders for later reference. For this purpose all orders made under section 4(2) must be formulated in precise terms, having regard to the decision of Reg. v Horsham, ex parte Farquharson [1982] 2 QB 762, and orders . . . must be committed to writing either by the judge personally or by the clerk of the court under the judge's directions. An order must state (a) its precise scope, (b) the time at which it shall cease to have effect, if appropriate, and (c) the specific purpose of making the order.

Courts will normally give notice to the press in some form that an order has been made . . . and court staff should be prepared to answer any enquiry about a specific case, but it is, and will remain, the responsibility of those reporting cases, and their editors, to ensure that no breach of any order occurs and the onus rests with them to make enquiry in any case of doubt.

(b) The requirements for making a postponement order

In the leading case on the requirements for making a postponement order, the Court of Appeal deleted restrictions which would have prevented the reporting of any material identifying the chief prosecution witness and of the closing speeches and summing-up in a trial for serious drugs offences, on the ground that these were not 'necessary' to avoid a substantial risk of prejudice to later trials of defendants for the same offences. The Lord Chief Justice formulated principles which have been applied in a number of subsequent cases.

---

[65] [1982] QB 782.

Extract 12.4.3
Ex parte The Telegraph plc **[1993] 1 WLR 980, at 984–5, 987–8 (CA)**

Lord Taylor CJ:

[Section 4 (2) of the Act] contains two requirements for the making of a postponement order, first that publication would create 'a substantial risk of prejudice to the administration of justice' and, second, that postponement of publication 'appears to be necessary for avoiding' that risk.

It has been said that there is a third requirement, derived from the word 'may' at the beginning of the subsection, namely, that a court, in the exercise of its discretion, having justify to the competing public interests of ensuring a fair trial and of open justice, considers it appropriate to make an order: see Reg. v Horsham Justices, Ex parte Farquharson [1982] Q.B. 762, 789D, per Lord Denning M.R.; Reg. v Saunders (unreported), 5 February 1990, per Henry J. and Reg. v Brooks (unreported), 31 July 1992, per Buckley J. It seems to us the discretion indicated by the use of the word 'may' in the provision is catered for by the second requirement that the court may only make an order where it appears to it to be 'necessary for avoiding' the substantial risk of prejudice to the administration of justice that it perceives. In forming a view whether it is necessary to make an order for avoiding such a risk a court will inevitably have regard to the competing public considerations of ensuring a fair trial and of open justice. It is noteworthy that whether the element of discretion is to be regarded as part of the 'necessity' test or as a third requirement, the courts as a matter of practice have tended to merge the requirement of necessity and the exercise of discretion: see, e.g., Reg. v Saunders, 5 February 1990, per Henry J.; Reg. v Brooks, 31 July 1992, per Buckley J.; Ex parte Central Television Plc. [1991] 1 W.L.R. 4, 8E, per Lord Lane C.J. and Reg. v Beck, Ex parte Daily Telegraph (1991) 94 Cr.App.R. 376, 379, 381, per Farquharson L.J.

As to the first of the two requirements, it should be noted that the risk of prejudice to the administration of justice must be 'substantial.'

As to the second of the requirements, the necessity for an order, it is a statutory recognition of the principle of open justice. There is an abundance of authority emphasising the importance of this principle in this context, and it is sufficient simply to mention some of the more important authorities in which it is expressed, namely: Attorney-General v Leveller Magazine Ltd. [1979] A.C. 440, 449H–450B, per Lord Diplock; Reg. v Horsham Justices, Ex parte Farquharson [1982] Q.B. 762, 793B–794G, 759B–C, per Lord Denning M.R.; Attorney-General v Guardian Newspapers Ltd. (No. 2) [1990] 1 A.C. 109, 183E–G, per Sir John Donaldson M.R. and Ex parte Central Television Plc. [1991] 1 W.L.R. 4, 8E, per Lord Lane C.J.

It was agreed by all the parties to these appeals that there would be a substantial risk of prejudice to the administration of justice in the subsequent trials of C., M., P. and H. if there were to be any reporting of proceedings in the first trial in the absence of the jury or of material identifying them. There were two other matters in issue.

The first, the subject of paragraph (3) of the judge's order, was whether the publication of material identifying Vukmirovic would create such a risk of prejudice. The judge found that it would, in the event of there being guilty verdicts in the first trial, because wide publicity given to such verdicts in accounts identifying him as the principal prosecution witness could improperly enhance his credibility when he comes to give evidence in the subsequent trials.

The second matter in issue, the subject of paragraph (4) of the judge's order, was whether the verdicts in the first trial should be reported before the conclusion of the later trials. The judge was of the view that they could be reported contemporaneously without risk of prejudice to the subsequent proceedings, but that the reporting of counsel's closing speeches and of his summing up could cause prejudice in the inevitable references to Vukmirovic's status as an accomplice and to his credibility which such speeches and summing up would contain.

The judge, having found that there would be a substantial risk of prejudice to the administration of justice in those four respects, should have proceeded to the second requirement of section 4 (2), namely, whether it was 'necessary' to make an order for avoiding such a risk. He did not do that. His approach was to investigate how the risk could be eliminated. He said:

'I now turn to the question whether, given the conclusion I have reached, there is any other course which I can take which would have the effect of eliminating the substantial nature of the risk of prejudice which I have identified.'

His answer to the question was that the risk could not be avoided by adopting other solutions, such as arranging for the subsequent trials to take place at another court, or by delaying them to give time for the publicity of the first trial to fade, or to reverse his decision as to separate trials. After considering and rejecting all of those options he returned to the question how, not whether, the risk of prejudice he had identified should be dealt with by way of an order under section 4(2). . . .

In determining whether publication of matter would cause a substantial risk of prejudice to a future trial, a court should credit the jury with the will and ability to abide by the judge's direction to decide the case only on the evidence before them. The court should also bear in mind that the staying power and detail of publicity, even in cases of notoriety, are limited and that the nature of a trial is to focus the jury's minds on the evidence put before them rather than on matters outside the courtroom: see Reg. v Kray (1969) 53 Cr.App.R. 412, 415–416, per Lawton J.; Reg. v Horsham Justices, Ex parte Farquharson [1982] Q.B. 762, 794, per Lord Denning M.R.; Attorney-General v News Group Newspapers Ltd. [1987] Q.B. 1, 16B–D, per Sir John Donaldson M.R. and Ex parte Central Television Plc. [1991] 1 W.L.R. 4, 8B–D, per Lord Lane C.J.

In this case we should also approach the matter on the basis that in each trial the judge will direct the jury clearly and firmly about the danger of convicting on Vukmirovic's evidence if uncorroborated, that there will be no public reporting of the names of C., H., M. or P. or of any material likely to identify them, and that, in compliance with section 4(1) of the Act of 1981, each of the trials will be reported fairly and accurately.

Having regard to all those considerations, we are of the view that there is only slight potential for prejudice flowing from such publicity as may be given to Vukmirovic's role and the verdicts in the first trial . . .

Even if, which we reject, there were a substantial risk of prejudice in the contemporaneous reporting of material likely to identify Vukmirovic and/or of the verdicts, the arguments of the media applicants on this issue are, in our view, well founded. The case is of importance and one in which there is a considerable and legitimate public interest because of the nature and quantity of the drug involved. It is the first major trial concerned with Ecstasy. Vukmirovic is alleged to have played a central role in the important events founding the prosecution against all the defendants. Any prohibition of contemporaneous reporting of material likely to identify him and his role in the case would make it almost impossible to report. It would also be very difficult for the media to identify what could properly be reported. Accordingly, it is a case in which the public interest in open trial would, in any event, outweigh any possible risk, substantial or not, of prejudice that might result from publication of Vukmirovic's role.

In *Beck*, where the defendants were social workers charged with serious offences of sexual abuse of children in their care at local authority homes, the Court of Appeal allowed an appeal against an order to postpone reporting of the first trial of the defendants which had been made on the ground that they also faced further charges to be considered later.[66] The Court of Appeal said that it might be possible to avoid the risk of prejudice, and hence the need for a postponement order, by extending the period of time between

---

[66] *R v Beck and others, ex parte Daily Telegraph* [1993] 2 All ER 177.

the first and any later trial, or by changing the venue of the later trial. Those courses might not be effective in this case to obviate the risk. However, in view of the horrific nature of the allegations, in which the public had a real interest, it would be wrong to postpone the reporting of the first trial; the freedom of the press to report the proceedings trumped the interests of the defendants.

A different result was reached in a more recent case, where the Court of Appeal distinguished *Beck* and appears to have given priority to the article 6 ECHR rights to a fair trial. Rafferty J had made an order prohibiting the reporting of the trial of a police officer for the murder of an unarmed man – a suspected drug dealer – during the course of a raid on his flat organised by the Sussex Police. After this trial had ended, three senior officers from the same force were to be tried for misconduct in public office; a crucial point is that the police officer would argue as part of his defence that there were serious failures in the organisation of the raid by a number of officers, including those who were facing trial. Indeed, it was for that reason that the judge had ordered severance of the trial of the senior officers from the murder trial.

Extract 12.4.4
Ex parte Telegraph Group plc **[2001] EWCA Crim 1075, [2002] EMLR 10, paras 19–22, 32–4**

EADY J:
19. The correct approach for the court to take on applications of this kind has been considered in a number of cases and we were invited to take account of the guidance given, in particular, in *R v Horsham Justices, ex parte Farquharson* [1982] Q.B. 762, *Re Central Independent Television Plc.* [1991] 1 W.L.R. 4, *R v Beck, ex parte Daily Telegraph Plc.* [1993] 2 All E.R. 177, *Ex parte The Telegraph Plc.* [1993] 1 W.L.R. 980, and *M.G.N. Pension Trustees Ltd. v. Bank of America National Trust and Savings Association* [1995] 2 All E.R. 355. We believe that from these authorities it is possible to derive a three stage series of tests by which to determine the matter on any given facts. We set out these three stages at paragraph 22 below.

20. Before turning to this, however, we should observe that care needs to be taken to avoid confusing the two senses in which the word 'necessary' is used in this context. First, the statute requires the court to address the question of whether a ban is necessary, in the light of the facts, to avoid the perceived risk of prejudice. Unless this is demonstrated, no such order should be made. Even if that hurdle has been overcome, however, it does not follow that the order has to be made. There then will arise the question of whether such an order is necessary in the second sense; that is to say the sense contemplated by Article 10(2) of the European Convention. Sometimes wider considerations of public policy will come into play such as to justify the refusal of a banning order even though there is no other way of eliminating the prejudice anticipated.

21. This is sometimes called the 'discretion stage', although the phrase can be misleading, since whether or not such an order is 'necessary in a democratic society' clearly involves consideration of objective criteria and the making of value judgments. There is a parallel with regard to the notion of 'discretion' in the law relating to the disclosure of journalists' sources under s.10 of the Contempt of Court Act . . .

22. These possible sources of confusion can perhaps be avoided if applications to restrict media coverage of court proceedings are approached in the following way:

(1) The first question is whether reporting would give rise to a 'not insubstantial' risk of prejudice to the administration of justice in the relevant proceedings. If not, that will be the end of the matter.

(2) If such a risk is perceived to exist, then the second question arises: would a s.4(2) order eliminate it? If not, obviously there could be no necessity to impose such a ban. Again, that would be the end of the matter. On the other hand, even if the judge is satisfied that an order would achieve the objective, he or she would still have to consider whether the risk could satisfactorily be overcome by some less restrictive means. If so, it could not be said to be 'necessary' to take the more drastic approach: see *Re Central Independent Television Plc.* [1991] 1 W.L.R. 4, 8D–G (*per* Lord Lane C.J.).

(3) Suppose that the judge concludes that there is indeed no other way of eliminating the perceived risk of prejudice; it still does not follow *necessarily* that an order has to be made. The judge may still have to ask whether the degree of risk contemplated should be regarded as tolerable in the sense of being 'the lesser of two evils'. It is at this stage that value judgments may have to be made as to the priority between 'competing public interests': see *Ex parte The Telegraph Plc.* [1993] 1 W.L.R. 980, 986B–C.

[In paras 23–31 the Court of Appeal considered the application of the first two questions. It was accepted by the media appellants and the prosecutor that the reporting would give rise to a substantial risk of prejudice to the trial of the senior officers. The Court also found that only a blanket ban would be likely to eliminate that risk, as a partial ban, precluding the reporting of the allegations about the serious failures of the senior officers, would present a distorted account of the trial. Other measures, such as postponing the second trial, would be ineffective, given the high profile of the incident and the likely impact of the murder trial.]

32. We need finally to decide, at the third stage, whether there is some overriding consideration of public policy which dictates that coverage should be permitted notwithstanding the undoubted risk it would generate that the three senior officers will not receive a fair trial on the charges of misfeasance. In other words, we need to make a value judgment as to 'competing public interests', as contemplated by Lord Taylor C.J. in *Ex parte The Telegraph Plc.*

33. It is fair to say that there are certain features that this case may be thought to have in common with *Beck*. It was there held that the trial judge had given too little weight to the importance of the need for media reporting of criminal trials, having regard to the widespread public concern over the circumstances in which persons in the public service had apparently been able to commit offences over a long period despite complaints having been made by some of the victims concerned (see especially at p. 182). There is clearly legitimate interest in these events too; all of the defendants were public servants. On the other hand, it is important to note that in *Beck* it was apparently conceded on behalf of the principal defendant that his later trial (if indeed it were to take place at all) would not be unfairly prejudiced by reporting of the first hearing if it was fair and accurate (see p. 180b). Moreover, there was real doubt as to whether the later trial would go ahead in the event that there were findings of guilt in the first. Of course, if he were acquitted there would have been little (if any) prejudice at a second trial.

34. Perhaps the single most important distinction, however, is that in this case (unlike in *Beck*) the evidence in the two trials is going to be inextricably linked for the reasons we have already addressed. Justice required the learned Judge to order severance. Publicity would inevitably defeat the object of that order. Against the background of this unusual combination of events, and of the offences charged, we are quite satisfied that the problems thereby created are incapable of being overcome by judicial directions to the second jury, however careful. After anxious consideration, we are left in no doubt that Rafferty J was entirely correct in the order she made. Any restriction of court reporting is regrettable and especially so in the case of such serious charges as these. Unfortunately, we have concluded that such an order is unavoidable in order to ensure that the three defendants in the second trial have a fair hearing in accordance with the rights guaranteed under Article 6 of the Convention.

The Court of Appeal seems to have extended the scope of the postponement power in the *Guardian Newspapers* case,[67] when it upheld an order by Poole J to ban any reports or republication of a newspaper article, the original publication of which had led to him halting the high profile trial of four defendants, including two Leeds United footballers, on grievous bodily harm charges, and ordering a retrial six months later. The Court of Appeal accepted the Crown's argument that any republication of the article was inextricably linked with the proceedings which had been halted and would be likely to prejudice the later trial of the defendants. The Court therefore had jurisdiction to make a postponement order under section 4(2) of the Contempt of Court Act, though arguably it would have been more appropriate to grant an injunction to prevent infringement of the strict liability rule under section 2(2) of that Act.

On the other hand, the Court of Appeal was more sympathetic to the arguments of the media in a more recent case. In *Re B*,[68] after one defendant, Barot, had pleaded guilty to conspiracy to murder in a high profile terrorist case, the judge granted a postponement order with regard to his sentencing hearing; his co-defendants argued successfully that reports of that hearing would prejudice their later trial on the same and other related charges. The judge considered that his reasons for sentencing Barot, the first Muslim to be sentenced in the UK for a terrorist crime involving the mass murder of civilians, would inevitably provoke public comment and therefore might prejudice the later trial. The Court of Appeal allowed the appeal brought by the BBC, Times Newspapers and Associated Press, holding that the postponement power should not be exercised to prevent prejudicial comment on Court proceedings; the media should be trusted to comment sensibly on them. In a striking passage, the Court of Appeal added that 'the jury will follow [appropriate directions], not only because they will loyally abide by the directions of law which they will be given by the judge, but also because the directions themselves will appeal directly to their own instinctive and fundamental belief in the need for the trial process to be fair'.[69] The spirit of this ruling seems quite different from that which animated the Court of Appeal's decision in 2001 in the *Telegraph* case (Extract 12.4.4).

Questions for discussion

1. How do the statutory requirements for a postponement order differ from those for the strict liability rule?
2. Does the decision of the Court of Appeal in *Ex parte Telegraph* (1993) give too much weight to the public interest in full reporting of criminal trials?
3. Is it possible to reconcile the decision in *Ex parte Telegraph* (2001) with other Court of Appeal rulings on exercise of the postponement power?

(c) Protection of the media

The Practice Direction (Extract 12.4.2) encourages courts to notify the press when they are considering whether to make a postponement order.[70] This course had already been encouraged by the Divisional Court.

---

[67] *R v Guardian Newspapers Ltd* [2001] EWCA Crim 1351: see Fenwick and Phillipson, 214–16.
[68] [2006] EWCA Crim 2692, [2007] EMLR 5.
[69] Ibid., para 31.
[70] Practice Direction of 2002 (Extract 12.4.2), para 3.2. This principle also applies to anonymity orders made under CCA 1981, s 11, discussed in Chapter 13, Section 13.5.

Extract 12.4.5
R v Clerkenwell Stipendiary Magistrate, ex parte The Telegraph **[1993] QB 462, at 470–1 (DC)**

MANN LJ:

In the absence of express provision it was my own practice when sitting in the Crown Court to hear any representations which the press desired to make in regard to a section 4(2) order and I believe that the practice of other judges has been, and is, the same. It is a practice which is recognised by the Court of Appeal: see Reg. v Beck, 94 Cr.App.R. 376, 381–382. The advantages of it are plain. The prosecution and the defence will frequently share as a prime concern the need to protect the integrity of the present and future proceedings and an application is often supported or not opposed by the other party. The interest which an order would adversely affect is best represented by the news media serving in their capacity as the eyes and ears of the public: see Attorney-General v Guardian Newspapers Ltd. (No. 2) [1990] 1 A.C. 109, 183F, per Sir John Donaldson M.R. They can argue, for example, that there is really no necessity, or no substantial risk, or that the public interest in knowing should be paramount in the circumstances.

Lord Williams [counsel for the applicant] submitted that it would be wrong if justices, who hear most of the criminal business in England and Wales, should be deprived of the assistance of representations from the news media when considering a section 4(2) order. He pointed to the absurdity of the contrast between an inability to hear such representations and the locus standi afforded to publishers in this court on a judicial review of any order made by the justices. Lord Williams suggested that a solution was to be found by treating the power to hear as inherent in the jurisdiction of magistrates' courts . . .

. . . The news media do not seek a right to be heard on the issue in the proceedings. They ask that they should be the subjects of a power to hear on consideration of reporting restrictions. In my judgment there is such a power in any court which is contemplating the exercise of powers under section 4(2) of the Contempt of Court Act 1981. I regard it as implicit in the enactment of section 4(2) that a court contemplating its use should be enabled to receive assistance from those who will, if there is no order, enjoy the right of making reports of the proceedings before the court. They are in particular the best qualified to represent that public interest in publicity which the court has to take into account when performing any balancing exercise which has to be undertaken. The need properly to operate section 4(2) requires that a court should be able to receive the best assistance available when considering the curtailment of the freedom to report. I accordingly conclude that the magistrate was wrong when on 17 July he decided that he had no power to hear the applicants and I would grant a declaration that on that day, and on 4 August, he had a power to hear the applicants.

The power which I have identified is a discretionary one. The occasion and manner of its exercise are matters for the court invested with the power, but I expect that the power will ordinarily be exercised when the media ask to be heard either on the making of an order or in regard to its continuance. The power will ordinarily be exercised because the court can expect to find assistance in representations from the news media. In practice it will be convenient if the press are able to present a single view thereby avoiding any need for the court to restrain repetition.

In the course of his judgment Mann LJ referred to the steps the media may now take to challenge postponement orders. In the *Horsham Justices* case[71] their recourse had been by way of an application for judicial review. However, on the general principles of judicial review, the Divisional (now the Administrative) Court can only review an order if it was made outside jurisdiction or was grossly unreasonable. Moreover, there can be no judicial review of an order made by a High Court or Crown Court judge to postpone the

[71] See n. 65.

reporting of a trial on indictment.[72] Initially, there was no provision for an appeal against a postponement order, a gap which led to an application to the European Commission of Human Rights on the basis that there was no effective domestic remedy for violation of the Convention.[73] Following this challenge, the government introduced a limited right of appeal.[74]

Extract 12.4.6
Criminal Justice Act 1988, section 159(1), (5)

159.—(1) A person aggrieved may appeal to the Court of Appeal, if that court grants leave, against—

(a) an order under section 4 or 11 of the Contempt of Court Act 1981 made in relation to a trial on indictment.

(b) any order restricting the access of the public to the whole or any part of a trial on indictment or to any proceedings ancillary to such a trial; and

(c) any order restricting the publication of any report of the whole or any part of a trial on indictment or any such ancillary proceedings, and the decision of the Court of Appeal shall be final.

. . .

(5) On the hearing of an appeal under this section the Court of Appeal shall have power—

(a) to stay any proceedings in any other court until after the appeal is disposed of;

(b) to confirm, reverse, or vary the order complained of; and

(c) [*Omitted*].

This right of appeal is frequently exercised by the media, and has led to many of the decisions referred to in this part of the book.[75] The extent of the Court of Appeal's powers on an appeal were made plain in *Ex parte The Telegraph* (1993), when Lord Taylor CJ, in a passage frequently cited in later decisions, said that the function of the Court of Appeal under section 159 of the Criminal Justice Act 1988 was to form its own view on the material, rather than simply to review the trial judge's decision. It could therefore confirm, reverse or vary his order.

There remain, however, some oddities and anomalies. First, strictly there is no *right* of appeal, for the Court of Appeal must give leave. Second, there is no further appeal to the Supreme Court: the Court of Appeal has the final word. There is a 'right' of appeal from orders made in relation to trials on indictment; but there remains only the more limited remedy of judicial review against an order postponing the reporting of summary proceedings. Equally hard to explain or justify is the absence of any possibility of appeal for a defendant whose request for a postponement order has been rejected, although apparently some appeals have been heard in this situation.[76] Despite its limitations, the provision in the Criminal Justice Act 1988 does provide some redress for the media whose freedom to report legal proceedings may have been seriously inhibited by a postponement order.

---

[72] Senior Courts Act 1981, s 29(3).

[73] See *Hodgson, Woolf Productions, NUJ, and Channel 4 v UK* (1987) 10 EHRR 503, where the Commission held admissible an application to challenge a court ban on television reconstruction of the Ponting secrecy trial.

[74] The right of appeal also applies to anonymity orders made under CCA 1981, s 11 and to orders restricting access to attend trials: see Chapter 13 for these orders.

[75] See for example the decisions in *R v Beck* (see n 66), *ex parte Telegraph* (1993) (Extract 12.4.3), *ex parte Telegraph* (2001) (Extract 12.4.4), and *Re B* (see n 68).

[76] For discussion, see I. Cram, 'Section 4(2) postponement orders: media reports of court proceedings under the Contempt of Court Act 1981' (1996) 2 *Yearbook of Media and Entertainment Law* 111, at 129–31.

12.5 PAYMENTS TO WITNESSES

The phenomenon of press payments to witnesses first emerged in the context of the famous Moors murder case in 1966 when two witnesses were offered money for their stories; the amount of payment was dependent on whether a conviction was obtained. The Phillimore Committee on Contempt of Court considered the practice sufficiently serious to warrant inquiry, although it did not think it should be covered by the law of contempt of court.[77] The practice again caused disquiet when it appeared that 19 witnesses in the Rosemary West murder trial had been offered or paid money. Indeed, these dealings formed one ground for her unsuccessful appeal against conviction.

Extract 12.5.1
R v West **(1996) 2 Cr App Rep 374, 388–9**

LORD TAYLOR CJ:

Mr Ferguson [counsel for Mrs West] submitted that the money received or contracts made by these four, who were important witnesses for the Crown, rendered their evidence tainted and suspect to the point of making the jury's verdicts unsafe. There was, he said, temptation for such witnesses to exaggerate. The more lurid their account the more valuable the contract. There might have been rehearsals before trial with journalists. Whereas a story given to a police officer would be monitored, logged and disclosed to the defence, statements given to journalists were not handled in that way. There might be a conscious or subconscious desire in the witness to fulfil the agreement with the media. He submitted this was particularly so in the case of Janet Leach. She said in her evidence-in-chief she had not received any money from the press. However, leading counsel for the Mirror Group contacted leading counsel for the Crown to disclose an agreement which had been made between Janet Leach and that Group. The defence were told immediately. In cross-examination Mrs Leach admitted both the contract and the receipt of money.

In reply Mr Leveson made clear that the prosecution deplored the payment of witnesses. Nevertheless, save in respect of Mrs Leach's contract of which the prosecution were unaware until the disclosure mentioned above, all the other contracts were disclosed to the defence before trial so that Mr Ferguson was able to cross-examine about them. The effect can only have been to weaken the Crown's case. Moreover, the trial judge painstakingly went through the contracts in detail in his summing-up and warned the jury to have regard to the commercial motive which the defence suggested these witnesses had.

. . .

We carefully considered the effect of these contracts with the media. We reached the conclusion that they did not in the circumstances of this particular case render the verdicts unsafe. That is not to say that we wish to condone the payment or promise of payment to witnesses in advance of a trial. Far from it. We believe that in some circumstances it could put justice at risk. For example, as Mr Leveson pointed out, in the present case Mrs Leach felt faint during her evidence and had to leave the witness box. That was before the disclosure that she had received payments from the media. Had she not been fit to return to the witness box, when she was able to be cross-examined about the payments she had received, the jury may well have been misled and the verdicts possibly put at risk.

In our view, the whole issue of media payments to witnesses requires to be reviewed – whether they should be prohibited, or if allowed, at what stage of criminal proceedings and with what, if any, control. It is not for us to answer those questions. We were told by Mr Leveson that the Attorney-General was apprised in October 1994 of the material concerning the press payments and that consideration is being given to the problems raised by such payments.

---

[77] Cmnd 7904 (1974), paras 78–9.

The conduct of the press in offering payments to potential witnesses in the West murder investigation also led to a complaint to the Press Complaints Commission (PCC).[78] As a result, its Code of Practice was strengthened. In addition to the requirement of an overriding need for payment for a witness's story, editors were obliged to show that there is a legitimate public interest at stake. Further, the payment to any witness who is cited to give evidence must be disclosed to the prosecution and defence.[79]

Following the *West* case the Lord Chancellor's Department issued a Consultation Paper to canvass views on its proposal to prohibit the practice of payments (and offers of payment) to witnesses, either by extension of contempt of court or by the institution of a specific offence. In its view legislation was necessary to deal with the threat posed by witness payments to the administration of justice. The government's preference then was to extend the strict liability rule, so that it covered payments or offers of payment to witnesses with the object of publication, where those payments created a substantial risk of serious prejudice to pending or imminent proceedings.[80] The National Heritage Committee of the House of Commons accepted this proposal, adding that, in its view, prejudice to the fairness of a trial is inherent in media payments to witnesses and that proof of the risk of prejudice should, therefore, not be required.[81] Early in 1998 the Lord Chancellor announced the government's intention to introduce legislation at a convenient time.

The *Gadd* (Gary Glitter) case in 1999 again highlighted the problem. The *News of the World* offered a substantial payment to a Ms Allison Brown, who had alleged that she had had sexual relations with Gadd when she was 14 and 15, for the publication of stories about this relationship; the offer was made in November 1997, apparently before Gadd was charged with an indecent assault on Ms Brown and for a number of child pornography offences. A further payment of £25,000 would be made for publication of her story, if Gadd were convicted of any offence relating to child pornography or to sexual relations with under-age girls. The trial judge, Butterfield J, deplored the arrangements, although they were not illegal. The PCC found that the newspaper has complied with the terms of the Code in most respects. When it made the contract, there were no current criminal proceedings and Ms Brown was neither a witness nor, in the PCC's view, a potential witness. Further, there was a substantial public interest for the publication, in that the stories obtained from Ms Brown exposed the commission of crime, and the arrangements had been disclosed to the jury. On the other hand, the PCC did find that the offer of payment conditional on Gadd's conviction infringed the Code, though at the time this particular practice was not explicitly banned. The adjudication showed the reluctance of the PCC to take a strong line on media payments to witnesses, and encouraged the government at that time to introduce legislation.

There was a further review in 2002 of the position by officials from the Lord Chancellor's department. Again, it found self-regulation in this area unsatisfactory and recommended the institution of a new offence, which would prohibit the making or receiving of payments, or entering into an agreement to make or receive payments, to a witness or potential witness in criminal proceedings with a view to publication of material, which is, or might be, relevant to them.[82] The offence would be one of strict liability, so there would be no need to prove any intent on the part of a newspaper to prejudice the proceedings; further, it should apply once proceedings are imminent or pending, as with common law contempt

---

[78] See Complaint against *Daily Mirror*, PCC Report No 40 (1997), 27–8.
[79] Former cl 16(i) of the PCC Code.
[80] LCD Consultation Paper, *Payments to Witnesses* (October 1996), paras 35–45.
[81] 2nd Report of National Heritage Committee for 1996–7, HC 86, paras 4–31.
[82] *Payments to Witnesses* (March 2002).

(see section 12.3 above). The government agreed with the view of the House of Commons National Heritage Committee that there should be no public interest defence, as there was at this time in the PCC Code. There could be no plausible public interest for paying witnesses to imminent legal proceedings.

Legislation to introduce these proposals seemed inevitable. However, the government agreed to give the press a final chance to outlaw the practice altogether. This was done by amendments to the PCC Code of Practice, which now contains an absolute ban on payments to witnesses or to likely witnesses in 'active' proceedings, and substantially limits their payment when proceedings are likely and foreseeable.

Extract 12.5.2
Press Complaints Commission Code of Practice, clause 15[83]

Witness payments in criminal trials

i. No payment or offer of payment to a witness – or any person who may reasonably be expected to be called as a witness – should be made in any case once proceedings are active as defined by the Contempt of Court Act 1981. This prohibition lasts until the suspect has been freed unconditionally by police without charge or bail or the proceedings are otherwise discontinued; or has entered a guilty plea to the court; or, in the event of a not guilty plea, the court has announced its verdict.

*ii. Where proceedings are not yet active but are likely and foreseeable, editors must not make or offer payment to any person who may reasonably be expected to be called as a witness, unless the information concerned ought demonstrably to be published in the public interest and there is an over-riding need to make or promise payment for this to be done; and all reasonable steps have been taken to ensure no financial dealings influence the evidence those witnesses give. In no circumstances should such payment be conditional on the outcome of a trial.

*iii. Any payment or offer of payment made to a person later cited to give evidence in proceedings must be disclosed to the prosecution and defence. The witness must be advised of this requirement.

Under this provision the PCC would probably now have to come to a different conclusion than it had reached in two notorious cases. In the first, it had dismissed claims that five national newspapers had paid or offered to pay young witnesses in the Amy Gehring indecency trial in breach of the clause prohibiting payments to witnesses. Gehring had been charged with indecent assault of under-age children at a school where she was a supply teacher. She was acquitted. For the PCC it was important that the approaches to, and offers to pay, the young children were made only after they had finished giving evidence, and, moreover, publication was in the public interest as it raised broad matters of education policy – the recruitment of overseas supply teachers – not at issue at the trial.[84] Neither of these factors would be relevant now. A complaint against the *News of the World* that it had made a payment to a potential witness in a court case involving an alleged attempt to kidnap Victoria Beckham was dismissed, because at the time the payment was made the defendants had not yet appeared in court and no charges had been brought in respect of the kidnapping.[85] In the PCC's view, proceedings were not 'current' at the time of payment,

---

[83] The clause was originally introduced in March 2003 as cl 16 of the Code. Clause 15(ii) and (iii) marked with an asterisk * are subject to the public interest defence (see Extract 2.3.1 above).
[84] PCC Report no 56/57, 25.
[85] PCC Report no 62/63, 20.

as required by the version of the Code then in force, although they were 'active' for the purposes of the rule now in force. Moreover, the PCC accepted that there was a public interest in the payment, as the newspaper had reasonable grounds for believing that Victoria Beckham was about to be kidnapped and that only by paying the witness money was he prepared to introduce its investigators to the gang of defendants.

However, the Press Complaints Commission may still dismiss a complaint in respect of payments to a potential witness, as shown in its disposition of a recent case which it investigated of its own volition.

Extract 12.5.3
Adjudication of an investigation into payment made by the *Daily Express*. Published 19 October 2010

The Press Complaints Commission has launched an own volition investigation into a payment made by Express Newspapers in April 2009 to Nicola Fisher. Ms Fisher had claimed to have been assaulted by a police officer on the second day of the G20 protests on 2 April 2009.

The Commission decided that there had been no breach of Clause 15 (Witness payments in criminal trials) of the Editors' Code of Practice.

The articles, which appeared on 17 April 2009 in the *Daily Star* and the *Daily Express*, were based on an interview with Ms Fisher in which she outlined the nature of her allegations against the police officer in question, later confirmed to be Sgt Delroy Smellie. Ms Fisher described the alleged assault in detail, claiming that the experience was 'like [she'd] been whipped by the Taliban', that she feared for her life and that the officer was a 'thug' who 'got his kicks out of hurting a woman'. Her injuries were described in the articles which included photographs of them. Ms Fisher was paid for her involvement in the story.

At the time of publication, the police officer had been suspended, but had not been arrested or charged with any offence. In September 2009 he was charged with common assault, pleading not guilty in November 2009. Sgt Smellie was subsequently cleared of the charge in March 2010. At his trial, Ms Fisher did not give evidence, apparently citing concerns that the defence would focus on her lifestyle and background.

The newspapers said that the incident with Ms Fisher, which left her badly injured, had occurred the day after the high-profile death of Ian Tomlinson, at a vigil and memorial for him. There had been extensive CCTV and mobile phone footage of each incident (which was placed immediately online).

At the time of the interview – while Ms Fisher had already spoken to the Independent Police Complaints Commission (IPCC) whose investigation was in its preliminary stges – proceedings against the officer were not active, not least because his identity had yet to become known. The CPS had been made aware of the payment to Ms Fisher – who would not have agreed to the interview without remuneration – through her representative. There was no question of her evidence being embellished (as she had already given her statement to the IPCC before her interview). In addition, the trial took place before a District Judge rather than a jury.

The newspapers said that the police tactics and conduct during the G20 protests was a matter of legitimate public interest: the IPCC had received over 270 complaints about the actions and Metropolitan, City of London and British Transport Police during the demonstrations. Given the actions of the police, including their controversial practice of 'kettling' and the death of Mr Tomlinson, it was right and proper that Ms Fisher's account be published. The footage of the incident had been widely disseminated on the internet and, at the trial, the officer did not deny the assault; rather, he defended his actions on the basis that he had used reasonable force in all the circumstances. While he had been acquitted of the charge, the decision had come in for some considerable public criticism.

Decision: Not Upheld

Adjudication:

Clause 15 of the Editors' Code imposes strict rules on payments to witnesses in criminal trials, in essence to avoid any threat, or perceived threat, to the integrity of the judicial process. It was significantly strengthened in 2003 to limit the circumstances in which payments could be made. The Commission receives relatively few complaints under this Clause (where the individual who receives payment is unlikely to complain) and is able proactively to launch an investigation of its own volition when legitimate concerns exist about the decision by a newspaper to make a payment. The Commission is committed to vigilance in this area, and will investigate any suggestion that Clause 15 is being breached by publications.

On this occasion, it became clear that the newspapers had paid Ms Fisher for the story, and she had subsequently not testified in court. The Commission wished to satisfy itself that due consideration had been given by the newspapers to ensuring that they had abided by the terms of the Code in its dealings with Ms Fisher.

Specifically, Clause 15 prohibits paying potential witnesses in circumstances where proceedings are not active, but are 'likely and foreseeable', unless 'the information ought demonstrably to be published in the public interest and there is an overriding need to make . . . payment for this to be done'.

It was arguable that proceedings in this case were likely, given the allegation of assault against a police officer. However, he had not yet publicly been identified at the time of publication. In those circumstances, Ms Fisher would certainly have been a witness for the prosecution and her evidence could have formed an essential part of the case, despite the existence of video evidence in the public domain.

The central question was whether the published information was in the public interest. The Commission considered that it was. Ms Fisher's experiences related to the allegedly violent behaviour of police at a vigil for Ian Tomlinson (who had himself notoriously been the victim of alleged assault by a police officer), which left her with visible injuries. Footage of the incident had been posted online, and the specific comments of the woman featured in it were – in the Commission's view – a key part of an ongoing story. There was no doubt that the behaviour of police at the demonstrations was a matter of intense and legitimate public discussion at the time, especially following the death of Mr Tomlinson. In these circumstances, the Commission was satisfied that there was a public interest in publishing Ms Fisher's own contribution, which she would not have apparently made without financial remuneration.

Of course, concerns may be raised about the fact that Ms Fisher did not subsequently attend the trial of the officer in question. The Commission was not in a position to comment upon her personal decision not to attend, and was aware of no evidence that the necessary disclosure about the payment had been the influencing factor. Clearly, if there had been such evidence, this would have been a matter of some concern to the Commission. In any case, the Commission believed that, at the time when the offer was made, there were sufficient public interest grounds (inherent in the subject matter of the story) to justify the newspapers' decision to pay her. It did not find a breach of the Code as a result.

Questions for discussion

1. Do you think that legislation should be introduced to restrict payments to witnesses or should the matter be left to the PCC?
2. If legislation is introduced, should it create a new head of strict liability contempt, or should it institute a discrete criminal offence, as recommended by the Lord Chancellor's Department Paper of 2002?

12.6 DISCLOSURE OF JURY DELIBERATIONS

Under the CCA 1981, section 8, it is almost always a contempt of court to disclose the jury's deliberations.

Extract 12.6.1
Contempt of Court Act 1981, section 8(1)–(2)

8.—(1) Subject to subsection (2) below, it is a contempt of court to obtain, disclose or solicit any particulars of statements made, opinions expressed, arguments advanced or votes cast by members of a jury in the course of their deliberations in any legal proceedings.

(2) This section shall not apply to any disclosure of any particulars—

(a) in the proceedings in question for the purpose of enabling the jury to arrive at their verdict, or in connection with the delivery of that verdict, or

(b) in evidence in any subsequent proceedings for an offence alleged to have been committed in relation to the jury in the first mentioned proceedings, or to the publication of any particulars so disclosed.

This provision has been considered by the courts, including the House of Lords, in a number of cases.[86] In *Attorney-General v Scotcher*[87] the House ruled that, properly interpreted, it is compatible with the right to freedom of expression guaranteed by article 10 of the ECHR, as it imposed a restriction necessary to prevent the disclosure of confidential information. The confidentiality of jury room deliberations has also been recognised in Strasbourg as a fundamental and legitimate feature of English trial law.[88] So in *Scotcher* there was a contempt of court when a juror wrote to the mother of two defendants, convicted by the jury by a majority verdict, informing her of some discussions in the jury room. Equally, it would have been a contempt of court to have revealed these discussions to the media, even if that was done in an attempt to reverse what a juror reasonably considered to have been a miscarriage of justice.

A leading media law case involved contempt proceedings in respect of an article in the *Mail on Sunday* revealing the deliberations of the jury in a serious fraud trial. It was written by the editor of the paper's City section, on the basis of information given him by 'researchers' who had interviewed members of the jury. The defendants argued that the provision only applied to disclosure by a juror, and not to the further publication by other persons, including the media, to whom a juror had disclosed the deliberations. The House of Lords rejected this argument, as well as the contention that it would be incompatible with article 10 of the ECHR to apply the provision to the press.

Extract 12.6.2
***Attorney-General v Associated Newspapers* [1994] 2 AC 238, at 259–60 (HL)**

LORD LOWRY:
Each party to the appeal advanced arguments based on the supposed absurdity of the other party's interpretation. The appellants contended that the Attorney-General's construction would render in contempt the reader of a newspaper who communicated a part of its contents to a neighbour who was then unaware of what the paper had said. In my view, my Lords, this

---

[86] In addition to the cases discussed below, see *R v Young (Stephen)* [1995] QB 324, CA, *R v Connor, R v Mizra* [2004] UKHL 2, [2004] 1 AC 1118. HL, and *R v Smith* [2005] UKHL 12, [2005] 1 WLR 704, HL.

[87] [2005] UKHL 36, [2005] 3 All ER 1.

[88] *Gregory v UK* [1997] 25 EHRR 577, para 44.

argument confuses disclosure with republication and I do not find it at all persuasive. If an item has been published in the paper, it has become a matter of public knowledge, and to describe the communication of that item of news as disclosure is, to my mind, a misuse of language.

Mr. Moses, on the other hand, who appeared with Mr. Havers for the Attorney-General, submitted that it would be absurd, when the long deplored activity was the publication of the jury's deliberations, if only the offending juror and his confidant were amenable, while the publisher went scot free. The act of a juror might be innocent and innocuous, whereas the release of the prohibited information to the public was bound to be much more harmful, actually or potentially, to the administration of justice. He further argued that it would be strange if Parliament hoped and intended to control the unwanted and harmful activities of powerful individuals and groups with an interest in the acquisition and dissemination of the prohibited information and the means to pay for it, if necessary, by merely enacting a prohibition and imposing sanctions on individual jurors.

One could instance the case of a jury-keeper who is told about or overhears the jury's deliberations. Can he not be guilty of disclosure if he reveals what he has heard to a newspaper? And are the newspaper's reporter and publisher immune if the deliberations are published? I scarcely think so. So far as the test of absurdity helps to decide the issue, my verdict is overwhelmingly on the side of the Attorney-General . . .

In order to get home, the appellants rely, as they must, on the submission that the word 'disclose' in its context is ambiguous, but I do not consider that this case poses for your Lordships an example of ambiguity. The appellants say that the word is ambiguous because it can refer either to disclosure by a juror or to disclosure through newspaper publication or by some other means. The true view is that the word 'disclose' describes and includes both (or all) kinds of disclosure. It is a comprehensive word.

This case was followed by the Divisional Court when the Attorney-General brought contempt proceedings against the foreman of a jury and Times Newspapers; the foreman had disclosed to the paper details of votes cast early in the jury discussions and of the arguments it considered in the course of its deliberations before convicting, by a 10–2 majority, a child-minder for killing a baby. Under the name of Frances Gibb, its Legal Editor, The *Times* published an article, which revealed these details and the unease of two members of the jury, including the foreman, with the part played by contentious medical evidence in its deliberations.

Extract 12.6.3

Attorney-General v Seckerson and Times Newspapers Ltd **[2009] EWHC 1023 (Admin), [2009] EMLR 20, paras 45, 50, 52–6**

PILL LJ:

45. I accept that Ms Frances Gibb followed the procedures laid down by the second defendants, proprietors of a highly reputable newspaper, before the article was published, including obtaining legal advice, which she followed. I accept that the second defendants' staff who gave that advice acted in good faith. Ms Gibb took up the story because she found it significant that two jurors had spoken out in a criminal case, which was obviously a serious case and one which had received considerable publicity. She clearly regarded the jurors' 'unprecedented move' as newsworthy.

. . .

50. There is no doubt that members of a jury, when so acting, form part of a judicial tribunal from whose members judicial standards are expected (Commission[89] and *Mirza*). The need to keep secret the deliberations of the jury, and the rationale for it, have been plainly stated in the cases:

(a) 'Free, uninhibited and unfettered discussion by the jury in the course of their deliberations is essential to the proper administration of a system of justice' (*Associated Newspapers*).

(b) 'Section 8 is aimed at keeping the secrets of the jury room inviolate in the interests of justice' (*Associated Newspapers*).

(c) 'It is an important element of that system that jurors should express themselves freely in the jury room without fear of outside disclosure of their views and opinions' (Commission).

(d) 'If a juror thought that what he said could subsequently become public, it is possible that he would bear in mind the future use to which his words might be put, and not just in the case in hand' (Commission).

(e) 'The unlimited prohibition on disclosure is then seen to be an inevitable protection for jurors' (Commission).

(f) 'The rule governing the secrecy of jury deliberations is a crucial and legitimate feature of English trial law . . . to guarantee open and frank deliberation by jurors on the evidence which they have heard' (*Gregory*).

(g) 'Confidentiality promotes candour and the kind of full and frank debate that is essential to this type of collegial decision-making' (*Mirza . . .*).

(h) 'The proper functioning of the jury system is dependent, at the very minimum, on a system that ensures the safety of jurors, their sense of security, as well as their privacy' (*Mirza . . .*).

. . .

52. It is the principle of the secrecy of the jury room which is at stake and which is central to the proper administration of justice in this jurisdiction, as stated in the authorities. It is not necessary to establish that the disclosure has led to injustice in the case concerned. Disclosures must be examined individually if the principle is to be maintained. Disclosures found to be in breach of the section do not obtain cover by being interwoven, whether intentionally or unintentionally interwoven, with expressions of general concern, which may legitimately be made by a juror. They do not obtain cover by the addition of favourable comments about how the jury functioned, as some of the disclosures in this case may have done. Indeed, disclosures incorporating favourable comment about other jurors could constitute a breach.

53. In my judgment, the disclosure of the 10–2 vote was a clear breach of section 8(1). It was a breach as disclosing a vote. Moreover, it revealed the opinions expressed by 10 members of the jury, at an early stage of a long deliberation. The reference to 'no going back' also revealed a firm intention on the part of those 10 members not to change their minds, a revelation of the opinions they held.

54. The paragraph dealing with common sense also constituted a breach. It was disclosed that the majority who convicted used a 'despicable enemy of correct and logical thinking'. That was the foreman's assessment of the opinions of and statements expressed by the majority members and he disclosed them by making those comments. The majority members were, in the opinion of the foreman, guilty of incorrect and illogical thinking, an accusation against them, combined with a disclosure of, their opinions.

55. It is disclosed that the majority members used that 'wonderfully persuasive device, common sense'. That is a disclosure of their approach to the evidence, which necessarily was based

---

[89] European Commission declaring inadmissible a challenge by Associated Newspapers to the decision of the House of Lords in Extract 12.6.2: Application No 24770/94.

on statements they had made or opinions they had expressed during the deliberations. If the foreman's assessment of their opinions was incorrect, it may add to the wrong done to them, but that is not material; the mischief is in the disclosure of the deliberations. It is not necessary to prove that the accusations made against fellow jurors were true.

56. The assumption is made in the foreman's disclosure that common sense is the enemy of correct thinking, and therefore of justice. That assumption can of course be questioned; common sense is generally perceived to be valuable and does not inevitably lead to the acceptance of expert medical evidence. Debate of the merits of common sense is not, however, in point for present purposes. What is relevant is that the disclosures reveal the approach of this jury to the evidence in this case; reliance on common sense and not correct and logical thinking. Whether or not that is a disclosure offensive to the majority members need not be decided; it was a disclosure of their approach, as assessed by the foreman, thereby revealing their opinions. It offended against the secrecy of the jury room, as that concept is viewed in the authorities. The foreman should not have disclosed the approach to the evidence of other jurors. What may be legitimate debate in the course of deliberations should not be revealed outside.

It would also be a contempt of court for a member of the jury to send an email, blog or otherwise use the Internet to reveal any aspect of the jury's deliberations.[90]

The prohibition on disclosure of jury deliberations is controversial,[91] in the first place because it is generally considered to inhibit, or even preclude, serious discussion in the media of particular jury decisions, as in the *Seckerson* case. It may also make more difficult research into the general working of the jury system, to investigate, for example, how far juries are influenced by prejudicial media publicity, whether the judge's directions are understood and followed, and whether juries discuss what their members may have discovered on the Internet, if they have improperly used it to conduct independent research.[92] The Review of Criminal Trials conducted by Lord Justice Auld described section 8 as 'unduly restrictive' of study of the jury system.[93] The provision does not, however, wholly preclude scholarly research into how juries work.[94] There is no legal objection to asking individual jurors about the impact, say, of media publicity; but section 8 of the Contempt of Court Act has created uncertainty about what jury research can be conducted.[95]

Questions for discussion

1. Are the arguments for the secrecy of the jury room sufficiently persuasive to justify section 8 of the Contempt of Court Act 1981?
2. Does this provision, as interpreted and applied by the English courts, wrongly inhibit the freedom of the media to discuss the merits of jury decisions?

---

[90] *Attorney-General* v *Joanne Fraill and Jamie Sewart* [2011] EWCA Crim 1570.

[91] Fenwick and Phillipson, 233–43, argue for reform of the provision to make it compatible with freedom of expression.

[92] The European Human Rights Court in *Seckerson* v *UK* and *Times Newspapers* v *UK* (2012) 54 EHRR SE 19 rejected the argument that CCA, s 8 infringed ECHR, art 10, while leaving open the possibility that it might be open to challenge if it were applied to penalise jury research.

[93] Published in October 2001, para 98.

[94] C. Thomas, 'Exposing the Myths of jury service' (2008) *Criminal Law Rev* 415–30.

[95] C. Thomas, 'Are juries fair?' (Ministry of Justice, Research Series 1/10, Feb 2010), 1.

Selected further reading

General

E. Barendt, *Freedom of Speech*, 2nd edn (Oxford: OUP, 2007) 312–37.

H. Fenwick and G. Phillipson, *Media Freedom Under the Human Rights Act* (Oxford: OUP, 2006), chs 4 and 6.

G. Robertson and A. Nicol, *Media Law*, 5th edn (London: Penguin Books, 2008), ch 7. All these books provide an overall treatment of the subject; Barendt's treatment offers comparative insights, while Fenwick and Phillipson focus on the impact of human rights arguments for contempt of court law.

The strict liability rule

J.A. Brandwood, 'You say "fair trial" and I say "free press": British and American approaches to protecting defendants' rights in high profile trials' (2000) 75 *New York Univ Law Rev* 1412–51 is critical of the Contempt of Court Act 1981 limits on press freedom.

M. Chesterman, 'OJ and the dingo: how media publicity for criminal cases is dealt with in Australia and America' (1997) 45 *American Journal of Comparative Law* 109–47 compares the US and common law approaches to the implications of media publicity.

D. Corker and M. Levi, 'Pre-trial publicity and its treatment in the English courts' (1996) *Criminal Law Rev* 622–32 explores the various measures courts can take to avoid the consequences of media publicity for fair trials.

I. Cram, *A Virtue Less Cloistered* (Oxford: Hart Publishing, 2002). Ch 3 compares the law in England, Scotland, the USA and Commonwealth countries.

C.J. Miller, *Contempt of Court*, 3rd edn (Oxford: OUP, 2000), chs 5–9 is the leading academic book on this topic.

G. Phillipson, 'Trial by media: the betrayal of the First Amendment's purpose' (2008) 71 *Law and Contemporary Problems* 15–29 is critical of US law.

C. Walker, 'Fundamental rights, fair trials and the new audio-visual media' (1996) 59 *Modern Law Rev* 517–39 explores the difficulties of regulating broadcasts and the Internet to protect fair trial rights, suggesting that self-regulation may offer better solutions.

C. Walker, 'Cyber-contempt: fair trials and the Internet' (1997) 3 *Yearbook of Media and Entertainment Law* 1–29 discusses the application of contempt of court law to the Internet.

The postponement power

I. Cram, 'Section 4(2): Media reports of court proceedings under the Contempt of Court Act 1981' (1996) 2 *Yearbook of Media and Entertainment Law* 111–32 looks at the case law on s 4(2) of the CCA.

The disclosure of jury deliberations

J. Jaconelli, *Open Justice: A Critique of the Public Trial* (Oxford: OUP, 2002). Chapter 7 examines the origins of CCA, s 8 and its implications for jury research.

C.J. Miller, *Contempt of Court*, 3rd edn (Oxford: OUP, 2000), paras 13.39–13.61 provides a full treatment of the interpretation of CCA, s 8.

C. Walker, I. Cram and D. Brogarth, 'The reporting of Crown Court proceedings and the Contempt of Court Act 1981' (1992) 55 *Modern Law Rev* 647–69 discusses the grounds on which courts exercise their powers under CCA, ss 4(2) and 11 to postpone or limit reports of their proceedings.

13 Reporting legal proceedings

13.1 INTRODUCTION

In its recent decision in *Al Rawi* v *Security Service*,[1] the Supreme Court, sitting with seven members in view of the importance of the case, emphasised the fundamental character of the common law principle of open justice. It held that in the absence of statutory authority, even in a case with significant repercussions for foreign relations and for the security services, the courts had no power to allow a closed material procedure under which evidence could be introduced without disclosure to one of the parties or to the media.[2] This chapter is concerned with this open justice principle and with aspects of the law concerning media reporting of legal proceedings. Other aspects were treated in the previous chapter on contempt of court; but the strict liability rule discussed there is more concerned with media publicity which may prejudice *future* proceedings than with reports of *contemporaneous* proceedings. The principal topics of this chapter are the right of journalists to attend legal proceedings and the extent to which courts may impose restrictions on this right and their freedom to report them.

English law generally adheres to a principle of open justice which requires the courts to sit in public. So under the principle the press and other media, as well as members of the public, are entitled to attend their proceedings. A further implication of open justice is that the media are usually entitled to report them in full: see Section 13.2.[3] Arguably, open justice now requires recognition of a right to film court proceedings, and broadcast these proceedings, or extracts from them, on television: see Section 13.3. The chapter also discusses a number of qualifications and exceptions to the principle, some established by common law, others created by statute. These are covered in Section 13.4, which deals with anonymity orders, and Section 13.5, which outlines some of the principal statutory restrictions on access and reporting rights.

Many of the qualifications to the open justice principle concern legal proceedings involving children and young persons, who, it is argued, should be protected against media publicity likely to harm their development. These qualifications are discussed in Section 13.6, in so far as they concern criminal proceedings affecting young persons as victims, as defendants or as witnesses. Section 13.7 is concerned with comparable restrictions to protect the privacy and welfare of children in family proceedings and public law proceedings in which local authorities apply to take care of children. As will be seen, the law draws a sharp distinction between proceedings involving adults, where there is a strong presumption in favour of open justice, and proceedings involving children, where it is usual for media access and reporting freedom to be significantly restricted. In many cases involving children (and also in some concerning adults) parties or witnesses invoke

---

[1] [2011] UKSC 34.

[2] The courts will have power to conduct civil proceedings under closed material procedures under the terms of the Justice and Security Act 2013, enactment of which will have significant repercussions for open justice; see 24th Report of Joint Committee on Human Rights for Session 2010–12, 27 March 2012, paras 193–217.

[3] Accurate contemporaneous reports of judicial proceedings are covered by the defence of absolute privilege to actions for libel (see Chapter 10, Section 10.5) and are immune from contempt proceedings under the strict liability rule: see Chapter 12, Section 12.4.

privacy rights, now guaranteed by article 8 of the European Convention on Human Rights (ECHR), so this chapter has some overlap with Chapter 11. Leading cases discussed in the chapter, notably *An Application by Guardian News and Media Ltd* (Extract 13.4.2 below) and *Re S (A Child)* (Extract 13.6.1 below) have been extensively cited and followed in the personal privacy cases discussed in Chapter 11.

As already indicated, there are at least two major limbs of the open justice principle; legal proceedings should be conducted in public, so the public and media are free to attend them, and the media should be free to report them. The second aspect is important, because few members of the public have the time to attend legal proceedings, so without the reporting freedom, they would know little or nothing about them. A third aspect has received less emphasis; open justice requires judgments to be published in full, so the parties and the general public are aware of the reasons for court decisions. It is wrong to redact or edit court judgments, unless this is required by an overwhelming argument of, say, national security.[4] It is important to keep these aspects of the open justice principle distinct. In some cases the media may be entitled to attend proceedings (for example, criminal cases involving children or prosecutions for sex offences) but there are significant statutory restrictions on freedom to report aspects of these proceedings. In other circumstances proceedings may be held in private, but there may be no restrictions on reporting evidence or other information disclosed in them; see Section 13.5 for discussion of these distinctions. These distinctions are one reason why this area of law is extremely complex; another is the bewildering variety of statutory restrictions on media freedom, which must be applied by the courts in conformity with the rights to freedom of expression and privacy guaranteed by the ECHR.

13.2 THE OPEN JUSTICE PRINCIPLE

There are many arguments for open justice. Publicity, as Jeremy Bentham argued, provides safeguards against injustice in the courts. Media coverage keeps judges and counsel on their toes, while witnesses may be more likely to tell the truth if they know that their evidence will be reported to the public who will spot any inaccuracies in it. More generally, it is important that the public knows about, and has confidence in, the legal process. Both the United States Supreme Court,[5] and the Supreme Court in Canada[6] have upheld media rights of access to, and to report, legal proceedings under the constitutional rights to freedom of speech or expression. However, it may be asked why the law should uphold a media right to attend legal proceedings, when there is no such right to attend, say, Cabinet or government committee meetings, which are of equal public importance and interest. Further, it is unusual for courts to uphold under a freedom of expression provision, such as ECHR, article 10, positive access rights – in this case to attend legal proceedings – when the provision normally covers only the freedom to impart information which the media has acquired.

The classic statement of the principle in English law is to be found in speeches in *Scott* v *Scott*. The particular issue before the House of Lords was whether the Court was entitled to hold Mrs Scott and her solicitor guilty of contempt for supplying Mr Scott's father with copies of notes of the nullity proceedings she had initiated against her husband. By order of the

---

[4] See *R (On Application of Mohamed)* v *Secretary of State for Foreign and Commonwealth Affairs* [2010] EWCA Civ 65, [2011] QB 218.
[5] *Richmond Newspapers* v *Virginia* 448 US 555 (1980).
[6] *Edmonton Journal* v *A-G of Alberta* [1989] 2 SCR 1326.

judge these proceedings had been held in private, or (to use the legal term then current) in camera; he held that it was, therefore, a contempt of court to publish a report of them. The House of Lords ruled that he had been wrong to hear the nullity petition in private.

Extract 13.2.1
Scott v *Scott* **[1913] AC 417, at 437–9 (HL)**

VISCOUNT HALDANE LC:

While the broad principle is that the Courts of this country must, as between parties, administer justice in public, this principle is subject to apparent exceptions, such as those to which I have referred. But the exceptions are themselves the outcome of a yet more fundamental principle that the chief object of Courts of justice must be to secure that justice is done. In the two cases of wards of Court and of lunatics the Court is really sitting primarily to guard the interests of the ward or the lunatic. Its jurisdiction is in this respect parental and administrative, and the disposal of controverted questions is an incident only in the jurisdiction. It may often be necessary, in order to attain its primary object, that the Court should exclude the public. The broad principle which ordinarily governs it therefore yields to the paramount duty, which is the care of the ward or the lunatic. The other case referred to, that of litigation as to a secret process, where the effect of publicity would be to destroy the subject-matter, illustrates a class which stands on a different footing. There it may well be that justice could not be done at all if it had to be done in public. As the paramount object must always be to do justice, the general rule as to publicity, after all only the means to an end, must accordingly yield. But the burden lies on those seeking to displace its application in the particular case to make out that the ordinary rule must as of necessity be superseded by this paramount consideration. The question is by no means one which, consistently with the spirit of our jurisprudence, can be dealt with by the judge as resting in his mere discretion as to what is expedient. The latter must treat it as one of principle, and as turning, not on convenience, but on necessity.

. . . But unless it be strictly necessary for the attainment of justice, there can be no power in the Court to hear in camera either a matrimonial cause or any other where there is contest between parties. He who maintains that by no other means than by such a hearing can justice be done may apply for an unusual procedure. But he must make out his case strictly, and bring it up to the standard which the underlying principle requires. He may be able to show that the evidence can be effectively brought before the Court in no other fashion. He may even be able to establish that subsequent publication must be prohibited for a time or altogether. But this further conclusion he will find more difficult in a matrimonial case than in the case of the secret process, where the objection to publication is not confined to the mere difficulty of giving testimony in open Court. In either case he must satisfy the Court that by nothing short of the exclusion of the public can justice be done. The mere consideration that the evidence is of an unsavoury character is not enough, any more than it would be in a criminal Court, and still less is it enough that the parties agree in being reluctant to have their case tried with open doors. My Lords, it may well be that in proceedings in the Divorce Court, whether the proceedings be for divorce, or for declaration of nullity, or for judicial separation, a case may come before the judge in which it is evident that the choice must be between a hearing in public and a defeat of the ends of justice. Such cases do not occur every day. If the evidence to be given is of such a character that it would be impracticable to force an unwilling witness to give it in public, the case may come within the exception to the principle that in these proceedings, and not the less because they involve an adjudication on status as distinguished from mere private right, a public hearing must be insisted on in accordance with the rules which govern the general procedure in English Courts of justice. A mere desire to consider feelings of delicacy or to exclude from publicity details which it would be desirable not to publish is not, I repeat, enough as the law now stands. I think that to justify an order for hearing in camera it must be shown that the paramount object of securing that justice is done would really be rendered doubtful of attainment if the order were not made.

Other members of the House of Lords were prepared to allow somewhat wider exceptions to the open justice principle, but all were agreed that there was a strong presumption in favour of public hearings, which the press (and public) are free to attend and to report. In the words of Lord Shaw, open justice was a 'sacred part of the constitution . . .'[7]

The open justice principle was fully considered by the House of Lords in the *Leveller Magazine* case. It was asked to decide whether it was a contempt to publish the name of a witness who had been permitted by magistrates, during proceedings under the official secrets legislation, to give evidence without disclosing his identity. Lord Diplock's doubts concerning the scope of the courts' powers to prohibit such a publication have now been resolved by the Contempt of Court Act 1981 (see Section 13.4), but his authoritative discussion of the open justice principle has been frequently cited in subsequent cases. The judgment was also important on the power of a court to allow evidence to be given anonymously in derogation from the open justice principle; this topic is considered below in Section 13.4.

Extract 13.2.2
***Attorney General* v *Leveller Magazine* [1979] AC 440, at 450–3 (HL)**

LORD DIPLOCK:

If the way that courts behave cannot be hidden from the public ear and eye this provides a safeguard against judicial arbitrariness or idiosyncrasy and maintains the public confidence in the administration of justice. The application of this principle of open justice has two aspects: as respects proceedings in the court itself it requires that they should be held in open court to which the press and public are admitted and that, in criminal cases at any rate, all evidence communicated to the court is communicated publicly. As respects the publication to a wider public of fair and accurate reports of proceedings that have taken place in court the principle requires that nothing should be done to discourage this.

However, since the purpose of the general rule is to serve the ends of justice it may be necessary to depart from it where the nature or circumstances of the particular proceeding are such that the application of the general rule in its entirety would frustrate or render impracticable the administration of justice or would damage some other public interest for whose protection Parliament has made some statutory derogation from the rule. Apart from statutory exceptions, however, where a court in the exercise of its inherent power to control the conduct of proceedings before it departs in any way from the general rule, the departure is justified to the extent and to no more than the extent that the court reasonably believes it to be necessary in order to serve the ends of justice . . .

In the instant case the only statutory provisions that have any relevance are section 8(4) of the Official Secrets Act 1920 and section 12(1)(c) of the Administration of Justice Act 1960. Both deal with the giving of evidence before a court sitting in camera. They do not apply to the evidence given by 'Colonel B' in the instant case. Their relevance is thus peripheral and I can dispose of them shortly.

Section 8(4) of the Act of 1920 applies to prosecutions under that Act and the Official Secrets Act 1911. It empowers but it does not compel a court to sit to hear evidence in private if the Crown applies for this on the ground that national safety would be prejudiced by its publication. Section 12(1) of the Act of 1960 defines and limits the circumstances in which the publication of information relating to proceedings before any court sitting in private is of itself contempt of court. The circumstance defined in section 12(1)(c) is

---

[7] [1913] AC 417, 473.

where the court sits in private for reasons of national security during that part of the proceedings about which the information in question is published . . .

So to report evidence in camera in a prosecution under the Official Secrets Act would be contempt of court.

In the instant case the magistrates would have had power to sit in camera to hear the whole or part of the evidence of 'Colonel B' if this had been requested by the prosecution; and although they would not have been bound to accede to such a request it would naturally and properly have carried great weight with them. So would the absence of any such request. Without it the magistrates, in my opinion, would have had no reasonable ground for believing that so drastic a derogation from the general principle of open justice as is involved in hearing evidence in a criminal case in camera was necessary in the interests of the due administration of justice.

In substitution for hearing 'Colonel B's' evidence in camera, which it could have asked for, the prosecution was content to treat a much less drastic derogation from the principle of open justice as adequate to protect the interests of national security. The witness's evidence was to be given in open court in the normal way except that he was to be referred to by the pseudonym of 'Colonel B' and evidence as to his real name and address was to be written down and disclosed only to the court, the defendants and their legal representatives.

I do not doubt that, applying their minds to the matter that it was their duty to consider – the interests of the due administration of justice – the magistrates had power to accede to this proposal for the very reason that it would involve less derogation from the general principle of open justice than would result from the Crown being driven to have recourse to the statutory procedure for hearing evidence in camera under section 8(4) of the Official Secrets Act 1920; but in adopting this particular device, which on the face of it related only to how proceedings within the courtroom were to be conducted it behoved the magistrates to make it clear what restrictions, if any, were intended by them to be imposed upon publishing outside the courtroom information relating to those proceedings and whether such restrictions were to be precatory only or enforceable by the sanction of proceedings for contempt of court.

My Lords, in the argument before this House little attempt was made to analyse the juristic basis on which a court can make a 'ruling', 'order' or 'direction' – call it what you will – relating to proceedings taking place before it which has the effect in law of restricting what may be done outside the courtroom by members of the public who are not engaged in those proceedings as parties or their legal representatives or as witnesses. The Court of Appeal of New Zealand in *Taylor* v *Attorney-General* [1975] 2 N.Z.L.R. 675 was clearly of opinion that a court had power to make an explicit order directed to and binding on the public ipso jure as to what might lawfully be published outside the courtroom in relation to proceedings held before it. For my part I am prepared to leave this as an open question in the instant case. It may be that a 'ruling' by the court as to the conduct of proceedings can have binding effect as such within the courtroom only, so that breach of it is not ipso facto a contempt of court unless it is committed there. Nevertheless where (1) the reason for a ruling which involves departing in some measure from the general principle of open justice within the courtroom is that the departure is necessary in the interests of the due administration of justice and (2) it would be apparent to anyone who was aware of the ruling that the result which the ruling is designed to achieve would be frustrated by a particular kind of act done outside the courtroom, the doing of such an act with knowledge of the ruling and of its purpose may constitute a contempt of court, not because it is a breach of the ruling but because it interferes with the due administration of justice.

So it does not seem to me to matter greatly in the instant case whether or not the magistrates were rightly advised that they had in law no power to give directions which would be binding as such upon members of the public as to what information relating to the proceedings taking place before them might be published outside the courtroom. What was incumbent upon them was to make it clear to anyone present at, or reading an accurate report of, the proceedings what in the interests of the due administration of justice was the result that was intended by them to be achieved by the limited derogation from the principle of open justice within the courtroom which they had authorised, and what kind of information derived from what happened in the courtroom would if it were published frustrate that result.

There may be many cases in which the result intended to be achieved by a ruling by the court as to what is to be done in court is so obvious as to speak for itself; it calls for no explicit statement. Sending the jury out of court during a trial within a trial is an example of this; so may be the common ruling in prosecutions for blackmail that a victim called as a witness be referred to in court by a pseudonym (see *Reg. v Socialist Worker Printers and Publishers Ltd., Ex parte Attorney-General* [1975] Q.B. 637); but, in the absence of any explicit statement by the Tottenham magistrates at the conclusion of the colonel's evidence that the purpose of their ruling would be frustrated if anything were published outside the courtroom that would be likely to lead to the identification of 'Colonel B' as the person who had given evidence in the case, I do not think that the instant case falls into this class.

Quite apart from the common law, open justice is guaranteed under the ECHR, now incorporated in UK law by the Human Rights Act 1998.

Extract 13.2.3
European Convention on Human Rights and Fundamental Freedoms, article 6(1)

In the determination of his civil rights and obligations or of any criminal charge against him, everyone is entitled to a fair and public hearing . . . Judgment shall be pronounced publicly but the press and public may be excluded from all or part of the trial in the interests of morals, public order or national security in a democratic society, where the interests of juveniles or the protection of the private life of the parties so require, or to the extent strictly necessary in the opinion of the court in special circumstances where publicity would prejudice the interests of justice.

However, this provision allows more exceptions than those permitted by the common law principle.[8] For example, it permits courts to exclude the press and public, when this step is necessary in the interests of public order, or when it is required to protect the private life of the parties. It might therefore have allowed the nullity proceedings in *Scott* to have been heard in camera to protect the husband's privacy. Another fundamental point is that ECHR, article 6 guarantees the rights of the *parties* to civil and criminal proceedings to a public hearing; it is not concerned with the interests or rights of the press and public to attend (and report details of) legal proceedings. That is covered by article 10 of the Convention. Although there is no decision of the Strasbourg Court on the point, it is unlikely to rule that the press have a right under the Convention to attend a trial, which a national court has considered appropriate, perhaps with the consent of the parties, to conduct in camera. In these circumstances an English court would have to rely on the common law open justice principle, rather than the Convention, to protect the media.

The value of the open justice principle has recently been considered by the Court of Appeal, when it rejected a government request to redact part of the reasoning in the courts'

---

[8] See Robertson and Nicol, para 1-014.

judgments in judicial review proceedings which had been brought by the applicant in connection with his complaints of serious ill-treatment by US authorities.[9] In the view of Lord Judge CJ, open justice represents an element of democratic accountability and is an exercise of freedom of expression; it depends for its effectiveness on the commitment of an independent media.[10] Open justice requires the full publication of court judgments, unless there are very powerful reasons against it. In this case there was a strong legitimate public interest in information about the mistreatment of detainees in Guantanamo Bay, so there was a significant public interest in full publication of the court's judgments.[11]

Questions for discussion

1. Why does English law attach great importance to open justice? Is it right to do this?
2. Should the press and other media have a right to attend legal proceedings, if the prosecution and the accused (or the parties in civil proceedings) would prefer them to be heard in private?

13.3 CAMERAS IN THE COURTROOM?

In the last few years the media have campaigned for the law to allow cameras in the courtroom to film proceedings, with a view to showing extracts from their coverage on television news and in other programmes. In England and Wales it has generally been assumed that their access is precluded by section 41 of the Criminal Justice Act 1925,[12] which prohibits the taking of photographs in court, or making there a sketch with a view to publication, of any person involved in the proceedings.[13] Cameras in the courtroom should perhaps now be allowed as an aspect of the open justice principle.[14] The argument is that otherwise the public will never become familiar with legal proceedings, for it relies increasingly on television for news. The press now lacks the financial resources to cover court trials; certainly, there is much less reporting of them, particularly in local newspapers, than there used to be fifty years ago. However, constitutional claims to film and broadcast legal proceedings have been rejected in Germany,[15] South Africa[16] and Canada; the Supreme Court of Canada held recently that bans on cameras in the courtroom were justified as necessary to protect the administration of justice.[17]

The following extract presents the case for allowing television cameras in the courtroom, while discussing arguments against that step.

---

[9] *R (On the application of Mohamed) v Secretary of State for Foreign and Commonwealth Affairs* [2010] EWCA Civ 65, [2011] QB 218.

[10] Ibid., paras 38–40.

[11] Ibid., paras 176–84 per Lord Neuberger MR.

[12] For a comprehensive study of this provision, see Jaconelli, 315–28.

[13] See the decision of the Chancellor, Judge Ellison, in the Salisbury Consistory Court, *Re St Andrew's, Heddington* [1978] Fam 121, holding that he could not permit BBC filming of its proceedings.

[14] See Robertson and Nicol, paras 8-111–8-114, and E. Thompson, 'Does the open justice principle require cameras to be permitted in the courtroom and the broadcasting of legal proceedings?' (2011) 3 *Journal of Media Law* 211.

[15] 103 BVerfGE 44 (2002), discussed in Barendt, 348.

[16] *South African Broadcasting Corporation Ltd v National Director of Public Prosecutions* 2007 (1) SA 523 (CC).

[17] *Canadian Broadcasting Corpn v AG for Canada* [2011] 1 SCR 19.

Extract 13.3.1
M. Dockray, 'Courts on Television' (1988) 51 *Modern Law Review* 593, at 598–602
(some footnotes omitted)

In contrast with the position in 1925, television is today thought to be the single most important source of news for the general public. It is undoubtedly the most important medium in which issues of general concern can be treated and public opinion formed and informed. One special value is its ability to provide a personal experience of current events rather than a merely secondhand reported version. The law itself recognises this value, in some cases preferring film or television to the written or spoken word.

These advantages are no small matter. They give television the potential to play both an important educational and an important political role. Educationally, regular coverage by television of court proceedings could have great value in developing wider public knowledge of the law and its workings. The importance of informing public opinion was recognised recently by the Master of the Rolls who said in the 1987 Court of Appeal (Civil Division) Annual Review that he believed:

> it to be crucially important that the judiciary should explain to the public what they are seeking to achieve, how they are seeking to achieve it, what problems they are encountering, what success is attending their efforts . . .

. . .

Television could also play an enhanced political role if courtroom proceedings could be recorded by making public scrutiny of the law and its institutions more informed and more effective. Improving the means of scrutiny is not necessarily unconstitutional or hostile to the judiciary. As the Master of the Rolls also said in his 1987 Review 'Independence is in no way inconsistent with public accountability . . .'

The potential benefits of television for the law are neither trivial nor illusory. They are matters of great public importance:[i]

> The democratic form of society demands of its members an active and intelligent participation in the affairs of their community . . . More and more it demands also an alert and informed participation not only in purely political processes but also in the efforts of the community to adjust its social and economic life to increasingly complex circumstances. Democratic society, therefore, needs a clear and truthful account of events, of their background and their causes . . .[ii]

Television has talents which enable it to provide just this type of account. It would be folly to fail to use those talents unless there are dangers in doing so which outweigh the potential advantages. What are the dangers?

Effect of cameras: judges and jurors

Fears in 1925 that the judiciary would be annoyed by cameras seem, in relation to television, to be over-solicitous. Members of the judiciary have appeared voluntarily on television without noticeable discomfort or resentment. It seems unlikely that a professional judge would be either embarrassed, intimidated or distracted by a video camera, provided physical disruption to the proceedings (see below) was controlled.

Jurors on the other hand, require special consideration. The danger of jurors being distressed by the presence of cameras is greater. Fear of criticism or desire for applause might tempt a juror to reach a popular decision, if television had made the identity of a jury widely known.[iii] It is undeniable that the presence of cameras might occasionally have some such insidious effect.[iv] But the legitimate desire to avoid this danger cannot possibly justify a ban on the use of cameras either in criminal proceedings in which a jury takes no part, or most civil cases[v] or in appellate proceedings. And even in jury cases, the danger could be avoided either barring coverage at the request of the jury, or locating cameras so that pictures of the jury could not be obtained.

Litigants

Here again Parliamentary fears that litigants generally go in terror of the camera seem to have been exaggerated in 1925. The vast majority of litigants have no reason to fear television coverage any more than they at present fear exposure in newspapers. It is ludicrous to imagine that litigants would abandon their rights wholesale if television coverage of courts was allowed. The possibility of being photographed by a newspaper on the way to or from court has not noticeably deterred droves of disputants.[vi]

There are no doubt some litigants each year who, for special reasons, would drop a case rather than see it broadcast on television. In some cases of this type, the court already has power to sit in private: where a court does sit in private, cameras could continue to be excluded. But where the court sits in public and press reports are permitted, the danger that a film report (as distinct from merely written coverage) will deter or harm litigants seems a very remote risk. The present total ban on cameras goes beyond what is needed to manage this risk. It would be sufficient if the court had power to prohibit television coverage on the application of any party who could show cause why this should be done.[vii] Evans J. adopted just this approach in *J. Barber & Sons* v *Lloyd's Underwriters*[viii] where the defendants sought to discharge an order made pursuant to a request from the California Superior Court that depositions be taken from the defendants before an examiner in England, and that the depositions be videotaped:

> As to discretion, I have heard strongly worded claims by the defendants that the presence of a camera would oppress them and cause additional stress. The defendants are Lloyd's underwriters. I have no evidence that they are not in good health or that they are subject to any personal disability. Of course it is a stressful matter to give evidence and the court is keen to protect those who are under any disability – especially the weak or the old. In the case of these four defendants I cannot accept that there will be additional stress, certainly not enough to outweigh the value and convenience of videotaping the proceedings . . . I can see therefore great value in having a video recording, which far outweighs the other matters. Courts in this country place great emphasis on the demeanour of witnesses, although opinions may differ as to its value. I will not vary the order to delete the reference to videotaping.

Witnesses

Where a court sits in public and there are no restrictions on newspaper reports, the danger that a film report will deter or prejudicially affect a witness also seems small.

Nevertheless, it is clearly possible that there are some witnesses who would not be affected by having to give evidence in public in the presence of newspaper reporters, but whose evidence would be affected if they were filmed while under oath. It is equally clear that this possibility is insufficient to justify a total ban on all cameras in all cases: it can scarcely justify the present rule in proceedings in which oral evidence is not heard. The danger to the particularly sensitive witness could be avoided without a general ban on cameras if a discretionary power (of the type mentioned above) was conferred on the court to prohibit filming of the testimony of any witness on good cause being shown.

The pillory of publicity[ix]

Another reason for banning photography which was mooted both in the debates which preceded the 1925 Act and earlier, was the desire to avoid unfairly pillorying those defendants in criminal cases in whom the press showed a special interest. But experience since 1925 suggests that this argument ought to receive little weight. Some cases, both civil and criminal, have continued to attract great public interest and consequent press attention despite the absence of cameras in court.

Permitting cameras in court would probably add very little to the burden of the participants in such a case. It might in fact ease the burden. If cameras were permitted in court under controlled conditions (see below) there would be no need for packs of photographers to haunt the doors of the court as they now do. Courtroom congestion might also be relieved. There is evidence from jurisdictions[x] in which filming in court is permitted which indicates that newspaper journalists often prefer to follow an important case on television from a press room rather than from the press bench in court.

Dignity

It has been said that it is not 'in keeping with the dignity of the court that it should be used as a studio'.[xi] This argument appears very dated today. Television coverage does not insult or impair the dignity of religious, Parliamentary or Royal occasions. Microphones and tape recorders, used to provide transcriptions, have not harmed the dignity of the Court. The use of video recorders and television monitors to present video evidence has not noticeably undermined respect for the law. There is no reason why a video camera should be any more harmful than a video recorder, provided that noise and physical disruption to the work of the court is kept within acceptable limits. In fact a bit of decent film taken under controlled conditions would be far more dignified than the 'out-of-court' sketches now used or the photographic scrimmage which now often occurs at the doors of the court.

Noise and physical disruption

This does not seem to have been regarded as an important factor in the debates preceding the 1925 ban. Probably this was because the courts already had quite adequate powers to deal with disruptive conduct.

But what about television? It is generally assumed that television cameras always require oppressive additional lighting; that cameras and recording equipment are invariably bulky and would leave courtrooms and corridors cluttered and confused; and that with television production a large noisy crew is inevitable.

None of these assumptions is necessarily true. At least in the views of one distinguished American judge, '. . . in the early days of television . . . I think perhaps the noise and lights and so on would have distorted and disrupted the proceedings. But as I understand the present technology, that is hardly a threat anymore . . .'[xii] In other words, today it is technically possible to obtain sound and pictures of a quality which are acceptable to a general audience without interfering with the smooth running of the court. The quality of the production may not match the standards which audiences have come to expect of broadcast television. But the important point is that material of appropriate quality can be obtained without interfering with the work of a court.

It would however be necessary to regulate in advance a number of matters. It would not be safe simply to throw open the doors of the court and leave everything to the discretion of any producer who came forward. Probably rules of court would be necessary.

---

[i] It has been objected that televising courts would not be educational because '. . . the news media chooses to cover only the sensational trials (and so) . . . warps public understanding of courtroom proceedings . . . The media would continue to select trials based upon their notoriety. In addition, programs would be edited, most likely to include the dramatic portions and remove the "dull or mundane"': Tongue & Lintott (1980) 16 Williamette L 777, 785. These criticisms cannot be fairly levelled against British television news and current affairs programmes which show a discriminating preference for legal cases of political, social and ethical concern. And the danger of editorial distortion is no greater in the case of film or videotape than it is in the case of traditional written or oral reporting.

[ii] Royal Commission on the Press, 1949, Cmd. 7700, para 362.

[iii] Zimmerman (1980) 4 Duke L 641 argues that available research evidence shows that cameras have little if any noteworthy impact on participants in trials. See also Netteburg (1980) 63 *Judicature* 467. Cf. *Estes* v *Texas* (1965) 381 U 532, 545.

[iv] The possible danger of members of a jury reviewing testimony each evening by watching television could be dealt with by warning to the jury or by prohibiting television coverage until the end of a trial. A similar warning to witnesses against watching the testimony of others would also be appropriate in some cases.

[v] In the House of Commons the 1925 Act was debated almost exclusively in the context of the criminal law: the few references to other types of proceedings were concerned for the most part with divorce cases.

[vi] Technical doubts about the meaning of 'precincts' (the legislation precludes the taking of photographs etc. in a courtroom or in the building or precincts of a building in which the court is held) have led to a

long-standing reluctance to prosecute where photographs are taken outside the court: the press and television have taken full advantage of this reluctance.

vii As originally drafted, cl 41 would have permitted photographs to be taken with leave of the judge (or the presiding or senior judge): this power was struck from the 1925 Bill at the committee stage of the House of Commons.

viii [1987] 1 QB 103.

ix The *Times*, leader, 28 February, 1924; HDeb vol 188, col 839 (Sir Wm. Joynson-Hicks).

x Davis (1980) 64 *Judicature* 85.

xi F. A. Broad, MP, HCDeb, vol 188, col 836.

xii Justice Potter Stewart (on retiring from the US Supreme Court): (1981) 67 ABAJ 954.

In many states in the USA cameras are permitted in the courtroom; for instance, the trials of O.J. Simpson and Louise Woodward were extensively televised. Since 2000, New Zealand has also allowed filming and broadcasting of legal proceedings, subject to the consent of the judge and safeguards for witnesses.[18] The ban in the Criminal Justice Act 1925 does not apply to Scotland, so in 1992 the courts there allowed on an experimental basis television filming of legal proceedings, albeit subject to conditions: for instance, the broadcast of current criminal trials was not permitted, and proceedings could only be filmed with the consent of the judge and all the parties involved.[19] On these principles, Lord Kirkwood in the High Court of Justiciary rejected an application by the BBC to televise the trial of the Lockerbie bombers; he held that ECHR, article 10 did not confer this right.[20] The Criminal Justice Act ban also does not apply to the Supreme Court,[21] which allows the filming and broadcasting of its proceedings in certain circumstances.

In 2012 the government announced its intention to relax the bans in the 1925 legislation and to permit the filming and broadcast of legal arguments in, and judgments of, the Court of Appeal. Eventually, the filming and broadcast of sentencing decisions in the Crown Court may be permitted; but the filming of victims, witnesses, jurors or defendants is not at present contemplated.[22] The Crime and Courts Act 2013, however, gives the Lord Chancellor power to extend by statutory order permission to film and broadcast legal proceedings; the Joint Committee on Human Rights has expressed concern that the scope of this power shows insufficient concern for the privacy and fair trial rights of witnesses, defendants, and other participants in legal proceedings.[23] The arguments about the merits of allowing cameras in the court room are far from over.

Questions for discussion

1. Do you find Dockray's arguments persuasive? Does the open justice principle require admission of the cameras into the courtroom?

2. Are the arguments against admission met by the imposition of strict conditions, for instance, prohibiting the filming of the faces of witnesses as they give evidence, and/or requiring the consent of the parties?

---

[18] See J. Burrows and U. Cheer, *Media Law in New Zealand*, 6th edn (Wellington, NZ: LexisNexis, 2010) 436–41.

[19] Jaconelli, 329–33.

[20] *Petititon No. 2 of the BBC* [2000] HRLR 423. On the other hand, the BBC was allowed to broadcast Al-Megrahi's appeal, subject to certain conditions.

[21] Constitutional Reform Act 2005, s 47.

[22] *Proposals to allow the broadcasting, filming, and recording of selected court proceedings* (Ministry of Justice, May 2012), 19–20.

[23] 5th Report of Joint Committee on Human Rights for 2012–13, HL Paper 67, HC 771, paras 50–61.

13.4 ANONYMITY ORDERS

(a) Introduction

In the *Leveller Magazine* case (see Extract 13.2.2 above) the magistrates had allowed a witness to give evidence anonymously, because revelation of his identity might have prejudiced national security. An anonymity order of this kind is to be distinguished from the automatic statutory anonymity to which the victims of sexual offences (Section 13.5) and children involved in legal proceedings (Sections 13.6 and 13.7) are entitled. Discretionary anonymity orders provide a less extreme measure than a direction that proceedings, or parts of proceedings, should be held in private. They are clearly justifiable in blackmail cases, where otherwise witnesses might be unwilling to give evidence,[24] and they may be similarly warranted in other sensitive criminal cases. The doubts expressed by Lord Diplock (and other members of the House) in *Leveller* whether this step can be supported by an order prohibiting the publication of the witness's name (or other information withheld during court proceedings) have now been resolved by section 11 of the Contempt of Court Act 1981: in cases when a court properly allows a witness to withhold his name (or other information), it may give directions to prevent the material being published by the media. So a court may in appropriate circumstances grant an anonymity order, which limits the information which journalists acquire through attendance in court, and also impose reporting restrictions which prevent evasion of that limitation.

Courts may be more prepared to grant anonymity in some types of case than in others. For example, witnesses at public inquiries should be allowed anonymity more readily than witnesses in criminal proceedings, because 'a defendant is entitled to know who is accusing him', a consideration which does not apply to tribunals set up under the Tribunals of Inquiry (Evidence) Act 1921.[25] The general principles governing anonymity orders were considered by the Court of Appeal when a firm of solicitors, seeking judicial review of the decision of the Legal Aid Board which had ended their franchise, applied for anonymity and for an order under section 11 of the 1981 Act. Kay J refused the application for anonymity, but granted a temporary order prohibiting publication of the name of the firm until the appeal had been heard. On appeal, the applicant argued that the firm should have anonymity in relation to the appeal itself, since it would be embarrassing for its name to be associated with the case.

Extract 13.4.1
***R v Legal Aid Board, ex parte Kaim Todner* [1998] 3 All ER 541, at 550–1 (CA)**

LORD WOOLF MR:
In deciding whether to accede to an application for protection from disclosure of the proceedings it is appropriate to take into account the extent of the interference with the general rule which is involved. If the interference is for a limited period that is less objectionable than a restriction on disclosure which is permanent. If the restriction relates only to the identity of a witness or a party this is less objectionable than a restriction which involves proceedings being conducted in whole or in part behind closed doors.

---

[24] See *R v Socialist Worker Printers and Publishers Ltd, ex parte Attorney General* [1975] QB 637 (DC).
[25] *R v Lord Saville of Newdigate, ex parte A and others* [1999] 4 All ER 860, para 68(3) per Lord Woolf MR. The Court of Appeal ruled that army officers giving evidence to the Bloody Sunday Inquiry should be allowed anonymity, because of the risk to their life and personal safety.

The nature of the proceedings is also relevant. If the application relates to an interlocutory application this is a less significant intrusion into the general rule than interfering with the public nature of the trial. Interlocutory hearings are normally of no interest to anyone other than the parties. The position can be the same in the case of financial and other family disputes. If proceedings are ex parte and involve serious allegations being made against another party who has no notice of those allegations, the interests of justice may require non-disclosure until such a time as a party against whom the allegations are made can be heard.

A distinction can also be made depending on whether what is being sought is anonymity for a plaintiff, a defendant or a third party. It is not unreasonable to regard the person who initiates the proceedings as having accepted the normal incidence of the public nature of court proceedings. If you are a defendant you may have an interest equal to that of the plaintiff in the outcome of the proceedings but you have not chosen to initiate court proceedings which are normally conducted in public. A witness who has no interest in the proceedings has the strongest claim to be protected by the court if he or she will be prejudiced by publicity, since the courts and parties may depend on their co-operation. In general, however parties and witnesses have to accept the embarrassment and damage to their reputation and the possible consequential loss which can be inherent in being involved in litigation. The protection to which they are entitled is normally provided by a judgment delivered in public which will refute unfounded allegations. Any other approach would result in wholly unacceptable inroads on the general rule.

There can however be situations where a party or witness can reasonably require protection. In prosecutions for rape and blackmail, it is well established that the victim can be entitled to protection. Outside the well-established cases where anonymity is provided, the reasonableness of the claim for protection is important. Although the foundation of the exceptions is the need to avoid frustrating the ability of the courts to do justice, a party cannot be allowed to achieve anonymity by insisting upon it as a condition for being involved in the proceedings irrespective of whether the demand is reasonable. There must be some objective foundation for the claim which is being made.

. . . This last point is particularly relevant to the claims for anonymity in this court which the appellants are putting forward. It is not a reasonable basis for seeking anonymity that you do not want to be associated with a decision of a court. Nor is it right for an appellant to seek to pre-empt the decision of this court by saying in effect we will not co-operate with the court unless the court binds itself to grant us anonymity. The appellant had secured anonymity until the end of the appeal and they could not reasonably ask for more.

It also cannot be reasonable for the legal profession to seek preferential treatment over other litigants. If the appellants had not raised the issue of anonymity, at the leave stage, it is not likely that their proceedings would have resulted in any publicity at least until the substantive hearing. If publicity did result from the substantive hearing then that publicity, so far as it was unfair, would be mitigated within a short time scale by the judgment of the court. If the judgment was adverse, then it is accepted on their behalf, that publicity could no longer be restrained since their alleged conduct should then be known. If the judgment was favourable, then the judgment would to a substantial extent provide the answer to any adverse publicity.

Kay J came to the right answer in deciding not to grant the application. The appeal against his decision will therefore be dismissed.

Lord Woolf distinguished the treatment of claimants and other applicants, of defendants, and of witnesses: courts might be less willing to grant anonymity to the first group, because they had chosen to come to court. Whatever the soundness of this argument, it is helpful to discuss the grant of anonymity orders under these three categories of case.

(b) Anonymity orders for claimants and other applicants

In some cases the courts are prepared to grant the claimant anonymity, for example, where it is clear that publication of the name would damage his or her mental stability.[26] Two recent Supreme Court decisions show how this issue is approached. In the first, the issue was whether anonymity should be granted to a number of individuals against whom the Treasury had made orders freezing their accounts, because they were suspected of involvement in terrorist acts. A number of media organisations challenged anonymity orders which had been made by Collins J.

Extract 13.4.2
An Application by Guardian News and Media Ltd, Re [2010] UKSC 1, [2010] EMLR 15, paras 63–76

LORD RODGER:

63. What's in a name? 'A lot', the press would answer. This is because stories about particular individuals are simply much more attractive to readers than stories about unidentified people. It is just human nature. And this is why, of course, even when reporting major disasters, journalists usually look for a story about how particular individuals are affected. Writing stories which capture the attention of readers is a matter of reporting technique, and the European Court holds that article 10 protects not only the substance of ideas and information but also the form in which they are conveyed: *News Verlags GmbH& Co KG* v *Austria* (2000) 31 EHRR 246, 256, para 39, quoted at para 35 above. More succinctly, Lord Hoffmann observed in *Campbell* v *MGN Ltd* [2004] 2 AC 457, 474, para 59, 'judges are not newspaper editors'. See also Lord Hope of Craighead in *In re British Broadcasting Corpn* [2009] 3 WLR 142, 152, para 25. This is not just a matter of deference to editorial independence. The judges are recognising that editors know best how to present material in a way that will interest the readers of their particular publication and so help them to absorb the information. A requirement to report it in some austere, abstract form, devoid of much of its human interest, could well mean that the report would not be read and the information would not be passed on. Ultimately, such an approach could threaten the viability of newspapers and magazines, which can only inform the public if they attract enough readers and make enough money to survive.

64. Lord Steyn put the point succinctly in *In re S* [2005] 1 AC 593, 608, para 34, when he stressed the importance of bearing in mind that

> from a newspaper's point of view a report of a sensational trial without revealing the identity of the defendant would be a very much disembodied trial. If the newspapers choose not to contest such an injunction, they are less likely to give prominence to reports of the trial. Certainly, readers will be less interested and editors will act accordingly. Informed debate about criminal justice will suffer.

Mutatis mutandis, the same applies in the present cases. A report of the proceedings challenging the freezing orders which did not reveal the identities of the appellants would be disembodied. Certainly, readers would be less interested and, realising that, editors would tend to give the report a lower priority. In that way informed debate about freezing orders would suffer.

65. On the other hand, if newspapers can identify the people concerned, they may be able to give a more vivid and compelling account which will stimulate discussion about the use of freezing orders and their impact on the communities in which the individuals live. Concealing their identities simply casts a shadow over entire communities.

---

[26] *H* v *Ministry of Defence* [1991] 2 All ER 834, CA (the claimant was seeking damages for injury to his genitals), and see Robertson and Nicol, para 8-074.

66. Importantly, a more open attitude would be consistent with the true view that freezing orders are merely indicative of suspicions about matters which the prosecuting authorities accept they cannot prove in a court of law. The identities of persons charged with offences are published, even though their trial may be many months off. In allowing this, the law proceeds on the basis that most members of the public understand that, even when charged with an offence, you are innocent unless and until proved guilty in a court of law. That understanding can be expected to apply, a fortiori, if you are someone whom the prosecuting authorities are not even in a position to charge with an offence and bring to court. But, by concealing the identities of the individuals who are subject to freezing orders, the courts are actually helping to foster an impression that the mere making of the orders justifies sinister conclusions about these individuals. That is particularly unfortunate when, as was emphasised on the appellants' behalf, they are unlikely to have any opportunity to challenge the alleged factual basis for making the orders.

67. It might be argued that, nevertheless, in this particular case naming M in any report would be an unnecessary luxury. After all, it could be said, what actually matter are the legal and constitutional issues raised in the proceedings and these can be understood and debated on the basis of an anonymised report. But the very fact that M and the other appellants are not accepting, but challenging, the whole system of freezing orders based on mere suspicion means that they are presenting the orders as wrongs done to them, rather than as indications that they themselves have done something wrong. Concealing their identities runs counter to the entire thrust of that case. Should their appeals be allowed, concealment would be even less appropriate. Not E but Mr John Entick of Stepney has gone down in history as the plaintiff in the great case of *Entick* v *Carrington* (1765) 19 Howell's State Trials 1030; 95 ER 807.

68. Certainly, the identities of the claimants cannot affect the answers that this Court gives to the legal questions in the substantive appeals. So those identities may not matter particularly to the judges. But the legitimate interest of the public is wider than the interest of judges qua judges or of lawyers qua lawyers. Irrespective of the outcome, the public has a legitimate interest in not being kept in the dark about who are challenging the TOs and the AQO. The case of HAY is instructive in this respect. Most people will be astonished, for example, to learn that, up until now, the courts have prevented them from discovering that one of the claimants, Mr Youssef, has already successfully sued the Home Secretary for wrongful detention after a failed attempt to deport him to Egypt. Equally importantly, even while the Treasury is defending these proceedings brought by him, the Government are trying to have his name removed from the 1267 Committee list. Meanwhile, he is busy writing and broadcasting from London on Middle East matters.

69. By lifting the anonymity order in HAY's case the court allows members of the public to receive relevant information about him which they can then use to make connexions between items of information in the public domain which otherwise appear to be unrelated. In this way the true position is revealed and the public can make an informed judgment. There may well, of course, be no similar revelations in the case of M. But, assuming that is so, this would, in itself, be important, since it would contribute to showing how the freezing-order system affects different people in different situations – a point to be considered in any debate on the merits of the system. At present, the courts are denying the public information which is relevant to that debate, even though the whole freezing-order system has been created and operated in their name.

70. Along with A, K and G, M has himself sought to enter the debate about the merits of freezing orders. After the judgment of Collins J in these proceedings in April 2008, his solicitors issued a press release which included the following:

> The five British nationals bringing this challenge who have been designated under the Orders have had their assets frozen, are only allowed to access enough money to meet basic expenses, and are compelled to account to a civil servant for every penny they spend. They are subject to unprecedented levels of intrusion and control without end or review. They require permission for all economic activity, however modest. The complex regime governed by permissions and licences is not merely harsh but at points

absurd. We have the madness of civil servants checking Tesco receipts, a child having to ask for a receipt every time it does a chore by running to the shops for a pint of milk and a neighbour possibly committing a criminal offence by lending a lawnmower . . .

The court ruling today has shown that the Government is willing to sacrifice the fundamental rights and liberties of its citizens, including the fundamental constitutional right that only Parliament can take away basic freedoms, when they think it convenient to do so. They have dishonoured their pledge of accountability and oversight through Parliament.

71. It is unusual, to say the least, for individuals to enter a debate, using highly charged language and accusing the Government of dishonouring a pledge, but at the same time to insist that they should have the right to hide behind a cloak of anonymity. It is also unusual for someone to assert the need for the press to respect his private and family life by not reporting his identity while simultaneously inviting them to report his version of the impact of the freezing orders on himself and members of his family. The public can hardly be expected to make an informed assessment of the argument if they are prevented from knowing who is making these points and, therefore, what his general stance is.

72. Of course, allowing the press to identify M and the other appellants would not be risk-free. It is conceivable that some of the press coverage might be outrageously hostile to M and the other appellants – even though nothing particularly significant appears to have been published when Mr al-Ghabra's identity was revealed. But the possibility of some sectors of the press abusing their freedom to report cannot, of itself, be a sufficient reason for curtailing that freedom for all members of the press. James Madison long ago pointed out that 'Some degree of abuse is inseparable from the proper use of everything, and in no instance is this more true than in that of the press': 'Report on the Virginia Resolutions' (1800), in *Letters and Other Writings of James Madison* (1865) Vol 4, p 544. The Press Complaints Commission is the appropriate body for dealing with any lapses in behaviour by the press. The possibility of abuse is therefore simply one factor to be taken into account when considering whether an anonymity order is a proportionate restriction on press freedom in this situation.

73. Although it has effects on the individual's private life, the purpose of a freezing order is public: it is to prevent the individual concerned from transferring funds to people who have nothing to do with his family life. So this is not a situation where the press are wanting to publish a story about some aspect of an individual's private life, whether trivial or significant. Rather, they are being prevented from publishing a complete account of an important public matter involving this particular individual, for fear of the incidental effect that it would have on M's private and family life.

74. So far as the potential effect on M's private and family life is concerned, the evidence is very general and, for that reason, not particularly compelling. The apparent lack of reaction to the naming of Mr al-Ghabra is relevant in this respect, since it suggests that the impact of identifying an individual on relationships with the local community is not likely to be as dramatic as the judges who made the orders appear to have anticipated. The fact that, through his solicitors, M has himself gone out of his way to put into the public domain what he says are the effects of the freezing order on his family life, is also significant.

75. On the other hand, publication of M's identity would make a material contribution to a debate of general interest.

. . .

76. In these circumstances, when carrying out the ultimate test of balancing all the factors relating to both M's article 8 rights and the article 10 rights of the press, we have come to the conclusion that there is indeed a powerful general, public interest in identifying M in any report of these important proceedings which justifies curtailment, to that extent, of his, and his family's, article 8 Convention rights to respect for their private and family life.

However, the Supreme Court did grant anonymity to an applicant, AP, who had challenged the terms of a control order under the terrorism legislation and was also challenging a deportation order.[27] Anonymity in this case was supported by the government on the ground that it allowed the police and other officials to discharge their responsibilities without attention or hostility from a local community. The reason for granting anonymity was that AP would be at risk of racist abuse, and perhaps of physical violence, if his identity were revealed. So the court ruled that the judgment in the control order proceedings should be published without naming him. However, the media had not made any submissions, so it did not think its decision should be regarded as laying down general principles for anonymity in control order cases.

(c) Anonymity for defendants in criminal cases

It is clear that anonymity will not be granted to a defendant, even though he may be acutely embarrassed or face financial ruin as a result of media publicity about criminal proceedings which may, of course, end in his acquittal.[28] In the *Evesham Justices* case, for example, the Divisional Court ruled that magistrates had been wrong to allow a defendant not to disclose his current address to prevent further harassment by his former wife.[29] The identity of a convicted criminal should not be concealed, even though its disclosure 'can bring misery, shame and disadvantage to their innocent children'.[30] However, until conviction, there is a stronger argument for allowing anonymity; the naming of a defendant could be considered incompatible with the presumption of innocence to which the accused is entitled.[31] The general principles for allowing defendants anonymity were recently considered by the Courts Martial Appeal Court. While it allowed an appeal by the media against an order by the Judge Advocate-General to hear in private proceedings against soldiers from the Special Forces charged with conspiracy to defraud, it allowed them anonymity. Such an order may be granted if otherwise the administration of justice would be seriously prejudiced or there is a real and immediate risk to the defendant's life.[32]

A successful challenge to an anonymity order was upheld by the House of Lords in *Re Attorney General's Reference (No 3 of 1999)*.[33] The BBC wanted to make a series of programmes concerning the abolition of the 'double jeopardy' rule, under which an acquitted defendant could not be retried for the same offence. An anonymity order had been made forbidding the naming by the media of D who had been acquitted on a charge of rape, and who was likely to be retried following abolition of the rule and after an earlier decision by the House of Lords that DNA evidence had been wrongly rejected by the judge at D's trial. In this case the House ruled that the balance between D's right to privacy and the BBC's freedom of expression should be struck in favour of the latter. The BBC was

---

[27] *Secretary of State for Home Department v AP (No 2)* [2010] UKSC 26.

[28] *R v Dover Justices, ex parte Dover DC* [1992] *Criminal Law Rev* 371, DC, where the court held it was wrong for magistrates to grant anonymity to a trader charged with public health offences.

[29] *R v Evesham Justices, ex parte McDonagh* [1988] QB 553.

[30] *Re Trinity Mirror plc* [2008] 2 All ER 1159, para 33 per Sir Igor Judge. The Court of Appeal allowed a media appeal against an order to stop them identifying someone convicted of making and possessing child pornography to protect the defendant's children, aged 6 and 8.

[31] R. Munday, 'Name suppression: an adjunct to the presumption of innocence and to mitigation of sentence' (1991) *Criminal Law Rev* 680–8 and 753–62.

[32] *Times Newspapers Ltd* and *Guardian News and Media Ltd v R* and *Soldiers, A, C, D, E and F* [2008] EWCA Crim 2559, paras 16–18.

[33] [2009] UKHL 34, [2010] 1 AC 145.

entitled to claim that their proposed series would lose much of its force unless it was free to discuss actual cases and mention the names of the parties involved.[34]

(d) Anonymity of witnesses

There is a powerful argument for allowing witnesses in some criminal proceedings to give evidence anonymously and for making orders which preclude the media and others from identifying them: otherwise witnesses might be unwilling to give evidence for fear of reprisal from the defendant or his associates. However, witness anonymity might hamper the defendant's ability to challenge the case against him, and so, as the House of Lords held in *R v Davis*,[35] deprive him of fair trial rights, guaranteed both by common law and by ECHR, article 6 (see Extract 13.2.3 above).[36] In response to that decision, the government introduced the Criminal Evidence (Witness Anonymity) Act 2008. Its provisions are now incorporated in the Coroners and Justice Act 2009.[37] Witness anonymity orders may only be granted if strict conditions specified in the legislation are met; in determining whether they have been the court must have regard to a number of considerations, among them the right of the defendant to know the identity of a witness in the proceedings, a right which reinforces the open justice principle.[38] An anonymity order cannot be granted merely because otherwise a witness would prefer not to give evidence.[39]

Arguments about media freedom in this context have understandably taken second place to arguments how to strike the right balance between fair trial rights and the need to protect witnesses. However, they might be made in a challenge to any measure taken by the court under its statutory powers to ensure that the identity of a witness granted anonymity is not disclosed in connection with any report of the proceedings.[40] The court may also support a grant of anonymity by issuing a direction under the provision in the Contempt of Court Act 1981, introduced to deal with the difficulty raised by the *Leveller* decision (see Extract 13.2.2 above).

(e) Contempt of Court Act 1981, section 11

Extract 13.4.3
Contempt of Court Act 1981, section 11

In any case where a court (having power to do so) allows a name or other matter to be withheld from the public in proceedings before the court, the court may give such directions prohibiting the publication of that name or matter in connection with the proceedings as appear to the court to be necessary for the purpose for which it was so withheld.

The provision does not clarify or extend the circumstances in which it is appropriate for a court to make an anonymity order in respect of a party or witness. The scope of that

---

[34] Ibid., paras 25–8 per Lord Hope.
[35] [2008] UKHL 36, [2008] 1 AC 1128.
[36] Article 6, 3(d) guarantees the right of anyone charged with a criminal offence 'to examine or have examined witnesses against him . . .'
[37] Sections 86–90.
[38] See the Court of Appeal in *R v Mayers* [200] EWCA Crim 2989, para 20. The decision is the leading authority on the interpretation of these provisions.
[39] Ibid., para 26.
[40] Coroners and Justice Act 2009, s 86.

power is determined by the existing common and statutory law considered above. If, but only if, the court exercises such power properly, it may further prohibit the media from publishing material covered by the anonymity order.[41] (However, the Youth Justice and Criminal Evidence Act 1999, section 46 gives the court power to restrict reports which would identify adult witnesses, for example, if a restriction is likely to improve the quality of evidence, otherwise diminished through fear or distress, even though that witness has not given evidence anonymously.) The *media* may appeal to the Court of Appeal against an order made under section 11, or against any order denying them access to legal proceedings or prohibiting them from reporting such proceedings: see Extract 12.4.6.

The scope of the section 11 power has been clarified in a handful of rulings. It cannot be used to stop the publication of a media report speculating on matter which might have been withheld in court proceedings. That would not amount to the publication of a name or other matter actually withheld.[42] Nor can the section be used to stop identification by the media of a defendant, when his name had not been withheld during a criminal trial.[43] The power supports a grant of anonymity; it is not an independent reporting restriction, similar to those discussed in the next section of this chapter. When, however, it is exercised appropriately, it may survive challenge on freedom of expression grounds. The European Commission dismissed a journalist's challenge to attend and report sentencing proceedings which had been held in private in order to safeguard the defendant's family.[44]

Questions for discussion

1. Do you agree with Lord Woolf MR that anonymity orders should be less readily granted to claimants, since in initiating proceedings they accept the likelihood of a public hearing?
2. In what circumstances should courts grant defendants anonymity? Should it be granted to protect a defendant from financial ruin, at least unless and until he has been convicted?
3. If a court grants an anonymity order, does it follow that it should also grant an order under section 11 of the Contempt of Court Act 1981?

13.5 RESTRICTIONS ON OPEN JUSTICE

A number of restrictions on open justice are imposed by statute, primarily to protect the privacy of the parties. Many of them concern the privacy and welfare of children; they are considered below in Sections 13.6 (criminal proceedings) and 13.7 (other proceedings, in particular family proceedings). This section discusses the principal restrictions on the open justice principle for the protection of adults. It should be emphasised that some provisions limit the access of the public and media to attend legal proceedings, while others restrict the freedom of the press and other media to report them. One might have expected that if proceedings are held in private, with access denied to the public and press, it automatically follows that the media are not free to report them, but that is not the position. It is clear

---

[41] No direction can be made in respect of a name or other material actually disclosed in court: *R v Arundel Justices, ex parte Westminster Press Ltd* [1985] 1 WLR 708 (DC).
[42] *Re Times Newspapers Ltd* [2007] EWCA Crim 1925, [2008] 1 All ER 343, para 31 per Lord Phillips CJ.
[43] *Re Trinity Mirror* (n. 30 above) paras 18–21.
[44] *Atkinson, Crook and the Independent* v UK (1990) 67 Decisions and Report 244.

from the terms of section 12 of the Administration of Justice Act 1960 (see Extract 13.5.3), as well as court decisions,[45] that the media are sometimes free to publish information concerning proceedings which are conducted in private. Equally, the press and public may be free to attend proceedings, and consequently to identify the parties, but there may be restrictions on their freedom to report them: see Section 13.5(c).

It is unclear whether there is any good explanation for this state of affairs. Reporting restrictions amount to a clearer interference with press freedom and the right of the public to receive information (guaranteed by ECHR, article 10) than do access restrictions. They also circumscribe the freedom of a party to proceedings who may want to reveal matters disclosed at a private hearing, perhaps to correct speculation or a false story about their character. Whatever the explanation, the divergence between the scope of access and reporting restrictions makes this area of media law exceptionally complex. A further introductory point is that courts must now take account not only of the competing Convention rights to respect for private life (ECHR, article 8) and freedom of the expression and the media (ECHR, article 10), but also of the right to a fair and public trial, guaranteed by ECHR, article 6 (see Extract 13.2.3). The correct balancing of these Convention rights has influenced court decisions in a number of leading English cases considered in this chapter, notably *Spencer* v *Spencer* (Extract 13.5.2) and *Re S* (Extract 13.6.1).

(a) Private hearings

As Viscount Haldane LC (and other Law Lords) intimated in *Scott* (Extract 13.2.1) the requirement that legal proceedings are open to the public is not absolute. Exceptions concerning trade secrets litigation and exercise of the wardship jurisdiction (now the inherent jurisdiction of the High Court with regard to children) have long been established by case law. Further, a few statutes enable the courts to sit in private for the whole or part of the proceedings. Evidence on sexual capacity in nullity proceedings should normally be heard in private, so reversing a major point in *Scott* itself.[46] The prosecution may apply to the court for it to hear the whole, or part, of proceedings under the official secrets legislation in private (see Extract 13.2.2).[47] Magistrates have discretion not to hear committal proceedings in public, where it appears 'that the ends of justice would not be served by their sitting in open court'.[48] Adoption proceedings in the High Court may, and in the County Court and Magistrates' Courts must, be heard in private.[49]

Under Rules (CPR) made under the Civil Procedure Act 1997 the general position is that a hearing should be in public, but the Rules provide that a hearing, or any part of it, may be conducted in private for a number of reasons: for example, if it involves national security matters or confidential information, if a private hearing is necessary to protect a child or patient, or more generally if publicity would defeat the object of the hearing or privacy is necessary in the interests of justice.[50] The opposite presumption applies to family proceedings. In *Re P-B (A Minor) (Child Cases: Hearings in Open Court)* the Court of Appeal held that, though a court has discretion to hear family proceedings in public, it is

---

[45] See in particular the decision of the Court of Appeal in *Clibbery* v *Allan* [2002] Fam 261.
[46] Matrimonial Causes Act 1973, s 48(2).
[47] Official Secrets Act 1920, s 8(4).
[48] Magistrates' Court Act 1980, s 4(2).
[49] Adoption and Children Act 2002, s 101; Magistrates' Courts Act 1980, s 69(3).
[50] SI 1998/3132: CPR r 39.2.

unlikely that it would hear evidence relating to the welfare of a child in open court.[51] As Thorpe LJ said in *Clibbery* v *Allan*,

> [i]n the family justice system, the designation 'in chambers' has always been accepted to mean strictly private. Judges, practitioners and court staff are vigilant to ensure that no one crosses the threshold of the court who has not got a direct involvement in the business of the day.[52]

However, the traditional privacy of family proceedings has been increasingly challenged in the last few years. The trend now is to allow greater openness, while protecting so far as possible the welfare and privacy of children involved in them.

In some circumstances, the law gives the press a general right of access to attend legal proceedings, from which members of the public may be excluded.[53] One example is a provision in the Magistrates' Courts Act 1980.

Extract 13.5.1
Magistrates Courts' Act 1980, section 69(2)

In the case of family proceedings in a magistrates' court other than proceedings under the Adoption and Children Act 2002, no person shall be present during the hearing and determination by the court of the proceedings except—

(a) officers of the court;
(b) parties to the case before the court . . . ;
(c) representatives of newspapers or news agencies;
(d) any other person whom the court may in its discretion permit to be present . . .

Under amendments to the Family Proceedings Rules made in 2009, 'duly accredited representatives of news gathering and reporting organizations' are allowed to attend family court proceedings conducted in private,[54] though under Rule 10.28(4) the court may exclude them when necessary in the interests of any child concerned in or connected with the proceedings, or for the safety of any party or witness in the proceedings, for their orderly conduct, or if otherwise justice will be impeded or prejudiced. The application of this new rule to family proceedings involving children will be discussed in Section 13.7, but their application to proceedings ancillary to a prominent society divorce was considered in *Spencer* v *Spencer*, where the judgment set out the convoluted origins of the rule. Proceedings involving the Countess and Earl Spencer attracted intense media interest. The judge noted that the new rules did not contain any provision about the reporting of private proceeding to which the media had access, although the parties would be free to apply for an injunction to stop their reporting; the court would then have to balance the Convention rights to privacy and to freedom of expression under the principles laid down by Lord Steyn in the House of Lords in *Re S* (see Extract 13.6.1).[55]

---

[51] [1997] 1 All ER 58, interpreting FPR r 4.16 (7) providing that a hearing shall be in chambers unless the court otherwise directs: see further, Section 7(a) below.
[52] See n. 45 above, para 93.
[53] Also see Children and Young Persons Act 1933, s 47(2). However, magistrates may now exclude the press from family proceedings, when they consider exclusion 'expedient in the interests of the child': Family Proceedings Court (Children Act 1989) Rules 1991 (SI 1991/1395), r 16(7), made under Children Act 1989, s 97(8).
[54] SI 2009/857, inserting new rule 10.28 into the FPR.
[55] It was also unlikely that AJA 1960, s 12 (Extract 13.5.3 below) would apply to ancillary divorce proceedings which would only indirectly involve children: *Spencer* v *Spencer*, paras 14–15.

Extract 13.5.2
Spencer v *Spencer* **[2009] EWHC 1529 (Fam), [2009] EMLR 25, paras 49–55, 59–66**

MUNBY J:

49. Can it be said that the media are to be excluded wholly from the generality of ancillary relief cases, whether proceeding in this Division or in other family courts? Surely not. That would be to set at naught the new public policy which underlies the recent change in the rules and would be to set at naught the clear statutory intention that the media should be allowed, as of right, to attend all such proceedings unless proper grounds can be shown for their exclusion within the limited circumstances identified in rule 10.28(4).

50. Is it then to be said that there is a justification for excluding the media from a case – and on one view of the arguments I have heard the present case comes very close to this – merely because the litigants in this case, unlike the litigants in an otherwise very similar case, are people in whom the media have an unusual interest? It seems to me that this is potentially dangerous, very dangerous, territory, because it has the potential to privilege one group of the community – those who attract the attention of the media – over and above another group who do not. Plainly the fact that the media are interested, if only because of the identity or character of the particular litigants rather than because of the nature of the underlying dispute, is a matter which is relevant. But it can hardly be determinative, unless we are to have one law for the celebrity and another law for those who live their lives in tranquillity and anonymity.

51. Mr. Mostyn put towards the forefront of his submissions the fact (and fact it is) that this is what he called a transitional case, that is to say a case where, as I have already mentioned, the petition was issued and the ancillary relief proceedings commenced long before the change in the law. He says that one must have regard to the fact that the driver for the change in the law was, as he suggests, concerns, particularly in the media, about so called 'secret' justice in the context of children cases – so the driving force behind the change in the law was not, he suggests, ancillary relief proceedings at all. He submits that the parties here, when they embarked upon these proceedings, had a legitimate, reasonable expectation of privacy and did not envisage that they would be overtaken by this radical change in the law. They would, he says, until very recently, have had every expectation that these proceedings would be carried on, as indeed they would have been before 27 April 2009, in private and without the attention of the media. That fact, he says, distinguishes this, and other transitional cases, from the general run of future ancillary relief cases where there will not of course be, at least in relation to those who issued their petition on or after 27 April 2009, any such expectation of privacy.

52. The fact, however, is that, although it may be that one of the major drivers, or indeed *the* major driver, behind the recent reform was perception of failings in the system so far as it related to children, the change actually implemented by the Family Proceedings (Amendment) (No. 2) Rules 2009 is quite clearly a change in relation to the rights of the media in relation to *all* family proceedings. It applies equally to ancillary relief proceedings as to children proceedings or, indeed, to any other type of family proceedings.

53. So far as concerns the argument based upon reasonable expectations, there is, as it happens, a feature in this case which, it seems to me, has to be borne in mind and reduces the extent to which the parties could in fact ever have had a confident expectation that the media would not be present.

54. As is well known, the Governmental process, culminating in the change of the law on 27 April 2009, began with the issue by the then Lord Chancellor, Lord Falconer, of a Green Paper 'Confidence and Confidentiality: Improving transparency and privacy in family courts', Cm 6886, which was published in July 2006 – that is, some two months *before* the petition was issued in the present case. In that consultation paper, the proposal put forward as reflecting Government policy was (see page 45) to 'pen up the family courts so that the media, in their role as a proxy

for the public, can attend all family courts as a matter of right, subject to the court's power to exclude if appropriate', a proposal, as was made clear, that would be applied 'in all family proceedings'. As is also well known, Lord Falconer performed what is popularly known as a U-turn when, in June 2007, he published a further Green Paper 'Confidence & confidentiality: Openness in family courts – a new approach', Cm 7131, announcing a radically different policy.

55. However, when his successor as Lord Chancellor, the Rt. Hon. Jack Straw MP, on 16 December 2008, issued the Government White Paper 'Family Justice in View', Cm 7502, he performed a second U-turn and, certainly so far as concerns the point with which I am currently concerned, in effect went back to the proposals announced as long ago as July 2006 by his predecessor. For, as was made clear in the White Paper, and in a statement which the Lord Chancellor made to the House of Commons the same day, the government's plan was (see page 31) to permit the media access to all family proceedings coupled with a judicial power to exclude in appropriate cases.

59. Whatever expectation or assumption the parties may have had in the present case, and I accept that, subject to the qualification I have mentioned, they did have at least some degree of expectation and hope until very recently that these proceedings would be held in private, that fact does not seem to me, either on its own or taken in conjunction with the other circumstances of the case, to suffice to bring the case within any of the relevant provisions of rule 10.28(4). To put it in Conventional terms, nor does either that consideration on its own or that consideration linked in with the other arguments based upon Article 8, suffice to tip the balance in favour of making the sweeping order which is sought, namely an order excluding the media altogether.

60. What then of the other important argument that this is a case which falls within at least one branch of the second limb of paragraph 5.4 in the Practice Direction? That in principle, as it seems to me, is a much more compelling argument if the factual premise which underlies that part of the Practice Direction is made out in the particular case. However, that feature is unlikely in the general run of such cases and certainly, in my judgment, in the present case is insufficient, to justify an order excluding the media from the proceedings altogether. This branch of paragraph 5.4 of the Practice Direction focusses upon the case of a specific witness who, there is credible reason to believe, will either not give evidence at all, or not give full or frank evidence, if the media are present. In other words if the case postulated by the Practice Direction arises it is, as it seems to me, properly a basis for excluding the media from that particular part of the proceedings where the condition is satisfied in relation to a particular witness. But it will not be in the general run of cases and in the present case certainly cannot be – indeed, I have some difficulty in seeing how it could ever realistically be – a reason for excluding the media from the hearing as a whole.

61. If it is to be said that this is a case in which a particular witness may be deterred from giving full and frank evidence because of the presence of the media, that is a matter to be considered further at the point when the problem arises. If a proper case for excluding the media is then demonstrated, the appropriate form of order is, in principle, an order requiring the media to remove themselves while that particular evidence is being given or that particular witness is giving evidence – rather than an order excluding them altogether.

62. At the end of the day, and leaving on one side the fact that this is a transitional case, this is in many ways, as both Mr. Mostyn and Mr. Marks were at pains to imply insofar as there is any such thing, a fairly routine big money case in this Division which involves no particular issues of principle or legal complexity. Is it to be said that, generally speaking, the media are to be excluded from such cases? Of course, every case must be determined on its own particular facts. As always, where the Convention applies, context is everything and, as Lord Steyn was at pains to point out in *In re S* at paragraph 17, the outcome in every such case will depend upon, and must be the result of, an 'intense focus' upon the circumstances of the particular case. However, that said, I cannot believe that it is consistent either with the legislative intent which lay

behind the change in the Rules nor consistent with the Rules themselves that the media should, as a matter of generality, be excluded from ancillary relief cases.

63. Truth be told, the only circumstance put forward in the present case for excluding the media from the hearing as a whole is the high public profile of the parties and the fact that they, unlike those who live less public lives, will be exposed, subject to whatever reporting restrictions there may be, to the publication of matters which they, no doubt like all litigants in ancillary relief proceedings, would prefer not to be exposed in public. It may be that, because of their public profile, they will not merely be exposed to the publication of facts and matters which they prefer to keep private, but also be exposed to comment of the kind which they would rather not be exposed to. But is that of itself to be a reason for making an order different from the order which one would make were that factor absent?

64. Of course, every case must depend upon its own particular facts. I am not, of course, suggesting that the fact of the public standing of the litigants in this particular case is an irrelevant consideration. Far from it. After all, one does not have to be unduly cynical to accept, fairly readily, the factual proposition which lies behind the argument that the media are present today only because of the identity of the parties involved. One could hardly move in the Royal Courts of Justice on 27 April 2009 without seeing some representative of the media, yet the fact is that the media, with the exception of only a few cases, have been conspicuously absent from family courts ever since. And certainly the fact is that, although I have been involved in ancillary relief cases since 27 April 2009, this is the first occasion that the media have appeared in my court in such a case – or, indeed, in any case. So I do not dispute, and am content to proceed on the basis of, the factual assumptions as to the reason for the media's interest which underlie the submissions from Mr. Marks and Mr. Mostyn.

65. But that is not, in my judgment, of itself sufficient to tip the balance. It is not, as the argument has so painfully demonstrated, sufficient to bring the case within any of the provisions of rule 10.28(4), save perhaps to a limited extent within the provisions of rule 10.28(4)(b) and even then only to the extent of perhaps justifying the exclusion of the media for part of the proceedings.

66. Accordingly, for all those reasons, as I announced this morning at the end of submissions, I refuse the only application which is currently before me – that is, the application that the media be excluded for the remainder of this hearing.

The judgment had an immediate impact. Counsel for the Countess indicated that he would apply for an injunction to stop any reporting of the proceedings, but before that could be considered, the parties applied for approval of a consent order under which the ancillary proceedings came to an end. Clearly the prospect of media publicity did not appeal to them.

The trend towards greater openness is also shown by a decision of the Court of Appeal,[56] upholding the permission granted by the Court of Protection for Independent News and Media to attend proceedings concerning the welfare of, and financial responsibilities for, a severely disabled adult, who nevertheless had become a musical prodigy. His life story had attracted considerable media interest. The Court of Appeal held that there was a legitimate public interest in the powers of the Court of Protection, and that this was a particularly appropriate hearing for the media to witness its processes.[57] The Court of Protection was right to permit the media to attend the hearing contrary to the wishes of the prodigy's relatives, despite the normal rule that its proceedings were heard in private.

---

[56] *Independent News and Media* v *A* [2010] EWCA Civ 343, [2010] EMLR 22.
[57] Ibid., para 23, per Lord Judge CJ. (The Court of Appeal was also composed of the Master of the Rolls and Sir Mark Potter, President of the Family Division.)

(b) Reporting of private proceedings

At common law the fact that a court sits in private does not necessarily prohibit the publication of information about those proceedings;[58] the media is free to publish information leaked, say, by one of the parties, unless perhaps it revealed trade secrets or concerned wards of court or mental patients.[59] The legal position is now governed by an important statutory provision, frequently discussed in court rulings on media freedom to report judicial proceedings.

Extract 13.5.3
Administration of Justice Act 1960 (AJA), section 12

12.—(1) The publication of information relating to proceedings before any court sitting in private shall not of itself be contempt of court except in the following cases, that is to say

(a) where the proceedings—
    (i)   relate to the exercise of the inherent jurisdiction of the High Court with respect to minors;
    (ii) are brought under the Children Act 1989; or
    (iii) otherwise relate wholly or mainly to the maintenance or upbringing of a minor;
(b) where the proceedings are brought under [certain provisions] of the Mental Health Act 1959 . . . ;
(c) where the court sits in private for reasons of national security during that part of the proceedings about which the information in question is published;
(d) where the information relates to a secret process . . . which is in issue in the proceedings;
(e) where the court (having power to do so) expressly prohibits the publication of all information relating to the proceedings or of information of the description which is published.

(2) Without prejudice to the foregoing subsection, the publication . . . of an order made by a court sitting in private shall not of itself be contempt of court except where the court (having power to do so) expressly prohibits the publication.

(3) [*Omitted*].

(4) Nothing in this section shall be construed as implying that any publication is punishable as contempt of court which would not be so punishable apart from this section.

The meaning of this complex provision has been clarified in a number of cases. In *Re F* the Court of Appeal allowed appeals by newspaper owners and editors who had been convicted of contempt when they published, without being aware of the connection, material which related to continuing wardship proceedings.[60] It ruled that the provision did not create a strict liability offence; the newspaper had to be aware that its publication related to proceedings held in private. On another important point, it was held that the term 'information relating to proceedings' in section 12(1) covered not only a report of the actual hearing, but documents such as the reports of the Official Solicitor and a social worker which were prepared for the court's use. Later decisions have established that the provision does not cover, or prevent the publication of, other information, such as the name of the parties or of children involved in the proceedings, or of the bare fact that private proceedings are taking place.[61]

---

[58] *Clibbery v Allan* [2002] Fam 261, para 51, per Dame Elizabeth Butler-Sloss, P.
[59] *Scott v Scott* [1913] AC 417, 444 per Earl Loreburn and 484 per Lord Shaw.
[60] The decision in *Re F* was approved by Lord Bridge in *Pickering v Liverpool Daily Post and Echo Newspapers plc* [1991] 2 AC 370, at 421–3 (HL).
[61] *Pickering v Liverpool Daily Post and Echo Newspapers* [1991] 2 AC 370, 421–3 per Lord Bridge; *Kelly v BBC* [2001] 1 All ER 323, 338–9 per Munby J; *Re B (A Child) (Disclosure)* [2004] EWHC 411 (Fam), [2004] 2 FLR 142, paras 68–82 per Munby J.

The courts have generally seemed anxious to limit the scope of AJA, section 12. Other statutory provisions, considered in Sections 13.6 and 13.7 below, prevent the media from identifying children involved in legal proceedings, while the courts have a jurisdiction, based on article 8 of the ECHR, to prevent unwarranted interferences with the privacy rights of individuals, whether adults or children (see the discussion of *Re S* (Extract 13.6.1 below). The availability of these other measures may have influenced the cautious approach of the courts to the application of section 12.

Two other Court of Appeal decisions should be mentioned to indicate judicial reluctance to impose reporting restrictions in respect of proceedings conducted in private. In *Hodgson* v *Imperial Tobacco Ltd*[62] it allowed an appeal against a 'gagging order' imposed by the judge to stop the parties and their advisers making comments to the media in relation to procedural directions he had issued in chambers in a controversial negligence action brought by cancer sufferers against cigarette manufacturers. Lord Woolf MR pointed out that a hearing in chambers was not identical to a private hearing, so the provision in the AJA did not apply; it was wrong for the judge to have made the 'gagging order', unless it was clearly necessary to safeguard the administration of justice. In *Clibbery* v *Allan*[63] the Court of Appeal held that family proceedings – here proceedings for an occupation order in respect of a flat owned by the appellant's company – could be heard in private, although no children were involved. However, the case did not concern the publication of confidential financial information disclosed to the court in the course of ancillary relief proceedings. None of the grounds for bringing contempt proceedings under the AJA applied. There was, therefore, no basis for any ban on *reporting* the proceedings, so the respondent, Glory Clibbery, was free to take her story, with extracts from an affidavit sworn by the appellant, to a newspaper for it to publish.

(c) Restrictions on reporting public proceedings

Under statute restrictions may be imposed on the reporting of all, or aspects of, judicial proceedings which are conducted in public. Some provisions give the court power to impose such a restriction when they consider this necessary for the administration of justice. One example is the power conferred by section 4(2) of the Contempt of Court Act 1981 to order that a report of proceedings be postponed to avoid a substantial risk of prejudice to those or to subsequent proceedings: see Section 12.4 above. Another example, discussed in Section 13.4(e), is the power under section 11 of the CCA 1981 to prohibit the reporting of a name or other matter withheld from the public in proceedings otherwise fully open to it.

Other statutory provisions impose automatic reporting bans, with perhaps a limited discretion for the court to dispense with it in specified circumstances. For example, only the bare details of committal proceedings or rulings at pre-trial hearing in summary proceedings before magistrates may be reported, for it is feared that otherwise the accused might be prejudiced by publication of the material, for example, evidence not introduced at the trial.[64]

Perhaps the best-known limit on media reporting protects the victims of rape and other sexual offences. They are entitled to anonymity. The initial statute (the Sexual Offences

---

[62] [1998] 2 All ER 673.
[63] See n 45 above.
[64] Magistrates' Courts Act 1980, ss 8–8C.

(Amendment) Act 1976) conferred anonymity only from the time a suspect was charged, but the law now protects the victim from the time the allegation was made. Originally confined to the victims of rape, anonymity was extended to the victims of a number of sexual offences in 1992. The protection is now contained in the Sexual Offences (Amendment) Act 1992, amended by the Youth Justice and Criminal Evidence Act 1999.

Extract 13.5.4
Sexual Offences (Amendment) Act 1992, section 1(1)

Where an allegation has been made that an offence to which this Act applies has been committed against a person, neither the name nor address, and no still or moving picture, of that person shall during that person's lifetime—
(a) be published in England and Wales in a written publication available to the public; or
(b) be included in a relevant programme for reception in England and Wales,
if it is likely to lead members of the public to identify that person as the person against whom the offence is alleged to have been committed.

The court may displace the anonymity rule in limited circumstances, for example, if a direction to that effect is necessary to induce potential witnesses to come forward and that without that direction the defence would be substantially prejudiced, or if the judge is satisfied that it is in the public interest to remove the restriction and that otherwise there would be a substantial and unreasonable restriction upon reporting.[65] However, the media are free to report the names and other details of the accused, unless publication is likely to lead to identification of the victim.[66]

One other statutory restriction should be mentioned. The Judicial Proceedings (Regulation of Reports) Act 1926 was introduced to some extent to placate George V, disgusted by the press publicity attending a prominent divorce case.[67] It bans the publication of any information in relation to divorce, nullity and judicial separation proceedings apart from the names and addresses of the parties, a concise statement of the charges and defences and the judge's summing up.[68] It also prohibits the publication in any judicial proceedings of any indecent matter or indecent medical or other details, '. . . the publication of which would be calculated to injure public morals'.[69] This latter provision is an unusual instance of a reporting ban imposed on grounds other than the privacy or welfare of individuals involved in the proceedings; it is unclear whether it would survive challenge now on freedom of expression grounds. The limit on reporting of divorce proceedings, etc. has had relatively little impact on press freedom, partly because the judge's summing up often referred to the parties' allegations in detail, and because divorce proceedings are invariably conducted in private – although the media may now be entitled to attend them under the recent change to the Family Proceedings Rules (see Section 13.5(a) above).[70]

---

[65] Sexual Offences (Amendment) Act 1992, s 3.
[66] The Criminal Justice Act 1988, s 158(5) repealed the provision in the 1976 legislation conferring anonymity on persons charged with rape.
[67] S. Cretney, ' "Disgusted, Buckingham Palace . . ." – The Judicial Proceedings (Regulation of Reports) Act 1926' (1997), 9 *Child and Family Law Quarterly* 43.
[68] Judicial Proceedings (Regulation of Reports) Act 1926, s 1(1)(b).
[69] Ibid., s 1(1)(a).
[70] Cretney (n. 67 above) 59–62. However, the Duchess of Argyll obtained an injunction to stop her husband publishing details of his divorce allegations against her on the basis of the 1926 Act; *Argyll* v *Argyll* [1967], Ch 302.

Questions for discussion

1. Does it make sense for the law to ban the access of the media to attend legal proceedings in some circumstances, but to impose no restriction on media reporting of these private proceedings?
2. Do you agree with the decision in *Spencer* v *Spencer*? Do the media have a legitimate interest in attending and reporting private family hearings involving celebrities such as the Spencers?
3. What arguments justify giving a victim of sexual offences anonymity? Why should an accused not enjoy the same protection from media publicity, at least unless and until he is convicted?

13.6 REPORTS OF PROCEEDINGS INVOLVING CHILDREN

(a) Introduction

The open justice principle is subject to a number of restrictions designed to protect children. While English law generally attaches much greater weight to open justice than it does to the privacy interests of adults, the reverse has seemed to be true with regard to children. The usual position is that a young person under the age of 18 cannot be named or identified in a report of criminal proceedings in which he is concerned as defendant, victim or witness (for further consideration, see Sections 13.6(b) and 13.6 below), while there have been significant restrictions on access to, and reporting of, family proceedings involving children (Section 13.7).

It is perhaps puzzling that the law draws this sharp distinction between the treatment of adults and children in this context. Why is it that the press is free to name an adult defendant in criminal proceedings for, say, burglary or arson, but cannot name or identify a co-defendant in the same proceedings, if he is under 18? On one view this position is incoherent; the protection afforded children suggests that the open justice principle can easily be sacrificed to accommodate privacy concerns.[71] On the other hand, there is the importance of allowing young people involved in criminal proceedings an opportunity to re-integrate in society as an adult, which might be endangered if they are named by the media. This interest has been recognised by international instruments, notably the UN Convention on the Rights of the Child (1989).[72] It may appear arbitrary to attach significant weight to this interest in respect of a defendant aged 16 or 17, but none at all in respect of a defendant aged 18 or 19, who may be just as immature and vulnerable as someone a little younger. However, the law has to draw lines in this context, as in others, even if that leads to results which appear hard to defend.

In the last few years the law has been much more careful to see that open justice is safeguarded so far as possible, even when the interests of children and young persons might be affected by media publicity. The relaxation of the absolute prohibition on media attendance at family proceedings is considered in Section 13.7. Here we should consider

---

[71] Jaconelli, 212–14.
[72] English courts have taken account of this Convention; see *McKerry* v *Teesdale and Wear Valley Justices* [2001] EMLR 5, paras 13–14 per Lord Bingham CJ; *R (On the Application of Y)* v *Aylesbury Crown Count* [2012] EWHC 1140 (Admin), [2012] EMLR 26, paras 35 per Hooper LJ (Extract 13.6.2 below).

the seminal decision of the House of Lords in *Re S (A Child)*,[73] a ruling of enormous importance in the context of media reporting of judicial proceedings affecting children. The mother of S, eight years old at the time of the proceedings, was charged with the murder of her other child. An order made in the course of the criminal proceedings against the mother under section 39 of the Children and Young Persons Act 1933 (see Section 13.6(b)) to prevent the identification of S was discharged on the ground that this provision did not apply; S was not a defendant, victim or witness in these proceedings. The question for the House of Lords was whether an injunction should be granted by the High Court to prohibit the publication of any material, including the names and photographs of his parents and of his dead brother, which would inevitably lead to the identification of S. In the only substantial speech in the House, Lord Steyn said that, after the HRA came into force, the courts had jurisdiction to protect the welfare of children in cases such as this on the basis of the Convention itself. The court need no longer refer to the complex case law on the inherent jurisdiction of the High Court to protect children.[74] The Court of Appeal had dismissed S's appeal from the decision of Hedley J, allowing various newspapers to identify the mother and to publish photographs of her and the dead brother.

Extract 13.6.1
Re S (A Child) (Identification: Restriction on Publication) **[2004] UKHL 47, [[2005] 1 AC 593, paras 30–8, HL**

LORD STEYN:

30. Dealing with the relative importance of the freedom of the press to report the proceedings in a criminal trial Hale LJ [dissenting in the Court of Appeal] drew a distinction. She observed (at para 56):

> The court must consider what restriction, if any, is needed to meet the legitimate aim of protecting the rights of CS. If prohibiting publication of the family name and photographs is needed, the court must consider how great an impact that will in fact have upon the freedom protected by Article 10. It is relevant here that restrictions on the identification of defendants before conviction are by no means unprecedented. The situation may well change if and when the mother is convicted. There is a much greater public interest in knowing the names of persons convicted of serious crime than of those who are merely suspected or charged. These considerations are also relevant to the extent of the interference with CS's rights.

I cannot accept these observations without substantial qualification. A criminal trial is a public event. The principle of open justice puts, as has often been said, the judge and all who participate in the trial under intense scrutiny. The glare of contemporaneous publicity ensures that trials are properly conducted. It is a valuable check on the criminal process. Moreover, the public interest may be as much involved in the circumstances of a remarkable acquittal as in a surprising conviction. Informed public debate is necessary about all such matters. Full contemporaneous reporting of criminal trials in progress promotes public confidence in the administration of justice. It promotes the values of the rule of law.

31. For these reasons I would, therefore, attribute greater importance to the freedom of the press to report the progress of a criminal trial without any restraint than Hale LJ did.
. . .

32. There are a number of specific consequences of the grant of an injunction as asked for in this case to be considered. First, while counsel for the child wanted to confine a ruling to the grant of an injunction restraining publication *to protect a child*, that will not do. The jurisdiction under the ECHR could equally be invoked by an adult non-party faced with possible damaging

---

[73] [2005] 1 AC 593.
[74] Ibid., paras 22–3.

publicity as a result of a trial of a parent, child or spouse. Adult non-parties to a criminal trial must therefore be added to the prospective pool of applicants who could apply for such injunctions. This would confront newspapers with an ever wider spectrum of potentially costly proceedings and would seriously inhibit the freedom of the press to report criminal trials.

33. Secondly, if such an injunction were to be granted in this case, it cannot be assumed that relief will only be sought in future in respect of the name of a defendant and a photograph of the defendant and the victim. It is easy to visualise circumstances in which attempts will be made to enjoin publicity of, for example, the gruesome circumstances of a crime. The process of piling exception upon exception to the principle of open justice would be encouraged and would gain in momentum.

34. Thirdly, it is important to bear in mind that from a newspaper's point of view a report of a sensational trial without revealing the identity of the defendant would be a very much disembodied trial. If the newspapers choose not to contest such an injunction, they are less likely to give prominence to reports of the trial. Certainly, readers will be less interested and editors will act accordingly. Informed debate about criminal justice will suffer.

35. Fourthly, it is true that newspapers can always contest an application for an injunction. Even for national newspapers that is, however, a costly matter which may involve proceedings at different judicial levels. Moreover, time constraints of an impending trial may not always permit such proceedings. Often it will be too late and the injunction will have had its negative effect on contemporary reporting.

36. Fifthly, it is easy to fall into the trap of considering the position from the point of view of national newspapers only. Local newspapers play a huge role. In the United Kingdom according to the website of The Newspaper Society there are 1301 regional and local newspapers which serve villages, towns and cities. Apparently, again according to the website of The Newspaper Society, over 85% of all British adults read a regional or local newspaper compared to 70% who read a national newspaper. Very often a sensational or serious criminal trial will be of great interest in the community where it took place. A regional or local newspaper is likely to give prominence to it. That happens every day up and down the country. For local newspapers, who do not have the financial resources of national newspapers, the spectre of being involved in costly legal proceedings is bound to have a chilling effect. If local newspapers are threatened with the prospect of an injunction such as is now under consideration it is likely that they will often be silenced. Prudently, the Romford Recorder, which has some 116,000 readers a week, chose not to contest these proceedings. The impact of such a new development on the regional and local press in the United Kingdom strongly militates against its adoption. If permitted, it would seriously impoverish public discussion of criminal justice.

. . .

37. In agreement with Hale LJ the majority of the Court of Appeal took the view that Hedley J had not analysed the case correctly in accordance with the provisions of the ECHR. I do not agree. In my view the judge analysed the case correctly under the ECHR. Given the weight traditionally given to the importance of open reporting of criminal proceedings it was in my view appropriate for him, in carrying out the balance required by the ECHR, to begin by acknowledging the force of the argument under article 10 before considering whether the right of the child under article 8 was sufficient to outweigh it. He went too far in saying that he would have come to the same conclusion even if he had been persuaded that this was a case where the child's welfare was indeed the paramount consideration under section 1(1) of the Children Act 1989. But that was not the shape of the case before him.

. . .

38. I would dismiss the appeal. The effect of the opinions delivered in the House today is that there is no injunction in respect of publication of the identity of the defendant or of photographs of the defendant or her deceased son.

The decision has been followed in a number of cases, where a court has declined to stop a newspaper from identifying an adult defendant in its report of criminal proceedings, even though its publication will be very distressing and painful for his children.[75] In a particularly complex case,[76] Munby J modified the terms of an injunction which had been granted to stop the publication of information relating to twin 8-year-old girls (both of whom suffered from a number of disabilities and were particularly vulnerable) and to their father, a reformed paedophile, in connection with the trial of the father's identical twin brother on charges of rape and indecent assault of young boys. The girls' father was a witness in his brother's trial. The injunction was maintained to stop the media reporting information relating to the two girls and their father's care for them, but was modified to enable the reporting of the criminal trial, except in so far as it referred to the two girls. However, they had to accept the risk that they might suffer indirectly as a result of reports of the criminal trial.[77] This judgment showed great care in balancing the girls' welfare against the public interest in full reporting of a criminal trial.

(b) Statutory restrictions on reporting proceedings concerning children

The Children and Young Persons Act 1933 (CYPA) has imposed restrictions on the reporting of legal proceedings involving children and young persons under 18. In the case of proceedings before youth (formerly juvenile) courts, that is, magistrates' courts dealing with criminal cases against young persons, there is an automatic ban on reporting which would disclose the name and other details identifying young persons concerned in them as defendant, victim or witness.[78] The Court has power to lift the ban in narrowly defined circumstances; in particular, following conviction of the child or young person, it may dispense with the restriction if it is in the public interest to do so.[79] In contrast, the protection of children involved in adult proceedings, whether as the accused, victim or witness has been more limited. Under section 39 of the 1933 legislation the Court has had a discretionary power to direct that reports and pictures identifying a young person under 18 should not be published; in the absence of a direction the media are free to publish such matters.[80] This provision applies to civil as well as criminal proceedings,[81] although their application to the latter is much more common. The distinction in principle between the two provisions is nicely illustrated in *Lee*,[82] where the Court of Appeal refused to review the lifting of an order which had restricted the identification of a boy, aged 14, convicted of robbery and (at an earlier trial) of rape. The Court of Appeal pointed out that the rule for adult proceedings is the reverse of that for proceedings in the Youth Court: there must be a good reason for imposing a restriction in the first place, rather than a justification for lifting a restriction on publicity.

---

[75] *R (On the Application of Gazette Media)* v *Teeside Crown Court* [2005] EWCA Crim 1983; *Re Trinity Mirror plc* [2008] EWCA Crim 50.

[76] *Re X and Y (Children)* [2004] EWHC 762 (Fam), [2004] EMLR 29.

[77] Ibid., para 96.

[78] Children and Young Persons Act 1933, s 49.

[79] Ibid., s 49(4A).

[80] Ibid., s 39(1).

[81] In *A (A Child)* v *Cambridge University Hospital NHS Foundation Trust* [2010] EWHC 454 (QB), [2011] EMLR 18, Tugendhat J made an order under s 39 CYPA directing the media not to identify a child in any report of the settlement of his personal injuries claim against the hospital.

[82] *R* v *Lee* [1993] 1 WLR 103.

The approach of the courts to the imposition of reporting bans under CYPA, section 39 is shown by a recent decision of the Divisional Court. On the application of a local newspaper, the Crown Court judge had varied an order restricting the publication of proceedings before him to allow the identification of a 16-year-old defendant who had pleaded guilty to an offence of arson in an area of High Wycombe. The police had supported the newspaper's application.

Extract 13.6.2
R (On the Application of Y) v Aylesbury Crown Court [2012] EWHC 1140 (Admin), [2012] EMLR 26, paras 18–19, 39–55

HOOPER LJ:

18. The judge's reasons for varying the order by allowing the publication of the claimant's name and address but not a photograph or other description appear, from this ruling, to have been two-fold:
i)   The claimant's identity is already known to local people;
ii)   The limited publication of the claimant's name and address together with the fact that he had pleaded guilty to one arson and sentenced accordingly would give the claimant, on his release, some protection from those who thought him to have been involved in more arsons.

19. It seems to us that neither reason is satisfactory. The fact that a defendant's identity is already known to some people in a locality is not necessarily a good reason for letting a very large number of others know about it. Secondly, it must be doubtful on the facts of this case whether it was permissible to allow publication in order, in some way, to help the claimant, particularly whilst at the same time letting many people know not only his name but also his address. In any event the judge did not, as he should have done, apply the relevant principles, to which we turn shortly. We would therefore quash the decision on the grounds of an error of law, namely the failure to give adequate reasons to justify the conclusion reached and the failure to apply the proper test.

. . .

39. How then should a court approach an application by a defendant to restrict publication under section 39?

40. The defendant will have to satisfy the court that there is a good reason to impose it. This is probably an evaluative exercise and would not involve the application of any burden or standard of proof (unless perhaps there is a factual dispute). See, for example, *O (FC) (Appellant)* v *Crown Court at Harrow* [2007] 1 AC 249, para 11.

41. In most cases the good reason upon which the defendant child or young person will rely is his or her welfare. Section 44 of the Children and Young Persons Act 1933 requires the court to have regard to his or her welfare when deciding a section 39 application. Having regard to the mandatory requirement of section 44, it is probably unnecessary to consider Article 8.

42. Because the defendant is a child or young person and not an adult, his or her future progress may well be assisted by restricting publication. Publication could well have a significant effect on the prospects and opportunities of the young person, and, therefore, on the likelihood of effective integration into society. Identifying a defendant in the media may constitute an additional and disproportionate punishment on the child or young person. In rare cases (and not in this case) the child or young person may be at serious personal risk if identified.

43. In reaching the decision upon an application by a defendant to restrict publication under section 39, the court must, in addition to having regard to the welfare of the child, have regard to the public interest and to Article 10 of the ECHR.

44. Amongst the possible public interests is the public interest in knowing the outcome of proceedings in court and the public interest in the valuable deterrent effect that the identification of those guilty of at least serious crimes may have on others.

45. In so far as Article 10 is concerned, in the words of the document entitled "Reporting Restrictions in the Crown Court", any order restricting publication must be necessary, proportionate and there must be a pressing social need for it.

46. The court must thus balance the welfare of the child or young person which is likely to favour a restriction on publication with the public interest and the requirements of Article 10 which are likely to favour no restriction on publication. Prior to conviction the welfare of the child or young person is likely to take precedence over the public interest. After conviction, the age of the defendant and the seriousness of the crime of which he or she has been convicted will be particularly relevant.

47. What the court should do is to identify the factors which would favour restriction on publication and the factors which would favour no restriction. The court may also decide, as the judge did in this case, to permit the publication of some details but not all.

48. If having conducted the balancing exercise between the welfare of the child or young person, on the one hand, and the public interest and the requirements of Article 10 on the other, the factors favouring a restriction on publication and the factors favouring publication are very evenly balanced, then it seems to us, for the reasons given by Lord Bingham CJ in *McKerry* v *Teesdale and Wear Valley Justices* [[2001] EMLR 5], that a court should make an order restricting publication.

49. We now apply this approach to this case.

50. Applying what we have set out in paragraph 42 above, it seems to us that the claimant's welfare would best be served by an order restricting publication.

51. Newsquest and the Thames Valley police submit that it is in the public interest to publish the claimant's name and address for the following reasons:

i)   the naming of the claimant would deter others 'from committing such a grave offence';
ii) the naming of the defendant is an additional necessary punishment for him;
iii) the naming not just of one offender but of both offenders demonstrates to the community that the police have done all that they could do in the face of a serious problem of gang related arson and intimidation and thus would restore the confidence of the community in the criminal justice system;
iv) the naming of not just one offender but of both offenders would encourage victims of arson attacks and other individuals, who are now frightened of the repercussions of coming forward, to feel confident about coming forward and give information about the some 100 other arsons.

52. It seems to us that each of these reasons given for identifying the claimant are reasons which a court would be entitled to take into account. In so far as (ii) is concerned, Simon Brown LJ appeared to accept in *R.* v *Winchester Crown Court* [[2001] 1 Crim App 11, Div Court] . . . that not making a section 39 order could be seen as part of the punishment.

53. If the claimant had been convicted of an offence or offences which showed that he was a party to a serious campaign of revenge arson, then it seems to us that a court would not make a section 39 order restricting publication.

54. But that is not this case. The claimant pleaded guilty to one count of simple arson committed when he was sixteen. Balancing the welfare of the claimant with the public interest, it seems to us that the public interest on the facts of this case does not take precedence. Most of the objectives sought by Newsquest and Thames Valley Police can be sufficiently met without naming the claimant.

55. We therefore allow the application and quash the decision.

The court referred to the ruling of the Divisional Court in *McKerry* v *Teesdale and Wear Valley Justices*,[83] in which it had dismissed an appeal against the decision of justices to lift reporting restrictions to allow the publication of the name (but not the address) of a young person of 15 who had pleaded guilty to a charge of taking a motor vehicle without consent. Although the Divisional Court thought there was no place for a policy of 'naming and shaming',[84] it declined to interfere with the decision of the magistrates, who had been influenced by the large number of the defendant's previous appearances before them; in their view he was a 'serious danger to the public'.[85] These two decisions perhaps indicate that the difference between the permissibility of full reporting in the two types of court proceedings is not as great in practice as it is in principle; the Divisional Court allowed the naming of an individual concerned in Youth Court proceedings, while it quashed the decision of the Crown Court judge allowing the naming of a young person involved in adult proceedings.

These reporting restrictions were tightened by provisions in the Youth Justice and Criminal Evidence Act 1999 (YJCEA). The 1933 legislation did not cover publicity before 'proceedings' began, a matter which was highlighted at the end of 1997 when it was unclear whether the press was free to identify the son of a Cabinet Minister suspected, but not charged, of a drugs offence. The YJCEA prohibits the publication of any 'matter relating to any person involved in [an] offence' while he is under 18 which is likely to identify him, whenever a criminal investigation has started in respect of an alleged offence.[86] However, it provides a defence, where a court is satisfied that the inclusion of the matter was in the public interest on the ground that otherwise the application of the prohibition would lead to a substantial and unreasonable restriction on reporting;[87] the defence does not apply where the young person was involved as a defendant, but is intended to cover the reporting of episodes such as the Dunblane shootings where there were a number of child victims.[88] Further, the provisions in the 1933 legislation restricting the reporting of criminal proceedings have been amended or replaced.[89] The press, however, persuaded the government not to bring these provisions into force, so the reporting restrictions in the 1933 legislation still apply.

Questions for discussion

1. Is the general ban on identifying persons under the age 18 involved in legal proceedings justifiable, given that there is no general restriction on naming adult defendants?
2. Do you agree with the decision of the House of Lords in *Re S*? Did Lord Steyn's speech show adequate concern for the welfare of the 8-year-old boy?
3. Was the Divisional Court right to quash the decision of the Aylesbury Crown Court?

---

[83] [2001] EMLR 5.
[84] Ibid., para 17.
[85] Ibid., para 24.
[86] Section 44. The ban covers publications identifying young persons as alleged victims of, or witnesses to the commission of, the offence, as well as suspects. The courts may dispense with the restriction if satisfied that is necessary in the interests of justice, taking into account the welfare of the young person involved.
[87] YJCEA, s 50(3).
[88] See Robertson and Nicol, para 8-034 for a full discussion on this point.
[89] CYPA s 49 has been amended by YJCEA Sch 2, and s 45 of the latter replaces CYPA s 39.

13.7 FAMILY PROCEEDINGS CONCERNING CHILDREN

(a) Introduction

The final section of the chapter discusses restrictions on access to, and the reporting of, family proceedings involving children. In this area of law there is often an acute conflict between the open justice principle and the privacy and welfare of children.[90] On the one hand, there are powerful arguments for the transparency of legal proceeding concerning the care of children and for public confidence in the ability of family courts to balance the claims of parents (which may themselves be in conflict) and the welfare of children involved in them. On the other hand there are understandable concerns that media publicity may discourage witnesses, including medical experts and social workers, from giving evidence or inhibit its frankness, and have an adverse impact on the welfare and development of children. The government has found it difficult to resolve this conflict: one Consultation Paper, issued in July 2006,[91] proposed greater openness in family proceedings, but another published a year later preferred to keep the traditional approach under which the media had no general right to attend family courts.[92] This ambivalence is perhaps reflected in the new rules on access to family courts introduced in 2009, which permit the media to attend their proceedings, but significantly qualify the entitlement in so far as children are concerned: this is discussed in Section 13.7(b) below.

Human rights arguments have exercised an important influence on judicial reasoning in this area of law. Courts must balance the competing rights under the Convention to freedom of expression and the media (ECHR article 10) and to respect for family and private life (ECHR article 8). The courts have recognised that parents and children may all claim the right to freedom of expression to reveal their stories to the media, although these rights must be balanced against the rights of other parties to have their privacy respected, so that their identity is not disclosed to the press and by it to the general public.[93] Article 6 of the Convention (Extract 13.2.3) is important in this context, as in others concerning the open justice principle. In *B v UK* the European Court of Human Rights held that there was no violation of article 6 when a county court heard an application by two fathers for residence orders under the Children Act 1989 in private.[94] Although article 6 guaranteed the right to a fair and public trial, that entitlement could be qualified to protect the interests of children or the private life of the parties or to avoid prejudice to the interests of justice. Further, it was legitimate for state law to designate an entire class of case as an exception to the general rule of open justice. It is therefore legitimate under the Convention to have special rules for family proceedings involving children, as is the case in English law. However, the Strasbourg Court emphasised that the Family Proceedings Rules did give the courts discretion to hold proceedings under the Children Act in public;[95] it is not clear whether it would have upheld an absolute rule for private hearings.

---

[90] For a discussion of this conflict, see M. Hanna, 'Irreconcilable differences: the attempts to increase media coverage of family courts in England and Wales' [2012] 4 *Journal of Media Law* 274–308.

[91] *Confidence and Confidentiality: Improving Transparency and Privacy in Family Courts*, Department of Constitutional Affairs Consultation Paper 11/06.

[92] *Openness in Family Courts – A New Approach*, Department of Constitutional Affairs Consultation Paper 10/07.

[93] *Kelly* v *BBC* [2001] 1 All ER 323, Munby J: *Re Angela Roddy (A Minor)* [2003] EWHC 2927 (Fam), [2004] EMLR 8, *Re Webster (A Child)* [2006] EWHC 2733, [2007] EMLR 7 (Extract 13.7.1).

[94] (2001) 11 BHRC 667, (2002) 34 EHRR 19. (The court upheld as compatible with the Convention the decision of the Court of Appeal in *Re P-B* (n 51 above)).

[95] Ibid., para 40.

(b) Media access to family proceedings concerning children

The approach of the family courts to media applications to attend these proceedings can be illustrated first by discussing the decision of Munby J, an enormously influential judge in this area of law, in *Re Webster (A Child)*.[96] The case concerned an application by the BBC and Associated Newspapers to attend, and to challenge drastic restrictions on the reporting of, care proceedings which had been brought by Norfolk County Council in respect of an infant boy, Brandon; three other children of his parents had already been taken into care and had later been adopted, following allegations of physical abuse by their parents. The allegations had always been denied by the parents, who claimed they had been the victims of a miscarriage of justice; their arguments had attracted considerable media publicity. Extract 13.7.1 discusses the principles to be applied in considering applications by the media to attend care proceedings, and the reasons Munby J relaxed the reporting restrictions imposed by Judge Curl (sitting as a High Court judge).

Extract 13.7.1
Re Webster (A Child) **[2006] EWHC 2733 (Fam), [2007] EMLR 7, paras 73–8, 99–104, 115**

MUNBY J:

73. Very recently the Strasbourg court has returned to the issue in *Moser* v *Austria* [2006] 3 FCR 107. That was a case in which the applicant's son had been taken into public care. The court held that there had been a breach of Article 6, inter alia on the ground that the hearing had not been in public. The court's reasoning is to be found in paras [96]–[97] (citations omitted):

'[96] The Court considers that there are a number of elements which distinguish the present case from *B* v *United Kingdom*. In that case, the Court attached weight to the fact that the courts had discretion under the Children Act to hold proceedings in public if merited by the special features of the case and a judge was obliged to consider whether or not to exercise his or her discretion in this respect if requested by one of the parties. The Court noted that in both cases the domestic courts had given reasons for their refusal to hear the case in public and that their decision was moreover subject to appeal. The Court notes that the Austrian Non-Contentious Proceedings Act now in force gives the judge discretion to hold family-law and guardianship proceedings in public and contains criteria for the exercise of such discretion. However, no such safeguards were provided for in the 1854 Non-Contentious Proceedings Act. It is therefore not decisive that the applicant did not request a public hearing, since domestic law did not provide for such a possibility and the courts' practice was to hold hearings in camera.

[97] Moreover, the case of *B* v *United Kingdom* concerned the parents' dispute over a child's residence, thus, a dispute between family members, i.e. individual parties. The present case concerns the transfer of custody of the first applicant's son to a public institution, namely the Youth Welfare Office, thus, opposing an individual to the State. The Court considers that in this sphere, the reasons for excluding a case from public scrutiny must be subject to careful examination. This was not the position in the present case, since the law was silent on the issue and the courts simply followed a long-established practice to hold hearings in camera without considering the special features of the case.'

74. I draw attention to the important distinction here drawn by the Strasbourg court between (to use our terminology) private law cases and public law cases. There are two aspects of the latter which in the present context, as it seems to me, are of fundamental importance. The first I have already touched upon. In a public law case the State – public authority – is seeking to intrude into family life and, indeed, very frequently is seeking to remove children from their families. The second is the point I made in *Re B (A Child) (Disclosure)* [2004] EWHC 411 (Fam), [2004] 2 FLR 142, at para [101]:

---

[96] [2006] EWHC 2733 (Fam), [2007] EMLR 7.

'As I pointed out in *Re L (Care: Assessment: Fair Trial)* [2002] EWHC 1379 (Fam), [2002] 2 FLR 730, at para [150]:

"... it must never be forgotten that, with the state's abandonment of the right to impose capital sentences, orders of the kind which judges of this Division are typically invited to make in public law proceedings are amongst the most drastic that any judge in any jurisdiction is ever empowered to make. It is a terrible thing to say to any parent – particularly, perhaps, to a mother – that he or she is to lose their child for ever."

When a family judge makes a freeing or an adoption order in relation to a 20-year-old mother's baby, the mother will have to live with the consequences of that decision for what may be upwards of 60 years, and the baby for what may be upwards of 80 years. We must be vigilant to guard against the risks.'

75. Just as I make no apology for repeating that observation, I make no apology for repeating what I said more recently in *Re X, London Borough of Barnet* v *Y and X* [2006] 2 FLR 998. Referring at para [166] to public law care cases, I said:

'Such cases, by definition, involve interference, intrusion, by the State, by local authorities, into family life. It might be thought that in this context at least the arguments in favour of publicity – in favour of openness, public scrutiny and public accountability – are particularly compelling.'

76. How then is the exercise required by *B* v *United Kingdom* (2001) 34 EHRR 529, [2001] 2 FLR 261, and by *Moser* v *Austria* [2006] 3 FCR 107 to be undertaken? By reference to what criteria is a judge to decide whether or not to accede to an application to disapply rule 4.16(7)? The answer can only be that the judge must apply the Convention, ensuring that his decision is Convention-compliant. Rule 4.16(7), after all, falls to be justified in accordance with the Article 6(1) tests of what is "required" or (as the case may be) what is 'strictly necessary'. And, as the decisions of the Strasbourg court in both *B* v *United Kingdom* (2001) 34 EHRR 529, [2001] 2 FLR 261, and *Moser* v *Austria* [2006] 3 FCR 107 make clear, such a blanket rule can be justified only if it remains 'subject to the court's control' and only if the court exercises a proper discretion in the circumstances of the particular case. Moreover in a public law case, as *Moser* v *Austria* [2006] 3 FCR 107 makes clear, 'the reasons for excluding a case from public scrutiny must be subject to careful examination' and the judge must 'consider . . . the special features of the case'.

77. In short the judge must, as it seems to me, adopt precisely the same 'parallel analysis' leading to the same 'ultimate balancing test', as described in *In re S* and *W*, which is applicable in deciding whether to relax on enhance reporting restrictions. I agree, therefore, with Mr Wolanski, when he submitted that rule 4.16(7) is properly to be regarded simply as a 'default provision' but not as a provision indicating some heavy presumption in favour of privacy. In my judgment, rule 4.16(7) must be read, construed and applied compatibly with the Convention. Once the point has been raised, the outcome must be determined in accordance with the Convention, 'balancing' all the various interests which are engaged and *not* giving any special pre-eminence to the claim to privacy. Moreover, and as Thorpe LJ pointed out, a judge must be alert to the dangers inherent in what he called the 'strong inherited convention of privacy' and careful not to be 'prejudiced by the tradition or an unconscious preference for the atmosphere created by a hearing in chambers'.

78. In relation to this last point, it is perhaps worth pointing out that 'representatives of newspapers or news agencies' have a statutory right under section 69(2)(c) of the Magistrates' Courts Act 1980 to attend hearings of the Family Proceedings Court except in the case of adoption proceedings or where the court has made an order either under section 69(4) (which permits the exclusion of the press if it is 'necessary in the interest of the administration of justice or of public decency' to exclude them 'during the taking of any indecent evidence') or under rule 16(7) of the Family Proceedings Courts (Children Act 1989) Rules 1991, SI 1991/1395 (which permits their exclusion 'if the court considers it expedient in the interests of the child'). So if the present care proceedings were still before the Family Proceedings Court the press would have a statutory *right* to be present!

. . .

99. Four factors in particular weigh heavily in my judgment in favour of the view that any greater degree of restraint than that which is being proposed by the applicants will indeed constitute a disproportionate – a significant and heavily disproportionate – interference with their rights: the claim that the case involves a miscarriage of justice, the parents' own wish for publicity, the very extensive publicity there has already been, and the need, in the circumstances, for the full facts and the 'truth' – whatever it may be – to emerge, and, moreover, to emerge in a way which will command public confidence. Two of these factors require a little elaboration.

100. As I observed in *Re B (A Child) (Disclosure)* [2004] EWHC 411 (Fam), [2004] 2 FLR 142, at para [99], parents – like the mother in that case and the parents in the present case – often want to speak out publicly. I repeat in this context the point I made in *Re Roddy (A Child) (Identification: Restriction on Publication)* [2003] EWHC 2927 (Fam), [2004] 2 FLR 949 at para [83]. In my judgment, the workings of the family justice system and, very importantly, the views about the system of the mothers and fathers caught up in it, are, as Balcombe LJ put it in *Re W (Wardship: Discharge: Publicity)* [1995] 2 FLR 466 at 474, 'matters of public interest which can and should be discussed publicly'. Many of the issues litigated in the family justice system require open and public debate in the media. I repeat what I said in *Harris v Harris; Attorney-General v Harris* [2001] 2 FLR 895 at paras [360]–[389] about the importance in a free society of parents who feel aggrieved at their experiences of the family justice system being able to express their views publicly about what they conceive to be failings on the part of individual judges or failings in the judicial system. And I repeat in this context what I said in the same case at para [368]:

> 'The freedom to publish things which judges might think should not be published is all the more important where the subject of what is being said is the judges themselves. Any judicial power to punish such publications requires the most cogent justification. Even more cogent must be the justification for giving the judges a power of prior restraint.'

101. The fact that the parents may not be the martyrs they claim to be – something which I am in absolutely no position to assess and on which I express no views at all – the fact that it may turn out that there was no miscarriage of justice, is not of itself any reason for denying the parents their voice.

102. In the first place, and in the very nature of things, the initial 'official' response to any allegation that there has been a miscarriage of justice is likely to be one of scepticism or worse. But that, it might be thought, is all the more reason why there should *not* be restraint, why the media should not be hindered in their vital role. I repeat what Lord Steyn said in *Simms*: 'In principle it is not easy to conceive of a more important function which free speech might fulfil.'

103. Moreover, freedom of speech is not something to be awarded to those who are thought deserving and denied to those who are thought undeserving. As Lord Oliver of Aylmerton robustly observed in *Attorney-General v Guardian Newspapers Ltd and Others; Attorney-General v Observer Ltd and Others; Attorney-General v Times Newspapers Ltd and Another* [1987] 1 WLR 1248 at page 1320:

> '. . . the liberty of the press is essential to the nature of a free state. The price that we pay is that that liberty may be and sometimes is harnessed to the carriage of liars and charlatans, but that cannot be avoided if the liberty is to be preserved.'

It is, after all, the underdog who is often most in need of the help afforded by a fearless, questioning and sceptical press.

104. The other element of great importance, as it seems to me, in the present case, is what I have referred to as the public interest in maintaining the confidence of the public at large in the courts and, specifically, in the family justice system. This is not merely a point of general application. It has, at it seems to me, a particular resonance in this particular case. Rightly or wrongly, correctly or otherwise – and for present purposes it matters not which – the media have

suggested that the parents and their children A, B and C have been, and that the parents and Brandon are at risk of being, the victims of a miscarriage of justice. In these circumstances there is a pressing need for public confidence to be restored – either by the public and convincing demonstration that there has *not* been a miscarriage of justice or, as the case may be, by public acknowledgement that there has been. That is not, of course, the purpose of the current proceedings, and it is very possible that the outcome of the judicial process, whatever it may be, will not be a clarity and certainty that all will accept. But as few obstacles as possible should be placed in the way of the media doing their job. For in the proper exercise by the media of their investigative and other functions there exists perhaps the best chance of the truth, whatever it may be, emerging at the end of the day. And that, at least in the circumstances of this case, points to the media having access not merely to more information than Judge Curl's order would permit them but access also to the forthcoming hearing.

. . .

115. I appreciate that the effect of the order I am proposing to make is that the family's true name – Webster – will for the first time be publicly known. But it seems to me that this alone will have little if any discernible impact upon Brandon. His first name and his photograph are already in the public domain, and those 'in the know' and, I suspect, many in his local community are well aware that Mr and Mrs Hardingham (as they have hitherto been referred to) are in fact Mr and Mrs Webster. There is, in my judgment, no disproportionate interference with Brandon's rights in permitting him and his parents to be identified by their true name. On the other hand, and in the particular circumstances of this case, it would, in my judgment, be a disproportionate interference with the parents' rights to deny them what they want, the right not merely to argue their case in public but to do so under their true name and not under a pseudonym.

In 2009 the Family Proceedings Rules (FPR) were amended[97] to permit 'duly accredited representatives of news gathering and reporting organizations'[98] to attend family proceedings held in private, although a court may direct that they do not attend them, or any part of them, when it is satisfied that this in the interests of a child concerned in or connected with the proceedings. (A direction may also be issued on other grounds in family cases where no children are concerned: see *Spencer* v *Spencer* (Extract 13.5.2 above). The amendments did not, however, make any new provision with regard to the reporting of family proceedings with respect to which the media may now have access.[99]

The principles to be applied in determining whether the media should be excluded in proceedings involving children were considered in *Re X (A Child)*,[100] from which Extract 13.7.2 is taken. The applicant father was a celebrity known both in this country and abroad, while the respondent mother had also been the focus of media attention. The father had brought residence and contact proceedings in respect of his young daughter, X, who lived with her respondent mother. The application of both parents to exclude the media was supported by evidence from a consultant child and adolescent psychiatrist and from a child welfare officer. In his judgment Sir Mark Potter, President of the Family Division, pointed out that even if the media were free to attend the private proceedings, they would not be entitled under AJA 1960, section 12 (Extract 13.5.3) to report the evidence, or to

---

[97] SI 2009//857, introducing new Rule 10.28 into the FPR.
[98] Rule 10.28(3)(f).
[99] The Children, Schools and Families Act 2010 introduced a very restrictive scheme for reporting family proceedings, but in the light of criticism of its provisions the Coalition government decided not to bring them into force: see L. Reed, 'Publication of information: Children, Schools and Families Act 2010' [2010] *Fam Law* 708, and Hanna (n 90 above) 294–5.
[100] [2009] EWHC 1728 (Fam), [2009] EMLR 26.

identify any child involved in the proceedings: Children Act 1989, section 97(2), considered in Section 7(c) below. The result of the amendment to the FPR might be that the media exercise a 'watchdog' role on behalf of the public, but 'are unable to report in their newspapers or programmes the identity of the parties or the details of the evidence which are likely to catch the eye and engage the interest of the average reader or viewer'.[101]

Extract 13.7.2
Re X (A Child) (Residence and Contact – Rights of Media Attendance) **[2009] EWHC 1728 (Fam), [2009] EMLR 26, paras 51–9**

SIR MARK POTTER P:

51. By way of general observation it is important to make the following matters clear. First, private law family cases concerning the children of celebrities are no different in principle from those involving the children of anyone else. An application by a celebrity who happens also to be a parent who is unable to agree with a former spouse or partner over the appropriate arrangements for their child(ren) is not governed by any principle or assumption more favourable to the privacy of the celebrity than that applied to any other parent caught up in the court process. In this respect, and in very different circumstances concerning the publication of the identity of a barrister who had been convicted of criminal offences, (*Crawford* v *CPS* [2008] EWHC 854 (Admin)), Thomas LJ rejected the submission that, in conducting the *Re S* balancing exercise there involved the Court should have regard to the public profile of the appellant:

> '[34] That is because it is fundamental that all persons are equal before the law of England and Wales, as embodied in our common law, our legislation and the Conventions to which this party (*sic*) has subscribed.

> [35] No person in this country can enjoy a different status because he holds a public position. It is important to stress that.'

52. However, in considering whether or not to exclude the press under Rule 10.28(4)(a)(i), the focus is upon the interests of the child and not the parents. It is almost axiomatic that the press interest in and surrounding the case will be more intense in the case of children of celebrities; and the need for protection of the child from intrusion or publicity, and the danger of leakage of information to the public will similarly be the more intense.

53. Second, Rule 10.28 provides that, in order to exclude the press on any of the grounds stated, the Court must be satisfied that it is *necessary* to do so. That is wording which picks up and reflects the provisions of the Convention relevant to the balancing act which the Court has to perform as set out in Articles 6(1), 8(2) and 10(2) of the Convention. We are here concerned with a restriction on the freedom of expression of the media under Article 10(1), (namely the right to receive and impart information and ideas without interference) for the purpose of the protection of the rights of the child to respect for her private and family life.

54. So far as necessity is concerned, as stated in *R* v *Shayler* [2003] 1 AC 247, 268, *per* Lord Bingham at para [23]:

> '"Necessary" has been strongly interpreted; it is not synonymous with "indispensable", neither has it the flexibility of such expressions as "admissible", "ordinary", "useful", "reasonable" or "desirable": *Handyside* v *United Kingdom* (1976) 1 EHRR 737, 754 para 48. One must consider whether the interference complained of corresponds to a pressing social need, whether it is proportionate to the legitimate aim pursued and whether the reasons given by the national authority to justify it are relevant and sufficient under Article 10 (2): *The Sunday Times* v *United Kingdom* (1979) 2 EHRR 245, 277–278 para 62.'

55. Third, since the ECHR has already held FPR Rule 4.16(7) to be Convention-compliant in a form which effectively excluded the press from admission, the introduction of a provision which gives the media the clear *prima facie* right to be present during the proceedings, subject only

---

[101] Ibid., para 38.

to exclusion on limited grounds is plainly Convention-compliant from the point of view of the media's Article 10 rights. In the light of the wording of Rule 10.28(4) and the Convention jurisprudence, the question of necessity in respect of the derogations from those rights must be approached on the basis set out by Lord Bingham above, in the context of the particular facts of the case, and with an eye to the question whether any information received in confidence is involved and therefore at risk by reason of press attendance . . .

56. Fourth, so far as the Practice Direction of 20 April 2009 is concerned, its reference to the exercise of the Court's *discretion* to exclude media representatives from all or part of the proceedings is, strictly speaking, not accurate. In *Interbrew SA* v *Financial Times* [2002] EWCA Civ 274 [2002] 2 Lloyd's Rep 229 at para [58] Sedley LJ made clear that where the Court has a duty to apply a test of necessity in relation to a series of questions as to legitimacy and proportionality the duty of the Court is to proceed though the balancing exercise making a value judgment as to the conflicts which arise rather than to regard the matter simply as an exercise of discretion as between two equally legitimate courses. Thus references to the Court's discretion in paragraph 3.1 and in the heading to paragraph 5 in the Practice Direction dated 20 April 2009 are a misnomer. Nonetheless, the balancing act involved in the weighing of the conflicting but interlocking rights and restraints embodied in Article 10 and Article 8 of the Convention are highly fact sensitive from case to case. Thus, in performing the necessary balancing act, and in particular the ultimate test of proportionality, it is the Judge dealing with the case who is the person best placed to make the necessary decision.

57. Fifth, the burden of satisfying the Court of the grounds set out in Rule 10.28 (4) is upon the party or parties who seek exclusion, or the Court itself in a case where it takes steps of its own motion, to exclude the press. This will be an easier burden to satisfy in the case of temporary exclusion in the course of the proceedings, in order to meet concerns arising from the evidence of the particular witness or witnesses.

58. Sixth, in deciding whether or not the grounds advanced for exclusion are sufficient to override the presumptive right of the press to be present and in particular whether or not an order for total exclusion is proportionate, it will be relevant to have regard to the nature and sensitivities of the evidence and the degree to which the watchdog function of the media may be engaged, or whether its apparent interests lie in observing, and reporting on matters relating to the child which may well be the object of interest, in the sense of curiosity, on the part of the public but which are confidential and private and do not themselves involve matters of public interest properly so called. However, while this may be a relevant consideration, it in no sense creates or places any burden of proof or justification upon the media. The burden lies upon the applicant to demonstrate that the matter cannot be appropriately dealt with by allowing the press to attend, subject as they are to the statutory safeguards in respect of identity and under the provisions of s.12 of the 1960 Act.

59. Moving to the question of the balancing exercise in this case, I have no doubt that, so far as the imminent hearing is concerned, a direction should be made that the media should be excluded from attending the proceedings, or any part of them, on the basis that such exercise is necessary in the interests of X as the child concerned in the proceedings: Rule 10.28(4)(a)(i). Also upon the basis that justice will otherwise be impeded: Rule 10.28(4)(b).

Sir Mark Potter P, was influenced by the consideration that media attendance would undermine the confidentiality of the exchanges between X and her psychiatrist and care officer and so endanger her long-term welfare. Reporting restrictions under the AJA and other legislation would not prevent that harm, nor would they apply to any reporting in the foreign media, which took some interest in the proceedings.[102] So he decided to exclude the media entirely from attending them.

---

[102] Ibid., paras 66–7.

(c) Reporting of family proceedings concerning children

The provision in the AJA (Extract 13.5.3) under which it may be a contempt of court to publish information about proceedings held in private clearly applies to proceedings concerning minors. A court may issue directions to ban reporting under section 39 of the Children and Young Persons Act 1933, which applies to civil (including family) proceedings as it does to criminal trials. Further, section 97(2) of the Children Act 1989 prohibits any publication intended, or likely, to identify any child involved in proceedings before the High Court, County Court, or a Magistrates' Court in which any power under that Act or the adoption legislation may be exercised in respect of any child.[103] This provision does not apply, however, to publications *after* the proceedings have been terminated. In *Clayton* v *Clayton*,[104] the Court of Appeal ruled that section 97(2) should be interpreted restrictively under section 3 of the Human Rights Act 1998 to conform with the right to freedom of expression; media freedom would be unduly restricted if the ban were not limited to the duration of the proceedings. However, the contempt of court provision in the AJA continues to apply after they had ended. Moreover, an application could always be made to the court for an injunction to stop a publication infringing the privacy of a child involved in judicial proceedings; the court would balance that right against the right to freedom of expression on the basis of the principles formulated by Lord Steyn in *Re S* (Extract 13.6.1 above).

(d) Anonymity of witnesses

Doctors and social workers giving evidence in family proceedings concerning children have sometimes claimed that they are entitled to anonymity. Their argument is that otherwise experts will be reluctant to assist the courts and may be inhibited from giving full and frank evidence. Against that point, there is a strong public interest in identifying discredited medical experts as well as in the general principle of open justice. The courts have refused to recognise that professional witnesses have a personal right to confidentiality in this context, though they have been prepared to grant anonymity in exceptional cases when this is in the public interest.[105] In *BBC* v *Rochdale MBC* Ryder J declined to grant a local authority, which had applied on behalf of two social workers, an injunction to stop the BBC from revealing their names, or any material leading to their identification, in a documentary about a notorious 'Satanic abuse' case which had occurred 15 years previously.[106] The judge in the earlier wardship proceedings had granted the social workers anonymity, as publication of their names then might have led to identification of the children involved. However, Ryder J held it would be wrong to grant in effect a permanent injunction, now that the wards were adult and were willing to talk about their experiences. Their rights and that of the BBC under ECHR article 10 reinforced by the public interest in scrutiny of the courts (ECHR article 6) trumped the social workers' rights under ECHR article 8.[107]

---

[103] Under s 97(4) a court may dispense with the ban, if dispensation is required by the 'welfare of the child'. This power must be construed generously in conformity with the right to freedom of expression: *Re Webster* (Extract 13.7.1 above), paras 57–62 per Munby, J.

[104] [2006] EWCA Civ 878, [2007] EMLR 3.

[105] *Re B(A Child) (Disclosure)* [2004] EWHC 411, [2004] 2 FLR 142.

[106] [2005] EWHC 2862 (Fam), [2006] EMLR 6.

[107] Ibid., paras 70–1.

The anonymity of expert witnesses has now been fully considered by the President of the Family Division in *Re X, Y and Z: Morgan* v *A Local Authority*.[108] Sir Nicholas Wall P, granted an application by Brian Morgan, a freelance journalist, for the media to name Dr M, a paediatrician whose report had been considered by the court in care proceedings. Though the President heard powerful arguments on behalf of the Royal College of Paediatrics and Child Health for anonymity, he was not persuaded that they outweighed the need for transparency in the family justice system. Conscientious expert medical witnesses should not be discouraged by the requirement of openness from giving evidence.[109] Anonymity, however, would be preserved, if disclosure of their name would discourage a child from participating in the process or undermine confidential relations between the child and doctors.[110] It was also held that Dr M's report could be published, appropriately edited to remove the names of the children or their parents. His report had been criticised by the judge in the care proceedings, so Sir Nicholas ruled that it should be published for there to be a real public debate about its merits. Two points emerge from this important ruling. First, witness anonymity will only be granted when this is necessary to protect the welfare of children involved in the proceedings. Second, the order that the report could be published shows that courts are willing to dispense with the AJA ban on reporting details of private proceedings (see Section 5(b) above). The statute is applied in conformity with freedom of expression and the values of public debate.

Questions for discussion

1. How should the importance of transparency in the family justice system and the privacy and welfare of children be balanced?
2. What is the point of allowing the press access to family proceedings, unless it is allowed fully to report them?
3. Should the courts be more willing to allow expert medical and other witnesses anonymity, because otherwise they might be reluctant to give evidence or submit a report?

Selected further reading

Open justice principle

J. Jaconelli, *Open Justice: A Critique of the Public Trial* (Oxford: OUP, 2002) esp. chs 1–3 and 5 examine the arguments for the open justice principle and the extent to which adherence to the principle is qualified.

B. McLachlin PC, 'Courts, transparency, and public confidence – to the better administration of justice' (2003) 8 *Deakin Law Rev* 111 is a stimulating discussion of the importance of open justice by a former Chief Justice of the Supreme Court of Canada.

J.J. Spigelman AC, 'The principle of open justice – a comparative perspective' (2006) 29 *University of New South Wales Law Journal* 147–66 suggests there is a close link between press freedom and open justice.

---

[108] [2011] EWHC 1157 (Fam), [2011] EMLR 26.
[109] Ibid., paras 74–85.
[110] Ibid., para 87.

Cameras in the courtroom

A. Biondi, 'TV cameras' access into the courtroom: a comparative note' (1996) 2 *Yearbook of Media and Entertainment Law* 133–50 discusses the law from a European, particularly Italian, perspective.

M. Dockray, 'Courts on television' (1988) 51 *Modern Law Review* 593–604 is a classic statement of the case for relaxing the ban on cameras in the courtroom.

J. Jaconelli, *Open Justice: A Critique of the Public Trial* (Oxford: OUP, 2002). Chapter 9 discusses the origins of the ban on cameras in courtrooms in England and the Scottish experiment to allow them.

D. Lepofsky, 'Cameras in the courtroom – not without my consent' (1996) 6 *National Journal of Constitutional Law* 161–232 is a vigorous statement by a leading Canadian lawyer of the case against cameras in the courtroom.

D. Stepniak, *Audio-Visual Coverage of Courts* (Cambridge: CUP, 2008) provides a comprehensive coverage of the issues from a comparative perspective, examining the laws in the UK, USA and Commonwealth countries.

T.H. Tongue and R.W. Lintott, 'The case against television in the courtroom' (1980) 16, *Williamette Law Rev* 777–801 is written in the context of US state law permitting the filming and broadcasting of legal proceedings.

Restrictions on media access and reporting

I. Cram, 'Automatic reporting restrictions in criminal proceedings and article 10 of the ECHR' (1998) 3 *European Human Rights Law Rev* 742–53 is critical of automatic restrictions, on the ground that they are imposed irrespective of whether reporting would endanger the fairness of the proceedings.

I. Cram, *A Virtue Less Cloistered* (Oxford: Hart Publishing, 2002). Chapter 4 discusses the restrictions on open justice in criminal proceedings concerning children.

R. Munday, 'Name suppression: an adjunct to the presumption of innocence and the mitigation of sentence' [1991] *Criminal Law Rev* 680–88, 753–62 argues for greater anonymity in the interest of defendants to criminal charges.

G. Robertson and A. Nicol, *Media Law*, 5th edn (London: Penguin Books, 2008). Chapter 8 offers a critical account of restrictions on media freedom in this area.

14 Investigative journalism: access to information and the privilege not to disclose sources

14.1 INTRODUCTION

In February 2011 the House of Lords Select Committee on Communications published a report: *The Future of Investigative Journalism*.[1] It found that investigative journalism performed an important role in putting otherwise unreported information before the public and so stimulating political and social debate, but it faced a number of challenges. As an expensive form of journalism it was threatened by rising economic costs.[2] Declining circulation and advertising revenue posed particular challenges for local and regional newspapers; they could no longer afford the costs of such journalism. Further, the traditional media increasingly faced competition from the providers of online content, which may fall outside effective legal and regulatory controls.[3] In contrast, the press and broadcasting media are subject to a number of restrictions which significantly hamper their ability to investigate stories of real public interest. These restrictions go beyond the laws of libel, privacy and contempt of court considered in Chapters 10–12 of this book. Significant restrictions are imposed by the criminal law and regulatory codes. The House of Lords Committee was particularly troubled by the failure of many laws to provide a 'public interest' defence which would enable a journalist to argue that he should not be convicted (or even prosecuted) for, say, infringing the official secrets legislation, because he was investigating a political story of real public importance.[4]

This chapter is concerned with a number of areas of law relevant to investigative journalism. The first is freedom of information law: to what extent do journalists have a right to obtain information from government and from other public authorities. This is discussed in Section 14.2. Section 14.3 is concerned with another access question which has occasionally come before the courts: do journalists have a right to interview prisoners, even though regulations proscribe an interview, unless the prison governor exercises discretion to permit one to take place? Laws providing for freedom of information, or for prison interviews, directly encourage investigative journalism. Such journalism is also indirectly protected by the privilege claimed by journalists and editors not to disclose their sources of information. This important topic, of enormous concern to individual journalists, is covered in Section 14.4. English courts have been less prepared than the European Court of Human Rights to recognise a broad freedom not to disclose sources of information, although they appear now more willing to recognise its importance for investigative journalism. Another area of concern to the media is the extent to which they must comply with warrants to search their premises or police requests to hand over

---

[1] 3rd Report of Session 2010–12, HL Paper 256.
[2] See N. Davies, *Flat Earth News* (London, Chatto & Windus, 2008) for an insightful analysis by a leading journalist of reasons for the decline in the quality of investigative journalism.
[3] Note 1, paras 59–63.
[4] Ibid., paras 80–8.

documents and photographs which would enable the identifications of people suspected, say, of committing public order offences at demonstrations. These questions are discussed in Section 14.5. A generous immunity from an obligation to hand over such material, or from search of media premises, would enable the press and broadcasters to engage with greater confidence in investigative journalism, knowing that they will not be required subsequently to hand over the fruits of their research to law enforcement authorities.

Before this chapter examines freedom of information, it briefly discusses the law's inconsistent treatment of 'public interest' defences in statutes which may impose criminal penalties on investigative journalists. The House of Lords Communications Committee pointed out that there is a public interest defence in the Data Protection Act 1998. The statute provides such a defence to the offence of knowing or reckless obtaining or disclosing of personal data,[5] as well as the broad exemption from compliance with most of the data protection principles for the processing of journalistic, literary or artistic material.[6] In contrast, there is no public interest defence in the Regulation of Investigatory Powers Act 2000, the Computer Misuse Act 1990 or the recent Bribery Act 2010. Perhaps the most disturbing example is the omission of a general public interest defence in the Official Secrets Act (OSA) 1989, under which a journalist might be prosecuted for, say, publishing information, disclosure of which is prohibited by the legislation, and to which he has been given access without lawful authority.[7] A journalist would commit the offence if he published information concerning, for example, a secret agreement between a British Prime Minister and another head of government, under which the Prime Minster agreed to commit British troops to military action undertaken by the other government – even though arguably such publication would be very much in the public interest.

However, the omission of an explicit public interest defence in the Official Secrets legislation, or other legislation, does not preclude a legal argument by the media that its publication was a legitimate exercise of freedom of expression (and the press) and so immune from conviction under the statute. The door was left open for such an argument by the leading decision of the House of Lords in *R v Shayler*, the first case in which an English court gave full consideration to the implications of incorporation into UK law of the right to freedom of expression guaranteed by the European Convention on Human Rights. In August 1997 The *Mail on Sunday* published an article written by the appellant, David Shayler, a former member of the Security Services, and other articles based on information disclosed by him; the information in these articles related to sensitive matters of security and intelligence.

Extract 14.1.1
R v Shayler **[2003] 1 AC 247, paras 18, 20–4, 27, 29–31, 36 (HL)**

LORD BINGHAM:

18. Section 1(1)(a) of the OSA 1989 imposes criminal liability on a member or former member of the security and intelligence services if, without lawful authority (as defined in section 7), he discloses any information or document relating to security or intelligence which is or has been in

---

[5] Data Protection Act 1998, s 55(2).
[6] Ibid., s 32, discussed in section 11.5.
[7] Official Secrets Act 1989, s 5. It would only be an offence if the publication was damaging and the journalist knew or had reasonable cause to believe it was damaging, although that qualification does not apply to a journalist's disclosure of any information or document which came into his possession as a result of a leak by a member of the security or intelligence services: ibid., s 5(6).

his possession by virtue of his position as a member of any of those services. The only defence expressly provided is, under subsection (5), that at the time of the disclosure he did not know and had no reasonable cause to believe that the information or documents in question related to security or intelligence. As already demonstrated, a member or former member of the security and intelligence services is treated differently under the Act from other persons, and information and documents relating to security and intelligence are treated differently from information and documents relating to other matters. Importantly, the section does not require the prosecution to prove that any disclosure made by a member or former member of the security and intelligence services was damaging to the interests of that service or the public service generally.

. . .

20. It is in my opinion plain, giving sections 1(1)(a) [and other provisions of the Act] their natural and ordinary meaning and reading them in the context of the OSA 1989 as a whole, that a defendant prosecuted under these sections is not entitled to be acquitted if he shows that it was or that he believed that it was in the public or national interest to make the disclosure in question or if the jury conclude that it may have been or that the defendant may have believed it to be in the public or national interest to make the disclosure in question. The sections impose no obligation on the prosecution to prove that the disclosure was not in the public interest and give the defendant no opportunity to show that the disclosure was in the public interest or that he thought it was . . .

. . .

21. The fundamental right of free expression has been recognised at common law for very many years: see, among many other statements to similar effect, *Attorney General* v *Guardian Newspapers Ltd* [1987] 1 WLR 1248, 1269B, 1320G; *Attorney General* v *Guardian Newspapers Ltd* (No 2) [1990] 1 AC 109, 178E, 218D, 220C, 226A, 283E; *R* v *Secretary of State for the Home Department, Ex p Simms* [2000] 2 AC 115, 126E; *McCartan Turkington Breen* v *Times Newspapers Ltd* [2001] 2 AC 277, 290G–291B. The reasons why the right to free expression is regarded as fundamental are familiar, but merit brief restatement in the present context. Modern democratic government means government of the people by the people for the people. But there can be no government by the people if they are ignorant of the issues to be resolved, the arguments for and against different solutions and the facts underlying those arguments. The business of government is not an activity about which only those professionally engaged are entitled to receive information and express opinions. It is, or should be, a participatory process. But there can be no assurance that government is carried out for the people unless the facts are made known, the issues publicly ventilated. Sometimes, inevitably, those involved in the conduct of government, as in any other walk of life, are guilty of error, incompetence, misbehaviour, dereliction of duty, even dishonesty and malpractice. Those concerned may very strongly wish that the facts relating to such matters are not made public. Publicity may reflect discredit on them or their predecessors. It may embarrass the authorities. It may impede the process of administration. Experience however shows, in this country and elsewhere, that publicity is a powerful disinfectant. Where abuses are exposed, they can be remedied. Even where abuses have already been remedied, the public may be entitled to know that they occurred. The role of the press in exposing abuses and miscarriages of justice has been a potent and honourable one. But the press cannot expose that of which it is denied knowledge.

22. Despite the high value placed by the common law on freedom of expression, it was not until incorporation of the European Convention into our domestic law by the Human Rights Act 1998 that this fundamental right was underpinned by statute. . . . Thus for purposes of the present proceedings the starting point must be that the appellant is entitled if he wishes to disclose information and documents in his possession unless the law imposes a valid restraint upon his doing so.

. . .

23. Despite the high importance attached to it, the right to free expression was never regarded in domestic law as absolute. Publication could render a party liable to civil or criminal penalties or restraints on a number of grounds which included, for instance, libel, breach of confidence, incitement to racial hatred, blasphemy, publication of pornography and, as noted above, disclosure of official secrets. The European Convention similarly recognises that the right is not absolute: article 10(2) qualifies the broad language of article 10(1) by providing, so far as relevant to this case:

> The exercise of these freedoms, since it carries with it duties and responsibilities, may be subject to such formalities, conditions, restrictions or penalties as are prescribed by law and are necessary in a democratic society, in the interests of national security, territorial integrity or public safety, for the prevention of disorder or crime . . . for the protection of the . . . rights of others, for preventing the disclosure of information received in confidence . . .

24. In the present case there can be no doubt but that the sections under which the appellant has been prosecuted, construed as I have construed them, restricted his prima facie right to free expression. There can equally be no doubt but that the restriction was directed to objectives specified in article 10(2) as quoted above. It was suggested in argument that the restriction was not prescribed by law because the procedure for obtaining authorisation was not precisely specified in the OSA 1989, but I cannot accept this. The restriction on disclosure is prescribed with complete clarity. A member or former member of any of the security or intelligence services wishing to obtain authority to disclose could be in no doubt but that he should seek authorisation from his superior or former superior in the relevant service or the head of that service, either of whom might no doubt refer the request to higher authority. It was common ground below, in my view, rightly, that the relevant restriction was prescribed by law. It is on the question of necessity, pressing social need and proportionality that the real issue between the parties arises.

. . .

27. The OSA 1989 imposes a ban on disclosure of information or documents relating to security or intelligence by a former member of the service. But it is not an absolute ban. It is a ban on disclosure without lawful authority. It is in effect a ban subject to two conditions. First of all, the former member may, under section 7(3)(a), make disclosure to a Crown servant for the purposes of his functions as such . . .

. . .

29. One would hope that, if disclosure were made to one or other of the persons listed above, effective action would be taken to ensure that abuses were remedied and offenders punished. But the possibility must exist that such action would not be taken when it should be taken or that, despite the taking of effective action to remedy past abuses and punish past delinquencies, there would remain facts which should in the public interest be revealed to a wider audience. This is where, under the OSA 1989 the second condition comes into play: the former member may seek official authorisation to make disclosure to a wider audience.

30. As already indicated, it is open to a former member of the service to seek authorisation from his former superior or the head of the service, who may no doubt seek authority from the secretary to the cabinet or a minister. Whoever is called upon to consider the grant of authorisation must consider with care the particular information or document which the former member seeks to disclose and weigh the merits of that request bearing in mind (and if necessary taking advice on) the object or objects which the statutory ban on disclosure seeks to achieve and the harm (if any) which would be done by the disclosure in question. If the information or document in question were liable to disclose the identity of agents or compromise the security of informers, one would not expect authorisation to be given. If, on the other hand, the document or information revealed matters which, however, scandalous or embarrassing, would not damage any security or intelligence interest or impede the effective discharge by the service

of its very important public functions, another decision might be appropriate. Consideration of a request for authorisation should never be a routine or mechanical process: it should be undertaken bearing in mind the importance attached to the right of free expression and the need for any restriction to be necessary, responsive to a pressing social need and proportionate.

31. One would, again, hope that requests for authorisation to disclose would be granted where no adequate justification existed for denying it and that authorisation would be refused only where such justification existed. But the possibility would of course exist that authority might be refused where no adequate justification existed for refusal, or at any rate where the former member firmly believed that no adequate justification existed. In this situation the former member is entitled to seek judicial review of the decision to refuse, a course which the OSA 1989 does not seek to inhibit. In considering an application for judicial review of a decision to refuse authorisation to disclose, the court must apply (albeit from a judicial standpoint, and on the evidence before it) the same tests as are described in the last paragraph. It also will bear in mind the importance attached to the convention right of free expression. It also will bear in mind the need for any restriction to be necessary to achieve one or more of the ends specified in article 10(2), to be responsive to a pressing social need and to be no more restrictive than is necessary to achieve that end.

. . .

36. The special position of those employed in the security and intelligence services, and the special nature of the work they carry out, impose duties and responsibilities on them within the meaning of article 10(2): *Engel* v *The Netherlands* (No 1) (1976) 1 EHRR 647, para 100; *Hadjianastassiou* v *Greece* (1992) 16 EHRR 219, para 46. These justify what Lord Griffiths called a bright line rule against disclosure of information of documents relating to security or intelligence obtained in the course of their duties by members or former members of those services . . . If, within this limited category of case, a defendant is prosecuted for making an unauthorised disclosure, it is necessary to relieve the prosecutor of the need to prove damage (beyond the damage inherent in disclosure by a former member of these services) and to deny the defendant a defence based on the public interest; otherwise the detailed facts concerning the disclosure and the arguments for and against making it would be canvassed before the court and the cure would be even worse than the disease. But it is plain that a sweeping, blanket ban, permitting of no exceptions, would be inconsistent with the general right guaranteed by article 10(1) and would not survive the rigorous and particular scrutiny required to give effect to article 10(2). The crux of this case is whether the safeguards built into the OSA 1989 are sufficient to ensure that unlawfulness and irregularity can be reported to those with the power and duty to take effective action, that the power to withhold authorisation to publish is not abused and that proper disclosures are not stifled. In my opinion the procedures discussed above, properly applied, provide sufficient and effective safeguards. It is, however, necessary that a member or former member of a relevant service should avail himself of the procedures available to him under the Act. A former member of a relevant service, prosecuted for making an unauthorised disclosure, cannot defend himself by contending that if he had made disclosure under section 7(3)(a) no notice or action would have been taken or that if he had sought authorisation under section 7(3)(b) it would have been refused. If a person who has given a binding undertaking of confidentiality seeks to be relieved, even in part, from that undertaking he must seek authorisation and, if so advised, challenge any refusal of authorisation. If that refusal is upheld by the courts, it must, however reluctantly, be accepted. I am satisfied that sections 1(1) and 4(1) and (3) of the OSA 1989 are compatible with article 10 of the convention; no question of reading those sections conformably with the convention or making a declaration of incompatibility therefore arises. On these crucial issues I am in agreement with both the judge and the Court of Appeal. They are issues on which the House can form its own opinion. But they are also issues on which Parliament has expressed a clear democratic judgment.

Although the argument from freedom of expression was rejected in *Shayler* itself, it might be harder for a court to resist it, if a prosecution under the official secrets legislation were brought against a journalist or broadcaster and there was a strong public interest in the story. It is difficult to believe, for example, that, given the state of public opinion, a prosecution could have been brought against the *Daily Telegraph* for publishing details of MPs' expenses claims, even if they had obtained the information as a result of a breach of the Official Secrets Act.[8] The Director of Public Prosecutions has issued guidelines explaining how freedom of expression considerations should be taken into account in determining whether a prosecution is in the public interest.[9] Nevertheless, the omission of an explicit public interest defence in the statute has been criticised,[10] and it is certainly damaging to investigative journalism.

14.2 ACCESS TO INFORMATION

(a) A fundamental right to freedom of information?

The question is whether there is a fundamental (human or constitutional) right to freedom of information either as a discrete right or as an aspect of freedom of expression. If there is, the media would have access to information, at least from government and other public authorities required to respect these rights. International conventions and national constitutions sometimes provide for a freedom to seek and receive information and ideas, as well as the freedom to impart them. For example, article 19 of the International Covenant on Civil and Political Rights states that the right to freedom of expression includes these freedoms, as does article 13 of the Inter-American Convention on Human Rights (IACHR). In contrast, article 10 of the ECHR explicitly covers the right to receive information and ideas, but not the freedom to *seek* them. That is also the position in the German Basic Law, which refers to the right of everyone 'freely to inform himself from generally accessible sources'.[11] In a landmark decision, the Inter-American Court of Human Rights upheld a right to request access to government information under the IACHR, and 'a positive obligation of the State to provide it', so that the individual either has access to it or must receive a justification for the government's refusal to supply it.[12] Moreover, restrictions on access must be compatible with the Convention, so they must be necessary in a democratic society to satisfy a compelling public interest.

Until recently the European Court declined to recognise a right to freedom of information under the guarantee of freedom of expression in article 10. For example, in *Leander* v *Sweden* it rejected the applicant's claim to have access to a secret file which the authorities had compiled about him; the freedom to receive information covered

---

[8] See the admission of Jeremy Hunt, MP, Secretary of State for Culture, Media and Sport in his evidence to the HL Communications Committee (n 1 above), para 77, and also see para 83.

[9] Interim guidelines for prosecutors on assessing the public interest in cases affecting the media, issued by the DPP on 18 April 2012, paras 31–2, available at: http://www.cps.gov.uk/consultations/mg_index.html (accessed 29 November 2012). Freedom of expression and other public interest arguments must be balanced against the degree of criminality in the alleged offence in deciding whether to prosecute.

[10] D. Feldman, *Civil Liberties and Human Rights in England and Wales*, 2nd edn (Oxford: OUP, 2002), 890–1, and Fenwick and Phillipson, 938–9.

[11] Article 5(1) (see Extract 1.1.1).

[12] *Marcel Claude Reyes et al.* v *Chile*, Judgment of 19 September 2006, para 77, on which see E.A. Bertoni, 'The Inter-American Court of Human Rights and the European Court of Human Rights: a dialogue on freedom of expression standards' (2009) *European Human Rights Law Review* 332, 347–8.

information which others wish to impart and did not impose an obligation on government services to disclose documents which they preferred to withhold.[13] On the other hand, in some circumstances the court has upheld an access right to information on the basis of the guarantee of the right to respect for private and family life, home and correspondence in article 8, ECHR.[14] This approach is surprising, because article 8, unlike article 10, does not explicitly provide for any right to information.[15] Further, it would have been of no use to the media, since it would be difficult for them to claim access to information under a privacy guarantee. However, in two recent decisions the Second Section of the Court in Strasbourg has upheld freedom of information claims under article 10. In the first case, the applicant, an association concerned to promote human rights and the rule of law, had been refused access to information about a challenge by a Member of Parliament to the constitutionality of drugs legislation in Hungary. It was argued that access to information was a pre-condition of freedom of expression; further, the association claimed to play a role similar to that of the press, for its work allowed the public to discover the views of political leaders concerning drugs policy.

Extract 14.2.1

Társaság A Szabadságjogokért v Hungary (2011) 53 EHRR 3, paras 26–9, 35–9

26. The Court has consistently recognised that the public has a right to receive information of general interest. Its case-law in this field has been developed in relation to press freedom which serves to impart information and ideas on such matters (see Observer *and* Guardian v *the United Kingdom*, 26 November 1991, §59, SeriesA no.216, and *Thorgeir Thorgeirson v Iceland*, 25 June 1992, §63, SeriesA no.239). In this connection, the most careful scrutiny on the part of the Court is called for when the measures taken by the national authority are capable of discouraging the participation of the press, one of society's 'watchdogs', in the public debate on matters of legitimate public concern (see Bladet Tromsø *and* Stensaas v *Norway* [GC], no. 21980/93, §64, ECHR 1999-III, and *Jersild* v *Denmark*, 23 September 1994, §35, Series A no. 298), even measures which merely make access to information more cumbersome.

27. In view of the interest protected by Article 10, the law cannot allow arbitrary restrictions which may become a form of indirect censorship should the authorities create obstacles to the gathering of information. For example, the latter activity is an essential preparatory step in journalism and is an inherent, protected part of press freedom (see *Dammann* v *Switzerland* (no.77551/01, §52, 25 April 2006). The function of the press includes the creation of forums for public debate. However, the realisation of this function is not limited to the media or professional journalists. In the present case, the preparation of the forum of public debate was conducted by a non-governmental organisation. The purpose of the applicant's activities can therefore be said to have been an essential element of informed public debate. The Court has repeatedly recognised civil society's important contribution to the discussion of public affairs (see, for example, *Steel and Morris* v *the United Kingdom* (no.68416/01, §89, ECHR 2005-II). The applicant is an association involved in human rights litigation with various objectives, including the protection of freedom of information. It may therefore be characterised, like the press, as a social 'watchdog' (see *Riolo* v *Italy*, no. 42211/07, §63, 17 July 2008; *Vides Aizsardzības Klubs* v *Latvia*, no. 57829/00, §42, 27 May 2004). In these circumstances, the Court is satisfied that its activities warrant similar Convention protection to that afforded to the press.

---

[13] (1987) 9 EHRR 433, para 74.
[14] See *Gaskin* v *UK* (1989) 12 EHRR 36; *Guerra* v *Italy* (1998) 26 EHRR 357.
[15] S. Sedley, 'Information as a human right' in *Freedom of Expression and Information: Essays in Honour of Sir David Williams*, J. Beatson and Y. Cripps (eds) (Oxford: OUP, 2000), 239, 245.

28. The subject matter of the instant dispute was the constitutionality of criminal legislation concerning drug-related offences. In the Court's view, the submission of an application for an *a posteriori* abstract review of this legislation, especially by a Member of Parliament, undoubtedly constituted a matter of public interest. Consequently, the Court finds that the applicant was involved in the legitimate gathering of information on a matter of public importance. It observes that the authorities interfered in the preparatory stage of this process by creating an administrative obstacle. The Constitutional Court's monopoly of information thus amounted to a form of censorship. Furthermore, given that the applicant's intention was to impart to the public the information gathered from the constitutional complaint in question, and thereby to contribute to the public debate concerning legislation on drug-related offences, its right to impart information was clearly impaired.

29. There has therefore been an interference with the applicant's rights enshrined in Article 10 §1 of the Convention.

. . .

35. The Court recalls at the outset that 'Article 10 does not . . . confer on the individual a right of access to a register containing information on his personal position, nor does it embody an obligation on the Government to impart such information to the individual' (*Leander* v *Sweden*, 26 March 1987, §74 *in fine*, SeriesA no.116) and that 'it is difficult to derive from the Convention a general right of access to administrative data and documents' (*Loiseau* v *France* (dec.), no. 46809/99, ECHR 2003-XII (extracts)). Nevertheless, the Court has recently advanced towards a broader interpretation of the notion of 'freedom to receive information' (see *Sdružení Jihočeské Matky c. la République tchèque* (dec.), no.19101/03, 10 July 2006) and thereby towards the recognition of a right of access to information.

36. In any event, the Court notes that 'the right to freedom to receive information basically prohibits a Government from restricting a person from receiving information that others wish or may be willing to impart to him' (*Leander*, *op. cit.*, §74). It considers that the present case essentially concerns an interference – by virtue of the censorial power of an information monopoly – with the exercise of the functions of a social watchdog, like the press, rather than a denial of a general right of access to official documents. In this connection, a comparison can be drawn with the Court's previous concerns that preliminary obstacles created by the authorities in the way of press functions call for the most careful scrutiny (see *Chauvy and Others* v *France*, no.64915/01, §66, ECHR 2004-VI). Moreover, the State's obligations in matters of freedom of the press include the elimination of barriers to the exercise of press functions where, in issues of public interest, such barriers exist solely because of an information monopoly held by the authorities. The Court notes at this juncture that the information sought by the applicant in the present case was ready and available (see, *a contrario*, *Guerra and Others* v *Italy*, 19 February 1998, §53 *in fine*, *Reports of Judgments and Decisions* 1998-I) and did not require the collection of any data by the Government. Therefore, the Court considers that the State had an obligation not to impede the flow of information sought by the applicant.

37. The Court observes that the applicant had requested information about the constitutional complaint eventually without the personal data of its author. Moreover, the Court finds it quite implausible that any reference to the private life of the MP, hence to a protected private sphere, could be discerned from his constitutional complaint. It is true that he had informed the press that he had lodged the complaint, and therefore his opinion on this public matter could, in principle, be identified with his person. However, the Court considers that it would be fatal for freedom of expression in the sphere of politics if public figures could censor the press and public debate in the name of their personality rights, alleging that their opinions on public matters are related to their person and therefore constitute private data which cannot be disclosed without consent. These considerations cannot justify, in the Court's view, the interference of which complaint is made in the present case.

38. The Court considers that obstacles created in order to hinder access to information of public interest may discourage those working in the media or related fields from pursuing such matters. As a result, they may no longer be able to play their vital role as 'public watchdogs' and their ability to provide accurate and reliable information may be adversely affected (see, *mutatis mutandis*, *Goodwin* v *the United Kingdom*, judgment of 27 March 1996, *Reports* 1996-II, p. 500, §39).

39. The foregoing considerations lead the Court to conclude that the interference with the applicant's freedom of expression in the present case cannot be regarded as having been necessary in a democratic society. It follows that there has been a violation of Article 10 of the Convention.

In the second case the same section of the court upheld a claim by an historian that Hungary had infringed article 10 when a government department refused, in violation of local court judgments, to allow him access for research purposes to documents in its possession.[16]

It is not clear whether these two decisions will be followed in later cases. In both of them the Hungarian government conceded that article 10 had been infringed, and the court did not clearly explain why it departed from its earlier rulings on freedom of information. The question may be asked whether courts, and in particular the European court of Human Rights, *should* recognise a right to freedom of information, given that the ECHR text does not explicitly provide for it, and that there are precedents both for and against upholding it. On one view, it seems odd to uphold freedom of information as an aspect of freedom of expression, when there is no willing speaker. Freedom of information imposes duties on the government to supply information, when it is unwilling to do this. Moreover, freedom of expression and of the media are usually regarded as liberties, with which the state should not interfere without good reason, rather than as claims which impose positive duties on it to provide documents or information.

On the other hand, it can be argued that unless the media, and other members of the public, do enjoy access to information, they will not be able to exercise their freedom of expression effectively. Many of the arguments which justify freedom of expression also justify freedom of information: both are necessary for the effective participation of the public in an open democracy. As Lord Bingham pointed out in *Shayler* (Extract 14.1.1 above, at para 21) the press cannot discharge its role in exposing miscarriages of justice, unless it has information to publish. Indeed, it has been argued that freedom of information should not be regarded as parasitic on other rights, such as freedom of speech or the right to privacy, but as an implicit foundational right; unless there is some access to information, it will never be known whether other rights have been infringed.[17] There is, therefore, a powerful argument for recognising freedom of information as a fundamental right. It does not necessarily follow, however, that the freedom is an aspect of a constitutional right to freedom of expression, let alone identical to it. Many legal systems do uphold freedom of information, but they do this by statute. For as the UK Freedom of Information Act 2000 shows, it is not enough simply to state the freedom; detailed provisions are necessary to specify the authorities which must provide information, and the circumstances in which it may legitimately be withheld.

---

[16] *Kenedi* v *Hungary* (2009) 27 BHRC 335.
[17] S. Sedley, 'Information as a human right' (n. 15 above) at 244 and 248.

Questions for discussion
1. Are you persuaded by the reasoning of the European Court in *Társaság* v *Hungary*?
2. Should the law recognise a fundamental right to freedom of information?

(b) The Freedom of Information Act 2000

Freedom of information (FOI) is a complex area of law, much of which is more appropriately covered in courses on law and government, than in media law courses. Moreover, it is the subject of several specialist works.[18] So this section of the chapter focuses on a few provisions of the Freedom of Information Act 2000 (FOIA), of specific concern to the media, and how they use the access rights conferred by it. The statute was enacted by the Labour government elected in May 1997 as one of its constitutional reforms along with the Human Rights Act 1998. However, the delay in its enactment showed some hesitation on the part of the new government, which was worried about its implications for public administration, while the final draft of the FOIA was criticised by advocates of freedom of information for diluting the original proposals.

The key provision of the FOIA entitles any person making a written request for information to a public authority to be informed in writing by the authority whether it holds information of the specified description and, if so, to have that information communicated to him.[19] There are, however, a number of exemptions from these entitlements and from the correlative duty on the part of the public authority to supply information; it is with regard to these areas of exemption that the law is most complex. Some of the exemptions are *absolute*. Of particular concern to the media are those provided by FOIA, section 32 (information held in some court records) and by section 40 (personal information: personal data concerning the applicant as the data subject, or concerning a third party where disclosure would breach the data protection principles).[20] In these circumstances the public authority need not comply with the request to provide information, whatever the merits of the application. Other exemptions are *qualified*. In those cases, the duty to disclose does not arise if 'in all the circumstances of the case, the public interest in maintaining the exemption outweighs the public interest in disclosing the information'.[21] Among the large number of qualified exemptions, the most important are that covering information relating to the formulation of government policy and ministerial communications (FOIA, section 35) and that covering information, the disclosure of which, in the reasonable opinion of a qualified person, would, or would be likely to, prejudice collective ministerial responsibility, inhibit the free and frank provision of advice, or otherwise prejudice the effective conduct of public affairs (FOIA, section 36).

Initial decisions on FOIA requests are taken by the Information Commissioner who also has jurisdiction over data processing disputes.[22] There is a full right of appeal (on the facts and law, and on the exercise of discretion whether to order disclosure) to the

---

[18] J. McDonald *et al.* (eds), *The Law of Freedom of Information*, 2nd edn (Oxford: OUP, 2009); P. Birkinshaw, *Freedom of Information*, 4th edn (Cambridge, CUP, 2010). Also see T. Pitt-Payne, 'Information law', ch 7 in D. Goldberg, G. Sutter and I. Walden (eds), *Media Law and Practice* (Oxford: OUP, 2009) to which this section is much indebted.

[19] S 1.

[20] For discussion of data protection principles, see Chapter 11, Section 5 above.

[21] FOIA, s 2(2)(b).

[22] See Chapter 11, Section 5 above.

Information Tribunal, now the Information Rights Tribunal,[23] with a further right of appeal on a point of law to the High Court (Administrative Court). In practice, Tribunal decisions form the most important sources of FOI law. The government does have a veto power over decisions of the Commissioner or Tribunal, but it has exercised it on only a handful of occasions, the best-known instance being the decision of Jack Straw, MP, in February 2009, when Minister of Justice, not to permit disclosure of Cabinet minutes and papers relating to discussion of legal advice from the Attorney-General before the invasion of Iraq.[24]

The FOIA provides for access rights to information held by *public* authorities, and provides in Schedule 1 to the Act an exhaustive list of those persons and bodies which are to be regarded as 'public authorities' for the purposes of the legislation. Some authorities are so listed only in relation to information held for particular purposes. The BBC, the public broadcasting corporation, is covered 'in respect of information held for purposes other than those of journalism, art or literature'.[25] The meaning of this provision was considered by the Supreme Court in a recent decision, which sheds light on the principles underlying the legislation and on the relationship between freedom of information and the freedom of the public broadcasting media. The applicant, Steven Sugar, a solicitor and supporter of Israel, requested from the BBC disclosure of a copy of a report prepared for it by a former editor of the Nine O'Clock News, Malcolm Balen, on its coverage of the Middle East. The Balen report was an internal briefing document for the use of the BBC's top management; the question was whether it was 'information held for purposes other than those of journalism . . .' If so, the BBC could be required to disclose it. In the Supreme Court Lord Wilson considered that if the Balen Report had been held *predominantly* for purposes other than journalism, the legislation on a proper construction required the BBC to disclose it; but that was not the case, for it had been prepared to enable the Corporation to monitor its coverage of the conflict in the Middle East. The other members of the court agreed with the Court of Appeal that the FOIA required only that the information was held for the purposes of journalism; it was immaterial whether it was held predominantly for other purposes. The applicant also argued in his appeal to the Supreme Court that the FOIA should be interpreted in conformity with recent decisions of the European Court which appeared to uphold a broad access right to information under ECHR, article 10 (see Section 14.2.1 above).

Extract 14.2.2
Sugar v *BBC* [2012] UKSC 4, [2012] EMLR 17, paras 75–9

LORD WALKER:

75. . . . In my judgment the correct view is that (as Lord Neuberger MR put it at para 44):

> once it is established that the information sought is held by the BBC for the purposes of journalism, it is effectively exempt from production under the Act, even if the information is also held by the BBC for other purposes.

---

[23] The Tribunal is part of the First-Tier Tribunal in the General Regulatory Chamber, formed as part of the new unified tribunal system under the Tribunals, Court and Enforcement Act 2007.
[24] Other vetoes concerned Cabinet committee minutes relating to discussion of devolution in 1997, and more recently an assessment of the risks of the Coalition government's controversial NHS reforms, and the contents of communications between the Prince of Wales and government ministers.
[25] FOIA, Sch 1, Part VI.

So in effect there are only two categories: one is information held for purposes that are in no way those of journalism, and the other is information held for the purposes of journalism, even if it is also held for other (possibly more important) purposes.

76. That conclusion follows both from FOIA's legislative purpose and from its language. First, legislative purpose. It is common ground that FOIA was enacted in order to promote an important public interest in access to information about public bodies. There are (as Schedule 1 to FOIA reveals) thousands of public authorities, large and small, which are paid for out of public funds, and whose actions or omissions may have a profound effect on citizens and residents of the United Kingdom. There is a strong public interest in the press and the general public having the right, subject to appropriate safeguards, to require public authorities to provide information about their activities. It adds to parliamentary scrutiny a further and more direct route to a measure of public accountability.

77. There is therefore force, in relation to FOIA as well as in relation to the Freedom of Information (Scotland) Act 2002, in the proposition 'that, as the whole purpose of the 2002 Act is the release of information, it should be construed in as liberal a manner as possible'. That is how it was put by Lord Marnoch in *Common Services Agency* v *Scottish Information Commissioner* [2006] CSIH 58, 2007 SC 231, para 32, approved by Lord Hope in the House of Lords [2008] UKHL 47, [2008] 1 WLR 1550, para 4. But Lord Hope continued:

> But that proposition must not be applied too widely, without regard to the way the Act was designed to operate in conjunction with the [Data Protection Act 1998]. It is obvious that not all government can be completely open, and special consideration also had to be given to the release of personal information relating to individuals. So while the entitlement to information is expressed initially in the broadest terms that are imaginable, it is qualified in respects that are equally significant and to which appropriate weight must also be given. The scope and nature of the various exemptions plays a key role within the Act's complex analytical framework.

(The *Commons Services Agency* case serves to explain the position on freedom of information in Scotland, which is not immediately apparent from FOIA itself. FOIA extends to Scotland and so applies to operations in Scotland of public authorities which operate throughout the United Kingdom; but Scotland also has its own statute applying to Scottish public authorities.)

78. In this case, there is a powerful public interest pulling in the opposite direction. It is that public service broadcasters, no less than the commercial media, should be free to gather, edit and publish news and comment on current affairs without the inhibition of an obligation to make public disclosure of or about their work in progress. They should also be free of inhibition in monitoring and reviewing their output in order to maintain standards and rectify lapses. A measure of protection might have been available under some of the qualified exemptions in Part II of FOIA, in particular those in sections 36 (Prejudice to effective conduct of public affairs), 41 (Information provided in confidence) and 43 (Commercial interests). But Parliament evidently decided that the BBC's important right to freedom of expression warranted a more general and unqualified protection for information held for the purposes of the BBC's journalistic, artistic and literary output. That being the purpose of the immunity, section 7 and Schedule 1 Part VI, as they apply to the BBC, would have failed to achieve their purpose if the coexistence of other non-journalistic purposes resulted in the loss of immunity.

79. That is confirmed by the language of these statutory provisions. The disclosable material is defined in terms ('held for purposes other than those of journalism, art or literature') which are positive in form but negative in substance. The real emphasis is on what is not disclosable – that is material held for the purposes of the BBC's broadcasting output. It is the most natural construction, which does not depend on reading in any words. That was the view formed both by Irwin J (see especially paras 55 to 58 and 63 to 65 of his *Sugar* judgment) and by Lord Neuberger MR (see especially paras 40 to 42, 44 to 46 and 49 of his judgment) . . .

Lord Brown considered whether ECHR, article 10 provides a broad right to freedom of information; in his view the recent decisions of the European Court of Human Rights, including *Társaság* v *Hungary* (Extract 14.2.1 above) were unpersuasive. Moreover, the Supreme Court appreciated that interpreting the FOIA to confer a right of access to information from the BBC might have deleterious consequences for its broadcasting freedom; it should be in the same position as commercial channels and other private media which are not subject to the freedom of information legislation.

An important decision of the Information Tribunal shows the use of the FOIA by the press to obtain minutes of government department meetings and the Tribunal's approach to the important qualified exemption conferred by section 35 of the Act; it must weigh the public interest in keeping confidential (and exempt from disclosure) information relating to the formation and development of government policy,[26] against the public interest in disclosure underlying the principle of freedom of information. The education correspondent of the *Evening Standard* requested the Department for Education and Skills (DFES) for all minutes of senior management meetings at the DFES from June 2002 to June 2003 regarding the setting of schools budgets in England. The Information Tribunal upheld the decision of the Information Commissioner ordering the DFES to supply the requested information.

Extract 14.2.3

DFES v *Information Commissioner and Evening Standard*, Appeal No EA/2006/0006, paras 61–4, 75–7

61. FOIA, in s.1, conferred an important new fundamental right to information held by public bodies. It is a right subject to exceptions, or conditions as they were termed by Lord Turnbull. Where such an exception is relied on by a public authority, it is for that authority to justify such reliance. If it says there is an absolute exemption, it must demonstrate it. If prejudice is a requisite factor, it must prove it.

62. We do not accept that the inclusion of information within such a class as s.35(1)(a) reflects the inevitability of damage to the public interest, in some degree, if it is disclosed. On the contrary, the wider such a provision as s.35(1)(a) is drawn, in accordance with the DFES argument which we have accepted, the more unreal such a contention becomes. The ready and entirely proper acceptance by the DFES that much of such material can be and is disclosed by the Department demonstrates the, at best, hypothetical nature of this argument.

63. In our judgement, inclusion within such a class of information simply indicates the need and the right of the public authority to examine the question of the balance of public interests when a request under s.1 is received. Often such examination will be very brief because disclosure poses no possible threat to good government.

64. Section 2(2)(b) is clear: the authority must disclose unless the public interest in withholding the information outweighs the public interest in disclosure. If the scales are level, it must disclose. Such an equilibrium may not be a purely theoretical result: there may be many cases where the apparent interests in disclosure and in maintaining the exemption are equally slight.

. . .

75. Having reflected on the competing arguments and the wealth of authorities with which we have been assisted, we conclude that the following principles should guide decisions as to disclosure in such a case as this:

[26] FOIA s 35(1)(a).

(i) The central question in every case is the content of the particular information in question. Every decision is specific to the particular facts and circumstances under consideration. Whether there may be significant indirect and wider consequences from the particular disclosure must be considered case by case.

(ii) No information within s.35(1) is exempt from the duty of disclosure simply on account of its status, of its classification as minutes or advice to a minister nor of the seniority of those whose actions are recorded.

(iii) Subject to principle (iv), which we regard as fundamental, the purpose of confidentiality, where the exemption is to be maintained, is the protection from compromise or unjust public opprobrium of civil servants, not ministers. Despite impressive evidence against this view, we were unable to discern the unfairness in exposing an elected politician, after the event, to challenge for having rejected a possible policy option in favour of a policy which is alleged to have failed.

(iv) The timing of a request is of paramount importance to the decision. We fully accept the DFES argument, supported by a wealth of evidence, that disclosure of discussions of policy options, whilst policy is in the process of formulation, is highly unlikely to be in the public interest, unless, for example, it would expose wrongdoing within government. Ministers and officials are entitled to time and space, in some instances to considerable time and space, to hammer out policy by exploring safe and radical options alike, without the threat of lurid headlines depicting that which has been merely broached as agreed policy . . .

(v) When the formulation or development of a particular policy is complete for the purposes of (iv) is a question of fact. However, s.35(2) and to a lesser extent 35(4), clearly assume that a policy is formulated, announced and, in many cases, superseded in due course. We think that a parliamentary statement announcing the policy, of which there are examples in this case, will normally mark the end of the process of formulation. There may be some interval before development. We do not imply by that that any public interest in maintaining the exemption disappears the moment that a minister rises to his or her feet in the House . . .

(vi) If the information requested is not in the public domain, we do not regard publication of other information relating to the same topic for consultation, information or other purposes as a significant factor in a decision as to disclosure.

(vii) In judging the likely consequences of disclosure on officials' future conduct, we are entitled to expect of them the courage and independence that has been the hallmark of our civil servants since the Northcote–Trevelyan reforms . . . The most senior officials are frequently identified before select committees, putting forward their department's position, whether or not it is their own.

(viii) On the other hand, there may be good reason in some cases for withholding the names of more junior civil servants who would never expect their roles to be exposed to public gaze. These are questions to be decided on the particular facts, not by blanket policy.

(ix) Similarly, notwithstanding past experiences which were recounted to us with a proper anonymity, we are entitled to expect of our politicians, when they assume power in a government department, a substantial measure of political sophistication and, of course, fair-mindedness. To reject or remove a senior official because he or she is identified, thanks to FOIA or for any other reason, with a policy which has now lost favour, whether through a change of administration or simply of minister, would plainly betray a serious misunderstanding of the way the executive should work. It would, moreover, be wholly unjust. . . .

(x) Likewise, decisions should not assume the worst of the public. The answer to ill-informed criticism of the perceived views of civil servants is to inform and educate the critic, however hard that task may be, not to deny information, simply through fear that it may reflect adversely and unfairly on a particular official.

(xi) A blanket policy of refusing to disclose the names of civil servants wherever they appear in departmental records cannot be justified because in many cases disclosure will do no harm to anyone, even if it does little good. Quite apart from cases falling within (iv) above, there will plainly be instances where an individual has advanced particularly sensitive or controversial advice which for whatever reason should not be attributed. It might be appropriate to disclose the advice with the name redacted. Again, each decision will depend on the facts of the case. There must, however, be a specific reason for omitting the name of the official where the document is otherwise disclosable. That reason may not need to be utterly compelling where, as will often be the case, there is little or no public interest in learning the name.

76. Applying such principles to the disputed information here, we regard the interest in maintaining the exemption, taking account of all the circumstances, as tenuous, at best . . .

77. We do not believe that disclosure of these minutes, having regard to both the general principles, we have sought to formulate, some of which are only marginally engaged here, and the content of this particular material would damage the public interest to any measurable degree.

In another decision the Tribunal, allowing an appeal against the Information Commissioner, required the BBC to release to the *Guardian* and Heather Brooke, a prominent FOI campaigner, the minutes of the meeting of its governors at which it considered the criticisms of the BBC by Lord Hutton in the Inquiry into the death of Dr David Kelly.[27] The Tribunal did not accept the BBC's argument that disclosure of the minutes would have a chilling effect on future deliberations of the governors. Moreover, the FOIA was based on the notion that disclosure of information served the general public interests in transparency, accountability and public debate.[28] Consequently, the BBC could not claim the qualified exemption from disclosure conferred by FOIA, section 36, allowing public authorities to refuse to provide information where disclosure would be likely to inhibit the free and frank exchange of views and that public interest outweighed the public interest in disclosure. Indeed, generally the Commissioner and Tribunal have declined to accept 'chilling effect' arguments against the release of public documents to the press or other freedom of information applicants.[29]

A study in 2006 showed that journalists are among the five main categories of FOI requestors, the others being MPs, campaign groups, researchers and private individuals.[30] The BBC and the *Guardian* made the most requests among the media applicants.[31] However, the press made a disproportionately high number of repeat requests for information of the same or similar kind to that originally requested. A survey conducted by the University College London Constitution Unit in 2009 estimated that journalists were responsible for 32 per cent of information requests – slightly more than those coming from individual members of the public (31 per cent) and from businesses (27 per cent).[32] Moreover, media requests tended to be time-consuming to deal with. There is some suspicion that journalists sometimes use FOI requests to 'fish' for stories necessary to sustain 24-hours news coverage, as an alternative to engaging in independent investigative

---

[27] EA/2006/0011 and EA/2006/0013.
[28] Ibid., para 87(5).
[29] See R. Hazell and D. Busfield-Birch, 'Opening the Cabinet door: freedom of information and government policy making' [2011] *Public Law* 260, 279–82.
[30] Report prepared by Frontier Economics, *Independent Review of the Freedom of Information Act* (2006), s 2.4.2.
[31] Ibid., Table 5.
[32] *FOI and local government; preliminary findings*, UCL Constitution Unit, October 2010.

journalism.[33] It would not be surprising if this did happen, since freedom of information requests cost the applicant nothing, while investigative journalism is expensive and time-consuming. The costs of answering FOI requests are met by the public authority to which the application is made. However, these points do not detract from the value of access to information for the media and the public. Journalists, particularly those with specialist knowledge of particular subjects, for example, health or penal policy, know what information is worth requesting, and can develop expertise in using the FOIA.[34] They played a prominent part in the revelations about MPs' expenses,[35] although the disclosures compelled by the FOIA were anticipated by leaks of fuller information to the *Daily Telegraph*. So FOI is certainly used to promote the values of investigative journalism, even if it may also be abused to acquire information of little public interest.

(c) Common law freedom of information and open justice

It is clear that English law common law has not recognised any general right to freedom of information. That is hardly surprising, given that freedom of expression and press freedom are generally negative liberties, with which government should not interfere, but which do not impose duties on the state.[36] In the absence of specific contractual or statutory rights, courts would not enforce any right to see public documents. However, there are exceptions to this in court procedures, where discovery of documents may be obtained by the parties; but this does not confer any rights for the media to publish information in these documents, unless perhaps they had been read out in court.[37]

However, in a recent decision the Court of Appeal has upheld at common law a claim by the *Guardian* to inspect and take copies of various documents, which had been supplied to a District Judge for the purpose of determining whether two defendants should be extradited to the United States for involvement in the bribery of Nigerian officials by a subsidiary of the US company, Halliburton. The judge had ruled that she did not have power to allow the newspaper's claim and her decision had been confirmed by the Administrative Court.

Extract 14.2.4
R (On the application of Guardian News and Media) v City of Westminster Magistrates' Court **[2012] EWCA Civ 420, [2012] EMLR 22, paras 72–7, 85**

TOULSON LJ:

72. The exclusion of court documents from the provisions of the Freedom of Information Act is in my view both unsurprising and irrelevant. Under the Act the Information Commissioner is made responsible for taking decisions about whether a public body should be ordered to

---

[33] Ministry of Justice Memorandum to the Justice Select Committee, *Post legislative assessment of the FOIA* (December 2011), para 205.

[34] See Pitt-Payne (n 18 above) at 260–1.

[35] The High Court confirmed the Tribunal's decision upholding the application by three journalists for disclosure by the House of Commons of information concerning MPs claims for housing expenses: *Corporate Office of the House of Commons* v *Information Commissioner, Brooke, Leapman and Thomas* [2008] EWHC 1084 (Admin).

[36] See Sir Anthony Mason, 'The relationship between freedom of expression and freedom of information' in *Freedom of Expression and Freedom of Information* (n 15 above), 225, 231–6.

[37] The media might benefit following the change in the Civil Procedure Rules after Harriet Harman's application to the European Human Rights Commission to challenge the decision of the HL in *Home Office* v *Harman* [1983] 1 AC 280 which held it a contempt of court for a party to show documents disclosed on discovery to third parties such as the media.

produce a document to a party requesting it. The Information Commissioner's decision is subject to appeal to a tribunal, whose decision is then subject to judicial review by the courts. It would be odd indeed if the question whether a court should allow access to a document lodged with the court should be determined in such a roundabout way.

73. More fundamentally, although the sovereignty of Parliament means that the responsibility of the courts for determining the scope of the open justice principle may be affected by an Act of Parliament, Parliament should not be taken to have legislated so as to limit or control the way in which the court decides such a question unless the language of the statute makes it plain beyond possible doubt that this was Parliament's intention.

74. It would be quite wrong in my judgment to infer from the exclusion of court documents from the Freedom of Information Act that Parliament thereby intended to preclude the court from permitting a non-party to have access to such documents if the court considered such access to be proper under the open justice principle. The Administrative Court's observation that no good reason had been shown why the checks and balances contained in the Act should be overridden by the common law was in my respectful view to approach the matter from the wrong direction. The question, rather, was whether the Act demonstrated unequivocally an intention to preclude the courts from determining in a particular case how the open justice principle should be applied.

75. Similarly, I do not consider that the provisions of the Criminal Procedure Rules are relevant to the central issue. The fact that the rules now lay down a procedure by which a person wanting access to documents of the kind sought by the Guardian should make his application is entirely consistent with the court having an underlying power to allow such an application. The power exists at common law; the rules set out a process.

76. I turn to the critical question of the merits of the Guardian's application. The application is for access to documents which were placed before the District Judge and referred to in the course of the extradition hearings. The practice of introducing documents for the judge's consideration in that way, without reading them fully in open court, has become commonplace in civil and, to a lesser extent, in criminal proceedings. The Guardian has a serious journalistic purpose in seeking access to the documents. It wants to be able to refer to them for the purpose of stimulating informed debate about the way in which the justice system deals with suspected international corruption and the system for extradition of British subjects to the USA.

77. Unless some strong contrary argument can be made out, the courts should assist rather than impede such an exercise. The reasons are not difficult to state. The way in which the justice system addresses international corruption and the operation of the Extradition Act are matters of public interest about which it is right that the public should be informed. The public is more likely to be engaged by an article which focuses on the facts of a particular case than by a more general or abstract discussion.

. . .

85. In a case where documents have been placed before a judge and referred to in the course of proceedings, in my judgment the default position should be that access should be permitted on the open justice principle; and where access is sought for a proper journalistic purpose, the case for allowing it will be particularly strong. However, there may be countervailing reasons. In company with the US Court of Appeals, 2nd Circuit, and the Constitutional Court of South Africa, I do not think that it is sensible or practical to look for a standard formula for determining how strong the grounds of opposition need to be in order to outweigh the merits of the application. The court has to carry out a proportionality exercise which will be fact-specific. Central to the court's evaluation will be the purpose of the open justice principle, the potential value of the material in advancing that purpose and, conversely, any risk of harm which access to the documents may cause to the legitimate interests of others.

It should be noted that the Court of Appeal upheld the claim on the basis of the common law principle of open justice, which was discussed in the previous chapter. It was immaterial that the FOIA had granted an absolute exemption from disclosure of documents placed in the custody of a court for the purpose of legal proceedings (or in the custody of a person conducting an inquiry or arbitration for comparable purposes).[38] Another noteworthy point is that it preferred to reach its judgment on the basis of common law, rather than on the strength of the Strasbourg jurisprudence (considered in subsection 2(a) above), which the Court of Appeal regarded as 'not entirely clear cut'.[39]

Questions for discussion

1. Is use of the FOI legislation by the media an important part of investigative journalism?
2. What light does the decision of the Supreme Court in *Sugar* v *BBC* shed on the principles underlying the Freedom of Information Act?
3. How significant is the decision of the Court of Appeal in the *Guardian News and Media* case? Does it suggest the development of a common law right to freedom of information?

14.3 INTERVIEWING PRISONERS

An important aspect of investigative journalism is exposing miscarriages of justice, so journalists may try to interview prisoners when it is unclear whether they have been rightly convicted or detained. In *R* v *Secretary of State for the Home Department, ex parte Simms*, the House of Lords recognised the value of investigative journalism in this context, when it held that a blanket ban on oral interviews of prisoners by journalists was incompatible with prisoners' fundamental right to freedom of expression, at least if the speech questioned the safety of their conviction.[40] Lord Steyn found unpersuasive the authority of a United States Supreme Court decision which had rejected a press claim that journalists had a right under the First Amendment to enter a prison to interview inmates;[41] in his view the Supreme Court deferred excessively to the judgment of the prison authorities that a press visit would be too disruptive.[42] Lord Steyn also said that '. . . investigative journalism, based on oral interviews with prisoners, fulfils an important corrective role, with wider implications than the undoing of particular miscarriages of justice.'[43] In the *Simms* case the challenge to the interpretation, or validity, of the Prison Service Standing Orders was made by two prisoners, but it might equally have been made by the journalists who wanted to interview them.

In 2012 the Administrative Court upheld a judicial review challenge brought by the BBC and one of its correspondents to the decision of the Secretary of State for Justice,

---

[38] FOIA, s 32: see *Kennedy* v *Information Commissioner* [2011] EWCA Civ 367, where it was held that the interpretation of this provision should be considered in the light of recent decisions of the European Human Rights Court.
[39] *Guardian News and Media* (Extract 14.2.4) para 89.
[40] [1999] 3 All ER 400.
[41] *Pell* v *Procunier* 417 US 817 (1974). Also see *Houchins* v *KQED* 438 US 1 (1978) (no right of access to prisons to film conditions there).
[42] See n 40 above, 411.
[43] Ibid., 410.

Kenneth Clarke, MP, refusing them permission to conduct a face-o-face interview with Babar Ahmad and to broadcast the interview. Ahmad had been detained in prison for eight years pending resolution of an application by the USA for his extradition to face charges for terrorism offences.

Extract 14.2.5
R (on the application of BBC and Dominic Casciani) v Secretary of State for Justice [2012] EWHC 13 (Admin), [2012] EMLR 18, paras 42–5, 76–82, 97

MR JUSTICE SINGH:

42. The Secretary of State fairly points out that in the present case he has not sought to impose a content-based restriction. He notes that Mr Ahmad and others speaking on his behalf have had plenty of opportunity to contribute to public debate about his case, for example in newspaper articles and on the internet, and may do so in the future. He also observes that there is nothing to prevent the claimants from making a programme about Mr Ahmad's case and the more general issues of public interest which it raises.

43. The claimants emphasise that the rights in article 10 include the right to choose not just the content of what is to be expressed but also the form of such expression. They submit that this is especially important as an aspect of journalistic and editorial freedom. In *News Verlags GmbH and Co KG v Austria* (2001) 31 EHRR 8, at para. 39, the European Court of Human Rights said:

> The Court recalls that it is not for the Court, or for the national courts for that matter, to substitute their own views for those of the press as to what technique of reporting should be adopted by journalists. Article 10 protects not only the substance of ideas and information but also the form in which they are conveyed.

44. The claimants submit that, in the present case, it is important for them to be able to exercise their professional judgment in deciding whether a face-to-face interview with Mr Ahmad is necessary and whether they should include extracts from that interview in a programme about his case. The Secretary of State submits that it is sufficient that they may correspond with Mr Ahmad in writing.

45. In this context it is worth recalling the particular power that television has in modern life. This can cut both ways. The claimants submit that a broadcast interview will bring home to the public the real human story of Mr Ahmad's case, for example the impact on his appearance, voice and manner of many years of detention without trial. On the other hand, the Secretary of State points out that it is precisely because of the greater impact that television can have that it needs to be more carefully regulated, for example because of the distress it could cause to the victim of a prisoner's crime. In *R (ProLife Alliance) v British Broadcasting Corporation* [2004] 1 AC 185, at para. 20, Lord Hoffmann explained that the power of the medium is the reason why broadcasting has been required to conform to standards of taste and decency which in the case of other media would nowadays be thought to be an unwarranted restriction on freedom of expression:

[*Quotation omitted*]

. . .

76. In our judgment, and even after giving appropriate weight to the views of the Secretary of State, the decision of 22 September 2011 constitutes a disproportionate interference with the right to freedom of expression in article 10. In the circumstances of this particular case, the justification for that interference has not been 'convincingly established', as the jurisprudence on article 10 requires.

77. The Secretary of State's own policy in PSI 37/2010 recognises that there may be instances where a face-to-face interview will be permitted. The policy does not envisage that permission to conduct such an interview will normally be refused. Rather, it envisages that there may well

be cases in which such an interview should be permitted either because its purpose is to highlight a potential miscarriage of justice or because there is some other sufficiently strong public interest: see para. 4.5 of PSI 37/2010. However, under the policy, permission for a face-to-face interview will only be given when the conditions set out in para. 4.6 are met.

78. In our judgment, the claimants have demonstrated on the evidence before the Court that they do require a face-to-face interview with Mr Ahmad and that they have achieved as much as they can by written correspondence . . .

79. The practical considerations which form part of the rationale for the Secretary of State's policy in PSI 37/2010 do not justify the decision in the present case, although they may well do so in many cases. It was essentially because of such practical considerations that the (former) European Commission of Human Rights held to be inadmissible the application in *Bamber* v *United Kingdom* (App. No. 33742/96, 11 September 1997, BAILII: [1997] ECHR 205).

80. If the decision of Mr Blunt [Parliamentary Under-Secretary of State for Prisons . . .] of 15 July 2011 had stood, there can be little doubt that the authorities would have found practical ways of permitting the face-to-face interview with Mr Ahmad to take place. As counsel for the Secretary of State fairly accepted during the hearing before us, the nub of the Secretary of State's reasoning for refusing the claimant's request in the present case can be found in paragraph 32 of [a] witness statement [submitted for the Secretary of State]. The two reasons which are given there are essentially reasons of principle and not ones that turn on practical considerations. They focus on the Secretary of State's policy that permission will normally be refused for the broadcasting of any interview where recording is allowed. It is because the claimants wished to broadcast the interview that the initial decision of 15 July 2011 to permit an interview was revoked on 22 September 2011.

81. Turning to the question of whether the claimants should be permitted to broadcast the product of any recorded interview, the policy in PSI 37/201 does envisage that this will normally be refused: see para. 4.27. However, the policy is not absolute, nor could it be as a matter of administrative law, since a rigid and inflexible policy would be unlawful. The policy on its face admits of the possibility in exceptional cases of permitting such an interview to be recorded for the purpose of broadcasting.

82. In our judgment, it is difficult to think of a case which would fall within the exception if not the present one. We accept the claimants' contention that, as a result of the particular combination of circumstances, this case is highly exceptional. By saying that we make it clear that we do not consider that the present case should be regarded as setting any precedent for other cases. It is because of the unusual combination of facts that the present case, in our view, justifies departure from the normal policy. More than that, in our view, the claimants' rights under article 10 require that departure in the exceptional circumstances of this case, and the Secretary of State has not been able to justify denying those rights on the facts of this case. However, the Secretary of State is entitled to maintain the policy which he does: no challenge has been made to his entitlement to have such a policy in principle and to apply it to the great majority of cases. It is on the unusual facts of the present case that its application constituted a disproportionate interference with the right to freedom of expression.

. . .

97. Turning to issue (iv), for reasons that we have already set out, we have come to the clear conclusion that the Secretary of State has not established that a fair balance has been maintained on the facts of this case. This is not a case where the public interest lies only on one side of the balance. The public interest in preventing distress to victims of terrorist offences is important, as is the public interest in maintaining confidence in the criminal justice system. However, there are powerful public interests on the other side of the balance too. Article 10 confers a right on the public to receive information, in particular about matters of public concern

in a democratic society, such as the treatment of a prisoner who has been in detention for a very long time without charge; and the extradition arrangements applied in this case. It is not for this Court to pronounce on the rights and wrongs of different views that may be held in debate about such matters. The importance of the rights in article 10 is that, in principle, the public should be able to engage in such debates and be as fully informed as possible and make their own minds up. For this reason too, the failure to maintain a fair balance, the Secretary of State's decision breaches the principle of proportionality.

Question for discussion

1. Do you agree with this decision? What were the circumstances which justified the right to conduct a face-to-face interview and to broadcast that interview?

14.4 PROTECTION OF JOURNALISTS' SOURCES

(a) General principles

When investigating stories, journalists commonly promise not to disclose their sources. Alternatively, they regard the promise as implicit in their discussions with informants. The media argue that unless they honour this commitment, people will be reluctant to come forward with information, generally for fear that if their identity is revealed, their employer will take steps to dismiss them. As a result it would be harder to acquire information, so stories of real public interest may never be published. Individual journalists consider they have an obligation, not only a right, to protect the confidentiality of their sources; this principle has been covered by the Codes of Practice of the National Union of Journalists and of the Press Complaints Commission.[44] They also regard the principle as an essential aspect of press freedom, so it would generally be wrong for a court in, say, criminal proceedings or a libel action, to order them to reveal their source. The law should therefore recognise a privilege for journalists (and perhaps others) not to disclose their sources, at least unless there is a pressing reason to compel them to do so.

At first glance this argument appears extremely persuasive.[45] It has been accepted, as will be seen, by leading courts. However, the case for a journalists' privilege not to disclose their sources of information is far from overwhelming. First, there is little evidence to show that without the privilege, sources would 'dry up', and stories of real public interest would never see the light of day.[46] Anthony Lewis, a distinguished columnist for the *New York Times* and commentator on press freedom, writing in 1979 doubted whether a privilege was necessary to enable journalists to engage in investigative journalism; he pointed to the impressive record of the London *Sunday Times* for such journalism, although English law at that time did not recognise the privilege.[47] Second, it is arguably a little paradoxical for the media to claim a privilege not to provide important information

---

[44] NUJ Code, cl 7; PCC Code, art 14.

[45] J. Brabyn, 'Protection against judicially compelled disclosure of the identity of news gatherers' confidential sources in common law jurisdictions' (2006) 69 *Modern Law Rev* 895, 926 argues that 'common human experience' shows that compelled disclosure of sources would have a chilling effect on press freedom.

[46] See the judgment of Sopinka J for the Supreme Court of Canada in *Moysa* v *Albeerta (Lahour Relations Board)* [1989] 60 DLR (4th), 1.

[47] 'A preferred position for journalism?' (1979) 7 *Hofstra Law Rev* 595, 616–17.

– the identity of their sources – when that information would give credibility to a story which otherwise might be understood as little more than speculation. Indeed, journalists may prefer to rely on information provided by named sources, because that enables them to publish a more authoritative story.

This last point gives rise to a difficult question: whose privilege is it? If it belongs to the journalist, is he or she entitled to waive it? In that event the press would be free to reveal the identity of its source, whenever it decides – in breach of any promise, explicit or implied – that this step would give the story greater credibility. The United States Supreme Court has however rejected a newspaper's claim of entitlement to break its promise to its source to keep his identity confidential and to reveal it as part of the story.[48] The better view is that the privilege belongs to the source, who is free to waive anonymity; but it is claimed by the press and other media on behalf of the public. A final point of general principle is that the privilege should not be equated with those claimed by lawyers, doctors and in some jurisdictions priests, not to disclose information given them in confidence by clients, patients or penitents. In all those instances, the privilege is claimed to keep particular information confidential, while the media claim a privilege to publish information, but not reveal the identity of their informant.

Whatever the merits of these reservations, many jurisdictions do recognise a privilege not to disclose the source of information. They differ, however, in the legal basis for recognition. In Germany, the privilege is upheld as an aspect of the constitutional right to freedom of expression and freedom of the press guaranteed by article 5 of the Basic Law.[49] A similar approach has been taken by the European Court of Human Rights in a number of leading decisions, notably *Goodwin* v *UK* (Extract 14.4.3 below) and *Financial Times* v *UK*.[50] However, other leading courts have rejected the argument for recognising the privilege as a matter of constitutional law. The United States Supreme Court distinguished freedom of speech and of the press to publish information, strongly protected by the First Amendment, and the freedom of the press to gather information, which is not so protected.[51] The freedom to investigate stories did not require special press privileges. It would be wrong to grant journalists, but not other writers or academic researchers, immunity from answering questions about their sources from a grand jury investigating criminal offences; one objection was that it would be necessary to define the categories of journalists covered by the privilege.

Recently, the Supreme Court of Canada has for similar reasons rejected the claim that the right to freedom of expression conferred by the Charter of Rights and Freedoms covers news gathering techniques, including a promise of confidentiality to media sources.[52] However, the court recognised that the law should sometimes accept the public interest in anonymity of sources as an important element in news gathering.[53] The decision whether to protect the confidentiality of sources should be left to the common law. In the USA 'shield' laws enacted in the various states protect journalists' privilege. These statutes determine, for example, whether only reporters working for the mass media enjoy the privilege or whether it also extends to freelancers, bloggers and citizen-journalists, and the law may also prescribe whether the privilege is absolute or qualified. In the latter case

---

[48] *Cohen* v *Cowles Media* 501 US 663 (1991).
[49] See the famous *Spiegel* case, 20 BVerfGE 162, 176 (1962), discussed in Barendt, 439–40.
[50] [2010] EMLR 21, discussed in Section 14.4(d) below.
[51] *Branzburg* v *Hayes* 408 US 665 (1972).
[52] *National Post, Fraser and McIntosh* v *HM The Queen* [2010] SCR 477, paras 37–41.
[53] Ibid., paras 33–4.

it may be outweighed in some circumstances by the public interest in revealing the identity of a source, for example, to protect national security or to ensure fair legal proceedings.[54] It is surely wise for statute to set out the general principles of the privilege, although weighing competing claims to confidentiality of sources against their disclosure in concrete cases must be done by the courts. As will now be explained, that is the position in UK law.

Questions for discussion

1. Are you persuaded by the arguments for the law to recognise a journalist's privilege not to disclose sources of information?
2. Whose privilege is it: the journalist's or the source's?

(b) The legal position in the United Kingdom: the Contempt of Court Act 1981

Common law declined to recognise journalists' privilege as an integral aspect of the right to freedom of speech and of the press. In the leading case the House of Lords by a majority of 4–1, with Lord Salmon dissenting, upheld an application by British Steel Corporation (BSC) to compel Granada Television to reveal the source, presumed to be an employee of the Corporation, who had sent Granada confidential documents quoted in a documentary about the management of BSC.[55] Lord Wilberforce in the leading speech recognised the public interest in investigative journalism, but that did not justify in his view any *right* to keep sources confidential. At most the public interest in the free flow of information was a factor to be taken into account when a court decided whether to order disclosure of the source's identity.[56] The legal position was changed after an amendment was introduced by Lord Scarman to the Contempt of Court Bill to give effect to Lord Salmon's dissenting speech in the British Steel case.

Extract 14.4.1
Contempt of Court Act 1981, section 10

No court may require a person to disclose, nor is any person guilty of contempt of court for refusing to disclose, the source of information contained in a publication for which he is responsible, unless it be established to the satisfaction of the court that disclosure is necessary in the interests of justice or national security or for the prevention of disorder or crime.

This provision clearly establishes a presumption in favour of immunity from disclosing the source of information, which may be rebutted when a court is satisfied that disclosure is necessary for one of the prescribed aims. However, this simple provision bristles with legal difficulties, some of which have been resolved satisfactorily by the courts in England; on other key points the approach of the courts has been found wanting by the European Court of Human Rights in Strasbourg, so the decisions of that court must be carefully considered in any account of this area of law in the UK.

---

[54] For a review of US state shield laws, see W.E. Lee, 'The priestly class: reflections on a journalist's privilege' (2006) 23 *Cardozo Arts and Entertainment Law Journal* 635.

[55] *British Steel Corpn* v *Granada Television* [1981] AC 1096.

[56] Under the procedure approved in *Norwich Pharmacal* v *Customs and Excise Commissioners* [1974] AC 133, HL, a person involved, however innocently, in the wrongful conduct of others, must assist the injured party by supplying him with full information about their identity.

We can first consider four points on which the law is now well settled. First, anyone responsible for a publication is entitled to claim the immunity; it is not confined to the traditional press and broadcasting media,[57] but covers citizen-journalists, bloggers and website operators, who publish information from sources to whom explicitly or implicitly they have promised anonymity.[58] So the common description 'journalists' privilege' is strictly a misnomer, although its use can be defended as journalists most frequently claim the privilege. Second, there is no need for the information already to have been published; it was accepted in the leading case, *X Ltd v Morgan Grampian Ltd*[59] that the immunity may be claimed whenever information has been supplied with a view to publication. A third point is that the immunity extends beyond the usual case of a refusal to name the source and covers a refusal to hand over documents or photographs from which the source could be identified. In *Secretary of State for Defence v Guardian Newspapers*,[60] the House of Lords held the newspaper could claim the protection of Contempt of Court Act (CCA), section 10, when it refused to hand over confidential documents sent anonymously to its editor, as their return would give the government a reasonable chance of finding out who had leaked them. (However, by 3–2 the House of Lords ordered the return of the documents, as disclosure of the source's identity was necessary in the interests of national security.)

The fourth point is linked to more complex questions concerning the weighing or balancing of the protection of sources against the interests prescribed in CCA, section 10 which may justify disclosure. Disclosure can only be ordered when the court is satisfied that this is *necessary* for the interests in, for example, justice or national security. It is clear from another decision of the House of Lords that ' "necessary" has a meaning that lies somewhere between "indispensable" on the one hand, and "useful" or "expedient" on the other . . .'[61] Arguably, an order for disclosure is not really 'necessary' if the applicant could identify the source from his own inquiries and investigations. Judges should consider whether the applicant or others have made any attempts to do this before they are prepared to hold that disclosure is necessary in the interests of justice, etc.[62]

The courts' interpretation of other aspects of the statutory provision has been more controversial. They have given a broad meaning to the interests, the protection of which may outweigh the value accorded protection of sources. Disclosure may be ordered 'in the interest of national security' if it would unmask the leaker of information, even though media publication of that particular information would not endanger national security; there is a risk that the source might later supply the media with really secret information.[63] The phrase 'for the prevention of disorder or crime' should not be narrowly construed to

---

[57] Lord Diplock in *Secretary of State for Defence v Guardian Newspapers* [1985] AC 339, 348, HL.

[58] However, it does not cover Internet Service Providers, as they do not take responsibility for the messages they carry over the Net: *Totalise v Motley Fool Ltd* [2001] EMLR 29, Owen J.

[59] [1991] 1 AC 1, 40 per Lord Bridge.

[60] [1985] AC 339. Also see *Handmade Films (Productions) Ltd v Express Newspapers plc* [1986] FSR 463, where Sir Nicholas Browne-Wilkinson V-C, held the privilege precluded an order to hand over photographs of Madonna and her husband, from which the identity of the source who had sent them to the paper could be discovered.

[61] *Re an Inquiry under the Company Securities (Insider Dealing) Act 1985* [1988] AC 660, 704, per Lord Griffiths.

[62] In *John v Express Newspapers* [2000] 3 All ER 257, the Court of Appeal held that disclosure should not be ordered against a newspaper which published pieced together confidential advice which a barrister had torn up and left in his Chambers' waste paper bin; the Chambers itself should have investigated who might have acquired the papers; also see *Special Hospitals Service Authority v Hyde* (1994) 20 BMLR 75, at 85, Peter Pain J; *Saunders v Punch* [1998] 1 All ER 234, at 245, Lindsay J.

[63] *Secretary of State for Defence v Guardian Newspapers* (n 57 above). The documents sent to the paper discussed the best way for the government to handle the controversy anticipated when news broke that Cruise missiles arrived in the UK – hardly a matter itself of national security.

permit disclosure of a source only when this was necessary to avert a *particular identifiable* crime; disclosure may be ordered when a court is satisfied that this is necessary to investigate suspected offences or deter the commission of crime in general.[64] On the other hand, the court will be disinclined to order disclosure if the applicant is not charged with the enforcement of the criminal law. A health authority, therefore, did not succeed in its application for disclosure of the source of a newspaper story that doctors in its employment suffered from AIDS.[65]

(c) In the interests of justice

Much the most difficult question has been the scope of 'interests of justice' as a justification for ordering disclosure. In the *Guardian* case, Lord Diplock suggested that the phrase referred to the administration of justice in legal proceedings. The implication was that disclosure could only be ordered if it was necessary for the disposition of particular proceedings. However, the House of Lords in *Morgan Grampian* gave the phrase a broader meaning. An anonymous source had telephoned a trainee journalist, William Goodwin, to give him information about the plaintiff company (later disclosed as Tetra Ltd), taken from a 'strictly confidential' document which had disappeared from its premises. The plaintiff obtained an injunction to stop publication of an article in *The Engineer* and an order requiring Goodwin to disclose the identity of the source and notes of the telephone conversation. Goodwin failed to comply with the order of the Court of Appeal to hand over the notes which were to remain secure in a sealed envelope until final determination of his appeal. Despite this contempt, the House of Lords heard the submissions made on his behalf. *Morgan Grampian* is also important because of the observations of Lord Bridge on the general approach courts should take to determining whether to order disclosure of the source.

> **Extract 14.4.2**
> ***X Ltd v Morgan Grampian Ltd* [1991] 1 AC 1, at 40–5 (HL)**
>
> LORD BRIDGE OF HARWICH:
> The courts have always recognised an important public interest in the free flow of information. How far and in what circumstances the maintenance of this public interest operated to confer on journalists any privilege from disclosure of their sources which the common law would recognise admitted of no short and simple answer on the authorities. But the matter is no longer governed by the common law and I do not think any assistance is to be gained from the authorities preceding the coming into force of section 10 of the Contempt of Court Act 1981 . . .
> It has been accepted in this case at all levels that the section applies to the circumstances of the instant case notwithstanding that the information obtained by Mr. Goodwin from the source has not been 'contained in a publication'. The information having been communicated and received for the purposes of publication, it is clearly right to treat it as subject to the rule which the section lays down, since the purpose underlying the statutory protection of sources of information is as much applicable before as after publication. It is also now clearly established that the section is to be given a wide, rather than a narrow, construction in the sense that the restriction on disclosure applies not only to direct orders to disclose the identity of a source but also to any order for disclosure of material which will indirectly identify the source and applies notwithstanding that the enforcement of the restriction may operate to defeat rights of property

---

[64] *Re an Inquiry under the Company Securities (Insider Dealing) Act 1985* (n 61 above).
[65] *X v– Y* [1988] 2 All ER 648, at 664–5, Rose J.

vested in the party who seeks to obtain that material: *Secretary of State for Defence* v *Guardian Newspapers Ltd.* [1984] Ch. 156, 166–167, *per* Griffiths L.J.; [1985] A.C. 339, 349–350, *per* Lord Diplock . . .

It follows then that, whenever disclosure is sought, as here, of a document which will disclose the identity of a source within the ambit of section 10, the statutory restriction operates unless the party seeking disclosure can satisfy the court that 'disclosure is necessary' in the interests of one of the four matters of public concern that are listed in the section. I think it is indisputable that where a judge asks himself the question: 'Can I be satisfied that disclosure of the source of *this* information is necessary to serve *this* interest?' he has to engage in a balancing exercise. He starts with the assumptions, first, that the protection of sources is itself a matter of high public importance, secondly, that nothing less than necessity will suffice to override it, thirdly, that the necessity can only arise out of concern for another matter of high public importance, being one of the four interests listed in the section . . .

These two public interests [national security and the prevention of crime] are of such overriding importance that once it is shown that disclosure will serve one of those interests, the necessity of disclosure follows almost automatically; though even here if a judge were asked to order disclosure of a source of information in the interests of the prevention of crime, he 'might properly refuse to do so if, for instance, the crime was of a trivial nature': [1988] A.C. 660, 703, *per* Lord Griffiths.

But the question whether disclosure is necessary in the interests of justice gives rise to a more difficult problem of weighing one public interest against another. A question arising under this part of section 10 has not previously come before your Lordships' House for decision. In discussing the section generally Lord Diplock said in *Secretary of State for Defence* v *Guardian Newspapers Ltd.* [1985] A.C. 339, 350:

> The exceptions include no reference to 'the public interest' generally and I would add that in my view the expression 'justice', the interests of which are entitled to protection, is not used in a general sense as the antonym of 'injustice' but in the technical sense of the administration of justice in the course of legal proceedings in a court of law, or, by reason of the extended definition of 'court' in section 19 of the Act of 1981 before a tribunal or body exercising the judicial power of the state.

I agree entirely with the first half of this dictum. To construe 'justice' as the antonym of 'injustice' in section 10 would be far too wide. But to confine it to 'the technical sense of the administration of justice in the course of legal proceedings in a court of law' seems to me, with all respect due to any dictum of the late Lord Diplock, to be too narrow. It is, in my opinion, 'in the interests of justice', in the sense in which this phrase is used in section 10, that persons should be enabled to exercise important legal rights and to protect themselves from serious legal wrongs whether or not resort to legal proceedings in a court of law will be necessary to attain these objectives. Thus, to take a very obvious example, if an employer of a large staff is suffering grave damage from the activities of an unidentified disloyal servant, it is undoubtedly in the interests of justice that he should be able to identify him in order to terminate his contract of employment, notwithstanding that no legal proceedings may be necessary to achieve that end.

Construing the phrase 'in the interests of justice' in this sense immediately emphasises the importance of the balancing exercise. It will not be sufficient, per se, for a party seeking disclosure of a source protected by section 10 to show merely that he will be unable without disclosure to exercise the legal right or avert the threatened legal wrong on which he bases his claim in order to establish the necessity of disclosure. The judge's task will always be to weigh in the scales the importance of enabling the ends of justice to be attained in the circumstances of the particular case on the one hand against the importance of protecting the source on the other hand. In this balancing exercise it is only if the judge is satisfied that disclosure in the interests of justice is of such preponderating importance as to override the statutory privilege against disclosure that the threshold of necessity will be reached.

Whether the necessity of disclosure in this sense is established is certainly a question of fact rather than an issue calling for the exercise of the judge's discretion, but, like many other questions of fact, such as the question whether somebody has acted reasonably in given circumstances, it will call for the exercise of a discriminating and sometimes difficult value judgment. In estimating the weight to be attached to the importance of disclosure in the interests of justice on the one hand and that of protection from disclosure in pursuance of the policy which underlies section 10 on the other hand, many factors will be relevant on both sides of the scale.

It would be foolish to attempt to give comprehensive guidance as to how the balancing exercise should be carried out. But it may not be out of place to indicate the kind of factors which will require consideration. In estimating the importance to be given to the case in favour of disclosure there will be a wide spectrum within which the particular case must be located. If the party seeking disclosure shows, for example, that his very livelihood depends upon it, this will put the case near one end of the spectrum. If he shows no more than that what he seeks to protect is a minor interest in property, this will put the case at or near the other end. On the other side the importance of protecting a source from disclosure in pursuance of the policy underlying the statute will also vary within a wide spectrum. One important factor will be the nature of the information obtained from the source. The greater the legitimate public interest in the information which the source has given to the publisher or intended publisher, the greater will be the importance of protecting the source. But another and perhaps more significant factor which will very much affect the importance of protecting the source will be the manner in which the information was itself obtained by the source. If it appears to the court that the information was obtained legitimately this will enhance the importance of protecting the source. Conversely, if it appears that the information was obtained illegally, this will diminish the importance of protecting the source unless, of course, this factor is counterbalanced by a clear public interest in publication of the information, as in the classic case where the source has acted for the purpose of exposing iniquity. I draw attention to these considerations by way of illustration only and I emphasise once again that they are in no way intended to be read as a code.

In the circumstances of the instant case, I have no doubt that Hoffmann J. and the Court of Appeal were right in finding that the necessity for disclosure of Mr. Goodwin's notes in the interests of justice was established. The importance to the plaintiffs of obtaining disclosure lies in the threat of severe damage to their business, and consequentially to the livelihood of their employees, which would arise from disclosure of the information contained in their corporate plan while their refinancing negotiations are still continuing . . . The importance of protecting the source on the other hand is much diminished by the source's complicity, at the very least, in a gross breach of confidentiality which is not counterbalanced by any legitimate interest which publication of the information was calculated to serve. Disclosure in the interests of justice is, on this view of the balance, clearly of preponderating importance so as to override the policy underlying the statutory protection of sources and the test of necessity for disclosure is satisfied.

Arguably, the interpretation of 'in the interests of justice' means the courts are always likely to order disclosure whenever it is likely that the source was a dishonest employee, whom the employer would like to unmask and dismiss. Although the House of Lords emphasised that balancing the confidentiality of sources against the interest in favour of disclosure involved the assessment of factors, rather than the exercise of discretion, it seems that courts do have a residual discretion not to order disclosure, even where an applicant has shown that this step was necessary to identify the dishonest employee who had leaked information to the press.[66] Section 10 of the CCA provides that '[n]o court *may*

---

[66] *Special Hospitals Service Authority v Hyde* (1994) 20 BLMR 75, 84–5, Peter Pain J.

require a person to disclose . . .' his source, unless it is satisfied that this is necessary for one of the prescribed aims, not that it must so require in these circumstances (emphasis added).

Questions for discussion

1. Do you agree with Lord Bridge's interpretation of the phrase, 'in the interests of justice'?
2. Does his approach to the 'balancing exercise' give adequate weight to the importance of freedom of the press and investigative journalism?

(d) The approach of the European Court of Human Rights

Goodwin took his case to Strasbourg. Six years after the House of Lords decision, the European Court of Human Rights by a majority of 11–7 held the decision infringed his right to freedom of expression under article 10 of the ECHR.

Extract 14.4.3
***Goodwin v United Kingdom* (1996) 22 EHRR 123, at 143–5 (ECHR) (footnotes omitted)**

The Court recalls that freedom of expression constitutes one of the essential foundations of a democratic society and that the safeguards to be afforded to the press are of particular importance.

Protection of journalistic sources is one of the basic conditions for press freedom, as is reflected in the laws and the professional codes of conduct in a number of Contracting States and is affirmed in several international instruments on journalistic freedoms. Without such protection, sources may be deterred from assisting the press in informing the public on matters of public interest. As a result the vital public watchdog role of the press may be undermined and the ability of the press to provide accurate and reliable information may be adversely affected. Having regard to the importance of the protection of journalistic sources for press freedom in a democratic society and the potentially chilling effect an order of source disclosure has on the exercise of that freedom, such a measure cannot be compatible with Article 10 of the Convention unless it is justified by an overriding requirement in the public interest.

These considerations are to be taken into account in applying to the facts of the present case the test of necessity in a democratic society under Article 10(2).

As a matter of general principle, the 'necessity' for any restriction on freedom of expression must be convincingly established. Admittedly, it is in the first place for the national authorities to assess whether there is a 'pressing social need' for the restriction and, in making their assessment, they enjoy a certain margin of appreciation. In the present context, however, the national margin of appreciation is circumscribed by the interest of democratic society in ensuring and maintaining a free press. Similarly, that interest will weigh heavily in the balance in determining, as must be done under Article 10(2), whether the restriction was proportionate to the legitimate aim pursued. In sum, limitations on the confidentiality of journalistic sources call for the most careful scrutiny by the Court.

The Court's task, in exercising its supervisory function, is not to take the place of the national authorities but rather to review under Article 10 the decisions they have taken pursuant to their power of appreciation. In so doing, the Court must look at the 'interference' complained of in the light of the case as a whole and determine whether the reasons adduced by the national authorities to justify it are 'relevant and sufficient'.

In the instant case, as appears from Lord Bridge's speech in the House of Lords, Tetra [the anonymous plaintiff in the previous extract] was granted an order for source disclosure primarily on the grounds of the threat of severe damage to their business, and consequently to the livelihood of their employees, which would arise from disclosure of the information in their corporate plan while their refinancing negotiations were still continuing . . .

In the Court's view, the justifications for the impugned disclosure order in the present case have to be seen in the broader context of the *ex parte* interim injunction which had earlier been granted to the company, restraining not only the applicant himself but also the publishers of *The Engineer* from publishing any information derived from the plan. That injunction had been notified to all the national newspapers and relevant journals. The purpose of the disclosure order was to a very large extent the same as that already being achieved by the injunction, namely to prevent dissemination of the confidential information contained in the plan. There was no doubt, according to Lord Donaldson in the Court of Appeal, that the injunction was effective in stopping dissemination of the confidential information by the press. Tetra's creditors, customers, suppliers and competitors would not therefore come to learn of the information through the press. A vital component of the threat of damage to the company had thus already largely been neutralised by the injunction. This being so, in the Court's opinion, in so far as the disclosure order merely served to reinforce the injunction, the additional restriction on freedom of expression which it entailed was not supported by sufficient reasons for the purposes of Article 10(2) of the Convention.

What remains to be ascertained by the Court is whether the further purposes served by the disclosure order provided sufficient justification.

In this respect it is true, as Lord Donaldson put it, that the injunction 'would not effectively prevent publication to [Tetra's] customers or competitors' directly by the applicant journalist's source (or that source's source). Unless aware of the identity of the source, Tetra would not be in a position to stop such further dissemination of the contents of the plan, notably by bringing proceedings against him or her for recovery of the missing document, for an injunction against further disclosure by him or her and for compensation for damage.

It also had a legitimate reason as a commercial enterprise in unmasking a disloyal employee or collaborator who might have continuing access to its premises in order to terminate his or her association with the company.

These are undoubtedly relevant reasons. However, as also recognised by the national courts, it will not be sufficient, *per se*, for a party seeking disclosure of a source to show merely that he or she will be unable without disclosure to exercise the legal right or avert the threatened legal wrong on which he or she bases his or her claim in order to establish the necessity of disclosure. In that connection, the Court would recall that the considerations to be taken into account by the Convention institutions for their review under Article 10(2) tip the balance of competing interests in favour of the interest of democratic society in securing a free press. On the facts of the present case, the Court cannot find that Tetra's interests in eliminating, by proceedings against the source, the residual threat of damage through dissemination of the confidential information otherwise than by the press, in obtaining compensation and in unmasking a disloyal employee or collaborator were, even if considered cumulatively, sufficient to outweigh the vital public interest in the protection of the applicant journalist's source. The Court does not therefore consider that the further purposes served by the disclosure order, when measured against the standards imposed by the Convention, amount to an overriding requirement in the public interest.

These principles have been affirmed by the Committee of Ministers of the Council of Europe,[67] and have been restated by the court itself in a number of subsequent decisions.[68] In the most notable of them, *Financial Times Ltd* v *United Kingdom*, it emphasised that

---

[67] Appendix to Recommendation No R (2000) 7, set out in *Voskuil* v *Netherlands* [2008] EMLR 14 at para 43.
[68] *Voskuil* v *Netherlands* (n 67 above), and see the decisions referred to in Section 14.5(c) below.

disclosure orders have a detrimental impact not only on the source, but on the media whose reputation may suffer if it reveals its source, and on members of the public who may be discouraged themselves from becoming sources.[69] The English courts had held in this case that the *Financial Times* should hand over documents to Interbrew SA, a Belgian brewing group, to identify the source of leaks about its plans to take over another brewery company and to protect the integrity of the share market.[70] The European Court ruled that this disclosure order infringed article 10 ECHR. In the court's view it would be wrong to attach weight to the source's allegedly improper purpose,[71] or to allegations that the leaked documents had been doctored. Moreover, disclosure orders could only be justified as necessary to prevent the risk of further leaks 'in exceptional circumstances', where no other step could be taken to prevent this risk and the risk was serious and clear.[72] Like *Goodwin*, the decision shows the high importance attached by the court to the confidentiality of sources; English courts must now take its approach into account under the Human Rights Act 1998.

Questions for discussion

1. Why does the European Human Rights Court ascribe such great importance to the journalistic protection of sources?
2. Why did the court in *Goodwin* dismiss the justifications put forward for the disclosure order?

(e) Post-HRA decisions of the English courts

The English courts accept that section 10 of the CCA must be applied in conformity with the guarantee of freedom of expression under ECHR, article 10. Both provisions 'have a common purpose in seeking to enhance the freedom of the press by protecting journalistic sources'.[73] The House of Lords has also accepted that disclosure orders have an undesirable chilling effect on press freedom and that normally courts should protect sources from identification.[74] The suggestions in one case decided after *Goodwin*, but before the Human Rights Act came into effect, that potential sources would be wise to consider that a court might order disclosure of their identity, and that it might be beneficial for them to be deterred from providing confidential material to the press would not be repeated now.[75] However, judicial acceptance in principle of the importance of protecting sources has not always been reflected in a reluctance to order disclosure in the particular case. Courts are sometimes ready to find that disclosure is justified in the special circumstances of the case. That happened in *Interbrew*, where the Court of Appeal ordered the return of documents

---

[69] [2010] EMLR 21, para 63.
[70] *Interbrew* v *Financial Times Ltd* [2002] EWCA Civ 274; [2002] EMLR 24, CA.
[71] For the Court of Appeal the apparently malicious motive of the source was crucial in its decision to uphold the disclosure order: ibid., para 55 per Sedley LJ. The European Court considered that the source's motive could not be established with sufficient certainty to warrant ascribing such importance to it: n. 69 above, para 66.
[72] Ibid., para 69.
[73] Lord Woolf CJ for the House of Lords in *Ashworth Hospital Authority* v *MGN Ltd* [2002] 1 WLR 2033, para 38.
[74] Ibid., para 61.
[75] See Thorpe LJ in *Camelot Group* v *Centaur Ltd* [1998] 1 All ER 251, 262, CA. The Court of Appeal upheld an order requiring a newspaper to return Camelot's draft accounts so it could discover the person who had leaked them. The material had been used in an article critical of payments made to Camelot's directors.

which it considered might have been doctored and leaked for malicious purposes; but as explained above the European Court of Human Rights found this decision infringed press freedom. Exceptional circumstances were also found in *Ashworth Hospital Authority v MGN Ltd*[76] to justify an order against the publisher of the *Daily Mirror* to reveal the identity of the person who had supplied the paper with medical records about Ian Brady, the Moors murderer; it was presumed this source was a member of the staff of the hospital where Brady was detained. Extracts from these records had been published by the paper. Upholding the disclosure orders made by the lower courts, the House of Lords emphasised the importance of deterring leaks of confidential medical information.

It had been assumed that compliance by the Mirror group with the disclosure order would reveal the original source. However, it revealed only the name of an intermediary, Robin Ackroyd, an experienced freelance journalist who specialised in investigative journalism about hospitals. Tugendhat J refused an application by the hospital authority for an order to compel him to disclose his source.[77] Among the facts he took into account, in circumstances which had changed in the four years since the House of Lords decision, were the absence of further leaks in that period, Ackroyd's record as a responsible investigative journalist, and the absence of any financial motive for the source to supply the medical records. The Court of Appeal upheld Tugendhat J's decision protecting the journalist's sources.

Extract 14.4.4
Mersey Care NHS Trust v Ackroyd (No 2) **[2008] EMLR 1, paras 17–24, 28–32, 80–5**

SIR ANTHONY CLARKE MR:

17. The question in each case to which section 10 of the 1981 Act or article 10 of the Convention applies is thus whether the claimant has shown that it is both necessary, in the sense of there being an overriding interest amounting to a pressing social need, and proportionate for the court to order the journalist to disclose the name of his source. As Lord Woolf put it at [[2002] 1 WLR 2033] [61], the requirements of necessity and proportionality are separate but substantially cover the same area.

18. In answering that question the judge must balance the interests of the claimant on the one hand and the interests of the journalist on the other hand. This can be seen from the approach of the House of Lords in the *MGN* case: see the speech of Lord Woolf at [61] to [67], especially at [63].

19. In this regard the judge discussed at [2006] EMLR 12 [87] to [101] the interests of justice and the rights of others. At [87] he held, applying the decision of the House of Lords in the *MGN* case, that the intention of the hospital to dismiss the source engaged the interests of justice. Protecting patient records is a legitimate aim of the hospital, and in principle such a measure may fulfil a pressing social need and be both necessary and proportionate. The judge correctly held that whether it does so on the facts of this case depends upon a consideration of those facts.

20. The judge said at [88], again in our opinion correctly,

> Where disclosure is sought from a journalist, he safeguards freedom of expression by seeking to keep his source private. The other right in issue is also a right to privacy, namely the claimant's right which the claimant is ultimately seeking to enforce against the source, once he is discovered. The claimant's right to maintain the privacy of his information is always a right under domestic law, whether or not it is also

---

[76] See n 73 above.
[77] *Mersey Care NHS Trust v Ackroyd* [2006] EWHC 107 (QB); [2006] EMLR 12.

a Convention right. In some cases, such as the present, even though the claimant is a corporation, there are also in issue the rights of third parties, namely the patients at the hospital.

21. The judge then considered in detail the rights of Mr Brady under article 8 of the Convention, to which we will further refer so far as necessary below. However, at [90] the judge noted Mr Millar's [counsel for Ackroyd] submission that, since the *MGN* proceedings, Mr Brady had altered his stance. In December 1999 Mr Brady's solicitors urged that there was engaged his right under article 8 of the Convention to respect for his private life with regard to medical information. By contrast the effect of a letter dated 6 January 2006 was that, if he had retained any privacy rights, he was no longer concerned to protect them. At [95] the judge accepted Mr Millar's submission that Mr Brady has now given consent to his notes (known as PACIS notes) for October 1999 being disclosed to all the world. However the judge did not accept Mr Millar's submission that all that was left were the rights which the hospital had to keep private communications between members of its staff.

22. The judge expressly accepted (as he was bound to do) that in the *MGN* case this court held that the hospital has both an interest in protecting the information in patient records and standing to bring this claim . . .

23. The judge considered the position of the hospital, as opposed to that of Mr Brady, at [95] to [101]. He quoted part of [57] of the decision of the European Court of Human Rights in *von Hannover* v *Germany* (2004) 16 BHRC 545 and held at [96] that the hospital was suing to safeguard the respect for the private lives of all its patients and that it would be unlawful for the court to act in a way which was incompatible with the rights of the patients at Ashworth: see section 6 of the HRA and the decision of Rose J in *X* v *Y* [1988] 2 All ER 648, where he explained the importance of confidentiality of medical records in terms similar to those used by Lord Woolf in the *MGN* case.

24. Having set out the terms of article 8, the judge said at [98] that medical records clearly come within the protection of article 8. Lord Woolf said at [63] that, although spoken in a different context, those paragraphs provided a useful guide to the significance of the wrongdoing which the House of Lords, in agreement with this court, held had occurred on the facts of the *MGN* case. We will return to those facts and how the facts found by the judge relate to them below. However, it is plain from the decision in the *MGN* case that the courts have regarded the confidentiality of medical records as of very high importance.

. . .

28. The English courts have thus regarded the protection of medical records as of considerable importance in carrying out the balancing exercise required in a case of this kind . . . There is, in our opinion, no doubt that the judge had these principles well in mind.

29. He also had in mind the correct approach to conflicting Convention rights. Thus he correctly directed himself by reference to this statement of principle in the speech of Lord Steyn in *In re S (A Child) (Identification: Restrictions on Publication)* [2005] 1 AC 593 (which was of course after the decision in the *MGN* case) at [17]:

> The interplay between articles 8 and 10 has been illuminated by the opinions in the House of Lords in *Campbell* v *MGN Ltd* [2004] 2 WLR 1232. For present purposes the decision of the House on the facts of *Campbell* and the differences between the majority and the minority are not material. What does, however, emerge clearly from the opinions are four propositions. First, neither article has as such precedence over the other. Secondly, where the values under the two articles are in conflict, an intense focus on the comparative importance of the specific rights being claimed in the individual case is necessary. Thirdly, the justifications for interfering with or restricting each right must be taken into account. Finally, the proportionality test must be applied to each. For convenience I will call this the ultimate balancing test. This is how I will approach the present case.

30. Between [105] and [119] the judge considered what he described as the value of the freedom of expression which Mr Millar was relying upon on behalf of Mr Ackroyd. As Lord Steyn put it in *R v Home Secretary, ex p Simms* [2000] 2 AC 115 at 127:

> The value of free speech in a particular case must be measured in specifics. Not all types of speech have an equal value.

We agree with the judge at [106] that some speech attracts a high degree of protection and some little or none at all; it varies from case to case: see e.g. *von Hannover* v *Germany* (2004) 16 BHRC 545 at [59], *Douglas v Hello!* [2005] EWCA Civ 596, at [87] and *R v Home Secretary ex p Simms* [2002] AC 115 per Lord Steyn at 125. The judge emphasised the significant role played by investigative journalism by reference to *McCartan, Turkington Breen* v *Times Newspapers Ltd* [2001] 2 AC 277, per Lord Bingham, *Reynolds* v *Times Newspapers Ltd* [2001] 2 AC 127 per Lord Nicholls at 200 G-H and *R v Shayler* [2003] 1 AC 247 at [21].

31. In this regard the judge drew a distinction between the evidence before him and the evidence in the *MGN* case. As the judge said at [111], in the *MGN* case the courts proceeded on the basis that the source was motivated by financial gain, whereas in this case Mr Ackroyd denied that that was the case and the hospital did not contend to the contrary . . .

32. Given the history of problems at the hospital in the 1990s (to which we refer further below) and the importance of investigative journalism in bringing them to light, the judge was in our opinion entitled to regard the freedom of expression invoked by Mr Ackroyd as being of a high order when put in the scales against the important consideration that medical records should be kept confidential.

. . .

80. As already stated, the question for the judge was whether he was persuaded by the hospital that it was necessary and proportionate to order Mr Ackroyd to disclose his source. That involved a balancing of considerations that could properly be urged on one side and the other. As explained above, the carrying out of that balance was essentially a matter for the judge, with whose conclusion this court, as an appellate court, should not interfere unless persuaded that he erred in principle in carrying out the balancing exercise, or that he reached a conclusion that a reasonable judge could not have reached after having had regard to all relevant considerations and having disregarded all irrelevant considerations.

81. It can be seen from the above discussion of the findings of the judge on the facts, and his conclusions based on them, that he took into account the key considerations on either side of the argument. In these circumstances we do not think that there is any basis on which we could properly interfere with the balance he struck. For the reasons the judge gave at [188], [189] and [197], the evidence before him and thus the facts he found were significantly different from the evidence given and the facts found in the *MGN* case and, by contrast with the position in that case, he was of course considering the position in 2006.

82. The judge was in our opinion quite entitled to hold that the position in 2006 was very different from that which it would have been if this action had come to trial in, say, 2000, when the *MGN* case came before Rougier J. Having explained the various differences, the judge said this at the end of [188] in a passage which we have already quoted:

> But, a source who misguidedly thought he or she was acting in the public interest in the extraordinary circumstances of October 1999 (when Ian Brady had a well-founded complaint of mistreatment by the hospital . . .), is not a person who can be said to present a significant risk of further disclosure, at least unless there were to be a repetition of events such as occurred on 30th September and 29th October 1999. No one suggests that that is likely to recur.

We see no reason to disagree with that analysis or (at least) to hold that it was not open to the judge.

83. Some key features of the evidence before the judge which he emphasised at [197] as being different from the evidence in the *MGN* case were that the purpose of the source was not to receive payment, that Mr Brady's stance had changed and that, although Mr Ackroyd was mixed up in the wrongdoing so as to engage the principle in the *Norwich Pharmacal* case, the disclosure of the notes was not in breach of a duty owed to Mr Brady. Mr Nelson submitted that those features of the case were not relevant distinguishing factors. We do not accept that submission. The conclusion that the source was paid for the information was regarded as a relevant factor in the *MGN* case and the stance of Mr Brady was naturally much relied upon by the hospital when it supported the hospital's position on disclosure. Indeed, Dr Collins continued to rely upon it in a statement dated 28 November 2005. In all the circumstances, the judge was in our opinion correct to hold that these were relevant factors. Mr Nelson further submitted that the judge placed too much weight upon them. However the weight to be given to a relevant factor in the overall balance was essentially a matter for the judge.

84. We should perhaps add that it was submitted on behalf of the hospital that the judge was wrong to hold that procedures were tightened as a result of the Fallon Report [into conditions at Ashworth Special Hospital]. However, the point made by the judge at [193(vi)] was that the necessity for a disclosure order had been lessened by the apparent success of the measures taken *since* the report, in order to impress upon those working at the hospital the need for patient records to be kept confidential and to avoid the serious faults which had occurred in the past. The judge was there emphasising the important point that the matter had to be judged in the light of the position as at 2006. We might add that we can see nothing in the judge's judgment which would encourage the source to disclose further confidential information now.

85. In all the circumstances, the judge was in our opinion entitled to hold that it was not convincingly established that there was in 2006 a pressing social need that the source or sources should be identified. He was also entitled to hold that an order for disclosure would not be proportionate to the pursuit of the hospital's legitimate aim to seek redress against the source, given the vital public interest in the protection of a journalist's source. It follows that we dismiss the appeal.

The decisions of Tugendhat J and the Court of Appeal suggest an increased willingness on the part of English courts to recognise the protection of sources as an essential element of press freedom and investigative journalism.

Questions for discussion

1. What factors do the courts now take into account in balancing the protection of sources against the interest of the applicant in disclosure of their identity?
2. How much weight should be accorded to the value of the publication or story, to which the information provided by the source contributes?

14.5 ACCESS TO JOURNALISTIC MATERIAL

(a) General principles

Press freedom arguments may be raised in other contexts. Journalists argue, for example, that they should enjoy immunity from standard police powers to search for, and seize, relevant evidence. Their ability to report public events might be inhibited, if the police were free to search newspaper premises for notes, photographs and other material collected for the purpose of reporting, which might be evidence of some crime. Media impartiality might be questioned if journalists too readily comply with police requests to hand over such material, while press photographers covering demonstrations might even be attacked for fear that the police might use their film to identity participants in public disorder. The United States Supreme Court has, however, rejected the claim of a student newspaper for protection under the First Amendment press guarantee against the search of its offices for photographs which would identify participants at a violent demonstration.[78] In contrast, as we will see in Section 14.5(c) below, the European Court of Human Rights has been more sympathetic to press freedom arguments in this context.

In principle section 10 of the CCA should apply if the police require the media to hand over documents in the course of an investigation;[79] in the *Guardian Newspapers* case[80] the House of Lords held that the provision applied to any proceedings where there was a reasonable chance that a court order might lead to disclosure of a source (see Section 14.4(b) above). However, it seems to have been assumed in a 1993 case that section 10 did not apply to an order under anti-terrorism legislation requiring Channel 4 to produce documents which might reveal the source of serious allegations canvassed in its *Dispatches* programme about collusion between the police and loyalist terrorists.[81] Under the HRA, legislation must now be interpreted compatibly with the right to freedom of expression, so it is doubtful whether provisions in the present terrorism legislation can properly be applied without taking account of article 10 ECHR, as interpreted by the European Court in *Goodwin* (Extract 14.4.3) and its subsequent decisions.

(b) Police and Criminal Evidence Act 1984

The Police and Criminal Evidence Act (PACE) 1984 takes account of the particular position of the media to a limited extent. A production order for police access to 'journalistic material', as defined in section 13 of PACE, may only be secured on application to a judge, provided the additional 'access conditions' in respect of 'excluded' or 'special procedure material' set out in Schedule 1 to the Act are satisfied.[82] Excluded material includes 'journalistic material' held in confidence;[83] access to it can only be obtained, if but for section 9(2) of PACE a warrant could have been issued to obtain it under earlier legislation.[84] In practice, the provisions with regard to obtaining 'special procedure' material, including journalistic material not held in confidence, are more important, and they are set out, together with the definition in PACE of 'journalistic material' in the next extract.

Extract 14.5.1
Police and Criminal Evidence Act 1984, s 13 and Sched 1, paras 1, 2 and 4

13.—(1) Subject to subsection (2) below, in this Act 'journalistic material' means material acquired or created for the purposes of journalism.
(2) Material is only journalistic material for the purposes of this Act if it is in possession of a person who acquired or created it for the purposes of journalism.

---

[78] *Zurcher* v *Stanford Daily* 436 US 547 (1978). White J for the majority doubted whether the procedure for obtaining a search warrant ex parte, rather than after a contested hearing, would inhibit press freedom.
[79] Fenwick and Phillipson, 376–7.
[80] See n 57 above.
[81] *DPP* v *Channel* 4 [1993] 2 All ER 517.
[82] PACE, s 9(1). For the definition of 'special procedure material', see PACE 1984, s 14.
[83] PACE s 11(3).
[84] Ibid., Sch 1, para 3(b).

(3) A person who receives material from someone who intends that the recipient shall use it for the purposes of journalism is to be taken to have acquired it for those purposes.

. . .

Schedule 1

1. If on an application made by a constable a circuit judge is satisfied that one or other of the sets of access conditions is fulfilled he may make an order under paragraph 4 below.[85]

2. The first set of access conditions is fulfilled if
(a) there are reasonable grounds for believing—
    (i)   that an indictable offence has been committed;
    (ii) that there is material which consists of special procedure material . . . on premises specified in the application;
    (iii) that the material is likely to be of substantial value . . . to the investigation . . . ; and
    (iv) that the material is likely to be relevant evidence;
(b) other methods of obtaining the material—
    (i)   have been tried without success; or
    (ii) have not been tried because it appeared that they were bound to fail; and
(c) it is in the public interest, having regard—
    (i)   to the benefit likely to accrue to the investigation if the material is obtained; and
    (ii) to the circumstances under which the person in possession of the material holds it, that the material should be produced or that access to it should be given.

. . .

4. An order under this paragraph is an order that the person who appears to the circuit judge to be in possession of the material to which the application relates shall—
(a) produce it to a constable for him to take it away; or
(b) give a constable access to it,
not later than the end of the period of seven days from the date of the order or the end of such longer period as the order may specify.

These provisions have been considered on a number of occasions, where the police wanted access to media film of demonstrations.[86] In a leading case, a newspaper publisher and press agency in Bristol applied for judicial review of an order requiring them to hand over unpublished photographs of riots in that city.

Extract 14.5.2
***R v Bristol Crown Court, ex parte Bristol Press and Picture Agency Ltd* (1987) 85 Cr App Rep 190, 195–6 (DC)**

GLIDEWELL LJ:
As to the public interest in subparagraph (c), the balancing exercise which has to be carried out is between the public interest in the investigation and prevention of crime and the public interest in the press being free to report and to photograph as much as they can of what is going on in our great cities, and particularly in the deprived areas of cities. There is also public interest in the press being able to go about that activity in safety. Both of these are matters about which Mr. Macdonald's clients [the newspaper and the press agency] expressed concern. The judge

---

[85] The second set of 'access conditions', not reproduced in the extract, concerns 'excluded material', including journalistic material held in confidence: see PACE 1984, s 11(1)(c).
[86] R. Costigan, 'Fleet Street Blues: police seizure of journalists' material' [1996] *Criminal Law Rev* 231 is very critical of the courts' application of the PACE provisions, particularly with regard to the protection of journalists' material.

took both into account. But Mr. Macdonald complains that he did not relate the public interest in the investigation of crime to the specific offences, but merely spoke of them generally. He submits that what must be in issue here is the public interest in relation to these particular crimes or suspected crimes.

The judge said:

> Is it in the public interest that the material should be produced, having regard (i) to the benefit likely to accrue to the investigation if the material is obtained? In my judgment it clearly is. There is a very great public interest that those guilty of crime, and particularly of serious crime involving widespread public disorder, should be brought to justice. Equally, there is great public interest that those who are innocent but who may be suspected of crime should be cleared and, if possible, eliminated from the criminal process. Photographs that are likely to advance either of these objects are of benefit to the investigation. Copies of two photographs published by the first respondents were shown to me. It is quite clear that these and similar photographs would be of great value.

If the judge had gone on to say that those general considerations, which apply to the investigation of all crime, of course apply to the investigation of the crimes committed here, I cannot think that Mr. Macdonald would have made his submission. The absence of those words is of no significance because of course they are to be implied. The learned judge in the next passage in his judgment on the following page weighed those interests against the other matters to which I have referred – the importance of the impartiality and independence of the press, the importance of ensuring that members of the press can photograph and report what is going on without fear of their personal safety – and, having done so, he concluded in favour of granting the application. If he applied the right test, it is not suggested that he was not entitled to weigh the various factors and come to a conclusion, it was a matter for his discretion. In my judgment he did apply the right test. He made no error of law. He directed himself correctly. He took account of relevant considerations. He did not take account of any irrelevant considerations. His decision is not susceptible of judicial review. The application should fail.

In a number of cases the courts have shown considerable sympathy for press concerns in this context. In *R v Central Criminal Court, ex parte Bright*[87] the Divisional Court declined (with one exception) to make production orders against the editors of the *Guardian* and the *Observer,* and a journalist working for the latter, in respect of material sent to the newspapers by David Shayler (see Extract 14.1.1). In the leading judgment, Judge LJ emphasised that judges should consider 'the potential stifling of public debate' before making a production order against the press to hand over journalistic material.[88] The court emphasised in another case that freedom of expression and the need to protect confidential journalist sources should be considered before production orders were made under the Terrorism Act 2000, though it upheld a decision to make the orders to ensure that a terrorist suspect had a fair trial.[89]

In perhaps its most important recent decision in this area, the Divisional Court upheld an application for judicial review of production orders granted by the Crown Court against a number of broadcasters and filmmakers to hand over footage recorded during the controversial evictions at Dale Farm, Basildon.[90] The court accepted that production orders may have an inhibiting impact on the media by creating the perception that they

---

[87] [2001] EMLR 4.
[88] Ibid., para 80.
[89] *Malik v Manchester Crown Court* [2008] EWHC 1362 (Admin); [2008] EMLR 19.
[90] *R (On the Application of BSkyB) v Chelmsford Crown Court* [2012] EWHC 1295 (Admin), [2012] EMLR 30. In addition to BSkyB the applicants included ITN, the BBC and an independent producer.

are working with the police and hence increasing the risk of violence to cameramen.[91] So orders should only be made when there is strong evidence indicating the importance of the footage to any police investigation and showing that the information it provided could not have been obtained in other ways; judges considering whether to make production orders must take account of ECHR, article 10.

(c) Decisions of the European Court

In *Ernst v Belgium* the European Court of Human Rights found that ECHR, article 10 had been infringed when the police conducted eight searches of newspaper offices and journalists' homes to discover the source of a leak of information in a sensitive criminal case.[92] The principles in that case and in the earlier *Goodwin* ruling (Extract 14.4.3) have now been developed by the Grand Chamber of the Court. Prosecutors required a weekly motor car magazine to hand over photographs which its journalists had taken of an illegal street race under guarantee that participants would not be identified; the police wanted the photos not to prosecute people for participating in the race, but to identify A and M, participants in the race, who were suspected of involvement in ram raids to remove cash dispensers.

Extract 14.5.3
Sanoma Uitgevers BV v Netherlands **[2011] EMLR 4, paras 64–72**

64. Turning to the present case, the Court is of the view that although the question has been the subject of much debate between the parties, it is not necessary to determine whether there actually existed an agreement binding the applicant company to confidentiality. The Court agrees with the applicant company that there is no need to require evidence of the existence of a confidentiality agreement beyond their claim that such an agreement existed. Like the Chamber, the Court sees no reason to disbelieve the applicant company's claim that a promise had been made to protect the cars and their owners from being identified.

65. As the Government correctly state, in the present case the authorities did not require the applicant company to disclose information for the purposes of the identification of the street race participants, but only to surrender photographs which in the applicant company's submission might, upon examination, lead to their identification. However, in *Nordisk Film & TV A/S v Denmark* (dec.), no.40485/02, ECHR 2005-XIII the Court held that the decision of the Danish Supreme Court to compel the applicant company to hand over unedited footage constituted an interference within the meaning of Article 10 §1 of the Convention despite the finding that the affected persons were not to be considered 'anonymous sources of information' within the meaning of the case-law of the Court (paragraphs 59 and 61 above). In its decision the Court accepted the possibility that Article 10 of the Convention might be applicable in such a situation and found that a compulsory handover of research material might have a chilling effect on the exercise of journalistic freedom of expression.

66. The Court further notes that in the present case the order concerned was not intended to identify the sources themselves in connection with their participation in the illegal street race and that indeed, no prosecution had been brought in relation to this race or even against A. and M., who were suspected of having committed grave crimes. The Court, however, does not consider this distinction to be crucial.

---

[91] Ibid., paras 25 per Eady J and 44 per Moses LJ.
[92] [2004] 39 EHRR 35. There was also a breach of art 8 guarantee of the right to respect for private life, the home and correspondence. Also see *Roemen and Schmitt v Luxembourg,* Decision of 25 February 2003.

67. In earlier case-law the Court has considered the extent to which the acts of compulsion resulted in the actual disclosure or prosecution of journalistic sources irrelevant for the purposes of determining whether there has been an interference with the right of journalists to protect them. In the case of *Roemen and Schmidt*, the information sought was not obtained as a result of the execution of the order for search and seizure in the journalist's workplace. This order was considered 'a more drastic measure than an order to divulge the source's identity . . . because investigators who raid a journalist's workplace unannounced and armed with search warrants have very wide investigative powers, as, by definition, they have access to all the documentation held by the journalist. It thus considers that the searches of the first applicant's home and workplace undermined the protection of sources to an even greater extent than the measures in issue in *Goodwin*' (*loc. cit.*, §57).

68. As previously observed, in the case of *Financial Times Ltd and Others v the United Kingdom*, cited above, §56, the fact that the disclosure order had not actually been enforced against the applicant company did not prevent the Court from finding that there had been an interference (see paragraph 63 above).

69. The Court observes, as the Chamber did, that unlike in other comparable cases – *Ernst and Others v Belgium*, cited above; *Roemen and Schmit v Luxembourg*, cited above; *Tillack v Belgium*, cited above – there was no search of the applicant company's premises. However, the public prosecutor and the police investigators clearly indicated their intention to carry out such a search unless the editors of *Autoweek* bowed to their will (see paragraph 18 above).

70. This threat – accompanied as it was by the arrest, for a brief period, of a journalist – was plainly a credible one; the Court must take it as seriously as it would have taken the authorities' actions had the threat been carried out. Not only the offices of *Autoweek* magazine's editors but those of other magazines published by the applicant company would have been exposed to a search which would have caused their offices to be closed down for a significant time; this might well have resulted in the magazines concerned being published correspondingly late, by which time news of current events (see paragraph 18 above) would have been stale. News is a perishable commodity and to delay its publication, even for a short period, may well deprive it of all its value and interest (see, for example, *Observer* and *Guardian v the United Kingdom*, 26 November 1991, §60, Series A no.216; *Sunday Times v the United Kingdom (no. 2)*, judgment of 26 November 1991, Series A no.217, §51; and *Association Ekin v France*, no. 39288/98, §56, ECHR 2001-VIII). This danger, it should be observed, is not limited to publications or periodicals that deal with issues of current affairs (cf. *Alınak v Turkey*, no.40287/98, §37, 29 March 2005).

71. While it is true that no search or seizure took place in the present case, the Court emphasises that a chilling effect will arise wherever journalists are seen to assist in the identification of anonymous sources (*mutatis mutandis*, *Financial Times Ltd and Others v the United Kingdom*, cited above, §70).

72. In sum, the Court considers that the present case concerns an order for the compulsory surrender of journalistic material which contained information capable of identifying journalistic sources. This suffices for the Court to find that this order constitutes, in itself, an interference with the applicant company's freedom to receive and impart information under Article 10 §1.

The court concluded that the law in the Netherlands did not provide sufficient safeguards to ensure that an independent decision balancing the needs of the criminal investigation against the protection of sources was conducted *prior* to handing the material over to the police and their inspection of it; the interference with press freedom did not meet the requirements of the rule of law and so was not 'prescribed by law', as required by ECHR, article 10(2).[93] The decision shows the great importance the court attaches to the protection of sources as a crucial aspect of media freedom.

[93] *Sanoma*, paras 88–100.

Questions for discussion

1. Why did the European Court in *Sanoma* hold that there was an interference with freedom of expression in that case? How does the ruling develop its earlier decisions in *Goodwin* and *Ernst*?
2. How should UK courts balance the public interest in investigating crime and in arresting, say, violent demonstrators against the interests of journalists and press photographers in providing a full report of public protest?

Selected further reading

Investigative journalism and freedom of information

P. Birkinshaw, *Freedom of Information*, 4th edn (Cambridge, CUP, 2010) is the leading academic book on freedom of information.

H. Fenwick and G. Phillipson, *Media Freedom under the Human Rights Act* (Oxford, OUP, 2006). Chapter 19 provides a good introductory discussion.

R. Hazell and D. Busfield-Birth, 'Opening the Cabinet door: freedom of information and government policy making' [2011] *Public Law* 260–83 examines the treatment in a number of jurisdictions of access to government papers.

House of Lords Select Committee on Communications, *The Future of Investigative Journalism*, 3rd Report of Session 2010–12, HL Paper 256 examines the pressures on investigative journalism in the present economic climate.

S. Sedley, 'Information as a human right' in J. Beatson and Y. Cripps (eds), *Freedom of Expression and Freedom of Information: Essays in Honour of Sir David Williams* (Oxford, OUP, 2000), 239–48 makes a strong case for upholding freedom of information as a foundational right.

Journalists' privilege not to reveal sources

J. Brabyn, 'Protection against judicially compelled disclosure of the identity of news gatherers' confidential sources in common law jurisdictions' [2006] 69 *Modern Law Review* 895–934 reviews case-law in a number of jurisdictions and argues for strong protection for the privilege not to disclose sources.

D. Carney, 'Theoretical underpinnings of the protection of journalists' confidential sources: why an absolute privilege cannot be justified' (2009) 1 *Journal of Media Law* 97–127 takes a more sceptical view of the privilege.

R. Costigan, 'The protection of journalistic sources' [2007] *Public Law* 464–87 is critical of the approach taken by English courts to the privilege in the light of the HRA.

D.J. Feldman, 'Press freedom and police access to journalistic material' (1995) 1 *Yearbook of Media and Entertainment Law* 43–80 provides a full review of the law on access to journalistic material under PACE.

H. Fenwick and G. Phillipson, *Media Freedom under the Human Rights Act* (Oxford, OUP, 2006). Chapter 7 is a comprehensive account of English and European court decisions on the privilege.

S. Palmer, 'Protecting journalists' sources: section 10, Contempt of Court Act 1981' [1992] *Public Law* 61–72 is critical of English law and argues for amendment to the statutory provision to give stronger protection for journalists' sources.

Index